AN INTRODUCTION TO INTERNATIONAL CRIMINAL LAW AND PROCEDURE

The international criminal courts and tribunals which deal with perpetrators of atrocities are an established part of the effort to bring an end to impunity for international crimes. This leading textbook gives an authoritative account of international criminal law, and focuses on what the student needs to know – the crimes that are dealt with by international courts and tribunals as well as the procedures that govern the investigation and prosecution of those crimes. The reader is guided through controversies with an accessible, yet sophisticated, approach. The four authors have rich experience as lawyers in this field, as teachers of the subject, and as negotiators at the establishment of the International Criminal Court (ICC). The book covers new developments in the case law and the practice and is essential reading for students and teachers of international criminal law and international relations. It is supplemented by a package of online resources (www.cambridge.org/law/cryer3), which offers convenient access to primary sources, excerpts for supplementary reading, problems and questions for reflection and discussion, and materials for exercises and simulations.

ROBERT CRYER is Professor of International and Criminal Law at the University of Birmingham.

HÅKAN FRIMAN is a Swedish lawyer and former Visiting Professor at University College London.

DARRYL ROBINSON is Professor of Law at Queen's University, Kingston, Canada.

ELIZABETH WILMSHURST is an associate fellow at Chatham House and former Visiting Professor at University College London.

AN INTRODUCTION TO INTERNATIONAL CRIMINAL LAW AND PROCEDURE

THIRD EDITION

ROBERT CRYER

HÅKAN FRIMAN

DARRYL ROBINSON

ELIZABETH WILMSHURST

CAMBRIDGE
UNIVERSITY PRESS

CAMBRIDGE
UNIVERSITY PRESS

University Printing House, Cambridge CB2 8BS, United Kingdom

Cambridge University Press is part of the University of Cambridge.

It furthers the University's mission by disseminating knowledge in the pursuit of
education, learning and research at the highest international levels of excellence.

www.cambridge.org
Information on this title: www.cambridge.org/9781107065901

First published 2007
Second edition 2010
Third edition 2014

Printed in the United Kingdom by TJ International Ltd. Padstow Cornwall

A catalogue record for this publication is available from the British Library

Library of Congress Cataloguing in Publication data
An introduction to international criminal law and procedure / Robert Cryer, Håkan Friman, Darryl Robinson,
Elizabeth Wilmshurst. – Third edition.
pages   cm
ISBN 978-1-107-06590-1 (hardback)
1. International crimes.   2. Criminal procedure (International law)   3. International criminal courts.   I. Cryer,
Robert, author.
KZ7000.I587   2014
345–dc23
2013048896

ISBN 978-1-107-06590-1 Hardback
ISBN 978-1-107-69883-3 Paperback

Contents

Preface to the Third Edition

Our intention for this third edition is the same as it was for the first two: to provide an accessible yet challenging explanation and appraisal of international criminal law and procedure for students, academics and practitioners. We focus on the crimes which are within the jurisdiction of international courts or tribunals – genocide, crimes against humanity, war crimes and aggression – and the means of prosecuting them. We also touch on terrorist offences, torture, and transnational crimes which are not within the jurisdiction of the principal international institutions.

International criminal law is now a vast subject, even in our circumscribed view of what it contains. This book is intended as a manageable and useful introduction to the field, and therefore does not attempt to delve into the entirety of the subject in the full detail it deserves. We welcome comments on possible improvements that could be made, and are grateful for those that we received on the first two editions. We have sought to be succinct rather than simplistic in our presentation. We have included references to academic commentary, both in the footnotes and in 'further reading' sections at the end of each chapter. However, there is a great deal of writing on international criminal law, and we could not refer to it all. We hope that this book piques the interest of those new to the subject to further investigations, including into the considerable and insightful literature which the developments in international criminal law have engendered.

While we hope that this book will appeal to practitioners as well as to students, the chapters are intended to cover the subjects which can be dealt with during a university Master's course in international criminal law. Part A is introductory. Following a discussion in Chapter 1 of what we mean by international criminal law, of some of its most fundamental principles and something of its philosophy, we consider in Chapter 2 the objectives of this body of law. Part B is concerned with prosecutions in national, rather than international, courts. Chapter 3 discusses the principles of jurisdiction as they relate to international crimes, Chapter 4 describes some instances of national prosecutions, and Chapter 5 concerns extradition, transfer of information and other means by which States cooperate to assist in bringing suspects to justice before national courts. Part C, which concerns international prosecutions, begins in Chapter 6 with a history of the trials following the Second World War, and Chapters 7 and 8 respectively discuss the ad hoc Tribunals and the International Criminal Court. Chapter 9 describes in brief other courts with an international element which have been established to investigate and prosecute international crimes. Part D discusses the substantive law of international crimes. Chapters 10 to 13 cover genocide, crimes against humanity, war crimes and aggression; Chapter 14 introduces the subject of 'transnational' crimes, and discusses briefly terrorist offences and torture. Chapters 15 and 16 introduce the principles of liability and defences, respectively. Part E is concerned with the processes of international prosecutions: Chapter 17 gives an expanded treatment of the procedures, Chapter 18 discusses the role of victims, and Chapter 19 deals with sentencing. Part F considers various aspects of the relationship between the national and international systems: State cooperation with the international courts and tribunals in Chapter 20; and immunities, in relation to both national and international jurisdictions in Chapter 21. Amnesties and other alternatives and complements to prosecutions are considered in Chapter 22. We end with our conclusions in Chapter 23, which contains our assessment of the development of international criminal law and its institutions and our forecast for the future.

The authors have all taught, to a greater or lesser extent, in international criminal law courses. Three of us took part in the negotiations on the International Criminal Court and participated at the Rome Conference as well as in the subsequent Preparatory Commission and in other advisory roles. Some of the comments in this book rely directly on our experience in this capacity.

We have all had an input into each chapter. Each of us drafted a number of chapters, which were circulated and commented upon by the other three. Each chapter has been the object of intensive discussion amongst all of us to achieve as much coherence among our views as possible. We have attempted to produce a book which reads as a coherent whole, rather than as a collection of separate papers from different writers. Of course, with four authors, complete consensus on every matter of substance was neither possible nor expected and the views expressed in individual chapters are therefore those of the author of that chapter, and not necessarily of the group as a whole.

The responsibility for Chapters 1, 2, 3, 6, 7, 15, 16 and 22 rests with Robert Cryer, for Chapters 5, 17, 18, 19 and 20 with Håkan Friman, for Chapters 11, 12 and 21 with Darryl Robinson and for Chapters 8, 10, 13, and 14 with Elizabeth Wilmshurst. Chapters 4, 9 and 23 have had input from various of us over the different editions. Elizabeth has taken a co-ordinating role. The chapters have been updated to reflect major developments since the second edition and with an increased focus on the International Criminal Court. Taking into account valuable comments that we have received on the earlier editions, we have expanded the discussion of issues such as the philosophy of international criminal law (Chapter 1) and the sources of international criminal procedures and the rights they incorporate (Chapter 17).

We express particular thanks to Sinéad Moloney of Cambridge University Press.

Robert Cryer
Håkan Friman
Darryl Robinson
Elizabeth Wilmshurst

Table of International Cases

European Court of Human Rights

International Court of Justice

International Criminal Tribunal for the Former Yugoslavia

International Military Tribunals

Permanent Court of International Justice

Residual Mechanism (MICT)

Special Tribunal for Lebanon

Table of National Cases

Argentina

Simón, Case No. 17.768, Decision 14.6.2005   574

Australia

Nulyarimma v. Thompson [1999] FCA 1192; 165 ALR 621   80
Polyukhović v. Australia [1991] HCA 32; 172 CLR 501   72, 80, 84, 88, 230

Austria

Dusko Cvetjković, Beschluss des Oberstern Gerichtshofs Os 99/94-6, 13.7.1994   66

Belgium

Sharon, Cour de Cassation, (2003) 127 ILR 110   550–1

Bosnia and Herzegovina

Boudellaa *et al.* v. Bosnia and Herzegovina *et al.*, 11.10.2002, reprinted in (2002) 23 *Human Rights Law Journal* 406   104

Canada

Meyer (Abbaye Ardenne case), IV LRTWC 97   377
Mugesera v. Canada [2005] 2 SCR 100   377
R v. Finta [1994] 1 SCR 701; 104 ILR 285   72, 84, 88, 243, 282, 414
Rose v. R (1947) 3 DLR 618   553
Suresh v. Canada [2002] SCC 1   339

United States

Table of Treaties and Other International Instruments

Abbreviations

A. Ch.	Appeals Chamber
AC	Appeal Cases (UK)
ACHPR	African Charter on Human and Peoples' Rights
ACHR	American Convention on Human Rights
AFRC	Armed Forces Revolutionary Council
AHRLR	African Human Rights Law Reports
All ER	All England Law Reports
AP	Additional Protocol (to the Geneva Conventions of 1949)
APMs	anti-personnel mines
ASEAN	Association of Southeast Asian Nations
ASIL	American Society of International Law
ASP	Assembly of States Parties (to the ICC)
AU	African Union
BFSP	British and Foreign State Papers
CARICOM	Caribbean Community
CAT	UN Convention against Torture and other Cruel, Inhuman and Degrading Treatment
CDF	Civil Defence Force
CIS	Commonwealth of Independent States
CJEU	Court of Justice of the European Communities
CLR	Commonwealth Law Reports
CMR	Court Martial Reports
DLR	Dominion Law Reports
DRC	Democratic Republic of the Congo
ECCC	Extraordinary Chambers in the Courts of Cambodia
ECHR	European Convention on Human Rights
ECJ	European Court of Justice (now the Court of Justice of the European Communities)
ECOSOC	UN Economic and Social Council
ECOWAS	Economic Community of West African States
ECtHR	European Court of Human Rights
ETS	European Treaty Series

EU	European Union
F Supp	Federal Supplement
FRY	Federal Republic of Yugoslavia
GA	UN General Assembly
GAOR	UN General Assembly Official Records
Hague Recueil	Recueil des cours de l'Academie de droit international
HL	House of Lords (UK)
HRC	UN Human Rights Committee
IACHR	Inter-American Human Rights Commission
IACtHR	Inter-American Court of Human Rights
ICC	International Criminal Court
ICCPR	International Covenant on Civil and Political Rights
ICJ	International Court of Justice
ICL	international criminal law
ICRC	International Committee of the Red Cross and Red Crescent
ICTR	International Criminal Tribunal for Rwanda
ICTY	International Criminal Tribunal for the former Yugoslavia
IFOR	Implementation Force (NATO)
IGAD	Intergovernmental Authority on Development (Eastern Africa)
IGC	Interim Governing Council
IHL	international humanitarian law
ILA	International Law Association
ILC	International Law Commission
ILM	International Legal Materials
ILR	International Law Reports
IMT	International Military Tribunal
JCE	joint criminal enterprise
KFOR	Kosovo Force (NATO)
LNTS	League of Nations Treaty Series
LRA	Lord's Resistance Army
LRTWC	Law Reports, Trials of War Criminals
MICT	Residual Mechanism (Mechanism for International Criminal Tribunals)
MINUSMA	UN Multidimensional Integrated Stabilization Mission in Mali
MONUC	UN Organization Mission in the Democratic Republic of the Congo
MONUSCO	UN Organization Stabilization Mission in the Democratic Republic of the Congo
OAS	Organization of American States
OAU	Organization of African Unity
OCIJ	Office of the Co-Investigative Judges (ECCC)
OHR	Office of the High Representative (Dayton Peace Agreement)
OIC	Organization of the Islamic Conference
OJ	Official Journal of the European Communities
OSCE	Organization for Security and Co-operation in Europe
OTP	Office of the Prosecutor (ICC)
PAUTS	Pan-American Union Treaty Series

PCIJ	Permanent Court of International Justice
PTC	Pre-Trial Chamber
PTJ	Pre-Trial Judge
RPE	Rules of Procedure and Evidence
RUF	Revolutionary United Front
SAARC	South Asian Association for Regional Cooperation
SADC	Southern African Development Community
SC	UN Security Council
SCC	Supreme Court Chamber (ECCC)
SCR	Supreme Court Reports
SCSL	Special Court for Sierra Leone
SFOR	Stability Force (NATO-led force, Bosnia)
STL	Special Tribunal for Lebanon
T. Ch.	Trial Chamber
TFV	Trust Fund for Victims (ICC)
TIAS	Treaties and Other International Acts Series
TWAIL	Third World Approaches to International Law
TWC	Trials of War Criminals
UKTS	United Kingdom Treaty Series
UNAMID	African Union/UN Hybrid operation in Darfur
UNICRI	UN Interregional Crime and Justice Research Institute
UNIIC	UN International Independent Commission
UNMIK	UN Mission in Kosovo
UNODC	UN Office on Drugs and Crime
UNTAET	UN Transitional Administration in East Timor
UNTS	United Nations Treaty Series
WLR	Weekly Law Reports

Abbreviations of Book Titles

The following abbreviated titles of books are used in the notes and in the 'Further reading' sections at the end of each chapter.

Boas, *Practitioner Library*, Vol. III	Gideon Boas, James L. Bischoff, Natalie L. Reid and B. Don Taylor III, *International Criminal Law Practitioner Library*, Vol. III (Cambridge, 2011)
Brown, *Research Handbook*	Bartram S. Brown (ed.), *Research Handbook on International Criminal Law* (Cheltenham, UK, and Northampton, MA, 2011)
Cassese, *Commentary*	Antonio Cassese, Paolo Gaeta and John R. W. D. Jones (eds.), *The Rome Statute of the International Criminal Court: A Commentary* (Oxford, 2002)
Doria, *Legal Regime*	José Doria, Hans-Peter Gasser and M. Cherif Bassiouni (eds.), *The Legal Regime of the International Criminal Court: Essays in Honour of Professor Igor Blishchenko* (Leiden, 2009)
Henckaerts and Doswald-Beck, *ICRC Customary Law*	Jean-Marie Henckaerts and Louise Doswald-Beck, *Customary International Humanitarian Law* (Cambridge, 2000), Vol. I
Lee, *Elements and Rules*	Roy Lee *et al.* (eds.), *The International Criminal Court–Elements of Crimes and Rules of Procedure and Evidence* (New York, 2001)
Lee, *The Making of the Rome Statute*	Roy Lee (ed.), *The International Criminal Court: The Making of the Rome Statute: Issues, Negotiations, Results* (The Hague, 1999)

McDonald and Goldman, *Substantive and Procedural Aspects*	Gabrielle Kirk McDonald and Olivia Swaak Goldman (eds.), *Substantive and Procedural Aspects of International Criminal Law: The Experience of International and National Courts* (Kluwer, 2000)
Schabas and Bernaz, *Routledge Handbook*	William A. Schabas and Nadia Bernaz (eds.), *Routledge Handbook of International Criminal Law* (London and New York, 2011)
Schabas, *Ashgate Research Companion*	William A. Schabas, Yvonne McDermott and Niamh Hayes (eds.), *The Ashgate Research Companion to International Criminal Law: Critical Perspectives* (Farnham, UK, and Burlington, VT, 2013)
Sluiter and Vasiliev, *International Criminal Procedure*	Göran Sluiter and Sergey Vasiliev (eds.), *International Criminal Procedure: Towards a Coherent Body of Law* (London, 2009)
Sluiter, *International Criminal Procedure*	Göran Sluiter, Håkan Friman, Suzannah Linton, Sergey Vasiliev and Salvatore Zappalà (eds.), *International Criminal Procedure: Principles and Rules* (Oxford, 2013)
Stahn and Sluiter, *Emerging Practice*	Carsten Stahn and Göran Sluiter (eds.), *The Emerging Practice of the International Criminal Court* (Leiden, 2009)
Triffterer, *Observers' Notes*	Otto Triffterer (ed.), *Commentary on the Rome Statute of the International Criminal Court. Observers' Notes*, 2nd edn (Munich, Oxford and Baden-Baden, 2008)

Part A

Introduction

1

Introduction: What Is International Criminal Law?

1.1   International criminal law

International law typically governs the rights and responsibilities of States;[1] criminal law, conversely, is paradigmatically concerned with prohibitions addressed to individuals, violations of which are subject to penal sanction by a State.[2] The two aspects are sometimes in tension. The development of a body of international criminal law which imposes responsibilities directly on individuals and punishes violations through international mechanisms is also relatively recent. Although there are historical precursors of and precedents in international criminal law,[3] it was not until the 1990s, with the establishment of the ad hoc Tribunals for the former Yugoslavia and Rwanda, that it could be said that an international criminal law regime had evolved. This is a relatively new body of law, which is not yet uniform, nor are its courts universal.

International criminal law developed from various sources. War crimes originate from the 'laws and customs of war', which accord certain protections to individuals in armed conflicts. Genocide and crimes against humanity evolved to protect persons from what are now often termed gross human rights abuses, including those committed by their own governments. With the possible exception of the crime of aggression with its focus on inter-State conflict, the concern of international criminal law is now with individuals and with their protection from wide-scale atrocities. As was said by the Appeals Chamber in the *Tadić* case in the International Criminal Tribunal for the former Yugoslavia (ICTY):

A State-sovereignty-oriented approach has been gradually supplanted by a human-being-oriented approach ... international law, while of course duly safeguarding the legitimate interests of States, must gradually turn to the protection of human beings.[4]

---

[1] See e.g. Robert Jennings and Arthur Watts (eds.), *Oppenheim's International Law*, 9th edn (London, 1994) 5–7.
[2] Glanville Williams, 'The Definition of Crime' (1955) 8 *Current Legal Problems* 107.
[3] See Chapter 6 and e.g. Timothy L. H. McCormack, 'From Sun Tzu to the Sixth Committee: The Evolution of an International Criminal Law Regime' in Timothy L. H. McCormack and Gerry J. Simpson (eds.), *The Law of War Crimes: National and International Approaches* (The Hague, 1997) 31.
[4] *Tadić*, ICTY A. Ch., 2 October 1995, para. 97.

The meaning of the phrase 'international criminal law' depends on its use, but there is a plethora of definitions, not all of which are consistent.[5] In 1950, the most dedicated chronicler of the uses of 'international criminal law', Georg Schwarzenberger,[6] described six different meanings that have been attributed to that term, all of which related to international law, criminal law and their interrelationship, but none of which referred to any existing body of international law which directly created criminal prohibitions addressed to individuals; Schwarzenberger believed that no such law existed at the time. 'An international crime', he said in reference to the question of the status of aggression, 'presupposes the existence of an international criminal law. Such a branch of international law does not exist.'[7]

Cherif Bassiouni,[8] on the other hand (and writing almost half a century later), listed twenty-five categories of international crimes, being crimes which affect a significant international interest or consist of egregious conduct offending commonly shared values, which involve more than the State because of differences of nationality of victims or perpetrators or the means employed, or which concern a lesser protected interest which cannot be defended without international criminalization. His categories include, as well as the more familiar ones, traffic in obscene materials, falsification and counterfeiting, damage to submarine cables and unlawful interference with mail.

Different meanings of international criminal law have their own utility for their different purposes, and there is no necessary reason to decide upon one meaning as the 'right' one.[9] Nevertheless, it is advisable from the outset to be clear about the sense in which the term is used in any particular situation. In this chapter, we shall attempt to elaborate the meaning which we give to the term for the purposes of this book and compare it with other definitions.

1.1.1   *Crimes within the jurisdiction of an international court or tribunal*

The approach taken in this book is to use 'international crime' to refer to those offences over which international courts or tribunals have been given jurisdiction under general international law. They comprise the so-called 'core' crimes of genocide, crimes against humanity, war crimes and the crime of aggression (sometimes known as the crime against peace). Our use thus does not include piracy, slavery, torture, terrorism, drug trafficking and many crimes which States Parties to various treaties are under an obligation to criminalize in their domestic law. But because a number of the practical issues surrounding the repression of these crimes are similar to those relating to international crimes (in the way we use the

---

[5] See Claus Kreß, 'International Criminal Law' in Rüdiger Wolfrum (ed.), *Max Planck Encyclopaedia of Public International Law* (Oxford, 2012) Vol. V, 717, 717–21. Kai Ambos, *Treatise on International Criminal Law*, Vol. I, *Foundations and General Part* (Oxford, 2013) 54–5.

[6] Georg Schwarzenberger, 'The Problem of an International Criminal Law' (1950) 3 *Current Legal Problems* 263.

[7] Georg Schwarzenberger, 'The Judgment of Nuremberg' (1947) 21 *Tulane Law Review* 329, 349.

[8] M. Cherif Bassiouni, 'International Crimes: The Ratione Materiae of International Criminal Law' in M. Cherif Bassiouni (ed.), *International Criminal Law*, 3rd edn (Leiden, 2008) Vol. I, 129, 134–5.

[9] But omnibus uses of 'international criminal law' risk implying that there is a structural unity to what is being referred to, and thus treating very different things as having similarities. For an example, see Barbara Yarnold, 'Doctrinal Basis for the International Criminalization Process' (1994) 4 *Temple International and Comparative Law Journal* 85.

term), they are discussed in this book, although only terrorist offences and torture will be discussed in any detail. Some of them (terrorist offences, drug trafficking and individual acts of torture) have been suggested as suitable for inclusion within the jurisdiction of the International Criminal Court (ICC)[10] and may therefore constitute international crimes within our meaning at some time in the future. Terrorism has been included in the jurisdiction of one 'internationalized' tribunal, the Special Tribunal for Lebanon, but this tribunal is intended to apply Lebanese domestic law on point, although its practice has been more equivocal (and controversial).[11]

Our approach does not differentiate the core crimes from others as a matter of principle, but only pragmatically, by reason of the fact that no other crimes are currently within the jurisdiction of international courts. However, it is clear that, since these crimes have a basis in international law, they are also regarded by the international community as violating or threatening values protected by general international law, as the Preamble to the Rome Statute of the International Criminal Court makes clear.[12]

'International criminal law', as used in this book, encompasses not only the law concerning genocide, crimes against humanity, war crimes and aggression, but also the principles and procedures governing the international investigation and prosecution of these crimes. As we shall see, in practice the greater part of the enforcement of international criminal law is undertaken by domestic authorities. The principle of complementarity, which is fundamental to the whole of international criminal law enforcement, shows that national courts both are, and are intended to be, an integral and essential part of the enforcement of international criminal law.[13] In this book, therefore, we shall cover not only the international prosecution of international crimes, but also various international aspects of their domestic investigation and prosecution. However, as mentioned above, this is only one way of conceiving of international criminal law; below we evaluate some of the other approaches to defining the subject.

1.2 Other concepts of international criminal law

1.2.1 Transnational criminal law

Until the establishment of the international courts and tribunals in the 1990s, the concept of international criminal law tended to be used to refer to those parts of a State's domestic criminal law which deal with transnational crimes, that is to say, crimes with actual or potential transborder effects. This body of law is now more appropriately termed 'transnational criminal law'.[14] A similar terminological distinction between 'international criminal

---

[10] See Final Act of the Rome Conference, UN Doc. A/CONF.183/10, Res. E.   [11] See further Chapters 9 and 14.
[12] See, in particular, preambular paras. 3–4, which affirm that such crimes threaten the 'peace, security and well-being of the world', and, as such, must be prosecuted.
[13] See Arts. 17 and 18 of the ICC Statute. As to the situation generally, Judges Higgins, Kooijmans and Buergenthal have stated: 'the international consensus that the perpetrators of international crimes should not go unpunished is being advanced by a flexible strategy, in which newly established international criminal tribunals, treaty obligations and national courts all have their part to play'. *Case Concerning the Arrest Warrant of 11 April 2000* (*Democratic Republic of the Congo* v. *Belgium*) 14 February 2002, Separate Opinion, para. 51.
[14] See Neil Boister, *An Introduction to Transnational Criminal Law* (Oxford, 2012).

law' (criminal aspects of international law) and 'transnational criminal law' (international aspects of national criminal laws) can also be found in other languages, such as German ('*Völkerstrafrecht*' compared with '*Internationales Strafrecht*'),[15] French ('*droit international pénal*' and '*droit pénal international*') and Spanish ('*derecho internacional penal*' and '*derecho penal internacional*').

Transnational criminal law includes the rules of national jurisdiction under which a State may enact and enforce its own criminal law where there is some transnational aspect of a crime. It also covers methods of cooperation among States to deal with domestic offences and offenders where there is a foreign element and the treaties which have been concluded to establish and encourage this inter-State cooperation. These treaties provide for mutual legal assistance and extradition between States in respect of crimes with a foreign element. Other treaties require States to criminalize certain types of conduct by creating offences in their domestic law, and to bring offenders to justice who are found on their territory, or to extradite them to States that will prosecute. While international law is thus the source of a part of this group of rules, the source of criminal prohibitions on individuals is national law.[16]

Until recently, there was not a clear distinction in the literature between international criminal law with its more restricted meaning and transnational criminal law. Transnational criminal law, with its focus on domestic criminal law and on inter-State cooperation in the sphere of criminal law, remains the body of 'international criminal law' with which national lawyers are most familiar. Providing full coverage of this body of law would not be possible within the remit of this work.[17] Our discussion of it will address only issues of State jurisdiction, such obstacles to national prosecution as immunities, and State cooperation in national proceedings relating to international crimes; we deal with 'transnational crimes' only in so far as they raise cognate issues to international crimes.

1.2.2   *International criminal law as a set of rules to protect the values of the international order*

Another, and more substantive, approach to determining the scope of 'international criminal law' is to look at the values which are protected by international law's prohibitions.[18] Under this approach, international crimes are considered to be those which are of concern to the international community as a whole (a description which is not of great precision), or acts which violate a fundamental interest protected by international law. Early examples include the suppression of the slave trade. The ICC Statute uses the term 'the most serious crimes of concern to the international community as a whole' almost as a

---

[15] Kai Ambos, *Internationales Strafrecht*, 3rd edn (Berlin, 2011).
[16] See generally Neil Boister, 'Transnational Criminal Law?' (2003) 14 *European Journal of International Law* 953, 967–77.
[17] See Boister, *Transnational.*
[18] For discussion in relation to the core crimes, see Bruce Broomhall, *International Justice and the International Criminal Court: Between Sovereignty and the Rule of Law* (Oxford, 2003) 44–51.

definition of the core crimes,[19] and recognizes that such crimes 'threaten the peace, security and well-being of the world'.[20]

It is of course true that those crimes which are regulated or created by international law are of concern to the international community; they are usually ones which threaten international interests or fundamental values.[21] But there can be a risk in defining international criminal law in this manner, as it implies a level of coherence in the international criminalization process which may not exist.[22] The behaviour which is directly or indirectly subject to international law is not easily reducible to abstract formulae. Even if it were, it is not clear that these formulae would be sufficiently determinate to provide a useful guide for the future development of law, although arguments from coherence with respect to the ambit of international criminal law can have an impact on the development of the law (as has occurred, *inter alia*, in relation to the law of war crimes in non-international armed conflict).[23]

1.2.3   *Involvement of a State*

Another approach to defining 'international crimes' relies upon State involvement in their commission.[24] There is some sense in this. For example, aggression is necessarily a crime of the State, committed by high-level State agents.[25] War crimes, genocide and crimes against humanity often, perhaps typically, have some element of State agency. But the subject-matter of international criminal law, as we use it, deals with the liability of individuals, mostly irrespective of whether or not they are agents of a State. In the definition of the crimes which we take as being constitutive of substantive international criminal law, the official status of the perpetrator is almost always irrelevant, with the main exception of the crime of aggression.[26]

1.2.4   *Crimes created by international law*

An international crime may also be defined as an offence which is created by international law itself, without requiring the intervention of domestic law. In the case of such crimes, international law imposes criminal responsibility directly on individuals. The classic statement of this form of international criminal law comes from the Nuremberg International Military Tribunal's seminal statement that:

---

[19] Arts. 1 and 5(1). The International Law Commission framed its investigation into international criminal law in the broad sense as being one into the 'Crimes against the Peace and Security of Mankind': Draft Code of Crimes against the Peace and Security of Mankind, in Report of The International Law Commission on the Work of its Forty-Eighth Session, UN Doc. A/51/10. See also Lyal Sunga, *The Emerging System of International Criminal Law* (The Hague, 1997).
[20] ICC Statute, Preamble, para. 3.
[21] M. Cherif Bassiouni, 'The Sources and Content of International Criminal Law' in M. Cherif Bassiouni (ed.), *International Criminal Law*, 2nd edn (New York, 1999) Vol. I, 3, 98.
[22] See Robert Cryer, 'The Doctrinal Foundations of the International Criminalization Process' in Bassiouni (ed.), *International Criminal Law*, Vol. I, 107.
[23] On such developments, see Chapter 12.
[24] See e.g. M. Cherif Bassiouni, *Crimes Against Humanity in International Criminal Law*, 2nd edn (The Hague, 1999) 243–6, 256.
[25] See Chapter 13.
[26] The reference in Art. 8(2)(b)(viii) of the ICC Statute to the transfer of population 'by the Occupying Power' would also seem to require that the perpetrator is a State agent.

crimes against international law are committed by men, not abstract entities, and only by punishing individuals who commit such crimes can the provisions of international law be enforced ... individuals have international duties which transcend the national obligations of obedience imposed by the individual state.[27]

The definition of an international crime as one created by international law is now in frequent use.[28] But this criterion may lead to unhelpful debate as to what is and what is not 'created' by international law.[29] The more pragmatic meaning used in this book, which we do not claim to be authoritative, excludes from detailed discussion certain conduct which has been suggested to be subject to direct liability in international criminal law but which others dispute, such as piracy and slavery,[30] a general offence of terrorism,[31] and individual acts of torture.[32]

Occasionally, the *sui generis* penal system of the international criminal tribunals and courts is described as 'supranational criminal law' in process of development.[33] This term, to the extent that it has a determinate meaning, is somewhat misleading since it is normally reserved for law imposed by supranational institutions and not treaty-based or customary international law;[34] the ICTY, International Criminal Tribunal for Rwanda (ICTR) and the ICC are not supranational in nature, neither as regards the laws they enforce nor, largely, as institutions.

1.3   Sources of international criminal law

As international criminal law is a subset of international law, its sources are those of international law. These are usually considered to be those enumerated in Article 38(1) (a)–(d) of the Statute of the International Court of Justice, in other words, treaty law, customary law, general principles of law and, as a subsidiary means of determining the law, judicial decisions and the writings of the most qualified publicists.[35] As will be seen, all of these have been used by the ad hoc Tribunals. They are available for use by national courts in so far as the relevant national system concerned will allow. The ICC Statute

---

[27] Nuremberg IMT, Judgment and Sentences, reprinted in (1947) 41 *American Journal of International Law* 172, 221.
[28] Broomhall, *International Justice and the International Criminal Court*, 9–10; Robert Cryer, *Prosecuting International Crimes: Selectivity and the International Criminal Law Regime* (Cambridge, 2005) 1; Hans-Heinrich Jescheck, *Die Verantwortlichkeit der Staatsorgane nach Völkerstrafrecht* (Bonn, 1951) 9; Otto Triffterer, *Dogmatische Untersuchungen zur Entwicklung des materiellen Völkerstrafrechts seit Nürnberg* (Freiburg im Breisgau, 1966) 34; Gerhard Werle, *Principles of International Criminal Law*, 2nd edn (The Hague, 2009) 29.
[29] A slightly different criterion of an international offence, one with a 'definition as a punishable offence in international (and usually conventional) law', leads to the inclusion of a much wider category of crimes, including hijacking, injury to submarine cables and drugs offences (Yoram Dinstein, 'International Criminal Law' (1975) 5 *Israel Yearbook of Human Rights* 55, 67). Many of these would fall, under our taxonomy, to be considered under the rubric of transnational criminal law.
[30] See e.g. Broomhall, *International Justice and the International Criminal Court*, 23–4; Jean Allain (ed.), *The Legal Understanding of Slavery* (Oxford, 2012); Robin Geiß and Anna Petrig, *Piracy and Armed Robbery at Sea* (Oxford, 2011).
[31] See e.g. Antonio Cassese and Paola Gaeta *et al.*, *Cassese's International Criminal Law*, 3rd edn (Oxford, 2013) Chapter 8.
[32] *Ibid.*, 132–5. For a counterpoint see Paola Gaeta, 'International Criminalization of Prohibited Conduct' in Antonio Cassese *et al.* (eds.), *The Oxford Companion to International Criminal Justice* (Oxford, 2009) 63, 68–9.
[33] E.g. Roelof Haverman, Olga Kavran and Julian Nicholls (eds.), *Supranational Criminal Law: A System Sui Generis* (Antwerp, 2003).
[34] See e.g. Werle, *Principles of International Criminal Law*, 38–9.
[35] See generally Dapo Akande, 'Sources of International Criminal Law' in Cassese *et al.* (eds.), *The Oxford Companion to International Criminal Justice*, 41.

contains its own set of sources for the ICC to apply, which are analogous, although by no means identical, to those in the ICJ Statute.[36]

1.3.1   Treaties

Treaty-based sources of international criminal law, either directly or as an aid to interpretation, include the 1907 Hague Regulations, the 1949 Geneva Conventions (and their Additional Protocols) and the 1948 Genocide Convention. They form the basis for many of the crimes within the jurisdiction of the ad hoc Tribunals and the ICC. The ICC Statute, which sets out the definitions of crimes within the jurisdiction of the ICC, is, of course, itself a treaty. Security Council Resolutions 827(2003) and 955(2004), which set up the ICTY and ICTR respectively, were adopted by the Security Council pursuant to its powers under Chapter VII of the UN Charter, and thus find their binding force in Article 25 of the Charter. The source of their binding nature is therefore a treaty. The Statutes of the ad hoc Tribunals have had an important effect on the substance of international criminal law both directly, as applied by the Tribunals, and indirectly as a source of inspiration for other international criminal law instruments;[37] the influence of the ICC Statute has so far largely been through its impact on national legislation.

It has been suggested that treaties might not suffice to place liability directly on individuals[38] and as such cannot be a direct source of international criminal law. Such arguments run up against long-standing practice in international humanitarian law, which has been to apply to individuals the 'laws and customs of war' as found in the relevant treaties, as well as in customary law. As the Permanent Court of International Justice noted over eighty years ago, treaties can operate directly on individuals, if that is the intent of the drafters.[39] The International Committee of the Red Cross and Red Crescent (ICRC) study on customary humanitarian law reports that 'the vast majority of practice does not limit the concept of war crimes to violations of customary international law. Almost all military manuals and criminal codes refer to violations of both customary law and applicable treaty law.'[40] That does not mean that every provision of the Geneva Conventions, for example, imposes direct criminal responsibility on individuals. Breach of some of them, for example those regarding the finest details of the treatment of detainees, would probably not constitute a war crime.[41]

It is only those treaties or provisions of a treaty which are intended to apply directly to an individual that can give rise to criminal responsibility. The 'suppression conventions', for

---

[36] Art. 21 of the ICC Statute. See Leena Grover, 'A Call to Arms:Fundamental Dilemmas Confronting the Interpretation of Crimes in the Rome Statute of the International Criminal Court' (2010) 21 *European Journal of International Law* 543; Robert Cryer, 'Royalism and The King: Article 21 of the Rome Statute and the Politics of Sources' (2009) 12 *New Criminal Law Review* 390. See also section 17.1.4.
[37] See Theodor Meron, 'War Crimes in Yugoslavia and the Development of International Law' (1994) 88 *American Journal of International Law* 78.
[38] Guénaël Mettraux, *International Crimes and the Ad Hoc Tribunals* (Oxford, 2005) 7–9.
[39] *Jurisdiction of the Courts in Danzig* Case, 1928 PCIJ Series B No. 15, 17. See Kate Partlett, *The Individual in the International Legal System: Continuity and Change in International Law* (Cambridge, 2011) 17–26. For a sceptical reading, see Roland Portmann, *Legal Personality in International Law* (Cambridge, 2010) 68–73.
[40] Jean-Marie Henckaerts and Louise Doswald-Beck, *Customary International Humanitarian Law* (Cambridge, 2005) 572.
[41] See Chapter 12.

example, which require States to criminalize conduct such as drug trafficking, hijacking and terror bombing,[42] are not generally regarded as creating individual criminal responsibility of themselves; the conduct covered by those treaties will be incorporated in national law by whatever constitutional method is used by the State concerned. Further, if a court is to apply the terms of a treaty directly to an individual, it will be necessary to show that the prohibited conduct has taken place in the territory of a State Party to the treaty or is otherwise subject to the law of such a party.[43] The practice of the ICTY has been, with occasional deviations,[44] to accept that treaties may suffice to found criminal liability. This began with the *Tadić* decision of 1995, and the position was reasserted in the *Kordić and Čerkez* appeal.[45] In the *Galić* case, the ICTY Appeals Chamber noted that the position of the Tribunal is that treaties suffice for criminal responsibility, although 'in practice the International Tribunal always ascertains that the relevant provision is also declaratory of custom'.[46] This is to adopt a 'belt and braces' approach rather than to require a customary basis for war crimes.[47] The proposition that treaties may found international criminal liability is inherent in the Statute of the ICTR, which criminalizes violations of Additional Protocol II (not all of which was at the time considered customary),[48] and is the most likely basis for aspects of the ICC's jurisdiction.[49]

1.3.2   *Customary international law*

The ICTY has accepted that, when its Statute does not regulate a matter, customary international law, and general principles, ought to be referred to.[50] Customary international law, that body of law which derives from the practice of States accompanied by *opinio iuris* (the belief that what is done is required by or in accordance with law),[51] has the disadvantage of all unwritten law in that it may be difficult to ascertain its content. This is not always the case, however, when the customary law originates with a treaty or other written instrument, for example a General Assembly resolution, which is accepted as reflecting custom, or has been recognized by a court as such.[52] Nevertheless, the use of customary international law in

---

[42] See Chapter 14.

[43] This problem will no longer arise in regard to crimes derived from the four Geneva Conventions which now have universal State participation.

[44] *Galić*, ICTY T. Ch. I, 5 December 2003, Separate and Partially Dissenting Opinion of Judge Nieto-Navia, paras. 109–12; *Milutinović, Sainović and Ojdanic*, ICTY A. Ch., 21 May 2003, paras. 10 *et seq.* See further Héctor Olásolo, 'A Note on the Principle of Legality in International Criminal Law' (2007) 19 *Criminal Law Forum* 301.

[45] *Kordić and Čerkez*, ICTY A. Ch., 17 December 2004, paras. 41–6, clarifying *Tadić*, ICTY A. Ch., 2 October 1995, para. 143.

[46] *Galić*, ICTY A. Ch., 30 January 2006, para. 85.

[47] Although at least two ICTY Appeals Chamber judges have taken the view that the ICTY only has jurisdiction over customary offences: Mohamed Shahabuddeen, *International Criminal Justice at the Yugoslav Tribunal: A Judge's Recollection* (Oxford, 2012) 61–70; *Galić*, ICTY A. Ch., 30 November 2006, Partially Dissenting Opinion of Judge Schomburg, para. 21.

[48] Art. 4 of the ICTR Statute; Report of the Secretary-General Pursuant to Paragraph 5 of Security Council Resolution 955(1994), UN Doc. S/1995/134, para. 12.

[49] Marko Milanovic, 'Is the Rome Statute Binding on Individuals? (And Why We Should Care)' (2011) 9 *Journal of International Criminal Justice* 25; Marko Milanovic, 'Aggression and Legality' (2012) 10 *Journal of International Criminal Justice* 165.

[50] *Kupreškić*, ICTY T. Ch. II, 14 January 2000, para. 591.

[51] An alternative description of customary international law dispenses with the need for *opinio iuris*, relying on the constant and uniform practice of States (Maurice Mendelson, 'The Formation of Customary Law' (1998) 272 *Hague Recueil* 159).

[52] E.g. para. 3(g) of the Definition on Aggression in GA Res. 3314(XXIX) of 14 December 1974; see section 13.2.3; and see Mendelson, 'The Formation of Customary Law', Chapter 5.

international criminal law has sometimes been criticized on the basis that it may be too vague to found criminal liability[53] or, even, that no law that is unwritten should suffice to found criminal liability. These claims will be discussed below at section 1.5.1 in relation to the principle of *nullum crimen sine lege*. Suffice it to say for the moment that this was not the position of the Nuremberg or Tokyo Tribunals, nor is it that of the ad hoc Tribunals.[54] Indeed, the President of the ICTY, Theodor Meron, has argued that 'customary international law now comes up in almost every international court and tribunal. [But] … it is in the international criminal tribunals … that the jurisprudence on customary law has been most rich'.[55] There is little question that the ICTY, in particular, has used customary law in an innovative fashion, to develop international criminal law in areas where its application was unclear or uncertain, and perhaps unforeseen.[56]

1.3.3 General principles of law and subsidiary means of determining the law

The ICTY has resorted to general principles of law to assist it in its search for applicable rules of international law.[57] Indeed, the Secretary-General's report that accompanied the creation of the ICTY expressly foresaw such a reliance, at least in the context of applicable defences.[58] Still, owing to the differences between international trials and trials at the national level, the ICTY has been chary of uncritical reliance on general principles taken from domestic legal systems and acontextual application of them to international trials.[59] That said, the ICTY and ICTR have both resorted to national laws to assist them in determining the relevant international law through this source. As was said in the *Furundžija* decision, however, care must be taken when using such legislation, not to look simply to one of the major legal systems of the world, as 'international courts must draw upon the general concepts and legal institutions common to all the major legal systems of the world'.[60] In relation to criminal law, general principles of law are not ideal. After all, they are, by their nature, general, and thus tend to be a last resort. Also, as the *Erdemović* case showed, at times there simply is no general principle to apply.[61] As regards the ICC, it is to apply, where the first two categories of law do not provide an answer:

---

[53] Vladimir Djuro-Degan, 'On the Sources of International Criminal Law' (2005) 4 *Chinese Journal of International Law* 45, 67. See also Olásolo, 'A Note', 301.

[54] For comments on custom before the ICTY, see Mary Fan, 'Custom and General Principles and the Great Architect Cassese' (2012) 10 *Journal of International Criminal Justice* 1063; Robert Cryer, 'International Criminal Tribunals and the Sources of International Law: Antonio Cassese's Contribution to the Canon' (2012) 10 *Journal of International Criminal Justice* 1045.

[55] Theodor Meron, *The Making of International Criminal Justice: A View from the Bench* (Oxford, 2011) 29.

[56] See generally Shane Darcy and Joseph Powderly (eds.), *Judicial Creativity at the International Criminal Tribunals* (Oxford, 2010); Beth van Schaak, 'Crimen Sine Lege: Judicial Lawmaking at the Intersection of Law and Morals' (2008) 97 *Georgetown Law Journal* 119; William Schabas, 'Customary Law or "Judge Made" Law: Judicial Creativity at the UN Criminal Tribunals' in José Doria, Hans-Peter Gasser and M. Cherif Bassiouni (eds.), *The Legal Regime of the International Criminal Court: Essays in Honour of Igor Blischenko* (Leiden, 2009) 77.

[57] See Fabián Raimondo, *General Principles of Law in the Decisions of International Criminal Courts and Tribunals* (The Hague, 2008).

[58] Report of the Secretary-General Pursuant to Paragraph 2 of Security Council Resolution 808, 3 May 1993, para. 58. See Shahabuddeen, *International Criminal Justice*, 54–5.

[59] *Erdemović*, ICTY A. Ch., 7 October 1997, Separate and Dissenting Opinion of President Cassese, para. 5.

[60] *Furundžija*, ICTY T. Ch. II, 10 December 1998, para. 178.

[61] *Erdemović*, ICTY A. Ch., 7 October 1997, Opinion of Judges McDonald and Vohrah, paras. 56–72.

general principles of law derived by the Court from national laws of legal systems of the world including, as appropriate, the national laws of States that would normally exercise jurisdiction over the crime, provided that those principles are not inconsistent with [the] Statute and with international law and internationally recognized norms and standards.[62]

The ICC may also apply 'principles and rules of law as interpreted in its previous decisions'.[63] The ICC is not, however, bound by its previous decisions; it has no equivalent to the common law principle of *stare decisis*. The ICTY has frequently had recourse to judicial decisions for determining issues of law, and has constructed a system of precedents for dealing with its own jurisprudence.[64] There has been considerable reliance on each other's case law between the ad hoc Tribunals, and the ICC has at times relied upon their jurisprudence too.[65] When looking at the work of the ad hoc Tribunals, however, it is important to bear in mind that their approach is, to some extent, reliant on the interpretation of their own foundational documents, rather than always making general statements on international law, and there are differences in approach between the Courts and the ad hoc Tribunals.[66]

The ICTY and ICTR have made reference to domestic, as well as international, case law.[67] Domestic case law is a major material source of evidence about international criminal law. However, a caveat must be entered in this regard. The assertions of international law in domestic cases can be affected by local idiosyncrasies. These can arise from the domestic statutes that are being evaluated or applied, or from a court seeing international criminal law through a distinctly national lens.[68]

Finally, although the writings of scholars are not, in themselves, sources of international criminal law, it is possible to have recourse to the views of scholars, which, at times, have been highly influential.[69] However, care must always be taken to ensure that the statements relied on are accurate statements of the law as it stands, rather than a statement of how the author would like the law to be; this is important, not least because of the *nullum crimen sine lege* principle.[70] Also, selection of scholars from only one, or a limited set of, legal tradition(s) can lead to a skewed view of what an inclusive approach to international criminal law would require.

---

[62] Art. 21(1)(c) of the ICC Statute. This and all other sources of law available to the ICC are qualified by Art. 21(3) which requires application and interpretation of the law to be consistent with internationally recognized human rights, and without adverse discrimination.

[63] *Ibid.*, Art. 21(2).

[64] *Aleksovski*, ICTY A. Ch., 24 March 2000, paras. 89–115. See Robert Cryer, 'Neither Here Nor There? The Status of International Criminal Jurisprudence in the International and UK Legal Orders' in Michael Bohlander and Kaiyan Kaikobad (eds.), *Law, Perspectives on Legal Order and Justice – Essays in Honour of Colin Warbrick* (Leiden, 2010) 155.

[65] Gilbert Bitti, 'Article 21 of the Statute of the International Criminal Court and the Treatment of Sources of Law in the Jurisprudence of the ICC' in Stahn and Sluiter, *Emerging Practice*; Volker Nehrlich 'The Status of ICTY and ICTR Precedent in Proceedings before the ICC' in *ibid.*, 305.

[66] See e.g. *Taylor*, SCSL A. Ch., 26 September 2013, paras. 472–80. On the issues that may arise with respect to the application of different forms of international criminal law, see Elies van Sliedregt, 'Pluralism in International Criminal Law' (2012) 25 *Leiden Journal of International Law* 847.

[67] See e.g. *Tadić*, ICTY A. Ch., 15 July 1999, paras. 255–70.

[68] See Leila Sadat Wexler, 'The Interpretation of the Nuremberg Principles by the French Court of Cassation: From Touvier to Barbie and Back Again' (1994) 32 *Columbia Journal of International Law* 289.

[69] E.g. *Krstić*, ICTY A. Ch., 19 April 2004, para. 10; *Stakić*, ICTY T. Ch. II, 31 July 2003, para. 519; *Katanga and Ngudjolo Chui*, ICC PTC, 30 September 2008, paras. 482, 485, 501.

[70] See section 1.5.1.

1.4   International criminal law and other areas of law

International criminal law relates to other areas of international law. The three areas for which an understanding is the most important are human rights law, international humanitarian law and the law relating to State responsibility.

1.4.1   International criminal law and human rights law

The development of crimes against humanity and the law of human rights was partially inspired by a wish to ensure that the atrocities that characterized Nazi Germany were not repeated. Thus, the modern law of human rights and a considerable part of international criminal law have a common base.[71] More recent developments in the enforcement of international criminal law, in particular the creation of the two ad hoc Tribunals, were introduced in response to mass abuses of human rights by States against their own citizens or others within their territory. Hence, parts of international criminal law have developed in this context to respond to egregious violations of human rights in the absence of effective alternative mechanisms for enforcing the most basic of humanitarian standards. Recently, international human rights bodies have taken a greater interest in international criminal law and its enforcement under their mandates;[72] such developments raise issues of coordination of their roles.[73]

Human rights obligations are imposed primarily on States, and it is frequently State agents who are the transgressors; where States are not implementing their human rights obligations, the principles of international criminal law are a useful and necessary alternative to State responsibility. The similarities in the objectives of both bodies of law are clear; both seek to provide a minimum standard of humane treatment. Both, unlike most other branches of international law, have a direct impact on individuals, albeit in somewhat different ways.

The Nuremberg International Military Tribunal (IMT) had an influence on the drafting of early human rights instruments.[74] Returning the compliment, the international instruments on human rights played an obvious part in the drafting of the Statutes of the two ad hoc Tribunals and in the ICC Statute.[75] And the ad hoc Tribunals have used human rights law, and decisions of international bodies applying that law, to assist them in their

---

[71] See e.g. R. Emilio Vinuesa, 'Interface, Correspondence and Convergence of Human Rights and International Humanitarian Law' (1998) 1 *Yearbook of International Humanitarian Law* 69, 70–6; William A. Schabas, 'Criminal Responsibility for Violations of Human Rights' in Janusz Symonides (ed.), *Human Rights, International Protection, Monitoring, Enforcement* (Aldershot, 2003) 281.

[72] See Alexandra Huneeus, 'International Criminal Law by Other Means:The Quasi-Criminal Jurisdiction of the Human Rights Courts' (2013) 107 *American Journal of International Law* 1; William Schabas, 'Synergy or Fragmentation? International Criminal Law and the European Convention on Human Rights' (2011) 9 *Journal of International Criminal Justice* 609.

[73] Emmanuel Decaux, 'The Place of Human Rights Courts and International Criminal Courts in the International System' (2011) 9 *Journal of International Criminal Justice* 597.

[74] Schabas, 'Synergy or Fragmentation?', 609–11.

[75] See e.g. the provisions on the rights of the accused in Art. 21 of the ICTY Statute and Art. 20 of the ICTR Statute, largely reproducing Art. 14(1), (2), (3) and (5) of the International Covenant on Civil and Political Rights; the procedures in the ICC Statute are very heavily influenced by human rights instruments, but see in particular Arts. 55 and 67.

interpretation of substantive international criminal law and in establishing new procedural concepts of law. For example, the ICTY in *Kunarac* explained its past practice thus:

> Because of the paucity of precedent in the field of international humanitarian law, the Tribunal has, on many occasions, had recourse to instruments and practices developed in the field of human rights law. Because of their resemblance, in terms of goals, values and terminology, such recourse is generally a welcome and needed assistance to determine the content of customary international law in the field of humanitarian law.[76]

The ICTR (particularly at trial level) has used human rights jurisprudence on hate speech and freedom of expression to assist it in drawing the boundaries of the offences of direct and public incitement of genocide and the crime against humanity of persecution in the cases of the Rwandan radio station RTLM,[77] and the musician Simon Bikindi.[78] The crime against humanity of persecution has fairly clear overlaps with human rights law, in that it can involve serious violations of fundamental rights under international law, which do not have to be international crimes in and of themselves. These can include severe violations of socio-economic, as well as civil and political, rights.[79]

In the area of international procedural law and, in particular, the right to a fair trial, the Tribunals have been especially ready to draw from human rights law. In *Dokmanović*, for example, the ICTY affirmed that an arrest must be made 'in accordance with procedures prescribed by law', as indicated in Article 5(1) of the European Convention for the Protection of Human Rights and Fundamental Freedoms and Article 9(1) of the International Covenant on Civil and Political Rights (ICCPR).[80] In *Tadić*, the Appeals Chamber recognized that a general principle of law may have its source in human rights instruments, in that case the principle that the Tribunal had to be 'established by law'.[81] This is discussed further in section 17.1 of Chapter 17 below.

Nonetheless, although there are overlaps between human rights law and international criminal law, the terms are not synonymous, and there are dangers in treating them as being so. Almost every international crime would be a violation of human rights law, but the converse does not apply. As the ICTY has said in the context of persecutions, 'although the realm of human rights is dynamic and expansive, not every denial of a human right may constitute a crime against humanity'.[82] The use of human rights standards by the Trial Chamber in the case of the Rwandan radio station RTLM with respect to direct and public incitement to genocide was upheld by the Appeals Chamber, but on the basis that the Trial Chamber was careful to distinguish hate speech, that may be a matter for human rights bodies, and that offence.[83] International criminal courts and tribunals do not exist to prosecute violations of the whole panoply of human rights. Further, human rights

---

[76] *Kunarac et al.*, ICTY T. Ch. II, 22 February 2001, para. 467. See Robert Cryer, 'The Interplay of Human Rights and Humanitarian Law: The Approach of the ICTY' (2009) 14 *Journal of Conflict and Security Law* 511.
[77] *Nahimana et al.*, ICTR T. Ch. I, 3 December 2003, paras. 983–1010.
[78] *Bikindi*, ICTR T. Ch. III, 2 December 2008, paras. 378–97.
[79] *Kupreškić*, ICTY T. Ch. II, 14 January 2000, paras. 608–15.
[80] See *Mrkšić et al.*, ICTY T. Ch. II, 22 October 1997, paras. 59–60.   [81] *Tadić*, ICTY A. Ch., 2 October 1995, paras. 42–7.
[82] *Kupreškić*, ICTY T. Ch. II, 14 January 2000, para. 618, see section 11.3.9.
[83] *Nahimana et al.* (the '*RTLM* Appeal'), ICTR A. Ch., 28 November 2007, paras. 692–6, 972–88 (although they were more

obligations are primarily imposed upon States, not individuals, and it is for States to decide how they will enforce them on their own agents; except in the case of the most serious abuses, this will not necessarily be by criminalizing the activity concerned. Finally, whereas human rights norms may be given a broad and liberal interpretation in order to achieve their objects and purposes, in international criminal law there are countervailing rights of suspects that are protected through principles requiring that the law be strictly construed and that ambiguity be resolved in favour of the accused.[84] As has been said elsewhere,

> The assumptions of human rights and humanitarian lawyers can also distort ICL [international criminal law] reasoning though substantive and structural conflation. Many of the prohibitions of ICL are drawn from, and similar to, prohibitions in human rights and humanitarian law. Faced with familiar-looking provisions, ICL practitioners often assume that the ICL norms are coextensive with their human rights or humanitarian law counterparts, and uncritically transplant concepts and jurisprudence from other domains to flesh out their content. Such assumptions overlook the fact that these bodies of law have different purposes and consequences and thus entail different philosophical commitments.[85]

As the case law of the two Tribunals and the ICC has grown, there is less of a need for these courts to have recourse to human rights jurisprudence to supplement the sources of international criminal law directly. Such a development ought not to be taken to be evidence of the fragmentation of international law, as it may also be evidence of appropriate contextual interpretation of both areas of law, which operate in harmony, rather than being unified in their roles. Furthermore, the influence of human rights law on international criminal law cannot be ignored or denied.[86] Article 21(3) of the ICC Statute, which has been described by one Judge of the ICC Appeals Chamber as being 'a fundamental provision of the Statute, in fact a cornerstone for both its application and interpretation',[87] requires that 'the application and interpretation of law pursuant to this article must be consistent with internationally recognised human rights', means this role is unlikely to end, especially, although not only, in procedural law. The practice of the ICC to date bears this out.[88]

1.4.2   International criminal law and international humanitarian law

International criminal law also shares common roots with international humanitarian law, the body of law designed to protect victims of armed conflict. Large areas of international humanitarian law are now criminalized as war crimes. Thus, international humanitarian law

---

circumspect on crimes against humanity of persecution). See also Partially Dissenting Opinion of Judge Shahabuddeen, paras. 18 *et seq*. However, see also the Partially Dissenting Opinion of Judge Meron, paras. 3–20, in relation to crimes against humanity of persecution.

[84] See e.g. Darryl Robinson, 'The Identity Crisis of International Criminal Law' (2008) 21 *Leiden Journal of International Law* 925; Allison Marston Danner and Jenny Martinez, 'Guilty Associations: Joint Criminal Enterprise, Command Responsibility and the Development of International Criminal Law' (2005) 93 *California Law Review* 75; *RTLM* Appeal, Partially Dissenting Opinion of Judge Meron, para. 8.

[85] Robinson, 'Identity Crisis', 946, although see also Hans-Peter Gasser, 'The Changing Relationship between International Criminal Law, Human Rights Law and Humanitarian Law' in Doria, *Legal Regime*, 1111, 1117.

[86] See e.g. Olivier de Frouville, 'The Influence of the European Court of Human Rights' Case Law on International Criminal Law of Torture and Inhuman or Degrading Treatment' (2011) 9 *Journal of International Criminal Justice* 633.

[87] Georghios M. Pikis, *The Rome Statute for the International Criminal Court* (Leiden, 2010) 89.

[88] See section 17.3. See also William Schabas, *The International Criminal Court: A Commentary on the Rome Statute* (Oxford, 2010) 397–400.

serves as a point of reference in understanding and interpreting the corresponding war crimes provisions. As with human rights norms, care must be taken before transposing all humanitarian law standards directly into international criminal law; the latter has distinct principles of interpretation. These issues are discussed further in Chapter 12. At this juncture, though, it is worth mentioning that there is a synergistic relationship between humanitarian law and international criminal law, especially the law of war crimes. Developments in humanitarian law are reflected in the law of war crimes but, especially when it comes to the customary law of armed conflict, decisions of international criminal tribunals also sometimes feed back into humanitarian law.[89] The 'humanization' of human-itarian law[90] has been assisted, if not driven, through the work of the ICTY in particular.[91]

1.4.3   International criminal law and State responsibility

International criminal law in the sense in which we use it concerns the criminal responsi-bility of individuals, not States.[92] The responsibility of a State under international law is a matter for a separate branch of international law, and is not dependent upon the legal responsibility of an individual. If an agent of a State is convicted of an international crime, the act in question may, depending upon the circumstances, be attributable to the State, in which case that State may also be internationally responsible.[93] The same act therefore can give rise to both individual criminal responsibility and State responsibility.[94] The important question is one of attributability of the conduct of the individual to the State. For aggression, this link is provided for in the definition of the crime, but it is not always so for other international crimes. Where the conduct of the individual *is* attributable to the State, the two responsibilities run in parallel. For example, an agent of Libya was convicted of (transnational) offences in relation to the aircraft explosion over Lockerbie in 1988, and the governments of the United Kingdom and the United States separately made claims for compensation from Libya.[95]

The question of State responsibility for international crimes was dealt with directly in the *Bosnian Genocide* case where, having determined that genocide had occurred in Srebrenica,

---

[89] See e.g. Robert Cryer, 'Of Custom, Treaties, Scholars and the Gavel: The Impact of the International Criminal Tribunals on the ICRC Customary Study' (2006) 11 *Journal of Conflict and Security Law* 239.

[90] Theodor Meron, 'The Humanization of Humanitarian Law' (2000) 94 *American Journal of International Law* 239.

[91] Tamás Hoffmann, 'The Gentle Civilizer of Humanitarian Law, Antonio Cassese and the Creation of the Customary Law of Non-International Armed Conflicts', in Carsten Stahn and Larissa van den Herik (eds.), *Future Perspectives on International Criminal Justice* (The Hague, 2010) 58.

[92] See generally André Nollkaemper, 'Concurrence between Individual Responsibility and State Responsibility in International Law' (2003) 52 *International and Comparative Law Quarterly* 615; Andrea Bianchi, 'State Responsibility and Criminal Liability of Individuals' in Cassese (ed.), *The Oxford Companion*, 16; Beatrice Bonafè, *The Relationship between State and Individual Responsibility for International Crimes* (Leiden, 2009).

[93] *Case Concerning the Application of the Convention on the Prevention and Punishment of the Crime of Genocide (Bosnia and Herzegovina v. Serbia and Montenegro)* (the '*Bosnian Genocide*' case), 26 February 2007, paras. 377–415. See generally Marko Milanović, 'State Responsibility for Genocide – A Follow-Up' (2007) 18 *European Journal of International Law* 669. For a critique see Paola Gaeta, 'On What Conditions Can a State Be Held Responsible for Genocide?' (2007) 18 *European Journal of International Law* 631; Antonio Cassese, 'On the Use of Criminal Law Notions in Determining State Responsibility for Genocide' (2007) 5 *Journal of International Criminal Justice* 875; Paola Gaeta, *The UN Genocide Convention: A Commentary* (Oxford, 2009) Part V.

[94] E.g. *Furundžija*, ICTY T. Ch. II, 10 December 1998, para. 142.   [95] See section 9.5.

the International Court of Justice (ICJ) decided that Serbia was not responsible for the perpetrators of that crime. Controversially, it rejected the standard for attributability of conduct to a State used by the ICTY, asserting that the relevant test may not always be the same between international criminal law and general international law.[96] However, given the State's relationship with the perpetrators, the ICJ determined that Serbia was separately responsible under Article I of the Genocide Convention for its own failures to prevent and punish that crime.[97]

The question of whether acts of a State can be categorized under international law as *criminal* acts is one which has caused controversy. The draft Articles on State responsibility prepared by the International Law Commission (ILC) in 1976 used the term 'international crime' to refer to an internationally wrongful act by a State which results from the breach by that State of an international obligation so essential for the protection of fundamental interests of the international community that its breach is recognized as a crime.[98] But there were objections to the concept of criminal responsibility, many being based on the nature of the State. It is difficult, although not completely impossible, to apply elements of criminal liability such as *mens rea* to States. There is also the problem of punishment. In practice, no international court or tribunal has ever provided for punishment of States different in kind from the law concerning tortious or delictual wrongs of a State. Also, States were not generally supportive of the concept of State criminal responsibility. The final version of the ILC's draft Articles on State responsibility no longer uses the concept of State crime, but characterizes the relevant acts as 'serious breaches of obligations under peremptory norms of general international law'.[99]

1.5   A body of criminal law

The two bodies of law that make up international criminal law (international law and criminal law) are compatible, although the relationship between the two can be fractious. International criminal law should be appraised from the standpoints of both bodies of law. Its sources are those of international law, but its consequences are penal.[100] As a body of international law, it requires an understanding of the sources and interpretation of international law. But it is also criminal law and as such needs substantive provisions that are clear and exact rather than the often more imprecise formulations of international law.[101] Further, the relevant international courts and tribunals require methods and procedures proper to a

---

[96] *Bosnian Genocide* case, para. 405. See e.g. Antonio Cassese, 'The Nicaragua and Tadić Tests Revisited in the Light of the ICJ Judgment on Genocide in Bosnia' (2007) 18 *European Journal of International Law* 649; Marina Spinedi, 'On the Non–Attribution of the Bosnian Serbs' Conduct to Serbia' (2007) 5 *Journal of International Criminal Justice* 829.

[97] *Bosnian Genocide* case, paras. 425–50.   [98] Art. 19.2 of the 1976 draft Articles.

[99] Arts. 40 and 41 of the draft Articles on Responsibility of States for Internationally Wrongful Acts (A/CN.4/L.602/Rev.1) (1976). See James Crawford, *State Responsibility* (Cambridge, 2013) 390–4.

[100] See e.g. Cassese, *International Criminal Law*, 5–9. On the nature of criminal law, see Glanville Williams, 'The Definition of Crime'.

[101] For a discussion of this, and a critique of the lack of attention paid by international criminal lawyers to this aspect of international criminal law, see George P. Fletcher, *The Grammar of Criminal Law, American, Comparative and International*, Vol. 1, Foundations (Oxford, 2007).

criminal court, with due regard to the rights of the accused at all stages of the investigation and court procedures. At a more abstract level, philosophical analyses of the appropriate ambit of criminal liability ought to be borne in mind whenever international crimes or their principles of liability are being appraised.[102]

Certain fundamental principles of national criminal law systems have now become entrenched in international law, and more particularly in human rights law. As we saw in section 1.4.1, international criminal law has been strongly influenced by human rights law. One aspect of human rights law with a close analogue in criminal law theory is the prohibition of retroactive criminal prohibitions and penalties (sometimes referred to together as the principle of legality or *nullum crimen, nulla poena, sine lege*).[103] As shown below, this principle is important both in the application of the law and in the drafting of the instruments of the international courts and tribunals. Owing to the relative imprecision of the nature and content of international law, the principle has greater prominence in international than in national courts.

1.5.1 *Nullum crimen sine lege*

The principle of *nullum crimen sine lege* has two aspects, non-retroactivity and clarity of the law, both of which seek to ensure that the law is reasonably publicized, so people can know whether their planned course of action is acceptable or not.[104] It is a fundamental principle of criminal law that criminal responsibility can only be based on a pre-existing prohibition of conduct that is understood to have criminal consequences. Article 15 of the ICCPR states that:

No one shall be held guilty on account of any act or omission which did not constitute a criminal offence, under national or international law, at the time when it was committed . . . Nothing in this article shall prejudice the trial of any person for any act or omission which, at the time it was committed, was criminal according to the general principles of law recognised by the community of nations.[105]

Claims that prosecutions for international crimes violated this principle predate the ICCPR. The Nuremberg and Tokyo IMTs both faced claims that prosecution of crimes against peace involved violations of the *nullum crimen* principle. The Nuremberg IMT, with which the Tokyo IMT agreed, responded by asserting that crimes against peace were already criminalized in international law[106] and that, anyway:

The maxim *nullum crimen sine lege* is not a limitation of sovereignty, but is in general a principle of justice. To assert that it is unjust to punish those who in defiance of treaties and assurances have attacked neighbouring States without warning is obviously untrue, for in such circumstances the

---

[102] For useful examples, see e.g. Mirjan Damaška, 'The Shadow Side of Command Responsibility' (2001) 49 *American Journal of Comparative Law* 455; Claus Kreß, 'The Crime of Genocide under International Law' (2006) 6 *International Criminal Law Review* 461. See further section 1.6.2 and Ambos, *Treatise*, 55.
[103] See generally A. P. Simester, J. Spencer, G. R. Sullivan and G. Virgo, *Simester and Sullivan's Criminal Law: Theory and Doctrine*, 5th edn (Oxford, 2012) Chapter 1.
[104] See generally Kenneth Gallant, *The Principle of Legality in International and Comparative Law* (Cambridge, 2009); Claus Kreß, 'Nulla Poena Nullum Crimen Sine Lege' in Rüdiger Wolfrum (ed.), *Max Planck Encyclopaedia of Public International Law* (Oxford, 2012) Vol. VII, 889.
[105] Art. 15 of the ICCPR.   [106] See section 13.1.2.

attacker must know that he is doing wrong, and so far from it being unjust to punish him, it would be unjust if his wrong was allowed to go unpunished.[107]

At the time, which was before the modern law of human rights, the Nuremberg IMT may have been correct about the law on point.[108] On the other hand, it is possible that the prohibition of retroactive criminal laws was a general principle of law by then,[109] and the *ex post facto* nature of liability for crimes against peace has been used to criticize the Nuremberg and Tokyo IMTs.[110]

When drafting the Statute of the ICTY, the UN Secretary-General was sensitive to such critiques, stating that:

The application of the principle of *nullum crimen sine lege* requires that the international tribunal should apply rules of international humanitarian law which are beyond any doubt part of customary law so that the problem of adherence of some but not all States to specific conventions does not arise. This would appear to be particularly important in the context of an international tribunal prosecuting persons responsible for serious violations of international humanitarian law.[111]

This statement emphasizes the fact that, if a rule reflects customary law, it will not be necessary for the relevant court to establish whether the parties to the conflict were parties to the relevant treaty. But it is misleading in its formulation. The important issue from the perspective of the *nullum crimen* principle is whether the treaty was applicable to the relevant armed conflict, not whether it reflected customary international law. There is nothing in the *nullum crimen* principle in general or in Article 15 of the ICCPR[112] that requires that any particular source of international law provide the prohibition.[113]

Suggestions that customary international law does not suffice to found criminal liability[114] are based on a strict construction of the *nullum crimen* principle (*nullum crimen sine lege scripta*),[115] which, whilst applicable in some domestic legal orders, is not the principle applicable in international law.[116] There is no reason in principle why customary international law cannot be used to form the relevant criminal law[117] and the ICTY has consistently taken this view.[118]

The general practice of the ICTY has been to adopt a fairly relaxed standard to the *nullum crimen* principle.[119] However, looking at the aspect of the principle that requires criminal laws to be sufficiently clear, in the *Vasiljević* case, a Trial Chamber asserted that:

---

[107] Nuremberg IMT, Judgment and Sentences, reprinted in (1947) 41 *American Journal of International Law* 172, 217.
[108] Although the versions of the Nuremberg judgment in different languages are not consistent on what precisely was meant here, see Guido Acquiva, 'At the Origins of Crimes against Humanity: Clues to a Proper Understanding of the Nullum Crimen Principle in the Nuremberg Judgment' (2011) 9 *Journal of International Criminal Justice* 881.
[109] See Gordon Ireland, 'Ex Post Facto from Rome to Tokyo' (1946) 21 *Temple Law Quarterly* 27; *contra* Susan Lamb, 'Nullum Crimen, Nulla Poena Sine Lege in International Criminal Law' in Cassese, *Commentary*, 733, 740.
[110] See section 6.3.2 and section 6.4.2.
[111] Report of the Secretary-General Pursuant to Paragraph 2 of Security Council Resolution 808, UN Doc. S/25704, para. 34.
[112] Nor in the ECHR, Art. 7.
[113] Machteld Boot, *Genocide, Crimes against Humanity, War Crimes: Nullum Crimen Sine Lege and the Subject-Matter Jurisdiction of the International Criminal Court* (Antwerp, 2002) 127–87.
[114] Djuro-Degan, 'On the Sources of International Criminal Law', 67; and see Olásolo, 'A Note', 301.
[115] 'No crime without written law.'   [116] Alain Pellet, 'Applicable Law' in Cassese, *Commentary*, 1051, 1057–8.
[117] *Ibid.*   [118] See e.g. *Tadić*, ICTY A. Ch., 2 October 1995, para. 94.
[119] William Schabas, *The UN International Criminal Tribunals: The Former Yugoslavia, Rwanda and Sierra Leone* (Cambridge, 2006) 63–7.

From the perspective of the *nullum crimen sine lege* principle, it would be wholly unacceptable for a Trial Chamber to convict an accused person on the basis of a prohibition which, taking into account the specificity of customary international law and allowing for the gradual clarification of the rules of criminal law is either insufficiently precise to determine conduct and distinguish the criminal from the permissible, or was not sufficiently accessible at the relevant time. A criminal conviction should indeed never be based upon a norm which an accused could not reasonably have been aware of at the time of his acts, and this norm must make it sufficiently clear what act or omission could engage his criminal responsibility.[120]

Owing to their view that customary law did not provide a definition of the offence of 'violence to life and person' that was clear enough, the Chamber refused to convict the defendant of that charge.[121] It is true that excessively vague offences can violate the *nullum crimen* principle, but it is questionable whether, in this particular case, the Tribunal's finding that the international law on the subject was excessively vague was correct.[122] This is particularly the case as clarification of the ambit of offences through case law does not inherently fall foul of the *nullum crimen* principle.[123] Judicial creation of crimes, which some have claimed the ICTY has done,[124] would. It must be said, however, that, when human rights courts have come to deal with the question of international crimes and the *nullum crimen* principle, they have generally been generous when appraising a State's prosecutions of international crimes.[125] For example, in the *Jorgić* case,[126] the European Court of Human Rights was willing to accept convictions in Germany for genocide on a broader interpretation of that crime than was later adopted by the ad hoc Tribunals, on the basis that it was at least arguable at the time of the conviction that the German courts' interpretation was correct.

The *nullum crimen* principle played an important role in the drafting of the ICC Statute. The ILC draft Statute with which the negotiations for the ICC Statute began[127] did not contain definitions of the crimes within the jurisdiction of the ICC, the ILC maintaining that the Statute should be 'primarily an adjectival and procedural instrument'.[128] There was soon, however, a move to define the crimes in the Statute with the clarity and precision needed for criminal law, and it was pursuant to that objective that the definitions of crimes and, later, the elements of crimes were set out. The wish of the negotiating States to ensure

---

[120] *Vasiljević*, ICTY T. Ch. I, 29 November 2002, para. 193.   [121] *Ibid.*, paras. 203–4.
[122] See Antonio Cassese, 'Black Letter Lawyering vs Constructive Interpretation: The Vasiljević Case' (2004) 2 *Journal of International Criminal Justice* 265.
[123] See Mohamed Shahabuddeen, 'Does the Principle of Legality Stand in the Way of Progressive Development of the Law?' (2004) 2 *Journal of International Criminal Justice* 1007; Ben Emmerson and Andrew Ashworth, *Human Rights and Criminal Justice* (London, 2001) 281–92.
[124] Mettraux, *International Crimes*, 13–18. The line between clarification and creation can be a fine one: see Joseph Powderly, 'Distinguishing Creativity from Activism: International Criminal Law and the 'Legitimacy' of Judicial Development of the Law' in Schabas, *The Ashgate Research Companion*, 223.
[125] For a (legally flawed) exception, see *Habré v. Republique de Senegal*, ECOWAS Court of Justice, 18 November 2010; for critique, see Valentine Spiga, 'Non-Retroactivity of Criminal Law: A New Chapter in the Hissène Habré Saga' (2011) 9 *Journal of International Criminal Justice* 5.
[126] *Jorgić* v. Germany, ECtHR, 12 July 2007, paras. 89–116.   [127] See section 8.2.
[128] Report of the International Law Commission on the work of its forty-sixth session, GAOR 49th Session Supp. No. 10, A/49/10 (1994) at 71.

that they knew exactly what they were signing up to may have been at least as strong a motivating factor as the principle of *nullum crimen* in this regard.

The Statute itself contains a strong restatement of the *nullum crimen* principle. Article 22 reads in part:[129]

1. A person shall not be criminally responsible under this Statute unless the conduct in question constitutes, at the time it takes place, a crime within the jurisdiction of the Court.
2. The definition of a crime shall be strictly construed and shall not be extended by analogy. In the case of ambiguity, the definition shall be interpreted in favour of the person being investigated, prosecuted or convicted.

The first sentence of the second paragraph was intended, rightly or wrongly, to prevent the ICC from engaging in expansions of criminal liability not mandated by the States Parties.

1.5.2   *Nulla poena sine lege*

This, related, principle requires that there are defined penalties attached to criminal prohibitions.[130] In customary law, the punishment for international crimes may include the death penalty[131] although many States have undertaken international obligations not to impose such a penalty, or may not permit that sentence in their domestic law.

It appears that concerns about the *nulla poena* principle also caused the Secretary-General, when drafting the ICTY Statute, to require the Tribunal to 'have recourse to the general practice regarding prison sentences in the Courts of the former Yugoslavia'.[132] The ICTR Statute has a similar provision, but with reference to Rwandan sentencing practices.[133] The fact that both States provided for the death penalty at the time of the offences, but the Tribunal cannot impose that sentence, has made this difficult to apply. The ICC Statute also contains an Article entitled 'Nulla poena sine lege' (Article 23). This states, uncontroversially: 'A person convicted by the Court may be punished only in accordance with this Statute.'[134] More generally, the principle in human rights law is more relaxed than the strict interpretation adopted by many civil law States, that require that specific provisions on sentencing are provided for all offences.[135]

1.6   International criminal law and philosophy

Perhaps as a testament to its maturity as an intellectual discipline, international criminal law is now an area of law that has become increasingly theorized.[136] Work has come from

---

[129] On which, see Bruce Broomhall, 'Article 22' in Triffterer, *Observers' Notes*, 713.
[130] See Chapter 19 and Kai Ambos, 'Nulla Poena Sine Lege in International Criminal Law' in Roelof Haveman and Olaoluwa Olusanya (eds.), *Sentencing and Sanctioning in International Criminal Law* (Antwerp, 2006) 17.
[131] *Klinge*, III Law Reports of Trials of War Criminals I at 3. See section 19.1.
[132] Art. 24 of the ICTY Statute; Lamb, 'Nullum Crimen', 758–9.   [133] Art. 23 of the ICTR Statute.
[134] See William Schabas, 'Article 23' in Triffterer, *Observers' Notes*, 730.   [135] Kreß, 'Nullum Poena', 898.
[136] For an overview, see Robert Cryer, 'The Philosophy of International Criminal Law' in Alexander Orakhelashvili (ed.), *Research Handbook on the History and Philosophy of International Law* (Cheltenham, 2012) 232. See also Larry May and Zachary Hoskins (eds.), *International Criminal Law and Philosophy* (Cambridge, 2010).

theoreticians of international law and criminal law, as well as from philosophers more generally.[137] Express theorization of international criminal law began, for the most part, in the era of the Nuremberg IMT. Two of the intellectual architects of that Tribunal, Quincy Wright and Sir Hersch Lauterpacht, both relied, to a greater or lesser extent, on natural law to justify the innovations in law that the Nuremberg IMT's Charter and judgment embodied.[138] Critics of the Tribunal tended to focus on arguments based on legal positivism to query the judgment, or the more general idea that international law could deal with individuals.[139] These critics tended, however, not to make their jurisprudential leanings clear. In the Tokyo IMT, the prosecution, defence and some of the judges relied expressly on philosophy, be it naturalistic or positivistic, in the formulation of their arguments and opinions, and the criticisms that each made of the other often fell upon these lines.[140] The practice of the more recent criminal tribunals can also be read through the lenses of disagreements along natural law and positivist approaches to international criminal law.[141]

Since the revival of international criminal law as an important area of international law from the early 1990s, philosophers of law have contributed considerably to the debates that have arisen. The philosophical approaches to international criminal law can be broadly separated into three 'fuzzy sets'. There are those that come from theories of international law, those that come from criminal law, and those that specifically relate to creating a philosophy of international criminal law. Many scholars would bristle at being 'pigeon-holed' in such a manner, and there are considerable overlaps between the approaches covered here.

1.6.1   *International criminal law and the philosophy of international law*

To look first to the theories of international criminal law that come from international law, even after the Nuremberg and Tokyo IMTs there have been those that, from an expressly positivist position, are heavily sceptical of the possibility that, structurally, international law can have a criminal side.[142] Such approaches, especially since the creation of the International Criminal Court, are now subject to critique on the basis that States have accepted that such a development has indeed occurred. There is nothing inherently contradictory between a positivist approach to law and accepting that entities other than States can be bearers of rights and responsibilities in international law. The point of positivism is that law is that which is 'posited' by a law-creating agency rather than inherent in nature. In international law, the main law-creating agents are States, and they have accepted the

---

[137] It is beyond the remit of this work to explain the intellectual backdrops to the various theories of law. For a primer, see Brian Bix, *Jurisprudence: Theory and Context*, 6th edn (London, 2012).

[138] Quincy Wright, 'Legal Positivism and the Nuremberg Judgment' (1948) 42 *American Journal of International Law* 405; Hersch Lauterpacht, 'The Law of Nations and the Punishment of War Crimes' (1944) 21 *British Yearbook of International Law* 58. See also Lord Wright, 'War Crimes under International Law' (1946) 62 *Law Quarterly Review* 40.

[139] Hans Ehard, 'The Nuremberg Trial against the Major War Criminals and International Law' (1947) 41 *American Journal of International Law* 37.

[140] See Neil Boister and Robert Cryer, *The Tokyo International Military Tribunal: A Reappraisal* (Oxford, 2008) Chapter 9.

[141] For an attempt at such a reading, see Cryer, 'Philosophy', 233–58. See also Cryer, 'International Criminal Tribunals'.

[142] Alfred Rubin, *Ethics and Authority in International Law* (Cambridge, 2007).

international criminal responsibility of individuals. In other words, States get the international law they want, and they have decided to create international criminal law. That, for positivists, ought to settle the question. The idea that the nature of the international legal order can trump this is a position that would find itself a more comfortable home in natural law, but natural lawyers have not made that argument. On the other hand, there is no question that the international legal order is one in which criminal law sits uncomfortably, the ICC Statute itself being an example of this tension.[143] These difficulties are practical, as well as philosophical.

International legal theorists have reflected upon international criminal law from various perspectives,[144] particularly from external perspectives such as critical legal studies, feminism and Third World Approaches to International Law (TWAIL). Critical scholars have queried the idea that there are clear rules of international criminal law, and investigated the extent to which the creation, application, and interpretation of international criminal law, in all its phases, reflects subjective premises, rather than coherent intellectual premises.[145] Others writing in this tradition have queried the extent to which international criminal law can balance its liberal ideals and the desire to engage in show trials.[146] Such critics tend not, however, to advocate the abolition of international criminal law, but self-reflection on the part of its participants, and a questioning of faith in its inherently 'progressive' nature.[147]

Turning to positions that relate to critical legal studies, feminist scholars have focused in particular on how sexual and gender-based crimes have not, at least until recently, received sufficient attention.[148] Other work from a gender perspective has shown how stereotypes and myths about masculinity have affected prosecution of sexual offences against men.[149] TWAIL, as an approach to international criminal law, has something of a pedigree, being traceable at least as far back as Judge Pal's famous dissent in the Tokyo IMT.[150] More recently, work based in TWAIL has spoken of the biased nature of international criminal law and its sources, which marginalize the interests of those in the Third World.[151] Critiques of the ICC and its practice in Africa have also come from TWAIL perspectives,[152] although

---

[143] Leila Sadat and Richard Carden, 'The New International Criminal Court: An Uneasy Revolution' (2000) 88 *Georgetown Law Journal* 381.

[144] The *American Journal of International Law* chose an issue of international criminal law (liability for war crimes in non-international armed conflict) for their influential Symposium on Method in International Law: (1999) 93 *American Journal of International Law* 291.

[145] E.g. Gerry Simpson, 'War Crimes: A Critical Introduction' in T. L. H. McCormack and G. J. Simpson (eds.), *The Law of War Crimes: National and International Approaches* (The Hague, 1997) 1.

[146] Martti Koskenniemi, 'Between Impunity and Show Trials' (2002) 6 *Max Planck Yearbook of United Nations Law* 1.

[147] Tor Krever, 'International Law: An Ideology Critique' (2013) 26 *Leiden Journal of International Law* 701; Immi Tallgren, 'The Sensibility and Sense of International Criminal Law' (2002) 13 *European Journal of International Law* 561.

[148] Christine Chinkin, 'Rape and Sexual Abuse of Women in International Law' (1994) 4 *European Journal of International Law* 329; Kelly Dawn Askin, *War Crimes against Women: Prosecution in International Tribunals* (The Hague, 1997). It has been argued that international criminal law has largely responded to such critiques (Noëlle Quénivet, *Sexual Offences in Armed Conflict in International Law* (New York, 2008)), but this remains controversial.

[149] Sandesh Sivakumaran, 'Sexual Violence against Men in Armed Conflict' (2007) 18 *European Journal of International Law* 253; Sandesh Sivakumaran, 'Lost in Translation: UN Responses to Sexual Violence against Men and Boys in Armed Conflict' (2010) 92 *International Review of the Red Cross* 259.

[150] See Chapter 6.

[151] Anthony Anghie and B. S. Chimni, 'Third World Approaches to International Law and Responsibility for Atrocities in International Armed Conflict' (2003) 2 *Chinese Journal of International Law* 77.

[152] Kamari Maxine Clarke, *Fictions of Justice: The International Criminal Court and the Challenge of Legal Pluralism in Sub-Saharan Africa* (Cambridge, 2009).

scholars coming from other perspectives have also questioned international criminal law's sensitivity to local cultures and ideas,[153] and sought to situate, and critique, international criminal law in a pluralistic world.[154]

Looking towards interdisciplinary work, international relations scholars, particularly those working in the constructivist tradition, have focused on the nature and functioning of international criminal courts and tribunals, and their place in the international order.[155] Others have looked at the question from the 'Grotian' or English School of international relations theory, which considers the interplay of realism and idealism in the international order,[156] the former tending to be more sceptical of international criminal law than the latter. Scholars working in the law and economics tradition have looked at the incentives that exist to obey or disobey international criminal law, to look at such issues as whether international criminal law can deter,[157] and, controversially, what the substance of international criminal law ought to be.[158]

1.6.2   *International criminal law and the philosophy of criminal law*

Economic, feminist and TWAIL approaches to international criminal law also often have comments to make on the substance of international criminal law.[159] Here, however, we are dealing with those who approach international criminal law from the point of view of the philosophy of criminal law. Such work is increasingly common in both the common law and civil law worlds. Much work has been based around explaining, justifying and critiquing international criminal law from the point of view of perspectives that draw on liberal approaches to criminal law. For example, Larry May has sought to show how genocide and crimes against humanity are legitimately criminalized at the international level owing to an international 'harm principle', which would be familiar to those working on criminalization at the domestic level.[160] Others have sought to use analogous principles, such as 'fair labelling' which requires crimes to appropriately reflect the specific harms and wrongs that it proscribes.[161] There have also been critiques on the basis that international criminal law

---

[153] José E. Alvarez, 'Crimes of States/Crimes of Hate: Lessons from Rwanda' (1999) 24 *Yale Journal of International Law* 365.
[154] Brad R. Roth 'Coming to Terms with Ruthlessness: Sovereign Equality, Global Pluralism and the Limits of International Criminal Law' (2010) 8 *Santa Clara Journal of International Law* 231.
[155] Stephen C. Roach (ed.), *Governance, Order and the International Criminal Court: Between Realpolitik and a Cosmopolitan Court* (Oxford, 2009).
[156] An excellent example is Jason Ralph, *Defending the Society of States: Why America Opposes the International Criminal Court and its Vision of World Society* (Oxford, 2009).
[157] Julian Ku and Jide Nzelibe, 'Do International Criminal Tribunals Deter or Exacerbate Humanitarian Atrocities?' (2006) 84 *Washington University Law Review* 777.
[158] Mark Osiel, *Making Sense of Mass Atrocity* (Cambridge, 2009) 10–15, 214–20.
[159] See above, and e.g. David Marcus, 'Famine Crimes in International Law' (2003) 97 *American Journal of International Law* 245.
[160] Larry May, *Crimes against Humanity: A Normative Account* (Cambridge, 2005) Chapter 5; Larry May, *Genocide: A Normative Account* (Cambridge, 2010) Chapters 4–5. See also Larry May, *War Crimes and Just War* (Cambridge, 2007); Larry May, *Aggression and Crimes against Peace* (Cambridge, 2008). For a useful primer on criminalization in criminal law theory, see Simester *et al.*, *Simester and Sullivan's Criminal Law*, Chapter 16.
[161] See e.g. Robert Cryer, 'General Principles of Liability in International Criminal Law' in Dominic McGoldrick, Peter Rowe and Eric Donnelly (eds.), *The Permanent International Criminal Court: Legal and Policy Issues* (Oxford, 2004) 233.

does not respect the principle of individual culpability, which again draw from the theory of criminal law.[162]

Theorists of criminal law influenced by civil law approaches to the theory of criminal law, in particular the *Dogmatik* approaches associated with German influenced systems of criminal law, have also contributed considerably to the theory of international criminal law.[163] Such approaches seek to provide taxonomical clarity for parts of criminal law, and deduce substantive results, and critique, from the application of fundamental principles of criminal law.[164] These approaches can be exceptionally sophisticated, and have been influential in international criminal law. However, they can also be unreflexive in their approach, insisting on theoretical purity over practical utility. In addition, as with all approaches 'read up' from national systems to the international sphere, there is a risk of applying ideas acontextually, even where, as has been the case, at the domestic level such theories have been developed with international crimes in mind.[165] As such, there have been calls for international criminal law to develop its own *Dogmatik*.[166]

1.6.3   *A separate(?) philosophy of international criminal law*

In part owing to the criticisms mentioned above about the utility of, but also the limitations of, transferring criminal law theories developed domestically to international criminal law, and the converse problem of applying theories of international law developed in a generally horizontal, State-based system to a penal system, there have been understandable calls for international criminal law to develop its own theories.[167] These, it is said, ought to reflect the collective nature of international crimes, which do not map easily to theories of criminal law developed domestically.[168] Such suggestions can overstate the differences, and approaches developed at the domestic level have the advantage of quite literally centuries of thought, which can, with sensitivity to context, inform the theory and practice of international criminal law.[169] Beyond that, however, significant work at the philosophical level on explaining why the international crimes that exist ought to be criminalized at that level, rather than simply domestically, has been undertaken.[170] Furthermore, similar work has been done by philosophers to explain and justify why and when international courts, or the

---

[162] George P. Fletcher and Jens David Ohlin, 'Reclaiming Fundamental Principles of Criminal Law in the Darfur Case' (2005) 3 *Journal of International Criminal Justice* 539; Darryl Robinson, 'How Command Responsibility Got So Complicated: A Culpability Contradiction, its Obfuscation and a Simple Solution' (2012) 13 *Melbourne Journal of International Law* 1.

[163] In this context, the term does not have the perjorative implication it may have in the English-speaking world. Roughly speaking, it means a systematic and coherent theory: see George P. Fletcher, 'The Theory of Criminal Liability and International Criminal Law' (2012) 10 *Journal of International Criminal Justice* 1029.

[164] For a recent example, see Kai Ambos, *Treatise on International Criminal Law*, Vol. I, *Foundations and General Part* (Oxford, 2013).

[165] Claus Roxin, 'Crimes as a Part of an Organized Power Structure' (2011) 9 *Journal of International Criminal Justice* 19; Thomas Wiegend, 'Perpetration through an Organization: The Unexpected Career of a German Legal Concept' (2011) 9 *Journal of International Criminal Justice* 91.

[166] Fletcher, 'Theory'.

[167] See e.g. Fletcher, 'Theory'; Darryl Robinson, 'A Cosmopolitan Liberal Account of International Criminal Law' (2013) 26 *Leiden Journal of International Law* 127.

[168] See e.g. Mark Drumbl, 'A Hard Look at the Soft Theory of International Criminal Law' in Leila N. Sadat and Michael P. Scharf (eds.), *The Theory and Practice of International Criminal Law: Essays in Honor of M. Cherif Bassiouni* (Leiden, 2010) 1.

[169] See e.g. David Luban, 'The Legacies of Nuremberg' (1987) 54 *Social Research* 779.   [170] See e.g. Ambos, *Treatise*, 57–60.

courts of States that are not directly affected third parties, have a right to punish such offences, and how this relates to the authority of a community beyond the State to define and punish crimes.[171]

Such considerations frequently implicate questions of the aims and objectives of international criminal justice, which the next chapter will discuss. This is indicative of a more general issue. Although theory in international criminal law has, in the past, tended to follow from practice, it now informs it. It would not be possible to elaborate all of the issues that arise in the abstract, but we have sought to integrate some of them throughout this book. This also underlines the fact that law, legal theory, and practice, exist in a synergistic fashion in modern international criminal law. Therefore, theoretical approaches ought to be seen as part and parcel of international criminal law rather than a distraction from its study.

Further reading

Dapo Akande, 'Sources of International Criminal Law' in Antonio Cassese *et al.* (eds.), *The Oxford Companion to International Criminal Justice* (Oxford, 2009) 41

Kai Ambos, *Treatise on International Criminal Law*, Vol. I, *Foundations and General Part* (Oxford, 2013) Chapter II

M. Cherif Bassiouni, *International Criminal Law*, 3rd edn (Leiden, 2008) Vol. I

Machteld Boot, *Genocide, Crimes against Humanity, War Crimes: Nullum Crimen Sine Lege and the Subject-Matter Jurisdiction of the International Criminal Court* (Antwerp, 2002) 127–87

Bruce Broomhall, *International Justice and the International Criminal Court: Between Sovereignty and the Rule of Law* (Oxford, 2003) Chapter 1

Antonio Cassese, 'The Influence of the European Court of Human Rights on International Criminal Tribunals: Some Methodological Remarks' in Morten Bergsmo (ed.), *Human Rights and Criminal Justice for the Downtrodden* (The Hague, 2003) Chapter II

Robert Cryer, *Prosecuting International Crimes: Selectivity and the International Criminal Law Regime* (Cambridge, 2005) Introduction, Chapters 1 and 5

Robert Cryer, 'The Philosophy of International Criminal Law' in Alexander Orakhelashvili (ed.), *Research Handbook on the History and Philosophy of International Law* (Cheltenham, 2012) 232

Vladimir Djuro-Degan, 'On the Sources of International Criminal Law' (2005) 4 *Chinese Journal of International Law* 45

George P. Fletcher, *The Grammar of Criminal Law: American, Comparative and International*, Vol. I, *Foundations* (Oxford, 2007)

Kenneth Gallant, *The Principle of Legality in International and Comparative Law* (Cambridge, 2009)

Nina H. B. Jørgensen, *The Responsibility of States for International Crimes* (Oxford, 2000)

Claus Kreß, 'International Criminal Law' in Rüdiger Wolfrum (ed.), *Max Planck Encyclopaedia of Public International Law* (Oxford, 2012) Vol. V, 717

---

[171] Alejandro Chehtman, *The Philosophical Foundations of Extraterritorial Punishment* (Oxford, 2010); Antony Duff, 'Can We Punish the Perpetrators of Atrocities?' in Thomas Brudghom and Thomas Cushman (eds.), *The Religious in Responses to Mass Atrocity* (Cambridge, 2009) 79; David Luban, 'Fairness to Rightness: Jurisdiction, Legality and the Legitimacy of International Criminal Law' in Samantha Besson and John Tasioulas (eds.), *The Philosophy of international Criminal Law* (Oxford, 2010) 569; Antony Duff, 'Authority and Responsibility in Internationl Criminal Law' in Besson and Tasioulas, *ibid.*, 589.

Timothy L. H. McCormack, 'From Sun Tzu to the Sixth Committee: The Evolution of an International Criminal Law Regime' in Timothy L. H. McCormack and Gerry J. Simpson (eds.), *The Law of War Crimes: National and International Approaches* (The Hague, 1997) 31

Erik Møse, 'Impact of Human Rights Conventions on the Two Ad Hoc Tribunals' in Morten Bergsmo (ed.), *Human Rights and Criminal Justice for the Downtrodden* (The Hague, 2003) Chapter VIII

Alain Pellet, 'Applicable Law' in Antonio Cassese, Paola Gaeta and John R. W. D. Jones (eds.), *The Rome Statute of the International Criminal Court: A Commentary* (Oxford, 2002) 1051

Alfred P. Rubin, *Ethics and Authority in International Law* (Cambridge, 1997)

Georg Schwarzenberger, 'The Problem of an International Criminal Law' (1950) 3 *Current Legal Problems* 263

2

The Aims, Objectives and Justifications
of International Criminal Law

2.1   Introduction

The assertion of criminal jurisdiction over a person is amongst the most coercive activities any society can undertake. Punishing a person involves depriving them of their liberty or another deliberate setting-back of their interests.[1] Such deprivations require justification.[2] Furthermore, criminal law is not, in itself, a good or a bad thing. It is a tool, to be employed to achieve certain ends. Some of those ends may be better pursued by means other than prosecutions.

It is the purpose of this chapter to introduce some of the justifications for punishment and the purposes it seeks to achieve.[3] It will also consider the wider goals which are claimed for international criminal law and discuss whether those goals can be met, alongside some of the challenges to international criminal law that have arisen. It should be noted at the outset, though, that different aspects of international criminal procedures may have different aims and objectives.[4] For example, the purpose of international criminal procedure may be to ensure the rule of law and fair trials,[5] and the implementation of sentences (rather than their imposition) may rely more on rehabilitative ideals than the general justifications of international criminal justice.[6] Here, we are looking at those general aims and justifications.

On a preliminary point, it has been suggested by some that the justifications for punishment may differ, or at least be differently interpreted, between international and domestic criminal law.[7] It is true that the general situations in which international criminal law is invoked are those of mass criminality, which are not the norm in domestic criminal law.[8]

---

[1] Indeed, in certain cases, unlawful imprisonment is, itself, an international crime. See e.g. Arts. 7 (1)(e) and 8(2)(a)(vii) of the ICC Statute.

[2] See generally Lucia Zedner, *Criminal Justice* (Oxford, 2004) 84–111.

[3] For more general surveys of the justification of punishment, see e.g. David Garland and Anthony Duff, *A Reader on Punishment* (Oxford, 1994); David Garland, *Punishment and Modern Society* (Oxford, 1990).

[4] Jens David Ohlin, 'Goals of International Criminal Justice and International Criminal Procedure' in G. Sluiter *et al.* (eds.), *International Criminal Procedure: Principles and Rules* (Oxford, 2012) 55.

[5] Jens David Ohlin, 'A Meta Theory of International Criminal Procedure: Vindicating the Rule of Law' (2009) 14 *UCLA Journal of International Law and Foreign Affairs* 77.

[6] Róisín Mulgrew, *Towards the Development of the International Penal System* (Cambridge, 2013) 207–9.

[7] See e.g. Mark Drumbl, 'Collective Violence and Individual Punishment: The Criminality of Mass Atrocity' (2004–5) 99 *Northwestern University Law Review* 539; Frederick Harhoff, 'Sense and Sensibility in Sentencing: Taking Stock of International Criminal Punishment' in Ola Engdahl and Pål Wrange (eds.), *Law at War: The Law as It Was and the Law as It Should Be: Liber Amicorum Ove Bring* (Leiden, 2008) 121.

[8] Although not all instances where international criminal law is relevant occur against this background: isolated, or relatively isolated, war crimes remain international crimes.

In addition, certain additional aims for international criminal law tend to be grafted onto those which are suggested for domestic systems of criminal law. These include the telling of the history of a conflict, distinguishing individual from group responsibility, reconciling societies and capacity building in domestic judicial systems.[9]

It is true that international society is not the same as domestic society. Nonetheless, much of the implementation of international criminal law is intended to be at the domestic level; therefore it is questionable whether the objectives of punishment ought to differ significantly between international and municipal criminal law. It has also been suggested that the justifications for punishment at the international level are inconsistent, and at times incoherent.[10] Even if this were the case (and it may well be), it would not necessarily undermine international criminal law. The same criticism could be made about the justifications for punishment at the domestic level, yet this has not led to widespread calls for the abolition of criminal law there.[11] It is true, however, that international criminal lawyers and the ad hoc Tribunals have at times been profligate in their assertions about the benefits and purposes of prosecutions. There is a risk in doing so of setting unreasonable expectations for what criminal law can do. If international criminal law is set impossible tasks, 'disenchantment and depression will set in when these goals are not being met'.[12] Some think this has occurred.[13]

It must also be remembered, at the outset, that the turn to criminal justice has not occurred in a vacuum. It has occurred in part as a response to dissatisfaction with the other methods of dealing with international criminals, which were either extrajudicial executions, or ignoring them. The first of these is clearly unlawful now.[14] The second, which was said by Robert Jackson to 'mock the dead and make cynics of the living',[15] is one which is rarely lawful.[16]

2.2   What international criminal justice is for

Broadly speaking, there are two approaches to justifying punishment: forward-looking (teleological); and those that focus on the crime itself (deontological).[17] In practice, most

---

[9] Antonio Cassese, 'Reflections on International Criminal Justice' (1998) 61 *Modern Law Review* 1, 6–7.

[10] See e.g. Immi Tallgren, 'The Sense and Sensibility of International Criminal Law' (2002) 13 *European Journal of International Law* 561; Mirjan Damaška, 'What Is the Point of International Criminal Justice' (2008) 83 *Chicago–Kent Law Review* 329, 331–5; but see Paul Roberts and Nesam McMillan, 'For Criminology in International Criminal Justice' (2003) 1 *Journal of International Criminal Justice* 315.

[11] Although see e.g. J. G. Murphy, 'Marxism and Retribution' (1973) 2 *Philosophy and Public Affairs* 217; Stanley Cohen, 'Alternatives to Punishment – The Abolitionist Case' (1991) 25 *Israel Law Review* 729; Philip Allott, *The Health of Nations* (Cambridge, 2003) 62–9.

[12] Iain Cameron, 'Individual Responsibility under National and International Law for the Conduct of Armed Conflict' in Engdahl and Wrange (eds.), *Law at War*, 58; Damaška, 'What Is the Point', 331.

[13] Florian Jessberger and Julia Geneuss, 'Down the Drain or Down to Earth? International Criminal Justice under Pressure' (2013) 11 *Journal of International Criminal Justice* 501; Payam Akhavan, 'The Rise, and Fall, and Rise, of International Criminal Justice' (2013) 11 *Journal of International Criminal Justice* 527.

[14] Additional Protocol I, Art. 75, which represents customary international law. See *Hamdan* v. *Rumsfeld*, 126 S Ct 2749, 2997 (2006); Geneva Conventions 1949, common Art. 3; ICCPR Art. 6; *Suarez de Guerrero* v. *Colombia* (Human Rights Committee 45/79); ECHR, Art. 2.

[15] Robert Jackson, 'Report to the President' (1945) 39 *American Journal of International Law* 178, 182.   [16] See section 4.3.

[17] For a useful introduction at the domestic level, see Stanley Cohen, 'An Introduction to the Theory, Justifications and Modern Manifestations of Criminal Punishment' (1981–2) 27 *McGill Law Journal* 73.

criminal justice systems tend to be defended on the basis of a mixture of the two.[18] There are a number of different aims that have been postulated for punishment in international criminal justice. The primary place in which the ICTY and ICTR have discussed their aims of punishment is in relation to their imposition of sentences.[19] The two main aims that the ICTY has asserted for its practice are retribution and deterrence.[20] It has also at times asserted the relevance of rehabilitation of offenders,[21] and other objectives, although it is fair to say that the precise relationship between the aims it has set out and the specific sentences given is unclear at best.[22]

2.2.1   Retribution

Retributive theories have a long history in criminal law, and are often associated with the philosophy of Immanuel Kant.[23] Retributive approaches focus on the necessity of punishing those who have violated societal norms, irrespective of the possible future benefits of prosecution, on the basis that the offenders deserve punishment for what they have done. The specific focus of this approach is the perpetrators themselves, on the basis that to treat them as a means to another end (as teleological approaches are wont to do) is to fail to respect them as full persons (i.e. reasoning moral agents). In other words, such theories claim that to refuse to focus on the autonomous actions of the perpetrators by holding them responsible for those actions, is to treat them as less than people, as responsibility is the concomitant of autonomy and full personhood.

Retribution has been considered by some to be particularly applicable to international criminal law, as other rationales for punishment asserted at the domestic level are less relevant at the international level.[24] Others, though, take the view that the nature of international crimes, in particular their complex nature and the diverse intuitions held by stakeholders in international criminal justice, render the utility of retributive justifications inapposite.[25] To a pure retributivist though, the consequential utility of prosecutions is irrelevant, as it is a deontological, not consequentialist, justification for punishment. Modern retributive theorists are careful to distinguish their position from that of simple vengeance. It is clear that the international criminal tribunals, when dealing with retributive justifications

---

[18] Which is acceptable: see H. L. A. Hart, *Punishment and Responsibility* (Oxford, 1968) Chapter 1.

[19] On which, see section 19.2 and William Schabas, *The UN International Criminal Tribunals: The Former Yugoslavia, Rwanda and Sierra Leone* (Cambridge, 2006) 554–61. The ICC has only issued one sentencing decision to date, in which it referred to the retributive and deterrent functions identified for the ICC in the Preamble to the Rome Statute: *Lubanga*, ICC T. Ch., 10 July 2012, para. 16.

[20] See e.g. *Alekšovski*, ICTY A. Ch., 24 March 2000, para. 185. See also SC Res. 827(1993) on the ICTY. To the extent to which it has discussed it, the ICC has not gone beyond these: *Lubanga, ibid.*

[21] *Momir Nikolić*, ICTY T. Ch. I, 2 December 2003, para. 85.

[22] Sylvia D'Ascoli, 'Reconciliation and Sentencing in the Practice of the Ad Hoc Tribunals' in Schabas *et al., Ashgate Research Companion*, 307, 311–14.

[23] See generally R. A. Duff and D. Garland, 'Thinking About Punishment' in Duff and Garland, *A Reader on Punishment*, 1, 2–3.

[24] Jens David Ohlin, 'Towards a Unique Theory of International Criminal Sentencing' in Göran Sluiter and Sergey Vasiliyev (eds.), *International Criminal Procedure: Towards a Coherent Body of Law* (London, 2009) 373.

[25] Andrew K. Woods. 'Moral Judgments and International Crimes: The Disutility of Desert' (2012) 52 *Virginia Journal of International Law* 632. One answer to this might be that those who hold different intuitions are incorrect, or are asking more of international criminal law than it can give, and their views are, thus, simply not salient to the question of what are the appropriate goals international criminal justice ought to have.

for punishment, have tried to avoid conflating the *lex talionis* and retributive justifications of punishment.[26] For example, the ICTY in the *Alekšovski* case asserted that retribution:

is not to be understood as fulfilling a desire for revenge but as duly expressing the outrage of the international community at these crimes. This factor has been widely recognised by Trial Chambers of this International Tribunal as well as Trial Chambers of the International Criminal Tribunal for Rwanda. Accordingly, a sentence of the International Tribunal should make plain the condemnation of the international community of the behaviour in question and show 'that the international community was not ready to tolerate serious violations of international humanitarian law and human rights'.[27]

Analogously, albeit in a passage that appears to place rather a lot under the rubric of retribution, the *Nikolić* case stated that:

In light of the purposes of the Tribunal and international humanitarian law generally, retribution is better understood as the expression of condemnation and outrage of the international community at such grave violations of, and disregard for, fundamental human rights at a time that people may be at their most vulnerable, namely during armed conflict. It is also recognition of the harm and suffering caused to the victims. Furthermore, within the context of international criminal justice, retribution is understood as a clear statement by the international community that crimes will be punished and impunity will not prevail.[28]

One positive aspect of retributivism was pointed out by the Trial Chamber in the *Todorović* case: it 'must be understood as reflecting a fair and balanced approach to the exaction of punishment for wrongdoing. This means that the penalty imposed must be proportionate to the wrongdoing, in other words, that the punishment be made to fit the crime.'[29] One difficulty with this is that it has been questioned whether punishments for international crimes can be proportionate to what can be enormous levels of wrongdoing and culpability.[30] A strong counter-argument to such assertions is given by Mark Osiel: 'There is a sense in which this argument is true, but trivial. After all, many ordinary offenders commit multiple offences for which they cannot "repay" . . . in fitting measure, within their remaining lifespan.'[31]

More specifically, though, a distinction between cardinal and ordinal proportionality ought to be recognized. Cardinal proportionality sets out the basic level of severity of response, such as minimum and maximum punishments, that a system can give for any crimes. Ordinal proportionality sets where a crime sits on the level of severity within that system. It may simply be that international criminal law and domestic criminal law have different cardinal points, and retributive theory is as much about ordinal proportionality as cardinal proportionality, which differs between States as well as between such systems and international criminal tribunals. That is not to say that it cannot throw up oddities, particularly between national jurisdictions and between national courts and international courts, but again that problem is not one which is unique to international criminal law.

---

[26] The *lex talionis* of the Biblical Old Testament is often expressed through the maxim 'an eye for an eye, a tooth for a tooth' (Deuteronomy 19:21).
[27] *Alekšovski*, ICTY A. Ch., 24 March 2000, para. 185.   [28] *Momir Nikolić*, ICTY T. Ch. I, 2 December 2003, paras. 86–7.
[29] *Todorović*, ICTY T. Ch. I, 31 July 2001, para. 29. See also *Plavšić*, ICTY T. Ch. III, 27 February 2003, para. 23.
[30] Harhoff, 'Sense and Sensibility', 125.
[31] Mark Osiel, 'Why Prosecute? Critics of Punishment for Mass Atrocity' (2000) 22 *Human Rights Quarterly* 118, 129.

Still, there are problems with a purely retributive approach. Some claim that it is important, for example, to move beyond a culture of blame.[32] Critics of retributivism may also argue that, as it appears to demand punishment without regard to cost, it sets impossibly high standards, particularly in relation to disadvantaged societies, and requires punishment even where it is pointless. There may be merit in this position, although a pure Kantian could respond that it misses the point; the important question is not what is practicable, but what is morally necessary. Even so, there is a risk of moral absolutism and insensitivity to context in such a position.

2.2.2   Deterrence

Deterrence is perhaps the best known of the justifications of punishment. Such theories were championed in particular by utilitarian political theorists such as Jeremy Bentham, who, in distinction to retributivists, focused on the future-related benefits of prosecution. It is a commonplace that punishment ought to be imposed to prevent both the offender and the population more generally from engaging in prohibited conduct. Equally, there are risks involved in deterrence. The first is that there is nothing inherent in utilitarianism that prevents exceedingly heavy punishment, and indeed punishment of the innocent, to achieve its goals. After all, it is likely that punishing close family members of a criminal for their misdeeds would quite possibly give a greater degree of deterrence than punishing criminals directly. Also, threatening torturous punishment for even minor violations of the law could prevent such breaches. But that is the mentality of the police State.

There are two other more general critiques of deterrence-based theories in international criminal law. The first is a philosophical one. Retributivists, in particular those of a Kantian persuasion, are right to point out that deterrence theories, especially those that look to general deterrence (i.e. deterrence of others, who see the punishment of others and decide not to engage in criminal conduct)[33] see people merely as a means to an end, which is inconsistent with their moral worth as human beings. The second is that deterrence-based approaches treat people as rational calculators, who carefully weigh up the costs and benefits of their actions, and this does not reflect the reality of the type of decision-making that often precedes decisions to commit crimes.[34] It is thought by many that the idea of fighting for a 'higher good', bigotry or more pressing concerns than possibly, at some point, being brought before a court or tribunal, are the determinative factors in the minds of those who commit international crimes.[35] This may be true in some situations, but the point probably underestimates the rational calculations of many high-ranking leaders who are not blinded by other considerations.[36]

---

[32] See e.g. Desmond Tutu, *No Future Without Forgiveness* (London, 1999).

[33] The other type of deterrence, particular deterrence, is based on preventing particular offenders engaging in such conduct again, as they become all too aware of the costs of such behaviour.

[34] David Wippman, 'Atrocities, Deterrence and the Limits of International Justice' (1999) *Fordham International Law Journal* 473; Drumbl, 'Collective Violence and Individual Punishment', 590–1.

[35] E.g. Jan Klabbers, 'Just Revenge? The Deterrence Argument in International Criminal Law' (2001)12 *Finnish Yearbook of International Law* 249; Harhoff, 'Sense and Sensibility', 127.

[36] Stephen Roach, 'Justice of the Peace? Future Challenges and Prospects for a Cosmopolitan Court' in Stephen Roach (ed.), *Governance, Order and the International Criminal Court* (Oxford, 2009) 225, 226–9; Jakob von Holderstein Holtermann, 'A Slice of Cheese – A Deterrence Argument in Favour of the International Criminal Court' (2010) 11 *Human Rights Review* 289, 306.

Whatever their merits, such critiques have led the ICTY to accept deterrence as a justification for punishment only within limits. For example, in the *Tadić* sentencing appeal, the Appeals Chamber, when referring to deterrence, said that 'it is a consideration that may legitimately be considered in sentencing ... Equally, the Appeals Chamber accepts that this factor must not be accorded undue prominence in the overall assessment of the sentences to be imposed on persons convicted by the International Tribunal.'[37]

Furthermore, the Appeals Chamber in the *Nikolić* case attempted to deal with some of the critiques of unmodified deterrence theories as follows:

During times of armed conflict, all persons must now be more aware of the obligations upon them in relation to fellow combatants and protected persons, particularly civilians. Thus, it is hoped that the Tribunal and other international courts are bringing about the development of a culture of *respect* for the rule of law and not simply the *fear* of the consequences of breaking the law, and thereby deterring the commission of crimes. One may ask whether the individuals who are called before this Tribunal as accused are simply an instrument to achieving the goal of the establishment of the rule of law. The answer is no. Indeed, the Appeals Chamber has held that deterrence should not be given undue prominence in the overall assessment of a sentence.[38]

Although the reasoning it contains is not a complete answer to the critiques above, as this quote implies, more sophisticated deterrence-based theories work on a more subtle level than some of their critics acknowledge. Those theories do not assert that deterrence works at the level of rational calculation, but at a preliminary stage, where people are (consciously or otherwise) setting up the available options. Where people simply think that certain options are not (in part, morally) open to them, they do not enter the second calculation of their costs and benefits, perhaps similarly to the way that now people simply do not think of settling disputes by duelling. This is linked to the denunciatory/educative function of punishment, which will be discussed below.[39]

Like many criminal theorists, the ICC Statute accepts that there is some role for deterrence in international criminal law.[40] Preambular paragraph 5 of the Statute asserts that the parties are '[d]etermined to put an end to impunity for the perpetrators of these crimes and thus to contribute to the prevention of such crimes'.[41] The Appeals Chamber of the ICC has picked up on this, and has referred to the Court's deterrent role in a normative fashion.[42] Furthermore, the ICC's Prosecutor has asserted that the ICC has had 'an impact' on the commission of certain crimes in Africa and on policies of many States.[43] Some scholars assert that a fairly direct deterrent function can be derived from prosecutions of international

---

[37] *Tadić*, ICTY A. Ch., 26 January 2000, para. 48. [38] *Momir Nikolić*, ICTY T. Ch. I, 2 December 2003, paras. 89–90.

[39] See Mark Drumbl, *Atrocity, Punishment and International Law* (Cambridge, 2007) 174.

[40] See also, more generally, Payam Akhavan, 'Can International Criminal Justice Prevent Future Atrocities?' (2001) 85 *American Journal of International Law* 7.

[41] See generally Hector Olásolo, *The Role of the International Criminal Court in Preventing Atrocity through Timely Intervention* (The Hague, 2011).

[42] *Situation in the Democratic Republic of the Congo*, Decision on the Prosecutor's Application for Warrants of Arrest Article 58, ICC-01/04–01/07, 10 February 2006, para. 55.

[43] Ben Schiff, 'The ICC's Potential for Doing Bad when Pursuing Good' (2012) 26 *Ethics and International Affairs* 73, 78.

crimes,[44] although others doubt their methodology or the extent to which their findings are transferable outside their context.[45] It ought to be noted that here is a significant body of sceptical opinion about deterrence in international criminal law.[46] That said, there is already an increasing amount of, admittedly anecdotal,[47] evidence of deterrence operating in relation to the international criminal tribunals, although there is no cause for triumphalism on the part of those basing their support of international criminal justice on its asserted deterrent function.[48]

It might be noted that, in the past, the absence of enforcement of international criminal law, and the small number of offenders that international criminal tribunals have prosecuted, undermined the goal of deterrence, as people do not think that they are likely to be punished.[49] Those doubting the possibility of deterrence in international criminal law have pointed to the fact that the creation of the ICTY did not stop crimes being committed in the former Yugoslavia between 1993 and 1995, and many other examples since the revival of international criminal justice where the possibility of prosecution has not prevented atrocities.[50] In relation to Yugoslavia, however, it might be noted that the Tribunal was a fledgling institution, with very few people in custody. Moreover, it was often thought that the Tribunal would be likely to be bargained away in a peace deal. Thus, the example may not be transferrable to international criminal law in general.[51] Other, more recent examples may not be so limited, however, and may reflect structural weaknesses in the enforcement of international criminal law,[52] which make prosecution often unlikely, and therefore less of a criterion weighing upon the mind of the rational international criminal.[53] Nonetheless, if a culture of accountability is created, and domestic courts play their part in prosecution of international crimes as the drafters of the ICC Statute intended, then this critique may become blunted over time.[54] Overall, the evidence is mixed, and interpreting it involves the factoring in of a large number of variables, of which the threat of criminal prosecution is only one, which renders clear conclusions very difficult, if not impossible, to reach.[55]

---

[44] Hunjoon Kim and Katherine Sikkink, 'Explaining the Deterrence Effect of Human Rights Prosecutions for Transitional Countries' (2010) 54 *International Studies Quarterly* 939.

[45] Pádraig McAuliffe, 'Suspended Disbelief? The Curious Endurance of the Deterrence Rationale in International Criminal Law' (2012) 10 *New Zealand Journal of Public and International Law* 227, 230, 254–6, 260–1.

[46] *Ibid.*

[47] Reliance on which is criticized by McAuliffe, 'Deterrence', 257–8, although the critique is more of over-reading it rather than using it at all.

[48] Harhoff, 'Sense and Sensibility', 128.

[49] See Tom Farer, 'Restraining the Barbarians: Can International Law Help?' (2000) 22 *Human Rights Quarterly* 90, 92–3.

[50] McAuliffe, 'Deterrence'; 234–7; Carsten Stahn, 'Between 'Faith' and 'Facts': By What Standard Should We Assess International Criminal Justice?' (2012) 25 *Leiden Journal of International Law* 251, 265.

[51] Paul Williams and Michael Scharf, *Peace with Justice: War Crimes and Accountability in the Former Yugoslavia* (Oxford, 2003) 21–2.

[52] Leslie P. Francis and John G. Francis, 'International Criminal Courts, the Rule of Law, and the Prevention of Harm: Building Justice in Times of Injustice' in Larry May and Zachary Hoskins (eds.), *International Criminal Law and Philosophy* (Cambridge, 2010) 58.

[53] McAuliffe, 'Deterrence', 236–7, 239.

[54] Harhoff accepts that the risk of prosecution is higher now than ever before: 'Sense and Sensibility', 128.

[55] James F. Alexander, 'The International Criminal Court and the Prevention of Atrocities: Predicting the Court's Impact' (2009) 54 *Villanova Law Review* 1, 42. Immi Tallgren, 'The Sense and Sensibility of International Criminal Law' (2002) 13 *European Journal of International Law* 561, 569.

2.2.3   *Incapacitation*

Incapacitation is another utilitarian justification of punishment. It has links to individual deterrence, in that it seeks to prevent crimes by keeping the relevant person in detention.[56] This has not had a great influence on international criminal law,[57] although Judge Röling, in the Tokyo IMT, asserted that the justification for prosecuting aggression, in spite of the fact that it was not previously criminal, was that the defendants were dangerous and their influence on Japan had to be excluded by their imprisonment.[58] Some of the arguments against amnesty, which rely on the idea that those who seek amnesties will not quietly retire, are linked to this justification of punishment. Incapacitative theories of punishment are controversial, as they rely on the imprecise science of determining who will reoffend and who will not. They do not focus on what has been done but, in effect, punish people for what they might do in the future.[59]

2.2.4   *Rehabilitation*

Rehabilitation is a theory of punishment which can trace its history back to the eighteenth century,[60] and is based on the idea that the point of criminal sanctions is reformation of the offender. It is a theory of punishment that has many advocates in the human rights community at the domestic level, in particular those who are supporters of restorative justice.[61] It has not made great advances in international criminal law, in part because many believe that the main perpetrators of international crimes are not the appropriate beneficiaries of rehabilitation. Nonetheless, this is not a universal view, in particular when it comes to the implementation of sentences,[62] and there are occasions upon which the international tribunals have mentioned rehabilitation in relation to lower-level offenders. Most notable in this regard is the decision of the Trial Chamber in the *Erdemović* case. Erdemović was a young Bosnian Croat who took part in the Srebrenica massacre under duress. In sentencing him to a relatively short five-year period of imprisonment, the Trial Chamber noted his 'corrigible personality' and that he was 'reformable and should be given a second chance to start his life afresh upon release, whilst still young enough to do so'.[63] The ICTY's practice seems to be that those who plead guilty ought to have their punishment carried out with a view to rehabilitation, although this is contingent on genuine remorse, and the rehabilitation may be more to do with that, and the admission of guilt, than the sentence itself.[64]

---

[56] See e.g. Zedner, *Criminal Justice*, 98–101.   [57] Drumbl, 'Collective Violence and Individual Punishment', 589.

[58] Dissenting Opinion of the Member from the Netherlands, 10–51; see Neil Boister and Robert Cryer, *Documents on the Tokyo International Tribunal* (Oxford, 2008) 684–703.

[59] Zedner, *Criminal Justice*, 100.

[60] *Ibid.*, 95–8. See also Andrew von Hirsch and Andrew Ashworth, *Principled Sentencing* (Oxford, 1998) Chapter 3.

[61] Interestingly, many such advocates at the domestic level are often far more retributivist when it comes to international crimes.

[62] Mulgrew, *Towards the Development of the International Penal System*.

[63] *Erdemović*, ICTY T. Ch., 5 March 1998, para. 16.   [64] Harhoff, 'Sense and Sensibility', 131.

2.2.5   *Denunciation/education*

One of the more modern theories designed to justify punishment, and one which has considerable support, is that of communication/denunciation.[65] Some of the most sophisticated defences of international criminal law adopt this defence of punishment for international crimes,[66] although sometimes on the basis that the other justifications have little plausibility.[67] Denunciatory and educative approaches view criminal procedures and punishment as 'an opportunity for communicating with the offender, the victim and wider society the nature of the wrong done'.[68] This is designed to engage offenders, and attempt to make them understand what was wrong with what they have done,[69] whilst also reaffirming the norm in the community and educating society about the unacceptable nature of the conduct condemned. Others add that it reaffirms faith in the rule of law.[70]

Some doubt this approach to punishment, criticizing the idea that international criminals are part of a relevant normative community with whom punishment is meant to communicate, on the basis that their acts or attitudes make it impossible or unlikely that they can or will heed the message. This contention is similarly applicable to domestic crimes, and a strong argument can be made that in international crimes the relevant normative community to which a person has to belong is humanity, rather than any thicker conception of community, and that the possibility of rejection of the message does not mean that it should not be attempted to be inculcated.[71] Also, those accused of international crimes are not the only audience for the message, which is also partly aimed at the wider community, to achieve general deterrence. There have though been suggestions as well that there are difficulties relating to what the moral message is when broad principles of liability which stretch individual culpability, such as joint criminal enterprise, are used.[72]

The ICTY has asserted the relevance of the didactic function in the *Kordić and Čerkez* case, referring to 'the educational function . . . [which] aims at conveying the message that rules of international humanitarian law have to be obeyed under all circumstances. In doing so, the sentence seeks to internalise these rules and the moral demands they are based on in the minds of the public.'[73] In some circumstances, where specific international crimes reflect a relatively recent moral consensus on point, the educative function of international criminal law may play a considerable role. Where people are unaware of prohibitions, they are less likely to live up to them. The prohibition of child soldiers may be an example of this.[74]

At a more nuanced level, the fact that there are lively debates over whether the term genocide may be applied to certain events implies that the expressive function of punishment

---

[65] Antony Duff, *Punishment, Communication and Community* (Oxford, 2001); Andrew von Hirsch, *Censure and Sanctions* (Oxford, 1993) Chapter 2; William Wilson, *Central Issues in Criminal Theory* (Oxford, 2002) 61–5.

[66] E.g. Darnaška, 'What Is the Point', 343; Antony Duff, 'Can We Punish the Perpetrators of Atrocities?' in Thomas Brudman and Thomas Cushman (eds.), *The Religious in Responses to Mass Atrocity* (Cambridge, 2008) 79.

[67] Stahn, 'Between Faith', 279.   [68] Zedner, *Criminal Justice*, 109.

[69] See Wilson, *Central Issues*, 62–3; Klaus Gunter, 'The Criminal Law of "Guilt" as a Subject of a Politics of Remembrance in Democracies' in Emilios Christodoulidis and Scott Veitch (eds.), *Lethe's Law: Justice, Law and Ethics in Reconciliation* (Oxford, 2001) 3.

[70] Drumbl, *Atrocity*, 173.   [71] Duff, 'Can We Punish', 85–100.   [72] Damaška, 'What Is the Point', 350–6.

[73] *Kordić and Čerkez*, ICTY A. Ch., 17 December 2004, paras. 1080–1.

[74] See Robert Cryer, 'The Role of International Criminal Prosecutions in Increasing Compliance with International Humanitarian Law' (forthcoming).

and labelling is important in international criminal law.[75] The relevance of the expressive function of punishment was seemingly accepted by the ICTY Appeals Chamber in the *Krštić* appeal when it said that:

Among the grievous crimes this Tribunal has the duty to punish, the crime of genocide is singled out for special condemnation and opprobrium. The gravity of genocide is reflected in the stringent requirements which must be satisfied before this conviction is imposed. These requirements – the demanding proof of specific intent and the showing that the group was targeted for destruction in its entirety or in substantial part – guard against a danger that convictions for this crime will be imposed lightly. Where these requirements are satisfied, however, the law must not shy away from referring to the crime committed by its proper name.[76]

Strongly related to the educative function, it has been suggested, with considerable practical and philosophical force, that the role of international criminal justice is, in spite of the extraordinary nature of international crimes, to normalize criminal law as the appropriate response. On this basis, the best way forward for international criminal law is to ensure that its utilization is just considered normal, rather than needing separate justification from criminal law in general.[77] This may not yet have come to pass, but, as things currently stand, the question best asked is whether progress has been achieved. The aims of international criminal justice ought not to be seen as short term goals.

2.3   Broader goals

2.3.1   *Vindicating the rights of victims*

There are certain other goals which have been suggested for international criminal law, all of which have a utilitarian focus, and relate in some ways to the future of the societies in which international crimes are committed. The first of these is that prosecutions may engender a sense of justice having been done, or 'closure' for victims,[78] either on the basis that seeing their persecutors prosecuted will have that result, or that the process of testifying will do so. Such a role in relation to victims was noted by the ICTY in the *Nikolić* case, which asserted that 'punishment must therefore reflect both the calls for justice from the persons who have – directly or indirectly – been victims of the crimes'.[79]

It can also be questioned whether criminal trials and punishment of offenders can have the suggested cathartic effects for victims.[80] It is doubtful, given the focus in international criminal tribunals on higher level offenders, that many victims will have an opportunity to see those people who committed the particular offences against them come to trial (although

---

[75] Diane Marie Amann, 'Group Mentality, Expressivism and Genocide' (2002) 2 *International Criminal Law Review* 93; see also Robert Sloane, 'The Expressive Capacity of International Punishment' (2007) 43 *Stanford Journal of International Law* 39.

[76] *Krštić*, ICTY A. Ch., 19 April 2004, paras. 36–7.

[77] David Luban, 'After the Honeymoon: Reflections on the Current State of International Criminal Justice' (2013)11 *Journal of International Criminal Justice* 505.

[78] On victims and their participation in international criminal tribunals more generally, see Chapter 18.

[79] *Momir Nikolić*, ICTY T. Ch. I, 2 December 2003, para. 86.

[80] Jamie O'Connell, 'Gambling with the Psyche: Does Prosecuting Human Rights Violators Console their Victims?' (2005) 46 *Harvard International Law Journal* 295.

national courts have a large role here). Evidence that the experience of testifying is helpful is mixed, with some victim–witnesses reporting that they were glad they had testified, whilst others did not.[81] The extent to which victims may be helped by prosecutions depends, *inter alia*, on the role they are permitted to play in the proceedings,[82] and, particularly at the national level, this is often minimal, and limited to the utilitarian goal of using them as witnesses.[83] There have been suggestions that the ICTY and ICTR have not always been exemplary in their treatment of victim–witnesses. Nonetheless, the ICC Statute has various provisions providing for victims' participation in proceedings and for reparations.[84]

2.3.2   Recording history

The next postulated goal is that of truth telling. The claim is that the process of subjecting evidence to forensic scrutiny will set down a permanent record of the crimes that will stand the test of time.[85] Some go further to suggest that trials should be structured to create a narrative which will be useful to the relevant post-conflict society.[86] The judgments of international criminal tribunals have often been lengthy, and have engaged in detailed discussion of the background of the conflicts which have led to the crimes, and have been criticized for doing so.[87] In the *Krstić* judgment, the intention of the tribunal to counter denial and create a record of the Srebrenica massacre was clear, and similar things can be said about the ICTR's characterization of the Rwandan genocide as being such.[88] The practice of the Tribunals is not entirely consistent; sometimes the Chambers of the Tribunals have disavowed an intention to write history. In the *Karadžić* case, the defendant sought to persuade the ICTY to find, if not for the purposes of legal evaluation then for the purposes of history, that he had been promised immunity from prosecution if he left politics. The Trial Chamber gave short shrift to such a suggestion, stating that '[t]he Trial Chamber rejects the Accuser's submission that not having an evidentiary hearing at this stage would be a disservice to history. The Chamber's purpose is not to serve the academic study of history.'[89]

The idea that criminal trials ought to serve truth-telling functions has been criticized. Some think that criminal trials are not always the best place to seek to write history.[90] There are various aspects to this claim. In relation to the Nuremberg and Tokyo IMTs, the claim, which was made, *inter alia*, by one of the judges of the Tokyo IMT, was that 'distortions of history did take place' in those Tribunals, at times for political reasons.[91] For the most part,

[81] Eric Stover, 'Witnesses and the Promise of the Hague' in Eric Stover and Harvey Weinstein (eds.), *My Neighbour, My Enemy: Justice and Community in the Aftermath of Mass Atrocity* (Cambridge, 2004) 104.
[82] Harhoff, 'Sense and Sensibility', 131; see Chapter 18.
[83] See e.g. A. T. Williams, *A Very British Killing* (London, 2012) 215–16.   [84] See Chapter 18.
[85] See e.g. Cassese, 'Reflections on International Criminal Justice', 6.
[86] Mark Osiel, *Mass Atrocity, Collective Memory and the Law* (New Brunswick, NJ, 1997).
[87] José Alvarez, 'Rush to Closure: Lessons of the Tadić Judgment' (1998) 96 *Michigan Law Review* 2061; José Alvarez, 'Lessons from the Akayesu Judgment' (1998–9) 5 *International Law Students' Association Journal of International and Comparative Law* 359.
[88] Drumbl, *Atrocity*, 175.   [89] *Karažić*, ICTY T. Ch. III, 8 July 2009, para. 46.
[90] Martha Minow, *Between Vengeance and Forgiveness* (Boston, 1998) 46–7.
[91] B. V. A. Röling, 'The Nuremberg and Tokyo Trials in Retrospect' in M. Cherif Bassiouni and Ved Nanda (eds.), *A Treatise on International Criminal Law* (Springfield, IL, 1973) 590, 600. See Donald Bloxham, *Genocide on Trial: War Crimes Trials and the Formation of Holocaust History and Memory* (Oxford, 2001); Richard Minear, *Victors' Justice* (Princeton, NJ, 1971); but see also Yasuaki Onuma, 'Beyond Victors' Justice' (1984) 9 *Japan Echo* 63, 66.

such comments relate to the findings on conspiracy and aggression, rather than war crimes and crimes against humanity.

There are more general points that may be made about criminal tribunals writing history. It is difficult to write the whole history of a period without straying beyond the bounds of the criminal trial, which is to try a specific person for specific conduct.[92] This gives rise to the concern that the trial may resolve into a political debate about the validity of the different historical accounts that are being told. It is indeed strange that, in long-running conflicts which are the context to the commission of many atrocities, a criminal court should be seen as the arbitrator between competing historical accounts.[93] Such events are not easily cognizable or interpretable through the medium of criminal law.[94] The rule-bound nature of criminal trials is not one designed to ensure a full discussion of history, and structures the evidence that can be brought before the tribunal.[95] To go beyond this, as Judge Röling put it, there is a difference between the 'real truth' and the 'trial truth'.[96] In addition, as the criminal standard of proof is required for a conviction before an international criminal tribunal, in some instances, where there have been acquittals before such tribunals, this has been taken as exoneration of both the defendants and the 'side' on whose behalf they acted. This may involve ignoring the nuances of a (frequently lengthy and carefully framed) judgment, but has occurred.

Nevertheless, the contextual elements of international crimes, in particular of crimes against humanity and genocide,[97] make it necessary that the larger context in which a person's actions must be placed is an issue at trial about which the defence is entitled to introduce evidence as well. Furthermore, the nature of a fair trial process is that it gives those responsible for international crimes the opportunity to raise political propaganda and to attempt to delegitimize the prosecution.[98] This may be a necessary aspect of such trials, since the alternative, that of silencing the defence, is unacceptable, but balancing the competing interests here is difficult.[99] The temporal, geographical and subject-matter jurisdiction of international criminal tribunals means that the story they can tell is by no means the full one,[100] even though some of the international criminal tribunals have used evidence of events outside their jurisdictional reach.[101]

While such critiques do not substantially undermine the work done by those tribunals in collecting and making public primary evidence such as documents and witness testimony, they do cast aspersions on the role of courts as presenters or interpreters of history. The

---

[92] Osiel, *Mass Atrocity*, Chapter 3; however, see also Ruti Teitel, *Transitional Justice* (Oxford, 2000) 74–5.

[93] See Martti Koskenniemi, 'Between Impunity and Show Trials' (2002) 6 *Max Planck Yearbook of United Nations Law* 1. Of course, sometimes a court itself is split over the history, as was the case, for example, in the Tokyo IMT. See Gerry Simpson, 'War Crimes: A Critical Introduction' in Timothy McCormack and Gerry Simpson (eds.), *The Law of War Crimes: National and International Approaches* (The Hague, 1997) 1, 26–8.

[94] Koskenniemi, 'Between Impunity', 12–13.

[95] See Laurence Douglas, *The Memory of Judgment: Making Law and History in the Trials of the Holocaust* (New Haven, CT, 2001); Richard A. Wilson, *Writing History in International Criminal Trials* (Cambridge, 2011).

[96] B. V. A. Röling and Antonio Cassese, *The Tokyo Trial and Beyond* (Cambridge, 1992) 50. Many would (rightly) query whether there is one form of 'real truth'.

[97] Both in customary law and in the ICC Statute and its concomitant Elements of Crimes: see Chapters 10 and 11.

[98] See generally Gerry Simpson, 'Politics, Sovereignty, Remembrance' in Dominic McGoldrick, Peter Rowe and Eric Donnelly (eds.), *The Permanent International Criminal Court: Legal and Policy Issues* (Oxford, 2004) 47, 49.

[99] See generally Koskenniemi, 'Between Impunity'.

[100] José E. Alvarez, 'Crimes of Hate/Crimes of State: Lessons from Rwanda' (1999) 23 *Yale Journal of International Law* 365, 375.

[101] *Nahimana, Barayagwiza and Ngeze*, ICTR T. Ch., 13 December 2003, paras. 100–4.

evidence brought before some tribunals can, however, be very useful in combating later denial of such crimes (as has occurred in relation to the practice of the Nuremberg IMT and the ICTR). The practice of 'plea bargaining' in the Tribunals has been said by some Trial Chambers of the ICTY to assist in the process of truth telling,[102] but other chambers have doubted that the full story can be told without full trials.[103] When it comes to writing the history of situations in which international crimes have been committed, it may be that truth commissions are better placed to write some aspects of that history, although they are not themselves a panacea.[104]

2.3.3   *Post-conflict reconciliation*

Linked both to the satisfaction of victims and to the telling of truths about international crimes, which has been said to form the basis of a society moving beyond its schisms, it has been claimed that providing a sense of justice through prosecutions for international crimes can facilitate societal reconciliation and provide the preconditions for a durable peace.[105] This is often expressed in the aphorism 'no peace without justice'.[106] Evidence from Latin America, where policies of amnesty were rife in the 1970s but where prosecutions have continuously been sought and are now beginning to occur, provides some support for that position.[107] There is, however, no clear empirical proof of this, and other societies have managed without trials[108] (although some would say that those societies are not reconciled).[109]

The Security Council provided significant support for the interconnection of peace and justice when it determined that, in the situations in the former Yugoslavia and Rwanda, prosecutions would assist in reconciliation and a return to peace in the area.[110] It is interesting that, in the *Tadić* jurisdictional appeal, the Appeals Chamber of the ICTY simply said that such a decision was within the competence of the Council to make, rather than entering into any discussion of the substantive merits of the point.[111] Later, in the *Nikolić* case, the ICTY gave the idea more direct support.[112]

Perhaps the high tide mark of support for the link between criminal justice and peace in the ICTY came in the *Plavšić* case. Biljana Plavšić was co-President of the Republika Srpska during 1992. She surrendered to the Tribunal and pleaded guilty to crimes against humanity, expressing her remorse and stating that in doing so she wished to 'offer some consolation to

---

[102]   *Jokić*, ICTY T. Ch. I, 18 March 2004, para. 77. See Mark Harmon, 'Plea Bargaining: The Uninvited Guest at the ICTY' in José Doria, Hans-Peter Gasser and M. Cherif Bassiouni (eds.), *The Legal Regime of the International Criminal Court: Essays in Honour of Igor Blischenko* (Leiden, 2009) 163, 177–9.

[103]   *Dragan Nikolić*, ICTY T. Ch. II, 18 December 2003, para. 122. See also Schabas, *The UN International Criminal Tribunals*, 427–8; Drumbl, *Atrocity*, 181–2.

[104]   For discussion, see Alison Bissett, *Truth Commissions and Criminal Trials* (Cambridge, 2012) Chapter 1.

[105]   See e.g. Cassese, 'Reflections on International Criminal Justice', 6.

[106]   Indeed, this is the name of one well-known NGO working in the area of international criminal law.

[107]   The politics of impunity, on the other hand, are often thought to inspire later crimes, even decades later: see e.g. Harmon, 'Plea Bargaining', 179–82; Jens Ohlin, 'Peace, Security and Prosecutorial Discretion' in Carsten Stahn and Göran Sluiter (eds.), *The Emerging Practice of the International Criminal Court* (Leiden, 2009) 185, 203–5.

[108]   See e.g. Priscilla Hayner, *Unspeakable Truths: Transitional Justice and the Challenge of Truth Commissions*, 2nd edn (London, 2011) Chapter 12.

[109]   See Richard Wilson, *The Politics of Truth and Reconciliation: Legitimizing the Post-Apartheid State* (Cambridge, 2001).

[110]   Although such a determination was necessary to invoke Chapter VII of the UN Charter to create the ICTY and ICTR.

[111]   See section 7.2.4.   [112]   ICTY T. Ch., 12 December 2003, para. 60.

the innocent victims – Muslim, Croat and Serb – of the war in Bosnia and Herzegovina'.[113] In sentencing Plavšić to eleven years' imprisonment, the Tribunal noted 'that acknowledgement and full disclosure of serious crimes are very important when establishing the truth in relation to such crimes. This, together with acceptance of responsibility for the committed wrongs, will promote reconciliation.'[114] It has been questioned whether this was accurate in the individual case, but the general point remains. The ICTY's practice on point has been characterized as 'incoherent', on the basis that, in other cases, the ICTY has refused to reduce sentences on the basis of contributions to the peace process.[115] Some of the most serious doubts that have been expressed about international criminal law relate to the claim that it promotes peace and reconciliation.[116] It has been suggested that to require prosecutions will simply cause parties to conflicts to fight to the last.[117] The parties to the ICC Statute affirmed, in the Preamble to that treaty, that the commission of international crimes threatens the 'peace, security and well being of the world'.[118] The ambivalent relationship between international criminal justice and peace is perhaps shown by the fact that the Security Council, using its powers to restore and maintain international peace and security under Chapter VII of the UN Charter, may not only refer a situation to the ICC, but also defer the activity of that court in certain circumstances.[119] There is some empirical evidence relating to the effect (or lack thereof) of the ICTY's role in promoting peace,[120] but it is simply too early to say, on the whole, whether the optimists or pessimists are correct on this. Transformation from a conflict, to post-conflict, then peaceful, stable, society may take many years, and, indeed, decades, if it occurs at all, and many factors contribute to the process. Criminal prosecutions are only one.[121]

2.3.4   *Further asserted benefits of international trials*

Certain other benefits have also been postulated, not of international criminal law in general, but of international trials. One of the most powerful of these is that international tribunals, with international judges, operating at a distance from the events themselves, are not as open to political manipulation or influence from actors in those societies, or unconscious bias on the part of the judges.[122] Nonetheless, there have been a number of claims before the ICTY, the ICTR and the Special Court for Sierra Leone (SCSL) that judges are biased.[123] Also, it is an often-made critique that the international tribunals are too distant from their primary audience, the victimized community.[124] It is also sometimes claimed that international judges are the best judges of international crimes.[125] There are two possible bases for these claims, the first

---

[113] *Plavšić*, ICTY T. Ch. III, 27 February 2003, para. 19.   [114] *Ibid.*, para. 80.   [115] Drumbl, *Atrocity*, 62.
[116] Anthony D'Amato, 'Peace v. Accountability in Bosnia' (1994) 88 *American Journal of International Law* 500; Ian Ward, *Justice, Humanity and the New World Order* (Aldershot, 2004) 131.
[117] Anonymous, 'Human Rights in Peace Negotiations' (1996) 18 *Human Rights Quarterly* 249.
[118] ICC Statute, Preamble, para. 3.   [119] Arts. 13 and 16 of the ICC Statute; see further sections 8.6 and 8.8.
[120] Janine N. Clark, 'The Limits of Retributive Justice – Findings of an Empirical Study in Bosnia and Hercegovina' (2009) 7 *Journal of International Criminal Justice* 463; Janine N. Clark, 'The ICTY and Reconciliation in Croatia: A Case-Study of Vukovar' (2012) 10 *Journal of International Criminal Justice* 397.
[121] See Janine N. Clark, 'Peace, Justice and the International Criminal Court: Limitations and Possibilities' (2011) 9 *Journal of International Criminal Justice* 521.
[122] Cassese, 'Reflections on International Criminal Justice', 4, 7.   [123] See section 17.2.2.   [124] See section 2.4.
[125] Cassese, 'Reflections on International Criminal Justice', 7.

being that international judges and tribunals are representative of the relevant community affected by international crimes, which is the community of all humanity. The second basis is more prosaic: that international judges are more familiar with the relevant law. It is true that domestic judges are less likely to be fully aware of the intricacies of international criminal law than some of their international counterparts. Indeed, some eminent and experienced international lawyers have sat on the international criminal tribunals. However, not all judges who have sat on international criminal tribunals go to them professing expertise in international criminal law; an in-depth knowledge of the workings of a criminal trial is an equally useful background for an international criminal judge.[126]

It has also been suggested that international tribunals are better able to investigate and prosecute offences which occur across State borders than domestic courts.[127] This may be the case, but the extent to which it is true depends on the extent of the tribunal's jurisdiction and investigatory powers, which differ between the various courts. Finally, it has been suggested that an international criminal court would provide for uniformity in the process and law for punishing international crimes.[128] There is some truth in this. Although there have been a number of different international criminal tribunals, with different procedures and different substantive law, the ICC Statute has promoted harmonization of the law at the domestic level. Equally, the value of uniformity is strongly linked to the merits of the law which becomes the standard.[129]

2.4   Other critiques of criminal accountability

Despite the functions which prosecutions may serve, there are also many critiques of criminal accountability, and international tribunals in particular. International tribunals are expensive. The ICTY and ICTR have, between them, cost about US$4 billion and the ICC has so far cost over €1billion. These are unquestionably huge sums of money, and the ICTR has been accused of financial irregularity.[130] To gain some perspective though, it might be noted that the annual base military budget in the United States in 2012 was in the region of US$700 billion. In addition, the international criminal courts prior to the ICC were set up almost completely from scratch, and international tribunals, unlike their domestic counterparts, are almost entire criminal justice systems in themselves.

International tribunals are also (with the exception of the SCSL) located far away from the places where the crimes occurred.[131] This means that they are inaccessible to many of the victims and seen as responding more to an international audience than the purported beneficiaries.[132] This gives succour to those who argue that the creation of the Tribunals

---

[126] The late ICTY judge, Sir Richard May, was a judge in the United Kingdom, and an acknowledged expert on (UK) evidence law prior to his appointment to the tribunal.

[127] Cassese, 'Reflections on International Criminal Justice', 8.   [128] *Ibid.*

[129] Robert Cryer, *Prosecuting International Crimes: Selectivity and the International Criminal Law Regime* (Cambridge, 2005) 167–84.

[130] See section 17.3.3.

[131] Alvarez, 'Crimes of Hate'. Even the Special Court for Sierra Leone in the Taylor case has moved the trial away from Sierra Leone, on security grounds.

[132] *Ibid.*

was more a sop to the conscience of those who failed to prevent or bring an end to the crimes now being punished.[133] The further from the *locus delicti* that trials are held, the more likely it is that they will encounter domestic resistance there, in part because of misrepresentation of their work and allegations of bias.[134] There is also a lack of 'ownership' of international tribunals at the local level. Given that such tribunals tend to focus on those most responsible, it is also the case that most victims will not see their immediate oppressors punished. In situations of large-scale commission of crimes, however, it is difficult to imagine any criminal justice system that could fulfil the task of ensuring that all international criminals were punished.[135]

More generally, it has been questioned whether criminal law is an adequate mechanism to comprehend events involving international crimes, particularly large-scale international crimes like genocide. The critique was perhaps most strongly made by Hannah Arendt,[136] but others have also made similar points. Martti Koskeniemmi, for example, has said that 'sometimes a tragedy may be so great, a series of events of such political or even metaphysical significance, that punishing an individual does not come close to measuring up to it'.[137] It could be queried whether trials are any worse at 'measuring up to it' than the other methods that have been suggested for dealing with such events, and Arendt was not against the prosecution of international crimes as such, although she was critical of aspects of some proceedings.[138] Still, it is true that most international crimes occur against the background of 'system criminality', where individual and collective responsibility is mixed. As such, individual liability can only be part of the answer.[139] Since individual criminal liability and State responsibility are largely separate, this need not be such a problem, as the existence of one does not negate the existence of the other.[140] The difficulty is finding ways that adequately express both the individual and collective contributions to international crimes.[141]

More generally, prosecutions of international crimes are open to the criticism that they are designed to legitimate those that create them. For example, the creation of the ICTY and ICTR may have allowed powerful States to cover their unwillingness to take more decisive action.[142] Prosecutions can also be used by States and successor governments to attempt to make the point that they are morally different from those on trial, even where there are international crimes that can be laid at their door too.[143] In addition, substantive international criminal law fails to deal with conduct very worthy of censure, thus providing some

---

[133] See Gary John Bass, *Stay the Hand of Vengeance: The Politics of War Crimes Tribunals* (Princeton, NJ, 2000) Chapter 6.
[134] Patrice McMahon and David Forsythe, 'The ICTY's Impact on Serbia: Judicial Romanticism Meets Network Politics' (2008) 30 *Human Rights Quarterly* 412.
[135] William Schabas, 'The Rwanda Case: Sometimes It's Impossible' in M. Cherif Bassiouni (ed.), *Post Conflict Justice* (New York, 2002) 499.
[136] Lotte Kohler and Hans Saner (eds.), *Hannah Arendt/Karl Jaspers: Correspondence* at 54, cited in Osiel, 'Why Prosecute?', 128.
[137] Koskeniemi, 'Between Impunity', 2.
[138] Hannah Arendt, *Eichmann in Jerusalem: A Report on the Banality of Evil* (Harmondsworth, 1994), epilogue.
[139] See André Nollkaemper and Harmen van der Wilt, 'Introduction' in André Nollkaemper and Harmen van der Wilt, *System Criminality in International Law* (Cambridge, 2009) 1, 4.
[140] Beatrice Bonafé, *The Relationship between State and Individual Responsibility for International Crimes* (Leiden, 2009), although on the overlaps and difficulties in entirely separating them, see also Gerry Simpson, 'Men and Abstract Entities' in Nollkaemper and van der Wilt, *System Criminality*, 69; Andrea Gattini, 'A Historical Perspective: From Collective to Individual Responsibility and Back' in *ibid.*, 101.
[141] Gattini, 'A Historical Perspective', 126.   [142] See section 7.2.
[143] Simpson, 'War Crimes: A Critical Introduction', 19–26.

form of legitimacy for it.[144] International trials and international criminal law ought not to serve as an excuse to the international community for not dealing with other more difficult and deep-seated problems.

International criminal justice, and international tribunals, reflect inequalities in the selection of cases. Selective justice is a problem from the point of view of the rule of law, and it can undermine many of the justifications of punishment.[145] For example, deterrence is unlikely to be possible if potential offenders take the view that they may be able to obtain exemption from prosecution. Retribution is not served well by selective punishment, and it causes the lessons that may be taught by international criminal law to be confused and equivocal.[146]

Some would go further than this, to argue that international criminal law is in some ways a Western construct, and that it is imposed on other societies.[147] With respect to the norms themselves, of genocide, crimes against humanity and war crimes, this is almost certainly overstated, in that genocide, crimes against humanity and most war crimes are considered contrary to universal norms. As has been said, 'modern writers on the subject correctly point to Chinese, Islamic and Hindu traditions that underscore the universal values enshrined in the prohibition of . . . crimes that shock the conscience of mankind'.[148] The treaties establishing the core of war crimes, the Geneva Conventions, have been ratified by probably every State in the world,[149] and the General Assembly has repeatedly and unanimously condemned genocide, crimes against humanity and war crimes.[150] Some scholars, however, have taken the view that, by using custom rather than treaties, the ad hoc Tribunals have preferred the interests of powerful States, which may have more weight in the creation of custom.[151]

When it comes to enforcement, selectivity arguments can take on a post-colonial aspect, i.e. that 'international prosecutions are instituted mainly against citizens of states that are weak actors in the international arena or fail to enjoy the support of powerful nations'.[152] It has also been claimed that decisions about what to do about international crimes are better left to national authorities.[153] The issues involved are not simple, but it might be noted that a number of post-colonial States (such as Rwanda, Uganda and the Democratic Republic of the Congo) have asked for international prosecutions of international crimes. Again, a synergistic relationship between national and international approaches to international crimes is probably the most helpful way forward.[154] On the former critique, selectivity is a major problem in international criminal law, although the strength of this critique is

---

[144] Simpson, 'Politics, Sovereignty, Remembrance', 56.
[145] Drumbl, 'Collective Violence and Individual Punishment', 593.   [146] See e.g. Damaška, 'What Is the Point', 361.
[147] Steven Ratner, Jason Abrams and James Bischoff, *Accountability for Human Rights Atrocities in International Law: Beyond the Nuremberg Paradigm*, 3rd edn (Oxford, 2009) 26.
[148] Leila Sadat, 'The Effect of Amnesties before Domestic and International Tribunals: Law, Morality, Politics' in Edel Hughes, William Schabas and Ramesh Thakur (eds.), *Atrocities and International Accountability* (Tokyo, 2007) 229.
[149] Kosovo is a controversial case, given the disagreements that surround its asserted statehood.
[150] E.g. GA Res. 47/131 (7 April 1993) and GA Res. 63/303 (23 July 2009).
[151] Anthony Anghie and B. S. Chimni, 'Third World Approaches to International Law and Individual Responsibility in Internal Armed Conflict' (2003) 2 *Chinese Journal of International Law* 77, 92–5.
[152] Damaška, 'What Is the Point', 361; Charles Chernor Jalloh, 'Regionalizing International Criminal Law?' (2009) 9 *International Criminal Law Review* 445.
[153] Anghie and Chimni, 'Third World Approaches', 91–2.
[154] See Ratner *et al.*, *Accountability*, 26. Alternatives to criminal prosecutions are evaluated in Chapter 22.

possibly diminishing.[155] The answer to such critiques is not to abandon punishment altogether, but to work towards non-selective application of the law. Even some enforcement is probably better than none, and powerful States are finding it more difficult to resist claims for criminal accountability of those who commit international crimes on their behalf.[156]

Further reading

Payam Akhavan, 'The Rise, and Fall, and Rise, of International Criminal Justice' (2013) 11 *Journal of International Criminal Justice* 527

José E. Alvarez, 'Crimes of Hate/Crimes of State: Lessons from Rwanda' (1999) 23 *Yale Journal of International Law* 365

Anthony Anghie and B. S. Chimni, 'Third World Approaches to International Law and Individual Responsibility in Internal Armed Conflict' (2003) 2 *Chinese Journal of International Law* 77

Antonio Cassese, 'On the Current Trend towards Criminal Prosecution and Punishment of Breaches of International Humanitarian Law' (1998) 9 *European Journal of International Law* 2

Mirjan Damaška, 'What Is the Point of International Criminal Justice' (2008) 83 *Chicago–Kent Law Review* 329

Mark Drumbl, *Atrocity, Punishment and International Law* (Cambridge, 2007)

Frederick Harhoff, 'Sense and Sensibility in Sentencing: Taking Stock of International Criminal Punishment' in Ola Engdahl and Pål Wrange (eds.), *Law at War: The Law as It Was and the Law as It Should Be: Liber Amicorum Ove Bring* (Leiden, 2008) 121

Martti Koskenniemi, 'Between Impunity and Show Trials' (2002) 6 *Max Planck Yearbook of United Nations Law* 1

David Luban, 'After the Honeymoon: Reflections on the Current State of International Criminal Justice' (2013) 11 *Journal of International Criminal Justice* 505

Jens Ohlin, 'Peace, Security and Prosecutorial Discretion' in Carsten Stahn and Göran Sluiter (eds.), *The Emerging Practice of the International Criminal Court* (Leiden, 2009) 185

Paul Roberts, 'Restoration and Retribution in International Criminal Justice' in Andrew von Hirsch *et al.* (eds.), *Restorative Justice and Criminal Justice: Competing or Reconcilable Paradigms?* (Oxford, 2004) 115

Robert Sloane, 'The Expressive Capacity of International Punishment' (2007) 43 *Stanford Journal of International Law* 39

Immi Tallgren, 'The Sense and Sensibility of International Criminal Law' (2002) 13 *European Journal of International Law* 561

---

[155] See Cryer, *Prosecuting International Crimes, passim.*   [156] Damaška, 'What Is the Point', 363.

Part B

Prosecutions in National Courts

3

Jurisdiction

3.1   Introduction

Jurisdiction is the power of the State to regulate affairs pursuant to its laws. Exercising jurisdiction involves asserting a form of sovereignty. This fact causes difficulties when jurisdiction is exercised extraterritorially. Where extraterritorial jurisdiction is asserted, sovereignties overlap, and general international law has not yet developed a hierarchy of lawful jurisdictional claims.[1] This chapter discusses the principles of jurisdiction as they relate to international crimes. International law tends to allow jurisdiction over international crimes on broader bases than it offers over other crimes. Therefore, this chapter must be read with the caveat that it is not intended to be a general discussion of the law of jurisdiction, but an explanation of jurisdiction over international crimes, a topic which is not coterminous with the general international law of jurisdiction.

3.2   The forms of jurisdiction

There are three ways in which jurisdiction may be asserted: legislative, adjudicative and executive. They will be considered in turn, although, as a matter of international law, in criminal cases 'jurisdiction to prescribe and jurisdiction to adjudicate in criminal matters are generally congruent in scope'.[2]

3.2.1   Legislative jurisdiction

This is the right of a State to pass laws that have a bearing on conduct. Some States take the view domestically that they are entitled to pass legislation covering matters which take place throughout the globe: hence the cliché that the UK Parliament could pass a statute making it a crime for a French person to smoke on the streets of Paris. However, enforcement of such a statute would be difficult from a practical point of view, as well as problematic in international law, owing to the principle of non-intervention. States are entitled to

---

[1] See section 3.5.4.
[2] Claus Kreß, 'Universal Jurisdiction over International Crimes and the Institut de Droit International' (2006) 4 *Journal of International Criminal Justice* 561, 564.

protest assertions of legislative jurisdiction which are unwarranted under international law, and there is an increasing trend towards them doing so. However, other States do not always consider their rights to be heavily affected by those claims until a specific case arises in which they are relied on.

3.2.2   *Adjudicative jurisdiction*

This is the extent to which domestic courts are able to take action to apply their State's laws and pass judgment on matters brought before them. At this point, other States may, rightly or wrongly, be more assertive in expressing their concerns about the exercise of jurisdiction, as an abstract (legislative) claim that may not directly affect a State crystallizes when a court actually asserts adjudicative jurisdiction over specific conduct.[3] By passing judgment over offences committed abroad, it is possible that courts, hence States, are intervening in the domestic jurisdiction of the State in which the offences were committed.

3.2.3   *Executive jurisdiction*

Executive (or enforcement) jurisdiction is the most intrusive of jurisdictional claims. It is the right to effect legal process coercively, such as to arrest someone, or undertake searches and seizures. The *Lotus* case,[4] which is generally accepted to reflect the international law on executive jurisdiction accurately, stated that:

> The first and foremost restriction imposed by international law upon a State is that – failing the existence of a permissive rule to the contrary – it may not exercise its power in any form in the territory of another State. In this sense jurisdiction is certainly territorial; it cannot be exercised by a State outside its territory.[5]

In the *Eichmann* case, it was accepted by Israel that, irrespective of the morality of its actions in abducting Adolf Eichmann from Argentina and taking him to Israel for trial, doing so without the consent of Argentina violated its sovereignty.[6] Care must be taken, however, to distinguish the exercise of executive jurisdiction over a person and the later exercise of adjudicative jurisdiction over them. That an arrest is illegal does not necessarily vitiate a court's adjudicative jurisdiction. The position is often referred to by the Latin aphorism *male captus bene detentus* (i.e. bad capture, good detention). The ICTY has come close to adopting this approach, by claiming that, in relation to its own jurisdiction:

> Apart from such exceptional circumstances [egregious human rights violations, not abduction *simpliciter*] however, the remedy of setting aside jurisdiction will … usually be disproportionate. The correct balance must therefore be maintained between the fundamental rights of the accused and

---

[3] For discussion of this in the context of the African Union and universal jurisdiction, see Roger O'Keefe, 'Domestic Courts as Agents of Development of the International Law of Jurisdiction' (2013) 26 *Leiden Journal of International Law* 541, 555.

[4] *SS Lotus* (*France* v. *Turkey*), 1927 PCIJ Series A No. 10.   [5] *Ibid.*, 18.

[6] *Attorney-General of Israel* v. *Eichmann*, 36 ILR 5, paras. 40–50 (District Court). For comment, see e.g. Helen Silving, 'In re Eichmann: A Dilemma of Law and Morality' (1961) 55 *American Journal of International Law* 307.

the essential interests of the international community in the prosecution of persons charged with serious violations of international humanitarian law.[7]

As the quote shows, though, the ICTY left itself some elbow room in extreme cases to refuse jurisdiction. Some national courts have adopted the position that abduction or human rights violations may, in very serious circumstances, make the assertion of jurisdiction inappropriate, as compounding an illegality.[8] Still, in spite of a trend towards such a position, it is not clear that there is an established principle of international law requiring them to do so,[9] and, as the ICTR found out, doing so in cases of international crimes can be politically contentious.[10]

3.3   Conceptual matters

3.3.1   The question of proof

It is often said that States are entitled to exercise jurisdiction unless there is a specific rule of international law that prevents them from doing so. The basis for this belief is the *Lotus* case's pronouncement that, 'far from laying down a general prohibition to the effect that States may not extend the application of their laws, and the jurisdiction of their courts to persons, property and acts outside their territory, [international law] leaves them in this respect a wide measure of discretion which is only limited in certain cases by prohibitive rules'.[11] However, even if that was the position in 1927 (which is doubtful), it does not reflect State practice since, which is to assert a positive ground for the exercise of jurisdiction, rather than to rely on the absence of a prohibition.[12] When the separate opinions in the first ICJ case on jurisdiction in which the '*Lotus* presumption' was relevant (the *Yerodia* case) came to deal with it, the judges disagreed on its continued relevance.[13]

3.3.2   Treaties and jurisdiction

It is important to note that States are entitled to pass jurisdiction to one another. The treaty-based transnational crimes are usually examples of where States have agreed between

---

[7] *Nikolić*, ICTY A. Ch., 5 June 2003, para. 30. See also *Barayagwiza*, ICTR A. Ch., 19 November 1999; *Barayagwiza*, ICTR A. Ch., 31 March 2000. See further section 17.7.3.

[8] See e.g. *R* v. *Horseferry Road Magistrates, ex parte Bennett* [1993] 2 All ER 318 (UK); *State* v. *Ebrahim* (1991) 1 South African Criminal Law Reports 307.

[9] See e.g. the decision of the Bundesverfassungsgericht (1986) *Neue Juristische Wochenschrift* 3021, denying the existence of an 'established principle of international law'; the arguments to the contrary are in Stephan Wilske, *Die völkerrechtswidrige Entführung und ihre Rechtsfolgen* (Berlin, 2000) 338–40.

[10] *Barayagwiza*, ICTR A. Ch., 19 November 1999; *Barayagwiza*, ICTR A. Ch., 31 March 2000.   [11] *SS Lotus*, at 19.

[12] See Michael Akehurst, 'Jurisdiction in International Law' (1972–3) 46 *British Yearbook of International Law* 145, 167; Vaughan Lowe and Christopher Staker, 'Jurisdiction' in Malcolm Evans (ed.), *International Law*, 3rd edn (Oxford, 2010) 315, 330. See generally Paola Gaeta, 'The Need Reasonably to Expand National Jurisdiction over International Crimes' in Antonio Cassese (ed.), *Realizing Utopia: The Future of International Law* (Oxford, 2012) 596, 598–601.

[13] *Case Concerning the Arrest Warrant of 11 April 2000* (*Democratic Republic of the Congo* v. *Belgium*), ICJ General List 121, 14 February 2002 (hereinafter '*Yerodia*'); see Separate Opinion of President Guillaume, paras. 13–14; Joint Separate Opinion of Judges Higgins, Koojimans and Buergenthal, paras. 49–51; Dissenting Opinion of Judge ad hoc Van den Wyngaert, paras. 48–51; however, see also Jean d'Aspremont, 'Multilateral versus Unilateral Exercises of Universal Jurisdiction' (2010) 43 *Israel Law Review* 301, 311–15.

themselves that they may exercise jurisdiction on each other's behalf.[14] An example of this is Article 5(1) and (2) of the 1979 International Convention against the Taking of Hostages.[15] Such treaties include obligations on (or permissions to) States Parties to criminalize certain conduct on quite broad jurisdictional bases, and either to extradite or prosecute suspects. These treaties are often seen, albeit somewhat inaccurately, as creating universal jurisdiction.[16] The jurisdiction conferred, strictly speaking, is only a matter of concessions between the parties, who agree that other States may exercise their jurisdiction on their behalf.[17] There is nothing unlawful about this. States are entitled to pass jurisdiction to one another.[18] However, if a State were to assert a right to prosecute someone on the basis of a treaty which is not referable to a concession of one of the accepted forms of jurisdiction by a State Party to the convention, it would violate international law, unless the convention can be regarded as reflective of custom.[19] Such claims of customary status are easier to make than prove. In the following sections, this chapter will concentrate on the jurisdiction States have pursuant to customary international law.

3.4   The 'traditional' heads of jurisdiction

3.4.1   The territoriality principle

The territoriality principle is the least controversial basis of jurisdiction. Under this principle, States have the right to exercise jurisdiction over all events on their territory, this includes their airspace and territorial waters, and also includes ships and aeroplanes which are registered in those countries as being what has been described as 'quasi-territorial' jurisdiction.[20] This is the position that the ICC Statute adopts too.[21] States also have quasi-territorial jurisdiction over areas which they are leasing (in accordance with the terms of that lease), or belligerently occupying.[22] How the ICC would deal with this, especially the latter situation, for its own purposes though, is an open question.

A State has jurisdiction over a crime when the crime originates abroad or is completed elsewhere, so long as at least one of the elements of the offence occurs in its territory. If it is the former, it is said to be 'objective' territorial jurisdiction, if it is the latter, then it is

---

[14] See section 14.1.2. A very useful discussion of this issue is included in Neil Boister, *An Introduction to Transnational Criminal Law* (Oxford, 2013) Chapter 12.

[15] 1316 UNTS 205.

[16] The ICJ is not immune from this trend: see *Questions Relating to the Obligation to Prosecute or Extradite* (*Belgium* v. *Senegal*), ICJ General List 144, 20 July 2012, para. 72. See also d'Aspremont, 'Multilateral versus Unilateral', 307, although the characterization of them as universal is based on an idiosyncratic concept of universal jurisdiction that is better considered as being mutual concessions of jurisdiction *inter partes* to the relevant treaties.

[17] Boister, *Transnational Criminal Law*, 147–50.

[18] Some doubt this: see e.g. Madeline Morris, 'High Crimes and Misconceptions: The ICC and Non Party States' (2000) 64 *Law and Contemporary Problems* 131. But there is considerable practice to support its legality: see e.g. Dapo Akande, 'The Jurisdiction of the International Criminal Court over Nationals of Non-Parties: Legal Basis and Limits' (2003) 1 *Journal of International Criminal Justice* 618, 620–34.

[19] See Lowe and Staker, 'Jurisdiction', 327–9; Anthony Colangelo, 'The Legal Limits of Universal Jurisdiction' (2006–7) 47 *Virginia Journal of International Law* 149, 166–9.

[20] Boister, *Transnational Criminal Law*, 139.   [21] Art. 12(2)(a).

[22] Bernard H. Oxman, 'Jurisdiction of States' in Rüdiger Wolfrum (ed.), *Max Planck Encyclopedia of Public International Law* Vol. VI, 547, 548.

'subjective' territoriality. An example is Article 14(2) of the Armenian Criminal Code, which provides that:

a crime is considered committed in the territory of the Republic of Armenia when:

1. it started, continued or finished in the territory of the Republic of Armenia;
2. it was committed in complicity with the persons who committed crimes in other countries.[23]

An example of objective and subjective territoriality in international criminal law would be where a rocket is fired from one State at a civilian object in another. The State in which the rocket was fired would have jurisdiction over the event on the basis of subjective territoriality, whilst the State in which the rocket landed would have jurisdiction over it on the basis of objective territoriality. Some would now go further and classify the 'ubiquity' principle as being an aspect of territorial jurisdiction. This principle is to the effect that, wherever a part of a crime (including complicity) occurs, there is territorial jurisdiction.[24] The Armenian Criminal Code quoted above adopts this position, and UK practice is even broader, as it asserts jurisdiction over (inchoate) conspiracies to commit crimes in the United Kingdom, even though all of the conduct occurs abroad, on the basis that the intended offence was to occur in the United Kingdom.[25]

The problem for international criminal law with the territoriality principle is not its existence or, for the most part, its extent, but the reluctance of many States to prosecute offences which occur on their territories, or, conversely, the extent to which fair trial guarantees are offered where such prosecutions occur. Examples of trials for international crimes based on territoriality include the Rwandan *gacaca* trials,[26] and the trials ongoing in the Bosnian War Crimes Chamber. These latter examples include cases originally investigated by the ICTY, but referred by it to the War Crimes Chamber.[27]

3.4.2   The nationality principle

The second generally accepted principle of jurisdiction is nationality (sometimes known as 'active nationality').[28] States are entitled under international law to legislate with respect to the conduct of their nationals abroad. Many States adopt this head of jurisdiction quite broadly. Article 12(2) of the Bosnia and Herzegovina Criminal Code, for example, states that '[t]he criminal legislation of Bosnia and Herzegovina shall be applied to a citizen of Bosnia and Herzegovina who, outside the territory of Bosnia and Herzegovina, perpetrates a criminal offence'.

Nationality is an important basis of jurisdiction in international criminal law, in particular in relation to armed forces (including peacekeepers) stationed overseas who, in the

---

[23] Available at www.nottingham.ac.uk/sharedl/shared_hrlcicju/Armeniai/Criminal_Code_English_.doc.
[24] Boister, *Transnational Criminal Law*, 140–1.   [25] *DPP* v. *Doot* [1973] AC 807.
[26] See Erin Daly, 'Between Punitive and Reconstructive Justice: The Gacaca Courts in Rwanda' (2001–2) 34 *New York University Journal of International Law and Politics* 355.
[27] E.g. *Stanković*, ICTY T. Ch., 17 May 2005; *Rašević and Todović*, ICTY T. Ch., 8 July 2005. See Chapter 9.
[28] For some of the benefits of nationality jurisdiction, see Paul Arnell, 'The Case for Nationality Based Jurisdiction' (2001) 50 *International and Comparative Law Quarterly* 955.

legislation of most States, 'carry the flag' abroad with them.[29] The principle, nonetheless, applies beyond the armed forces, and also covers civilians. An example of this is section 9 of the United Kingdom's Offences against the Person Act 1861, which, as an exception to the usual preference of common law countries for territoriality jurisdiction, also asserts jurisdiction over murders committed by British nationals irrespective of the place of commission.

Nationality jurisdiction relies on the link between a national and the State to which he or she owes allegiance. For the most part, the question of who is a national is relatively uncontroversial and dealt with by the legislation of the State granting nationality. Equally, the extent to which other States are required to accept that nationality (and thus any jurisdiction based on it) is limited by international law.[30] One test for nationality in international law was given in the *Nottebohm* case: that the person with the purported nationality must have a 'genuine connection' with the State of which he or she is an alleged national.[31]

Some doubt that the *Nottebohm* test is the appropriate test for nationality jurisdiction. They do so on the basis that the *Nottebohm* case was dealing not with a jurisdictional matter, but with the extent to which a State could rely on its own grant of nationality to exercise diplomatic protection with respect to a person who had sought that nationality.[32] These are strong reasons, although it must be noted that others are happy to draw the analogy,[33] and, where jurisdiction is being asserted on the basis of the nationality of the offender, the *locus delicti* is being required to accept the jurisdiction of a foreign State over events on its territory, so there are some parallels that may legitimately be drawn. Nonetheless, the broad jurisdiction accepted by international law in relation to international crimes (when compared to ordinary domestic crimes) means that this will rarely be an issue, unless a person who denies nationality is being prosecuted on the basis of legislation that does not adopt those broader jurisdictional claims.

For nationality jurisdiction, it is often required that the person over whom that jurisdiction is being asserted was a national at the time of the offence rather than after. Otherwise, it has been claimed, a violation of the *nullum crimen sine lege* principle could occur.[34] Nevertheless, some States provide for jurisdiction in the situation where suspects later acquire their nationality.[35] Those States tend to view such an exercise of the jurisdiction as being a vicarious use of the authority of the *locus delicti*.[36] As a result, the lawfulness of

---

[29] This is important as often, under Status of Forces agreements, territorial States agree to waive their jurisdiction over foreign forces in their territory. See generally Rain Livoja, *An Axiom of Military Law: Applicability of National Criminal Law to Military Personnel and Associated Civilians Abroad* (Helsinki, 2011).
[30] Lowe and Staker, 'Jurisdiction', 324–5.   [31] *Liechtenstein v. Guatemala* (1955) ICJ Reports 4.
[32] Lowe and Staker, 'Jurisdiction', 324–5. More generally, see Chittharanjan Amerasinghe, *Diplomatic Protection* (Oxford, 2008) 92–6, 113–16.
[33] Bruno Simma and Andreas Th. Müller, 'Exercise and Limits of Jurisdiction' in James Crawford and Martti Koskenniemi (eds.), *The Cambridge Companion to International Law* (Cambridge, 2012) 134, 142.
[34] See Roger O'Keefe, 'Universal Jurisdiction: Clarifying the Basic Concept' (2004) 2 *Journal of International Criminal Justice* 735, 742–3.
[35] See e.g. Swedish Penal Code, Chapter 2, s. 2.
[36] This is justified on the basis that many States adopting such a position refuse to extradite their nationals.

any such use depends on whether the conduct for which the suspect is prosecuted was criminal in the *locus delicti* (or in international law) at the time of its commission.[37]

A number of States assert jurisdiction over the activities of their permanent residents even when they are abroad. This is an expanded form of nationality jurisdiction,[38] but one which is acceptable under international law, as those who have chosen to reside permanently in a State are clearly analogous to its nationals. A similar consideration applies to non-nationals who serve a State's armed forces.

One of the most well-known uses of nationality jurisdiction was the US prosecution of Lieutenant William Calley for his role in the My Lai massacre in Vietnam.[39] This case also provides an example of one of the criticisms often laid at the door of nationality jurisdiction, that prosecutions by States of their own nationals for war crimes may tend to be overly lenient.[40]

3.4.3   *The passive personality principle*

Passive personality jurisdiction is jurisdiction exercised by a State over crimes committed against its nationals whilst they are abroad. In most instances, the assertion of such jurisdiction is controversial. All of the judges who expressed an opinion on the matter in the *Lotus* case took the view that customary international law does not accept such a principle.[41] There has been an increase in the use of passive personality jurisdiction, particularly by the United States, in relation to terrorist offences,[42] and there is increasing support for it.[43] However, considerable disagreement remains surrounding the lawfulness of its application.[44] There are fears that passive personality jurisdiction favours powerful States at the expense of weaker States. Concerns have also been raised that passive personality jurisdiction could lead to people being subjected simultaneously to the laws of many different States, which would include prohibitions of which they were understandably unaware.[45]

The latter problem only arises where the law differs between States. The problem ought not to apply to international crimes, as its prohibitions apply across States rather than reflecting national oddities. One of the few areas in which passive personality jurisdiction has traditionally been accepted is in relation to war crimes.[46] Thus, States have the right to prosecute war crimes committed against their nationals. One of many examples is the

---

[37] If it was not, then a violation of the *nullum crimen* principle would result, unless the allegation was one of an international crime.

[38] See further James Crawford, *Brownlie's Principles of Public International Law*, 8th edn (Oxford, 2012) 459–60.

[39] *United States* v. *Calley* (1969) 41 CMR 96; (1973) 46 CMR 1131; (1973) 48 CMR 19.

[40] See Timothy L. H. McCormack, 'Their Atrocities and our Misdemeanours: The Reticence of States to Try their "own Nationals" for International Crimes' in Philippe Sands and Mark Lattimer (eds.), *Justice for Crimes against Humanity* (Oxford, 2003) 107.

[41] See e.g. David J. Harris, *Cases and Materials on International Law*, 6th edn (London, 2005) 281; the judgment itself, however, does not contain a ruling on the matter.

[42] One example is *United States* v. *Yunis* (1991) 30 ILM 403.   [43] Simma and Müller, 'Exercise', 142–3.

[44] See Lowe and Staker, 'Jurisdiction', 330.

[45] James L. Brierly, 'The "Lotus Case"' (1928) 44 *Law Quarterly Review* 154, 161.

[46] E.g. *Rohrig, Brunner and Heinze* (1950) 17 ILR 393.

Almelo case,[47] in which a German national was prosecuted by a British military court for killing a UK national in the Netherlands. International law goes beyond this, however, to permit prosecution of offences committed against the nationals of co-belligerent States. For example, in the *Velpke Baby Home* case the United Kingdom prosecuted German nationals for neglect and mistreatment of Polish children which took place in Germany.[48]

Where passive personality jurisdiction is asserted over international crimes, the same questions arise in relation to determining nationality as for nationality jurisdiction. The relevant time for determining nationality is generally considered to be the time of the offence. Consequently, the fact that a person later gains the nationality of a State that wishes to prosecute offences against him or her does not grant that State passive personality jurisdiction. As with nationality jurisdiction, however, the broader jurisdiction applicable to international crimes means that this will not normally be a problem. For example, Israel sought to assert passive personality jurisdiction in the *Eichmann* case on behalf of Eichmann's Jewish victims. Its claims on this basis, in relation to the victims, who were not Israeli nationals at the time of Eichmann's offences, has been severely criticized,[49] although Israel's right to try Eichmann on the basis of the universality principle was generally accepted.

3.4.4   The protective principle

A State is entitled to assert protective jurisdiction over extraterritorial activities that threaten State security, such as the selling of a State's secrets, spying or the counterfeiting of its currency or official seal. Although the principle could be used to justify the assertion of jurisdiction over aggression, and was asserted by Israel as one of the bases of jurisdiction over Adolf Eichmann,[50] practically all its imaginable uses in relation to international criminal law overlap with territorial, nationality or passive personality jurisdiction. The assertion of the protective principle in *Eichmann* was criticized on the basis that, irrespective of its right to prosecute him, the State of Israel did not exist at the time of the commission of the offences.[51]

3.5   Universal jurisdiction

3.5.1   Introduction

Universal jurisdiction is probably the most controversial principle of jurisdiction in international criminal law. It is certainly the most talked-about.[52] The term 'universal jurisdiction'

---

[47] I LRTWC 35.
[48] George Brand, *Trial of Heinrich Gerike* (London, 1950). Lauterpacht ('Foreword', *ibid.*, xv) went further, to assert that the trial was based on universality, but see George Brand, 'Introduction', *ibid.*, xxix.
[49] James E. S. Fawcett, 'The Eichmann Case' (1962) 38 *British Yearbook of International Law* 181, 190–2.
[50] *Attorney-General of Israel v. Eichmann*, 36 ILR 18, 54–7, 304.
[51] David Lasok, 'The Eichmann Trial' (1962) 11 *International and Comparative Law Quarterly* 355, 364.
[52] For a useful overview of the voluminous literature on the subject at the turn of the millennium, see A. Hays Butler, 'The Doctrine of Universal Jurisdiction: A Review of the Literature' (2000) 11 *Criminal Law Forum* 353.

refers to jurisdiction established over a crime without reference to the place of perpetration, the nationality of the suspect or the victim or any other recognized linking point between the crime and the prosecuting State. It is a principle of jurisdiction limited to specific crimes. There are those who deny that universal jurisdiction exists at all.[53] However, the view more consistent with current practice is that – other than piracy, which is subject to universal jurisdiction owing to its occurring, by definition, on the high seas[54] – States are entitled to assert universal jurisdiction over war crimes, crimes against humanity, genocide and torture,[55] as those crimes are defined in customary law.[56] There are no examples of universal jurisdiction prosecutions for aggression.[57]

Jurisdiction tends to inhere in States for the purpose of protecting their own interests. The purpose of universal jurisdiction, on the other hand, is linked to the idea that international crimes affect the international legal order as a whole.[58] Owing to the recognition that such offences affect all States and peoples, and awareness that territorial and nationality States do not always respond fairly and effectively to allegations of international crimes, international law grants all States the right to prosecute international crimes. The precise conditions under which a State may do so, however, are controversial, and matters are not helped by a tendency to roll together the issues of whether universal jurisdiction exists and whether or not there is a duty to exercise such jurisdiction. This is compounded by a conflation of two other questions, namely, whether States may exercise universal jurisdiction and whether they ought to do so. The discussion below relates to whether States are entitled to assert universal jurisdiction as there is no real evidence that, outside treaty obligations, States are obliged to do so.

3.5.2 *Approaches to universal jurisdiction*

Universal jurisdiction has often, at least since the ICJ's decision in the *Yerodia* case,[59] been separated into two questionable subcategories. These are what is often termed 'absolute' or 'pure' universal jurisdiction (also known as 'universal jurisdiction *in absentia*') and 'conditional' universal jurisdiction (sometimes known as 'universal jurisdiction with presence').

---

[53] See e.g. Alfred Rubin, 'Actio Popularis, Jus Cogens and Offences Erga Omnes' (2001) 35 *New England Law Review* 265; Marc Henzelin, *Le Principe de l'Universalité en Droit Pénal Internationale* (Brussels, 2000).

[54] Some question whether piracy is an appropriate analogy for modern assertions of universal jurisdiction: see Eugene Kontorovich, 'The Piracy Analogy: Modern Universal Jurisdiction's Hollow Foundation' (2004) 45 *Harvard International Law Journal* 183. Even if this is the case, it does not, however, undermine State practice in the area.

[55] See Institut de Droit International, *Seventeenth Commission, Universal Jurisdiction over Genocide, Crimes against Humanity and War Crimes* (Cracow, 2005) 2. See Kreß, 'Universal Jurisdiction'. On torture, see *Furundžija*, ICTY T. Ch. II, 10 December 1998, para. 156.

[56] Colangelo, 'Legal Limits'.

[57] Attempts to persuade German prosecutors to take on the question of aggression with respect to Iraq have failed: see e.g. Claus Kreß, 'The German Chief Federal Prosecutor's Decision Not to Investigate the Alleged Crime of Preparing Aggression against Iraq' (2003) 2 *Journal of International Criminal Justice* 245.

[58] Rosalyn Higgins, *Problems and Process: International Law and How We Use It* (Oxford, 1994) 56–63; Andreas Zimmermann, 'Violations of Fundamental Norms of International Law and the Exercise of Universal Jurisdiction in Criminal Matters' in Christian Tomuschat and Jean-Marc Thouvenin (eds.), *The Fundamental Rules of the International Legal Order* (Leiden, 2006) 335; Simma and Müller, 'Exercise', 144; Alejandro Chehtman, *The Philosophical Foundations of Extraterritorial Punishment* (Oxford, 2010).

[59] *Case Concerning the Arrest Warrant of 11 April 2000 (Democratic Republic of the Congo v. Belgium)*, ICJ General List 121, 14 February 2002.

Pure universal jurisdiction is when a State seeks to assert jurisdiction over an international crime (usually by investigating it and/or requesting extradition of the suspect) even when the suspect is not present in the territory of the investigating State. Conditional universal jurisdiction is universal jurisdiction exercised when the suspect is already in the State asserting jurisdiction.

The distinction has gathered considerable acceptance in academic literature,[60] but, although the matter is not entirely not beyond controversy, the better view is that the distinction is non-existent at a conceptual level.[61] That said, many States limit their use of universal jurisdiction to where a person is present on their territory;[62] this can, at least in part, be explained on the basis that adopting pure universal jurisdiction 'may show a lack of international courtesy'.[63] Where States have adopted such a limit, it appears that some of them have done so as a matter of practical prudence, or as the result of political pressure, rather than as a matter of law.

The resolution on universal jurisdiction of the Institut de Droit International attempts to tread a middle path between the approaches by providing that, '[a]part from acts of investigation and requests for extradition, the exercise of universal jurisdiction requires the presence of the alleged offender in the territory of the prosecuting State ... or other lawful form of control over the alleged offender'.[64] However, the Institut's resolution appears to mix questions of jurisdiction and whether States are entitled, under human rights law, to try people *in absentia*.[65] It is also questionable whether adjudicative jurisdiction can be split up between extradition and trial in the manner the Institut suggests,[66] in particular as those asserting the distinction between absolute and conditional universal jurisdiction in *Yerodia* were discussing an arrest warrant, which was intended as a precursor to extradition.[67]

3.5.3   The rise of universal jurisdiction

The possibility of universal jurisdiction being exercised over war crimes was mooted during the Second World War.[68] A number of cases prosecuted after the Second World War could be justified or explained on the basis of universal jurisdiction.[69] The United Nations War Crimes

[60] See e.g. Antonio Cassese, 'Is the Bell Tolling for Universality? A Plea for a Sensible Notion of Universal Jurisdiction' (2003) 1 *Journal of International Criminal Justice* 589, 592–3; Georges Abi-Saab, 'The Proper Role of Universal Jurisdiction' (2003) 1 *Journal of International Criminal Justice* 596, 601.
[61] O'Keefe, 'Universal Jurisdiction: Clarifying the Basic Concept', is a particularly powerful argument to this effect. See also Thomas Weigend, 'Grund und Grenzen universaler Gerichtsbarkeit', in Jörg Arnold *et al.* (eds.), *Festschrift für Albin Eser* (Munich, 2005) 955; Kreß, 'Universal Jurisdiction', 576–8; Crawford, *Brownlie's Principles*, 469.
[62] Fannie Lafontaine, 'Universal Jurisdiction – The Realistic Utopia' (2012) 10 *Journal of International Criminal Justice* 1277, 1280–3.
[63] *Yerodia*, Separate Opinion of Judge ad hoc Van den Wyngaert, para. 3.   [64] Resolution, para. 3(b).
[65] Kreß, 'Universal Jurisdiction', 578–9.   [66] *Ibid.*, 576–8.
[67] The position for non-coercive acts of investigation, such as requests for information, however, may be differentiated, on the basis that they can be refused at will. The ICJ in the *Certain Criminal Proceedings* Case (*Djibouti* v. *France*), paras. 170–1, considered a request for information to a person who was immune not to violate international law, as it was not a coercive measure.
[68] Willard Cowles, 'Universality of Jurisdiction over War Crimes' (1945) 33 *California Law Review* 177.
[69] E.g. *Tesch and Others* (the 'Zyklon B case'), I LRTWC 93.

Commission[70] took the view that 'the right to punish war crimes ... is possessed by any independent State whatsoever'.[71] Equally those cases could be justified on the basis of the expanded passive personality jurisdiction international law accepts for war crimes.

In 1949 the Geneva Conventions provided a treaty-based analogue to universal jurisdiction in relation to their grave breaches provisions. Article 49 of Geneva Convention I (to which the other three conventions have similar provisions) reads:

Each High Contracting Party shall be under the obligation to search for persons alleged to have committed, or to have ordered to be committed, such grave breaches and shall bring such persons, regardless of their nationality, before its own courts [or hand them over to another High Contracting Party].[72]

The grave breaches regime is often considered a paradigmatic case of universal jurisdiction, and in practice is exceptionally similar to it. Still, it should be noted that the Conventions speak of 'grave breaches' of their own provisions. Given that (other than common Article 3) the Conventions only apply to conflicts between High Contracting Parties,[73] by their own terms the grave breaches provisions only have *inter partes* effect as a matter of treaty law.[74] Still, the fact that essentially every State in the world has ratified the Conventions makes this a distinction of form rather than substance.[75]

Probably the most famous exercise of universal jurisdiction was the Israeli prosecution of Adolf Eichmann. Eichmann was abducted from Argentina in 1960 by the Israeli security service, Mossad, and flown to Jerusalem to be tried.[76] The District Court in Jerusalem, in affirming Israel's right to prosecute him, stated that:

The abhorrent crimes defined under this Law are not crimes under Israeli law alone. These crimes, which struck at the whole of mankind and shocked the conscience of nations, are grave offences against the law of nations itself (*delicta juris gentium*). Therefore, so far from international law negating or limiting the jurisdiction of countries with respect to such crimes, international law is, in the absence of an international court, in need of the judicial and legislative organs of every country to give effect to its criminal interdictions and to bring the criminals to trial. The jurisdiction to try crimes under international law is universal.[77]

It might be noted that, in spite of its comments about an international criminal court which, in light of the principle of complementarity, now seem anachronistic, the District Court's opinion is a strong affirmation of a right (and perhaps even a duty) to establish universal

---

[70] Which, for clarity's sake, it should be noted was an inter-Allied body, rather than the (practically) universal international organization.

[71] XV LRTWC 26 (Commentary).

[72] See Richard van Elst, 'Implementing Universal Jurisdiction over Grave Breaches of the Geneva Conventions' (2000) 13 *Leiden Journal of International Law* 815.

[73] The Geneva Conventions, common Art. 2.   [74] Their prohibitions, however, clearly reflect customary law.

[75] The situation with respect to grave breaches of Additional Protocol I is a little more complex, as it is less (although still broadly) ratified. Most, if not all, of the grave breaches provisions of Additional Protocol I, however, reflect customary law.

[76] Israel originally claimed that the 'rendition' (in modern terminology) was undertaken by public-spirited private Israeli citizens, but its assertion was not widely believed. See also section 3.2.3.

[77] (1968) 36 ILR 5, para. 12 (District Court).

jurisdiction over international crimes. Israel did rely on other bases of jurisdiction, but its primary jurisdictional claim was universality, as the Israeli Supreme Court explained:

if in our judgment we have concentrated on the international and universal character of the crimes . . . one of the reasons for our so doing is that some of them were directed against non-Jewish groups.[78]

After *Eichmann*, there was little evidence of any political will to engage in universal jurisdiction prosecutions until 1985, when Israel requested the extradition of John Demjanjuk from the United States. Demjanjuk was suspected of being a notorious camp guard in Treblinka known as 'Ivan the Terrible'. The United States agreed to extradite Demjanjuk,[79] who stood trial in Israel, but was acquitted on the basis that, although he was a guard at Sobibor and Trawniki camps, he was not 'Ivan the Terrible'.[80]

Other examples of assertions of universal jurisdiction around this time were legislative Acts such as the United Kingdom's War Crimes Act 1991[81] and Australia's War Crimes Amendment Act 1988,[82] both of which dealt with offences committed in the Second World War by those acting on behalf of the Axis but who later became residents of those two countries. As jurisdiction crystallizes at the time of the offence, these Acts, and the (limited) prosecutions under them, are best seen as based on universal jurisdiction.[83] This is because later residence *per se* is not a head of jurisdiction, and the basis of jurisdiction is not territoriality or nationality.[84]

The conflicts in Yugoslavia and Rwanda (which notably gave rise to the ICTY and ICTR) led to a number of prosecutions, in particular of people who had come to countries such as Germany and Switzerland as refugees.[85] A number of prosecutions were undertaken in Belgium, pursuant to its Law of 16 June 1993 Relating to the Repression of Grave Breaches of the Geneva Conventions of 12 August 1949 and their Protocols I and II of 8 June 1977,[86] which criminalized certain violations of those treaties without regard to the place of their commission.[87]

By 1999, it appeared that universal jurisdiction was developing considerable momentum. The *Pinochet* litigation throughout Europe,[88] for example, was thought by careful commentators to represent 'the globalization of human rights law through the affirmation that the

---

[78] (1968) 36 ILR 277, para. 12 (Supreme Court).
[79] *Demjanjuk v. Petrovsky*, 776 F 2d 571 (USCA 6th Cir. 1985); cert. den. 475 US 1016 (1986); 628 F Supp 1370 (1986); 784 F 2d 1254 (1986).
[80] See Jonathan M. Weinig, 'Enforcing the Lessons of History: Israel Judges the Holocaust' in Timothy L. H. McCormack and Gerry J. Simpson (eds.), *The Law of War Crimes: National and International Approaches* (The Hague, 1997) 103, 115–18. Demjanjuk was finally convicted by a Munich court in 2011 for crimes committed as a guard in Sobibor in 1943. He was sentenced to five years' imprisonment but set free pending an appeal. He died on 17 March 2012.
[81] War Crimes Act 1991, s. 1(a). On the Act, see Christopher Greenwood, 'The War Crimes Act 1991' in Hazel Fox and Michael A. Meyer (eds.), *Armed Conflict and the New Law: Effecting Compliance* (London, 1993) 215.
[82] War Crimes Amendment Act 1988, s. 5. See generally Gillian Triggs, 'Australia's War Crimes Trials: A Moral Necessity or Legal Minefield?' (1987) 16 *Melbourne University Law Review* 382.
[83] See Chapter 4.
[84] It would be possible to argue that jurisdiction could be co-belligerent (or passive personal jurisdiction), but the Acts do not limit themselves to victims who were nationals of the Allied powers.
[85] Andreas Ziegler, 'International Decisions: In re G' (1998) 82 *American Journal of International Law* 78; Luc Reydams, *Universal Jurisdiction: International and Municipal Legal Perspectives* (Oxford, 2003) 196–200.
[86] *Moniteur Belge*, 5 August 1993.   [87] See Reydams, *Universal Jurisdiction*, 109–16.
[88] See the comments on the various cases in (1999) 93 *American Journal of International Law* 690–711.

consequences of, and jurisdiction over, gross violations are not limited to the State in which they (mostly) occur, or of that of the nationality of the majority of the victims'.[89] In the same year, Belgium revised its 1993 legislation on grave breaches to add to it jurisdiction over genocide and crimes against humanity 'irrespective of where such breaches have been committed'.[90] The presence of the suspect in Belgium was not required for the initiation of proceedings, which could be brought by private parties. The 1999 law also declared that immunities were inapplicable in proceedings relating to the Act.[91]

3.5.4 The retrenchment of universal jurisdiction?

Although the 1993 statute gave rise to a number of proceedings relating to Rwanda, which did not upset the Rwandan government,[92] the Belgian law proved to be politically controversial. Proceedings were brought – though never completed – against, amongst others, Ariel Sharon, Yasser Arafat, Fidel Castro and Hashemi Rafsanjani.[93] These proceedings all led to political embarrassment for Belgium. The case against Abduldaye Yerodia Ndombasi led to a challenge to the Belgian law in the International Court of Justice.

The Yerodia case

Abduldaye Yerodia, then foreign minister of the Democratic Republic of the Congo (DRC), was the subject of an international arrest warrant issued by Damien Vandermeersch, a Belgian investigating judge, on 11 April 2000. Six months later, the DRC brought a suit against Belgium in the ICJ, alleging that Belgium had acted unlawfully by asserting universal jurisdiction over Yerodia and ignoring his immunity as a foreign minister.[94] Late in the proceedings the DRC dropped the claim relating to universal jurisdiction, and concentrated on the issue of immunities, on which the ICJ eventually found in its favour.[95]

Owing to the DRC's litigation strategy, the majority decided that the ICJ did not need to determine the lawfulness of Belgium's assertion of universal jurisdiction. The majority was criticized for this by a number of the judges, including the President of the Court, Gilbert Guillaume,[96] Judges Higgins, Koojimans and Buergenthal,[97] and the Belgian ad hoc judge, Christine Van den Wyngaert.[98] Their critiques are telling: logically the question of

[89] Christine Chinkin, 'R v. Bow Street Stipendiary Magistrate, Ex Parte Pinochet (No. 3) [1999] 2 WLR 827' (1999) 93 *American Journal of International Law* 703, 711. The precise bases of jurisdiction were made more complex by the fact that jurisdiction under general international law was supplemented in a number of States with arguments based on the Torture Convention.
[90] (1999) ILM 921, Art. 7. For an overview, see Damien Vandermeersch, 'Prosecuting International Crimes in Belgium' (2005) 3 *Journal of International Criminal Justice* 400.
[91] (1999) ILM 921, Art. 5(3).
[92] See Luc Reydams, 'Belgium's First Application of Universal Jurisdiction: The Butare Four Case' (2003) 1 *Journal of International Criminal Justice* 428.
[93] See Steven R. Ratner, 'Belgium's War Crimes Statute: A Postmortem' (2003) 97 *American Journal of International Law* 888, 890.
[94] *Yerodia.* See Neil Boister, 'The ICJ in the Belgian Arrest Warrant Case: Arresting the Development of International Criminal Law' (2002) 7 *Journal of Conflict and Security Law* 293; O'Keefe, 'Universal Jurisdiction: Clarifying the Basic Concept'.
[95] See Chapter 21. [96] *Yerodia,* Separate Opinion of the President, para. 1.
[97] *Ibid.,* Joint Separate Opinion of Judges Higgins, Koojimans and Buergenthal, paras. 3–5.
[98] *Ibid.,* Dissenting Opinion of Judge ad hoc Van den Wyngaert, para. 41.

jurisdiction precedes that of immunity (as there must be immunity from something).[99] Also, the arguments about immunity may have been affected by the arguments about universal jurisdiction (in particular those relating to *ius cogens*).

Unlike the majority decision, a number of the separate and dissenting opinions dealt with universal jurisdiction in detail. They revealed a deeply divided court. Four judges (President Guillaume, Judges Ranjeva, Rezek and Judge ad hoc Bula-Bula) were opposed to the assertion of jurisdiction, whereas six judges (Judge Koroma, Judges Higgins, Buergenthal and Koojimans in their joint opinion, Judge al-Khasawneh and Judge ad hoc Van den Wyngaert) supported it (Judge al-Khasawneh at least implicitly took that view).[100] Although many saw this case as a blow to universal jurisdiction, it must be noted that the majority of judges who expressed a view on the matter upheld the universality principle and only one of the judges questioned the use of universal jurisdiction where the person is found in the territory of the State asserting jurisdiction. Three of the four judges who criticized universal jurisdiction appear only to be referring to such jurisdiction being asserted *in absentia*.[101] Only President Guillaume appeared hostile to any sort of universal jurisdiction outside of piracy and treaty regimes.[102]

Limiting universality

Belgium's political problems with its law did not end with the *Yerodia* case. Following attempts to indict ex-President George H. W. Bush, Vice-President Dick Cheney and Colin Powell for war crimes alleged to have been committed by them in the Gulf War in 1991, Belgium came under heavy pressure from the United States to alter its legislation.[103] In response, Belgium altered its legislation twice in 2003 to limit its jurisdiction and reintroduce immunities.[104] Some saw the Belgian action as signalling the demise of broad notions of universality.[105] The Belgian law is no longer as wide, but it retains some universal jurisdiction elements. For example, jurisdiction may be exercised if a perpetrator later becomes a Belgian resident.[106] It is also clear that the Belgian position is not that universal jurisdiction *in absentia* is unlawful. Its stated reason for repealing the Act was that it had been abused. After 2003, Belgium sought the extradition of Hissène Habré, the ex-dictator of Chad, pursuant to a complaint made before the Act was amended, on the basis of absolute universality. This implies that its view is that universal jurisdiction remains available in international law.[107]

---

[99] *Yerodia*, para. 46.   [100] Judge Oda also seemed sympathetic: *ibid.*, Dissenting Opinion of Judge Oda, para. 12.
[101] Alain Winants, 'The Yerodia Ruling of the International Court of Justice and the 1993/1999 Belgian Law on Universal Jurisdiction' (2003) 16 *Leiden Journal of International Law* 491, 500.
[102] *Yerodia*, Separate Opinion of President Guillaume, para. 16.   [103] Ratner, 'A Postmortem'.
[104] See *ibid.*; and see Luc Reydams, 'Belgium Reneges on Universality: The 5 August 2003 Act on Grave Breaches of International Humanitarian Law' (2003) 1 *Journal of International Criminal Justice* 679.
[105] Cassese, 'Is the Bell Tolling?'   [106] Criminal Procedure Code, Art. 6.1°*bis*.
[107] Although in the particular case the extradition request was refused and Senegal agreed to try Habré itself. The proceedings have moved very slowly, and in 2012 the ICJ determined that these delays meant that Senegal was violating its duty to prosecute under the Torture Convention: *Questions Relating to the Obligation to Prosecute or Extradite (Belgium v. Senegal)*, ICJ General List 144, 20 July 2012.

The other State whose use of universal jurisdiction appeared to have been reined in somewhat is Spain. Spain was the first State to ask the United Kingdom to extradite General Pinochet.[108] It has, since 1999, also indicted (and in one instance convicted) a number of ex-members of military juntas from Latin America. Although the Pinochet case failed to lead to an extradition owing to the UK Home Secretary's determination that the defendant's ill-health prevented it, Spain has used universal jurisdiction successfully in other cases. It has obtained the extradition of Ricardo Cavallo, accused of torture in Argentina, and convicted Adolfo Scilingo for crimes against humanity for his role in torture and killings in Argentina after he went to Spain to testify about his actions in another case.[109]

A number of cases since 2000 did, however, place a fairly restrictive interpretation on universal jurisdiction, requiring that Spanish universal jurisdiction be 'subsidiary' to the jurisdiction of the territorial State, with Spain only having jurisdiction if there is no effort to prosecute by that State. This may be a sensible practical limit, but is not required by international law.[110] The Spanish cases also appeared to require the presence of the suspect in Spain, although presence pursuant to extradition, as in the Cavallo case, seemed sufficient.[111] A firm reaffirmation of universal jurisdiction, without any of the limitations suggested in the previous cases, came from the Spanish Constitutional Tribunal in the *Guatemala Genocide* case, which expressly repudiated the earlier, more limited, jurisprudence.[112] However, after a number of controversial attempts to prosecute, *inter alia*, American officials, similar pressures to those that were brought to bear on Belgium led the Spanish parliament to include subsidiarity-based limitations on Spanish exercises of universal jurisdiction.[113]

Other practice

It is common to tie, to a greater or lesser extent, the fate of universal jurisdiction to the Belgian, and sometimes the Spanish, experience(s),[114] however, there are many other States

---

[108] Although it ought to be noted that some, but not all, of the victims of the conduct for which Spain sought to extradite Pinochet were Spanish.

[109] See Christian Tomuschat, 'Issues of Universal Jurisdiction in the Scilingo Case' (2005) 3 *Journal of International Criminal Justice* 1074; Alicia Gil Gil, 'The Flaws of the Scilingo Judgment' (2005) 3 *Journal of International Criminal Justice* 1082; Guilia Pinzanuti, 'An Instance of Reasonable Universality' (2005) 3 *Journal of International Criminal Justice* 1092.

[110] *Guatemalan Generals* case, Tribunal Supremo, Sala de lo Penal, Sentencia 327/2003. See Hervé Ascensio, 'Are Spanish Courts Backing Down on Universality? The Supreme Tribunal's Decision in Guatemalan Generals' (2003) 1 *Journal of International Criminal Justice* 690, 695–7. For a (persuasive) argument that this has not become customary, even though as a matter of policy it is very sensible, see Cedric Ryngaert, 'Applying the Rome Statutes Complementarity Principle: Drawing Lessons from the Prosecution of Core Crimes by States Acting under the Universality Principle' (2008) 19 *Criminal Law Forum* 153, 173–7; see also Lafontaine, 'Universal Jurisdiction', 1286–1302; however, see also Kreß, 'Universal Jurisdiction', 579–81.

[111] Cassese, 'Is the Bell Tolling?', 590.

[112] Naomi Roht-Arriaza, 'Guatemala Genocide Case' (2006) 100 *American Journal of International Law* 207; Hervé Ascensio, 'The Spanish Constitutional Tribunal's Decision in Guatemalan Generals' (2006) 4 *Journal of International Criminal Justice* 586.

[113] *Ley Organcia del Poder Judicial*, 4 November 2009. See generally Enrique Carnero Rojo, 'National Legislation Providing for the Prosecution and Punishment of International Crimes in Spain' (2011) 9 *Journal of International Criminal Justice* 699.

[114] See e.g. Luc Reydams, 'The Rise and Fall of Universal Jurisdiction' in William Schabas and Nadia Bernaz (eds.), *The Routledge Research Handbook on International Criminal Law* (London, 2011) 337.

and organizations that have engaged with universal jurisdiction.[115] First, having become parties to the Statute of the International Criminal Court, a number of countries have introduced international crimes into their domestic law and, when doing so, have also adopted universal jurisdiction over them. Some States, such as New Zealand, have not included any residence or other requirement in their legislation and have thus adopted absolute universality.[116] Germany has adopted similar legislation, although a prosecutor is entitled to dismiss the case if there is no linking point to Germany or it is being investigated by a more closely related State or an international criminal court.[117] The United Kingdom and Canada have both included jurisdiction over offences committed by non-nationals who later become linked to them in specified ways. It suffices for Canada's War Crimes and Crimes against Humanity Act that the person is later present in Canada (section 8). For prosecution in the United Kingdom, the relevant legislation requires the person later to become a resident of the United Kingdom.[118] Nonetheless, given that the United Kingdom does not extradite to States on bases of jurisdiction it considers to be in excess of international law, by providing (in section 72) for extradition to States which have broader extraterritorial jurisdiction than it takes over international crimes itself, the United Kingdom seems to have accepted that international law allows States to adopt universal jurisdiction over war crimes, genocide and crimes against humanity. Owing to the fact that the ICC Statute does not require States to take universal jurisdiction (or even mention it), this acceptance must be based on the position in customary international law.[119]

Other States that have adopted universal jurisdiction legislation include Trinidad and Tobago,[120] the Netherlands (which has engaged in a number of prosecutions on this basis)[121] and Senegal.[122] Even the United States, no frequent friend of universal jurisdiction on the basis of customary law,[123] has adopted universal jurisdiction over some war crimes, including the use of child soldiers, which is not created by a treaty to which the United States is a party.[124] The Peruvian Constitutional Court has also affirmed the existence of universal jurisdiction over international crimes.[125]

---

[115] For useful case studies, see Maximo Langer, 'The Diplomacy of Universal Jurisdiction: The Political Branches and the Transnational Prosecution of International Crimes' (2011) 105 *American Journal of International Law* 1; Joseph Rikhof, 'Fewer Places to Hide? The Impact of Domestic War Crimes Prosecutions on International Impunity' (2009) 20 *Criminal Law Forum* 1.

[116] International Crimes and International Criminal Court Act 2000, ss. 8–11.

[117] Code of Crimes against International Law, s. I; Criminal Code, s. 153f. On practice relating to this, see Kai Ambos, 'International Core Crimes, Universal Jurisdiction and § 153F of the German Criminal Procedure Code' (2007) 18 *Criminal Law Forum* 43.

[118] International Criminal Court Act 2001, s. 68(1). On the definition of 'resident' as amended by the Coroners and Justice Act 2009, see Robert Cryer and Paul David Mora, 'The Coroners and Justice Act 2009 and International Criminal Law: Backing into the Future?' (2010) 59 *International and Comparative Law Quarterly* 803, 810–13.

[119] Although in its comments on universal jurisdiction to the Sixth Committee of the General Assembly, the United Kingdom was equivocal on universal jurisdiction over crimes against humanity and genocide: The Scope and Application of the Principle of Universal Jurisdiction, Report of the Secretary-General, UN Doc. A/66/93, 20 June 2011, 10.

[120] International Criminal Court Act 2006, s. 8.

[121] International Crimes Act 2003, s. 2. See Erwin van der Borght, 'Prosecution of International Crimes in the Netherlands: An Analysis of Recent Case Law' (2007) 28 *Criminal Law Forum* 87.

[122] Art. 2 of Loi No. 2007-05 (12 February 2007), Penal Code, Ar. 431, Constitution of Senegal, Art. 9.

[123] See John Bellinger, 'US Initial Reactions to ICRC Study on Customary International Law'.

[124] Child Soldiers Accountability Act 2007, S2135.   [125] Decision 01271-2008-PHC/TC, 8 August 2008, para. 6.

A particularly notable example of practice is the declaration of the African Union of 2008 on the abuse of universal jurisdiction; in this, the Assembly of Heads of State and Government, in spite of condemning the abuse of universal jurisdiction,[126] 'recognis[ed] that universal jurisdiction is a principle of international law whose purpose is to ensure that individuals who commit grave offences such as war crimes and crimes against humanity do not do so with impunity and are brought to justice, which is in line with ... the Constitutive Act of the African Union'.[127] This is a significant official statement by fifty-three States, a number of which have had officials investigated on the basis of universal jurisdiction, which recognizes the lawfulness of such jurisdiction. The concern was with the abuse, not the existence, of the jurisdiction.

Nonetheless, the African Union has been very critical of some uses of universal jurisdiction. Its expressions of concern about universal jurisdiction have engendered considerable debate,[128] but a careful reading of its practice reveals that the primary concern is immunities, rather than the existence of universal jurisdiction, and that 'contrary to appearances ... universal jurisdiction is unobjectionable to this bloc'.[129] Indeed, the African Union has recently adopted a draft model law on universal jurisdiction that, in addition to war crimes, suggests African States adopt universal jurisdiction over crimes against humanity and genocide, as well as piracy, drug trafficking and terrorism.[130] In part in response to African Union concerns, the Sixth Committee of the UN General Assembly has been studying the question since 2009, and, although States have reaffirmed the validity of the principle, controversies remain.[131]

Turning to the views of the international (and internationalized) criminal tribunals, both the ICTY and ICTR have asserted that States may exercise universal jurisdiction,[132] as has the Special Court for Sierra Leone.[133] Outside this context, the European Court of Human Rights has also accepted that universal jurisdiction exists, at least for genocide,[134] whilst the Inter-American Commission on Human Rights considers such jurisdiction to exist over crimes against international law.[135] Against this background, reports of the death of universal jurisdiction are greatly exaggerated, although it remains controversial, and some, perhaps excessive, expectations have remained unfulfilled.

---

[126] In particular, the indictment of high-level Rwandan officials by France.

[127] Decision on the Report of the Commission on the Abuse of Universal Jurisdiction (Assembly/AU/14/(XI)), annexed to Letter from the AU Permanent Observer to the President of the Security Council, UN Doc. S/2008/465.

[128] For detailed reviews, see Harmen van der Wilt, 'Universal Jurisdiction under Attack: An Assessment of African Misgivings towards International Criminal Justice as Administered by Western States' (2011) 9 *Journal of International Criminal Justice* 1043; Charles Chernoh Jalloh, 'Universal Jurisdiction: Universal Prescription? A Preliminary Assessment of the African Union Perspective on Universal Jurisdiction' (2010) 21 *Criminal Law Forum* 1.

[129] O'Keefe, 'Role of Domestic Courts', 555–6.   [130] EXP/MIN/Legal/VI, Arts. 4, 9–14.

[131] GA Res. 64/117, 16 December 2009; *The Scope and Application of the Principle of Universal Jurisdiction: Report of the Secretary-General Prepared on the Basis of Comments and Observations of Governments*, UN Doc. A/65/181, 29 July 2010; *The Scope and Application of the Principle of Universal Jurisdiction: Report of the Secretary-General*, UN Doc. A/66/93/ Ade.1, 16 August 2011; *The Scope and Application of the Principle of Universal Jurisdiction: Report of the Secretary-General*, UN Doc. A/67/116, 28 June 2012.

[132] *Tadić*, ICTY A. Ch., 2 October 1995, para. 62; *Ntuyuhaga*, ICTR T. Ch. I, 18 March 1999 (in relation to genocide).

[133] *Kallon and Kamara*, SCSL A. Ch., 13 March 2004, paras. 67–71.

[134] *Jorgić* v. *Germany*, ECtHR, 12 July 2007, paras. 67–70.   [135] Res. 1/03, 24 October 2003.

3.5.5   *Universal jurisdiction's practical problems*

One of the major problems with undertaking prosecutions on the basis of universal jurisdiction is that the existence of jurisdiction *per se* does not give rise to any obligations on
behalf of the territorial or nationality State to assist in any investigation, provide evidence or
extradite suspects.[136] The matter of cooperation falls to treaty obligations or comity.[137] It is
perhaps unsurprising that some of the most successful prosecutions on the basis of universal
jurisdiction, the Belgian prosecution of the 'Butare Four', the Niyontenze case in
Switzerland and the UK prosecutions of the Afghan warlord, Faryadi Zardad[138] and Nazi
war criminal Anthony Sawoniuk, occurred with the concurrence, if not the support, of the
relevant territorial States. Those States permitted investigations and on-site visits, as well as
providing witnesses to testify in the forum State. Although, in some prosecutions on the
basis of universal jurisdiction, witnesses are found in the forum State among the refugee
community,[139] the availability of evidence, both human and physical, cannot be presumed.
A number of cases based on universal jurisdiction have failed to achieve the standard of
proof for a criminal conviction.[140]

Even where witnesses are available, problems of inter-cultural understanding can arise.
Translation difficulties, as well as difficulties of appraising the credibility of witnesses
testifying through interpreters and from different cultural backgrounds, make the appraisal
of witness evidence very difficult. In some cases (the Sawoniuk case being an example),[141]
this problem is mitigated by on-site visits by the fact-finders, who can thereby achieve a
better understanding of the witnesses' cultural and material context.

There is also the possible problem of 'forum shopping', in which victims or NGOs may
seek to initiate prosecutions in multiple forums, to maximize the possibility of a conviction.
This can raise the important issue of the rights of defendants, who could be prosecuted (and
have to defend themselves) repeatedly in relation to the same facts, something which, if
done in one State, would violate the *ne bis in idem* principle.[142] The absence of such a
principle operating between States makes this a possibility, albeit one which is not unique to
universal jurisdiction nor one which has occurred in practice.[143]

---

[136] See Bruce Broomhall, *International Justice and the International Criminal Court: Between Sovereignty and the Rule of Law* (Oxford, 2003) 119–23.

[137] See Chapter 4.

[138] See Robert Cryer, 'Zardad' in A. Cassese *et al.* (eds.), *The Oxford Companion to International Criminal Justice* (Oxford, 2009) 978–9.

[139] Dusko Tadić, who achieved notoriety as the first defendant before the ICTY, was originally proceeded against in Germany, having been recognized by other refugees. The case was discontinued after his transfer to the ICTY.

[140] E.g. the Dusko Cvetković prosecution in Austria and *In re Gabrez* in Switzerland.

[141] Other examples of this include two recent genocide trials, where Scandinavian courts conducted part of their proceedings in Rwanda: *Public Prosecutor* v. *Bazarama*, District Court of Porvoo Ita-Uusimaa (Finland), Case No. R 09/04, judgment 11 June 2010 (see Minna Kimpimäki, 'Genocide in Rwanda: Is It Really Finland's Concern?' (2011) 11 *International Criminal Law Review* 1550); and *Public Prosecutor* v. *Mbanenande*, Stockholm District Court (Sweden), Case No. B-18271-11, judgment 20 June 2013.

[142] George Fletcher, 'Against Universal Jurisdiction' (2003) I *Journal of International Criminal Justice* 580.

[143] See Albin Eser, 'For Universal Jurisdiction: Against Fletcher's Antagonism' (2003–4) 39 *Tulsa Law Review* 955, 957–8, 963–71; Ryngaert, 'Applying the Rome Statute', 155–6.

3.5.6 *Policy-based/political criticisms of universal jurisdiction*

There have been a number of arguments of policy brought against universal jurisdiction, which are of varying persuasiveness. The first of these is that prosecutions on the basis of universal jurisdiction may impact upon foreign policy. Such concerns have led the executive in a number of States to impose additional hurdles, such as consent of a government lawyer prior to issuing proceedings on this basis.[144] Universal jurisdiction prosecutions may also upset the balance struck between prosecution and amnesty in an emerging democracy, where amnesties have been used.[145] This critique has more purchase when applied to processes such as South Africa's than when compared to General Pinochet's self-granted immunity.[146] On the other hand, international crimes are not simply the concern of one State alone. Crimes against humanity, genocide and (probably most) war crimes violate *erga omnes* obligations; therefore all States have some form of interest in the response to such offences.[147] From a purely legal point of view, domestic amnesty legislation does not bind any other State, and the problem is, again, not one unique to universal jurisdiction.[148]

The practical ability of more powerful nations both to assert jurisdiction beyond their borders and to pressure other countries into leaving their nationals alone has led to claims that universal jurisdiction can be selective in its application. As President Guillaume argued in *Yerodia*, to support universal jurisdiction would be to 'encourage the arbitrary for the purposes of the powerful, purportedly acting for an ill-defined "international community"'.[149]

This argument frequently takes on a neocolonial twist, as in Judge Rezek's opinion in the same case: '[I]t is not without reason that the Parties before the court have discussed the question of how certain European countries would react if a judge from the Congo had indicted their officials for crimes supposedly committed on their orders in Africa.'[150] As this quote shows, however, this would apply in relation to territorial jurisdiction in a similar manner to universal jurisdiction. Judge ad hoc Bula-Bula, however, made the criticism directly on the basis that the exercise of universal jurisdiction was a form of neocolonial intervention by Belgium in its former colony.[151]

There is no evidence that universal jurisdiction prosecutions are directed by States for nefarious political reasons (or at least no more than on other heads of jurisdiction).[152] Indeed, some of the attempted prosecutions have caused political difficulties for States in

---

[144] Langer, 'Diplomacy', 1–7. In the United Kingdom, this has led to legislative reform on the question of arrest warrants being sought by private parties: see Police Reform and Social Responsibility Act 2011, s. 153, on which, see Sarah Williams, 'Arresting Developments? Restricting the Enforcement of the UK's Universal Jurisdiction Provisions' (2012) 75 *Modern Law Review* 368.

[145] Henry Kissinger, 'The Pitfalls of Universal Jurisdiction' (2001) 80 *Foreign Affairs* 86, 90–1; Eugene Kontorovich, 'The Inefficiencies of Universal Jurisdiction' (2008) *University of Illinois Law Review* 389.

[146] Kenneth Roth, 'The Case for Universal Jurisdiction' (2001) 80 *Foreign Affairs* 150, 153.

[147] *Furundžija*, ICTY T. Ch. II, 10 December 1998, para. 156; *Legality of the Threat or Use of Nuclear Weapons*, Advisory Opinion (1996) ICJ Reports 226, para. 79; *Kupreškić et al.*, ICTY T. Ch. II, 14 January 2000, para. 520 (although this last case goes a little far in asserting that all norms of humanitarian law have this status).

[148] See further Chapter 22.   [149] *Yerodia*, Separate Opinion of President Guillaume, para. 15.

[150] *Ibid.*, Separate Opinion of Judge Rezek, para. 9 (translation in Reydams, *Universal Jurisdiction*, 229).

[151] *Yerodia*, Separate Opinion of Judge Bula-Bula.

[152] 'Final Report on the Exercise of Universal Jurisdiction in Relation to Gross Human Rights Abuses' in ILA, *Report of the Sixty-Ninth Conference, held in London* (London, ILA, 2000) 403, 422; Ryngaert, 'Applying the Rome Statute', 155–6.

which indictments have been sought,[153] and, indeed, recent practice tends to be that States have (re)asserted executive control over judges and prosecutors to rein in such applications.[154] Even so, where non-governmental actors have sought to bring proceedings, they normally have to bring sufficient evidence to persuade a court or a prosecutor to take the matter on.[155] Actual prosecutions on the basis of universal jurisdiction to date have centred on those who have not been proceeded against in their territorial or nationality States,[156] and have focused mostly on ex-Nazis, Rwandans and former Yugoslavs, where there have been international prosecutions. In such cases, there is a high degree of agreement in principle on the appropriateness of the prosecution of such offenders.[157]

Other offenders that have actually faced courts have tended to be those who are not considered to be representatives of, or protected by, powerful States.[158] This, when added to increased executive control over who is prosecuted on the basis of universal jurisdiction does give rise to rule of law issues.[159] Selective enforcement, nonetheless, remains a problem in relation to international crimes, whatever the principle of jurisdiction invoked. Some of these problems could be mitigated by the adoption of an international agreement on the exercise of universal jurisdiction,[160] although there are no official proposals for such a treaty at present, and, without universal ratification, such a treaty might further muddy the waters of this form of jurisdiction, and call into question the existing customary law on point.[161]

Further reading

Michael Akehurst, 'Jurisdiction in International Law' (1972–3) 46 *British Yearbook of International Law* 145

Jean d'Asprement, 'Multilateral versus Unilateral Exercises of Universal Jurisdiction' (2010) 43 *Israel Law Review* 301

Alejandro Chehtman, *The Philosophical Foundations of Extraterritorial Punishment* (Oxford, 2010)

Anthony Colangelo, 'The Legal Limits of Universal Jurisdiction' (2006–7) 47 *Virginia Journal of International Law* 149

Robert Cryer, *Prosecuting International Crimes: Selectivity and the International Criminal Law Regime* (Cambridge, 2005) 75–101

---

[153] E.g. Christine Bakker, 'Universal Jurisdiction of Spanish Courts over Genocide in Tibet: Can It Work?' (2006) 4 *Journal of International Criminal Justice* 595, 599–601; Jonny Paul, 'Peres Slams UK Law Jeopardizing IDF Officers', *Jerusalem Post*, 23 November 2008.

[154] Langer, 'Diplomacy', 1–7.

[155] Prosecutors frequently have discretion in this regard, even in States where this is not a norm: see e.g. Salvatore Zappalà, 'The German Federal Prosecutor's Decision Not to Prosecute a Former Uzbek Minister: Missed Opportunity or Prosecutorial Wisdom?' (2006) 4 *Journal of International Criminal Justice* 602.

[156] See van der Wilt, 'Universal Jurisdiction', 1064–6.   [157] Langer, 'Diplomacy', 9.   [158] *Ibid.*   [159] *Ibid.*, 47–9.

[160] Such a course of action is suggested in Cassese, 'Is the Bell Tolling?', 595.

[161] Although d'Asprement, 'Multilateral', 309 *et seq.*, considers any non-treaty-based assertion of universal jurisdiction to have legitimacy problems. However, this is no more or less of a problem than with any assertion of customary law, and d'Asprement's approach comes from an approach to jurisdiction that rejects the idea that international law allocates jurisdiction between States, an approach he accepts is far from the majority of scholarship (*ibid.*, 314), to which may be added most States' views too.

Edwin D. Dickinson (Reporter), 'Harvard Draft Convention on Jurisdiction with Commentary' (1935) 29 *American Journal of International Law Supplement* 439

Menno T. Kamminga, 'Lessons Learned from the Exercise of Universal Jurisdiction over Gross Human Rights Abuses' (2001) 23 *Human Rights Quarterly* 940

Henry Kissinger, 'The Pitfalls of Universal Jurisdiction' (2001) 80 *Foreign Affairs* 86

Claus Kreß, 'Universal Jurisdiction over International Crimes and the Institut de Droit International' (2006) 4 *Journal of International Criminal Justice* 561

Maximo Langer, 'The Diplomacy of Universal Jurisdiction: The Political Branches and the Transnational Prosecution of International Crimes' (2011) 105 *American Journal of International Law* 1

Vaughan Lowe and Christopher Staker, 'Jurisdiction' in Malcolm Evans (ed.), *International Law*, 3rd edn (Oxford, 2010) 330

Steven Macedo (ed.), *Universal Jurisdiction: National Courts and the Prosecution of Serious Crimes under International Law* (Philadelphia, 2003)

Roger O'Keefe, 'Universal Jurisdiction: Clarifying the Basic Concept' (2004) 2 *Journal of International Criminal Justice* 735

Bernard H. Oxman, 'Jurisdiction of States' in Rüdiger Wolfrum (ed.), *Max Planck Encyclopedia of Public International Law* (Oxford, 2012), Vol. VI, 547

Kenneth C. Randall, 'Universal Jurisdiction under International Law' (1988) 65 *Texas Law Review* 785

Luc Reydams, *Universal Jurisdiction: International and Municipal Legal Perspectives* (Oxford, 2003)

Cedric Ryngaert, *Jurisdiction in International Law* (Oxford, 2008)

4

National Prosecutions of International Crimes

4.1   Introduction

International crimes are primarily intended to be prosecuted at the domestic level. Although the 1948 Genocide Convention foresaw a possible 'international penal tribunal as may have jurisdiction with respect to those Contracting Parties which shall have accepted its jurisdiction',[1] the International Criminal Court regime, through its system of complementarity, sees national courts as the courts of first resort.[2] This has been described as an 'indirect enforcement system' whereby international criminal law is to be enforced through national systems.[3] National prosecutions are not only the primary vehicle for the enforcement of international crimes, they are also often considered a preferable option – in political, sociological, practical and legitimacy terms – to international prosecutions.[4]

But, although the world vowed after the Second World War never again to allow such atrocities to occur, they continue to be committed in many places around the world, yet domestic prosecutions are sparse. Indeed, the international criminal courts and tribunals have been created to counter the impunity that tends to exist domestically. This chapter will address international obligations in this regard and some major legal issues that arise concerning national prosecutions of international crimes. Among the complicating factors, insufficient legislation, *ne bis in idem* (double jeopardy) and statutory limitations are addressed here, while amnesties are dealt with in Chapter 22, State cooperation in Chapter 5 and immunities in Chapter 21.

4.2   National prosecutions

Of the international crimes that are the subject of this book, war crimes have been regulated in domestic law the longest and have been prosecuted most often.[5] Early examples are prosecutions with respect to the American Civil War in the 1860s and the Anglo-Boer Wars in the late nineteenth and early twentieth centuries. The quite reluctant prosecutions in Germany and Turkey after the First World War, the Leipzig trials and the Istanbul

---

[1] Art. 6 of the Genocide Convention. See also Art. 5 of the 1973 Apartheid Convention.   [2] See Chapter 8.
[3] See e.g. M. Cherif Bassiouni, *Introduction to International Criminal Law*, 2nd edn (Leiden, 2013) 487.
[4] See Chapters 2 and 7.   [5] For national case law, see the ICRC webpage, www.icrc.org/ihl-nat.

(Constantinople) trials in the 1920s, related to war crimes and were conducted under domestic laws.[6]

No conflict has generated as many national prosecutions as the Second World War, sometimes for international crimes, but in many instances for 'ordinary' crimes under national penal law. Apart from the (literally) thousands of cases in Germany,[7] and the trials by Allied States in the Pacific sphere,[8] many other European States have instituted prosecutions.[9] The most well known are the French cases against Klaus Barbie (head of the Gestapo in Lyons), Paul Touvier (a pro-Nazi militiaman), and Maurice Papon (a high-ranking official of the French Vichy regime), who were convicted for crimes against humanity in 1987, 1994 and 1998 respectively, after very long proceedings plagued with difficulties.[10] Prosecutions have also taken place, *inter alia*, in Italy (for example, the *Hass and Priebke* case),[11] Austria, the Netherlands, and former Eastern Bloc countries. In the United Kingdom, after the many prosecutions directly after the war, only one Second World War case, *R* v. *Sawoniuk*, has resulted in a conviction for war crimes in the recent past.[12]

Second World War crimes have also been prosecuted elsewhere, most notably by Israel. The seminal *Eichmann* case addressed not only important issues of jurisdiction,[13] including the exercise of jurisdiction upon abduction of the accused from another State,[14] but also criminal defences (superior orders and the 'act of State' doctrine) and the principle of non-retroactivity of criminal law.[15] Adolf Eichmann stood trial for 'crimes against the Jewish people', crimes against humanity and war crimes. He was found guilty, sentenced to death and executed in 1962. Jurisdictional issues were also considered when US courts decided to extradite John Demjanjuk to Israel to stand trial for war crimes and crimes against humanity.[16] Before the Israeli courts, however, evidentiary matters came to the forefront, and Demjanjuk was finally acquitted because of doubts in respect of his identity

---

[6] See section 6.2. See also Timothy McCormack, 'Their Atrocities and our Misdemeanours: The Reticence of States to Try their "own Nationals" for International Crimes' in Mark Lattimer and Philippe Sands (eds.), *Justice for Crimes against Humanity* (Oxford, 2003) 121–5.

[7] For German judgments concerning Nazi crimes, see Christiaan Rüter and Dick de Mildt (eds.), *Justiz und NS-Verbrechen: Sammlung (west-)deutscher Strafurteile wegen nationalsozialistischer Tötungsverbrechen 1945–2012* (Amsterdam and Munich, 1968–2012), and *DDR-Justiz und NS-Verbrechen: Sammlung (ost-)deutscher Strafurteile wegen nationalsozialist-ischer Tötungsverbrechen 1945–1998* (Amsterdam and Munich, 2002–9). Such trials have not ended, on one recent controversial case, see Sabine Swoboda, 'Paying the Debts – Late Nazi Trials before German Courts: The Case of Heinrich Boere' (2011) 9 *Journal of International Criminal Justice* 243.

[8] See section 6.5.

[9] See generally Axel Marschik, 'The Politics of Prosecution: European National Approaches to War Crimes' in Timothy L. H. McCormack and Gerry Simpson (eds.), *The Law of War Crimes: National and International Approaches* (The Hague, 1997) 65–101.

[10] See Leila Sadat Wexler, 'The French Experience' in M. Cherif Bassiouni (ed.), *International Criminal Law*, 3rd edn (Leiden, 2008) Vol. III, 329.

[11] Convictions for war crimes and crimes against humanity: Rome Military Tribunal, 22 July 1997; Military Court of Appeal, 7 March 1998; and Supreme Court of Cassation, 16 November 1998. See Paola Gaeta, 'War Crimes Trials before Italian Criminal Courts: New Trends' in Horst Fischer *et al.*, *International and National Prosecution of Crimes under International Law: Current Developments* (Berlin, 2001) 751–68. On other Italian trials, see also Pier Paolo Rivello, 'The Prosecution of War Crimes Committed by Nazi Forces in Italy' (2005) 3 *Journal of International Criminal Justice* 422.

[12] [2000] 2 Crim App Rep 220. [13] See Chapter 3. [14] See section 5.4.7.

[15] *Attorney-General of Israel* v. *Eichmann* (1968) 36 ILR 5 (District Court) and *Attorney-General of Israel* v. *Eichmann* (1968) 36 ILR 277 (Supreme Court); see Matthew Lippman, 'Genocide:The Trial of Adolf Eichmann and the Quest for Global Justice' (2002) 8 *Buffalo Human Rights Law Review* 45.

[16] *Demjanjuk*, US District Court (ND Ohio), 15 April 1985; and *Demjanjuk* v. *Petrovsky et al.*, US Court of Appeals (Sixth Circuit), 31 October 1985; see Jonathan Wenig, 'Enforcing the Lessons of History: Israel Judges the Holocaust' in McCormack and Simpson, *Law of War Crimes*, 115–18. See also section 3.5.3.

(as the concentration camp guard 'Ivan the Terrible' of Treblinka).[17] In 2009, though, Demjanjuk was extradited to Germany to face trial for his wartime activities, and convicted in 2011.

Other interesting cases are the Canadian *Finta* case, where very strict mental and material requirements for crimes against humanity and war crimes were introduced,[18] and the Australian *Polyukhovic* case, where the constitutional validity of war crimes legislation was challenged with respect to jurisdiction and retroactivity.[19] In both cases, evidentiary insufficiency, in part owing to the length of time between the events and the trials, meant that they ended in acquittals.

Conflicts after the Second World War did not produce many national criminal proceedings. A few examples are the US court martials concerning the infamous My Lai massacre during the Vietnam War, albeit for domestic rather than international crimes,[20] some cases in Romania and Ethiopia where reference was made to 'genocide',[21] a show trial in Cambodia of Pol Pot and the Khmer Rouge in 1979,[22] and more recently controversial prosecutions of crimes committed during the 1971 Pakistan–Bangladesh war.[23]

It was not until the 1990s, with the renewed focus on international criminal justice in general, and the establishment of the ad hoc Tribunals in particular, that the frequency of national prosecutions increased. This is particularly true in Rwanda and the States of the former Yugoslavia. Rwanda introduced new legislation on genocide in 1996 – dividing genocide into three categories based on the gravity of the crime, carrying different penalties – and started a large number of prosecutions. But, with a huge number of detainees awaiting trial, said to be more than 100,000 people, the criminal system had to be reformed and traditional *gacaca* courts were introduced in 2001.[24] After more than ten years, these semiformal courts came to an end. In spite of their considerable successes, the standards of justice they meted out have caused concern.[25]

In the former Yugoslavia, the Dayton Peace Agreement laid the ground for interaction between the ICTY, having primary jurisdiction over the relevant offences, and national authorities.[26] These relationships improved over time and the ICTY has referred cases (where no ICTY indictment was issued) to courts in Croatia and Serbia. With respect to Bosnia and Herzegovina, a special scheme applied until 2004 (called 'Rules of the Road') whereby the ICTY Prosecutor in effect vetted national cases before a domestic arrest warrant

---

[17] Israel Supreme Court, 29 July 1993.
[18] Supreme Court of Canada, 24 March 1994; see Irwin Cotler, 'Bringing Nazi War Criminals in Canada to Justice: A Case Study' (1997) *ASIL Proceedings* 262; and Leslie C. Green, 'Canadian Law, War Crimes and Crimes against Humanity' (1988) 59 *British Yearbook of International Law* 217.
[19] High Court of Australia, 14 August 1991.
[20] *United States* v. *Calley*, conviction of 29 March 1971 (sentence, 31 March 1971); and US Military Court of Appeals decision, 21 December 1973. However, Lieutenant Calley's commander, Captain Medina, was acquitted by court martial on 22 September 1971.
[21] See William Schabas, 'National Courts Finally Begin to Prosecute Genocide, the Crime of Crimes' (2003) 1 *Journal of International Criminal Justice* 39; Firew Kebede Tiba, 'The Mengistu Genocide Trial in Ethiopia' (2007) 5 *Journal of International Criminal Justice* 513, 518.
[22] UN Doc. A/34/491 (20 September 1979).
[23] See M. Cherif Bassiouni, *Crimes against Humanity in International Law*, 2nd edn (The Hague, 1999) 549–51.
[24] See e.g. William Schabas, 'Genocide Trials and Gacaca Courts' (2005) 3 *Journal of International Criminal Justice* 879.
[25] E.g. Gerald Gahima, *Transitional Justice in Rwanda* (London, 2013) Chapter 6.
[26] See McCormack, 'Their Atrocities', 127–34.

for war crimes was issued.[27] As part of the completion strategies of the ICTY and ICTR, cases where the Tribunal had issued an indictment could also be referred to national jurisdictions.[28]

In addition, prosecutions of crimes committed in Rwanda and the former Yugoslavia have taken place in third States, such as Austria, Belgium, Denmark, Finland, Germany, Norway, Sweden and Switzerland. For example, the *Tadić* case originated as a domestic case in Germany but was taken over by the ICTY,[29] while the 'Butare Four' case in Belgium proceeded after the ICTR had declined to exercise jurisdiction.[30]

The trend has extended beyond these two conflict situations. A number of cases, often based on private complaints, have commenced in domestic courts, particularly in Europe[31] and Latin America,[32] regarding different conflicts all around the world. In some countries, however, for example the United States and Canada, denaturalization and deportation under the citizenship and immigration legislation have been preferred to criminal prosecution,[33] but in 2009 the first successful Canadian prosecution for genocide, crimes against humanity and war crimes (committed in Rwanda) led to a conviction.[34] Specialized domestic courts for international crimes, sometimes referred to as 'internationalized courts', have been established in some countries with international assistance.[35]

National prosecutions of international crimes have been highly selective and, generally, States have been unwilling to prosecute their own nationals.[36] There are examples to the contrary, however, and the numerous post-Second World War prosecutions of nationals in West and East Germany, the more recent prosecutions in the former Yugoslavia[37] and Rwanda, as well as the court martials in the United States and the United Kingdom of a number of soldiers for abusing (and in one case killing) detainees in Iraq,[38] are notable

---

[27] On the relationship between the ICTY and the Bosnian courts, see William W. Burke-White, 'The Domestic Impact of International Criminal Tribunals: The International Criminal Tribunal for the Former Yugoslavia and the State Court of Bosnia and Herzegovina' (2007–8) 46 *Columbia Journal of Transnational Law* 279.

[28] *Ibid.* See also section 7.2.4 and section 9.3.2.

[29] See e.g. Jan MacLean, 'The Enforcement of Sentence in the Tadić Case' in Fischer *et al.*, *International and National Prosecution*, 727–31.

[30] See e.g. Luc Reydams, 'Belgium's First Application of Universal Jurisdiction: The Butare Four Case' (2003) 1 *Journal of International Criminal Justice* 428; and Damien Vandermeersch, 'Prosecuting International Crimes in Belgium' (2005) 3 *Journal of International Criminal Justice* 400.

[31] For a survey, see e.g. Human Rights Watch, *Universal Jurisdiction in Europe: The State of the Art* (June 2006), available at www. hrw.org; and Redress/FIDH, *Extraterritorial Jurisdiction in the European Union: A Study of the Law and Practice in the 27 Member States of the European Union* (December 2010), available at www.fidh.org.

[32] See the surveys on Argentina, Brazil, Chile, Colombia, Mexico, Peru and Uruguay in (2010) 10 *International Criminal Law Review* 491–618.

[33] See e.g. Irwin Cotler, 'R v. Finta' (1996) 90 *American Journal of International Law* 460; and Matthew Lippman, 'The Pursuit of Nazi War Criminals in the United States and Other Anglo-American Legal Systems' (1998) 29 *California Western International Law Journal* 1.

[34] See e.g. Robert Currie and Ion Stancu, 'R v. Munyaneza: Pondering Canada's First Core Crimes Conviction' (2010) 10 *International Criminal Law Review* 829; and Fannie Lafontaine, 'Canada's Crimes against Humanity and War Crimes Act on Trial: An Analysis of the Munyaneza Trial' (2010) 8 *Journal of International Criminal Justice* 269.

[35] See Chapter 9.   [36] See McCormack, 'Their Atrocities', 107–42.

[37] See section 9.3.2 (Bosnia and Herzegovina) and section 9.4.2 (Serbia); and Ivo Josipović, 'Responsibility for War Crimes before National Courts in Croatia' (2006) 88:(861) *International Review of the Red Cross* 145.

[38] In the United States, see Roberta Arnold, 'The Abu-Ghraib Misdeeds:Will there Be Justice in the Name of the Geneva Conventions?' (2004) 2 *Journal of International Criminal Justice* 999. In the United Kingdom, see Nathan Rasiah, 'The Court-Martial of Corporal Payne and Others and the Future Landscape of International Criminal Justice' (2009) 7 *Journal of International Criminal Justice* 177.

exceptions.[39] A high degree of selectiveness within one and the same conflict may project the message that all other activities were legal, or the non-prosecuted parties acted in an irreproachable way.[40] The political willingness to pursue national prosecutions is decisive.[41] A case regarding crimes committed in the prosecuting State may well end up putting the State itself on trial. The Barbie trial, for example, led to embarrassing questions about the French State's collaboration with the Nazis and the commission of international crimes in the conflict in Algeria.[42] There are also other political considerations which either prevent national prosecutions altogether or make them highly selective.[43] Serious questions of legality present themselves (selectivity, vagueness of the law, retroactivity and very long time periods between crime and prosecution).[44] Even where true will exists, the costs involved and other criminal justice priorities may be impediments.

Another problem is that national courts often expose uneasiness and insecurity when dealing with international crimes. For example, national courts frequently refer to 'customary international law', but without an accompanying attempt to demonstrate the existence of such norms. The legal reasoning in some of the judgments has been criticized as 'lightweight and generally superficial', at least when compared with the ICTY and ICTR judgments.[45] Domestic courts are sometimes subject to contradictory imperatives, seeking to apply national and international law when it comes to international crimes.[46]

4.3　　State obligations to prosecute or extradite

4.3.1　Treaty obligations

A number of international treaties, which address international (or transnational) crimes, oblige the States Parties to investigate and prosecute the offence in question, or to extradite suspects to another State Party willing to do so: the so-called *aut dedere aut judicare* ('to extradite or prosecute') principle.[47] Examples can be found in the four Geneva Conventions

---

[39] Although it is notable that prosecutions on the basis of universal jurisdiction have tended to concentrate on those conflicts where there have been international tribunals, but there are other examples too: see Maximo Langer, 'The Diplomacy of Universal Jurisdiction: The Political Branches and the Transnational Prosecution of International Crimes' (2011) 105 *American Journal of International Law* 1, 9.

[40] Gerry Simpson, 'War Crimes: A Critical Introduction' in McCormack and Simpson, *Law of War Crimes*, 21–6.

[41] Marschik, 'The Politics of Prosecution', 100; Peter Burbidge, 'Waking the Dead of the Spanish Civil War: Judge Baltasar Garzón and the Spanish Law of Historical Memory' (2011) 9 *Journal of International Criminal Justice* 753.

[42] See Guyora Binder, 'Representing Nazism: Advocacy and Identity in the Trial of Klaus Barbie' (1989) 98 *Yale Law Journal* 1321.

[43] See the examples regarding Italy after the Second World War, and Pakistan and Bangladesh after the 1971 Cessation War; Bassiouni, *Crimes against Humanity*, 548–51. But also more recently, see Neil J. Mitchell, *Democracy's Blameless Leaders: From Dresden to Abu Ghraib: How Leaders Evade Accountability for Abuse, Atrocity and Killing* (New York and London, 2012).

[44] See e.g. Simpson, 'War Crimes: A Critical Introduction', 1–30.　　[45] Schabas, 'National Courts', 63.

[46] Yaël Ronen, 'Silent Enim Leges Inter Arma – But Beware the Background Noise: Domestic Courts as Agents of Development of the Law on the Conduct of Hostilities' (2013) 26 *Leiden Journal of International Law* 599; Eyal Benvenisti, 'Judicial Misgivings regarding the Application of International Norms: An Analysis of Attitudes of National Courts' (1993) 4 *European Journal of International Law* 159. For a general study, see André Nollkaemper, *National Courts and the International Rule of Law* (Oxford, 2011). See also Roger O'Keefe, 'Domestic Courts as Agents of Development of the International Law of Jurisdiction' (2013) 26 *Leiden Journal of International Law* 541.

[47] This maxim was originally devised by Hugo Grotius (*De Jure Belli ac Pacis*, 1624) as '*aut dedere . . . aut punire*' ('to extradite or punish'). For an extensive study, see M. Cherif Bassiouni and Edward Wise, *Aut Dedere, Aut Judicare: A Duty to Extradite or Prosecute in International Law* (Dordrecht, 1995).

and Additional Protocol I,[48] covering war crimes that constitute 'grave breaches' under these instruments. The provisions are phrased in the imperative:

Each High Contracting Party shall be under the obligation to search for persons alleged to have committed, or to have ordered to be committed, such grave breaches and shall bring such persons, regardless of their nationality, before its own courts [or hand them over to another High Contracting Party].

For other serious violations of the Geneva Conventions, which are not 'grave breaches', the principle does not apply under the treaty scheme, but States still have a right, although not a duty, to prosecute such violations.[49]

The principle also exists, *inter alia*, in the 1984 Torture Convention, the Convention on Enforced Disappearances,[50] and many terrorism-related treaties.[51] Such treaty clauses are often, although not entirely accurately, considered as allowing States to exercise 'universal jurisdiction',[52] and are normally phrased in mandatory terms.[53] Newer provisions require States to 'submit' cases of alleged violations to the 'competent authorities for the purpose of prosecution', which is a wording that takes into account modern fair trial rights, such as the presumption of innocence, but which should not be understood to lessen the duty to prosecute if the evidence is there;[54] one should also note that many civil law jurisdictions provide for compulsory prosecutions when an evidentiary threshold is met. However, the obligations are only applicable between the parties to the particular treaty.

The nature and extent of the obligations contained in the Torture Convention were the subject of the *Habré* case in the ICJ in 2012.[55] The case related to the continued delays encountered in the Senegalese prosecution of the ex-head of State of Chad, Hissène Habré, against the backdrop of a Belgian request for his extradition to face charges, *inter alia*, of torture. The Court held that parties to the Torture Convention are obliged to criminalize torture on the basis of universal jurisdiction.[56] By failing to implement universal jurisdiction over torture until 2007 (seven years after complaints had been made against Habré in Senegal), the Court determined that Senegal had breached its obligations to conduct a timely preliminary investigation and submission of the matters to its competent authorities.

---

[48] Arts. 49–50 of Geneva Convention I; Arts. 50–51 of Geneva Convention II; Arts. 129–130 of Geneva Convention III; Arts. 146–147 of Geneva Convention IV; Arts. 11, 85–86 and 88 of Additional Protocol I.

[49] See Theodor Meron, 'Is International Law Moving towards Criminalization?' (1998) 9 *European Journal of International Law* 18, 23.

[50] International Convention for the Protection of All Persons from Enforced Disappearances, GA Res 61/177 Annex, Arts. 9, 11.

[51] See Chapter 14.   [52] See section 3.5.

[53] Exceptions to this, however, are Art. 5 of the 1973 Apartheid Convention, and Art. 105 of the 1982 Law of the Sea Convention (piracy on the high seas), where the exercise of jurisdiction is instead phrased in permissive terms ('may').

[54] Michael Scharf, 'The Letter of the Law: The Scope of the International Legal Obligation to Prosecute Human Rights Crimes' (1996) 59 *Law and Contemporary Problems* 41, 46–7.

[55] *Questions Relating to the Obligation to Extradite or Prosecute* (*Belgium* v. *Senegal*), ICJ, 20 July 12 (the '*Habré*' case). See e.g. Mads Andenas and Thomas Weatherall, 'Questions Relating to the Obligation to Extradite or Prosecute (Belgium v. Senegal)' (2013) 62 *International and Comparative Law Quarterly* 753; André Nollkamper, 'Whither Aut Dedere? The Obligation to Extradite or Prosecute after the ICJ's Judgment in Belgium v. Senegal' (2013) 4 *Journal of International Dispute Settlement* 501.

[56] *Habré*, paras. 74–5, although, as mentioned above, the term 'universal' jurisdiction is something of a misnomer here.

The Court also took the view that the duty to conduct a preliminary inquiry arises as soon as the State has reason to suspect that a person in the State's territory is responsible for torture.[57] At the latest, this is when a complaint is submitted to the authorities.[58] The duty to do this (and to submit the matter to the competent authorities) is not contingent on the receipt of a request for extradition.[59] The Court also said that, although States have a choice in how to conduct their investigations, they must establish the relevant facts, to the same standard as is involved in standard domestic cases, and this may involve seeking the cooperation of other States.[60]

As for the obligation to extradite or prosecute, the ICJ determined that the obligation is not necessarily to prosecute, but rather to submit the matter to its competent authorities, who should determine whether or not a prosecution should go ahead on the same basis as they would a domestic case.[61] Perhaps controversially, the ICJ determined that the primary duty on the State is to submit the matter for prosecution; extradition is an option given to the State which would relieve it of its obligation.[62] The case, alongside the recent work of the ILC on the principle,[63] has provided welcome clarity, and perhaps development, in the area. Although the Court's comments are limited to the Torture Convention, they are likely to be very useful for interpreting similarly worded provisions in other treaties. However, the *aut dedere aut judicare* principle is formulated differently in different conventions, as are other treaty provisions, and thus a case-by-case examination is necessary.

The 1948 Genocide Convention, unlike the Torture Convention, includes an undertaking by the States Parties to prevent and punish genocide, but the jurisdictional scope is restricted to the courts of 'the State in the territory of which the act was committed',[64] and there is no explicit *aut dedere aut judicare* provision.[65] Nonetheless, some argue that the Convention may be read to include an obligation to prosecute or extradite.[66] Support for broader duties than those explicitly set out in the Convention has also been sought in ICJ jurisprudence, but such conclusions have been questioned,[67] and obtained little succour in the Court in the merits phase of the *Bosnian Genocide* case. The Court expressly found the obligation to prosecute to be territorially limited, although the obligation to cooperate with relevant accepted international criminal tribunals was considered not to be so limited where fugitives are found on the territory of the State.[68] In the latter situation, the Court seemed to accept that

---

[57] *Ibid.*, para. 88.   [58] *Ibid.*, para. 86.   [59] *Ibid.*, paras. 94–5.   [60] *Ibid.*, paras. 83–6.   [61] *Habré*, paras. 90, 94.

[62] *Ibid.*, para. 95. For discussion, see Andenas and Weatherall, 'Questions', 767–8.

[63] See e.g. Report of the Working Group I the Obligation to Extradite or Prosecute (Aut Dedere Aut Judicare), UN Doc. A/CN.4/L.829, 22 July 2013.

[64] Art. 6 of the Genocide Convention; see also Arts. 1, 4 and 5.

[65] The States Parties do agree, however, to grant extradition and not consider genocide a 'political crime': *ibid.*, Art. 7 (see section 5.4.3).

[66] See e.g. Eric David, *Principes de droit des conflits armés*, 2nd edn (Brussels, 1999) 667–8 (a modern interpretation of the Convention in light of Art. 1); and Lee A. Steven, 'Genocide and the Duty to Extradite or Prosecute: Why the United States Is in Breach of its International Obligations' (1999) 39 *Virginia Journal of International Law* 425, 460–1 (interpretation of Arts. 1 and 4–7).

[67] Antonio Cassese, Paolo Gaeta *et al.*, *Cassese's International Criminal Law*, 3rd edn (Oxford, 2013), referring to the ICJ's opinion of 28 May 1951 in the *Genocide* case, para. 23; and the *Bosnian Genocide* case, ICJ, Judgment, 11 July 1996, para. 31; cf. William Schabas, *Genocide in International Law*, 2nd edn (Cambridge, 2009) 475–8; and Robert Cryer, *Prosecuting International Crimes: Selectivity and the International Criminal Law Regime* (Cambridge, 2005) 102–3.

[68] *Bosnian Genocide* case, paras. 442, 449. See Anja Siebert-Fohr, *Prosecuting Serious Human Rights Violations* (Oxford, 2009) 154.

prosecution of extraterritorial instances of genocide would suffice to fulfil this duty, probably on the basis that they were thinking of complementarity and the ICC. Domestic prosecution of crimes against humanity is not treaty-regulated except for torture and enforced disappearance (as separate crimes), and apartheid.

4.3.2   Human rights law obligations

As well as treaties explicitly covering international crimes, some have argued that, since States have duties to 'respect and ensure'[69] the rights granted in the various human rights conventions, it could be that the latter clause implies a duty to prosecute certain serious violations of human rights. All acts constituting genocide and crimes against humanity would be serious violations of human rights when governments are responsible for them, as would most war crimes. This may be supported by some case law from the Inter-American Court of Human Rights, in particular the *Velasquez-Rodriguez* v. *Honduras* case,[70] and more recently the *Barrios Altos* case, which takes a very dim view of amnesties.[71] It is difficult to say, however, that these cases on positive duties under human rights treaties can be read as creating an absolute duty to prosecute all international crimes in all circumstances.[72] Cases from the Inter-American system are in advance of the jurisprudence of those of, for example, the European Court of Human Rights and the UN Human Rights Committee,[73] and responded to the specific circumstances the Inter-American institutions were dealing with. Therefore, the jurisprudence of the Inter-American Court should not be borrowed directly, in its uncompromising formula and legal reasoning, by other human rights bodies for situations which are structurally different.[74]

4.3.3   Customary obligations and ius cogens arguments

Beyond treaty obligations, genocide, crimes against humanity and, at least in part, war crimes are also criminalized in customary international law.[75] As mentioned above, some national prosecutions have taken place, but these are quite rare and actual State practice does not support the position that States have a general duty to prosecute international crimes. In legal commentary, it has been suggested that a duty to prosecute or extradite nevertheless

---

[69] E.g. Art. 2 of the ICCPR.

[70] *Velasquez-Rodriguez* v. *Honduras*, IACtHR, 29 July 1988. The classic statement of the argument is Diane Orentlicher, 'Settling Accounts: The Duty to Prosecute Violations of a Prior Regime' (1991) 100 *Yale Law Journal* 2537.

[71] *Barrios Altos* case (*Chumbipuma Aguirre et al.* v. *Peru*), IACtHR, 14 March 2001. See e.g. Lisa J. Laplante, 'Outlawing Amnesty: The Return of Criminal Justice in Transitional Schemes' (2009) 49 *Virginia Journal of International Law* 915. See further Chapter 22.

[72] E.g. Michael Scharf, 'The Letter of the Law: The Scope of the International Legal Obligation to Prosecute Human Rights Crimes' (1996) 59 *Law and Contemporary Problems* 1; Bruce Broomhall, *International Justice and the International Criminal Court* (Oxford, 2003) 98–100; Cryer, *Prosecuting International Crimes*, 103–5.

[73] See the comprehensive review in Siebert-Fohr, *Prosecuting Serious Human Rights Violations*.

[74] *Ibid.*, 109. See further section 22.2.1. But, for a contrary view, see e.g. James L. Cavallaro and Stephanie Erin Brewer, 'Reevaluating Regional Human Rights Litigation in the Twenty-First Century: The Case of the Inter-American Court' (2008) 102 *American Journal of International Law* 768.

[75] See further Chapters 10–12.

exists in customary international law; if correct, the duty would bind States regardless of whether they are parties to the relevant treaty. The claim is sometimes made by reference to a particular crime, but sometimes by reference to all international crimes.

There are expressions in support of a customary duty. The 1996 ILC Draft Code of Crimes against the Peace and Security of Mankind, for example, advocated a duty to prosecute or extradite individuals accused of genocide, crimes against humanity and war crimes, as defined in the Code, and to prohibit such crimes regardless of where or by whom the crime was committed.[76] The ICTY Appeals Chamber in *Blaškić* has stated that there is a customary obligation to prosecute or extradite those who have allegedly committed grave breaches of international humanitarian law, but without developing the argument further.[77] The Preamble to the ICC Statute 'recall[s] the duty of every State to exercise its criminal jurisdiction over those responsible for international crimes', although without clarifying the jurisdictional scope of this 'duty' or being reinforced by any operative provision in the Statute. It is unlikely that the Statute can be read as creating a positive duty to prosecute at the national level; there are some claims to the contrary,[78] but these expressly rely on mixing the *lex lata* and *lex ferenda* (law is it is, and law is it should be).[79]

In making the case for a customary duty, reference has been made to certain General Assembly resolutions as an expression of *opinio iuris*.[80] But close scrutiny of the wording and voting record gives rise to doubts about their authority, and the majority of State practice, particularly on amnesties, speaks against an existing customary duty to prosecute international crimes.[81] A good case can be made, however, that such a duty is emerging concerning prosecutions based on territoriality, and perhaps nationality, jurisdiction.[82]

Another line of argument is that a duty to prosecute follows from the nature of international crimes: the core crimes of international criminal law rest on norms of *ius cogens* (peremptory norms)[83] and as such give rise to obligations *erga omnes* (towards the entire international community).[84] Advocating this position, Bassiouni has argued that the *erga omnes* obligation is not to grant impunity to violators of such crimes and thus to prosecute or extradite, and this argument wins support in ICJ case law so far as genocide is concerned.[85] A linked hypothesis is the existence of an international community (a *civitas maxima*) with a common interest in repressing international crimes which, combined with the right of every

---

[76] Arts. 8–9. See also the 1996 ILC Report, at 42–50.

[77] *Blaškić*, ICTY A. Ch., 29 October 1997, para. 29. Cf. *Furundžija*, ICTY T. Ch. II, 10 December 1998, paras. 153–7, where the implication of torture being a *ius cogens* crime was discussed, but not with respect to a duty to prosecute or extradite.

[78] For an argument that there is a customary obligation for core crimes, see Raphaël van Steenberghe, 'The Obligation to Extradite or Prosecute: Clarifying its Nature' (2011) 9 *Journal of International Criminal Justice* 1089, 1091–1115. The reticence of the ICJ to discuss the matter in *Habré*, and the lack of actual practice on this basis, speak strongly the other way.

[79] Payam Akhavan, 'Whither National Courts? The Rome Statute's Missing Half, towards an Express and Enforceable Obligation for the Domestic Repression of International Crimes' (2010) 8 *Journal of International Criminal Justice* 1045.

[80] GA Res. 2840(XXVI) of 18 December 1971 and 3074(XXVIII) of 3 December 1973; see Jordan Paust, *International Law as Law of the United States* (Durham, NC, 1996) 405.

[81] See e.g. Cryer, *Prosecuting International Crimes*, 105–10.

[82] See e.g. Darryl Robinson, 'Serving the Interests of Justice: Amnesties, Truth Commissions and the International Criminal Court' (2003) 14 *European Journal of International Law* 481; Siebert-Fohr, *Prosecuting Serious Human Rights Violations*, Chapter 7.

[83] See Art. 53 of the Vienna Convention on the Law of Treaties.

[84] See the *Barcelona Traction* case, ICJ, 5 February 1970, at 32.

[85] M. Cherif Bassiouni, 'International Crimes: Jus Cogens and Obligatio Erga Omnes' (1996) 59 *Law and Contemporary Problems* 63. See also the ICJ in the *Genocide* case, 28 May 1951, para. 23; and the *Bosnian Genocide* case, 11 July 1996, para. 31.

State to prosecute international crimes, has led to a duty to prosecute or extradite. Hence, shared moral values have turned into a legal obligation. Taken together, the proponents assert that a customary duty exists in spite of the fact that there is no consistent State practice or *opinio iuris* in support of this view. Unsurprisingly, others reject or question this conclusion and many of its underlying assumptions.[86]

The conclusion that there is a duty to prosecute or extradite does not automatically resolve the scope of criminal jurisdiction to be exercised by States, in particular third States. But, as we have seen in Chapter 3, it is widely held that these crimes are subject to permissive universal jurisdiction by States. An argument of mandatory universal jurisdiction (due to the *ius cogens* status of the crimes or otherwise) would in fact result in most States being in constant breach of the obligation, which brings into question whether State practice does indeed indicate the existence of such a customary obligation.

4.4   Domestic criminal law and criminal jurisdiction

4.4.1   *Domestic legislation*

Of course, national prosecutions presuppose that there is applicable criminal law and criminal jurisdiction.[87] The Genocide and Geneva Conventions explicitly require that the States Parties enact necessary legislation.[88] Some States adopt implementing legislation, while others rely upon direct application of international law in the domestic system; hence, not all States will need domestic legislation to meet their treaty obligations. A number of States have enacted special penal law on war crimes and genocide, either in a civil or a military penal system or both. Prior to the ICC Statute, there was no generally accepted convention on crimes against humanity, and thus these crimes were only rarely provided for as distinct crimes in domestic law. Aggression is criminalized in a minority of States.[89]

Most of the underlying offences that can constitute genocide or crimes against humanity have long been criminalized and prosecuted under domestic law, but as ordinary crimes and not in the qualified form of genocide or crimes against humanity. This posed an obstacle to prosecutions in France until the Court of Cassation in *Barbie* established that crimes against humanity, as embodied in the Nuremberg Charter, were directly applicable in France.[90] The ruling paved the way for further prosecutions of Second World War crimes and for subsequent French legislation on genocide and other '*crimes contre l'humanité*'.

Reliance upon 'ordinary crimes' may fall short of criminalization in international law, and thus the State may violate its duty to enact with the manifestation of seriousness that is

---

[86] See Cryer, *Prosecuting International Crimes*, 110–17; however, see also Akhavan, 'Whither National Courts?', 1259–62. For arguments for and against, see Bassiouni and Wise, *Aut Dedere, Aut Judicare*.

[87] On jurisdiction, see Chapter 3.

[88] Art. V of the Genocide Convention; Art. 49 of Geneva Convention I; Art. 50 of Geneva Convention II; Art. 129 of Geneva Convention III; and Art. 146 of Geneva Convention IV.

[89] See Chapter 13.

[90] Court of Cassation, 26 January 1984, rejecting an earlier ruling by the same court in *Touvier*, 30 June 1976, where crimes against humanity were considered 'ordinary crimes'; see Sadat Wexler, 'The French Experience', 293–4.

embedded in the international crimes.[91] In Australia, the approach of relying on ordinary crimes in meeting the obligations under the Genocide Convention led a domestic court to the conclusion that genocide was not recognized domestically and could not be prosecuted in Australian courts.[92]

In some cases, the special legislation that is introduced is unsatisfactory. And, even if the definitions correspond to those of international law, other aspects such as the modes of liability set forth in the Genocide Convention are sometimes overlooked or inadequately addressed by the application of ordinary domestic criminal law principles.[93] Customary international law is rarely reflected.[94] This will hinder prosecution of crimes that are based on customary law alone.[95] Some States (for example, Germany) do not accept non-written criminal law, due to a strict interpretation of the legality principle. Other States do accept such law (for example, common law jurisdictions like the United Kingdom), and also direct application of customary international law by national courts, but not that customary international law is capable of creating offences in domestic law;[96] as the power to create new crimes should be reserved for the democratic process and elected assemblies.[97]

Moreover, national legislation has sometimes been carefully designed or interpreted to have a selective application. Perhaps the most criticized feature of the *Barbie* case was the imposition by the Court of Cassation of the (additional) requirement that crimes against humanity be committed 'in the name of a State practising a hegemonic political ideology'.[98] This requirement, which also affected subsequent French trials, excluded its application to crimes during France's own decolonization conflicts in Indochina and Algeria. Likewise, earlier Australian law on war crimes, as interpreted in the *Polyukhovic* case, excluded crimes in East Timor.[99] In Israel, the Nazis and Nazi Collaborators (Punishment) Act of 1950, providing for crimes against humanity, war crimes and 'crimes against the Jewish people', is solely retroactive.[100] Yet another example is the 1991 War Crimes Act in the United Kingdom which was restricted to violations of the laws of war when committed on German or German-occupied territory between 1939 and 1945; an Act that the House of Lords rejected twice with reference to retroactivity and selectivity before it was passed.[101]

---

[91] This approach has hindered referral of cases from the Tribunals; *Bagaragaza*, ICTR A. Ch., 30 August 2006. But compare *Hadžihasanović et al.*, ICTY T. Ch. II, 15 March 2006, paras. 253–60 (no duty under conventional or customary law to prosecute war crimes as international crimes and not as ordinary crimes).

[92] *Nulyarimma v. Thompson* [1999] FCA 1192.

[93] See Art. III of the Genocide Convention; see also Schabas, *Genocide*, 350–2.

[94] See, however, the Canadian Crimes against Humanity and War Crimes Act 2000, s. 4(4), which allows for custom; and the German Code of Crimes against International Law 2002, which incorporates rules of customary international law into the definitions of certain crimes.

[95] See Helmut Kreicker, 'National Prosecution of Genocide from a Comparative Perspective' (2005) 5 *International Criminal Law Review* 313, 319–20. Note, however, that French courts in *Barbie* and other cases accepted criminal responsibility grounded on customary international law.

[96] See e.g. *R v. Bow Street Metropolitan Stipendiary Magistrate, ex parte Pinochet Ugarte (No. 3)* [2000] 1 AC 147; and *Nulyarimma v. Thompson* [1999] FCA 1192.

[97] The UK House of Lords has held that customary international law can no longer create crimes in the UK legal order; *R v. Jones* [2006] UKHL 16; see Patrick Capps, 'The Court as Gatekeeper: Customary International Law in English Courts' (2007) 70 *Modern Law Review* 458. A small door may have been left open, however, in relation to war crimes.

[98] French Court of Cassation, 20 December 1985, although, see also Caroline Fournet, *Genocide and Crimes against Humanity: Confusions and Misconceptions in French Law and Practice* (Oxford, 2013).

[99] High Court of Australia, 14 August 1991.   [100] See further Wenig, 'Enforcing the Lessons of History', 102–22.

[101] See e.g. A. T. Richardson, 'War Crimes Act 1991' (1992) 55 *Modern Law Review* 73, 77; and Marschik, 'The Politics of Prosecution', 87–9.

Even when national courts interpret international law in good faith, there is a significant chance that judges not well versed in international law may misunderstand what it requires.[102] On the other hand, the use of domestic law offences, although more familiar to municipal judges, can sometimes lead to standards being imposed that are narrower than those set by international law.[103]

4.4.2   The ICC as a catalyst for domestic legislation

The fundamental principle that the ICC is to assume jurisdiction only when States fail to do so, the complementarity principle,[104] provides a strong incentive for States to enact the crimes laid down in the ICC Statute and, to a greater or lesser extent, assume jurisdiction over crimes committed abroad.[105] Although not a legal obligation under the Statute, States will want to meet the 'complementarity test'.[106] It is also an opportunity to express a commitment to combating impunity for international crimes. This has already led to new penal legislation being passed in a number of States, sometimes in spite of having been parties to the relevant conventions for a long time, and the process is under way in others.[107] In turn, this has generated criminal investigations and prosecutions in, for example, the DRC and Uganda.[108]

The introduction of such laws is a complex task, however, and requires careful political and legal considerations. When it is politically important to ensure criminalization that coincides with that of the ICC, and thus to prevent the ICC from intervening in future cases, the safest option is to adopt the offences as defined in the ICC Statute. This is the approach taken by, *inter alia*, Argentina, Australia, Canada, New Zealand, South Africa and the United Kingdom.[109] Another approach is to transform the offences into the normal legal terminology of the national system as has been done, for example, in Germany.[110] In this

---

[102] See e.g. the Italian *Lozano* case (*Italy* v. *Lozano*, Rome Court of Assize, 25 October 2007, and Court of Cassation, 24 July 2008); and Antonio Cassese, 'The Italian Court of Cassation Misapprehends the Notion of War Crimes: The Lozano Case' (2008) 6 *Journal of International Criminal Justice* 1077.

[103] See e.g. Nathan Rasiah, 'The Court Martial of Corporal Payne and Others'. Although, as he notes at 198, elsewhere the converse may also be the case.

[104] See section 8.6.

[105] See e.g. Katherine Doherty and Timothy McCormack, 'Complementarity as a Catalyst for Comprehensive Domestic Penal Legislation' (1999) 5 *UC Davis Journal of International Law and Policy* 147; Mark Ellis, 'The International Criminal Court and its Implications for Domestic Law and National Capacity Building' (2002) 15 *Florida Journal of International Law* 215; Broomhall, *International Justice and the International Criminal Court*, 86–93; Darryl Robinson, 'The Rome Statute and its Impact on National Law' in Cassese, *Commentary*, 1849–69; Julio Bachio Terracino, 'National Implementation of the ICC Crimes: Impact on National Jurisdictions and the ICC' (2007) 5 *Journal of International Criminal Justice* 421.

[106] But see section 8.6.2 for cases of uncontested admissibility. For the argument that an effective and comprehensive system of international criminal justice requires a duty on States to prosecute core international crimes (and cooperation obligations among States), see Akhavan, 'Whither National Courts?'

[107] For a useful discussion, see Olympia Bekou, 'Crimes at Crossroads: Incorporating International Crimes at the National Level' (2012) 10 *Journal of International Criminal Justice* 677.

[108] See Max Du Plessis, Antoinette Louw and Ottilia Maunganidze, *African Efforts to Close the Impunity Gap*, Institute for Security Studies Paper 241 (Pretoria, 2012).

[109] See David Turns, 'Aspects of National Implementation of the Rome Statute: The United Kingdom and Selected Other States' in Dominic McGoldrick *et al.* (eds.), *The Permanent International Criminal Court: Legal and Policy Issues* (Oxford, 2003) 337–87; on Latin America, see the contributions by Elizabeth S. Vargas (genocide), Ramiro G. Falconi (crimes against humanity) and Salvador H. Carrasco (war crimes) in (2010) 10 *International Criminal Law Review* 441–73.

[110] See e.g. Helmut Satzger, 'German Criminal Law and the Rome Statute: A Critical Analysis of the New German Code of Crimes against International Law' (2002) 2 *International Criminal Law Review* 261.

process, however, States must also take into account their other international obligations concerning international crimes. Accordingly, the German approach has been also to focus on customary international law offences.[111] Yet another approach is to ensure that 'ordinary' domestic offences cover all conduct that also falls within the crimes of the Statute. Neither the 'complementarity test' nor the related *ne bis in idem* provisions (see section 4.7) require that the State and the ICC make the same legal characterization of the underlying conduct (i.e. that national law also includes genocide, crimes against humanity and war crimes as specific offences and relevant conduct is prosecuted as such).

In this process, the scope of national criminal jurisdiction as well as the applicable principles of criminal law and penalties must also be considered. States are free to choose solutions other than those provided for the ICC, but again the choice may affect the capacity to meet the 'complementarity test'; and other international obligations must also be adhered to.

4.4.3   *Impact of domestic and international case law*

National courts consider foreign case law to a greater or lesser extent. While it is natural in common law jurisdictions to pay attention to decisions from other (common law) jurisdictions, civil law jurisdictions often have a more reluctant approach to jurisprudence as a source of law. But the persuasive effect of court decisions, particularly those of higher courts, is similar. Domestic jurisprudence may also have an impact as a source of law for international criminal courts, as the practice of the ICTY and ICTR shows.[112] Such decisions may serve as tools for the interpretation of treaties, identification and interpretation of rules of customary international law or general principles of law, and perhaps even as independent authorities.

Decisions of international courts are a recognized, but formally a subsidiary, means for determining international law. In practice, these decisions have made very important contributions to the development of international criminal law, from the Nuremberg and Tokyo IMTs to the ICC. Not least, the ICTY and ICTR have made a lasting impact by operating for many years and providing important clarifications of various issues. To what extent international jurisprudence is considered by national courts depends upon how international law is generally integrated into and applied within the domestic legal order. Some domestic legislation, such as that in the United Kingdom, explicitly requires that national courts take into account decisions and judgments of the ICC and any other relevant international jurisprudence.[113] In other States which have incorporated international crimes into domestic

---

[111] However, this approach entails risks of going further than other States would accept, or not going far enough to meet the 'complementarity test'; see Robinson, 'The Rome Statute', 1861–2.

[112] See André Nollkaemper, 'Decisions of National Courts as Sources of International Law: An Analysis of the Practice of the ICTY' in William Schabas and Gideon Boas (eds.), *International Criminal Law Developments in the Case Law of the ICTY* (Leiden, 2003) 277–96.

[113] International Criminal Court Act 2001, s. 66(4) (UK). See generally Robert Cryer, 'Neither Here Nor There? The Status of International Criminal Jurisprudence in the International and UK Legal Orders' in Michael Bohlander and Kaiyan Kaikobad (eds.), *International Law and Power: Perspectives on Legal Order and Justice: Essays in Honour of Colin Warbrick* (The Hague, 2010) 183.

law, national courts will normally be under an obligation to interpret the domestic provisions in accordance with the interpretation of equivalent international provisions, including that made by international criminal tribunals.[114]

4.5   Statutory limitations

Most domestic systems know of statutory limitations, or prescription (i.e. time limitations on prosecution). While most civil law jurisdictions provide for a general application, most common law jurisdictions exclude murder and other serious crimes. Neither the post-Second World War trials, nor the Geneva Conventions or the Genocide Convention, address the issue, but subsequently there has been much debate regarding the application of statutory limitations with respect to genocide, crimes against humanity and war crimes. Statutory limitations aim to prevent unjust delays between the commission of the offence and prosecution (or punishment), but could, if applicable, lead to impunity for the most heinous international crimes. In order to close this possible 'technical' escape from liability, treaties on the non-applicability of statutory limitations to genocide, crimes against humanity and war crimes were adopted under the auspices of the UN and the Council of Europe.[115] Some States have also passed laws which make statutory limitations inapplicable to such crimes, but these laws vary in scope. There is also some municipal and international case law to the effect that statutory limitations shall not apply to international crimes, for example the ICTY ruling regarding torture in *Furundžija*.[116] The ICC Statute explicitly provides that statutory limitations do not apply before it.[117] The Enforced Disappearances Convention, although stopping short of disapplying statutes of limitation for individual disappearances,[118] provides that any limitation shall take into account the exceptional seriousness of disappearances and shall only run from the end of the offence, given its continuing nature.[119]

But statutes of limitations have been obstacles in national prosecutions.[120] In the *Barbie* case,[121] for example, the French law on non-application of such limitations was strictly interpreted to apply only to crimes against humanity, thus barring prosecution for war crimes. Similarly, prescription concerning war crimes also led to the acquittal by Italian courts in the *Hass and Priebke* case, where the accused had admitted to a massacre of hundreds of civilians during the Second World War. Still, war crimes carrying life imprisonment under Italian law were considered exempt from statutory limitations. In 1976, Swiss

---

[114] See e.g. the *Jorgić* case, German Federal Constitutional Court, 12 December 2000.

[115] Convention on the Non-Applicability of Statutory Limitations to War Crimes and Crimes against Humanity of 26 November 1968; European Convention on the Non-Applicability of Statutory Limitations to Crimes against Humanity and War Crimes of 25 January 1974.

[116] *Furundžija*, ICTY T. Ch. II, 10 December 1998, para. 157. See also the *Barrios Altos* case, IACtHR, 14 March 2001, para. 41; and *Kononov* v. *Latvia*, ECtHR, 17 May 2010, paras. 231–3. An example of a domestic decision is the *Sandoval* case, Supreme Court of Chile, 17 November 2004 (on enforced disappearances).

[117] Art. 29 of the ICC Statute.

[118] Art. 5 of the Enforced Disappearances Convention provides a savings clause for crimes against humanity of enforced disappearance.

[119] *Ibid.*, Art. 8(1)(b).

[120] See further Christine Van den Wyngaert, 'War Crimes, Genocide and Crimes against Humanity – Are States Taking National Prosecutions Seriously?' in M. Cherif Bassiouni (ed.), *International Criminal Law*, 2nd edn (New York, 1999) Vol. III, 233–5.

[121] French Court of Cassation, 26 January 1984.

authorities had to refuse extradition to the Netherlands of Second World War criminal Pieter Menten due to statutory limitations (and were also prevented from prosecuting the case),[122] as did the lower Argentine courts when considering the extradition of Erich Priebke to Italy, although he was eventually extradited to face trial, and was convicted. Statutory limitations have also been an issue in Spanish prosecutions of Francoist-era crimes. Sometimes the concept of 'continuing crimes' has provided a way of circumventing national limitations on prosecution.[123]

It has been claimed that the non-applicability of statutory limitations to war crimes has developed into a norm of customary international law.[124] Others restrict the claim of a customary rule to genocide, crimes against humanity and torture.[125] While there is clearly a move towards an acceptance that statutory limitations shall not apply, the fact remains that many States still apply such limitations to international crimes in their domestic legal orders and that the two conventions have a modest number of States Parties.[126] For example, both German and Dutch law retain statutory limitations for the least serious war crimes, even against the general non-applicability of such limitations in the ICC Statute.[127] The assertion of a customary norm may thus be premature.[128] However, it is important to note that domestic legislation does not affect liability under international law, and there is no positive rule of international law providing for the prescription of liability for international crimes, and, as such, liability under international law is not subject to prescription.

4.6   The non-retroactivity principle

Related to statutory limitations is the principle of non-retroactivity of criminal law, which in turn forms part of the legality principle.[129] The question of compatibility with the non-retroactivity principle arises when a limitation period is extended or set aside retroactively or when extraterritorial jurisdiction is introduced retrospectively. National courts have accepted retroactive criminality with respect to Second World War crimes, in so far as the crimes were considered covered by conventional or customary international law at the time the offence was committed. Both the Supreme Court of Canada in *Finta* and the High Court of Australia in *Polyukhovic* accepted this regarding crimes committed abroad; the French Court of Cassation in *Barbie* resolved the issue by considering crimes against humanity as directly applicable international crimes. States will consider statutory limitations as either

---

[122] See Andreas Ziegler, 'Domestic Prosecution and International Cooperation with Regard to Violations of International Humanitarian Law: The Case of Switzerland' (1997) 7 *Schweizerische Zeitschrift für internationales und europäisches Recht* 561, 570–1.

[123] E.g. Samantha Salsench i Linares, 'Francoism Facing Justice: Enforced Disappearances before Spanish Courts' (2013) 11 *Journal of International Criminal Justice* 463.

[124] Henckaerts and Doswald-Beck, *ICRC Customary Law*, 614–18.   [125] See e.g. Cassese, *International Criminal Law*.

[126] In September 2013, the UN Convention had fifty-four States Parties and the European Convention had seven Parties (and one signatory).

[127] See Harry Verweij and Martijn Groenleer, 'The Netherlands' Legislative Measures to Implement the ICC Statute' in R. S. Lee, *States' Responses to Issues Arising from the ICC Statute: Constitutional, Sovereignty, Judicial Cooperation and Criminal Law* (New York, 2005) 97; and Satzger, 'German Criminal Law and the Rome Statute', 272–3. Cf. Sweden, which as of 1 July 2010 repealed the statutory limitations, *inter alia*, for international crimes (see Chapter 35, s. 2, of the Swedish Penal Code).

[128] See also Gaeta, 'War Crimes Trials', 766.   [129] See section 1.5.1.

substantive or procedural rules, and the principle of legality is only applicable to the former, but there must in any case be grounds for concluding that the crime existed at the time of its commission.[130] Similarly, the European Court of Human Rights has accepted that a conviction in 2004 for war crimes committed in 1944 did not violate the legality provision in Article 7 of the European Convention on Human Rights (ECHR).[131]

Some ICC-related legislation addresses the question of retroactivity. According to the Canadian Crimes against Humanity and War Crimes Act 2000, for example, crimes committed outside Canada may be prosecuted retrospectively, but prosecution of crimes committed before the adoption of the ICC Statute (on 17 July 1998) is allowed only in so far as the crimes correspond to the state of customary law at the time of their commission.[132] The Act also clarifies that the crimes defined in the ICC Statute are deemed to reflect customary law at the latest when the Statute was adopted, possibly earlier, and that crimes against humanity were criminal according to customary international law or general principles of law recognized by civilized nations prior to the Nuremberg IMT Charter or the Tokyo IMT Charter.[133] The New Zealand International Crimes and International Criminal Courts Act 2000 establishes start dates for jurisdiction over genocide and crimes against humanity,[134] which reflect the date when New Zealand ratified the Genocide Convention (for genocide) and the date when the jurisdiction of the ICTY commenced (for crimes against humanity). Similar provisions exist in the United Kingdom which retrospectively gave UK courts jurisdiction over certain customary international crimes that have occurred since 1 January 1991.[135]

4.7   *Ne bis in idem* or double jeopardy

4.7.1   *Application between States*

The principle that no one shall be tried or punished more than once for the same offence, expressed as *ne bis in idem* or double jeopardy, is reflected in the major human rights treaties,[136] and is an expression of the broader principle of finality and the binding effect of judgments (the doctrine of *res judicata*).[137] Reasons of fairness to defendants and the interest of thorough investigations and preparations of cases by the prosecutorial authorities motivate the principle. The principle also applies in the context of international cooperation in criminal matters.[138]

---

[130] See Van den Wyngaert, *National Prosecutions*, 235–7.   [131] *Kononov* v. *Latvia*, ECtHR, 17 May 2010, paras. 205–27.

[132] Crimes against Humanity and War Crimes Act 2000, s. 6.

[133] *Ibid*. The Charters were adopted on 8 August 1945 and 19 January 1946 respectively.

[134] International Crimes and International Criminal Court Act 2000, s. 8(4).

[135] Coroners and Justice Act 2009. Section 70 provides for jurisdiction over genocide, war crimes and crimes against humanity committed since 1991. See Robert Cryer and Paul David Mora, 'The Coroners and Justice Act 2009 and International Criminal Law: Backing into the Future?' (2010) 58 *International and Comparative Law Quarterly* 803.

[136] E.g. Art. 14(7) of the ICCPR; and Art. 4 of Protocol 7 to the ECHR.

[137] For a concise overview, see José Luis de la Cuesta, 'Concurrent National and International Criminal Jurisdiction and the Principle of "Ne Bis in Idem": General Report' (2002) 73 *International Review of Penal Law* 707. See also Gerard Coffey, 'Resolving Conflicts of Jurisdiction in Criminal Proceedings: Interpreting Ne Bis in Idem in Conjunction with the Principle of Complementarity' (2013) 4 *New Journal of European Criminal Law* 59.

[138] See section 5.3.3.

But these provisions relate only to proceedings in one and the same State.[139] Hence, it is lawful for a State to prosecute a person for an offence for which he or she has been prosecuted, and even punished, elsewhere. Part of this is an outcropping of the principle of sovereign equality. One State's courts cannot bind another. Different States view the effects of a foreign criminal judgment differently. In many common law jurisdictions, for example, the plea of *autrefois acquit, autrefois convict* is not restricted to a previous acquittal or conviction in the same domestic jurisdiction.[140] In other States, the practice ranges from almost complete recognition of foreign judgments to no recognition at all, while most States recognize some foreign judgments to a limited extent. When retrials are allowed, municipal law sometimes demands that a penalty imposed and served abroad is taken into account in sentencing.

Basic differences in the common law and civil law traditions, on issues such as the finality of a judgment, appeals against acquittals and determination of the same act or 'object of the trial' (*idem*), influence the application of the principle.[141] While some States apply a narrow interpretation of *idem*, covering only the conduct in law ('the offence'), other States give it a broader meaning whereby the conduct both in law and in fact is covered. Exceptions may apply, however, and difficult questions arise with respect to conduct that constitutes multiple offences, or continuing offences. When interpreting the principle, the European Court of Human Rights has arrived at different conclusions,[142] and the Court of Justice of the European Communities has accepted that the principle is applied differently by different EU Member States.[143] There is also no general consensus as to what decisions (*bis*), apart from convictions and acquittals, may bar new proceedings. Candidates are other decisions which prevent further proceedings, based on abuse of process, 'extinction' of the right to prosecute, certain out-of-court settlements and, more controversially, plea-bargaining agreements and decisions not to prosecute.[144]

Thus, although the principle applies internally in almost all domestic systems, its cross-border application remains controversial[145] and is not recognized as a customary rule or a general principle of law.[146] It is sometimes argued, however, that a customary rule concerning cross-border application of the principle is evolving, at least with regard to international

---

[139] See e.g. Christine Van den Wyngaert and Guy Stessens, 'The International Non Bis in Idem Principle: Resolving Some of the Unanswered Questions' (1999) 48 *International and Comparative Law Quarterly* 779. However, some argue that this is a serious lacuna in the protection of individual human rights, e.g. Alexander Poels, 'A Need for Transnational Non Bis in Idem Protection in International Human Rights Law' (2005) 23 *Netherlands Quarterly of Human Rights* 329.

[140] See e.g. *Treacy* v. *DPP* [1971] AC 537.

[141] Christine Van den Wyngaert and Tom Ongena, 'Ne Bis in Idem Principle, Including the Issue of Amnesty' in Cassese, *Commentary*, 710–15.

[142] On Art. 4 of Protocol 7 to the ECHR: see e.g. *Gradinger* v. *Austria*, ECtHR, 23 October 1995; and *Fischer* v. *Austria*, ECtHR, 29 August 2001 (broad interpretations of *idem*); *Oliveira* v. *Switzerland*, ECtHR, 30 July 1998 (more narrow interpretation). An authoritative interpretation is now provided in *Zolotukhin* v. *Russia*, ECtHR, 10 February 2009, paras. 70–84 (focusing on the broader 'same conduct' or *idem factum*).

[143] On Art. 54 of the 1990 Convention Implementing the Schengen Agreement, see e.g. *Gözütok and Brügge*, ECJ, 11 February 2003, paras. 31–3; *Miraglia*, ECJ, 10 March 2005; and *Van Esbroeck*, ECJ, 9 March 2006, paras. 25–42 (also applying a broad interpretation of *idem*).

[144] In this sense, the CJEU has adopted a quite far-reaching approach: see the cases referred to in the previous footnote. Cf. Art. 8(4) of the ACHR, which only applies to acquittals.

[145] For one example, see the *Boere* case (Regional Court Aachen, 23 March 2010); Swoboda, 'Paying', 261–9.

[146] See e.g. Gerard Convay, 'Ne Bis in Idem in International Law' (2003) 3 *International Criminal Law Review* 217. Cf. *Karemera et al.*, ICTR T. Ch. III, 16 July 2008, para. 4 (double jeopardy is an 'accepted principle of international law').

crimes,[147] as a corollary to the right to exercise universal jurisdiction. Rather than (even more) complex *ne bis in idem* provisions, which provide a 'first come first served' solution, the EU has adopted a mechanism for avoiding parallel proceedings.[148] In support of the evolving norm there, the provisions of the ICTY, ICTR and ICC Statutes all establish that the principle shall apply both ways in the relationship between the international and national courts.

4.7.2   Application vis-à-vis *international criminal jurisdictions*

The establishment of international criminal jurisdictions adds another dimension to the *ne bis in idem* principle.[149] In line with their primary jurisdiction *vis-à-vis* States,[150] the ICTY and ICTR Statutes provide that no one may be tried for the same conduct after he or she has been prosecuted at the Tribunal, but the Tribunals are not hindered by domestic proceedings in certain circumstances;[151] the set criteria relate both to the quality of the national proceedings and to the interest of enjoining the seriousness of international crimes. Only finalized national proceedings can bar prosecution before the Tribunal.[152] The 'deduction of sentence' principle applies in the event that the Tribunal retries the person.

The jurisdiction of the ICC, on the other hand, is complementary to that of States, which calls for a different *ne bis in idem* regime.[153] Apart from barring subsequent ICC proceedings regarding the same (factual) conduct,[154] convictions and acquittals by the ICC preclude the person being tried by a national (or another international) court 'for a crime referred to in Article 5' that was subject to the conviction or acquittal. Interestingly, it seems that owing to the latter provision, although national courts cannot prosecute a person for an international crime after he or she has been prosecuted for it at the ICC, they could prosecute him or her, on the basis of the same conduct, for a domestic crime.[155] It may be understandable that States would want to preserve the right to try a person for murder after an unsuccessful war crimes charge at the ICC, for example when no armed conflict could be established, but as worded the provisions would also allow a subsequent national murder trial in spite of a war crimes conviction on the same facts by the ICC.

The ICC Statute also provides that national decisions concerning 'conduct also proscribed under Article 6, 7 or 8' (of the Statute) hinder prospective ICC prosecutions, but with certain

---

[147] See e.g. Cassese, *International Criminal Law*.
[148] Council Framework Decision (2009/948/JHA) on prevention and settlement of conflicts of exercise of jurisdiction in criminal proceedings of 30 November 2009, OJ L328, 15 December 2009, p. 42.
[149] See e.g. Diane Bernard, 'Ne Bis in Idem – Protector of Defendants' Rights or Jurisdictional Pointman' (2011) 9 *Journal of International Criminal Justice* 863. See generally Håkan Friman, Helen Brady, Matteo Costi, Fabricio Guariglia and Carl-Friedrich Stuckenberg, 'Charges' in Sluter, *International Criminal Procedure*, 436–46 and 452–4.
[150] See Chapter 7.
[151] Art. 10 of the ICTY Statute; and Art. 9 of the ICTR Statute. The same applies between the SCSL and Sierra Leone: see Arts. 8–9 of the SCSL Statute.
[152] *Tadić*, ICTY T. Ch. II, 14 November 1995; *Musema*, ICTR T. Ch. I, 12 March 1996, para. 12.
[153] Art. 20 of the ICC Statute.
[154] This provision is subject to exceptions as provided in the ICC Statute, for example revision of conviction or sentence (Art. 84) and, according to some, appeals against an acquittal (Art. 81).
[155] Immi Tallgren and Astrid Reisinger Coracini, 'Article 20' in Triffterer, *Observers' Notes*, 669; Van den Wyngaert and Ongena, 'Ne Bis in Idem Principle', 723–4; Friman, 'Charges', 442.

exceptions. Again 'sham trials' do not bar subsequent international proceedings. There is, however, no exception for cases where the national court has dealt with the matter as an 'ordinary crime'; it is the underlying facts, not the legal characterization, that are decisive. Moreover, the ICC is required to assess whether the national proceedings were conducted independently and impartially 'in accordance with the norms of due process recognised by international law'. The ICC Statute does not require the Court to apply the 'deduction of sentence' principle, but provides instead for discretionary deduction of time spent in detention 'in connection with conduct underlying the crime'.[156]

4.8   Practical obstacles to national prosecutions

Where national prosecution is of crimes committed abroad, there are special demands relating to security, logistics and international cooperation. Some countries have established specialized police and prosecution units to deal with crimes of this kind, for example Canada, Denmark, the Netherlands, Norway, Sweden and the United Kingdom.

Where international cooperation is required, it may have attendant problems. In many cases, proceedings have been extended due to problems concerning apprehension of the accused.[157] Eichmann was abducted in another State, Barbie was 'expelled' (but not 'extradited') from Bolivia, Touvier was, for a long time, in hiding in France, and many others have escaped justice because of extradition requirements. Documentary and physical evidence is normally difficult to secure and witness evidence is therefore crucial. The investigation often must be conducted in the country where the crime was committed, and sometimes parts of the trials too.[158]

National prosecutions have regularly taken place long after the event. This may make live evidence impossible to obtain or may affect the reliability of the statements made; key witnesses may have forgotten critical events and misidentified the accused, as in the *Polyukhovich* and *Demjanjuk* cases. The difficulty of obtaining evidence may also affect fair trial rights, and some national courts have applied rules of evidence more liberally to defence evidence as a protection against unjust convictions. Examples include the *Finta* case in Canada and the *Demjanjuk* case in Israel.[159] Furthermore, old defendants may no longer be fit to stand trial or to serve a prison sentence; for example, the *Papon* case and the abandoned UK trial against Szyman Serafinowicz.[160] But domestic prosecutions are the backbone of international criminal law enforcement, since international tribunals cannot undertake prosecution of even a minority of international crimes, and as such one of their major functions is to encourage prosecutions at the domestic level.

---

[156] Art. 78(2) of the ICC Statute.   [157] See Chapter 5.

[158] See the Finnish *Bazaramba* case (District Court of Itä-Uusimaa/Porvoo, 11 June 2010, upheld on appeal) and the Swedish *Mbanenande* case (Stockholm District Court, 20 June 2013; currently on appeal). On the former, see Minna Kimpimäki, 'Genocide in Rwanda: Is It Really Finland's Concern?' (2011) 11 *International Criminal Law Review* 155.

[159] Richard May, 'The Collection and Admissibility of Evidence and the Rights of the Accused' in Lattimer and Sands (eds.), *Justice for Crimes*, 167–9.

[160] See Jane Garwood-Cutler, 'The British Experience' in Bassiouni, *International Criminal Law*, 325–6. See also Susanne Beck, 'Does Age Prevent Punishment? The Struggles of the German Judicial System with Alleged Nazi Criminals: Commentary on the Criminal Proceedings against John Demjanjuk and Heinrich Boere' (2010) 11 *German Law Journal* 347.

Further reading

Horst Fischer, Claus Kreß and Sascha Rolf Lüder (eds.), *International and National Prosecution of Crimes under International Law: Current Developments* (Berlin, 2001)

Roy S. Lee (ed.), *States' Responses to Issues Arising from the ICC Statute: Constitutional, Sovereignty, Judicial Cooperation and Criminal Law* (New York, 2005)

Steven R. Ratner, Jason S. Abrams and James L. Bischoff, *Accountability for Human Rights Atrocities in International Law: Beyond the Nuremberg Legacy*, 3rd edn (Oxford, 2009) Chapter 8

Joseph Rikhof, 'Fewer Places to Hide? The Impact of Domestic War Crimes Prosecutions on International Impunity' (2009) 20 *Criminal Law Forum* 1

William Schabas, *Genocide in International Law*, 2nd edn (Cambridge, 2008)

David Turns, 'Aspects of National Implementation of the Rome Statute: The United Kingdom and Selected Other States' in Dominic McGoldrick, Peter Rowe and Eric Donnelly (eds.), *The Permanent International Criminal Court: Legal and Policy Issues* (Oxford, 2003) 337–87

Christine Van den Wyngaert and Tom Ongena, 'Ne Bis in Idem Principle, Including the Issue of Amnesty' in Antonio Cassese, Paolo Gaeta and John R. W. D. Jones (eds.), *The Rome Statute of the International Criminal Court: A Commentary* (Oxford, 2002) 705–29

The ICRC collects and makes available national legislation and case law (www.icrc.org), with updates also published in the *International Review of the Red Cross*. National legislation and case law are also available in the ICC Legal Tools Database (www.legal-tools.org).

5

State Cooperation with Respect to National Proceedings

5.1   Introduction

Criminal law and proceedings are at the heart of State sovereignty, and cooperation in criminal matters is a voluntary undertaking; a State is not obliged to cooperate with others in criminal matters unless it has agreed to do so. But, over time, the parochial view that criminal law, including its effects, is local in nature has given way to an ever-growing need for and actual regulation of international legal cooperation. Influential factors in this regard are increased cross-border activities, including the commission of crimes, international terrorism and the development of human rights.

International crimes are of concern to all States and therefore lend themselves to efforts at cooperation. A commitment to cooperate, in the form of extradition, is the alternative to prosecution in accordance with the *aut dedere aut judicare* principle, when applicable.[1] Cooperation is particularly important when the State is exercising jurisdiction over crimes committed abroad, but may also be necessary when a State is investigating and prosecuting crimes committed on its own territory. Prosecution of genocide, crimes against humanity and war crimes is no exception.

But international law, treaty and custom, has not (yet) developed a special regime for State-to-State cooperation concerning these international crimes.[2] The Geneva Conventions and Additional Protocol I, for example, explicitly refer to cooperation in accordance with domestic legislation.[3] A recent attempt in the UN Commission on Crime Prevention and Criminal Justice to create a special cooperation instrument for such crimes, in furtherance of the ICC complementarity principle (Chapter 8), was rejected on formal grounds, but clearly also the substance was considered controversial.[4] One must therefore resort to general principles and provisions of international and domestic law on international cooperation

---

[1] The International Law Commission is currently considering the obligation to extradite or prosecute (*aut dedere aut judicare*): see ILC Report, A/68/10 (2011). The principle has also been subject to adjudication by the ICJ: see *Questions Relating to the Obligation to Prosecute or Extradite* (*Belgium v. Senegal*), ICJ General List 144, 20 July 2012. See further Chapter 4.

[2] See, however, e.g. GA Res. 3074(XXVIII) of 3 December 1973, which establishes a special regime but does not reflect custom.

[3] Art. 49 of Geneva Convention I; Art. 50 of Geneva Convention II; Art. 129 of Geneva Convention III; Art. 146 of Geneva Convention IV; and Art. 88 of Additional Protocol I.

[4] Commission on Crime Prevention and Criminal Justice, 22nd Session, Vienna, 22–26 April 2013 (Res. E/CN.15/2013/L.5, which was ultimately withdrawn).

in criminal matters. In relation to the ICTY, ICTR and ICC, however, State cooperation is subject to separate regimes to which we shall return in Chapter 20.

Traditional forms of legal cooperation[5] are: extradition, mutual legal assistance, transfer of criminal proceedings and enforcement of foreign penalties. In addition, there is an ever-increasing degree of cooperation, at various levels of formality, between police and other law enforcement authorities in different States.

5.2　　International agreements

Originally informal, extradition was the first form of legal cooperation to be regulated by international (bilateral and later multilateral) agreements. Other forms of cooperation were subsequently added, first as auxiliary measures to extradition and only later as independent forms of assistance. In the 1960s, further steps were taken, especially within the Council of Europe, to extend the cooperation into transfer of criminal proceedings (delegation of prosecution) and post-conviction measures.

Most States require a bilateral or multilateral agreement as a condition for providing cooperation, and thus reciprocity, but States can also grant assistance unilaterally. However, the quantity and quality of international agreements and, to an even greater degree, domestic legislation on legal cooperation is unevenly distributed across the world. Some States have concluded a great number of bilateral agreements. Increasingly, States that long did not do so, like China, now seek agreements.[6] Some regions have very advanced multilateral regimes, for example in Europe where both the Council of Europe and the EU are very active in this field,[7] and also within the Commonwealth. But there is no global extradition or mutual legal assistance treaty of general application, and many States rely on international and national regimes that are rudimentary, outdated or restricted to special crimes. In order to assist States, the UN has developed Model Treaties concerning all major forms of cooperation.[8] Assistance with implementing legislation is also provided by the UN, other organizations and individual States.

State cooperation is addressed in various multilateral treaties, the primary function of which is to codify international or transnational crimes and oblige the States Parties to combat them by criminalizing certain acts and provide for criminal jurisdiction. The older treaties, however, address cooperation only in very general terms. For example, the

---

[5] The terminology in this field is subject to some controversy. Civil law jurisdictions seem to prefer the term 'international judicial assistance', which reflects the judicial involvement in criminal investigations in these countries, while common law jurisdictions rather refer to 'international or mutual legal assistance'. Other distinctions have been suggested between assistance (to a foreign criminal investigation or trial) and transfer (of proceedings or penalty enforcement), and between extradition and other (lesser) forms of assistance.

[6] See Matthew Bloom, 'A Comparative Analysis of United States's Response to Extradition Requests from China' (2008) 33 *Yale Journal of International Law* 177.

[7] Regional and sub-regional treaties have also been adopted under the auspices of, *inter alia*, the Organization of American States (OAS), the League of Arab States, the Commonwealth of Independent States (CIS), the Southern African Development Community (SADC), the Economic Community of Central African States (ECCAS) and the East African Intergovernmental Authority on Development (IGAD).

[8] On 14 December 1990, the UN General Assembly adopted Model Treaties on extradition (Res. 45/116), mutual assistance in criminal matters (Res. 45/117), transfer of proceedings in criminal matters (Res. 45/118) and transfer of supervision of those conditionally sentenced or conditionally released (Res. 45/119).

contracting parties to the 1948 Genocide Convention 'pledge themselves … to grant extradition in accordance with their laws and treaties';[9] the 1977 Additional Protocol I to the Geneva Conventions,[10] as well as the 1984 Torture Convention,[11] require the parties to afford each other 'the greatest measure of assistance'. Additionally, many treaties explicitly provide that the relevant crime shall be an extraditable offence and that the treaty may satisfy domestic conditions that a treaty obligation for extradition exists.

More recent treaties, however, elaborate further on legal cooperation in criminal matters and include more or less complete regimes for extradition, mutual legal assistance and sometimes other forms of legal cooperation. Examples of multilateral UN treaties are the 1988 Drug Trafficking Convention,[12] the 2000 Transnational Organized Crime Convention (the Palermo Convention)[13] and the 2003 Corruption Convention.[14] Less detailed, and with a particular focus on extradition (and temporary transfer of detainees and prisoners), are the 1997 Terrorist Bombings Convention[15] and the 1999 Terrorist Financing Convention.[16]

With respect to terrorism, however, there are also some examples where the Security Council has ordered a State to surrender suspects for prosecution in another State, and thereby circumvented the normal requirements for extradition, including that of a treaty base.[17]

Some specialized organizations operate in this area. Most well known is the International Criminal Police Organization (Interpol), originally established in 1923 and with 190 member countries, which provides a police communications system, databases (of, *inter alia*, criminals, stolen property, firearms, fingerprints and DNA profiles), and operational police support services. Other examples are the European Police Office (Europol) and the EU's Judicial Cooperation Unit (Eurojust), both created within the EU. In addition, different networks exist, including the European network of contact points for investigation of genocide, crimes against humanity and war crimes.[18]

5.3   Some basic features

Both in law and in practice, cooperation in criminal matters is characterized by a dichotomy between State sovereignty, and hence a preference for one's own system, and a common interest and solidarity among States in combating crimes, which in turn requires trust in the legal systems of others. State-to-State cooperation is horizontal in nature – each State is considered sovereign and equal – which is manifested, *inter alia*, by reciprocity requirements and extensive grounds to refuse a request for cooperation.

---

[9] Art. 7. See also Art. 49 of Geneva Convention I; Art. 50 of Geneva Convention II; Art. 129 of Geneva Convention III; and Art. 146 of Geneva Convention IV.
[10] Art. 88.   [11] Art. 9.   [12] Arts. 6–11.   [13] Arts. 13–14, 16–21.
[14] Arts. 43–50. In addition, the Convention entails an advanced scheme for cooperation concerning asset recovery: Arts. 51–59.
[15] Arts. 8–14.   [16] Arts. 9–17.
[17] See Chapter 14; see also Michael Plachta, 'The Lockerbie Case: The Role of the Security Council in Enforcing the Principle Aut Dedere Aut Judicare' (2001) 12 *European Journal of International Law* 125.
[18] EU Council Decision 2002/494/JHA of 13 June 2002; and Council Decision 2003/335/JHA of 8 May 2003.

There is also an obvious link between international legal cooperation and the exercise of extraterritorial criminal jurisdiction.[19] The more far-reaching the extraterritorial jurisdiction is, the more problematic the issue of competing, concurrent jurisdictions will be, and this in turn will often hamper cooperation.

5.3.1   Traditional assistance and 'mutual recognition'

Traditionally, the requesting State asks for assistance with a certain measure (or seeks a particular result) and the requested State, if granting the request, takes the measure according to the conditions and the procedures prescribed by its domestic law. Strict formalities and lengthy procedures often plague cooperation and a scheme of this kind does not always produce results that are useful in the requesting State, particularly if the laws are very different or if strict conditions apply regarding, for example, the admissibility of evidence. Efforts have therefore been made to improve this traditional format, *inter alia*, by allowing the requesting State to prescribe procedural requirements and to participate when measures are taken on its behalf.[20] There is also a move away from the traditional, and often inefficient, diplomatic channel for cooperation requests in favour of specialized central authorities in the States, often located within the Ministry of Justice or Home Office, or even direct communications between the judicial authorities in the different States.

Within the EU, a further, and more radical, step has been taken with the introduction of a principle of 'mutual recognition' of foreign judicial decisions as the cornerstone for legal cooperation among the Member States.[21] This development of the horizontal approach to cooperation includes an *ipso facto* recognition and execution of foreign orders or requests with a minimum of formality. The concept rests on a high level of mutual trust and similar, or at least well known, procedural principles and human rights standards; the 'approximation' of laws (the politically correct term within the EU for 'harmonization') is a closely related issue. First articulated as a general principle in 1999, it has subsequently been implemented in different instruments, most notably regarding the European Arrest Warrant.[22]

5.3.2   Double criminality, rule of specialty and statutory limitations

Although cooperation originates from a common interest in combating crime, international agreements and domestic laws impose strict requirements for cooperation, and States retain broad powers to refuse requests from other States.

---

[19] See e.g. Christopher Blakesley and Otto Lagodny, 'Finding Harmony amidst Disagreement over Extradition, the Role of Human Rights, and Issues of Extraterritoriality under International Criminal Law' (1991) 24 *Vanderbilt Journal of Transnational Law* 1.

[20] See e.g. Art. 18 of the 2000 Palermo Convention and Arts. 2 and 8 of the 2001 Additional Protocol II to the 1959 European Convention on Mutual Assistance in Criminal Matters.

[21] See generally e.g. Ilias Bantekas, 'The Principle of Mutual Recognition in EU Criminal Law' (2007) 32 *European Law Review* 365.

[22] Council Framework Decision of 13 June 2002 on the European Arrest Warrant and the Surrender Procedures between Member States, OJ L190, 18 July 2002, pp. 1–20. See section 5.4.1.

The principle of 'double criminality' (or 'dual criminality') has long been applied, requiring that the underlying act (or omission) is criminal in both the requesting and the requested State. The principle stems from the principle of legality (*nulla poena sine lege*), but is also closely linked to State sovereignty and reciprocity.[23] It is often asserted that the requirement, although sometimes discretionary, constitutes a major obstacle to effective cooperation, and many commentators argue that it is no longer necessary; other grounds for refusal, such as *ordre public*, offer sufficient protection of State interests.[24] But the assertion is not empirically proven, and others argue that the double-criminality requirement serves to protect human rights.[25] Many newer instruments, particularly in the EU, seek to abolish the requirement, at least partially; the European Arrest Warrant, for example, does not require double criminality regarding selected crimes, including 'crimes within the jurisdiction of the International Criminal Court'.[26] This so-called 'list approach' was thereafter applied in many subsequent EU instruments. Some older examples exist too, regarding States with similar laws and a long tradition of close cooperation, for example extradition among the Nordic States.[27]

Moreover, the double-criminality rule is applied differently. Some States require identical crimes, while others are satisfied if the underlying facts constitute any crime (of sufficient gravity, if required) in both legal systems. However, this could entail not only a comparison of the definition of the crime (*in abstracto*), but also applicable grounds for excluding criminal responsibility in the case at hand (*in concreto*). A further restriction is the requirement in some countries that not only the conduct but also the applicable criminal jurisdiction of the requesting State must be equivalent to that of the requested State; the exercise of jurisdiction in the requesting State must also have been possible in the requested State.[28] The latter practice hinders cooperation when the requesting State applies extraterritorial jurisdiction and the jurisdiction of the requested State is primarily based upon territoriality, as is normally the case in common law jurisdictions. In addition to these conditions, the double-criminality rule also has a temporal aspect: the House of Lords in the *Pinochet* case controversially established that the double-criminality requirement must be met at the time of the offence and not (only) at the time of the extradition request.[29]

---

[23] See generally Nils Jareborg (ed.), *Double Criminality – Studies in International Criminal Law* (Uppsala, 1989); and Wendy De Bondt, 'Double Criminality in International Cooperation in Criminal Matters' in Gert Vermeulen, Wendy De Bondt and Charlotte Ryckman, *Rethinking International Cooperation in Criminal Matters in the EU: Moving Beyond Actors, Bringing Logic Back, Footed in Reality* (Antwerp and Apeldoorn, 2012) 106–84.

[24] See e.g. Thomas Weigend, 'Grundsätze und Probleme des Deutschen Auslieferungsrecht' (2000) 40/2 *Juristische Schulung* 105, 107.

[25] See e.g. Michael Plachta, 'The Role of Double Criminality in International Cooperation in Penal Matters' in Jareborg, *Double Criminality*, 128–9.

[26] Art. 2 of the Framework Decision on the European Arrest Warrant; see also the 1996 EU Extradition Convention (Art. 7).

[27] As a result of legislative cooperation, extradition laws with substantively the same content were enacted by Denmark, Finland, Norway and Sweden in 1959–61 (double criminality is not required except for extradition of nationals and political offences). Similarly, witnesses are required to give evidence before a court of another Nordic State without any double-criminality requirement. The extradition scheme has since been replaced by the Nordic Arrest Warrant, established by the Convention on Surrender for Crime between the Nordic States of 15 December 2005. See Gjermund Mathisen, 'Nordic Cooperation and the European Arrest Warrant: Intra-Nordic Extradition, the Nordic Arrest Warrant and Beyond' (2010) 79 *Nordic Journal of International Law* 1.

[28] See also the Framework Decision on the European Arrest Warrant, Art. 4(7)(b).

[29] *R v. Bow Street Metropolitan Stipendiary Magistrate, ex parte Pinochet Ugarte (No. 3)* [1999] 2 All ER 97, HL. See Colin Warbrick, 'Extradition Aspects of Pinochet 3' (1999) 48 *International and Comparative Law Quarterly* 958.

With respect to genocide, crimes against humanity and war crimes, the ICC Statute and the incentive to enact domestic legislation that the complementarity principle provides, offer hope for improved cooperation even if a double-criminality requirement is retained among States. Many have adopted, or are considering, similar, if not identical, crimes and broader criminal jurisdiction in national law, which should reduce the room for refusals on double-criminality grounds.

The rule of specialty, which is common in extradition treaties,[30] restricts the requesting State to bringing proceedings only with respect to the crimes for which the suspect was extradited; the double-criminality principle and other conditions for extradition, such as the political offence exception, would otherwise easily be defeated. However, the requested State could always consent to prosecution of other offences, and, within the EU and the Council of Europe, some agreements provide a presumption of consent under certain circumstances as well as a possibility for the suspect to waive entitlement of the specialty rule.[31] For mutual legal assistance, the imposition of conditions on the use or transmission of information and material furnished by the requested State, may serve the same purpose.[32]

Also linked to the double-criminality requirement are statutory limitations, which in some domestic systems apply generally and may bar cooperation; concerning extradition, some agreements, such as the 1957 European Extradition Convention,[33] explicitly allow statutory limitations as a discretionary ground for refusal. In other systems, like the United Kingdom, serious offences are not subject to such limitations, but extradition may still be refused because the passage of time would make it 'unjust and oppressive' (a *habeas corpus* ground).[34] As we have seen in Chapter 4, this also applies to international crimes in many States and no customary rule prevents this practice. However, more recent international developments go towards abandoning lapse of time due to statutory limitations in the requested State as a ground, at least a mandatory one, to refuse extradition.[35]

5.3.3   Ne bis in idem *or double jeopardy*

As described in section 4.7, the principle of *ne bis in idem* is a general criminal law principle in most national systems, but one that is normally confined to application within the same system. However, so long as criminal proceedings are not prevented by a judgment (or other final decision) in another State, criminal proceedings concerning the same person and

---

[30] E.g. Arts. 14–15 of the 1957 European Extradition Convention, as amended by the 2012 Fourth Additional Protocol to the Convention (Art. 3); and Art. 18(1) and (2) of the 2003 UK–US Extradition Treaty.

[31] E.g. Art. 10 of the 1996 EU Extradition Convention, Art. 27 of the Framework Decision on the European Arrest Warrant, and Arts. 4–5 of the 2010 Third Additional Protocol to the 1957 European Extradition Convention. See also *Leymann and Pustovarov*, ECJ, 1 December 2008.

[32] E.g. Art. 18(19) of the 2000 Palermo Convention.   [33] Art. 10 of the 1957 European Extradition Convention.

[34] Extradition Act 2003, ss. 11, 14, 79 and 82 (UK).

[35] E.g. the 1990 Convention Implementing the Schengen Agreement (Art. 62), the 1996 EU Extradition Convention (Art. 8) and the 2012 Fourth Additional Protocol to the 1957 European Extradition Convention (Art. 1). See also the Revised Manual to the UN Model Treaty on Extradition.

criminal act (or omission) might already be finalized in the requested State when the request is made. This is even more likely regarding offences over which States exercise extraterritorial jurisdiction.

Traditionally, international extradition agreements acknowledge the principle with regard to the requested State by prohibiting extradition if that State has already passed a final judgment against the fugitive. The 1957 European Extradition Convention and, more recently, the European Arrest Warrant provide such grounds for refusal.[36] Similarly, this ground for refusal is provided for other forms of cooperation; while some treaties aim at preventing double punishment only,[37] others seek to prevent double prosecutions too.[38]

Furthermore, there is a trend towards giving the principle a broader application, especially in the EU with the commitment to recognize each other's judicial decisions (mutual recognition). Not only evidence gathering and seizure but also arrests are now subject to such recognition. Consequently, the EU States are allowed, under certain conditions, to refuse execution of a European Arrest Warrant if the fugitive has already been finally adjudged by a third State concerning the same act.[39] Such provisions exist also in some bilateral agreements.[40] This increases the scope for rejecting a request and preserves the common law plea of *autrefois acquit, autrefois convict* without a special reservation to the international instrument.[41] Nonetheless, there is no general rule of international law preventing extradition because of a judgment in a third State.

However, the lack of common standards for the application of the *ne bis in idem* principle (see section 4.7) complicates cooperation and increasingly international courts such as the European Court of Human Rights and the Court of Justice of the European Communities have had to address how it should be applied to different forms of cooperation.[42]

5.3.4   *Human rights and legal cooperation*

In criminal law there is often a tension between the fundamental human rights afforded to individuals and the State interest in efficient law enforcement and prosecution; international cooperation in criminal matters is no exception. Extradition laws and treaties have traditionally been interpreted in favour of the request. In common law jurisdictions the 'rule of non-inquiry' has often discouraged the courts from inquiring into the fairness of the

---

[36] Art. 9 of the 1957 European Extradition Convention (and the 1975 Additional Protocol) and Art. 3(2) of the Framework Decision on the European Arrest Warrant.

[37] See e.g. Arts. 35–37 of the 1972 European Convention on Transfer of Proceedings in Criminal Matters (mandatory ground for refusal) and Art. 18(1)(e) of the 1990 European Proceeds from Crime Convention (optional ground for refusal).

[38] See e.g. Arts. 54–58 of the 1990 Convention Implementing the Schengen Agreement (albeit with certain exceptions).

[39] Art. 4(5) of the Framework Decision on the European Arrest Warrant.

[40] E.g. the 2003 UK–US Extradition Treaty, Art. 5(2).

[41] The United Kingdom made a formal reservation to Art. 9 of the 1957 European Extradition Convention.

[42] See e.g. John Vervaele, 'The Transnational Ne Bis in Idem Principle in the EU: Mutual Recognition and Equivalent Protection of Human Rights' (2005) 1 *Utrecht Law Review* 100; André Klip, *European Criminal Law: An Integrative Approach*, 2nd edn (Antwerp, Oxford and Portland, OR, 2012) 249–64; Wolfgang Schomburg, Otto Lagodny, Sabine Gless and Thomas Hackner, *Internationale Rechtshilfe in Strafsachen*, 5th edn (Munich, 2012); and Gerhard Coffey, 'Resolving Conflicts of Jurisdiction in Criminal Proceedings:Interpreting Ne Bis in Idem in Conjunction with the Principle of Complementarity' (2013) 4 *New Journal of European Criminal Law* 59.

proceedings of the requesting State.[43] One argument for the 'rule of non-inquiry' is that it promotes cooperation.[44] But, while the general trend is to limit the grounds for refusing cooperation, human rights considerations point in the opposite direction: cooperation, particularly extradition, should not be granted if the fundamental human rights of the person concerned would be at risk.

The development in Europe attempts to reconcile the two approaches. Indeed, one important prerequisite for the more far-reaching cooperation in Europe, and the underlying level of confidence in each other's legal systems, is the adherence to common and well-developed human rights standards. But, in addition to measures to improve cooperation within the EU, there are calls for better safeguards, a task that is complicated by the separate system of the Council of Europe, to which all EU Member States belong, but not yet the EU itself; in April 2013, a draft agreement between the Council of Europe Member States and the EU was finalized, allowing the EU to accede to the ECHR. In addition, EU directives for strengthening procedural rights for suspected or accused persons (for example, the right to interpretation and translation and the right to access to a lawyer) are being developed.[45] Such efforts are particularly important today when the international fight against terrorism, which includes improved cooperation, is challenged for violating and eroding fundamental human rights.[46]

An early expression of the human rights concerns is the *non-refoulement* principle which applies in refugee law and provides that a refugee should not be returned to a country where he or she is likely to be persecuted, as established in the 1951 Refugee Convention; a principle to which exception is made, however, concerning those who have committed a 'crime against peace, a war crime, or a crime against humanity' or 'a serious non-political crime'.[47]

That domestic human rights protection, constitutional or otherwise, is applicable also to legal cooperation is natural and established by courts in many States. It was long unclear, however, whether international human rights obligations would apply, and even trump, international cooperation obligations. But in the groundbreaking *Soering* decision of 1989, the European Court of Human Rights established that States Parties to the ECHR have certain obligations to protect individuals against a serious breach of their human rights in another State: 'knowingly to surrender a fugitive to another State where there were substantial grounds for believing that he would be in danger of being subjected to torture', or to inhuman or degrading treatment, would be a violation of the ECHR.[48] Also, 'a flagrant denial of a fair trial' in the requesting country may hinder extradition.[49] The UN Human Rights Committee has followed suit when interpreting the ICCPR.[50]

---

[43] E.g. the United States takes a strict approach to the rule of non-inquiry; John T. Parry, 'International Extradition, the Rule of Non-Inquiry, and the Problem of Sovereignty' (2010) 90 *Boston University Law Review* 1973, 1975.

[44] For a sceptical view, see William Magnuson, 'The Domestic Politics of International Extradition' (2012) 52 *Virginia Journal of International Law* 839, 888.

[45] See Resolution of the Council of 30 November 2009 on a Roadmap for strengthening procedural rights of suspected or accused persons in criminal proceedings, OJ C295, 4 December 2009, pp. 1–3.

[46] See generally Chapter 14; and Helen Duffy, *The 'War on Terror' and the Framework of International Law* (Cambridge, 2005).

[47] Art. 1 of the 1951 Refugee Convention.   [48] *Soering* v. *United Kingdom*, ECtHR, 7 July 1989, para. 88.

[49] *Ibid.*, para. 113. See section 5.4.5.

[50] See e.g. *Ng* v. *Canada*, HRC, 5 November 1993. See further Joanna Harrington, 'The Absent Dialogue: Extradition and the International Covenant on Civil and Political Rights' (2006) 32 *Queen's Law Journal* 82.

However, the international human rights bodies only apply the treaties they are established to protect and do not have to choose between conflicting treaty obligations or apply the domestic laws[51] by which these obligations are implemented. The opposite is true for domestic courts. In some countries, the courts can rely upon the constitution, or laws which take precedence over other laws, for example a law incorporating the ECHR, to afford priority to human rights considerations, while in other countries this is reflected in the legislation on international cooperation in criminal matters. From an international law perspective, however, the justification must be sought elsewhere; it has been suggested that certain human rights norms have higher status, based on *ius cogens* notions, and that multilateral human rights conventions have primacy over other international agreements on *ordre public* grounds.[52] But this is controversial and would in any case not go beyond the most serious violations, such as torture, and general primacy of human rights over extradition does not yet exist.[53]

Human rights standards do not only play a role in extradition. Material that has been obtained abroad through mutual legal assistance could also be affected by violations, for example evidence obtained by torture,[54] and therefore be inadmissible in the requesting State. Other obstacles relate to data protection concerning transferred information and third party rights in case of the seizure or freezing of property.

5.4   Extradition

Extradition is the surrender of a person by one State to another, the person being either accused of an (extraditable) crime in the requesting State or unlawfully at large after conviction. This is a considerable intrusion into the liberty of the person concerned, but one which is justified by the common interest of States in combating crimes and expunging safe havens for fugitives. The standard term being 'extradition', terms such as 'surrender' or 'transfer' are sometimes used, often with a view to signalling a substantive difference.[55]

Extradition is one option to meet the obligation of *aut dedere aut judicare*, but the principle is phrased differently in various treaties which, taken together with other treaty provisions, impacts on the interpretation of the obligation.[56] As pointed out in Chapter 4, it has been argued that the principle, in one form or another, has customary status in relation to international offences.[57] Put differently, the question is whether States have an obligation to extradite the offender of an international crime without such a duty following from a treaty

---

[51] The ECtHR has nonetheless assumed certain powers to review the compliance with domestic law, which also applied to detention pending extradition; see e.g. *Bordovskiy* v. *Russia*, ECtHR, 8 May 2005, paras. 41–4.

[52] Dugard and Van den Wyngaert, 'Reconciling Extradition', 194–5.

[53] *Ibid.*, 205–6; but see Art. 1(3) of the Framework Decision on the European Arrest Warrant.

[54] See e.g. *A (FC)* v. *Secretary of State for the Home Department (No. 2)* [2005] UKHL 71; [2006] 2 AC 221; and *El Haski* v. *Belgium*, ECtHR, 25 September 2012 (with references to ECtHR case law).

[55] See e.g. Michael Plachta, '"Surrender" in the context of the International Criminal Court and the European Union' (2004) 19 *Nouvelles études pénales* 465.

[56] See e.g. 'Survey of Multilateral Conventions Which May Be of Relevance for the Work of the International Law Commission on the Topic "The Obligation to Extradite or Prosecute (Aut Dedere Aut Judicare)", Study by the Secretariat', UN Doc. A/CN.4/630 of 18 June 2010.

[57] *Ibid.*, 20–50; and Raphaël van Steenberghe, 'The Obligation to Extradite or Prosecute: Clarifying Its Nature' (2011) 9 *Journal of International Criminal Justice* 1092.

(and unless the State prosecutes the fugitive instead). But, as also noted, State practice does not support this view, which should thus rather be seen as *de lege ferenda*. Moreover, extradition is only an alternative to prosecution when a request for this course of action exists, regardless of how the obligation is formulated. While the State facing the option to prosecute or extradite has discretion to choose, it has been suggested that extradition to a more interested State should be given priority when that is possible.[58] As to the flip side of the coin, or whether a duty to prosecute also includes a duty to seek extradition of a fugitive abroad, the prosecutorial determinations and the executive's foreign policy considerations are also subject to broad discretion, albeit that a decision not to seek extradition may be subject to judicial review.[59]

Extradition is normally subject to strict requirements. The already mentioned principle of double criminality and the rule of specialty apply, and the offences must also be of a certain gravity to be extraditable. The requested State may deny extradition with reference to *ne bis in idem*, which sometimes also covers a pardon or an amnesty in that State or a third State.[60]

Additionally, numerous grounds for refusal apply and conditions may be imposed. By allowing States to grant extradition in accordance with domestic law and applicable treaties, as is the case in the 1949 Geneva Conventions, the *aut dedere aut judicare* obligation is qualified. Hence, the States may apply the same conditions as for all other crimes. The provisions of the 1984 Torture Convention may, however, differ in this respect and it is sometimes argued that a condition such as non-extradition of nationals (see section 5.4.4) may not be invoked to refuse extradition concerning torture; but in practice many States do refuse extradition of nationals even in torture cases.[61] In addition, other requirements may be prescribed in international law.[62] With all these hurdles, requests for extradition are not always successful.

5.4.1 Extradition agreements and the European Arrest Warrant

Many States insist on reciprocity and require an international agreement for extradition. Apart from numerous bilateral agreements, the basic multilateral treaty in Europe is the 1957 European Extradition Convention and its Additional Protocols, adopted by the Council of Europe, which represent a traditional scheme. The EU has followed suit and adopted two conventions in 1995 and 1996, which provide for simplified proceedings and reduced grounds for refusal but they are not widely ratified.[63]

---

[58] E.g. *ibid.*, 1110–15.

[59] See e.g. *El-Masri*, Cologne Administrative Court, 7 December 2010; Peter Wilkitzki, 'German Government Not Obliged to Seek Extradition of CIA Agents for "Extraordinary Rendition"' (2011) 9 *Journal of International Criminal Justice* 1117.

[60] The 1975 Additional Protocol (Chapter II.2) and the 1978 Second Additional Protocol (Chapter IV.4) to the 1957 European Extradition Convention.

[61] See e.g. Arnd Düker, 'The Extradition of Nationals: Comments on the Extradition Request for Alberto Fujimori' (2003) 4 *German Law Journal* 1165.

[62] E.g. Art. 49 of Geneva Convention I, Art. 50 of Geneva Convention II, Art. 129 of Geneva Convention III and Art. 146 of Geneva Convention IV, all require that the requesting State has made 'a *prima facie* case'. See also *Questions Relating to the Obligation to Prosecute or Extradite (Belgium v. Senegal)*, ICJ General List 144, 20 July 2012, para. 120 (implying as a condition that the requesting State must have jurisdiction to prosecute and try the fugitive).

[63] The 1995 EU Convention on Simplified Extradition Procedures and the 1996 EU Extradition Convention.

Among the EU Member States, however, the European Arrest Warrant has replaced the traditional extradition scheme and introduced a system whereby a warrant in one State shall be recognized and enforced (arrest and surrender) in all other Member States. Building upon the principle of mutual recognition of judicial decisions, the European Arrest Warrant restricts many traditional grounds for refusal.[64] This has prompted amendments to domestic laws, either by special legislation (for example, Sweden) or amendments to the existing extradition legislation (for example, the United Kingdom). The scheme is generally perceived as successful, at least from a law enforcement perspective. But critical voices have been raised regarding sufficient safeguards, such as for protection of fair trial rights and prevention of 'overuse'.

In relation to non-EU States, however, extradition still applies in accordance with multilateral or bilateral agreements and domestic extradition legislation. Efforts are also made to harmonize extradition law for external relations, with the 2003 EU–US Extradition Agreement as the first example.[65] The Agreement supplements and modifies bilateral extradition agreements between EU Member States and the United States which otherwise continue to apply.

As mentioned in section 5.2, global penal law conventions and anti-terrorism conventions include provisions on extradition. A common provision is that States, which make extradition conditional on the existence of a treaty, may accept the convention as the legal basis for such cooperation.

5.4.2   *Extradition procedures*

The extradition procedures follow the law and practice of the requested State and applicable extradition agreements. Traditionally, the requesting State requests the arrest and extradition, or provisional arrest to be followed within a certain time by a surrender request, of the accused or convicted person. The requested State institutes proceedings to execute the request. In most States, both the executive and the judiciary have a role to play in the proceedings: a court considers the formal requirements and the actual surrender is an executive decision. The European Arrest Warrant, on the other hand, is to be recognized and enforced as such in the other Member States with minimal formalities. This scheme is also an example of a general trend towards a primarily judicial process.

The framing of the procedures depends upon the view taken on the extradition process as such.[66] Traditionally, it is seen as exclusively an arrangement between sovereign States, which will check the formal requirements and protect fundamental rights and fairness; the individual will play an insignificant role being merely the object of the proceedings. The opposite view, inspired by the development of human rights, is that the process entails rights

---

[64] See e.g. Nicola Vennemann, 'The European Arrest Warrant and its Human Rights Implications' (2003) 63 *Zeitschrift für ausländisches öffentliches Recht und Völkerrecht* 103.

[65] Agreement on Extradition between the European Union and the United States of America, 25 June 2003, OJ L181, 19 July 2003, pp. 27–32.

[66] For further discussion, see M. Cherif Bassiouni, *International Extradition: United States Law and Practice*, 5th edn (New York, 2007) 33–47.

that the fugitive may claim individually. Hence, the proceedings can be more or less extensive and time-consuming in different States. In common law countries, the *habeas corpus* principle extends also to extradition and offers an additional ground to challenge a foreign request.[67] Linked to this, these countries also require that the prosecution evidence against the fugitive justifies the trial for which extradition is sought; supporting evidence is required and a *prima facie* test is applied. While the United Kingdom has made exceptions to this requirement in recent years – *vis-à-vis* EU Member States and certain other countries, including the United States[68] – it still applies in many other common law jurisdictions.

Moreover, courts in many common law jurisdictions have long applied a rule of non-inquiry regarding the good faith and motive behind the extradition request or the standards of criminal justice of the requesting State;[69] it would conflict with the principle of comity if courts were to 'assume the responsibility for supervising the integrity of the judicial system of another sovereign nation'.[70] Instead, such considerations of justice and international relations form part of the executive decision whether to extradite. A consequence is that the fugitive may not bring evidence concerning discrimination or other possible human rights violations, a practice that has been criticized.[71] In the United Kingdom and Ireland, the European Arrest Warrant has prompted mandatory judicial considerations of human rights issues.[72] In civil law jurisdictions as well, the presumption is that the extradition request is made in good faith, but the courts often accept challenges by the fugitive regarding human rights violations.

5.4.3 *Extraditable and non-extraditable offences*

Extradition is normally restricted to serious offences, often by reference to a minimum level of punishment,[73] which might simplify, but does not do away with, a double-criminality requirement. In practice, international and transnational crimes are regularly extraditable, regardless of whether the *aut dedere aut judicare* principle of a particular treaty or a general requirement of gravity applies.

In addition, certain classes of offences are typically excluded from extradition. Most agreements, and thus domestic legislation, provide, as the main rule, that offences of a

---

[67] On UK law, see e.g. Nicholls *et al.*, *The Law of Extradition and Mutual Assistance*, 164–9.   [68] Extradition Act 2003.
[69] For jurisprudence, see Dugard and Van den Wyngaert, 'Reconciling Extradition', 189–91; and Bassiouni, *International Extradition*, 604–42.
[70] *Jhirad* v. *Ferrandina*, US Court of Appeals (2nd Cir.), 12 April 1976, para. 22. See also e.g. *Hoxha* v. *Levi*, US Court of Appeals (3rd Cir.), 3 October 2006.
[71] See e.g. Richard J. Wilson, 'Toward the Enforcement of Universal Human Rights through Abrogation of the Rule of Non-Inquiry in Extradition' (1997) 3 *ILSA Journal of International and Comparative Law* 751; David B. Sullivan, 'Abandoning the Rule of Non-Inquiry in International Extradition' (1999) 15 *Hastings International and Comparative Law Review* 111.
[72] See Susie Alegre and Marisa Leaf, 'Mutual Recognition in European Judicial Cooperation: A Step Too Far Too Soon? Case Study – The European Arrest Warrant' (2004) 10 *European Law Journal* 200, 203–5.
[73] Some countries, e.g. the United Kingdom and the United States, have traditionally referred to a list of offences, with the drawback of repeatedly requiring amendments, but this approach is giving way to the minimum penalty and double-criminality requirements.

political nature are non-extraditable;[74] the requested State avoids getting involved in conflicts abroad and preserves its right to grant political asylum. What will be considered a 'political offence' is not internationally defined, however, which leaves room for considerable discretion.[75] It has been criticized as being 'a "blackbox" for cases in which the requested state wants neither to extradite nor to reveal the actual grounds for the refusal'.[76] The scope of application is potentially broad but it has been reduced in some domestic jurisdictions by distinguishing between 'absolute' and 'relative' political offences where only the former will always prevent extradition. Today, however, a number of terrorism treaties explicitly provide that the crimes in question shall not be regarded as a political offence for the purpose of extradition.[77] The 1948 Genocide Convention[78] also has such a clause and, in Europe, the 1975 Additional Protocol to the 1957 European Extradition Convention clarifies that genocide and certain war crimes shall not prevent extradition by being considered political offences.[79] The scope for applying the political offence exception to international crimes is thus restricted and the trend is increasingly to consider 'freedom fighters' as criminals, which is due, not the least, to more ruthless and violent methods being employed. The European Arrest Warrant applies to offences of certain gravity, including the crimes under the ICC Statute, and does not include a political offence exception.

Another, often excluded, group of offences is military offences.[80] These are offences according to military law, but not ordinary criminal law, and should not hinder extradition for international crimes such as war crimes. Fiscal offences are also traditionally exempt from extradition.

5.4.4   Non-extradition of nationals

Many States, primarily civil law jurisdictions, prohibit the extradition of their own nationals; the principle is based on a historical duty of the State to protect its citizens, sovereignty, and indeed distrust in foreign legal systems, and it is often constitutionally protected.[81] As a counterweight, many of these States provide for extensive criminal jurisdiction over offences committed abroad. This in turn may prevent extradition, however, if the national is in a third State and that State considers the applied theory of jurisdiction when determining the

---

[74] E.g. extradition from the United States to the United Kingdom was denied in a number of cases involving members of the Irish Republican Army; see Bassiouni, *International Extradition*, 679–701.

[75] See e.g. Bert Swart, 'Human Rights and the Abolition of Traditional Principles' in A. Eser and O. Lagodny (eds.), *Principles and Procedures for a New Transnational Criminal Law* (Freiburg, 1992) 505–34. See generally Christine Van den Wyngaert, *The Political Offence Exception to Extradition: The Delicate Problem of Balancing the Rights of the Individual and the International Public Order* (The Hague, 1980).

[76] Blakesley and Lagodny, 'Finding Harmony amidst Disagreement', 46–7.

[77] Instead of the political offence exception, many terrorism treaties contain a so-called 'discrimination clause': a request for extradition (and mutual legal assistance) may be rejected if made 'for the purpose of prosecuting or punishing a person on account of that person's race, religion, nationality, ethnic origin or political opinion or that compliance with the request would cause prejudice to that person's position for any of these reasons'; e.g. Art. 12 of the 1997 Terrorist Bombings Convention and Art. 15 of the 1999 Terrorism Financing Convention. Also older conventions contain similar provisions, e.g. Art. 3(2) of the 1957 European Extradition Convention. On terrorism, see further Chapter 14.

[78] Art. 7.   [79] Art. 3 of the Additional Protocol.   [80] E.g. Art. 4 of the 1957 European Extradition Convention.

[81] See e.g. Michael Plachta, '(Non-)Extradition of Nationals: A Never-Ending Story?' (1999) 13 *Emory International Law Review* 77.

double-criminality requirement (see section 5.3.2) and also takes a restrictive view on jurisdiction, which is often the case in common law countries. This was a key issue in the *Pinochet* case in the United Kingdom where the House of Lords accepted the jurisdiction of the requesting State (Spain) only from the date when the United Kingdom had implemented the 1984 Torture Convention (and thus accepted extraterritorial jurisdiction).[82]

Within the EU, efforts have been made to do away with nationality as a ground for refusal.[83] The European Arrest Warrant is an example, which has prompted constitutional discussions and amendments in Member States. As a result, the requested State retains a right to refuse surrender if it chooses to exercise jurisdiction itself, or it may request the return of the fugitive for service of any custodial sentence or detention order.[84] Similarly, the 2000 Palermo Convention acknowledges the condition that an extradited national of the requested State be returned for the service of any sentence imposed.[85]

5.4.5   *Death penalty, life imprisonment and other human rights grounds*

Many States that have abolished capital punishment domestically also prohibit extradition when the fugitive may face the death penalty, unless the requesting State undertakes not to impose this penalty in the case at hand or at least not to enforce it.[86] This is in keeping with commitments made in certain human rights treaties and the *Soering* principle that a State is bound by its human rights obligations with respect to extradition. Some international treaties also enshrine this extradition condition.[87] But the penalty as such is not banned under customary international law (see section 19.1), and hence the *Soering* case addressed the matter as a part of the prohibition of torture or inhumane or degrading treatment or punishment.[88] In some jurisdictions, however, the above-mentioned rule of non-inquiry may mean that extradition is not prevented even if the fugitive risks execution and even so when this punishment would not be applicable in the extraditing State.[89]

The 1984 Torture Convention also provides that extradition is not allowed to a country where the fugitive would be in danger of torture.[90] Inhumane and degrading treatment or punishment is a less clear and thus more difficult concept. While the *Soering* case found that 'the death-row phenomenon' falls under the prohibition, the UN Human Rights Committee

---

[82] *R v. Bow Street Metropolitan Stipendiary Magistrate, ex parte Pinochet Ugarte (No. 3)* [1999] 2 All ER 97, 107 and 135–6. For a critical view, see Warbrick, 'Extradition Aspects of Pinochet 3'.
[83] See e.g. Zsuzsanna Deen-Racsmány and Rob Blekxtoon, 'The Decline of the Nationality Exception in European Extradition? The Impact of the Regulation of (Non-)Surrender of Nationals and Dual Criminality under the European Arrest Warrant' (2005) 13 *European Journal of Crime, Criminal Law and Criminal Justice* 317.
[84] Arts. 4(6) and 5(3) of the Framework Decision on the European Arrest Warrant.   [85] Art. 16(11).
[86] See William Schabas, 'Indirect Abolition: Capital Punishment's Role in Extradition Law and Practice' (2003) 25 *Loyola of Los Angeles International and Comparative Law Review* 581.
[87] E.g. Art. 11 of the 1957 European Extradition Convention.
[88] Art. 3 of the ECHR. See also *Öcalan* v. *Turkey* (2005) ECHR 282, paras. 162–75 (also considerations under Art. 2 of the ECHR regarding unfair proceedings and the death penalty).
[89] See *Prasopat* v. *Banov*, US Court of Appeal (9th Cir.), 31 August 2005. For a critical view, see Andrew Parmenter, 'Death by Non-Inquiry: The Ninth Circuit Permits the Extradition of a US Citizen Facing the Death Penalty for a Non-Violent Drug Offense [Prasoprat v. Benov, 421 F 3d 1009 (9th Cir. 2005)]' (2006) 45 *Washburn Law Journal* 657.
[90] Art. 3(1); see Chapter 14. See also Art. 3(f) of the UN Model Treaty on Extradition.

has not so found and instead attacked the methods of execution.[91] Corporal punishment, poor prison conditions, lack of appropriate medical care, and harsh interrogation methods may also meet the criteria for refusal.[92] However, the fact that the fugitive will face potentially very high penalties and possible detention in solitary confinement in a maximum security facility is not necessarily sufficient.[93]

Life imprisonment is also a problematic concept in some States, and even unconstitutional, and there are regional examples where life imprisonment prevents extradition.[94] The European Court of Human Rights, with reference to domestic examples, has established that a grossly disproportionate sentence amounts to a human rights violation (ill-treatment) and thus prevents extradition, which applies also to life sentences.[95] One solution, provided by the European Arrest Warrant, is to allow States to make the surrender conditional on the issuing State providing for review of life sentences.[96]

A common clause in international agreements, inspired by the *non-refoulement* principle, prevents extradition when there are substantial grounds for believing that there is a discriminatory purpose behind the prosecution or punishment in the requesting State.[97] The UN Model Treaty on Extradition 1990 extends this prohibition to cases where the fugitive does not receive the minimum guarantees in criminal proceedings according to the ICCPR.[98] But without any qualifications this condition would be difficult to apply and it could seriously hamper cooperation.

The European Court of Human Rights, beginning with the *Soering* decision, is instead requiring that the fugitive has suffered or risks suffering a flagrant denial of justice. Potential future violations are more difficult to establish than already suffered violations. While a refusal of extradition based upon a judgment *in absentia*, which cannot be appealed, already has support in some extradition agreements[99] and accords with the case law of the European Court of Human Rights,[100] there has been a reluctance to conclude that there has been a flagrant denial of justice in a concrete case. The Court had indicated various forms of unfairness that under certain conditions could meet this rather high threshold – trials *in absentia*, summary trials, detention without access to an independent tribunal, and refusal to have access to a lawyer – but the first finding of a violation on this ground came only in

---

[91]   See *Ng* v. *Canada*, HRC, 5 November 1993; and *Kindler* v. *Canada*, HRC, 11 November 1993.
[92]   See e.g. *Tyrer* v. *United Kingdom*, ECtHR, 25 April 1978; *Ireland* v. *United Kingdom*, ECtHR, 18 January 1978; *Musiał* v. *Poland*, ECtHR, 20 January 2009; *Grzywaczewski* v. *Poland*, ECtHR, 31 May 2012; *Torreggiani and Others* v. *Italy*, ECtHR, 8 January 2013; and *Boudellaa et al.* v. *Bosnia and Herzegovina et al.*, Human Rights Chamber for Bosnia and Herzegovina, 11 October 2002.
[93]   *Babar Ahmad and Others* v. *United Kingdom*, ECtHR, 10 April 2012, paras. 200–24, 235–44; and *Aswat* v. *United Kingdom*, ECtHR, 16 April 2013, paras. 57–8 (but the fugitive's severe mental illness meant that extradition would violate the prohibition).
[94]   E.g. Art. 9 of the 1981 Inter-American Extradition Convention.
[95]   *Harkins and Edwards* v. *United Kingdom*, ECtHR, 17 January 2012, paras. 132–8.
[96]   Art. 5(2) of the Framework Decision on the European Arrest Warrant.
[97]   E.g. Art. 11 of the 1957 European Extradition Convention; Art. 9 of the 1979 Hostage Convention; Art. 4(5) of the 1981 Inter-American Extradition Convention; and the 1990 Commonwealth Scheme for the Rendition of Fugitive Offenders.
[98]   Art. 3(f) of the UN Model Treaty.
[99]   E.g. Art. 3 of the 1978 Second Additional Protocol to the 1957 European Extradition Convention. Cf. the conditional surrender provided for in the Framework Decision on the European Arrest Warrant, as amended by the Council Framework Decision of 26 February 2009 which harmonizes the grounds of non-recognition due to *in absentia* proceedings; see also *Melloni*, CJEU, 26 February 2013.
[100]   E.g. *Stoichkov* v. *Bulgaria*, ECtHR, 24 June 2005, paras. 53–8.

2012.[101] Increasingly, national courts in Europe consider allegations that extradition will result in a serious breach of human rights, at least when the fugitive can support the claim; the mere fact that the requesting State is also party to the ECHR is not sufficient *per se* for ruling out potential violations.[102] Denying extradition would arguably be consistent with the right to decline cooperation on *ordre public* grounds. Following the European Arrest Warrant,[103] judicial human rights considerations are now mandatory in the extradition proceedings of some countries, for example the United Kingdom and Ireland. It does mean, however, that the courts will have to make difficult decisions on complex political and legal systems, often on the basis of incomplete evidence. In practice, diplomatic assurances by the requesting State often make extradition possible in spite of human rights concerns – non-application or non-enforcement of the death penalty,[104] guarantees against torture, the right to a new trial, etc. But such assurances are difficult to follow up and normally without sanctions if breached. Hence, a thorough assessment must be made in each case as to whether they offer sufficient protection, and conditional extradition is not always a solution.[105]

In a spate of cases, extradition of genocide suspects to Rwanda was declined by a number of European States (for example, Finland, France, Germany, Switzerland and the United Kingdom)[106] with reference to decisions by the ICTR refusing the referral of proceedings to Rwanda under Rule 11*bis* of the ICTR Rules (see Chapter 7). Likely violations of fair trial rights were raised against extradition, particularly with respect to difficulties in securing the attendance of defence witnesses. But the standard applied by the ICTR is different from that required by the ECHR and Rwanda has reformed its system in order to make ICTR referrals and extradition possible. Hence, in July 2009, Sweden granted extradition to Rwanda in a genocide case.[107] After the European Court of Human Rights agreed that the extradition to Rwanda would not violate the ECHR,[108] other States have followed suit.[109]

5.4.6   Re-extradition

In order to observe all the conditions for extradition, and often as part of the rule of specialty, the requesting State is generally not allowed to re-extradite the fugitive to a third State

---

[101] *Othman (Abu Qatada)* v. *United Kingdom*, ECtHR, 17 January 2012, paras. 258–87 (violation with reference to the use of evidence obtained by torture).

[102] See Vennemann, 'The European Arrest Warrant', 117–19.

[103] See Art. 1(3) of the Framework Decision on the European Arrest Warrant.

[104] E.g. *Nivette* v. *France*, ECtHR, 14 December 2000; and *Harkins and Edwards* v. *United Kingdom*, ECtHR, 17 January 2012.

[105] The ECtHR has set forth a number of factors to be considered when assessing the quality of the assurance; *Othman (Abu Qatada)* v. *United Kingdom*, ECtHR, 17 January 2012, para. 189. See also *Chahal* v. *United Kingdom*, ECtHR, 15 November 1996, para. 105; and *Alzery* v. *Sweden*, HRC, 10 November 2006, paras. 11.3–11.5. See further Dugard and Van den Wyngaert, 'Reconciling Extradition', 206–8; and Lena Skoglund, 'Diplomatic Assurances against Torture – An Effective Strategy?' (2008) 77 *Nordic Journal of International Law* 319.

[106] E.g. *Brown (aka Banyani) and Ors* v. *Government of Rwanda* [2009] EWCA 770. For a critical view, see Mark Drumbl, 'Prosecution of Genocide v. the Fair Trial Principle: Comments on Brown and Others v. The Government of Rwanda and the UK Secretary of State for the Home Department' (2010) 8 *Journal of International Criminal Justice* 289.

[107] Decision by the government of Sweden concerning extradition to Rwanda, 9 July 2009; see also the Decision by the Swedish Supreme Court of 26 May 2009 (Case Ö1082–09).

[108] *Ahorugeze* v. *Sweden*, ECtHR, 27 October 2011. However, the suspect had already been released by the Swedish Supreme Court and left the country when the ECtHR handed down its decision, preventing the actual extradition.

[109] E.g. Canada, Denmark and Norway. In the United Kingdom, the suspects regarding whom a Rwandan extradition request was previously denied are now subject to new extradition proceedings.

without the consent of the requested State. This is provided, for example, in the 1957 European Extradition Convention concerning re-extradition for offences committed before the surrender to the requesting State[110] and in many bilateral treaties. However, the European Arrest Warrant allows re-extradition to another EU State without consent in some cases and also provides that a general waiver from the remaining consent requirement may be made; but re-extradition to a third State will always require consent.[111] In practice, this means that the third State seeking re-extradition will have to meet the conditions both in the original requesting and requested States. There are examples, however, where the requirements for re-extradition have, in effect, been circumvented by instead deporting the fugitive under immigration laws (see the next section).[112]

5.4.7   *Abduction, rendition or expulsion*

When there are no extradition arrangements, or these are inapplicable (for example, the political offence exception) or seen as ineffective, some States will resort to other measures in order to apprehend the fugitive – abduction or 'irregular rendition'. This may be conducted in a particular case, such as the *Eichmann* case,[113] or even as a State policy for certain cases, such as the United States' anti-terrorist rendition programme. Such activities often violate international law with respect to the territorial sovereignty of another State and the human rights of the individual concerned.[114] Additionally, international humanitarian law may also be invoked in case of an 'armed conflict' (see Chapter 12). However, less dramatic actions, such as luring the fugitive out of his home country, are less likely to violate international law.[115]

In accordance with the maxim *male captus, bene detentus*, national courts have long been prepared to try accused persons regardless of how they came under the jurisdiction of the court, even if the arrest and surrender of the person was unlawful under national or international law. Hence, in the *Eichmann* case, the District Court of Jerusalem saw no obstacle to trying the accused even though he had been abducted from Argentina, without that State's consent, by Israeli agents. While this principle still applies in some States, notably the United States, it is being replaced in other States by the so-called abuse of process

---

[110] Art. 15.

[111] Art. 28 of the Framework Decision on the European Arrest Warrant; see Samuli Miettinen, 'Onward Transfer under the European Arrest Warrant: Is the EU Moving towards the Free Movement of Prisoners?' (2013) 4 *New Journal of European Criminal Law* 99. See also Art. 12 of the 1996 EU Extradition Convention, which removed the consent requirement among the EU States but which never entered into force.

[112] See e.g. *Bozano* v. *France*, ECtHR, 18 December 1986.

[113] See Chapter 3; see also P. O'Higgins, 'Unlawful Seizure and Irregular Rendition' (1960) 36 *British Yearbook of International Law* 279.

[114] See e.g. Silvia Borelli, 'Extraordinary Rendition' in Ben Saul (ed.), *Research Handbook on International Law and Terrorism* (Cheltenham, UK, and Northampton, MA, 2013) Chapter 19. The Venice Commission, *Opinion on the International Legal Obligations of Council of Europe Member States in Respect of Secret Detention Facilities and Inter-State Transport of Prisoners*, 17 March 2006 (www.venice.coe.int); and *El-Masri* v. *Former Yugoslav Republic of Macedonia*, ECtHR, 13 December 2012.

[115] This conclusion was made by the German Constitutional Court: see Matthias Hartwig, 'The German Federal Constitutional Court and the Extradition of Alleged Terrorists to the United States' (2004) 5 *German Law Journal* 185.

doctrine.[116] Originally established by the House of Lords, the doctrine has been applied by courts, *inter alia*, in the United Kingdom, New Zealand, Australia, South Africa and Zimbabwe, refusing to exercise jurisdiction due to irregularities when the fugitive was apprehended and transferred. But the case law is inconsistent and different factors have had an impact on the decision whether to decline jurisdiction due to abuse of process: involvement by officials of the forum State, the nationality of the accused, protests by the injured State, the possibility of seeking extradition, the treatment of the accused and the gravity of the crimes.[117] In addition, an 'Eichmann exception' has been argued concerning 'universally condemned offences'.[118]

State authorities sometimes choose to deport a fugitive under immigration laws instead of dealing with the matter as extradition.[119] This is usually much faster and the surrender normally unconditional. But, as the South African Constitutional Court has stated,[120] deportation and extradition serve different purposes and the former method must not, as in that case, be used unlawfully and with the effect that no undertaking was obtained regarding the non-imposition of the death penalty. As for human rights protection, the European Court of Human Rights has ruled that the *Soering* principle also applies to deportation and other forms of expulsion.[121] Deportation, as a disguised form of extradition when the latter was not possible, may also amount to a violation of the ECHR.[122]

The way in which the fugitive is apprehended and surrendered may also violate his or her right to liberty and to security under international human rights law. It is important to note, however, that instruments such as the ECHR do not regulate extradition or deportation as such, nor do they prevent cooperation in criminal matters as long as such cooperation does not interfere with any specific rights.[123] Hence, atypical measures are not contrary *per se* to these instruments and the lawfulness of the detention must be assessed against national law and the purpose behind the relevant human rights provision.

5.5   Mutual legal assistance

Mutual legal assistance developed from the so-called 'letters rogatory',[124] a comity-based system of requests for assistance with the taking of evidence, but is mainly treaty based

---

[116] For a survey of national case law, see *Dragan Nikolić*, ICTY T. Ch. II, 9 October 2002, paras. 79–93. See also e.g. Silvia Borelli, 'Terrorism and Human Rights', 808–10; Bassiouni, *International Extradition*, 273–347; and Robert Currie, 'Abducted Criminals before the International Criminal Court: Problems and Prospects' (2007) 18 *Criminal Law Forum* 349.

[117] *Dragan Nikolić*, ICTY T. Ch. II, 9 October 2002, para. 95.

[118] See Rosalyn Higgins, *Problems and Process: International Law and How We Use It* (Oxford, 1994) 72–3. See also section 17.7.3.

[119] Quite apart from such practice in individual cases, some States have opted, as a matter of policy, to deal with war criminals through deportation and denaturalization rather than criminal prosecution and extradition. The most notable example is the US policy concerning Nazi war criminals; see e.g. Matthew Lippman, 'The Pursuit of Nazi War Criminals in the United States and in Other Anglo-American Legal Systems' (1998) 29 *California Western International Law Journal* 1, 50–3 (and examples).

[120] *Mohamed and Dalvie* v. *President of the Republic of South Africa and Six Others*, 2001 (1) SA 893, Constitutional Court.

[121] See e.g. *Chahal* v. *United Kingdom*, ECtHR, 15 November 1996.

[122] E.g. *Bolzano* v. *France*, ECtHR, 18 December 1986, para. 60.

[123] See *Öcalan* v. *Turkey*, ECtHR, 12 May 2005, paras. 83–90.

[124] Among some States, the practice of sending delegations to another State to conduct its own investigation ('Commission Rogatory') also existed.

today and covers a wide range of measures.[125] These may relate to a criminal investigation, prosecution or trial, and include, for example, the taking of witness statements, search and seizure, service of documents, and tracing of persons and information.

The usefulness of such assistance in the requesting State depends in part upon the nature of its criminal procedures. The more adversarial the proceedings, the greater the importance normally attached to witnesses appearing in the courtroom and being subject to cross-examination. Evidence obtained abroad by foreign authorities thus becomes less attractive.[126] In inquisitorial systems, where written evidence is more relied upon, the problem is reduced, although there might be concerns that the evidence was not obtained in a required manner. Consequently, common law jurisdictions were traditionally more hesitant than civil law jurisdictions to make use of mutual legal assistance. But this position has changed and the cooperation is now generally seen as a very important tool for combating crimes; increasingly, the focus is on the proceedings for which the assistance is sought.

Many States require an agreement and only a few dispense with this condition. In addition to pre-concluded bilateral or multilateral agreements, the assistance may also be based upon an ad hoc agreement for the case at hand.

In Europe, the basic multilateral instrument[127] is the 1959 Council of Europe Convention on Mutual Assistance in Criminal Matters, to which Additional Protocols have been adopted in 1978 and 2001. The Protocols were developed to improve cooperation and reflect progress elsewhere, particularly in the 2000 EU Convention on Mutual Assistance in Criminal Matters between the Member States of the European Union. This introduced new forms of cooperation and simplified many procedures. Some of the new measures involve both judicial and law enforcement cooperation, for example 'joint investigation teams',[128] and the use of modern technology such as video and audio conferencing. In the EU, the principle of mutual recognition also applies to certain measures, *inter alia*, the Framework Decision on the execution in the EU of orders freezing property and evidence[129] and the European Evidence Warrant.[130] With respect to replacing traditional forms of cooperation with the principle of mutual recognition, however, mutual legal assistance is so far the least developed area and the two systems apply side by side which complicates matters. Negotiations regarding a European Investigation Order are being finalized, aiming to replace mutual legal assistance regarding almost all investigative measures, but this is a complex task and not all are convinced that such a radical shift is possible or even desirable.[131] A new feature is the agreements between the EU and its

---

[125] For a comprehensive survey of multilateral treaties in Europe, see McClean, *International Co-operation*.

[126] See Christopher Gane and Mark Mackarel, 'Admitting Irregularly or Illegally Obtained Evidence from Abroad into Criminal Proceedings – A Common Law Approach' (1997) *Criminal Law Review* 720–9.

[127] In addition, many States have concluded bilateral agreements with other countries, and there are also sub-regional agreements, for example between the Nordic States.

[128] First introduced in the 2000 Palermo Convention, and thereafter adopted in different EU and Council of Europe instruments; see Michael Plachta, 'Joint Investigation Teams' (2005) 13 *European Journal of Crime, Criminal Law and Criminal Justice* 284.

[129] OJ L196, 2 August 2003, pp. 45–55.

[130] Framework Decision on the European evidence warrant for the purpose of obtaining objects, documents and data for use in proceedings in criminal matters, OJ L350, 30 December 2008, pp. 72–92.

[131] See e.g. Peter Rackow and Cornelius Birr, 'Recent Developments in Legal Assistance in Criminal Matters' (2010) 2 *Goettingen Journal of International Law* 1087; Lorena Bachmaier Winter, 'European Investigation Order for Obtaining Evidence in the

Member States and third countries; mixed multilateral and bilateral agreements have been concluded with the United States in 2003,[132] as well as an agreement with Japan in 2009.[133] Through a separate agreement, Iceland and Norway have partly acceded to the 2000 EU Convention on Mutual Assistance and its 2001 Additional Protocol.[134]

Regional conventions on mutual legal assistance also exist among States in the Americas (OAS), the Caribbean (CARICOM), Western Africa (ECOWAS), Central Africa (ECCAS), Eastern Africa (IGAD), Southern Africa (SADC), the Commonwealth of Independent States (CIS), Southeast Asia (ASEAN) and South Asia (SAARC).[135] Hence, there is a fairly extensive network of treaties, operating within regions but not between them. However, the 1959 European Convention is also open to non-members of the Council of Europe, and a few such States have adhered to the Convention. The Commonwealth Scheme on Mutual Assistance (the Harare Scheme)[136] is an example of an arrangement that is not confined to a geographic region. In addition, many bilateral agreements exist. Many States have implemented the treaties by special legislation. Globally, advanced schemes for mutual legal assistance are provided in more recent treaties on transnational crimes, for example the 1998 Drug Trafficking Convention, the 2000 Palermo Convention and the 2003 Corruption Convention;[137] other treaties such as the 1984 Torture Convention and the 1999 Terrorist Financing Convention mainly contain a general obligation to cooperate.

Mutual legal assistance is circumscribed by conditions, or grounds for refusal, which are similar to those applicable to extradition. Although treaties often phrase such exceptions in facultative rather than mandatory terms,[138] many States have insisted on applying them. But here too there is a trend to do away with, or at least restrict, the various grounds for refusal.[139]

In spite of improvements such as allowing the requesting State to prescribe procedures to be followed, differences in the procedures of the different countries still create problems. Apart from procedural incompatibility, issues may arise as to whether sufficient fair trial rights are provided. Different views as to whether the accused may give testimony or the scope for witness testimonies are two examples. Another shortcoming is that, so far, the accused cannot independently seek assistance from a foreign State; it has to be done between public authorities or courts in the different States.[140] Claims of immunity may also hamper

---

Criminal Proceedings' (2010):9 *Zeitschrift für Internationale Strafrechtsdogmatik* 580; and Frank Zimmermann, Sanja Glaser and Andreas Motz, 'Mutual Recognition and its Implications for the Gathering of Evidence in Criminal Proceedings: A Critical Analysis of the Initiative for a European Investigation Order' (2011) *European Criminal Law Review* 55.

[132] OJ L181, 19 July 2003, pp. 34–43.   [133] OJ L39, 12 February 2010, pp. 20–39.   [134] OJ L26, 29 January 2004, pp. 3–9.

[135] Inter-American Convention on Mutual Legal Assistance in Criminal Matters, 23 May 1992; Caribbean Mutual Legal Assistance Treaty in Serious Criminal Matters, 6 July 2005; Economic Community of West African States Convention on Mutual Assistance in Criminal Matters, 29 July 1992; ECCAS Mutual Assistance Pact, 24 February 2002; IGAD Mutual Legal Assistance Convention, 8 December 2009; Minsk Convention on Legal Assistance and Legal Relations in Civil, Family and Criminal Matters, 22 January 1993; Kishinev (Chishinau) Convention, 7 October 2002; SADC Protocol on Mutual Legal Assistance in Criminal Matters, 3 October 2002; ASEAN Treaty on Mutual Assistance in Criminal Matters, 29 November 2004; SAARC Convention on Mutual Legal Assistance in Criminal Matters, 3 August 2008.

[136] Scheme Relating to Mutual Assistance in Criminal Matters within the Commonwealth (Harare Scheme), 28 July–1 August 1986, (1986) 12 *Commonwealth Law Bulletin* 1118–24 (later amended in April 1990, November 2002 and October 2005).

[137] An interesting regional treaty is the 2001 Cyber Crime Convention (Council of Europe).

[138] See e.g. the 1959 European Convention on Mutual Assistance in Criminal Matters.

[139] See e.g. the 2000 EU Convention on Mutual Assistance in Criminal Matters and its 2001 Additional Protocol; and the 2000 Palermo Convention.

[140] The refusal to seek measures abroad at the request of the accused may, however, affect the fairness of the subsequent trial, e.g. *Papageorgiou* v. *Greece*, ECtHR, 9 May 2003.

cooperation.[141] But the major obstacle is that the process is slow and cumbersome and fraught by practical problems, often due to ineffective implementation, indirect communications, and poor translations and language skills.

5.6   Transfer of proceedings

With diverging views on criminal jurisdiction and all the restrictions and difficulties concerning international legal cooperation, alternative solutions have been considered. One model is the transfer of criminal proceedings from one State to another, both of which have jurisdiction over the offence; a double-criminality requirement always applies and, due to the nature of the cooperation, is often far-reaching. Most well known is a multilateral convention adopted by the Council of Europe.[142] But States tend to insist on reciprocity and the measure is infrequently used since only a few States have ratified the instruments.

Transfer of proceedings is not primarily a device for giving priority to particular jurisdictional grounds; the motive is rather that the accused has ties to the requesting State or that proceedings there would be more convenient. Coordination between the different proceedings is important and many agreements include *ne bis in idem* provisions, albeit often optional instead of mandatory ones. Furthermore, numerous grounds for refusal apply and a transfer of proceedings could be difficult in practice; for example, prosecutorial and judicial decisions taken in the transferring State have little effect, if any, and evidence collected may be inadmissible in the requesting State.

5.7   Enforcement of penalties

While States have historically been reluctant to recognize foreign criminal judgments formally, cooperation does exist regarding enforcement of foreign prison sentences and other penalties. Apart from humanitarian aspects, this possibility sometimes facilitates extradition: an otherwise reluctant State may accept extradition on condition that the fugitive is returned to serve any sentence imposed.[143]

Both bilateral and multilateral agreements on the point have been concluded. In Europe, the Council of Europe took the lead with the 1970 European Convention on the International Validity of Criminal Judgments and the 1983 Convention on the Transfer of Sentenced Persons (and its 1997 Additional Protocol). The penalty will either be converted into a new

---

[141] See e.g. *Case Concerning Certain Questions of Mutual Legal Assistance in Criminal Matters (Djibouti v. France)*, ICJ, 4 June 2008. For a comment, see Robert Cryer and Ioannis Kalpouzos, 'International Court of Justice, Certain Questions of Mutual Assistance in Criminal Matters (Djibouti v. France) Judgment of 4 June 2008' (2010) 59 *International and Comparative Law Quarterly* 193. A domestic example is *Khurts Bat v. Investigating Judge of the German Federal Court*, 29 November 2011 [2011] EWHK 2029 (Admin); see Andrew Sanger, 'Immunity of State Officials from the Criminal Jurisdiction of a Foreign State' (2013) 62 *International and Comparative Law Quarterly* 193. On immunities, see further Chapter 21.

[142] The 1972 European Convention on the Transfer of Proceedings in Criminal Matters. See also the 1990 UN Model Treaty on Transfer of Proceedings in Criminal Matters. Transfer of criminal proceedings is also referred to in other multilateral treaties, such as the 1988 Narcotic Drugs Convention (Art. 8).

[143] See generally Michael Plachta, *Transfer of Prisoners under International Instruments and Domestic Legislation: A Comparative Study* (Freiburg, 1993).

penalty in the administering State, after which it is enforced there, or continued enforcement of the sentence will take place. A mandatory double-criminality requirement applies, as do numerous conditions and grounds for refusal. In addition various initiatives have been taken within the EU based on the principle of mutual recognition regarding fines and confiscation orders, as well as custodial and other non-custodial sentences.[144]

Further reading

M. Cherif Bassiouni (ed.), *International Extradition: United States Law and Practice*, 5th edn (New York, 2007)

M. Cherif Bassiouni (ed.), *International Criminal Law,* Vol. II, *Multilateral and Bilateral Enforcement Mechanisms*, 3rd edn (Leiden, 2008)

Rob Blekxtoon and Wouter van Ballegooij (eds.), *Handbook on the European Arrest Warrant* (The Hague, 2005)

Silvia Borelli, 'Terrorism and Human Rights: Treatment of Terrorist Suspects and Limits on International Cooperation' (2003) 16 *Leiden Journal of International Law* 803

Iain Cameron, Malin Thunberg Schunke, Karin Påle-Bartes, Christoffer Wong and Petter Asp, *International Criminal Law from a Swedish Perspective* (Antwerp, Oxford and Portland, 2011)

Gilles de Kerchove and Anne Weyembergh (eds.), *La confiance mutuelle dans l'espace pénal européen / Mutual Trust in the European Criminal Area* (Brussels, 2005)

John Dugard and Christine Van den Wyngaert, 'Reconciling Extradition with Human Rights' (1998) 92 *American Journal of International Law* 187

Albin Eser, Otto Lagodny and Christopher Blakesley, *The Individual as Subject of International Cooperation in Criminal Matters: A Comparative Study* (Baden-Baden, 2002)

Geoff Gilbert, 'Extradition' in Craig Barker and John Grant (eds.), *Harvard Research in International Law: Contemporary Analysis and Appraisal* (Buffalo, NY, 2007) 247–74

André Klip, *European Criminal Law: An Integrative Approach*, 2nd edn (Antwerp, Oxford and Portland, OR, 2012)

David McClean, *International Co-operation in Civil and Criminal Matters*, 3rd edn (Oxford, 2012)

Clive Nicholls, Claire Montgomery, Julian Knowles, Anand Doobay and Mark Summers, *The Law of Extradition and Mutual Assistance*, 3rd edn (Oxford, 2013)

Wolfgang Schomburg, Otto Lagodny, Sabine Gless and Thomas Hackner, *Internationale Rechtshilfe in Strafsachen*, 5th edn (Munich, 2012)

United Nations Office on Drugs and Crime (UNODC), *Manual on Mutual Legal Assistance and Extradition* (New York, 2012), www.unodc.org/documents/organized-crime/ Publications/Mutual_Legal_Assistance_Ebook_E.pdf

---

[144] Council Framework Decision of 24 February 2005 on financial penalties, OJ L76, 22 March 2005, pp. 16–30; Council Framework Decision of 6 October 2006 on confiscation orders, OJ L328, 24 November 2006, pp. 59–78; Council Framework Decision of 27 November 2008 on custodial sentences, OJ L327, 5 December 2008, pp. 27–46; and Council Framework Decision of 27 November 2008 on supervision of probation and alternative sanctions, OJ L337, 16 December 2008, pp. 102–22.

Part C

International Prosecution

6

The History of International Criminal Prosecutions: Nuremberg and Tokyo

6.1   Introduction

International criminal law, or something similar to it, has a very long history.[1] Its closest European precursor prior to the modern era was the chivalric system that applied in the medieval era.[2] The most notable of the trials that were related to this system was that of Peter von Hagenbach in Breisach in 1474.[3] Although its status as a legal precedent is highly limited, the issues involved at that trial, superior orders, sexual offences, cooperation in evidence gathering, and pleas as to the jurisdiction of the court, have clear present-day relevance.[4] The purpose of this chapter, however, is to introduce the modern history of international criminal prosecutions rather than provide a comprehensive overview of the entire history of the subject. Therefore, we shall start in the early part of the twentieth century, at the end of the First World War.

6.2   The commission on the responsibility of the authors of the war

After the First World War, the Allies set up a fifteen-member commission to investigate the responsibility for the start of the war, violations of the laws of war and what tribunal would be appropriate for trials.[5] It reported in March 1919, determining that the central powers were responsible for starting the war[6] and that there were violations of the laws of war and humanity.[7] It recommended that high officials, including the Kaiser, be tried for ordering such crimes and on the basis of command responsibility.[8]

---

[1] See Timothy L. H. McCormack, 'From Sun Tzu to the Sixth Committee, The Evolution of an International Criminal Law Regime' in Timothy L. H. McCormack and Gerry J. Simpson (eds.), *The Law of War Crimes: National and International Approaches* (The Hague, 1997) 31; M.Cherif Bassiouni, 'From Versailles to Rwanda in Seventy-Five Years: The Need to Establish an International Criminal Court' (1997) 10 *Harvard Human Rights Law Journal* 11.

[2] See e.g. Maurice H. Keen, *The Laws of War in the Late Middle Ages* (London, 1965); Theodor Meron, *Bloody Constraint: Crimes and Accountability in Shakespeare* (New York, 1998).

[3] See Georg Schwarzenberger, *International Law as Applied by International Courts and Tribunals* (London, 1968) Vol. II, Chapter 39.

[4] See e.g. Robert Cryer, *Prosecuting International Crimes: Selectivity and the International Criminal Law Regime* (Cambridge, 2005) Chapter I.

[5] Report of the Commission to the Preliminary Peace Conference, reprinted in (1920) 14 *American Journal of International Law* 95.

[6] *Ibid.*, 107.   [7] *Ibid.*, 114–15.   [8] *Ibid.*, 116–17, 121.

Further to this, the commission suggested the setting up of an Allied 'High Tribunal' with members from all of the allied countries to try violations of the laws and customs of war and the laws of humanity.[9] This aspect was criticized by the commission's US and Japanese members. The US members said that they knew 'of no international statute or convention making violation of the laws and customs of war – not to speak of the laws or principles of humanity – an international crime'.[10] The Japanese representatives questioned 'whether international law recognises a penal law applicable to those who are guilty'.[11] The majority, however, clearly considered there to be a body of international criminal law, albeit one which did not include aggression as a crime.[12]

As a result, the Treaty of Versailles provided, in Article 227, that the Kaiser was to be 'publicly arraigned' for 'a supreme offence against international morality and the sanctity of treaties' before an international tribunal. It was never implemented as the Netherlands refused to hand the Kaiser over to the Allies on the basis that the offence was a political one.[13] Articles 228 and 229 of the Treaty of Versailles also provided for prosecutions of German nationals for war crimes before Allied courts, including mixed commissions where the victims came from more than one State. These provisions, however, were never put into practice. Some prosecutions, but far fewer than the Allies wanted, were undertaken by Germany itself in Leipzig between 1921 and 1923. The proceedings were characterized by bias towards the defendants, questionable acquittals and lenient sentences.[14] However, two of these cases later formed important precedents in international criminal law,[15] and the report of the commission accurately presaged many of the difficulties modern international criminal law has faced.

6.3   The Nuremberg International Military Tribunal

6.3.1   The creation of the Tribunal

Although in 1937 a treaty to create an international criminal court to try terrorist offences was negotiated,[16] this was not supported by States, and never came into force. The real leap forward in international criminal law came about at the end of the Second World War. The Allies initially issued a declaration in Moscow in 1943, which promised punishment for Axis war criminals, but stated that this was 'without prejudice to the case of the major criminals whose offences have no particular geographical location and who will be punished

---

[9] *Ibid.*, 122.   [10] *Ibid.*, 144–6.   [11] *Ibid.*, 152.

[12] *Ibid.*, 118. See Kirsten Sellars, *'Crimes against Peace' and International Law* (Cambridge, 2013) 2–11.

[13] See M. Cherif Bassiouni, 'World War I: "The War to End All Wars" and the Birth of a Handicapped International Criminal Justice System' (2002) 30 *Denver Journal of International Law and Policy* 244, 269–73.

[14] Claus Kreß, 'Versailles – Nuremberg – The Hague: Germany and International Criminal Law' (2006) 40 *International Lawyer* 15, 16–20. On the report, see Gerry Simpson, 'International Criminal Law and the Past' in Gideon Boas, William Schabas and Michael Scharf (eds.), *International Criminal Justice: Legitimacy and Coherence* (Cheltenham, 2012) 123, 123–4, 132–5.

[15] *The Dover Castle* (1922) 16 *American Journal of International Law* 704; *The Llandovery Castle* (1922) 16 *American Journal of International Law* 708. See Kreß, 'Versailles – Nuremberg – The Hague', 16–18.

[16] 1937 Convention for the Creation of an International Criminal Court. See Manley O. Hudson, 'The Proposed International Criminal Court' (1938) 32 *American Journal of International Law* 549.

by a joint declaration of the governments of the Allies'.[17] After considerable discussion amongst the Allies during the war, Churchill was persuaded by the United States and the Soviet Union that a trial of such persons was preferable to their summary execution.[18] As a result, France, the United Kingdom, the United States and the Soviet Union met in London to draft the charter of an international tribunal. The negotiations leading to the London charter, which formed the basis of the Nuremberg IMT, were tense, in particular as the US and Soviet representatives clashed over a number of important issues. The representatives of the Soviet Union thought that the purpose of the tribunal was simply to determine the punishment to be meted out to the defendants, who they thought were to be presumed guilty. This was unacceptable to the United States. Differences between the civil law States (France and the Soviet Union) and their common law counterparts (the United Kingdom and the United States) on the appropriate procedures for the trial also caused considerable difficulties.[19] Nonetheless, on 8 August 1945, the four Allies signed the London Agreement, which created the Tribunal.[20] Nineteen other States also adhered to the charter later.

6.3.2 The Tribunal and the trial

The Tribunal had eight judges, four principal judges, one for each of the major Allies (France, the Soviet Union, the United Kingdom and the United States) and four alternates (understudies drawn from the same States). The President of the Tribunal was Lord Justice Geoffrey Lawrence from the United Kingdom, who exercised a firm, but largely fair, hand over the proceedings. Each of the main Allies was entitled to appoint a chief prosecutor. The defence was undertaken by a number of German lawyers, the leading lights of whom were Hermann Jahreiss, an international lawyer from Cologne, and Otto Kranzbühler, a talented naval judge-advocate.

The indictment was received by the Tribunal on 10 October 1945, at its official seat in Berlin. It contained four main charges, all of which were based on Article 6 of the IMT's Charter. Count one was the overall conspiracy, which was handled by the US prosecution team. Count two concerned crimes against peace. This count was dealt with by the UK prosecutors. Count three charged war crimes and count four concerned crimes against humanity. The prosecution of these two offences was split between the French and Soviet prosecutors, the French dealing with the western zone of conflict, the Soviet with the eastern. Twenty-four defendants were arraigned before the tribunal.[21] There were also prosecutions

---

[17] Declaration of Moscow, 1 November 1943.
[18] See Arieh Kochavi, *Prelude to Nuremberg: Allied War Crimes Policy and the Question of Punishment* (Durham, NC, 1998).
[19] Robert Jackson, *Report to the President of Robert H. Jackson, US Delegate to the International Conference on Military Trials* (London, 1945); Sellars, *Crimes*, Chapter 3.
[20] 1945 London Agreement for the IMT, 82 UNTS 279.
[21] Karl Dönitz, Hans Frank, Wilhelm Frick, Hans Fritzsche, Walter Funk, Hermann Göring, Rudolf Hess, Alfred Jodl, Ernst Kaltenbrunner, Wilhelm Keitel, Konstantin von Neurath, Franz von Papen, Willem Raeder, Joachim von Ribbentrop, Alfred Rosenberg, Fritz Saukel, Hjalmar Schacht, Baldur von Schirach, Arthur Seyss-Inquart, Albert Speer and Julius Streicher. Martin Bormann was tried *in absentia*; Gustav Krupp was declared mentally incapable of standing trial; and Robert Ley committed suicide in custody prior to the trial.

of six criminal organizations.[22] Having received the indictment, the Tribunal moved to the city it is now associated with, Nuremberg.[23]

In the opening session, the US Chief Prosecutor, Justice Robert Jackson (who had represented the United States at the London negotiations),[24] began the prosecution case with a stirring speech, embodying many of the ideas that have later been adopted into the ideals of international criminal law. Jackson described the Tribunal as 'the greatest tribute ever paid by power to reason', and sought to deflect concerns about the fairness of the trial and the non-prosecution of Allied nationals by saying that, 'while this law is first applied against German aggressors, the law includes, and if it is to serve a useful purpose it must condemn, aggression by any other nations, including those which sit here now in judgment'.[25]

The trial took place over ten months, and 403 open sessions. In the end, three of the defendants (Schacht, Fritzsche and von Papen) were acquitted, as were three of the six indicted organizations (the SA, the High Command and the Reich Cabinet). Of the remaining defendants, twelve were sentenced to death and seven to periods of imprisonment ranging from ten years to life. The Soviet judge, Major-General Nikitchenko, dissented from all the acquittals and the life sentence for Rudolf Hess. He would have declared all the defendants and organizations guilty, and sentenced Hess to death.[26]

The judgment of the Tribunal, in addition to its findings on the facts, represented a considerable contribution to international law. The judgment dealt at some length with the defence contention that the prosecution of crimes against peace was contrary to the *nullum crimen sine lege* principle. In spite of the fact that the judgment took the view that the Tribunal's Charter was binding as to what law the Tribunal ought to apply, the judgment engaged in a detailed, if in the final analysis unconvincing, review of pre-war developments, in particular the 1928 Kellogg–Briand Pact.[27] It used that treaty (which was not intended to create criminal liability) and a number of non-binding sources to create a case that aggressive war was criminalized by customary international law.[28] The Tribunal may have been on more solid ground in relation to positive international law when it asserted that the *nullum crimen* principle was not established as an absolute principle in international law at the time.[29] Probably the Tribunal's most famous holding, however, is its firm affirmation of direct liability under international law, which has become a foundational statement in international criminal law:

crimes against international law are committed by men, not abstract entities, and only by punishing individuals who commit such crimes can the provisions of international law be enforced ...

---

[22] See Telford Taylor, *The Anatomy of the Nuremberg Trial* (London, 1993) 501–33.

[23] See generally Guénaël Mettraux (ed.), *Perspectives on the Nuremberg Trial* (Oxford, 2008).

[24] The Russian judge (Nikitchenko) had also represented his country at the negotiations.

[25] 1 *Trial of Major War Criminals, Nuremberg* (London, 1946) 85. See Matthew Lippmann, 'Nuremberg Forty-Five Years Later' (1991) 7 *Connecticut Journal of International Law* 1, 39.

[26] 21 *Trial of Major War Criminals, Nuremberg* (London, 1946) 531–47.   [27] (1929) UKTS 29.

[28] See further Chapter 13; Sellars, *Crimes*, Chapters 4–5; and Sheldon Glueck, *War Criminals: Their Prosecution and Punishment* (New York, 1944); *contra* Sheldon Glueck, *The Nuremberg Trial and Aggressive War* (New York, 1946). For the Tribunal's views on superior orders, see section 16.8.

[29] Nuremberg IMT, Judgment and Sentences, reprinted in (1947) 41 *American Journal of International Law* 172, 217.

individuals have international duties which transcend the national obligations of obedience imposed by the individual state.[30]

The 'principles' of the IMT's charter and judgment were quickly affirmed by the General Assembly in its Resolution 95(1).[31] Although some aspects of the Tribunal's decision were controversial in international law,[32] others have proved highly influential, especially its holding that the 1907 Hague Regulations represented customary international law.[33]

6.3.3 Assessment of the Nuremberg IMT

The Nuremberg IMT is often accused of being an example of 'victor's justice', although it is not always clear precisely what this concept is. It contains a number of linked, but different allegations. These are that the trial itself was not fair, in particular that the judges were biased against the accused,[34] that the applicable law was designed to guarantee a conviction, and that similar acts were committed by the prosecuting State(s) but were not prosecuted (i.e. a plea of *tu quoque*).[35]

With respect to the first issue, some aspects of the Nuremberg trial were imperfect. There was, for example, a heavy reliance on affidavit evidence,[36] and a huge disparity in resources between the prosecution and the defence. However, given the standards applicable to trials at the time, the proceedings were, basically, fairly run.[37] Even so, a reasonable case can be made that the presence of neutral judges, or a judge from Germany, would have increased the legitimacy of the proceedings.[38] In relation to the critiques of the law, it is true that the law on crimes against humanity and peace was defined by the Allies in London, with the actions of the Nazis in mind,[39] and at least in relation to crimes against peace the Charter was, in essence, *ex post facto* legislation. It might be doubted, however, whether the Nazis truly thought that their actions were not criminal according to principles of law recognized by the community of nations, especially after the Moscow declaration of 1943. If this was the relevant standard at the time, the critiques of the Nuremberg IMT on point become less convincing.

The final aspect of the victor's justice critique, that similar acts by the Allies were not prosecuted, has some purchase, although the Allies had not committed mass crimes of the magnitude of the Holocaust. The defence were not permitted to raise the issue of crimes committed by the Allies, although Kranzbühler cleverly raised the *tu quoque*

---

[30] *Ibid.*, 221.   [31] UN Doc. A/64/Add.1.

[32] In addition to the debate about crimes against peace, considerable controversy surrounds the determination of the Tribunal that conspiracy existed as a mode of liability in international criminal law. It is doubtful that it did at the time.

[33] See e.g. *Legal Consequences of the Construction of a Wall in the Occupied Palestinian Territory* (2004) ICJ Reports 136, para. 89; *Case Concerning Armed Activities on the Territory of the Congo* (*Democratic Republic of the Congo v. Uganda*), Merits, (2005) ICJ Reports; ICJ General List 116, para. 217. Michael J. Kelly and Timothy L. H. McCormack, 'Contributions of the Nuremberg Trial to the Subsequent Development of International Law' in David A. Blumenthal and Timothy L. H. McCormack (eds.), *The Legacy of Nuremberg: Civilising Influence or Institutionalized Vengeance?* (Leiden, 2008) 101.

[34] Richard H. Minear, *Victor's Justice: The Tokyo War Crimes Trial* (Princeton, NJ, 1971) 74–124.

[35] See Cryer, *Prosecuting International Crimes*, Chapter 4.   [36] Lippmann, 'Nuremberg', 27.   [37] *Ibid.*, 39.

[38] But see Arthur Goodhart, 'Questions and Answers Concerning the Nuremberg Trials' (1947) 1 *International Law Quarterly* 525, 527.

[39] See e.g. M. Cherif Bassiouni, *Crimes against Humanity in International Criminal Law*, 2nd edn (The Hague, 1999) 9–10.

issue as one of law, by alleging that unrestricted submarine warfare was permitted by customary international law, as the US Chief of the Pacific Navy, Chester Nimitz, had admitted that US practice in that sphere was the same as that charged against the naval defendants.[40] The judges did not agree with that proposition of law, but because of the Allied practices they refrained from assessing the sentences of Dönitz and Raeder by reference to the war crimes charges relating to submarine warfare. The *tu quoque* argument also had an interesting effect on the indictments. Owing to the devastation visited upon Germany by Allied (in particular UK) bombing, no charges related to the Blitz over the United Kingdom were brought.[41] Soviet conduct in the Soviet Union, Poland and, late in the war, Germany made other charges difficult to bring without implicitly inviting *tu quoque* claims.

There are criticisms of the Nuremberg IMT which do not relate to allegations of 'victor's justice'. Particular amongst these is that the prosecution, in particular the US section, saw the trial as being primarily one of aggression, rather than of the Holocaust.[42] This is supported by the judgment's statement that aggression was the 'supreme international crime'.[43] However, the Tribunal is primarily remembered now as a trial of atrocities rather than of aggression,[44] and the overall judgment on Nuremberg, and its promised legacy of accountability,[45] tends to be quite favourable.

6.4   The Tokyo International Military Tribunal

6.4.1   The creation of the Tribunal

The Nuremberg IMT's sibling, the International Military Tribunal for the Far East (Tokyo IMT) was set up in January 1946 by a proclamation of General Douglas MacArthur.[46] MacArthur's actions were authorized by powers granted to him by the allied States as Supreme Commander, Allied Powers, to implement the Potsdam declaration,[47] principle 10 of which promised 'stern justice' for war criminals. The declaration had been accepted by Japan in its instrument of surrender. The setting up of the Tokyo IMT on the basis of principle 10 led to a challenge to the jurisdiction of the Tribunal relating to crimes against peace, a challenge which was rejected on the basis that the majority judgment found that, at

---

[40] 18 *Trial of Major War Criminals, Nuremberg* (London, 1948) 26–8.

[41] Chris af Jochnik and Roger Normand, 'The Legitimation of Violence: A Critical History of the Law of War' (1994) 35 *Harvard International Law Journal* 49, 91–2.

[42] Mark Osiel, *Mass Atrocity, Collective Memory and the Law* (New Brunswick, NJ, 1997) 225–6.

[43] Nuremberg IMT, Judgment and Sentences, reprinted in (1947) 41 *American Journal of International Law* 172, 186.

[44] Osiel, *Mass Atrocity,* 225–6.

[45] See M. Cherif Bassiouni, 'The Nuremberg Legacy' in M. Cherif Bassiouni (ed.), *International Criminal Law*, 2nd edn (New York, 1999) Vol. III, 195; David Luban, 'The Legacies of Nuremberg' (1987) 54 *Social Research* 779. However, see also Mark Aarons, 'Justice Betrayed: Post-1945 Responses to Genocide' in Blumenthal and McCormack, *Legacy,* 69.

[46] Special Proclamation, Establishment of an International Military Tribunal for the Far East, 19 January 1946, TIAS No. 1589, at 3. See generally Neil Boister and Robert Cryer, *The Tokyo International Military Tribunal: A Reappraisal* (Oxford, 2008); Neil Boister and Robert Cryer (eds.), *Documents on the Tokyo International Military Tribunal: Charter, Indictment and Judgments* (Oxford, 2008); Yuma Totani, *The Tokyo War Crimes Trial: The Pursuit of Justice in the Wake of World War II* (Cambridge, MA, 2008); Sellars, *Crimes,* Chapter 6.

[47] See *Hirota* v. *MacArthur,* 335 US 876; 93 L Ed. 1903.

the time of the surrender, the Japanese government understood that the term 'war criminals' included those responsible for initiating the war.[48]

6.4.2   The Tribunal and the trial

The Tribunal was made up of eleven judges, nine from the signatory States to the Japanese surrender (Australia, Canada, China, France, New Zealand, the Netherlands, the United Kingdom, the United States and the Soviet Union), together with one each from India and the Philippines.[49] This unwieldy bench was overseen by the Australian Judge, Sir William Webb, whose conduct of the trial has been criticized.[50] The United States was entitled to appoint the chief prosecutor, whilst the other countries were only permitted to appoint associate prosecutors.[51] The US choice, Joseph Keenan, was unsuited to the task, and his professionalism open to serious challenge.[52] The defence was undertaken by a number of Japanese and American lawyers, the most well known of whom were Kenzo Takayanagi, a professor of Anglo-American law from Tokyo, and Ichiro Kiyose, a politician and lawyer.

The huge trial began with the submission of the indictment to the Tribunal on 29 April 1946. The indictment, in fifty-five counts, charged the twenty-eight defendants[53] with crimes against peace and attendant conspiracies, war crimes, and murders, the last on the basis of a prosecution theory that all killings (including those of combatants) in an unlawful war were murders.[54] The trial lasted nearly two and a half years, with the majority judgment being pronounced in November 1948. The judgment found all the accused who remained before the IMT at the time of judgment guilty, although not on all the counts with which they had been charged. It sentenced seven defendants to death, one to twenty years' imprisonment, one to seven years' imprisonment, and the rest to incarceration for life. In addition to this there were three dissenting judgments, one concurring judgment, and one separate opinion.

The majority judgment, as a number of Allied governments had indicated to their judges that they wanted them to,[55] followed the Nuremberg IMT's opinion on practically all aspects of the law, expressly adopting its reasoning in relation to the binding nature of the Tribunal's

---

[48] Tokyo IMT, reprinted in Neil Boister and Robert Cryer, *Documents on the Tokyo International Military Tribunal* (Oxford, 2008) 48,440–1.

[49] On the bench, see Yuki Tanaka, Tim McCormack and Gerry Simpson (eds.), *Beyond Victor's Justice: The Tokyo War Crimes Trial Revisited* (Leiden, 2011) Part 3.

[50] See e.g. R. John Pritchard, 'An Overview of the Historical Importance of the Tokyo War Trial' in Chihiro Hosoya, Yasuaki Onuma, Nisuke Ando and Richard Minear (eds.), *The Tokyo Trial: An International Symposium* (Tokyo, 1986) 90, 92; Boister and Cryer, *Tokyo: A Reappraisal*, Chapter 4.

[51] Tokyo IMT Charter, Art. 8.   [52]   B. V. A. Röling and Antonio Cassese, *The Tokyo Trial and Beyond* (Cambridge, 1992) 16.

[53] Kenji Dohihara, Koki Hirota, Seishiro Itagaki, Heitaro Kimura, Iwane Matsui, Akira Muto, Hideki Tojo, Sadao Araki, Kingoro Hashimoto, Shunroko Hata, Kiichiro Hiranuma, Naoki Hoshino, Okinori Kaya, Koichi Kido, Kuniaki Koiso, Jiro Minami, Takasumi Oka, Hiroshi Oshima, Kenryo Sato, Shigetaro Shimada, Toshi Shiratori, Teiichi Suzuki, Yoshijiro Umezu, Shigenori Togo, Mamoru Shigemitsu. Yosuke Matsuoka and Osami Nagano died during the trial. Shumei Okawa was declared mentally unfit to stand trial. See Tokyo IMT, reprinted in Neil Boister and Robert Cryer, *Documents on the Tokyo International Military Tribunal* (Oxford, 2008) 48,425. On the selection, see Awaya Kentaro, 'Selecting Defendants at the Tokyo Trial' in Tanaka, McCormack and Simpson (eds.), *Beyond*, 57.

[54] These charges were not decided upon, as they were seen as cumulative to the crimes against peace charges. See Boister and Cryer, *Tokyo: A Reappraisal*, Chapter 6.

[55] Sellars, *Crimes*, 234–41, 249.

charter, the criminality of aggressive war and the abolition of the absolute defence of superior orders.[56] Perhaps the only major difference was that, unlike the Nuremberg IMT, which did not find it necessary to deal with command responsibility, the Tokyo IMT discussed that principle of liability in some detail, and applied it to both military and civilian defendants.[57] In relation to the facts, the judgment decided that there was an overarching conspiracy to initiate aggressive wars, and impose Japanese authority over Asia. It also, less controversially, determined that war crimes were committed both against Allied prisoners-of-war and civilians, perhaps most notably in the Rape of Nanking in 1937.

The President of the Tribunal gave a separate opinion, in which he gave his own views on the law, in particular that the criminality of aggressive war could be based on natural law.[58] Webb also asserted that, as the Emperor was responsible for initiating such wars, his absence ought to be reflected in the sentences meted out to the defendants.[59] Judge Bernard of France also considered that crimes against peace could be based on natural law.[60] He took a more sophisticated approach to command responsibility than the majority.[61] Nonetheless, he considered the trial to have progressed in such a manner that he was not able to reach a judgment on the responsibility of the defendants.[62]

The two major dissenting judgments were given by the judges from the Netherlands and from India, Judges Röling and Pal. Judge Röling disagreed with the majority (and with the Nuremberg Tribunal) on the question of crimes against peace, taking the view that there was no individual criminal liability for aggression in international law; he was, however, of the view that occupying powers were entitled to imprison those responsible for initiating wars, as they threatened occupying powers' security.[63] He supported this view by pointing out that the Tribunal had sentenced no one to death for committing a crime against peace alone.[64] While that fact does not prove that the majority saw their sentencing practice in that light, he was right to express doubt about the broad way in which the majority derived a criminal conspiracy from the facts (some of which he contested), and the way they applied command responsibility.[65] He argued that a number of the defendants, most notably Shigemitsu and Hirota, should have been acquitted.[66] He took a stern line on war crimes though, and would have imposed death sentences on more of the defendants found guilty of those crimes.[67]

Judge Pal gave the longest and most well known of the dissenting judgments. He denied that crimes against peace were a part of existing international law and noted that, in the absence of a clear definition, the concept of aggression was open to 'interested interpretation'.[68] Pal also gave an interpretation of the facts completely at variance with that of the majority, largely accepting defence arguments that Japan's actions were only ever ad hoc

[56] Tokyo IMT, reprinted in Neil Boister and Robert Cryer, *Documents on the Tokyo International Military Tribunal* (Oxford, 2008) 48,437–9.
[57] *Ibid.*, 48,442–7.   [58] Separate Opinion of the President, at 6.
[59] *Ibid.*, 19–20. On the non-indictment of the Emperor, see Yoriko Otomo, 'The Decision Not to Prosecute the Emperor' in Tanaka, McCormack and Simpson (eds.), *Beyond Victor's Justice*, 63.
[60] Dissenting Opinion of the Member from France, at 10.   [61] *Ibid.*, 12–18.   [62] *Ibid.*, 22.
[63] Dissenting Opinion of the Member from the Netherlands, 10–51.   [64] *Ibid.*, 48–9.   [65] *Ibid.*, 54–135.
[66] *Ibid.*, 178–249.   [67] *Ibid.*, 178.   [68] Dissenting Opinion of the Member from India, at 69–153, 227–79.

reactions to provocations by Western powers or explained by fear of communism in China.[69] He gave a lengthy critique of the fairness of the trial proceedings[70] and made clear that he saw the prosecution as hypocritical, owing to the record of many of the prosecuting States in colonialism, and the use of nuclear weapons against Hiroshima and Nagasaki.[71] As a result, he would have acquitted all the defendants, including of the war crimes charges.[72] His opinion was criticized in Judge Jaranilla's concurring opinion. Jaranilla, the Philippine judge, said that Pal ought to have accepted the Charter's provisions on the law, as he accepted an appointment under the Charter.[73] He also asserted that the trial proceedings were fair, and that the atomic bombings were justified, as they brought an end to the war.[74] Jaranilla's appointment was controversial, as he had been a victim of the Bataan Death march, and he therefore ought not to have sat, on the basis that he might have been biased against the defendants.[75] His view that the sentences imposed were too lenient did little to dispel this suspicion.[76]

6.4.3 *Assessment of the Tribunal*

The view of the Tokyo IMT traditionally adopted by most international criminal lawyers was summed up by the title of the most well-known book on the trial, Richard Minear's *Victor's Justice*.[77] There is something to be said for such a view. Where the Tokyo IMT agreed with its Nuremberg counterpart on the law, the same critiques are applicable to both, although in relation to both conspiracy and command responsibility the Tokyo IMT went further, and, in the judgment of many, too far. The majority's view of the facts was unsubtle, and the idea of 'an all-inclusive seventeen-year criminal conspiracy involving all the accused strained credulity . . . [and] betrayed an underlying inability to grasp the dynamics of Japanese politics or a misplaced determination to force, after the fact, unrelated and fortuitous events into a preconceived thesis'.[78] On the other hand, Judge Pal's contrasting view of many of the facts was similarly unconvincing, as he was unduly credulous of the defence's claims that Japan was acting altruistically, to liberate Asia from Western colonialism.[79] In addition, the majority were on stronger ground in relation to the war crimes counts.[80]

In spite of the efforts of some of the judges, there were considerable flaws in the trial process. Also, not only was the *tu quoque* argument given some purchase by the bombing of Hiroshima and Nagasaki, it was also raised by one of the judges themselves. Cultural misunderstandings and insensitivities affected the trial, and some of the judges appeared to be biased. Evidence of Unit 731, the Japanese chemical and biological weapons unit

---

[69] *Ibid.*, 349–1014.   [70] *Ibid.*, 280–348.   [71] *Ibid.*, 1231–5.   [72] *Ibid.*, 1226.
[73] Concurring Opinion of the Member from the Philippines, at 28–32.   [74] *Ibid.*, 24–7.
[75] IMTFE Paper 141, 10 June 1946, Motion Suggesting the Disqualification and Personal Bias of the Philippine Justice of the Tribunal.
[76] Concurring Opinion of the Member from the Philippines, 32–5.
[77] R. Minear, *Victor's Justice: The Tokyo War Crimes Trial* (Princeton, NJ, 1971).
[78] John Piccigallo, *The Japanese on Trial* (Austin, TX, 1979) 212.   [79] Boister and Cryer, *Documents*, lxxx–lxxxi.
[80] Boister and Cryer, *Tokyo: A Reappraisal*, 202–4.

which engaged in human vivisection, was kept from the Tribunal, as the United States had promised its members immunity in return for information about their experiments.[81] But simple dismissals of the Tokyo IMT as a show trial are un-nuanced.[82] There was far too much disagreement between the judges for it to have been a show trial.[83] Many of the findings on war crimes were accurate, and many of the heavily criticized delays in the trial were occasioned by genuine difficulties, such as difficulties in translating Japanese to English.[84]

It is unquestionable, however, that politics entered into the indictment process and the release policies for those imprisoned. The Emperor was not indicted, on the ground that his immunity was necessary for Japan's post-war stability, and he was deliberately not mentioned by the prosecution nor (with the exception of one slip) the defence.[85] Cold War considerations led to the United States (whose views were largely determinative on this matter) acquiescing in the release of all those imprisoned by 1955.[86]

In spite of the acceptance of the judgment by the Japanese government in Article 11 of the 1952 Peace Treaty, it has been questioned whether its findings were accepted by all parts of Japanese society. However, the question of memories and views of the Second World War in Japan is a complex and contested one both inside and outside Japan.[87] In the West, the Tribunal has, until recently, been largely ignored,[88] and knowledge of it in Japan is waning. Amongst those in Japan with knowledge of the trial, however, there is less support for Japanese actions in the war,[89] and the Tokyo IMT remains a staple of debate amongst those discussing the question of war responsibility in Japan.[90]

6.5   Control Council Law No. 10 trials and military commissions in the Pacific sphere

In addition to the Nuremberg IMT, the Allied powers occupying Germany also engaged in a large-scale policy of prosecuting war crimes in their respective occupation zones. These were undertaken under the authority of Control Council Law No. 10, which provided for domestic prosecutions of war crimes, crimes against humanity and crimes against peace.

---

[81] Röling and Cassese, *Tokyo Trial*, at 48–50. On 'Forgotten Crines' in the Tokyo IMT, see Tanaka, McCormack and Simpson, *Beyond Victor's Justice*, Parts 5–7.

[82] See e.g. Yasuaki Onuma, 'Beyond Victor's Justice' (1984) 11 *Japan Echo* 63; Fujita Hisaku, 'The Tokyo Trial: Humanity's Justice v. Victors' Justice' in Tanaka, McCormack and Simpson, *Beyond Victor's Justice*, 3; Totani, *The Tokyo War Crimes Trial*, provides a useful counterpoint to Minear, *Victor's Justice*.

[83] See e.g. Totani, *The Tokyo War Crimes Trial*; Boister and Cryer, *Tokyo: A Reappraisal*.

[84] Tokyo IMT, reprinted in Neil Boister and Robert Cryer, *Documents on the Tokyo International Military Tribunal* (Oxford, 2008) 48,429–30.

[85] Herbert P. Bix, *Hirohito and the Making of Modern Japan* (London, 2000) Chapter 15.

[86] R. John Pritchard, 'The International Military Tribunal for the Far East and the Allied National War Crimes Trials in Asia' in Bassiouni, *International Criminal Law*, Vol. III, 142.

[87] See Ian Buruma, *The Wages of Guilt: Memories of War in Germany and Japan* (New York, 1994). For a very useful empirical modern study of Japanese views, see Madaoka Futamura, *War Crimes Tribunals and Transitional Justice: The Tokyo Trial and the Nuremberg Legacy* (London, 2007). See further Boister and Cryer, *Tokyo: A Reappraisal*, Chapter 11.

[88] Although there has been an upsurge in interest: see e.g. Sarah Finnin and Tim McCormack, 'Tokyo's Continuing Relevance' in Tanaka, McCormack and Simpson, *Beyond Victor's Justice*, 353.

[89] 'Poll Shows Ignorance of Tokyo Tribunal', *Asahi Shimbun*, 5 March 2006.

[90] Futamura, *War Crimes Tribunals and Transitional Justice*; Boister and Cryer, *Tokyo: A Reappraisal*, Chapter 11.

Twelve major US trials that took place in Nuremberg after the IMT had concluded its business, were known as the 'subsequent proceedings'. These included trials of Nazi doctors and judges, the *Einsatzgruppen* and members of the German High Command. These trials have had a considerable influence on international criminal law.[91] Proceedings in the British zone of Germany were carried out under the Royal Warrant of 1946.[92] There were also proceedings in the French and Soviet zones of Germany. The trials were guided, to varying degrees, by the findings of the Nuremberg IMT.[93]

In the Pacific sphere, a large number of trials were undertaken by the Allies, including the United Kingdom, the United States, Australia, China and the Philippines.[94] These were on the basis of various domestic war crimes provisions. In the United Kingdom, this was the Royal Warrant. Even though there were literally thousands of such proceedings, the trials are on the whole rather less well known than those in the European sphere of the Second World War.[95] The most famous of the trials is the US prosecution of General Yamashita,[96] which was an early modern use of the principle of command responsibility. Other interesting trials of the era include the proceedings against Admiral Toyoda before a mixed panel of Allied judges.

Further reading

Neil Boister and Robert Cryer, *The Tokyo International Military Tribunal: A Reappraisal* (Oxford, 2008)

Neil Boister and Robert Cryer (eds.), *Documents on the Tokyo International Military Tribunal: Charter, Indictment and Judgments* (Oxford, 2008)

Hans Ehard, 'The Nuremberg Trial against the Major War Criminals and International Law' (1949) 43 *American Journal of International Law* 223

Madaoka Futamura, *War Crimes Tribunals and Transitional Justice: The Tokyo Trial and the Nuremberg Legacy* (London, 2007)

George Ginsburgs and Vladimir Kudriavstsev (eds.), *The Nuremberg Trial and International Law* (Dordrecht, 1990)

Kevin Jon Heller, *The Nuremberg Military Tribunals and the Origins of International Criminal Law* (Oxford, 2011)

---

[91] For a comprehensive analysis, see Kevin Jon Heller, *The Nuremberg Military Tribunals and the Origins of International Criminal Law* (Oxford, 2011). See also Howard Levie, *Terrorism in War: The Law of War Crimes* (New York, 1992) 72–98; Matthew Lippman, 'The Other Nuremberg, American Prosecutions of Nazi War Criminals in Occupied Germany' (1992) 3 *Indiana International and Comparative Law Review* 1.

[92] See Anthony P. V. Rogers, 'War Crimes Trials under the Royal Warrant: British Practice 1945–1949' (1990) 39 *International and Comparative Law Quarterly* 780. On the British trials in Hong Kong, see Suzannah Linton, 'Rediscovering the War Crimes Trials in Hong Kong, 1946–48' (2012) 13 *Melbourne Journal of International Law* 284.

[93] See Adam Basak, 'The Influence of the Nuremberg Judgment on the Practice of the Allied Courts in Germany' (1977–8) 9 *Polish Yearbook of International Law* 161.

[94] See Levie, *Terrorism*, 155–83; Piccigallo, *The Japanese*; Robert W. Miller, 'War Crimes Trials at Yokohama' (1948–9) 15 *Brooklyn Law Review* 19; Michael Carrol, 'Australia's Prosecution of Japanese War Criminals: Stimuli and Constraints' in Blumenthal and McCormack, *Legacy*, 239.

[95] Although some are reported in the *Law Reports, Trials of War Criminals* series. On their links to contemporary international criminal justice, see Robert Cryer, 'International Criminal Justice in Historical Context: The Post-Second World War Trials and Modern International Criminal Justice' in Boas, Schabas and Scharf (eds.), *International Criminal Justice*, 145.

[96] *United States* v. *Yamashita*, 327 US 1.

Hans Kelsen, 'Will the Judgment in the Nuremberg Trial Constitute a Precedent in International Law?' (1947) 1 *International Law Quarterly* 153

Otto Kranzbühler, 'Nuremberg: Eighteen Years Afterwards' (1965) 14 *De Paul Law Review* 333

Matthew Lippmann, 'Nuremberg Forty-Five Years Later' (1991) 7 *Connecticut Journal of International Law* 1

Guénaël Mettraux, *Perspectives on the Nuremberg Trial* (Oxford, 2008)

Richard H. Minear, *Victor's Justice: The Tokyo War Crimes Trial* (Princeton, NJ, 1971)

A. Frank Reel, *The Case of General Yamashita* (Chicago, 1949)

B. V. A. Röling and Antonio Cassese, *The Tokyo Trial and Beyond* (Cambridge, 1992)

Georg Schwarzenberger, 'The Judgment of Nuremberg' (1947) 21 *Tulane Law Review* 329

Kirsten Sellars, *'Crimes against Peace' and International Law* (Cambridge, 2013)

Yuki Tanaka, Tim McCormack and Gerry Simpson (eds.), *Beyond Victor's Justice: The Tokyo War Crimes Trial Revisited* (Leiden, 2011)

Telford Taylor, *The Anatomy of the Nuremberg Trial* (London, 1993)

Yuma Totani, *The Tokyo War Crimes Trial: The Pursuit of Justice in the Wake of World War II* (Cambridge, MA, 2008)

Quincy Wright, 'The Law of the Nuremberg Trial' (1947) 41 *American Journal of International Law* 37

7

The Ad Hoc International Criminal Tribunals

7.1   Introduction

Until the early 1990s, it seemed unlikely that any progeny of the Nuremberg and Tokyo IMTs would appear soon. However, in response to two conflicts in the 1990s (the Yugoslav wars of dissolution and the Rwandan genocide of 1994), the United Nations revived the idea of international criminal tribunals. This chapter will introduce those Tribunals, and explain their practice. Although both Tribunals are now winding down, it is too early to come to any final conclusions about them, but this chapter will draw out some of the plaudits and criticisms that have attended the operation of the Tribunals to date. This chapter does not, however, attempt to provide a comprehensive analysis of the jurisprudence of the Tribunals, as their output is analysed elsewhere in this book.[1]

7.2   The International Criminal Tribunal for Yugoslavia

7.2.1   The creation of the ICTY

Although some of the roots of the dissolution of Yugoslavia go back to the Second World War if not further, political developments in what was then the Socialist Federal Republic of Yugoslavia in the 1980s led that country to break up through a number of linked armed conflicts starting in 1991.[2] The conflicts were characterized by large-scale violations of international criminal law committed especially against civilians, most notably sexual offences and the practice of 'ethnic cleansing'. Pictures of concentration camps in Bosnia, which evoked memories of the Holocaust, caused public outcry and led to demands that something be done about the situation.

Even before the conflict was formally brought to an end in December 1995, the Security Council had taken action in relation to prosecuting those crimes. The Council approached

---

[1] See also generally William Schabas, *The UN International Criminal Tribunals: The Former Yugoslavia, Rwanda and Sierra Leone* (Cambridge, 2006). The decisions of the Tribunals are regularly noted and explained in the 'Current Developments in the Ad Hoc Tribunals' section of the *Journal of International Criminal Justice*. See also Geoffrey Watson, 'The Changing Jurisprudence of the International Criminal Tribunal for the Former Yugoslavia' (2002–2003) 37 *New England Law Review* 871; Payam Akhavan, 'The Crime of Genocide in the ICTR Jurisprudence' (2005) 3 *Journal of International Criminal Justice* 989.

[2] See e.g. Laura Silber and Alan Little, *The Death of Yugoslavia* (Harmondsworth, 1996).

the Rubicon to prosecution in autumn 1992, with Resolution 780(1992), which created a commission to investigate allegations of international crimes in Yugoslavia.[3] The commission did not obtain significant State support, materially or financially, so its first chairman, Frits Kalshoven, resigned. Under its second chairman, M. Cherif Bassiouni, the commission obtained financing from private sources and engaged in considerable evidence gathering in the former Yugoslavia.[4] It reported in 1994.[5]

While the commission was still at work, the Secretary-General consulted States about the creation of a possible future tribunal as a Security Council organ, at that time an entirely novel concept. In response to a request by the Council in Resolution 808(1993), the Secretary-General recommended that it create a tribunal by resolution.[6] The possibility of creating the tribunal by treaty was canvassed, but rejected on the basis that it would take too long, and there was no guarantee that all the relevant States (in particular, those in what was by then the former Yugoslavia) would ratify it.[7] The report annexed a draft Statute for the tribunal, modelled in some ways on the Nuremberg IMT's Charter, but also creating a cooperation regime which was to be streamlined when compared to inter-State cooperation, and mandatory in nature.[8] The Security Council adopted the draft Statute in Resolution 827(1993),[9] although some States and commentators questioned whether the Security Council had the power to set up such a tribunal.[10] Although there is no real evidence of interference by the Council in the operation of the ICTY,[11] the question of the extent to which a political organ such as the Security Council ought to be able to act in this area is a controversial one, and one which has also arisen in relation to the ICC.

Resolution 827(1993) set out the aims of the Security Council in establishing the ICTY; these were that, in the circumstances in Yugoslavia, the Tribunal could 'put an end to such crimes and take effective measures to bring to justice the persons who are responsible for them', and thus 'contribute to the restoration and maintenance of peace'.[12] The Council further asserted that it believed that creating the ICTY would 'contribute to ensuring that such violations are halted and effectively redressed'.[13] Such goals were certainly broad and optimistic, and perhaps overstated the extent to which criminal punishment, alone, can create international peace and security, although the Council only asserted that the ICTY would contribute to, rather than single-handedly create, reconciliation in the former Yugoslavia.

---

[3] SC Res. 780(1992) of 6 October 1992.
[4] See generally M. Cherif Bassiouni, 'The United Nations Commission of Experts Established Pursuant to Security Council Resolution 780' (1994) 88 *American Journal of International Law* 784.
[5] Final Report of the Commission of Experts Established Pursuant to Security Council Resolution 780(1992), UN Doc. S/1994/674 of 27 May 1994.
[6] Report of the Secretary-General Pursuant to Paragraph 2 in Security Council Resolution 808(1993), UN Doc.S/25704 of 3 May 1993, para. 20.
[7] *Ibid.*
[8] See generally Larry D. Johnson, 'Ten Years Later: Reflections on the Drafting' (2004) 2 *Journal of International Criminal Justice* 368.
[9] SC Res. 827(1993) of 25 May 1993.
[10] S.PV/3217, 20–2. Alfred P. Rubin, 'An International Criminal Tribunal for the Former Yugoslavia' (1994) 6 *Pace International Law Review* 7. Most of these doubts were laid to rest after *Tadić*, ICTY A. Ch., 2 October 1995.
[11] The only possible exception is the completion strategy: see section 7.2.4.   [12] SC Res. 827(1993). Preamble.
[13] *Ibid.* See also Michael Scharf, 'The Tools for Enforcing International Criminal Justice in the New Millennium: Lessons from the Yugoslavia Tribunal' (1999) 49 *DePaul Law Review* 925, 928–33.

7.2.2   The structure of the ICTY

There are three main organs of the ICTY: the Registry, the Office of the Prosecutor and the Chambers.[14] The Registry is responsible for the administrative management of the Tribunal, including, for example, the victims and witnesses programme, transport of accused, their conditions of detention and public affairs. The Office of the Prosecutor is the organ whose responsibility it is to investigate allegations, issue indictments (which have to be confirmed by a judge) and bring matters to trial. The final organ of the ICTY is the Chambers. The Trial Chambers each consist of a presiding judge and two other judges;[15] they are subject to the appellate control of the Appeals Chamber. This seven-member chamber (which sits in a panel of five) is headed by the President and is the final authority on matters of law in the Tribunal.[16]

7.2.3   The jurisdiction of the ICTY and its relationship to national courts

The ICTY has jurisdiction over war crimes, crimes against humanity and genocide committed after 1 January 1991 on the territory of the former Yugoslavia.[17] Article 2 grants the Tribunal jurisdiction over grave breaches of the Geneva Conventions (which only apply in international armed conflicts),[18] whilst Article 3 provides the Tribunal with jurisdiction over a non-exhaustive list of violations of the laws or customs of war. The Tribunal decided in 1995 that this provision covered war crimes in both international and non-international armed conflicts,[19] a decision that paved the way for some of the Tribunal's most innovative jurisprudence.[20] The Tribunal has jurisdiction over genocide and crimes against humanity pursuant to Articles 4 and 5 of its Statute respectively. Aggression is not included in the jurisdiction of the ICTY. The open-ended nature of the temporal jurisdiction of the Tribunal means that it has jurisdiction over the later conflicts in Kosovo and the former Yugoslav Republic of Macedonia,[21] and over peacekeepers in the area, which was not anticipated by the drafters.

The ICTY has primacy over national courts.[22] Pursuant to this principle, the Tribunal may require States to defer to it any proceedings they were contemplating or undertaking.[23] The situations when deferral is justified are given in Rule 9 of the Rules of Procedure and Evidence. Those situations are when the conduct is not charged as an international crime,

---

[14] For an overview of the structure and personnel, see Mohamed Shahabuddeen, *International Criminal Justice at the Yugoslav Tribunal: A Judge's Recollection* (Oxford, 2012). 33–49.

[15] Art. 11 of the ICTY Statute.

[16] The *ratio decidendi* of its decisions bind the Trial Chambers: see *Aleksovski*, ICTY A. Ch., 24 March 2000, para. 112. The Appeals Chamber does not bind itself, but will only depart from its previous jurisprudence if there are 'cogent reasons in the interests of justice' to do so: *ibid.*, para. 107. Trial Chambers do not bind one another: *ibid.*, para. 113.

[17] Arts. 1 and 8 of the ICTY Statute.   [18] *Tadić*, ICTY A. Ch., 2 October 1995, paras. 79–85.   [19] *Ibid.*, paras. 86–93.

[20] See Chapter 12.

[21] See SC Res. 1160(1998); *Multinović et al.*, ICTY A. Ch., 8 June 2004; *In re the Republic of Macedonia*, ICTY T. Ch. I, 4 October 2002.

[22] Art. 9(1) of the ICTY Statute. Göran Sluiter, *International Criminal Adjudication and the Collection of Evidence: Obligations of States* (Antwerp, 2002) 81–8.

[23] E.g. *Karadžić et al.*, ICTY T. Ch., 16 May 1995. Compare the relationship between the ICC and national courts: section 8.6.

where the proceedings are not fair or impartial, or what is in issue is closely related to, or otherwise involves, significant factual or legal questions which may have implications for investigations or prosecutions before the Tribunal.[24] The last is a very broad provision, effectively allowing the ICTY to demand transfer of cases at will. As the Tribunal winds up its work, however, it has gone from taking cases from domestic jurisdictions to referring them back.

7.2.4   *Milestones in the practice of the ICTY*[25]

Beginnings and the Tadić case

It is fair to say that the ICTY began slowly. A skeleton staff, beset with funding and cash-flow problems, had to create an international criminal court effectively from nothing.[26] When they began, investigations were hampered by the continuing armed conflicts in Yugoslavia.[27] In the absence of indictments or defendants, there was relatively little for the judges to do other than write and refine the Rules of Procedure and Evidence.[28] The first major breakthrough occurred in April 1995, when Germany deferred its own proceedings against a (low-ranking) Bosnian Serb accused of various international crimes, Duško Tadić, and transferred him to the ICTY for trial.[29]

Tadić challenged the ICTY's jurisdiction over him. This led to the seminal Interlocutory Appeal decision of October 1995.[30] Tadić had asserted that the Security Council had no authority to set up a criminal court, that the ICTY's primacy over national courts was unlawful, and that anyway the Tribunal had no jurisdiction over the crimes he was alleged to have committed.[31]

First, Tadić's challenge required the ICTY to decide whether it had the authority to pass on the legality of its own creation, a matter made more sensitive by the fact that the question. of judicial review of the actions of the Security Council was an area in which the ICJ had, soon before, feared to tread too heavily.[32] Given this, and the fact that the ICTY is formally a subsidiary body of the Security Council, it was perhaps unsurprising that the Trial Chamber in the *Tadić* jurisdictional case simply denied that it had the authority to rule on the legality of its parent's actions, stating that its powers were limited to passing judgment on crimes in the former Yugoslavia.[33]

---

[24] Rule 9(i)–(iii) of the ICTY RPE.
[25] Detailed statements of the ICTY's practice may be found in the annual reports which the ICTY submits to the Security Council.
[26] The financial problems arose because of a disagreement between the Security Council and the General Assembly over the appropriate budget from which to fund it. See generally Annual Report of the ICTY 1994, UN Doc. S/1994/1007, paras. 34–6, 143–9.
[27] Annual Report of the ICTY 1995, UN Doc. S/1995/728, paras. 4, 194–6.
[28] On the Rules, see Annual Report of the ICTY 1994, paras. 52–97; for frustration with the lack of visible progress, see Annual Report of the ICTY 1995, paras. 171–8.
[29] Annual Report of the ICTY 1995, paras. 179–84.   [30] *Tadić*, ICTY A. Ch., 2 October 1995.   [31] *Ibid.*, para. 8.
[32] *Questions of Interpretation and Application of the 1971 Montreal Convention Arising from the Aerial Incident at Lockerbie (Libya v. US; Libya v. UK)* (1992) ICJ Reports 114.
[33] *Tadić*, ICTY T. Ch. II, 10 August 1995, paras. 8, 16.

The Appeals Chamber, by contrast, decided that it had the authority to determine the legality of its own creation.[34] It decided this on the basis that it had an inherent power to do so, in order to determine if it could lawfully exercise its primary jurisdiction over criminal cases.[35] The Tribunal's claim that it had incidental jurisdiction over something that it could not exercise primary jurisdiction to decide was bold.[36]

In his separate opinion, Judge Sidhwa provided one of the stronger arguments for the Tribunal's decision, noting that, unlike the ICJ, the ICTY is a criminal court with mandatory jurisdiction over individuals, and this militated in favour of review.[37] Judge Li, on the other hand, took the view that, since there was no express power granted to the ICTY to do so, and it did not have the expertise to determine the appropriateness of the Security Council's action, the review was 'worthless both in fact and in law'.[38]

Judge Li's comments relate not only to the power of the Tribunal, but also to whether the question was a political one which, as a court, the Tribunal ought to decline to answer. The majority, on the authority of a number of ICJ decisions, in particular the *Certain Expenses* advisory opinion,[39] responded that the notions of 'political questions and non-justiciable disputes' were an anachronism in international adjudication, and that, so long as a question has a legal answer, it may be given.[40] The majority had a point; the ICJ has shown itself willing to deal with the legal sides of disputes which have considerable political dimensions, including the use of force,[41] nuclear weapons[42] and aspects of the Middle East situation,[43] in the face of claims that they were political rather than legal questions.

When reviewing the actions of the Council, the majority in *Tadić* adopted a deferential standard. First, it said that it was clear that the Security Council was entitled to invoke its powers under Chapter VII of the UN Charter, as there was an armed conflict in Yugoslavia at the relevant time.[44] This is correct, but it is not clear that the Council based the determination of a threat to the peace in Resolution 827 on the armed conflict. That resolution, after expressing its grave alarm at violations of humanitarian law, determined that 'this situation' was a threat to peace. Equally, the Council had the right to invoke Chapter VII over such events regardless of circumstances.

Next, the Tribunal determined that the Council could set up a court. It based the authority of the Council to do this on Article 41 of the UN Charter. Although Article 41 does not

---

[34] *Tadić*, ICTY A. Ch., 2 October 1995, paras. 14–25. See generally José E. Alvarez, 'Nuremberg Revisited: The Tadić Case' (1996) 7 *European Journal of International Law* 245.

[35] *Tadić*, ICTY A. Ch., 2 October 1995, para. 20.

[36] See Colin Warbrick, 'The International Criminal Tribunal for Yugoslavia: The Decision of the Appeals Chamber on the Interlocutory Appeal on Jurisdiction in the Tadić Case' (1996) 45 *International and Comparative Law Quarterly* 691, 691–2.

[37] *Tadić*, ICTY A. Ch., 2 October 1995, Separate Opinion of Judge Sidhwa, para. 34. For discussion, see George Aldrich, 'Jurisdiction of the International Criminal Tribunal for the Former Yugoslavia' (1993) 90 *American Journal of International Law* 64, 65; Alvarez, 'Nuremberg Revisited', 251, 255.

[38] *Tadić*, ICTY A. Ch., 2 October 1995, Separate and Dissenting Opinion of Judge Li, paras. 2–4.

[39] *Certain Expenses of the United Nations* (1962) ICJ Reports 151.   [40] *Tadić*, ICTY A. Ch., 2 October 1995, paras. 24–5.

[41] See e.g. *Case Concerning Military and Paramilitary Activities in and against Nicaragua* (*Nicaragua* v. *USA*) (1986) ICJ Reports 14.

[42] *Legality of the Threat or Use of Nuclear Weapons*, Advisory Opinion (1996) ICJ Reports 226.

[43] *Legal Consequences of the Construction of a Wall in Palestinian Territory*, ICJ General List 131, (2004) 43 ILM 1009.

[44] *Tadić*, ICTY A. Ch., 2 October 1995, para. 30. Judge Sidhwa agreed, adding that the appraisal of the evidence leading to the determination was 'based on a proper appraisal of the evidence, and was reasonable and fair and not arbitrary or capricious'. Separate Opinion of Judge Sidhwa, para. 61.

expressly state that the Council can do so, this did not trouble the Appeals Chamber, as the list of measures it contains is not exhaustive.[45] The Tribunal also rejected the idea that the Council could not create a court as it had no judicial functions to pass to such a body. Its reasoning was that the Council did not purport to do such a thing, but to create a court in the exercise of its functions in relation to peace and security, in an analogous manner to the General Assembly's creation of an administrative tribunal, an action which received the sanction of the ICJ.[46] Finally, the majority refused to second-guess the Security Council's belief that the establishment of a court could help restore international peace and security as, it said, an *ex post facto* evaluation as to whether or not this belief was correct would be inappropriate.[47] The question was not if that belief was correct, but whether it was held. On these points, the Chamber was right.

Further, the Tribunal also determined that, owing to the membership of the former Yugoslav States in the UN, primacy did not violate the sovereignty of the former Yugoslav States,[48] or the (non-existent) right of the defendant to be tried before his own domestic courts.[49] The Chamber also dealt with the suggestion that, under human rights law, the ICTY was not 'established by law'. The Appeals Chamber, rather generously, took the view that, although human rights treaties were not directly applicable to the Tribunal, the requirement that a tribunal be set up by law was a general principle of law, thus binding on the Tribunal.[50] With some justification, the Chamber asserted that this principle could not be applied in an unadulterated fashion without respect for the specific situation of an international tribunal: it only required at the international level that the Tribunal be set up with sufficient safeguards for fair trial, which the Tribunal was.[51]

The Dayton Peace Agreement, which formally brought to an end the Yugoslav wars of dissolution,[52] included an obligation on all the former Yugoslav States to cooperate with the ICTY,[53] and provided that international forces in the former Yugoslavia had the authority to arrest those indicted by the ICTY.[54] Cooperation from the States of the former Yugoslavia, other than Bosnia and Herzegovina, was still not forthcoming.[55]

Kosovo, Milošević and NATO

By 1996, its judicial workload led the ICTY to ask for the creation of a second Trial Chamber.[56] This prospect was boosted when international forces began to arrest indictees in 1997.[57] The Federal Republic of Yugoslavia remained uncooperative. Croatia transferred one defendant that year.[58] Owing to the increased violence in Kosovo, the Security Council requested that the Prosecutor look into events there.[59] This led, in May 1999, to the ICTY

---

[45] *Tadić*, ICTY A. Ch., 2 October 1995, paras. 34–5.

[46] *Ibid.*, paras. 37–8, referring to *Effect of Awards of Compensation Made by the United Nations Administrative Tribunal* (1954) ICJ Reports 47, 61.

[47] *Tadić*, ICTY A. Ch., 2 October 1995, para. 39.   [48] *Ibid.*, paras. 55–60.   [49] *Ibid.*, paras. 61–4.

[50] *Tadić*, ICTY A. Ch., 2 October 1995, para. 42.   [51] *Ibid.*, para. 46.   [52] (1996) 35 ILM 75.   [53] Art. X, Annex 1A.

[54] Art. IV(4), Annex IA; see Paolu Gaeta, 'Is NATO Authorized or Obliged to Arrest Persons Indicted by the International Criminal Tribunal for Former Yugoslavia?' (1998) 9 *European Journal of International Law* 174.

[55] Annual Report of the ICTY 1997, UN Doc. S/1997/729, paras. 167–71.   [56] *Ibid.*, para. 72.

[57] *Ibid.*, para. 190. Darryl Robinson, 'Trials, Tribulations and Triumphs: Major Developments in 1997 at the International Criminal Tribunal for Yugoslavia' (1997) 35 *Canadian Yearbook of International Law* 179.

[58] Annual Report of the ICTY 1997, para. 183.   [59] SC Res. 1160, Annual Report of the ICTY 1998, para. 118.

indicting Slobodan Milošević,[60] for alleged crimes in Kosovo. The Prosecutor was assisted in this process by considerable evidence made available to her by Western States.[61]

In 1999, the Prosecutor was asked by a number of people and groups to investigate NATO States for alleged war crimes during NATO's air campaign in relation to Kosovo. In response, the Prosecutor set up a committee to carry out a preliminary assessment of the evidence presented and to advise her on whether or not to initiate a full investigation. Even this action caused consternation in some circles.[62] The committee recommended in June 2000 that no full investigation be undertaken.[63] This recommendation was accepted by the Prosecutor and caused considerable controversy.[64] Whether or not this decision reflected an unwillingness to investigate NATO officials, and whether or not the conclusions reached in the report are sound, aspects of the report's reasoning are certainly open to challenge.[65]

The completion strategy and the process of winding down

Around 2000, the judges of the ICTY concluded that their work could take them until at least 2016 to complete.[66] This was considered to be too long, so the ICTY suggested to the Security Council that there be a 'completion strategy'.[67] This involved a number of steps. The first was the creation of *ad litem* judges, peripatetic judges who would sit for one case.[68] This was achieved when a set of twenty-seven such judges were authorized by Security Council Resolution 1329(2000).[69] The next step was getting senior lawyers to deal with some pre-trial matters rather than judges.[70] The third step of the plan was to expand the Appeals Chamber, a move that was also accepted in Resolution 1329(2000).

The visibility and perceived effectiveness of the Tribunal increased considerably in 2001, when the Federal Republic of Yugoslavia began, after considerable economic and political pressure, sporadic cooperation with the Tribunal, most notably with the surrender of ex-President Milošević to the ICTY in June 2001. Just over a month later, the ICTY handed down its first conviction for genocide, of General Radislav Krštić, for his role in the Srebrenica massacre.[71] During this period, the Prosecutor undertook a number of initiatives to ensure that investigations would be completed by the end of 2004.[72] These involved, *inter alia,*

---

[60] *Milošević et al.*, ICTY Indictment, 24 May 1999.

[61] Annual Report of the ICTY 1999, UN Doc. S/1999/846, paras. 126, 128.

[62] See e.g. Rachel Kerr, *The International Criminal Tribunal for Former Yugoslavia: An Exercise in Law, Politics and Diplomacy* (Oxford, 2004) 202–3.

[63] Final Report to the Prosecutor by the Committee Established to Review the NATO Bombing Campaign against the Federal Republic of Yugoslavia, 8 June 2000, para. 90; (2000) 39 ILM 1257.

[64] See, in favour of the decision, Kerr, *International Criminal Tribunal*, 199–204. (Strongly) against, see Michael Mandel, 'Politics and Human Rights in International Criminal Law: Our Case against NATO and the Lessons to be Learnt from It' (2001–2) 25 *Fordham International Law Journal* 95.

[65] See Paolo Benvenuti, 'The ICTY Prosecutor and the Review of the NATO Bombing against the Federal Republic of Yugoslavia' (2001) 12 *European Journal of International Law* 503; Michael Bothe, 'The Protection of the Civilian Population and NATO Bombing on Yugoslavia: Comments on a Report to the Prosecutor of the ICTY' (2001) 12 *European Journal of International Law* 531.

[66] Annual Report of the ICTY 2000, UN Doc. S/2000/777, para. 336.

[67] See generally Dominic Raab, 'Evaluating the ICTY and its Completion Strategy' (2005) 3 *Journal of International Criminal Justice* 82.

[68] Annual Report of the ICTY 2000, para. 340.

[69] SC Res. 1329(2000) of 30 November 2009. The roles of such judges have gradually expanded.

[70] Annual Report of the ICTY 2001, UN Doc. S/2001/865, para. 4.   [71] *Krštić*, ICTY T. Ch. I, 2 August 2001.

[72] Annual Report of the ICTY 2002, UN Doc. S/2002/985, para. 7.

focusing on high-level offenders, as lower-level offenders could be tried at the domestic level.[73] It was hoped that this would permit the Tribunal to complete its trial-level work by 2008, although this was contingent on State cooperation in transferring evidence and indictees.[74]

The possibility of the Tribunal living up to its timetable was, at the time, thought to be assisted by three factors. First, increasing numbers of defendants were willing to plead guilty, in particular, in October 2002, Biljana Plavšić, a wartime president of the Republika Srpska.[75] Second, the Federal Republic of Yugoslavia increased its cooperation with the Tribunal, although the two highest profile fugitives, Radovan Karadžić and Ratko Mladić remained at liberty.[76] Finally, more indictees began to surrender voluntarily to the ICTY.[77] On its side, the ICTY revised Rule 11*bis* of the Rules of Procedure and Evidence to permit the ICTY to transfer indictments, and later, cases, after it had considered the appropriateness of doing so, taking into account, *inter alia*, the gravity of the crime, the role of the accused, and the fair trial guarantees that would be accorded to the accused.[78]

A major development occurred in August 2003, when the Security Council explained its approach to the ICTY's completion strategy in Resolution 1503. In addition to the Prosecutor completing investigations by 2004, the Trial Chambers were required to complete their business by 2008 and appeals were to end by 2010.[79] Scepticism about the ability of the Tribunal to keep to this timetable was not unfounded.[80] Nonetheless, the Security Council adopted Resolution 1534(2004), which required the Tribunal's judges to check that any new indictment focused on 'the most senior leaders suspected of being most responsible for crimes' in the Tribunal's jurisdiction.[81] Some have questioned whether this is consistent with the requirements of prosecutorial independence.[82] Although such critiques are worth taking seriously, it is unlikely that it altered the Prosecutor's strategy in a practical way, as she had already been focusing on such offenders for some time.

On the other hand, one of the ICTY's own judges issued a stinging critique of the completion strategy from the viewpoint of the fair trial rights of the defendants. Judge Hunt asserted that the international community expected trials to be in accordance with fair trial rights, but were unwilling to give the time and money necessary. However, the answer was not to curtail defence rights, since '[t]his Tribunal will not be judged by the number of convictions which it enters, or by the speed with which it concludes the Completion Strategy which the Security Council has endorsed, but by the fairness of its trials. The ... [decisions] in which the Completion Strategy has been given priority over the rights of

---

[73] *Ibid.*, para. 218.   [74] *Ibid.*, para. 328.
[75] Annual Report of the ICTY 2003, UN Doc. S/2003/829, para. 2. See *Plavšić*, ICTY T. Ch. III, 23 November 2003.
[76] Annual Report of the ICTY 2003, para. 8.   [77] *Ibid.*, para. 232.
[78] See generally Michael Bohlander, 'Referring an Indictment from the ICTY and ICTR to Another Court – Rule 11*bis* and the Consequences for the Law of Extradition' (2006) 55 *International and Comparative Law Quarterly* 219. See Chapters 5 and 9.
[79] SC Res. 1503(2003) of 28 August 2003. See also Raab, 'Completion Strategy', 85–6.
[80] Raab, 'Completion Strategy', 86, 95.
[81] SC Res. 1534(2004) of 26 March 2004; see Rule 28(A) of the ICTY RPE. See further section 17.8.1.
[82] Darryl A. Mundis, 'The Judicial Effects of the "Completion Strategies" on the Ad Hoc International Criminal Tribunals' (2005) 99 *American Journal of International Law* 142; Larry D. Johnson, 'Closing an International Criminal Tribunal while Maintaining International Human Rights Standards and Excluding Impunity' (2005) 99 *American Journal of International Law* 158.

the accused will leave a spreading stain on this Tribunal's reputation.'[83] Whether or not this is accepted,[84] it is true that the completion strategy has led to a number of procedural innovations, and an increased use of documentary evidence.[85]

Against a backdrop of the majority of trials proceeding at least towards judgment, the Secretary-General reported on the afterlife of the Tribunals in 2009.[86] Picking up on this in 2010, the Security Council looked towards the closure of the ICTY. However, it was aware of the fact that there are matters, such as supervision of prison sentences, release, and the possible trial of fugitives or contempt cases, and reopening of cases that will last beyond the lifespan of the ICTY. It therefore decided, in Resolution 1966(2010), to establish a 'Residual Mechanism' to perform these functions for the ICTY and ICTR, with branches in Arusha and The Hague.[87]

This is, in essence, a pared-down version of the Tribunals, and is to 'continue the material, territorial, temporal and personal jurisdiction' of the Tribunals,[88] and, as appropriate, to refer cases to national jurisdictions.[89] It also has the express power to punish contempt.[90] Appeals made on or after 1 July 2013, as well as any retrials, will be handled by the Mechanism. The bulk of its work is likely to be related to its function of supervising the implementation of sentences, alongside questions of pardon or commutation of sentence.[91] Like the ICTY, the Residual Mechanism has an Office of the Prosecutor, Chambers and Registry.[92] It also has a President, currently Theodor Meron (who is also the President of the ICTY).[93] It began its work on the ICTY in July 2013, when it took over supervision of ICTY sentences. After 2016, the work of the Residual Mechanism is to be reviewed on a biannual basis, with a view to reducing its functions and staff over time.[94]

As of August 2013, the ICTY had, of the 161 people charged, completed proceedings against 136 accused with 69 convictions and 18 acquittals. It is continuing proceedings against 25 accused (others have had their indictments withdrawn, the proceedings referred to domestic courts under Rule 11*bis*, or died). The death of the most (in)famous of these, Slobodan Milošević, in 2006, just before the end of his lengthy and often controversial trial, robbed the Tribunal of the possibility of completing proceedings against one of the main leaders involved in the wars of 1991–5.[95] With the transfer of the final two fugitives from the ICTY, Ratko Mladić and Göran Hadžić to the Tribunal in 2011, the Tribunal had obtained

---

[83] *Milošević*, ICTY, Dissenting Opinion of Judge David Hunt on Admissibility of Evidence in Chief in the Form of Written Statement (Majority Decision Given 30 September 2003), 21 October 2003, paras. 21–2.

[84] See Fausto Pocar, 'Completion or Continuation Strategy?' (2008) 6 *Journal of International Criminal Justice* 655, 657–8; 'Discussion' (2008) 6 *Journal of International Criminal Justice* 681, 682–7.

[85] O-Gon Kwon, 'The Challenge of the International Criminal Trial as Seen from the Bench' (2007) 5 *Journal of International Criminal Justice* 360.

[86] Report of the Secretary-General, UN Doc. S/2009/258, 21 May 2009. See also Gabriël Oosthuizen and Robert Schaeffer, 'Complete Justice: Residual Functions and Potential Residual Mechanisms of the ICTY, ICTR and SCSL' (2008) 3 *Hague Justice Journal* 48.

[87] SC Res. 1966(2010) of 22 December 2010. On the background, see Guido Acquaviva, '"Best before Date Shown": Residual Mechanisms at the ICTY' in Bert Swart, Alexander Zahar and Göran Sluiter (eds.), *The Legacy of the International Criminal Tribunal for the Former Yugoslavia* (Oxford, 2011) 507–36. The Residual Mechanism has identified its ad hoc functions as being the tracking and prosecution of fugitives, appeals, retrials, trials for contempt and perjury, and review proceedings. Its continuing functions are victim and witness protection, supervising sentences, assisting national jurisdictions and archive preservation.

[88] See generally the symposium in (2011) 9 *Journal of International Criminal Justice* 787 *et seq.*

[89] Art. 6 of the MICT Statute.   [90] *Ibid.*, Art. 1(4).   [91] *Ibid.*, Arts. 25–26.   [92] *Ibid.*, Art. 4.

[93] The Prosecutor is Hasan Bubacar Jallow, the current Prosecutor of the ICTR.   [94] Res. 1966.

[95] Gideon Boas, *The Milošević Trial: Lessons for the Conduct of Complex International Criminal Proceedings* (Cambridge, 2007);

custody over all indictees over whom it asserted jurisdiction.[96] The Tribunal is currently working on completing its proceedings, but the number of accused currently still undergoing proceedings at the ICTY makes it unlikely that the Tribunal will close before at least 2016. Ironically, given the staffing problems at the outset of the ICTY's history, the impending closure of the ICTY has led to difficulties again, as people leave for more secure employment elsewhere.[97]

The ICTY's eye has also increasingly turned to what it terms its 'legacy', which includes ensuring that large amounts of its judicial and other materials are properly archived and available,[98] creating a compilation of its practices[99] and undertaking capacity building in domestic jurisdictions.[100] However, in late 2012 and early 2013, controversial acquittals, *inter alia*, in the *Gotovina* and *Perisić* cases, led to outrage in some quarters,[101] and disquiet amongst some of the judges. This led one judge to criticize the decisions and the President of the ICTY publicly, which in turn led to disqualification proceedings against that judge in the *Šešelj* case.[102] Both the acquittals and the judicial response to them have, for some, raised questions about the legacy the ICTY will leave.

7.2.5   Appraisal of the ICTY

The ICTY itself has set out a number of its achievements. These are, *inter alia*, that it has promoted accountability rather than impunity, including with respect to leaders, established the facts of the crimes in the former Yugoslavia, brought justice for victims and given them a voice, developed international law and strengthened the rule of law.[103] The Tribunal has, to some extent, fulfilled these goals.

It is true that the creation of the ICTY has contributed to the trend against impunity, not least as its creation and Statute provided a direct precedent for the ICTR, and a slightly less direct one for the ICC.[104] Also, the ICTY showed that international prosecutions were possible outside the situation of a complete defeat of one side in a conflict. Equally, at times the Tribunal has struggled to contain the size of trials against high-ranking defendants, and has similarly had difficulty containing the disruptive activities of a number of

---

Maya Steinitz, 'The Milošević Trial – Live! An Iconical Analysis of International Law's Claim to Legitimate Authority' (2005) 3 *Journal of International Criminal Justice* 310. The leaders of Croatia and Bosnia in the relevant periods, Franjo Tudjman and Alija Izetbegović respectively, died unindicted, if not uninvestigated.

[96] Radovan Karadžić having been transferred to the Tribunal in 2008.
[97] Report to the Security Council, 18 May 2009, UN Doc. S/2009/252, para. 43.
[98] The preservation and management of the ICTR and ICTY's archives is also an important responsibility for the Residual Mechanism, Art. 27 of the MICT Statute.
[99] ICTY/UNICRI, *ICTY Manual on Developed Practices* (Turin, 2009); also available at http://wcjp.unicri.it/proceedings/docs/ UNICRI_ICTY_manual_on_developed_practices_eng.pdf.
[100] *Ibid.*, para. 53.
[101] *Gotovina and Markač*, ICTY A. Ch., 16 November 2012. *Perisić*, ICTY A. Ch., 13 February 2013. On the former, see Janine Natalya Clarke, 'Courting Controversy: The ICTY's Acquittal of Croatian Generals Gotovina and Markač' (2013) 11 *Journal of International Criminal Justice* 399. Note also the acquittal in *Stanišić and Simatović*, ICTY T. Ch., 30 May 2013, under appeal at the time of writing.
[102] *Šešelj*, ICTY Chamber convened by the Vice-President, 28 August 2013. The consequences of this decision for other cases continue to be the subject of proceedings at the time of writing.
[103] See the ICTY webpage at www.icty.org/sid/324.
[104] Ralph Zacklin, 'The Failings of Ad Hoc International Tribunals' (2004) 2 *Journal of International Criminal Justice* 541.

defendants.[105] The Tribunal has taken considerable pains to determine what happened in the former Yugoslavia accurately, even if its approach has been criticized.[106] The Tribunal spent considerable time and resources to attempt to bring (corrective) justice to victims, even if its practice has not always been perfect by the exacting standards of victims' rights advocates,[107] nor the experiences of victims appearing before it uniformly positive.[108]

It is difficult, if not impossible, to doubt the ICTY's impact on international law.[109] Although the Tribunal has been accused of being too quick to decide that aspects of the law are customary,[110] and of seeking always to expand its own authority,[111] most of its decisions are well reasoned, and have not been criticized by States.[112] Although it might be queried whether all of the ICTY's decisions on custom have been irreproachable, it is not clear that they have violated the *nullum crimen sine lege* principle.[113] The more recent judgments of the ICTY may be less discursive of larger issues of law than earlier decisions such as *Tadić*; as the major issues were decided in the earlier decisions, there is less scope for iconic case law from the ICTY now.

On the downside, the ICTY has been accused, with varying degrees of accuracy, of various sins against international law and justice.[114] Some accusations, such as that it has been systematically biased towards or against one of the sides in the Yugoslav wars of dissolution, are easily dismissable,[115] even though the necessity of obtaining cooperation from States has probably led to some necessary diplomatic manoeuvring by the prosecutors.[116] Other critiques have included that the Tribunal has been too expensive and bureaucratic,[117] that its trials are characterized by delay,[118] violate the rights of defendants,[119] and

---

[105] See e.g. Göran Sluiter, 'Compromising the Authority of International Criminal Justice: How Vojislav Šešelj Runs his Trial' (2007) 5 *Journal of International Criminal Justice* 529; Michael P. Scharf, 'Chaos in the Courtroom: Controlling Disruptive Defendants and Contumacious Counsel in War Crimes Trials' (2006–2007) 39 *Case Western Reserve Journal of International Law* 155; Robert Cryer, 'Prosecuting the Leaders: Promises, Politics and Practicalities' (2009) 1 *Göttingen Journal of International Law* 45, at 72–4.

[106] José E. Alvarez, 'Rush to Closure: Lessons of the Tadić Judgment' (1998) 96 *Michigan Law Review* 2031.

[107] Marie-Bénédict Dembour and Emily Haslam, 'Silencing Hearings? Victim–Witnesses at War Crimes Trials' (2004) 15 *European Journal of International Law* 151.

[108] Eric Stover, *The Witnesses* (New York, 2007).

[109] See e.g. Robert Cryer, 'Of Custom, Treaties, Scholars and the Gavel: The Influence of the International Criminal Tribunals on the ICRC Customary Study' (2006) 11 *Journal of Conflict and Security Law* 239; Shane Darcy and Joseph Powderly (eds.), *Judicial Creativity at the International Criminal Tribunal* (Oxford, 2010); Swart *et al.*, *Legacy*.

[110] See Guénaël Mettraux, *International Crimes and the Ad Hoc Tribunals* (Oxford, 2005) 13–8.

[111] See e.g. Gregory Lombardi, 'Legitimacy and the Expanding Power of the ICTY' (2002–3) 37 *New England Law Review* 887. A counterexample would be the *Blaškić* decision: see Chapter 20.

[112] One exception is *Kupreškić et al.*, ICTY T. Ch. II, 14 January 2000, paras. 521–36, which rather unconvincingly derived the prohibition of practically all reprisals from contradictory practice and a bold interpretation of the Martens clause. See Christopher Greenwood, 'Belligerent Reprisals in the Jurisprudence of the International Criminal Tribunal for the Former Yugoslavia' in Horst Fischer *et al.* (eds.), *National and International Prosecution of Crimes under International Law* (Berlin, 2001) 539. The Tribunal has, however, now, in essence, overturned this decision: see section 16.9.2.

[113] See generally Mohamed Shahabuddeen, 'Does the Principle of Legality Stand in the Way of Progressive Development of the Law?' (2004) 2 *Journal of International Criminal Justice* 1007.

[114] On the more general questions about criminal prosecution here, see section 2.4.

[115] Although see also footnotes 66–9 above and the corresponding text on the critiques in relation to the NATO/Kosovo Report.

[116] Victor Peskin, *International Justice in Rwanda and the Balkans: Virtual Trials and the Struggle for State Cooperation* (Cambridge, 2008); Carla del Ponte, *Madame Prosecutor* (New York, 2009).

[117] Zacklin, 'Failings', 543–4.

[118] See e.g. Patrick L. Robinson, 'Ensuring Fair and Expeditious Trials at the ICTY' (2000) 11 *European Journal of International Law* 569.

[119] *Ibid.*

are far removed from the populations of the former Yugoslavia.[120] More generally, it has been alleged that the Tribunal was created in place of more effective action to prevent crimes in the former Yugoslavia.[121]

All of these critiques have some purchase. The ICTY is expensive. Since 1993, the ICTY has cost over US$2 billion. It may simply be that international justice is expensive;[122] equally, excessive bureaucracy in the UN contributing to both cost and delay is not unprecedented. Trials have taken a long time, although some delays have been referable to attempts to ensure fair trials for defendants. Nonetheless, some of the decisions of the Tribunal have been controversial in relation to fair trial. Notable in this regard has been the use of anonymous witnesses. Although understandable witness protection issues arise in relation to prosecutions of international crimes, the practice of the Trial Chamber in the *Tadić* case of granting witnesses complete anonymity proved very controversial, in particular owing to the false testimony of one such protected witness, Dragan Opacić.[123]

The question of distance from the relevant populations is a difficult one, but the ICTY did not initially give such matters sufficient consideration in its early practice, which allowed local actors to distort matters,[124] a point the Tribunal has attempted to rectify by setting up various 'outreach' programmes.[125] In defence of the Tribunal, it can be said that the relationship between the media and international justice is not simple, in particular as proceedings are rarely akin to the court dramas many are used to watching and there are other calls on their attention.[126] In addition, the security situation in the former Yugoslavia would not have permitted the ICTY to have sat there, at least until recently. In relation to the final critique mentioned above, that the ICTY was created in place of more effective action to prevent crimes in the former Yugoslavia, it raises an important issue, although it is likely that the best available option was to create a tribunal. If it had not been created, there would not have been any more effective response to the crimes in the former Yugoslavia forthcoming. Equally, a more general issue, that of selectivity, certainly arises whenever an ad hoc tribunal is set up.[127]

---

[120] Laurel E. Fletcher and Harvey Weinstein, 'A World unto Itself: The Application of International Criminal Justice in Former Yugoslavia' in Eric Stover and Harvey Weinstein (eds.), *My Neighbour, My Enemy: Justice and Community in the Aftermath of Mass Atrocity* (Cambridge, 2004) 29.

[121] See e.g. David Forsythe, *Human Rights in International Relations* (Cambridge, 2000) 221.

[122] David Wipmann, 'The Costs of International Justice' (2006) 100 *American Journal of International Law* 861.

[123] *Tadić*, ICTY T. Ch. II, 7 May 1997, paras. 553–4. See section 18.3.

[124] Mirko Klarin, 'The Impact of the ICTY Trials on Public Opinion in the Former Yugoslavia' (2009) 7 *Journal of International Criminal Justice* 89.

[125] David Tolbert, 'The International Criminal Tribunal for the Former Yugoslavia: Unforeseen Successes and Foreseeable Shortcomings' (2002) 26(2) *Fletcher Forum of World Affairs* 7, 13–14; Gabrielle Kirk McDonald, 'Problems, Obstacles and Achievements of the ICTY' (2004) 2 *Journal of International Criminal Justice* 558, 569–70.

[126] Marlise Simons, 'International Criminal Tribunals and the Media' (2009) 7 *Journal of International Criminal Justice* 83.

[127] Gerry Simpson, 'War Crimes: A Critical Introduction' in Timothy McCormack and Gerry Simpson (eds.), *The Law of War Crimes: National and International Approaches* (The Hague, 1997) 1, 8.

7.3   The International Criminal Tribunal for Rwanda

7.3.1   *The creation of the ICTR*

Fears of selectivity fed into the decision to create the ICTR. Given the creation of the ICTY for a European conflict, when genocide clearly occurred in Africa, it was considered necessary and appropriate to create an analogous tribunal for crimes committed there.[128] The UN and its members (who reduced the number of peacekeepers in Rwanda at the start of the genocide in April 1994)[129] treated the creation of a tribunal for Rwanda largely as they treated the ICTY, beginning with condemnation, then setting up a commission of experts and, before they reported, deciding to set up an international tribunal.[130]

Unlike the ICTY Statute, the ICTR Statute was drafted by the members of the Security Council, following closely the model of the ICTY Statute. While Rwanda, then a member of the Council, was initially supportive, it did not succeed in including the death penalty, excluding crimes other than genocide from the court's jurisdiction or granting the court jurisdiction before 1994, and therefore voted against the creation of the ICTR.[131] This does not affect the legality of the creation of the Tribunal, which finds its basis, like the ICTY, in Chapter VII of the UN Charter.[132]

7.3.2   *The structure of the ICTR*

The structure of the ICTR is very similar to that of the ICTY; it too has an Office of the Prosecutor, a Registry, and one Trial Chamber, which have the same functions as their counterparts in The Hague. To ensure a consistent jurisprudence between the ICTY and ICTR, they share a joint Appeals Chamber (based in The Hague).[133] Originally, the Appeals Chamber was staffed only by judges from the ICTY. This gave rise to a feeling that the ICTR was the 'poor cousin' of the ICTY, but was rectified in late 2000 when two ICTR judges were appointed to that Chamber. Originally, the ICTY and ICTR shared a prosecutor. However, the job was split in 2003 and a separate prosecutor for the ICTR was appointed. The ICTR has always had its own president.

7.3.3   *The jurisdiction of the ICTR and its relationship to national courts*

The ICTR, like the ICTY, has jurisdiction over war crimes, crimes against humanity and genocide,[134] although the definitions of the last two crimes are different from those in the ICTY. In particular, the definition of crimes against humanity has an additional requirement

---

[128] Payam Akhavan, 'The International Criminal Tribunal for Rwanda: The Politics and Pragmatics of Punishment' (1996) 90 *American Journal of International Law* 501.
[129] See SC Res. 912(1994) of 21 April 1994. More generally, see e.g. Gerard Prunier, *The Rwanda Crisis* (London, 1997).
[130] SC Res. 935(1994), 1 July 1994 (Commission) and 955(1994) of 8 November 1994 (Court).
[131] UN Doc. S/PV.3453, 2, 10–12. China abstained on the resolution.
[132] The ICTR affirmed the legality of its own creation in *Kanyabashi*, ICTR T. Ch. II, 18 June 1997. The decision is, however, terse and amounts to little more than a refusal to investigate the legality of Security Council actions.
[133] Art. 12(2) of the ICTR Statute.   [134] *Ibid.*, Arts. 2, 3 and 4 respectively.

of discrimination for all crimes against humanity (Article 3), and the jurisdiction of the ICTR over war crimes is limited to those in non-international armed conflicts (Article 4). The ICTR's jurisdiction over these crimes is limited to where they occurred in Rwanda, or were committed by Rwandans in neighbouring States, between 1 January and 31 December 1994.[135] The ICTR has primacy over domestic courts, in the same way as the ICTY.[136] Like the ICTY, it has also adopted a Rule 11*bis*, which allows it to refer cases to domestic jurisdictions.

7.3.4   The practice of the ICTR[137]

Teething troubles

The ICTR began at a snail's pace. Its seat, in Arusha, Tanzania, was only decided upon in February 1995.[138] Also, staffing was a problem, recruitment being difficult and slow.[139] Even so, the first indictment was confirmed in November 1995.[140] Early cooperation from some African States was quite quick, and proceedings opened against Georges Rutaganda and Jean-Paul Akayesu on 30 May 1996.[141] Rwanda, however, remained rather lukewarm in its relations with the Tribunal.

Although funding for the Tribunal at the time was inadequate,[142] there were also concerns about the extent to which resources, and the Tribunal as a whole, were being managed.[143] A highly critical report of the UN Office of Internal Oversight Services of 6 February 1997[144] accepted that sporadic funding for the Tribunal limited its effectiveness,[145] and decided that the 'evidence adduced did not confirm allegations of corrupt practices or misuse of funds';[146] but the report uncovered 'mismanagement in almost all areas of the Tribunal, and frequent violations of United Nations rules and regulations'.[147] The Registry was singled out for very heavy criticism, in particular for financial irregularities, employing under-qualified staff and weak asset management.[148] The Office of the Prosecutor was considered inefficient, and beset by leadership failure by the Deputy Prosecutor.[149] Of the three organs, only the Chambers escaped serious critique.[150] As a result of the report, both the Registrar's and the Deputy Prosecutor's resignations were sought, and obtained.[151] Also, attempts were made to recruit appropriate people to managerial positions and to improve financial discipline.[152]

Moving forward

The ICTR's fortunes took a turn for the better in May 1998, when Jean Kambanda, the Prime Minister of the government that presided over the genocide, pleaded guilty to genocide. Notwithstanding his guilty plea, which recognized, importantly, that genocide had occurred

---

[135] *Ibid.*, Art. 1.   [136] *Ibid.*, Art. 8(1).
[137] For an interesting perspective, from the ex-Rwandan minister of Justice, see Gerald Gahima, *Transitional Justice in Rwanda: Accountability for Atrocity* (London, 2013) Chapter 4.
[138] SC Res. 977(1995) of 22 February 1995.   [139] Annual Report of the ICTR 1996, UN Doc. S/1996/778, para. 12.
[140] *Ibid.*, para. 31.   [141] *Ibid.*, para. 39.   [142] *Ibid.*, para. 77.   [143] GA Res. 52/213 C.
[144] Report of the Secretary-General on the Activities of the Office of Internal Oversight Services, UN Doc. A/51/789 of 6 February 1997.
[145] *Ibid.*, para. 5.   [146] *Ibid.*, para. 6.   [147] *Ibid.*   [148] *Ibid.*, paras. 11–33.   [149] *Ibid.*, paras. 55–9.
[150] *Ibid.*, paras. 60–3.   [151] Annual Report of the ICTR 1997, UN Doc. S/1997/868, para. 57.   [152] *Ibid.*

in Rwanda, he was sentenced to life imprisonment.[153] In spite of continuing technical, logistical and resourcing problems, the Tribunal moved into a phase of increased trial work, which led the Security Council to increase the number of Trial Chambers to three in April 1998.[154] The first full trial ended in September 1998, with the conviction of Akayesu for genocide, in a judgment that not only offered the first express application of the Genocide Convention by an international tribunal, but also determined that sexual offences could form the *actus reus* of genocide.[155]

Trials were moving slowly but forward during 1999, when the relationship between the ICTR and Rwanda collapsed. The reason for this was the decision of the Appeals Chamber that the pre-trial detention of Jean-Bosco Barayagwiza, one of the mass media advocates of the genocide, violated his human rights, and so the Tribunal should use its inherent power to decline jurisdiction over him.[156] Rwanda was outraged, and suspended cooperation with the Tribunal, which owing to the vast majority of evidence and witnesses being located in Rwanda made progress with trials very difficult. The Appeals Chamber quickly revisited its decision on the point and determined that, on the basis of further factual submissions by the Prosecutor, the Tribunal ought to continue to exercise jurisdiction over him, but he ought to receive a reduction in any sentence he received if he were to be convicted, to take into account his pre-trial predicament.[157] Although relations between the ICTR and Rwanda improved, many thought that politics, more than law, was involved in the decision.[158]

Nonetheless, the position of the ICTR was improved in 2001 when, pursuant to Security Council Resolution 1329,[159] *ad litem* judges were appointed to assist in trials. By early 2001, it was thought that the Prosecutor would complete her investigative work by 2005.[160] Trial work remained slow, however,[161] and pre-trial detention of suspects remained very long.

The completion strategy and the process of winding down

As the ICTR began to think in terms of completion, plans were formulated to pass up to forty cases to national jurisdictions (including Rwanda) rather than have them prosecuted by the ICTR.[162] Thus, in July 2002 the ICTR adopted its own Rule 11*bis*, permitting the transfer of cases to national jurisdictions. To assist the ICTR in completing its judicial business (which was still taking a great deal of time), the Security Council adopted Resolution 1431 on 14 August 2002, which set up a pool of eighteen *ad litem*

---

[153] *Kambanda*, ICTR T. Ch. I, 4 September 1998. Kambanda unsuccessfully appealed; *Kambanda*, ICTR A. Ch., 19 October 2000.
[154] SC Res. 1165(1998) of 30 April 1998. See Annual Report of the ICTR 1999, UN Doc. S/1999/943, paras. 5, 126.
[155] *Akayesu*, ICTR T. Ch. I, 2 September 1998; see section 10.3.1.   [156] *Barayagwiza*, ICTR A. Ch., 3 November 1999.
[157] *Barayagwiza*, ICTR A. Ch., 31 March 2000. In the event, he was convicted, and sentenced to thirty-five years' imprisonment, unlike his co-defendants, both of whom were sentenced to life. *Nahimana, Barayagwiza and Ngeze*, ICTR T. Ch. I, 3 December 2003, paras. 1106–7. His sentence was reduced to thirty-two years on appeal.
[158] William A. Schabas, 'Prosecutor v. Barayagwiza' (2000) 94 *American Journal of International Law* 563, 565.
[159] 5 December 2000.   [160] Annual Report of the ICTR 2002, UN Doc. S/2002/733, para. 121.   [161] *Ibid.*, paras. 1–6.
[162] *Ibid.*, para. 10. The ICTR had, early on in its practice, unsuccessfully attempted such an approach, with respect to Bernard Ntuyuhaga: *Ntuyuhaga*, ICTR T. Ch. I, 18 March 1999.

judges.[163] Although the ICTR was assisted by a number of States, relations with Rwanda remained less than friendly.[164]

In August 2003, Security Council Resolution 1503(2003) set out the Security Council's timetable for completion, which was the same as that for the ICTY. This resolution also split the role of the Prosecutor in two, creating separate positions of ICTY and ICTR Prosecutor on the stated basis that the job was too large for one person and thus Rwanda was being overlooked.[165] The completion strategy was expanded upon by Resolution 1534, which required both Tribunals to review their caseloads to determine which cases could be tried at the domestic level.[166] The ICTR declared its ability to meet the various deadlines (subject to State cooperation) in 2005.[167] Its ability to do so was, it was hoped, to be assisted by negotiations with Rwanda to facilitate transfer of cases from the ICTR to Kigali.[168] There have been transfers of cases to France[169] and, although initially the ICTR has been critical of the possibility of fair trials in Rwanda and of the standards of imprisonment there, transfers of cases to Rwanda were ordered in 2011 and 2012.[170]

These transfers meant that the trial work of the ICTR ended in December 2012, when the last trial judgment was given. The ICTR expects to complete its appellate work in 2015–16.[171] The cases against three high-ranking fugitives from the ICTR have been handed over to the Residual Mechanism for trial, and the Mechanism has re-issued arrest warrants for them.[172] The Residual Mechanism started work with respect to the ICTR in July 2012, and is now fully functional. It is monitoring trials referred under Rule 11*bis*, engaging in witness protection and overseeing the implementation of sentences.[173] As such, it is increasingly taking over the functions of the ICTR, which is, accordingly, reducing its role. Like the ICTY, the winding-up of its activities has led to staff leaving the ICTR for more permanent employment, whilst it is working on analogous 'legacy' activities.[174]

7.3.5   *Appraisal of the ICTR*

The Tribunal has come in for a great deal of criticism in the past,[175] but the picture has, over the years become rosier than critics would suggest. The ICTR has had notable success in

---

[163] See Annual Report of the ICTR 2003, UN Doc. S/2003/707, paras. 7–8; Annual Report of the ICTR 2005, UN Doc. S/2005/534, para. 5.

[164] *Ibid.*, para. 63.

[165] SC Res. 1503(2003) of 28 August 2003. For the view that this was more to do with del Ponte's stated willingness to begin investigating allegations against the Rwandan Patriotic Front, see Luc Reydams, 'The ICTR Ten Years On: Back to the Nuremberg Paradigm?' (2005) 3 *Journal of International Criminal Justice* 977; and del Ponte, *Madame Prosecutor*, Chapter 9.

[166] SC Res. 1434(2004) of 26 March 2004.   [167] UN Doc. S/2005/336.   [168] Annual Report of the ICTR 2005, para. 49.

[169] *Buchiybaruta*, ICTR T. Ch., 20 November 2007; *Munyeshaka*, ICTR T. Ch., 20 November 2007.

[170] Report on the Completion Strategy of the International Criminal Tribunal for Rwanda (as at May 2013), UN Doc. S/20130/310, Annex II.

[171] *Ibid.*, Annex IV.   [172] *Ibid.*, Annex III.

[173] Progress Report of the President of the Residual Mechanism for Criminal Tribunals, Judge Theodor Meron, for the Period from 15 November 2012 to 23 May 2013, UN Doc. S/2013/309, paras. 4, 12.

[174] Report on the Completion Strategy of the International Criminal Tribunal for Rwanda (as at 4 May 2009), UN Doc. S/2009/247, paras. 46, 66–8.

[175] See e.g. Todd Howland and William Calathes, 'The UN's International Criminal Tribunal: Is It Justice or Jingoism for Rwanda? A Call for Transformation' (1998) 39 *Virginia Journal of International Law* 135. For an early (positive) appraisal, see Djiena Wembou, 'The ICTR: Its Role in the African Context' (1997) 321 *International Review of the Red Cross* 685.

obtaining, and trying, high-level suspects. Although it has not obtained all of the ringleaders of the genocide, it has many of them, both civilian and military, and they are being prosecuted or have been convicted.[176] Its successes on this point are perhaps greater than those of the ICTY. The early *Akayesu* decision formed an important authoritative determination that genocide had occurred in Rwanda, a point that some in the mid 1990s denied or tried to minimize.[177] Indeed, the ICTR now takes juridical notice of the fact that there was genocide in Rwanda in 1994.[178]

The Tribunal has assisted in the development of international criminal law, perhaps most notably by its treatment of sexual offences,[179] but also in relation to the responsibility of controllers of mass media for incitement to commit genocide.[180] It is nonetheless true that the quality of the legal reasoning contained in judgments of the ICTR has been variable.[181]

Trials at the ICTR have taken an extremely long time, and have been subject to manifold delays. These are, in part, because of the difficulties involved in translation of Kinyarwanda into English and French,[182] and the awkward logistics of having the Tribunal based in Arusha, and the Office of the Prosecutor based in Kigali, neither of which are cities with a strong infrastructure.[183] Problems relating to repeated changes of defence counsel by the defendants have also contributed to the dilatory nature of trials,[184] but the judges too have not always helped to move things along speedily.[185] Also, attempts to assist victims, although laudable,[186] have not always been effective, and treatment of victims by the Tribunal has not always lived up to its aspirations, or, on occasion, basic standards.[187]

One of the major critiques that has been made of the ICTR is its failure to prosecute alleged offences committed by the Rwandan Patriotic Front after the genocide in 2004. The ICTR has undertaken some investigations into the Rwandan Patriotic Front,[188] but referred some allegations back to Rwanda after investigation and the establishment of a *prima facie* case.[189] The necessity of ensuring Rwandan cooperation for prosecutions of *génocidaires* may have been relevant here, although the Prosecutor has said that it is owing to the fact that

[176] Larissa J. van den Herik, *The Contribution of the Rwanda Tribunal to the Development of International Law* (The Hague, 2005) 263; these include Kambanda and top-ranking military officials such as Théoneste Bagosora; *Bagosora et al.*, ICTR T. Ch. I, 18 December 2008; and (on appeal) *Bagosora and Nsengiyumva*, ICTR A. Ch., 14 December 2011.
[177] See Prunier, *The Rwanda Crisis*, 345.
[178] *Karemera, Ngirumpatse and Nzirorera*, ICTR A. Ch., 16 June 2006. Some are critical of this, however: see Kevin Jon Heller, 'Prosecutor v. Karemera' (2007) 101 *American Journal of International Law* 157.
[179] Kelly Askin, 'Gender Crimes at the ICTR: Positive Developments' (2005) 3 *Journal of International Criminal Justice* 1007. On other aspects of the ICTR's practice on sexual offences, see Annual Report of the ICTR 2000, UN Doc. S/2000/927, para. 133; Annual Report of the ICTR 2001, UN Doc. S/2001/863, para. 108; Annual Report of the ICTR 2002, UN Doc. S/2002/733, para. 75; Annual Report of the ICTR 2004, UN Doc. S/2004/601, paras. 59–61.
[180] *Nahimana, Barayagwiza and Ngeze*, ICTR T. Ch. I, 3 December 2003; and (on appeal) ICTR A. Ch., 28 November 2007; although, see also Dina Temple-Raston, *Justice on the Grass* (New York, 2005).
[181] See van den Herik, *The Contribution of the Rwanda Tribunal*, 261.
[182] About which the Tribunal has been candid: see e.g. *Akayesu*, ICTR T. Ch. I, 2 September 1998, para. 145.
[183] Eric Møse, 'The Main Achievements of the ICTR' (2005) 3 *Journal of International Criminal Justice* 920, 923, 927.
[184] Annual Report of the ICTR 2001, para. 14.
[185] Alison des Forges and Timothy Longman, 'Legal Responses to the Genocide in Rwanda' in Stover and Weinstein, *My Neighbour, My Enemy*, 53–5.
[186] See Møse, 'The Main Achievements', 937; see also the Annual Report of the ICTR 1999, UN Doc. S/1999/943, para. 113.
[187] Göran Sluiter, 'The ICTR and the Protection of Witnesses' (2005) 3 *Journal of International Criminal Justice* 962.
[188] Report of the ICTR to the Security Council 12 May 2008, UN Doc. S/2008/322, para. 45.
[189] Eric Møse, 'The ICTR's Completion Strategy: Challenges and Possible Solutions' (2008) 6 *Journal of International Criminal Justice* 667, 674.

the allegations are less serious than those against Hutu defendants and because of the completion strategy.[190]

It has been suggested that the ICTR is both geographically and metaphorically too distant from the people of Rwanda, who remain for the most part uninformed about and unaffected by the Tribunal.[191] The Tribunal created an outreach programme, which included a visitors' centre in Rwanda, radio broadcasts and the creation of a satellite television station,[192] but whether these proved effective is a matter of controversy.[193] A linked critique is the cost of the ICTR, which has been high (although lower than the cost of the ICTY).[194] Some have suggested that the money spent on the ICTR would have been put to better use supporting Rwandan justice efforts.[195] Whether or not that would have been the case, similar levels of funding would not have materialized if a call had instead gone out for assistance to rebuild the Rwandan justice system.

Further reading

The websites of both Tribunals are very useful. They may be found at www.icty.org and www.ictr.org. Useful symposia on the ICTY can be found at (2004) 2 *Journal of International Criminal Justice* 353–597 and (2002–3) 37 *New England Law Review* 865–1080. Similarly, on the ICTR, see (1997) 321 *International Review of the Red Cross* 665–732 and (2005) 3 *Journal of International Criminal Justice* 801–1033. The completion strategy is the subject of discussion in a symposium in (2008) 6 *Journal of International Criminal Justice* 655–709, and the Residual Mechanism is discussed in the symposium in (2011) 9 *Journal of International Criminal Justice* 787–837.

M. Cherif Bassiouni and Peter Manikas, *The Law of the International Criminal Tribunal for Yugoslavia* (Ardsley, NY, 1996)

Gideon Boas, *The Milošević Trial: Lessons for the Conduct of Complex International Criminal Proceedings* (Cambridge, 2007)

Shane Darcy and Joseph Powderly (eds.), *Judicial Creativity at the International Criminal Tribunal* (Oxford, 2010)

Gerald Gahima, *Transitional Justice in Rwanda: Accountability for Atrocity* (London, 2013) Chapter 4

John Hagan, *Justice in the Hague: Prosecuting War Crimes in the Balkans* (Chicago, 2003)

Pierre Hazan, *Justice in a Time of War: The True Story behind the International Criminal Tribunal for the Former Yugoslavia*, James Snyder (trans.) (College Station, TX, 2004)

---

[190] Peskin, *International Justice in Rwanda*, Chapter 8; Vanessa Thalman, 'French Justice's Endeavors to Substitute for the ICTR' (2008) 6 *Journal of International Criminal Justice* 995, 1001–2.

[191] José E. Alvarez, 'Crimes of Hate/Crimes of State, Lessons from Rwanda' (1999) 24 *Yale Journal of International Law* 365, 403–18, 459–62. See also Sigall Horovit, 'The Impact of the International Criminal Tribunal for Rwanda and the Special Court for Sierra Leone on Impunity in Rwanda and Sierra Leone' in Vincent Nmehielle (ed.), *Africa and International Criminal Justice* (The Hague, 2012) 15.

[192] See generally Annual Report of the ICTR 1999, para. 1208; Annual Report of the ICTR 2001, paras. 135 *et seq.*; Annual Report of the ICTR 2004, para. 55; Annual Report of the ICTR 2005, paras. 61–3.

[193] See Timothy Longman *et al.*, 'Connecting Justice to Human Experience: Attitudes towards Accountability and Reconciliation in Rwanda' in Stover and Weinstein, *My Neighbour, My Enemy*, 206.

[194] The ICTR's annual budget for 2008–9 was approximately US$270 million, the ICTY's US$342 million.

[195] Alvarez, 'Crimes of Hate', 461.

Rachel Kerr, *The International Criminal Tribunal for Former Yugoslavia: An Exercise in Law, Politics and Diplomacy* (Oxford, 2004)

Virginia Morris and Michael P. Scharf, *An Insider's Guide to the International Criminal Tribunal for Former Yugoslavia* (New York, 1995)

Virginia Morris and Michael P. Scharf, *The International Criminal Tribunal for Rwanda* (New York, 1998)

John C. O'Brien, 'The International Tribunal for Violations of International Humanitarian Law in the Former Yugoslavia' (1993) 77 *American Journal of International Law* 639

Victor Peskin, *International Justice in Rwanda and the Balkans: Virtual Trials and the Struggle for State Cooperation* (Cambridge, 2008)

Alfred Rubin, 'An International Criminal Tribunal for the Former Yugoslavia' (1994) 6 *Pace International Law Review* 7

William Schabas, *The UN International Criminal Tribunals: The Former Yugoslavia, Rwanda and Sierra Leone* (Cambridge, 2006)

Mohamed Shahabuddeen, *International Criminal Justice at the Yugoslav Tribunal: A Judge's Recollection* (Oxford, 2012)

Bert Swart, Alexander Zahar and Göran Sluiter (eds.), *The Legacy of the International Criminal Tribunal for the Former Yugoslavia* (Oxford, 2011)

Larissa J. van den Herik, *The Contribution of the Rwanda Tribunal to the Development of International Law* (The Hague, 2005)

8

The International Criminal Court

8.1   Introduction

The creation of a permanent international criminal court with potentially worldwide jurisdiction is one of the most important developments in international criminal law. The Statute of the International Criminal Court (ICC) has not only established a judicial institution to investigate and try international crimes, but has also set out a code of international criminal law. This chapter describes the steps leading to the establishment of the ICC, its principal features and early practice, and the challenges the Court confronts.

8.2   The creation of the ICC

In spite of the so-called Nuremberg promise that the trials after the Second World War would set a precedent for others,[1] there was no early successor to the Nuremberg and Tokyo IMTs to prosecute international crimes at the international level. There had been earlier proposals for a permanent international criminal court,[2] and a proposal was discussed during the negotiations on the Genocide Convention, but the Convention as agreed foresaw only the possibility of such a court in the future.[3]

When it approved the Genocide Convention in 1948, the United Nations General Assembly also requested the International Law Commission to study the desirability and possibility of establishing an international judicial organ for the prosecution of, *inter alia*, the crime of genocide.[4] A draft statute for a permanent court was produced by a special committee appointed in 1950, but the General Assembly postponed the matter until

---

[1] See section 6.3.2.
[2] The first serious proposal for an international court was probably that made in 1872 by Gustav Moynier, one of the founders of the International Committee of the Red Cross, who was concerned that national judges would not be able fairly to judge offences committed in wars in which their countries had been involved: Christopher Keith Hall, 'The First Proposal for a Permanent International Criminal Court' (1998) 322 *International Review of the Red Cross* 57.
[3] Art. VI provides that persons charged with genocide are to be tried by a court in the territory where the act was committed or 'by such international penal tribunal as may have jurisdiction with respect to those Contracting Parties which shall have accepted its jurisdiction'.
[4] GA Res. 260(III)B. This study was to be undertaken by the ILC in parallel with its drafting of the substantive rules of international criminal law.

consideration of the definition of aggression and the draft Code of Offences was complete.[5] In turn, progress on the draft Code stalled. The concept of a permanent international criminal court had not received universal support, and during the Cold War allegations of the commission of international crimes were usually regarded as largely propagandistic. Attention was turned to the development of more effective means of inter-State cooperation in the *national* prosecution of crimes, under treaties providing for extradition or prosecution and for legal assistance from one State to another.[6]

It was a proposal in 1989 by Trinidad and Tobago that put the creation of a permanent criminal court back on the agenda of the United Nations. A major concern of Trinidad and Tobago was to secure international prosecutions for drugs offences – although the ICC as finally established does not have jurisdiction over these offences. Responding to the proposal, the General Assembly asked the International Law Commission to draft a statute for a court, and the Commission responded swiftly, producing a final text[7] in 1994.

The draft Statute proposed by the ILC would have given the court jurisdiction over more offences than the ICC has now: as well as the four categories in the ICC Statute, there was a list of 'treaty crimes' which included offences under the multilateral terrorism conventions and the 1988 UN drugs convention.[8] But in most respects the ILC draft was more protective of States' sovereignty than the eventual ICC Statute. Only States Parties and the Security Council could refer situations to the proposed court; the Prosecutor was not able to initiate investigations on his or her own initiative. In respect of most of the crimes,[9] and in the absence of a referral by the Security Council, the court would have jurisdiction only if *both* the State with custody of the alleged offender and the State on whose territory the alleged crime had been committed had accepted the jurisdiction of the court for the purpose of that crime. This was the so-called opt-in provision: States were not required, by becoming parties to the Statute, to accept the jurisdiction of the court for their nationals or for crimes occurring on their territory in respect of any crime except genocide; they were free to opt in for additional specific crimes, or for none at all. The ILC draft also had a provision which precluded the court from taking jurisdiction over a situation which was on the agenda of the Security Council under Chapter VII of the UN Charter, unless the Council agreed. This provision would have allowed the Council to prevent court action by putting any matter on its agenda under its peace and security mandate.

---

[5] GA Res. 898(IX). It was not until 1994 that the ILC produced a draft Code of Offences; see Lyal Sunga, *The Emerging System of International Criminal Law: Developments in Codification and Implementation* (The Hague, 1997). The Code has been largely ignored by governments since 1988 in view of the more detailed codification of international crimes undertaken in the ICC Statute.

[6] Roger Clark, 'Offenses of International Concern: Multilateral State Treaty Practice in the Forty Years since Nuremberg' (1988) 57 *Nordic Journal of International Law* 49.

[7] *Report of the International Law Commission on the Work of its Forty-Sixth Session*, GAOR 49th Session Supp. No. 10, UN Doc. A/49/10 (1994); included, without commentary, in M. Cherif Bassiouni, *The Statute of the International Criminal Court: A Documentary History* (New York, 1998) 657. The drafting of the ILC's draft Statute is discussed in James Crawford, 'The Making of the Rome Statute' in Philippe Sands (ed.), *From Nuremberg to the Hague: The Future of International Criminal Justice* (Cambridge, 2003) 109.

[8] The full list of treaty crimes comprised grave breaches of the Geneva Conventions and its Additional Protocol 1, and offences under six terrorism instruments, the Apartheid Convention, and the UN Drugs Convention.

[9] There was worldwide jurisdiction over genocide, provided that a complaint was lodged by a State which was a party both to the court's Statute and to the Genocide Convention.

The 1994 ILC draft Statute was completed at a fortunate time in international relations: Cold War divisions had thawed, there was enthusiasm for international criminal tribunals, and the international community had embarked on several treaty-based initiatives strengthening human rights and humanitarian law. Scepticism about the prospects for a permanent international criminal court was diminishing. A significant number of States, however, still doubted the wisdom of creating a new court, both in principle and with respect to the specific details of the project. An ad hoc committee was established by the UN General Assembly to examine the issues more closely,[10] and within a year there was enough support to set up a Preparatory Committee[11] to prepare a text of a draft convention. Starting from the ILC's draft Statute, the Preparatory Committee progressed beyond it and put together a draft statute for a new court with hundreds of different alternative proposals. This draft served as the basis for negotiation at the conference in Rome in the summer of 1998.[12]

8.2.1   The 1998 Rome Conference

In the five weeks allocated to the conference to draft the ICC Statute, there was a cornucopia of controversies, from the highly political, like the role of the Security Council, to detailed aspects of criminal procedure negotiated by criminal lawyers from very diverse legal systems. Of the various objectives of the negotiators, two of the strongest were the conflicting aims, often reflected within a single government delegation, of ensuring the prosecution of those responsible for the world's worst atrocities but avoiding undue exposure of national leaders to the new Court. The sixty-strong Like-Minded Group, composed of States supportive of the Court, was influential both in driving forward the process as a whole and in seeking specific proposals for some aspects of the text. Other groupings of States such as the European Union, the Southern African Development Community, and the Non-Aligned Movement all met at different times during the conference and formulated coordinated positions on various of the provisions of the Statute.[13] Non-governmental organizations were represented in large numbers; although they could not take part directly in the negotiations, they helped to maintain the impetus for the establishment of the Court.

By the last week of the conference most of the technical matters had been settled, but a few major questions remained. The most difficult issues related to the jurisdiction of the new Court and, in particular, which States would have to consent before the Court could exercise its jurisdiction. In the absence of agreement and with two days left before the end of the conference, it fell to the Bureau of the Committee of the Whole and associated delegates, under the Chairman, Philippe Kirsch, to propose a compromise on these controversial issues. Their proposal, including the texts of the controversial Articles 12 and 124, was

---

[10] The Ad Hoc Committee on the Establishment of an International Criminal Court, convened by GA Res. 49/53, met for two sessions in 1995 and produced a report (GAOR A/50/22) which records the early discussions on the major features of the court.

[11] Convened by GA Res. 50/46 and with its mandate reaffirmed in GA Res. 51/207 and 52/160, the Preparatory Committee on the Establishment of an International Criminal Court met for six sessions during the years 1995 to 1998; its reports may be found in GAOR A/51/22 and in the conference records at UN Doc. A/CONF.183/13 (Vol. III) 5.

[12] UN Doc. A/CONF.183/13 (Vol. III) 5.

[13] Many States belonging to each of these groups were also members of the Like-Minded Group.

put forward with the rest of the negotiated Statute on the penultimate day in an attempt to balance the conflicting positions of different delegations.

While most delegations supported the text, some were not prepared to accept it as it stood and chose to put their own amendments to the vote. The delegation of India asked for a vote on its proposals to include a crime related to the use of weapons of mass destruction and to exclude any role for the Security Council.[14] The United States called for a vote on their amendments to the jurisdiction provision, which would have required the consent of the State of nationality of the suspect, the territorial State and, if the suspect was committing official acts which were acknowledged as such by the State concerned, the consent of that State.[15] Only the adoption of a 'no-action motion' for both sets of amendments avoided the text of the Statute being broken apart.[16] The Statute was finally adopted by a vote of 120 to 7, with 21 abstentions.[17] There is reason to think that, had the Statute not been adopted at the Rome Conference in 1998, the process would have stalled.

It is not necessary to revisit in detail the course of the Rome Conference, but an understanding of how the Statute was negotiated helps to explain some of the difficulties in the text. Much of the negotiation of specific provisions was carried out in informal committees or in even more informal groups. The work was done without voting and by consensus, so compromises had to be reached, even where the issues concerned technical but important subjects such as the general principles of criminal law. The methods of work adopted by the conference led to disconnections among some parts of the Statute and to different usages in terminology. Had there been more time, the drafting committee would have been able to draw attention to inconsistencies and ambiguities in the text, rather than simply reconciling some of the linguistic differences, as they did.[18] But the pressure of time and the fact that some of the major issues were left until the last two days resulted in problems of interpretation of the Statute.[19]

Another result of the informal process of negotiation is that there are only limited written records of the conference.[20] Further, some of the provisions result from the negotiations during the Preparatory Committee in New York, rather than during the conference. Except for those few provisions which follow the draft prepared by the International Law Commission, therefore, the history of which is to be found in the formal conference records, there is a marked absence of the *travaux préparatoires* which are usually to be expected in the drafting of a major treaty and which may be relied upon as a supplementary means of

---

[14] UN Doc. A/CONF.183/C.1/L.94 and UN Doc. A/CONF.183/C.1/L.95.

[15] UN Doc. A/CONF.183/C.1/L.70 and UN Doc. A/CONF.183/C.1/L.90.

[16] This procedural device was a means of allowing delegations to vote against putting the amendments to the vote, an easier step for many to take than voting against the amendments themselves.

[17] The votes were not officially recorded, but China, Israel and the United States announced that they had been among those who voted against.

[18] Even the linguistic differences could not all be resolved at the conference, and the final text of the Statute had to undergo a large number of more or less technical corrections after it had been signed by a number of States. The official text – in all languages – is slightly different from the one voted on at the conference.

[19] See Shabtai Rosenne, 'Poor Drafting and Imperfect Organization: Flaws to Overcome in the Rome Statute' (2000) 41 *Virginia Journal of International Law* 164, which addresses the discrepancy between the wording of Arts. 9 and 21 with regard to the weight to be attached by the Court to the Elements of Crimes.

[20] For the official records, see UN Doc. A/CONF.183/13 (Vols. I to III).

interpreting a treaty.[21] The reasoning behind most of the texts which emerged from New York and from Rome is not to be found in the record of the views of delegates who argued for them or in an examination of the written proposals for amendments. The lack of standard *travaux préparatoires* means that those seeking help with the meaning of a difficult or controversial provision of the Statute will have to place more reliance than would normally be the case on written commentaries and books about the ICC;[22] if these record the recollections of the negotiators at the conference, they are the nearest things to *travaux* that we have, although they cannot always be relied upon to be neutral.

8.2.2   Preparations for the Court

The closing session of the Rome Conference adopted both the text of the Statute and a number of resolutions, one of which set up a Preparatory Commission to prepare the subsidiary documents necessary for the establishment of the Court.

Sixty States were required to become parties to the Statute before it came into force. The pace of ratifications was quicker than expected, and the Statute came into force on 1 July 2002, bringing the Court formally into existence. The Assembly of States Parties, created by the Statute to oversee the administration of the Court, then met and adopted the Elements of Crimes, the Rules of Procedure and Evidence and the Agreement on the Privileges and Immunities of the Court,[23] all of which had been negotiated by the Preparatory Commission.

8.3   Structure and composition of the ICC

The judges of the Court are divided into Pre-Trial, Trial and Appeals Chambers; the inclusion of a Pre-Trial Chamber is a compromise between the common law prosecutorial system and the French system of *juges d'instruction*, providing a contrast with the largely common law character of the pre-trial stage at the ad hoc Tribunals.[24] The Presidency, composed of the President and two Vice-Presidents and elected by the judges from among their number, is responsible for the administration of the Court, while the Registry provides the 'non-judicial aspects' of administration.[25] The Registry is also responsible for the Victims and Witnesses Unit, which provides, in consultation with the Office of the Prosecutor, measures of protection and security; as well as for the Office of Public Counsel for the Defence and Office of Public Counsel for Victims.[26] The Office of the Prosecutor is an integral part of the Court; care needs to be taken in referring to the 'Court' when only the judicial arm is intended. The inclusion of the prosecution in the Court

---

[21] See Arts. 31 and 32 of the Vienna Convention on the Law of Treaties.

[22] The two most comprehensive of those written immediately after the conference are R. S. Lee, *The International Criminal Court: The Making of the Rome Statute* (The Hague, 1999) and Triffterer, *Observers' Notes*.

[23] The Rules of Procedure and Evidence have since been amended by the Assembly of States Parties. The documents may all be found on the website of the ICC at www.icc-cpi.int.

[24] See Chapter 17 for a description of the procedures of the Court.

[25] The composition and administration of the Court are dealt with in Part 4 of the Statute.

[26] Art. 43(6) of the Statute, and rr. 16–19 of the RPE; regs. 77 and 81 of the ICC Regulations.

structure, but not the defence, can be argued to create an imbalance between the parties and gives rise to administrative difficulties owing to the need to ensure the independence of the Office of the Prosecutor.

In recognition of the importance for the success of the Court in having judges of the highest possible calibre, the Statute sets out detailed provisions for the qualifications of candidates for the judiciary. Article 36(3) requires candidates to have competence in criminal law or in relevant areas of international law. This requirement for professional qualifications is combined with a duty for States selecting the judges to 'take into account' the need for representation of the principal legal systems of the world, equitable geographical representation and, for the first time in criteria for the composition of an international tribunal, the need for a fair representation of female and male judges.[27] The complex voting rules agreed upon for the election of the eighteen judges of the Court[28] by the Assembly of States Parties takes into account all of these criteria except for the representation of the world's legal systems (an exclusion justified on the basis that this criterion would largely be met if geographical representation were equitable). The Assembly has also established an advisory committee on nominations of judges,[29] which is intended to facilitate the election of the best qualified judges.

8.4   Crimes within the jurisdiction of the ICC

The Court has jurisdiction over 'the most serious crimes of international concern': genocide, crimes against humanity, war crimes and aggression (Article 5(1)); the Court cannot, however, exercise jurisdiction over the crime of aggression until the amendments to the Statute adopted in 2010 have come into force. Unlike the Statutes of the two ad hoc Tribunals, the ICC Statute goes into some detail in defining the crimes subject to its jurisdiction. The definitions are to be 'strictly construed and shall not be extended by analogy' (Article 22(2)), no doubt indicating a concern to avoid too much judicial creativity. The definitions must be read with the general principles of liability and defences in Part 3 of the Statute (see Chapter 15 and 16) and are further elaborated in the Elements of Crimes which are to be used by the Court in the interpretation and application of the provisions on offences (Articles 9 and 21).[30]

The oft-stated aim of the process of definition was to codify existing customary law for the purpose of the new Court and the definitions of the crimes are therefore by and large conservative. But, in crystallizing and clarifying those provisions which had not been previously expressed as written criminal law, the process inevitably moved the law along.[31] There are provisions which arguably go beyond a mere codification of existing law as it

---

[27] Art. 36(8) of the ICC Statute.
[28] ICC-ASP/3/Res.6, as amended by ICC-ASP/5/Res.5. A list of the judges currently on the Court, as well as those chosen in past elections, may be found on the website of the ICC at www.icc-cpi.int.
[29] See ICC-ASP/10/Res.5, as provided for in Art. 36(4)(c) of the ICC Statute.   [30] See section 8.5 below.
[31] For discussion of the process, see Leila Sadat, *The International Criminal Court and the Transformation of International Law* (New York, 2002) 12,261–74; Darryl Robinson, 'Crimes against Humanity: Reflections on State Sovereignty, Legal Precision and the Dictates of the Public Conscience' in Flavia Lattanzi and William Schabas (eds.), *Essays on the Rome Statute of the International Criminal Court* (Il Sirente, 1999) Vol. I, 140–4.

stood in 1998,[32] but some of them have since been referred to as customary law in the jurisprudence.[33] The ICC Statute has thus contributed to the development of customary law.

On the other hand, there are provisions which are arguably not as extensive as customary law allows.[34] Article 10 attempts to address this point by providing that the Statute does not limit or prejudice existing or developing rules of international law 'for purposes other than this Statute'. This both mitigates the concern that the Statute will in some way freeze the development of customary international law and confirms that so far as the Court is concerned it must apply the provisions in the Statute even if customary law creates wider offences.

The status of the ICC Statute is perhaps best described by an ICTY Trial Chamber in the *Furundžija* case:

> In many areas the Statute may be regarded as indicative of the legal views, i.e. *opinio juris* of a great number of States. Notwithstanding article 10 of the Statute, the purpose of which is to ensure that existing or developing law is not 'limited' or 'prejudiced' by the Statute's provisions, resort may be had *cum grano salis* to these provisions to help elucidate customary international law. Depending on the matter at issue, the Rome Statute may be taken to restate, reflect or clarify customary rules or crystallise them, whereas in some areas it creates new law or modifies existing law. At any event, the Rome Statute by and large may be taken as constituting an authoritative expression of the legal views of a great number of States.[35]

The offences are further discussed in Chapters 10 to 13 of this book.

8.4.1   Other crimes

During the negotiations for the ICC Statute, proposals were made for other crimes to be added to the list but they were unsuccessful.[36] Crimes may be added to the Statute by amendments adopted in accordance with Article 121.[37] States Parties, however, do not

---

[32] E.g. the provision on child soldiers: see Herman von Hebel and Darryl Robinson, 'Crimes within the Jurisdiction of the Court' in Lee, *The Making of the Rome Statute*, 117–18.

[33] E.g. the Special Court for Sierra Leone decided that recruitment of child soldiers was a crime in customary law (*Norman*, SCSL A. Ch., 13 March 2004, paras. 30–53); but see Justice Robertson's view that, 'until the Rome Treaty itself, the rule against child recruitment was a human rights principle and an obligation upon States, but did not entail individual criminal liability in international law. It did so for the first time when the Treaty was concluded and approved on 17th July 1998' (Dissenting Opinion at para. 38).

[34] E.g. the commentary to Rule 156 in Henckaerts and Doswald-Beck, *ICRC Customary Law*, 586, maintains that a list of war crimes not mentioned in the ICC Statute forms part of customary international law. In addition, there is no crime regarding the use of biological or chemical weapons in the Statute, not because there were strong views against regarding this as customary law but because there was no agreement for the inclusion of nuclear weapons (see von Hebel and Robinson, 'Crimes within the Jurisdiction', 113–16).

[35] *Furundžija*, ICTY T. Ch. II, 10 December 1998, para. 227, supported in *Tadić*, ICTY A. Ch., 15 July 1999, para. 223, although Judge Shahabuddeen reserved his position on the matter (Separate Opinion of Judge Shahabuddeen, para. 3). See also *Kupreškić et al.*, where the Trial Chamber said that, 'although the Statute of the ICC may be indicative of the *opinio juris* of many States, Article 7(1)(h) is not consonant with customary international law' (ICTY T. Ch. II, 14 January 2000, para. 580); and *Hadžihasanović et al.*, where the Appeals Chamber considered that the fact that the Rome Conference voted for Art. 28, though not legally conclusive of the matter, at least cast doubt on views opposing the law contained in that text, and that the fact that 'the Rome Statute embodied a number of compromises among the States parties that drafted and adopted it hardly undermines its significance. The same is true of most major multilateral conventions' (ICTY A. Ch., 16 July 2003, para. 53).

[36] Proposals included terrorist offences and drugs offences. See Patrick Robinson, 'The Missing Crimes' in Cassese, *Commentary*, 497.

[37] A Working Group on Amendments has been established by the Assembly of States Parties to consider any proposals for amendments before they are formally submitted. For the difficulties in the use of the amendment procedure for the addition of the amendments on aggression, see Chapter 13.

have to accept the jurisdiction of the Court for any additional crimes in relation to their own nationals or crimes committed on their own territory if they do not wish to do so (Article 121(5)). At the Kampala Review Conference in 2010, some new war crimes in non-international armed conflict were added at the same time as the new provisions on the crime of aggression.

8.5   Applicable law[38]

Article 21 requires the Court to apply 'in the first place' the Statute, the Elements of Crimes and its Rules of Procedure and Evidence. As regards the Elements, the wording of Article 9 (Elements 'shall assist' the Court) appears to conflict with a requirement to *apply* them, but the Court has not had difficulty in reconciling these provisions. The Pre-Trial Chamber in the *Al Bashir* arrest warrant case has found that 'the Elements of Crimes and the Rules must be applied unless the competent Chamber finds an irreconcilable contradiction between these documents on the one hand, and the Statute on the other hand'. The Chamber found that a fully discretionary power to apply the Elements would be inconsistent with the principle of *nullum crimen sine lege* and on that basis went on to apply a controversial part of the Elements on genocide.[39]

The Court is also required to apply 'in the second place' treaties and principles and rules of international law, and, 'failing that', general principles of law, including national laws consistent with the Statute and with internationally recognized norms and standards. The Court has indicated that these other sources of law 'can only be resorted to when the following two conditions are met: (i) there is a lacuna in the written law contained in the Statute, the Elements of Crimes and the Rules; and (ii) such lacuna cannot be filled by the application of the criteria of interpretation provided in articles 31 and 32 of the Vienna Convention on the Law of Treaties and article 21(3) of the Statute'.[40] The sources of law are further discussed in Chapter 17.

Article 21(2) authorizes (but does not compel) the Court to apply principles and rules of law established in its previous decisions, and Article 21(3) requires the Court to apply and interpret applicable law consistent with 'internationally recognized human rights' and without discrimination on a number of enumerated grounds.

---

[38] See further Gilbert Bitti, 'Article 21 of the Statute of the International Criminal Court and the Treatment of Sources of Law in the Jurisprudence of the ICC' in Carsten Stahn and Göran Sluiter (eds.) *The Emerging Practice of the International Criminal Court* (Leiden, 2009).

[39] *Al Bashir*, ICC PTC I, 4 March 2009, paras. 128–32. But see the Separate and Partially Dissenting Judgment of Judge Ušacka, who seemed to prefer the view that the Elements are not binding on the Court; whether or not they are, she considered that the contextual element for genocide was met, so that the element's consistency with the definition of genocide did not have to be decided (paras. 16–20). For discussion of the majority view, see Robert Cryer, 'The Definitions of International Crimes in the Al Bashir Arrest Warrant Decision' (2009) 7 *Journal of International Criminal Justice* 283; and Claus Kreß, 'The Crime of Genocide and Contextual Elements' (2009) 7 *Journal of International Criminal Justice* 297. For the background to the wording of the different Statute provisions regarding the Elements, see Herman von Hebel, 'The Making of the Elements of Crimes' in Lee, *Elements and Rules*, 7–8.

[40] *Al Bashir*, ICC PTC I, 4 March 2009, para. 44.

8.6   Complementarity and other grounds of inadmissibility

8.6.1   *The complementarity principle*

The ICC is intended to be a court of last resort, supplementing not supplanting national jurisdictions; the Preamble to the ICC Statute recognizes that every State has a responsibility to exercise its own criminal jurisdiction over international crimes.[41] The first Article of the Statute describes the Court as being 'complementary' to national criminal jurisdictions. The principle of complementarity is based not only on respect for the primary jurisdiction of States but also on practical considerations of efficiency and effectiveness, since States will generally have the best access to evidence and witnesses and the resources to carry out proceedings. An international court is only one way to enforce international criminal law and it may not in every instance be the best one.[42]

The concept of complementarity originated in the ILC draft but was substantially remodelled during the negotiations. It was crucial for the success of the negotiations that the complementarity principle be settled at an early stage; before they could agree to support the establishment of a new international court, States which were content with their own administration of justice had to be satisfied that the new court would not be able to take over cases which were being dealt with perfectly well at home. The provision which is now Article 17 was therefore substantially agreed before the Rome Conference even began.

A case will be inadmissible, and the Court will not be able to exercise its jurisdiction, if a national authority is investigating or prosecuting the case or has already done so, unless the circumstances indicate that the State is nevertheless unwilling or unable to carry out proceedings genuinely. There is therefore a 'two-step test' in considering the issue of complementarity: (i) whether there is an ongoing investigation or prosecution of the case at the national level; and, if so, (ii) whether the State is unwilling or unable genuinely to carry out that investigation or prosecution.[43]

8.6.2   *First step: are there proceedings at the national level?*

A case is only inadmissible on the ground of complementarity if it is being investigated or prosecuted or it has been investigated by a State with jurisdiction over it (Article 17(1)(a) and (b)). Article 17(1)(c) contemplates the further possibility that both an investigation and a trial have been completed, in which case the principle of *ne bis in idem* governs the situation (see section 8.6.6). Where no State has taken any action in relation to the case, none of these criteria for inadmissibility is met, and thus a claim to inadmissibility on the ground of complementarity must fail. It is only where national authorities are engaged or

[41] Para. 6 of the Preamble.
[42] For discussion of the relative merits of international and national trials, see sections 2.3.4 and 2.4.
[43] *Katanga and Ngudjolo Chui*, ICC A. Ch., 25 September 2009, paras. 1 and 75–9.

have been engaged in apparent exercise of their own jurisdiction that the exceptions of 'unwillingness' or 'inability' may be considered.[44]

The two-step test is applicable regardless of what 'trigger mechanism' is employed, including the instances where a State refers a situation in its own territory to the Court.[45] In *Katanga and Ngudjolo Chui* the DRC stated that it did not intend to investigate the charges against the defendant, which simplified the admissibility proceedings before the Court.[46] Following the issue of a warrant of arrest against Mr Bemba Gombo in the Central African Republic situation, which had been referred to the ICC by the government, an admissibility challenge was lodged by Mr Bemba on the ground that there had been an effective national investigation, followed by domestic proceedings; the challenge was rejected on the ground that the proceedings had been discontinued by the Cour de Cassation. (While recognizing that it was strictly unnecessary, the Pre-Trial Chamber went on to apply also the second limb of the complementarity test, holding that the national courts were unable to pursue the proceedings; among other things the budget of the Ministry of Justice was described as 'ridiculously insignificant'.)[47] The requirement of national proceedings in relation to the 'case' raises the question of how broadly 'case' is to be interpreted. Questions of admissibility have to be considered at different stages: before the Prosecutor opens an investigation and before she chooses a case to prosecute. At the stage of initiating an investigation, the Prosecutor may not have identified specific 'cases' and thus the assessment of inadmissibility will necessarily have a less specific focus. Accordingly, admissibility is assessed by looking at the set of likely cases for ICC prosecution.[48] Once the Prosecutor seeks an arrest warrant, she has identified a specific 'case', and thus the test can be applied more specifically. The ICC has held that, for a national proceeding to concern the same 'case', the 'national investigations must cover the same individual and substantially the same conduct as alleged in the proceedings before the Court'.[49] In *Lubanga*, for example, the ICC's first arrested suspect had been detained in the Democratic Republic of the Congo before transfer and had been (formally) charged with other crimes. The Pre-Trial Chamber laid down the same person/same conduct test, now part of the Court's settled jurisprudence, and held that the DRC was not acting in relation to the specific charge before the Court (conscription of children) and thus that it was not proceeding in relation to the 'case'; hence the case was admissible before the Court.[50]

---

[44] *Ibid.*, paras. 1 and 74–9. The ruling of the Appeals Chamber has put to rest a contrary argument that the Court must in every case establish whether the unwillingness or inability criteria are met, whether or not there are or have been national proceedings; see e.g. Mahnoush Arsanjani and Michael Reisman, 'The Law-in-Action of the International Criminal Court' (2005) 99 *American Journal of International Law* 385, 395–7.

[45] See the discussion of 'self-referrals' at section 8.7.4.

[46] *Katanga and Ngudjolo Chui*, ICC T. Ch. II, 16 June 2009, para. 95; and ICC A. Ch., 25 September 2009. See William Burke-White, 'Complementarity in Practice: The International Criminal Court as Part of a System of Multi-Level Global Governance in the Democratic Republic of the Congo' (2005) 18 *Leiden Journal of International Law* 557, 567–8.

[47] *Bemba Gombo*, ICC T. Ch. III, 24 June 2010, paras. 21 and 245.

[48] *Situation in the Republic of Kenya*, ICC PTC II, 31 March 2010, paras. 50, 182 and 188.

[49] *Ruto et al.*, ICC A. Ch., 30 August 2011, para. 1.

[50] *Lubanga*, ICC PTC I, 10 February 2006, paras. 31–9. Pre-Trial Chambers have made admissibility determinations on their own motion in the course of their decisions to issue arrest warrants under Art. 58(1), but it has since been held by the Appeals Chamber that, for the issue of a warrant of arrest, an admissibility assessment is not a requirement and it will be only in appropriate instances that a Pre-Trial Chamber should exercise its discretion to address admissibility at that stage of the proceedings: *Situation in the DRC*, ICC A. Ch., 13 July 2006, paras. 42–53.

The 'same conduct' test has been criticized as requiring a State to divine exactly what case the ICC will bring if the State wishes to challenge admissibility. The Appeals Chamber expressed the test more flexibly in the *Situation in Kenya*, referring to 'substantially' the same conduct.[51] The Pre-Trial Chamber in the *Gaddafi* case also adopted a more flexible approach; the Chamber did not require that the national proceedings concern the same incidents but rather the same gravamen or essence of the crime.[52]

Of course, a State may wish to pursue an accused for a case other than the one contemplated by the ICC. Part 9 of the Statute allows the State and the Court to consult as to the sequencing of their respective cases.[53] Article 17 addresses competing proceedings concerning the same 'case'. If national proceedings relate only to 'ordinary crimes', that alone is not determinative of an admissibility challenge. If the proceedings cover the same conduct as the subject of the ICC proceedings, that will be sufficient.[54]

Another question that arises is whether *any* State with jurisdiction may bring proceedings and thus oust the jurisdiction of the ICC. Many States take wide or universal jurisdiction over the Statute crimes. The Statute does not prioritize between bases of jurisdiction. It is enough to render a case inadmissible if any State 'with jurisdiction' takes criminal proceedings, whatever the basis for jurisdiction may be. There has not, however, been any indication that States are disposed to exercise universal jurisdiction rather than allowing the ICC to take proceedings.

8.6.3   *Second step: unwillingness or inability to carry out proceedings genuinely*

Article 17(1) renders a case inadmissible before the ICC if a State is investigating or prosecuting the case, *unless* the Prosecutor can show that the State is in reality 'unwilling' or 'unable' to carry out the ostensible proceedings genuinely. The term 'genuinely' was chosen in preference to other terms, such as 'effectively': the latter could have given the impression that a case would be admissible if the national system was, for example, proceeding more slowly (less effectively) than the ICC would or if the ICC could do a better job.[55] Where national efforts are underway, the case will be admissible only where those efforts cannot be considered genuine. It is for the Court itself to decide whether these conditions are met, not the national authorities.[56]

In determining whether a case is inadmissible by reason of 'unwillingness', the Court must consider whether one of the following factors exists:

---

[51] *Muthaura et al.*, ICC A. Ch., 30 August 2011, para. 76. For further discussion of the 'same' (or substantially the same) conduct, see Rod Rastan, 'Situations and Cases: Defining the Parameters' in Carsten Stahn and Mohamed El Zeidy (eds.), *The International Criminal Court and Complementarity* (Cambridge, 2011) 421–58; Sarah Nouwen, 'Fine-Tuning Complementarity' in Brown, *Research Handbook*, 206–31.

[52] *Gaddafi and Al-Senussi*, ICC PTC I, 31 May 2013, paras. 73–83. See also on this point the Prosecutor's response to Libya's appeal (ICC-01/11-01/11-384, 22 July 2013, paras. 45 *et seq.*).

[53] Arts. 89(4), 94(1) and 97 of the ICC Statute.   [54] *Gaddafi and Al-Senussi*, ICC PTC I, 31 May 2013, para. 88.

[55] John Holmes, 'Complementarity: National Courts versus the ICC' in Cassese, *Commentary*, 674.

[56] At the Rome Conference, an alternative approach was suggested by the representative of Mexico who proposed a text which read: 'The court has no jurisdiction where the case in question is being investigated or prosecuted, or has been prosecuted, by a State which has jurisdiction over it' (Vol. III of the Official Records of the Conference at p. 28).

(a) The proceedings were or are being undertaken or the national decision was made for the purpose of shielding the person concerned from criminal responsibility for crimes within the jurisdiction of the court referred to in Article 5;

(b) There has been an unjustified delay in the proceedings which in the circumstances is inconsistent with an intent to bring the person concerned to justice;

(c) The proceedings were not or are not being conducted independently or impartially, and they were or are being conducted in a manner which, in the circumstances, is inconsistent with an intent to bring the person concerned to justice.[57]

The first criterion gives the Court the difficult task of assessing the motives of the national authorities (whether judicial, executive or legislative); the second two more clearly allow inferences to be drawn from objective factors.[58] All the criteria are based on procedural and institutional factors, not the substantive outcome of a case or an investigation. A case will not be admissible by reason only of the closure of the investigation or an acquittal of an apparently guilty accused. In taking its decisions on the complementarity principle, the Court is to have regard to the principles of due process recognized by international law, and may have before it information submitted by a State showing that its courts meet internationally recognized standards for the prosecution of similar conduct.[59]

Arguments have been made that the Court is thus given a general role in monitoring the human rights standards of domestic authorities.[60] The better view is that delay and lack of independence are relevant in so far as either of them indicates an intention to shield the person concerned from justice, but as a general rule fair trial rights under national law are not part of the Court's assessment of admissibility; this is not a human rights court.[61] In an extreme case, however, the lack of a fair trial may mean that there is effectively no trial at all, and if the lack of human rights protections impedes the ability of national courts to undertake domestic proceedings in a situation where the judicial system is 'unavailable' within the meaning of Article 17(3), that may be a factor showing the inability of the State and thus the admissibility of the case.[62]

The assessment of inability may be easier than that of unwillingness, since the concept depends upon objective criteria which do not demand that motives be inferred. Article 17(3) reads:

---

[57] Art. 17(2).

[58] For differing views as to whether the criteria are or are not exhaustive, see Markus Benzing, 'The Complementarity Regime of the International Criminal Court: International Criminal Justice between State Sovereignty and the Fight against Impunity' (2003) 7 *Max Planck Yearbook of United Nations Law* 591, 606; Holmes, 'Complementarity: National Courts', 675; and Darryl Robinson, 'Serving the Interests of Justice: Amnesties, Truth Commissions and the International Criminal Court' (2003) 14 *European Journal of International Law* 481, 500.

[59] Rule 51 of the ICC RPE.

[60] See e.g. Federica Gioia, 'State Sovereignty, Jurisdiction and "Modern" International Law: The Principle of Complementarity in the International Criminal Court' (2006) 19 *Leiden Journal of International Law* 1095, 1110–13. Arguments that lack of fair trial rendered the case admissible were presented by the defence in *Gaddafi*, but the Pre-Trial Chamber did not rule upon them since it was not necessary for its decision; see section 8.6.4.

[61] For the extent to which the Court may take into account the fairness of the national proceedings, see Enrique Rojo, 'The Role of Fair Trial Considerations in the Complementarity Regime of the International Criminal Court: From "No Peace without Justice" to "No Peace with Victor's Justice"?' (2005) 18 *Leiden Journal of International Law* 829; Benzing, 'The Complementarity Regime of the International Criminal Court', 606–7; Frédéric Mégret and Marika Giles Samson, 'Holding the Line on Complementarity in Libya: The Case for Tolerating Flawed Domestic Trials' (2013) 11 *Journal of International Criminal Justice* 57; and Kevin Jon Heller, 'The Shadow Side of Complementarity: The Effect of Article 17 of the Rome Statute on National Due Process' (2006) 17 *Criminal Law Forum* 255.

[62] See *Gaddafi and Al-Senussi*, ICC PTC I, 3 May 2013, paras. 212–15.

In order to determine inability in a particular case, the Court shall consider whether, due to a total or substantial collapse or unavailability of its national judicial system, the State is unable to obtain the accused or the necessary evidence and testimony or otherwise unable to carry out its proceedings.

The last three criteria (inability to obtain the accused or the evidence and testimony, or other inability to carry out the proceedings) must result from the collapse or unavailability of the legal system, not from any other factor (such as absence of an extradition agreement resulting in difficulties in obtaining the presence of the accused). Absence of the necessary legislation to enable prosecution may give rise to 'inability' in the sense of Article 17(3).

8.6.4   Two cases

These principles are illustrated in two of the more recent admissibility challenges launched under Article 19 by the States in which the alleged crimes were committed, Kenya and Libya.

Six warrants of arrest were issued by the ICC in the *Situation in Kenya* as a result of inter-communal violence occurring in Kenya after the elections in 2007/8. In launching a challenge to admissibility on the ground that national proceedings were ongoing, the government of Kenya asserted that it could not be right that, for a case to be inadmissible, the persons being investigated by the Prosecutor must always be exactly the same as those being investigated by the State; this was particularly so where, as here, the State did not hold the same evidence as the Prosecutor, since the Prosecutor had not disclosed his evidence to Kenya in case the latter was involved in witness intimidation. Kenya also claimed that the national authorities were anyway pursuing investigations against the named suspects. The Appeals Chamber ruled that after arrest warrants had been issued, national investigations must indeed 'cover the same individual and substantially the same conduct as alleged in the proceedings before the Court'.[63] As to whether the national proceedings were actually being pursued, the Pre-Trial Chamber did not regard as sufficient the fact that the Kenyan authorities opened police files on the suspects after the ICC warrants were issued. The Chamber required proof that Kenya was taking specific steps to investigate the suspects. The Appeals Chamber confirmed that the term 'being investigated' requires that a State take concrete steps, and that a State must show that it is indeed investigating the case, and not simply providing general assurances that it is prepared to investigate in future.[64]

In the case of *Gaddafi*, a warrant of arrest was issued against a son of Colonel Gaddafi for crimes against humanity of murder and persecution allegedly committed during the revolution in Libya in February 2011. The government of post-revolution Libya challenged the admissibility of the case on the ground that its authorities were actively investigating Mr Gaddafi for multiple acts of murder and persecution, which amounted to crimes against humanity. Libya also argued that, in its transition to democracy, the Court should be prepared to afford Libya more time to develop its judicial system and improve its security situation, so as to allow it to

[63] *Ruto et al.*, ICC A. Ch., 30 August 2011, paras. 1, 41; and *Muthaura et al.*, ICC A. Ch., 30 August 2011, paras. 1, 40.
[64] *Muthaura et al.*, ICC A. Ch., 30 August 2011, paras. 1, 2, 40.

mount its own proceedings. The Pre-Trial Chamber considered a great deal of evidence submitted to it by the Libyan authorities but held that, although national investigative steps had been taken 'with respect to certain discrete aspects that arguably relate to the conduct' covered by the ICC proceedings, 'the actual contours of the national case' were not such that 'the scope of the domestic investigation could be said to cover the same case' as that set out in the ICC warrant of arrest.[65] Having given the authorities three opportunities to submit evidence regarding national proceedings, the Chamber did not consider that there was any need to delay further its decision that there were no ongoing national proceedings for the purpose of complementarity. The Chamber could have stopped there, but went on to hold that in any event Libya was *unable* to carry out national proceedings because its judicial system was 'unavailable' within the meaning of Article 17(3) of the Statute. This unavailability led to lack of capacity to obtain the necessary evidence due to the inability of judicial and governmental authorities to provide adequate witness protection, inability to appoint defence counsel (national lawyers were intimidated from acting) and inability to secure the transfer of the suspect from the Zintan militia into State custody.[66]

In finding the case admissible, the Chamber made some important rulings. It did not regard the absence of Libyan legislation specifically incorporating 'international crimes' as a decisive factor. In basing part of its decision on 'inability', the Chamber ruled that the Libyan 'system cannot yet be applied in full in areas or aspects relevant to the case', and it was this unavailability of the system that led to the inability to carry out proceedings.[67] And, while the Chamber did not find it necessary to address the defence argument that the case was admissible because Gaddafi would not get a fair trial in Libya, it held that the difficulty of finding a local lawyer was an impediment to national proceedings (and was therefore part of the 'inability' finding) since it stopped the trial proceeding in accordance with the rights and protections afforded by the Libyan system.

8.6.5   *Amnesties and truth and reconciliation commissions*

The Statute does not address the relationship between the jurisdiction of the Court and non-judicial approaches to past atrocities, such as amnesties and truth and reconciliation commissions.[68] If a State emerging from a bitter internal conflict decides to grant amnesties, would these amnesties preclude the Court from taking jurisdiction? Should they? The Rome Conference did not consider itself able to deal with the issue explicitly[69] and the issue will therefore be left to the application of the admissibility provisions and the powers of the Prosecutor and Chambers.[70]

---

[65] *Gaddafi and Al-Senussi*, ICC PTC I, 31 May 2013, paras. 134, 135.   [66] *Ibid.*, paras. 204–15.   [67] *Ibid.*, para. 205.
[68] Amnesties and truth and reconciliation commissions generally are dealt with in sections 22.2 and 22.3.
[69] Questions of amnesties and pardons were addressed at Art. 19 and footnote 47 in the draft Statute submitted to the conference (Vol. III, p. 27, of the Official Records; the brief recorded discussion in the Committee of the Whole is at Vol. II, pp. 213–21).
[70] See section 22.2.2; and Darryl Robinson, 'Serving the Interests of Justice: Amnesties, Truth Commissions and the International Criminal Court' (2003) 14 *European Journal of International Law* 481; Michael Scharf, 'The Amnesty Exception to the Jurisdiction of the International Criminal Court' (1999) 32 *Cornell International Law Journal* 507; Jessica Gavron, 'Amnesties

At first sight, a case involving a crime covered by an amnesty would clearly be admissible before the Court in that there would have been no national investigation or prosecution or, if there had been, it would have been 'for the purpose of shielding the person concerned from criminal responsibility'.[71] It has been argued, however, that, if amnesties are accompanied by some form of inquiry (as with the South African Truth and Reconciliation Commission), that could constitute an investigation sufficient to render the case inadmissible before the Court.[72] The counterview is that the wording of Article 17(2)(a) and (c) makes clear that the investigation must be for the purpose of bringing the person concerned to justice. It would only be if the term 'justice' could be interpreted so as to include forms of justice alternative to criminal justice that such a case might be inadmissible;[73] in view of the reference to 'national judicial system' in Article 17(3) and the wording of the fourth and sixth preambular paragraphs of the Statute, such an interpretation would seem unlikely.[74]

The Prosecutor may, however, decide, having regard to a particular amnesty, that there would be 'substantial reasons to believe that an investigation would not serve the interests of justice', taking into account 'the gravity of the crime and the interests of victims'.[75] But, if a decision not to initiate an investigation is taken solely on the ground that it would be against the interests of justice, the Prosecutor must inform the Pre-Trial Chamber, which may decide to review the decision.[76]

8.6.6   Other grounds for inadmissibility

Ne bis in idem

The principle of *ne bis in idem*[77] protects a person from being tried before the ICC for conduct which has already been tried by the Court itself or by other courts in previous proceedings.[78] The exceptions to the principle with regard to proceedings in other courts are in very similar terms to two of the criteria for 'unwillingness' in Article 17(2). A case will be admissible therefore if the purpose of the completed proceedings was to shield the person from criminal responsibility or they were otherwise not independent and were inconsistent

in the Light of Developments in International Law and the Establishment of the International Criminal Court' (2002) 51 *International and Comparative Law Quarterly* 91; Anja Seibert-Fohr, 'The Relevance of the Rome Statute of the International Criminal Court for Amnesties and Truth Commissions' (2003) 7 *Max Planck Yearbook of United Nations Law* 553.

[71] The power to 'overturn' amnesties has been criticized by some as interfering in democratic decision-making: John Bolton, 'The Risks and Weaknesses of the International Criminal Court from America's Perspective' (2000–1) 41 *Virginia Journal of International Law* 199–200.

[72] Seibert-Fohr, 'The Relevance of the Rome Statute', 569; Robinson, 'Serving the Interests of Justice', 500.

[73] Carsten Stahn, 'Complementarity, Amnesties and Alternative Forms of Justice: Some Interpretative Guidelines for the International Criminal Court' (2005) 3 *Journal of International Criminal Justice* 695, 716.

[74] See, however, the declaration made on ratification of the Statute by Colombia, which expresses the view of that State that none of the Statute's provisions prevent Colombia from granting amnesties, reprieves or judicial pardons for political crimes if they are in conformity with the Colombian constitution and with international law principles accepted by Colombia (5 August 2002). Since reservations are not permitted by the Statute, that declaration may have to be assessed in accordance with the provisions of the Statute.

[75] Art. 53(1)(c) of the ICC Statute; and note that Art. 53(2)(c) relating to the initiation of a prosecution is in similar but not identical terms; see further Chapter 17. See Stahn, 'Complementarity, Amnesties', 718, for the view that Art. 53 does not allow the Prosecutor the scope to weigh the interests of national reconciliation against the interests of individual accountability, since the concept of interests of justice under that Article is linked to individual and case-related considerations. The former Prosecutor, in his *Policy Paper on the Interests of Justice*, has stated that 'the broader matter of international peace and security is not the responsibility of the Prosecutor; it falls within the mandate of other institutions'. September 2007, p. 9.

[76] Art. 53(1) and (3)(b) of the ICC Statute.   [77] See section 4.7.   [78] Arts. 17(1)(c) and 20(1) and (3) of the ICC Statute.

with an intent to bring the person to justice.[79] A difficulty arises with regard to the grant of pardons for purely political reasons, akin to the grant of an amnesty. If such a pardon follows apparently genuine proceedings, the case would not appear to be admissible before the Court, unless an inference can be drawn from all the circumstances that the original proceedings in fact came within the exceptions just mentioned.[80]

'Not of sufficient gravity'

A final ground for inadmissibility is that a case 'is not of sufficient gravity to justify further action by the Court'.[81] While all crimes within the Statute are 'grave', Article 17 contemplates an additional threshold of gravity for the selection of situations and cases.

Gravity, like other grounds for inadmissibility, is considered by the Prosecutor at the situation-selection stage as well as at the case-selection stage. The Office of the Prosecutor has stated that it regards factors relevant in assessing gravity as including the scale of the crimes, the nature of the crimes, the manner of their commission and their impact.[82]

So far, all situations in which investigations have been initiated involved hundreds or thousands of the gravest forms of crimes (such as murder or sexual violence). In his letter in response to communications concerning alleged crimes committed in Iraq in the 2003 conflict, the former Prosecutor concluded that in the context of the hundreds and thousands of victims in the other situations he was investigating, '4 to 12 victims of wilful killing and a limited number of victims of inhuman treatment' was not sufficient to initiate an investigation.[83]

Gravity is also considered in the selection of specific cases within a situation. In the Darfur situation, a case was brought concerning war crimes causing the death of 'only' twelve peacekeepers and severe wounding of eight; the Prosecutor's view that the nature, manner and impact of the crimes were critical factors in assessing gravity was approved by the Pre-Trial Chamber in its confirmation decision.[84]

The meaning of the gravity criterion was examined by the Appeals Chamber in the case of *Ntaganda*. The Pre-Trial Chamber had held that three criteria must be met: first, the conduct concerned must be systematic or large scale and the social alarm caused to the community should be taken into account; second, the suspect should be one of the most senior leaders in the situation under investigation; third, regard should be had to the role played by him and the role played by the State or organization in the overall commission of crimes. The Appeals Chamber found that none of these tests was in conformity with the Statute: the first because it blurred the distinction between the jurisdictional requirements for war crimes and crimes against humanity, and the 'social alarm' test had no source in the Statute, the second and third because there was nothing in the Statute to restrict the level of perpetrator.[85] The Appeals Chamber did not produce its own criteria for gravity. It is often noted that the

---

[79] Art. 20(3).   [80] John Holmes, 'The Principle of Complementarity' in Lee, *The Making of the Rome Statute*, 76, 77.
[81] Arts. 17(1)(d) and 53(1)(c).   [82] Office of the Prosecutor, *Report on Prosecutorial Strategy*, 14 September 2006, 5.
[83] Office of the Prosecutor's response to communications received concerning Iraq, 10 February 2006, available on the website of the ICC at www.icc-cpi.int. For criticism of the former Prosecutor's approach to the gravity criterion, see William Schabas, 'Prosecutorial Discretion v. Judicial Activism at the International Criminal Court' (2008) 6 *Journal of International Criminal Justice* 731.
[84] *Abu Garda*, ICC PTC, 8 February 2010, paras. 30–4. However, the Chamber declined to confirm the charges.
[85] *Situation in the DRC*, ICC A. Ch., 13 July 2006, paras. 66–82.

gravity of a case should not be assessed only from a quantitative perspective by a simple consideration of the number of victims.[86]

The stated policy of the Office of the Prosecutor of bringing charges against those bearing the *greatest responsibility* for the crimes within the ICC's jurisdiction[87] is a sensible one in view of the limitations of resources of an international court. Neither the Office of the Prosecutor nor the Appeals Chamber regards it as a *legal* limitation on the power of the Court.[88]

8.6.7   *Challenges to admissibility*

The Statute provides procedures ensuring that all States which can take jurisdiction themselves will hear of the possibility of ICC proceedings at the earliest opportunity. When deciding to initiate an investigation *proprio motu* or after a State Party referral, the Prosecutor is required to notify all States Parties and other States which, 'taking into account the information available, would normally exercise jurisdiction over the crimes concerned'.[89]

The admissibility of a case may be challenged by an accused or a person subject to an arrest warrant,[90] a State with jurisdiction if it is investigating or prosecuting the case itself, and any other State from which acceptance of jurisdiction is required under Article 12.[91] It is not only States Parties to the Statute which have the right to make a challenge; States which are not parties may also do so (but are not under any obligation of cooperation to comply with requests for information and other such matters).[92] The aim of complementarity is to ensure that some judicial system is dealing with a case; so long as the proceedings are being carried out genuinely it does not matter whether they are in a State Party or not.

8.6.8   *The ICC Statute as an incentive for national legislation*

One of the results of the principle of complementarity is that States are encouraged to improve standards of investigations and trials in their own domestic systems. While the assertion that States Parties are *obliged* to introduce the Statute offences into their own law[93] puts too much weight on the effect of preambular paragraph 6 of the Statute, States do have

---

[86] *Abu Garda*, ICC PTC, 8 February 2010, para. 31.
[87] *Paper on Some Policy Issues before the Office of the Prosecutor*, September 2003, 7, on the website of the ICC at www.icc-cpi.int.
[88] See Ignaz Stegmiller, 'The Gravity Threshold under the ICC Statute: Gravity Back and Forth in Lubanga and Ntaganda' (2009) 9 *International Criminal Law Review* 547, which makes a distinction between 'two gravity facets', one legal and one relative (or discretionary).
[89] Art. 18(1) of the ICC Statute. The Article also sets out procedures for the deferral of an ICC investigation if relevant national authorities are exercising jurisdiction, subject to appeal by the Prosecutor to the Pre-Trial Chamber. For the negotiating history and the interpretation of the term 'normally exercise jurisdiction', see Hector Olasolo, *The Triggering Procedure of the International Criminal Court* (Leiden, 2005) 72–5. For further discussion, see section 17.4 below.
[90] E.g. the challenge to admissibility made by Katanga, *Katanga and Ngudjolo Chui*, ICC T. Ch. II, 16 June 2009; see also ICC A. Ch., 25 September 2009.
[91] Art. 19(2) of the ICC Statute; see section 17.4 below.
[92] Unless the non-State Party has accepted the Court's jurisdiction in accordance with Art. 12(3) or has agreed separately to cooperate.
[93] See Kleffner, 'Complementarity in the Rome Statute', Chapter VI; and Payam Akhavan, 'Whither National Courts? Towards an Express and Enforceable Obligation for the National Repression of International Crimes' (2010) 8 *Journal of International Criminal Justice* 1245.

an *interest* in incorporating the offences if they wish to allow their own nationals to be investigated in their home country rather than by the ICC.[94] The admissibility criteria may also have the effect of encouraging improvements in procedural standards. Such national legislation should not be seen as an inappropriate avoidance scheme since national and international jurisdictions may thus together provide the means of bringing offenders to justice. This 'positive complementarity' means that the Office of the Prosecutor 'will encourage genuine national proceedings where possible'.[95] The frequently cited statement of the first Prosecutor of the Court, while arguably exaggerated in its aspiration for an absence of cases for the Court, reflects this view:

The effectiveness of the International Criminal Court should not be measured by the number of cases that reach the Court. On the contrary, the absence of trials by the ICC, as a consequence of the effective functioning of national systems, would be a major success.[96]

8.7 Initiation of proceedings (the 'trigger mechanisms')

There are three means of bringing a matter before the Court:[97] a referral by a State Party, a referral by the Security Council acting under Chapter VII of the UN Charter, and the institution of an investigation by the Prosecutor acting on his own initiative (Article 13). States and the Security Council may only refer a 'situation' to the Court: it is for the Prosecutor, not for political bodies, to determine which specific cases and suspects warrant investigation.

8.7.1 States Parties

Only States which are parties to the Statute may refer situations to the Court. Those which are not may seek a referral by the Security Council if the situation threatens international peace and security, or may pass information to the Prosecutor in the hope that the Prosecutor will begin an investigation on his own motion.

Some of the first parties to the Statute were States on whose territories large-scale atrocities were being committed. Four referrals to the Court have been made by States Parties in relation to situations on their own territories – Uganda, the Democratic Republic of the Congo, the Central African Republic and Mali.[98] One referral has been made in relation to an incident occurring on a ship registered in a State Party: Comoros referred to the Court the situation arising in May 2010 regarding a flotilla of ships bound for Gaza with humanitarian aid.[99]

---

[94] See section 4.4.2.   [95] *Prosecutorial Strategy 2009–2012*, 1 February 2010, 17.
[96] *Paper on Some Policy Issues before the Office of the Prosecutor*, September 2003, 4, on the website of the ICC at www.icc-cpi.int.
[97] For the negotiations at the conference: on referral by States, see Philippe Kirsch and Darryl Robinson, 'Referral by States Parties' in Cassese, *Commentary*, 619; on the Prosecutor's authority, see Silvia Fernández de Gurmendi, 'The Role of the International Prosecutor' in Lee, *The Making of the Rome Statute*, 175; and Morten Bergsmo and Jelena Pejic, 'Article 15: Prosecutor' in Triffterer, *Observers' Notes*, 581; on referral by the Security Council, see Lionel Yee, 'The International Criminal Court and the Security Council: Articles 13(b) and 16' in Lee, *The Making of the Rome Statute*, 143.
[98] See section 8.7.4 on 'self-referrals'.
[99] There were deaths and serious injuries as a result of action by the Israeli Defence Forces. Since the situation also extended to the ships of two other States Parties, it is being investigated by the Prosecutor as *Situation on Registered Vessels of the Union of the Comoros, the Hellenic Republic and the Kingdom of Cambodia.*

8.7.2   Security Council

While there was some opposition during the negotiation of the Statute to the role of the Security Council in referring situations to the Court, it was widely recognized that such a role would be both useful and appropriate. The Statute does not 'confer' any such role on the Council; it could not add to the powers which the Council is given by the UN Charter. But the establishment of the ad hoc Tribunals has already illustrated that the Council can have a role in international criminal justice when international peace and security are threatened. When the Council refers situations to the ICC, it is not establishing a new institution as it did with the ICTY and the ICTR; the situation is being referred to the ICC as it stands, with all the powers and responsibilities laid down by the Statute.[100] It is open to the Council to impose additional obligations on States – for example, the obligation to cooperate with the Court – but the Court itself is an independent institution and its powers conferred by treaty cannot be changed by the Council.

The situation in Darfur in Sudan was referred to the ICC by the Security Council under Resolution 1593(2005). This was a welcome example of the United States allowing, indeed welcoming, the invocation of the Court's jurisdiction, in spite of its then firm objections to the Court. Cases are pending as a result of the referral, but arrest warrants have not been executed and the Security Council has taken no action to follow up its own referral of the situation. And the resolution itself presented a number of problems. It required that no funding for the ICC investigations should come from the UN, in spite of Article 115 of the ICC Statute; it had unnecessary and meaningless references to Article 16 and to the bilateral non-surrender agreements of the US;[101] and, in its paragraph 6, it granted troop-contributing States which are not parties to the Statute exclusive jurisdiction over their nationals.[102] The situation in Libya was referred to the Court by Resolution 1970(2011), adopted by the Council by consensus. The resolution followed the Darfur precedent in including a meaningless reference to Article 16, exclusive jurisdiction for non-States Parties and a denial of UN funding.

8.7.3   Prosecutor's power to initiate an investigation

A major point of controversy in the negotiation of the trigger mechanisms related to the power of the Prosecutor to begin investigations *proprio motu* – on his or her own initiative. On the one hand, there were concerns that, if a provision to this effect were included in the Statute, the Prosecutor might institute politically motivated investigations and would not be subject to the oversight which national authorities have of their own prosecutors. On the

---

[100] Agreement on this proposition does not, however, resolve all difficulties: see the different conclusions reached regarding the application of Art. 27 of the Statute to President Al-Bashir, in Dapo Akande, 'The Legal Nature of Security Council Referrals to the ICC and its Impact on Al Bashir's Immunities' (2009) 7 *Journal of International Criminal Justice* 333 and Paola Gaeta, 'Does President Al Bashir Enjoy Immunity from Arrest?' (2009) 7 *Journal of International Criminal Justice* 315.

[101] See statement of the US on adoption of the resolution at UN Doc. S/PV.5158, at 4. The representatives of Denmark and Brazil made statements attempting to limit the effect of this reference: *ibid.*, at 6 and 11 respectively.

[102] For a comment on the resolution see Robert Cryer, 'Sudan, Resolution 1593 and International Criminal Justice' (2006) 19 *Leiden Journal of International Law* 195. For further discussion of US actions in opposition to the ICC see section 8.11.3.

other hand, there was a desire that the Court should not be entirely dependent on the decisions of external actors to trigger its work. Article 15 provides that the Prosecutor may initiate prosecutions without a State Party or Security Council referral, but to do so requires the authorization of the Pre-Trial Chamber. In addition, the procedures for investigation and prosecution which ensure both that the case is a proper one for the Court in terms of evidence and jurisdiction, and that national courts are not genuinely handling the case, have the effect of restricting the Prosecutor's authority, while not infringing on his independence.[103] The complex admissibility requirements in particular, including the requirement that the Prosecutor inform all States with jurisdiction before beginning an investigation,[104] address concerns about a Prosecutor with a personal agenda.

The Prosecutor has received thousands of communications from individuals and organizations who want ICC investigations to be opened into crimes in various parts of the world.[105] Having assessed the seriousness of the information, the Office of the Prosecutor may open a preliminary examination into a situation brought to its attention in order to decide whether 'there is a reasonable basis to proceed with an investigation'. As with situations referred by a State or the Security Council the Prosecutor will examine whether there is a reasonable basis to believe that a crime within the jurisdiction of the Court has been committed, whether the case would be admissible and whether the interests of justice would not be served (Article 53(1)).[106] Preliminary examinations have been started in respect of situations in Afghanistan, Colombia, Comoros, Georgia, Guinea, Honduras, the Republic of Korea and Nigeria. In relation to allegations of crimes in Iraq, Venezuela and Palestine the Prosecutor decided that the requirements for opening investigations had not been met.[107] In relation to crimes committed in Colombia, the Prosecutor has issued an interim report which indicates that developments in national proceedings will continue to be the focus of attention.[108]

The Prosecutor has initiated two investigations *proprio motu* (in Kenya and Côte d'Ivoire), the remainder of the investigations having followed referrals by States Parties or the Security Council. The decision by the Prosecutor to await or to seek referrals rather than use *proprio motu* powers liberally may reflect the view that explicit demonstrations of support can generate cooperation exceeding the Statute obligations of cooperation, and that strong State support is needed to enable the effective carrying out of the Prosecutor's responsibilities.[109]

---

[103] See Allison Marston Banner, 'Enhancing the Legitimacy and Accountability of Prosecutorial Discretion at the International Criminal Court' (2003) 97 *American Journal of International Law* 510.
[104] Art. 18.   [105] See the OTP's annual reports on preliminary examination activities.
[106] Annex to the *Paper on Some Policy Issues before the Office of the Prosecutor*, 'Referrals and Communications', on the website of the ICC at www.icc-cpi.int. See also regs. 25–31 of the Regulations of the Office of the Prosecutor.
[107] See Prosecutor's letters of 9 February 2006; these and the Prosecutor's decision on Palestine may be found on the website of the ICC at www.icc-cpi.int. For criticism of the Prosecutor's approach to the allegations on Iraq, see Schabas, 'Prosecutorial Discretion'. New complaints about UK actions in Iraq were reportedly made in 2014.
[108] *Situation in Colombia: Interim Report*, November 2012, on the website of the ICC at www.icc-cpi.int. See generally Kai Ambos, *The Colombian Peace Process and the Principle of Complementarity of the International Criminal Court* (Dordrecht, 2010).
[109] See Banner, 'Enhancing the Legitimacy', 518.

8.7.4   'Self-referrals'

The first situations to be dealt with by the Court were referred to it by States in relation to crimes committed on their own territories. While some commentators have doubted whether 'self-referral' is contemplated in the Statute,[110] the wording of the Statute suggests otherwise. The Statute simply says that 'a State Party may refer to the Prosecutor a situation', without any limitations.[111] Moreover, the drafting history shows that referrals by 'interested' States, such as territorial States, were specifically foreseen and even preferred.[112] A self-referral can be of benefit to the Court; it may indicate that, far from an international investigation being intrusive, it is welcomed and will be supported by full cooperation by the State concerned, including by granting protection to investigators and witnesses. The Prosecutor has indeed expressed the intention to 'seek where possible to make this support [from a State] explicit through a referral'.[113]

There are risks, however.[114] A government of a divided country may use a referral to seek the Court's intervention against its own political opponents.[115] The referral by Uganda in 2003 concerned the 'situation concerning the Lord's Resistance Army' but the Prosecutor had to make it clear that this would be interpreted as covering crimes 'within the situation of northern Uganda by whomever committed'.[116]

Self-referrals may also present the risk that States will overburden the Court with cases they could handle themselves. And, as argued by the defendant in *Katanga*, 'if States are granted an unconditional right not to prosecute, this would seriously jeopardise any encouragement of States to prosecute domestically and would negate this persisting and primary responsibility for States to prosecute international crimes'.[117] The Prosecutor is not, however, obliged to initiate an investigation when a referral is made, and may decline to take a case on grounds such as lack of gravity, complementarity and the interests of justice.

8.8   Jurisdiction: personal, territorial and temporal

The Court has *potentially* worldwide jurisdiction, but this will be fully realized only after all States become parties to its Statute. In the meantime, Article 12(2) provides:

---

[110] See e.g. William Schabas, 'First Prosecutions at the International Criminal Court' (2006) 27 *Human Rights Law Journal* 25, 32.

[111] Art. 14(1).

[112] See Darryl Robinson, 'The Controversy over Territorial State Referrals and Reflections on ICL Discourse' (2011) 9 *Journal of International Criminal Justice* 355. The debate in the negotiations was whether States Parties who were *not* 'interested States' (territorial, nationality or custodial) should be allowed to make referrals. See e.g. UN Doc. A/AC.249/1, paras. 162–3; UN Doc. A/CONF.183/2/Add.1, p. 36.

[113] Annex to the *Paper on Some Policy Issues before the Office of the Prosecutor*, 'Referrals and Communications', at section D, on the website of the ICC at www.icc-cpi.int.

[114] Claus Kreß, 'Self-Referrals and Waivers of Complementarity: Some Considerations in Law and Policy' (2004) 2 *Journal of International Criminal Justice* 944; Mahnoush Arsanjani and Michael Reisman, 'The Law-in-Action of the International Criminal Court' (2005) 99 *American Journal of International Law* 385, 392.

[115] See also William Burke-White, 'Complementarity in Practice: The International Criminal Court as Part of a System of Multi-Level Global Governance in the Democratic Republic of the Congo' (2005) 18 *Leiden Journal of International Law* 557, 567–8.

[116] Letter of the Prosecutor of 17 June 2004 attached to the Presidency Decision to assign the situation in Uganda to Pre-Trial Chamber II. See more generally, Payam Akhavan, 'The Lord's Resistance Army Case: Uganda's Submission of the First State Referral to the International Criminal Court' (2005) 99 *American Journal of International Law* 403; Schabas, 'First Prosecutions', 31.

[117] *Katanga and Ngudjolo Chui*, ICC A. Ch., 25 September 2009, para. 63.

the Court may exercise its jurisdiction if one or more of the following States are Parties to this Statute or have accepted the jurisdiction of the Court in accordance with paragraph 3:

(a) The State on the territory of which the conduct in question occurred or, if the crime was committed on board a vessel or aircraft, the State of registration of that vessel or aircraft;

(b) The State of which the person accused of the crime is a national.

Article 12(3) allows a State not party to declare that it accepts the jurisdiction of the Court with respect to the crime in question. The modifications to these rules on jurisdiction which have been agreed with respect to the crime of aggression at the Kampala Review Conference are discussed in Chapter 13 below.

The Court also has jurisdiction where a situation has been referred to the Court by the Security Council under Chapter VII of the UN Charter.[118] In the event of referral by the Council, the Court has jurisdiction even if none of the relevant States is a party to the Statute or gives its consent.[119]

The rationale for requiring the consent of the territorial State or the State of nationality is that these are the two most uncontroversial bases for the jurisdiction of States themselves.[120] The consent of one of these States therefore gives a solid basis for the taking of international jurisdiction. But these are not of course the only bases of State jurisdiction; the crimes listed in the Statute are ones over which universal jurisdiction may be taken by States. Why was a narrower jurisdiction agreed upon for the Court? As previously described,[121] the ILC draft Statute, with which the negotiations on the Court began, made large concessions to State sovereignty. For all crimes except genocide,[122] the ILC model of a court had jurisdiction only if *both* the State with custody of the suspect *and* the territorial State had accepted the jurisdiction of the court *in respect of that category of crime*. During the negotiations, various different proposals emerged. The most ambitious was a German proposal[123] to give unlimited jurisdiction to the Court, wherever the crime was committed, whether or not in the territory of a State Party and of whatever nationality the suspect. An alternative was a South Korean proposal[124] to confer jurisdiction on the Court with the acceptance of any one of four States: those with territorial jurisdiction, or active nationality jurisdiction, or passive nationality jurisdiction, or with custody of the suspect. At the other end of the spectrum, the United States argued that the consent of *both* the territorial and the nationality State ought to be required. The South Korean proposal had a great deal of support, but a compromise text was accepted by the conference and is now reflected in Article 12; it gives a more limited jurisdiction to the Court, but one which was thought to entail a greater likelihood of acceptance by the Rome Conference as a whole.[125]

---

[118] This is the Chapter of the Charter under which the Council takes decisions, binding on States, to maintain or restore international peace and security; it was under this Chapter that the Council established the two ad hoc Tribunals.

[119] As in the situations in Darfur and Libya referred to the Court by SC Res. 1593(2005) and Res. 1970(2011) respectively.

[120] See Chapter 3. [121] See section 8.2.

[122] The ICC had jurisdiction over genocide whenever a complaint was brought by a State Party which was also a party to the Genocide Convention; this was a form of universal jurisdiction.

[123] The German proposal, with many additional proposals on this issue, was contained in the draft text of the Statute submitted to the conference by the Preparatory Committee (UN Doc. A/CONF.183/13 (Vol. III)).

[124] UN Doc. A/CONF.183/C.I/L.6.

[125] For the history of the negotiations, see Sharon Williams and William Schabas, 'Article 12' in Triffterer, *Observers' Notes*, 547; Elizabeth Wilmshurst, 'Jurisdiction of the Court' in Lee, *The Making of the Rome Statute*, 127.

Under the ILC draft Statute, ratification of the Statute did not in itself entail acceptance of jurisdiction; a State could choose whether to 'opt in' to any crime (except in respect of genocide, for which there was a form of universal jurisdiction). As it became clear during the course of the negotiations that the list of crimes would include only the 'core crimes', the 'opt-in' regime was seen to be less necessary and, over time, the great majority of the negotiators came to favour 'automatic jurisdiction', meaning that a State upon ratification signified its acceptance of jurisdiction for all core crimes.

The Statute thus follows the automatic acceptance model, meaning that a State upon ratification accepts jurisdiction over all core crimes; there is however an exception to this in Article 124, which allows a State, upon ratification of the Statute, not to accept the jurisdiction of the ICC over war crimes with regard to its nationals or to crimes committed on its territory for a period of seven years. This provision, which has no justification other than as a concession necessary to secure agreement on the final text of the Statute,[126] could have created a serious obstacle to the exercise of the Court's jurisdiction, but has not proved to be so. Of the first 110 States Parties, only two, France and Colombia, took advantage of the opt-out regime; France later withdrew its declaration under Article 124 and Colombia's has expired.[127] In 2010, the Kampala Review Conference declined however to remove the Article from the Statute and decided to remit it for review to the Assembly of States Parties.[128]

8.8.1   'Ad hoc' acceptance of jurisdiction

An acceptance of the jurisdiction of the Court under Article 12(3) by a State not party to the Statute extends the territorial and personal jurisdiction of the Court. It does not constitute a referral to the Court; indeed, States that are not parties may not refer situations to the Court. Following or before the making of the declaration of acceptance, there will therefore need to be either a referral by a State or, more likely, the initiation of an investigation by the Prosecutor under his own powers, before the Court may exercise its jurisdiction.[129] The legal effect of a declaration is simply to put a non-State Party on the same jurisdictional basis as a State Party, but in practice the declaration will indicate to the Prosecutor that the State concerned is willing to have the particular situation dealt with by the Court. There is, however, no obligation on the Prosecutor to begin an investigation.[130] The cooperation obligations of Part 9 of the Statute will apply to the State making the declaration.

It is important to note that the declaration accepting jurisdiction 'with respect to the crime in question' has as a consequence the acceptance of jurisdiction for *all* the crimes relevant to

---

[126] For criticism of the French attempt at justification of the provision, see Alain Pellet, 'Entry into Force and Amendment of the Statute' in Cassese, *Commentary*, 145, 168–9.

[127] The French withdrawal was with effect from 15 June 2008; Colombia's declaration expired on 1 November 2009.

[128] During the 1,4181th session of the Assembly of States Parties: RC/Res.4.

[129] For the procedures applicable to such a declaration, see Carsten Stahn, Mohamed el-Zeidy and Héctor Olásolo, 'The International Criminal Court's Ad Hoc Jurisdiction Revisited' (2005) 99 *American Journal of International Law* 421.

[130] E.g. Côte d'Ivoire lodged a declaration under Art. 12(3) on 18 April 2003 but the Prosecutor did not seek authorization for the opening of an investigation until 23 June 2011.

the situation.[131] This avoids the possibility of a non-State Party consenting to the Court's jurisdiction with regard to enemy nationals, while shielding its own.

Article 12(3) allows only 'States' to make a declaration. The declaration lodged by the Palestinian National Authority on 22 January 2009 obliged the Prosecutor to take a decision on whether Palestine was a State for this purpose. He invited submissions on the question,[132] and decided eventually that the declaration was not acceptable since the UN General Assembly had not accepted Palestine as being 'a State'. Following the General Assembly resolution of 29 November 2012, which accorded Palestine the status of an observer State, a different conclusion would be likely in the event of a renewal of the declaration or indeed accession to the Statute.[133]

8.8.2   *Persons over the age of 18*

The Court's jurisdiction is limited to persons over the age of 18 at the time the alleged offence was committed.[134] Turning the question of age into a jurisdictional issue avoids having to choose between different national age limits for criminal responsibility.[135] Prosecuting minors would have required the provision of a special regime and was not considered to be a sensible use of the Court's slender resources. This does not of course exclude national jurisdiction over minors for the commission of international crimes.

8.8.3   *Temporal jurisdiction*

The ICC does not have jurisdiction over offences committed before the entry into force of the Statute on 1 July 2002. States were unwilling to allow the ICC to deal with past practices. If a State becomes a party to the Statute after its entry into force, the Court may exercise jurisdiction only with respect to crimes committed after the Statute has entered into force for that State (Article 11); the State may, however, make a declaration under Article 12(3) to fill this temporal gap – and the declaration of Cote d'Ivoire was retroactive.[136] Crimes committed before 1 July 2002 may not be tried by the ICC under any circumstance.[137]

---

[131] Rule 44(2) of the ICC RPE.   [132] A summary of submissions is on the website of the ICC at www.icc-cpi.int.

[133] For a discussion of the legal effects of the Palestinian declaration in the new circumstances, see Andreas Zimmermann, 'Palestine and the International Criminal Court Quo Vadis? Reach and Limits of Declarations under Article 12(3)' (2013) 11 *Journal of International Criminal Justice* 303.

[134] See Roger Clark and Otto Triffterer, 'Article 26' in Triffterer, *Observers' Notes*, 771.

[135] Per Saland, 'International Criminal Law Principles' in Lee, *The Making of the Rome Statute*, 189, 200–2.

[136] For critique of retroactive effect, see Andreas Zimmermann, 'Palestine and the International Criminal Court Quo Vadis?' (2013) 11 *Journal of International Criminal Justice* 303.

[137] Even if the Security Council were minded to refer a situation to the ICC in which the alleged crimes were committed before the entry into force of the Statute, the Court would not be able to exercise its jurisdiction, since it is a creature of the Statute, not of the Security Council, and, although the Council's resolutions may override the treaty obligations of States (Art. 103 of the Charter), they cannot change the powers of an independent organization.

8.9   Deferral of investigation or prosecution: Article 16

Article 16 reads as follows:

No investigation or prosecution may be commenced or proceeded with under the Statute for a period of 12 months after the Security Council, in a resolution adopted under Chapter VII of the Charter of the United Nations, has requested the Court to that effect; that request may be renewed by the Council under the same conditions.

This Article originates in an even wider restriction on the Court's jurisdiction which was contained in the ILC draft Statute; that provision would have removed jurisdiction over any matter which was being considered by the Security Council unless the Council agreed otherwise. The draft was reversed by the negotiators, who saw it as unacceptably subordinating the ICC to the Security Council.[138] Thus, instead of requiring a positive Council decision (necessitating nine positive votes and no veto by a permanent member) to *allow* the ICC to proceed in such circumstances, Article 16 requires a positive decision to *defer* a proceeding. The Council has to act under Chapter VII of the Charter, which applies only where there is a 'threat to the peace, breach of the peace or act of aggression'. The Council request for deferral has effect for twelve months and may be renewed.

     The intervention in judicial proceedings of a political organ in this way requires some explanation.[139] The purpose was to allow the Council, under its primary responsibility for the maintenance of peace and security, to set aside the demands of justice at a time when it considered the demands of peace to be overriding; if the suspension of legal proceedings against a leader will allow a peace treaty to be concluded, precedence may be given to peace. Any suspension of the proceedings is only temporary.

     There are no criteria in the Statute for the use of Article 16. Assessments of whether the demands of peace processes should occasion the suspension of Court proceedings may differ. From time to time, requests have been made to the Council in the perceived interests of peace to suspend proceedings in relation to the situations in northern Uganda and in Kenya, and in relation to the arrest warrant against the President of Sudan. All such requests have been unsuccessful and the Council has taken no action in relation to them. The adoption by the Council of resolutions suspending non-existent proceedings in 2002 and 2003, at the behest of the previous US administration, was a surprising and controversial use of Article 16.[140]

8.10   Enforcement of the ICC's decisions

A national court may rely on local police to arrest suspects for the purpose of trial, and on local detention facilities to imprison them on conviction. The ICC has to rely entirely on the international community for these matters. Part 9 of the Statute requires States Parties to

[138] Morten Bergsmo and Jelena Pejic, 'Article 16' in Triffterer, *Observers' Notes*, 595, 597–9.
[139] See Franklin Berman, 'The Relationship between the International Criminal Court and the Security Council' in H. von Hebel, J. Lammers and J. Schukking (eds.), *Reflections on the International Criminal Court* (The Hague, 1999).
[140] The relevant resolutions are discussed at section 8.11.3.

cooperate with the Court in providing various forms of assistance such as the taking of evidence and the tracing of assets. Article 89(1) imposes the all-important obligation to surrender any person found within a State's territory when the Court so requests. The limitations on the Court in making such requests where the person concerned enjoys immunity or where there is a relevant international agreement are described in Article 98. As regards sentences of imprisonment imposed by the Court, there is no obligation on States to provide prison facilities, and sentences will be served in a State selected by the Court from a list of those that have declared their willingness to accept sentenced persons (Article 103).[141]

If a State Party fails to comply with a request from the Court to cooperate, in breach of its obligations under the Statute, the Court may refer the matter to the Assembly of States Parties or, in the case of a referral by the Security Council, to the Council.[142] For example, in 2010 a Pre-Trial Chamber decided to inform the Security Council of Sudan's lack of cooperation with the Court.[143] In 2011, the authorities of Chad and Malawi, both parties to the ICC Statute, refused to cooperate with ICC requests for the arrest and surrender of President Al Bashir of Sudan when he visited those countries; the Court issued two decisions with findings of the failure to cooperate, ordering that the decisions be transmitted to the Security Council and the Assembly of States Parties.[144] No action has been taken by the Security Council. The Assembly has no powers of enforcement and relies on public expressions of concern and informal good offices.

The Prosecutor has to conduct investigations in situations of ongoing violence or actual conflict where security is a problem, presenting considerable challenges to the investigators and witnesses in the field. The possibilities of collecting evidence are often limited. Although the commission of atrocities may be common knowledge, information about incidents and command structures may be very difficult to obtain: local governments may be unwilling or unable to provide significant assistance; humanitarian organizations in the field may be reluctant to assist so as not to put at risk their continued presence; international peacekeeping missions may not have a wide enough mandate or may wish to avoid prejudicing their neutrality; other governments may not wish to disclose evidence obtained by their intelligence services or may have their own political interests in the region which conflict with their interests in the enforcement of international criminal justice. Seen against such difficulties as these, the provisions of the Statute enforcing the Court's requests and decisions have been described as 'paltry, at best'.[145]

For discussion of State cooperation with the ICC and a comparison with the cooperation requirements of the two ad hoc Tribunals, see Chapter 20. Chapter 21 deals with the way in which the Court handles the issue of immunities.

---

[141] See Chapter 19. [142] Art. 87(7) of the Statute. [143] *Harun and Ali Kushayb*, ICC PTC I, 25 May 2010.
[144] *Al Bashir*, ICC PTC I, 12 December 2011 (Malawi) and 13 December 2011 (Chad). Chad has since continued to receive visits from Al Bashir. Other approaches taken by the Court, when informed about an ongoing or approaching visit by a fugitive, are to order publicly the State to arrest and surrender the fugitive (e.g. *Al Bashir*, ICC PTC II, 15 July 2013) or order the Registry to make inquiries about the visit and to remind the State about its obligations (e.g. *Hussein*, ICC PTC II, 26 April 2013).
[145] Leila Sadat and Richard Garden, 'The New International Criminal Court: An Uneasy Revolution' (2000) 88 *Georgetown Law Journal* 381, 389.

8.11   Opposition to the ICC

At the time its Statute was adopted, the ICC enjoyed strong support from much of the
international community. It was clear, however, that the Court in the form that had been
agreed would not soon achieve universal acceptance.[146] Various objections on legal and
political grounds have been expressed to the ICC Statute. A frequently expressed criticism is
that the ICC is given jurisdiction over nationals of a State not a party to the Statute without
that State's consent.[147] The claim that this is contrary to international law is made first by
reference to the Vienna Convention on the Law of Treaties, Article 34 of which provides:
'A treaty does not create either obligations or rights for a third State without its consent.'
However, the Statute clearly does not create obligations for States not party to it. The fact
that a foreign court or tribunal may have jurisdiction over a State's nationals, on grounds
such as territorial jurisdiction, is nothing new, and does not entail any 'obligations'. While it
undoubtedly affects a State's *interests* that the Court may have jurisdiction over its nationals,
that is not a ground for claiming that the Statute is contrary to international law. It is also
asserted in this context that there is nothing in customary international law to justify the
delegation of jurisdiction over the nationals of non-States Parties to an international court.
However, international law does not preclude States from acting collectively in delegating to
an international court the jurisdiction which they would be entitled to exercise themselves,[148] and there is no requirement for a positive rule of international law allowing
States to exercise their jurisdiction collectively in this manner. On the contrary, any
suggestion that there is such a rule would be contrary to the principle of territorial jurisdiction and generally retrogressive.

   There are other provisions of the Statute which have given rise to controversy, although the
arguments here are less of law than of perceived legitimacy.[149] Some arguments are based on a
general mistrust of the ICC.[150] They include the criticism that States with effective legal
systems cannot be sure that the Court will not take over the prosecutions of their nationals,
because the Statute leaves it to the Court itself to judge whether the national court is 'unable or
unwilling' genuinely to deal with a case. On this view, the complementarity principle is not a

---

[146] See generally Dominic McGoldrick, 'Political and Legal Responses to the International Criminal Court' in McGoldrick *et al.*
(eds.), *The Permanent International Criminal Court*, 389.

[147] Under Art. 12. There is an extensive literature on the arguments; see e.g. Eve La Haye, 'The Jurisdiction of the International
Criminal Court' (1999) 46 *Netherlands International Law Review* 1; M. Scharf, 'The ICC's Jurisdiction over the Nationals of
Non-Party States: A Critique of the US Position' (2001) 64 *Law and Contemporary Problems* 98; Madeline Morris, 'High
Crimes and Misconceptions: The ICC and Non Party States' (2000) 64 *Law and Contemporary Problems* 131; Frédéric Mégret,
'Epilogue to an Endless Debate: The International Criminal Court's Third Party Jurisdiction and the Looming Revolution of
International Law' (2001) 12 *European Journal of International Law* 241; Dapo Akande, 'The Jurisdiction of the International
Criminal Court over Nationals of Non-Parties: Legal Basis and Limits' (2003) 1 *Journal of International Criminal Justice* 618.

[148] The Nuremberg judgment decided that that trial was justified on the basis that what States could do alone could be done
together: '[T]hey have done together what any one of them might have done singly; for it is not to be doubted that any nation has
the right thus to set up special courts to administer law' (Nuremberg IMT, Judgment and Sentences, reprinted in (1947) 41
American Journal of International Law 172, 216).

[149] See e.g. Michael Lohr and William Lietzau, 'One Road Away from Rome: Concerns Regarding the International Criminal
Court' (1999) 9 *US Air Force Journal of Legal Studies* 33.

[150] John Bolton, 'The Risks and Weaknesses of the International Criminal Court from an American Perspective' (2000–1) 41
Virginia Journal of International Law 186; David Forsythe, 'The United States and International Criminal Justice' (2002) 24
Human Rights Quarterly 974.

reliable safeguard since the ICC cannot be trusted to apply it without political bias. A further concern is that the Prosecutor, unlike national prosecutors, is accountable to no outside agency or authority in exercising his power of initiating investigations.

The arguments overlook or downplay the various restraints and limits on the Prosecutor's actions which are provided throughout the Statute system, and formal and informal methods of securing accountability.[151] They also fail to take fully into account the ability of States not party to the Statute to avoid the exercise of the ICC's jurisdiction by prosecuting Statute crimes themselves; although if such States wish to take advantage of the complementarity principle they will have to ensure that their own legislation gives them jurisdiction over all the conduct with which the ICC may become concerned.[152]

The United States was by no means the only State to oppose the creation of the Court.[153] But, because it was the most open and vocal in expressing its opposition and in taking action to maintain its policy, its early practice is considered here. We also discuss briefly the attitude of the African Union: while more than 60 per cent of its members are parties to the ICC Statute, it has expressed strong concerns about aspects of the Court's practice.

8.11.1   *The early practice of the United States*

The United States, under the Clinton administration, signed the Statute on 31 December 2000, the last day that it was possible to do so. Its signature may be attributed to the fact that the United States was not in principle opposed to the creation of a new court to dispense international criminal justice, and hoped to resolve some of the points of difficulty by means of changes to the rules of procedure and other documents. Signature imposed an obligation on the United States under Article 18 of the Vienna Convention on the Law of Treaties: a signatory State may not 'defeat the object and purpose of a treaty prior to its entry into force' unless it has made clear its intention not to become a party to the treaty. The advent of the Bush administration brought fiercer opposition to the ICC and, in order to avoid the obligation under Article 18, the United States made clear its intention not to ratify the Statute in a communication to the UN Secretariat on 6 May 2002. Israel followed suit, in respect of its own signature, on 28 August 2002.[154]

The US opposition to the ICC led them to make various attempts to prevent the possibility of US nationals being tried by the Court. Their action on the international front was supported and partially instigated by domestic legislation. The American Servicemembers' Protection Act prohibits various forms of US cooperation with the ICC, provides for the cessation of

---

[151] See Banner, 'Enhancing the Legitimacy'. The arguments on informal means of accountability may, however, understate the importance of prosecutorial independence.

[152] See Thomas Pittman and Matthew Heaphy, 'Does the United States Really Prosecute its Service Members for War Crimes? Implications for Complementarity before the International Criminal Court' (2008) 21 *Leiden Journal of International Law* 165.

[153] For discussion of the opposition of some other States, see Lu Jianping and Wang Zhixiang, 'China's Attitude towards the ICC' (2005) 3 *Journal of International Criminal Justice* 608; Bakhtiyar Tuzmukhamedov, 'The ICC and Russian Constitutional Problems', *ibid.*, 621; Usha Ramanathan, 'India and the ICC', *ibid.*, 621; Hirad Abtahi, 'The Islamic Republic of Iran and the ICC', *ibid.*, 635.

[154] Sudan made a similar communication on 26 August 2008. The various communications are available at http://treaties.un.org/Pages/ViewDetails.aspx?src=TREATY&mtdsg_no=XVIII-10&chapter=18&lang=en.

military and other aid to States Parties which do not sign a non-surrender agreement with the United States, and authorizes the use of 'all means necessary, including military force', to release persons arrested by the ICC.[155]

In the months immediately prior to the entry into force of the ICC Statute, the United States looked to the possibility of using a Security Council resolution to exempt US nationals from the Court's jurisdiction. This involved an unexpected reference to Article 16 of the Statute: Security Council Resolution 1422(2002), pushed through the Council by the United States with the threat of refusal to support a peacekeeping operation, requested the ICC to defer any exercise of its jurisdiction for twelve months 'if a case arises involving current or former officials or personnel from a contributing State not a party to the Rome Statute over acts or omissions relating to a United Nations established or authorised operation'. A further resolution asking for suspension for another twelve months was adopted in 2003 (Resolution 1487(2003)). The following year, however, support for the US action had dwindled and there was not the necessary majority in the Security Council to adopt another resolution in the series.

The two resolutions have been highly controversial and doubts have been expressed as to their compatibility with the UN Charter as well as their effectiveness under the ICC Statute.[156] The negotiating history of Article 16 indicates that the intention was that the Council would consider, on a case-by-case basis, whether the continuation of ICC proceedings would prejudice the maintenance of international peace and security; a request for the suspension of hypothetical proceedings which might arise at some time in the future would not appear to come within the objective of Article 16 even though it fell within its wording.[157] While there has been a great deal of academic debate about the resolutions, they have had no practical impact on the Court, no case having arisen in the relevant period. It is to be hoped that they are now of historical interest only.

In a further approach to seeking exemption from the ICC's jurisdiction over its personnel, the United States promoted the decision in Resolution 1497(2003) that personnel from a State which is not a party to the ICC Statute will be subject to the exclusive jurisdiction of that State for all acts related to the multinational force or United Nations force in Liberia.[158] This was used as a precedent in the resolutions referring to the ICC the situations in Darfur, Sudan, and in Libya.[159] These decisions relating to particular situations have the aim of shielding a group

---

[155] 2002 Supplemental Appropriations Act for Further Recovery from and Response to Terrorist Attacks on the United States, as amended; see Sean Murphy, 'Contemporary Practice of the United States' (2002) 96 *American Journal of International Law* 975. Other US legislation, the Foreign Relations Authorization Act (HR 3427), Public Law No. 106-113, §§ 705–706, of 29 November 1999 also bans US funding of the Court.

[156] See e.g. Aly Mokhtar, 'The Fine Art of Arm-Twisting: The US, Resolution 1422 and Security Council Deferral Power under the Rome Statute' (2002) 3 *International Criminal Law Review* 295; Neha Jain, 'A Separate Law for Peacekeepers: The Clash between the Security Council and the International Criminal Court' (2005) 16 *European Journal of International Law* 239; Carsten Stahn, 'The Ambiguities of Security Council Resolution 1422(2002)' (2003) 14 *European Journal of International Law* 85; Dominic McGoldrick, 'Political and Legal Responses to the ICC' in McGoldrick *et al.* (eds.), *The Permanent International Criminal Court*, 415–22; see also statements by representatives of Canada and Jordan at the Security Council meeting on 10 July 2002 (UN Doc. S/PV.4568).

[157] See statement of New Zealand at the Security Council meeting on 10 July 2002 (UN Doc. S/PV.4568).

[158] Para. 7 of the resolution. Mexico, France and Germany abstained, asserting that the paragraph not only undermined the ICC but also prevented countries from exercising jurisdiction over persons accused of murdering their citizens (UN Doc. S/PV.4803).

[159] SC Res. 1593(2005), para. 6 (Darfur). Brazil explained that this paragraph was one of the reasons for its abstention from the vote (UN Doc. S/PV.5158); and Res. 1970(2011), para. 6 (Libya).

of persons from any courts save those of their own States. In purporting to set aside the jurisdiction not only of the ICC but also of national courts, they attempt to interfere with treaties – the ICC Statute as well as the Geneva Conventions, since the latter require all States to exercise jurisdiction over grave breaches of international humanitarian law wherever they occur. The Charter obligation on States to comply with binding Security Council resolutions and the hierarchy of treaties established by Article 103 of the Charter ensure that the resolutions will be effective to prevent a State from taking jurisdiction over persons covered by their provisions. The ICC, however, is not a Council organ and is not itself bound by Council resolutions; as the Relationship Agreement between the ICC and the UN recognizes, it is an independent institution with international legal personality. The resolutions would not therefore have any restrictive effect on the jurisdiction of the ICC;[160] it is a matter for argument whether they would preclude States from surrendering suspects to the Court.

In a further attempt to keep US nationals from the ICC, the United States under the Bush administration negotiated bilateral agreements with other States, some of them parties to the Statute, others not, which provide that no nationals, current or former officials, or military personnel of either party may be surrendered or transferred by the other State to the ICC for any purpose.[161] The United States referred to Article 98(2) of the Statute as the basis for these agreements, maintaining that the ICC will not be able to request a State to surrender a US national to the Court, once that State has entered into such an agreement with the United States.

The agreements will of course only be effective in preventing the Court from making such a request if they are in truth compatible with the Statute. Article 98(2) precludes the Court from asking for the surrender of a suspect if that would require the requested State 'to act inconsistently with its obligations under international agreements pursuant to which the consent of a sending State is required to surrender a person of the State to the Court'. The provision was inserted in the Statute to address the problem of conflicting obligations where, for example, a State in which foreign military personnel are stationed has agreed under a status of forces agreement (SOFA) to accord the right to the sending State to exercise criminal jurisdiction over its troops for certain kinds of offences. Without Article 98(2), such an agreement would conflict with the obligation in the ICC Statute to surrender suspects to the Court when so requested.[162] In assessing the compatibility of the US agreements with the ICC Statute, it should be noted that the key to the interpretation of Article 98(2) is in the phrase 'sending State'. There is nothing in the provision to prevent the Court requesting the surrender of a person who has not been 'sent' by one State to another State. But the US agreements cover

---

[160] Other (weak) arguments as to the efficacy of para. 6 of SC Res. 1593(2005) in relation to the ICC include that preambular para. 2 has a reference to Art. 16 of the Rome Statute; but this does not turn it into a request to the Court to defer investigations under that Article: it is not worded as a request to the ICC and does not seek temporary deferral. Nor can the resolution be regarded as a referral of a situation *minus* the activities of peacekeepers and other personnel: see Cryer, 'Sudan, Resolution 1593', 17–18; for reasoning to the contrary, see David Scheffer, 'Staying the Course with the International Criminal Court' (2001–2) 35 *Cornell International Law Journal* 47, 90.

[161] For the text of one example, that of East Timor, see (2003) 97 *American Journal of International Law* 201–2.

[162] Another example of an agreement covered by the provision is an extradition arrangement under which the rule of specialty would require the State receiving a suspect extradited from another State to obtain the consent of that State before dealing with the suspect in any other way than prosecuting him for the offence for which his extradition was requested.

all US nationals. Tourists and businessmen can by no stretch of the imagination be regarded as persons 'sent' by one State to another. The agreements entered into by the United States therefore do not fall within the terms of Article 98(2) and would not have the effect of preventing the ICC from requesting surrender.[163] The requested State Party will continue to be obliged to cooperate with the ICC by surrendering the person concerned and will have the problem of attempting to reconcile conflicting treaty obligations.

During the second term of the Bush administration, US relations with the Court thawed somewhat, and, with a change of administration in 2009, a more positive attitude to the Court has come about on the part of the United States. There is, however, no indication that the United States will become a party to the ICC Statute in the foreseeable future.

8.11.2   *The African Union*

While the number of African States which are parties to the ICC Statute is large,[164] the African Union (AU) has adopted resolutions that are critical of the Court and that have on occasion demanded action by its members which is inconsistent with the obligations many of them have under the Statute. Resolutions of the AU Assembly have criticized the arrest warrant against President Al Bashir, noting 'the unfortunate consequences that the indictment has had on the delicate peace processes underway in the Sudan';[165] asked for the adoption by the Security Council of resolutions requesting the deferral of the proceedings against Al Bashir, and the proceedings in the Libyan and Kenyan situations;[166] decided that Member States should not cooperate in the execution of the arrest warrant against Al Bashir;[167] expressed concern at the impact of the charges against the President and Deputy President of Kenya on peace efforts in Kenya and the region and asked for the referral back to Kenya of the cases.[168]

The concerns underlying the resolutions are reflected in allegations of the Court's double standards, with its focus on atrocities committed in Africa, the possible impact on peace and security in the region and a perhaps genuine difference of view on whether or not heads of States which are not parties to the Statute enjoy immunity from court proceedings.[169] The AU has expressed its disagreement with the Court's view of immunity, stating that countries refusing to arrest Al Bashir did so in conformity with their obligations to the AU and with Article 98 of the ICC Statute.

---

[163] This is the view generally reflected in the guidelines agreed upon by the EU Council, binding upon all EU Member States: EU Council of Ministers 2459th Session, GAER Doc. 12134/02 30 September 2002; reprinted in McGoldrick *et al.* (eds.), *The Permanent International Criminal Court*, 430–1. On the subject generally, see David Scheffer, 'Article 98(2) of the Rome Statute: America's Original Intent' (2005) 3 *Journal of International Criminal Justice* 333; Markus Benzing, 'US Bilateral Non-Surrender Agreements and Article 98 of the Statute of the International Criminal Court: An Exercise in the Law of Treaties' (2004) 8 *Max Planck Yearbook of United Nations Law*, 182; Herman van der Wilt, 'Bilateral Agreements between the US and States Parties to the Rome Statute' (2005) 18 *Leiden Journal of International Law* 93; Opinion by James Crawford SC, Philippe Sands QC and Ralph Wilde available at www.iccnow.org/documents/SandsCrawfordBIA14June03.pdf.
[164] Thirty-four as at the end of 2013.   [165] Assembly/AU/December/3(XIII), 2009.
[166] See Assembly/AU/December/366(XVII), 2011.
[167] *Ibid.* The AU Assembly has on various occasions affirmed that countries refusing to arrest Al Bashir on visits to their countries did so in conformity with AU obligations.
[168] Assembly/AU/13(XXI), 2013.   [169] See Chapter 21.

Allegations of bias on the part of the Court neglect the fact that only two of the current proceedings were instituted under the Prosecutor's *proprio motu* powers and of these the Court's intervention in the Kenya situation was based on government acceptance that the Court would act if local authorities failed to do so. Of the remaining situations, four followed the referral by the African countries in which the crimes took place. Two were referred by the Security Council, but one of those (Libya) was at the request of the new authorities. A further point is that the Court's involvement is in support of African victims;[170] the interests of the victims are not mentioned in the AU resolutions, which may lead to the impression that the governments behind them are not necessarily reflecting the views of all of their citizens but are seeking to protect their leaders. The long neglect of crimes in the region was the impetus for so many African States to support the creation of the ICC. Current accusations of neocolonialist intervention should be assessed in the context of the previous accusations that *failure* to act was a sign of Western racism, indifference and double standards.[171] In spite of the adoption of the AU resolutions over the years, many AU members are opposed to them, and there continue to be cooperation and interaction with the Court in most instances.[172]

8.12   Appraisal

With the Court's first decade behind it, assessments of its record and of the state of inter-national criminal justice abound.[173] Expectations for the Court were high – perhaps too high if they foresaw an early deterrent effect on the conduct of armed conflict. The failure to meet some other expectations may be due less to the practice of the Court itself than to other factors and actors. The Court cannot be blamed for the fact that it has to operate in a conflict or post-conflict environment with all the practical problems that brings, nor for the fact that the Security Council retains the veto for its permanent members and is selective in the situations which it refers to the Court, nor for the lack of an international police force to execute the Court's arrest warrants and other orders. The international community is still governed by sovereign States; the ICC was not intended to transform international law nor the global political system in which it operates.

The Court faces severe challenges. Its future success will depend in part on the extent to which States are prepared to take ownership of the Court. They will need to lend it their cooperation and support not only through strict and willing compliance with their obligations to the Court, but also by multilateral measures such as enlarging the mandates of Security Council peacekeeping missions and proactively assisting with evidence by incorporating

---

[170] See e.g. Fatou Bensouda, 'The ICC: A Response to African Concerns', 10 October 2012, available on the website of the ICC at www.icc-cpi.int.

[171] See e.g. Makau Mutua, 'Never Again: Questioning the Yugoslav and Rwanda Tribunals' (1997) 11 *Temple International and Comparative Law Journal* 167; Kingsley Chiedu Moghalu, 'Image and Reality of War Crimes Justice: External Perceptions of the International Criminal Tribunal for Rwanda' (2002) 26 *Fletcher Forum of World Affairs* 21.

[172] At the time of writing, however, there is a real possibility that Kenya will withdraw from the Statute. For futher analysis, see section 23.2.

[173] One issue of the *Journal of International Criminal Justice* focuses on such assessments and the many problems facing international criminal justice: (2013) Volume 11, issue 3. See also Chapter 23 below.

assistance to the Court into their intelligence-gathering capabilities. The opposition of the African Union is a challenge not only for the Court but for all the States Parties. The Court is dependent on the international community to ensure cooperation by reluctant States and to implement arrest warrants. The ability of President Al Bashir to travel to many countries without apparent fear of arrest, the continued failure to execute the first arrest warrants of the Court for members of the Lord's Resistance Army, the reluctance of the Security Council to follow up its referrals of situations to the Court[174] are all matters of concern.

The Court – and the international community – will continue to face the challenge posed to international criminal justice generally by the so-called peace and justice dilemma. The statement is often quoted that 'Justice, peace and democracy are not mutually exclusive objectives, but rather mutually reinforcing imperatives',[175] but there have been demands in particular situations that justice should be subordinated either temporarily or indefinitely to the needs of a peace process. In Uganda, the opening of the investigation and the subsequent refusal to withdraw the arrest warrants against the LRA leaders were criticized for impeding the peace process and for impeding efforts to persuade members of the LRA to defect.[176] The arrest warrant against President Al Bashir, as we have seen, gave rise to demands that, where peace and justice clash, as here allegedly, peace should be put first.[177] A similar argument was raised in relation to the warrants issued against the persons who became President and Deputy President of Kenya. Is international peace and security the responsibility of the Prosecutor? Not at first sight, but some have argued that the Prosecutor should indeed take account of peace processes within her inherent prosecutorial discretion, and avoid bringing politically destablizing cases for a necessary period.[178] Issuing arrest warrants against serving heads of State or government necessarily has political repercussions in the country concerned and perhaps in the wider region, but, if persons at the top of the command structure are the ones who should be dealt with by such a court as this, a political impact is inevitable. The way in which such dilemmas are handled by both the Prosecutor and the wider international community will provide a further marker for the success or failure of the Court.

The exercise of the Prosecutor's discretion more generally is a further test for the Court. The Prosecutor necessarily has to make choices among situations to investigate and among cases within situations referred to the Court. These selections will inevitably be met by criticisms from those who would have selected differently, bringing challenges to the Court's legitimacy. The allegations made by the African Union about the double standards

---

[174] The Presidential statement of 16 June 2008 urging Sudan to cooperate with the Court was a rare exception (S/PRST/2008/21).

[175] Report of the Secretary-General on the Rule of Law and Transitional Justice, 23 August 2004 (UN Doc. S/2004/616), introduction. There was a discussion on peace and justice at the ICC Review Conference: for a summary, see www.icc-cpi. int/iccdocs/asp_docs/RC2010/RC-11-Annex.V.b-ENG.pdf.

[176] See the discussion in Payam Akhavan, 'The Lord's Resistance Army Case: Uganda's Submission of the First State Referral to the International Criminal Court' (2005) 99 *American Journal of International Law* 403, 416–21; Manisuli Ssenyonjo, 'Accountability of Non-State Actors in Uganda for War Crimes and Human Rights Violations: Between Amnesty and the ICC' (2005) 10 *Journal of Conflict and Security Law* 405.

[177] See 2009 AU resolution (Assembly/AU/December/3(XIII)). For arguments to the contrary, see Christopher Gosnell, 'The Request for an Arrest Warrant in Al Bashir. Idealistic Posturing or Calculated Plan?' (2008) 6 *Journal of International Criminal Justice* 841.

[178] See e.g. Kenneth Rodman, 'Is Peace in the Interests of Justice? The Case for Broad Prosecutorial Discretion at the International Criminal Court' (2009) 22 *Leiden Journal of International Law* 99.

employed by the ICC in its focus on Africa may in part be dismissed as reflecting only the voice of State elites and ignoring victims, but the neglect of situations elsewhere in the world seems to give plausibility to the complaints of those African States who are opposed to the Court on other grounds.[179]

Other challenges for the Court are found in the length of pre-trial and trial procedures, including for victims, the arrangements for the protection of witnesses, and the quality of the candidates for election to the judiciary. There have been improvements in all of these areas but they have to continue to be addressed. A further problem lies in the funding for the Court; the Court has to struggle with a measure of under-funding. International criminal justice is expensive, although set in context the costs are not so high.[180]

The effect which the Court has had on the increase in national legislation and ability to prosecute for atrocities is real but as a contribution to international justice it can be overstated: for situations such as those before the Court there is no real alternative to an international trial, either because of the political unwillingness of the national system or because lack of resources or insecurity rules out national proceedings. The Court has, however, contributed to the development of the increasing acceptance by States of the essential normality of accountability for mass atrocities.

Further reading

The website of the ICC is useful; see www.icc-cpi.int.

Bruce Broomhall, *International Justice and the International Criminal Court: Between Sovereignty and the Rule of Law* (Oxford, 2003)

Antonio Cassese, Paola Gaeta and John R. W. D. Jones (eds.), *The Rome Statute of the International Criminal Court: A Commentary* (Oxford, 2002)

José Doria, M. Cherif Bassiouni and Hans-Peter Gasser (eds.), *The Legal Regime of the International Criminal Court* (Leiden, 2009)

Philippe Kirsch and John Holmes, 'The Rome Conference of an International Criminal Court: The Negotiating Process' (1999) 93 *American Journal of International Law* 2

Jann Kleffner, *Complementarity in the Rome Statute and National Criminal Jurisdictions* (Oxford, 2008)

Mark Lattimer and Philippe Sands (eds.), *Justice for Crimes against Humanity* (Oxford, 2003)

Roy Lee (ed.), *The International Criminal Court: The Making of the Rome Statute* (The Hague, 1999)

Conor McCarthy, *Reparations and Victim Support in the International Criminal Court* (Cambridge, 2012)

Dominic McGoldrick, Peter Rowe and Eric Donnelly (eds.), *The Permanent International Criminal Court: Legal and Policy Issues* (Oxford, 2004)

Sarah Nouwen, *Complementarity in the Line of Fire: The Catalysing Effect of the International Criminal Court in Uganda and Sudan* (Cambridge, 2013)

---

[179] See John Dugard, 'Palestine and the International Criminal Court: Institutional Failure or Bias?' (2013) 11 *Journal of International Criminal Justice* 563, for the view that failure to open an investigation into crimes allegedly committed by Israel and Hamas during Operation Cast Lead reinforces the AU's claim that the OTP has chosen to focus attention only on Africa.

[180] An interesting comparison is available in Daniel McLaughlin, *International Criminal Tribunals: A Visual Overview* (Leitner Center for International Law and Justice, 2013) 77, www.leitnercenter.org/files/International%20Criminal%20Tribunals.pdf.

Georgios Pikis, *The Rome Statute for the International Criminal Court* (Leiden, 2010)

Steven Roach, *Governance, Order and the International Criminal Court: Between Realpolitik and a Cosmopolitan Court* (Oxford, 2009)

Leila Sadat, *The International Criminal Court and the Transformation of International Law* (New York, 2002)

Philippe Sands (ed.), *From Nuremberg to the Hague: The Future of International Criminal Justice* (Cambridge, 2003) Chapters 2 and 4

William Schabas, *The International Criminal Court: A Commentary on the Rome Statute* (Oxford, 2010)

Benjamin Schiff, *Building the International Criminal Court* (Cambridge, 2008)

Carsten Stahn and Göran Sluiter (eds.), *The Emerging Practice of the International Criminal Court* (Leiden, 2009)

Carsten Stahn and Mohamed el-Zeidy (eds.), *The International Criminal Court and Complementarity* (Cambridge, 2011)

Otto Triffterer (ed.), *The Rome Statute of the International Criminal Court: Observers' Notes, Article by Article*, 2nd edn (Baden-Baden, 2008)

9

Other Courts with International Elements

9.1 Introduction

In a parallel development to the establishment of international criminal tribunals and courts, other courts with international elements, sometimes labelled 'internationalized courts' or 'hybrid courts', have been set up. In part, they represent a reaction to the large and expensive international tribunals, which have a limited capacity and are located away from the State in question for security and other reasons. It was hoped that these internationalized courts would better address sovereignty concerns, promote local ownership, legitimacy and victim involvement, build capacity in post-conflict societies, and deliver credible but less expensive justice.[1]

Different models for courts with international elements have been developed. Each model is different, as were their political backgrounds and the legal bases for establishing them. For Sierra Leone, Cambodia and Lebanon, special courts were created by agreement between the UN and the post-conflict government, although the agreement with Lebanon entered into force by a Security Council resolution. These courts have both international and national officials, but, while the Cambodian and Senegalese courts explicitly form part of the domestic system, the other two are separate entities. Further, the subject-matter jurisdiction differs; unlike the other three, the Special Court for Lebanon is not designed to adjudicate genocide, crimes against humanity or war crimes. These four models are briefly outlined in this chapter.

In other instances, the courts were established by the UN or another international administration. In East Timor (Timor Leste) and Kosovo, the courts were created as a direct result of international intervention and installation of an international transitional administration. A specialized court in Bosnia and Herzegovina was also established by an international agency, mandated by a peace agreement. These are, or were, domestic courts with jurisdiction over both international and domestic crimes and with international as well as national judges and prosecutors. They are discussed below.

Other models are based on more limited international assistance to domestic efforts. In Iraq, a special national court was originally created by the occupying powers and later by the

---

[1] E.g. Laura A. Dickinson, 'The Promise of Hybrid Courts' (2003) 97 *American Journal of International Law* 295, 302–7.

State itself. Another example is a specialized court in Serbia. These domestic courts with jurisdiction over international crimes, and national judges only, will also be described as examples of yet different approaches. In addition, one domestic court established for a particular trial concerning domestic crimes (the Lockerbie trial) will also be mentioned as a separate model of international involvement.

While the permanent ICC is intended to be the preferred option for international criminal adjudication, the limitations with respect to its temporal jurisdiction have sometimes required alternative solutions. Other options may also be preferred for practical and/or political reasons. This in turn may prompt questions concerning the principle of complementarity (see section 9.6).

9.2   Courts established by agreement between the United Nations or the African Union and a State

9.2.1   *Special Court for Sierra Leone*

Almost a decade of very violent civil war began in 1991 when a rebel group, the Revolutionary United Front (RUF), entered Sierra Leone from neighbouring Liberia, aiming to overthrow the government. The ensuing stages of the conflict featured all forms of gross human rights violations, but it was particularly characterized by the use of child soldiers and widespread mutilation of civilians by amputation of arms and other limbs. The conflict ended in 2000 with the intervention of a British force and a large UN peacekeeping presence.

The Special Court for Sierra Leone (SCSL) was established by treaty between Sierra Leone and the UN. A request from the President of Sierra Leone to the Security Council for the creation of a special court to deal with crimes committed in the civil war led to a Council resolution[2] requesting the Secretary-General to enter into negotiations with Sierra Leone. An agreement between the government and the UN Secretary-General, attaching the Statute of the Court, was concluded on 16 January 2002.[3] Thereafter, Sierra Leone adopted implementing legislation,[4] and the SCSL began work in July 2002.

The UN Secretary-General has described the SCSL as 'a treaty-based *sui generis* court of mixed jurisdiction and composition'.[5] The international judges, who were appointed by the UN Secretary-General, form a majority; a minority was appointed by the government of Sierra Leone. The UN also appointed the Prosecutor and the Registrar, and Sierra Leone a Deputy Prosecutor.

---

[2] SC Res. 1315(2000) of 14 August 2000.
[3] The agreement, and the Statute of the SCSL, are available at the Court's website, www.sc-sl.org.
[4] The Special Court Agreement (2002) Ratification Act, Supplement to Sierra Leone Official Gazette, Vol. 130, No. 2, 7 March 2002 (as amended).
[5] Report by the Secretary-General on the Establishment of a Special Court for Sierra Leone, UN Doc. S/2000/915 of 4 October 2000, para. 9 ('Secretary-General's Report'). See further Stuart Beresford and A. S. Müller, 'The Special Court for Sierra Leone: An Initial Comment' (2001) 14 *Leiden Journal of International Law* 635; and Robert Cryer, 'A "Special Court" for Sierra Leone' (2001) 50 *International and Comparative Law Quarterly* 435.

The SCSL was not a subsidiary organ of the UN Security Council but a separate international institution and, as clarified in the Sierra Leonean implementing legislation, nor was it part of the Sierra Leonean legal system. The Court applied its own Statute and Rules of Procedure and Evidence, but these make reference to international instruments and some national laws.[6] The Statute provides that the SCSL and national courts of Sierra Leone have concurrent jurisdiction, but the SCSL has primacy.[7]

The SCSL, having established its competence to determine its own jurisdiction, dismissed several challenges, which included the competence of the Sierra Leonean government and the UN Secretary-General to agree to the Court and the compatibility with the Lomé Peace Agreement.[8] Not without controversy, the SCSL also established that it is an international court, and that consequently, by reference to the ICJ *Yerodia* case, State immunity does not bar prosecution of a head of State.[9] It also confirmed that the amnesty granted in the Lomé Peace Agreement did not bar prosecution of international crimes at the SCSL;[10] in fact, this was one motive behind seeking an internationalized solution.

The SCSL had jurisdiction to prosecute persons 'who bear the greatest responsibility for serious violations of international humanitarian law and Sierra Leonean law' committed in the territory of Sierra Leone since 30 November 1996.[11] The reference to 'greatest responsibility' was intended as guidance for a prosecutorial policy rather than a formal limitation of jurisdiction;[12] the objective was that the SCSL should target a limited number of perpetrators and have a short period of operation. Offences by peacekeepers and related personnel were, with some exceptions, left to the jurisdiction of the sending State.[13] A very controversial issue was what to do with the many child soldiers who had committed serious crimes during the civil war; the solution finally chosen was to exclude jurisdiction over children under the age of 15 at the time of the crime and to include special provisions about treatment before and after conviction of juvenile offenders (between 15 and 18 years of age).[14]

Owing to the nature of the conflict, the subject-matter jurisdiction of the SCSL was confined to crimes against humanity and to war crimes committed in a non-international armed conflict.[15] Genocide and war crimes in an international armed conflict were not included. The Court decided, however, that the war crimes within its jurisdiction might be

---

[6] Art. 14 of the SCSL Statute (which refers to the ICTR RPE; these, however, have been substantively amended by the SCSL judges). The Appeals Chamber is also to be guided by the decisions of the ICTY and the ICTR Appeals Chambers: Art. 20.3.
[7] Art. 8 of the SCSL Statute. See also Art. 9 on *ne bis in idem*.
[8] *Kallon, Norman and Kamara*, SCSL A. Ch., 13 March 2004; *Kallon and Kamara*, SCSL A. Ch., 13 March 2004; *Fofana*, SCSL A. Ch., 25 May 2004 (UN competence); and *Gbao*, SCSL A. Ch., 25 May 2004. See also Peace Agreement between the Government of Sierra Leone and the Revolutionary United Front of Sierra Leone (RUF), signed on 7 July 1999 after a meeting in Lomé, Togo (Lomé Peace Agreement). A peculiarity of the SCSL, intended to speed up the process, is that jurisdictional challenges are heard by the Appeals Chamber as the first and last instance; r. 72 of the SCSL RPE.
[9] *Taylor*, SCSL A. Ch., 31 May 2004; see further Chapter 21. See also *Case Concerning the Arrest Warrant of 11 April 2000* (*Democratic Republic of the Congo v. Belgium*), Judgment, 14 February 2002, (2002) ICJ Reports. For a commentary, see Micaela Frulli, 'The Question of Charles Taylor's Immunity' (2004) 2 *Journal of International Criminal Justice* 1118.
[10] Art. 10 of the SCSL Statute; and *Kallon and Kamara*, SCSL A. Ch., 13 March 2004. Cf. Art. IX of the Lomé Peace Agreement.
[11] Art. 1(1) of the SCSL Statute. The date relates to an earlier peace agreement between the government of Sierra Leone and the RUF, signed in Abidjan on 30 November 1996 (Abidjan Peace Agreement).
[12] Secretary-General's Report, para. 30; and see *Kallon, Kamara and Kanu*, SCSL A. Ch., 3 March 2008, paras. 272–85. See also David M. Crane, 'Dancing with the Devil: Prosecuting West Africa's Warlords: Building Initial Prosecutorial Strategy for an International Tribunal after Third World Armed Conflicts' (2005) 37 *Case Western Reserve Journal of International Law* 1.
[13] Art. 1(2) and (3) of the SCSL Statute.   [14] *Ibid.*, Arts. 7, 15(5) and 19(1).   [15] *Ibid.*, Arts. 2–4.

prosecuted regardless of whether the armed conflict was international or non-international in nature.[16] The Court's jurisdiction also covered some specified crimes under Sierra Leonean law.[17]

The definition of crimes against humanity was inspired by, but not identical to, the definition in the ICTR Statute; there is no reference to discriminatory intent as a general requirement for the crime, and some of the underlying acts – sexual offences and persecution – have been further developed for the SCSL.[18] As to war crimes, Article 3 of the Statute regarding violations of Article 3 common to the Geneva Conventions and of Additional Protocol II, reproduced almost *verbatim* the war crimes provisions of the ICTR Statute. In addition, however, the SCSL Statute lists certain other serious violations of international humanitarian law, reflecting only some of the equivalent violations included in the ICC Statute. The inclusion of recruitment of child soldiers in the list was challenged as a breach of the principle of legality, but the Court determined that this was a war crime under customary international law before November 1996.[19]

The Court indicted a total of thirteen suspects (although two indictments were withdrawn owing to the death of the accused). Three joint trials of nine accused were held,[20] and eight persons were convicted on charges of war crimes and crimes against humanity, one having died in custody. On appeal, the convictions and sentences in two of the cases were largely upheld.[21] The third case, against members of the government-associated Civil Defence Force (CDF), was more controversial; while the majority found the accused guilty of some of the charges, one Sierra Leonean judge argued for full acquittals on the basis, *inter alia*, that the actions of the CDF were primarily dictated by necessity.[22] The relatively lenient sentences imposed were disputed.[23] The Appeals Chamber, also by majority, reversed the judgment with respect to some counts and increased the sentences substantially; again, one Sierra Leonean judge wanted to acquit and keep the lenient sentences since it was a 'fight for the restoration of the democratically elected Government'.[24] The Appeals Chamber thus honoured the principle that 'all parties in a conflict must abide by the same rules and be subject to the same punishments'.[25]

The last defendant was the former President of Liberia, Charles Taylor, who was convicted on all eleven counts of crimes against humanity and war crimes by the Trial

---

[16] *Fofana*, SCSL A. Ch., 25 May 2004 (war crimes).   [17] Art. 5 of the SCSL Statute.

[18] The elaboration of sexual offences and persecution is clearly influenced by the ICC Statute. The definition also departs from the ICTY Statute in that no nexus to an armed conflict is required. See further Chapter 11.

[19] *Norman*, SCSL A. Ch., 31 May 2004; cf. Judge Robertson who, in a dissenting opinion, asserted that non-forcible enlistment had first entered international criminal law with the ICC Statute in 1998.

[20] The trials were of members of the Civil Defence Force (CDF), the RUF and the Armed Forces Revolutionary Council (AFRC). For an account of the establishment of the Court, and the indictments and their background, see Stephen Rapp, 'The Compact Model in International Criminal Justice: The Special Court for Sierra Leone' (2008) 57 *Drake Law Review* 11.

[21] *Brima, Kamara and Kanu*, SCSL T. Ch. II, 20 June 2007, and SCSL A. Ch., 22 February 2008; *Sesay, Kallon and Gbao*, SCSL T. Ch. I, 2 March 2009, and SCSL A. Ch., 26 October 2009.

[22] *Fofana and Kondewa*, SCSL T. Ch. I, 2 August 2007; cf. Separate Concurring and Partially Dissenting Opinion of Hon. Justice Bankole Thompson, para. 100.

[23] *Fofana and Kondewa*, SCSL T. Ch. I, 9 October 2007.

[24] *Fofana and Kondewa*, SCSL A. Ch., 28 May 2008; cf. Partially Dissenting Opinion of Hon. Justice George Gelaga King, para. 93. Dissenting opinions were also filed by another Sierra Leonean judge, regarding the sentence, and by one international judge.

[25] Gill Wigglesworth, 'The End of Impunity? Lessons from Sierra Leone' (2008) 84 *International Affairs* 809, 823.

Chamber and sentenced to fifty years' imprisonment.[26] The trial was held at the premises of the ICC in The Hague, by special arrangement due to security concerns.[27] One accused remains at large, and arrangements have been made for his trial in another jurisdiction if he is ever captured.[28] Taylor's conviction and sentence were reaffirmed on appeal,[29] and, hence, the SCSL has completed all its trials.

Commentators have concluded that the SCSL, although plagued by funding problems throughout its existence, has contributed significantly to the clarification of international law concepts and principles, new developments on war crimes and crimes against humanity, and by institutional and procedural innovations.[30] Located in Sierra Leone, it was intended to contribute to national peace and stability and to the long-lasting development of the domestic justice system and national institutions through so-called 'legacy projects'. As in the case of the ICTY and ICTR, different mechanisms have been discussed for the residual functions of the Court, such as conducting reviews of verdicts and sentences, supervision of the enforcement of sentences, providing witness and victim protection, and maintaining the archives. The solution was the establishment, by agreement between the UN and Sierra Leone,[31] of a Residual Special Court for Sierra Leone (RSCSL) to handle these tasks at the closure of the SCSL. The Court's primary seat is in Sierra Leone, but it has an interim seat in the Netherlands with a sub-office in Sierra Leone.[32] It has a roster of both international and national judges, and the Prosecutor and Registrar are appointed by the UN Secretary-General.[33]

9.2.2 Cambodia: Extraordinary Chambers

Another approach was followed to deal with the atrocities committed during the Khmer Rouge rule in Cambodia under Pol Pot, which lasted from 1975 to 1979 when the regime was ousted by invading Vietnamese forces. During these years an estimated 1.7 million people are believed to have died by execution, starvation and forced labour.

The introduction of so-called Extraordinary Chambers in the domestic courts is the culmination of a long process which began by a request from Cambodia to the UN for assistance in bringing Khmer Rouge officials to justice, followed by a UN expert group report recommending the establishment of an ad hoc Tribunal.[34] Cambodia insisted on a domestic solution, however, and negotiations between the Cambodian government and the

---

[26] *Taylor*, SCSL T. Ch. II, 26 April 2012 (summary judgment), 18 May 2012 (written judgment) and 30 May 2012 (sentencing judgment).
[27] See SC Res. 1688(2006) of 16 June 2006.　　[28] Rule 11*bis*, added to the SCSL RPE on 27 May 2008.
[29] *Taylor*, SCSL A. Ch., 26 September 2013.
[30] E.g. Chacha Murungu, 'Prosecution and Punishment of International Crimes by the Special Court for Sierra Leone' in Chacha Murungu and Japhet Biegon (eds.), *Prosecuting International Crimes in Africa* (Pretoria, 2011) 97–118; Vincent Nhemielle (ed.), *Africa and the Future of International Justice* (The Hague, 2012); and Charles Chernor Jallow, *The Sierra Leone Special Court and its Legacy: The Impact for Africa and International Criminal Law* (Cambridge, 2013).
[31] Agreement between the United Nations and the Government of Sierra Leone on the Establishment of a Residual Special Court for Sierra Leone of 11 August 2010, ratified by Sierra Leone through the Residual Special Court for Sierra Leone (Ratification) Act, 2011. Annexed to the agreement is the Residual SCSL Statute.
[32] Art. 6 of the Residual SCSL Statute.　　[33] *Ibid.*, Arts. 13–15.
[34] See e.g. Helen Horsington, 'The Cambodian Khmer Rouge Tribunal: The Promise of a Hybrid Tribunal' (2004) 5 *Melbourne Journal of International Law* 462.

UN started in 1999. They broke down in 2002 and the UN Secretary-General withdrew from the process having concluded that the Cambodian court, as then envisaged, would not guarantee the required independence, impartiality and objectivity, and that Cambodia refused to accept that UN assistance would be governed by a UN–Cambodian agreement.

Nevertheless, later in 2002 the UN General Assembly requested the Secretary-General to resume negotiations towards establishing domestic Chambers,[35] with a model based on Cambodian law. An agreement between the UN and Cambodia was adopted by the General Assembly in May 2003,[36] and ratified by the Cambodian National Assembly in October 2004.[37] It is an international agreement which is subject to the law of treaties and cannot be circumvented by Cambodian legislation.

Unlike the SCSL, the Extraordinary Chambers in the Courts of Cambodia (ECCC) form part of the domestic system of Cambodia and apply municipal law. The Pre-Trial Chamber has, however, concluded that the ECCC has distinctive features and is an entirely 'independent entity within the Cambodian court structure'.[38] The Chambers are to try 'senior leaders of Democratic Kampuchea and those most responsible for the crimes and serious violations of Cambodian penal law, international humanitarian law and custom, and international conventions recognised by Cambodia'; the offences include genocide under the 1948 Genocide Convention, crimes against humanity as defined in the ICC Statute, grave breaches of the Geneva Conventions, and certain other crimes under Cambodian law.[39] War crimes in non-international armed conflicts are not covered; Cambodia was not party to the Additional Protocols before 1980 and there were doubts as to the customary status of these crimes in the 1970s when the crimes were committed.[40] The temporal jurisdiction is exclusively retroactive and limited to crimes committed between 17 April 1975 and 6 January 1979. Of course, the death of Pol Pot in April 1998 means that the one person probably most responsible will never stand trial.

The mixed composition of the ECCC and the prosecution was a matter of dispute during the negotiations with the UN. The Cambodian side insisted on supremacy and, therefore, the national judges are in the majority both in the Trial Chamber and in the Supreme Court Chamber. For balance a qualified majority is required for any decision,[41] a difficult solution which could result in deadlock and, arguably, an acquittal even if all the international judges vote for a conviction. The agreement stipulates that the ECCC's procedures shall be in accordance with Cambodian procedural law.[42] Owing to the civil law origin of the Cambodian criminal procedures, investigative judges are responsible for the investigations; one international and one local judge operate together, with disagreements being resolved by

[35] GA Res. 57/228A of 18 December 2002.
[36] GA Res. 57/228B of 13 May 2003 (to which the UN–Cambodia Agreement is attached).
[37] Arts. 2 and 31 of the UN–Cambodia Agreement. The agreement is implemented by Cambodian national legislation under which the ECCC operate: the Law on the Establishment of Extraordinary Chambers in the Courts of Cambodia for the Prosecution of Crimes Committed during the Period of Democratic Kampuchea, NS/RKM/1004/006 (2004).
[38] *Kaing Guek Eav ('Duch')*, ECCC PTC, 3 December 2007, paras. 17–20.
[39] Arts. 1 and 9 of the UN–Cambodia Agreement.
[40] Report of the Group of Experts for Cambodia Established Pursuant to General Assembly Resolution 52/135, UN Doc. A/53/850, paras. 72–5.
[41] Arts. 3 and 4 of the UN–Cambodia Agreement.   [42] *Ibid.*, Art. 12.

a Pre-Trial Chamber, again with local judges in the majority.[43] A similar scheme applies to the two co-prosecutors.[44] All the judges and prosecutors are appointed by the Cambodian Supreme Council of Magistracy, although the international officials are nominated by the UN Secretary-General.

Hence, a distinct feature of the ECCC is being domestic in nature both with respect to the majority of local judges and regarding applicable law. There is however a 'super-majority' required for decision-making and the agreement allows guidance to be sought from 'procedural rules established at the international level' under certain conditions.[45] A lack of clarity concerning the sources of Cambodian procedural law, paired with fair trial concerns, prompted the ECCC judges to adopt Internal Rules;[46] the implicit rule-making power of the judges has been questioned, but the ECCC has upheld the constitutionality and superiority of the Internal Rules *vis-à-vis* Cambodian law.[47] The Internal Rules may help to remove some of the potential for blocks in the system, but still concerns are being expressed about the independence, impartiality and efficiency of the ECCC and their future activities.[48] In part, this is because of other distinguishing features: the very pronounced division between national and international officials, as well as civil law procedures in combination with a largely adversarial trial which give rise to both 'a full-length judicial investigation and a full-length trial'.[49]

With the trial of 'Duch',[50] the ECCC began their first proceedings. Four other persons have been charged with genocide, crimes against humanity and war crimes. One of these is former Foreign Minister, Ieng Sary, who was accorded a royal pardon and amnesty following his conviction *in absentia* for genocide after the fall of the Khmer Rouge in 1979. The agreement with the UN includes a commitment by the Cambodian government not to request amnesties or pardons and leaves to the Chambers to decide the scope of previously granted pardons.[51] The co-investigating judges held that the amnesty and pardon granted to Ieng Sary did not cover the offences subject to the jurisdiction of the ECCC and was therefore no bar to the proceedings against him, but the Pre-Trial Chamber was less clear, ruling that it was 'not manifest or evident' that the amnesty or pardon would prevent his conviction for genocide.[52] After Ieng Sary's death in March 2013 and the Court finding

[43] *Ibid.*, Arts. 5 and 7.   [44] *Ibid.*, Art. 6 and Rule 71 of the Internal Rules.   [45] *Ibid.*, Art. 12.
[46] See e.g. Robert Petit and Anees Ahmed, 'A Review of the Jurisprudence of the Khmer Rouge Tribunal' (2010) 8 *Northwestern Journal of International Human Rights* 165, 167–9.
[47] E.g. *Nuon Chea*, ECCC PTC, 26 August 2008, paras. 14–5, and 25 February 2009.
[48] See e.g. Sarah Williams, 'The Cambodian Extraordinary Chambers: A Dangerous Precedent for International Justice?' (2004) 53 *International and Comparative Law Quarterly* 227. See also Göran Sluiter, 'Due Process and Criminal Procedure in the Cambodian Extraordinary Chambers' (2006) 4 *Journal of International Criminal Justice* 314.
[49] Alex Bates, *Transitional Justice in Cambodia: Analytical Report* (Atlas Project, 2010) 134. See also John D. Ciorciari and Anne Heindel, 'Experiments in International Criminal Justice: Lessons from the Khmer Rouge Tribunal' (2014) 35 *Michigan Journal of International Law* (forthcoming).
[50] *Kaing Guek Eav*, ECCC SCC, 3 February 2012. Kaing Guek Eav, otherwise known as Duch, was convicted of crimes against humanity, war crimes and the domestic offences of murder and torture, and directed the site called S21, the headquarters of the secret police special branch under the Khmer Rouge. Duch has been in a Cambodian prison since 1999, and in the end he was sentenced to life imprisonment.
[51] Art. 11 of the UN–Cambodia Agreement.
[52] *Ieng Sary*, ECCC OCIJ, 14 November 2007, and ECCC PTC, 17 October 2008, paras. 57–9. However, insofar as doubt remains, there may be room to raise the issue anew in accordance with a ruling in another case that a Trial Chamber is not bound by the decision of a Pre-Trial Chamber: see *Kiang Guek Eav*, ECCC T. Ch., 23 September 2009, para. 12.

his wife, Ieng Thirith, unfit to stand trial in November 2011, only two accused remain in the case. The trial is conducted in several separate parts and the first trial was concluded in October 2013.

The co-prosecutors were divided as to whether these five persons were to be the only ones to be tried by the ECCC, and their disagreement went to the Pre-Trial Chamber. The Chamber was unable to reach the required 'super-majority',[53] and it was therefore possible to open the new investigations. Both the co-prosecutors and the Chamber were split along national/ international lines. Later, during the investigation of Case 003 and Case 004 (the identity of the suspects remains confidential), this split continued, creating the perception that the Cambodian judges do not act impartially with respect to further investigations and prosecutions. The conflict became particularly acrimonious at the level of the co-investigating judges, resulting in the resignation of two international co-investigative judges, and other international staff, and the refusal by Cambodian authorities to recognize a third international judge who also left the Court. In June 2012, the UN Secretary-General appointed a fourth international co-investigative judge (as well as one reserve judge) who is now investigating the cases, although reportedly with little assistance from the Cambodian court officials. The division is likely to continue in spite of the serious harm it is causing the ECCC.

9.2.3   Special Tribunal for Lebanon

Upon the killing of Lebanon's former Prime Minister, Rafiq Hariri, on 14 February 2005, the Security Council established a commission to assist the Lebanese authorities in their investigation of the assassination, including the links to neighbouring Syria.[54] Lebanon requested the creation of an international tribunal, and the Secretary-General was asked by the Security Council to negotiate an agreement with the government of Lebanon on a 'tribunal of an international character'.[55] After negotiations with Lebanon and the members of the Security Council, the Secretary-General presented a draft agreement and Statute for a tribunal, which were accepted by the Security Council.[56] The government of Lebanon signed the agreement but because of constitutional difficulties the agreement could not come into force in accordance with its terms; the Security Council therefore brought its provisions into force, at the request of the Lebanese Prime Minister, by means of a Chapter VII resolution.[57]

Like the Special Court for Sierra Leone, the Special Tribunal for Lebanon (STL) is treaty-based and is not a subsidiary organ of the UN (although its provisions were brought into

---

[53] Cases 003 and 004, ECCC PTC, 18 August 2009.

[54] SC Res. 1595(2005) of 7 April 2005 established the UN International Independent Investigation Commission (UNIIC). SC Res. 1636(2005) of 31 October 2005 and 1644(2005) of 15 December 2005 required Syria to cooperate with the UNIIC.

[55] SC Res. 1664(2006) of 29 March 2006. Both the UNIIC and the Tribunal were part of the Council's global counter-terrorism strategy: see D. A. Bellemare, 'Bringing Terrorists before International Justice: A View from the Front Lines' (2012) 23 *Criminal Law Forum* 425.

[56] See the Report of the Secretary-General on the Establishment of a Special Tribunal for Lebanon, UN Doc. S/2006/893 of 15 November 2006; and Letter dated 21 November 2006 from the President of the Security Council addressed to the Secretary-General, UN Doc. S/2006/911 of 24 November 2006.

[57] SC Res. 1757(2007) of 30 May 2007. The five members of the Council who abstained on the vote on the resolution criticized the use of a Chapter VII resolution to bypass national constitutional procedures.

force by Security Council resolution). It does not form part of the Lebanese court system. It sits in The Hague and has a majority of international judges, including an international pre-trial judge, an international chief prosecutor and a Lebanese deputy prosecutor, a registry and a defence office. The STL is established for a specific trial or trials with jurisdiction covering those responsible for the attack on Hariri and other related crimes of a similar nature and gravity committed within a limited time period.[58]

The Tribunal applies Lebanese law, with some modifications such as the inapplicability of the death penalty; crimes within its jurisdiction are crimes under Lebanese criminal law relating to terrorism and 'offences against life and personal integrity, illicit associations and failure to report crimes and offences'.[59] It does not have jurisdiction over international crimes.[60] The Tribunal has primacy over national courts in Lebanon. In November 2011, the Appeals Chamber took the unusual step of issuing a decision at the request of the Pre-Trial Judge on the applicable law concerning terrorism, conspiracy, homicide, perpetration and cumulative charging.[61] Instead of merely supplementing Lebanese law with international law, the Chamber interpreted the former in the context of 'international obligations undertaken by Lebanon with which, in the absence of very clear language, it is presumed any legislation complies'.[62]

The agreement establishing the STL came into force on 10 June 2007, and after a period of transition from UN International Independent Commission (UNIIC) to the Office of the Prosecutor, the Prosecutor continued the investigations begun by the Commission. Rules of Procedure and Evidence were adopted. Shortly after the beginning of the Tribunal's work in March 2009, the pre-trial judge requested the Lebanese court to defer to the Tribunal's competence, and to refer to the Prosecutor the results of any investigation and the court's records on the case concerning the assassination of Hariri.[63] The pre-trial judge then ordered the release of four Lebanese generals with ties to Syrian security services, who had spent nearly four years in Lebanese custody.[64]

Thereafter attention has been directed elsewhere, and on 28 June 2011 an indictment was confirmed and arrest warrants issued against four accused with links to the powerful political and military organization Hezbollah,[65] which in turn had political repercussions in Lebanon.

---

[58] In addition to the attack of 14 February 2005, the Tribunal has jurisdiction over other attacks in Lebanon between 1 October 2004 and 12 December 2005 if it finds that they are connected with, and are of similar nature and gravity to, the February attack. The UN and the Lebanese government can decide to fix a date later than 12 December 2005 to extend jurisdiction to other 'connected' crimes, subject to the approval of the Security Council.

[59] Art. 2(a) of the STL Statute. The Statute is set out in SC Res. 1757(2007).

[60] The inclusion of crimes against humanity, to be defined in the Statute, was considered but later rejected due to insufficient support within the Security Council; see the Report, UN Doc. S/2006/893, paras. 23–5.

[61] See *Ayyash et al.*, STL A. Ch., 16 February 2011.

[62] *Ibid.*, paras. 19–20. For substantive and procedural criticism, see e.g. Kai Ambos, 'Judicial Creativity at the Special Tribunal for Lebanon: Is there a Crime of Terrorism under International Law?' (2011) 24 *Leiden Journal of International Law* 655; and Ben Saul, 'The Special Tribunal for Lebanon and Terrorism as an International Crime: Reflections on the Judicial Function' in Schabas, *Ashgate Research Companion*, 79–100. On terrorism, see further Chapter 14.

[63] *In the Matter of El Sayed*, STL PTJ, 27 March 2009 (issued without reference to any named suspect).

[64] *In the Matter of El Sayed*, STL PTJ, 29 April 2009 (issued without reference to any named suspect). One of the generals is now pursuing a case on disclosure of documents with the ultimate aim to bring proceedings in national courts on wrongful detention and libel (*In the Matter of El Sayed*).

[65] *Ayyash et al.*, STL PTJ, 28 June 2011. The arrest warrants were issued in separate decisions the same day, and international arrest warrants were issued against each accused on 8 July 2011.

The arrest warrants were not executed and the Trial Chamber decided to hold the trial *in absentia*, concluding that each of the accused 'has absconded or otherwise cannot be found'.[66] The accused have court-appointed defence counsel and the trial opened in January 2014. There have been numerous pre-trial motions and unsuccessful challenges to the jurisdiction and legality of the Tribunal.[67] In addition, the STL has opened a case concerning three related attacks on 1 October 2004 (Marwan Hamadeh), 21 June 2005 (George Hawi) and 12 July 2005 (Elias El-Murr), and has issued deferral orders to Lebanese judicial authorities at the request of the Prosecutor.[68]

The STL, with a staff of almost 400 people, is financed by voluntary contributions from the international community (51 per cent) and by Lebanon (49 per cent). The mandate is limited, and the current President has stated that the Tribunal is expected to finish its work by 2015.

9.2.4   Senegal: Extraordinary African Chambers

The presidency of Hissène Habré in Chad between 1982 and 1990 was characterized by serious human rights violations. Since 2000 various attempts have been made to bring Habré to justice, including in Senegal where he resides. In the wake of a ruling by the Court of Justice of the Economic Community of West African States (ECOWAS), declaring that Habré must be tried in accordance with a 'special ad hoc procedure of an international character',[69] and the ICJ's judgment in *Questions Relating to the Obligation to Prosecute or Extradite* (*Belgium* v. *Senegal*), ordering Senegal to prosecute Habré without further delay,[70] an agreement was concluded between the African Union (AU) and Senegal to establish Extraordinary African Chambers in the courts of Senegal.[71]

The Chambers are tasked with the prosecution of those most responsible for genocide, crimes against humanity, war crimes and torture committed in Chad between 7 June 1982 and 1 December 1990, that is to say, under Habré's rule.[72] They consist of one Investigative Chamber, one Indicting Chamber, one Trial Chamber and one Appeals Chamber, all within existing Senegalese courts and composed mainly of Senegalese judges who are nominated by Senegal and appointed by the Chairperson of the AU Commission; the presiding judge of

---

[66] Art. 22 of the STL Statute and r. 106 of the STL RPE; *Ayyash et al.*, STL T. Ch., 1 February 2012. A later request for reconsideration of the decision was dismissed, which was also upheld on appeal: *Ayyash et al.*, STL T. Ch., 11 July 2012 and STL A. Ch., 1 November 2012.

[67] *Ayyash et al.*, STL T. Ch., 27 July 2012 and STL A. Ch., 24 October 2012. The rejected claims were that that the STL was illegally established by the Security Council, that its establishment infringes the sovereignty of Lebanon, that it is unconstitutional under Lebanese law, and that it is not 'established by law' since it infringes the fundamental human rights of the accused. For a critical view, see José Alvarez, 'Tadić Revisited: The Ayyash Decisions of the Special Tribunal for Lebanon' (2013) 11 *Journal of International Criminal Justice* 291.

[68] Connected Cases, *Hamadeh, Hawi and El-Murr*, STL PTJ, 19 August 2011 (three separate orders).

[69] *Hissein Habré* v. *Republique du Senegal*, Court of Justice of ECOWAS, 18 November 2010, para. 61. According to the Court, the principle of non-retroactivity would otherwise be violated; for a critical view, see Jan Arno Hessbruegge, 'ECOWAS Court Judgment in Habré v. Senegal Complicates Prosecution in the Name of Africa' (2010) 15(4) *ASIL Insights* (3 February 2010).

[70] *Questions Relating to the Obligation to Prosecute or Extradite* (*Belgium* v. *Senegal*), ICJ General List 144, 20 July 2012. See Chapter 4.

[71] Agreement of 22 August 2012. In December 2012, the Senegalese National Assembly adopted a law establishing the Chambers. See Sangeeta Shah, 'Questions Relating to the Obligation to Prosecute or Extradite (Belgium v. Senegal)' (2013) 13 *Human Rights Law Review* 351.

[72] Arts. 3–8 of the Extraordinary African Chambers Statute. An unofficial English version of the Statute is available at the website of Human Rights Watch, www.hrw.org.

the Trial and Appeals Chambers respectively are to be a national of another AU Member State.[73] The prosecutors, in a separate Office of the Prosecutor, must be Senegalese and are nominated and appointed in the same way.[74] An Administrator and the Registry are appointed by the Minister of Justice of Senegal.[75] The Chambers, which were inaugurated in February 2013, apply their Statute and Senegalese law. The funding is primarily from international (voluntary) donors.

On 2 July 2013, Habré was charged with crimes against humanity, torture and war crimes, and ordered to be held in pre-trial detention. The jurisdiction is not restricted to Habré, however, and the Prosecutor has made public that he has requested the indictment of five former officials of Habré's administration, although none of them is in Senegal. Senegal and Chad have concluded a special agreement on judicial cooperation.[76] Chad had already in 2002 waived Habré's immunity from prosecution abroad, but the Statute of the Chambers explicitly rules out immunity (or an amnesty) as a bar to prosecution.[77] The Statute provides for the dissolution of the Chambers once all judgments are final.[78]

9.3 Courts established by the United Nations or other international administration

9.3.1 *Kosovo and East Timor: special panels*

Following Security Council resolutions in 1999, the UN temporarily assumed the sovereign activities of the previous authorities in East Timor and Kosovo, both territories having suffered violence during struggles for independence. The UN Mission in Kosovo (UNMIK)[79] was empowered to exercise all executive and legislative authority in that territory, including the administration of justice. The UN Transitional Administration in East Timor (UNTAET)[80] had similar powers. The essentially State-building mandates to establish law and order, and a credible and fair justice system, included powers to repeal and rewrite laws and to administer courts, develop legal policy, draft legislation, assess the quality of justice and address allegations of human rights violations.[81] Questions have been raised as to the legal authority for taking the far-reaching measures, the competence of UN missions to fulfil such tasks and the democratic deficiency of the administrations.[82]

---

[73] *Ibid.*, Arts. 2 and 11.   [74] *Ibid.*, Art. 12.   [75] *Ibid.*, Arts. 13 and 15.

[76] Judicial Cooperation Agreement between the Republic of Chad and the Republic of Senegal for the Prosecution of International Crimes Committed in Chad between 7 June 1982 to 1 December 1990, 3 May 2013.

[77] Arts. 10(3) and 20 of the Extraordinary African Chambers Statute. Interestingly, in 2011 Habré was reportedly convicted *in absentia* in Chad and, thus, questions relating to *ne bis in idem* may arise: *ibid.*, Art. 19 (see also Art. 18(2) on the transfer of criminal prosecutions, which may apply if the judgment is not final).

[78] *Ibid.*, Art. 37.   [79] Established by SC Res. 1244(1999) of 10 June 1999.

[80] Established by SC Res. 1272(1999) of 25 October 1999.

[81] See further Hansjörg Strohmeyer, 'Collapse and Reconstruction of a Judicial System: The United Nations Missions in Kosovo and East Timor' (2001) 95 *American Journal of International Law* 46.

[82] See e.g. M. Brand, 'Institution Building and Human Rights Protection in Kosovo in the Light of UNMIK Legislation' (2001) 70 *Nordic Journal of International Law* 461; David Marshall and Shelley Inglis, 'The Disempowerment of Human Rights-Based Justice in the United Nations Mission in Kosovo' (2003) 16 *Harvard Human Rights Journal* 95; Carsten Stahn, 'Justice under Transitional Administration: Contours and Critique of a Paradigm' (2005) 27 *Houston Journal of International Law* 311.

Both territories experienced the destruction of infrastructure, a shortage of qualified lawyers, a compelling security situation and a history of ethnic discrimination. But, since the creation of the special courts had different aims, the institutional solutions differed. In Kosovo, where the ICTY (and the Residual Mechanism) also has jurisdiction,[83] the main purpose was to support more peaceful relations between different groups in society and to address a broader range of crimes, while the East Timor scheme was intended mainly to prosecute international crimes. In both cases, more ambitious proposals were rejected.[84]

In Kosovo, the appointment of new domestic judges and prosecutors did not quell discriminatory practices and international judges and prosecutors were embedded in the ordinary courts.[85] UNMIK also assumed the power to assign an international prosecutor, an international investigative judge, or a court panel with a majority of international judges – so-called 'Regulation 64 Panels' – to a particular case, when this was considered necessary 'to ensure the independence and impartiality of the judiciary or the proper administration of justice'.[86] The panels, being domestic courts, initially applied pre-existing domestic law, but later UNMIK introduced new legislation including provisional criminal and criminal procedure codes[87] which also included modern definitions of international crimes. The panels tried a large number of major or high-profile cases, including war crimes trials against Kosovar Serbs, and internationalized panels of the Supreme Court overturned questionable convictions by lower courts. But, while the international presence improved the appearance of objectivity, the legal quality of the work was criticized and there were other problems relating to detention, defence representation, witness protection and sentencing.[88]

The declaration of independence by the Kosovo Assembly in February 2008 led to a replacement of some of the functions of UNMIK by an EU presence, EULEX.[89] The Kosovo Assembly has substituted the 'Regulation 64 Panels' with a law under which EULEX judges and prosecutors operate, either separately or in mixed composition, within the national system.[90] In particular, EULEX judges have competence concerning cases investigated and prosecuted by the Special Prosecution Office of the Republic of Kosovo,[91] which deals with all war crimes and terrorism cases; EULEX prosecutors also have authority to investigate and prosecute such cases.[92] The current EULEX mandate runs until 14 June 2014.

---

[83] This jurisdiction was exercised in *Milutinović et al.*, ICTY T. Ch. III, 6 May 2003.

[84] The Kosovo War and Ethnic Crimes Court (KWECC), proposed by a Technical Advisory Commission (UNMIK Regulation 1999/5 of 7 September 1999), and an international criminal tribunal for East Timor, suggested in the Report of the International Commission of Inquiry on East Timor to the Secretary-General, UN Doc. A/54/726, UN Doc. S/2002/59 (2000) at 153.

[85] UNMIK Regulation 2000/6 of 15 February 2000 and Regulation 2000/34 of 29 May 2000.

[86] UNMIK Regulation 2000/64 on Assignment of International Judges/Prosecutors and/or Change of Venue, of 15 December 2000 (the time limit for its application was extended).

[87] UNMIK Regulation 2003/25 and Regulation 2003/26, both of 6 July 2003. Subsequently, these provisional codes have been replaced by legislation adopted by the Republic of Kosovo.

[88] See e.g. in reports by the OSCE Mission in Kosovo, Legal System Monitoring Section; available at www.osce.org/kosovo.

[89] The European Union Rule of Law Mission in Kosovo.

[90] Law No. 03/L-053 on the Jurisdiction, Case Selection and Case Allocation of EULEX Judges and Prosecutors in Kosovo, adopted on 13 March 2008.

[91] Law No. 03/L-052 on the Special Prosecution Office of the Republic of Kosovo, adopted on 13 March 2008.

[92] Law No. 03/L-053, Arts. 3.1 and 8.1; and Law No. 03/L-052.

In East Timor, UNTAET began with the creation of a new court system consisting of six district courts and a Court of Appeal, all with jurisdiction in both criminal and civil cases.[93] This was soon followed by the establishment of 'Serious Crimes Panels' of the District Court in Dili (the capital) and the Court of Appeal, similar to an abandoned model for Kosovo, with exclusive jurisdiction over certain serious criminal offences and with a mixed composition of East Timorese and international judges.[94] On each panel, the international judges were in the majority. UNTAET also established a national prosecution service for the prosecution of crimes before the 'Serious Crimes Chambers', with both local and international prosecutors.[95]

The jurisdiction of the 'Serious Crimes Panels' covered genocide, crimes against humanity and war crimes, as well as certain domestic crimes (murder, sexual offences and torture), the international crimes being defined in the UNTAET Regulation together with provisions on general principles of criminal law and penalties.[96] The jurisdiction covered crimes in East Timor, or elsewhere if committed against an East Timorese citizen, during a limited time period (1 January–25 October 1999).[97] The panels applied domestic law,[98] UNTAET Regulations, including a provisional Code of Criminal Procedure,[99] and, where appropriate, applicable treaties and recognized principles and norms of international law.[100] After primarily prosecuting domestic crimes, later cases also led to convictions for crimes against humanity, many of them based on guilty pleas. But difficult questions were not always sufficiently addressed by the panels, such as the characterization of the conflict for the purpose of war crimes, the prerequisites for crimes against humanity, and the legal import of duress and superior orders.[101]

After general and presidential elections, the UN handed over its authority to the new democratic institutions of East Timor in 2002, and UNTAET was replaced by another UN mission with a consultative mandate. The UNTAET Regulations continued to apply provisionally and the 'Serious Crimes Panels' functioned under the authority of the new East Timorese Constitution. Gradually the Regulations were replaced, and in May 2005 the 'Serious Crimes Panels' suspended operations indefinitely. The international judges and prosecutors departed, and the ordinary courts now handle cases involving international crimes.

---

[93] UNTAET Regulation 2000/11 of 6 March 2000 (later amended).   [94] UNTAET Regulation 2000/15 of 5 July 2000.
[95] UNTAET Regulation 2000/16 of 5 July 2000. A legal aid service, including public defenders, was also created: UNTAET Regulation 2001/24 of 5 September 2001.
[96] UNTAET Regulation 2000/15 of 5 July 2000, ss. 4–6 (and torture, s. 7) and ss. 10–21.   [97] *Ibid.*, s. 2(3).
[98] Adding to the complexity, the Court of Appeals rejected Indonesian law as 'domestic law', arguing that the Indonesian occupation of East Timor was illegal, and ruled that the law of the former colonial power, Portugal, should be applied instead; *Armando Dos Santos*, Court of Appeals, East Timor, 15 July 2003; for a critical view, see e.g. Sylvia de Bertodano, 'Current Developments in Internationalized Courts: East Timor – Justice Denied' (2004) 2 *Journal of International Criminal Justice* 910.
[99] UNTAET Regulation 2000/30 of 25 September 2000 (subsequently amended).   [100] *Ibid.*, s. 3.
[101] See e.g. Suzannah Linton, 'Prosecuting Atrocities at the District Court of Dili' (2001) 2 *Melbourne Journal of International Law* 414; Suzannah Linton and Caitlin Reiger, 'The Evolving Jurisprudence and Practice of East Timor's Special Panels for Serious Crimes on Admission of Guilt, Duress and Superior Orders' (2001) 4 *Yearbook of International Humanitarian Law* 1; Claus Kreß, 'The 1999 Crisis in East Timor and the Threshold of the Law on War Crimes' (2002) 13 *Criminal Law Forum* 409; Kai Ambos and Steffen Wirth, 'The Current Law of Crimes against Humanity: An Analysis of UNTAET Regulation 15/2000' (2002) 13 *Criminal Law Forum* 1; Guy Cumes, 'Murder as a Crime against Humanity in International Law: Choice of Law and Prosecution of Murder in East Timor' (2003) 11 *European Journal of Crime, Criminal Law and Criminal Justice* 40.

In both situations, these domestic institutions depended upon the respective home States to secure international cooperation, requiring accession to international agreements as well as adoption of domestic legislation. In practice, lack of cooperation hindered efforts to prosecute. This was particularly pronounced in East Timor since Indonesia refused to cooperate, in spite of a bilateral agreement, and instead pursued some proceedings before a much criticized ad hoc tribunal in Jakarta.[102]

9.3.2   Bosnia and Herzegovina: the War Crimes Chamber

During the demise of the former Yugoslavia, tens of thousands of people died and perhaps a million people were displaced in Bosnia and Herzegovina. With the 1995 Dayton Peace Agreement, a complex political structure and two 'entities' were created, the Federation of Bosnia and Herzegovina, and Republika Srpska. The Office of the High Representative (OHR) oversees the civilian aspects of the agreement on behalf of the international community. The Court of Bosnia and Herzegovina, with jurisdiction over both entities, and within that court a War Crimes Chamber was established as a domestic institution with international components.[103] The Chamber, which began its work in March 2005, stems from a joint initiative of the ICTY and the OHR. Individual States provided the initial funding, with responsibility now being transferred to the national budget, although the Court still receives international donations.

As well as being part of the reform of the national justice system by the OHR,[104] the Chamber was also an essential element of the ICTY completion strategy,[105] being a domestic court to which the ICTY could refer cases against lower-level perpetrators in accordance with Rule 11*bis* of the ICTY's Rules of Procedure and Evidence.[106] This rule allows the referral of an indictment against an accused, regardless of whether he is in the ICTY's custody or not, to any State which has jurisdiction and which is willing and adequately prepared to accept such a case. The ICTY will consider the gravity of the crime and the level of responsibility of the

---

[102]   See e.g. Suzannah Linton, 'Unravelling the First Three Trials at Indonesia's Ad Hoc Court for Human Rights Violations in East Timor' (2004) 17 *Leiden Journal of International Law* 303. East Timor and Indonesia did, however, establish a joint Commission of Truth and Friendship to report on violence in 1999: see Commission of Truth and Friendship's Final Report on the 1999 Atrocities in East Timor.

[103]   See e.g. Bogdan Ivanišević, *The War Crimes Chamber in Bosnia and Herzegovina: From Hybrid to Domestic Court* (International Center for Transitional Justice, 2008), available at www.ictj.org/images/content/1/0/1088.pdf; Clair Garbett, 'Localising Criminal Justice: An Overview of National Prosecutions at the War Crimes Chamber of the Court of Bosnia and Herzegovina' (2010) 10 *Human Rights Law Review* 558; and Louise Mallinder, 'War Crimes Chamber of the Court of Bosnia and Herzegovina' in Lavinia Stan and Nadya Nedelsky (eds.), *Encyclopedia of Transitional Justice* (Cambridge, 2012) Vol. 3, 484–8.

[104]   For critical assessments, see e.g. Alejandro Chehtman, 'Developing Bosnia and Herzegovina's Capacity to Process War Crimes Cases: Critical Notes on a "Success Story"' (2011) 9 *Journal of International Criminal Justice* 547; Kateřina Uhlířovà, 'War Crimes Chamber of the Court of Bosnia and Herzegovina: Seeding "International Standards of Justice"?' in Kristjansdottir (ed.), *International Law in Domestic Courts*, 195–217; and Olga Martin-Ortega, 'Prosecuting War Crimes at Home: Lessons from the War Crimes Chamber in the State Court of Bosnia and Herzegovina' (2012) 12 *International Criminal Law Review* 589.

[105]   See e.g. the Completion Strategy Report of the ICTY of 14 May 2009 (S/2009/589).

[106]   See Michael Bohlander, 'Referring an Indictment from the ICTY and ICTR to Another Court – Rule 11*bis* and the Consequences for the Law of Extradition' (2006) 55 *International and Comparative Law Quarterly* 219 (also noting that the Tribunals under this scheme may issue an arrest warrant and direct States to surrender the accused to another State). Arts. 1(4) and 6 of the MICT Statute also mandate the referral of cases to national jurisdictions, but, since the ICTY has not transferred any case to MICT, this mechanism will not be utilized *vis-à-vis* the Balkan States. See also Chapter 7.

perpetrator; it must also be satisfied that the accused would receive a fair trial and that the death penalty would not be imposed. Six cases have been referred, and ten accused transferred, to Bosnia and Herzegovina from the ICTY.[107]

The Chamber operates under national law, including new criminal and criminal procedure codes introduced by the OHR,[108] and deals with the most serious war-related crimes in Bosnia. But it does not have exclusive or superior jurisdiction over war crimes, which are also prosecuted in the district or cantonal courts. The criminal code applied by the Chamber defines, *inter alia*, genocide, crimes against humanity and war crimes, regulates general criminal law principles such as command responsibility and provides for far-reaching criminal jurisdiction.

Apart from the international involvement in the establishment of the institution and the adoption of applicable law, the Chamber had international judges at both trial and appeal levels. The Office of the Prosecutor of the State Court has a Special Department for War Crimes, which had both international and local prosecutors and other staff, and an organization to accept ICTY referrals. International defence counsel are also provided for. However, the intention from the outset was to terminate the Chamber's international features relatively quickly. Initially, the international judges and prosecutors were appointed by the OHR, but from July 2006 they were appointed locally in accordance with national procedures. Until 2008, each of the five trial panels and the appellate panel included two international members and one national member but the balance of composition was then reversed, with national judges in a majority. In 2012, the international prosecutors and judges were phased out altogether.

Adoption of a national war crimes prosecution strategy will assist in tackling the huge domestic caseload still remaining.[109] International legal cooperation is crucial, though often difficult. Bosnia has adhered to certain European cooperation treaties, but cooperation with neighbouring States has been difficult, particularly having regard to constitutional bans on extraditing nationals. However, in recent years regional cooperation has improved and various agreements have been concluded.

9.4 Courts established by a State with international support

9.4.1 *Iraq: the Iraqi High Tribunal*

During Saddam Hussein's authoritarian regime, lasting for over thirty-five years, individuals and ethnic communities were violently suppressed and wars were fought against Iraq's neighbours, Iran and Kuwait. In the wake of his removal from power by coalition forces, a

---

[107] See e.g. *Janković and Stanković*, ICTY A. Ch., 1 September 2005. All cases have been adjudicated by the War Crimes Chamber. In addition, referral motions against four accused were refused by the ICTY.

[108] Criminal Code of Bosnia and Herzegovina, Official Gazette No. 37/03, and Criminal Procedure Code of Bosnia and Herzegovina, Official Gazette No. 36/03, both of 24 January 2003 (with amendments).

[109] See paras. 29–38 of the Thirty-Fifth Report of the High Representative for Bosnia and Herzegovina to the UN Secretary-General (S/2009/206).

specialized court for genocide, crimes against humanity and war crimes was created in Iraq, primarily to deal with crimes of the old regime. As a domestic court, and not being established by the Security Council, by a UN administration, by treaty, or directly by occupying powers like the post-Second World War Tribunals, the international aspects are distinctly different, and limited, compared with the courts previously mentioned.

The court began as the Iraqi Special Tribunal, which was established by the Iraqi Interim Governing Council (IGC) on 10 December 2003, authorized by the body representing the occupying powers, the Coalition Provisional Authority (CPA). The Statute was drawn up with considerable international input.[110] Concerns were raised about the legal basis for the Tribunal and its legitimacy.[111] These were put to rest by a new law, adopted by the Iraqi Transitional National Assembly in 2005,[112] which provides a new Statute for the Tribunal, now called the Iraqi High Tribunal (or Supreme Iraqi Criminal Court).

The Tribunal has jurisdiction over certain crimes committed in Iraq or elsewhere between 16 July 1968 (the Ba'athist *coup d'état*) and 1 May 2003 (the 'end of major combat operations') by Iraqi nationals or residents; members of the coalition are thus excluded, as are juridical persons.[113] The subject-matter jurisdiction covers genocide, crimes against humanity and war crimes, all defined almost exactly as in the ICC Statute but not previously included in Iraqi law,[114] and some crimes under domestic law relating to abuse of power.[115] Interestingly, one of the domestic crimes, 'the pursuit of policies that may lead to the threat of war or use of the armed forces of Iraq against an Arab country', could apply as a kind of crime of aggression, though not in relation to the 2003 intervention in Iraq itself.[116] The Tribunal has concurrent jurisdiction with, but also primacy over, all other Iraqi courts, and it may under certain circumstances try someone who has already been tried by another Iraqi court.[117] The judges and prosecutors of the Iraqi High Tribunal are all Iraqi nationals; the Statute allows the appointment of non-Iraqi judges, appointed by a national authority, but only if one of the parties in the case is a State.[118] Nonetheless, international advisers, observers, and defence co-counsel may work in the Tribunal,[119] and many did so, particularly in the early days. Coalition members also provided substantial support with regard to funding, training, security and personnel. However, the Tribunal's power to impose the death penalty had the consequence that many States and international human rights groups were not willing to support it or cooperate with it.[120]

---

[110] Coalition Provisional Authority Order No. 48 of 10 December 2003 (to which the Iraqi Special Tribunal Statute was attached).

[111] See e.g. Ilias Bantekas, 'The Iraqi Special Tribunal for Crimes against Humanity' (2004) 54 *International and Comparative Law Quarterly* 237; and Cherif Bassiouni, 'Post-Conflict Justice in Iraq: An Appraisal of the Iraq Special Tribunal' (2005) 38 *Cornell International Law Journal* 327.

[112] The Law on the Iraqi High Tribunal was signed by the Iraqi President on 11 October 2005. See Charles Garraway, 'The Statute of the Iraqi Special Tribunal' in Susan Breau and Agnieszka Jachec-Neale (eds.), *Testing the Boundaries of International Humanitarian Law* (London, 2006) 155–89.

[113] Art. 1 of the Statute.

[114] See e.g. Yuval Shany, 'Does One Size Fit All?' (2004) 2 *Journal of International Criminal Justice* 338.

[115] Arts. 11–14 of the Statute.

[116] See Claus Kreß, 'The Iraqi Special Tribunal and the Crime of Aggression' (2004) 2 *Journal of International Criminal Justice* 347. See Chapter 13.

[117] Arts. 29–30 of the Statute.   [118] *Ibid.*, Arts. 4(3) and 28.   [119] *Ibid.*, Arts. 7(2)–(3), 8(10), 9(7)–(8) and 18(3).

[120] See e.g. Tom Parker, 'Prosecuting Saddam: The Coalition Provisional Authority and the Evolution of the Iraqi Special Tribunal' (2005) 38 *Cornell International Law Journal* 899.

The first trial before the Tribunal was of Saddam Hussein and other former top-ranking officials; Saddam Hussein was sentenced to death for crimes against humanity, albeit not the most notorious crimes that he allegedly committed, and later hanged (the '*Dujail* case').[121] The Tribunal continues its work, which includes several convictions of Ali Hassan al-Majid (or 'Chemical Ali') concerning, *inter alia*, large-scale attacks against the Kurdish population in 1988 (the *Anfal* case). The trials have been subjected to international criticism for lack of judicial independence, weak guarantees of fair trial, administrative failures, and a lack of outreach to the Iraqi public.[122] However understandable the wish to try national criminals in a national court, the Tribunal illustrates the difficulties of a domestic court within a post-conflict situation, dealing, without previous experience, with vast and complex international crimes.

9.4.2 Serbia: the War Crimes Chamber

The War Crimes Chamber of the Belgrade District Court in Serbia is another example of a specialized court for international crimes that was created with international assistance, primarily the OSCE, but which is entirely national in nature.[123] The Chamber and a specialized Prosecutor's Office for War Crimes were both established in 2003. Jurisdiction extends to crimes committed anywhere in the former Socialist Federal Republic of Yugoslavia, regardless of the citizenship of the perpetrator or victims. The ICTY has referred some cases to the Chamber, including crimes in Vukovar (Croatia) and Zvomik (Bosnia and Herzegovina), primarily in cases where no ICTY indictment was issued but also one post-indictment referral under Rule 11*bis* of the ICTY Rules of Procedure and Evidence.[124] The Chamber, and the Belgrade Court of Appeals (War Crimes Department), continue to handle war crimes cases, but critical voices argue, *inter alia*, that the number of new indictments are declining, 'the big fish' escape justice, and that the protection of victims and witnesses is insufficient.[125]

---

[121] English translations of the judgments in the *Dujail* case, T. Ch. I, 5 November 2006, and A. Ch., 26 December 2006 (and the subsequent *Anfal* case, T. Ch. II, 24 June 2007, and A. Ch., 4 September 2007) are available, together with other documents, at http://gjpi.org/2009/09/13/iraqi-high-tribunal (Global Justice Project: Iraq, S. J. Quinney College of Law, University of Utah).

[122] For discussion of some of the trials, see e.g. Miranda Sissons and Ari Bassin, 'Was the Dujail Trial Fair?' (2007) 5 *Journal of International Criminal Justice* 272; M. Cherif Bassiouni and Michael Hanna, 'Ceding the High Ground: The Iraqi High Criminal Court Statute and the Trial of Saddam Hussein' (2006–7) 39 *Case Western Reserve Journal of International Law* 21; Michael Newton, 'Implementing International Law: A Qualified Defense of the Al Dujail Trial' (2006) 9 *Yearbook of International Humanitarian Law* 117; Nehal Bhuta, 'Fatal Errors: The Trial and Appeal Judgments in the Dujail Case' (2008) 6 *Journal of International Criminal Justice* 39; Jennifer Trahan, 'A Critical Guide to the Iraqi High Tribunal's Anfal Judgment: Genocide against the Kurds' (2009) 30 *Michigan Journal of International Law* 305. For a wider discussion of the Hussein trial and its background, see Michael Newton and Michael Scharf, *Enemy of the State* (New York, 2008).

[123] Law on Organization and Competence of Government Authorities in War Crimes Proceedings, Official Gazette of the Republic of Serbia No. 67/2003. See Mark Ellis, 'Coming to Terms with its Past: Serbia's New Court for the Prosecution of War Crimes' (2004) 22 *Berkeley Journal of International Law* 165; Bogdan Ivanišević, *Against the Current – War Crimes Prosecutions in Serbia* (International Center for Transitional Justice, 2007); and Miodrag Majić and Dušan Ignjatović, *Ten Lessons from Serbia's Experience in War Crimes Issues* (FICHL Policy Brief Series No. 9, 2012).

[124] See *Vladimir Kovačević*, ICTY Referral Bench, 17 November 2006.

[125] See *Report on War Crimes Trials in Serbia in 2012* (Humanitarian Law Center, Belgrade, 2013), available at www.hlc-rdc.org/wp-content/uploads/2013/02/Report-on-war-crimes-trials-in-Serbia-in-2012-ENG-FF.pdf.

9.5   Lockerbie: an ad hoc solution for a particular incident

Yet another solution, although not for dealing with international crimes, was chosen for the prosecution of two Libyan nationals accused of the 1988 bombing of Pan Am flight 103 over Lockerbie in Scotland. The surrender of the accused from Libya, in return for the suspension of sanctions imposed by the Security Council against Libya under Chapter VII of the UN Charter,[126] was secured only by coming to a special arrangement for the criminal proceedings. The court, prosecution and applicable law were all Scottish, but the court sat in a neutral venue in the Netherlands rather than in Scotland.

The compromise was worked out by the UN, Libya, the United States and the United Kingdom. Scots law had to be amended to allow the Scottish High Court of Justiciary to sit abroad without a jury;[127] an agreement also had to be concluded between the United Kingdom and the Netherlands following the adoption of a Security Council resolution under Chapter VII of the Charter.[128] The indictment was confined to charges of murder. Criminal jurisdiction was based on territoriality. On 31 January 2001, the High Court convicted one and acquitted one of the accused,[129] a verdict that was upheld on appeal on 14 March 2002.[130] This is not an example of an international court or of international crimes, but an ad hoc arrangement relating to a domestic trial brokered at the international level.[131]

9.6   Relationship with the ICC

An interesting question is how these internationalized or hybrid courts relate to the ICC. In many of the examples mentioned in this chapter, there is no jurisdictional conflict between the court and the ICC; even where the territorial, personal and subject-matter jurisdictions overlap, the non-retroactive jurisdiction of the ICC prevents it from dealing with many past crimes. But some of the internationalized courts, for example those in East Timor and Kosovo, have not been confined to dealing with past crimes, and other internationalized courts may be established in the future.

Since most of the courts, so far, form part of the domestic system, the scheme of Article 17 of the ICC Statute (the complementarity principle) will apply to them, and if the ICC has jurisdiction it will be only complementary.[132] Other specialized domestic courts have also

---

[126] SC Res. 731(1992) of 21 January 1992; SC Res. 748(1992) of 31 March 1992; SC Res. 883(1993) of 11 November 1993; and SC Res. 1192(1998) of 27 August 1998. See Chapter 14.
[127] High Court of Justiciary (Proceedings in the Netherlands) (United Nations) Order 1998.
[128] Agreement of 18 September 1998, reprinted in (1999) 38 ILM 926, following the adoption of SC Res. 1192(1998).
[129] *HM Advocate* v. *Al Megrahi* (High Court of Justiciary at Camp Zeist).
[130] *Al Megrahi* v. *HM Advocate*, 2002 SCCR 509; the case was then referred back to the appeal court in Edinburgh by the Scottish Criminal Cases Review Commission. Al Megrahi served part of his sentence but did not proceed with the appeal; he was released on compassionate grounds in 2009 since he was suffering from a terminal illness. He died in 2012.
[131] For a critique of the arrangements, see Donna Arzt, 'The Lockerbie "Extradition by Analogy" Agreement: "Exceptional Measure" or Template for Transnational Criminal Justice?' (2002) 18 *American University International Law Review* 163.
[132] See Chapter 8. See also e.g. Markus Benzing and Morten Bergsmo, 'Some Tentative Remarks on the Relationship between Internationalized Criminal Jurisdictions and the International Criminal Court' in Romano *et al.*, *Internationalized Criminal Courts*, 407–16; and Carsten Stahn, 'The Geometry of Transitional Justice: Choices of Institutional Design' (2005) 18 *Leiden Journal of International Law* 425, 462–5.

been established, for example in Uganda,[133] or suggested, for example regarding Sudan and Burundi,[134] with a varying degree of international involvement and sometimes as a direct response to the complementarity principle. Also, multilateral court arrangements have been discussed, although they are not explicitly covered by Article 17; it has been proposed to extend the jurisdiction of existing regional judicial bodies in Africa to international crimes.[135] It is not impossible that the ICC would apply the principle of complementarity by analogy, and it is argued by some that local and regional arrangements should be accepted and recognized to the greatest extent possible as long as they entail some kind of accountability.[136]

9.7   An appraisal

The use of these arrangements, rather than international courts, does not of course indicate that there is a hierarchy of atrocities, with one level meriting less effort and expenditure from the international community. Indeed, the crimes prosecuted in most of the courts discussed in this chapter are among the worst in the post-Second World War era. The Cambodia Chambers, for example, are having to address, in however limited a way, responsibility for the 'killing fields of Cambodia', and the atrocities dealt with by the Special Court for Sierra Leone were such that the Court could not recall 'any other conflict in the history of warfare in which innocent civilians were subjected to such savage and inhumane treatment'.[137]

The models for the internationalized courts discussed in this chapter have their disadvantages compared with tribunals established by a Security Council resolution under Chapter VII of the UN Charter. A problem common to almost all of them is the shortage of financial and other resources. Their resources consist chiefly of voluntary contributions by States, in money, personnel and equipment.[138] Indeed, cost-related considerations played a major role

---

[133] The International Crimes Division of Uganda's High Court was set up as an attempt, although unsuccessful, to get LRA leader Joseph Kony to sign a peace agreement in spite of an ICC arrest warrant; see Human Rights Watch, *Justice for Serious Crimes before National Courts: Uganda's International Crimes Division* (2012), and *Kony et al.*, ICC PTC II, 10 March 2009.

[134] The report of the Mbeki Panel, established by the AU, recommended a hybrid criminal chamber within the Sudanese justice system; see Robert Cryer, 'Sudan, Resolution 1593, and International Criminal Justice' (2006) 19 *Leiden Journal of International Law* 195; and Lutz Oette, 'The African Union High-Level Panel on Darfur: A Precedent for Regional Solutions to the Challenges Facing International Criminal Justice?' in Nhemielle, *Africa and the Future of International Criminal Justice*, 353–74. Another proposed initiative was a special war crimes chamber in the Burundi court system (see UN Doc. S/2005/158 of 11 March 2005, paras. 57–66; and SC Res. 1606(2005) of 20 June 2005); rejected by the government in favour of a special tribunal, the future establishment of any such institution is uncertain. On Burundi, see Matteo Crippa, 'A Long Path toward Reconciliation and Accountability: A Truth and Reconciliation Commission and a Special Chamber for Burundi?' (2012) 12 *International Criminal Law Review* 71.

[135] The AU is considering extending the jurisdiction of the future African Court of Justice and Human Rights: see Decision by the 19th Ordinary Session of the AU Assembly 15–16 July 2012, Doc.Assembly/AU/13 XIX(a). In addition, the East African Community (EAC) contemplates extending the jurisdiction of the East African Court of Justice. See further Kai Ambos and O. A. Maunganidze (eds.), *Power and Prosecution: Challenges and Opportunities for International Criminal Justice in Sub-Saharan Africa* (Göttingen, 2012) 11–12; and Max Du Plessis, *Implications of the AU Decision to Give the African Court Jurisdiction over International Crimes* (Institute for Security Studies Paper No. 235, Pretoria, 2012) 11.

[136] E.g. Kai Ambos, 'Expanding the Focus on the "African Criminal Court"' in Schabas, *Ashgate Research Companion*, 499, 528.

[137] *Brima, Kamara and Kanu*, SCSL T. Ch. II, 19 July 2007, paras. 34–5. The AFRC defendants were found responsible 'for some of the most heinous, brutal and atrocious crimes ever recorded in human history'.

[138] See e.g. Thordis Ingadottir, 'The Financing of Internationalized Criminal Courts and Tribunals' in Romano *et al.* (eds.), *Internationalized Criminal Courts*, 271–89.

when decisions were taken to opt for the various hybrid models instead of international criminal tribunals. Funding difficulties may have a detrimental impact not only on the effectiveness and efficiency of the tribunal concerned, but also on the rights of the accused to a fair trial; the independence and impartiality of the institution may even be questioned, as was (unsuccessfully) argued before the Special Court for Sierra Leone.[139] Having to rely on voluntary funding by States, rather than on UN-assessed contributions, has led to a precarious existence for some institutions, with court staff having to spend a great deal of time fundraising. At various periods of their existence, the SCSL, ECCC and STL have come near to having their work terminated for lack of funding.

A further potential problem is that courts which are largely domestic may suffer from the influence of their national systems, political or otherwise, where the judiciary and the legal system are not strong. This is particularly so in those cases where the international element is less powerful than the national one, as with the ECCC, or almost non-existent, as with the Iraqi High Tribunal.

These courts may suffer from the disadvantage of difficulties in securing cooperation from other States. Because the Security Council has not created them by Chapter VII resolution, there is no legal requirement for other States to proffer cooperation;[140] the court or State concerned has to attempt to establish voluntary arrangements with regional States or rely on existing agreements. This has led to difficulties for the SCSL and the Bosnia War Crimes Chamber, and has the potential to block the work of the Special Tribunal for Lebanon.

Nevertheless, there are advantages. The creation of these courts is expected to have positive influences on the relevant domestic legal system,[141] and the criminal process may be adapted to the domestic system.[142] Unlike the ICTY and the ICTR (and perhaps the ICC),[143] most courts sit in the country in question and, with the exception of Sierra Leone and Lebanon, operate within existing or newly created domestic judicial structures. Some form part of the restoration of the domestic system, and all of them are intended to assist in building local capacity, enhancing respect for the rule of law and providing independent, impartial and fair criminal proceedings for past crimes as well as an example for the future. Outreach programmes are established to assist with these goals, and the domestic impact will depend on how dedicated are these efforts of engagement with the local communities.[144] The courts are also contributing to case law on international criminal law. For example, the SCSL

---

[139] *Norman*, SCSL A. Ch., 13 March 2004.
[140] Chapter VII resolutions were necessary in the course of the establishment of both the Special Tribunal for Lebanon and the Lockerbie court, and these resolutions required the cooperation of certain States.
[141] See e.g. Laura Dickinson, 'The Promise of Hybrid Courts' (2003) 97 *European Journal of International Law* 295. For a critical view, see Sigall Horovitz, 'Impact of the International Criminal Tribunal for Rwanda and the Special Court for Sierra Leone on Impunity in Rwanda and Sierra Leone' in Nhemielle, *Africa and the Future of International Criminal Justice*, 15.
[142] The procedural laws of the SCSL, the ECCC, the STL and the Special Panels in East Timor are further analysed in Sluiter, *International Criminal Procedure*.
[143] See Arts. 3 and 62 of the ICC Statute (the ICC may sit elsewhere than at its seat in The Hague). Rule 4 of the ICTY RPE and of the ICTR RPE respectively also allows those Tribunals to exercise their functions away from the seat, but this has rarely happened in practice. See Chapter 20.
[144] For the necessity of good outreach programmes, particularly in relation to the ECCC, see Norman Pentelovitch, 'Seeing Justice Done: The Importance of Prioritizing Outreach Efforts at International Criminal Tribunals' (2008) 39 *Georgetown Journal of International Law* 445.

has added significantly to jurisprudence on the war crime of conscripting or enlisting children under the age of 15 years into the armed forces and on the crime against humanity of forced marriage.[145] The courts discussed in this chapter, each of which has been chosen to suit a particular situation, add to the network of arrangements to combat impunity; their success will be judged by the results.

Only one new 'internationalized court' has been created more recently, and most of those covered in this chapter are either gone or winding down. But, in spite of the shortcomings and the existence of the permanent ICC, to declare the demise of this phenomenon as such would probably be wrong. In line with the ICC's complementarity principle, international support to domestic efforts will continue and regional or sub-regional courts that are specialized on international crimes might appear.[146] Nonetheless, the appetite for such ambitious projects as the SCSL, ECCC and STL is very small today and one may predict that anything similar, if ever recurring, will be reserved for very special occasions.

Further reading

The following websites are useful:

- Special Court for Sierra Leone: www.sc-sl.org
- Extraordinary Chambers in the Courts of Cambodia: www.eccc.gov.kh/english
- Special Tribunal for Lebanon: www.stl-tsl.org
- Bosnia War Crimes Chamber: www.sudbih.gov.ba/?jezik=e
- Serbia Office of the War Crimes Prosecutor: www.tuzilastvorz.org.rs/html_trz/pocetna_eng.htm
- EULEX in Kosovo: www.eulex-kosovo.eu/training/?id=13

Kai Ambos and Mohamed Othman (eds.), *New Approaches in International Criminal Justice: Kosovo, East Timor, Sierra Leone and Cambodia* (Freiburg im Breisgau, 2003)

Hervé Ascensio, Elisabeth Lambert-Abdelgawad and Jean-Marc Sorel (eds.), *Les jurisdictions pénales internationalisées (Cambodge, Kosovo, Sierra Leone, Timor Leste)* (Paris, 2006)

M. Cherif Bassiouni (ed.), *Post-Conflict Justice* (New York, 2002)

William W. Burke-White, 'The Domestic Influence of International Criminal Tribunals: The International Criminal Tribunal for the Former Yugoslavia and the Creation of the State Court of Bosnia and Herzegovina' (2008) 46 *Columbia Journal of Transnational Law* 279

Charles Chernor Jallow (ed.), *The Sierra Leone Special Court and its Legacy: The Impact for Africa and International Criminal Law* (Cambridge, 2013)

Edda Kristjansdottir, André Nollkaemper and Cedric Ryngaert (eds.), *International Law in Domestic Courts: Rule of Law Reform in Post-Conflict States* (Cambridge, Antwerp and Portland, OR, 2012)

---

[145] On forced marriage, see e.g. *Brima, Kamara and Kanu*, SCSL A. Ch., 22 February 2008, para. 195; on the recruitment of child soldiers, see *Norman*, SCSL A. Ch., 31 May 2004.

[146] E.g. under the auspices of the African Union or the East African Community, see section 9.6.

Suzannah Linton, 'Cambodia, East Timor and Sierra Leone: Experiments in International
    Justice' (2001) 12 *Criminal Law Forum* 414
Daryl Mundis, 'New Mechanisms for the Enforcement of International Humanitarian Law'
    (2001) 95 *American Journal of International Law* 934
Cesare Romano, André Nollkaemper and Jann Kleffner (eds.), *Internationalized Criminal
    Courts: Sierra Leone, East Timor, Kosovo, and Cambodia* (Oxford, 2004)
Sarah Williams, *Hybrid and Internationalized Criminal Tribunals: Selected Jurisdictional
    Issues* (Oxford, 2012)

Part D

Substantive Law of International Crimes

10

Genocide

10.1 Introduction

10.1.1 Overview

Genocide 'is a denial of the right of existence of entire human groups, as homicide is the denial of the right to live of individual human beings'.[1] It is a crime simultaneously directed against individual victims, the group to which they belong, and human diversity. What gives the crime its particular horror is the intention to destroy a group of people. This form of intent, a necessary element of the crime, marks it out from all other international crimes. It explains why genocide is regarded as having a particular seriousness, and has been referred to as the 'crime of crimes'.[2] The seriousness of the crime is underlined by the fact that its prohibition has attained the status of a *ius cogens* norm[3] and an *erga omnes* obligation on States (owed to the international community as a whole).[4]

The legal concept of genocide is narrowly circumscribed, the term 'genocide' being reserved in law for a particular subset of atrocities which are committed with the intent to destroy groups, even if colloquially the word is used for any large-scale killings. Most of the crimes committed by the Pol Pot regime in Cambodia in 1975–8, for example, are atrocities which do not readily fit within the narrow definition, however dreadful the suffering they caused.[5]

The definition has been criticized as being too narrow. Victims' groups have wanted to appropriate the term for atrocities which may fall outside the definition. There is a wish to attract the mobilizing power of the label, reference being made to the obligation imposed by

---

[1] GA Res. 96(1).
[2] *Kambanda*, ICTR T. Ch., 4 September 1998, para. 16. But note the statement of the International Commission of Inquiry on Darfur: genocide 'is not necessarily the most serious international crime. Depending upon the circumstances, such international offences as crimes against humanity or large scale war crimes may be no less serious and heinous than genocide' (UN Doc. S/2005/60, para. 522).
[3] *Case Concerning Armed Activities on the Territory of the Congo* (*Democratic Republic of the Congo* v. *Rwanda*), Jurisdiction of the Court and Admissibility of the Application, ICJ, 3 February 2006, para. 64.
[4] *Reservations to the Convention on the Prevention and Punishment of the Crime of Genocide*, Advisory Opinion (1951) ICJ Reports 15, 23.
[5] The Extraordinary Chambers in the Courts of Cambodia have jurisdiction over genocide, as defined by the Genocide Convention; the co-investigating judges have restricted the charges of genocide to the crimes committed against the Cham and the Vietnamese ethnic minorities (closing order in Case 002/19-09-2007, 15 September 2012, paras. 1336–49), not charging as genocide the much larger massacres of the Khmer on political grounds.

the Genocide Convention (Article I) to prevent genocide and the possibility (mentioned in Article VIII) of involving the United Nations if genocide is committed. Further, if the crime of genocide is said to stand at the apex of international criminality, there will be emotional or political reasons for wishing to use the label for all particularly serious atrocities. Not to use the term may seem like a judgment on the suffering of a group of victims.[6] The response is that if the classification is to be meaningful, the term should be precisely and carefully used, both on legal grounds and on the ground that if we stretch its meaning we reduce its capacity to evoke a unique form of devastation; it belittles the scale and intensity of unmistakable forms of genocide such as the Holocaust. A decision that a particular atrocity is not 'genocide' does not of course remove the moral or legal guilt for conduct that falls within the definition of other international crimes such as crimes against humanity.

When the conduct constituting the offence is attributable to a State, genocide, like other international crimes, is not only a crime of individual responsibility: it also engages State responsibility. In the *Bosnian Genocide* case, Bosnia took proceedings in the ICJ alleging breaches of the Genocide Convention[7] by Serbia in attempting to destroy protected groups, in particular the Muslim population. The Court confirmed that the Convention not only imposes on States a duty to prevent and punish genocide but also an obligation to refrain from genocide.[8] This is not to introduce a concept of State crime or State criminal responsibility; the obligation is one of State responsibility under general international law.[9]

The standard definition of genocide is contained in Article II of the Genocide Convention, which is adopted *verbatim* in the Statutes of the ad hoc Tribunals and of the ICC. It is:

any of the following acts committed with the intent to destroy, in whole or in part, a national, ethnical, racial or religious group, as such:

(a) Killing members of the group;
(b) Causing serious bodily or mental harm to members of the group;
(c) Deliberately inflicting on the group conditions of life calculated to bring about its physical destruction in whole or in part;
(d) Imposing measures intended to prevent births within the group;
(e) Forcibly transferring children of the group to another group.

Almost every word of this definition has raised difficulties of interpretation. It is the purpose of this chapter to explain some of these controversies, and the way in which academics and courts have attempted to deal with them.

---

[6] For the debate on the power of the label and the meaning it is said to confer on suffering and injustice, as well as the dangers of such labeling, see Payam Akhavan, *Reducing Genocide to Law* (Cambridge, 2012).

[7] The Convention on the Prevention and Punishment of the Crime of Genocide, adopted by the General Assembly on 9 December 1948.

[8] *Case Concerning the Application of the Convention on the Prevention and Punishment of the Crime of Genocide* (*Bosnia and Herzegovina* v. *Serbia and Montenegro*), ICJ, 26 February 2007 (the '*Bosnian Genocide*' case), paras. 162–6. The Court also held that Art. III obliges States to refrain from engaging in conspiracy, incitement, attempt and complicity in genocide (para. 167). For comment on the case, see Claus Kreß. 'The International Court of Justice and the Elements of the Crime of Genocide' (2007) 18 *European Journal of International Law* 619; Richard Goldstone and Rebecca Hamilton, 'Bosnia v. Serbia: Lessons from the Encounter of the International Court of Justice with the International Criminal Tribunal for Former Yugoslavia' (2008) 21 *Leiden Journal of International Law* 95.

[9] *Bosnian Genocide* case, para. 170.

10.1.2 Historical development

The identification of genocide as an international crime came as a response to the Holocaust. Massacres with the purpose of exterminating national or ethnic minorities were not a twentieth-century novelty, but the term 'genocide' was not coined until 1944 by Raphael Lemkin, a Polish lawyer.[10] The indictment of the defendants at Nuremberg stated that they had conducted 'deliberate and systematic genocide, viz, the extermination of racial and national groups, against the civilian population of certain occupied territories in order to destroy particular races and classes of people, and national, racial or religious groups, particularly Jews, Poles, and Gypsies'.[11] But genocide as such was not a crime within the jurisdiction of the Nuremberg Tribunal, and the term was not mentioned in its judgment. As the ICTR said many years later: 'The crimes prosecuted by the Nuremberg Tribunal, namely the holocaust of the Jews or the "Final Solution", were very much constitutive of genocide, but they could not be defined as such because the crime of genocide was not defined until later.'[12]

All of the crimes prosecuted by the Nuremberg Tribunal and its immediate successors were defined as having a connection with war. It was because of this restriction in the definition of crimes against humanity that it was necessary to recognize the crime of genocide as a separate international crime. This was done in General Assembly Resolution 96(1) of 11 December 1946. Two years later, the Genocide Convention was concluded, having been drafted largely by the Sixth Committee of the UN General Assembly; it came into force on 12 January 1951. In the same year, the ICJ declared that the prohibitions contained in the Convention constituted customary international law.[13]

Although Article VI of the Convention refers to the possibility of an international court being available to try cases of genocide, it was not until the establishment of the ad hoc Tribunals in 1993 and 1994 that this became a reality. The first conviction for genocide by an international court was recorded on 2 September 1998 by the ICTR, of Jean-Paul Akayesu, a Rwandan mayor. Two days after that, Jean Kambanda, the former Prime Minister of Rwanda, was sentenced to life imprisonment after pleading guilty to genocide, conspiracy, incitement and complicity in genocide, as well as crimes against humanity.

10.1.3 Relationship to crimes against humanity

Genocide has obvious similarities to crimes against humanity. As mentioned in section 10.1.2, the Nuremberg defendants were charged with war crimes and crimes against

---

[10] Raphael Lemkin, *Axis Rule in Occupied Europe: Laws of Occupation, Analysis of Government, Proposals for Redress* (Washington DC, 1944) 79.

[11] *The Trial of German Major War Criminals* (London, 1946), part I, 22; Indictment presented to the International Military Tribunal, Cmd 6696, 14. For the development of the concept of genocide in the cases brought under Control Council Law No. 10, see Matthew Lippman, 'The Convention on the Prevention and Punishment of the Crime of Genocide: Fifty Years Later' (1998) 15 *Arizona Journal of International and Comparative Law* 415.

[12] *Kambanda*, ICTR T. Ch. I, 4 September 1998, para. 16.

[13] *Reservations to the Convention on the Prevention and Punishment of the Crime of Genocide*, Advisory Opinion (1951) ICJ Reports 15, 23.

humanity for what would now be prosecuted as genocide. The Genocide Convention makes clear in Article I that genocide can be committed in time of peace as in war, and now that there is no longer a nexus between crimes against humanity and armed conflict[14] it is even clearer that genocide can be, indeed typically is, a form of crimes against humanity.[15]

The chief difference between the two categories of crimes is the intent to destroy the whole or part of a group, which is a necessary element of genocide. And the interests protected by the law against genocide are narrower than for crimes against humanity. The law against genocide protects the rights of certain groups to survival, and thus human diversity,[16] but the similar crime against humanity – persecution 'against any identifiable group or collectivity on political, racial, national, ethnic, cultural, religious, gender ... or other grounds that are universally recognised as impermissible under international law' – protects groups from discrimination rather than elimination. Thus, 'when persecution escalates to the extreme form of wilful and deliberate acts designed to destroy a group or part of a group, it can be held that such persecution amounts to genocide'.[17]

Unlike crimes against humanity, the crime of genocide does not explicitly include any objective requirement of scale. The threshold for a crime against humanity is its connection to a widespread or systematic attack directed against a civilian population, and, for a war crime, its commission during an armed conflict. The required elements for the latter two crimes therefore include an objectively existing situation of scale and gravity in which civilians are at risk. In contrast, the gravity of genocide is primarily marked by the subjective *mens rea*, the intent to destroy a national, ethnic, racial or religious group as such.

10.1.4   *The nature of genocide*

The significance of the genocidal intent in the definition of the crime raises important questions about the nature of genocide and its status as the 'crime of crimes'. Can it be 'genocide' where an isolated individual acts with a fervent, albeit unrealistic, intent to destroy a group? During the negotiation of the ICC Elements of Crimes, for example, the US delegation pointed out that an isolated hate crime, if committed with the requisite intent, would satisfy the description in the Genocide Convention, and yet it would seem absurd to label a single murder by an isolated individual as a 'genocide'.[18]

Further, does there need to be a collective plan to commit genocide before the crime is committed? In *Jelisić*, an ICTY Trial Chamber stated that killings committed by a single perpetrator are enough 'to establish the material element of the crime of genocide and it is *a priori* possible to conceive that the accused harboured the plan to exterminate an entire group without this intent having been supported by any organisation in which other individuals participated'. The Chamber 'did not discount the possibility of a lone individual

[14] See section 11.2.1.   [15] *Kayishema*, ICTR T. Ch., 21 May 1999, para. 89.

[16] 'Those who devise and implement genocide seek to deprive humanity of the manifold richness its nationalities, races, ethnicities and religions provide': *Krstić*, ICTY A. Ch., 19 April 2004, para. 36.

[17] *Kupreskić et al.*, ICTY T. Ch. II, 14 January 2000, para. 636.

[18] Valerie Oosterveld, 'Context of Genocide' in Roy Lee *et al.* (eds.), *The International Criminal Court: Elements or Crimes and Rules of Procedure and Evidence* (Ardsley, NY, 2001) 44, 45.

seeking to destroy a group as such'.[19] Such a view is not supported consistently in the case law, or in academic writing.[20] William Schabas, for example, described the possibility as 'little more than a sophomoric *hypothèse d'école*'.[21] Others go further, taking the view that the very nature of genocide requires a structural element.[22]

To include in the scope of genocide an isolated crime, committed in the absence of any attack or genocidal context, even if legally possible, risks overly expanding the concept of genocide, and effacing the profound stigma and mobilizing power of the term. As the ICTY prosecution has warned:

> in the interests of international justice, genocide should not be diluted or belittled by too broad an interpretation. Indeed, it should be reserved only for acts of exceptional gravity and magnitude which shock the conscience of humankind and which, therefore, justify the appellation of genocide as the 'ultimate crime'.[23]

It is ordinarily assumed therefore that several protagonists are involved in the crime of genocide.[24] Although it is not a formal element of the crime that there be a genocidal plan,[25] the Tribunals have noted that it would be difficult to commit genocide without one.[26] The only realistic exception may be where others were committing crimes against humanity – without genocidal intent – but a single perpetrator had the intent to eliminate a group while committing the same atrocities. In such a situation, the surrounding crimes against humanity would already provide the pattern of mass atrocities, so it might be conceivable for an individual with the necessary intent to carry out acts that could be described as 'genocide'.

But, if genocide generally has a collective nature, and is to be limited to serious situations, how is this reflected in the elements of the offence when a court is assessing the guilt or innocence of one individual accused? Two different ways have been proposed for addressing the issue: in the material elements of the crime; and in the mental element.[27]

The first approach is that taken by the Elements of Crimes adopted for the ICC, which add a 'contextual element' to the *actus reus*, requiring that the conduct for which the defendant is on trial takes place in the context of 'a manifest pattern of similar conduct' or is of itself able to destroy the group or part of it. This contextual element rules out most situations of isolated crimes by requiring either a broader pattern of crimes or a concrete threat to the group. It is discussed in more detail in section 10.3.2.

---

[19] *Jelisić*, ICTY T. Ch., 19 December 1999, para. 400.

[20] Even in *Jelisić* the Trial Chamber went on to say, at para. 78: '[T]he Trial Chamber will have to verify that there was both an intentional attack against a group and an intention on the part of the accused to participate in or carry out this attack.' And see *Kayishema*, ICTR T. Ch. II, 21 May 1999, paras. 94, 276. On both sides of the academic debate, see William Schabas, 'The Jelisić Case and the Mens Rea of the Crime of Genocide' (2001) 14 *Leiden Journal of International Law* 125; Otto Triffterer. 'Genocide: Its Particular Intent to Destroy in Whole or in Part the Group as Such' (2001) 14 *Leiden Journal of International Law* 399; J. Quigley, *The Genocide Convention: An International Law Analysis* (Aldershot, 2006) 164–70.

[21] William Schabas, 'Darfur and the "Odious Scourge": The Commission of Inquiry's Findings on Genocide' (2005) 18 *Leiden Journal of International Law* 871, 877.

[22] Hans Vest, 'A Structure-Based Concept of Genocidal Intent' (2007) 5 *Journal of International Criminal Justice* 781.

[23] *Karadžić and Mladić*, ICTY T. Ch. (transcript of hearing), 27 June 1996, 15–16.

[24] *Krstić*, ICTY T. Ch. I, 2 August 2001, para. 549.   [25] *Jelisić*, ICTY A. Ch., 19 July 2001, para. 48.

[26] *Kayishema*, ICTR T. Ch. II, 21 May 1999, para. 94; *Jelisić*, ICTY T. Ch., 19 December 1999, para. 101.

[27] Schabas, 'The Jelisić Case', 133–8.

The alternative approach, proposed in the context of the intent requirement, is that there must be an organized and widespread plan to exterminate a group and the perpetrator must act with knowledge that the commission of the individual act would, or would be likely to, further the implementation of the plan.[28] This approach, not as yet accepted by any court, is discussed at the end of section 10.4.1.

10.2   The protected groups

Not all groups of people are protected by the Genocide Convention. The Convention lists only national, ethnic, racial and religious groups, and the list is a closed one. During the negotiation of the Convention, attempts were made to include others, such as social and political groups, but these failed.[29] Ever since the conclusion of the Convention there have been criticisms of its narrow focus, and proposals have been made to expand it, but these have all been similarly unsuccessful.[30] It has also been suggested that other groups come within the scope of genocide by virtue of customary international law.[31] Another approach has been to interpret expansively the existing terms so as to include other groups within the definition. For example, the ICTR Trial Chamber sitting in the *Akayesu* case determined on the basis of a (mis)reading of the *travaux préparatoires* that the drafters of the Convention intended to protect any stable and permanent group, rather than simply the groups specifically mentioned.[32] This approach was followed by the Commission of Inquiry established at the request of the Security Council to investigate violations of international humanitarian law and human rights in Darfur.[33] The Commission stated that this expansive interpretation had 'become part and parcel of international customary law'.[34]

But, while stability and permanence were certainly used as criteria by some delegates in the Sixth Committee to argue for or against the inclusion of a particular group in the drafting of the Convention, there is no evidence at all that the criteria were adopted as an open-ended description of protected groups. All the evidence is that the enumerated list of groups was intended to be exhaustive. The view that the Convention's list of groups is not exhaustive is not supported by case law other than *Akayesu*, nor by general State practice and *opinio iuris*, and cannot be seen as reflective of current law. No other Trial Chamber of the two ad hoc

---

[28] See John R. W. D. Jones, 'Whose Intent Is It Anyway?' in Lal Chand Vohrah *et al.* (eds.), *Man's Inhumanity to Man: Essays in Honour of Antonio Cassese* (The Hague, 2003) 467.

[29] GAOR, 3rd Session, 6th Committee, p. 664; see Schabas, *Genocide*, 153–71.

[30] For attempts made during the ICC negotiations, see *Report of the Ad Hoc Commission on the Establishment of an International Criminal Court*, GAOR 50th Session, Supp. No. 22, UN Doc. A/50/22 (1995), paras. 60–1; and *Report of the Preparatory Committee on the Establishment of an International Criminal Court*, Vol. I, GAOR, 51st Session, Supp. No. 22, UN Doc. A/51/22 (1996), paras. 59–60.

[31] Beth Van Schaack, 'The Crime of Political Genocide: Repairing the Genocide Convention's Blind Spot' (1997) 106 *Yale Law Journal* 2259.

[32] *Akayesu*, ICTR T. Ch. I, 2 September 1998, para. 516. For critique, see Schabas, *Genocide*, 151–3. In support, see Diane Marie Amann, 'International Decisions: Prosecutor v. Akayesu' (1999) 93 *American Journal of International Law* 195.

[33] Res. 1564(2004) of 18 September 2004. The Commission (the 'Darfur Commission') was established by the UN Secretary-General 'to investigate reports of violations of international humanitarian law and human rights law in Darfur by all parties, to determine also whether or not acts of genocide have occurred, and to identify the perpetrators of such violations with a view to ensuring that those responsible are held accountable'.

[34] *Report of the International Commission of Inquiry on Violations of International Humanitarian Law and Human Rights Law in Darfur*, UN Doc.S/2005/60, para. 501.

Tribunals has followed the *Akayesu* approach, and the Appeals Chamber has consistently, albeit quietly, kept to the view that the four groups are the exclusive focus of the Genocide Convention.[35] The ICC, in its early practice, has adopted the same view.[36]

There are national jurisdictions that have adopted wider formulations of the protected groups in their domestic law.[37] At the domestic level, States are entitled to use broader definitions but other States are not required to accept those definitions.[38] It has been rightly said that it is precisely because of the rigours of the definition, and because of its focus on crimes aimed at the eradication of particular groups, that genocide is especially stigmatized.[39]

10.2.1 *National, ethnical, racial and religious groups*

Given that these four groups are the exclusive beneficiaries of the protection of the Genocide Convention, it is unfortunate that there is no internationally recognized definition of any of them. It is difficult to attribute a distinct meaning to each, since they overlap considerably.[40] The ICTR has attempted to give each one a meaning. In past judgments it has described a national group as a 'collection of people who are perceived to share a legal bond based on common citizenship, coupled with reciprocity of rights and duties';[41] what it describes as the 'conventional definition' of racial group 'is based on the hereditary physical traits often identified with a geographical region, irrespective of linguistic, cultural, national or religious factors';[42] an ethnic group it described as 'a group whose members share a common language or culture';[43] and 'a religious group includes denomination or mode of worship or a group sharing common beliefs'.[44]

But to attempt to give each term its own definition risks missing the wood for the trees. The ICTR Trial Chamber in *Akayesu* ran into difficulties in assessing whether the Tutsi were a protected group in the context of the widespread massacres in Rwanda.[45] Having defined an ethnic group as sharing a common language or culture, the evidence before the Chamber made it clear that it was not thus that the Tutsi were distinguished from the Hutu. The Chamber had to rely on the fact that Rwandans were required to carry identification cards indicating the ethnicity of the bearer as Hutu, Tutsi or Twa and that the Tutsi constituted a

---

[35] *Krstić*, ICTY A. Ch., 19 April 2004, paras. 6–8; see Guglielmo Verdirame, 'The Genocide Definition in the Jurisprudence of the Ad Hoc Tribunals' (2000) 49 *International and Comparative Law Quarterly* 579, 588–92.

[36] *Situation in Darfur (Al Bashir* arrest warrant case), ICC PTC I, 4 March 2009, paras. 134–7.

[37] E.g. see the Spanish *Pinochet* case, noted at (1999) 93 *American Journal of International Law* 690, especially 693. A further example is the Ethiopian law which defines as genocide acts designed to eliminate 'political groups' and 'population transfer or dispersion'; see Firew Kebede Tiba; 'The Mengistu Genocide Trial in Ethiopia' (2007) 5 *Journal of International Criminal Justice* 513, 518.

[38] Genocide charges against General Pinochet were not considered in the extradition process in the United Kingdom, on the basis that they relied on an interpretation of genocide broader than that in international law; see David Turns, 'Pinochet's Fallout: Jurisdiction and Immunity for Criminal Violations of International Law' (2000) 20 *Legal Studies* 566, 567–8.

[39] Schabas, *Genocide*, 10.

[40] For a powerful argument in *favour* of identifying separate meanings, see Claus Kreß, 'The Crime of Genocide under International Law' (2006) 6 *International Criminal Law Review* 461.

[41] *Akayesu*, ICTR T. Ch. I, 2 September 1998, para. 511. [42] *Ibid.*, para. 513.

[43] *Ibid.*, paras. 512–15; and see *Kayishema*, ICTR T. Ch. II, 21 May 1999, para. 98. [44] *Ibid.*, para. 98.

[45] For critique of the Chamber's reasoning, see Payam Akhavan, 'The Crime of Genocide in the ICTR Jurisprudence' (2005) 3 *Journal of International Criminal Justice* 989.

group referred to as 'ethnic' in official classifications. It was only by virtue of its determination that any 'stable and permanent' group was covered by the Convention, and therefore by the ICTR Statute, that the Chamber was able to find that the Tutsi were a protected group.[46] As mentioned above, the decision on this point is not legally defensible. That would not, however, change the outcome in this case, as the Tutsi are considered an ethnic group on the correct interpretation of the Convention and the ICTR has taken judicial notice of the fact.[47]

The better approach, followed by the *Krstić* Trial Chamber, is to recognize that the list is exhaustive but to accept that the four groups were not given distinct and different meanings in the Convention:

European instruments on human rights use the term 'national minorities', while universal instruments more commonly make reference to 'ethnic, religious or linguistic minorities'; the two expressions appear to embrace the same goals. In a study conducted for the Sub-Commission on Prevention of Discrimination and Protection of Minorities in 1979, F. Capotorti commented that 'the Sub-Commission on Prevention of Discrimination and Protection of Minorities decided, in 1950, to replace the word "racial" by the word "ethnic" in all references to minority groups described by their ethnic origin'. The International Convention on the Elimination of All Forms of Racial Discrimination defines racial discrimination as 'any distinction, exclusion, restriction or preference based on race, colour, descent, or national or ethnic origin'. The preparatory work on the Genocide Convention also reflects that the term 'ethnical' was added at a later stage in order to better define the type of groups protected by the Convention and ensure that the term 'national' would not be understood as encompassing purely political groups.

The preparatory work of the Convention shows that setting out such a list was designed more to describe a single phenomenon, roughly corresponding to what was recognised, before the second world war, as 'national minorities', rather than to refer to several distinct prototypes of human groups. To attempt to differentiate each of the named groups on the basis of scientifically objective criteria would thus be inconsistent with the object and purpose of the Convention.[48]

The groups also 'help to define each other, operating much as four corner posts that delimit an area within which a myriad of groups covered by the Convention find protection'.[49] This 'four corners' approach avoids the difficulties of fitting a group such as the Tutsis precisely into one of the listed categories, but ensures that it comes within the area of protection that was intended by the negotiators, while also respecting the negotiators' intent that the list be a closed one.

10.2.2 *Identification of the group and its members*

As is clear from the wording of the different parts of the *actus reus* of the offence, the acts must be directed at members of the group. However, determination of the groups and their members is not a simple matter; it is certainly more difficult than the drafters of the

---

[46] *Akayesu*, ICTR T. Ch. I, 2 September 1998, para. 702.   [47] *Karemera*, ICTR T. Ch. III, 11 December 2006, final paragraph.

[48] *Krstić*, ICTY T. Ch. I, 2 August 2001, paras. 555–6 (footnotes not included); the Chamber followed the approach in Schabas, *Genocide*, 128–32; and see *Rutaganda*, ICTR T. Ch., 19 December 1999, para. 56. See also *Fourth Report on the Draft Code of Offences against the Peace and Security of Mankind*, by Doudou Thiam, Special Rapporteur, UN Doc. A/CN.4/398, para. 56.

[49] Schabas, *Genocide*, 129.

Convention, working against the presuppositions (and perhaps prejudices) of their era, thought. There are genuine difficulties in deciding if a person is a member of the group, and the complex question of who ought to be able to make that determination arises.[50] A subjective approach has its attractions: that is to say, the criterion for the identification of members of the group is that a perpetrator considers the victims to be members of a group he or she is targeting. The most significant factor in a particular case may be that the perpetrators have the specific intent to destroy a group identified by themselves. As was said in the *Bagilishema* case:

A group may not have precisely defined boundaries and there may be occasions when it is difficult to give a definitive answer as to whether or not a victim was a member of a protected group. Moreover, the perpetrators of genocide may characterize the targeted group in ways that do not fully correspond to conceptions of the group shared generally, or by other segments of society. In such a case, the Chamber is of the opinion that, on the evidence, if a victim was perceived by a perpetrator as belonging to a protected group, the victim should be considered by the Chamber as a member of the protected group, for the purposes of genocide.[51]

It is by no means clear that groups intended to be protected by the Genocide Convention always have an objective existence in the manner which the drafters thought. Groups are often social constructs, rather than scientific facts. This problem was discussed by the Darfur Commission, owing to the fact that, although the United States had described the crimes committed in Darfur as 'genocide',[52] on close analysis the question of group existence in Darfur was complicated. The Commission found that the Fur, Masalit and Zaghawa groups did not appear to make up ethnic groups distinct from those to which their attackers belonged. They had the same religion, and the same language, though the 'Africans' spoke their own dialect in addition to Arabic, while the 'Arabs' spoke only Arabic. Years of inter-marriage and coexistence had blurred the distinction between the groups. The sedentary or nomadic character of the groups appeared to constitute one of the main distinctions between them.[53] The Commission relied upon a partially subjective concept of groups in deciding that the victim groups nevertheless came within the scope of the crime of genocide. Victims and perpetrators had 'come to perceive themselves as either "African" or "Arab"'. A 'self-perception of two distinct groups' had emerged.[54] When the same question came before the ICC Pre-Trial Chamber in the *Al Bashir* arrest warrant case, the majority found that each of the three groups had 'its own language, its own tribal customs and its own traditional links to its lands' and was therefore a distinct ethnic group. The majority did not consider it necessary to explore the subjective or objective approach to the definition of groups.[55] Interestingly, Judge Ušaka, in dissent, argued that the three groups

---

[50] In the human rights context, see the decision of the Human Rights Committee in *Lovelace* v. *Canada*, Human Rights Committee (22/47).

[51] *Bagilishema*, ICTR T. Ch. I, 7 June 2001, para. 65.

[52] House Concurrent Resolution 467, Senate Concurrent Resolution 133, 22 July 2004.

[53] Report, UN Doc. S/2005/60, para. 508.   [54] *Ibid.*, paras. 510–11.

[55] *Al Bashir* arrest warrant case, ICC PTC, 14 March 2009, para. 137 and footnote 152. Judge Ušacka adopted the mixed objective/ subjective approach that the ICTY and ICTR now use: Partially Dissenting Opinion of Judge Ušacka, para. 23. The decision of the majority was accepted in the second arrest warrant case, ICC PTC, 12 July 2010, para. 9.

ought to be taken together as, in the Darfurian context, the ethnic faultline was considered to fall along the grounds of 'Arab' and 'African', the latter encompassing all three groups.[56]

Reliance on a purely subjective approach is uncomfortable, but it may be that with racism there is not always an objective basis: perceptions may be based on imagined distinctions rather than genuine ones.[57] While the ad hoc Tribunals have in some cases appeared to use an entirely subjective approach,[58] the better view is that the group must have some form of objective existence in the first place; otherwise the Convention could be used to protect entirely fictitious national, ethnic, racial or religious groups. It now seems settled that the identification of members of the group cannot be *solely* subjective. To overcome the problems of purely objective and purely subjective approaches, the Tribunals have adopted an approach that blends the two, but with sensitivity to the fact that the idea of a separate group may not have a basis in objective fact, but can be a set of reified beliefs about difference. Thus, whether a group is a protected one should be 'assessed on a case-by-case basis by reference to the *objective* particulars of a given social or historical context, and by the *subjective* perceptions of the perpetrators'.[59]

In addition, it is now well established that, notwithstanding some case law to the contrary,[60] a group cannot be defined 'negatively', i.e. by identifying persons *not* sharing the group characteristics of the perpetrators, for example, 'non-Serbs'.[61] It is also the case that where a person has a mixed identity, if he or she is targeted on the basis of membership of the protected group, the person so targeting them may be guilty of genocide. Thus, in the *Ndindabahizi* case, the ICTR accepted that a half-Belgian, half-Rwandan man, who was targeted as a Tutsi in the Rwandan genocide, was a member of the targeted group of Tutsis and thus was a victim of the crime of genocide.[62]

10.3   Material elements

10.3.1   *The prohibited acts*

Not every act committed with the intention to destroy, in whole or in part, a protected group will lead to a conviction for genocide. Only those which are mentioned in Article II of the Genocide Convention may form the *actus reus* of genocide. Further, it is important to remember that to prove the crime it is not necessary to show that the relevant act assisted in destroying a protected group: what is needed is that it was committed with the *intent* to destroy. Although all of the underlying crimes are defined by reference to victims in the plural, the ICC Elements of Crimes state that even one victim suffices, if the relevant act is

---

[56] *Ibid.*, paras. 24–6.   [57] See Schabas, 'Darfur and the "Odious Scourge"', 879.

[58] *Kayishema*, ICTR T. Ch. II, 21 May 1999, para. 98; *Jelisić*, ICTY T. Ch., 14 December 1999, paras. 69–72.

[59] *Semanza*, ICTR T. Ch., 15 May 2003, para. 317. For a critique, see Richard Wilson, *Writing History in International Criminal Tribunals* (Cambridge, 2011) Chapter 7.

[60] *Jelisić*, ICTY T. Ch., 14 December 1999, paras. 70, 71; and see Judge Shahabudeen's powerful dissent in *Stakić*, ICTY A. Ch., 22 March 2006, paras. 8–18.

[61] *Stakić*, ICTY T. Ch. II, 31 July 2003, para. 512; ICTY A. Ch., 22 March 2006, paras. 19–28. See also *Bosnian Genocide* case, paras. 193–4.

[62] *Ndindabahizi*, ICTR T. Ch., 15 July 2004, paras. 467–9. The conviction was overturned on appeal, on factual rather than legal grounds: *Ndindabahizi*, ICTR A. Ch., 16 January 2007, para. 117.

committed with the necessary intent. This is a controversial conclusion in relation to subparagraph (c) of Article II, which refers to inflicting conditions of life on the 'group'.

Killing

Article II(a) covers what is the paradigmatic conduct that amounts to genocide: killing members of the group. However, there are certain interpretative problems which have had to be resolved. The English term 'killing' (which the ICC Elements of Crimes state is interchangeable with 'caused death') is neutral as to whether the killing is intentional, or whether reckless (or perhaps even negligent) causing of death suffices. The term used in the French version of the Genocide Convention, '*meurtre*', is more precise. In *Kayishema*, the Appeals Chamber confirmed the Trial Chamber's view that there is virtually no difference between the terms in the English and French versions *in the context* of genocidal intent.[63] The act must be intentional but not necessarily premeditated.[64] Owing to the operation of Article 30 of the ICC Statute, genocidal killings must be intentional in proceedings before the ICC. If there is doubt about the intention to kill, rather than the intention to cause serious harm, it is of course possible to charge the defendant pursuant to Article II(b) of the Convention for the conduct that led to the death.

Causing serious bodily or mental harm to members of the group

In spite of the popular understanding of genocide as being confined to conduct causing death, the drafters of the Genocide Convention were not so limited in their understanding of the crime. Article II(b) of the Convention also criminalizes the causing of serious bodily or mental harm to victims. In the *Eichmann* case, the District Court of Jerusalem said that serious bodily and mental harm could be caused 'by the enslavement, starvation, deportation and persecution of people ... and by their detention in ghettos, transit camps and concentration camps in conditions which were designed to cause their degradation, deprivation of their rights as human beings and to suppress them and cause them inhumane suffering and torture'.[65] The ICTR in the *Akayesu* case broke new ground in deciding that acts of sexual violence and rape can constitute genocide; sexual violence was found to be an integral part of the process of destruction in the Rwanda genocide.[66] The ICC Elements of Crimes follow this approach.[67]

Owing to its concerns about the possible breadth of the *mental* harm aspect of genocide, the United States entered an 'understanding' to the Convention on ratifying, which stated that the term 'means permanent impairment of mental faculties through drugs, torture or similar techniques'. Serious mental harm does mean more than minor or

---

[63] *Kayishema*, ICTR A. Ch., 1 June 2001, para. 151; for a critique, see David Nersessian, 'The Contours of Genocidal Intent: Troubling Jurisprudence from the International Criminal Tribunals' (2002) 37 *Texas International Law Journal* 231.
[64] See e.g. *Stakić*, ICTY T. Ch. II, 31 July 2003, para. 515.
[65] *Attorney-General of Israel v. Eichmann* (1968) 36 ILR 5 (DC) 340.
[66] *Akayesu*, ICTR T. Ch. I, 2 September 1998, para. 731.   [67] ICC Elements of Crimes, Art. 6(b), footnote 3.

temporary impairment of mental faculties,[68] but neither mental nor physical harm need be permanent or irremediable.[69] Obviously, as the term 'serious' is one which involves a value judgment, there will be differing views on what treatment is included. In *Kayishema*, it was held that decisions on what is meant by serious bodily or mental harm should be made on a case-by-case basis.[70]

> *Deliberately inflicting on the group conditions of life calculated to bring about its physical destruction in whole or in part*

This category of prohibited acts comprises methods of destruction whereby the perpetrator does not immediately kill the members of the group, but which seek to bring about their physical destruction in the end.[71] The ICC Elements of Crimes interpret the term 'conditions of life' as including, but 'not necessarily restricted to, deliberate deprivation of resources indispensable for survival, such as food or medical services, or systematic expulsion from homes'.[72] Thus, one of the counts of genocide against President Al Bashir of Sudan includes contamination of the wells and water-pumps in the towns and villages primarily inhabited by the protected groups.[73] Unlike the two previous categories, this is not a result-based form of the crime[74] but it requires that the conditions are 'calculated' to achieve the result.[75]

The question of the forced migration of people, commonly known by the ugly term 'ethnic cleansing', has been addressed under this subparagraph of Article II. This practice, when committed by the Serbs to eliminate the Muslim presence in large parts of Bosnia and Herzegovina, was regarded by Judge ad hoc Lauterpacht in the ICJ provisional measures ruling of 13 September 1993 as constituting genocide,[76] though his view was not shared by the majority. As seen above, the ICC Elements of Crimes give 'systematic expulsion from homes' as one of the illustrations of this category of prohibited act.

But ethnic cleansing does not necessarily constitute genocide. In the *Eichmann* case, the District Court of Jerusalem found that, before 1941, Nazi persecution of the Jews was aimed at persuading them to leave Germany. Only later did the policy develop into one for their destruction. Since the court doubted that there was a specific intent to exterminate before 1941, Eichmann was acquitted of genocide for acts before that date.[77]

Eichmann is authority for the proposition that, if and in so far as the objective of a forced migration is 'only' to remove a group or part of it from a territory, it differs from that of genocide. In *Brđanin*, for example, the Trial Chamber found a 'consistent, coherent and

---

[68] *Semanza*, ICTR T. Ch., 15 May 2003, para. 321.

[69] *Akayesu*, ICTR T. Ch. I, 2 September 1998, para. 502. The *Kayishema* Trial Chamber gave perhaps a narrower interpretation as 'harm that seriously injures the health, causes disfigurement or causes any serious injury to the external, internal organs or senses': *Kayishema*, ICTR T. Ch. II, 21 May 1999, para. 109.

[70] *Ibid.*, para. 110. Examples of mental harm were given in *Blagovejić*, T. Ch. I, 17 January 2005, para. 647.

[71] *Akayesu*, ICTR T. Ch. I, 2 September 1998, para. 505.   [72] ICC Elements of Crimes, Art. 6(c), footnote 4.

[73] See *Al Bashir*, second arrest warrant decision, ICC PTC, 12 July 2010, paras. 32–9.

[74] See e.g. *Stakić*, ICTY T. Ch. II, 31 July 2003, para. 517.

[75] As pointed out in Kreß, 'The Crime of Genocide', 481–3, 'calculated' and 'physical destruction' are difficult concepts.

[76] *Application of the Convention on the Prevention and Punishment of the Crime of Genocide (Bosnia and Herzegovina* v. *Yugoslavia (Serbia and Montenegro))* (1993) ICJ Reports 325, 431–2. Ethnic cleansing was also considered genocide by the ICTY in the decision confirming the second indictment in *Karadžić and Mladić*: Review of the Indictments Pursuant to Rule 61 of the Rules of Procedure and Evidence, ICTY T. Ch. I, 11 July 1996, para. 94.

[77] *Attorney-General of Israel* v. *Eichmann* (1968) 36 ILR 5 (DC). See Schabas, *Genocide*, 233–4.

criminal strategy of cleansing the Bosnian Krajina' but determined that the crimes had been committed with 'the sole purpose of driving people away'.[78] There was no evidence that they had been committed with the intent required for genocide.[79] The fact of forced migration alone is not enough for a court to deduce the special intent of destruction of the group.

The matter was usefully summed up by the ICJ in the *Bosnian Genocide* case:

Neither the intent, as a matter of policy, to render an area 'ethnically homogeneous', nor the operations that may be carried out to implement such policy, can *as such* be designated as genocide: the intent that characterizes genocide is 'to destroy, in whole or in part' a particular group, and deportation or displacement of the members of a group, even if effected by force, is not necessarily equivalent to destruction of that group, nor is such destruction an automatic consequence of the displacement. This is not to say that acts described as 'ethnic cleansing' may never constitute genocide, if they are such as to be characterized as, for example, 'deliberately inflicting on the group conditions of life calculated to bring about its physical destruction in whole or in part', contrary to Article II, paragraph (c), of the Convention, provided such action is carried out with the necessary specific intent (*dolus specialis*), that is to say with a view to the destruction of the group, as distinct from its removal from the region . . . whether a particular operation described as 'ethnic cleansing' amounts to genocide depends on the presence or absence of acts listed in Article II of the Genocide Convention, and of the intent to destroy the group as such. In fact, in the context of the Convention, the term 'ethnic cleansing' has no legal significance of its own. That said, it is clear that acts of 'ethnic cleansing' may occur in parallel to acts prohibited by Article II of the Convention, and may be significant as indicative of the presence of a specific intent (*dolus specialis*) inspiring those acts.[80]

Imposing measures intended to prevent births within the group

This provision (Article II(d) of the Genocide Convention) was inspired by the Nazis' practice of forced sterilization before and during the Second World War. Examples of these measures given by the ICTR Trial Chamber in *Akayesu* are sexual mutilation, sterilization, forced birth control, separation of the sexes and prohibition of marriages.[81] The Trial Chamber added:

In patriarchal societies, where membership of a group is determined by the identity of the father, an example of a measure intended to prevent births within a group is the case where, during rape, a woman of the said group is deliberately impregnated by a man of another group, with the intent to have her give birth to a child who will consequently not belong to its mother's group. Furthermore, the Chamber notes that measures intended to prevent births within the group may be physical, but can also be mental. For instance, rape can be a measure intended to prevent births when the person raped subsequently refuses to procreate, in the same way that members can be led, through threats or trauma, not to procreate.[82]

[78] *Brdanin*, ICTY T. Ch. II, 1 September 2004, para. 118.
[79] *Ibid.*, para. 989. See also *Stakić*, ICTY T. Ch. II, 31 July 2003, paras. 519, 557; *Stakić*, ICTY A. Ch., 22 March 2006, paras. 46–8.
[80] *Bosnian Genocide* case, para. 190.   [81] *Akayesu*, ICTR T. Ch. I, 2 September 1998, para. 507.   [82] *Ibid.*, paras. 507–8.

While this may stray into the separate crime of forced impregnation, it is not too broad, given that both genocidal intent, and the intent to prevent births within the group, must also be proved.

Forcibly transferring children of the group to another group

This is a form of genocide which has received little judicial consideration.[83] Probably the most authoritative interpretative source on the point is to be found in the ICC Elements of Crimes, defining children as being those below 18 and noting that '[t]he term "forcibly" is not restricted to physical force, but may include threat of force or coercion, such as that caused by fear of violence, duress, detention, psychological oppression or abuse of power, against such person or persons or another person, or by taking advantage of a coercive environment'.

The provision (Article II(e)) was included in the Genocide Convention as a compromise for the exclusion of cultural genocide. In 1997, the Australian Human Rights and Equal Opportunities Commission controversially decided that the forcible transfer of Aboriginal children to non-indigenous institutions and families constituted genocide.[84] The wording of the Commission's findings indicated, however, that it was 'cultural genocide' that was in mind, since the objective of the transfers was to assimilate the children into non-Aboriginal society. Cultural genocide is not within the scope of the Convention,[85] nor in customary law,[86] although forcibly transferring children can be close to such a concept.

10.3.2   The 'contextual element'

The ICC Elements of Crimes have an additional material element, which was introduced to avoid the problem that isolated hate crimes could fall within the Convention definition, diluting the seriousness of the term 'genocide'.[87] In relation to each prohibited act, the element requires that:

> The conduct took place in the context of a manifest pattern of similar conduct directed against that group or was conduct that could itself effect such destruction.[88]

The first branch of this element reflects the more likely situation, where the individual accused is acting within a broader context in which others are also committing acts of

---

[83] Although see *Akayesu*, ICTR T. Ch. I, 2 September 1998, para. 509. In the *Bosnian Genocide* case, Bosnia claimed that forced pregnancy constituted this form of genocide since rape was used as a means of affecting the demographic balance; children born as a result of the forced pregnancies would not be considered to be part of the protected group and the intent of the perpetrators was to transfer the unborn children to the group of Bosnian Serbs. The ICJ found that the evidence did not establish any form of policy of forced pregnancy, 'nor that there was any aim to transfer children of the protected group to another group within the meaning of Article II (*e*) of the Convention': paras. 362–7.

[84] Cited in Schabas, *Genocide*, 205.   [85] See section 10.4.1.

[86] *Krstić*, ICTY T. Ch. I, 2 August 2001, para. 580; *Krstić*, ICTY A. Ch., 19 April 2004, para. 25.   [87] See section 10.1.4.

[88] See Valerie Oosterveld and Charles Garraway, 'The Elements of Genocide' in Roy Lee *et al.* (eds.), *The International Criminal Court: Elements of Crimes and Rules of Procedure and Evidence* (New York, 2001) 41, 44, 45.

genocide (or crimes against humanity) against the targeted group.[89] The adjective 'manifest', included at the insistence of the United States, means that the pattern must be a clear one and not one of a few isolated crimes occurring over a period of years.[90] The second branch applies where the conduct in question 'could itself effect such destruction'. Although by far the less likely, this could occur where a group is particularly small or where the accused has access to powerful means of destruction (such as the use of a nuclear or biological weapon) with genocidal intent. In such a case, there is no need for a pattern of similar conduct, since the accused is in a position to pose a real threat to a protected group. The provision would be relevant for prosecutions of ringleaders and instigators. It would also capture those who had the means to destroy a group but for whatever reason managed to cause only a single death or a few deaths, such that there would be no objective 'pattern'.[91]

The contextual element does not exclude entirely the possibility of a 'lone *génocidaire*', since it requires similar *conduct* not similar *intent*;[92] the second clause of the element also envisages a single perpetrator with the means to destroy the group or part of it. It does however require either a pattern of crimes, or a concrete danger to a group, thereby ruling out isolated hate crimes.

The Elements of Crimes are equivocal on the mental element attaching to this element:

Notwithstanding the normal requirement for a mental element provided for in article 30, and recognizing that knowledge of the circumstances will usually be addressed in proving genocidal intent, the appropriate requirement, if any, for a mental element regarding this circumstance will need to be decided by the Court on a case-by-case basis.[93]

The 'contextual element' was not drawn directly from Tribunal jurisprudence; it was based very loosely on two passages in the *Akayesu* trial judgment.[94] The ICTY Trial Chamber in *Krstić* adopted the element although it was not of course obliged to,[95] but the Appeals Chamber was hostile to the Trial Chamber's view:

The Trial Chamber relied on the definition of genocide in the Elements of Crimes adopted by the ICC. This definition, stated the Trial Chamber, 'indicates clearly that genocide requires that "the conduct took place in the context of a manifest pattern of similar conduct."' The Trial Chamber's reliance on the definition of genocide given in the ICC's Elements of Crimes is inapposite . . . the requirement that the prohibited conduct be part of a widespread or systematic attack does not appear in the Genocide Convention and was not mandated by customary international law. Because the definition adopted by the Elements of Crimes did not reflect customary law as it existed at the time Krstić committed his crimes, it cannot be used to support the Trial Chamber's conclusion.[96]

[89] Or, if the other perpetrators do not have the genocidal intent, they may be committing crimes against humanity rather than genocide, while still in a 'manifest pattern of similar conduct'.
[90] Oosterveld and Garraway, 'The Elements of Genocide', 47.
[91] Wiebke Ruckert and Georg Witschel, 'Genocide and Crimes against Humanity in the Elements of Crimes' in H. Fischer, C. Kreß and S. R. Lüder (eds.), *International and National Prosecution of Crimes under International Law* (Berlin, 2000) 66.
[92] Oosterveld, 'Context of Genocide', 47–8.   [93] Elements of Crimes, Art. 6, Introduction, para. 3.
[94] *Akayesu*, ICTR T. Ch. I, 2 September 1998, paras. 520 and 523.   [95] *Krstić*, ICTY T. Ch. I, 2 August 2001, para. 682.
[96] *Krstić*, ICTY A. Ch., 19 April 2004, para. 224.

After *Krstić*, the Tribunals will not be accepting the contextual element within their own jurisprudence.

In the ICC, on the other hand, a majority in a Pre-Trial Chamber has taken the view that the contextual provision in the Elements is not inconsistent with the ICC Statute (which includes the Genocide Convention definition) and it has therefore applied it.[97] The Chamber took the view that the contextual element was 'fully consistent with the traditional consideration of the crime of genocide as the "crime of crimes"'.[98] Indeed, if genocide is to be seen as a particularly serious crime, some threshold of objective 'scale and gravity'[99] must be maintained, and the ICC Elements of Crimes provision offers a formulation which has been accepted and adopted by consensus by the international community.

10.4   Mental elements

The mental elements of genocide comprise both the requisite intention to commit the underlying prohibited act (such as killing) and the intent special to genocide. It is the special intent 'to destroy in whole or in part [a protected group] as such' that distinguishes genocide from other crimes.[100] But the meaning to be attributed to this intent requirement is a matter of some difficulty. There are four aspects to be considered, and they are interconnected. Does every perpetrator have to have a specific intent to destroy or is it sufficient, either for all, or at least for non-leaders, that they have knowledge of a collective plan and foresee that their conduct will further it? What is the meaning of 'destroy' for the purpose of the special intent? What is the 'whole' or 'part' of a group? What is the meaning of 'as such': is motive relevant? These four issues are considered below.

10.4.1   *Intent*

It is worth emphasizing that, unlike the crime of aggression, genocide is not a crime that may be committed only by those who lead and plan a campaign of destruction. The rank and file may also be principal perpetrators of genocide, provided they have the requisite intent.[101] The special intent required for genocide necessitates each individual perpetrator, whether leader or foot soldier, having the intention to destroy the group or part of it when committing any of the prohibited acts.[102] It differs from the 'normal' intent in criminal law, as exemplified in Article 30 of the ICC Statute. That Article provides that, in relation to

---

[97] *Al Bashir* arrest warrant case, ICC PTC I, 4 March 2009, paras. 117–33; and *Al Bashir*, second arrest warrant decision, ICC PTC, 12 July 2010, para. 13. But the majority's conclusion (in the first decision) that the contextual element means that 'the relevant conduct presents a concrete threat to the existence of the targeted group' imposes a requirement not included in the element; see Separate and Partly Dissenting Opinion of Judge Anita Ušacka, para. 19, footnote 26. See also Claus Kreß, 'The Crime of Genocide and Contextual Elements: A Comment on the ICC Pre-Trial Chamber's Decision in the Al Bashir Case' (2009) *Journal of International Criminal Justice* 1; and Robert Cryer, 'The Definitions of International Crimes in Al Bashir Arrest Warrant Decision' (2009) 7 *Journal of International Criminal Justice* 283.
[98] *Al Bashir* arrest warrant case, para. 133.   [99] *Krstić*, ICTY T. Ch. I, 2 August 2001, para. 549.
[100] *Kambanda*, ICTR T. Ch. I, 4 September 1998, para. 16; *Kayishema*, ICTR T. Ch. II, 21 May 1999, para. 91.
[101] *Kayishema*, ICTR A. Ch., 1 June 2001, para. 170.
[102] See e.g. *Akayesu*, ICTR T. Ch. I, 2 September 1998, para. 498; *Kayishema*, ICTR T. Ch. II, 21 May 1999, para. 91; *Musema*, ICTR T. Ch. I, 27 January 2000, para. 164.

conduct, the individual must mean to engage in the conduct, and, in relation to a consequence, the individual must mean to cause that consequence 'or is aware that it will occur in the ordinary course of events'. That is a less stringent requirement than the special intent for genocide; Article 30 is however relevant to the underlying acts and to some other forms of liability in relation to genocide.[103]

In time of armed conflict, where the intention is to defeat the opposing side, it may be difficult to assess whether mass killings are committed with a genocidal intent or with the intent of winning the war. The findings of the ICTY in the *Krstić* case and of the Commission of Inquiry on Darfur provide useful illustrations. The defence in *Krstić* argued that the purpose of the killings in Srebrenica was not to destroy the group as such, but to remove a military threat; this was evidenced by the fact that men of military age had been targeted. The Trial Chamber held, however, as affirmed by the Appeals Chamber, that the killings did constitute genocide. Its reasoning, which was upheld on appeal,[104] deserves setting out in detail:

the Bosnian Serb forces could not have failed to know, by the time they decided to kill all the men, that this selective destruction of the group would have a lasting impact upon the entire group. Their death precluded any effective attempt by the Bosnian Muslims to recapture the territory. Furthermore, the Bosnian Serb forces had to be aware of the catastrophic impact that the disappearance of two or three generations of men would have on the survival of a traditionally patriarchal society ... The Bosnian Serb forces knew by the time they decided to kill all of the military aged men, that the combination of those killings with the forcible transfer of the women, children and elderly would inevitably result in the physical disappearance of the Bosnian Muslim population at Srebrenica. Intent by the Bosnian Serb forces to target the Bosnian Muslims of Srebrenica as a group is further evidenced by their destroying homes of Bosnian Muslims in Srebrenica and Potocari and the principal mosque in Srebrenica soon after the attack. Finally, there is a strong indication of the intent to destroy the group as such in the concealment of the bodies in mass graves, which were later dug up, the bodies mutilated and reburied in other mass graves ... By killing all the military aged men, the Bosnian Serb forces effectively destroyed the community of the Bosnian Muslims in Srebrenica and eliminated all likelihood that it could ever re-establish itself on that territory.[105]

On the other hand, General Krstić himself, the Appeals Chamber decided, did not have a genocidal intent:

His own particular intent was directed to a forcible displacement. Some other members of the VRS Main Staff harboured the same intent to carry out forcible displacement, but viewed this displacement as a step in the accomplishment of their genocidal objective ... all that the evidence can establish is that Krstić was aware of the intent to commit genocide on the part of some members of the VRS Main Staff, and with that knowledge, he did nothing to prevent the use of Drina Corps personnel and resources to facilitate those killings. This knowledge on his part alone cannot support an inference of genocidal intent.

---

[103] For other forms of participation in genocide, see section 15.4. [104] *Krstić*, ICTY A. Ch., 19 April 2004, paras. 24–38.
[105] *Krstić*, ICTY T. Ch. I, 2 August 2001, paras. 595–7.

Genocide is one of the worst crimes known to humankind, and its gravity is reflected in the stringent requirement of specific intent. Convictions for genocide can be entered only where that intent has been unequivocally established. There was a demonstrable failure by the Trial Chamber to supply adequate proof that Radislav Krštić possessed the genocidal intent. Krštić, therefore, is not guilty of genocide as a principal perpetrator.[106]

In the same direction, the Darfur Commission of Inquiry decided that the policy of attacking, killing and forcibly displacing members of some tribes in Darfur did not show the special intent of genocide, but rather the intent 'to drive the victims from their homes, primarily for purposes of counter-insurgency warfare'.[107] The material elements of genocide – the killing and other prohibited acts, and the existence of a protected group – were present, but not the special intent, and the Commission therefore found that the government of Sudan had not pursued a policy of genocide.[108] The Commission's finding was not of course binding on the ICC, and the Prosecutor made an application to a Pre-Trial Chamber in 2009 for an arrest warrant against President Al Bashir, alleging genocide among other crimes. The Chamber at first refused to grant a warrant in respect of genocide, while allowing it for war crimes and crimes against humanity. The counts of genocide were excluded because 'the existence of reasonable grounds to believe that the [government of Sudan] acted with a *dolus specialis* specific intent to destroy in whole or in part the Fur, Masalit and Zaghawa groups is not the only reasonable conclusion that can be drawn' from the facts described by the Prosecutor. That finding was overturned on appeal,[109] and the Pre-Trial Chamber went on to issue a warrant of arrest for genocide.[110]

Proof of special intent

Direct evidence of genocidal intent may not be available. In the absence of such, the Tribunals have been prepared to deduce intent from circumstantial evidence including the actions and words of the perpetrator. In *Seromba*, for example, the defendant, a priest, had approved the decision to destroy a church to kill those inside it, had shown the bulldozer driver the weakest side of the church and directed him to destroy it. The Appeals Chamber found that Seromba 'knew that there were approximately 1,500 Tutsis in the church and that the destruction of the church would necessarily cause their death'. In the context of Seromba's previous actions and statements with regard to the Tutsis, the Chamber found that he had the requisite specific intent (and had directly participated in acts of genocide); the

---

[106] *Krštić*, ICTY A. Ch., 19 April 2004, paras. 133, 134. See also *Stakić*, ICTY A. Ch., 22 March 2006, para. 47: no genocidal intent existed when the defendant's 'intention was only to displace the Bosnian Muslim population and not to destroy it'.
[107] Report, UN Doc. S/2005/60, para. 518.
[108] For a useful comment on the Commission's report, see Schabas, 'Darfur and the "Odious Scourge"'; see also Kreß, 'The Crime of Genocide'.
[109] *Al Bashir* arrest warrant case, ICC PTC I, 4 March 2009, para. 205, and ICC A. Ch., 3 February 2010, paras. 20–42.
[110] *Al Bashir*, second arrest warrant decision, ICC PTC, 12 July 2010. President Al Bashir had not been arrested at the time of writing.

Chamber replaced Seromba's conviction of aiding and abetting genocide with that of perpetration of genocide.[111]

Less reasonably, the ICTR has also stated that intent may be deduced from the behaviour of *others*; it may be deduced, the *Akayesu* Trial Chamber said, from:

the general context of the perpetration of other culpable acts systematically directed against that same group, whether these acts were committed by the same offender or by others. Other factors, such as the scale of atrocities committed, their general nature, in a region or a country, or furthermore, the fact of deliberately and systematically targeting victims on account of their membership of a particular group, while excluding the members of other groups, can enable the Chamber to infer the genocidal intent of a particular act.[112]

This was somewhat tempered by the Appeals Chamber in *Stakić*, which noted that the Trial Chamber in that case 'considered whether the apparent intentions of others . . . could provide indirect evidence of the Appellant's own intentions when he agreed with those others to undertake criminal plans'.[113] As the Appeals Chamber also noted, all the evidence (such as the type of attacks, discriminatory animus, the use of derogatory slurs, attacks on religious sites and 'targeting of . . . leaders for death or slander')[114] must be taken together when determining intent since, looking at each piece individually rather than cumulatively, as the Trial Chamber did, 'obscured the proper inquiry'.[115] In spite of this error, however, the Appeals Chamber did not consider that the prosecution had shown that the Trial Chamber had such evidence before it that it was obliged to find genocidal intent.[116]

Intent, not knowledge

The interpretation of the special intent element given above has been criticized. It is said that simple foot soldiers will normally follow orders without necessarily having an intent to destroy a whole group[117] and that it would not be realistic to look for an intent from one individual to destroy the group through his own conduct. In relation to an accused who participated in a genocidal campaign, courts may therefore face the difficult choice between acquittal for lack of evidence of the special intent as normally defined and 'squeezing ambiguous fact patterns into the specific intent paradigm'.[118] Courts will be tempted to ease the requirements of evidence by drawing wide deductions from the facts, as indicated above, thus establishing the special intent 'by the evidentiary backdoor'.[119] These difficulties have led commentators to propose alternative formulations of the intent necessary for genocide. In particular, Greenawalt has suggested:

---

[111] *Seromba*, ICTR A. Ch., 12 March 2008, paras. 177–82. The Chamber in this case also adopted a wide definition of 'perpetration'; see section 15.2.
[112] *Akayesu*, ICTR T. Ch. I, 2 September 1998, para. 523.   [113] *Stakić*, ICTY A. Ch., 22 March 2006, para. 40.
[114] *Ibid.*, para. 53.   [115] *Ibid.*, para. 55.   [116] *Ibid.*, para. 56.
[117] Harmen van der Wilt, 'Complicity in Genocide and International v. Domestic Jurisdiction' (2006) 4 *Journal of International Criminal Justice* 242.
[118] Alexander Greenawalt, 'Rethinking Genocidal Intent: The Case for a Knowledge-Based Interpretation' (1999) 99 *Columbia Law Review* 2265, 2281.
[119] Claus Kreß, 'The Darfur Report and Genocidal Intent' (2005) 3 *Journal of International Criminal Justice* 565, 572.

In cases where a perpetrator is otherwise liable for a genocidal act, the requirement of genocidal intent should be satisfied if the perpetrator acted in furtherance of a campaign targeting members of a protected group and knew that the goal or manifest effect of the campaign was the destruction of the group in whole or in part.[120]

This 'knowledge-based' approach, which is more akin to what is required by Article 30 of the ICC Statute, is to be distinguished from the 'purpose-based' approach used by the Tribunals and the ICC in interpreting the crime of genocide. Some commentators argue that the purpose-based approach goes beyond what is envisaged in the Genocide Convention.[121] They distinguish between the collective intent, manifested in an overall genocidal plan or campaign, and the individual intent which, in their view, need involve only knowledge of the plan on the part of the individual perpetrator together with foresight or recklessness as to the occurrence of the planned destruction.[122]

   As indicated above,[123] if such an approach were to be adopted, it would reflect the nature of genocide as a collective crime. It was illustrated in *Kayishema* where the Trial Chamber first found that there was a genocidal plan, and went on to say:

The killers had the common intent to exterminate the ethnic group and Kayishema was instrumental in the realisation of that intent.[124]

In *Krštić*, however, the Appeals Chamber, while noting that the intent to destroy must be discernible in the joint participation of the crime itself, held that individual participants must each have the necessary intent.[125] This insistence on the special intent for each individual perpetrator remains the standard required for the crime of genocide by the case law and may be seen as correctly reflecting the need to reserve genocide convictions only for those who have the highest degree of criminal intent. In practice, however, the approach of the Tribunals to modes of liability which do not require a special intent, such as aiding and abetting and joint criminal enterprise, has led to a blurring of the lines.[126] General Krštić himself was acquitted of genocide, as lacking the specific intent to destroy, but he was convicted of aiding and abetting acts of genocide. Prosecutors who are not sure of being able to prove the special intent are likely to charge such lesser modes of liability rather than genocide as a principal perpetrator.

10.4.2 'To destroy'

The intent is to destroy. The destruction specified here is physical or biological, although the means of causing the destruction of the group may be by acts short of causing the death of individuals.[127] Other forms of destruction, for example, the social assimilation of a group

---

[120] Greenawalt, 'Rethinking Genocidal Intent', 2288; and see Alicia Gil Gil, *Derecho penal internacional: Especial consideratión del delito de genocidio* (Madrid, 1999); Kreß, 'The Darfur Report', 577.
[121] Otto Triffterer, 'Genocide: Its Particular Intent to Destroy in Whole or in Part the Group as Such' (2001) 14 *Leiden Journal of International Law* 399; Jones, 'Whose Intent?'. 478.
[122] See Jones, 'Whose Intent?'; Kreß, 'The Darfur Report', 576–7.   [123] See section 10.1.4.
[124] *Kayishema*, ICTR T. Ch. II, 21 May 1999, paras. 533, 535.   [125] *Krštić*, ICTY A. Ch., 19 April 2004, para. 549.
[126] See section 15.4.   [127] *Kayishema*, ICTR T. Ch. II, 21 May 1999, para. 95.

into another, or attacks on cultural characteristics which give a group its own identity, do not constitute genocide if they are not related to physical or biological destruction. While the Preamble to General Assembly Resolution 96(1) stated that genocide 'results in great losses to humanity in the form of cultural and other contributions represented by these human groups', this did not suggest that cultural loss, in the absence of physical destruction, can amount to genocide. The *travaux préparatoires* of the Convention indicate that the inclusion of cultural genocide was hotly debated and eventually rejected.[128]

Some national jurisdictions have extended the meaning of genocide to cover other forms of destruction within their own law.[129] But, as the Trial Chamber in *Krstić* (which was quoted approvingly on appeal) put it:

despite recent developments, customary international law limits the definition of genocide to those acts seeking the physical or biological destruction of all or part of the group. An enterprise attacking only the cultural or sociological characteristics of a human group in order to annihilate these elements which give to that group its own identity distinct from the rest of the community would not fall under the definition of genocide.[130]

The Trial Chamber in the later case of *Blagojević* appears to have departed from this in finding that 'the forcible transfer of individuals could lead to the material destruction of the group, since the group ceases to exist as a group, or at least as the group was'. It emphasized 'that its reasoning and conclusion are not an argument for cultural genocide, but rather an attempt to clarify the meaning of physical and biological destruction',[131] but this looks like an attempt to square the circle. In the *Bosnian Genocide* case, the ICJ confirmed that genocide was limited to physical or biological destruction of a group;[132] if the transfer of members of a group results in the splitting up of the group, that is not genocide unless done with an intent to physically destroy the group. However, acts of ethnic cleansing – and attacks on cultural and religious property – may be significant evidence towards establishing the intent to destroy.

10.4.3   'In whole or in part'

There must be an intent to destroy the protected group in whole or in part. This aspect of the intention[133] is one which has caused considerable controversy. This is because the ambit of the protections granted by the prohibition of genocide is quite heavily dependent on how broadly or narrowly the relevant group is conceptualized. The first issue is a geographical one. To take an example from a clear case of genocide – Rwanda – the Hutu *génocidaires* did not appear to want to destroy all Tutsis everywhere, but only in Rwanda.[134] The relevant

---

[128] Summarized in Schabas, *Genocide*, 207–14.
[129] See e.g. the decision of the German Federal Constitutional Court, 2 BvR 290/99, 12 December 2000, para. III(4)(a)(aa).
[130] *Krstić*, ICTY T. Ch. I, 2 August 2001, para. 580; *Krstić*, ICTY A. Ch., 19 April 2004, para. 25.
[131] *Blagojević and Jokić*, ICTY T. Ch. I, 17 January 2005, para. 666.   [132] *Bosnian Genocide* case, para. 344.
[133] It is worth emphasizing that this part of the offence is a part of the mental element, not the material elements, of genocide – it is not necessary to establish whether all or part of a group was actually destroyed to prove genocide.
[134] *Krstić*, ICTY A. Ch., 19 April 2004, para. 13.

group could be conceived of as Tutsis everywhere, in which case Rwandan Tutsis were protected only as a 'part' of that group. Or it could be thought that the relevant group was the Rwandan Tutsis. This difference matters as, in the latter instance, an intention to destroy all the Tutsis in part of Rwanda could fulfil this aspect of the mental element of genocide. In the former, it could not. According to the ICJ, 'it is widely accepted that genocide may be found to have been committed where the intent is to destroy the group within a geographically limited area'.[135]

A further issue is the meaning of 'part' of a group. The case law of the Tribunals has established that it is not genocide if the intention is to target a part which is less than 'substantial',[136] and this has been confirmed by the ICJ:

the intent must be to destroy at least a substantial part of the particular group. That is demanded by the very nature of the crime of genocide: since the object and purpose of the Convention as a whole is to prevent the intentional destruction of groups, the part targeted must be significant enough to have an impact on the group as a whole.[137]

The findings in *Krstić* illustrate the difficulties of determining both the whole and the substantial part of the group for the purpose of assessing whether the special intent is present. The Trial Chamber determined that the Bosnian Muslims constituted the protected group and 'the Bosnian Muslims of Srebrenica or the Bosnian Muslims of Eastern Bosnia constitute a part of the protected group'.[138] This finding was affirmed by the Appeals Chamber, which also pointed out that, in determining what a 'substantial' part was, the prominence of the targeted individuals within the group as well as the number targeted (in absolute and in relative terms) could also be relevant; hence, both qualitative and quantitative criteria should be considered. 'If a specific part of the group is emblematic of the overall group, or is essential to its survival, that may support a finding that the part qualifies as substantial.'[139] Here the fate of the Srebrenica Muslims was emblematic of that of all Bosnian Muslims.

The decision has been criticized as having set too low a threshold for the scale of genocide.[140] The killings were of 7,000–8,000 men, and it therefore appeared that the people targeted formed a part of a part of a group. However, the Chamber also took into account the fact that women and children were transferred from the area, to argue that the 'part' of the group was the Bosnian Muslims of Srebrenica. The prosecution had urged the ICTY to take the view that the Bosnian Muslims of Srebrenica were the relevant whole group.[141] If the Chamber had accepted this, it would have made proving genocide

---

[135] *Bosnian Genocide* case, para. 199.
[136] *Kayishema*, ICTR T. Ch. II, 21 May 1999, para. 96; *Bagilishema*, ICTR T. Ch. I, 7 June 2001, para. 64; *Semanza*, ICTR T. Ch., 15 May 2003, para. 316.
[137] *Bosnian Genocide* case, para. 198.   [138] *Krstić*, ICTY T. Ch. I, 2 August 2001, para. 560.
[139] *Krstić*, ICTY A. Ch., 19 April 2004, para. 12.
[140] William Schabas, 'Was Genocide Committed in Bosnia and Herzegovina? First Judgments of the International Criminal Tribunal for the Former Yugoslavia' (2002) 25 *Fordham International Law Journal* 23, 45–7: '[C]ategorising [the atrocities] as "genocide" seems to distort the definition unreasonably.' And see Katherine Southwick, 'Srebrenica as Genocide? The Krstić Decision and the Language of the Unspeakable' (2005) 8 *Yale Human Rights and Development Law Journal* 188, 206–11.
[141] *Krstić*, ICTY T. Ch. I, 2 August 2001, para. 545.

considerably simpler for the prosecution, as the Bosnian Muslim men of military age could have been seen as a substantial part of the group. This would, however, have diluted the concept of genocide considerably.

10.4.4 'As such'

There must be an intent to destroy the group, or part of it, 'as such'. During the negotiation of the Convention, there were those who wanted to include *motive* as a necessary element of genocide. Others did not. The compromise which allowed agreement to be reached was to exclude any explicit reference to motive, but to include the words 'as such'.[142] While these words are therefore relied upon by some as evidence of the need for motive,[143] the *travaux préparatoires* disclose that that was not the meaning that all the negotiators attached to the words.

The motive for which a crime is committed, as opposed to the intention with which it is committed, is ordinarily irrelevant to guilt in criminal law. But the discriminatory nature of genocide seems to require a motive: the victims are singled out not by reason of their individual identity but *because* of their membership of a national, ethnic, racial or religious group.[144] It is not surprising therefore that decisions by the ad hoc Tribunals have sometimes used the language of motive, referring to the need for the accused to 'seek' or 'aim at' the destruction of the group.[145] If it is possible to untangle the sometimes apparently conflicting case law of the Tribunals, it can be said that the Tribunals do distinguish between motive and genocidal intent[146] – personal motivation (such as a wish to profit financially from the genocide) for the perpetrator's participation in the crime is not relevant – but having a discriminatory purpose for the crime is intrinsic to the special intent.[147] Further, in cases where a set of facts and their consequences may have different explanations, it may be that a consideration of motive may be relevant in assessing intent, even though it will not itself be decisive.[148]

10.5   Other modes of participation

The 'other acts' of participation in genocide listed in Article III of the Convention – conspiracy, 'direct and public incitement', attempt and complicity – are expressly incorporated in the Statutes of the ad hoc Tribunals. The ICC, on the other hand, relies on the general

---

[142] The negotiations are well summarized in A. Greenawalt, 'Rethinking Genocidal Intent: The Case for a Knowledge-Based Interpretation' (1999) 99 *Columbia Law Review* 2259, 2274–9; and Schabas, *Genocide*, 294–306.

[143] See the discussion in Quigley, *The Genocide Convention*, 120–6.

[144] *Niyitegeka*, ICTR A. Ch., 9 July 2004, para. 53; *Musema*, ICTR A. Ch., 16 November 2001, para. 165.

[145] See e.g. *Jelisić*, ICTY A. Ch., 5 July 2001, para. 46; *Rutaganda*, ICTR A. Ch., 26 May 2003, para. 524.

[146] *Krštić*, ICTY T. Ch. I, 2 August 2001, para. 561; and see *Tadić*, ICTY A. Ch., 15 July 1999, paras. 269, 270.

[147] *Krštić*, ICTY T. Ch. I, 2 August 2001, para. 545; *Krštić*, ICTY A. Ch., 19 April 2004, para. 45; *Kayishema and Ruzindana*, ICTR A. Ch., 1 June 2001, para. 161; *Stakić*, ICTY A. Ch., 22 March 2006, para. 45; *Jelisić*, ICTY A. Ch., 5 July 2001, para. 49.

[148] See criticism of the *Krštić* case on the ground that the Trial Chamber did not take any account of motive, in Southwick, 'Srebrenica as Genocide?' See further Paul Behrens, 'Genocide and the Question of Motive' (2012) 10.

principles of law in Part 3 of its Statute, which apply to all of the crimes within the jurisdiction of the Court, for all these forms of liability. The exception is incitement to genocide, for which specific provision was made in Article 25(3)(e) of the ICC Statute. For the ICC, the omission of conspiracy, due to hesitations of civil law countries, has left a gap, although the Statute provision on contribution to a common purpose may largely fill it. Further discussion of these other acts and of command responsibility in relation to genocide may be found in Chapter 15.

Further reading

Hirad Abtahi and Philippa Webb, *The Genocide Convention: The Travaux Préparatoires*, 2 Vols. (The Hague, 2008)

Payam Akhavan, *Reducing Genocide to Law* (Cambridge, 2012)

Paul Behrens and Ralph Henham (eds.), *Elements of Genocide* (Abingdon and New York, 2013)

Antonio Cassese, 'Genocide' in A. Cassese, P. Gaeta and J. R. W. D. Jones (eds.), *The Rome Statute of the International Criminal Court: A Commentary* (Oxford, 2002) 335

Caroline Fournet, *Genocide and Crimes against Humanity* (Oxford, 2013)

Alexander Greenawalt, 'Rethinking Genocidal Intent: The Case for a Knowledge-Based Interpretation' (1999) 99 *Columbia Law Review* 2259

Nina Jørgensen, 'The Definition of Genocide: Joining the Dots in the Light of Recent Practice' (2001) 1 *International Criminal Law Review* 285

Claus Kreß, 'The Crime of Genocide under International Law' (2006) 6 *International Criminal Law Review* 461

Laurence J. Le Blanc, 'The Intent to Destroy Groups in the Genocide Convention: The Proposed US Understanding' (1984) 78 *American Journal of International Law* 369

Raphael Lemkin, *Axis Rule in Occupied Europe: Laws of Occupation, Analysis of Government, Proposals for Redress* (Washington DC, 1944)

Raphael Lemkin, 'Genocide as a Crime under International Law' (1947) 41 *American Journal of International Law* 145

Matthew Lippman, 'The Convention on the Prevention and Punishment of the Crime of Genocide: Fifty Years Later' (1998) 15 *Arizona Journal of International and Comparative Law* 415

Guénaël Mettraux, *International Crimes and the Ad Hoc Tribunals* (Oxford, 2005) Chapter 6

John Quigley, *The Genocide Convention: An International Law Analysis* (Aldershot, 2006)

William Schabas, *Genocide in International Law*, 2nd edn (Cambridge, 2009)

Malcolm Shaw, 'Genocide in International Law' in Yoram Dinstein (ed.), *International Law at a Time of Perplexity* (Dordrecht, 1989) 797

Dinah Shelton (ed.), *The Encyclopaedia of Genocide and Crimes against Humanity* (Farmington Hills, MI, 2005)

11

Crimes against Humanity

11.1   Introduction

11.1.1   Overview

Crimes against humanity are as old as humanity itself.[1] However, it is only in the last century that the international legal prohibition of crimes against humanity has emerged, and it is only in the last twenty years that the precise contours of the crime have been clarified.

Whereas genocide and war crimes have been codified in conventions with widely accepted definitions, crimes against humanity have appeared in a series of instruments with somewhat inconsistent definitions. The law of crimes against humanity was initially created to fill certain gaps in the law of war crimes, but many parameters were left undefined. The recent increase in the application of international criminal law has produced a fruitful interplay between international instruments, national jurisprudence, international jurisprudence and academic commentaries, leading to a more coherent picture of the scope and definition of crimes against humanity today.

A crime against humanity involves the commission of certain inhumane acts, such as murder, torture, rape, sexual slavery, persecution and other inhumane acts, in a certain *context*: they must be part of a widespread or systematic attack directed against a civilian population. It is this context that elevates crimes that might otherwise fall exclusively under national jurisdiction to crimes of concern to the international community as a whole. An individual may be liable for crimes against humanity if he or she commits one or more inhumane acts within that broader context. It is not required that the individual be a ringleader or architect of the broader campaign.

11.1.2   Historical development

The most significant early reference to 'crimes against humanity' as a legal concept was a joint declaration by France, Great Britain and Russia in 1915. Responding to the massacre of Armenians by Turkey, the joint declaration denounced 'crimes against humanity and

---

[1] Jean Graven, 'Les crimes contre l'humanité' (1950) 76 *Hague Recueil* 427, 433.

civilization' and warned of personal accountability.[2] After the First World War, an international war crimes commission recommended the creation of an international tribunal to try not only war crimes but also 'violations of the laws of humanity'.[3] However, the US representative objected to the references to the laws of humanity on the grounds that these were not yet precise enough for criminal law, and the concept was not pursued at that time.[4]

In the wake of the Second World War, the drafters of the Nuremberg Charter were confronted with the question of how to respond to the Holocaust and the massive crimes committed by the Nazi regime. The classic definition of war crimes did not include crimes committed by a government against its own citizens. The drafters therefore included 'crimes against humanity', defined in Article 6(c) as:

murder, extermination, enslavement, deportation and other inhumane acts committed against any civilian population, before or during the war, or persecutions on political, racial or religious grounds in execution of or in connection with any crime within the jurisdiction of the Tribunal, whether or not in violation of the law of the country where perpetrated.

Three major features may be noted. First, the reference to 'any' civilian population meant that even crimes committed against a country's own population were included. This was a major advancement, given that, at that time, prior to the advent of the human rights movement, international law generally regulated conduct *between* States and said little about a government's treatment of its own citizens. Second, the requirement of connection to war crimes or the crime of aggression meant in effect that crimes against humanity could occur only with some 'nexus' to armed conflict.[5] Third, the reference to 'population' was understood to create some requirement of scale, but the precise threshold was specified neither in the Charter nor in the Nuremberg judgment.[6]

It remains controversial whether the Nuremberg Charter created new law, or whether it recognized an existing crime.[7] Among those concluding that it was a new crime, many argued that the principle of non-retroactivity had to give way to the overriding need for accountability for large-scale murder and atrocities recognized as criminal by all nations.[8] Perhaps because of this uncertainty in the status of crimes against humanity, the Nuremberg

---

[2] For more information on these historical developments, see United Nations War Crimes Commission, *History of the United Nations War Crimes Commission and the Development of the Laws of War* (London, 1948); Roger Clark, 'Crimes against Humanity' in G. Ginsburgs and V. N. Kudriavstsev (eds.), *The Nuremberg Trial and International Law* (Dordrecht, Boston and London, 1990); Egon Schwelb, 'Crimes against Humanity' (1946) 23 *British Yearbook of International Law* 178.

[3] The Inter-Allied Commission on the Responsibility on the Authors of the War. See section 6.1.

[4] War Crimes Commission, *History*.

[5] The text as originally adopted contained a semi-colon following the word 'war', which would give rise to the interpretation that the connection requirement applied only to persecution. This was promptly amended by the Berlin Protocol of 6 October 1945, which replaced the semi-colon with a comma, thereby supporting the interpretation that the connection requirement applied to all crimes against humanity. See Clark, 'Crimes', 190–2.

[6] War Crimes Commission, *History*, 192–3.

[7] See e.g. M. Cherif Bassiouni, *Crimes against Humanity: Historical Evolution and Contemporary Application* (Cambridge, 2011).

[8] Hans Kelsen, 'Will the Judgment in the Nuremberg Trial Constitute a Precedent in International Law?' (1947) 1 *International Law Quarterly* 153 especially at 165; see also E. Schwelb, 'Crimes against Humanity' (1946) 23 *British Yearbook of International Law* 178; and see the treatment of the question in *R v. Finta* [1994] 1 SCR 701; *Polyukhovic* [1991] HCA 32; (1991) 172 CLR 501, 661–2, High Court of Australia; *Eichmann*, 36 ILR 277, 283, SC.

judgment tended to blur discussion of crimes against humanity and war crimes and provided very little guidance on the particular elements of the crime.[9]

The Tokyo Charter included a similar definition with some modifications.[10] The Allied Control Council, creating law for occupied Germany, adopted Control Council Law No. 10 with a similar definition. Control Council Law No. 10 added rape, imprisonment and torture to the list of inhumane acts, and did not require a connection to war crimes or aggression.

The concept of crimes against humanity was promptly endorsed by the UN General Assembly,[11] but in the decades that followed there was only a limited body of national cases[12] as well as a few treaties and instruments recognizing enforced disappearance and apartheid as crimes against humanity.[13] The International Law Commission also developed several definitions as part of its work on a draft code of international crimes.

A major advance occurred when the Security Council created the ICTY and ICTR in response to mass crimes in the former Yugoslavia and in Rwanda. The Statute of each Tribunal contained a list of acts based on the Control Council Law No. 10 list. The ICTY Statute (Article 5) defined the contextual threshold as 'when committed in armed conflict, whether international or internal in character, and directed against any civilian population'. The Tribunal itself, referring to previous authorities, interpreted this threshold as requiring a 'widespread or systematic attack'.[14] The ICTR Statute (Article 3) defined the context as 'when committed as part of a widespread or systematic attack against any civilian population on national, political, ethnic, racial or religious grounds'. Thus, the definitions are similar, except that the ICTY Statute requires armed conflict and the ICTR Statute requires discriminatory grounds.

The ICC Statute, adopted in 1998, recognizes the same contextual threshold in Article 7: 'when committed as part of a widespread or systematic attack directed against any civilian population'. The ICC Statute rejects both the armed conflict requirement and the requirement of discriminatory grounds, as these were not considered to be required in customary international law. The ICC Statute requires a 'State or organizational policy', which is controversial, as is discussed below. The ICC Statute contains the same list of acts as previous instruments, but adds forced transfer of population, sexual slavery, enforced prostitution, forced pregnancy, enforced sterilization, sexual violence, enforced

---

[9] Nuremberg IMT, Judgment and Sentences, reprinted in (1947) 41 *American Journal of International Law* 172, especially at 248–9.

[10] Art. 5(c) of the Tokyo Charter included the same definition with the omission of racial and religious persecution, on the ground that such crimes had not occurred in that theatre of conflict. The term 'any civilian population' was also deleted, on which basis the prosecution argued that all killing during an aggressive war was murder. Such arguments were rejected at Nuremberg and Tokyo, as they would undermine the distinction between the law governing *justification for* armed conflict and the law governing *conduct during* armed conflict. See Chapter 12.

[11] GA Res. 95(I), UN Doc. A/64/Add.1 (1946).

[12] Including cases in France, the Netherlands, Israel, Canada and Australia, as discussed at section 11.2.3. See also Joseph Rikhof, 'Crimes against Humanity, Customary International Law and the International Tribunals for Bosnia and Rwanda' (1995) 6 *National Journal of Constitutional Law* 231; Matthew Lippman, 'Crimes against Humanity' (1997) 17 *Boston College Third World Law Journal* 171; Leila Sadat Wexler, 'The Interpretation of the Nuremberg Principles by the French Court of Cassation: From Touvier to Barbie and Back Again' (1994) 32 *Columbia Journal of Transnational Law* 289.

[13] Examples include the Convention on the Non-Applicability of Statutory Limitations to War Crimes and Crimes against Humanity 1968, the Apartheid Convention 1973, the Inter-American Convention on Enforced Disappearance 1994 and the UN Declaration on Enforced Disappearance 1992.

[14] *Tadić*, ICTY T. Ch. II, 7 May 1997, para. 644; *Tadić*, ICTY A. Ch., 15 July 1999, para. 248.

disappearance and the crime of apartheid.[15] The ICC Statute includes supplementary definitions in Article 7(2), some of which have been generally welcomed as helpful clarifications, whereas others have been controversial, as will be discussed later.

Additional sources on the definition of crimes against humanity may now be found in national and international jurisprudence, the ICC Elements of Crimes, and instruments of other tribunals, such as the SCSL. Each of these includes a comparable list of acts as well as the now-standard requirement of widespread or systematic attack directed against any civilian population. In addition, discussions are underway about a possible convention on crimes against humanity, to affirm the obligations of States to prevent and punish such crimes.[16]

11.1.3   Relationship to other crimes

War crimes and crimes against humanity can and do frequently overlap. For example, a mass killing of civilians during an armed conflict could constitute both types of crimes. There are, however, significant differences. First, unlike war crimes, crimes against humanity may occur even in the absence of armed conflict. Second, crimes against humanity require a context of widespread or systematic commission, whereas war crimes do not; a single isolated incident can constitute a war crime. Third, war crimes law was originally based on reciprocal promises between parties to a conflict, and hence primarily focuses on protecting 'enemy' nationals or persons affiliated with the other party to the conflict. The law of crimes against humanity protects victims regardless of their nationality or affiliation. Fourth, war crimes law regulates conduct even on the battlefield and against military objectives,[17] whereas the law of crimes against humanity concerns actions directed primarily against civilian populations.[18]

Thus, the 'international dimension' of war crimes arises from the armed conflict, and the 'international dimension' of crimes against humanity arises from the attack on a civilian population. Cumulatively, the two bodies of law, working together, penalize atrocities committed during armed conflict or committed on a widespread or systematic basis.

Isolated crimes occurring in the absence of armed conflict continue to be governed by national criminal law. War crimes law is sometimes useful to interpret the law of crimes against humanity, so that the two bodies of law function coherently.[19]

Genocide was initially regarded as a particularly odious form of crime against humanity,[20] in that it was a crime against humanity committed with the intent to destroy, in whole or in part, a national, ethnical, racial or religious group as such. Over time, however, the

---

[15] See Art. 7 of the ICC Statute.
[16] See the Crimes against Humanity initiative, discussed in Leila Nadya Sadat (ed.), *Forging a Convention on Crimes against Humanity* (Cambridge, 2011); and, earlier, see M. Cherif Bassiouni, 'Crimes against Humanity: The Need for a Specialized Convention' (1994) 31 *Columbia Journal of Transnational Law* 457. In 2013, the ILC decided to put the issue on its agenda.
[17] See Chapter 12.   [18] See section 11.2.4.
[19] Of course, care must be taken when extending humanitarian law concepts outside the context of armed conflicts. See section 11.2.4; and see Payam Akhavan, 'Reconciling Crimes against Humanity with the Laws of War' (2008) 6 *Journal of International Criminal Justice* 21.
[20] War Crimes Commission, *History*, 196–7.

definitions of the two crimes have evolved and pose differing requirements. Therefore, it is no longer useful to describe genocide as a subset of crimes against humanity. Nonetheless, almost any conceivable example of genocide would also satisfy the requirements of crimes against humanity.[21]

11.2   Common elements (the contextual threshold)

As already noted, the contemporary definition of a crime against humanity entails the commission of a listed inhumane act, in a certain context: the listed act must be committed as part of a 'widespread or systematic attack directed against a civilian population'.

11.2.1   *Aspects not required*

No nexus to armed conflict

The Nuremberg and Tokyo Charters both required a connection to war crimes or to aggression, in effect requiring some nexus to armed conflict.[22] On the other hand, Control Council Law No. 10 did not include such a requirement. Subsequent case law of military tribunals split over whether such a nexus must be read into the definition, or was not required. For example, the *Flick* and *Weizsäcker* cases imported the requirement from the Nuremberg Charter, whereas the *Ohlendorf* and *Altstötter* decisions concluded that it was unnecessary.[23]

Subsequent international conventions[24] indicated that a nexus to armed conflict was not required. However, the ICTY Statute, adopted in 1993 by the Security Council, restricted crimes against humanity to those 'committed in armed conflict, whether international or internal in character' (Article 5). The Security Council promptly reversed this position in 1994, when it adopted the ICTR Statute without such a requirement (Article 3). Finally, after extensive debates at the 1998 Rome Conference, agreement was reached on a definition of crimes against humanity rejecting any such requirement (Article 7).[25]

Today, it seems well settled that a nexus to armed conflict is not required. The majority of instruments and precedents oppose such a requirement. The limitation in the Nuremberg Charter is generally seen as a jurisdictional limitation only,[26] and the ICTY Statute definition appears to be the anomaly. Indeed, the jurisprudence of the ICTY itself concludes that the requirement is a deviation from customary law.[27] This view is also supported by national

---

[21] See section 10.1.3.   [22] See e.g. Bassiouni, *Crimes against Humanity*, 136–46.

[23] *United States* v. *Ohlendorf et al.*, 4 TWC 411; *United States* v. *Altstötter et al.* (the 'Justice Trial'), VI LRTWC I; *United States* v. *Flick*, IX LRTWC 1; *United States* v. *Weizsäcker* (the 'Ministries Trial'), 14 TWC 1.

[24] Including the Genocide Convention, the Convention on the Non-Applicability of Statutory Limitations to War Crimes and Crimes against Humanity 1968, the Apartheid Convention 1973 and the Inter-American Convention on Enforced Disappearance 1994.

[25] Darryl Robinson, 'Defining Crimes against Humanity at the Rome Conference' (1999) 93 *American Journal of International Law* 43.

[26] War Crimes Commission, *History*, 192–3; see also Clark, 'Crimes', 196; Diane Orentlicher, 'Settling Accounts: The Duty to Prosecute Human Rights Violations of a Prior Regime' (1991) 100 *Yale Law Journal* 2537, 2588–90.

[27] *Tadić*, ICTY T. Ch. II, 7 May 1997, para. 627; *Tadić*, ICTY A. Ch., 15 July 1999, paras. 282–8.

case law, international bodies of experts, and the writings of commentators.[28] No requirement of armed conflict has appeared in subsequent definitions of crimes against humanity.

No requirement of discriminatory animus

Article 3 of the ICTR Statute requires that crimes against humanity be committed on 'national, ethnic, racial or religious grounds'.[29] Such a requirement was supported by a few cases in France, but did not appear in most precedents.[30]

Although an early ICTY trial decision reluctantly adopted the 'discriminatory grounds' requirement for the purposes of consistency, it explicitly noted that it was not supported in previous authorities, and the ICTY Appeals Chamber subsequently ruled that discrimination is not a requirement.[31] The ICC Statute, adopted in 1998, rejected a discrimination requirement. It appears reasonably well settled today that discriminatory animus is not a requirement, and it has not been included in subsequent instruments (Sierra Leone, Iraq). The ICTR Appeals Chamber has held that the restriction in the ICTR Statute relates only to the Tribunal, and also that the requirement relates to the attack as a whole; thus discriminatory intent of the perpetrator is not required.[32]

Thus, it would appear that discriminatory grounds are not required in customary law, except for the specific crime of persecution, discussed in section 11.3.9.

11.2.2   *'Widespread or systematic'*

The concept of 'widespread or systematic attack directed against any civilian population' emerged in the 1990s as the accepted formulation for the contextual threshold. The emergence of a generally accepted formulation, elaborating upon the laconic Nuremberg definition, has contributed to clarity and consistency in this area of law. Nonetheless, some aspects of the definition of these terms remain to be resolved.

The 'widespread or systematic' test is disjunctive;[33] a prosecutor need only satisfy one or the other threshold. However, in addition to 'widespread or systematic', there must also be an 'attack'. As will be discussed below, some authorities indicate that an 'attack directed against a civilian population' necessarily entails at least some modest degree of scale and

---

[28] *Eichmann* (1968) 36 ILR 5, 49 (DC); *Barbie* (1990) 78 ILR 124, 136 (Cour de Cassation); ILC Report 1996, UN Doc. A/51/10 (1996) p. 96; Orentlicher, 'Settling Accounts', 2588–90; Theodor Meron, 'International Criminalization of Internal Atrocities' (1995) 89 *American Journal of International Law* 554; Beth van Schack, 'The Definition of Crimes against Humanity: Resolving the Incoherence' (1999) 37 *Columbia Journal of Transnational Law* 787.

[29] For discussion, see David Scheffer, *All the Missing Souls: A Personal History of the War Crimes Tribunals* (Princeton, NJ, 2012).

[30] Some French cases, including *Barbie*, 78 ILR 124 (Cour de Cassation) and *Touvier*, 100 ILR 338 (Cour d'Appel), suggested that a policy of discrimination is required.

[31] *Tadić*, ICTY T. Ch. II, 7 May 1997, para. 652; *Tadić*, ICTY A. Ch., 15 July 1999, paras. 282–305.

[32] *Akayesu*, ICTR A. Ch., 1 June 2001, paras. 461–9.

[33] The French version of the ICTR Statute referred to the requirements conjunctively (*généralisée et systématique*), but this was held to be a simple error: *Akayesu*, ICTR T. Ch. I, 2 September 1998, para. 579.

organization.[34] This would mean that, while the rigorous thresholds of 'widespread' or 'systematic' are disjunctive, the 'attack' requires at least some minimal aspect of each.

The term 'widespread' has been defined in various ways, and generally connotes the 'large-scale nature of the attack and the number of victims'.[35] No specific numerical limit has been set; the issue must be decided on the facts. While 'widespread' typically refers to the cumulative effect of numerous inhumane acts, it could also be satisfied by a singular act of exceptional magnitude.[36]

The term 'systematic' has also been defined in various ways. Early decisions set high thresholds: in *Akayesu*, it was defined as (1) thoroughly organized, (2) following a regular pattern, (3) on the basis of a common policy and (4) involving substantial public or private resources.[37] It is understandable to pose a significant threshold, especially given that non-widespread crimes should not lightly be labelled as a crime against humanity, but this definition may set the bar too high.[38] In *Blaškić*, it was defined by reference to four factors: (1) a plan or objective, (2) large-scale or continuous commission of linked crimes, (3) significant resources, and (4) implication of high-level authorities.[39] Other cases refer more simply to 'pattern or methodical plan', 'organised nature of the acts' or 'organised pattern of conduct'.[40] The most recent cases seem to be settling on 'the organised nature of the acts of violence and the improbability of their random occurrence'.[41] Consistent with the ordinary meaning of the term, it may be that the hallmark of 'systematic' is the high degree of organization, and that features such as patterns, continuous commission, use of resources, planning, and political objectives are important factors.

11.2.3 'Attack'

The term 'attack' is not used in the same sense as in the law of war crimes. An 'attack' need not involve the use of armed force, and can encompass mistreatment of the civilian population.[42] It refers to the broader course of conduct, involving prohibited acts, of which the acts of the accused form part.[43]

---

[34] See Art. 7(2)(a) of the ICC Statute; and see *Haradinaj et al.*, ICTY T. Ch. I, 3 April 2008, para. 122.

[35] *Tadić*, ICTY T. Ch. II, 7 May 1997, para. 206; *Kunarac et al.*, ICTY T. Ch. II, 22 February 2001, para. 428; *Nahimana*, ICTR A. Ch., 28 November 2007, para. 920; *Situation in Darfur (Al Bashir* arrest warrant case), ICC PTC I, 4 March 2009, para. 81; *Taylor*, SCSL T. Ch., 18 May 2012, para. 511.

[36] *Kordić and Čerkez*, ICTY T. Ch., 26 February 2001, para. 176; *Blaškić*, ICTY T. Ch. I, 3 March 2000, para. 206; ILC Draft Code, pp. 94–5.

[37] *Akayesu*, ICTR T. Ch. I, 2 September 1998, para. 580.

[38] See also Kai Ambos and Steffen Wirth, 'The Current Law of Crimes against Humanity: An Analysis of UNTAET Regulation 15/2000' (2002) 13 *Criminal Law Forum* 1, 18–20.

[39] *Blaškić*, ICTY T. Ch., 3 March 2000, para. 203.

[40] *Tadić*, ICTY T. Ch. II, 7 May 1997, para. 648; *Kunarac et al.*, ICTY T. Ch. II, 22 February 2001, para. 429; *Ntakirutimana et al.*, ICTR T. Ch. I, 21 February 2003, para. 804.

[41] See e.g. *Nahimana et al.*, ICTR A. Ch., 28 November 2007, para. 920; *Al Bashir* arrest warrant case, ICC PTC I, 4 April 2009, para. 81; *Taylor*, SCSL T. Ch. II, 18 May 2012, para. 511. As will be suggested below, improbability of random occurrence arguably should not only be an aspect of the disjunctive 'systematic' test, it should already be inherent in the concept of an 'attack'; otherwise widespread but random crime would constitute a crime against humanity.

[42] ICC Elements of Crimes, Crimes against Humanity Introduction, para. 3; *Kunarac et al.*, ICTY A. Ch., 12 June 2002, para. 86; *Akayesu*, ICTR T. Ch. I, 2 September 1998, para. 581; *Taylor*, SCSL T. Ch., 18 May 2012, para. 506.

[43] Art. 7(2)(a) of the ICC Statute; *Tadić*, ICTY T. Ch. II, 7 May 1997, para. 644; *Akayesu*, ICTR T. Ch. I, 2 September 1998, para. 205.

The ICC Statute defines 'attack' in Article 7(2)(a): 'a course of conduct involving the multiple commission of acts referred to in paragraph 1 against any civilian population, pursuant to or in furtherance of a State or organisational policy to commit such attack'. This definition requires that there must be at least some minimal level of scale ('multiple' acts) and some minimal level of collectivity (the 'policy' element). In addition, there must be a high level of scale ('widespread') or a high level of collective coordination ('systematic'). The definition screens out truly isolated crimes ('multiple') and truly unconnected crimes ('policy').

The requirement of 'multiple' crimes has not been particularly controversial. Tribunal jurisprudence also indicates there must at least be multiple acts or multiple victims in order to warrant the label 'attack directed against a civilian population'.[44] These acts may be all of the same type or of different types, for example murder, rape and deportation.[45] A single event (planting a bomb) can constitute a 'multiple' commission of prohibited acts (for example, murders).[46] Recall also that the multiple crimes requirement applies to the attack, not the accused; it suffices that the accused commit a single act within the context of an attack. The requirement of 'multiple acts' is not synonymous with 'widespread'. Both terms measure scale, but 'multiple' is a low threshold and 'widespread' is a high threshold.

The controversy concerning the policy element

The controversial aspect is the 'policy' element. The deeper question underlying this issue is what links different acts together so that they constitute an 'attack'. Crime, even on a 'widespread' basis – for example, a crime wave, or anarchy following a natural disaster – does not by itself constitute a crime against humanity. The random acts of individuals are not sufficient; some thread of connection between acts is needed so that they can accurately be described collectively as an *attack directed* against a civilian population. Some authorities seek to make this proposition explicit by indicating that there must be an underlying governmental or organizational policy that directs, instigates or encourages the crimes. Other authorities reject such a requirement. It is therefore controversial whether the policy element is a necessary component of crimes against humanity.

The divide in the authorities

National jurisprudence on crimes against humanity following the Second World War frequently indicated that governmental policy is a requirement.[47] In the 1990s, the very same authorities that established the 'widespread or systematic' test also coupled this with a

---

[44] Art. 7(2)(a) of the ICC Statute; *Kunarac et al.*, ICTY T. Ch. II, 22 February 2001, para. 415; *Krnojelac*, ICTY T. Ch. II, 15 March 2002, para. 54.

[45] *Kayishema*, ICTR T. Ch. II, 21 May 1999, para. 122.

[46] *Kordić*, ICTY T. Ch., 26 February 2001, para. 176; *Blaškić*, ICTY T. Ch. I, 3 March 2000, para. 206; ILC Draft Code, pp. 94–5.

[47] Examples include: the Justice Trial, VI LRTWC I; *Brandt* (the 'Doctors Trial'), IV LRTWC 91 (US Military Tribunal); *Barbie*, 78 ILR 124 (Court of Cassation), 6 December 1983 (France); *Menten*, 75 ILR 362–3 (Netherlands); *R v. Finta* [1994] 1 SCR 701, 814 (Canada); *Polyukhovic* (1991) 172 CLR 501 (Australia); *Pinochet (No. 3)* [1999] 2 All ER 97 (United Kingdom) (Lord Hope and Lord Millett; but see *contra* Lord Browne-Wilkinson).

requirement of policy or of direction, instigation or encouragement by a State or organization.[48] Early Tribunal cases tended to follow this approach.[49]

At the Rome Conference, there was considerable opposition to an unqualified disjunctive 'widespread or systematic' test, on the grounds that it would incorrectly include widespread but unconnected crimes, such as a crime wave. It was argued in response that the customary law concept of an 'attack' excluded random crimes. Agreement was reached on the disjunctive 'widespread or systematic' test, provided that the definition of 'attack' included this clarification. Article 7(2)(a) therefore defines 'attack' and includes a policy element, which was based on the *Tadić* decision and related authorities. 'Policy' was understood as a low threshold which could be inferred from the manner in which the acts occur.[50] The definition followed recent authorities indicating that the policy need not be that of a government, but could also be that of an organization.

Strong concerns were already growing about the policy element, both in Tribunal jurisprudence and in the ICC negotiations. The major concerns were that it imposed a novel burden, that it would be difficult to prove, and that it contradicted the disjunctive test.[51] Tribunal cases began to split, with some supporting, then some declining to take a position, and then some expressing doubt.[52] Finally, in *Kunarac*, the ICTY Appeals Chamber held, rather categorically, that 'nothing in the Statute or in customary international law ... required proof of the existence of a plan or policy to commit these crimes'.[53] Whereas decisions on other issues of customary law have tended to involve an extensive review of precedents, the Appeals Chamber resolved this major controversy with reasoning appearing only in a single footnote, and declining to address (or acknowledge) most of the contrary authorities.[54]

Thus, the main indicators of customary law are now divided. On the one hand, the ICC Statute indicates that policy is required. The Statute was adopted by a great number of

---

[48] Commission of Experts (the Former Yugoslavia), *Final Report of the Commission of Experts Established Pursuant to Security Council Resolution 780(1992)*, UN Doc. S/1994/674, 23; Commission of Experts (Rwanda), *Final Report of the Commission of Experts Established Pursuant to Security Council Resolution 935(1994)*, UN Doc. G/SO 214, para. 135; ILC, Report on the Work of its Forty-Eighth Session (ILC draft Code), UN Doc. A/51/10, 93 and 95–6; and see Final Report on Systematic Rape, Sexual Slavery and Slavery-Like Practices during Armed Conflict, UN Doc. E/CN.4/Sub.2/1992/13 (1998).

[49] *Tadić*, ICTY T. Ch. II, 7 May 1997, para. 644; *Bagilishema*, ICTR T. Ch. I, 7 June 2001, para. 78.

[50] *Tadić*, ICTY T. Ch. II, 7 May 1997, paras. 653–5; Robinson, 'Defining Crimes against Humanity', 50–1; Timothy H. L. McCormack, 'Crimes against Humanity' in Dominic McGoldrick, Peter Rowe and Eric Donnelly (eds.), *The Permanent International Criminal Court: Legal and Policy Issues* (Oxford, 2004) 186–9.

[51] See Margaret McAuliffe de Guzman, 'The Road from Rome: The Developing Law of Crimes against Humanity' (2000) 22 *Human Rights Quarterly* 335; Phyllis Hwang, 'Defining Crimes against Humanity in the Rome Statute of the International Criminal Court' (1998) 22 *Fordham International Law Journal* 457. The most thorough argument against the policy element appears in Guénaël Mettraux, 'The Definition of Crimes against Humanity and the Question of a "Policy" Element' in Sadat, *Forging a Convention*.

[52] *Kupreškić et al.*, ICTY T. Ch. II, 14 January 2000, paras. 554–5; *Kunarac et al.*, ICTY T. Ch. II, 22 February 2001, para. 432; *Kordić and Čerkez*, ICTY T. Ch., 26 February 2001, paras. 181–2; *Krnojelac*, ICTY T. Ch. II, 15 March 2002, para. 58.

[53] *Kunarac et al.*, ICTY A. Ch., 12 June 2002, para. 98. The reasoning of the Chamber is strikingly similar to that in Guénaël Mettraux, 'Crimes against Humanity in the Jurisprudence of the International Criminal Tribunals for the Former Yugoslavia and Rwanda' (2002) 43 *Harvard International Law Journal* 237, 270–82.

[54] For commentary critical of the Chamber's claims about past precedents, see Claus Kreß, 'On the Outer Limits of Crimes against Humanity: The Concept of Organization within the Policy Requirement: Some Reflections on the March 2010 ICC Kenya Decision' (2010) 23 *Leiden Journal of International Law* 855; William Schabas, 'State Policy as an Element of International Crimes' (2008) 98 *Journal of Criminal Law and Criminology* 953; M. Cherif Bassiouni, 'Revisiting the Architecture of Crimes against Humanity: Almost a Century in the Making, with Gaps and Ambiguities Remaining – The Need for a Specialized Convention' in Leila Nadya Sadat (ed.), *Forging a Crime against Humanity* (Cambridge, 2011) 43.

States purporting to codify existing customary law, and hence it is a strong indicator of customary law. A similar requirement appears in much national jurisprudence, and in legislation based on the ICC Statute definitions, which will also shape State practice. On the other hand, Tribunal jurisprudence, which also purports to reflect customary law, and which is also a strong indicator, rejects the policy element. Moreover, Article 10 of the ICC Statute indicates that its definitions 'shall not be interpreted as limiting or prejudicing in any way existing or developing rules of international law for purposes other than this Statute'.

Much of the controversy over the policy element may result from differing understandings of what the element *means*.[55] Some commentators reject the policy element, but agree that random criminality of individuals does not amount to an 'attack'.[56] To other commentators, that is precisely what the policy element means:[57] indeed, the necessary logical corollary of excluding acts of individuals on their own initiative is to require some instigation or encouragement by something *other than* individuals, namely, a State or organization. Some scholars argue that the collective character reflected in the policy element is the fundamental essence of crimes against humanity; they are 'politics gone cancerous'.[58]

Implications for jurisdictions rejecting a policy element

For those jurisdictions that have rejected the term 'policy', it is essential not to lose sight of the principle that unconnected random acts cannot constitute an 'attack'.[59] Tribunal jurisprudence often asserts that unconnected random acts are excluded, but does not seem to have any legal element that actually performs this function. (The requirement of 'widespread' crime does not suffice, because crimes in a region may be widespread and yet unconnected.) Recent Tribunal jurisprudence mentions the element of 'improbability of random occurrence', but only as part of the definition of 'systematic'.[60] However, the element of improbability of random occurrence must be inherent in all 'attacks'.[61] In the absence of some such clarification, a literal and mechanistic application of Tribunal definitions would encompass widespread but random crimes of individuals, which reflects either a failure to describe the crime accurately, or else a loss of the basic conceptual foundation for crimes against humanity.[62]

---

[55] See e.g. Mettraux, 'Crimes', 275, rejecting some authorities as precedent for a policy element because all they meant is to exclude isolated crimes. See also Hwang, 'Defining Crimes', 502–3, fearing that 'policy' might be misinterpreted as more stringent than 'systematic'.

[56] Mettraux, 'Crimes', 254, 273 and 275.

[57] See e.g. Yoram Dinstein, 'Crimes against Humanity after Tadić' (2000) 13 *Leiden Journal of International Law* 273, 389; Simon Chesterman, 'An Altogether Different Order: Defining the Elements of Crimes against Humanity' (2000) *Duke Journal of Comparative and International Law* 283, 316.

[58] See e.g. David Luban, 'A Theory of Crimes against Humanity' (2004) 29 *Yale Law Journal* 85, 90; see also Ambos and Wirth, 'The Current Law', 26–34; William Schabas, 'State Policy as an Element of International Crimes' (2008) 98 *Journal of Criminal Law and Criminology* 953.

[59] *Kunarac et al.*, ICTY T. Ch. II, 22 February 2001, para. 422.

[60] *Kunarac et al.*, ICTY T. Ch. II, 22 February 2001, para. 429; *Krnojelac*, ICTY T. Ch. II, 15 March 2002, para. 57.

[61] Ambos and Wirth, 'The Current Law', 30–1.

[62] See e.g. David Luban, 'A Theory of Crimes against Humanity' (2004) 29 *Yale Law Journal* 85; Ambos and Wirth, 'The Current Law', 30–1; Geoffrey Robertson, *Crimes against Humanity: The Struggle for Global Justice* (London, 1999) 311 and 314.

Although Tribunal jurisprudence overtly rejects a policy element, it may indirectly re-inject something similar with its requirements to examine whether an 'identifiable population' was 'targeted' or was a 'primary object', all of which imply some direction or coordination from some source.[63]

Implications for jurisdictions requiring a policy element

For those jurisdictions that apply a policy element, the element must be interpreted, in accordance with previous jurisprudence, as a modest threshold that excludes random action.[64] First, as noted in the jurisprudence, a 'policy' need not be formally adopted, nor expressly declared, nor even stated clearly and precisely.[65] Thus, it must be given an ordinary meaning such as 'a course of action adopted as advantageous or expedient',[66] rather than any connotation of a formal and official strategy. Second, the element may be satisfied by inference from the manner in which the acts occur;[67] it is sufficient to show the improbability of random occurrence. Third, it is not required to show *action* by a State or organization; case law indicates that the requirement is satisfied by 'explicit or implicit approval or endorsement' or that the conduct is 'clearly encouraged' or 'clearly fits within' a general policy.[68] Thus, inaction designed to encourage the crimes would also suffice.[69]

Significant concerns have been raised about early Pre-Trial Chamber decisions applying an exceptionally stringent conception of the policy element.[70] For example, some decisions have defined the policy element in a manner tantamount to 'systematic', requiring that the attack be 'thoroughly organised'.[71] Such an interpretation neglects past authorities that the element can be satisfied by active or passive encouragement.[72] It also creates a contradiction within Article 7, by requiring 'systematic' in all cases; the coherence of the provision requires that the policy element be a more modest requirement than 'systematic'. In another example, a majority of the ICC Pre-Trial Chamber examining the charges against Laurent Gbagbo, President of Côte d'Ivoire, requested proof of the formal adoption of the policy,

---

[63] See e.g. *Kunarac et al.*, ICTY A. Ch., 12 June 2002, paras. 90–2; *Stakić*, ICTY T. Ch., 31 July 2003, para. 627; *Stakić*, ICTY A. Ch., 22 March 2006, para. 247. In *Haradinaj et al.*, ICTY T. Ch. I, 3 April 2008, a Chamber found that a 'relatively small number of incidents', lacking scale or frequency, and without significant evidence of structure, organization or targeting, did not amount to an attack directed against a civilian population.

[64] McAuliffe de Guzman, 'Road from Rome', 374.

[65] *Tadić*, ICTY T. Ch. II, 7 May 1997, para. 653; *Blaškić*, ICTY T. Ch. I, 3 March 2000, paras. 204–5; *Bemba Gombo*, ICC PTC II, 15 June 2009, para. 81; *Katanga and Ngudjolo Chui*, ICC PTC I, 30 September 2008, para. 396 (albeit also requiring, contradictorily, that an attack must be 'thoroughly organised').

[66] *Oxford English Dictionary*, 2nd edn (Oxford, 1989) Vol. XII, 27, provides this as the 'chief living sense'.

[67] *Tadić*, ICTY T. Ch. II, 7 May 1997, para. 653; *Blaškić*, ICTY T. Ch. I, 3 March 2000, para. 204; *Bemba Gombo*, ICC PTC II, 15 June 2009, para. 81.

[68] *Kupreškić*, ICTY T. Ch. II, 14 January 2000, paras. 554–5.

[69] Commission of Experts (the Former Yugoslavia), *Final Report*, 23. The ICC Elements of Crimes, footnote 6, reach this result but in a particularly tortured manner, twice emphasizing a need for action, before acknowledging, in a restrictive manner, the possibility of passive encouragement. The ICC Elements of Crimes also add that inaction alone is not enough to infer a policy; this cannot be interpreted as repudiating the preceding sentence. Rather, it acknowledges that there may be other reasons for inaction (lack of knowledge of crimes, lack of ability), and hence policy should not be inferred without considering alternative explanations.

[70] Leila Sadat, 'Crimes against Humanity in the Modern Age' (2013) 107 *American Journal of International Law* 334.

[71] *Katanga and Ngudjolo Chui*, ICC PTC I, 30 September 2008, para. 396; *Gbagbo*, ICC PTC III, 30 November 2009, para. 37.

[72] *Kupreškić*, ICTY T. Ch. II, 14 January 2000, paras. 554–5; ICC Elements of Crimes, footnote 6; Ambos and Wirth, 'Current Law', 31–4.

including dates of relevant meetings.[73] Past jurisprudence has consistently held that formal adoption is not required and that a policy may be inferred from events.

State or organization

The newest and most interesting controversy with respect to the policy element (for those jurisdictions that recognize it) concerns the interpretation of 'State or organisation'. This seemingly technical issue brings to the fore the essence of the crime. The issue arose in the ICC examination of the Kenya situation. The situation involved over a thousand killings and hundreds of rapes, orchestrated by political parties. The Pre-Trial Chamber split as to whether political parties constitute an 'organization'.[74] The majority took a broad approach, adopting a factor-based test that would include any organization capable of directing mass crimes. Judge Kaul, in dissent, argued that an organization must be 'State-like'. There are merits in both views. Views differ as to whether crimes against humanity should include crimes by terrorist organizations, criminal organizations, slavery rings and so on. How one interprets 'organization' reflects one's understanding of the dividing line between crimes against humanity and 'ordinary' crimes. The narrower view, requiring States or State-like organizations, may see crimes against humanity as involving a betrayal of a responsibility to protect.[75] The broader view sees crimes against humanity as any collective effort to inflict massive crimes on a civilian population.[76] The broader view seems to be supported in other decisions of the ICC.[77] It is also compatible with the ordinary meaning of the term 'organization',[78] as well as the purpose of the policy element, which is to exclude random acts of individuals acting on their own initiative.[79]

11.2.4 *'Any civilian population'*

The word 'any' highlights the central innovation and *raison d'être* of crimes against humanity. The law of crimes against humanity not only protects enemy nationals, it also covers, for example, crimes by a State against its own subjects.[80] The nationality or affiliation of the victim is irrelevant.

The term 'civilian' connotes crimes directed against non-combatants rather than combatants, while the term 'population' indicates that 'a larger body of victims is visualised', and that 'single or isolated acts against individuals' fall outside the scope of the concept.[81] The

---

[73] *Gbagbo*, ICC PTC I, 3 June 2013, para. 44. See also the stringent approach applied in *Mbarushimana*, ICC PTC I, 16 December 2011, paras. 242–67, declining to find a policy despite documentary evidence, oral testimony and circumstantial evidence.
[74] *Situation in Kenya*, ICC PTC II, 31 March 2010.
[75] Claus Kreß, 'Outer Limits'; William Schabas, 'Prosecuting Dr Strangelove, Goldfinger, and the Joker at the International Criminal Court: Closing the Loopholes' (2010) 23 *Leiden Journal of International Law* 847.
[76] Sadat, 'Crimes against Humanity'; Charles Jalloh, 'What Makes a Crime against Humanity a Crime against Humanity?' (2013) 28 *American University International Law Review* 381.
[77] *Bemba Gombo*, ICC PTC II, 15 June 2009, para. 81; *Katanga and Ngudjolo Chui*, ICC PTC I, 30 September 2008, para. 396; *Situation in Côte d'Ivoire*, ICC PTC III, 3 October 2011.
[78] Gerhard Werle and Boris Burghardt, 'Do Crimes against Humanity Require the Participation of a State or a "State-Like" Organization?' (2012) 10 *Journal of International Criminal Justice* 1151.
[79] As suggested above in this section.   [80] War Crimes Commission, *History*, 193.   [81] *Ibid.*

reference to population implies 'crimes of a collective nature' but does not require that the entire population be targeted.[82]

Antonio Cassese has put forward a significant argument that, in customary international law, the crime is not restricted to 'civilian' populations, relying on Second World War cases that identified crimes against military personnel as crimes against humanity.[83] Those cases are important. However, the major precedents – including the seminal Nuremberg Charter as well as the ICTY, ICTR, ICC and SCSL Statutes and the great majority of case law – not only refer to 'civilian population' but regard it as a defining ('time-honoured')[84] feature of crimes against humanity. Moreover, current international law clearly *permits* widespread and systematic attacks directed against military targets, in accordance with humanitarian law, even if it involves killing and injury.

It is nonetheless possible that the law of crimes against humanity can address crimes against military personnel outside combat situations. The population need only be '*predominantly* civilian in nature'; the 'presence of certain non-civilians in their midst does not change the character of the population'.[85] Furthermore, it is not required that each individual victim is civilian.[86] These authorities allow prosecution of crimes against detained military personnel if they are part of a broader context.

What if an attack is directed *entirely* against former combatants, such as prisoners-of-war? We must examine the word 'civilian'. Several early decisions of Trial Chambers of the ad hoc Tribunals interpreted the term 'civilian' to include all those no longer taking part in hostilities at the time the crimes were committed. This includes former combatants who had been decommissioned, as well as combatants placed *hors de combat* (wounded or detained).[87]

Examining these cases, it is possible to form a hypothesis that the 'civilian' reference serves a functional purpose, which is simply to *exclude military actions against legitimate military objectives in accordance with international humanitarian law*. This would provide a coherent underlying rationale for the requirement. Given that the laws of war are a special regime in which killing, wounding and destruction can be allowed, attacks on military targets are more appropriately assessed under that law.[88] This theory is consistent with Tribunal jurisprudence which requires that the civilian population be the 'primary object' of the attack,[89] and which considers compliance with the laws of war as an indicator of whether there was an attack against a civilian population.[90] Patterns of

---

[82] *Tadić*, ICTY T. Ch. II, 7 May 1997, para. 644; *Kunarac et al.*, ICTY T. Ch. II, 22 February 2001, para. 425.

[83] A. Cassese, 'Crimes against Humanity' in Cassese, *Commentary*, 375.

[84] Dinstein, 'Crimes against Humanity after Tadić' (2000) 13 *Leiden Journal of International Law* 273, 381–2.

[85] *Tadić*, ICTY T. Ch. II, 7 May 1997, para. 638; see also *Kordić and Čerkez*, ICTY T. Ch. III, 26 February 2001, para. 180.

[86] See e.g. *Martić*, ICTY A. Ch., para. 307; *Mrskić*, ICTY A. Ch., 5 May 2009, paras. 30–3.

[87] *Akayesu*, ICTR T. Ch., 2 September 1998, para. 582; *Tadić*, ICTY T. Ch. II, 7 May 1997, para. 643; *Kordić and Čerkez*, ICTY T. Ch. III, 26 February 2001, para. 180; *Blaškić*, ICTY T. Ch., 3 March 2000, para. 214. See also Ambos and Wirth, 'The Current Law', 22–6. Note that a current member of an armed force or organization remains a combatant even in moments when he or she is not armed or in combat, and thus may be lawfully attacked by an enemy party to the conflict. See e.g. *Blaškić*, ICTY A. Ch., 29 July 2004, para. 114.

[88] See e.g. Ambos and Wirth, 'The Current Law', 22–6; and, on a related theme, see Akhavan, 'Reconciling'.

[89] *Kunarac et al.*, ICTY A. Ch., 12 June 2002, para. 91.

[90] *Ibid.* See also *Fofana and Kondewa*, SCSL A. Ch., 28 May 2008, paras. 300–8; Mettraux, 'Crimes', 245–50.

indiscriminate or clearly excessive attacks could indicate that the attacks were in reality directed against a civilian population.[91]

Unfortunately, more recent ICTY cases complicate this picture. In *Martić*, the Appeals Chamber concluded that 'civilian' has the same meaning as in Article 50 of Additional Protocol I, and hence does not include persons *hors de combat* (such as prisoners-of-war).[92] The Chamber affirmed that persons *hors de combat* could be victims of crimes against humanity, but only where the broader attack was directed at civilians in the narrower sense.[93] The effect of this interpretation is that large-scale extermination or torture directed entirely against prisoners-of-war would not constitute crimes against humanity.[94]

There are reasons to doubt that the definition from Additional Protocol I, an international humanitarian law instrument, should be transplanted into the law of crimes against humanity. First, 'attack against a civilian population' is already given a different meaning in crimes against humanity than it receives in war crimes, since it does not require actual force but can refer to a series of non-violent acts amounting to inhumane acts.[95] Second, the definition of 'civilian' in Additional Protocol I arises in a detailed legislative regime that already grants protection to prisoners-of-war. The term 'civilian' in crimes against humanity arose decades earlier, and likely harked to a simpler bifurcation between those taking part in hostilities and those who are not. Third, the Appeals Chamber relied on the principle of distinction,[96] but a deliberate targeting of prisoners-of-war is equally prohibited under the principle of distinction. It may be hoped that other jurisdictions such as the ICC will critically examine the Tribunal's reasoning before following the same path.[97]

11.2.5 *The link between the accused and the attack*

The rigorous requirements relating to the attack must be distinguished from the requirements relating to the accused's conduct. With respect to the individual accused, all that is required is that the accused committed a prohibited act, that the act objectively falls within the broader attack, and that the accused was aware of this broader context.[98]

Only the attack, not the acts of the individual accused, needs to be widespread or systematic.[99] A single act by the accused may constitute a crime against humanity if it

---

[91] Chile Eboe-Osuji, 'Crimes against Humanity: Directing Attacks against a Civilian Population' (2008) 2 *African Journal of Legal Studies* 118.

[92] *Martić*, ICTY A. Ch., 8 October 2008, paras. 296–302.

[93] *Ibid.*, paras. 301–14. See also *Mrkšić, Radić and Šljvančanin*, ICTY A. Ch., 5 May 2009, paras. 29–33.

[94] See the discussion in the *Mrskić* trial judgment, which concerned attacks on the Vukovar hospital: *Mrkšić, Radić and Šljvančanin*, ICTY T. Ch. II, 27 September 2007, paras. 443–64.

[95] See e.g. *Nahimana*, ICTR A. Ch., 28 November 2007, para. 918.   [96] *Martić*, ICTY A. Ch., 8 October 2008, footnote 806.

[97] At the SCSL in the *Taylor* case, both the prosecution and the defence agreed that 'civilian' means 'non-combatants', yet the Trial Chamber opted to follow the narrower approach of the ICTY: *Taylor*, SCSL T. Ch., 18 May 2012, paras. 508–10.

[98] *Tadić*, ICTY A. Ch., 15 July 1999, para. 271. To determine if an act is 'part of' an attack, one may consider its characteristics, aims, nature or consequence: *Semanza*, ICTR T. Ch., 15 May 2003, para. 326. A crime may be committed several months after, or several kilometres away from, the main attack, and still, if sufficiently connected, be part of the attack: *Krnojelac*, ICTY T. Ch. II, 15 March 2002, para. 127.

[99] *Kunarac*, ICTY A. Ch., 12 June 2002, para. 96; *Blaškić*, ICTY A. Ch., 29 July 2004, para. 101.

forms part of the attack.[100] The act of the accused may also in itself *constitute* the attack, if it is of great magnitude, for example, the use of a biological weapon against a civilian population.[101] The accused need not be an architect of the attack, need not be involved in the formation of any policy, and need not be affiliated with any State or organization nor even share in the ideological goals of the attack, so long as there is a nexus between the conduct of the defendant and the attack.[102]

Furthermore, the acts of the accused need not be of the same type as other acts committed during the attack. For example, if a group launches a killing campaign, and a person commits sexual violence in the execution of that campaign, the person is guilty of the crime against humanity of sexual violence. It is irrelevant whether the State or organization encouraged sexual violence, since the necessary contextual element is already satisfied because of the attack based on killing.[103]

11.2.6 *Awareness of context*

In addition to the requisite mental elements for the particular offences, the accused must also be aware of the 'broader context in which his actions occur', namely, the attack directed against a civilian population.[104] It is the context of a widespread or systematic attack against a civilian population that makes an act a crime against humanity, and hence knowledge of this context is necessary in order to make one culpable for a crime against humanity as opposed to an ordinary crime or a war crime.[105]

Tribunal cases indicate that awareness, wilful blindness, or knowingly taking the risk that one's act is part of an attack, will suffice.[106] The ICC approach is yet to be determined; the Court might apply the mental element specified in Article 30, or it could conclude that the term 'with knowledge of the attack' refers to the more inclusive approach (risk) in previous authorities.[107] The ICC Elements of Crimes suggest that the mental element required for 'contextual elements' is modest.[108] It is not required that the perpetrator had detailed knowledge of the attack or its characteristics or of the policy.[109] In most conceivable circumstances, the existence of a widespread or systematic attack would be notorious and

---

[100] *Kunarac*, ICTY A. Ch., 12 June 2002, para. 96; *Blaškić*, ICTY A. Ch., 29 July 2004, para. 101.
[101] *Blaškić*, ICTY T. Ch. I, 3 March 2000, para. 206.   [102] See the denunciation cases at section 11.2.6.
[103] Art. 7(2)(a) of the ICC Statute.
[104] *Tadić*, ICTY A. Ch., 15 July 1999, para. 248; *Kupreškić et al.*, ICTY T. Ch. II, 14 January 2000, para. 134.
[105] *Tadić*, ICTY T. Ch. II, 7 May 1997, para. 656; *Kupreškić et al.*, ICTY T. Ch. II, 14 January 2000, para. 138; *Semanza*, ICTR T. Ch., 15 May 2003, para. 332; and see also *R v. Finta* [1994] 1 SCR 701, 819: '[T]he mental element of a crime against humanity must involve an awareness of the facts or circumstances which would bring the acts within the definition of a crime against humanity.'
[106] *Tadić*, ICTY T. Ch. II, 7 May 1997, para. 657; *Kunarac et al.*, ICTY A. Ch., 12 June 2002, para. 102; *Blaškić*, ICTY T. Ch. I, 3 March 2000, para. 251; *Krnojelac*, ICTY T. Ch. II, 15 March 2002, para. 59; see also *R v. Finta* [1994] 1 SCR 701, 819.
[107] Ambos and Wirth, 'The Current Law', 36–42.
[108] See e.g. Maria Kelt and Herman von Hebel, 'General Principles of Criminal Law and the Elements of Crimes' in Lee, *Elements and Rules*, 34–5.
[109] ICC Elements of Crimes, Crimes against Humanity Introduction, para. 2, states that it is not required that the perpetrator 'had knowledge of all characteristics of the attack or the precise details of the plan or policy of the State or organisation'; see also *Blaškić*, ICTY T. Ch. I, 3 March 2000, para. 251; *Kunarac et al.*, ICTY A. Ch., 12 June 2002, para. 102; *Taylor*, SCSL T. Ch. II, 18 May 2012, paras. 513 and 515; *Bemba Gombo*, ICC PTC II, 15 June 2009, para. 88.

knowledge could not credibly be denied. Thus, knowledge may be inferred from the relevant facts and circumstances.[110]

The perpetrator need not share in the purpose or goals of the overall attack.[111] The mental requirement relates to knowledge of the context, not motive.[112] After the Second World War, several cases dealt with instances where individuals had denounced others to the Nazi regime, for personal opportunistic reasons. Such persons were held liable for crimes against humanity, because, even though they acted out of personal motives, their actions were objectively part of the persecutory system, and they acted with knowledge of the system and the likely consequences.[113]

11.3   Prohibited acts

11.3.1   The list of prohibited acts

The foregoing sections discussed the 'contextual elements': the surrounding backdrop of the widespread or systematic attack. We shall now look at the 'prohibited acts': the crimes carried out by perpetrators within that broader context.

The list of prohibited acts has gradually evolved over the decades. The first list, appearing in the Nuremberg Charter, comprised murder, extermination, enslavement, deportation, persecution and other inhumane acts. Shortly thereafter, Control Council Law No. 10 added rape, imprisonment and torture. The ICTY and ICTR Statutes follow the same expanded list.

In 1998, the ICC Statute added sexual slavery, enforced prostitution, forced pregnancy, other sexual violence, enforced disappearance and apartheid. At first glance, this may seem to be an expansion on existing customary law. However, the list of prohibited acts in the previous precedents ended with the residual clause 'or other inhumane acts'. If sexual slavery and these other acts are inhumane acts, which they surely are, then Article 7 simply codified explicitly what was already contained implicitly in the residual clause. The view that these acts were already inhumane acts is supported by the following considerations. First, each of these acts was already recognized as an inhumane act or crime against humanity in previous international instruments. Second, the agreed objective of States at the Rome Conference was to reflect, not to expand, existing customary law, and thus Article 7 reflects a simultaneous statement of *opinio iuris* by 120 States.[114] Third, their status has been supported in subsequent jurisprudence and instruments.[115]

For each of the following crimes, where no specific observations are made about the mental element, the normal mental element applies. Thus, the relevant conduct must be

[110] ICC Elements of Crimes, General Introduction, para. 3.   [111] *Kunarac et al.*, ICTY A. Ch. II, 22 February 2001, para. 103.
[112] *Tadić*, ICTY A. Ch., 15 July 1999, paras. 271–2, overturning a suggestion to the contrary by the Trial Chamber.
[113] See the cases discussed in *Tadić*, ICTY A. Ch., 15 July 1999, paras. 255–69.
[114] Richard Baxter, 'Multilateral Treaties as Evidence of Customary International Law' (1965) 41 *British Yearbook of International Law* 275.
[115] See e.g. *Kvočka et al.*, ICTY T. Ch. I, 2 November 2001, para. 208, and *Kupreškić et al.*, ICTY T. Ch. II, 14 January 2000, para. 566, recognizing enforced disappearance, sexual violence, forced prostitution and forced transfer of populations. Art. 2 of the SCSL Statute recognizes the sexual violence offences, and the Iraq Special Tribunal Statute includes each of the ICC Statute crimes other than apartheid and enforced sterilization.

committed intentionally and with knowledge of the relevant circumstances.[116] With respect to legal requirements (for example, 'unlawful') or other normative requirements (for example, 'inhumane', 'severe'), it is not required that the perpetrator personally considered the conduct inhumane or severe; it is sufficient that the perpetrator was aware of the underlying facts.[117]

11.3.2 Murder

The crime of murder is well known to all legal systems and is an archetypal form of crime against humanity. There is general conformity between Tribunal jurisprudence and the ICC Elements of Crimes that murder refers to unlawfully and intentionally causing the death of a human being.[118]

Tribunal jurisprudence, consistent with jurisprudence in many national systems, indicates that the mental element is satisfied if the perpetrator intends to kill, or intends to inflict grievous bodily harm likely to cause death and is reckless as to whether death ensues.[119] It is unclear whether the ICC will be able to adopt the same approach, in light of the different wording of Article 30 of the ICC Statute (mental element), although it may be possible to interpret the Statute consistently with previous authorities.[120]

The conduct element of murder (crime against humanity) and wilful killing (war crime) is the same; the difference is the contextual element. The distinction between murder and extermination is discussed in the next section.

11.3.3 Extermination

The major issue with the crime of extermination has been how to distinguish it from the crime against humanity of murder. Both involve killing, but 'extermination' connotes killing on a large scale. Is extermination distinct from murder on the basis that the perpetrator must carry out killing on a large scale, or is there another way to distinguish between the two? Rather than requiring that the accused personally carried out or directed large-scale killing, both Tribunal jurisprudence and the ICC Elements of Crimes indicate that extermination involves killing by the accused *within a context* of mass killing.[121]

Thus, the first and major difference between murder and extermination is that extermination requires a surrounding circumstance of mass killing.[122] The perpetrator need not carry out the mass killing personally; he only needs to know of the context of mass killing.

---

[116] See e.g. Art. 30 of the ICC Statute.

[117] See e.g. Art. 32(2) of the ICC Statute; ICC Elements of Crimes, General Introduction, para. 4.

[118] ICC Elements of Crimes, Art. 7(1) (a); *Akayesu*, ICTR T. Ch. I, 2 September 1998, para. 589; *Jelisić*, ICTY T. Ch. I, 14 December 1999, para. 35; *Kupreškić et al.*, ICTY T. Ch. II, 14 January 2000, paras. 560–1.

[119] See e.g. *Čelebići*, ICTY T. Ch. II, 16 November 1998, para. 439; *Akayesu*, ICTR T. Ch. I, 2 September 1998, para. 589; *Kordić and Čerkez*, ICTY T. Ch., 26 February 2001, para. 236.

[120] C. K. Hall, 'Article 7' in Triffterer, *Observers' Notes*, 188–9.

[121] ICC Elements of Crimes, Art. 7(1)(b); *Kayishema and Ruzindana*, ICTR T. Ch. II, 21 May 1999, para. 147.

[122] Whereas a crime against humanity of murder can occur on the basis of a single killing, committed in the context of a widespread or systematic attack based on other crimes.

A second difference is that extermination expressly includes indirect means of causing death. This distinction was recognized as early as the 1948 UN War Crimes Commission, which included 'implication in the policy of extermination without any direct connection with actual acts of murder'.[123] Tribunal jurisprudence also includes indirect means of causing death,[124] as does the ICC Statute. Article 7(2)(b) of the ICC Statute expressly includes 'inflicting conditions of life . . . calculated to bring about the destruction of part of a population', a phrase adapted from the Genocide Convention.[125]

It is not required that the accused personally be responsible for a substantial number of deaths. Some early cases held that 'responsibility for one or for a limited number of killings is insufficient'.[126] However, the ICTY Appeals Chamber concluded that a single killing is sufficient provided that the accused is aware of the necessary context of mass killing.[127] The ICC Elements of Crimes also follow the latter interpretation.[128]

There are also significant overlaps between extermination and the crime of genocide. Indeed, the concepts of killing or inflicting conditions of life calculated to bring about the destruction of part of a population are common to both extermination and genocide. The major difference between the two crimes is the requisite special intent for the crime of genocide (the intent to destroy a group as such). Moreover, genocide can only be committed where there is an intent to target one of four types of groups (national, ethnical, racial or religious).[129]

11.3.4 Enslavement

The accepted definition of enslavement is 'exercising the powers attaching to the right of ownership' over one or more persons. This definition is drawn from the 1926 Slavery Convention and the 1956 Supplementary Slavery Convention, and has been adopted in the ICC Statute (Article 7(2)(c)) and in Tribunal jurisprudence.[130]

Enslavement may take various forms. It includes the traditional concept of 'chattel slavery', that is to say, the treatment of persons as chattels, as in the slave trade. It also includes other practices, which are not limited to these 'transactional' or 'chattel slavery' examples, but which also involve exercising powers attaching to the right of ownership.[131]

First, with respect to 'chattel slavery', the Slavery Convention definition of 'slave trade' refers to the capture, acquisition, sale, exchange, transport or disposal of persons with intent to reduce them to slavery or to sell or exchange them.[132] The ICC Elements of Crimes also list, as examples, such transactions as 'purchasing, selling, lending or bartering'.

---

[123] War Crimes Commission, *History*, 194.
[124] *Rutaganda*, ICTR T. Ch., 6 December 1999, para. 81; *Kayishema and Ruzindana*, ICTR T. Ch. II, 21 May 1999, para. 146.
[125] Art. 2(c) of the Genocide Convention 1948.   [126] *Vasiljević*, ICTY T. Ch. I, 29 November 2002, para. 228.
[127] *Stakić*, ICTY A. Ch., 22 March 2006, paras. 260–1; see also *Kayishema and Ruzindana*, ICTR T. Ch. II, 21 May 1999, para. 147.
[128] ICC Elements of Crimes, Art. 7(1)(b), Element 1.   [129] See Chapter 10.
[130] 1926 Slavery Convention, Art. 1; 1956 Supplementary Slavery Convention; *Kunarac*, ICTY T. Ch. II, 22 February 2001, para. 539; *Krnojelac*, ICTY T. Ch. II, 15 March 2002, para. 353. See also Jean Allain (ed.), *The Legal Understanding of Slavery* (Oxford, 2012).
[131] Valerie Oosterveld, 'Sexual Slavery and the International Criminal Court: Advancing International Criminal Law' (2003) 25 *Michigan Journal of International Law* 605, 643.
[132] 1926 Slavery Convention, Art. 1(2).

Second, the ICC Statute explicitly mentions the example of trafficking in persons, in particular women and children (Article 7(2)(c)).[133]

Third, as noted in the ICC Elements of Crimes, enslavement also includes 'reducing a person to a servile status' as defined in the 1956 Supplementary Slavery Convention. This includes practices of debt bondage, serfdom, forced marriage and child exploitation, as defined in that Convention.[134]

Fourth, forced labour can also constitute enslavement.[135] In determining whether labour is 'forced' as prohibited under customary law, regard may be had to instruments such as the 1949 Geneva Convention III (Articles 49–57), the ICCPR (Article 8(3)(c)) and the 1930 Forced or Compulsory Labour Convention. In general, these instruments prohibit forced or compulsory labour, with various recognized exceptions, such as military and national service, normal civic obligations, hard labour as lawful punishment for crime, and certain forms of labour for prisoners-of-war.[136] In *Krnojelac*, the Appeals Chamber held that severely overcrowded conditions, deplorable sanitation, insufficient food, locked doors, frequent beatings, psychological abuse, and brutal living conditions rendered it impossible for detainees to consent to work and that their labour was indeed forced.[137]

Fifth, other activities may also amount to enslavement. The ICTY Appeals Chamber in the *Kunarac* decision indicated that relevant factors include 'control of someone's movement, control of physical environment, psychological control, measures taken to prevent or deter escape, force, threat of force or coercion, duration, assertion of exclusivity, subjection to cruel treatment and abuse, control of sexuality and forced labour'.[138] A specific form of enslavement, namely, sexual slavery, is discussed in section 11.3.8.

In *Kunarac*,[139] the victims were kept in an abandoned house for approximately six months, where they were raped and sexually assaulted whenever the soldiers returned to the house. The Chamber found that they were constantly and continuously raped, forced to do household chores and obey all demands. Although at some point they were given the keys to the house, they had nowhere to go or to hide, and hence:

no realistic option whatsoever to flee the house . . . or to escape their assailants. They were subjected to other mistreatments, such as Kunarac inviting a soldier into the house so that he could rape [the victim] for 100 Deutschmark if he so wished . . . The two women were treated as . . . personal property.

The two men responsible were found guilty of enslavement.

11.3.5 *Deportation or forcible transfer*

Deportation and forcible transfer of population are frequently seen examples of crimes against humanity, particularly in contexts of 'ethnic cleansing'. The terms refer to forced

---

[133] See also Tom Obokata, 'Trafficking of Human Beings as a Crime against Humanity' (2005) 54 *International and Comparative Law Quarterly* 445.

[134] ICC Elements of Crimes, footnote 11; 1956 Supplementary Slavery Convention, Art. 1.

[135] ICC Elements of Crimes, footnote 11.   [136] See e.g. Geneva Convention III 1949, Arts. 49–57; Art. 8(3) of the ICCPR.

[137] *Krnojeiac*, ICTY T. Ch. II, 15 March 2002, paras. 193–5.   [138] *Kunarac et al.*, ICTY A. Ch., 12 June 2002, para. 119.

[139] *Kunarac et al.*, ICTY T. Ch. II, 22 February 2001, paras. 732–42.

displacement of persons by expulsion or other coercive acts from the area in which they are lawfully present, without grounds permitted under international law.[140]

'Deportation' is generally regarded as referring to displacement across a border, whereas 'forcible transfer' is generally regarded as referring to internal displacement.[141] ICTY jurisprudence follows this distinction. In the *Stakić* case, the Appeals Chamber confirmed that 'deportation' must be across a border, usually a *de jure* border, or in some circumstances a *de facto* border, but in any event crossing of 'constantly changing frontlines' would not suffice.[142]

The deportation or transfer must be *forced* in order to be a crime against humanity.[143] This does not require actual physical force, but may also include the threat of force or coercion, psychological oppression, or other means of rendering displacement involuntary.[144] Thus, if a group flees of its own genuine volition, for example to escape a conflict zone, that would not be forced displacement.[145] On the other hand, if a group flees to escape deliberate violence and persecution, they would not be exercising a genuine choice.[146]

The forced displacement must also be *unlawful* under international law. Most or all States carry out legitimate acts of deportation on a frequent basis. Deportation of aliens not lawfully present in the territory is an established practice of States.[147] International humanitarian law, for example, allows transfers when the security of the population or imperative military reasons so demand. Such transfers must meet certain stringent conditions and humanitarian safeguards.[148]

11.3.6   Imprisonment

Although imprisonment did not appear in the Nuremberg or Tokyo Charters, it was listed in Control Council Law No. 10 and subsequent definitions. The term 'imprisonment' is broadly construed, capturing not only detention in prison-like conditions but other serious forms of confinement and detention. Out of an abundance of caution, the ICC Statute added 'or other severe deprivation of physical liberty' to ensure that a narrow definition was not applied, and that situations such as house arrest were included.[149] It remains to be determined precisely how restrictive or how long a confinement must be in order to constitute imprisonment or severe deprivation of physical liberty.

---

[140] Art. 7(2)(d) of the ICC Statute; *Stakić*, ICTY A. Ch., 22 March 2006, para. 278.   [141] ILC draft Code, 1996, p. 100.

[142] *Stakić*, ICTY A. Ch., 22 March 2006, para. 300. The Appeals Chamber therefore allowed the appeal from an anomalous Trial Chamber decision which had held that 'deportation' could be internal. The Appeals Chamber did not clarify the circumstances in which crossing a *de facto* border would suffice. For other cases, see *Kršktić*, ICTY T. Ch. I, 2 August 2001, para. 521; *Krnojelac et al.*, ICTY T. Ch. II, 15 March 2002, para. 474; *Kupreškić et al.*, ICTY T. Ch. II, 14 January 2000, para. 566.

[143] ICC Statute, Art. 7(2)(d); *Krstić*, ICTY T. Ch. I, 2 August 2001, para. 528; *Krnojelac*, ICTY T. Ch. II, 15 March 2002, para. 475.

[144] ICC Elements of Crimes, Art. 7(1)(d); *Stakić*, ICTY A. Ch., 22 March 2006, para. 281; *Krnojelac*, ICTY T. Ch. II, 15 March 2002, para. 475; *Kunarac et al.*, ICTY T. Ch. II, 22 February 2001, para. 129.

[145] Jean Pictet, *Commentary on Geneva Convention IV* (Geneva, 1960) 279; Akhavan, 'Reconciling', 34–5.

[146] *Krstić*, ICTY T. Ch. I, 2 August 2001, para. 530.

[147] The question whether an individual was 'lawfully' present would probably be assessed under international as well as national law. For example, a government could not circumvent the definition of this crime through an arbitrary legislative act declaring members of a group not lawfully present.

[148] Art. 49 of the Geneva Convention IV 1949; Art. 87 of Additional Protocol I.   [149] Hall, 'Article 7', 202.

The imprisonment must be arbitrary to constitute a crime against humanity. After all, there are many contexts in which persons may be lawfully detained, including following lawful arrest, conviction following trial, lawful deportation or extradition procedures, quarantine, and, during armed conflict, assigned residence, internment on security grounds and internment of prisoners-of-war.[150] Tribunal jurisprudence refers to imprisonment without due process of law.[151] Article 7(1)(e) of the ICC Statute refers to deprivation 'in violation of fundamental rules of international law'.

The requirement that the imprisonment be 'arbitrary' does not mean that a minor procedural defect would expose all involved to international prosecution; significant failings are required. For this reason, the ICC Elements of Crimes refer to the 'gravity of the conduct' being such as to violate fundamental rules of international law.[152] Tribunal jurisprudence states that deprivation will be arbitrary and unlawful 'if no legal basis can be called upon to justify the initial deprivation of liberty'.[153] Even where the initial detention was justified, imprisonment will become arbitrary if the legal basis ceases to apply and the person remains imprisoned.[154]

While caution must always be used when relying on human rights standards in a criminal law context,[155] the three categories suggested by the UN Working Group on Arbitrary Detention seem to capture the forms of this crime admirably: (1) absence of any legal basis for the deprivation of liberty; (2) deprivation of liberty resulting from exercise of specified rights and freedoms (that is to say, political prisoners); and (3) 'when the total or partial non-observance of the international human rights norms relating to the right to a fair trial . . . is of such gravity as to give the deprivation of imprisonment an arbitrary character'.[156]

The material elements of arbitrary imprisonment are comparable to the material elements for unlawful confinement (war crime); the difference between the two is the contextual element (armed conflict or widespread or systematic attack).

11.3.7 *Torture*

The crime of torture appeared in Control Council Law No. 10 and subsequent definitions of crimes against humanity. The prohibition against torture is well established in numerous conventions and instruments, including the Universal Declaration of Human Rights, the International Covenant on Civil and Political Rights, the European Convention on Human Rights, the American Convention on Human Rights, the African Charter on Human and Peoples' Rights, the Convention against Torture, the Inter-American Convention to Prevent and Punish Torture, and the Geneva Conventions and the Additional Protocols thereto. It is well recognized as a norm of customary law and amounts to *ius cogens*.[157]

---

[150] Arts. 5, 42 and 43 of the Geneva Convention IV 1949; Arts. 21–32 of the Geneva Convention III 1949.
[151] *Kordić and Čerkez*, ICTY T. Ch. III, 26 February 2001, para. 302; *Krnojelac*, ICTY T. Ch. II, 15 March 2002, para. 113.
[152] ICC Elements of Crimes, Art. 7(1)(e), Element 2.   [153] *Krnojelac*, ICTY T. Ch. II, 15 March 2002, para. 114.
[154] E.g. if the procedural safeguards of Art. 43 of the Geneva Convention IV 1949 for internment of civilians are disregarded: *Kordić and Čerkez*, ICTY T. Ch. III, 26 February 2001, para. 286; *Čelebići*, ICTY T. Ch. II, 16 November 1998, para. 579.
[155] See section 1.4.1.   [156] Report of the UN Working Group on Arbitrary Detention, UN Doc. E/CN.4/1998/44, para. 8.
[157] *Čelebići*, ICTY T. Ch. II, 16 November 1998, para. 454. For discussion of the crime of torture under the Convention against Torture, see section 14.3.

Much of the definition in the 1984 Convention against Torture (CAT) is also accepted as the core definition for torture as a crime against humanity or war crime: the intentional infliction of severe pain or suffering, whether physical or mental, upon a person.[158] There are, however, several open questions.

The first open question is that of official capacity. The CAT definition requires that the pain or suffering be 'inflicted by or at the instigation of or with the consent or acquiescence of a public official or other person acting in an official capacity'.[159] Early Tribunal cases adopted the requirement of official instigation or acquiescence.[160] However, in *Kunarac*, the Trial Chamber departed from this approach, noting structural differences between international criminal law and human rights law.[161] Human rights law focuses on the State because it regulates State treatment of human beings. International criminal law holds individuals accountable for crimes, and applies to everyone whether or not affiliated with a State. Similarly, the ICC Statute and the ICC Elements of Crimes do not require a linkage between the act of torture and a public official.[162] Thus, torture by rebel groups, paramilitaries and others is included.

The second is the 'purpose' element. The CAT definition requires a specific purpose, such as 'obtaining from him or a third person information or a confession, punishing him for an act he or a third person has committed or is suspected of having committed, or intimidating or coercing him or a third person, or for any reason based on discrimination of any kind'.[163] It is not yet settled whether the customary law crime against humanity of torture requires the act to be committed with a specific purpose.

Many authorities, including the CAT and related international instruments, as well as Tribunal jurisprudence, regard the purpose element as a defining feature of torture.[164] On this approach, the presence of prohibited purpose distinguishes torture from inhuman treatment.[165] The purpose need not be the sole or predominant purpose, but must be part of the motivation.[166] The list is illustrative and some cases suggest the addition of 'humiliation' as a prohibited purpose.[167]

In other authorities, such as the jurisprudence of the European Court of Human Rights, the difference between torture and lesser violations, such as inhuman treatment, is *severity*: the special stigma of torture requires infliction of 'very serious and cruel suffering'.[168] Article 7 of the ICC Statute followed this approach, and did not include a purpose element.

---

[158] Art. 1 of the CAT.   [159] *Ibid.*
[160] *Akayesu*, ICTR T. Ch. I, 2 September 1998, para. 594; *Furundžija*, ICTY T. Ch. II, 10 December 1998, para. 162.
[161] *Kunarac et al.*, ICTY T. Ch. II, 22 February 2001, paras. 387–91.
[162] Art. 7(2)(e) of the ICC Statute; but see Art. 7(2)(a) which appears to require some sort of linkage between a State or organization and the attack as a whole, albeit not the particular crimes of the accused.
[163] Art. 7(2)(e) of the ICC Statute.
[164] *Akayesu*, ICTR T. Ch. I, 2 September 1998, paras. 593–5; *Čelebići*, ICTY T. Ch. II, 16 November 1998, para. 459; *Furundžija*, ICTY T. Ch. II, 10 December 1998, para. 161; *Krnojelac*, ICTY T. Ch. II, 15 March 2002, para. 180.
[165] *Čelebići*, ICTY T. Ch. II, 16 November 1998, para. 469; *Krštić*, ICTY T. Ch. I, 2 August 2001, para. 516.
[166] *Kunarac et al.*, ICTY A. Ch., 12 June 2002, para. 155; *Kvočka et al.*, ICTY T. Ch. I, 2 November 2001, para. 153; *Čelebići*, ICTY T. Ch. II, 16 November 1998, para. 470.
[167] *Furundžija*, ICTY T. Ch. II, 10 December 1998, para. 162; but see *Krnojelac*, ICTY T. Ch. II, 15 March 2002, para. 186, doubting the customary law status of this extension.
[168] *Ireland* v. *United Kingdom*, ECtHR, 18 January 1978, para. 167; *Selmouni* v. *France*, ECtHR, 28 July 1999, para. 105; *Aydin* v. *Turkey*, ECtHR, 25 September 1997, para. 82.

Further adding to the uncertainty, the ICC Elements of Crimes adopted the 'purpose' requirement with respect to the war crime of torture but not with respect to the crime against humanity of torture.[169] Thus, it would seem that the divergent treatment in the Elements must either be given a principled explanation or else regarded as an anomaly.

Third, the ICC Statute, while dropping any requirements of purpose or link to an official, adds a requirement that the victim be in the 'custody or control' of the perpetrator. The requirement should not be onerous to prove since, as a practical matter, torture entails such custody or control. Various explanations have been offered for this addition, including establishing a link of power or control given the deletion of a link to a public official, or excluding the use of force against military objectives during armed conflict.[170]

It should also be noted that most definitions of torture, including the CAT and the ICC Statute, expressly exclude 'pain or suffering arising only from, inherent in or incidental to, lawful sanctions'. 'Lawful' in this context would appear to mean lawful in accordance with national law, provided, however, that the national law is not in violation of international law.[171]

Tribunal jurisprudence and regional human rights bodies have recognized that rape can constitute a form of torture.[172] Rape causes severe pain and suffering, both physical and psychological. In *Furundžija*, the accused was convicted of torture for acts during an interrogation, including sexual threats, rapes and forced nudity, inflicted on the victim for purposes of intimidation, humiliation and extracting confession.[173]

11.3.8 *Rape and other forms of sexual violence*

The crime of rape appeared in Control Council Law No. 10 and subsequent instruments, including the ICTY and ICTR Statutes. The 1996 draft Code of Crimes prepared by the International Law Commission proposed that the definition be updated by adding enforced prostitution and other forms of sexual abuse.[174] The ICC Statute took up the idea of modernizing the definition, by including 'rape, sexual slavery, forced pregnancy, enforced sterilisation, or any other form of sexual violence of comparable gravity' (Article 7(1) (g)).[175] The inclusion was seen not as an expansion but rather as an acknowledgment that these acts, which have persisted in history, including during the violence in

---

[169] Delegates followed Tribunal precedents with respect to war crimes, but they did not do so for crimes against humanity, out of fidelity to the decision taken at the Rome Conference not to require such an element for the crime against humanity of torture. Footnote 14 to the ICC Elements of Crimes therefore specifies that no purpose element is required.

[170] Darryl Robinson, 'Elements of Crimes against Humanity' in Lee, *Elements and Rules*, 90; Hall, 'Article 7', 253.

[171] Report of the ICC UN Special Rapporteur on Torture, UN Doc. E/CN.4/1988/17, para. 42.

[172] *Akayesu*, ICTR T. Ch. I, 2 September 1998, para. 597; *Kunarac et al.*, ICTY A. Ch., 12 June 2002, para. 150; *Semanza*, ICTR T. Ch., 15 May 2003, para. 482; *Čelebići*, ICTY T. Ch. II, 16 November 1998, para. 495; *Fernando and Racquel Mejia v. Peru*, Inter-American Commission on Human Rights, 1 March 1996; *Aydin v. Turkey*, ECtHR, 25 September 1997, para. 86.

[173] *Furundžija*, ICTY T. Ch. II, 10 December 1998, para. 267.

[174] Report of the International Law Commission on the Work of its Forty-Eighth Session, 1996, GAOR 51st Session, Supp. No. 10 (A/51/10) at 102–3.

[175] See e.g. Vienna Declaration, World Conference on Human Rights, UN Doc. A/CONF.157/24 (1993) Part I, para. 28, and Part II, para. 38; Beijing Declaration and Platform for Action, Fourth World Conference on Women, 15 September 1995, UN Doc. A/CONF.177/20 (1995) and UN Doc. A/CONF.177/20/Add.1 (1995) Chapter II, paras. 114–15*bis*.

the former Yugoslavia and Rwanda, are inhumane acts falling within the definition of crimes against humanity.[176]

The same definitions apply both in crimes against humanity and in war crimes, so the relevant issues for both war crimes and crimes against humanity will be discussed here.

Rape

The crime of rape has two components. The first is a physical invasion of a sexual nature. The second component is, according to some authorities, the presence of coercive circumstances or, according to other authorities, the absence of consent.

The first component, the conduct element, was described in *Akayesu*, the first case defining the crime against humanity of rape. The ICTR Trial Chamber held that rape 'is a form of aggression and ... cannot be captured in a mechanical description of objects and body parts', which led it to the definition 'a physical invasion of a sexual nature, committed on a person in circumstances which are coercive'.[177] A slight rift emerged in Tribunal jurisprudence, however, when a subsequent decision of an ICTY Trial Chamber (*Furundžija*) concluded that greater clarity was needed, and defined the physical element (rather mechanically) as: the sexual penetration, however slight, of (a) the vagina or anus of the victim by the penis of the perpetrator or any other object, or (b) the mouth of the victim by the penis of the perpetrator.[178] This definition was subsequently endorsed by the Appeals Chamber in *Kunarac*.[179]

The ICC Elements of Crimes falls in between the two definitions:

The perpetrator invaded the body of a person by conduct resulting in penetration, however slight, of any part of the body of the victim or of the perpetrator with a sexual organ, or of the anal or genital opening of the victim with any object or any other part of the body.[180]

This definition is closer to the later Tribunal jurisprudence, in that it is comparably specific, yet it is slightly broader and gender neutral.

The second component is less settled; some sources focus on coercive circumstances and some focus on absence of consent. Early Tribunal jurisprudence required coercive circumstances, that is to say, coercion or force or threat of force against the victim or a third person.[181] This approach was followed in the ICC Elements of Crimes, albeit significantly expanded:

The invasion was committed by force, or by threat of force or coercion, such as that caused by fear of violence, duress, detention, psychological oppression or abuse of power, against such person or another person, or by taking advantage of a coercive environment, or the invasion was committed against a person incapable of giving genuine consent.[182]

---

[176] For a more detailed overview of the advances and difficulties, see Kelly Askin, 'Prosecuting Wartime Rape and Other Gender-Related Crimes under International Law: Extraordinary Advances, Enduring Obstacles' (2003) 21 *Berkeley Journal International Law* 288.

[177] *Akayesu*, ICTR T. Ch. I, 2 September 1998, paras. 597–8.   [178] *Furundžija*, ICTY T. Ch. II, 10 December 1998, para. 185.

[179] *Kunarac et al.*, ICTY T. Ch. II, 22 February 2001, para. 127.   [180] ICC Elements of Crimes, Art. 7(1)(g)–1, Element 1.

[181] *Akayesu*, ICTR T. Ch. I, 2 September 1998, para. 598; *Furundžija*, ICTY T. Ch. II, 10 December 1998, para. 185.

[182] ICC Elements of Crimes, Art. 7(1)(g)–1, Element 2.

This definition more thoroughly encompasses the possible coercive circumstances.

More recently, Tribunal jurisprudence has moved away from cataloguing coercive circumstances and has adopted a simpler element, known in most or all legal systems: the lack of consent of the victim. In *Kunarac*, the Trial Chamber analysed various legal systems and concluded that the correct element was lack of consent of the victim. This was the true common denominator and reflected the basic principle of penalizing violations of sexual autonomy.[183] The Appeals Chamber confirmed this approach, and held that force or threat of force may be relevant, in providing clear evidence of non-consent, but force is not an element *per se* of rape.[184]

Strong arguments can be made that the new line of cases better reflects national legal systems and indeed the underlying principle of sexual autonomy,[185] and that the newer interpretation is also more compatible with the ICC Rules of Procedure and Evidence.[186]

In a plausible counter-argument, Catharine MacKinnon argues that the 'coercion' approach is preferable to the 'non-consent' approach.[187] She argues that, in circumstances of 'mass sexual coercion', an inquiry into consent is decontextualized and unreal.[188] War crimes and crimes against humanity of sexual violence are almost invariably committed in coercive circumstances where consent or reasonable belief in consent is simply not a credible possibility. Where such circumstances are shown, inquiry into consent should not be necessary.[189]

On either approach, it is desirable to adopt procedural and evidentiary rules to limit how the issue of consent may be raised, in order to prevent harassment of witnesses and spurious lines of questioning (see section 17.10).

Sexual slavery

Sexual slavery is a particularly serious form of enslavement.[190] The first element of sexual slavery is therefore identical to enslavement.[191] The additional requirement is that the perpetrator caused the victim to engage in one or more acts of a sexual nature.[192] Particularly egregious examples include the 'comfort stations' maintained by the Japanese

---

[183] *Kunarac et al.*, ICTY T. Ch. II, 22 February 2001, paras. 440–60.

[184] *Kunarac et al.*, ICTY A. Ch., 12 June 2002, para. 129.

[185] Kristen Boon, 'Rape and Forced Pregnancy under the ICC Statute: Human Dignity, Autonomy and Consent' (2001) 32 *Columbia Human Rights Law Review* 625.

[186] The ICC RPE contain rules on evidence of consent in cases of sexual violence, and yet the current elements do not refer to consent as a significant factor.

[187] Catharine MacKinnon, 'Defining Rape Internationally: A Comment on *Akayesu*' (2005/6) 44 *Columbia Journal of International Law* 940.

[188] *Ibid.*, 950.

[189] See section 16.9.1, text of footnote 129, which discusses consent as a defence and concludes that 'In most cases relating to international crimes it is difficult to think of situations in which consent would be a genuine issue.' Suggestions have at times been made to go further, to legally exclude entirely the relevance of consent in any context of armed conflict. If such an approach were adopted, and consent were deemed irrelevant, then even consensual relations between long-standing sexual partners would become 'war crimes'. One might argue that 'prosecutorial discretion' is the solution to such problems, but the fact of liability in such circumstances indicates that the suggested rule is too broad. It therefore seems more appropriate to restrict consent defences to those circumstances where there is no air of reality to such a claim.

[190] Special Rapporteur, *Final Report on Systematic Rape, Sexual Slavery and Slavery-Like Practices during Armed Conflict*, UN Doc. E/CN.4/Sub.2/1998/13, 22 June 1998, para. 30.

[191] ICC Elements of Crimes, Art. 7(1)(g)–2, Element 1.   [192] ICC Elements of Crimes, Art. 7(1)(g)–2, Element 2.

in the Second World War and the 'rape camps' in the former Yugoslavia.[193] The examples of enslavement from the Tribunal cases, discussed above,[194] would clearly qualify as sexual slavery.

Sexual slavery includes many acts that in the past would have been categorized as 'enforced prostitution'.[195] The latter concept is, however, problematic in that it obscures the violence involved and in that it degrades the victim. Thus, 'sexual slavery' is generally preferred as properly reflecting the nature and seriousness of the crime.[196] The SCSL was the first tribunal to enter convictions for sexual slavery; in doing so the Court has explored overlaps with the concept of 'forced marriage', discussed in section 11.3.12.[197]

Enforced prostitution

Enforced prostitution is prohibited in Geneva Convention IV, but as an example of an attack upon a woman's honour; in Additional Protocol I, it is prohibited as an outrage upon personal dignity.[198] The ICC Statute lists it as a crime against humanity and war crime in its own right, removing the outdated linkage to 'honour'.

The ICC Elements of Crimes refer to (1) causing one or more persons to engage in one or more acts of a sexual nature, (2) by force or by threat of force (or under the coercive circumstances, as noted above in the discussion of rape).[199] In addition, pursuant to a US proposal, it is required that (3) 'the perpetrator or another person obtained or expected to obtain pecuniary or other advantage in exchange for or in connection with the acts of a sexual nature'.[200] There were considerable misgivings among some delegations concerning the paucity of precedent for this element. In the end, however, it was adopted, in order to create some distinction from sexual slavery and in light of the ordinary meaning of the term 'prostitution'. In the absence of such anticipated advantage, the relevant conduct could still be prosecuted as sexual slavery or sexual violence.

Forced pregnancy

The inclusion of 'forced pregnancy' was the subject of intense debate in the negotiation of the ICC Statute.[201] It had previously been recognized in instruments such as the Vienna Declaration and Programme of Action and the Beijing Declaration and Platform for Action.[202] The inclusion recognized a particular harm inflicted on women, including during

---

[193] *Final Report on Systematic Rape*, para. 30.   [194] See section 11.3.4.   [195] *Final Report on Systematic Rape*, para. 31.
[196] Oosterveld, 'Sexual Slavery'; Kelly D. Askin, 'Women and International Humanitarian Law' in Kelly D. Askin and Dorean M. Koening (eds.), *Women and International Human Rights Law* (Brill, 1999) Vol. I, 48; Rhonda Copelon, 'Surfacing Gender: Re-Engraving Crimes against Women in Humanitarian Law' (1994) 5 *Hastings Law Journal* 243.
[197] *Sesay, Kallon and Gbao* (RUF case), SCSL T.Ch I 2 March 2009; *Taylor*, SCSL T.Ch II 18 May 2012.
[198] Art. 27 of Geneva Convention IV 1949: 'Women shall be especially protected against any attack on their honour, in particular against rape, enforced prostitution, or any form of indecent assault.'
[199] ICC Elements of Crimes, Art. 7(1)(g)–3, Element 1.   [200] ICC Elements of Crimes, Art. 7(1)(g)–3, Element 2.
[201] Cate Steains, 'Gender Issues' in Lee, *The Making of the Rome Statute*, 363–9.
[202] Vienna Declaration, World Conference on Human Rights, UN Doc. A/CONF.157/24 (1993) Part II, para. 38; Beijing Declaration and Platform for Action, Fourth World Conference on Women, 15 September 1995, UN Doc. A/CONF.177/20 (1995) and UN Doc. A/CONF.177/20/Add.1 (1995) Chapter II, para. 115.

the conflicts in the former Yugoslavia, where captors indicated that they tried to impregnate women and hold them until it was too late to obtain an abortion.[203]

However, some delegations were concerned that the concept would be used to criminalize national systems that did not provide a right to abortion, which would conflict with their religious convictions and their constitutional provisions. It was agreed that discussion of the right to abortion will continue in a human rights context[204] but was not part of the crimes against humanity debate. Agreement was reached on the following definition: (1) unlawful confinement (2) of a woman forcibly made pregnant (3) with the intent of affecting the ethnic composition of a population or carrying out other grave violations of international law.[205] The reference to grave violations of international law includes, for example, biological experiments. For greater clarity, Article 7(2)(f) states that '[t]his definition shall not in any way be interpreted as affecting national laws relating to pregnancy'.

Enforced sterilization

The ICC Statute is the first treaty expressly recognizing enforced sterilization as a crime against humanity and war crime. The conduct has, however, been prosecuted before, in the context of unlawful medical experiments such as were seen in the Second World War.[206] The ICC Elements of Crimes require that (1) the perpetrator deprived one or more persons of biological reproductive capacity and (2) that the conduct was neither justified by the medical or hospital treatment of the persons concerned nor carried out with their genuine consent.[207] This definition is not restricted to medical operations, but could also include an intentional use of chemicals for this effect.[208] The concept of 'genuine consent' excludes consent obtained by deception.[209]

Enforced sterilization can also satisfy the conduct requirements of genocide (Article 6(e) of the ICC Statute) and can amount to genocide where genocidal intent is present.

Other sexual violence

The ICC Statute also includes 'other sexual violence of comparable gravity'. The ICC Elements of Crimes elaborate the following elements: (1) the perpetrator committed an act of a sexual nature against one or more persons *or* caused one or more persons to engage in an act of a sexual nature, (2) by force or threat of force or coercion[210] and (3) the gravity of the conduct was comparable to the other offences in Article 7(1)(g).[211]

The first element covers both acts against the victim as well as forcing the victim to perform sexual acts. It is not restricted to cases of assault, and therefore can include

[203] Commission of Experts (the Former Yugoslavia), *Report*, paras. 248–50.
[204] On the difference between human rights and crimes against humanity, see section 1.4.1.
[205] Art. 7(2)(f) of the ICC Statute.   [206] *Brandt* (the 'Doctors Trial'), IV LRTWC 91.
[207] ICC Elements of Crimes, Art. 7(1)(g)–5, Elements 1 and 2.
[208] Eve La Haye, 'Sexual Violence' in Lee, *Elements and Rules*, 195. The ICC Elements of Crimes exclude 'birth control measures with a non-permanent effect'.
[209] ICC Elements of Crimes, footnote 55.
[210] With the same list of coercive circumstances discussed above in the context of rape.
[211] ICC Elements of Crimes, Art. 7(1)(g)–6, Elements 1 and 2.

examples of forced nudity.[212] The second element, coercive circumstances, is discussed above in the context of rape. The third element creates a threshold of seriousness, so that the acts warrant being described as crimes against humanity.[213]

The UN Special Rapporteur on systematic rape, sexual slavery and slavery-like practices observed that sexual violence includes:

any violence, physical or psychological, carried out by sexual means or targeting sexuality. Sexual violence covers both physical and psychological attacks directed at a person's sexual characteristics, such as forcing a person to strip naked in public, mutilating a person's genitals or slicing off a woman's breasts. Sexual violence also characterizes situations in which two victims are forced to perform sexual acts on one another or to harm one another in a sexual manner.[214]

11.3.9   *Persecution*

Persecution involves the intentional and severe deprivation of fundamental rights, against an identifiable group or collectivity on prohibited discriminatory grounds. In addition, the ICC Statute requires that persecution be committed in connection with another crime or at least one inhumane act.

Severe deprivation of fundamental rights

Until recently, the crime of persecution was not well defined, and the need for adequate precision was highlighted both in Tribunal jurisprudence and in the drafting of the ICC Statute.[215] The test developed in Tribunal jurisprudence requires (1) a gross or blatant denial, (2) on discriminatory grounds, (3) of a fundamental right, laid down in international customary or treaty law, (4) reaching the same level of gravity as other crimes against humanity.[216] Although there is some different terminology, this is generally compatible with the ICC definition, which refers to intentional and severe deprivation of fundamental rights, on specified discriminatory grounds.

The emergent definition, with the notions of fundamental rights, severe deprivation, and discriminatory grounds, provides the needed precision for criminal law. Nonetheless, the test necessarily remains somewhat open with respect to the particular *acts* that may constitute persecution, as it is impossible to anticipate all future examples. Tribunal jurisprudence has noted that:

neither international treaty law nor case law provides a comprehensive list of illegal acts encompassed by the charge of persecution, and persecution as such is not known in the world's major criminal justice

---

[212] La Haye, 'Sexual Violence', 198; *Final Report on Systematic Rape*, paras. 21–2.

[213] In the context of war crimes, the requirement refers to gravity comparable to a grave breach (or common Art. 3 in the case of internal armed conflicts) of the Geneva Conventions.

[214] *Final Report on Systematic Rape*, paras. 21–2.

[215] *Kupreškić et al.*, ICTY T. Ch. II, 14 January 2000, para. 618: 'However, this Trial Chamber holds the view that in order for persecution to amount to a crime against humanity it is not enough to define a core assortment of acts and to leave peripheral acts in a state of uncertainty. There must be clearly defined limits on the types of acts which qualify as persecution. Although the realm of human rights is dynamic and expansive, not every denial of a human right may constitute a crime against humanity.'

[216] See e.g. *Kupreškić et al.*, ICTY T. Ch. II, 14 January 2000, para. 621.

systems. [Thus] the crime of persecution needs careful and sensitive development in light of the principle of *nullum crimen sine lege*.[217]

Gravity or severity

Tribunal jurisprudence indicates that persecution requires a gravity comparable to other crimes against humanity;[218] in the ICC definition this requirement may be subsumed in the requirements of 'severe' deprivation.

Discriminatory grounds

The fundamental feature of persecution is that it be committed on discriminatory grounds. The ICTY and ICTR Statutes refer to persecution on political, racial or religious grounds.[219] The ICC Statute contains an updated and more inclusive list of prohibited grounds: political, racial, national, ethnic, cultural, religious or gender.[220] In addition, the ICC list is cautiously open-ended in referring to 'other grounds that are universally recognised as impermissible under international law'.[221] The standard of 'universal' means that the threshold required to read in additional grounds is a high one, but a high standard was considered necessary in order to satisfy the principle of legality.

Connection to other acts

The ICC Statute contains an additional requirement, that persecution be committed in connection with (a) any crime within the jurisdiction of the Court or (b) any other act listed in Article 7(1). This requirement was included because of the concern of several States about the possible elasticity of the concept of persecution. The fear was that any practices of discrimination, more suitably addressed by human rights bodies, would be labelled as 'persecution', giving rise to international prosecutions. The connection requirement was inserted to ensure at least a context of more recognized forms of criminality. Although the original proposal was to require a link to another crime within the jurisdiction of the Court, this was widened to include a link to any other act referred to in Article 7(1).

   The customary law status of this requirement is open to doubt. Such a requirement is not applied in Tribunal jurisprudence; in *Kupreškić*, an ICTY Trial Chamber found that, 'although the Statute of the ICC may be indicative of the *opinio juris* of many States, Article 7(1)(h) is not consonant with customary international law'.[222] In any event, the requirement should not pose a significant obstacle for legitimate prosecutions of persecution, since it is satisfied by a linkage to even *one* other recognized act (a killing or other inhumane act), which one would expect to find in a situation warranting international

---

[217] *Kordić and Čerkez*, ICTY T. Ch., 26 February 2001, para. 694.
[218] See e.g. *Kupreškić et al.*, ICTY T. Ch. II, 14 January 2000, paras. 619 and 621; *Kvočka et al.*, ICTY T. Ch. I, 2 November 2001, para. 185; *Ruggio*, ICTR T. Ch., 1 June 2000, para. 21.
[219] Art. 5(h) of the ICTY Statute; Art. 3(h) of the ICTR Statute.   [220] Art. 7(1)(h) of the ICC Statute.   [221] *Ibid.*
[222] *Kupreškić et al.*, ICTY T. Ch. II, 14 January 2000, para. 580. Antonio Cassese argues persuasively that the requirement is inconsistent with the elimination of the general nexus requirement in the Nuremberg Charter and therefore is a restriction on customary law: Cassese, 'Crimes against Humanity', 376.

prosecution. In so far as such an element exists, it is purely an objective element to ensure the seriousness of the situation, and does not require any mental element.[223]

Mental element

In addition to the normal mental element relating to the conduct and the broader context, persecution requires a particular intent to target a person or group on prohibited grounds of discrimination.[224] Tribunal jurisprudence indicates that a particular *intent* to discriminate is required, not simply a *knowledge* that one is acting in a discriminatory way.[225] With respect to the requirement in the ICC Statute of a 'connection' to other crimes or prohibited acts, this requirement is purely objective and no mental element is required.[226]

Relationship to other crimes

Persecution and genocide each require a particular discriminatory intent. In the case of genocide, however, the intent is more specific: it must be an intent to destroy a group as such, and the target must be a national, ethnical, racial or religious group. Genocide can only be based on the listed acts (see, for example, Article 6 of the ICC Statute) whereas the conduct potentially amounting to persecution is broader. Acts amounting to other crimes against humanity can constitute persecution if the additional aggravating element of discriminatory intent is present.

Examples of persecutory acts

Persecutory acts include the prohibited acts already listed in the definition of crimes against humanity, when committed with discriminatory intent.[227] Examples that have been prosecuted include murder, extermination, imprisonment, deportation, transfer of populations, torture, enslavement and beatings (inhumane acts).[228] In addition, they can include other conduct that severely deprives political, civil, economic or social rights. Examples include the passing of discriminatory laws, restriction of movement and seclusion in ghettos, the exclusion of members of an ethnic or religious group from aspects of social, political and economic life, including exclusion from professions, business, educational institutions, public service and inter-marriage.[229] It also includes overt violence such as burning of homes and terrorization.[230] The ICTR Appeals Chamber has held that, while hate speech alone does not constitute persecution, hate speech and calls to violence, contributing to acts of violence, and in a broader context of persecution, can be of comparable gravity to other crimes and hence constitute acts of persecution.[231]

Attacks on property can constitute persecution. This includes 'systematic destruction of monuments or buildings representative of a particular social, religious, cultural or other

---

[223] ICC Elements of Crimes, footnote 22.
[224] ICC Elements of Crimes, Art. 7(1)(h), Element 3; *Kordić and Čerkez*, ICTY T. Ch., 26 February 2001, para. 212.
[225] *Krnojelac*, ICTY T. Ch. II, 15 March 2002, para. 435; *Kordić and Čerkez*, ICTY T. Ch., 26 February 2001, para. 212.
[226] ICC Elements of Crimes, footnote 22.   [227] *Kupreškić et al.*, ICTY T. Ch. II, 14 January 2000, paras. 593–607.
[228] *Tadić*, ICTY T. Ch. II, 7 May 1997, paras. 704–10; *Kupreškić*, ICTY T. Ch. II, 14 January 2000, para. 594.
[229] *Kupreškić et al., ibid.*, paras. 608–15.   [230] *Krstić*, ICTY T. Ch. I, 2 August 2001, para. 537.
[231] *Nahimana et al.*, ICTR A. Ch., 28 November 2007, paras. 986–8.

group',[232] and destruction of homes and means of livelihood.[233] The *Tadić* decision noted doubts about whether attacks on purely industrial property would suffice, but thought economic measures with personal effects, including deprivation of livelihood, would suffice.[234] The *Blaškić* decision affirmed that persecution includes 'targeting property, so long as the victimised persons were specially selected on grounds linked to their belonging to a particular community'.[235] This may be seen in destruction of private dwellings, businesses, symbolic buildings, looting and plunder of businesses and private property, boycott of businesses and shops, and forcing the group out of economic life.[236]

11.3.10 Enforced disappearance

The ICC Statute expressly includes enforced disappearance as a crime against humanity. Enforced disappearance was recognized previously as an international crime and indeed as a crime against humanity. It was exemplified in the 'Night and Fog Decree' issued by the Nazis, to execute people and to provide no information to the families as to their whereabouts or fate.[237] It was also a prevalent feature under military regimes in Latin America in the 1980s, and is still practised today in various regimes around the world. Enforced disappearance is expressly recognized as a crime against humanity in the 1992 UN Declaration on the Protection of All Persons from Enforced Disappearance, the 1994 Inter-American Convention on the Forced Disappearance of Persons and, more recently, in the 2005 International Convention on the Protection of All Persons from Enforced Disappearance.[238]

The definition in the ICC Statute is based on the UN Declaration and the Inter-American Convention,[239] and refers to the 'arrest, detention or abduction of persons by, or with the authorisation, support or acquiescence of, a State or political organisation, followed by a refusal to acknowledge that deprivation of freedom or to give information on the fate or whereabouts of those persons, with the intention of removing them from the protection of law for a prolonged period of time'.[240]

A welcome development in the negotiation of the ICC Elements of Crimes was the realization that there are various ways in which an *individual* may be liable for this crime. Previous definitions simply described the whole system of enforced disappearance, but it is unlikely that a single individual would be involved in the arrest, detention or abduction phase, as well as the refusal to acknowledge the deprivation or to provide information. Enforced disappearance typically involves many actors. Therefore, the ICC Elements of Crimes recognize that the crime may be committed (a) by arresting, detaining or abducting a

---

[232] ILC Report, 1991, p. 268.   [233] *Kordić and Čerkez*, ICTY T. Ch. III, 26 February 2001, para. 205.
[234] *Tadić*, ICTY T. Ch. II, 7 May 1997, para. 707.   [235] *Blaškić*, ICTY T. Ch. I, 3 March 2000, para. 233.
[236] *Ibid.*, paras. 220–33.
[237] Nuremberg IMT, Judgment and Sentences, reprinted in (1947) 41 *American Journal of International Law* 172, 230.
[238] Preamble, paras. 4, 5 and 6 of the respective instruments.
[239] Preamble, para. 3 of the UN Declaration and Art. 2 of the Inter-American Convention.   [240] Art. 7(2)(i) of the ICC Statute.

person, with knowledge that a refusal to acknowledge or give information would be likely to follow in the ordinary course of events, or (b) by refusing to acknowledge the deprivation of freedom or to provide information on the fate or whereabouts, with knowledge that such deprivation had occurred.[241] In addition, the crime of enforced disappearance requires a particular intention, to remove a person from the protection of the law.

Previous instruments required commission, authorization, support or acquiescence from the State. The ICC Statute expanded this to refer as well to 'political organisations', consistent with the fundamental proposition that crimes against humanity may be committed by non-State actors.

Enforced disappearance may involve other crimes such as killing, torture or arbitrary imprisonment. The essence of the crime, however, is that the friends and families of the direct victims do not know whether the persons concerned are alive or dead. It is this uncertainty that is the hallmark of enforced disappearance, and indeed the friends and families of the direct victims are also the special victims of this crime.

11.3.11 Apartheid

The ICC Statute includes the crime of apartheid as a crime against humanity. Apartheid was recognized as a crime against humanity in instruments such as the 1968 Convention on the Non-Applicability of Statutory Limitations to War Crimes and Crimes against Humanity and the 1973 Apartheid Convention.[242]

The definition was generalized to refer not only to the situation which had prevailed in South Africa, but also any similar situations in the future. Article 7(2)(h) of the ICC Statute defines it as 'inhumane acts of a character similar to those referred to in paragraph 1, committed in the context of an institutionalised racial regime of systematic oppression and domination by one racial group over any other racial group and committed with the intention of maintaining that regime'.

The definition of crimes against humanity has always included a residual clause encompassing other inhumane acts of a similar character. Thus, by requiring in the definition of the crime of apartheid that the inhumane acts be 'of a character similar to those referred to in paragraph 1', the drafters ensured that they did not exceed existing law. What the ICC Statute provides is simply an express recognition of the crime of apartheid where inhumane acts are committed in the context of an institutionalized racial regime of systematic oppression and domination.

Most or all of the acts listed in the Apartheid Convention are captured by the ICC definition. The requirement of 'similar character' to other inhumane acts naturally covers acts of *identical* character,[243] and hence murder, torture, arbitrary imprisonment and

---

[241] Georg Witschel and Wiebke Rückert, 'Crime against Humanity of Enforced Disappearance of Persons' in Lee, *Elements and Rules*, 98–103.
[242] Art. 1(b) of the Convention on Statutory Limitations, quoted in Apartheid Convention, Preamble, para. 5.
[243] A point clarified in the ICC Elements of Crimes, Art. 7(1)(j), Element 2.

persecution are clearly included. In addition, inflicting conditions calculated to cause physical destruction of a group; legislative measures to prevent a racial group from participating in political, social, economic and cultural life; legislative measures to divide the population through ghettos, prohibiting mixed marriage, and expropriating property; and forced labour, appear to be of character similar to 'persecution' and 'other inhumane acts' and therefore would be covered. The significant difference between the two definitions is that the ICC Statute specifies that the crime must be committed 'in the context of an institutionalised regime of systematic oppression and domination by one racial group over any other racial group or groups'. To constitute the crime of apartheid, the conduct must be committed with the particular intent of maintaining the regime.

11.3.12 Other inhumane acts

All definitions of crimes against humanity close with the general residual clause 'or other inhumane acts'. A residual clause remains necessary because:

However much care were taken in establishing all the various forms of infliction, one would never be able to catch up with the imagination of future torturers who wished to satisfy their bestial instincts; and the more specific and complete a list tries to be, the more restrictive it becomes.[244]

Jurists have, however, been aware that any such residual clause must be infused with adequate precision to satisfy the criminal law principle of legality. The ICC Statute provides the necessary threshold by requiring that the inhumane acts (1) be of a similar character to other prohibited acts and (2) that they cause great suffering or serious injury to body or to mental or physical health.[245] Tribunal jurisprudence provides the threshold by requiring 'similar gravity and seriousness' to other prohibited acts.[246]

The accused must carry out the conduct intentionally. It is not required that the accused considered his or her actions 'inhumane', it is sufficient that the accused was aware of the factual circumstances that established the character of the act.[247] The accused must intend to inflict serious bodily or mental harm.[248]

Tribunals have held the conduct element of 'inhumane acts' to be synonymous with the conduct element of the war crime of 'cruel treatment'.[249]

The Tribunal Statutes, unlike the ICC Statute, do not expressly include forced disappearance, sexual violence, forced prostitution and forced transfer of populations in their list of prohibited acts, and hence Tribunal jurisprudence has found that each of these are encompassed in the Tribunal Statutes under 'other inhumane acts'.[250] Other acts that have been

---

[244] *Blaškić*, ICTY T. Ch., 13 March 2000, para. 237, referring to Jean Pictet, *Commentary on Geneva Convention IV* (Geneva, 1960) 54.
[245] Art. 7(1)(k) of the ICC Statute.   [246] See e.g. *Kayishema and Ruzindana*, ICTR A. Ch., 1 June 2001, para. 583.
[247] ICC Elements of Crimes, Art. 7(1)(k), Element 3; *Čelebići*, ICTY T. Ch. II, 16 November 1998, para. 543.
[248] ICC Elements of Crimes, Art. 7(1)(k); *Blaškić*, ICTY T. Ch. I, 3 March 2000, para. 243.
[249] *Jelisić*, ICTY T. Ch., 14 December 1999, para. 52. The ICC Elements of Crimes use different terms for the two crimes, so it remains to be seen whether the ICC will adopt the same approach.
[250] *Kvočka et al.*, ICTY T. Ch. I, 2 November 2001, para. 208; *Kupreškić et al.*, ICTY T. Ch. II, 14 January 2000, para. 566.

characterized as inhumane acts include mutilation, severe bodily harm, beatings, serious physical and mental injury, inhumane or degrading treatment falling short of the definition of torture, imposing inhumane conditions in concentration camps, forced nudity and forced marriage.[251] More recently, the SCSL has recognized the phenomenon in which women and girls are abducted and forced to serve as 'bush wives' as an inhumane act. One chamber recognized 'forced marriage' as an 'inhumane act', and defined it as 'forced conjugal association with another person resulting in great suffering, or serious physical or mental injury on the part of the victim'.[252] Another chamber preferred not to use the term 'forced marriage', on the ground that marriage was a misnomer for what happened to the victims, describing it instead as 'conjugal slavery' and holding that the phenomenon is already encompassed within the crime of sexual slavery.[253]

Further reading

Kai Ambos and Steffen Wirth, 'The Current Law of Crimes against Humanity: An Analysis of UNTAET Regulation 15/2000' (2002) 13 *Criminal Law Forum* 1

M. Cherif Bassiouni, *Crimes against Humanity: Historical Evolution and Contemporary Application* (Cambridge, 2011)

Machteld Boot, *Genocide, Crimes against Humanity and War Crimes* (Oxford, 2002)

Machteld Boot, Rodney Dixon and Christopher K. Hall, 'Article 7' in Triffterer, *Observers' Notes*

Antonio Cassese, 'Crimes against Humanity' in Cassese, *Commentary*

Simon Chesterman, 'An Altogether Different Order: Defining the Elements of Crimes against Humanity' (2000) *Duke Journal of Comparative and International Law* 283

Roger Clark, 'Crimes against Humanity' in G. Ginsburgs and V. N. Kudriavstsev (eds.), *The Nuremberg Trial and International Law* (Dordrecht, Boston and London, 1990)

Phyllis Hwang, 'Defining Crimes against Humanity in the Rome Statute of the International Criminal Court' (1998) 22 *Fordham International Law Journal* 457

Claus Kreß, 'On the Outer Limits of Crimes against Humanity: The Concept of Organization within the Policy Requirement: Some Reflections on the March 2010 ICC Kenya Decision' (2010) 23 *Leiden Journal of International Law* 855

David Luban, 'A Theory of Crimes against Humanity' (2004) 29 *Yale Law Journal* 85

Timothy McCormack, 'Crimes against Humanity' in Dominic McGoldrick, Peter Rowe and Eric Donnelly (eds.), *The Permanent International Criminal Court: Legal and Policy Issues* (Oxford, 2004)

Joseph Rikhof, 'Crimes against Humanity, Customary International Law and the International Tribunals for Bosnia and Rwanda' (1995) 6 *National Journal of Constitutional Law* 231

Darryl Robinson, Georg Witschel and Wiebke Rückert, 'Elements of Crimes against Humanity' in Lee, *Elements and Rules*

---

[251] *Akayesu*, ICTR T. Ch. I, 2 September 1998, paras. 685–97; *Tadić*, ICTY T. Ch. II, 7 May 1997, para. 730; *Blaškić*, ICTY T. Ch. I, 3 March 2000, para. 239; *Kvočka et al.*, ICTY T. Ch. I, 2 November 2001, para. 209; *Čelebići*, ICTY T. Ch. II, 16 November 1998, paras. 554–8.

[252] *Brima, Kamara and Kanu*, SCSL A. Ch., 22 February 2008, para. 195.

[253] *Taylor*, SCSL T. Ch. II, 18 May 2012, paras. 424–8. Valerie Oosterveld, 'Gender and the Charles Taylor Case at the Special Court for Sierra Leone' (2012) 19 *William and Mary Journal of Women and the Law* 7.

Leila Sadat, 'Crimes against Humanity in the Modern Age' (2013) 107 *American Journal of International Law* 334

William Schabas, 'State Policy as an Element of International Crimes' (2008) 98 *Journal of Criminal Law and Criminology* 953

Beth van Schack, 'The Definition of Crimes against Humanity: Resolving the Incoherence' (1999) 37 *Columbia Journal of Transnational Law* 787

Egon Schwelb, 'Crimes against Humanity' (1946) 23 *British Yearbook of International Law* 178

12

War Crimes

12.1 Introduction

12.1.1 Overview

A war crime is a serious violation of the laws and customs applicable in armed conflict (also known as international humanitarian law, or IHL) which gives rise to individual criminal responsibility under international law. Because the law of war crimes is based on international humanitarian law, the present section will explain the relevant underlying principles of international humanitarian law and the development of war crimes law. Section 12.2 will review issues common to all war crimes, namely, the existence of armed conflict, the nexus between the conduct and the armed conflict, and the role of the perpetrator and victim. Section 12.3 will survey the specific offences constituting war crimes.

Unlike crimes against humanity, war crimes have no requirement of widespread or systematic commission. A single isolated act can constitute a war crime. For war crimes law, it is the situation of armed conflict that justifies international concern.

12.1.2 A brief history of humanitarian law

Laws and customs regulating warfare may be traced back to ancient times. While such norms have varied between civilizations and centuries, and were often shockingly lax by modern standards, it is significant that diverse cultures around the globe have recorded agreements, religious edicts and military instructions laying out ground rules for military conflict.[1]

Codification and progressive development at the international level was spurred in part by the efforts of one individual. In 1859, Henri Dunant, a businessman from Geneva, witnessed the aftermath of the Battle of Solferino, and was shocked by the horrors of wounded soldiers left to die on the battlefield. He published a poignant and evocative account of the carnage,

---

[1] See e.g. Leslie Green, *The Contemporary Law of Armed Conflict* (Manchester, 2000) 20–53; Christopher Greenwood, 'Historical Development and Legal Basis' in Dieter Fleck (ed.), *Handbook of International Humanitarian Law*, 2nd edn (Oxford, 2008) 1–44; M. Sassoli and A. Bouvier, *How Does Law Protect in War? Cases, Documents and Teaching Materials on Contemporary Practice in International Humanitarian Law* (Geneva, 1999) 97–104.

urging measures to reduce such unnecessary suffering.[2] This appeal led promptly to the creation of the International Committee of the Red Cross in 1863 and the adoption of the first Geneva Convention.[3]

Since then, there have been many treaties developing IHL. These are sometimes divided into 'Hague law' and 'Geneva law'. The Hague Conventions limit the methods and means of warfare to reduce unnecessary destruction and suffering. The most important of these is the 1907 Hague Regulations, which recognized that 'the right of belligerents to adopt means of injuring the enemy is not unlimited', and laid down many provisions on the means and methods of warfare that are now recognized as customary law.

The Geneva Conventions primarily focus on protecting civilians and others who are not active combatants. The four Geneva Conventions of 1949, adopted in response to the inhumanities of the Second World War, considerably added to and updated previous Geneva Conventions. The 1949 Conventions deal with sick and wounded in the field ('Geneva Convention I'), the wounded, sick and shipwrecked at sea ('Geneva Convention II'), prisoners-of-war ('Geneva Convention III') and civilians ('Geneva Convention IV'). In 1977, these rules were again updated by two Additional Protocols, the first concerning international armed conflicts ('AP I') and the second, non-international (hereinafter, for the sake of brevity, 'internal') armed conflicts ('AP II'). AP I combines elements of 'Hague law' and 'Geneva law', making this traditional distinction less relevant.

Other significant treaty developments have strengthened the protection of cultural property,[4] the prohibition or regulation of certain weapons (such as biological and chemical weapons and anti-personnel mines),[5] and the prohibition on the use of child soldiers.[6]

The provisions of the 1907 Hague Regulations as well as much of the 1949 Geneva Conventions have come to be recognized as customary law; hence they apply regardless of whether parties to the conflicts have ratified those conventions.[7] Some, but not all, provisions of the Additional Protocols have obtained recognition as customary law.[8]

---

[2] Henri Dunant, *Un Souvenir de Solférino* (Geneva, 1862).

[3] 1864 Geneva Convention for the Amelioration of the Condition of the Wounded in Armies in the Field.

[4] 1954 Hague Convention for the Protection of Cultural Property in the Event of an Armed Conflict, 14 May 1954, and two protocols thereto, the 1954 First Hague Protocol, 24 May 1954, and the 1999 Second Hague Protocol, 29 March 1999.

[5] Convention on the Prohibition of the Development, Production and Stockpiling of Bacteriological (Biological) and Toxin Weapons and on their Destruction, 10 April 1972; Convention on Prohibitions or Restrictions on the Use of Certain Conventional Weapons Which May Be Deemed to Be Excessively Injurious or to Have Indiscriminate Effects, 10 October 1980; four protocols thereto including Convention on the Prohibition of the Development, Production, Stockpiling and Use of Chemical Weapons and on their Destruction, 13 January 1993; Convention on the Prohibition of the Use, Stockpiling, Production and Transfer of Anti-Personnel Mines and on their Destruction, 18 September 1997.

[6] Optional Protocol to the Convention on the Rights of the Child on the involvement of children in armed conflict, adopted and opened for signature, ratification and accession by GA Res. A/RES/54/263 of 25 May 2000.

[7] Theodor Meron, *Human Rights and Humanitarian Norms as Customary Law* (Oxford, 1999) 41–62.

[8] See e.g. *Hamdan v. Rumsfeld*, 126 S Ct 2749 (2006) (regarding Art. 75 of AP I); *Strugar*, ICTY A. Ch., 22 November 2002, para. 9 (regarding Arts. 51 and 52 of AP I); Meron, *Customary Law*, 62–78.

12.1.3   *Key principles of humanitarian law*

The resulting principles may be summarized in different ways, but key elements include:

- Non-combatants are to be spared from various forms of harm; this category includes not only civilians but also former combatants, such as prisoners-of-war and fighters rendered *hors de combat* because they are wounded, sick, shipwrecked or have surrendered.
- Combatants must distinguish between military objectives and the civilian population, and attack only military objectives (the principle of distinction).
- In attacking military objectives, combatants must take measures to avoid or minimize collateral civilian damage and refrain from attacks that would cause excessive civilian damage (the principle of proportionality).
- There are restrictions on the means and methods of war, to reduce unnecessary suffering and to maintain respect for humanitarian principles.

IHL is triggered by the outbreak of armed conflict and seeks to regulate how such conflict is conducted. The goal of abolishing armed conflict altogether is left to other legal and political domains.[9]

Indeed, a fundamental principle of IHL is the complete separation of the *ius ad bellum* (the law regarding resort to armed conflict) and the *ius in bello* (the law governing conduct during the armed conflict). In previous centuries, some scholars had suggested that the party fighting a 'just' war should benefit from more permissive IHL provisions.[10] The obvious difficulty with this proposition is that both sides claim to be fighting with just cause, leading to confusion and obfuscation as to the applicable rules. Moreover, the victims of armed conflict still need protection regardless of the purpose of the conflict. In order to advance the fundamental humanitarian aims of IHL, it is now a clearly established principle that IHL applies equally and uniformly, irrespective of the origins of or reasons for the conflict.[11] *Ius ad bellum* considerations have no bearing on the interpretation or application of IHL in a conflict. Hence, it cannot be argued, for example, that a war was unjustified and therefore that all killings of combatants were war crimes or that all attacks were disproportionate.[12] Conversely, even if forces are fighting in legitimate self-defence of their country, they are still fully accountable for war crimes.[13] The question whether the decision to resort to force

---

[9] See e.g. Preamble to and Arts. 1 and 2 of the 1907 Hague Regulations: 'Seeing that while seeking means to preserve peace and prevent armed conflicts between nations, it is likewise necessary to bear in mind the case where the appeal to arms has been brought about by events which their care was unable to avert; Animated by the desire to serve, even in this extreme case, the interests of humanity and the ever progressive needs of civilization ... '.

[10] See e.g. Hugo Grotius, *De Jure Belli ac Pacis* (1625); Peter Haggenmacher, *Grotius et la doctrine de la guerre juste* (Paris, 1983) 597–612.

[11] See e.g. Preamble, para. 5, of AP I: 'provisions ... must be fully applied in all circumstances ... without any adverse distinctions based on the nature or origin of the conflict or on the causes espoused by or attributed to the parties to the conflict'; and see Sassoli and Bouvier, *How Does Law Protect*, 83–8, 681–2; *United States v. List* (the 'Hostages case'), VIII LRTWC at 59; François Bugnion, 'Guerre juste, guerre d'agression et droit international humanitaire' (2002) 84 *Revue International de la Croix-Rouge* 523. See, however, discussion of Art. 1(4) AP I in section 12.2.2.

[12] See e.g. Sassoli and Bouvier, *How Does Law Protect*, 665; *United States v. Altstötter* (the 'Justice Trial'), VI LRTWC 1, 52.

[13] *Boskoski and Tarculovski*, ICTY A. Ch., 19 May 2010, para. 51; *Fofana and Kondewa*, SCSL A. Ch., 28 May 2008, paras. 531–4.

was legal or illegal is addressed under other law such as the UN Charter (and some day, perhaps, the crime of aggression).[14]

12.1.4 The challenge of regulating warfare

The effort to regulate the exceptional situation of armed conflict is rife with difficulty. Indeed, war in many ways seems to be the antithesis of law, leading to the mistaken saying that *silent enim leges inter arma* (law is silent in war). Normal rules – including the fundamental legal and moral prohibitions on killing and destruction – are to some extent displaced in armed conflict, and combatants cannot be punished for lawful acts of war. Nonetheless, the outbreak of armed conflict does not create a legal vacuum. The law that grants a right to engage in conduct that would normally be criminal also imposes limits on such conduct. Militaries are still subject to discipline, and compliance with IHL norms is required. But enforcement of international norms, which can be challenging in the best of circumstances, is all the more difficult in the context of a deadly struggle among armed groups.[15] International criminal justice is one means of deterring violations and educating people that some basic laws apply in all circumstances.

Permeating the development and interpretation of IHL and war crimes law is the tension between military and humanitarian considerations. Combatants may put too great a weight on military imperatives at the expense of humanitarian considerations. Conversely, it would also be an error to place all emphasis on harm avoidance and to discount military considerations.

When appraising war crimes law, it is important to consider the chaotic situations faced in armed conflict and the requirements of military strategy and tactics. Destruction and death will occur even in lawfully conducted conflict. Mistakes may occur, with tragic consequences, without necessarily amounting to war crimes.

While IHL involves a balancing of military and humanitarian considerations, it is also clear that the weight assigned to these considerations has been shifting over the years in a progressive direction. This process has been aptly referred to as 'the humanization of humanitarian law'.[16] Many factors have contributed to this process, including the increasing emphasis in international law and international relations on protecting human beings as opposed to an exclusive focus on State interests. The result has been stricter rules of conduct, protecting more classes of victims and applying in more circumstances, including during internal armed conflicts.

In addition, while egregious violations remain common in many conflicts, the practice among many States has been to place greater and greater weight on humanitarian considerations. The phenomena of mass media, democratization and globalization mean that images of civilian suffering are more readily available (although censorship and propaganda remain ubiquitous). In addition, technological advances have raised expectations about

---

[14] See Chapter 13.
[15] Hersch Lauterpacht, 'The Problem of the Revision of the Law of War' (1952) 29 *British Yearbook of International Law* 360, 382.
[16] Theodor Meron, 'The Humanization of Humanitarian Law' (2000) 94 *American Journal of International Law* 239.

precision attacks.[17] Those who plan operations know that incidents causing significant civilian casualties can erode support from domestic populations, coalition partners and the international community. Anecdotal evidence also indicates that awareness of international criminal justice institutions is inducing greater compliance among military leaders.[18] Conversely, the difficulties of 'asymmetric' warfare against non-State actors with no regard for humanitarian law have at times led some governments to seek to deny or restrict the application of IHL, creating new points of tension.[19]

12.1.5   The relationship between war crimes and IHL

War crimes law criminalizes a narrower subset of IHL.[20] The major question is which of the rules of IHL constitutes a criminal offence when violated.

Some treaties, such as the Geneva Conventions, expressly criminalize violations of identified fundamental provisions.[21] War crimes may also be found in customary law even in the absence of a treaty provision criminalizing the norm. For example, the Nuremberg Tribunal held that key provisions of the 1907 Hague Regulations reflected customary law and that violations amounted to crimes, even though the 1907 Hague Regulations did not expressly criminalize such violations.[22]

In the seminal *Tadić* decision on jurisdiction, the Appeals Chamber interpreted the ICTY Statute provision on 'violations of the laws or customs of war', giving guidance on how to identify the content of war crimes law. The decision confirmed that not every IHL violation amounts to a war crime.[23] Such a conclusion is clearly correct, since IHL includes a great many technical regulations that would be inappropriate for criminalization.[24] For example, Geneva Convention III requires that prisoners-of-war have a canteen where they may purchase foodstuffs, soap and tobacco at local market prices, and that they be given a specific monthly advance of pay depending on rank;[25] an unavailability of tobacco would be a breach of IHL, but it is not a war crime.

The Appeals Chamber in *Tadić* set the following requirements for war crimes within the jurisdiction of the Tribunal: (1) the violation must infringe a rule of IHL; (2) that rule must be found in customary law or applicable treaty law; (3) the violation must be 'serious', in that the rule protects important values and the breach involves grave consequences for the victim; and (4) the violation must entail individual criminal responsibility.[26]

---

[17] Michael N. Schmitt, 'Precision Attack and International Humanitarian Law' (2005) 87 *International Review of the Red Cross* 445.

[18] See Chapter 2.

[19] Toni Pfanner, 'Asymmetric Warfare from the Perspective of Humanitarian Law and Humanitarian Action' (2005) 87 *International Review of the Red Cross* 149; Luisa Vierucci, 'Prisoners of War or Protected Persons Qua Unlawful Combatants? The Judicial Safeguards to which Guantanamo Bay Detainees Are Entitled' (2003) 1 *Journal of International Criminal Justice* 284.

[20] M. Bothe, 'War Crimes' in Cassese, *Commentary*, 387–8.   [21] See section 12.1.6.

[22] Nuremberg IMT, Judgment and Sentences, reprinted in (1947) 41 *American Journal of International Law* 172, 218 and 248–9; *United States* v. *von Leeb*, XII LRTWC 1, 61–2 and 86–92.

[23] *Tadić*, ICTY A. Ch., 2 October 1995, para. 94.

[24] See e.g. Henckaerts and Doswald-Beck, *ICRC Customary Law*, 568; and Hersch Lauterpacht, 'The Law of Nations and the Punishment of War Crimes' (1944) 21 *British Yearbook of International Law* 58, 78–9.

[25] Arts. 28 and 60 of Geneva Convention III.   [26] *Tadić*, ICTY A. Ch., 2 October 1995, para. 94.

This test has been applied in subsequent Tribunal cases.[27] Questions have been raised as to whether the fourth requirement is in reality redundant, since the evidence presented of criminalization has typically been sparse, and it may simply be that all serious violations are criminalized.[28] It has also been argued, though, that simply applying the adjective 'serious' is question-begging and is not operational as a distinguishing criterion;[29] hence more may be needed to elaborate upon the requirement. In an article presaging the *Tadić* decision, Theodor Meron referred to factors such as whether the norm is directed to individuals, whether it is unequivocal in character, the gravity of the act and the interests of the international community.[30] In any event, the approach of recognizing serious violations of IHL as war crimes largely inspired the selection of crimes in the ICC Statute.[31]

Since war crimes are serious violations of IHL, it is often necessary to refer to the relevant principles of IHL to interpret international criminal law in this area.[32] This is why the chapeau of Article 8(2)(a) of the ICC Statute refers to the provisions of the relevant Geneva Conventions, and the chapeau of Article 8(2)(b) refers to 'the established framework of international law'. Some uncertainties have been expressed as to the interpretation of the latter provision,[33] but it is simply a *renvoi* to the relevant rules of IHL to aid in the interpretation of the various provisions.[34]

IHL and war crimes law have similar aims but somewhat different scopes and consequences. IHL is addressed to governments and other parties to a conflict; it sets out standards expected in armed conflict, and violations can culminate in compensation or other satisfaction. War crimes law is addressed to individuals, it addresses the most serious crimes of concern to the international community as a whole, and it can culminate in imprisonment of a person as a war criminal. For these reasons, similar provisions may warrant a more restrictive interpretation in the context of war crimes law, consistent with the narrower focus of war crimes law on the most serious violations as well as general principles of criminal law (strict construction). For example, IHL requires that, before any sentencing of protected persons, a party must provide a fair trial affording all indispensable judicial guarantees.[35] A minor breach of even one such right would fall below this standard and

---

[27] See e.g. *Galić*, ICTY T. Ch., 5 December 2003, paras. 13–32; *Galić*, ICTY A. Ch., 30 November 2006, paras. 86–98, applying the test to find a war crime of committing acts of violence with the primary purpose of spreading terror among the civilian population. See also Chapter 14; and Robert Cryer, '*Prosecutor* v. *Galić* and the War Crime of Terror Bombing' (2005–6) 2 *Israel Defence Forces Law Review* 73.

[28] *Ibid.*, 91–5.

[29] Georges Abi-Saab, 'The Concept of War Crimes' in Sienho Yee and Wang Tieya (eds.), *International Law and the Post-Cold War World: Essays in Memory of Li Haopei* (London, 2001) 112.

[30] Theodor Meron, 'International Criminalization of Internal Atrocities' (1995) 89 *American Journal of International Law* 554, 562.

[31] Herman von Hebel and Darryl Robinson, 'Crimes within the Jurisdiction of the Court' in Lee, *The Making of the Rome Statute*, 103–5.

[32] Peter Rowe, 'War Crimes' in Dominic McGoldrick, Peter Rowe and Eric Donnelly (eds.), *The Permanent International Criminal Court: Legal and Policy Issues* (Oxford, 2004) 217–19.

[33] Antonio Cassese, 'The Statute of the International Criminal Court: Some Preliminary Reflections' (1999) 10 *European Journal of International Law* 149, 150–2, expresses concern that it may require proof of customary law status, while preferring an interpretation that it reflects the drafters' view that the crimes are already customary law. See also Machteld Boot, *Genocide, Crimes against Humanity and War Crimes* (Oxford, 2002) 564–6.

[34] This understanding is now confirmed in ICC Elements of Crimes, Introduction to War Crimes, para. 2, and dovetails with Art. 21(1)(b) of the ICC Statute.

[35] Common Art. 3 to the Geneva Conventions.

violate IHL, requiring an appropriate remedy. However, it would be incorrect to say that as a consequence all involved in conducting the trial should thereby be branded as war criminals. For the purpose of war crimes law, it is necessary to look at the cumulative effect of shortcomings to see whether there was a deprivation of fair trial amounting to a war crime.[36]

12.1.6   *A brief history of the law of war crimes*

War crimes law deals with the *criminal responsibility of individuals* for serious violations of international humanitarian law. National laws have long provided for prosecution of war crimes.[37] For example, the Lieber Code recognized criminal liability of individuals for violations of its strictures, and similar provisions are in the military manuals of many countries.[38] Following some prominent historical examples of war crimes prosecutions,[39] and after abortive efforts to conduct international trials at the end of the First World War,[40] the Nuremberg Charter gave form to the international law of war crimes. Article 6(b) of the Charter included:

War crimes: namely, violations of the laws or customs of war. Such violations shall include, but not be limited to, murder, ill-treatment or deportation to slave labour or for any purpose of civilian population of or in occupied territory, murder or ill-treatment of prisoners-of-war or persons on the seas, killing of hostages, plunder of public or private property, wanton destruction of cities, towns or villages, or devastation not justified by military necessity.

Within the scope of 'war crimes' the Nuremberg Tribunal included key provisions of the 1907 Hague Regulations, which it held gave rise to individual criminal responsibility under customary law.[41]

The four Geneva Conventions of 1949 included 'grave breach' provisions, expressly recognizing certain violations as crimes subject to universal jurisdiction.[42] These provisions have come to be regarded as reflective of customary international law.[43] Additional Protocol I to those Conventions ('AP I'), adopted in 1977, introduced additional 'grave breaches', although not all of these have attained recognition as customary law.[44]

The ICTY Statute included grave breaches of the Geneva Conventions (Article 2 of the ICTY Statute) as well as violations of other laws or customs of war, featuring an open-ended

---

[36] ICC Elements of Crimes, footnote 59; Knut Dörman, 'Article 8' in Triffterer, *Observers' Notes* at 316.

[37] Timothy L. H. McCormack, 'From Sun Tzu to the Sixth Committee: The Evolution of an International Criminal Law Regime' in Timothy L. H. McCormack and Gerry. J. Simpson (eds.), *The Law of War Crimes: National and International Approaches* (The Hague, 1997); Leslie Green, *The Contemporary Law of Armed Conflict* (Manchester, 2000) 286–90.

[38] Instructions for the Government Armies of the United States in the Field, General Orders No. 100, 24 April 1863.

[39] E.g. the 1474 trial of Peter von Hagenbach for crimes during the occupation of Breisach.   [40] See Chapter 6.

[41] Nuremberg IMT, Judgment and Sentences, reprinted in (1947) 41 *American Journal of International Law* 172, 218; von Leeb, XII LRTWC 1, 86–92.

[42] Art. 49 of Geneva Convention I; Art. 51 of Geneva Convention II; Art. 130 of Geneva Convention III; and Art. 147 of Geneva Convention IV. See Chapter 3 for a discussion of whether these provisions confer universal jurisdiction strictly so called.

[43] See Art. 2 of the ICTY Statute; Art. 8(2)(a) of the ICC Statute; and *Legality of the Threat or Use of Nuclear Weapons*, Advisory Opinion (1996) ICJ Reports 226, 8 July 1996, at paras. 79 and 82.

[44] Art. 85 AP I. But see the study of customary law undertaken under ICRC auspices: Henckaerts and Doswald-Beck, *ICRC Customary Law*.

list with five examples.[45] The ICTR Statute, designed to deal with an internal armed conflict, included serious violations of common Article 3 and Additional Protocol II of 1977 ('AP II'), featuring an open-ended list with eight examples.[46]

The ICC Statute, adopted in 1998, contains the longest and most comprehensive list of war crimes of any of the Tribunal Statutes. Unlike previous lists, however, the list in Article 8 is exhaustive. Some States, such as the United States, which had been quite content to impose an open-ended list upon others (Nuremberg, ICTY, ICTR) had a notable change of heart when confronted with a permanent court that could potentially apply to their own forces.[47] There may also have been a concern to avoid the initiatives of judge-made law within the ad hoc Tribunals.[48] In any event, despite the seeming double standards, an exhaustive list is certainly more consistent with criminal law principles, particularly the principle *nullum crimen sine lege*.

The ICC Statute contains an extensive list of fifty offences, including grave breaches of the Geneva Conventions, serious violations of common Article 3 and other serious violations drawn from various sources. Since the goal of the drafters was to reflect customary law rather than to create new law, many provisions from previous instruments were excluded because of a lack of consensus on their customary law status. The ICC list, while lengthy, does not include all war crimes recognized in customary law; an example often cited is the general prohibition on the use of chemical or biological weapons.[49] As expressly noted in Article 10 of the ICC Statute, the absence of a provision in the ICC Statute list does not affect its status as existing or developing international law.

The SCSL Statute and the Iraq Special Tribunal Statute included some of the key provisions in the ICC list. Article 14 of the Iraq Special Tribunal Statute copies the ICC Statute definitions, providing another instance of State practice confirming those definitions. The SCSL Statute includes violations of common Article 3 and a short list of other serious violations, reflecting certain crimes from the ICC Statute, namely, attacks directed against civilians, attacks on humanitarian aid workers and child conscription.[50]

In addition to the extensive list of war crimes in the ICC Statute, other war crimes may be identified in customary law and treaty law. As mentioned above, the ICC Statute is not a complete codification of all crimes in customary law, and hence other provisions may be identified applying the *Tadić* test, described in section 12.1.5. Moreover, war crimes may be established under treaty law – for example, among parties to AP I, the entire set of grave breaches in that Protocol is applicable as a matter of treaty law, regardless of whether they are also customary law.

---

[45] Art. 3 of the ICTY Statute. The list included use of poisonous weapons or weapons calculated to cause unnecessary suffering; wanton destruction; attack on undefended places; seizure or destruction of historic monuments, works of art, or institutions dedicated to certain purposes; and plunder.

[46] Art. 4 of the ICTR Statute. The list included murder, cruel treatment, torture, mutilation, collective punishments, hostage taking, terrorism, and outrages on dignity which includes rape, enforced prostitution and indecent assault, pillage, and passing sentences without proper trial.

[47] See Robert Cryer, *Prosecuting International Crimes* (Cambridge, 2005) 263–9.

[48] See William Schabas, *Introduction to the International Criminal Court* (Cambridge, 2001) 54.

[49] See section 12.3.7. Poisonous and asphyxiating gases are however included: Art. 8(2)(b)(xviii).

[50] Arts. 3 and 4 of the SCSL Statute.

12.1.7   *War crimes in internal armed conflicts*

Traditionally, neither IHL nor war crimes law applied in non-international armed conflicts. Before the advent of human rights law, States were regarded as entitled to deal with their own citizens more or less as they pleased, including in situations of rebellion and insurrection. This was an 'internal affair', in which other States should have no say. States sought to preserve latitude in putting down rebels, and they did not wish to bestow any possible recognition on rebel groups. Exceptionally, States involved in intense internal conflicts occasionally recognized a situation of 'belligerency', in which case IHL was applied to the conflict.[51]

During the negotiation of the four Geneva Conventions of 1949, several delegations pressed for recognition of rules in internal conflicts, a proposal strongly opposed by others.[52] After intense discussions, agreement was reached to include in each Convention a common Article – Article 3 – laying out some very basic norms recognized to apply even in internal armed conflicts. Even this very modest provision was an achievement.

Regulation of internal armed conflict was expanded significantly in AP II of 1977. Again, the negotiation was difficult, with many States opposing regulation. Agreement was reached on a short list of provisions, expanding upon and developing those rules in common Article 3 but still falling far short of that applicable to international armed conflict.[53]

Significantly, common Article 3 and AP II contained no grave breaches provisions, leading many to the conclusion that violations of those provisions were not criminalized. As of 1990, it was widely accepted that the law of war crimes did not apply in internal armed conflict.[54]

By the 1990s, the gap in coverage had become increasingly problematic, and several factors converged to precipitate a necessary legal evolution. First, internal conflicts had increased in magnitude and duration, causing vastly more civilian deaths than in previous centuries.[55] Second, internal conflicts had become more prevalent than international conflicts,[56] making change necessary if war crimes law was to have relevance for victims of conflict. Third, the increasing interdependence of States meant that internal conflicts had greater consequences for surrounding regions, increasing the urgency of regulating the conflicts. Fourth, the increased prioritization of human rights and human security meant

---

[51]   See e.g. Eric David, *Principes de droit des conflits armés*, 2nd edn (Brussels, 1999) 124–7; Lindsay Moir, *The Law of Internal Armed Conflict* (Cambridge, 2002) 3–21.

[52]   Jean Pictet, *Commentary to I Geneva Convention* (Geneva, 1952) 38–48.

[53]   Howard S. Levie, *The Law of Non-International Armed Conflict* (Dordrecht, 1987) 27–90; Michael Bothe, *New Rules for Victims of Armed Conflict* (The Hague, 1982) 605–8; Yves Sandoz *et al.*, *Commentary on the Additional Protocols of 8 June 1977* (Geneva, 1987) 1336.

[54]   '[A]ccording to humanitarian law as it stands today, the notion of war crimes is limited to situations of international armed conflict': ICRC DDM/JUR442 b, 25 March 1993, para. 4 (cited in the Separate Opinion of Judge Li, *Tadić*, ICTY A. Ch., 2 October 1995, para. 7); Denise Plattner, 'The Penal Repression of Violation of International Humanitarian Law' (1990) 30 *International Review of the Red Cross* 409.

[55]   UN Development Programme, *Human Development Report 2005* (UNDP, 2005) 153–61.

[56]   Human Security Centre, *Human Security Report 2005* (Oxford, 2005) 22–5.

that States were more willing to insist on extending protection even in contexts previously considered an 'internal affair'.[57]

The Security Council took the first major step forward when it adopted the ICTR Statute. Because the conflict in Rwanda was internal, the Council was confronted with the question of war crimes in internal conflict. The Council included in the Statute serious violations of common Article 3 and core provisions of AP II, thus expressly recognizing a criminalization of these prohibitions.

The *Tadić* decision on jurisdiction by the ICTY Appeals Chamber had a considerable impact on the development of the law in this area.[58] The decision reviewed State practice, resolutions of the League of Nations, General Assembly, Security Council and European Union, ICJ decisions, military codes of conduct, and agreements and understandings, and concluded that the traditional stark dichotomy between international and internal conflicts was becoming blurred, and that some war crimes provisions were now applicable in internal armed conflicts. The Chamber held that there had not been a wholesale transposition or a complete convergence, but rather that '*only a number of rules* and principles ... have gradually been extended to apply to internal conflicts'.[59] Moreover, 'this extension has not taken place in the form of a full and mechanical transplant of those rules to internal conflicts; rather, *the general essence* of those rules, and not the detailed regulation they may contain, has become applicable to internal conflicts'.[60] To determine whether a norm also applies in internal armed conflict, one must consider: whether there is clear and unequivocal recognition of the norm, State practice indicating an intention to criminalize the norm, the gravity of the acts, and the interest of the international community in their prohibition.[61]

The *Tadić* decision was seen as groundbreaking at the time,[62] but it was rapidly digested by the international community. The approach was followed soon afterward by the ICTR,[63] and, more significantly, it received a remarkable level of State acceptance during the negotiation of the ICC Statute.[64] Although a determined minority in Rome strongly opposed the inclusion of war crimes in internal conflicts, a clear majority was equally strongly committed to their inclusion. Opposition gave way to acceptance of common Article 3 and a limited list of other fundamental provisions in the Statute. Significantly, the approach taken by the Rome Conference largely followed that of *Tadić*: identifying fundamental prohibitions and transposing them to internal conflicts.[65]

---

[57] *Tadić*, ICTY A. Ch., 2 October 1995, paras. 94–6; and see the discussion in e.g. Theodor Meron, 'International Criminalization of Internal Atrocities' (1995) 89 *American Journal of International Law* 554; Darryl Robinson and Herman von Hebel, 'War Crimes in Internal Conflicts: Art. 8 of the ICC Statute' (1999) 2 *Yearbook of International Humanitarian Law* 193.

[58] *Tadić*, ICTY A. Ch., 2 October 1995.   [59] *Ibid.*, para. 126.   [60] *Ibid.*   [61] *Ibid.*, paras. 128 and 129.

[62] See e.g. Christopher Greenwood, 'International Humanitarian Law and the Tadić Case' (1996) 7 *European Journal of International Law* 265; George Aldrich, 'Jurisdiction of the International Criminal Tribunal for the Former Yugoslavia' (1996) 90 *American Journal of International Law* 64; Geoffrey Watson, 'The Humanitarian Law of the Yugoslavia War Crimes Tribunal: Jurisdiction in Prosecutor v. Tadić' (1996) 36 *Virginia Journal of International Law* 687.

[63] *Kanyabashi*, ICTR T. Ch. II, 18 June 1997, para. 8.

[64] In effect, the theory of partial convergence of the law of international and internal armed conflicts was put to the international community: Claus Kreß, 'War Crimes Committed in Non-International Armed Conflict and the Emerging System of International Criminal Justice' (2001) 30 *Israel Yearbook on Human Rights* 1, 5; Moir, *Law of Internal Conflict*, 160–7.

[65] Robinson and von Hebel, 'War Crimes', 197–200.

In the result, roughly half of the provisions from international conflicts were transplanted to internal conflicts in the ICC Statute. For other provisions, there was not consensus that they were so fundamental that customary law at that point recognized them in internal conflicts. While the recognition of half of the provisions was a remarkable achievement in 1998, there is good reason to believe that the list of war crimes in Article 8(2)(e) falls short of the list that the *Tadić* test would permit. For example, the prohibition of starvation as a means of warfare, the use of chemical weapons, attacking civilian objects, and launching disproportionate attacks, are all fundamental provisions with long recognition in the laws and customs of war, and hence merit recognition in internal conflicts.[66] Indeed, the incompleteness of the list in Article 8(2)(e) produces a number of strange consequences.[67] As noted in section 12.1.6, Article 10 affirms that nothing in the ICC Statute limits or prejudices the development of other international law.

It has been suggested that the ICC Statute is 'retrograde' in that it did not abolish completely the international–internal distinction.[68] However, while the trend certainly favours continued convergence, State practice and *opinio iuris* do not currently support the view that the two regimes have become identical. Indeed, even the trend-leading *Tadić* decision did not assert that there had been a full and mechanical transplant of rules from international conflicts to their internal counterparts, but rather that the essence of some of the most important rules was applicable. Moreover, some provisions from international armed conflict simply would not make sense in internal conflict, particularly provisions concerning occupied territory and prisoners-of-war.[69]

The law does, however, continue to move towards increased convergence. A major ICRC study of customary law suggested a large degree of convergence in the law for different types of conflicts.[70] In 2010, the Kampala Review Conference amended the ICC Statute to reflect that poisoned weapons, asphyxiating gases, and 'dum-dum' bullets (see section 12.3.6) are prohibited in internal armed conflict as well as international armed conflict.[71]

Given the convergence already recognized, it would already at this point in time be useful in any future catalogues of war crimes to consolidate those provisions that are common to both internal and international conflicts. The bifurcated structure in the current Statutes can create unnecessary complications, because it requires a determination of the character of an armed conflict in order to know which provisions to charge (for example, Article 8(2)(b) or 8(2)(e)), even where the provisions are similar or identical. It may be necessary to collect evidence and litigate on complex issues, such as the role of third States,[72] which are quite irrelevant to the role and liability of the perpetrator and the gravamen of the offence. Indeed,

---

[66] Kreß, 'War Crimes', 37, 39.   [67] *Ibid.*

[68] Antonio Cassese, 'The Statute of the International Criminal Court: Some Preliminary Reflections' (1999) 10 *European Journal of International Law* 149, 150.

[69] Sandesh Sivakumaran, 'Re-Envisaging the International Law of Internal Armed Conflict' (2011) 22 *European Journal of International Law* 219, discusses the limits of transposing rules from international to internal armed conflict, and the need to consider differences, such as the capabilities of non-State armed groups. See also Sandesh Sivakumaran, *The Law of Non-International Armed Conflict* (Oxford, 2012) especially at 65–77.

[70] Henckaerts and Doswald-Beck, *ICRC Customary Law.*

[71] Amal Alamuddin and Philippa Webb, 'Expanding Jurisdiction over War Crimes under Article 8 of the ICC Statute' (2010) 8 *Journal of International Criminal Justice* 1219.

[72] See section 12.2.2.

this problem has already arisen in the first case to be tried by the ICC, the *Lubanga* case. The Prosecutor characterized the conflict as internal, the Pre-Trial Chamber recharacterized the conflict as international, and the Trial Chamber concluded it was an internal armed conflict, all of which was irrelevant to the criminal wrongdoing, yet necessary to determine whether charges should fall under Article 8(2)(b) or 8(2)(e).[73]

The ICTY has partially sidestepped such problems by relying heavily on common Article 3 and other provisions applicable in internal conflicts, on the ground that these more limited provisions apply in all conflicts.[74] In any future catalogue of war crimes, it would be more efficient to establish one list of crimes applicable in both international and internal conflicts, and a short list of those crimes applicable only in international conflict.[75] Such a list would not entail any change in customary law, but would simply be a clearer presentation of the existing legal situation.

12.2   Common issues

12.2.1   *Armed conflict*

The essential element for any war crime is the nexus with armed conflict. It is the insecure and volatile situation of armed conflict that warrants international interest and gives rise to international jurisdiction over the crime. Whereas early IHL depended on a declaration of a state of war, this was problematic in that parties to conflict might raise formalistic arguments denying a state of war.[76] Current IHL and war crimes law therefore focus on the objective existence of armed conflict, even if one or both of the parties deny the state of war.[77]

In the case of internal conflict, a certain threshold of intensity and organization must be met, in order to distinguish armed conflict from mere internal disturbances and riots, as is discussed below.[78] In the case of State-to-State conflict, most authorities indicate that *any* resort to force involving military forces amounts to armed conflict.[79]

---

[73] *Lubanga*, ICC PTC I, 29 January 2007, paras. 200–37; *Lubanga*, ICC T. Ch. I, 14 March 2012, paras. 503–67.

[74] *Delalic*, ICTY A. Ch., 20 February 2001, para. 150 (holding that prohibitions from internal armed conflict also apply in international armed conflict since the latter has broader regulation). See also the *Nicaragua* case of the ICJ, holding that common Art. 3 applies to all forms of conflict: *Case Concerning Military and Paramilitary Activities in and against Nicaragua (Nicaragua v. USA)*, Merits, (1986) ICJ Reports 14, para. 218. And see S. Boelaert-Suominen, 'The Yugoslavia Tribunal and the Common Core of Humanitarian Law Applicable to All Armed Conflicts' (2000) 13 *Journal of International Law* 619.

[75] As a model, see the German Code of Crimes against International Law, reproduced in e.g. Gerhard Werle, *Principles of International Criminal Law* (The Hague, 2005) 428–33.

[76] Pictet, *Commentary to I Geneva Convention*, 32–3.   [77] See e.g. common Art. 2 to the Geneva Conventions.

[78] See section 12.2.3.

[79] Tribunal jurisprudence requires 'protracted' violence for internal conflict but not for State-to-State conflict: *Tadić*, ICTY A. Ch., 2 October 1995, para. 70. According to the ICRC commentary on the Geneva Conventions, the concept of armed conflict includes 'any difference arising between two States and leading to the intervention of members of the armed forces': Pictet, *Commentary to I Geneva Convention*, 20; and see the discussion in Claus Kreß, 'The 1999 Crisis in East Timor and the Threshold of the Law of War Crimes' (2002) 13 *Criminal Law Forum* 409, 412–13; Dapo Akande, 'Classification of Armed Conflicts: Relevant Legal Concepts' in Elizabeth Wilmshurst (ed.), *International Law and the Classification of Conflict* (Oxford, 2012) 32, 41.

The concept of armed conflict includes not only the application of force between armed forces, but also an invasion that meets no resistance,[80] aerial bombing, or an unauthorized border crossing by armed forces.

The state of armed conflict does not end with each particular ceasefire; rather, it continues until the 'general close of military operations'.[81] According to Tribunal jurisprudence, the state of armed conflict extends 'until a general conclusion of peace is reached, or in the case of internal armed conflict, until a peaceful settlement is achieved'.[82] The state of conflict may also be ended by a decisive close of military operations even without an agreement.[83] The state of armed conflict also applies during occupation, that is to say, when territory is placed under the authority of a hostile army.[84]

12.2.2   *Distinguishing between international and internal conflicts*

The paradigmatic situation of international armed conflict is the resort to force between the military forces of States. Complex issues arise outside this paradigm, with respect to wars of national liberation, UN enforcement operations and foreign intervention through proxy forces.[85]

Wars of national liberation

According to Article 1(4) of AP I, the concept of international armed conflict also includes conflicts in which 'peoples are fighting against colonial domination and alien occupation and against racist regimes in the exercise of their right of self-determination'. This definition applies, as a matter of treaty law, to any prosecutions based on the grave breaches regime of AP I.[86]

The more difficult question is whether this expansion of the concept of international armed conflict also applies in the general law of war crimes.[87] On the one hand, if the question is answered in the negative, parties to AP I would be simultaneously subject to two regimes: an international conflict regime under AP I and an internal conflict regime under (for example) the ICC Statute, which would seem an undesirable result. On the other hand, if the question is answered in the affirmative, the AP I definition might be applied in conflicts where the parties had not ratified AP I, which would also seem undesirable.

---

[80] Art. 2 of Geneva Convention I.   [81] Art. 6 of Geneva Convention IV.
[82] *Tadić*, ICTY A. Ch., 2 October 1995, para. 70. In addition, '[u]ntil that moment, international humanitarian law continues to apply in the whole territory of the warring States or, in the case of internal conflicts, the whole territory under control of a party, whether or not actual combat takes place there'.
[83] Art. 6 of Geneva Convention IV; Christopher Greenwood, 'The Scope of Application of Humanitarian Law' in Fleck, *Handbook*, 72; see also SC Res. 95(1951), finding an interdiction by Egypt to be contrary to an armistice agreement (even without a general peace treaty).
[84] See e.g. Art. 52 of the 1907 Hague Regulations; Art. 6 of Geneva Convention IV; ICC Elements of Crimes, footnote 34; *Naletilić*, ICTY T. Ch. I, 31 March 2003, paras. 214–17.
[85] The complexities of these distinctions have further strengthened calls for a single body of IHL applicable in all conflicts: James Stewart, 'Toward a Single Definition of Armed Conflict in International Humanitarian Law: A Critique of Internationalized Armed Conflict' (2003) 85 *International Review of the Red Cross* 313.
[86] Art. 85 of AP I.   [87] See e.g. discussion in Andreas Zimmerman, 'Article 8' in Triffterer, *Observers' Notes*, 479–80.

The answer to the question seems to hinge on whether the AP I definition can be regarded as customary law.[88] The scant State practice makes it prudent to avoid any hasty pronouncements on that provision's customary status. The paradigmatic case of a people with a clear historic national identity resisting colonial domination can be more readily seen as 'international'. On the other hand, a conflict involving local oppressed groups fighting against a discriminatory regime, may well be a worthy cause but it would seem counterfactual to describe it as 'international'.[89]

UN forces

Another interesting question is the legal effect of intervention by UN enforcement operations. It was once questioned whether IHL applies at all to such forces. After all, the UN is an international organization and hence not party *per se* to the Geneva Conventions and other IHL treaties. It is now recognized that the law of armed conflict applies to the operations of UN forces: the UN has accepted and declared that the fundamental principles and rules of IHL apply to UN forces.[90] Participants in a conflict cannot be exempted from basic principles of IHL because they are fighting in a just cause (maintenance of international peace and security). Experience shows, regrettably, that even peacekeeping forces may be involved in IHL violations and war crimes.

The remaining question is whether the intervention of UN forces – whether operations under the UN flag or simply approved by the UN – can render a previously internal conflict an international one. The law on this point does not appear to be settled. To regard UN forces as being 'parties to a conflict' may seem inimical to the role of the UN, and one could argue that an otherwise internal conflict remains internal.[91] However, this may be blurring the issue of the justness of the cause with the issue of whether forces are in fact engaged in armed conflict. The practice on this question is ambiguous.[92] Where UN forces intervene with a State's consent in order to support it, the conflict may remain internal (as there is no clash between States); conversely, where UN troops apply significant force *against* a State's forces, the conflict would seem to be international.[93]

---

[88] The ICC might be able to avoid the problem by insisting that it applies only the terms of Arts. 8(2)(d) and (f), which do not include 'national liberation' as a factor. The fact that Art. 8 repeatedly refers to the 'established framework of international law' may, however, drive the Court back into an analysis of customary international law.

[89] Doubting the customary law status, see Akande, 'Classification of Armed Conflict' at 49. On the fundamental separation between 'just cause' and IHL, see section 12.1.3.

[90] Secretary-General's Bulletin: Observance by United Nations Forces of International Humanitarian Law, 6 August 1999, UN Doc. ST/SGB/1999/13; Ray Murphy, 'United Nations Military Operations and International Humanitarian Law: What Rules Apply to Peacekeepers?' (2003) 14 *Criminal Law Forum* 153.

[91] See e.g. Dietrich Schindler, 'The Different Types of Armed Conflicts According to the Geneva Conventions and Protocols' (1979) 163 *Hague Recueil* 121, 151.

[92] Christopher Greenwood, 'International Humanitarian Law and United Nations Military Operations' (1998) 3 *Yearbook of International Humanitarian Law* 3.

[93] Akande, 'Classification of Armed Conflicts', 64–70. Where UN peacekeepers are not engaged in a major enforcement measure, but simply use force in self-defence, they are arguably not engaged in armed conflict: *Abu Garda*, ICC PTC I, 8 February 2010, para. 83.

Proxy forces

A seemingly internal conflict may be rendered international where it is found that local armed groups are in fact acting on behalf of an external State. For example, in the *Tadić* case, the determination of whether the grave breaches provision applied depended on whether the conflict was international, which in turn depended on whether acts of certain forces in Bosnia (the VRS) were attributable to the Federal Republic of Yugoslavia. The Federal Republic of Yugoslavia (FRY) had purported to withdraw its forces (the JNA) from Bosnia, but left behind the VRS, composed of former JNA soldiers of Bosnian origin, with the same officers, the same weapons, the same equipment, the same suppliers and the same objectives, with funding still coming from the FRY.

The majority of the Trial Chamber referred to the ICJ's decision in the *Nicaragua* case, which had adopted a stringent 'effective control' test to determine whether acts of an armed band could be attributed to a State.[94] The majority in the Trial Chamber found that, while the FRY had the capacity to direct operations, there was no evidence of specific orders or that the FRY had actually directed operations.[95] The decision was criticized in a powerful dissent and in commentary for not reflecting the reality of the situation.[96]

The Appeals Chamber replaced the test of 'effective control' with a more flexible test of 'overall control' over armed groups.[97] Under the 'overall control' test, it is not necessary to produce evidence of specific orders or instructions relating to particular military actions.[98] It is sufficient to establish 'overall control going beyond the mere financing and equipping of such forces and involving also participation in the planning and supervision of military operations'.[99] The Appeals Chamber's approach has been adopted by others as the test for determining whether external involvement internationalizes a conflict,[100] but the decision has raised some controversies,[101] and the matter is not necessarily settled.[102]

Transnational conflict

Another contemporary situation that is not well addressed by the Geneva Conventions is where a State engages in conflict with a non-State armed group on the territory of another State.[103] Examples include the conflict between Uganda and armed groups roaming in the the Democratic Republic of the Congo, or US attacks on Al Qaeda personnel in Pakistan. On

[94] *Case Concerning Military and Paramilitary Activities in and against Nicaragua (Nicaragua v. USA)*, Merits, (1986) ICJ Reports 14, para. 115.
[95] *Tadić*, ICTY T. Ch. II, 7 May 1997, paras. 588–607.
[96] McDonald, Dissent in *Tadić*, ICTY T. Ch. II, 7 May 1997; see e.g. Theodor Meron, 'Classification of Armed Conflict in the Former Yugoslavia: *Nicaragua's* Fallout' (1998) 92 *American Journal of International Law* 236.
[97] *Tadić*, ICTY A. Ch., 15 July 1999, para. 137.   [98] *Ibid.*, para. 145.   [99] *Ibid.*
[100] The test has been adopted by the ICC: see e.g. *Lubanga*, ICC T. Ch. I, 14 March 2012, para. 540.
[101] In a subsequent case, the ICJ disapproved of the ICTY Appeals Chamber's purported distinguishing of *Nicaragua* and its pronouncements on general international law. The ICJ conceded, without deciding, that 'overall control' may be an appropriate test for determining the character of armed conflict in international criminal law, but it is not an appropriate test for determining the responsibility of States under general international law: *Case Concerning the Application of the Convention on the Prevention and Punishment of Genocide (Bosnia and Herzegovina v. Serbia and Montenegro)*, ICJ General List 91, paras. 402–7.
[102] James Crawford, *State Responsibility: The General Part* (Cambridge, 2013) 145–56.
[103] See generally Claus Kreß, 'Some Reflections on the International Legal Framework Governing Transnational Armed Conflicts' (2010) 15 *Journal of Conflict and Security Law* 245.

the one hand, such a conflict does not involve a clash between the forces of two States, and hence does not seem 'international'. On the other hand, the conflict is not entirely within the territory of a single State, and thus it is not purely 'internal' in the classic sense. Where the intervening State is engaging only with the armed group, and the armed group is not affiliated with the territorial State, views differ on the correct characterization. There is some State practice and jurisprudence in favour of treating such conflicts as non-international.[104] This may sound counter-intuitive, because the action crosses borders and affects the interests of another State, but it may be the most plausible approach, given that an armed group cannot necessarily fulfil all of the obligations applicable in international armed conflicts.

12.2.3 *Distinguishing internal conflict from riots and disturbances*

The previous section discussed the line between international and internal armed conflict. There is also a lower threshold, dividing situations of sufficient intensity to be called 'armed conflict' from lesser situations of riots and disturbances, which are insufficient to activate IHL and the law of war crimes. It is sometimes difficult to determine the point at which mere civil strife crosses the threshold to amount to internal armed conflict.

The widely accepted test to distinguish armed conflicts from mere riots or disturbances focuses on two criteria: (1) the intensity of the conflict and (2) the organization of the parties. The test was first elaborated by the ICTY Appeals Chamber in the *Tadić* case, which stated that 'armed conflict exists whenever there is a resort to armed force between States or *protracted armed violence* between governmental authorities and *organised armed groups* or between such groups within a State'.[105] The test has been adopted by the ICTR, the SCSL and the ICC, and is widely accepted as the applicable test.[106]

The 'intensity' requirement is that the armed violence be 'protracted' rather than sporadic or isolated. Relevant factors include the seriousness of attacks, their geographic spread and temporal persistence, the mobilization of government forces, the distribution of weapons and whether the situation has attracted the attention of the UN Security Council.[107] It is worth repeating that the intensity threshold is not required in conflicts between States, where any resort to force warrants regulation by IHL (see section 12.2.2); it is required in internal

---

[104] *Lubanga*, ICC T. Ch. I, 14 March 2012, para. 541; *Hamdan* v. *Rumsfeld*, 126 S Ct 2749, 2757 (2006); and see the examples in Sivakumaran, *Non-International Armed Conflict*, 228–32. But see also Akande, 'Classification of Armed Conflict', 70–9, for authorities for the position that the conflict would be international. Some scholars suggest that transnational armed conflicts require a distinct legal regime.

[105] *Tadić*, ICTY A. Ch., 2 October 1995, para. 70 (emphasis added).

[106] See e.g. *Akayesu*, ICTR T. Ch., 12 September 1998, paras. 619–20; *Taylor*, SCSL T. Ch., 18 May 2012, paras. 563–4; *Lubanga*, ICC T. Ch., 14 March 2012, paras. 534–8.

[107] *Tadić*, ICTY T. Ch. II, 7 May 1997, paras. 562–7; *Akayesu*, ICTR T. Ch., 12 September 1998, paras. 619–20; *Lubanga*, ICC T. Ch. I, 14 March 2012, para. 538. The Inter-American Human Rights Commission appears to have applied a rather lower threshold for the 'protracted' nature of the conflict. An attack by forty-two persons on military barracks, resulting in a military response to retake the barracks, lasting around thirty hours and resulting in the deaths of twenty-nine attackers and several State agents, was found sufficient to constitute an armed conflict: *La Tablada*, IACHR Report No. 55/97, Case No. 11.137, Argentina; OEA/L/V/II.97, Doc. 38, 20 October 1997.

armed conflicts, in order to distinguish them from banditry, terrorism or short-lived insurrections.

As for the 'organisation of the parties' requirement, courts have looked at various non-exhaustive factors. For example, in the *Haradinaj* case, an ICTY Chamber referred to factors such as the existence of a command structure, disciplinary mechanisms, head-quarters, control of territory, access to weapons, military training, ability to plan and carry out military operations, and ability to speak with one voice and negotiate and conclude agreements such as ceasefire or peace accords.[108] In the *Lubanga* case, an ICC Chamber summarized past jurisprudence as referring to factors such as internal hierarchy, command structure, equipment and weapons, ability to plan and carry out military operations, and extent of military involvement.[109]

A slightly higher threshold appears in Additional Protocol II, which led to the question of whether the customary law of war crimes might entail different thresholds for different crimes (for example, common Article 3 and AP II crimes). AP II stipulates that it only applies to armed conflicts:

which take place in the territory of a High Contracting Party between its armed forces and dissident armed forces or other organized groups which, under responsible command, exercise such control over a part of its territory as to enable them to carry out sustained and concerted military operations and to implement this protocol.[110]

Among the unique requirements in AP II are that one party must be a State (as opposed to group versus group conflict) and that the armed group must have control over territory. While those requirements apply under AP II as a matter of treaty law, they have not been accepted as part of the general customary international law of war crimes. Tribunal juris-prudence and the ICC Statute recognize armed conflict entirely between armed groups.[111] Control of territory has been accepted as an indicative factor as to the existence of an armed conflict, but it was rejected as a requirement in Tribunal jurisprudence and the ICC Statute, although it has been recognized as an important *indicative factor*.[112] Thus, these restrictions may continue to limit the applicability of AP II as a matter of treaty law, but they do not affect the interpretation of 'armed conflict' in the customary law of war crimes.[113]

---

[108] *Haradinaj*, ICTY T. Ch., 3 April 2008, paras. 37–60. Helpful indicators are also listed in *Boskoski and Tarculovski*, ICTY T. Ch., 10 July 2008, paras. 175–205.

[109] *Lubanga*, ICC T. Ch. I, 14 March 2012, para. 537. For a more thorough review of the jurisprudence, see Sivakumaran, Non-International Armed Conflict 167–80.

[110] Art. 1(1) of AP II. Green, *Contemporary Law*, 67, regards the test as 'so high that it would exclude most revolutions and rebellions'.

[111] Art. 8(2)(f) of the ICC Statute; *Tadić*, ICTY A. Ch., 2 October 1995, para. 70.

[112] Art. 8(2)(f) of the ICC Statute; *Akayesu*, ICTR T. Ch. I, 2 September 1998, paras. 619–20. An ICC Pre-Trial Chamber referred to control of territory as a 'key' factor (*Situation in Darfur (Al Bashir* arrest warrant case), ICC PTC I, 4 March 2009, para. 60) which is an unfortunate wording in so far as it may suggest the factor is almost indispensable, given that it was expressly rejected by the ICC Statute drafters. See e.g. Robert Cryer, 'International Crimes in the Al Bashir Arrest Warrant Decision' (2009) 7 *Journal of International Criminal Justice* 283, 285–6. The *Lubanga* Pre-Trial Chamber confirmed that territorial control is not a requirement: *Lubanga*, ICC PTC I, 29 January 2007, para. 233.

[113] As discussed in cases such as *Tadić*, ICTY A. Ch., 2 October 1995, para. 70; *Akayesu*, ICTR T. Ch. I, 2 September 1998, paras. 619–20; *Lubanga*, ICC PTC I, 29 January 2007, para. 233.

Similarly, Article 8(2)(f) of the ICC Statute lays out what may appear to be an additional threshold for war crimes other than those in common Article 3, as it refers to 'protracted armed *conflict*'[114] rather than 'protracted *violence*'. This appears to have been a straightforward drafting error, since the intent was to incorporate the threshold from *Tadić*, not to exclude a class of armed conflicts.[115] The French version of the Statute indicates that the intent was to refer to the established concept of 'protracted violence', which is already applicable to all war crimes in internal conflict.[116] Indeed, early ICC cases have interpreted the term in the same manner as Tribunal jurisprudence.[117] Thus, it should not be interpreted as creating different thresholds for different crimes.[118]

In summary, the jurisprudence of the various international criminal tribunals, as well as other authorities, agree on the 'intensity' and 'organisation' tests and a single, consistent threshold to identify internal armed conflicts.[119]

12.2.4   *Nexus between conduct and conflict*

In order to constitute a war crime, conduct must be linked to an armed conflict. For example, the ICC Elements of Crimes require that the conduct be committed 'in the context of and associated with' an armed conflict.[120]

The term 'in the context of' refers to the temporal and geographic context in a broad sense: the conduct occurred during an armed conflict and on a territory in which there is an armed conflict.[121] This requirement is very general, since a state of armed conflict is recognized throughout the territory, beyond the time and place of the hostilities.[122] There is no need for military activities at the time and place of the crime; crimes can be temporally and geographically remote from the actual fighting.[123]

The phrase 'associated with' refers to the specific nexus between the conduct of the perpetrator and the conflict, and matches the ICTY requirement that the conduct be 'closely related to' the conflict.[124] Not all criminal activity on a territory experiencing armed conflict amounts to a war crime. For example, if a person kills a neighbour purely out of jealousy or

---

[114] Art. 8(2)(f).

[115] Kreß, 'War Crimes', 15–17. See also Sandesh Sivakumaran, 'Identifying an Armed Conflict Not of an International Character' in Stahn and Sluiter, *Emerging Practice*, 363.

[116] *Tadić*, ICTY A. Ch., 2 October 1995, para. 70.

[117] *Lubanga*, ICC PTC I, 29 January 2007, para. 234; *Al Bashir* arrest warrant case, ICC PTC I, 4 March 2009, para. 60.

[118] Kreß, 'War Crimes', 15–17; Meron, 'Humanization', 260; Sandesh Sivakumaran, 'Identifying an Armed Conflict Not of an International Character' in Stahn and Sluiter, *Emerging Practice*, 363.

[119] In a similar vein, see International Committee of the Red Cross, Opinion Paper, 'How Is the Term "Armed Conflict" Defined in International Law', March 2008, available at www.icrc.org.

[120] See e.g. ICC Elements of Crimes, Art. 8(2)(a)–I. The test was referenced by the ICTR in *Kayishema*, ICTR T. Ch. II, 21 May 1999, para. 187, although the Chamber ultimately declined to articulate a legal test: *ibid.*, para. 188.

[121] Knut Dörmann, Eve La Haye and Herman von Hebel, 'War Crimes' in Lee, *Elements and Rules*, 120–1.

[122] *Tadić*, ICTY A. Ch., 2 October 1995, para. 70.   [123] *Kunarac*, ICTY A. Ch., 12 June 2002, para. 57.

[124] *Tadić*, ICTY A. Ch., 2 October 1995, para. 70. While some nexus is needed, the crime need not be committed during combat, nor need it be part of a policy or practice or in the interests of a party to the conflict: *Tadić*, ICTY T. Ch. II, 7 May 1997, paras. 572–3.

because of a private dispute over land, and this happens to occur during an armed conflict, that is not a war crime.[125]

In the *Kunarac* judgment, the ICTY Appeals Chamber provided a helpful elaboration of this test, focusing on whether the existence of conflict played a substantial part in the perpetrator's *ability* to commit a crime, his *decision* to commit it, the *manner* in which it was committed or the *purpose* for which it was committed.[126] Hence, it is sufficient that the perpetrator acted in furtherance of or under the guise of the armed conflict.[127] In assessing these questions, one may take into account, *inter alia*, the following factors: the status of perpetrator (for example, combatant); the status of the victim (for example, non-combatant, combatant of opposing party); whether the act serves a goal of a military campaign; and whether it was committed in the context of the perpetrator's official duties.[128]

12.2.5   The perpetrator

The law of war crimes does not govern only members of armed forces or groups and their leaders. The fact that a perpetrator is a member of an armed force does help to establish the nexus to armed conflict, but it is not a requirement.[129] The conduct of civilians can be a war crime even if it is not imputable to a party to the conflict, provided that the nexus requirement is met.[130]

A more difficult question is whether the perpetrator must have some awareness of the armed conflict. Early Tribunal jurisprudence did not inquire into knowledge of the conflict,[131] which suggests either that the judges saw the existence of the conflict as a purely jurisdictional matter or that they saw the knowledge as obvious. In *Kordić* and subsequent cases, the ICTY Appeals Chamber indicated that the knowledge of the accused of the fact of armed conflict is indeed required, as the conflict is an element of the crime.[132]

Similarly, the ICC Elements of Crimes[133] indicate that a person cannot be convicted as a war criminal unless he or she has the necessary awareness of the factual circumstances that make the conduct a war crime. The final element for each war crime requires that the perpetrator was 'aware of factual circumstances that established the existence of an armed conflict'.[134] The knowledge requirement in the Elements is clarified or attenuated in three ways. First, the Introduction to War Crimes clarifies that no *legal*

---

[125] Knut Dörmann, *Elements of War Crimes under the Rome Statute of the International Criminal Court* (Cambridge, 2003) 19–20.

[126] See *Kunarac*, ICTY A. Ch., 12 June 2002, para. 58.   [127] *Ibid.*

[128] *Kunarac*, ICTY A. Ch., 12 June 2002, para. 59; *Rutaganda*, ICTR A. Ch., 26 May 2003, para. 569.

[129] *Akayesu*, ICTR A. Ch., 1 June 2001, paras. 444–5.

[130] See e.g. the *Essen Lynching Trial*, I LRTWC 88; *Tesch* (the 'Zyklon B case'), I LRTWC 93.

[131] *Tadić*, ICTY T. Ch. II, 7 May 1997, para. 572.

[132] *Kordić*, ICTY A. Ch., 17 December 2004, para. 311; *Naletilić*, ICTY A. Ch., 3 May 2006, paras. 116–20. In both cases, the Appeals Chamber required knowledge of 'the *factual* circumstances, e.g. that a foreign state was involved in the armed conflict' (emphasis in original). This test is more onerous than that in the ICC Elements of Crimes, where knowledge of the international character of the conflict is not required: ICC Elements of Crimes, Introduction to War Crimes, para. 3.

[133] Dörmann, La Haye and von Hebel, 'War Crimes' in Lee, *Elements and Rules*, 121–3. Some national jurisprudence reaches the same conclusion: see e.g. the Supreme Court of Canada decision of *R v. Finta* [1994] 1 SCR 701, 820.

[134] See e.g. ICC Elements of Crimes, Art. 8(2)(a)(i), Element 5.

evaluation by the perpetrator is required; it is sufficient that the accused be aware of the facts.[135] Second, the Introduction clarifies that there is no requirement of awareness of the factual circumstances establishing the *character* of the conflict as international or internal.[136] Third, and most remarkably, the Introduction states that:

There is only a requirement for the awareness of the factual circumstances that established the existence of an armed conflict that is implicit in the terms 'took place in the context of and was associated with'.

The result is not a model of legislative clarity, but it appears to require only sufficient factual awareness so that the crime may be said objectively to meet the 'associated with' or 'closely related' test.[137] The judges are left ample room to clarify based on relevant facts. In any event, the issue seems to be of theoretical interest rather than practical importance, since it is difficult to conceive of situations where a perpetrator's conduct could satisfy the nexus to conflict, while the perpetrator was somehow unaware of the armed conflict going on around him or her.

12.2.6 *The victim or object of the crime*

The definitions of many war crimes include certain criteria with respect to the victim (or object) of the crime. For example, for grave breaches of the Geneva Conventions, the crime must affect 'protected persons or objects'.[138] Protected persons include civilians, prisoners-of-war and combatants who are no longer able to fight because they are sick, wounded or shipwrecked.[139] Similarly, common Article 3 protects 'persons no longer taking active part in hostilities, including members of armed forces who have laid down their arms and those placed *hors de combat* by sickness, wounds, detention or other cause'. These restrictions are necessary because some acts, such as wilful killing, are not a crime when committed against a combatant.

Other war crimes specify a particular victim or object of the crime (for example, civilian population, civilian objects, persons involved in humanitarian assistance, undefended towns, etc.).[140] Some war crimes regulate battlefield conduct, to reduce unnecessary suffering of combatants, and hence even combatants are protected as victims of the crime.[141]

Because IHL originally developed as a series of reciprocal promises between parties to a conflict, most of IHL regulates conduct towards those affiliated with the 'enemy'.[142] For this reason, many war crimes require that the victim be 'in the hands of'[143] or 'in the power

---

[135] ICC Elements of Crimes, Introduction to War Crimes, para. 3. [136] *Ibid.* [137] See section 12.2.4.
[138] See e.g. Art. 147 of Geneva Convention IV; Art. 8(2)(a) of the ICC Statute; and Art. 2 of the ICTY Statute.
[139] See e.g. Arts. 12 and 13 of Geneva Convention I; Arts. 12 and 13 of Geneva Convention II; Art. 4 of Geneva Convention III; and Art. 4 of Geneva Convention IV.
[140] Art. 8(2)(b)(i)–(v) of the ICC Statute. [141] See e.g. Art. 8(2)(b)(vi), (vii), (xi), (xii) and (xvii)–(xx).
[142] There are exceptions; for example, Art. 75 of AP I protects *all* persons in the hands of a party to conflict; and see section 12.3.8 concerning child soldiers. As the emphasis has shifted to the duty of any party towards victims of conflict, the role of reciprocity is diminishing in IHL, although it is still significant: see René Provost, *International Human Rights and Humanitarian Law* (Cambridge, 2002) 121–238. Sivakumaran, *Non-International Armed Conflict*, 246–9, argues that many IHL provisions now protect persons on the 'same side'.
[143] Art. 4 of Geneva Convention IV.

of'[144] an adverse party.[145] Some of the most important protections for civilians arise in Geneva Convention IV, which protects persons 'who find themselves, in case of a conflict or occupation, in the hands of a Party to the conflict or Occupying Power of which they are not nationals'.[146] This provision was drafted bearing in mind a classic State-to-State international armed conflict.

However, recent history has shown that conflicts can be far more complex. The armed conflict in Bosnia was international in character, due to the involvement of neighbouring States, yet it was also predominantly an ethnic conflict. Persons were frequently detained by, and abused by, persons of another ethnic group, that is to say, a different party to the conflict, yet they were all of the same nationality. Applying the Geneva Conventions literally, the victims would not be entitled to protection, because all concerned held the same passport, even though they were in fact hostile forces.

In the *Tadić* decision, the ICTY Appeals Chamber held that the crucial test is allegiance, and that ethnicity rather than nationality may become the ground of allegiance.[147] Thus, the Chamber chose to look at the substance of the relations rather than formalities.[148]

12.2.7   *The 'jurisdictional' threshold in the ICC Statute*

Article 8(1) of the ICC Statute provides that the ICC 'shall have jurisdiction in respect of war crimes in particular when committed as part of a plan or policy or as part of a large-scale commission of such crimes'. It must be emphasized that this is not an element of a war crime; unlike crimes against humanity, even a single isolated act can constitute a war crime. Article 8(1) is rather an indicator to the ICC as to how it ought to exercise its jurisdiction; namely, to focus its resources not on isolated war crimes but on the most serious situations. The term 'large scale' is either synonymous with, or less demanding than, the 'widespread' element of crimes against humanity, and 'plan or policy' is less demanding than 'systematic', corresponding instead to the lower threshold in Article 7(2)(a).[149] The words 'in particular' indicate that this is a guide rather than a requirement.[150] Thus, the ICC may still act with respect to isolated war crimes which are of sufficient gravity to warrant action, such as crimes with a particularly grave impact.

---

[144] See e.g. Art. 4 of Geneva Convention III; ICC Elements of Crimes, Art. 8(2)(b)(x)–I, Element 4.

[145] It has been suggested that the requirement of 'in the hands of' or 'in the power of' is also needed to distinguish Geneva-type provisions from provisions regulating methods and means of combat. For example, it might be anticipated that an aerial bombing of a military target will cause a civilian death, but this is not a 'wilful killing' since the civilian is not 'in the hands' of the attacking party. On this view, a comparable requirement should be imported into internal conflicts: Kreß, 'War Crimes'.

[146] Art. 4 of Geneva Convention IV.   [147] *Tadić*, ICTY A. Ch., 2 October 1995, para. 166.   [148] *Ibid.*, para. 168.

[149] Chapter 11. The Appeals Chamber in *Ntaganda*, ICC A. Ch., 13 July 2006, para. 70, also notes that Art. 8(1) does not refer to 'systematic'.

[150] Art. 8(1) was discussed by the Appeals Chamber in *Ntaganda*, ICC A. Ch., 13 July 2006, paras. 70–1, and by the ICC Office of the Prosecutor, Response to Communications Concerning the Situation in Iraq, 10 February 2006, available at www.icc-cpi.int (under 'Structure of the Court', 'Office of the Prosecutor', 'Communications and Referrals', 'Iraq').

12.3   Specific offences

12.3.1   *The lists of war crimes in the Statutes of the Tribunals and the ICC*

This section examines the specific offences constituting war crimes. This examination will start with some observations on the lists of war crimes in the relevant instruments.

The ICTY Statute lists grave breaches of the Geneva Conventions (Article 2), and other violations of the laws and customs of war, drawing on other customary law sources (Article 3).[151] The ICTR Statute lists only serious violations of common Article 3 and AP I (Article 4). The ICC Statute follows the same approach of listing by source, and is the most elaborate. It features four lists: grave breaches of the Geneva Conventions (Article 8(2)(a)), other serious violations of the laws and customs applicable in international armed conflict (Article 8(2)(b)), serious violations of common Article 3 (Article 8(2)(c)), and other serious violations of the laws and customs applicable in non-international armed conflict (Article 8 (2)(e)). The 'other serious violations' lists in Article 8(2)(b) and (e) are drawn from various sources that were accepted as customary law, including provisions from Geneva law,[152] Hague law and other sources.

Because of the desire to adhere to customary law, and to reach agreement, the drafters of the ICC Statute relied on provisions from well-accepted instruments. Even when there was overlap, provisions were often included to avoid missing any customary norms. The drafters also declined to attempt to consolidate overlapping provisions, as this would have been seen as legislating. As a result of this reliance on various sources, there is considerable duplication. Furthermore, the order of the provisions in Article 8(2)(b) and (e) largely reflects the original instruments and the order of proposals, and the dynamics of reaching agreement did not allow for technical review and thematic re-sequencing. The list has been described as 'unwieldy',[153] a 'hodgepodge',[154] lacking 'a clear and analytically convincing structure',[155] and not readily comprehensible to commanders.[156]

While there are many possible ways to group and order the specific war crimes, this chapter will present them in the following order, regardless of the original source of the norm. First, we examine provisions protecting non-combatants (section 12.3.2) and then two provisions governing attacks by combatants: the principle of distinction (section 12.3.3) and proportionality (section 12.3.4). We shall then examine prohibitions relating to property (section 12.3.5), which reflect some of the overlaps in these principles (protecting rights of non-combatants and the principles of distinction and proportionality). This will be followed

---

[151] Report of the Secretary-General Pursuant to Paragraph 2 of Security Council Resolution 808(1993), Presented 3 May 1993, UN Doc. S/25704.
[152] Including some grave breaches from AP I and some other provisions of the Geneva Conventions not listed as grave breaches.
[153] M. Cherif Bassiouni, 'Negotiating the Treaty of Rome on the Establishment of an International Criminal Court' (1999) 32 *Cornell International Law Journal* 462.
[154] Bothe, 'War Crimes' in Cassese, *Commentary*, 396.   [155] Kreß, 'War Crimes', 29.
[156] While recognizing that sticking to traditional text made Art. 8 acceptable, Sunga notes that it would have been desirable to consolidate the provisions and build coherence, rather than following *lex lata* so literally, and that the result makes the list less comprehensible to commanders, thereby hindering compliance among even the most cooperative: Lyal Sunga, 'The Crimes within the Jurisdiction of the International Criminal Court' (1998) 6/4 *European Journal of Crime, Criminal Law and Criminal Justice* 377, 393–4.

by an explanation of provisions regulating the means (section 12.3.6) and methods (section 12.3.7) of warfare. Finally, there are two significant war crimes provisions that do not fall neatly into the above categories, as they protect other interests (section 12.3.8).

12.3.2   Crimes against non-combatants

Violence and mistreatment

At the heart of war crimes law is a series of prohibitions of violence against and mistreatment of non-combatants (including civilians, prisoners-of-war and wounded or sick former combatants). These prohibitions are derived from the basic principle that non-combatants must be treated humanely. While these provisions are legally and conceptually straightforward, they are frequently violated in armed conflict, sometimes as practice or policy and sometimes as acts of individual soldiers. Deliberate and blatant violations of these provisions make up the majority of war crimes charges that have been brought in national and international jurisdictions.

The war crime of murdering or wilfully killing protected persons is well recognized in international and internal armed conflict.[157] Killing of *combatants* is of course permitted in lawfully conducted operations; moreover, civilians may also die as a consequence of military actions against military objectives, and such deaths must be assessed using the more specific tools of the prohibition on disproportionate collateral damage. While the international armed conflict provisions refer to 'wilful killing' and the internal armed conflict provisions refer to 'murder', the basic elements of the crime are the same, and correspond to those for the crime against humanity of murder, as already discussed.[158]

Torture, inhuman treatment, mutilation, and biological, medical or scientific experiments are also prohibited in any armed conflict.[159] Different instruments present the crimes with different structures, but the basic prohibitions are the same.[160]

The elements of torture and inhuman treatment have been discussed, in relation to crimes against humanity. However, unlike in the context of crimes against humanity,[161] the war crime of torture has a purpose requirement – that the perpetrator inflicted pain or suffering 'for such purposes as obtaining information or a confession, punishment, intimidation or coercion or for any reason based on discrimination of any kind'.[162] In the absence of such a purpose, the conduct could still amount to inhuman treatment.

---

[157] Art. 8(2)(a)(i) and (c)(i) of the ICC Statute; Art. 2(a) of the ICTY Statute; Art. 4(a) of the ICTR Statute; Art. 147 of Geneva Convention IV; common Art. 3 to the Geneva Conventions.

[158] See Chapter 2.

[159] Art. 8(2)(a)(ii), (b)(x), (c)(i) and (e)(xi) of the ICC Statute; Art. 2(b) of the ICTY Statute, reflecting the grave breach provisions (e.g. Art. 147 of Geneva Convention IV); common Art. 3 to the Geneva Conventions; and Art. 11 of AP I.

[160] Compare *inter se* Art. 8(2)(a)(ii) (grave breach) of the ICC Statute, Art. 8(2)(b)(x) of AP I, Art. 8(2)(c)(i) of common Art. 3 to the Geneva Conventions and Art. 8(2)(e)(xi) of AP I.

[161] See Chapter 11.

[162] See ICC Elements of Crimes, Art. 8(2)(a)(ii)–1, Element 2; *Delalić*, ICTY T. Ch. II, 16 November 1998, para. 459; and *Kunarac*, ICTY T. Ch. II, 22 February 2001, para. 485.

Various forms of experimentation are prohibited in different instruments.[163] The prohibitions contain comparable requirements of endangering the physical or mental health or integrity of persons, not being justified by medical reasons (the treatment of the person) and not being carried out in the person's interest.[164]

The war crime of wilfully causing great suffering or serious injury to body or health arises from the grave breach provisions of the Geneva Conventions.[165] It can include actions deliberately causing long-lasting and serious harm without satisfying the elements of torture.[166]

The war crime of committing outrages upon personal dignity, in particular humiliating and degrading treatment, is drawn from common Article 3 and the Additional Protocols,[167] and therefore applies in any armed conflict. The prohibition is broader than the previously mentioned prohibitions, in that it also covers acts which, without directly causing harm to the integrity and physical and mental well-being of persons, are aimed at humiliating and ridiculing them, or forcing them to perform degrading acts.[168] The conduct must meet a certain objective level of seriousness to be considered an outrage upon personal dignity. Indignities against corpses can fall within the prohibition, as can deliberately debasing prisoners by forcing them to violate religious requirements.[169]

The most important development in this area is the recognition that various forms of sexual violence amount to war crimes. Until recently, international law has done a poor job of dealing with the sexual abuses routinely committed against women.[170] In most military cultures in the past, and in some military cultures today, licence to rape was seen as a reward for troops, an expected occurrence after the taking of a city or village, and a means of terrorizing and demoralizing the enemy.[171] In such a climate, sexual violence has been pervasive in armed conflicts.[172] While IHL has criminalized rape for centuries, this was not always explicit, and it was rarely prosecuted. IHL treaties, negotiated by men, tended to reflect the perspectives and concerns of men, and thus did not explicitly recognize sexual violence as a form of war crime.[173] Article 27 of Geneva Convention IV stipulated that women should be protected against rape, but did not make rape a grave breach. Sexual

---

[163] Biological experiments appear in the Geneva Convention grave breach provisions, and medical or scientific experiments appear in AP I.

[164] See e.g. ICC Elements of Crimes, Arts. 8(2)(a)(ii)–3 and 8(2)(b)(x)–2.

[165] See e.g. Art. 8(2)(a)(iii) of the ICC Statute; Art. 2(c) of the ICTY Statute; Art. 147 of Geneva Convention IV. Under the ICC Statute, the provision applies only in international armed conflict.

[166] *Delalić*, ICTY T. Ch. II, 16 November 1998, paras. 508–11; *Akayesu*, ICTR T. Ch. I, 2 September 1998, para. 502; *Blaškić*, ICTY T. Ch. I, 3 March 2000, para. 156; *Kordić*, ICTY T. Ch., 26 February 2001, para. 245.

[167] Common Art. 3 to the Geneva Conventions; Art. 95 of Geneva Convention IV; Arts. 75(2)(b) and 85(4)(c) AP I; Art. 4(2)(e) AP II; Art. 8(2)(b)(xxi) and (c)(ii) of the ICC Statute.

[168] Jean Pictet *et al.*, *Commentary to Additional Protocol I* (Geneva, 1987) 873; *Alekšovski*, ICTY T. Ch., 25 June 1999, para. 56; *Kunarac*, ICTY T. Ch. II, 22 February 2001, paras. 501–4.

[169] See e.g. ICC Elements of Crimes, footnote 49.

[170] Elizabeth Odio-Benito, 'Sexual Violence as a War Crime' in Pablo Antonio Fernandez-Sánchez, *The New Challenges of Humanitarian Law in Armed Conflict* (The Hague, 2005).

[171] See e.g. Kelly Askin, *War Crimes against Women: Prosecution in International Tribunals* (The Hague, 1997) especially at 12–42.

[172] See e.g. Susan Brownmiller, *Against our Will: Men, Women and Rape* (New York, 1975); Christine Chinkin, 'Rape and Sexual Abuse of Women in International Law' (1994) 5 *European Journal of International Law* 1.

[173] Some military codes did recognize sexual violence as a punishable war crime; for example, the Lieber Code provided the death penalty for rape.

violence was mentioned again in the Additional Protocols, but not as a crime.[174] Moreover, it was listed as an example of 'outrages upon personal dignity', which in the view of many treated rape as an attack on 'honour', trivializing the nature of the violation.

The ICTY Statute did not list rape as a war crime (although it was listed as a crime against humanity). This lacuna triggered the efforts to establish that rape could fall within the definition of grave breaches, such as 'torture' or 'inhuman treatment'.[175] It also reinforced the need to establish that rape is a war crime *per se*.[176] The ICTR Statute was an improvement, in that its war crimes provision expressly included rape, enforced prostitution and other forms of sexual violence.[177] However, mirroring the language of Additional Protocol II, these were included as 'outrages upon personal dignity'. The ICC Statute took the further step, explicitly recognizing rape, sexual slavery, enforced prostitution, forced pregnancy, enforced sterilization and other sexual violence as war crimes.[178] The ICC Statute also confirms that sexual violence can amount to grave breaches of the Geneva Conventions.[179] For the elements of these offences, see the discussion in Chapter 11.

Further compounding the historical lack of legal recognition of crimes of sexual violence, an additional problem was that prosecutors shied away from bringing charges of sexual violence even when applicable law did recognize the crime. For example, in the Nuremberg proceedings, where there was ample evidence of widespread use of rape as a weapon of war, the French prosecutor simply submitted a dossier and asked forgiveness 'if I avoid citing the atrocious details' – even though many atrocious details were scrutinized thoroughly in relation to other charges.[180] As a result there were no convictions for sexual violence in the Nuremberg proceedings. The record of the Tokyo Tribunal was somewhat better, as there were war crimes convictions of leaders for rapes and sexual violence, including in relation to the 'Rape of Nanking', in which Japanese soldiers raped approximately 20,000 women and children.[181] The sexual slavery of women as 'comfort women' by the Japanese military was, however, largely overlooked.[182] In response to these experiences, many NGOs, academics and lawyers have successfully engaged with the ICTY and ICTR to ensure that crimes of sexual violence are diligently investigated and prosecuted.[183] These efforts have culminated in rules of procedure sensitive to victims, gender advisers on staff, and several landmark decisions. In the same spirit, the ICC Statute has a number of provisions to ensure the

---

[174] Art. 4(2)(e) of AP II, referring to rape, enforced prostitution and indecent assault; Art. 75(2)(b) AP I, referring to enforced prostitution and indecent assault.

[175] Patricia Viseur Sellers and Kaoru Okuizumi, 'International Prosecution of Sexual Assaults' (1997) 7 *Transnational Legal and Contemporary Problems* 45; see *Akayesu*, ICTR T. Ch. I, 2 September 1998, para. 731 (rape and sexual violence can constitute the *actus reus* of other crimes); *Delalić*, ICTY T. Ch. II, 16 November 1998, paras. 475–96 (rape can constitute torture where the elements of torture are satisfied).

[176] Theodor Meron, 'Rape as a Crime under International Humanitarian Law' (1993) 87 *American Journal of International Law* 424.

[177] Art. 4(e) of the ICTR Statute.   [178] Art. 8(2)(b)(xxii) of the ICC Statute.   [179] *Ibid.*

[180] Gabrielle Kirk McDonald, 'Crimes of Sexual Violence: The Experience of the International Criminal Tribunal' (2000) 39 *Columbia Journal of Transnational Law* 1, 10.

[181] *Ibid.*

[182] *Ibid.* The crime was mentioned only in Tokyo IMT, reprinted in Neil Boister and Robert Cryer, *Documents on the Tokyo International Military Tribunal* (Oxford, 2008) 49,617.

[183] Christine Chinkin, 'Women: The Forgotten Victims of Armed Conflict' in Helen Durham and Timothy L. H. McCormack, *The Changing Face of Conflict and the Efficacy of International Humanitarian Law* (The Hague, 1999).

effective investigation and prosecution of such crimes, while preserving the safety, dignity and privacy of victims and witnesses.[184]

Other legal interests of protected persons

In addition to prohibiting violence against and mistreatment of protected persons, war crimes law also protects other rights of persons. For example, several provisions protect liberty and mobility rights. In international conflicts, the unlawful deportation, transfer or confinement of civilians is a grave breach.[185] In internal conflicts, there is a more modest prohibition on displacement of the civilian population for reasons unrelated to the conflict.[186] Since IHL permits the transfer and/or confinement of civilians under certain conditions, it is necessary to refer to IHL to determine whether a particular act is unlawful.[187]

The taking of hostages is a war crime in international or internal conflicts.[188] Tribunal jurisprudence requires an unlawful deprivation of freedom perpetrated in order to obtain a concession or to gain an advantage,[189] and the ICC Elements of Crimes contain a comparable but more detailed definition drawing on the Hostages Convention 1979.[190]

Unjustified delay in the repatriation of prisoners-of-war and civilians is identified as a grave breach in AP I,[191] which therefore applies as a matter of treaty law for parties to that Protocol. The provision was not included in the ICC Statute, due to lack of agreement on the customary law status of the provision. This lack of agreement at the Rome Conference is not conclusive as to the customary status of the provision for jurisdictions other than the ICC.[192]

Other provisions protect the legal rights of persons. Punishment of protected persons without a regular trial is a grave breach (international conflict) and a serious violation of common Article 3 (internal conflict).[193] In international conflict, it is also a war crime to declare abolished, suspended or inadmissible the rights and actions of nationals of a hostile party.[194]

---

[184] Art. 36(8)(b) (judges with expertise in violence against women and children), Art. 42(6) (advisers on sexual and gender violence and violence against children), Art. 44(2) (staff with such expertise), Art. 54(1)(b) (prosecutor to respect interests of victims and witnesses and take into account sexual violence, gender violence and violence against children), and Art. 68 (protection of victims and witnesses and participation in proceedings). See e.g. Valerie Oosterveld, 'The Making of a Gender-Sensitive International Criminal Court' (1999) 1 *International Law FORUM du droit international* 38.

[185] See Art. 8(2)(a)(vii) of the ICC Statute; Art. 2(g) of the ICTY Statute; and Art. 147 of Geneva Convention IV. Significantly, this provision appears only in Geneva Convention IV, allowing the conclusion that only civilians may be victims of this offence.

[186] See Art. 8(2)(e)(viii) of the ICC Statute; Art. 17(1) of AP II.

[187] See e.g. Arts. 41–43, 68, 78 and 79–141 of Geneva Convention IV.

[188] See e.g. Art. 8(2)(a)(viii) and (c)(iii) of the ICC Statute; Arts. 34(4) and 147 of Geneva Convention IV; Art. 75(2)(c) AP I; and Art. 4(2)(c) AP II. See also *United States* v. *Altstötter* (the 'Justice Trial'), VI LRTWC 1.

[189] *Blaškić*, ICTY T. Ch. I, 3 March 2000, para. 158.

[190] Art. 8(2)(a)(viii) of the ICC Elements of Crimes: 'The perpetrator intended to compel a State, an international organisation, a natural or legal person or a group of persons to act or refrain from acting as an explicit or implicit condition for the safety or the release of [the detained persons].'

[191] Art. 85(4)(b) of AP I.   [192] Art. 10 of the ICC Statute.

[193] Art. 8(2)(a)(vi) and (c)(iv) of the ICC Statute; Art. 2(f) of the ICTY Statute; Art. 3(g) of the ICTR Statute; Art. 130 of Geneva Convention III; Art. 147 of Geneva Convention IV; common Art. 3(1)(d) to the Geneva Conventions. See *Hamdan* v. *Rumsfeld*, 126 S Ct 2749 (2006), finding that military tribunals established by the US government, allowing the exclusion of the accused from his own trial, did not meet the common Art. 3 standard.

[194] Art. 8(2)(b)(xiv) of the ICC Statute; Art. 23(h) of the 1907 Hague Regulations. On the ambiguous drafting of the 1907 Hague Regulations, see Michael Cottier, 'Article 8' in Triffterer, *Observers' Notes*, 232–5.

Two closely related provisions, one from Geneva law, the other from Hague law, protect persons from being compelled to fight against their own side during international conflicts. It is a grave breach to compel a prisoner-of-war or civilian to serve in the forces of a hostile power,[195] and it is also a war crime to compel persons to participate in operations of war against their own country.[196] The two provisions overlap but have some different scope of application; one focuses on conscription into forces (fighting against any party) and the other focuses on the forced breach of loyalty in fighting one's own country (whether or not as part of military forces).[197]

Slavery and forced labour, while not listed as war crimes in the ICC Statute, have been recognized as war crimes in Tribunal jurisprudence.[198] It is necessary to make reference to IHL, which permits parties to require prisoners-of-war to carry out work under certain conditions, to determine the ambit of these prohibitions.[199]

12.3.3   *Attacks on prohibited targets (principle of distinction)*

With respect to the conduct of military operations, perhaps the most fundamental principle is the principle of distinction: belligerents are required to distinguish between military objectives and the population and objects, and to 'direct their operations only against military objectives'.[200] As already explained in section 12.1.3, this is a cardinal principle of IHL.[201]

The relevant IHL instruments provide guidance on the differences between civilians, civilian population and objects, and military objectives. In case of doubt whether a person is a civilian, that person shall be considered to be a civilian.[202] With respect to 'civilian population', '[t]he presence within the civilian population of individuals who do not come within the definition of civilians does not deprive the population of its civilian character'.[203] The population must be of a 'predominantly civilian nature'.[204] Civilian objects are 'all objects which are not military objectives'.[205]

Military objectives include combatants, whether on or off duty, as well as objects:

which by their nature, location, purpose or use make an effective contribution to military action and whose total or partial destruction, capture or neutralization, in the circumstances ruling at the time, offers a definite military advantage.[206]

---

[195] Art. 8(2)(a)(v) of the ICC Statute; Art. 130 of Geneva Convention III; Art. 147 of Geneva Convention IV.

[196] Art. 8(2)(b)(xv) of the ICC Statute; Art. 23(h) of the 1907 Hague Regulations.

[197] The ICC Elements of Crimes combine both aspects in the elements of Art. 8(2)(a)(v).

[198] *Krnojelac*, ICTY T. Ch. II, 15 March 2002, paras. 350–60; *Naletilić*, ICTY T. Ch., 31 March 2003, paras. 250–61.

[199] See Arts. 49–57 of Geneva Convention III on authorized work and working conditions.

[200] Art. 48 AP I; see also Art. 51 AP I and Art. 13 AP II. For a discussion on the law of targeting, see Michael N. Schmitt, 'Fault Lines in the Law of Attack' in Susan C. Breau and Agnieszka Jachec-Neale (eds.), *Testing the Boundaries of International Humanitarian Law* (London, 2006) 277–92.

[201] *Legality of the Threat or Use of Nuclear Weapons*, Advisory Opinion (1996) 1 ICJ Reports 226, 257 (8 July 1996), para. 78.

[202] Art. 50(1) AP I.   [203] Art. 50(3) AP I.

[204] *Tadić*, ICTY T. Ch. II, 7 May 1997, para. 638; *Blaškić*, ICTY T. Ch., 13 March 2000, para. 214; *Strugar*, ICTY T. Ch. II, 31 January 2005, para. 282.

[205] Art. 50(3) AP I; also *Blaškić*, ICTY T. Ch., 13 March 2000, para. 180; *Kordić*, ICTY T. Ch., 26 February 2001, para. 53; *Strugar*, ICTY T. Ch. II, 31 January 2005, para. 282.

[206] This definition, found in Art. 52(2) AP I, is widely accepted as reflecting customary law. For further discussion of this two-part test, see e.g. Yoram Dinstein, 'Legitimate Military Objectives under the Current Jus in Bello' (2001) 31 *Israel Yearbook on Human Rights* 1–34; Pictet *et al.*, *Commentary to Additional Protocol I*, 635–7, footnotes 2014–18. The definition can still give

The war crimes of directing attacks against civilians or the civilian population,[207] or against civilian objects,[208] are the most elementary and straightforward expression of these principles.[209]

The other 'prohibited target' provisions are simply examples of this prohibition, focusing on certain specially protected objects or interests. These include: attacking or bombarding undefended towns, villages, dwellings or buildings which are not military objectives;[210] intentionally directing attacks against buildings dedicated to 'religion, education, art, science or charitable purposes, historic monuments, hospitals and places where the sick and wounded are collected, provided they are not military objectives';[211] and directing attacks against buildings, transport and personnel using the distinctive emblems of the Geneva Conventions.[212] The first two examples are early illustrations recognized in Hague law and reproduced in the ICTY, ICTR and ICC Statutes. The third arises from the Geneva Conventions, which have particular provisions emphasizing the protection to be accorded to these distinctive emblems, so that personnel of these organizations may carry out their work of ameliorating the suffering of victims of warfare.[213]

The ICC Statute also specifically prohibits attacks on personnel, installations and vehicles involved in a humanitarian assistance mission or peacekeeping mission in accordance with the UN Charter.[214] This provision may, at first glance, appear to extend beyond existing customary law; however, since it only protects those 'entitled to the protection given to civilians', it is evident that it is simply a specific illustration of the undisputed prohibition on attacking civilians.[215] The inclusion of this provision was inspired by the same considerations that led to the 1994 Convention on Safety of UN and Associated Personnel,[216] and specifically addresses attacks on those who risk their lives to bring humanitarian aid. Such attacks may cause the failure of or withdrawal of humanitarian missions, with grave repercussions for the affected population.

The 'prohibited target' offences all concern deliberate targeting. However, Tribunal jurisprudence has often considered the mental element to be satisfied by recklessness or *dolus eventualis*. This means that the offence could be satisfied where there is an attack on a

---

rise to disagreement as to its application; see e.g. the controversial analysis of attacks on TV stations in the ICTY, Final Report to the Prosecutor by the Committee Established to Review the NATO Bombing, 13 June 2000, available at www.icty.org/sid/10052.

[207] Art. 8(2)(b)(i) and (e)(i) of the ICC Statute; Art. 51(2) AP I; Art. 13(2) AP II.

[208] Art. 8(2)(b)(ii) of the ICC Statute; Art. 62(1) AP I.

[209] In internal armed conflicts, the ICC Statute recognizes the prohibition on attacking civilians but not civilian objects; thus attacks on civilian objects are covered only if they are specially protected objects (buildings dedicated to certain purposes, or objects under the Geneva Conventions symbols or a humanitarian mission).

[210] Art. 8(2)(b)(v) of the ICC Statute; Art. 3(c) of the ICTY Statute; Art. 25 of the 1907 Hague Regulations; Art. 59(1) AP I.

[211] Art. 8(2)(b)(ix) and (e)(iv) of the ICC Statute; Arts. 27 and 56 of the 1907 Hague Regulations; and see the 1954 Hague Convention on Cultural Property and the 1999 Second Hague Protocol. For analysis, see Roger O'Keefe, 'Protection of Cultural Property under International Criminal Law' (2010) *Melbourne Journal of International Law* 339.

[212] Art. 8(2)(b)(xxiv) and (e)(ii) of the ICC Statute.

[213] Arts. 38–44 of Geneva Convention I; Arts. 41–45 of Geneva Convention II.

[214] Art. 8(2)(b)(iii) and (e)(iii) of the ICC Statute; see also Art. 4(b) of the SCSL Statute.

[215] The restriction to those with civilian status means that peacekeepers engaged in military operations under Chapter VII are not protected. This is a necessary outcome consistent with general principles of IHL; otherwise, for one side of the conflict, killing combatants would be a crime.

[216] 2051 UNTS (1999) 391.

legitimate military objective with a high risk of hitting civilian targets.[217] While the use of concepts such as recklessness is generally understandable in criminal law, it is problematic with respect to these offences, because they are concerned with attacks *directed against* prohibited targets.[218] An attack directed against a *military* objective which may cause incidental civilian injury should be assessed under the more relevant law (*lex specialis*) of disproportionate attacks (section 12.3.4).

Two other prohibitions flow from the principle of sparing the civilian population. First, it is prohibited to use the starvation of civilians as a method of war, including wilfully impeding relief supplies.[219] Second, under Tribunal jurisprudence, it is a war crime to commit acts of violence primarily intended to spread terror among the civilian population.[220] The *Taylor* decision of the SCSL explored the potentially gendered dimension of the latter offence, with the use of sexual violence and sexual slavery as a means of terrorizing a population.[221]

12.3.4 *Attacks inflicting excessive civilian damage*

The principle of proportionality

The companion to the principle of distinction is the principle of proportionality: even where an attack is directed against a military objective, the anticipated incidental civilian damage must not be disproportionate to the anticipated military advantage.[222] This principle is well established as customary law.[223]

No other principle of IHL illustrates so clearly the tension between military and humanitarian considerations. The various prohibitions on mistreatment of civilians are important but they are legally and conceptually straightforward, whereas the prohibition on disproportionate attacks poses problems of interpretation even for – indeed, *particularly* for – military forces striving to comply fully with IHL. Even with precision weapons and sophisticated intelligence, military strikes often result in significant civilian casualties, injuries and property damage. As the prohibition on disproportionate attacks brings to the fore many complex and sensitive questions, this chapter will examine it in some detail.

---

[217] A careful review of the *Galić, Blaškić, Kordić* and *Strugar* cases is provided in Jens Ohlin, 'Targeting and the Concept of Intent' (2013) 34 *Michigan Journal of International Law* (forthcoming).

[218] Ohlin, *ibid*. Note that the Tribunals also deal with a customary law war crime of *indiscriminate* attacks, which are launched without regard for whether the target is military or civilian.

[219] Art. 8(2)(b)(xxv) of the ICC Statute; Art. 54 AP I; see also, on the general duty not to impede relief, Arts. 10, 23, 59–63 and 108–111 of Geneva Convention IV and Arts. 70–71 AP I. Under the ICC Statute the provision is recognized only in international conflicts, although it would appear to meet the *Tadić* test; see also Art. 14 AP I.

[220] *Galić*, ICTY T. Ch., 5 December 2003, paras. 87–138; *Galić*, ICTY A. Ch., 30 November 2006, paras. 87–104. See Art. 51(2) AP I and Art. 13(2) AP II: '[a]cts or threats of violence the primary purpose of which is to spread terror among the civilian population are prohibited'; Robert Cryer, 'War Crime of Terror Bombing', 73. For further discussion of the crime of terrorism, see Chapter 14.

[221] *Taylor*, SCSL T. Ch. II, 18 May 2012, para. 2035; Valerie Oosterveld, 'Gender and the Charles Taylor Case at the Special Court for Sierra Leone' (2012) 19 *William and Mary Journal of Women and the Law* 7.

[222] Art. 51(5)(b) AP I.

[223] Henckaerts and Doswald-Beck, *ICRC Customary Law*, 46–50; *Kupreškić*, ICTY T. Ch. II, 14 January 2000, paras. 522–6; Schmitt, 'Fault Lines', 292.

The prohibition is criminalized in Article 85(3)(b) of AP I and in Article 8(2)(b)(iv) of the ICC Statute. Article 8(2)(b)(iv) of the ICC Statute criminalizes:

Intentionally launching an attack in the knowledge that such attack will cause incidental loss of life or injury to civilians or damage to civilian objects or widespread, long-term and severe damage to the natural environment which would be clearly[224] excessive in relation to the concrete and direct overall military advantage anticipated.

The application of this test therefore requires an assessment of:

(a) the anticipated civilian damage or injury;
(b) the anticipated military advantage; and
(c) whether (a) was excessive in relation to (b).

Article 8(2)(b)(iv) requires the launching of such an attack, with the requisite knowledge, but does not appear to require that any particular *result* occur;[225] whereas the Geneva Conventions and Tribunal jurisprudence require that the attack actually results in harm.[226] The ICC Statute lists this provision only in the context of international conflicts; however, the prohibition relates to one of the most fundamental principles of IHL and hence would appear to meet the *Tadić* test for customary law war crimes in internal armed conflicts.[227]

First side of the equation: harm to civilians, civilian objects and the environment

The terms 'civilian', 'civilian population' and 'civilian object' are discussed in section 12.3.3.

Article 8(2)(b)(iv) of the ICC Statute differs from Article 85(3)(b) of AP I in that it also includes damage to the environment in the assessment. The terminology is drawn from Article 35(3) of AP I, which prohibits attacks causing 'widespread, long-term and severe damage to the natural environment'.[228] The ICC Statute has been criticized on the grounds that it is more restrictive than Article 35(3) of AP I, since the damage must satisfy not only the 'widespread, long-term and severe' requirement but also the disproportionality test.[229] This overlooks, however, that the prohibition in Article 35(3), while absolute, was not criminalized in AP I, and it is unclear if the prohibition can be criminalized to the extent that it goes further than the prohibition of wanton devastation or disproportionate attacks. The

---

[224] The AP I standard is 'excessive' whereas the ICC Statute standard is 'clearly excessive'. On the one hand, the adjective seems to raise the standard required under AP I. On the other hand, the difference may not be significant in practice since prosecution would not be viable or appropriate except in clear cases: see below in this section.

[225] The chapeau of Art. 85(3) AP I requires that the attack must have caused death or serious injury to body or health; this requirement could arguably be incorporated by virtue of the chapeau of Art. 8(2) ('within the established framework of international law'). However, during the negotiation of the Elements of Crimes, the decision was reached not to include a result requirement. Daniel Frank, 'Article 8(2)(b)(i)' in Lee, *Elements and Rules*, 141.

[226] *Kordić*, ICTY A. Ch., 17 December 2004, paras. 55–68. An attack that would have been excessive based on the available information, but which unexpectedly caused no harm, could, however, still be prosecuted as an attempt.

[227] The *Tadić* decision refers specifically to proportionality in relation to internal armed conflicts: *Tadić*, ICTY A. Ch., 2 October 1995, para. 111. See also *Kupreškić*, ICTY T. Ch. II, 14 January 2000, paras. 521 *et seq.*

[228] On these terms, see ILC, GAOR, 46th Session, Supp. No. 10 (A/46/10) 276; and Dörmann, *Elements of War Crimes under the Rome Statute*, 175. More generally, see Jay E. Austin and Carl E. Bruch, *The Environmental Consequences of War* (Cambridge, 2000); Karen Hulme, *War Torn Environment: Interpreting the Legal Threshold* (The Hague, 2004).

[229] Cassese describes the environmental provision as 'a huge leap backwards': Antonio Cassese, *International Criminal Law*, 2nd edn (Oxford, 2008) 96.

ICC Statute recognizes individual criminal liability, but in connection with the well-established principle of proportionality. The inclusion of environmental considerations in the proportionality assessment is consistent with other authorities.[230] The dual threshold in Article 8(2)(b)(iv) does, however, mean that environmental damage will only be considered in the criminal law context where it is both widespread, long-term and severe *and* disproportionate to the military advantage.

Second side of the equation: military advantage

Military objectives include combatants, whether they are on or off duty, unless and until they have surrendered, are sick or wounded, or have ceased to take part in hostilities.[231] Objects may also be military objectives, as defined above.[232] Article 8(2)(b)(iv) also requires an assessment of the 'concrete and direct overall military advantage anticipated'.[233] The obvious tension between these modifiers ('concrete and direct', 'overall') is addressed in footnote 36 of the Elements of Crimes:

The expression 'concrete and direct overall military advantage' refers to a military advantage that is foreseeable by the perpetrator at the relevant time. Such advantage may or may not be temporally or geographically related to the object of the attack.[234]

One example of an anticipated advantage that is specific and foreseeable, yet not temporally or geographically linked to the target, could be a feint. For example, in the Second World War, the Allies attacked military targets in the Pas de Calais, but the greater intended contribution was to deceive Germany into believing that the amphibious assault would take place in the Pas de Calais rather than in Normandy.[235]

Comparing the two sides of the equation: the proportionality test

It is comparatively simple to state the proportionality test in the abstract, yet it is profoundly difficult to assess compliance with it in practice, given that: (1) assessing the anticipated civilian damage is a difficult task, requiring a prediction of consequences based on variables and probabilities, relying on available information under circumstances of urgency; (2) assessing the anticipated military advantage involves the same problems of variables and uncertainties, taking into account the broader military strategy and possible future ramifications of the action; and (3) comparing the two is even more challenging, given that they are entirely unlike properties with no common unit of measurement.[236]

---

[230] *Legality of the Threat or Use of Nuclear Weapons*, Advisory Opinion (1996) 1 ICJ Reports 226 (8 July 1996), para. 30; ICTY, Final Report to the Prosecutor by the Committee Established to Review the NATO Bombing, para. 15.

[231] Arts. 43, 48 and 51(3) AP I.   [232] See section 12.3.3.

[233] On 'concrete and direct', see Jean Pictet, *Commentary on the Additional Protocols* (Geneva, 1987), para. 2209. On 'overall', see statements of understanding of Belgium, Canada, Germany, Italy, the Netherlands, New Zealand, Switzerland and the United Kingdom, available in A. Roberts and R. Guelff (eds.), *Documents of the Laws of War*, 3rd edn (Oxford, 2000) 499–512.

[234] ICC Elements of Crimes, footnote 36. The footnote was the subject of intense negotiations.

[235] Dormann, *Elements of War Crimes under the Rome Statute*, 171.

[236] Michael Bothe, 'War Crimes' in Cassese, *Commentary*, 398; see also ICTY, Final Report to the Prosecutor by the Committee Established to Review the NATO Bombing, para. 48; W. J. Fenrick, 'Targeting and Proportionality during the NATO Bombing Campaign against Yugoslavia' (2001) 12 *European Journal of International Law* 489, 499; Schmitt, 'Fault Lines', 292–8.

Because of these difficulties, it is generally recognized that decision-makers must be allowed a 'considerable margin of appreciation'.[237] During the negotiation of the ICC Statute, many States were concerned about the inclusion of Article 8(2)(b)(iv) on the grounds that the officials and judges of the ICC would not be likely to have military experience and hence would apply an incorrectly onerous standard, and that the Court would be reviewing decisions *ex post facto* with the benefit of hindsight, failing to take into account the 'fog of war' (incomplete information, urgency, confusion, limited time for critical decisions).[238]

To address these concerns, and to reflect the concept of a margin of appreciation, the term 'clearly' was inserted, so that the ICC will act only with respect to cases that are 'clearly excessive'.[239] This may well be seen as an unwarranted restriction on the standard in AP I, a view bolstered by the fact that Tribunal jurisprudence has not as of this point endorsed the 'clearly excessive' standard.[240] Alternatively, it may be seen as an appropriate clarification given that the Statute deals not with the basic ground rules for the parties to a conflict, but rather with the criminalization of individual behaviour.[241] Some commentators, including the ICRC study on customary law and the ICTY report on NATO bombing, have concluded that inclusion of the word 'clearly' does not entail a significant new hurdle, since prosecution would in any event be viable only in cases where the proportionality requirement was clearly breached.[242]

Some authorities indicate that proportionality must be assessed from the point of view of a 'reasonable military commander'[243] or 'a reasonably well-informed person in the circumstances of the actual perpetrator, making reasonable use of the information available to him'.[244] However, even such points of reference do not provide measurable ratios of military advantage and civilian damage that would be considered disproportionate.[245] A review of State practice, even among States with traditions of IHL compliance and political incentive to minimize collateral damage, suggests that significant numbers of casualties can be inflicted in pursuit of military advantages without falling foul of the prohibition. Further clarity, through State practice or jurisprudence, would help give valuable content to the prohibition. To assess compliance, it may also be useful to examine the

---

[237] Stefan Oeter, 'Methods and Means of Combat' in Fleck, *Handbook*, 205; see also Fenrick, 'Targeting and Proportionality', 499.

[238] The provision has therefore been highlighted as creating undue exposure. See e.g. David Scheffer, 'Statement in the 6th Committee of the General Assembly', 21 October 1998, US Mission to the UN, Press Release No. 179; Cassandra Jeu, 'A Successful Permanent International Criminal Court – Isn't It Pretty to Think So?' (2004) 26 *Houston Journal of International Law* 411.

[239] Von Hebel and Robinson, 'Crimes within the Jurisdiction', 111.   [240] Cryer, *Prosecuting*, 277–9.

[241] D. Pfirter, 'Article 8(2)(b)(iv)' in Lee, *Elements and Rules*, 148.

[242] Henckaerts and Doswald-Beck, *ICRC Customary Law*, 576–7; ICTY, Final Report to the Prosecutor by the Committee Established to Review the NATO Bombing, para. 21; Roberta Arnold, 'Article 8' in Triffterer, *Observer's Notes* at 341.

[243] ICTY, Final Report to the Prosecutor by the Committee Established to Review the NATO Bombing, 13 June 2000, para. 50. See the comments on this standard in Paolo Benvenuti, 'The ICTY Prosecutor and the Review of the NATO Bombing Campaign against the Federal Republic of Yugoslavia' (2001) 12 *European Journal of International Law* 503, 517; and Michael Bothe, 'The Protection of the Civilian Population and NATO Bombing on Yugoslavia: Comments on a Report to the Prosecutor of the ICTY' (2001) 12 *European Journal of International Law* 531, 535.

[244] *Galić*, ICTY T. Ch., 5 December 2003, para. 8.

[245] One of the few relevant cases is *Galić*, where shells were fired in the midst of a football tournament. The Trial Chamber noted the presence of some soldiers at the game, but found that an attack on a crowd of approximately 200 people, including numerous children, was excessive in relation to the military advantage anticipated: *Galić*, ICTY T. Ch., 5 December 2003, para. 387.

actual *conduct* of the parties: were target selections reviewed? Were decision-makers advised by military lawyers? Were efforts taken to reduce incidental damage? Were precautionary measures taken? And were precision weapons used when the targets so required?[246]

At times, tribunals and investigative bodies are confronted with a pattern of damage (for example, artillery impacts) and must attempt to draw appropriate conclusions.[247] Because civilian objects may be hit even when all appropriate precautions are taken, it can be difficult to assess whether the persons launching the attack (1) targeted civilian objects, (2) were indiscriminate between military and civilian objects, (3) targeted military objects but with excessive foreseeable collateral damage, or (4) targeted military objects and the damage was proportionate or reasonably unanticipated. In the *Gotovina* decision, the Trial Chamber used as a factor whether there were military objectives within 200 metres of artillery impacts, but the Appeals Chamber disagreed with this approach and entered an acquittal.[248] The acquittal was highly controversial (the trial decision may not have used the factor as rigidly as the Appeals Chamber suggested).[249] Development of reliable forensic metrics in this area would be helpful. Nonetheless, despite the present difficulties in measuring compliance with this provision, it does at least allow a criminal law response to the most glaringly disproportionate attacks.[250]

The mental element

A critical element is the knowledge of the perpetrator at the time of launching the attack.[251] The Elements of Crimes clarify that the information available to the perpetrator at the time is central.[252] This is consistent with general principles of criminal law[253] and with State practice.[254]

It is clear that a perpetrator must have awareness of the extent of the anticipated harm and military advantage. The more difficult issue is whether the perpetrator must also consider the former clearly excessive in relation to the latter, or whether that determination is to be made by the ICC on an objective basis.[255] Footnote 37 to the ICC Elements of Crimes indicates that this crime requires that the perpetrator personally completes a particular value

---

[246] The ICC Office of the Prosecutor appears to have taken such considerations into account in its analysis of allegations against States Parties operating in Iraq: Iraq ICC Office of the Prosecutor, Response to Communications Concerning the Situation in Iraq, 10 February 2006, pp. 6–7, available at www.icc-cpi.int (under 'Structure of the Court', 'Office of the Prosecutor', 'Communications and Referrals', 'Iraq').

[247] See e.g. the Office of the Prosecutor's report on Iraq situation, *ibid.*; ICTY, Final Report to the Prosecutor by the Committee Established to Review the NATO Bombing; Report of the United Nations Fact Finding Mission on the Gaza Conflict, UN Doc. A/HRC/12/48, 15 September 2009; *Gotovina*, ICTY A. Ch., 16 November 2012.

[248] *Gotovina*, ICTY A. Ch., 16 November 2012.

[249] Janine Clark, 'Courting Controversy: The ICTY's Acquittal of Croatian General Gotovina and Markac' (2013) 11 *Journal of International Criminal Justice* 399.

[250] See e.g. *Galić*, ICTY T. Ch., 5 December 2003, para. 387; ICTY, Final Report to the Prosecutor by the Committee Established to Review the NATO Bombing, para. 21. The Report of the International Commission of Inquiry on Darfur, 25 January 2005, para. 260, observes that the principle of proportionality 'remains a largely subjective standard' but it 'nevertheless plays an important role, first of all it must be applied in good faith, and secondly because its application may involve the prohibition of at least the most glaringly disproportionate injuries to civilians'.

[251] ICC Elements of Crimes, Art. 8(2)(b)(iv), para. 3.   [252] ICC Elements of Crimes, footnote 37, second sentence.

[253] Art. 30 (mental element) and Art. 32 (mistake of fact) of the ICC Statute.

[254] See e.g. declarations by Algeria, Australia, Belgium, Canada, Egypt, Germany, Ireland, the Netherlands, New Zealand, Spain and the United Kingdom that what is relevant is 'the information available to them at the relevant time'.

[255] Pfirter, 'Article 8(2)(b)(iv)', 151.

judgment.[256] As the ICC Elements of Crimes reflect a consensus statement by the international community as to the content of the crimes, their provisions should not lightly be disregarded. Nonetheless, this particular footnote was included at the last minute of the negotiations, without discussion in the working group, and there are grave reasons to doubt its compatibility with general principles and hence the ICC Statute,[257] since it seems to make the 'perpetrator, in a way, the judge in his own cause'.[258] Other commentators have suggested that the provision should be interpreted as reflecting the need for a margin of appreciation, but not as insulating reckless or incredible assessments.[259]

12.3.5   War crimes against property

Several war crimes provisions address crimes involving property, namely, the destruction, appropriation, seizure and pillage of property.[260] These provisions flow from different instruments, and protect slightly different interests, but in practice they overlap considerably. The ICC Statute includes destruction, appropriation, seizure and pillage in international conflict, but in internal conflict it includes only the long-established prohibition on pillage.

The grave breach regime includes 'extensive destruction and appropriation of property, not justified by military necessity and carried out unlawfully and wantonly'.[261] The 1907 Hague Regulations prohibit 'destroying or seizing the enemy's property unless such destruction or seizure be imperatively demanded by the necessities of war'.[262] These two provisions are similar in scope, although they arise from different interests. The Geneva provisions protect property from the vantage point of upholding the rights of protected persons (including their property), whereas the Hague provisions protect property from the vantage point of the proper conduct of hostilities – military force should be applied for military aims and with minimal impact on the civilian population and objects. The Hague law provision simply requires an assessment of military necessity, whereas the Geneva law provision contains additional elements of 'excessive' and 'wanton'. The ICC Statute includes both provisions, since the Hague provision is more inclusive and hence more useful, whereas excluding the Geneva provision would have meant an incomplete list of grave breaches of the Geneva Conventions.

In addition, *pillage* of property is also a war crime.[263] Pillage is distinct from appropriation or seizure because it refers to taking for private or personal use[264] as opposed to taking

---

[256] ICC Elements of Crimes, footnote 37. This is a departure from the principle in the General Introduction, para. 4, that value judgments of the perpetrator are not relevant; it is sufficient that a perpetrator is aware of the relevant facts.
[257] Art. 9 of the ICC Statute requires that the ICC Elements of Crimes be consistent with the ICC Statute.
[258] Bothe, 'War Crimes' in Cassese, *Commentary*, 400.
[259] Pfirter, 'War Crimes' in Lee, *Elements and Rules*, 151; see also Dörmann, *Elements of War Crimes under the Rome Statute*, 165.
[260] See e.g. Art. 8(2)(a)(iv), (b)(xiii), (e)(xii), (b)(xvi) and (e)(v) of the ICC Statute.
[261] See e.g. Art. 8(2)(a)(iv) of the ICC Statute; Art. 2(d) of the ICTY Statute.
[262] See e.g. Art. 8(2)(b)(xiii) of the ICC Statute; Art. 23(g) of the 1907 Hague Regulations.
[263] Art. 8(2)(b)(xvi) and (e)(v) of the ICC Statute; Art. 4(f) of the ICTR Statute; Art. 3(e) of the ICTY Statute (plunder being synonymous with pillage); Art. 28 of the 1907 Hague Regulations; Art. 33 of Geneva Convention IV.
[264] ICC Elements of Crimes, Art. 8(2)(b)(xvi), Element 2.

for military purposes. It is more akin to the domestic crime of theft. This is why, for appropriation or seizure, one must consider excessiveness and military necessity, whereas, for pillage, there is no 'balancing' test, since the property is not taken for military reasons. Tribunal jurisprudence indicates that, to be criminalized, pillage must be serious; hence, for example, the theft of a single loaf of bread would not be considered a war crime.[265]

The result is a set of overlapping provisions. The *destruction* of property may be examined under the above-mentioned Article 8(2)(a)(iv) or 8(2)(b)(xii), which require a review of military necessity, or under the generic provision on disproportionate attacks (Article 8(2)(b)(iv)) or, where an attack is deliberately directed against civilian property without any military purpose, it can be assessed simply as an attack on a prohibited target (for example, Article 8(2)(b)(ii)). Where property is *appropriated or seized* for military purposes, then it must be assessed under Article 8(2)(a)(iv) or Article 8(2)(b)(xiii). Where property is taken for personal or private use, it is pillage, which is a war crime (Article 8(2)(b)(xvi)).

12.3.6   Prohibited means of warfare (weapons)

Each of the foregoing provisions was aimed primarily at sparing *non-combatants* and their property as far as possible from the effects of war. War crimes law also contains provisions that regulate the methods and means of conducting hostilities. These provisions are distinct in that *combatants* are also beneficiaries of the protections granted.

This section examines prohibited means of warfare, that is to say, prohibited weapons.[266] The prohibition on certain weapons flows from two rationales. One is to protect civilians: some weapons are *inherently indiscriminate* – that is to say, they cannot be used in a manner distinguishing civilian and military. The other is to protect combatants: some weapons are of a nature to cause superfluous injury or *unnecessary suffering.*[267]

Although the ICC Statute contains war crimes provisions on prohibited weapons only in the context of international conflicts, there is ample support for the recognition of such war crimes in internal conflict as well.[268]

Weapons which have been banned from the battlefield on the ground of unnecessary suffering include poison and poisoned weapons;[269] asphyxiating or poisonous gases and analogous liquids, materials or devices;[270] and 'dum-dum' bullets (bullets which expand or flatten easily upon impact).[271] Use of these weapons was recognized as a war crime in the

---

[265] *Tadić*, ICTY A. Ch., 2 October 1995, para. 94.
[266] Art. 8(2)(b)(xvi)–(xix) of the ICC Statute; Art. 3(a) of the ICTY Statute.
[267] Note here the underlying peculiarity of IHL and war crimes law. It is accepted that one may kill combatants, and that combat operations may inflict great suffering on combatants, so the rather modest objective is to reduce *superfluous* injury or *unnecessary* suffering. In regulating weapons, States therefore examine the military efficacy of a particular weapon as well as its consequences to determine if it inflicts *unnecessary* suffering, which can be a rather fine question.
[268] See e.g. *Tadić*, ICTY A. Ch., 2 October 1995, paras. 119–24 (specifically finding weapons prohibitions applicable in internal conflicts).
[269] Art. 8(2)(b)(xvii) of the ICC Statute; Art. 23(a) of the 1907 Hague Regulations.
[270] Art. 8(2)(b)(xviii) of the ICC Statute; Geneva Chemical Weapons Protocol, 17 June 1925.
[271] Art. 8(2)(b)(xix) of the ICC Statute; Declaration on the Use of Bullets Which Expand or Flatten Easily in the Human Body, 29 July 1899.

ICC Statute; more recently, at the Kampala Review Conference in 2010, the Statute was amended to recognize these war crimes in internal armed conflict as well.[272]

Equally prohibited under the customary law of war crimes are chemical weapons and biological and toxic weapons.[273] However, even though the customary law status of these crimes was not disputed at the Rome Conference, these crimes were excluded from the ICC Statute due to a stand-off with respect to nuclear weapons. At the conference, some delegations, most notably India, insisted on the inclusion of nuclear weapons in the list of prohibited weapons.[274] However, nuclear weapons could not be included because there was no agreement that such weapons were prohibited *per se* under customary law. Indeed, the International Court of Justice had specifically found that nuclear weapons are not prohibited *per se*.[275] A large number of delegations then insisted that it was unfair to exclude nuclear weapons – 'the rich man's weapons of mass destruction' – but to include biological and chemical weapons – 'the poor man's weapons of mass destruction'.[276] When no break-through could be found for this impasse, the drafters deferred the whole issue: no such weapons were included in Article 8, but a placeholder was inserted, inviting review of the question once the Statute is open for amendment at a future review conference.[277]

While chemical,[278] biological and nuclear weapons are not prohibited *per se* in the ICC Statute, their use can still constitute a war crime if they are employed in a manner contravening other provisions (such as Article 8(2)(b)(i) or (iv)). Indeed, the ICJ has noted that in most imaginable circumstances the use of nuclear weapons would be likely to fall foul of one of the existing prohibitions.[279]

Other weapons are frequently mentioned as candidates for a comprehensive prohibition. Perhaps the closest to achieving a status as a war crime is the use of anti-personnel mines (APMs). APMs cannot distinguish between combatants and civilians, and remain long after the conflict has ended, causing a great toll of suffering for civilians. APMs are the subject of a widely ratified convention,[280] and therefore the use of such weapons may be on its way to becoming a war crime under customary law. Before concluding that the use of APMs is a

---

[272] Now Art. 8(2)(e)(xiii)–(xv) of the ICC Statute.

[273] See e.g. Henckaerts and Doswald-Beck, *ICRC Customary Law*, 1607–1770; Bacteriological and Toxin Weapons Convention 1972; Chemical Weapons Convention 1993.

[274] Explanation of Vote by Mr Dilip Lahiri, Head of Delegation of India, on the Adoption of the Statute of the International Court, 17 July 1998, *United Nations Diplomatic Conference of Plenipotentiaries on the Establishment of an International Criminal Court Rome, 15 June–17 July 1998, Official Records*, Vol. II, 122.

[275] *Legality of the Threat or Use of Nuclear Weapons*, Advisory Opinion (1996) 1 ICJ Reports 226 (8 July 1996), paras. 52 and 74.

[276] Michael Cottier, 'Article 8' in Triffterer, *Observers' Notes*, 412; von Hebel and Robinson, 'Crimes within the Jurisdiction', 113–16; for detailed discussion of the history and its implications, see Roger S. Clark, 'The Rome Statute of the International Criminal Court and Weapons of a Nature to Cause Superfluous Injury or Unnecessary Suffering, or Which Are Inherently Indiscriminate' in John Carey, William V. Dunlap and P. John Pritchard (eds.), *International Humanitarian Law: Challenges* (Ardsley, NY, 2003).

[277] Arts. 8(2)(b)(xx), 121 and 123 of the ICC Statute.

[278] Some chemical weapons would fall within the definition of Art. 8(2)(b)(xviii) and hence would be prohibited under the ICC Statute.

[279] *Legality of the Threat or Use of Nuclear Weapons*, Advisory Opinion (1996) 1 ICJ Reports 226 (8 July 1996), held that the use of nuclear weapons would be illegal if they were used in contravention of specific rules, such as the principle of proportionality. The ICJ indicated that, in most conceivable circumstances, the use of nuclear weapons would contravene a rule of IHL (para. 95), but it did not rule out the possibility of a legal use (para. 97).

[280] 1997 Ottawa Convention on the Prohibition of the Use, Stockpiling, Production and Transfer of Anti-Personnel Mines and on their Destruction, 2056 UNTS 241.

war crime under customary law, one would have to consider the large number of States that have not accepted the norm, and the contrary State practice among major military powers.

Strong concerns are often raised about the use of cluster bombs[281] and depleted uranium projectiles,[282] but again caution must be shown before one declares that there is a customary law prohibition on their use, let alone a criminalization of their use.[283] A ban on many forms of cluster munitions has come a significant step closer with the recent adoption of a Convention on Cluster Munitions.[284]

12.3.7   *Prohibited methods of warfare*

In addition to the prohibition on certain *means* of warfare (weapons), war crimes law also prohibits certain *methods* of warfare. Many of these provisions find their origin in traditions of chivalry, namely, codes of fair conduct to be respected even among combatants. Such rules are based not only on notions of honour and humanity, but also on preventing deliberate abuse of the rules of IHL to obtain advantage over the enemy, since this would rapidly undermine compliance with IHL.

It is a war crime to kill or wound a combatant who has surrendered or is otherwise *hors de combat* ('out of the fight'),[285] a prohibition which is drawn from the 1907 Hague Regulations and AP I.[286] The provision ensures there is no gap in protection between the moment of becoming *hors de combat* and the moment of being taken into custody as a prisoner-of-war.[287] Compliance with this norm not only shows respect for IHL and the humanity of the surrendering combatant, but also helps to encourage surrender rather than fights to the death.

The war crime of 'declaring that no quarter will be given' refers to orders or announcements that no prisoners will be taken or that there will be no survivors.[288] Such orders violate the duty to spare persons who are *hors de combat* or who are civilians. It is a crime whether the declaration is made publicly, that is to say, to threaten the enemy, or as a private order, namely, to conduct hostilities on the basis that there be no survivors.[289]

---

[281] Cluster bombs drop numerous bomblets and hence are valued by the military for attacking soft targets over a certain area (e.g. vehicles). However, because of their area effect, they can cause significant incidental damage. In addition, some bomblets fail to detonate on impact, remaining behind as a continuing hazard to civilians.

[282] Depleted uranium projectiles are particularly dense and hence are effective in penetrating armour. However, there are concerns about radioactive dust created upon impact as well as the effects of spent projectiles remaining in the soil.

[283] See ICTY, Final Report to the Prosecutor by the Committee Established to Review the NATO Bombing, paras. 26 and 27. Similarly, the ICC OTP in its Iraq analysis held that the use of cluster munitions was not *per se* a war crime under the ICC Statute, but it examined whether such weapons were used in a manner satisfying the definition of other war crimes, such as attacks on civilians or excessive attacks: ICC Office of the Prosecutor, Response to Communications Concerning the Situation in Iraq, 10 February 2006, p. 5, available at www.icc-cpi.int (under 'Structure of the Court', 'Office of the Prosecutor', 'Communications and Referrals', 'Iraq').

[284] Convention on Cluster Munitions, Dublin, 30 May 2008. The Convention will enter into force six months after thirty States become parties to it.

[285] Art. 8(2)(b)(vi) of the ICC Statute, as clarified in the ICC Elements of Crimes.

[286] Art. 23(c) of the 1907 Hague Regulations; Arts. 41 and 42 AP I.

[287] Pictet *et al., Commentary to Additional Protocol I*, 481–2.

[288] Art. 8(2)(b)(xii) and (e)(x) of the ICC Statute; Art. 23(d) of the 1907 Hague Regulations; see also Art. 40 AP I.

[289] ICC Elements of Crimes, Art. 8(2)(b)(xii); Art. 40 AP I.

The war crime of 'killing or wounding treacherously a combatant adversary' is drawn from the 1907 Hague Regulations.[290] This antiquated language raises the question, what is killing 'treacherously' during combat, when enemy forces are making all efforts to deceive and kill each other? The answer is found in the concept of 'perfidy', that is to say, 'inviting the confidence of an adversary to lead him to believe that he is entitled to, or obliged to accord protection' under the rules of IHL, with intent to betray that confidence.[291] Thus, it is not deception *per se* that makes an act perfidious. Deception and ruses are a sound aspect of military strategy and tactics. Ruses – such as the use of camouflage, decoys, mock operations and misinformation – mislead the adversary but do not invite the confidence of the adversary with respect to the protection of IHL.[292]

Perfidy, however, involves a false promise to bestow protection, or an invitation to accord protection with an intent to betray that confidence. Examples of perfidy include feigning an intent to negotiate under a flag of truce, feigning an intent to surrender, feigning incapacitation by wounds or sickness, feigning civilian or non-combatant status, and feigning protected status by use of signs or emblems of the United Nations, neutral States or the recognized emblems of the Geneva Conventions.[293] Thus, to pretend to surrender in order to attack the enemy off-guard is a war crime, as is promising to take persons prisoner in order to massacre them once they relinquish their weapons. Perfidy not only breaches a code of honour, it also undermines compliance with IHL, as adversaries learn that compliance with IHL will be used against them, with grave consequences for efforts to reduce suffering in war.

The war crime of 'making improper use of a flag of truce, of the flag or of the military insignia and uniform of the enemy or of the United Nations, as well as of the distinctive emblems of the Geneva Conventions, resulting in death or serious personal injury' also addresses the problem of perfidy.[294] Whereas 'treacherous killing' focuses on the *result* (wounding or killing by any perfidious means), the 'improper use' offences focus on a particular *means* – using particular symbols, emblems or uniforms. For example, the laws of war require combatants not to attack or disrupt those working under the emblem of the ICRC, so that they can, *inter alia*, help to deliver relief supplies and check on detainees.[295] The protective force of these symbols would be greatly eroded if combatants were to use those symbols to conceal military operations, leading the adversary to distrust such symbols or to respect them at their own peril. On permissible and impermissible uses of such symbols, flags, emblems and uniforms, one must refer to relevant IHL rules. The regimes may be open to interpretation,[296] giving rise to questions about when it is fair to hold persons criminally accountable for misuse, and indeed the ICC Elements of Crimes suggest a certain

[290] Art. 8(2)(b)(xi) and (e)(ix) of the ICC Statute; Art. 23(b) of the 1907 Hague Regulations; see also Art. 37 AP I.
[291] ICC Elements of Crimes, Art. 8(2)(b)(xi), Elements 1 and 2; Art. 37 AP I.   [292] Art. 37(2) AP I.
[293] Arts. 23(c) and (f), 24, 33, 34, 35, 40 and 41 of the 1907 Hague Regulations; Arts. 37, 38, 39 and 85(3)(f) AP I.
[294] Art. 8(2)(b)(vii) of the ICC Statute; Art. 23(f) of the 1907 Hague Regulations, adding also UN insignia in accordance with Arts. 37 and 38 AP I.
[295] See e.g. Art. 8(2)(b)(iii) and (xxiv).
[296] See e.g. Art. 39(2) AP I: enemy uniforms may not be worn while engaged in attack, but might be used in other circumstances, such as espionage.

hesitation on the part of the drafters to hold persons criminally accountable when the relevant regime on the use of certain symbols and emblems may be unclear.[297]

Finally, it is a war crime to use 'human shields', that is to say, to utilize 'the presence of a civilian or other protected person to render certain points, areas or military forces immune from military operations'.[298] The Geneva Conventions do not expressly criminalize this conduct, but it was recognized as criminal in the ICC Statute on the ground that it satisfies the *Tadić* test for identifying war crimes, due to its seriousness. It has been recognized as a war crime in Tribunal jurisprudence.[299] The use of human shields improperly abuses the adversary's respect for IHL, including the principle of proportionality, to frustrate attacks on legitimate targets. The prohibition covers both bringing civilians to the military targets and bringing military targets to civilians.[300] The fact that an adversary is illegally using human shields does not relieve the attacking force from the duty not to launch attacks causing excessive incidental harm.[301]

The ICC Statute recognizes each of the above crimes in international armed conflict, whereas in internal armed conflict it recognizes treacherous killing and declaring no quarter but not killing a combatant *hors de combat*,[302] improper use of flags and symbols, and use of human shields.

12.3.8 *War crime provisions protecting other values*

Finally, there are two war crimes provisions that do not originate in classic concerns of reciprocal protection of persons and property affiliated with the 'other side', and may be characterized as protecting interests and values other than those listed above.

Transfer of population into occupied territory

It is a war crime for an occupying power to transfer parts of its own civilian population into the territory it occupies.[303] This provision protects an interest or value distinct from the other 'transfer' crimes because it is not aimed at protecting enemy civilians who have fallen under a party's power; it refers to transfer of a party's own nationals, and does not require that the transfer be forcible. The purpose of this provision is to ensure respect for the temporary nature of occupation, and to prevent an occupying power from changing the demographic composition of a territory in order to make the occupation permanent.

---

[297] ICC Elements of Crimes, footnotes 39, 40 and 41, requiring knowledge (or constructive knowledge) of the prohibited nature of the use, and actual knowledge of the prohibited nature of the use with respect to UN flags because of the variable and regulatory nature of the prohibition. While mistake of law is not a defence under the ICC Statute, the Statute does permit some scope where a mistake as to another body of law negates the mental element for a crime: see Art. 32(2) of the ICC Statute and Chapter 15. See also C. H. B. Garraway, 'War Crimes' in Lee, *Elements and Rules* at 157–9. Bothe suggests that a solution is to focus on perfidy and perfidious intent: Bothe, 'War Crimes' in Cassese, *Commentary*, 404–5.

[298] Art. 8(2)(b)(xxiii) of the ICC Statute, drawing from Art. 23(1) of Geneva Convention III, Art. 28 of Geneva Convention IV and Arts. 51(7) and 58 AP I.

[299] See e.g. *Blaškić*, ICTY T. Ch. I, 3 March 2000, paras. 742–3.   [300] Art. 51(7) AP I.   [301] Art. 51(8) AP I.

[302] Although killing a combatant *hors de combat* would most likely be captured anyway under Art. 8(2)(c)(i).

[303] Art. 8(2)(b)(viii) of the ICC Statute; Art. 85(4)(a) AP I; Art. 49 of Geneva Convention IV. The second variation of this war crime, transferring 'all or parts of the population of the occupied territory within or outside this territory', is more akin to the other transfer-related war crimes, since it protects the original population, although this provision is also intended to prevent ethnic cleansing.

The inclusion of this provision was controversial during the Rome Conference, with Israel voicing strong opposition.[304] It is undoubtedly true that some of the Arab delegations insisting on inclusion of the provision were seeking to highlight activities by Israel in its occupied territories. However, the majority of delegations at the conference agreed to its inclusion because the *legal* basis for the provision was well established: the provision was based on Article 85(4)(a) of AP I, which in turn was based on Article 49 of Geneva Convention IV.

A particular point of controversy related to the departure from the wording of the Geneva Convention provision by the insertion of 'directly or indirectly' in Article 8, with some arguing it was inherent in the definition and others arguing that it expanded the definition. This controversy was put to rest when a footnote was added to the ICC Elements of Crimes, clarifying that the term 'transfer' is to be interpreted in accordance with existing IHL,[305] enabling the ICC Elements of Crimes to be adopted by consensus.

Child soldiers

A comparatively recent addition to the corpus of war crimes law is the use of child soldiers, namely, 'conscripting or enlisting children under the age of fifteen years into armed forces or groups or using them to participate actively in hostilities'.[306]

The proliferation of inexpensive and light weapons, which can be carried and wielded by children, has led to a great increase in the use of child soldiers, who are seen as cheap, malleable and expendable. Of ongoing or recently ended conflicts, 80 per cent include fighters under the age of 15. Child soldiers are often used for the most dangerous missions and for tasks such as detecting land mines.[307] The use of child soldiers has been addressed in cases of the SCSL and was the subject of the *Lubanga* case, the first trial before the ICC.

This provision serves a distinct interest and value, because it is not aimed solely at protecting enemy civilians who have fallen under a party's power; its primary purpose is to protect all children. The prohibition on the use of child soldiers is a norm of both IHL and human rights law.[308]

The recognition of this crime was initially somewhat controversial during the negotiations of the ICC Statute, because it had not previously been recognized expressly as a criminalized prohibition. However, agreement was reached to include it in the ICC Statute

[304] Statement by the Head of the Delegation of Israel, Judge Eli Nathan, 17 July 1998, *United Nations Diplomatic Conference of Plenipotentiaries on the Establishment of an International Criminal Court Rome, 15 June–17 July 1998, Official Records*, Vol. II, 122.
[305] ICC Elements of Crimes, footnote 44; Michael Cottier, 'Article 8' in Triffterer, *Observers' Notes*, 369; von Hebel, 'War Crimes', 158–62.
[306] Art. 8(2)(e)(vii) and (b)(xxvi) of the ICC Statute; Art. 4(c) of the SCSL Statute. Art. 8(2)(b)(xxvi) contains an additional restriction, so that it applies only to recruitment into 'national' armed forces, which may appear to exclude armed groups. Such a restriction is not found in any other instruments and seems rather inconsonant with general principles of humanitarian law, and there is therefore reason to doubt its applicability for other jurisdictions: Art. 10 of the ICC Statute.
[307] P. W. Singer, *Children at War* (New York, 2005); *Report of the Special Representative of the Secretary-General for Children and Armed Conflict*, UN Doc. A/60/335,7 September 2005; *Children and Armed Conflict, Report of the Secretary-General*, UN Doc. A/59/695 – S/20005/72, 9 February 2005; Human Security Centre, *Human Security Report 2005* (Oxford, 2005); Coalition to Stop the Use of Child Soldiers, *Child Soldiers Global Report 2008*, available www.childsoldiersglobalreport.org.
[308] Art. 4(3)(c) AP II; and Art. 38(3) of the Convention on the Rights of the Child 1989.

because it was a well-established prohibition (appearing in Article 77(2) of AP I, Article 4(3)(c) of AP II and Article 38(3) of the Convention on the Rights of the Child) and it was a serious violation protecting important values and warranting criminalization. The crime was also recognized in Article 4(c) of the SCSL Statute. In a split decision, the SCSL held that the provision was already customary international law prior to the adoption of the ICC Statute in 1998; that is to say, that the ICC Statute codified an existing customary norm rather than forming a new one.[309]

The provision recognizes three distinct offences: conscripting, enlisting, and using children to participate actively in hostilities. The term 'conscripting' refers to forcible recruitment, whereas 'enlisting' encompasses 'voluntary' recruitment,[310] to the extent that decisions of children under 15, usually living in circumstances of poverty, hardship and armed conflict, may be described as 'voluntary'. 'Enlisting' includes 'any conduct accepting the child as part of the militia'.[311]

The term 'using children to participate actively in hostilities' obviously includes participation in combat. It also includes more indirect contributions to hostilities, and is somewhat broader than the IHL term of art, 'direct participation in hostilities', which is used to determine when a person loses civilian immunity and can be lawfully targeted.[312] Decisions of the SCSL have held that the term includes support functions such as 'carrying loads for the fighting faction, finding and/or acquiring food, ammunition or equipment, acting as decoys, carrying messages, making trails or finding routes, manning checkpoints or acting as human shields'.[313] The *Lubanga* judgment of the ICC listed similar activities but added that the key factor is whether the indirect support exposed the child to real danger as a potential target.[314] The use of 'risk' as a factor has raised some concerns, as it may confuse the issue of when persons in indirect support roles may be targeted.[315] Judge Odio Benito, in dissent, would have included the sexual violence and sexual enslavement of girl soldiers in the concept of 'active participation'.[316]

The ICC Elements of Crimes apply a modified mental element for this crime, namely, that the perpetrator 'knew or should have known' that the persons were under the age of 15 years. The modified standard was adopted in SCSL jurisprudence as well.[317] The first judicial treatment by the ICC interpreted the provision, plausibly, as covering situations where the

---

[309] *Norman*, SCSL A. Ch., 31 May 2004. See also the dissent of Judge Robertson.
[310] *Lubanga*, ICC PTC I, 29 January 2007, paras. 246–7; *Fofana and Kondewa*, SCSL A. Ch., 28 May 2008, para. 140; *Taylor*, SCSL T. Ch., 18 May 2012, paras. 442–3; *Lubanga*, ICC T. Ch., 14 March 2012, paras. 607–18.
[311] *Fofana and Kondewa*, SCSL A. Ch., 28 May 2008, para. 144.   [312] *Lubanga*, ICC T. Ch., 14 March 2012, para. 627.
[313] *Taylor*, SCSL T. Ch., 18 May 2012, para. 444; *Brima, Kamara and Kanu* (the 'AFRC case'), SCSL T. Ch., 20 June 2007, para. 737.
[314] *Lubanga*, ICC T. Ch., 14 March 2012, paras. 628 and 820.
[315] Roman Graf, 'The International Criminal Court and Child Soldiers' (2012) 10 *Journal of International Criminal Justice* 945; Thomas Liefländer, 'The Lubanga Judgment of the ICC: More than Just the First Step?' (2012) 1 *Cambridge Journal of International and Comparative Law* 191.
[316] *Lubanga*, ICC T. Ch., 14 March 2012, Dissenting Opinion of Judge Odio Benito. Sexual violence and sexual enslavement were prominently recounted by witnesses, and yet were not among the charges brought by the Prosecutor, and thus this approach would air this important dimension of the case. However, the counter-argument is that doing so would distort concepts of participation in hostilities and the preferable solution would have been to bring charges concerning sexual violence.
[317] See e.g. *Taylor*, SCSL T. Ch., 18 May 2012, para. 439.

perpetrator failed to know the age because of a failure to exercise due diligence in the circumstances.[318] Some commentators have expressed concern that 'should have known' is an inappropriate standard in criminal law.[319] However, criminal law routinely imposes duties on individuals, and a failure to carry out the duty can satisfy the requisite elements, including mental elements.[320] In crimes designed to protect children, it is not uncommon to impose a duty to take reasonable steps to ascertain age.[321] It is entirely plausible that parties to a conflict have a positive duty to verify the age of children before recruiting them or using them in hostilities.[322]

In 2000, an Optional Protocol to the Convention on the Rights of the Child was adopted, raising the minimum ages for conscription and for participation in hostilities to 18.[323] However, the *criminal* prohibition continues to deal with those who use child soldiers under 15 years of age, since the new limits are treaty law and have not developed into customary law, let alone customary criminal law.

Further reading

Dapo Akande, 'Classification of Armed Conflicts: Relevant Legal Concepts' in Elizabeth Wilmshurst (ed.), *International Law and the Classification of Conflict* (Oxford, 2012) 32

Roberta Arnold *et al.*, 'Article 8' in Triffterer, *Observers' Notes*, 275–504

Kelly Askin, *War Crimes against Women: Prosecution in International Tribunals* (The Hague, 1997)

Machteld Boot, *Genocide, Crimes against Humanity and War Crimes* (Oxford, 2002)

Michael Bothe, 'War Crimes' in Cassese, *Commentary*

Knut Dörmann, *Elements of War Crimes under the Rome Statute of the International Criminal Court* (Cambridge, 2003)

Knut Dörmann *et al.*, 'War Crimes' in Lee, *Elements and Rules*, 109–218

Dieter Fleck, *Handbook of International Humanitarian Law*, 2nd edn (Oxford, 2008)

Leslie Green, *The Contemporary Law of Armed Conflict* (Manchester, 2000)

Jean-Marie Henckaerts and Louise Doswald-Beck, *Customary International Humanitarian Law* (Cambridge, 2000)

---

[318] *Ibid.*, para. 358.

[319] Bothe, 'War Crimes' in Cassese, *Commentary*, 117–18. Some commentators also query whether the Elements can provide for a modified mental element. Art. 30 provides a default mental element 'unless otherwise provided'. The question is whether the Elements can so 'provide'. The view endorsed in *Lubanga* (para. 359), and by the Assembly of States Parties (Elements of Crimes, General Introduction, para. 2), is that the Elements can 'provide otherwise'; see also Donald Piragoff and Darryl Robinson, 'Article 30' in Triffterer, *Observers' Notes*, 856; Roger Clark, 'The Mental Element in International Criminal Law: The Rome Statute of the International Criminal Court and the Elements of Offences' (2001) 12 *Criminal Law Forum* 291.

[320] See e.g. the principle of command responsibility, which also imposes duties of inquiry and hence a 'should have known' standard: Art. 28 of the ICC Statute.

[321] As an example, see Canada's Criminal Code, RSC 1985, C-46, ss. 150(4), (5) and (6), providing, in the context of sexual assault, that it is no defence that the accused believed that a person was over 16 unless the accused 'took all reasonable steps to ascertain the age' of the person.

[322] Garraway, 'War Crimes', 207.

[323] Optional Protocol to the Convention on the Rights of the Child on the Involvement of Children in Armed Conflict, adopted and opened for signature, ratification and accession by GA Res. A/RES/54/263 of 25 May 2000. The age for voluntary recruitment may be set at any age above 15, but specified conditions are to be followed.

Howard M. Hense (ed.), *The Law of Armed Conflict: Constraints on the Contemporary Use of Military Force* (Aldershot, 2005)

Claus Kreß, 'War Crimes Committed in Non-International Armed Conflict and the Emerging System of International Criminal Justice' (2001) 30 *Israel Yearbook on Human Rights* 1

Timothy L. H. McCormack and Gerry J. Simpson (eds.), *The Law of War Crimes: National and International Approaches* (The Hague, 1997)

Theodor Meron, *War Crimes Law Comes of Age* (Oxford, 1998)

Theodor Meron, 'The Humanization of Humanitarian Law' (2000) 94 *American Journal of International Law* 239

Lindsay Moir, *The Law of Internal Armed Conflict* (Cambridge, 2002)

Adam Roberts and Richard Guelff, *Documents of the Laws of War*, 3rd edn (Oxford, 2000)

Anthony Rogers, *Law on the Battlefield*, 2nd edn (Manchester, 2004)

Marco Sassoli and Antoine A. Bouvier, *How Does Law Protect in War?* (Geneva, 1999) 97–104

Sandesh Sivakumaran, *The Law of Non-International Armed Conflict* (Oxford, 2012)

UK Ministry of Defence, *Manual of the Law of Armed Conflict* (Oxford, 2005)

13

Aggression

13.1 Introduction

13.1.1 Overview

The crime of aggression, or 'crime against peace' as it was referred to by the Nuremberg Tribunal, is committed by a leader or policy-maker of a State who participates in an act of aggression carried out by the State. The prevention of acts of aggression is one of the primary purposes of the United Nations.

The crime of aggression differs from all others within the scope of this book in being inextricably linked to an unlawful act of a State against another State. The use of a country's troops against its own population does not come within the crime, nor attacks on a State by a non-State group. Such operations might involve other crimes within the Court's jurisdiction such as crimes against humanity and war crimes, but not aggression. The crime of aggression can be said to protect State sovereignty by punishing attacks on States, but also to encroach on sovereignty by going behind the State to make individual leaders directly accountable under international law.

13.1.2 Historical development

Leaving aside historical curiosities,[1] the first international trial for aggression, under the name of 'crimes against peace', was before the Nuremberg International Military Tribunal following the Second World War.[2] There was an attempt at a trial after the First World War: the 1919 Treaty of Versailles provided for the establishment of a special tribunal to try Kaiser Wilhelm II. The intention was to try him not for 'aggression', but for 'a supreme offence against international morality and the sanctity of treaties',[3] a provision that was explained as having 'not a juridical character as regards its substance, but only in its form. The ex-Emperor is arraigned as a matter of high international policy.'[4] The Kaiser, however, took refuge in the Netherlands and was never put on trial.

---

[1] E.g. the trial of Conradin von Hohenstaufen in 1268 for what now would be termed waging aggressive war.
[2] See further section 6.3.   [3] Art. 227. See section 6.2.
[4] *Reply of the Allied and Associated Powers to the Observations of the German Delegation and the Conditions of Peace* (HMSO Misc. No. 4, 1919).

During the Second World War, the discussions in the United Nations War Crimes Commission and elsewhere which preceded the drafting of the London Charter setting up the Nuremberg IMT showed that it was by no means a widely held view that there existed a crime of aggression under international law as it then stood.[5] Nevertheless, agreement was reached on Article 6(a) of the Charter, which gave the Nuremberg IMT jurisdiction over 'crimes against peace', defined as the 'planning, preparation, initiation, or waging of a war of aggression, or a war in violation of international treaties, agreements, or assurances, or participation in a common plan or conspiracy for the accomplishment of any of the foregoing'. The equivalent provisions in the Charter for the Tokyo IMT and in Control Council Law No. 10 were very similar.[6]

The Nuremberg IMT had to deal with the objection of the accused that, in its reference to crimes against peace, the Charter created new law and that the Tribunal was applying law *ex post facto*. The Tribunal dismissed this claim by ruling that, ever since the 1928 Kellogg–Briand Pact,[7] aggressive war had been a crime under international law:

In the opinion of the Tribunal, the solemn renunciation of war as an instrument of national policy necessarily involves the proposition that such a war is illegal in international law; and that those who plan and wage such a war, with its inevitable and terrible consequences, are committing a crime in so doing.[8]

This reasoning was followed in the judgment of the Tokyo Tribunal, although Judges Röling, Bernard and Pal in their dissenting judgments disagreed with it.[9] Indeed, the Kellogg–Briand Pact had not intended to give rise to individual criminal responsibility.[10] But whatever the merits of the decisions by the two Tribunals as to the status of the crime after the Second World War, it is widely accepted that there is now a crime of aggression under customary international law.[11] The customary law crime remains as in the jurisprudence of Nuremberg, supplemented by the subsequent proceedings under Control Council Law No. 10 and by the Tokyo IMT.

Following the judgment of the Nuremberg Tribunal, the recently formed United Nations was quick to endorse the law as laid down in the judgment. The General Assembly affirmed 'the principles of international law' recognized by the London Charter and the Nuremberg

---

[5] See Ian Brownlie, *International Law and the Use of Force by States* (Oxford, 1963) 159–66.

[6] The Charter for the Tokyo IMT defined crimes against peace as 'the planning, preparation, initiation, or waging of a declared or undeclared war of aggression, or a war in violation of international law, treaties, agreements or assurances'; Control Council Law No. 10, Art. II(a), began: 'Initiation of invasions of other countries and wars of aggression in violation of international laws and treaties, including but not limited to planning . . .' (as in the London Charter).

[7] The General Treaty for the Renunciation of War, 27 August 1928.

[8] Nuremberg IMT, Judgment and Sentences, reprinted in (1947) 41 *American Journal of International Law* 172, 218.

[9] Tokyo IMT, reprinted in Neil Boister and Robert Cryer, *Documents on the Tokyo International Military Tribunal* (Oxford, 2008) 48,437–9. Judge Röling did, however, agree that the occupiers were entitled to prosecute for the initiation of wars on the basis that they threatened their security. See section 6.4.2.

[10] See further section 6.3.2. For an overview of the critical responses on this ground immediately following the judgment, see Thomas Weigend, '"In General a Principle of Justice"' (2012) 10 *Journal of International Criminal Justice* 41.

[11] See Brownlie, *International Law and the Use of Force*, 185–94; Yoram Dinstein, *War, Aggression and Self-Defence*, 5th edn (Cambridge, 2011). That was not, however, the universal view in 1950 when the Nuremberg principles were discussed in the Sixth Committee of the GA (GAOR 5th Session, 6th Committee, 231st meeting); and see Christian Tomuschat, 'Crimes against the Peace and Security of Mankind and the Recalcitrant Third State' (1995) 24 *Israel Yearbook on Human Rights* 41, 53. In the UK case of *R* v. *Jones* [2006] UKHL 16, the House of Lords unanimously held that aggression was a crime under customary international law (though not a part of the law of England and Wales).

judgment, and in 1947 directed the new International Law Commission to formulate those principles and to prepare a code of offences against the peace and security of mankind.[12] Thereafter, progress stalled. The ILC's draft principles, which described aggression in the same way as the London Charter, were neither accepted nor rejected by the General Assembly.[13] In 1950, the ILC was requested to elaborate a definition of aggression[14] but did not succeed in reaching agreement, the Special Rapporteur indeed deciding that aggression 'by its very essence, is not susceptible of definition'.[15] Although the ILC included a provision on aggression in its 1954 draft code of crimes, the General Assembly decided that the code raised problems 'closely related to that of the definition of aggression' and postponed further consideration until the special committee, established by the General Assembly in 1952 to consider the definition of aggression, had reported.[16]

After protracted intergovernmental negotiations,[17] made difficult by the tensions of the Cold War in which they were conducted, a 'definition of aggression' was finally adopted in 1974 by General Assembly Resolution 3314[18] and recommended to the Security Council as guidance for the Council. It begins with a broad definition of aggression by States and then lists specific examples.[19] It is clear that the resolution does not as such provide a customary law definition for the individual crime of aggression.[20] Article 5.2 provides:

A war of aggression is a crime against international peace. Aggression gives rise to international responsibility.

This distinguishes between a war of aggression, participation in which engages individual criminal responsibility, and acts of aggression, engaging the responsibility of States.[21] After

[12] Res. 95(1) of 11 December 1946 and Res. 177(11) of 21 November 1947.   [13] See Res. 488(V) of 12 December 1950.
[14] Res. 378B(V) of 17 November 1950. See further Ahmed Rifaat, *International Aggression* (Stockholm, 1979).
[15] UN Doc. A/CN.4/44, 69.
[16] Res. 897(IX) of 4 December 1954. The definition of aggression in the draft code read in part: 'Any act of aggression, including the employment by the authorities of a State of armed force against another State for any purpose other than national or collective self-defence or in pursuance of a decision or recommendation of a competent organ of the United Nations'; threats were also included.
[17] The special committee established in 1952 was to draft 'definitions of aggression or draft statements of the notion of aggression' (Res. 688(VII)). Neither this committee nor two subsequent ones (created by Res. 895(IX) and Res. 118(XII)) reached agreement on a definition. It required the establishment of a fourth special committee (Res. 2330(XXII)) and sixteen more years before a definition of aggression was finally adopted.
[18] GA Res. 3314(XXIX) of 14 December 1974. The definition is contained in the annex to the resolution. On the negotiation of the definition, see Rifaat, *International Aggression*, Chapter 15; Julius Stone, 'Hopes and Loopholes in the 1974 Definition of Aggression' (1977) 71 *American Journal of International Law* 224; Benjamin Ferencz, *Defining International Aggression* (New York, 1975) Vol. II.
[19] See section 13.2.3.
[20] As the ILC noted in its commentary on its 1994 draft Statute for an international criminal court, the resolution 'deals with aggression by States, not with the crimes of individuals, and is designed as a guide for the Security Council, not as a definition for judicial use. But, given the provisions of Article 2(4) of the Charter of the United Nations, that resolution offers some guidance.' For the view that the resolution *does* provide a customary law definition of the crime, see e.g. Mohammed Gomaa, 'The Definition of the Crime of Aggression and the ICC Jurisdiction over that Crime' in Mauro Politi and Giuseppe Nesi (eds.), *The International Criminal Court and the Crime of Aggression* (Aldershot, 2004) 56.
[21] For the negotiating history on this point, see Bengt Broms, 'The Definition of Aggression' (1977) 154 *Hague Recueil* 299; Benjamin Ferencz, *Defining International Aggression* (New York, 1975) Vol. II, 45; Rifaat, *International Aggression*, 275, 276. The Friendly Relations Declaration has a similar provision: 'A war of aggression constitutes a crime against the peace, for which there is responsibility under international law'. Declaration on Principles of International Law Concerning Friendly Relations and Cooperation Among States in Accordance with the Charter of the United Nations (Resolution 2625(XXV) of 24 October 1970), Annex, para. I.

a revival of its earlier mandate,[22] the ILC adopted a draft Code of Crimes against the Peace and Security of Mankind in 1996, which included the crime of aggression but without a definition.[23] The ILC stated in its commentary that individual responsibility for the crime was incurred only if the conduct of the State was 'a sufficiently serious violation of the prohibition' in Article 2(4) of the UN Charter.[24] The Code was not adopted by governments, their attention being absorbed by the negotiations on the crimes within the jurisdiction of the ICC.

The international criminal court negotiations

The international negotiations to establish the ICC began on the basis of the draft Statute proposed by the ILC in 1994.[25] This included the crime of aggression (undefined) within the jurisdiction of the court, but on the condition that no complaint of an act of aggression could be brought before the court unless the Security Council had first determined that a State had committed that act.[26] The provision was controversial and, during the negotiations for the ICC, opinion was divided on three issues: whether the crime of aggression should be included in the Statute at all, how it should be defined, and how and whether a role for the Security Council should be reflected in the Statute.[27]

Different proposals incorporating the crime of aggression were transmitted to the Rome Conference,[28] but there was again failure to reach agreement on the definition and on a role for the Security Council.[29] The final compromise was reflected in Article 5(1) and (2) of the ICC Statute. Article 5(1)(d) includes aggression in the jurisdiction of the court, but Article 5(2) provides that:

> The Court shall exercise jurisdiction over the crime of aggression once a provision is adopted in accordance with Articles 121 and 123 defining the crime and setting out the conditions under which the Court shall exercise jurisdiction with respect to this crime. Such a provision shall be consistent with the relevant provisions of the Charter of the United Nations.

Accordingly, the ICC was not able to try any case of aggression until the States Parties to the Statute reached agreement on this further provision.

Following subsequent lengthy negotiations,[30] the Review Conference of the ICC Statute, held in Kampala in 2010, adopted by consensus amendments to the Statute which delete

---

[22] GA Res. 36/106 of 10 December 1981, by which the ILC was invited to resume its work on the draft Code of Offences against the Peace and Security of Mankind.

[23] *Yearbook of the International Law Commission 1996*, Vol. II, Part Two, 42.   [24] *Ibid.*   [25] See section 8.2.

[26] Art. 23(2).

[27] For the early discussions, see Report of the Ad Hoc Committee on the Establishment of an International Criminal Court, GAOR 50th Session, Supp. No. 22 (A/50/22), paras. 63–71; Report of the Preparatory Committee on the Establishment of an International Criminal Court, Vol. I, GAOR 51st Session, Supp. No. 22 (A/51/22).

[28] The proposals can be found in the Report of the Prepcom on the Establishment of an International Criminal Court, UN Doc. A/CONF.183/2, included in the official records of the conference (UN Doc. A/CONF.183/13 (Vol. III)) at 14–15.

[29] For a brief description of the negotiations at Rome, see Herman von Hebel and Darryl Robinson, 'Crimes within the Jurisdiction of the Court' in Lee, *The Making of the Rome Statute*, 79, 81–5.

[30] Negotiations were carried out first in the Preparatory Commission established by the Rome Conference, and then in the Special Working Group on the Crime of Aggression, established by the Assembly of States Parties (ICC-ASP/1/Res.1 of 9 September 2002). For a summary of the negotiations in the Prepcom, see Silvia Fernandez de Gurmendi, 'The Working Group on Aggression at the Preparatory Commission for the International Criminal Court' (2002) 25 *Fordham International Law Journal* 589; and see Roger Clark, 'Rethinking Aggression as a Crime and Formulating its Elements: The Final Work-

Article 5(2) from the Statute and which set out a definition of aggression (in new Article 8*bis*) and arrangements for the Court to exercise its jurisdiction over it (in new Articles 15*bis* and 15*ter*); new Elements for the crime were also adopted.[31] The amendments ('the Kampala amendments') were accompanied by seven 'understandings' incorporating agreed interpretations. The Court will not be able to exercise its jurisdiction over aggression until a further decision allowing it to do so is taken after 1 January 2017 by a two-thirds majority of States Parties.

Although the draft definition of aggression put before the conference had been negotiated beforehand, the proceedings at the conference were complex and difficult.[32] The resulting amendments, the means of bringing them into force and the 'understandings' all provide material for an unusually high degree of disagreement and difference of interpretation, as will be discussed below.

13.1.3 *The definition in the ICC Statute*

The crime of aggression is defined in what will be Article 8*bis* of the Statute as:

the planning, preparation, initiation or execution, by a person in a position effectively to exercise control over or to direct the political or military action of a State, of an act of aggression which, by its character, gravity and scale, constitutes a manifest violation of the Charter of the United Nations.

In its turn, 'act of aggression' is defined as:

the use of armed force by a State against the sovereignty, territorial integrity or political independence of another State, or in any other manner inconsistent with the Charter of the United Nations. Any of the following acts, regardless of a declaration of war, shall in accordance with the United Nations General Assembly Resolution 3314(XXIX) of 14 December 1974, qualify as an act of aggression: [the amendment then lists the acts set out in that resolution].

The definition of aggression thus incorporates all three of the different approaches which had been discussed in the early part of the negotiations. One school of thought had favoured using as a definition the list of acts of aggression in General Assembly Resolution 3314. This met with arguments that the list was illustrative only, thus conflicting with the *nullum crimen* principle[33] if it was used to define the crime, and that the purpose of the resolution was to provide guidance for the Security Council in its determinations of aggression by States,[34] not to provide a definition for the purpose of individual responsibility. A second approach to the definition was to specify that participation in *any* unlawful use of force by a State under

---

Product of the Preparatory Commission for the International Criminal Court' (2002) 15 *Leiden Journal of International Law* 859. For the proposals before the Special Working Group and the Kampala Review Conference, see Stefan Barraga and Claus Kreß (eds.), *The Travaux Préparatoires of the Crime of Aggression* (Cambridge, 2011).

[31] Annex II to RC/Res.6. A new Art. 25(3*bis*) was also added to ensure that the provision in the Statute on superior responsibility applies only to those leaders who are included in the definition of aggression as perpetrators of the crime.

[32] For details of the negotiations at Kampala, see Claus Kreß and Leonie von Holtzendorff, 'The Kampala Compromise on the Crime of Aggression' (2010) 8 *Journal of International Criminal Justice* 1179, 1201–17.

[33] See section 1.5.1.   [34] Para. 4 of the resolution.

the UN Charter was criminal. Both of these approaches found their way into the definition. A third category of proposals started from the proposition that only participation in a 'war' of aggression reflected customary law. To deal with the fact that war is now uncommon, suggestions were made to define aggression as the unlawful use of force but to add an unlawful purpose such as military occupation or annexation or a 'threshold' of manifest illegality. The definition as finally agreed does not have a requirement of purpose but includes a threshold which needs to be crossed before the ICC can try the crime: the act of aggression must be one which 'by its character, gravity and scale, constitutes a manifest violation of the Charter of the United Nations'.

Discussion of the elements of the crime – material and mental – in sections 13.2 and 13.3 below is based on the definition adopted at Kampala ('the ICC definition') and the new Elements, although those amendments have not yet been brought into force; we also refer to the case law of the post-Second World War tribunals which were the last international tribunals to try the crime.

13.1.4   Relationship to other crimes

Aggression provides an *occasion* for the commission of the other crimes. In the view of the Nuremberg Tribunal, '[t]o initiate a war of aggression . . . is not only an international crime; it is the supreme international crime differing only from other war crimes in that it contains within itself the accumulated evil of the whole'.[35] Armed conflict on a major scale causes great suffering and frequently (if not always) it involves the commission of atrocities. Genocide has now been described as the 'crime of crimes',[36] but there cannot be any need to engage in an abstract competition for the title of the worst international crime.

Aggression differs markedly from genocide, crimes against humanity and war crimes in that, unlike those crimes, it concerns the *ius ad bellum* (the law governing recourse to armed conflict), and therefore raises questions of international law regarding State responsibility for aggressive acts.[37] To understand the crime, it is necessary to understand the rules of international law on these questions; they are discussed briefly in section 13.2.2, where we consider the elements of the crime.

A further distinction from the other crimes is that, while genocide, crimes against humanity and war crimes may be committed by members of the armed forces of a State or by those affiliated with a State, aggression can *only* be committed on behalf of a State and as part of a State plan or policy. Expansion of the crime to acts by non-State entities has not been widely supported.[38] Further, unlike other international crimes, aggression is a

---

[35] Nuremberg IMT, Judgment and Sentences, reprinted in (1947) 41 *American Journal of International Law* 172, 186.
[36] *Kambanda*, ICTR T. Ch., 14 September 1998, para. 16.
[37] See further Yoram Dinstein, 'The Distinction between War Crimes and Crimes against Peace' (1995) 24 *Israel Yearbook on Human Rights* 1.
[38] But see Mark Drumbl, 'The Push to Criminalize Aggression: Something Lost Amid the Gains?' (2009) 41 *Case Western Reserve Journal of International Law* 291. There is an African treaty, the 2006 Protocol on Non-Aggression and Mutual Defence in the Great Lakes Region, which defines aggression as including acts by non-State actors, and requires States to criminalize acts of aggression as so defined. But this extension of the definition of the crime to persons representing non-State actors does not reflect customary international law.

leadership crime and is only committed by persons in policy-making positions in a State.[39]

Aggression was the last of the crimes considered in this book to be formally defined, and it will be the last to be brought within the active jurisdiction of an international tribunal. Of the courts and tribunals discussed in this book, only the ICC has jurisdiction, and when the Kampala amendments are brought into force only the ICC will be able to prosecute it.

13.2   Material elements

The collective act of aggression by a State is the point of reference for the act of the individual perpetrator. Under the ICC definition, the crime is committed (1) by a perpetrator in a leadership position in a State (2) who has participated (3) in an act of aggression by the State (4) which 'by its character, gravity and scale, constitutes a manifest violation of the Charter of the United Nations'. Each of these aspects of the material elements of the crime is described below.[40]

13.2.1   *Perpetrators*

Aggression is a 'leadership crime': it is committed only by leaders and high-level policy-makers. Thus, the ICC definition and Elements require that a person be 'in a position effectively to exercise control over or to direct the political or military action' of the State which committed the act of aggression. While the reference in the London Charter to the 'waging' of a war of aggression seems to imply that *all* persons carrying out the State's acts of aggression are individually responsible, from the general down to the foot soldier, that is not how the Charter was interpreted in practice.[41] The point is well illustrated by *Von Leeb and Others* (the 'High Command case'), tried before an American Military Tribunal constituted under Control Council Law No. 10.[42] The fourteen accused were all in positions of high military authority: thirteen generals and one admiral. But they were acquitted of the charge of crimes against peace on the ground that 'the criminality which attaches to the waging of an aggressive war should be confined to those who participate in it at the policy level'.[43] In spite of their senior military positions, the defendants were not at the required policy level and they were not criminalized by not having refused to implement the aggressive plans. Accordingly, in countries where the military are largely kept out of the political decisions on the initiation of force, it will less often be the military who are responsible for the crime of aggression than their political superiors. The exact threshold

---

[39] See section 13.2.1.
[40] And see more generally Carrie McDougall, *The Crime of Aggression under the Rome Statute of the International Criminal Court* (Cambridge, 2013).
[41] See G. Brand, 'The War Crimes Trials and the Laws of War' (1949) 26 *British Yearbook of International Law* 414, 419. For a useful compilation of relevant sections of the post-Second World War case law, see the UN Secretariat paper, 'Historical Review of Developments Relating to Aggression', PCNICC/2002/WGCA/L.1.
[42] XII LRTWC 1.
[43] *Ibid.*, 67. One defendant committed suicide and no judgment was given. Eleven of the accused were convicted of war crimes and crimes against humanity.

of criminal responsibility is not clear and there may not have been complete consistency in the findings of the Nuremberg IMT and in the subsequent proceedings.[44] But somewhere 'between the Dictator and Supreme Commander of the military forces of the nation and the common soldier is the boundary between the criminal and the excusable participation in the waging of an aggressive war by an individual engaged in it'.[45]

The relevant levels of policy-making in the post-Second World War tribunals were not necessarily confined to government or the military. Some of the accused in the proceedings subsequent to Nuremberg were industrialists, not part of the government but closely associated with it. In *Krauch and Others* (the 'IG Farben case'),[46] the accused were, however, acquitted on the ground that, like Albert Speer, one of the Nuremberg IMT defendants, their efforts 'were in aid of the war effort in the same way that other productive enterprises aid in the waging of war';[47] their responsibility was below that of planning and leading. The ICC definition, however, appears to retreat from the earlier case law, in that it excludes persons who are not political leaders but nonetheless have power to shape and influence policy.[48]

The crime of aggression constitutes participation in a collective act by a State against another State. Neither the ICC definition nor customary law extends the crime to acts committed by individual mercenaries not sponsored by a State, nor to other non-State actors, even though the devastation caused by such acts may be comparable to inter-State military intervention.[49]

13.2.2   *Planning, preparation, initiation or execution*

The nexus between the State's act of aggression and the act of the individual leader or other high-level policy-maker is described in the ICC definition as 'planning, preparation, initiation or execution', following closely Article 6 of the Nuremberg Charter which referred to the 'planning, preparation, initiation or waging' of an aggressive war. The Charter also included 'participation in a common plan or conspiracy', but conspiracy is not included in the ICC definition – as interpreted by the Nuremberg IMT, conspiracy differed little from planning and preparation[50] and the charge of conspiracy was in effect superfluous.[51] It is difficult to distinguish planning from preparation in the jurisprudence. Preparation had to be

[44] Brownlie, *International Law and the Use of Force*, 205.   [45] XII LRTWC 67.
[46] X LRTWC 1; see also *Krupp and Others*, X LRTWC 69.
[47] Nuremberg IMT, Judgment and Sentences, reprinted in (1947) 41 *American Journal of International Law* 172 321.
[48] See Kevin Heller, 'Retreat from Nuremberg: The Leadership Requirement in the Crime of Aggression' (2007) 18 *European Journal of International Law* 477.
[49] The African Union has, however, adopted an extensive definition of aggression which appears to include acts by non-State actors (African Union Non-Aggression and Common Defence Pact 2005; see also Protocol on Non-Aggression and Mutual Defence in the Great Lakes Region 2006).
[50] Quincy Wright, (1947) 41 *American Journal of International Law* 38, 68.
[51] See Brownlie, *International Law and the Use of Force*, 201. Charges of conspiracy were more important to the Tokyo IMT, which relied on the concept of inchoate conspiracy; its rulings have also come in for extensive criticism; see the comment and authorities cited in Neil Boister and Robert Cryer, *The Tokyo International Military Tribunal: A Reappraisal* (Oxford, 2008) Chapter 8.

closely linked with planning; preparation for some vague future programme of aggression was not sufficient.[52]

Participation in *threats* to use military force does not come within the crime of aggression. The collective act must have been completed in order to found criminal responsibility. For the ICC this is confirmed in Element 3. The threat of aggression was not included in the Charters of the Nuremberg or Tokyo IMTs, nor in Control Council Law No. 10. The unopposed invasions of Austria and Czechoslovakia, following the successful threat of aggressive force, were treated as evidence of the aggressive conspiracy but were not charged as crimes against peace before the Nuremberg IMT. They were, however, charged in indictments under Control Council Law No. 10 (which included 'invasions' within the jurisdiction of the tribunals constituted under it).[53]

For the ICC, the question will arise as to the applicability of the modes of liability provisions in Article 25 of the Statute. For the crime of aggression, that Article has been amended only in respect of superior responsibility: new Article 25(3*bis*) provides that the concept applies only to those leaders who are included in the definition of aggression as perpetrators of the crime. But there has been no amendment to the rest of the Article. The Prosecutor will have to show that an accused planned, prepared, initiated or executed an act of aggression that was in fact committed, *and* that the accused fulfilled the elements of a mode of liability under Article 25.

As for defences to the crime, the provisions of the ICC Statute for other crimes (in Article 31) will apply also to individuals charged with aggression. In addition, the defences under public international law relating to the collective act of aggression will be available to the defendant in arguing that the State concerned did not commit an act of aggression; it would have been preferable had this been made clearer in the Kampala amendments, but, as indicated below, it is a necessary inference from their wording.

13.2.3 Act of aggression

The collective act in which the individual participates is the act of aggression of a State committed against another State. The ICC definition, in paragraph 1, describes this collective act as 'the use of armed force by a State against the sovereignty, territorial integrity or political independence of another State, or in any other manner inconsistent with the Charter of the United Nations'. Here the wording is similar (though not identical) to Article 2(4) of the Charter,[54] thus requiring reference to the rules of international law regarding the unlawful use of force by States. The effect of paragraph 1 is that any unlawful use of force by a State is defined as an 'act of aggression' for the purpose of the ICC definition.

---

[52] Nuremberg IMT, Judgment and Sentences, reprinted in (1947) 41 *American Journal of International Law* 172, 222.

[53] E.g. in the case of *United States* v. *Weizsäcker et al.* (the 'Ministries Trial'), the tribunal held: 'The fact that the aggressor was here able to so overawe the invaded countries does not detract in the slightest from the enormity of the aggression, in reality perpetrated. The invader here employed an act of war.' Judgment, 11–13 April 1949, *Trials of War Criminals before the Nuremberg Military Tribunals* (United States Government Printing Office), Vol. XIV, 330.

[54] For the differences between Art. 1 of the Definition and Art. 2(4) of the Charter, see Dinstein, *War, Aggression*, 101, 102.

Paragraph 2 gives examples. It lists the acts set out in General Assembly Resolution 3314 (XXIX) of 1974 and provides that any of these acts, 'in accordance with' that resolution, qualifies as an act of aggression for the purpose of the ICC definition. The list of acts includes invasion, bombardment and annexation of another State's territory, attack on another State's armed forces, and sending armed groups which commit aggressive acts against another State. The definition makes clear that this is a non-exhaustive list.

The incorporation in the ICC definition of a major part of the 1974 General Assembly definition does not lead to an entirely comfortable result. The 1974 definition, adopted by the General Assembly to provide guidance to the Security Council,[55] states that the Council may conclude that in specific circumstances a listed act does *not* constitute aggression,[56] for example if 'the acts concerned or their consequences are not of sufficient gravity' (Article 2). It should also be noted that the list in the General Assembly resolution, now incorporated in the ICC definition, does not limit 'act of aggression' to instances of major, serious or large-scale use of force. On its face, the list includes border skirmishes and infringements of maritime limits or air space, which would not necessarily be regarded as aggression under international law.[57] Further, the description of each of the acts in the 1974 resolution as an act of aggression appears to indicate that a listed use of force is aggression even though there may be a justifiable defence under public international law.[58]

These problems can mostly be resolved by sensible application of the provisions of the ICC definition. First, the reference to the list of acts qualifying as aggression 'in accordance with' the 1974 resolution can be interpreted to mean that any relevant conditions and qualifications in the 1974 definition are incorporated. By this means, for example, Article 6 of the 1974 definition,[59] which can be regarded as preserving Charter provisions on the legality of certain acts, can be applied so as to import international law defences to allegations of aggressive acts. Second, it is not the State's act of aggression (whether in the 1974 list or not) which founds individual criminality, but only an act which 'constitutes a manifest violation' of the Charter.

Whether an act of aggression has been committed by a State, a necessary part of the crime of aggression as we have seen will need to be determined under public international law – the *ius ad bellum*. We give a brief overview of this area of public international law below.

International law regarding the use of force by a State[60]

Article 2(4) of the Charter of the United Nations reads as follows:

[55] See e.g. para. 4 of Res. 3314.   [56] Arts. 2 and 4.
[57] See e.g. Theodor Meron, 'Defining Aggression for the International Criminal Court' (2001) 25 *Suffolk Transnational Law Review* 1, 4.
[58] See comment in Michael Glennon, 'The Blank-Prose Crime of Aggression' (2009) 35 *Yale Journal of International Law* 71, 88–90. For other difficulties arising from the transposition of the resolution to the ICC definition, see Claus Kreß, 'The Crime of Aggression before the First Review of the ICC Statute' (2007) 20 *Leiden Journal of International Law* 851, 857.
[59] 'Nothing in this Definition shall be construed as in any way enlarging or diminishing the scope of the Charter, including its provisions concerning cases in which the use of force is lawful.'
[60] What follows is an extremely brief discussion of this area of public international law. For useful summaries of the law, see Humphrey Waldock, 'The Regulation of the Use of Force by Individual States in International Law' (1952) 81 (II) *Hague*

All Members shall refrain in their international relations from the threat or use of force against the territorial integrity or political independence of any State, or in any other manner inconsistent with the purposes of the United Nations.

The Charter put in place a new structure for international peace and security, requiring the settlement of disputes by peaceful means and introducing a collective system for States to act through the UN to suppress aggression and other breaches of international peace. While the collective system has developed in a different direction from that envisaged by the drafters, the prohibition on the use of force remains as set out in Article 2(4). This is the fundamental legal principle governing the use of force and it reflects customary international law.[61]

Although the provision is at the heart of the rules of international law on the use of force, its interpretation and application are not easy. In particular, there are differences of view as to the exceptions to the prohibition. The only exceptions universally admitted are, first, individual or collective self-defence and, second, force authorized by the Security Council acting under Chapter VII of the Charter. There is controversy over whether there is also an exception for humanitarian intervention.

Self-defence

The relevant provision of the Charter is Article 51, which provides in part:

Nothing in the present Charter shall impair the inherent right of individual or collective self-defence if an armed attack occurs against a Member of the United Nations, until the Security Council has taken measures necessary to maintain international peace and security . . .

The Charter does not elaborate on the conditions for a lawful use of force in self-defence, but international law requires that self-defence is lawful only if it is *necessary* to use force, and only if that force is *proportionate*, that is to say, it is not excessive in relation to the need to avert or respond to the attack.[62] A classic formulation of the applicable rules is that of US Secretary of State Webster in the 1837 *Caroline* incident.[63] In an exchange of correspondence with the British, he stated that, for action to be lawful, there must be a 'necessity of self-defence, instant, overwhelming, leaving no choice of means, and no moment for deliberation' and that the action must not be 'unreasonable or excessive; since the act justified by the necessity of self-defence, must be limited by that necessity, and kept clearly within it'.

Commentators differ as to whether force may be used in anticipatory self-defence, that is to say, against an attack that is threatened and not ongoing. On one view, the right to

---

Recueil 455; Malcolm Shaw, *International Law*, 6th edn (Cambridge, 2008) Chapter 20; see further Brownlie, *International Law and the Use of Force*; Dinstein, *War, Aggression*; and Christine Gray, *International Law and the Use of Force*, 3rd edn (Oxford, 2008) Chapters 2, 4 and 6.

[61] *Case Concerning Military and Paramilitary Activities in and against Nicaragua* (*Nicaragua* v. *USA*) (1986) ICJ Reports 14, paras. 188–90.

[62] The requirement of necessity and proportionality has been confirmed by the ICJ; see e.g. *Case Concerning Armed Activities on the Territory of the Congo* (*Democratic Republic of the Congo* v. *Uganda*) (2005) ICJ Reports, para. 147.

[63] The incident concerned the destruction over the Niagara Falls of a steamer thought to be supplying Canadian rebels against the British. See Robert Jennings, 'The Caroline and Macleod Cases' (1938) 32 *American Journal of International Law* 86.

self-defence applies only once an armed attack has begun.[64] The contrary view, that States have a right to act in order to avert the threat of an imminent attack, is supported not least by the practical argument that it is unrealistic in all cases to await an actual attack; this consideration applies particularly to threats from weapons of mass destruction.[65] The ICJ has left open the issue of the lawfulness of a response to the threat of an imminent armed attack.[66] However, the claim to 'pre-emptive self-defence' to prevent the emergence of a security threat is widely rejected as impermissible under international law.[67] Further controversial questions about the right to self-defence are whether force may be used to rescue a State's nationals in a State which is unable or unwilling to protect them,[68] and whether the 'armed attack' must cross some threshold of intensity before self-defence is justified.[69]

One of the frequent questions of modern times is whether there is a right of self-defence against non-State organizations operating from another State;[70] for example, whether military force may lawfully be used by a threatened State against terrorist groups who are in the territory of another State. Commentators differ as to whether, if force may be used against such groups, it is lawful if the State from which they are operating is not complicit with or tolerating the actions of those groups; developing State practice seems to support the view that States have the right of self-defence against terrorist groups in other States where the 'harbouring' States are unable or unwilling to deal with the threat themselves.[71]

---

[64] See Brownlie, *International Law and the Use of Force*, 275–8; Dinstein, *War, Aggression*, 201–5 (but giving a wide interpretation of what constitutes the start of the attack justifying self-defence).

[65] See e.g. Waldock, 'The Regulation of the Use of Force', 495–505; Derek Bowett, *Self-Defence in International Law* (Manchester, 1958) 184–93; Christopher Greenwood, 'International Law and the United States' Air Operation against Libya' (1987) 89 *West Virginia Law Review* 933, 942; Bruno Simma *et al.* (eds.), *The Charter of the United Nations: A Commentary*, 3rd edn (Oxford, 2012) 1423, 1424.

[66] *Case Concerning Military and Paramilitary Activities in and against Nicaragua (Nicaragua v. USA)* (1986) ICJ Reports 14, para. 194. See also *Case Concerning Armed Activities on the Territory of the Congo (Democratic Republic of the Congo v. Uganda)* (2005) ICJ Reports, para. 143.

[67] The claim is made in the 2002 'National Security Strategy of the United States' (2002) 41 ILM 1478; see Christopher Greenwood, 'International Law and the Pre-emptive Use of Force: Afghanistan, Al-Quaida and Iraq' (2003) 4 *San Diego International Law Journal* 7; for a contrary view, see Ruth Wedgwood, 'The Fall of Saddam Hussein: Security Council Mandates and Preemptive Self-Defense' (2003) 97 *American Journal of International Law* 576, 582–5.

[68] See Gray, *International Law and the Use of Force*, 156–60; Dinstein, *War, Aggression*, 231–4.

[69] See *Case Concerning Military and Paramilitary Activities in and against Nicaragua (Nicaragua v. USA)* (1986) ICJ Reports 14, paras. 191 and 195; and *Oil Platforms (Islamic Republic of Iran v. USA)* (2003) ICJ Reports, paras. 51, 63–4 and 72; for critique of this point, see Oscar Schachter, 'In Defense of International Rules on the Use of Force' (1986) 53 *University of Chicago Law Review* 113.

[70] For arguments in favour of the right to self-defence in such circumstances, see Christopher Greenwood, 'International Law and the "War on Terrorism"' (2002) 78 *International Affairs* 301; Michael Byers, 'Terrorism, the Use of Force and International Law after 11 September' (2002) 51 *International and Comparative Law Quarterly* 401; for arguments against, see Antonio Cassese, 'Terrorism Is Also Disrupting Some Crucial Legal Categories in International Law' (2001) 12 *European Journal of International Law* 993; Eric Myjer and Nigel White, 'The Twin Towers Attack: An Unlimited Right to Self-Defence?' (2002) 7 *Journal of Conflict and Security Law* 5; J. Kammerhofer, 'Armed Activities Case and Non-State Actors in Self-Defence Law' (2007) 20 *Leiden Journal of International Law* 89. See also *Legal Consequences of the Construction of a Wall in the Occupied Palestinian Territory*, Advisory Opinion (2004) ICJ Reports 36, para. 139; and *Case Concerning Armed Activities on the Territory of the Congo (Democratic Republic of the Congo v. Uganda)* (2005) ICJ Reports, paras. 146, 147; the majority decisions in both cases have been criticized for disregarding the possibility of self-defence against non-State actors: see e.g. Separate Opinions, in the former case by Judge Higgins, paras. 33–6, in the latter by Judge Kooijmans, paras. 26–30 and Judge Simma, paras. 7–12; and see Sean Murphy, 'Self-Defence and the Israeli Wall Advisory Opinion: An Ipse Dixit' (2005) 99 *American Journal of International Law* 62.

[71] For useful overviews of State practice, see Christian Tams, 'The Use of Force against Terrorists' (2009) 20 *European Journal of International Law* 1; and Tom Ruys, *'Armed Attack' and Article 51 of the UN Charter: Evolutions in Customary Law and Practice* (Cambridge, 2010) 419.

Authorization under Chapter VII

The Security Council, acting under Chapter VII of the UN Charter, may authorize the use of force, either by UN peacekeeping or peace-enforcement missions ('blue helmets') or by coalitions of forces of States. Such authorizations provide an undoubted exception to the prohibition on the use of force set out in Article 2(4). Even here there may be controversy. For example, the legal justification put forward by the United Kingdom and the United States for the military intervention in 2003 in Iraq was that their military action had been authorized by the Security Council; the argument, which is widely accepted as having little substance, interpreted Resolution 1441(2002) as reviving the authorization (given in Resolution 678 (1991)) to use military action to counter Iraq's invasion of Kuwait in 1990, without the need for any further decision by the Council.[72]

Humanitarian intervention

This term is given to military action taken for humanitarian purposes but without Security Council authorization and without the agreement of the State concerned. On its face such action breaches the prohibition on the use of force set out in Article 2(4), but commentators differ as to whether interventions such as that in 1991 in northern Iraq, and in 1999 by NATO in Kosovo, are nevertheless lawful. The conservative, and perhaps the better, view is that humanitarian intervention is contrary to international law; a few doubtful examples of humanitarian practice cannot constitute a new rule of customary international law. Other commentators state either that there is an emerging norm of customary law which allows the implementation by the international community of the responsibility to protect, or that such intervention is already lawful under existing international law; these views rely on arguments about the interpretation of Article 2(4), and as to the continued existence of a customary law right which has not been displaced by the Charter.[73] Military interventions such as these remain a difficulty in defining the crime of aggression.[74]

---

[72] On these and other arguments for and against the legality of the intervention, see the papers in 'Agora: Future Implications of the Iraq Conflict' (2003) 97 *American Journal of International Law*, 553–642; Sean Murphy, 'Assessing the Legality of Invading Iraq' (2004) 92 *Georgetown Law Journal* 173.

[73] All of these views are discussed in J. L. Hozgrefe and Robert Keohane (eds.), *Humanitarian Intervention* (Cambridge, 2003); see also Bruno Simma, 'NATO, the UN and the Use of Force: Legal Aspects' (1999) 10 *European Journal of International Law* 1; Nico Krisch, 'Unilateral Enforcement of the Collective Will: Kosovo, Iraq, and the Security Council' (1999) 3 *Max Planck Yearbook of United Nations Law* 59; Adam Roberts, 'The So-Called "Right" of Humanitarian Intervention' (2000) 3 *Yearbook of International Humanitarian Law* 3; International Development Research Centre, *The Responsibility to Protect: Report of the International Commission on Intervention and State Sovereignty* (Ottawa, 2001); Danish Institute of International Affairs, *Humanitarian Intervention: Legal and Political Aspects* (Copenhagen, 1999); Gray, *International Law and the Use of Force*, 33–53.

[74] For the view that humanitarian intervention is included within the draft definition of aggression, see Kriangsak Kittichaisaree, 'The NATO Military Action and the Potential Impact of the International Criminal Court' (2000) 4 *Singapore Journal of International and Comparative Law* 498, 506, 507.

13.2.4 '[A] manifest violation of the Charter'

As we have seen, the ICC definition as agreed in Kampala effectively encompasses every unlawful use of force by a State within the term 'act of aggression'. But the commission by a State of an act of aggression does not in itself criminalize the participation in that act by the State's leaders. The crime is constituted by participation (in the manner and by the persons discussed above)[75] in an act which 'by its character, gravity and scale, constitutes a manifest violation of the Charter of the United Nations'. The origin of this threshold needs explanation.

The crime of aggression under customary international law is generally regarded as being limited to participation in a 'war' of aggression.[76] Although declared war is now uncommon and the term is not employed in the legal regimes of the UN Charter and the Geneva Conventions, it is possible to give the term content even when it has lost its currency in international relations.[77] There were accordingly attempts during the course of the negotiations for the ICC Statute to include within the definition only such uses of force which could be regarded as equating to a 'war', whether because they were large scale or because of the aggressive aim or intention of the leadership.[78] For example, one of the proposals put forward by Germany in the negotiations referred to the unlawful use of force carried out 'with the object or result of establishing a military occupation of, or annexing' the foreign territory.[79] Those purposes would, however, have excluded acts which might be regarded as properly coming within the criminal category,[80] for example aggressive wars to extract economic or political advantages of some kind. The ICC definition as finally agreed did not include reference to the purpose of the use of force, nor a special intent (as in genocide).

Instead, the threshold of 'manifest violation' was included. It raises obvious difficulties of interpretation.[81] 'Manifest', according to the *Oxford English Dictionary*, means 'evident to the eye, mind or judgment; obvious'. We may say that even a minor border skirmish may be evident and obvious. But the reference to gravity and scale appears to exclude even obvious violations if they are of insufficient severity.

[75] See section 3.2.1 and section 3.2.2.
[76] See e.g. T. Bruha, *Die Definition der Aggression* (Berlin, 1980) 126; Dinstein, *War, Aggression*, 130–5; Claus Kreß, 'The German Chief Federal Prosecutor's Decision Not to Investigate the Alleged Crime of Preparing Aggression against Iraq' (2004) 2 *Journal of International Criminal Justice* 245, 249. See to the contrary Richard Griffiths, 'International Law, the Crime of Aggression and the Ius ad Bellum' (2002) 2 *International Criminal Law Review* 301, 303–4; Mary Ellen O'Connell and Mirakmal Niyazmatov, 'What Is the Crime of Aggression? Comparing the Ius ad Bellum and the ICC Statute' (2012) 10 *Journal of International Criminal Justice* 189.
[77] See e.g. Dinstein, *War, Aggression*, Chapter 6.
[78] This is variously described as a special intent required for participants in aggression, or as a material element of the crime: Stefan Glaser, 'Quelques remarques sur la définition de l'aggression en droit international pénal' in S. Hohenleitner *et al.* (eds.), *Festschrift für Theodor Rittler* (Aalen, 1957) 383; Brownlie, *International Law and the Use of Force*, 213; Kreß, 'The German Prosecutor's Decision', 256; Kreß, 'Time for Decision: Some Thoughts on the Immediate Future of the Crime of Aggression: A Reply to Andreas Paulus' (2009) 20 *European Journal of International Law* 1129, 1136–42; Cassese, 'On Some Problematic Aspects of the Crime of Aggression' (2007) 20 *Leiden Journal of International Law* 841, 848.
[79] PCNICC/1999/DP.13.   [80] Clark, 'Rethinking Aggression as a Crime', 878.
[81] For a critique of the term and the rest of the definition, see Andreas Paulus, 'Second Thoughts on the Crime of Aggression' (2009) 20 *European Journal of International Law* 1117, 1119–25.

Two of the 'understandings' which were adopted at Kampala as a means of interpretation of the amendments[82] relate to this threshold. The first states that 'aggression is the most serious and dangerous form of illegal use of force, and that a determination whether an act of aggression has been committed requires consideration of all the circumstances of each particular case, including the gravity of the acts concerned and their consequences, in accordance with the Charter of the United Nations'.[83]

The second understanding states:

the three components of character, gravity and scale must be sufficient to justify a 'manifest' determination. No one component can be significant enough to satisfy the manifest standard by itself.[84]

In spite of the poor drafting of this understanding, it is apparent from the reading of the definition of the crime itself that there must be a finding with respect to each one of the three elements of character, gravity and scale, although the meaning of 'character' may be difficult to agree upon.

The reference to 'gravity and scale', and the first understanding set out above, do make it clear that 'manifest violation' does, at the least, include only violations that are manifestly serious in scale and effect. It has also been suggested that the term means 'manifestly unlawful', with the intention of excluding grey areas of public international law on the use of force including such controversial uses of force as humanitarian intervention, self-defence against terrorist groups in other States, and anticipatory self-defence.[85] (It should be noted, however, that a proposal by the US delegation at Kampala that there should be a specific exclusion of force used for humanitarian intervention was not accepted by the conference.[86]) That 'manifest violation' refers to both seriousness and manifest illegality would appear to be supported in the *travaux préparatoires*.[87] And the amended Elements make clear that the violation must be 'manifest' to the Court, not simply to the aggressor or victim States.[88]

A great deal however is being demanded of the term 'manifest violation'. The law lacks the necessary certainty if State leaders cannot predict in advance whether they will be vulnerable to prosecution, or not, depending upon the meaning eventually ascribed by the ICC to the term and upon whether the ICC concludes that the law is sufficiently controversial, or the State's act is not sufficiently serious, for the violation not to be regarded as 'manifest'.

---

[82] For discussion of the legal status of the understandings, see Kevin Heller, 'The Uncertain Legal Status of the Aggression Understandings' (2012) 10 *Journal of International Criminal Justice* 229.

[83] RC/Res.6, Annex III, Understanding No. 6.   [84] *Ibid.*, Understanding No. 7.

[85] See e.g. Claus Kreß, 'The Crime of Aggression before the First Review of the ICC Statute' (2007) 20 *Leiden Journal of International Law* 851; the term 'fully accords with the goal of the Statute's drafters to confine the Court's jurisdiction to atrocious behaviour that indisputably violates general customary international law' (at 859). Although written before the Review Conference, this comment refers to the text as agreed. See also the discussion in Kreß, 'The German Prosecutor's Decision', 259.

[86] Note that the view of Kreß on the reason for non-acceptance of the US proposal for exclusion was that there was not necessarily disagreement on the substance but that 'it would not be appropriate to address key issues of current international security law in the form of understandings drafted not with all due care, but in the haste of the final hours of diplomatic negotiations'. Kreß and von Holtzendorff, 'The Kampala Compromise on the Crime of Aggression' at 1205.

[87] E.g. para. 24 of the 2008 Report of the Special Working Group reads as follows: 'Delegations supporting this threshold clause noted that it would appropriately limit the Court's jurisdiction to the most serious acts of aggression under customary international law, thus excluding cases of insufficient gravity and falling within a grey area.'

[88] The 'term "manifest" is an objective qualification'. RC/Res.6, Annex II, Introduction, para. 3.

13.3   Mental elements

The amendments to the ICC Elements of Crimes adopted at the Kampala Review Conference include two mental elements, Elements 4 and 6. Element 4 requires that the perpetrator is aware of the factual circumstances establishing the inconsistency of the use of armed force by the State with the Charter of the United Nations. Element 6 requires that the perpetrator is aware of the factual circumstances establishing the manifest violation of the Charter. There is no requirement to prove that the perpetrator knew of the illegality, or made a legal evaluation of the act's inconsistency with the Charter or of its 'manifest' nature.[89] Provided, therefore, that the perpetrator intended to lead his country into a conflict and knew of the circumstances surrounding the conflict, it is not necessary that he knew that the conflict was unlawful.

The post-Second World War case law indicates that the intent to participate in the aggressive act was present if the perpetrator had knowledge of the collective intent to initiate and wage aggressive war but continued to participate. Two examples from the Nuremberg trial will suffice. Schacht was at some relevant periods President of the Reichsbank and a central figure in Germany's rearmament programme. 'But', said the Tribunal, 'rearmament of itself is not criminal under the Charter. To be a crime against peace under Article 6 of the Charter it must be shown that Schacht carried out this rearmament as part of the Nazi plans to wage aggressive wars.'[90] He was acquitted since it could not be inferred from the evidence that he knew of the plans for aggressive war. Bormann rose to a position of great power and was finally of great influence over Hitler. But the evidence did not show that he knew of the plans; he did not attend the crucial planning meetings. He was acquitted of the crimes against peace charged against him.[91]

13.4   Prosecution of aggression in the ICC

It is only as a result of the amendments adopted at the Review Conference in Kampala that the ICC will be able to try the crime of aggression. But the compromise provisions agreed upon at Kampala include two preliminary hurdles. First, the Court may only exercise jurisdiction 'subject to a decision to be taken after 1 January 2017 by the same majority of States Parties as is required for the adoption of an amendment to the Statute'[92] (that is, probably, by a two-thirds majority). So theoretically (though unlikely in practice) the Kampala amendments could yet be rejected. Second, the ICC may only exercise jurisdiction over an alleged crime committed more than one year after thirty States have ratified or accepted the amendments.[93] The meaning of the provisions is not entirely clear, but two 'understandings' adopted at the conference[94] appear to give them a cumulative effect: that is to say, the ICC will only have jurisdiction in respect of crimes committed after the

---

[89] Introduction, paras. 2 and 4.
[90] Nuremberg IMT, Judgment and Sentences, reprinted in (1947) 41 *American Journal of International Law* 172, 300.
[91] *Ibid.*, 329.   [92] RC/Res.6, Annex I, Art. 15*bis*, para. 3; Art. 15*ter*, para. 3.
[93] RC/Res.6, Annex I, Art. 15*bis*, para. 2; Art. 15*ter*, para. 2.   [94] RC/Res.6, Annex III, Understandings Nos. 1 and 3.

affirmative decision of the States Parties in 2017 or later. It will not have jurisdiction over crimes committed in earlier years, even if thirty States ratify or accept the amendments before 2017.

These aspects of the provisions adopted at Kampala were included in order to reach agreement by consensus on a package of amendments which have to be considered as a whole. The discussion below of the jurisdiction of the Court and the conditions under which it will exercise that jurisdiction is subject to these two hurdles. Until they are surmounted, the Court will not be able to exercise its jurisdiction over the crime of aggression.

13.4.1   *Jurisdiction of the ICC*

As a result of the provisions of the Statute and of the Kampala amendments, the rules for ICC jurisdiction over the crime of aggression differ from those for other crimes. Recall that for the other three crimes the general rule in Article 12 is that the Court has jurisdiction if the alleged crime was committed by a national of a State Party or on the territory of a State Party; there is no possibility for States Parties of opting out; and jurisdiction can extend to the nationals or territory of non-States Parties if the conditions of Article 12 are met. But, for aggression, States Parties have a choice as to the jurisdiction they wish to accept (although it is not entirely clear how that choice is made, or how wide it is, as discussed below) and there is no jurisdiction over aggression when it is committed by the nationals of a non-State Party or committed on the territory of such a State. This is a departure from the general jurisdictional regime of Article 12. There will be jurisdiction without these qualifications if the Security Council refers a situation of aggression to the Court: there is no need for any State to have accepted the amendments.[95] And of course the possibility of accepting jurisdiction ad hoc under Article 12(3) still applies.

The Kampala amendments have left uncertainties about aspects of the Court's jurisdiction; these uncertainties result from disagreements at the Review Conference about which amendment procedures to use, and the decisions taken to resolve them. The principal difficulty is whether the nationals or territory of a State which does not accept the amendments are subject to the Court's jurisdiction. On the one hand, the amendments provide that a State Party may make a declaration that it does not accept the jurisdiction of the Court in respect of acts of aggression it commits (Article 15*bis*(4)). But this has to be contrasted with Article 121(5) of the existing Statute, the second sentence of which provides that, for a State Party which has not accepted an amendment relating to the crimes subject to the Court's jurisdiction, there will be no jurisdiction when the crime covered by the amendment is committed by that State Party's nationals or on its territory. On their face, these two provisions, Article 15*bis*(4) and Article 121(5), conflict. The former appears to be based on an assumption that there will be jurisdiction, once the amendments have entered into force, unless a State Party accepts the amendments and then opts out, with the further oddity that the opt-out seems to extend only to acts of aggression committed by the opting-out

---

[95] RC/Res.6, Annex I, Art. 15*ter*.

State. But the natural interpretation of Article 121(5) of the existing Statute leaves the nationals and territory of a State Party which does not accept the Kampala amendments unaffected by the Court's jurisdiction.[96]

Commentators differ on the explanations for the conflicting provisions and their interpretation.[97] The better view, in accordance with the relatively clear wording of Article 121(5) and its history, would seem to be that the nationals and territory of a State Party are not exposed to the Court's jurisdiction over the crime of aggression until the State ratifies or accepts the Kampala amendments; if a State Party accepts the amendments it then has the choice of opting out, under Article 15*bis*, but only in relation to acts of aggression it commits itself.

The contrary view is that States Parties will have to accept the amendments and then opt out if they do not want their nationals to be tried for aggression. It has to be recognized that such an interpretation of the Article 121 amendment procedures effectively amends Article 121 itself, a step not possible except through the amendment procedures set out in Article 121(4).[98] Accepting this interpretation would have an effect not only for the amendments on aggression but also for other amendments to the crimes in the Statute. The interpretation circumvents what had been intended as a safeguard for States which did not want to have new crimes included without their consent, and allows new amendments to be adopted in the future by a two-thirds majority or under whatever procedures the Assembly of States Parties may choose. It would be advisable for the States Parties to resolve this problem when the Assembly of States Parties takes the necessary further decision in 2017; otherwise the continuing uncertainty may have to be settled by the Court.

Another issue of contention relates to non-States Parties. The amendments provide that the Court has no jurisdiction over the crime of aggression with respect to a State that is not a party to the Statute 'when committed by that State's nationals or on its territory'.[99] The result is that the Court cannot try any of their nationals for the crime of aggression nor any aggression committed on their territory by others – unless the Security Council refers the situation to the Court. The removal of States not party to the Statute from the ambit of the Court's aggression jurisdiction, although perhaps politically desirable, involves an amendment to the Statute which should have been effected by the slower procedure of Article 121(4).

---

[96] RC/Res.6, para. 1, provides that the amendments shall enter into force in accordance with Art. 121(5), confirming that the conference considered that this provision applies even though the amendments went wider than amendments to Art. 5.

[97] For a useful and critical analysis, see Andreas Zimmerman, 'Amending the Amendment Provisions of the Rome Statute' (2012) 10 *Journal of International Criminal Justice* 209. For a differing account, see Kreß and von Holtzendorff, 'The Kampala Compromise' (2010) 8 *Journal of International Criminal Justice* 1179; among other points, the authors describe an interpretative approach by which Art. 121(5) does not preclude ICC jurisdiction over a national of a non-ratifying State Party when the alleged aggression was committed within the territory of a State Party that *has* ratified or accepted the amendment. This approach relies on Art. 12(2) of the Statute (which allows the Court to exercise its jurisdiction over the nationals of States that are not parties to the Statute whenever their acts are committed on the territory of a State Party) and conflicts with the history of the ICC Statute; see e.g. Mauro Politi, 'The ICC and the Crime of Aggression' (2012) 10 *Journal of International Criminal Justice* 267, 280. See also Sean Murphy, 'The Crime of Aggression at the ICC' in Marc Weller (ed.), *Oxford Handbook on the Use of Force* (forthcoming, 2013).

[98] For reference to statements by Japan at the Review Conference and France at the subsequent Assembly of States Parties, expressing disagreement with the procedures used, see Politi, 'The ICC and the Crime of Aggression' at 281–2.

[99] RC/Res.6, Annex I, Art. 15*bis*, para. 5.

Whether or not this attempt to amend the Statute has been successful may, like the other defects of the amendments, have to be determined by the Court.

13.4.2   *The role of the Security Council*

The crime of aggression presupposes that an aggressive act has been committed by a State. When the ILC included aggression in its draft Statute, it considered that it was not appropriate for the ICC to try individuals in the absence of a finding of aggression against the State concerned.[100] To hold an individual responsible for a crime of participation in a State's act condemns the State itself. The ILC proposed that, in view of the Security Council's responsibilities under the UN Charter, the way to resolve the problem was to require that, before the ICC could exercise its jurisdiction, there had to be a prior determination by the Security Council that a State had committed the act of aggression which was the subject of the proceedings.[101] The legal effect of any such determination would be for the ICC itself to decide.

As we have seen,[102] this provision was not included in the ICC Statute, and Article 5(2) left the whole question for further negotiations. The requirement in that Article that the conditions for the exercise of the ICC's jurisdiction must be 'consistent with the relevant provisions of the Charter of the United Nations' was interpreted by some as requiring a determination by the Council, prior to ICC prosecution, that the State concerned had committed aggression.[103] But those opposing a Security Council filter were in a large majority. The arguments were largely of a political or practical nature. On the one hand, to require the Court to act only after the Council's determination would have given the permanent members of the Council an effective veto over prosecutions relating to themselves and their allies. The Court ought to be allowed to act without Council interference.[104] The Council has in fact very rarely made a determination of aggression,[105] and if this inaction continued there would be a risk that the Court would be blocked from ever considering a case of aggression. On the other hand, if the ICC, in the absence of a Security Council determination, had to decide that an act of aggression had taken place, it might infringe on the responsibilities of the Council with regard to the actions of the State concerned. There could be a risk that investigations undertaken by the ICC for an act of aggression without a prior Council authorization might bring about an escalation of the

---

[100] James Crawford, 'The ILC's Draft Statute for an International Criminal Tribunal' (1994) 88 *American Journal of International Law* 134, 147.

[101] Art. 23(2) of the ILC draft Statute. See Crawford, 'The ILC's Draft Statute'; and James Crawford, 'The ILC Adopts a Statute for an International Criminal Court' (1995) 89 *American Journal of International Law* 404, 411.

[102] In section 13.1.2.

[103] This was the understanding of the United Kingdom, as indicated in its statement made on the adoption of the Statute on 17 July 1998 (UN Doc. A/CONF.183/13 (Vol. II) at p. 124); see also Zimmerman in Triffterer, *Observers' Notes*, 140, 144; see also Rolf Fife, 'Criminalizing Individuals for Acts of Aggression Committed by States' in Morten Bergsmo (ed.), *Human Rights and Criminal Justice for the Downtrodden* (Leiden and Boston, 2003) 53, at 67.

[104] See e.g. Antonio Cassese, 'The Statute of the International Criminal Court: Some Preliminary Reflections' (1999) 10 *European Journal of International Law* 144, 147.

[105] Although in relation to several situations the Council has described certain conduct as acts of aggression: see 'Historical Review', PCNICC/2002/WGCA/L.1, paras. 381–404.

situation.[106] To avoid the Council blocking a case through inertia, it was suggested that if the Council failed to act the UN General Assembly, or the ICJ under its advisory jurisdiction, should be able to make a determination of responsibility by a State prior to trial of an individual by the ICC.

At the Review Conference, the question whether there should be a role for a UN organ was one of the most contentious. Agreement on a final text was secured by linking the issue of the Security Council role with the jurisdictional reach of the Court over the crime, as discussed in the previous section. The final result, as set out in new Articles 15*bis* and 15*ter*, is that, if the Security Council refers to the ICC a situation of aggression, the ICC will have jurisdiction as for the other crimes in the Statute and there is no need for a Council determination of an act of aggression by a State. If the situation is referred to the Court by a State Party, or if the Prosecutor exercises his or her own power to begin an investigation, the Prosecutor must notify the UN Secretary-General and ascertain whether the Security Council has made a determination of an act of aggression by the State concerned. If the Council has done so, the Prosecutor may proceed with the investigation. If no such determination has been made within six months of the notification, the Prosecutor may proceed but must secure authorization for the investigation from the Pre-Trial Division.[107] The Security Council may also ask for a suspension of proceedings under Article 16 in the usual way.

13.4.3   Implications of the prosecution of aggression before the ICC

The outcome of the Kampala Review Conference was greeted with great enthusiasm.[108] More than sixty years after the Nuremberg judgment the international community had finally reached agreement on the future prosecution of the crime of aggression. But, before joining the chorus, it is wise to consider the concerns which have been expressed about the implications of prosecuting the crime.

As we have seen, there is concern about the ambiguity and indeed indeterminacy of the definition. Some have expressed this in strong terms:

> The definition's ambiguity broadens its potential reach to the point that, had it been in effect for the last several decades, every US President since John F. Kennedy, hundreds of US legislators and military leaders, as well as innumerable military and political leaders from other countries could have been subject to prosecution.[109]

[106] See e.g. Andreas Zimmerman, 'The Creation of a Permanent International Criminal Court' (1998) 2 *Max Planck Yearbook of International Law* 169, 203.
[107] The amendment (Art. 15*bis*, para. 8) specifies the Division rather than a Pre-Trial Chamber. For comment, see Politi, 'The ICC and the Crime of Aggression'.
[108] Kreß and von Holtzendorff, 'The Kampala Compromise on the Crime of Aggression' at 1180: the amendments were adopted with 'an outburst of collective joy'.
[109] Michael Glennon, 'The Blank-Prose Crime of Aggression' (2010) 35 *Yale Journal of International Law*, written before the adoption of the Kampala amendments but making reference to the definition there adopted.

Others, while recognizing the problem, point out that the extent of uncertainty is not unique among other international or domestic crimes and that the ICC will have to resolve the outstanding matters – though needing to exercise its discretion with great care.[110]

Another concern relates to what might amount, in effect, to the invocation of criminal law to regulate the use of force by States. To turn the ICC into a forum for litigating disputes between States risks harm both to the Court and to the maintenance of international peace and security.[111] The determination of whether there has been an act of aggression by a State will be a necessary part of the Court's decision on an individual's criminal responsibility, and such determinations – by a criminal court – will be likely to have repercussions for the maintenance of international peace and security.

Further, the ICC will need to enter into highly political and controversial questions of public international law.[112] The legal principles of the *ius ad bellum* give rise to significantly more controversy than the *ius in bello*. The Court is not best placed to settle controversies about the content of international law on the use of force which have dogged the international community for decades.[113] This leads to a related concern that the prosecution of aggression may have 'collateral implications' for public international law outside the context of criminal law. The understanding adopted at Kampala seeks to lessen the possibility:

It is understood that the amendments that address the definition of the act of aggression and the crime of aggression do so for the purpose of this Statute only. The amendments shall, in accordance with article 10 of the Rome Statute, not be interpreted as limiting or prejudicing in any way existing or developing rules of international law for purposes other than this Statute.

But the future practice of the ICC in prosecuting or not prosecuting particular acts may, it has been argued, influence existing views of the justifiability or not of certain uses of force under the ius ad bellum, and the higher threshold given in the definition of the crime of aggression may seem to condone lesser uses of force by a State.[114]

The practical difficulties for the ICC in particular cases are likely to be severe. The constitution and procedures of the ICC are designed for the determination of individual, not State, responsibility.[115] The concept of complementarity, fundamental to the success of the

---

[110] Marko Milanovic, 'Aggression and Legality: Custom in Kampala' (2012) 10 *Journal of International Criminal Justice* 165.

[111] Fife, 'Criminalizing Individuals', 70–3.

[112] Meron, 'Defining Aggression', 1. See also Erin Creegan, 'Justified Uses of Force and the Crime of Aggression' (2012) 10 *Journal of International Criminal Justice* 59.

[113] See e.g. Claus Kreß, 'The Crime of Aggression before the First Review of the ICC Statute' (2007) 20 *Leiden Journal of International Law* 851. International criminal law is 'ill-equipped to decide major controversies about the content of existing legal rules' (at 851). See also Creegan, 'Justified Uses of Force', concluding therefore that 'the crime of aggression must be excluded from the jurisdiction of the ICC and the understanding of good or bad uses of force trusted to the development of state practice and the political judgment of states' (at 82).

[114] The first concern is expressed by Murphy, 'The Crime of Aggression at the ICC'; the second by Mary Ellen O'Connell and Mirakmal Niyazmatov, 'What Is the Crime of Aggression? Comparing the Ius ad Bellum and the ICC Statute' (2012) 10 *Journal of International Criminal Justice* 189.

[115] One important aspect of the ICC Statute is the attention given to the needs of victims of crimes; for example they are accorded rights of participation in trials and rights of protection and reparation. Whereas the victims of the other crimes within the jurisdiction of the Court are individuals, the victim of an act of aggression is in reality a State. See James Boeving, 'Aggression, International Law, and the ICC: An Argument for the Withdrawal of Aggression from the Rome Statute' (2005) 43 *Columbia Journal of Transnational Law* 557, 583–8.

ICC, does not fit well with the crime of aggression.[116] Except where the documents of a defeated State are available to the international community, as with Germany and Japan in the Second World War – when the Tribunals had a glut of the defeated governments' most secret papers[117] – there will be difficulties of access to evidence.

Before the adoption of the Kampala amendments, some commentators expressed doubts about the inclusion of aggression in the ICC Statute at all,[118] and about whether its inclusion would be more than pure symbolism.[119] If one prediction may be safely made, it is that there will not be many prosecutions for aggression before the Court. But, if the existence of ICC jurisdiction acts as a deterrent to even a few war-mongering presidents and prime ministers, it has the potential thereby to save many lives.

Further reading

The definition of aggression and the other amendments adopted at Kampala may be found on the website of the ICC, www.icc-cpi.int. One issue of the *Journal of International Criminal Justice* (2012, number 10) is devoted entirely to articles on the crime of aggression in light of the Kampala amendments.

M. Cherif Bassiouni and Benjamin Ferencz, 'The Crime against Peace' in M. Cherif Bassiouni (ed.), *International Criminal Law*, 2nd edn (New York, 1999) Vol. I, 313

Neil Boister and Robert Cryer, *The Tokyo International Military Tribunal: A Reappraisal* (Oxford, 2008)

Ian Brownlie, *International Law and the Use of Force by States* (Oxford, 1963)

Yoram Dinstein, *War, Aggression and Self-Defence*, 5th edn (Cambridge, 2011)

Rolf Einar Fife, 'Criminalizing Individuals for Acts of Aggression Committed by States' in Morten Bergsmo (ed.), *Human Rights and Criminal Justice for the Downtrodden* (Leiden and Boston, 2003) 53

Ahmed Rifaat, *International Aggression* (Stockholm, 1979)

Kirsten Sellars, *Crimes against Peace in International Law* (Cambridge, 2013)

---

[116] Indeed, Beth van Schaack, 'Par in Parem Imperium Non Habet' (2012) 10 *Journal of International Criminal Justice* 133, argues that the ICC be allowed to exercise *de facto* primacy over the crime of aggression.

[117] In Japan, however, many of the relevant papers had been burnt.

[118] See e.g. Antonio Cassese, 'The Statute of the ICC: Some Preliminary Reflections' (1999) 10 *European Journal of International Law* 144, 146; a suggestion to delete aggression from the Statute was made in Matthias Schuster, 'The Rome Statute of an International Criminal Court and the Crime of Aggression: A Gordian Knot in Search of a Sword' (2003) 14 *Criminal Law Forum* 1.

[119] William Schabas, 'The Unfinished Work of Defining Aggression: How Many Times Must the Cannonballs Fly, before They Are Forever Banned?' in D. McGoldrick, P. Rowe and E. Donnelly (eds.), *The Permanent International Criminal Court* (Oxford and Portland, OR, 2004) 124, 141.

14

Transnational Crimes, Terrorism and Torture

14.1   Introduction

14.1.1   Overview

To focus only on the 'core crimes' and their prosecution would be to ignore a substantial area of criminal law with international implications; there are other crimes of international concern which have a huge impact on global economic development and on people's general welfare.[1] Crimes which are the subject of international suppression conventions, but for which there is as yet no international criminal jurisdiction, are the focus of this chapter. They are here termed 'transnational crimes'.[2] These are crimes which have actual or potential transboundary effects. We include torture in this chapter because, although it does not have a cross-border element, it is dealt with by the international community in the same way as transnational crimes properly so-called.[3]

The prevention and punishment of transnational crimes requires cooperation among governments and among law enforcement agencies. A growing number of agreements are being concluded to provide for this in relation to such crimes as drugs trafficking,[4] piracy,[5] slavery,[6]

---

[1] In Res. 56/120, the UN General Assembly expressed deep concern over 'the impact of transnational organised crime on the political, social and economic stability and development of societies'. UN Doc. A/RES/56/120 (2002).

[2] As, to some extent, with 'international criminal law', there is no real conceptual basis for this term; it is, however, now in common use. See further Chapter 1.

[3] Neil Boister, 'Transnational Criminal Law?' (2003) 14 *European Journal of International Law* 953, 967–77. Boister, *An Introduction to Transnational Criminal Law* (Oxford, 2012), states that '[t]ransnational crime is now a commonly used criminological term to describe cross-border or potentially cross-border crime'. He does not include torture within his classification of transnational crimes.

[4] UN Convention against Illicit Trafficking in Narcotic Drugs and Psychotropic Substances 1988.

[5] Arts. 100–105 of the UN Law of the Sea Convention 1982. Although the modern recurrence of piracy has led to suggestions that the crime be placed within the jurisdiction of an international court, assistance with national prosecutions would appear to be the better way forward; for a useful discussion of the options, see Report of the Secretary-General on possible options to further the aim of prosecuting and imprisoning persons responsible for acts of piracy and armed robbery at sea off the coast of Somalia, including, in particular, options for creating special domestic chambers possibly with international components, a regional tribunal or an international tribunal and corresponding imprisonment arrangements of 26 July 2010 (S/2010/39). See also Douglas Guilfoyle, 'Prosecuting Somali Pirates: A Critical Evaluation of the Options' (2012) 10 *Journal of International Criminal Justice* 767. For discussion of piracy prosecutions more generally, see 'Agora: Piracy Prosecutions' (2010) 104 *American Journal of International Law* 397.

[6] Among the more recent agreements on slavery are the 1926 Slavery Convention; the UN Supplementary Convention on the Abolition of Slavery, the Slave Trade and Institutions and Practices Similar to Slavery 1956; the UN Convention on the Law of the Sea 1982, Art. 99.

terrorism offences,[7] torture,[8] apartheid,[9] enforced disappearances,[10] corruption,[11] transnational organized crime including people trafficking, smuggling migrants and illegal arms trafficking.[12] Some of these are also covered by customary international law or are international crimes when committed in certain circumstances (for example, as crimes against humanity).[13] They include those which were listed as 'treaty crimes' in the ILC draft of the ICC Statute, but which were excluded from the final Rome Statute in the course of the negotiations.[14] Particular transnational crimes may in the future come to be dealt with as international crimes within the jurisdiction of an international court,[15] if States believe that the values they conflict with are sufficiently important to the international community and that international prosecution is an effective way of dealing with them.[16] New transnational crimes emerge, as States develop new suppression conventions.[17] While each transnational crime deserves a chapter to itself, for reasons of space only two categories, terrorism and torture, will be covered in this chapter, at sections 14.2 and 14.3 respectively; both of them, when committed under certain conditions, may also constitute international crimes within the jurisdiction of the international courts and tribunals.

14.1.2   *International suppression conventions*

Transnational criminal law relies on domestic legal systems for the prosecution of transnational crimes, rather than international courts and tribunals. To facilitate effective domestic prosecution, as well as to cooperate in the suppression of the crimes, States have concluded international agreements providing for the possibility of cooperation among States which otherwise might have few law enforcement concerns in common.[18] Transnational criminal law therefore consists, on the one hand, of treaty obligations between States and, on the other, the application of criminal law by those States to individuals in implementation of those treaty obligations.[19] The typical agreement requires States to create criminal offences of the relevant conduct in their domestic law, and defines the material and mental elements as a 'standard designed to produce the degree of correspondence between national definitions of crimes sufficient to enable international cooperation'.[20] The agreement will also

---

[7] See section 14.2.   [8] See section 14.3.
[9] International Convention on the Suppression and Punishment of the Crime of Apartheid 1973.
[10] International Convention for the Protection of All Persons from Enforced Disappearance 2006.
[11] UN Convention against Corruption 2003.
[12] UN Convention against Transnational Organized Crime 2000; Protocol to Prevent, Suppress and Punish Trafficking in Persons, Especially Women and Children, supplementing that Convention; Protocol against the Smuggling of Migrants by Land, Air and Sea, supplementing that Convention; Protocol against the Illicit Manufacturing of and Trafficking in Firearms, their Parts and Components and Ammunition, supplementing that Convention.
[13] For an interesting discussion in relation to the Tokyo Tribunal, see Neil Boister, 'Punishing Japan's "Opium War-Making" in China: The Relationship between Transnational Crime and Aggression' in Yuki Tanaka, Tim McCormack and Gerry Simpson (eds.), *Beyond Victor's Justice: The Tokyo War Crimes Trial Revisited* (Leiden, 2011).
[14] See section 8.2.
[15] Terrorism (under Lebanese law) already comes within the jurisdiction of one internationalized court, the Special Tribunal for Lebanon; see below for the decision of that Tribunal that it is an international crime under customary international law.
[16] See Neil Boister, 'International Tribunals for Transnational Crimes: Towards a Transnational Criminal Court?' (2012) 23(4) *Criminal Law Forum* 295–318.
[17] See Boister, *An Introduction*, Chapter 10 ('Emerging Transnational Crimes').
[18] See Ethan A. Nadelmann, 'Global Prohibition Regimes: The Evolution of Norms in International Society' (1990) 44 *International Organization* 479, 481.
[19] Boister, *An Introduction*, 13.   [20] Boister, *An Introduction*.

require States to take the necessary jurisdiction for the purpose of prosecution, and to provide penalties which take into account the gravity of the offences. States are also required either to extradite an offender or to consider the case for prosecution (*aut dedere aut judicare*), and to provide each other with mutual legal assistance for the purpose of prosecution or extradition.[21] All of these features are to be seen in the agreements on terrorist offences discussed in section 14.2.2.

The jurisdiction which States are required to take differs from one agreement to another, but in each case there is a link between the suspect and the State concerned. Most agreements require States to take jurisdiction based on territory and nationality. Some provide other options on grounds such as the nationality of the victim. For example, in the 1997 Convention for the Suppression of Terrorist Bombings, each State is *required* to take jurisdiction where the offence is committed in its territory, on its ships or aircraft, or by its nationals; it is *permitted* to take jurisdiction when the offence is committed against a national or against a State or government facility, by a stateless person, or in an attempt to compel the State to action or inaction, or when committed on an aircraft operated by the State.[22] The suppression conventions also require States to take jurisdiction so that they can prosecute if they do not extradite a suspect on their territory, wherever the crime was committed. This is a 'last resort universal jurisdiction'[23] *as between States Parties*, which is dependent on the presence of the suspect. In effect, the States Parties delegate authority to the other parties to exercise jurisdiction on their behalf.[24]

Because these agreements require that the crimes be prosecuted under domestic law, they do not themselves prescribe in detail the material and mental elements of the offences; many States, however, adopt the definitions they contain *verbatim* in their national law rather than further elaborate upon their definitions.[25] As a unified system of enforcement and suppression they are weak.[26] An additional criticism is that, since they largely rely on domestic legal systems to provide the necessary procedural rights for the accused during investigation and prosecution, this leaves scope for human rights violations in those States which do not have adequate fair trial and other such protections. In their concern with law and order, States Parties to the agreements have neglected human rights requirements.[27]

14.2   Terrorism

14.2.1   Introduction

The phenomenon of terrorism presents a number of difficulties of legal categorization. The problem of *defining* terrorism is not unique to lawyers: 'one man's terrorist is the other man's

---

[21] For discussion of *aut dedere aut judicare* obligations, see Chapter 4; for extradition and mutual legal assistance, see Chapter 5.
[22] Art. 6(1) and (2).
[23] See e.g. Art. 6(4) of the International Convention for the Suppression of Terrorist Bombings (the Terrorist Bombing Convention). See Roger Clark, 'Offences of International Concern: Multilateral Treaty Practice in the Forty Years since Nuremberg' (1988) 57 *Nordic Journal of International Law* 49, 58.
[24] See further section 3.3.2.   [25] See Clark, 'Offences of International Concern', 72, for further discussion.
[26] See Boister, *An Introduction*, Chapters 21 and 22.
[27] See Neil Boister, 'Human Rights Protections in the Suppression Conventions' (2002) 2 *Human Rights Law Review* 199.

freedom fighter' is a cliché which describes a genuine conceptual difficulty common to most commentators. Beyond this, it is important to consider whether 'terrorism' is a useful or necessary legal term.[28] Terrorism may be regarded as simply the commission of 'ordinary', though serious, criminal acts with a particular purpose. Some States, including the United Kingdom, do not have a specific offence of 'terrorism' in domestic law but use the criminal law to prosecute offences associated with terrorism.[29] Some would argue that the categorization of terrorism is positively dangerous, in that it may encourage counter-measures that disregard human rights.

A further question is the extent to which it is necessary – and justifiable – to use armed force against terrorists in those cases where terrorism cannot be adequately addressed solely by the criminal law. The lawfulness of the use of force and military detention to counter terrorism is beyond the scope of this chapter.[30] But some of the responses to terrorism have led one commentator to conclude that it is 'perhaps the ultimate paradox of the "war on terror" that the horrendous acts of lawlessness witnessed on 11 September 2001 have been relied upon to justify repeated violations and further disregard for the international rule of law'.[31]

The fight against terrorism is now multifaceted[32] and includes measures imposed by the UN Security Council, including financial sanctions. But the primary paradigm to address terrorism remains criminal law, and terrorist acts, in one form or another, constitute criminal offences. There remains the difficulty, for national and international systems alike, of classifying and defining who is a terrorist and who is not, for the purposes of criminal law. The question of definition is discussed at section 14.2.3.

Terrorist acts can be prosecuted in an international court at present only if they amount to war crimes or crimes against humanity. It is true that one internationalized court, the Special Tribunal for Lebanon, has jurisdiction over terrorist acts (see Chapter 9), but this jurisdiction is expressed in its Statute to be over crimes under Lebanese, not international,

---

[28] 'We have cause to regret that a legal concept of "terrorism" was ever inflicted upon us. The term . . . serves no operative legal purpose': R. R. Baxter, 'A Sceptical Look at the Concept of Terrorism' (1973/4) 7 *Akron Law Review* 380. 'Terrorism is a term without legal significance . . . The term is at once a shorthand to allude to a variety of problems with some common elements and a method of indicating community condemnation for the conduct concerned': Rosalyn Higgins, in discussing early attempts at a definition of terrorism in Rosalyn Higgins and Maurice Flory (eds.), *Terrorism and International Law* (London, 1997) 28.

[29] A whole raft of offences under UK legislation depend upon the definition of terrorism which is set out in the Terrorism Act 2000, s. 1, as amended by the Terrorism Act 2006 and the Counter-Terrorism Act 2008: terrorism means the use or threat of action which involves serious violence against a person or serious danger to property, endangers a person's life, creates a serious risk to public health or safety, or is designed seriously to interfere with or disrupt an electronic system where 'the use or threat is designed to influence the government or an intergovernmental organisation or to intimidate the public or a section of the public', and it is made 'for the purpose of advancing a political, religious, racial or ideological cause'. The offences which depend upon this definition include crimes associated with membership or support for a proscribed organization, encouraging or glorifying terrorist acts, funding and financing terrorist activities, and offences such as weapons training for terrorist purposes.

[30] For some of the extensive literature, see Jutta Brunnée and Stephen Toope, 'The Use of Force after Iraq' (2004) 53 *International and Comparative Law Quarterly* 785; Gilbert Guillaume, 'Terrorism and International Law' (2004) 53 *International and Comparative Law Quarterly* 537; Sean Murphy, 'Terrorism and the Concept of "Armed Attack" in Article 51 of the UN Charter' (2002) 43 *Harvard International Law Journal* 41; Tal Becker, *Terrorism and the State* (Oxford, 2006).

[31] Helen Duffy, *The 'War on Terror' and the Framework of International Law*, 2nd edn (Cambridge, forthcoming, 2014).

[32] See John P. Grant, 'Beyond the Montreal Convention' (2004) 36 *Case Western Reserve Journal of International Law* 453, 472. In the United Kingdom, the term 'the war on terror' was not used in the literal sense of an armed conflict; see the response of the Parliamentary Under-Secretary of State, Foreign and Commonwealth Office (Baroness Amos): 'The term "the war against terrorism" has been used to describe the whole campaign against terrorism, including military, political, financial, legislative and law enforcement measures' (Hansard, 22 November 2001, col. WA 53).

law.[33] Although the Appeals Chamber of the Special Tribunal for Lebanon has, controversially, determined that terrorism is already a crime under customary international law and that there is already a customary law definition of terrorism,[34] this chapter discusses terrorism within the category of 'transnational' rather than international crimes and discusses international cooperation with the purpose of securing prosecution in *national* courts. Brief consideration is, however, given at section 14.2.5 to the circumstances in which terrorist acts may also constitute international crimes which can be prosecuted by international jurisdictions.

14.2.2 *Development of international cooperation against terrorism*

One of the earliest attempts at agreeing on an international prohibition of terrorism was the 1937 Convention for the Prevention and Punishment of Terrorism, which was negotiated within the League of Nations following the assassination of King Alexander I of Yugoslavia in 1934. The Convention defined acts of terrorism as 'criminal acts directed against a State and intended or calculated to create a state of terror in the minds of particular persons, or a group of persons or the general public', and listed acts to be criminalized by States Parties, including those causing death, serious injury or loss of liberty to heads of State and public officials, damage to public property of another State, and risk to the lives of members of the public. The Convention did not receive sufficient ratifications to enter into force.[35] The United Nations took on the task of defining and prohibiting terrorism when the General Assembly set up a committee on terrorism in 1972, but although the committee met until 1979 it failed to reach agreement. There was disagreement as to whether acts committed by national liberation movements for causes such as decolonization should be excluded from any definition of terrorism, and there were related arguments that there should be no international ban on terrorist activities unless at the same time the causes of terrorism were understood and resolved.

Global counter-terrorism agreements

The impossibility of securing international agreement on an unqualified condemnation of terrorism led to the adoption of a 'thematic' approach to cooperation to prevent and

---

[33] Art. 2 of the STL Statute. However, the Special Tribunal for Lebanon, in *Ayyash et al.*, STL A. Ch., 16 February 2011, decided to apply Lebanese law in accordance with what it determined to be international customary law (see section 14.2.3).

[34] *Ibid*. The case, decided when Antonio Cassese was the President of the Chamber, followed the view expressed in his academic writings, e.g. 'Terrorism as an International Crime' in Andrea Bianchi (ed.), *Enforcing International Law Norms against Terrorism* (Oxford, 2004) 213; and in 'The Multifaceted Criminal Notion of Terrorism in International Law' (2006) 4 *Journal of International Criminal Justice* 1. The ruling is criticized in Ben Saul, 'Legislating from a Radical Hague: The United Nations Special Tribunal for Lebanon Invents an International Crime of Transnational Terrorism' (2011) 24 *Leiden Journal of International Law* 677; see also critique by Kai Ambos, 'Judicial Creativity at the Special Tribunal for Lebanon: Is there a Crime of Terrorism under International Law?' (2011) 24 *Leiden Journal of International Law* 655. To the contrary, see Manuel Ventura, 'Terrorism According to the Special Tribunal for Lebanon's Interlocutory Decision on the Applicable Law: A Defining Moment or a Moment of Defining?' (2011) 9 *Journal of International Criminal Justice* 1021.

[35] League of Nations Doc. C.546(1).M.383(1).1937.V. For an interesting review of its negotiation, see Ben Saul, 'The Legal Response of the League of Nations to Terrorism' (2006) 4 *Journal of International Criminal Justice* 78.

criminalize terrorist acts. International agreements were negotiated on specific areas of terrorist activity, each separately defined. There are eleven of these agreements, each of them negotiated to deal with specific kinds of terrorist threats prevalent at the time the agreements were concluded.[36] For example, two of the earliest conventions, the Hague and Montreal Conventions, deal with the safety of civil aviation, following instances of terrorist hijacking and other offences against air travel at the time.[37] The impetus for the drafting of the 1988 Convention on the Suppression of Unlawful Acts against the Safety of Maritime Navigation, on the other hand, was the hijacking in 1985 of the *Achille Lauro*, an Italian cruise ship, and the accompanying murder of an elderly disabled US citizen of Jewish origin.

The eleven agreements have as their purpose the effective *national* prosecution of specified acts, and thus their better prevention. They share the main features of the model already described,[38] incorporating the principle *aut dedere aut judicare* and imposing obligations on States Parties to give assistance in criminal and extradition proceedings. In their provisions on extradition, the three most recent agreements, unlike the early ones, specify that the offence in question may not be regarded as a political offence for the purpose of extradition or mutual legal assistance.[39]

With the conclusion of the Terrorist Bombing Convention in 1997, most kinds of 'terrorist' conduct had been covered in one or other of these agreements. For better or worse, however, a proposal was then introduced to negotiate a 'comprehensive' convention to address explicitly all forms of terrorism; as such it would of course require a definition of terrorism.[40] The hope of finally agreeing upon a definition of terrorism for the purpose of such a convention had received some impetus from a General Assembly resolution of 1994,[41] adopted by consensus, which annexed a Declaration on Terrorism containing the following provision:

---

[36] There are at present thirteen agreements altogether, but two of them, as explained below, do not follow the same model of State cooperation. The eleven agreements are: the 1970 Convention for the Suppression of Unlawful Seizure of Aircraft (the Hague Convention); the 1971 Convention for the Suppression of Unlawful Acts against the Safety of Civil Aviation (the Montreal Convention) and its 1988 Protocol for the Suppression of Unlawful Acts of Violence at Airports Serving International Civil Aviation; the 1973 Convention on the Prevention and Punishment of Crimes against Internationally Protected Persons, including Diplomatic Agents; the 1979 International Convention against the Taking of Hostages; the 1980 Convention on the Physical Protection of Nuclear Material; the 1988 Convention on the Suppression of Unlawful Acts against the Safety of Maritime Navigation (the SUA Convention) and its 1988 Protocol for the Suppression of Unlawful Acts against the Safety of Fixed Platforms Located on the Continental Shelf; the 1997 International Convention for the Suppression of Terrorist Bombings (the Terrorist Bombing Convention); the 1999 International Convention for the Suppression of the Financing of Terrorism (the Terrorist Financing Convention); and the 2005 International Convention for the Suppression of Acts of Nuclear Terrorism (the Nuclear Terrorism Convention). Within the list of global terrorism agreements are often included the 1963 Convention on Offences and Certain Other Acts Committed on Board Aircraft (the Tokyo Convention) and the 1991 Convention on the Marking of Plastic Explosives for the Purpose of Detection, but these two differ from the others: the objective of the Tokyo Convention is primarily to assign powers and jurisdiction to different States and persons in relation to activities on board aircraft, while the Plastic Explosives Convention provides for the marking of explosives and the prevention of possession and transfer of unmarked explosives. The UN Convention on the Safety of United Nations and Associated Personnel 1994 (annexed to GA Res. 49/59) is sometimes added to the list: although not drafted primarily as an instrument against terrorism, it follows the same model as the terrorism agreements.

[37] See Christopher Joyner and Robert Friedlander, 'International Civil Aviation' in M. Cherif Bassiouni (ed.), *International Criminal Law*, 2nd edn (New York, 1999) Vol. I, 837.

[38] At section 14.1.2.

[39] Art. 11 of the Terrorist Bombing Convention 1997; Art. 14 of the Terrorist Financing Convention 1999; and Art. 15 of the Nuclear Terrorism Convention 2005. See Chapter 5.

[40] The proposal was made by India in 1996: UN Doc. A/C.6/51/6.

[41] Declaration on Measures to Eliminate International Terrorism (1994), annexed to GA Res. 49/60 of 9 December 1994.

Criminal acts intended or calculated to provoke a state of terror in the general public, a group of persons or particular persons for political purposes are in any circumstances unjustifiable, whatever the considerations of a political, philosophical, ideological, racial, ethnic, religious or other nature which may be invoked to justify them.

The resolution, unlike previous ones, had no preambular reference to acts committed by a national liberation movement; it made quite clear that terrorism was condemned whatever the motivation and by whomever it was committed. Unfortunately, the hope that a similarly unqualified definition could be agreed was not fulfilled, and the negotiation of a comprehensive convention has been stalled for years.[42] The difficulties of reaching agreement on a definition relate largely to two connected questions: are there causes which justify acts otherwise classed as terrorism, which should therefore be excluded? And should 'State terrorism' be included?

Regional counter-terrorism agreements

There are a number of international counter-terrorism agreements which have been concluded within the forums of regional organizations.[43] Like the global conventions, these agreements are generally focused on methods of international cooperation with the aim of national prosecution. Another regional initiative is the European Union's Framework Decision on Combating Terrorism, adopted on 13 June 2002 in implementation of Security Council Resolution 1373(2001).[44] The Council Decision requires that a list of acts must be deemed to be terrorist offences; directing and participating in the activities of a terrorist group is also to be punishable. The differing formulations in these regional instruments illustrate the problem of defining terrorism.

Security Council resolutions

After the occurrence of specific instances of terrorism, the Security Council determined that suppression of international terrorism was essential for the maintenance of international peace and security and took decisions requiring the surrender to justice of persons accused of terrorist acts. On 21 December 1988, Pan Am flight 103, bound from London to New York, exploded over the Scottish town of Lockerbie. The blast killed all 259 people on board and eleven people on the ground. The suspects identified in the Scottish investigation that

---

[42] For a study of the negotiations, see Tal Becker, *Terrorism and the State* (Oxford, 2006) 84–118. For the text of the draft convention and the state of the negotiations in 2013, see Report of the Ad Hoc Committee established by General Assembly Resolution 51/210 of 17 December 1996 (16th Session), UN Doc. A/68/37.

[43] Arab Convention on the Suppression of Terrorism 1998 (the Arab Convention); Convention of the Organization of the Islamic Conference on Combating International Terrorism 1999; European Convention on the Suppression of Terrorism 1977; Organization of American States Convention to Prevent and Punish Acts of Terrorism Taking the Form of Crimes against Persons and Related Extortion that Are of International Significance 1971; OAU Convention on the Prevention and Combating of Terrorism 1999; South Asian Association for Regional Co-operation, Regional Convention on Suppression of Terrorism 1987; Treaty on Cooperation among the States Members of the Commonwealth of Independent States in Combating Terrorism 1999 (the CIS Convention); European Convention on the Prevention of Terrorism 2005.

[44] 2002/475/JHA, OJ L164/3, 22 June 2002, as amended by Decision 2008/919/JHA, OJ L330, 9 December 2008, p. 21.

followed were believed to be Libyan State agents, and the governments requiring the suspects to be brought to justice did not proceed under the Montreal Convention on the ground that the Convention, with its focus on national proceedings, did not cover State-sponsored terrorism.[45] The Security Council required Libya to surrender the suspects, and imposed sanctions when the request was not acceded to.[46] Examples of similar Council resolutions are those requiring Sudan to hand over the persons accused of attempting to assassinate the President of Egypt,[47] and requiring the Taliban to transfer Osama bin Laden to countries which had indicted him.[48] In another part of its role in countering international terrorism, the Council has imposed economic and other sanctions on persons associated with Al Qaeda and the Taliban.[49] The Security Council has also determined that international terrorism more generally is a threat to international peace and security. Resolution 1368(2001), adopted the day after 11 September 2001, stated that the terrorist attacks in Washington and New York were, 'like any act of international terrorism … a threat to international peace and security'. The Council went further in Resolution 1373(2001), adopted under Chapter VII of the Charter, and imposed extensive obligations on States in relation to the suppression of terrorist acts, including the financing of terrorism. The resolution covers some of the same ground as the global terrorism conventions, in particular the Terrorist Financing Convention. The resolution, which was controversial when adopted,[50] decides, *inter alia*, that all States must ensure that any person who participates in financing, planning, preparing for, perpetrating or supporting terrorist acts is brought to justice, and States must establish such acts as serious criminal offences in their law with appropriately serious penalties (paragraph 2(e)). But, although it imposes binding obligations, establishes the Counter-Terrorism Committee to monitor their implementation, and is a significant part of the international counter-terrorism effort, the resolution contains no definition of terrorism.

14.2.3   The definition of terrorism

As yet, no definition of terrorism has been agreed for the purpose of a *global* prohibition of terrorist acts in a legally binding instrument. None of the eleven global conventions defines terrorism except the Terrorist Financing Convention, and that is only for a secondary purpose.[51] Many of the agreements do not even mention the word 'terrorism', thus

[45] See Higgins, in Higgins and Flory, *Terrorism and International Law*, 23.
[46] SC Res. 731(1992) and 748(1992). For the end of the story, see section 9.5, and Michael Plachta, 'The Lockerbie Case: The Role of the Security Council in Enforcing the Principle Aut Dedere Aut Judicare' (2001) 12 *European Journal of International Law* 125.
[47] Following their flight to Sudan; Res. 1044(1966) and 1054(1966).   [48] SC Res. 1267(1999) and 1333(2000).
[49] There is a long string of Security Council resolutions on the subject; see e.g. Res. 2082(2012) and 2983(2012).
[50] Res. 1373(2001) was criticized as Security Council 'legislation' in a field which is the preserve of intergovernmental agreement; for discussion, see Matthew Happold, 'Security Council Resolution 1373 and the Constitution of the United Nations' (2003) 16 *Leiden Journal of International Law* 593; Paul Szasz, 'The Security Council Starts Legislating' (2002) 96 *American Journal of International Law* 901; Stefan Talmon, 'The Security Council as World Legislature' (2005) 99 *American Journal of International Law* 175.
[51] Art. 2 of the Convention refers to the offence of financing acts of terrorism, which are defined as acts covered by the terrorism conventions and 'any other act intended to cause death or serious bodily injury to a civilian, or to any other person not taking an active part in the hostilities in a situation of armed conflict, when the purpose of such act, by its nature or context, is to intimidate a population, or to compel a Government or an international organisation to do or to abstain from doing any act'.

exemplifying the view that it is possible to deal with terrorism without creating specific 'terrorist' offences. There are, however, definitions of a kind. Each of the regional counter-terrorism agreements has a definition of terrorism for the purpose of the agreement; while some merely list the offences covered by the global conventions with or without other serious offences,[52] others create their own generic definitions.[53] Security Council Resolution 1566(2004) has a description of terrorism (said not to be a 'definition');[54] it covers only the acts included in the global conventions, and specifies that they are commit-ted with 'the purpose to provoke a state of terror … intimidate a population or compel a government or an international organisation to do or to abstain from doing any act'.

The difficulties of negotiating a universally agreed definition raise the question whether the effort is worthwhile. Each of the underlying acts which go to make up a terrorist offence is already criminalized in the various agreements. It might make more sense for the focus in the UN to revert to the range of acts that all States regard as impermissible in all circum-stances.[55] However, a definition of some kind is needed if there is to be a comprehensive international prohibition on 'terrorism' and a requirement for multilateral cooperation including extradition; a definition is also needed if terrorism is to be added to the jurisdiction of the International Criminal Court. Further, existing instruments imposing obligations in relation to counter-terrorism, for example Resolution 1373(2001), need a definition to ensure uniform implementation and effective monitoring. But, even if a solution is reached for the purpose of a comprehensive convention, the drafting compromises that will be needed in order to reach agreement are unlikely to result in a definition suitable for all purposes. And the tendency exhibited in the negotiations on the Convention to seek a broad definition may lead to 'ordinary' criminals being included within the definition and thus being subjected to the full range of domestic and international counter-terrorism measures.

Human rights considerations are important in drafting definitions of terrorism, whether national or international. Terrorist offences are likely to carry higher penalties than other offences, national systems may have more invasive means of investigation for terrorist offences, the political offence exception in extradition agreements may be disapplied and applications for asylum may be refused. If the criminal acts included in a definition of terrorism are not of a very serious nature, and if the purposes for which those acts are committed are defined too broadly, there is a danger that the serious consequences of being a terrorist suspect in national law will be applied to conduct which is 'merely' criminal, and political opponents or even petty criminals may be treated as terrorists. Minor damage to property committed in the course of a political demonstration, for example, ought not to attract the stigma and legal consequences of being classed as terrorism.[56] Further, wide and

---

[52] See e.g. the European Convention on the Suppression of Terrorism 1977 and the European Convention on the Prevention of Terrorism 2005.

[53] See e.g. the Arab Convention on the Suppression of Terrorism 1998.

[54] See, in particular, the remarks of the representative of Brazil on the adoption of the resolution (UN Doc. S/PV 3053).

[55] G. Levitt, 'Is "Terrorism" Worth Defining?' (1986) 13 *Ohio Northern University Law Review* 97; John Murphy, 'Defining International Terrorism: A Way Out of the Quagmire' (1989) 19 *Israel Yearbook on Human Rights* 13.

[56] The South African legislation usefully excepts from the definition of terrorism certain kinds of acts committed in pursuance of protests or industrial action if they are not intended to cause particular kinds of harm: Protection of Constitutional Democracy against Terrorist and Related Activities Act 2004, s. 1(3).

ambiguous definitions of terrorism leave undue discretion to State authorities, risking abuse by them. Human rights considerations have motivated the 'UN Special Rapporteur on the promotion and protection of human rights and fundamental freedoms while countering terrorism' to suggest a limited model definition of terrorism, comprising acts intended to cause death or serious bodily injury, involving lethal or serious physical violence or the taking of hostages, provided that the acts are committed with the intention of provoking a state of terror, or compelling a government or international organization to action or inaction and the acts come within the definition of a serious offence in national law.[57]

In discussing the elements of an existing 'transnational' crime of terrorism, comparison can be made between the descriptions of terrorist acts in the different multilateral instruments.[58] But, like the suppression conventions for other transnational crimes, the eleven global terrorism conventions do not make detailed provision for the material and mental elements of the crimes they cover, leaving these to the domestic law of the States Parties. The same is true of the regional agreements. Leaving aside the early terrorism conventions, the practice indicates that there are generally two or more tiers to the terrorism definitions used by States in national and international instruments: first, the underlying act, which is generally a criminal offence in itself; and, second, the purpose of coercion of a State or international organization, and/or the purpose of causing alarm among the population. There is sometimes added a requirement of political or ideological motive and, in relation to international terrorism, a transnational character to the underlying act (which should not be limited in its effects to one country). While there is particular controversy about the authors of terrorism – whether freedom fighters and State agents are excluded – the practice diverges in relation to *all* aspects of the definition.[59]

Material elements

The *actus reus* of the crime of terrorism is the underlying act. With the exception of the Terrorist Financing Convention, the eleven global terrorism agreements require or imply that the underlying act must be an offence in itself.[60] The regional agreements mostly do the same, either by listing the offences covered by the global agreements, or within their own

---

[57] *Report of the Special Rapporteur on the Promotion and Protection of Human Rights and Fundamental Freedoms while Countering Terrorism – Ten Areas of Best Practices in Countering Terrorism*, 22 December 2010 (A/HRC/16/51), paras. 26–8.

[58] For a more thorough discussion of the elements of the eleven global agreements, see Reuven Young, 'Defining Terrorism: The Evolution of Terrorism as a Legal Concept in International Law and its Influence on Definitions in Domestic Legislation' (2006) 29 *Boston College International and Comparative Law Review* 23.

[59] See the discussion in Robert Kolb, 'The Exercise of Criminal Jurisdiction over International Terrorists' in Bianchi, *Enforcing International Law Norms*, 227. But see Antonio Cassese, 'Terrorism as an International Crime' in Bianchi, *Enforcing International Law Norms*, 213, and in Cassese, 'The Multifaceted Criminal Notion of Terrorism in International Law' (2006) 4 *Journal of International Criminal Justice* 1, for the view that the practice shows a consistent approach and that it is therefore a misconception to allege that there is no generally agreed definition of terrorism; he followed this view when President of the Special Tribunal for Lebanon in finding that there *was* an international customary law definition of terrorism in *Ayyash et al.*, STL A. Ch., 16 February 2011.

[60] See e.g. Art. 2(1) of the Terrorist Bombing Convention 1997 which lists acts committed 'unlawfully and intentionally'. The Terrorist Financing Convention 1999 prohibits the provision or collection of funds (the underlying act) with the intention that the funds should be used for terrorist acts. In the definition of terrorism in the United Kingdom's Terrorism Act 2000, the underlying acts are not specified as offences: see footnote 29 above.

generic definitions. Some of the latter, however, are broad and ambiguous. The 1999 Convention of the OAU (now the African Union), for example, includes 'any act which is a violation of the criminal laws of a State Party and which . . . may cause damage to public or private property, natural resources, environmental or cultural heritage'.[61] This appears to cover relatively minor criminal conduct. The underlying act of a terrorist offence should be a *serious* offence, if it is to capture what is generally regarded as terrorism. The draft comprehensive convention lists the underlying acts of causing death or serious personal injury, serious damage to property including public transport or the environment, or (lesser) damage to property or systems which results in major economic loss.[62]

There is divergent practice with regard to the description of those who commit terrorism. In spite of the unqualified condemnation of terrorism in the 1994 General Assembly declaration,[63] the Arab, OIC and OAU Conventions, concluded subsequent to that declaration, include an exception for acts committed by peoples struggling against foreign occupation or for national liberation in accordance with the principles of international law.[64] It is not clear whether the reference to international law in these instruments is only to the *ius ad bellum* (as the wording in at least the first two mentioned agreements would indicate) or also to international humanitarian law (as is sometimes claimed).[65] If the latter is a permissible interpretation of these agreements, those committing terrorist acts would be excluded from the exemption since terrorism is prohibited by international humanitarian law.

It ought to be acknowledged by all that the targeting of civilians, however just the cause of the conflict, is unacceptable. Attempts have therefore been made to solve the problem of definition by specifying that only civilians are the targets of terrorism (as in Article 2(1)(b) of the Terrorist Financing Convention).[66] As a complete solution this is defective. What after all is the definition of 'civilian' in peacetime? And it does not address the question of how to deal with insurgents of various kinds, as either combatants or common criminals[67] – but admittedly this is a very difficult issue.

Linked to the question of national liberation movements is that of 'State terrorism'. The long-standing Western position in the UN has been that wrongful acts by States, whether properly termed State terrorism or not, are more appropriately regulated by the ordinary

---

[61] Art. 1(3). The Arab Convention 1998 and the OIC Convention 1991 have similarly wide formulations: Art. 1(2) of the former and Art. 1(2) of the latter.

[62] See footnote 35. For a critique of individual elements of the draft Convention's elements, see Alexandra Orlova and James Moore, '"Umbrellas" or "Building Blocks"? Defining International Terrorism and Transnational Organized Crime in International Law' (2005) 27 *Houston Journal of International Law* 267, 271–6.

[63] See section 14.2.2.

[64] Art. 3(1) of the OAU Convention; Preamble to and Art. 2(a) of the Arab Convention; Art. 2 of the OIC Convention.

[65] See Mahmoud Hmoud, 'The Organization of the Islamic Conference' in Nesi, *International Cooperation in Counter-Terrorism*, 166; see also Michael de Feo, 'The Political Offence Concept in Regional and International Conventions Relating to Terrorism' in *ibid.*, 116–19. It is interesting to note that the South African legislation implementing the AU agreement adopts this interpretation, referring 'especially' to international humanitarian law: Protection of Constitutional Democracy against Terrorist and Related Activities Act 2004.

[66] The Supreme Court of Canada has stated that this definition 'catches the essence of what the world understands by terrorism' (*Suresh* v. *Canada* [2002] SCC 1, para. 98). And see para. 164 of the Report of the Secretary-General's High-Level Panel on Threats, Challenges and Change (UN Doc. A/59/565).

[67] See Jan Klabbers, 'Rebel with a Cause? Terrorists and Humanitarian Law' (2003) 14 *European Journal of International Law* 299.

rules of State responsibility rather than under criminal law.[68] This was also the view of the former UN Secretary-General in his report, 'In Larger Freedom';[69] it is also reflected in Article 19(2) of the Terrorist Bombing Convention, for example. The opposing point of view that terrorism is prohibited 'by whomever committed',[70] including State actors, is being put forward in the negotiations on the comprehensive convention.[71]

Mental elements

The aspect distinguishing terrorism from other crimes is the purpose with which the under-lying acts are committed. Like genocide, terrorism in its most typical form is a compound offence and needs both the *mens rea* appropriate to the underlying offence, and a special intent for terrorism itself (which, departing from the normal practice of distinguishing between purpose and intention under criminal law, often uses the terms interchangeably). There are two kinds of victims of terrorism: both the targets of the underlying offence and the 'real' targets, those in whom terror has been induced.

Most of the eleven terrorism agreements mentioned in section 14.2.2, in avoiding a definition of terrorism, also avoid specifying an intent or purpose for which the criminal acts are committed.[72] For them, there is no special intent. This approach made possible the conclusion of these agreements, but it does have the disadvantage that they therefore implicitly include acts committed for merely personal or commercial reasons, and thus miss the unique feature of terrorism. Other terrorism agreements differ in their descrip-tions of the special intent. Spreading terror[73] would seem the most obvious purpose, but it is wide and may be difficult to prove. The draft comprehensive convention uses the same formulation as the Terrorist Financing Convention, specifying a purpose or intention of intimidating a population or persuading a government to act.[74] Some instruments go wider. The EU Framework Decision includes the 'aim' of 'seriously destabilising or destroying the fundamental political, constitutional, economic or social structures of a country or an international organisation' (which would mean that a protest against the World Trade Organization, for example, would constitute terrorism if it caused damage); the OAU Convention includes the intention to 'create general insurrection in a State'.[75]

---

[68] See e.g. the statement of the UK representative in the Security Council of 18 January 2002: 'None of these seminal texts [the global terrorism agreements] refer to State terrorism, which is not an international legal concept. We must be careful not to get caught up in the rhetoric of political conflict. If States abuse their power, they should be judged against the international conventions and other instruments dealing with . . . humanitarian law' (UN Doc. S/PV.4453 (2002), paras. 24–5).

[69] 'It is time to set aside debates on so-called "State terrorism". The use of force by States is already thoroughly regulated under international law' (UN Doc. A/59/2005, para. 91).

[70] GA Res. 49/60(1994).

[71] And it was also the view of Oscar Schachter, 'The Lawful Use of Force by a State against Terrorists in Another Country' (1989) 19 *Israel Yearbook on Human Rights* 209, 210.

[72] The exception is the Hostages Convention, Art. 1 (since the imposition of conditions of release is an intrinsic part of the offence of hostage-taking); and see Art. 2 of the Terrorist Financing Convention; see also the rather odd references to terrorist acts committed for certain purposes in Art. 5 of the Terrorist Bombing Convention and Art. 6 of the Nuclear Terrorism Convention.

[73] The definition in the CIS Convention includes terrorizing the population as one of the purposes for which terrorist acts are committed. See also Art. 51(2) of Additional Protocol I.

[74] See footnote 45.   [75] OAU Convention on the Preventing and Combating of Terrorism 1999.

Intent must be distinguished from motive. While some national definitions include a motive with which the terrorist act is committed,[76] most international formulations, including the draft comprehensive convention, do not. Motive cannot be a justification of terrorist action, and, if the purpose or intention is specified, it is perhaps unnecessary to limit the offence further by requiring the action to have a political, religious or other motive.

A customary law definition of an international crime?

The Appeals Chamber of the Special Tribunal for Lebanon has determined that there is indeed a crime of terrorism under customary international law:

> a number of treaties, UN resolutions, and the legislative and judicial practice of States evince the formation of a general *opinio juris* in the international community, accompanied by a practice consistent with such *opinio*, to the effect that a customary rule of international law regarding the international crime of terrorism, at least *in time of peace*, has indeed emerged. This customary rule requires the following three key elements: (i) the perpetration of a criminal act (such as murder, kidnapping, hostage-taking, arson, and so on), or threatening such an act; (ii) the intent to spread fear among the population (which would generally entail the creation of public danger) or directly or indirectly coerce a national or international authority to take some action, or to refrain from taking it; (iii) when the act involves a transnational element.[77]

It must be doubted whether there is indeed State practice treating terrorism, as so defined, as an international crime, directly criminalized by international law. The decision takes a very questionable view of the national legislation, judicial decisions, treaties, and UN resolutions it cites; indeed, one commentator is of the view that the Appeals Chamber's 'conclusion has scant empirical grounding in state practice, its reasoning is poorly substantiated, and it ultimately plays fast and loose with custom formation'.[78] This may be a harsh assessment, but that does not mean it is an unfair one. The position of the Special Tribunal for Lebanon has, however, been quoted approvingly in UK courts for the proposition that there is a defined international crime of terrorism.[79] But the idea has, as of yet, remained unpersuasive.

14.2.4   Prosecution and other national measures

The multilateral conventions, like other suppression conventions, focus on international cooperation and include *aut dedere aut judicare* obligations. The goal is national prosecution. Information about how many prosecutions or extraditions have taken place on the

---

[76] See e.g. the UK definition at footnote 29 above, and the South African at footnote 56 above.

[77] *Ayyash et al.*, STL A. Ch., 16 February 2011, para. 85. The Tribunal then went on to 'interpret and apply' Lebanese law (which was the only applicable law under its Statute) in accordance with the customary rule as found by the Tribunal, thereby significantly broadening the provisions of Lebanese law.

[78] Ben Saul, 'Legislating from a Radical Hague: The United Nations Special Tribunal for Lebanon Invents an International Crime of Transnational Terrorism' (2011) 24 *Leiden Journal of International Law* 677, 678.

[79] *R* v. *Gul*, UK Court of Appeal, 22 February 2012.

basis of the conventions is hard to secure. In one notorious case of aviation terrorism, the Lockerbie bombing, the prosecution was on the basis of ordinary murder charges, not charges under the Montreal Convention. In another case in the United Kingdom, Zardad, an Afghan warlord, was convicted in 2004 for conspiracy to take hostages under the legislation implementing the Hostages Convention (he was convicted also of conspiracy to torture).[80]

One of the major challenges of dealing with terrorist offences is to strike a balance between, on the one hand, the protection of the community from acts of terrorism and, on the other hand, the maintenance of the rights of all citizens, including suspected terrorists. Some national legislation imposing criminal sanctions for offences connected with terrorism has been widely criticized on human rights grounds.[81] There are rights which cannot be balanced against any other interest; chief among these is protection from torture. As is indicated below,[82] there is an absolute prohibition on torture by a State's officials, and on the transfer of an individual to a country where there are substantial grounds for believing that he would be in danger of being tortured.

National prosecutions for terrorism-related offences can meet with a number of problems. They may have to grapple with the difficulties of definition, particularly if national law incorporates international law.[83] Another major difficulty arises from the nature of the evidence on which the charges may be based, for example where the evidence comes from intercepted material or is otherwise intelligence-based. In the United Kingdom, where such difficulties are perceived to stand in the way of effective prosecutions, other means of detaining terrorist suspects have been devised, not all of which have been found by the courts to be compatible with human rights law.[84] A further problem may arise from the perceived difficulties of preparing criminal charges in sufficient time to satisfy procedural and human rights obligations regarding the early bringing of suspects before a judge. In the United Kingdom, this has led to successive attempts to extend periods of pre-charge detention, which again have to be analysed against human rights obligations.[85]

---

[80] *R v. Faryadi Sarwar Zardad*, UK Court of Appeal, 7 February 2007. For a digest of terrorism cases generally, see UNODC *Digest of Terrorist Cases* (Vienna, 2010), www.unodc.org/documents/terrorism/Publications/Digest_of_Terrorist_Cases/English.pdf.

[81] See Helen Duffy, *The War on Terror and the Framework of International Law*, 2nd edn (Cambridge, forthcoming, 2014) Chapter 7; Kalliopi Koufa, 'The UN, Human Rights and Counter-Terrorism' in Nesi, *International Cooperation in Counter-Terrorism*, 45. For a discussion of the impact which post-September 11 counter-terrorist legislation has had on human rights in a few common law jurisdictions, see Ben Golder and George Williams, 'Balancing National Security and Human Rights: Assessing the Legal Response of Common Law Nations to the Threat of Terrorism' (2006) 8 *Journal of Comparative Policy Analysis* 43.

[82] See section 14.3.1.

[83] For a discussion of an illustrative case in Italy's Supreme Court of Cassation, see Lucia Aleni, 'Distinguishing Terrorism from Wars of National Liberation in the Light of International Law' (2008) 6 *Journal of International Criminal Justice* 525.

[84] Legislation allowing the detention, pending deportation, of persons suspected of being international terrorists was ruled to be incompatible with human rights obligations by the House of Lords in *A (FC) v. Secretary of State for the Home Department* [2004] UKHL 56. Following the adoption of further legislation giving the power to make 'control orders' in relation to terrorist suspects, the House of Lords held in *Secretary of State for the Home Department v. AF (FC) and Another* [2009] UKHL 28, that, where a person subject to a control order was not given sufficient information about the allegations against him (on the basis that the information was too sensitive to be disclosed), he was deprived of the right to a fair trial. Control orders have been superseded by Terrorism Prevention and Investigation Measures, which in their turn are likely to be subjected to scrutiny under human rights legislation.

[85] The Terrorism Act 2006 extended the permitted length of pre-charge detention to twenty-eight days; current legislation changed the permitted length to fourteen days.

In the United States, there is wide-ranging legislation regarding the prevention and prosecution of domestic and international terrorism. There has been ambivalence about whether to detain suspected terrorists indefinitely as enemy combatants in the 'war against terror' or to prosecute them.[86] With the attempt to close the Guantanamo Bay camps, however, the criminal law model is gaining in importance. Under the Military Commissions Act of 2009 'alien unlawful enemy combatants' engaged in hostilities against the United States can be tried for violations of the laws of war and other offences triable by military commission; these include the crime of terrorism, which is thus being tried as a war crime. Prosecutions by military commission have been criticized, but President Obama's attempts to use civilian courts for prosecutions were negated by congressional legislation effectively precluding trials of Guantanamo Bay detainees in US civilian courts.[87]

Both the UN General Assembly and the Security Council have stressed that, in taking counter-terrorism measures, States should comply with international human rights law.[88] Some of the global terrorism conventions require expressly that the terrorist suspect be treated fairly in proceedings against him, and provide that there is no obligation to extradite where a State has substantial grounds for believing that the extradition request has been made for the purpose of punishing on the basis of race, religion or political opinion.[89] But, for the most part, the agreements leave to national systems the responsibility of protecting the rights of the accused, a responsibility which must be exercised in accordance with international human rights obligations.

14.2.5 Terrorism as an international crime

There is no international court or tribunal which has jurisdiction over a crime of terrorism as such.[90] The offences covered by the global terrorism conventions were included in the list of treaty crimes in the ILC draft for the new international criminal court, and there was some support for including terrorism within the jurisdiction of the ICC. But the ICC was not given jurisdiction, since the existing network of treaties providing for national prosecutions was regarded as adequate and it would not in any event have been possible to negotiate an agreed definition when the General Assembly had failed to do so. Resolution F of the ICC Final Act recommended that a review conference consider crimes of terrorism 'with a view to arriving at an acceptable definition and their inclusion in the list of crimes within the jurisdiction of the court', but the Kampala Review Conference in 2010 was not asked to take a decision on the matter. A proposal to give the ICC jurisdiction remains on the table.[91]

A terrorist act may be an international crime within the meaning used in this book if it falls within one of the established categories of crimes against humanity or war crimes. The

---

[86] For the position under the Bush administration, see Steven Less, 'Country Report on the USA' in Christian Walter *et al.* (eds.), *Terrorism as a Challenge for National and International Law: Security versus Liberty?* (Berlin, 2004) 633.
[87] See 'Contemporary Practice of the United States' (2011) 105 *American Journal of International Law* at 596.
[88] See e.g. GA Res. 51/210 of 17 December 1996, para. 3; SC Res. 1456(2003), para. 6 of the Annex.
[89] See e.g. Arts. 12 and 16 of the Nuclear Terrorism Convention 2005.
[90] As we have seen, terrorism does come within the jurisdiction of the Special Tribunal for Lebanon, an internationalized court.
[91] See proposal of the Netherlands, Annex 3 to report of the Working Group on Amendments, ICC-ASP/10/32.

organized use of terror was considered as both a war crime and a crime against humanity by the Nuremberg Tribunal.[92]

Terrorism as a war crime

Acts of terrorism are prohibited by international humanitarian law and may constitute war crimes. Article 51(2) of Additional Protocol I provides:

> The civilian population as such, as well as individual civilians, shall not be the object of attack. Acts or threats of violence the primary purpose of which is to spread terror among the civilian population are prohibited.[93]

This prohibition and its criminalization are part of customary international law.[94] While acts of terrorism are included specifically in the list of violations of common Article 3 in the Statutes of the ICTR and of the Special Court for Sierra Leone,[95] the ICTY has no such explicit wording in its Statute. But the ICTY has held that it has jurisdiction by virtue of the general wording of Article 3 of its Statute (violation of the laws and customs of war).[96] Terrorism is not within the list of war crimes in Article 8 of the ICC Statute, and the ICC therefore does not have jurisdiction in respect of it; in the ICC, attacks on civilians committed with the specific intent to terrorize will be a factor in sentencing only.

In the first case involving terrorism before an international court, the ICTY convicted General Galić on the war crimes charge of 'acts of violence the primary purpose of which is to spread terror among the civilian population', based upon command responsibility for a protracted campaign of shelling and sniping in civilian areas of Sarajevo.[97] Evidence was given that civilians were attacked while attending funerals, while in ambulances and buses, while gardening and while shopping in markets; the main thoroughfare of Sarajevo became known as 'Sniper Alley'. The Tribunal found that the campaign was intended to terrorize the civilian population; it had no discernible military significance.

The Trial Chamber first had to show that the war crime of terror was within its jurisdiction as being a 'violation of the laws and customs of war' and prohibited and criminalized at the time of the commission of the alleged offence. For reasons relating to the perceived need to consider only 'serious' violations of treaty law as war crimes (equating to grave breaches), it specifically left to one side the question whether it had jurisdiction over acts of violence which did not cause death or injury, thus apparently coming up with a hybrid crime drawing on both parts of Article 51(2) of Additional Protocol I.[98] The Appeals Chamber has explained this reticence to deal with threats and acts not causing death or injury by stating

---

[92] Nuremberg IMT, Judgment and Sentences, reprinted in (1947) 41 *American Journal of International Law* 172 at e.g. 229, 231, 289 and 319.

[93] Art. 51(2) of Additional Protocol I; Art. 33(1) of Geneva Convention IV; Arts. 4(2)(d) and 13(2) of Additional Protocol II.

[94] *Galić*, ICTY A. Ch., 30 November 2006, paras. 87–98. Judge Shahabudeen in his Separate Opinion noted that the Appeals Chamber was not suggesting, in this finding, that a comprehensive definition of terror was known to customary international law; only the 'core concept'.

[95] Art. 4(d) of the ICTR Statute; and Art. 3(d) of the SCSL Statute.   [96] In *Galić*, ICTY T. Ch., 5 December 2003.

[97] *Ibid.* For lengthy discussion of the war crime of terrorism in a later case, see *D. Milošević*, ICTY A. Ch., 12 November 2009.

[98] Robert Cryer, 'Prosecutor v. Galić and the War Crime of Terror Bombing' (2005–6) 2 *Israel Defence Force Law Review* 73.

that that question was not before the Trial Chamber.[99] The SCSL has found that it is indeed unnecessary to prove actual death or injury in order to constitute this war crime.[100]

The war crime does not consist in *causing* terror: it is to be expected that *all* acts of war will result in general fear in the country concerned. In *Galić*, the Appeals Chamber confirmed that actual terrorization of a civilian population is not an element of the crime.[101] As regards the mental element, the Trial Chamber required the prosecution 'to prove not only that the accused accepted the likelihood that terror would result from the illegal acts – or, in other words, that he was aware of the possibility that terror would result – but that that was the result which he specifically intended. The crime of terror is a specific-intent crime.' The spreading of terror does not have to be the only purpose of the acts,[102] but it does have to be the *primary* purpose. In *Brima, Kamara and Kanu* (the 'AFRC case'), the SCSL held that the use of child soldiers, abduction and forced labour were committed primarily for military purposes, and thus did not constitute the war crime of terrorism, while the brutal amputations of the hands or arms of civilians were committed primarily to spread terror.[103]

In sum, the international case law shows that there are three elements in the war crime of acts of terrorism: (1) acts or threats of violence; (2) the accused wilfully made the civilian population or individual civilians not taking direct part in hostilities the objects of those acts or threats of violence; and (3) the acts or threats were carried out with the specific intent of spreading terror among the civilian population.

Terrorism as a crime against humanity

Terrorist acts are not listed as crimes against humanity in the Statutes of the ad hoc Tribunals or the ICC. It is, however, clear that acts falling within the definition of crimes against humanity in the Statutes are not excluded from that definition merely because they are also committed with the intention of terrorizing the population and with a particular political or other ideological purpose. In *Galić*, the accused was charged with and convicted of crimes against humanity of murder and inhumane acts on the basis of the same facts as the war crime of terror.[104]

After 11 September 2001, statements were made by public figures condemning the terrorist acts in New York and Washington as crimes against humanity.[105] There were obvious difficulties with any suggestion that the crimes should therefore be tried by the ICC: the State primarily concerned was opposed to such an idea and the principle of

---

[99] *Galić*, ICTY A. Ch., 30 November 2006, para. 100.
[100] *Fofana and Kondewa*, SCSL A. Ch., 28 May 2008, paras. 350–2.
[101] *Galić*, ICTY A. Ch., 30 November 2006, para. 104.   [102] *Ibid.*
[103] The case against members of the Armed Forces Revolutionary Council: *Brima, Kamara and Kanu*, SCSL T. Ch. II, 20 June 2007, paras. 1447–64; upheld on appeal, SCSL A. Ch., 22 February 2008.
[104] *Galić*, ICTY T. Ch., 5 December 2003. See also *Krštić*, ICTY T. Ch. I, 2 August 2001, paras. 607, 653.
[105] Antonio Cassese, 'Terrorism Is Also Disrupting Some Crucial Legal Categories of International Law' (2001) 12 *European Journal of International Law* 993, 994; see also Frédéric Mégret, 'Justice in Times of Violence' (2003) 14 *European Journal of International Law* 327, 332–4.

complementarity would have stood in the way even if there was otherwise jurisdiction. But the acts were arguably within the subject-matter jurisdiction of the ICC.[106]

14.3   Torture

14.3.1   Introduction

There can be few issues on which international legal opinion is more clear than on the condemnation of torture. Offenders have been recognised as the 'common enemies of mankind'.[107]

There is an absolute prohibition of torture in international law, both in treaty and customary law.[108] The prohibition applies even in times of national emergencies or wars, and there are no exceptions or justifications.[109] It amounts to *ius cogens*[110] and States incur international responsibility if their officials commit torture.[111] While torture is not an international crime as that term is used in this book[112] since it is not punishable *as such* by any international court or tribunal, under certain conditions it may constitute a crime against humanity or a war crime.[113] There is no necessary transnational element to the crime, but it offends against a fundamental value of the international community and States have concluded a suppression convention, the Convention against Torture and Other Cruel, Inhuman and Degrading Treatment or Punishment of 1984 (widely referred to by its acronym, CAT).[114]

14.3.2   UN Convention against Torture

The UN Convention against Torture was concluded to 'make more effective' the already existing prohibition under international law.[115] It follows the same pattern as the model discussed above.[116] It requires States Parties to criminalize the offence of torture in their domestic law, including attempts and complicity as well as participation (Article 4).[117] The

---

[106] See Roberta Arnold, 'Terrorism as a Crime against Humanity under the ICC Statute' in Nesi, *International Cooperation in Counter-Terrorism*, 121; see to the contrary William Schabas, 'Is Terrorism a Crime against Humanity?' (2002) 8 *International Peacekeeping: The Yearbook of International Peace Operations* 255.

[107] Lord Bingham in the House of Lords case of *A (FC) and Others (FC)* v. *Secretary of State for the Home Department* [2005] UKHL 71, para. 33.

[108] For a list of international instruments prohibiting torture, see section 11.3.7.

[109] Art. 2(2) of the 1984 UN Convention against Torture: 'No exceptional circumstances whatsoever, whether a state of war or a threat of war, internal political instability or other public emergency, may be invoked as a justification for torture.' The classic argument that torture is sometimes justifiable may be found in Alan M. Dershowitz, *Why Terrorism Works: Understanding the Threat, Responding to the Challenge* (New Haven, CT, 2002); for a response to such claims, see Paola Gaeta, 'May Necessity Be Available as a Defence against Torture in the Interrogation of Suspected Terrorists?' (2004) 2 *Journal of International Criminal Justice* 762.

[110] Affirmed in *Questions Relating to the Obligation to Prosecute or Extradite* (*Belgium* v. *Senegal*), ICJ General List 144, 20 July 2012, para. 99.

[111] *Furundžija*, ICTY T. Ch. II, 10 December 1998, para. 153.

[112] In some classifications torture is an international crime; the House of Lords in *Pinochet (No. 3)* regarded it as such (*R* v. *Bow Street Metropolitan Stipendiary Magistrate, ex parte Pinochet Ugarte (No. 3)* [1999] 2 All ER 97, 198, 249, 260, 288) though their Lordships' remarks are not always easy to follow. In *Cassese's International Criminal Law*, 3rd edn (Oxford, 2013) 132–4, torture is described as an international crime.

[113] See section 11.3.7 and section 12.3.2 above.   [114] Boister, 'Transnational Criminal Law?', 967.

[115] Preamble to the Convention.   [116] See section 14.1.2.

[117] See N. Rodley and M. Pollard, 'Criminalisation of Torture: State Obligations under the United Nations Convention against Torture and Other Cruel, Inhuman and Degrading Treatment or Punishment' (2006) 2 *European Human Rights Law Review* 115 at footnote 17.

Committee against Torture, established by the CAT, has confirmed that States must define torture as a separate offence in their criminal law, but they do not have to reproduce the Convention definition *verbatim*; they may adopt a wider definition.

Material elements

As defined in the CAT – and for the purpose of the CAT – the crime has two objective elements. First, it comprises 'any act by which severe pain or suffering, physical or mental', is inflicted on a person; and second, it is committed 'by or at the instigation of or with the consent or acquiescence of a public official or other person acting in an official capacity'. The second element is not present in some other definitions of torture. The Inter-American Convention to Prevent and Punish Torture 1985 provides a wider definition, which does not specify a purpose, nor a level of pain and suffering; indeed, it does not have an element of pain or suffering at all if the act is intended 'to obliterate the personality of the victim or to diminish his physical or mental capacities'.[118] Early commentators have stated that Article 1(1) of the CAT 'gives a *description* of torture for the purpose of understanding and implementing the *Convention* rather than a legal definition for direct application in criminal law and criminal procedure'.[119] The ICTY has pronounced the definition as reflecting customary international law, but only for the purpose of State obligations under the CAT, not as regards the meaning of the crime more generally.[120]

The assessment of whether particular ill-treatment is of a degree to amount to the crime of torture can be a difficult one since the severity threshold qualifies the pain and suffering of the victim, not the treatment itself. Legal memoranda written for the US administration in 2002 and 2003, which provided an excessively restrictive interpretation of the obligations of the United States under the CAT, and the treatment of detainees during the so-called 'war on terror', occasioned a great deal of debate about what kind of treatment constitutes torture.[121] The memorandum of August 2002 from the Office of the Legal Counsel in the US Department of Justice,[122] which was later withdrawn, was written to interpret a US statute enacted to implement the Convention. In describing what pain amounted to torture, it stated that 'it must be equivalent in intensity to that which accompanies serious physical injury, such as organ failure, impairment of bodily function, or even death'. The defence in the *Brđanin* case before the ICTY on appeal claimed that the international definition of torture was as interpreted in this memorandum. The Court had no hesitation in dismissing this

---

[118] Arts. 1(2), 2 and 3. For the definition and the case law, see Laurence Burgorgue-Larsen and Amaya Ubeda de Torres, *The Inter-American Court of Human Rights: Case Law and Commentary* (Oxford, 2011) 369.

[119] J. H. Burgers and H. Danelius, *The United Nations Convention against Torture: A Handbook on the Convention against Torture and Other Cruel, Inhuman or Degrading Treatment or Punishment* (Leiden, 1988) 122.

[120] *Kunarac et al.*, ICTY A. Ch., 12 June 2002, paras. 146, 147 (and the other cases there cited); and *Kvočka et al.*, ICTY A. Ch., 28 February 2005, para. 284.

[121] The memoranda are set out in Karen Greenberg and Joshua Dretel, *The Torture Papers: The Road to Abu Ghraib* (Cambridge, 2005). See Mary Ellen O'Connell, 'Affirming the Ban on Harsh Interrogation' (2005) 66 *Ohio State Law Journal* 1231; Marcy Strauss, 'The Lessons of Abu Ghraib' *ibid.*, 1269; Seth Kreimer, '"Torture Lite," "Full Bodied" Torture, and the Insulation of Legal Conscience' (2005) 1 *Journal of National Security Law and Policy* 187. The Executive Order issued by President Obama on 22 January 2009 prohibits reliance, in conducting interrogations, upon any Department of Justice memorandum interpreting the Torture Convention issued between 11 September 2001 and 20 January 2009.

[122] 'The Bybee/Yoo Memorandum': Memorandum from the Office of the Legal Counsel, Department of Justice, to Alberto R. Gonzales, Re: Standards of Conduct for Interrogation under 18 USC 2340–2340A (1 August 2002).

argument. 'No matter how powerful or influential a country is, its practice does not automatically become customary international law.'[123]

There is difficulty in assessing when ill-treatment is to be distinguished from 'cruel, inhuman or degrading treatment or punishment', as that term is used in Article 16 of the CAT and, of course, in human rights provisions such as Article 3 of the European Convention on Human Rights. On one view, the severity of pain or suffering, although it constitutes an essential element of the definition of torture, is not a criterion distinguishing torture from cruel and inhuman treatment; the distinction is in the purpose for which the pain or suffering is inflicted.[124] Practice under the UN human rights conventions and regional agreements such as the European Convention on Human Rights may be used in the context of criminal law;[125] the case law of the ad hoc Tribunals in relation to war crimes and crimes against humanity is also relevant in assessing the level of pain and suffering which amounts to torture.

It is not useful to attempt a catalogue of conduct amounting to torture,[126] but the following points are indicative of some current trends in the case law. The five interrogation techniques in use by the British security forces in the 1970s, namely, 'wall standing, hooding, subjection to noise, deprivation of sleep and deprivation of food and drink', were held by the European Court of Human Rights in 1978 to be inhuman treatment, not torture,[127] but there are indications by the same Court that this kind of treatment may now be regarded as torture.[128] Some acts establish *per se* the suffering of those upon whom they were inflicted, so that the level of pain or suffering need not be proved. Sexual violence 'necessarily gives rise to severe pain or suffering, whether physical or mental';[129] 'rape involves the infliction of suffering at a requisite level of severity to place it in the category of torture'.[130] Solitary confinement may be torture 'to the extent that the confinement of the victim can be shown to pursue one of the prohibited purposes of torture and to have caused the victim severe pain or suffering';[131] 'waterboarding' has been widely acknowledged to constitute torture.[132] There is no absolute threshold level of pain or suffering.[133]

The CAT definition refers to acts but not to omissions. Does that exclude from the definition omissions such as failure to provide a prisoner with food or water? Such an interpretation would be contrary to common sense, if all the other elements of intention, purpose and connection with a public official are present.[134]

---

[123] *Brdanin*, ICTY A. Ch., 20 February 2001, para. 247.
[124] Manfred Nowak and Elizabeth Arthur, *The United Nations Convention against Torture* (Oxford, 2008) 69.
[125] *Furundžija*, ICTY A. Ch. II, 10 December 1998, para. 159, although see the warning in *Kunarac*, ICTY T. Ch., 22 February 2001, para. 471, not to transpose too easily concepts developed in a different legal context.
[126] N. Rodley, *The Treatment of Prisoners under International Law*, 3rd edn (Oxford, 2009), reviews the authorities at Chapter 3 ('What Constitutes Torture and Other Ill-Treatment?'); and see *Delalić et al.*, ICTY T. Ch. II, 16 November 98, paras. 461–9.
[127] *Ireland* v. *United Kingdom*, ECtHR, 18 January 1978.
[128] *Selmouni* v. *France*, ECtHR, 28 July 1999; and see Nigel Rodley, 'The Definition(s) of Torture in International Law' (2002) 55 *Current Legal Problems* 467, 476–7.
[129] *Kunarac et al.*, ICTY A. Ch., 12 June 2002, para. 150.   [130] *Delalić et al.*, ICTY T. Ch. II, 16 November 1998, para. 489.
[131] *Krnojelac*, ICTY T. Ch. II, 15 March 2002, para. 183.
[132] E.g. by US Attorney-General Holder in his confirmation hearing in January 2009.
[133] *Kunarac et al.*, ICTY A. Ch., 12 June 2002, para. 149.
[134] Burgers and Danelius, *The United Nations Convention*, 118; and *Delalić et al.*, ICTY T. Ch. II, 16 November 1998, para. 468.

Pain or suffering arising only from lawful punishment, or incidental to it, is excluded from the definition of torture.[135] In recognition of the loophole this leaves in the CAT, there was an attempt in the negotiations for the Convention to specify that the punishment must be limited 'to the extent consistent with' the UN Standard Minimum Rules for the Treatment of Prisoners. This was rejected on the grounds that the Rules are not legally binding, and apply only to prisoners.[136] Article 1(2) makes clear that, by excluding from its definition of torture various means of punishment, the CAT does not legitimize any act which would be contrary to some other provision of international law.

The CAT definition of torture is limited to acts committed by 'a public official or other person acting in an official capacity'.[137] That limitation is not included in the definition of torture as a crime against humanity, nor, as now confirmed by the ICTY, in the requirements for war crimes.[138]

Mental elements

The pain or suffering must be 'intentionally' inflicted. A further necessary element of the crime as defined in the CAT is that it is committed against a person 'for such purposes as obtaining from him or a third person information or a confession, punishing him for an act he or a third person has committed or is suspected of having committed, or intimidating him or a third person, or for any reason based on discrimination of any kind' (Article 1(1)). The list is narrow. While it is not exhaustive, the wording demands that other purposes must be of the same kind as those in the list. If the act is committed for essentially private purposes, out of sheer sadism, it would appear not to be covered, although it might be expected that a court interpreting the words would strive to bring any such act within the ambit of the definition.[139] States implementing the CAT in domestic law are not obliged to confine the offence to acts committed only with the listed purposes; the United Kingdom, for example, has not included any requirement of purpose.[140]

14.3.3 *Prosecution and other national measures*

The CAT incorporates the *aut dedere aut judicare* principle (Article 7), requiring States to take a wide jurisdiction to prosecute and, if they do not prosecute, to extradite to anywhere in the

---

[135] Art. 1 of the CAT. For the view that there is no meaningful scope of application of this exclusion and that it must therefore simply be ignored, see Nowak, *Commentary* at 84.

[136] Burgers and Danelius, *The United Nations Convention*, 46–7 and 121–2.

[137] The term clearly goes beyond State officials. For discussion of its meaning, see Sandesh Sivakumaran, 'Torture in International Human Rights and International Humanitarian Law: The Actor and the Ad Hoc Tribunals' (2005) 18 *Leiden Journal of International Law* 541.

[138] See section 11.3.7 and section 12.3.2.

[139] Burgers and Danelius maintain that the common element in the list is the existence of a State interest or policy, but that even where the purpose is sadistic there is usually an aspect of punishment or intimidation to bring it within the list: Burgers and Danelius, *The United Nations Convention*, 119.

[140] See the Criminal Justice Act 1988, s. 134.

world.[141] There is generally recognized to be a basis under customary international law for universal jurisdiction in respect of acts of torture.[142] Article 5(2) of the CAT requires a State Party to 'establish its jurisdiction' over acts of torture when the alleged offender is 'present in any territory under its jurisdiction' and the State does not extradite him. Article 6(2) and Article 7(1) respectively require a State Party, when a person who has allegedly committed an act of torture is found on its territory, to hold a preliminary inquiry into the facts and, if it does not extradite him, to 'submit the case to its competent authorities for the purpose of prosecution'. In *Questions Relating to the Obligation to Prosecute or Extradite* (*Belgium* v. *Senegal*),[143] the International Court of Justice considered the meaning of the obligations in the CAT:

if the State in whose territory the suspect is present has received a request for extradition in any of the cases envisaged in the provisions of the Convention, it can relieve itself of its obligation to prosecute by acceding to that request. It follows that the choice between extradition or submission for prosecution, pursuant to the Convention, does not mean that the two alternatives are to be given the same weight. Extradition is an option offered to the State by the Convention, whereas prosecution is an international obligation under the Convention, the violation of which is a wrongful act engaging the responsibility of the State.[144]

The Convention imposes other obligations; for example, States may not use in legal proceedings information obtained by torture (Article 15);[145] States must afford effective remedies and adequate reparation to the victims (Article 14); they may not deport, extradite or otherwise transfer a person to a country where there are substantial grounds for believing that he would be in danger of being tortured (Article 3).[146]

In the first prosecution brought in the United Kingdom under legislation implementing the CAT, an Afghan warlord was convicted of conspiracy to torture, although he was not an official of the Afghan government. His faction, however, controlled an area of Afghanistan, and the Convention was held to include *de facto* officials where their organization exercises effective control over territory and quasi-governmental authority.[147]

14.3.4   *Torture as an international crime*

Like terrorism, torture is within the jurisdiction of the ad hoc Tribunals and the ICC only if committed under certain conditions: it is included expressly within the categories of crimes

---

[141] Some commentators suggest that the Convention requires States to take universal jurisdiction to allow them to prosecute an act of torture, regardless of whether the State where the act was committed, or the State of nationality of the victim or suspect, is a State Party or not: Rodley and Pollard, 'Criminalisation of Torture', 131. This approach would conflict with the ordinary principles of treaty interpretation. See generally on universal jurisdiction section 3.5.

[142] See section 3.5.1.

[143] *Questions Relating to the Obligation to Prosecute or Extradite* (*Belgium* v. *Senegal*), ICJ General List 144, 20 July 2012.

[144] *Ibid.*, para. 95.

[145] For the application of this provision in UK law, see Lord Bingham in the House of Lords case of *A (FC) and Others (FC)* v. *Secretary of State for the Home Department* [2005] UKHL 71. And see Tobias Thienel, 'The Admissibility of Evidence Obtained by Torture under International Law' (2006) 17 *European Journal of International Law* 349.

[146] See also case law on the interpretation of Art. 3 of the European Convention on Human Rights, which makes clear that it is not possible to balance other rights and interests against the protection of a person from being deported to a country where he will be subjected to torture or ill-treatment (e.g. *Saadi* v. *Italy*, 37201/06, 28 February 2008).

[147] *R* v. *Sarwar Zardad*, preparatory hearing, 7 April 2004. The prosecution was brought under s. 134 of the Criminal Justice Act 1988 and the defendant was convicted of conspiracy to torture (and conspiracy to take hostages).

against humanity and war crimes in the relevant Statutes.[148] Although the 'core' part of the CAT definition (the intentional infliction of severe pain or suffering) is also a constituent element of torture as a crime against humanity and as a war crime, in some other respects the definitions differ. Perpetrators are not limited to persons acting in an official capacity, and the list of prohibited purposes is extended – indeed, a requirement of purpose is omitted altogether for the prosecution of crimes against humanity before the ICC.

Further reading

Transnational crimes

M. Cherif Bassiouni (ed.), *International Criminal Law*, 3rd edn (New York, 2008) Vol. I

Neil Boister, *An Introduction to Transnational Criminal Law* (Oxford, 2012)

Roger Clark, 'Offences of International Concern: Multilateral Treaty Practice in the Forty Years since Nuremberg' (1988) 57 *Nordic Journal of International Law* 49

Robert Currie, *International and Transnational Criminal Law* (Toronto, 2010)

Alexandra Orlova and James Moore, '"Umbrellas" or "Building Blocks"? Defining International Terrorism and Transnational Organized Crime in International Law' (2005) 27 *Houston Journal of International Law* 267

Terrorism

Andrea Bianchi (ed.), *Enforcing International Law Norms against Terrorism* (Oxford, 2004)

Helen Duffy, *The 'War on Terror' and the Framework of International Law*, 2nd edn (Cambridge, 2013)

John Dugard, 'International Terrorism and the Just War' (1977) 12 *Stanford Journal of International Studies* 21

Rosalyn Higgins and Maurice Flory (eds.), *Terrorism and International Law* (London, 1997)

Christopher Joyner, 'Suppression of Terrorism on the High Seas: The 1988 IMO Convention on the Safety of Maritime Navigation' (1989) 19 *Israel Journal on Human Rights* 343

Nicola McGarrity, Andrew Lynch and George Williams (eds.), *Counter-Terrorism and Beyond: The Culture of Law and Justice after 9/11* (London, 2010)

Giuseppe Nesi (ed.), *International Cooperation in Counter-Terrorism* (Aldershot, 2006)

Eric Rosand, 'Security Council Resolution 1373, the Counter-Terrorism Committee, and the Fight against Terrorism' (2003) 97 *American Journal of International Law* 333

Robert Rosenstock, 'International Convention against the Taking of Hostages: Another International Community Step against Terrorism' (1980) 9 *Denver Journal of International Law and Policy* 169

Nicolas Rostov, 'Before and After: The Changed UN Response to Terrorism since September 11th' (2002) 35 *Cornell International Law Journal* 475

Ben Saul, *Defining Terrorism in International Law* (Oxford, 2006)

---

[148] For discussion of torture as a crime against humanity and as a war crime, see section 11.3.7 and section 12.3.2.

Sami Shubber, 'The International Convention against the Taking of Hostages' (1981) 52 *British Yearbook of International Law* 205

Surya P. Subedi, 'The UN Response to International Terrorism in the Aftermath of the Terrorist Attacks in America and the Problem of the Definition of Terrorism in International Law' (2002) 4 *International Law FORUM du droit international* 159

Christian Walter *et al.* (eds.), *Terrorism as a Challenge for National and International Law: Security versus Liberty?* (Berlin, 2004)

Samuel M. Witten, 'The International Convention for the Suppression of Terrorist Bombings' (1998) 92 *American Journal of International Law* 774

Michael Wood, 'The Convention on the Prevention and Punishment of Crimes against Internationally Protected Persons, Including Diplomatic Agents' (1974) 23 *International and Comparative Law Quarterly* 791

On the prosecution of terrorist cases, see the UNODC website, www.unodc.org/unodc/en/terrorism/technical-assistance-tools.html.

Torture

Ahcene Boulesbaa, *The UN Convention on Torture and the Prospects for Enforcement* (The Hague, 1999)

J. Herman Burgers and Hans Danelius, *The United Nations Convention against Torture: A Handbook on the Convention against Torture and Other Cruel, Inhuman or Degrading Treatment or Punishment* (Leiden, 1988)

Manfred Nowak and Elizabeth Arthur, *The United Nations Convention against Torture* (Oxford, 2008)

Nigel Rodley, *The Treatment of Prisoners under International Law*, 3rd edn (Oxford, 2009)

Nigel Rodley and Matt Pollard, 'Criminalisation of Torture: State Obligations under the United Nations Convention against Torture and Other Cruel, Inhuman and Degrading Treatment or Punishment' (2006) 2 *European Human Rights Law Review* 115

Lene Wendland, *A Handbook on State Obligations under the UN Convention against Torture* (Geneva, 2002)

15

General Principles of Liability

15.1   Introduction

The substantive definitions of crimes discussed in Chapters 10–13 provide only a part of the picture of criminal liability. The general principles of liability apply across the various different offences and provide for the doctrines by which a person may commit, participate in, or otherwise be found responsible for those crimes. They include forms of liability such as aiding and abetting, which are familiar to all domestic criminal lawyers, as well as principles like command responsibility, which are specific to international criminal law. It is important to note at the outset that the various forms of liability not only have different conduct elements, but also different mental elements, and the extent to which principles of accomplice liability have been used in some cases to avoid high *mens rea* requirements for primary commission of international crimes has been controversial. Unlike in domestic law, where the traditional image of a criminal is the primary perpetrator, such as the person who pulls the trigger, in international criminal law, the paradigmatic offender is often the person who orders, masterminds, or takes part in a plan at a high level.[1] This also reflects the fact that international crimes tend to occur against a backdrop of collective criminality.[2] As a result, principles of liability play a comparatively large role in international criminal law.[3]

This chapter will discuss the principles of liability from two points of view, the ambit of liability recognized in customary and conventional international law,[4] alongside the appropriateness of those principles from the point of view of foundational principles of criminal law.[5] Admittedly those principles remain perhaps underdeveloped directly in international

---

[1] Such persons are often referred to as 'those bearing greatest responsibility' for international crimes (see e.g. Art. 1 of the SCSL Statute) or 'the most senior leaders suspected of being most responsible for' international crimes (SC Res. 1534(2004)). See further section 17.5 and section 17.8.1.

[2] See e.g. Elies van Sledregt, *Individual Criminal Responsibility in International Criminal Law* (Oxford, 2012) Chapter 2; André Nollkaemper and Harmen van der Wilt (eds.), *System Criminality in International Law* (Cambridge, 2009).

[3] See William Schabas, 'Enforcing Individual Criminal Responsibility in International Criminal Law: Prosecuting the Accomplices' (2001) 843 *International Review of the Red Cross* 439. Equally, as we shall see, some forms of liability in international criminal law allow people who would traditionally be seen as accomplices to be viewed as principal perpetrators. See also Héctor Olásolo, *The Criminal Responsibility of Senior Political and Military Leaders as Principals to International Crimes* (Oxford, 2009) Chapter 1.

[4] As was mentioned in section 8.4, the ICC Statute ought not to be taken straightforwardly as determinative of customary international criminal law.

[5] See further on this point, Robert Cryer, 'General Principles of Liability in International Criminal Law' in Dominic McGoldrick, Peter Rowe and Eric Donnelly (eds.), *The International Criminal Court: Legal and Policy Issues* (Oxford, 2004) 233.

criminal law, but they have proved important mechanisms for critique in this area.[6] It must be noted at the outset though, that the principles of liability are not watertight compartments, and there are overlaps between them, a complication that is not assisted by sometimes loose use of language by the Courts.[7] Where they overlap, the ICTY has suggested that 'the Trial Chamber has a discretion to choose which is the most appropriate head of responsibility under which to attach criminal responsibility to the accused'.[8] When exercising such discretion, Trial Chambers have 'entered a conviction under the head of responsibility which better characterises the criminal conduct of the accused'.[9] It also ought to be noted at the outset that the Genocide Convention adopts slightly different, additional, principles on aspects of liability for genocide.

15.2   Perpetration/commission

The concept of commission (which in all likelihood is synonymous with 'perpetration')[10] is, unsurprisingly, well established in international criminal law. For example, in the *Jaluit Atoll* case in 1945, three Japanese soldiers were convicted of personally shooting prisoners-of-war.[11] Article 7(1) of the ICTY Statute (to which Article 6(1) of the ICTR Statute and Article 6(1) of the SCSL Statute conform in all material respects) makes this clear, imposing liability, *inter alia*, on any 'person … [who] committed' an international crime. This description is, however, deceptively simple, as it begs the question of precisely who can be considered to have 'committed' a crime. As the ICTY has said, this primarily refers to 'the physical perpetration of a crime by the offender himself, or the culpable omission of an act that was mandated by a rule of criminal law'.[12]

This is not the only form that commission can take; there are other forms of commission that exist in treaty and custom. For example, in *Seromba*, the ICTR Appeals Chamber took a broad approach to 'commission', rejecting, for genocide, the idea that it was limited to the physical commission of crimes: '"direct and physical perpetration" need not mean physical killing, other acts can constitute direct participation in the *actus reus* of the crime'.[13] Unfortunately, the Appeals Chamber did not provide a detailed explanation of

[6] For a variety of views, see George Fletcher, 'The Theory of Criminal Liability and International Criminal Law' (2012) 10 *Journal of International Criminal Justice* 1029; Darryl Robinson, 'A Cosmopolitan Liberal Account of International Criminal Law' (2013) 26 *Leiden Journal of International Law* 127; James Stewart, 'The End of Modes of Liability for International Crimes' (2012) 25 *Leiden Journal of International Law* 165; Markus Dubber, 'Common Civility: The Culture of Alegality in International Criminal Law' (2011) 24 *Leiden Journal of International Law* 923; Elies van Sliedregt, 'The Curious Case of International Criminal Liability' (2012) 10 *Journal of International Criminal Justice* 1171; Schachar Eldar, 'Exploring International Criminal Law's Reluctance to Resort to Modalities of Group Responsibility: Five Challenges to International Prosecutions and their Impact on Broader Forms of Responsibility' (2013) 11 *Journal of International Criminal Justice* 331. For a recent attempt to create a comprehensive study postulating the bases for such doctrine, see Kai Ambos, *Treatise on International Criminal Law*, Vol. 1, *Foundations and General Part* (Oxford, 2013).
[7] Mohamed Shahabuddeen, *International Criminal Justice at the Yugoslav Tribunal: A Judge's Recollection* (Oxford, 2012) 216–17.
[8] *Krnojelac*, ICTY T. Ch. II, 15 March 2002, para. 173.
[9] *Stakić*, ICTY T. Ch. II, 31 July 2003, para. 463. See also Chapter 17 concerning indictments.
[10] The two will be used interchangeably here.   [11] *United States* v. *Masuda and Others* (the 'Jaluit Atoll case'), I LRTWC 71.
[12] *Tadić*, ICTY A. Ch., 15 July 1999, para. 188. See similarly *Kvočka et al.*, ICTY T. Ch. I, 2 November 2001, para. 251.
[13] *Seromba*, ICTR A. Ch., 12 March 2008, para. 161. See Flavia Zorzi Giustiniani, 'Stretching the Boundaries of Commission Liability' (2008) 6 *Journal of International Criminal Justice* 783; as noted at 787–8, a majority of the Appeals Chamber also thought that this would apply to the crime against humanity of extermination. The ICTR in *Gacumbitsi*, ICTR A. Ch., 7 July

what else would amount to 'commission' beyond stating that Seromba's actions (which largely amounted to agreeing, as a priest, to the use of bulldozers to destroy a church in which about 1,500 Tutsis had hidden) were 'as much an integral part of the genocide as were the killings which [they] enabled'.[14] In contrast, in *Kalimanzira*, it was held that it was 'not unreasonable' to define a defendant's tacit approval of a call for killing of Tutsis, alongside luring victims to an area where he brought armed perpetrators, as aiding and abetting rather than commission.[15] At no point have the Chambers of the ad hoc Tribunals given detailed proof of the customary law nature of this form of commission, but their jurisprudence seems settled.[16]

Article 25(3)(a) of the ICC Statute defines perpetration in a more detailed fashion, criminalizing a person who '[c]ommits such a crime whether as an individual, jointly with another or through another person, regardless of whether that other person is criminally responsible'. This formulation raises some of the important issues relating to the concept of perpetration. The first issue is whether or not perpetration can occur by omission. In customary law this is certainly the case, so long as the charge relates to a failure to live up to a duty to act, and the omission has a 'concrete influence' on the crime.[17] Although, owing to the fact that an Article criminalizing omissions was dropped at Rome,[18] some doubt that perpetration by omission is recognized in the ICC Statute,[19] the better view is that liability for omissions was not categorically excluded by the drafters. The ICC Elements of Crimes deliberately avoid the term 'acts' in favour of 'conduct', on the ground that the latter term includes acts or omissions.[20]

In the context of Article 25(3)(a), the ICC has identified three forms of perpetration: where the defendant:

a. physically carries out all elements of the offence (commission of the crime as an individual);
b. has, together with others, control over the offence by reason of the essential tasks assigned to him (commission of the crime jointly with others); or
c. has control over the will of those who carry out the objective elements of the offence (commission of the crime through another person).[21]

2006, para. 60, asserted, however, that 'In the context of genocide, however, direct and physical perpetration need not mean physical killing; other acts can constitute direct perpetration in the *actus reus* of the crime.' See also the Separate Opinion of Judge Schomberg, paras. 2–4.
[14] *Seromba*, ICTR A. Ch., 12 March 2008, para. 161, citing *Gacumbitsi*, ICTR A. Ch., 7 July 2006, para. 60. See Giustiniani, 'Stretching the Boundaries', 796–9.
[15] *Kalimanzira*, ICTR A. Ch., 20 October 2010, paras. 219–20.   [16] Ambos, *Treatise*, 121.
[17] *Orić*, ICTY A. Ch., 3 July 2008, para. 94. See generally Ambos, *Treatise*, 180–97 (where it is suggested that it is a general principle rather than custom). For a list of positive obligations in humanitarian law, see Yves Sandoz, Christoph Swiniarski and Bruno Zimmermann (eds.), *Commentary on the Additional Protocols of 8 June 1977 to the Geneva Conventions of 8 August 1949* (Geneva, 1987) 1009. One example of a conviction for an omission is *Delalić et al.*, ICTY T. Ch. II, 16 November 1998, paras. 1092–6, 1101–5.
[18] Per Saland, 'International Criminal Law Principles' in Lee, *Making of the Rome Statute*, 212.
[19] See e.g. Kai Ambos, 'Article 25' in Triffterer, *Observers' Notes*, 475, 492; Kerstin Weltz, *Die Unterlassungshaftung im Völkerstrafrecht* (Freiburg im Breisgau, 2004) 320 *et seq.*
[20] See e.g. Maria Kelt and Hermann von Hebel, 'The Making of the Elements of Crimes' in Lee, *Elements and Rules*, 14.
[21] *Katanga and Ngudjolo Chui*, ICC PTC I, 30 September 2008, para. 488.

This first is basic perpetration. The second is co-perpetration, the third is 'vertical'/indirect perpetration. The first is relatively simple (although subject to the above). The second and third will be dealt with in turn, and then the controversial issue of a hybrid of those two forms of liability–indirect co-perpetration will be evaluated. First, however, it is necessary to canvass the form of commission known as 'joint criminal enterprise', as it has been developed by the ICTY, ICTR and other courts and tribunals relying on customary law.

15.2.1   *Joint criminal enterprise*[22]

The Charters of the Nuremberg and Tokyo IMTs both provided that those who participated in a 'common plan or conspiracy to commit any of the foregoing crimes are responsible for all acts performed by any person in execution of such a plan'.[23] The form of liability contained in these provisions, which both Tribunals determined only applied to crimes against peace,[24] is often called conspiracy.[25] The use of 'conspiracy' in this regard is misleading, as it is apt to cause confusion between this type of liability and the separate (common law) offence of conspiracy, which is an agreement to commit an offence, and does not require that any further action is taken in pursuance of that agreement.[26] In international criminal law, this inchoate crime only exists in relation to genocide.[27] The Nuremberg and Tokyo IMTs, whilst both using the term 'conspiracy', were dealing with the situation where the plans were put into effect. Whilst the Nuremberg IMT interpreted the principle quite narrowly,[28] the Tokyo IMT took a very broad approach to it, and was criticized for doing so.[29]

Article 7(1) of the ICTY Statute, Article 6(1) of the ICTR Statute and Article 6(1) of the SCSL Statute do not contain any express provision on this form of liability. Nor do they contain analogous wording to that in Article 25(3)(a) of the ICC Statute about how commission may occur.[30] Nonetheless, the ICTY has developed a detailed jurisprudence on what it terms 'joint criminal enterprise' (or common purpose) liability. The leading judgment on the point is in *Tadić*. Tadić had been acquitted at trial level of involvement in the killing of five civilians in the village of Jaskići in June 1992 by the armed group he was a member of, as there was no evidence he was involved directly in the killing himself.

---

[22] For a useful overview, see Elies van Sliedregt, *The Criminal Responsibility of Individuals for Violations of International Humanitarian Law* (The Hague, 2003) 94–110. See also the symposium and anthology in (2007) 5 *Journal of International Criminal Justice* 67–244.

[23] Art. 6 of the Nuremberg IMT Statute; Art. 5(c) of the Tokyo IMT Statute.

[24] Nuremberg IMT, Judgment and Sentences, reprinted in (1947) 41 *American Journal of International Law* 172, 221–2; Tokyo IMT, reprinted in Neil Boister and Robert Cryer, *Documents on the Tokyo International Military Tribunal* (Oxford, 2008) 48,449, Judges Bernard and Jaranilla dissented on this: Dissenting Opinion of the Member from France, at 5–7; Concurring Opinion of the Member from the Philippines, 1–7.

[25] Including by the Tribunals themselves.   [26] *Milutinović et al.*, ICTY A. Ch., 21 May 2003, para. 23.

[27] Art. 3(d) of the 1948 Genocide Convention. See William Schabas, *Genocide in International Law*, 2nd edn (Cambridge, 2008) Chapter 6.

[28] Nuremberg IMT, Judgment and Sentences, reprinted in (1947) 41 *American Journal of International Law* 172 222.

[29] Ian Brownlie, *International Law and the Use of Force by States* (Oxford, 1962) 203; John Piccigallo, *The Japanese on Trial* (Austin, TX, 1979) 21; Neil Boister and Robert Cryer, *The Tokyo International Military Tribunal: A Reappraisal* (Oxford, 2008) Chapter 8.

[30] See, for discussion, Harmen van der Wilt, 'Joint Criminal Enterprise: Possibilities and Limits' (2007) 5 *Journal of International Criminal Justice* 91, 102–8.

The Appeals Chamber overturned this acquittal, and set out its understanding of commission by virtue of participation in a joint criminal enterprise (JCE). The Chamber began by looking at Article 7(1) of the ICTY Statute. It decided, on the basis of a teleological interpretation, that, as the purpose of the Statute was to cover all those responsible for international crimes in the former Yugoslavia, Article 7(1) 'does not exclude those modes of participating in the commission of crimes which occur where several persons having a common purpose embark on criminal activity that is then carried out either jointly or by some members of this plurality of persons'.[31] It supported this finding by pointing to the nature of many international crimes, in particular that they are committed jointly by large numbers of people.[32] Since the *actus reus* and *mens rea* were not set out in the ICTY Statute, the Appeals Chamber looked to customary law, primarily as evidenced in case law.

Actus reus

Having reviewed post-Second World War proceedings,[33] such as the *Almelo* case[34] and the *Essen Lynching Trial*,[35] the Appeals Chamber in *Tadić* determined that there was a customary basis for such liability in three classes of cases: (1) 'co-perpetration, where all participants in the common design possess the same criminal intent to commit a crime (and one or more of them actually perpetrate the crime, with intent)' (JCE I); (2) so-called 'concentration camp cases' (JCE II); and (3) 'type three' JCE, where crimes are committed by members of the group, outside its common purpose, but as a foreseeable incident of it (JCE III).[36] It further determined that all three types shared a common *actus reus*, namely, that there was:

i.   A plurality of persons.
ii. The existence of a common plan, design or purpose which amounts to or involves the commission of a crime provided for in the Statute.
iii. Participation of the accused in the common design involving the perpetration of one of the crimes provided for in the Statute.[37]

The Appeals Chamber in *Tadić* elaborated on these criteria. For example, the plurality 'need not be organised in a military, political or administrative structure'.[38] 'There is no necessity for this plan, design or purpose to have been previously arranged or formulated. The common plan or purpose may materialise extemporaneously and be inferred from the fact that a plurality of persons acts in unison to put into effect a joint criminal enterprise.'[39] Participation in the common design 'need not involve commission of a specific crime under one of those provisions ... but may take the form of assistance in, or contribution to, the

---

[31] *Tadić*, ICTY A. Ch., 15 July 1999, paras. 189–90. Another case has, controversially, determined that Art. 7(1) is not exhaustive: *Milutinović et al.*, ICTY A. Ch., 21 May 2003, para. 20. Still, the Appeals Chamber in *Stakić* appeared to frown on new doctrines being introduced into the Tribunal's jurisprudence: *Stakić*, ICTY A. Ch., 22 March 2006, para. 59.
[32] *Tadić*, ICTY A. Ch., 15 July 1999, para. 191.
[33] Not all of which, it must be noted, firmly based their forms of liability in international law.
[34] *Otto Sandrock*, I LRTWC 35.   [35] *Erich Heyer*, I LRTWC 88.
[36] *Tadić*, ICTY A. Ch., 15 July 1999, para. 220. See also *Gacumbitsi*, ICTR A. Ch., 7 July 2006, Separate Opinion of Judge Shahabuddeen, para. 40.
[37] *Tadić*, ICTY A. Ch., 15 July 1999, para. 227.   [38] *Ibid.*   [39] *Ibid.*

execution of the common plan or purpose'.[40] It also said that the conduct must be 'in some way … directed to the furthering of the common plan or purpose'.[41]

Later cases have also contributed to an understanding of the *actus reus*. It is clear, for example, that membership in the group *per se* is not enough to ground liability on this basis.[42] There has to be some form of action by the defendant to contribute to the implementation of the plan.[43] Equally, both direct and indirect participation suffice.[44] There is no requirement that the contribution made by the defendant is a 'necessary or substantial' one,[45] but a later Appeals Chamber decision in the *Brđanin and Talić* case said that it needs to be 'significant'.[46] The Appeals Chamber in that case took the view that the direct perpetrators 'on the ground' do not have to be a part of the enterprise, so long as the crimes can be imputed to one member of the enterprise, who is acting pursuant to the common plan when he or she uses those direct perpetrators to commit crimes.[47] Furthermore:

Factors indicative of such a link include evidence that the JCE member explicitly or implicitly requested the non-JCE member to commit such a crime or instigated, ordered, encouraged, or otherwise availed himself of the non-JCE member to commit the crime. However, it is not determinative whether the non-JCE member shared the *mens rea* of the JCE member or that he knew of the existence of the JCE.[48]

There is sense in the Appeals Chamber's position, in that the usual collective nature of the crimes means that it would be practically impossible to prove the *mens rea* of all of the direct perpetrators when trying high-level participants.[49] In asserting this position, though, the ICTY has opened itself up to criticism on the ground that it is stretching liability beyond the appropriate bounds of culpability.[50]

If the common plan or purpose fundamentally alters, then this is a new plan or purpose, not simply a continuation/mutation of the old one,[51] and a person is only responsible for crimes which relate to the plan or purpose he or she subscribed to;[52] if they agree to the expansion, they can be responsible for the new crimes. In this circumstance, too, 'it is not necessary to show that the JCE members *explicitly* agreed to the expansion of criminal

---

[40] *Ibid*. See also *Krajišnik*, ICTY A. Ch., 17 March 2009, para. 695.
[41] *Tadić*, ICTY A. Ch., 15 July 1999, para. 229, The requirement is not exactly clear, however.
[42] *Milutinović*, ICTY A. Ch., 21 May 2003, para. 26; *Brđanin and Talić*, ICTY T. Ch. II, 1 September 2004, para. 263.
[43] *Brđanin and Talić*, ICTY T. Ch. II, 1 September 2004, para. 263.   [44] *Ibid*.
[45] *Kvočka et al.*, ICTY A. Ch., 28 February 2005, para. 97.
[46] *Brđanin and Talić*, ICTY A. Ch., 3 April 2007, para. 430. The exact difference between 'substantial' and 'significant' is not entirely clear, but has been repeated; see *Krajišnik*, ICTY A. Ch., 17 March 2009, para. 215.
[47] *Brđanin and Talić*, ICTY A. Ch., 3 April 2007, paras. 410–14, but see the Dissenting Opinion of Judge Shahabuddeen, paras. 4–20. Nor does there have to be an agreement with the direct perpetrator for them to commit the crime: *ibid.*, paras. 418–19.
[48] *Krajišnik*, ICTY A. Ch., 17 March 2009, para. 226.
[49] In *ibid.*, para. 156, the Appeals Chamber noted that not all members have to be named; reference by group may be enough in some circumstances, but the 'rank and file consist[ing] of local politicians, military and police commanders, paramilitary leaders, and others' was too vague.
[50] E.g. Harmen van der Wilt, 'Joint Criminal Enterprise: Possibilities and Limits' (2007) 5 *Journal of International Criminal Justice* 91.
[51] *Blagojević and Jokić*, ICTY T. Ch. I, 7 January 2005, para. 700.
[52] *Krajišnik*, ICTY T. Ch. I, 27 September 2006, para. 1903. See also *ibid.*, para. 701, footnote 2157, although, if the later plan or purpose is broader, he or she may still be liable for those crimes that fall within the narrower aspect agreed to.

means; this agreement may materialise extemporaneously and be inferred from circumstantial evidence'.[53]

Mens rea

Although the conduct element of all of the forms of joint criminal enterprise liability is the same, the distinction between them comes in via the mental element. The Appeals Chamber in *Tadić* is the standard reference on the point:

> the *mens rea* element differs according to the category of common design under consideration. With regard to the first category, what is required is the intent to perpetrate a certain crime (this being the shared intent on the part of all co-perpetrators). With regard to the second category (which ... is really a variant of the first),[54] personal knowledge of the system of ill-treatment is required (whether proved by express testimony or a matter of reasonable inference from the accused's position of authority), as well as the intent to further this common concerted system of ill-treatment. With regard to the third category, what is required is the *intention* to participate in and further the criminal activity or the criminal purpose of a group and to contribute to the joint criminal enterprise or in any event to the commission of a crime by the group. In addition, responsibility for a crime other than the one agreed upon in the common plan arises only if, under the circumstances of the case, (i) it was *foreseeable* that such a crime might be perpetrated by one or other members of the group and (ii) the accused *willingly took that risk*.[55]

As ought to be clear, the first category of JCE (JCE I) is close to the concept of joint perpetration: the various participants share the intention to commit the crime that occurs. This is possibly slightly diluted in the second type (JCE II), where knowledge of the system of ill-treatment suffices rather than the intent to commit the specific crime (if knowledge and intention are entirely separable concepts).[56] The broadest form of liability comes in JCE III, where the foreseeability of a crime is said to be the test.

It might be thought that, by using the term 'foreseeable' rather than 'foreseen' in relation to JCE III, the Appeals Chamber was imposing a negligence standard. That would be inaccurate, as the second aspect of the test – that the accused 'willingly took that risk' – clearly shows that the test is whether the person was subjectively reckless (or, in civil law terms, had *dolus eventualis*) in relation to such a crime.[57] It is also important to note that any inference must take into account what the particular person knew: 'What is natural and foreseeable to one person participating in a systemic joint criminal enterprise, might not be natural and foreseeable to another, depending on the information available to them.'[58] If this

---

[53] *Krajišnik*, ICTY A. Ch., 17 March 2009, para. 163. See also *Ayyash et al.*, STL A. Ch., 16 February 2011, para. 246.
[54] But see *Kvočka et al.*, ICTY A. Ch., 28 February 2005, para. 86; Steven Powles, 'Joint Criminal Enterprise: Criminal Liability by Prosecutorial Ingenuity and Judicial Creativity?' (2004) 2 *Journal of International Criminal Justice* 606, 609–10.
[55] *Tadić*, ICTY A. Ch., 15 July 1999, para. 228.
[56] Although in both instances the Appeals Chamber has said the participants must share the physical perpetrator's *mens rea*: *Krnojelac*, ICTY A. Ch., 17 September 2003, para. 83.
[57] See *Tadić*, ICTY A. Ch., 15 July 1999, para. 220; *Stakić*, ICTY A. Ch., 22 March 2006, paras. 99–103.
[58] *Kvočka et al.*, ICTY A. Ch., 28 February 2005, para. 86.

is shown, however, 'a person may be found responsible for such acts, even if it is not proved that he or she knew they had occurred'.[59]

The nature of joint criminal enterprise liability

The Appeals Chamber in *Mulutinović*, somewhat controversially, determined that joint criminal enterprise liability is a form of 'committing', in the language of Article 7(1).[60] Even if the other two forms can be considered a form of primary liability,[61] which is also not beyond controversy, it might be questioned whether JCE III liability could really be seen as a form of 'commission'.[62]

The nature of joint criminal enterprise liability is important. For example, if JCE is considered a primary form of liability, participants in the enterprise can be aided and abetted by those outside it.[63] If it is a form of secondary liability, then they could not. Also, from the point of view of the principle of fair labelling, the omnibus nature of treating joint criminal enterprise liability as 'committing', runs together rather different levels of culpability, not expressing a distinction between those who are in essence joint perpetrators, but with a simple division of labour, from those who are far closer to aiders and abettors than primary perpetrators. This is particularly the case if '[r]egardless of the role each played in its commission, all of the participants in the enterprise are guilty of the same crime'.[64] The Appeals Chamber has admitted that this may be disquieting, but claimed that such matters can be dealt with satisfactorily in sentencing.[65]

Perhaps unsurprisingly, this form of liability has proved very controversial. The Appeals Chamber did rely upon a rather small number of post-War trials and two treaties (one of which was not directly applicable to international crimes).[66] Academics[67] and later judicial decisions have been critical of the ICTY's approach to establishing the law here. The Pre-Trial Chamber of the ECCC, for example, has determined, through a review of the same materials as the ICTY relied upon, that customary law did not contain a broad principle of joint enterprise liability equivalent to JCE III between 1975 and 1979.[68] On JCE III, the

---

[59] *Milošević*, ICTY T. Ch. III, 16 June 2004, para. 150.
[60] *Milutinović et al.*, ICTY A. Ch., 21 May 2003, para. 20; *Kvočka et al.*, ICTY A. Ch., 28 February 2005 paras. 79–80.
[61] Aspects of joint criminal enterprise can perhaps appropriately be seen as forms of commission, given the often large-scale perpetration of international crimes; see e.g. Jens Ohlin, 'Three Conceptual Problems with the Doctrine of Joint Criminal Enterprise' (2007) 5 *Journal of International Criminal Justice* 69, 70, 72–4.
[62] See also *ibid.*, 85–8.   [63] *Vasiljević*, ICTY A. Ch., 25 February 2004, para. 102.
[64] *Blagojević and Jokić*, ICTY T. Ch. I, 17 January 2005, para. 702, referring, *inter alia*, to *Vasiljević*, ICTY A. Ch., 25 February 2004, para. 111. See also Ohlin, 'Three Conceptual Problems', 76–7; and Kai Ambos, 'Joint Criminal Enterprise and Command Responsibility' (2007) 5 *Journal of International Criminal Justice* 159, 167–76. For a defence, see Antonio Cassese, 'The Proper Limits of Criminal Liability under the Doctrine of Joint Criminal Enterprise' (2007) 5 *Journal of International Criminal Justice* 109, 114–15.
[65] *Brđanin and Talić*, ICTY A. Ch., 3 April 2007, para. 432.
[66] *Tadić*, ICTY A. Ch., 15 July 1999, paras. 195–226. Admittedly, the ICC Statute is applicable to international crimes, but, as we shall see, it does not adopt such a broad approach to JCE as the ICTY.
[67] Robert C. Clark, 'Return to Borkum Island: Extended Joint Criminal Enterprise Responsibility in the Wake of World War II' (2011) 9 *Journal of International Criminal Justice* 839. Alison Marston Danner and Jenny S. Martinez, 'Guilty Associations: Joint Criminal Enterprise, Command Responsibility and the Development of International Criminal Law' (2005) 93 *California Law Review* 75, 110–17; Powles, 'Joint Criminal Enterprise', 614–17; Ohlin, 'Three Conceptual Problems', 75–6; Olásolo, *Criminal Responsibility*, Chapter 2.
[68] *Ieng Sary et al.*, ECCC PTC, 20 May 2010, paras. 75–88.

Chamber specifically refuted the reasoning of the ICTY, criticizing, in particular, its reliance on British cases such as *Borkum Island* and the *Essen Lynching* cases, as they were unreasoned, and thus too thin a basis for it.[69] The Chamber also dismissed the Italian cases, as they were applying domestic principles of liability.[70] In spite of this, the ICTY Appeals Chamber has been unimpressed by such critiques, and repeatedly reaffirmed its earlier holdings.[71]

From the point of view of fairness to the defendant, the vague, 'elastic' nature of the doctrine has led to claims that it is overbroad, thus reliant on prosecutorial discretion rather than law to keep it in check.[72] This is particularly the case where large-scale enterprises are charged.[73] Fears have also been expressed about the extent to which it encourages prosecutors to bring indictments that assert joint enterprises in a very general manner, making preparation difficult for the defence.[74] Turning to the *mens rea*, a person may be convicted before the ICTY and ICTR of specific intent crimes such as genocide even if that person did not have the relevant *mens rea* for that offence, but the crimes were a natural and foreseen incident of the enterprise he or she was involved in on the basis of JCE.[75] This has led to criticisms of JCE liability, as allowing the prosecution to circumvent the proper *mens rea* requirements for such serious crimes.[76] The principle, however, remains popular with the ICTY Prosecutor,[77] and does go some way to describing the joint nature of many international crimes and explaining the culpability of some participants not otherwise easily brought under the ambit of criminality, in spite of their blameworthiness.[78]

Other than Judge Cassese,[79] Judge Shahabuddeen has also defended JCE as the requirement that the accused willingly took the risk of the offence occurring within the scope of the joint enterprise is a significant limitation.[80] In addition, the policy considerations relating to the danger of collective activity and attributing liability in such circumstances means that JCE is justifiable.[81] Whether these considerations answer the question of whether liability

---

[69] *Ibid.*, paras. 79–81.   [70] *Ibid.*, para. 82.

[71] *Ibid.*, paras. 29, 40–3; *Martić*, ICTY A. Ch., 8 October 2008, paras. 80–1; *Krajišnik*, ICTY A. Ch., 17 March 2009, paras. 652–72.

[72] Mark Osiel, 'The Banality of Good: Aligning Incentives against Mass Atrocity' (2005) 105 *Columbia Law Review* 1751, 1799–1802; Danner and Martinez, 'Guilty Associations', 135–46; Mohamed Elawa Badar, 'Just Convict Everyone! – Joint Perpetration from Tadić to Stakić and Back Again' (2006) 6 *International Criminal Law Review* 302. Equally, see Katrina Gustafson, 'The Requirement of an "Express Agreement" for Joint Criminal Enterprise Liability: A Critique of Brđanin' (2007) 5 *Journal of International Criminal Justice* 134; Cassese, 'Proper Limits', 116–23; and *Brđanin and Talić*, ICTY A. Ch., 3 April 2007, paras. 426–32.

[73] Which they may be: *Brđanin and Talić*, ICTY A. Ch., 3 April 2007, paras. 420–5.

[74] Guénaël Mettraux, *International Crimes and the Ad Hoc Tribunals* (Oxford, 2005) 293; Osiel, 'The Banality of Good', 1803. Although the ICTY does not think this problematic: see *Limaj et al.*, ICTY A. Ch., 27 September 2007, para. 104.

[75] *Karemera et al.*, ICTR A. Ch., 22 October 2004, paras. 30–1. However, this position has been rejected by the Special Tribunal for Lebanon: *Ayyash et al.*, STL A. Ch., 16 February 2011, para. 248.

[76] Mettraux, *International Crimes*, 265; Osiel, 'The Banality of Good', 1796. For a defence, see Elies van Sliedregt, 'Joint Criminal Enterprise as a Pathway to Convicting Individuals for Genocide' (2007) 5 *Journal of International Criminal Justice* 184.

[77] See e.g. Nicola Piacente, 'Importance of the Joint Criminal Enterprise Doctrine for ICTY Prosecutorial Policy' (2004) 2 *Journal of International Criminal Justice* 446.

[78] Mettraux, *International Crimes*, 292; Osiel, 'The Banality of Good', 1786–90, but see 1802; Danner and Martinez, 'Guilty Associations', 132–4.

[79] Cassese, 'Proper Limits'.

[80] Shahabuddeen, *International Criminal Justice*, 222–3; Antonio Cassese *et al.*, *Cassese's International Criminal Law*, 3rd edn (Oxford, 2013) 170.

[81] *Ibid.*, pp. 224–6.

ought to be attributed in such circumstances is debatable.[82] Owing to the fact that JCE III does not fall under the jurisdiction of the ICC, its significance is likely to evanesce over time, although it may retain relevance for prosecutions that are based on customary law.

The ICC Statute recognizes an attenuated form of joint enterprise liability.[83] Article 25(3) (d) provides for liability for someone who:

contributes to the commission or attempted commission of such a crime by a group of persons acting with a common purpose. Such contribution shall be intentional and shall either

   i. Be made with the aim of furthering the criminal activity or criminal purpose of the group, where such activity or purpose involves the commission of a crime within the jurisdiction of the Court; or
  ii. Be made in the knowledge of the intention of the group to commit the crime.

It seems clear that this does not recognize recklessness (as it requires an intentional contribution, and at least knowledge of the intention of the group),[84] and therefore does not provide for liability on a basis akin to JCE III.[85] That said, it does not seem to require a 'significant' contribution to the plan, requiring only that the participation be 'in any other way' than those identified in Articles 25(3)(a)–(c).[86] Pre-Trial Chamber I of the ICC has determined, distinguishing liability under Article 25(3)(a) and (d), that the contribution made by the alleged perpetrator need not be 'essential', but merely 'significant'.[87] Relevant factors in determining this have been said to be:

(i) the sustained nature of the participation after acquiring knowledge of the criminality of the group's common purpose, (ii) any efforts made to prevent criminal activity or to impede the efficient functioning of the group's crimes, (iii) whether the person creates or merely executes the criminal plan, (iv) the position of the suspect in the group or relative to the group, and (v) perhaps most importantly, the role the suspect played *vis-à-vis* the seriousness and scope of the crimes committed.[88]

Such factors are by no means exhaustive.

Separately, Pre-Trial Chamber I held that the suspect does not need to be a member of the group that acts with the common purpose for liability to arise under this provision.[89] It has further determined that the 'group acting with a common purpose' meant the same as it did in the context of Article 25(3)(a) (that there be a common plan between at least two people), which is discussed below.[90] With respect to the first criterion (of a non-essential

---

[82] For critique, see Wayne Jordash, 'Joint Criminal Enterprise Liability: Result Oriented Justice' in Schabas, *Ashgate Research Companion*, 133.

[83] Cassese *et al.* (*Cassese's International Criminal Law*, 175) assert that, rather than Art. 25(3)(d), Art. 25(3)(a) of the ICC Statute, by providing for liability for those committing crimes 'jointly with another', 'implicitly permits' JCE liability, but the ICC has not taken this path, and this remains very much a minority view.

[84] *Mbarushimana*, ICC PTC I, 16 December 2011, paras. 288–9.

[85] Jens David Ohlin, 'Joint Criminal Confusion' (2009) 2 *New Criminal Law Review* 406, 410–16. See also Ambos, *Treatise*.122–3.

[86] Van Sliedregt, *Individual*, 146.

[87] *Mbarushimana*, ICC PTC I, 16 December 2011, paras. 276–84. The Chamber, in spite of differentiating the concepts, drew upon ICTY jurisprudence in relation to JCE to derive this standard. The Chamber also found that such assistance can also occur after the crimes have been committed, so long as the contribution was agreed prior to the commission of the crime: paras. 286–7. Owing to the circumstances of the case, the majority of the Appeals Chamber did not express an opinion: *Mbarushimana*, ICC A. Ch., 30 May 2012, paras. 64–9.

[88] *Mbarushimana*, ICC PTC I, 16 December 2011, para. 284.   [89] *Ibid.*, paras. 273–5.   [90] *Ibid.*, para. 271.

contribution), the fact that, as will be seen, this condition is controversial in relation to Article 25(3)(a) means that the issue cannot, as yet, be considered settled. The Chamber did make clear, though, that Article 25(3)(d) covers, largely, what is caught under JCE I and II. An important difference between this provision and JCE is that, whereas JCE is considered a form of perpetration, liability under Article 25(3)(d) is a form of complicity.

15.2.2 Co-perpetration

The second type of perpetration noted by the ICC is commonly known as co-perpetration. It performs an analogous function to JCE, although is probably not as broad. Co-perpetration in general:

is originally rooted in the idea that when the sum of the coordinated individual contributions of a plurality of persons results in the realisation of all the objective elements of a crime, any person making a contribution can be held vicariously responsible for the contributions of all the others and, as a result, can be considered as a principal to the whole crime.[91]

There was an attempt by at least one Trial Chamber in the ICTY to introduce a form of 'co-perpetratorship',[92] which took a broad approach to what amounts to commission into the law of the ad hoc Tribunals. In the *Stakić* case, the Trial Chamber found that there was a form of liability that consisted of:

An explicit agreement or silent consent to reach a common goal by coordinated cooperation and joint control over the criminal conduct … These can be described as shared acts which when brought together achieve the shared goal based on the same degree of control over the execution of the common acts.[93]

Its support for this came from doctrine and national analogies, rather than direct sources of international law. The Appeals Chamber in that case determined that there was no such concept of co-perpetratorship, stating that '[t]his mode of liability, as defined and applied by the Trial Chamber, does not have support in customary international law or in the settled jurisprudence of this Tribunal'.[94] The Appeals Chamber preferred to see such a form of co-perpetratorship as being a form of joint criminal enterprise liability.[95] The Trial Chamber itself admitted that it was 'aware that the end result of its definition of co-perpetration approaches that of the aforementioned joint criminal enterprise and even overlaps in part'.[96]

---

[91] *Lubanga*, ICC PTC I, 29 January 2007, para. 326.
[92] Care must be taken when reading judgments on this point, as sometimes such a term is used to mean joint perpetration or the liability of a person participating in a joint criminal enterprise. See, for the former, e.g. *Furundžija*, ICTY T. Ch. II, 10 December 1998, para. 252; for the latter, see e.g. *Vasiljević*, ICTY A. Ch., 25 February 2004, para. 102; *Kvočka et al.*, ICTY A. Ch., 28 February 2005, para. 90.
[93] *Stakić*, ICTY T. Ch. II, 31 July 2003, para. 440.
[94] *Stakić*, ICTY A. Ch., 22 March 2006, para. 62. See also *Multinović et al.*, ICTY T. Ch. III, 22 March 2006.
[95] *Stakić*, ICTY A. Ch., 22 March 2006, paras. 62–3.   [96] *Stakić*, ICTY T. Ch. II, 31 July 2003, para. 441.

In spite of the doubts about the customary status of co-perpetration, it has played a large part in the early practice of the ICC. Even so, the basis and ambit of the principle remain contentious.[97]

The jurisprudence on direct co-perpetration formed the basis of the ICC's first conviction, in the *Lubanga* case.[98] The basic requirements were identified in the majority decision in the *Lubanga* trial judgment (which claimed to follow the Pre-Trial Chamber's views on point, owing to the fact that they were the basis upon which the trial proceeded) and are that:

  (i)   there was an agreement or common plan between the accused and at least one other co-perpetrator that, once implemented, will result in the commission of the relevant crime in the ordinary course of events;
 (ii)   the accused provided an essential contribution to the common plan that resulted in the commission of the relevant crime;
(iii)   the accused meant to . . . [commit the relevant crime] or he was aware that by implementing the common plan these consequences 'will occur in the ordinary course of events'; [and]
 (iv)   the accused was aware that he provided an essential contribution to the implementation of the common plan.[99]

Actus reus

Let us take the requirements in turn. The first, that there is a common plan is analogous to that in JCE liability,[100] and case law has established that the plan need not be express;[101] it may be inferred from later concerted action.[102] There may be some inconsistency in the jurisprudence of the ICC on whether or not the plan has to be directed to committing a crime,[103] but the Pre-Trial Chamber in *Lubanga* accepted that:

It suffices: (i) that the co-perpetrators have agreed (a) to start the implementation of the common plan to achieve a non-criminal goal, and (b) to only commit the crime if certain conditions are met, or (ii) that the co-perpetrators are aware (a) of the risk that implementing the common plan (which is specifically directed at the achievement of a non-criminal goal) will result in the commission of the crime and (b) accept such an outcome.[104]

This would also be consistent with ICTY jurisprudence on JCE,[105] although the two are by no means coterminous. The requirement that the plan objectively 'will' lead to crimes has been criticized,[106] and some question whether it exists.[107] The framing of the issue by the

[97] See the symposium at (2011) 9 *Journal of International Criminal Justice* 85–226.
[98] *Lubanga*, ICC T. Ch. I, 14 March 2012, para. 994. The decision has not gone uncriticized on point: Steffen Wirth, 'Co-Perpetratorship in the Lubanga Trial Judgment' (2012) 10 *Journal of International Criminal Justice* 971, 984–5.
[99] *Ibid.*, para. 1018. The Chamber asserted that they were, for reasons of fairness, following the definition given by the Pre-Trial Chamber in that case. In fact, there are differences. The subjective elements identified by the Pre-Trial Chamber were: (1) the suspect fulfils the subjective elements of the relevant offence (i.e. the war crime, crime against humanity or genocide); (2) the co-perpetrators must be mutually aware and accept that implementing the common plan may . . . result in the realization of the objective elements of the crime; and (3) the suspect is aware of the circumstances that enable him or her to jointly control the crime, *Lubanga*, ICC PTC I, 29 January 2007, paras. 349–67.
[100] Wirth, 'Co-Perpetration', 986; van Sliedregt, *Individual*, 100.   [101] *Lubanga*, ICC PTC I, 29 January 2007, para. 348.
[102] *Ibid.*, para. 345.   [103] Van Sliedregt, *Individual*, 100.   [104] *Lubanga*, ICC PTC I, 29 January 2007, para. 344.
[105] *Ibid.*   [106] Wirth, 'Co-Perpetration', 986.
[107] *Ngudjolo Chui*, ICC T. Ch. II, 18 December 2012, Concurring Opinion of Judge Van den Wyngaert, paras. 31–9; *Lubanga*, ICC T. Ch. I, 14 March 2012, Separate Opinion of Judge Fulford, para. 15.

Pre-Trial Chamber implies that the risk of crimes occurring suffices. The Trial Chamber did not seem to disagree, asserting that, although the plan does not need to be 'intrinsically criminal', it needs, at a minimum, to include a 'critical element of criminality', in that if it is implemented the plan carries a 'sufficient risk that, if events follow the ordinary course, a crime will be committed'.[108] Some question whether this is too low a requirement,[109] but much depends on the *mens rea* of the participants: if they believe implementation will lead to the offence being committed, then the critique is significantly avoided.

The majority of judicial views given so far about the conduct of the co-perpetrator require that the contribution must be essential to the commission of the objective elements of the crime, in that he or she could frustrate the commission of the crime by not undertaking his or her part.[110] The 'essential contribution' requirement comes from the alleged basis of co-perpetration being the joint control of the crime.[111] This requirement was largely developed along the lines of German criminal law theory (*Dogmatik*), in particular that of Claus Roxin.[112] This has been criticized, in particular by Judge Fulford in the *Lubanga* case, and, more recently, Judge Van den Wyngaert in the *Ngudjolo* judgment on the basis that it directly imports theories developed in one particular domestic jurisdiction into international criminal law.[113] This is particularly important in the context of the ICC which, as Judge Van den Wyngaert has noted, has a universalist bent, which means that 'the Court should refrain from relying on particular national models, however sophisticated they may be'.[114]

The 'essential contribution' requirement has been supported on the basis that this is a form of perpetration, rather than complicity, and, according to the requirement's supporters, Article 25(3) creates a hierarchy of forms of participation, with perpetration (in Article 25(3)(a) – including co-perpetration) being more serious than other forms of liability.[115] Hence, it ought to have higher thresholds. Although it is possible to derive such a hierarchy from the structure of the ICC Statute,[116] the forms of liability overlap, and there is nothing in the Statute or its *travaux* that indicates that the drafters of the ICC Statute intended such a rigid hierarchy.[117] Furthermore, the 'essential' criterion can lead

---

[108] *Lubanga*, ICC T. Ch. I, 14 March 2012, para. 984.   [109] Ambos, *Treatise*, 152.

[110] *Lubanga*, ICC PTC I, 29 January 2007, paras. 347–8. In *Katanga and Ngudjolo Chui*, ICC PTC I, 30 September 2008, para. 526, the Chamber held that '[d]esigning the attack, supplying weapons and ammunitions, exercising the power to move the previously recruited and trained troops to the fields; and/or coordinating and monitoring the activities of those troops, may constitute contributions that must be considered essential regardless of whether are they exercised (before or during the execution stage of the crime)'.

[111] For detailed elaboration of this idea, see Hector Olásolo, *The Responsibility of Senior Political and Military Leaders as Principals to International Crimes* (Oxford, 2009) Chapters 4–5.

[112] For details, see e.g. Thomas Weigend, 'Perpetration through an Organization: The Unexpected Career of a German Legal Concept' (2011) 9 *Journal of International Criminal Justice* 91; van Sliedregt, *Individual*, 83–8.

[113] Fulford in *Lubanga*, ICC T. Ch. I, 14 March 2012, paras. 8–12. Weigend, *ibid.*, 105–6.

[114] Van den Wyngaert in *Ngudjolo Chui*, ICC T. Ch. II, 18 December 2012, para. 5. See also Stefano Manacorda and Chantal Meloni, 'Indirect Perpetration versus Joint Criminal Enterprise: Concurring Approaches in the Practice of International Criminal Law' (2011) 9 *Journal of International Criminal Justice* 159, 170.

[115] *Lubanga*, ICC T. Ch. I, 14 March 2012, paras. 996–9.   [116] See Ambos, *Treatise*, 146–8, 152–3.

[117] Fulford in *Lubanga*, ICC T. Ch. I, 14 March 2012, paras. 6–9; Van den Wyngaert in *Ngudjolo Chui*, ICC T. Ch. II, 18 December 2012, paras. 12–15, 66–70; van Sliedregt, *Individual*, 85–6.

to artificial counterfactual speculations, especially in the complex situations in which international crimes often occur.[118]

Concentrating on the language of the Statute itself, both Judges Fulford and Van den Wyngaert found no reason to require more than a contribution of the conduct of the accused to the offence.[119] So Judge Fulford would accept liability as long as there was a causal link between the contribution and the crime.[120] Judge Van den Wyngaert wanted something more, namely, that the contribution be 'direct', i.e. that it had an 'immediate impact on the way in which the material elements of the crimes are realised'.[121] It was common ground between all of the judges in *Lubanga*, and Van den Wyngaert in *Ngudjolo Chui*, that this did not require physical presence at the scene of the crime, nor need it occur at the time of the offence *per se*.[122]

Mens rea

Turning to the subjective elements, although the Pre-Trial Chamber in *Lubanga* required it,[123] the Trial Chamber in *Lubanga* did not make entirely clear that the co-perpetrators, including the accused, must have the mental element for the relevant crime. However, it seems implicit in the opinion,[124] and has been supported in other decisions of the ICC.[125] It might be thought that this is subsumed within the requirement that the co-perpetrator 'meant' to commit the crime or was aware that it would occur in the ordinary course of events. Where, however, there are special intent offences, such as genocide, this implies that knowledge may suffice for co-perpetration where it would not for perpetration in its traditional sense. The Chamber also did not deal with the question of whether or not the mental element of co-perpetrators is a necessary element, although it did not really arise in the *Lubanga* case.[126]

The second aspect of the mental element has also proved controversial. At the pre-trial level in *Lubanga*, it was determined that it sufficed if the co-perpetrator realized that the implementation of the plan 'may' lead to the commission of a relevant crime. This mental element was set at the level of advertent recklessness/*dolus eventualis*.[127] This would bring the mental elements close to those of JCE III. Whatever the merits of this approach, it sits ill with Article 30 of the ICC Statute.[128] As a result, the fact that the Trial Chamber in *Lubanga* required that the co-perpetrator was aware that the crimes 'will' occur[129] is a welcome finding, and one consistent with other decisions of the ICC.[130]

---

[118] Fulford, *ibid.*, para. 17. For academic support, which is largely convincing, see Wirth, 'Co-Perpetration', 986–8.
[119] Fulford, *ibid.*, para. 15; Van den Wyngaert in *Ngudjolo Chui*, ICC T. Ch. II, 18 December 2012, paras. 40–2. For discussion, see Jens David Ohlin, Elies van Sliedregt and Thomas Weigend, 'Assessing the Control-Theory' (2013) 26 *Leiden Journal of International Law* 725, 728–34.
[120] Fulford, *ibid.*, para. 16.   [121] Van den Wyngaert, *Ngudjolo Chui*, ICC T. Ch. II, 18 December 2012, paras. 44–6.
[122] Van den Wyngaert, *ibid.*, para. 47; Fulford in *Lubanga*, ICC T. Ch. I, 14 March 2012, para. 15; *Lubanga*, ICC PTC I, 29 January 2007, paras. 347–8.
[123] *Lubanga*, ICC PTC I, 29 January 2007, paras. 349–60.   [124] Wirth, 'Co-Perpetration', 972.
[125] *Bemba Gombo*, ICC PTC II, 15 September 2009, para. 351; *Ruto et al.*, ICC PTC II, 23 January 2012, paras. 291–2.
[126] Wirth, 'Co-Perpetration', 989.   [127] *Lubanga*, ICC PTC I, 29 January 2007, para. 361.   [128] See below.
[129] *Lubanga*, ICC T. Ch. I, 14 March 2012, para. 1018.
[130] E.g. *Ruto et al.*, ICC PTC II, 23 January 2012, paras. 291–2 and authorities cited therein.

The third element is that the accused was aware that he or she made a contribution, 'essential' or otherwise, to the implementation of the common plan.

15.2.3   Indirect perpetration/perpetration through another person

The third form of perpetration identified by the ICC case was perpetration through another, where the person controls the will of that other. The concept of commission through another person recognizes the concept of 'innocent agency' by which a person commits a crime through an unwitting person, who cannot be considered to have any culpable part in the crime, for example because they were incapable of understanding the nature of their acts, or because they were an inadvertent participant or were acting under duress. Someone who persuades children under the age of criminal responsibility to commit crimes, or one who does something similar with respect to those who are mentally incompetent, would be considered by practically all domestic systems as the primary perpetrator. In that situation, there is no question of those legally incompetent people having exercised any form of choice, the concept which underlies criminal responsibility at the most basic level.[131]

Article 25(3)(a) enters more controversial waters, however, by recognizing the possibility of perpetration through a guilty agent separate from joint perpetration. This appears to be close to the concept in German law of the '*Hintermann*' (roughly, 'background man') perpetrator, where the mastermind of an operation who controls the will of those who directly commit the offence is taken to be a direct perpetrator rather than an accomplice.[132]

Expansion of the concept of perpetration is necessary in legal systems where accomplices may only be given a lower sentence than is available for principal perpetrators. As this is not the case in international criminal law it may be questionable whether it was necessary to include this form of liability as a form of commission,[133] especially as it might be thought to downgrade the gravity of the acts committed by those closest to the crime.[134] Nonetheless, the principle has significant defenders,[135] and it does reflect the dynamics that often characterize international crimes.[136] This is what is known as 'indirect' or 'vertical' perpetration.

The ICC has also held that this form of perpetration may occur through control of an organization.[137] This, based expressly on Roxin's theory of *Organisationsherrschaft*,[138] is the idea that control over an organization can lead to perpetration through that organization.

---

[131] See e.g. Andrew Simester *et al.*, *Simester and Sullivan's Criminal Law: Theory and Doctrine*, 5th edn (Oxford, 2013) 108.

[132] See e.g. Claus Kreß, 'Claus Roxin's Lehre von der Organisationsherrschaft und das Völkerstrafrecht' (2006) *Goltdammers Archiv für Strafrecht* 304. For support in the ICTR, see *Gacumbitsi*, ICTR A. Ch., 7 July 2006, Separate Opinion of Judge Schomburg, paras. 14–23; but see Separate Opinion of Judge Shahabuddeen, paras. 42–52, and Partially Dissenting Opinion of Judge Güney, paras. 2–9.

[133] See *Krnojelac*, ICTY T. Ch. II, 15 March 2002, paras. 74–5.

[134] Some of the problems this caused for the prosecution in the Frankfurt Auschwitz trial are discussed in Devin Pendas, *The Frankfurt Auschwitz Trial 1963–1965: Genocide, History and the Limits of Law* (Cambridge, 2006).

[135] Albin Eser, 'Individual Criminal Responsibility' in Cassese, *Commentary*, 793–5; Osiel, 'The Banality of Good', 1831–7. See also Judge Schomberg in *Gacumbitsi*, ICTR A. Ch., 7 July 2006, paras. 16–21.

[136] *Katanga and Ngudjolo Chui*, ICC PTC I, 30 September 2008, paras. 501–3.   [137] *Ibid.*, paras. 500–10.

[138] See Claus Roxin, 'Crimes as Part of Organized Power Structures' (2011) 9 *Journal of International Criminal Justice* 193, as adopted in *Katanga and Ngudjolo Chui*, ICC PTC I, 30 September 2008, para. 498.

In such circumstances, although the crimes are committed in the first instance by others, they are attributed to the controller of the organization. For liability to accrue this way, the defendant must control (or be in 'functional domination' of) an organization, which must be hierarchically organized, with sufficient subordinates that if the orders are not carried out by one subordinate, another will do so nearly automatically,[139] and:

> it is critical that the chief, or the leader, exercises authority and control over the apparatus and that his authority and control are manifest in subordinates' compliance with his orders. His means for exercising control may include his capacity to hire, train, impose discipline, and provide resources to his subordinates.[140]

In other words, '[t]he leader must use his control over the apparatus to execute crimes, which means that the leader, as the perpetrator behind the perpetrator, mobilises his authority and power within the organisation to secure compliance with his orders'.[141] In this instance, for liability to accrue, the person needs to be aware of the nature of their organization and their role within it, and the facts that meant their compliance with their orders would be 'near automatic'.[142] They also need to have the *mens rea* of the underlying crime. This derives from the simple fact that, if they are to be considered the perpetrator through others, they must have the *mens rea* for the offence.

Overall, it may be said that Roxin's theory, although having achieved some measure of acceptance in German courts, has been the subject of considerable criticism in Germany for setting high standards such as 'domination' of an organization, a condition that may not be appropriate to do the normative work Roxin hoped, even domestically.[143] A related critique is that, even if it was appropriate in the domestic context in which it was developed (Nazi criminality), it may not be more generally applicable,[144] in particular in less formal settings such as modern conflicts involving non-State actors and militias, such as those that have characterized modern African conflicts.[145]

15.2.4   *Indirect co-perpetration*

Co-perpetration has been the subject of further expansion, *inter alia*, through the *Lubanga* and *Katanga and Ngudjolo Chui* cases, by mixing the two types of perpetration described above.[146] The idea being that a horizontal co-perpetrator in that organization can be co-responsible for the crimes committed by those for whom another co-perpetrator is vertically responsible through indirect perpetration. To take an example, a foreign minister may be a participant in a common plan with a minister of defence that will lead to the commission of war crimes. The minister of defence is in control of the armed forces, but the foreign minister is not. On the basis of the common plan, the foreign minister could be held responsible by indirect co-perpetration for the offences of the armed forces, as the criminality of the defence minister would be attributed to the foreign minister, and this would include the defence

---

[139] *Ibid.*, paras. 515–17.   [140] *Ibid.*, para. 513.   [141] *Ibid.*, para. 514.   [142] *Ibid.*, para. 534.
[143] Weigend, 'Perpetration', 94–101.   [144] *Ibid.*, 107.   [145] Manacorda and Meloni, 'Indirect Perpetration', 171.
[146] See Ambos, *Treatise*, 156–60.

minister's indirect perpetration of the offences by the armed forces. This is said, helpfully, to mix vertical and horizontal perpetration, and acts in a manner similar to JCE, since the *Brđanin and Talić* case determined that the physical perpetrators did not have to be members of the JCE.[147]

The ICC has set out the requirements of indirect co-perpetration as follows:

  (i) the suspect must be part of a common plan or an agreement with one or more persons;
 (ii) the suspect and the other co-perpetrator(s) must carry out essential contributions in a coordinated manner which result in the fulfillment of the material elements of the crime;
(iii) the suspect must have control over the organization;
 (iv) the organization must consist of an organized and hierarchal apparatus of power;
  (v) the execution of the crimes must be secured by almost automatic compliance with the orders issued by the suspect;
 (vi) the suspect must satisfy the subjective elements of the crimes;
(vii) the suspect and the other co-perpetrators must be mutually aware and accept that implementing the common plan will result in the fulfillment of the material elements of the crimes; and
(viii) the suspect must be aware of the factual circumstances enabling him to exercise joint control over the commission of the crime through another person(s).[148]

As can be seen, requirements (i) to (vii) are very much an amalgam of the requirements of co-perpetration and indirect perpetration. This is unsurprising. The final part comes from indirect perpetration, but requires too much of those who are accused on the basis of joint control of the crime theories.[149] This is because the co-perpetrator who is not in control of forces will not have joint control over the commission of crimes committed by their co-perpetrator's subordinates, so cannot be aware of a fact that does not exist. It seems that the matter is probably one of loose terminology. Perhaps the way forward would be to accept that the knowledge has to be of the suspect's part in the plan, and the ability of other co-perpetrators to control the organization that is being used to commit the crimes on the ground.

The customary basis of this type of liability has been rejected on a number of occasions.[150] However, this is not a fatal objection to co-perpetration, as it is said to be a creature of the ICC Statute which, pursuant to Article 21 of the Statute, is the primary source of law for the ICC.[151] A more directed critique has come from Judge Van den Wyngaert, who has said that 'co-perpetration through another person' cannot be expanded out to the organizational context on the interpretation of the ICC Statute.[152] She cites the Pre-Trial Chamber's view that:

---

[147] See Jens Ohlin, 'Second Order Linking Principles: Combining Vertical and Horizontal Forms of Liability' (2012) 25 *Leiden Journal of International Law* 771.
[148] *Ruto et al.*, ICC PTC II, 23 January 2012, para. 292, relying on *Bemba Gombo*, ICC PTC II, 15 June 2009, paras. 350–1; *Katanga and Ngudjolo Chui*, ICC PTC I, 30 September 2008, paras. 500–14, 527–39; *Al Bashir*, ICC PTC I, 4 March 2009, paras. 209–13.
[149] Ambos, *Treatise*, 154.
[150] E.g. *Stakić*, ICTY A. Ch., 22 March 2006, para. 62; *Ayyash et al.*, STL A. Ch., 16 February 2011, para. 256.
[151] See e.g. *Ruto et al.*, ICC PTC II, 23 January 2012, para. 289.
[152] Van den Wyngaert in *Ngudjolo Chui*, ICC T. Ch. II, 18 December 2012, paras. 52–64.

An individual who has no control over the person through whom the crime would be committed cannot be said to commit the crime by means of that other person. However, if he acts jointly with another individual – one who controls the person used as an instrument – these crimes can be attributed to him on the basis of mutual attribution.

This, in her view, was an unwarranted and 'radical expansion of Article 25(3)(a) of the Statute, and indeed is a totally new mode of liability'.[153] Some of these criticisms have met with responses on the basis of a notionally logical or systematic approach to the ICC Statute and postulations about the intentions of the drafters,[154] but these were points which were the subject of critique by Judges Fulford and Van den Wyngaert, mentioned above, and have also provoked academic controversy.[155] The basis for such a form of liability has gathered academic support, however, although the need for clearer elaboration of this by the ICC is necessary.[156]

So long as the ICC sticks, *inter alia*, to requiring intention for co-perpetration (i.e. foresight that crimes 'will' occur) and requiring more than a minimal contribution to the plan, this ICC form of liability probably balances quite well the countervailing requirements of representing the dynamics of the commission of international crimes and maintaining a strong link to individual culpability. Where contributions and mental elements fall below this level, there are also principles of liability such as aiding and abetting that may be used to fill any gaps. After all, the concept of co-perpetration, direct and indirect, is one of 'commission' of international crimes rather than complicity. The relationship between indirect co-perpetration and liability under Article 25(3)(d) has been emphasized by the fact that the ICC has decided to recharacterize the form of liability under which one defendant is to be judged from the former to the latter.[157]

15.3   Aiding and abetting

Liability for aiding and abetting (or 'encouraging') international crimes is not new. A notable example of a prosecution for aiding a war crime was the *Zyklon B* case,[158] in which two German industrialists were convicted of supplying poison gas for use in concentration camp killings. The existence of liability for aiding and abetting is uncontroversial; it is recognized, for example in Article 7(1) of the ICTY Statute, Article 6(1) of the ICTR Statute and Article 6(1) of the SCSL Statute, all of which criminalize 'a person . . . who aided and abetted in the planning, preparation or execution' of an international crime. There have been, and remain, greater controversies about its precise ambit than its existence.[159] There are also overlaps between this form of liability and joint criminal

---

[153] *Ibid.*, para. 61, referring to *Katanga and Ngudjolo Chui*, ICC PTC I, 30 September 2008, para. 493.
[154] Wirth, 'Co-Perpetration', 978–9.   [155] Van Sliedregt, *Individual*, 85; *contra* Wirth, 'Co-Perpetration', 978–9.
[156] Ohlin, 'Second Order', 783–97; Ohlin *et al.*, 'Assessing', 735–7.
[157] *Katanga and Ngudjolo Chui*, ICC T. Ch. II, 21 November 2012. See section 17.8.4.   [158] *Tesch and Others*, I LRTWC 93.
[159] There is also a question as to whether complicity in genocide, criminalized in Art. 3(e) of the Genocide Convention, is different from this form of liability; the Appeals Chamber in *Krstić*, ICTY A. Ch., 19 April 2004, paras. 138–44, hinted that the two differ. Since then the case has been read by the Appeals Chamber as establishing that 'the prohibited act of complicity in genocide, which is included in the Genocide Convention and in Article 2 of the Statute, encompasses aiding and abetting'. *Ntakirutimana*

enterprise,[160] although the ICTY has said that, where people have participated in a joint criminal enterprise, to convict them 'only as an aider and abettor might understate the degree of their criminal responsibility',[161] and thus 'aiding and abetting is a form of responsibility which generally warrants lower sentences than responsibility as a co-perpetrator'.[162] The use of the term 'generally' in this context is important: there is no *a priori* reason why an aider or abettor cannot be as responsible as a perpetrator. The views of the ICTY here also need to be understood against the background of its broad interpretation of what perpetration entails, namely, as including participation in a joint criminal enterprise.[163]

The law on aiding and abetting in the ad hoc Tribunals is largely explained by the *Tadić* appeal judgment of 1999. This set out the requirements as follows: 'The aider and abettor carries out acts specifically directed to assist, encourage or lend moral support to the perpetration of a certain specific crime ... and this support has a substantial effect upon the perpetration of the crime ... the requisite mental element is knowledge that the acts performed by the aider and abettor assist the commission of a specific crime by the principal.'[164]

There are a number of things worth noting about this definition. To begin with, the conduct which aids or abets must have a direct and 'substantial' effect on the commission of the crime. However, this should not be taken as setting a particularly high standard: the ICTY has seen it more as meaning any assistance which is more than *de minimis*.[165] As the SCSL has said, 'International Tribunals never required that, as a matter of law, an aider and abettor must provide assistance in a particular manner such as providing assistance to the physical actor that is then used in the commission of the crime.'[166] It is also the case that the conduct itself need not be intrinsically criminal, it is the factual effect of the conduct that is the test.[167]

The Tribunals have accepted, amongst other things,[168] that standing near victims whilst armed to prevent them escaping amounts to aiding,[169] as does providing weapons to a

---

and Ntakirutimana, ICTR A. Ch., 13 December 2004, paras. 371 and 500, however, leaves the door open for 'other forms of complicity' than aiding and abetting. However, see *Blagojević and Jokić*, ICTY T. Ch. I, 7 January 2005, para. 679. See Chile Eboe-Osuji, '"Complicity in Genocide" versus "Aiding and Abetting Genocide"' (2005) 3 *Journal of International Criminal Justice* 56; Payam Akhavan, 'The Crime of Genocide in the ICTR Jurisprudence' (2005) 3 *Journal of International Criminal Justice* 989.

[160] The similarities and differences are discussed in *Tadić*, ICTY A. Ch., 15 July 1999, para. 229, and *Kvočka et al.*, ICTY A. Ch., 28 February 2005, para. 90: the main differences are that an aider or abettor does not need to know of any common plan, but his or her assistance must be substantial (but see below in this section on this criterion). An aider or abettor is only responsible for crimes known about (again, see below in this section), whereas foresight by the defendant suffices for liability for crimes committed pursuant to a joint criminal enterprise.

[161] *Tadić*, ICTY A. Ch., 15 July 1999, para. 192.

[162] *Vasiljević*, ICTY A. Ch., 25 February 2004, para. 182; *Orić*, ICTY T. Ch. II, 30 June 2006, para. 281. See also *Tadić*, ICTY A. Ch., 15 July 1999, para. 191.

[163] See *Orić*, ICTY T. Ch. II, 30 June 2006, para. 282.

[164] *Tadić*, ICTY A. Ch., 15 July 1999, para. 229. *Orić*, ICTY T. Ch. II, 30 June 2006, para. 288, took the view that 'the intention must contain a cognitive element of knowledge and a volitional element of acceptance, whereby the aider and abettor may be considered as accepting the criminal result of his conduct if he is aware that in consequence of his contribution, the commission is more likely than not'. The Trial Chamber in *Halilović*, ICTY T. Ch. I, 16 November 2005, para. 286, asserts that 'recent judgments also demand some sort of acceptance of the final result'. There is no express requirement in *Blaškić*, ICTY A. Ch., 29 July 2004, para. 46, but, in relation to ordering, the Appeals Chamber said that ordering 'with the awareness of the substantial likelihood that a crime will be committed ... has to be regarded as accepting that crime': *ibid.*, para. 42.

[165] See e.g. Kai Ambos, 'Article 25' in Triffterer, *Observers' Notes*, 481.

[166] *Taylor*, SCSL A. Ch., 26 September 2013, para. 371.   [167] *Ibid.*, para. 395.

[168] For a useful overview of some of the conduct that has been held to aid or abet, see *ibid.*, para. 369.

[169] *Vasiljević*, ICTY A. Ch., 25 February 2004, para. 134. Judge Shahabuddeen in that case considered this to suffice for co-perpetratorship through joint criminal enterprise liability: see Partially Dissenting Opinion of Judge Shahabuddeen, para. 40.

principal,[170] or taking principals to the scene of a crime and pointing at people to be killed.[171] Allowing resources for which a person is responsible to be used for crimes may also suffice.[172] Amongst other things, although presence *per se* does not amount to encouragement,[173] the presence of a superior at the scene of an offence may suffice for liability for abetment by tacit approval.[174] Omissions may suffice for aiding or abetting, provided that there is a legal obligation on the defendant to prevent the crime and the ability to intervene.[175] Although there is no necessity that the principal offender know of the assistance for liability for aiding to arise,[176] it would be essentially impossible to abet someone without their being aware of the abetting behaviour. Moreover, 'the lending of practical assistance, encouragement, or moral support may occur before, during, or after the crime or underlying offence occurs'.[177]

Although the *Tadić* Appeals Chamber said that the conduct needs to be 'specifically directed' towards aiding or abetting the relevant crimes, for a long time this statement played little substantive part in the jurisprudence of the ad hoc Tribunals. For example, the statement was repeated in some judgments, but ignored or said not to be essential in others (most notably the *Mrksić and Slijvančanin* case).[178] It had not been treated as determinative, or even important, in any case up until the *Perišić* trial judgment, which convicted the defendants in part on the basis of their rejection of the specific direction standard.[179] This finding was successfully challenged on appeal. The Appeals Chamber determined that the *Tadić* formula stood because, on its sometimes stretched interpretation, no appeal decision had expressly rejected the specific direction standard as part of the *actus reus* of aiding and abetting.[180] The majority also distinguished earlier ICTY cases that did not require a separate showing of specific direction on the basis that they were not dealing with remote assistance, as they were here.[181] In such cases, the Appeals Chamber held that it was necessary to show specific direction.[182]

Judge Liu disagreed, concluding that:

Given that specific direction has not been applied in past cases with any rigor, to insist on such a requirement now effectively raises the threshold for aiding and abetting liability. This shift risks undermining the very purpose of aiding and abetting liability by allowing those responsible for knowingly facilitating the most grievous crimes to evade responsibility for their acts. The present appeal is a case in point.[183]

---

[170] *Ntakirutimana and Ntakirutimana*, ICTR A. Ch., 13 December 2004, para. 530.   [171] *Ibid.*, para. 532.
[172] *Krštić*, ICTY A. Ch., 19 April 2004, para. 137.   [173] *Orić*, ICTY T. Ch. II, 30 June 2006, para. 283.
[174] *Alekšovski*, ICTY A. Ch., 24 March 2000, paras. 36–7; *Brđanin and Talić*, ICTY A. Ch., 3 April 2007, para. 273. Whether or not the obligation has to be imposed by the criminal law is an open question: *Mrksić and Šlijvančanin*, ICTY A. Ch., 5 May 2009, paras. 148–52.
[175] *Orić*, ICTY T. Ch. II, 30 June 2006, para. 283; *Milutinović et al.*, ICTY T. Ch. III, 26 February 2009, para. 90.
[176] *Tadić*, ICTY A. Ch., 15 July 1999, para. 229.   [177] *Milutinović et al.*, ICTY T. Ch. III, 26 February 2009, para. 91.
[178] *Mrksić and Šlijvančanin*, ICTY A. Ch., 5 May 2009, para. 159. A detailed history of those cases that discussed it may be found in *Perišić*, ICTY A. Ch., 28 February 2013, paras. 28–31.
[179] *Perišić*, ICTY T. Ch. I, 6 September 2011, para. 126. Judge Moloto dissented.
[180] *Perišić*, ICTY A. Ch., 28 February 2013, paras. 25–40. Judge Liu dissented.
[181] The assistance in *Perišić* was the provision of arms and other material from Belgrade to Bosnian Serb forces.
[182] *Perišić*, ICTY A. Ch., 28 February 2013, paras. 38–40.   [183] *Ibid.*, Partially Dissenting Opinion of Judge Liu, para. 3.

The Appeals Chamber acquitted Perišić. The acquittal has been criticized on grounds similar to those raised by Judge Liu, that is to say, that the requirement is unsupported in other cases and commentary, and national law;[184] it seems to conflate *actus reus* and *mens rea* considerations;[185] and also seems to create a separate form of aiding and abetting in 'remote' cases, which is 'retrogressive'.[186] It is also thought that it could lead to high-ranking figures providing assistance to rebels and others with impunity.[187] Such concerns were not allayed by the later acquittals in the *Stanišić and Simantović* case, decided on the ground that the defendants had not specifically directed their assistance to criminal conduct.[188]

The specific direction standard was before the SCSL Appeals Chamber barely six months after *Perišić*, in the *Taylor* case. Here, despite acknowledging that they were not bound by *Perišić*, the judges rejected the standard in firm terms.[189] Characterizing it as 'novel',[190] the SCSL Appeals Chamber criticized the ICTY for not having expressly set out the customary basis upon which the specific direction standard lay, including in *Tadić*.[191] On the contrary, they held that:

> The Appeals Chamber has independently reviewed the post-Second World War jurisprudence, and is satisfied that those cases did not require an *actus reus* element of 'specific direction' in addition to proof that the accused's acts and conduct had a substantial effect on the commission of the crimes. Similarly, the Appeals Chamber has examined the ILC Draft Code of Crimes and state practice, and is satisfied that they do not require such an element.[192]

In an extraordinary development, however, in early 2014 a differently constituted Appeals Chamber of the ICTY, in the *Šainović et al.* case,[193] came to the conclusion that *Perišić* was 'unequivocally' wrong, and the specific direction requirement was not part of customary law.[194] This followed a detailed review of the post-War jurisprudence and national laws on point. Whichever view is taken on the more appropriate standard, the recent disjuncture between the jurisprudence of the Tribunals and between differently constituted Appeals Chambers of the ICTY at such a late stage in their existence is not a welcome development.

As to the *mens rea*, what is expressly required is that the aider and abettor knows that his or her conduct assists a specific crime. In spite of the 'specific direction' standard canvassed above, which confuses the matter somewhat and may imply a higher standard, the *mens rea*

---

[184] James Stewart, 'Specific Direction Is Unprecedented: Results from Two Empirical Studies', available at www.ejiltalk.org/specific-direction-is-unprecedented-reults-from-two-empirical-studies. Although see Kai Ambos and Ousman Njikam, 'Charles Taylor's Criminal Responsibility' (2013) 11 *Journal of International Criminal Justice* 789.

[185] *Perišić*, ICTY A. Ch., 28 February 2013, Separate Opinion of Judge Ramaronson. In their Separate Opinion (paras. 3–4), Judges Meron and Agius almost admit this, saying that, were they to qualify the matter outside precedent, they would do so as a matter of *mens rea*.

[186] James Stewart, 'The ICTY Loses its Way on Complicity' available at http://opiniojuris.org/2013/04/03/guest-post-the-icty-loses-its-way-on-complicity-part-1.

[187] Judge Liu, Dissenting Opinion, in *Perišić*, ICTY A. Ch., 28 February 2013, para. 3. The majority had admitted the issue (para. 72), but they provided no convincing answer to the problem. Judge Harhoff's incautious criticism of the requirement on this basis, though, led to disqualification proceedings against him in later cases: see *Sešelj*, ICTY Chamber convened by order of the Vice-President, 28 August 2013.

[188] *Stanišić and Simantović*, ICTY T. Ch. I, 30 May 2013.

[189] Judge Avis Fischer was particularly trenchant: *Taylor*, SCSL A. Ch., 26 September 2013, paras. 716–20. Judge Winter agreed.

[190] *Taylor*, SCSL A. Ch., 26 September 2013, para. 479.   [191] *Ibid.*, paras. 477–8.   [192] *Ibid.*, para. 474.

[193] *Šainović*, ICTY A. Ch., 23 January 2014, paras. 1617–50.   [194] *Ibid.*, para. 1650.

standard that remains accepted is knowledge, not purpose.[195] The SCSL has consistently held that this includes 'awareness of the substantial likelihood' of an offence occurring.[196] But they are alone in seeing knowledge this way. There is, in addition, the question of how much knowledge about a crime is necessary. For example, does the aider or abettor have to know who or what is going to be attacked or in what way? The Appeals Chamber in *Tadić* asserted that 'awareness . . . of the essential elements of the crime committed by the principal would suffice'.[197] When a person knows that more than one crime might be committed, the ICTY has said that:

> it is not necessary that the aider and abettor should know the precise crime that was intended and which in the event was committed. If he is aware that one of a number of crimes will probably be committed, and one of those crimes is in fact committed, he has intended to facilitate the commission of that crime, and is guilty as an aider and abettor.[198]

Some have criticized a knowledge-based version of *mens rea* in relation to the crime of genocide, on the basis that it dilutes the special intent that characterizes that offence.[199] These critiques have force. Still, the Tribunals have had no compunction in convicting people of aiding and abetting genocide on the basis of knowledge of the genocidal intentions of others.[200]

The definition of aiding and abetting in the ICC Statute is slightly different from that used by the ICTY and ICTR, the ICC Statute criminalizing anyone who '[f]or the purpose of facilitating the commission of such a crime, aids, abets, or otherwise assists in its commission or its attempted commission, including providing the means for its commission'.[201] Although there is no express requirement that the assistance or encouragement make a substantial contribution to the crime, the ICC has taken the view that assistance does have to reach that level.[202] More important is the *mens rea*, which is that the accomplice's conduct was 'for the purpose' of assisting. This is a higher requirement than the 'knowledge' required by the ICTY and ICTR, and one which will involve some difficult determinations of motive.[203] It will certainly complicate prosecuting those who sell or otherwise supply arms or other war *matériel* which is used for international crimes.[204] Even if an arms dealer knew weapons that he sold to a country were destined to be used for the commission of international crimes, liability would not arise if the sole purpose for selling them was making a profit. It will cause further problems for prosecuting acts which, on their face, are neutral or professional acts such as providing chemicals that may be used for an innocent purpose as well as to make chemical weapons. Equally, a broad approach to what amounts to

---

[195] *Taylor*, SCSL A. Ch., 26 September 2013, paras. 413–37.   [196] *Ibid.*, para. 438.
[197] *Tadić*, ICTY A. Ch., 15 July 1999, para. 164. See also *Orić*, ICTY T. Ch. II, 30 June 2006, para. 288.
[198] *Furundžija*, ICTY T. Ch. II, 10 December 1998, para. 246. Approved in *Blaškić*, ICTY A. Ch., 29 July 2004, para. 50.
[199] Mettraux, *International Crimes*, 286–7; Larissa van den Herik and Elies van Sliedregt, 'Ten Years Later, the Rwanda Tribunal Still Faces Legal Complexities: Some Comments on the Vagueness of the Indictment, Complicity in Genocide, and the Nexus Requirement for War Crimes' (2004) 17 *Leiden Journal of International Law* 537, 544–51.
[200] *Krstić*, ICTY A. Ch., 19 April 2004, para. 140.   [201] Art. 25(3)(c) of the ICC Statute.
[202] *Mbarushimana*, ICC PTC I, 16 December 2011, para. 280.   [203] See Cryer, 'General Principles', 248.
[204] For a (slightly) more sanguine view, see Schabas, 'Enforcing International Humanitarian Law'.

participation in a joint criminal enterprise liability could undermine this high threshold in some circumstances.

15.4 Ordering, instigating, soliciting, inducing and inciting[205]

15.4.1 *Ordering*

Because many international crimes are committed by a large number of people acting together, it is frequently the case that such crimes are committed at the behest of a superior authority. If defendants in war crimes trials are to be believed, almost every crime is committed pursuant to orders. It has never really been questioned that those ordering international crimes are responsible for them. The reason given by those supporting a defence of superior orders in the early nineteenth century was that liability was more appropriately placed on the person who gave the order than the person who carried it out.[206] However, even though reliance on the defence of superior orders was barred in the Nuremberg IMT, that Tribunal had no compunction in imposing liability for giving orders.[207] Although some see those giving orders to commit international crimes as perpetrators acting through innocent or guilty agents,[208] the ICC Statute and the Statutes of the ICTY, ICTR and SCSL all treat it as a separate form of liability.[209] The core aspect of the crime of ordering, as interpreted by the ICTY and ICTR, is that a 'person in a position of authority uses it to convince another to commit an offence'.[210]

This requires three things: a superior/subordinate relationship; the transmission of an order; and the relevant mental element. In relation to the first of these, it is not necessary that the relationship be a legal one; the point is whether there is, factually, 'some position of authority on the part of the accused that would compel another to commit a crime in following the accused's order'.[211] The transmission of an order can be established by circumstantial evidence.[212] An example of this would be when there are a remarkable number of similar actions over a disparate area in a short time. A court does not need a paper copy of an order or a tape of it to convict on this basis. A person does not have to be the author of an order to become liable for ordering in international criminal law: passing it down the chain of command can be enough.[213] Similarly, nor does a person who issues an order have to pass it directly to the person who commits the crime: it may go through a

[205] See generally van Sliedregt, *Individual*, 102–9.
[206] See e.g. Lassa Oppenheim, *International Law* (London, 1906) Vol. II, 264–5.
[207] See e.g. Nuremberg IMT, Judgment and Sentences, reprinted in (1947) 41 *American Journal of International Law* 172, 274 (Göring), 282 (Keitel), 284 (Kaltenbrunner), 289–90 (Frank), 292 (Frick), 312 (Saukel), 315 (Jodl), 320 (Seyss-Inquart), 325 (von Neurath), 329 (Bormann).
[208] Ambos, 'Article 25', 480, 491.
[209] Art. 25(3)(b) of the ICC Statute; Art. 7(1) of the ICTY Statute; Art. 6(1) of the ICTR Statute; Art. 6(1) of the SCSL Statute.
[210] *Akayesu*, ICTR T. Ch. I, 2 September 1998, para. 483; *Blaškić*, ICTY T. Ch. I, 3 March 2000, para. 601.
[211] *Semanza*, ICTR A. Ch., 20 May 2005, para. 361. See also *Kordić and Čerkez*, ICTY T. Ch. III, 26 February 2001, para. 388, and ICTY A. Ch., 17 December 2004, para. 28. In *Gacumbitsi*, ICTR A. Ch., 7 July 2009, para. 182, the Appeals Chamber noted that this is not the same as the requirement in command responsibility of effective control, as it 'requires merely authority to order, a more subjective criterion depends on the circumstances and the perceptions of the listener'.
[212] *Blaškić*, ICTY T. Ch. I, 3 March 2000, para. 281.
[213] Nuremberg IMT, Judgment and Sentences, reprinted in (1947) 41 *American Journal of International Law* 172, 282; *Kupreškić et al.*, ICTY T. Ch. II, 14 January 2000, para. 862.

number of intermediaries' hands first.[214] This form of liability cannot attach to a pure omission,[215] and the order must substantially contribute to the commission of the crime (but need not be a *sine qua non*).[216]

The mental element of ordering has been set out by the ICTY as being 'the awareness of the substantial likelihood that a crime will be committed in the execution of that order ... Ordering with such awareness has to be regarded as accepting that crime.'[217] That said, it is not necessary that an order is illegal on its face for a person to become liable for giving it.[218] This is consonant with the point that a mistake of law that does not affect *mens rea* is not exculpatory, and a mistake about whether certain conduct is criminal does not *per se* affect *mens rea*.[219] The *mens rea* of the person who issued (or passed on) the order is determinative of what particular crime he or she is responsible for ordering, not the *mens rea* of the person who carries it out.[220]

Article 25(3)(b) of the ICC Statute appears to see ordering as a form of secondary liability, as it provides for responsibility only when the ordered crime 'occurs or is attempted'. The ICTY and ICTR have also conceptualized ordering in this way.[221] It is questionable whether this was necessary or appropriate. Post-Second World War cases such as *von Falkenhorst* imposed liability for issuing orders which were not implemented.[222] There are those who claim that ordering offences should be seen as a form of perpetration by means.[223] Conceptualizing ordering in such a manner would have the advantage of allowing the issuance of orders which were not acted upon to be considered attempts.[224] However, there are specific wrongs involved in ordering which are also not quite captured by such a manner of conceptualization, which may be a form of responsibility all of its own,[225] and difficult problems of demarcation between the two may arise.[226]

15.4.2   *Instigating, soliciting, inducing and inciting*[227]

Instigation, which the ICTY has described as 'prompting',[228] and the ICTR as 'urging or encouraging'[229] another to commit a crime, seems to be largely the same as soliciting or inducing in Article 25(3)(b) of the ICC Statute.[230] As the Trial Chamber in *Blaškić* put it '[t]he essence of instigating is that the accused causes another person to commit a crime. Although it must be proved that the instigation was a clear contributing factor to the

---

[214] *Blaškić*, ICTY T. Ch. I, 3 March 2000, para. 282.   [215] *Galić*, ICTY A. Ch., 30 November 2006, para. 176.
[216] E.g. *Milutinović et al.*, ICTY T. Ch. III, 26 February 2009, para. 88.   [217] *Blaškić*, ICTY A. Ch., 29 July 2004, para. 42.
[218] *Blaškić*, ICTY T. Ch. I, 3 March 2000, para. 282.   [219] See Chapter 16.
[220] *Blaškić*, ICTY T. Ch. I, 3 March 2000, para. 282.
[221] *Ibid.*, paras. 281–2; *Kordić and Čerkez*, ICTY T. Ch. III, 26 February 2001, para. 388; *Akayesu*, ICTR T. Ch. I, 2 September 1998, para. 483.
[222] XI LRTWC 18.   [223] Eser, 'Individual Criminal Responsibility', 797; van Sliedregt, *Individual*, 109.
[224] And, lest we forget, there is an obligation on subordinates to disobey, at the least, manifestly unlawful orders: see Art. 33 of the ICC Statute.
[225] See Cryer, 'General Principles', 242–7.   [226] Kreß, 'Claus Roxin's'.
[227] As Mettraux, *International Crimes*, 281, notes, there is considerable overlap here between instigation and abetting.
[228] *Blaškić*, ICTY T. Ch. I, 3 March 2000, para. 280.   [229] *Bagilishema*, ICTR A. Ch., 2 July 2002, para. 30.
[230] See e.g. van Sliedregt, *Individual*, 108.

commission of the crime, it need not be a *conditio sine qua non*'.[231] The Chamber also clarified that '[i]nstigation can take many different forms; it can be express or implied, and entail both acts and omissions'.[232] The instigation must have been a substantially contributing factor (but need not be the only cause) of the physical element of the crime.[233] In other words:

It requires some kind of influencing the principal perpetrator . . . [but] does not necessarily presuppose that the original idea or plan to commit the crime was generated by the instigator. Even if the principal perpetrator was already pondering on committing a crime, the final determination can still be brought about by persuasion or strong encouragement of the instigator. However, if the principal perpetrator . . . has definitely decided to commit the crime, further encouragement or moral support may merely, though still, qualify as aiding and abetting.[234]

Turning to the mental element, rather like for ordering, the ICTY has said that 'a person who instigates another person to commit an act or omission with the awareness of the substantial likelihood that a crime will be committed in the execution of that instigation, has the requisite *mens rea* for establishing responsibility . . . [for] instigating. Instigating with such awareness has to be regarded as accepting that crime.'[235] Some cases have seen the giving of orders which are not carried out as a form of incitement/instigation.[236]

Direct and public incitement to genocide is specifically criminalized, in essentially the same terms, by Article 3(c) of the Genocide Convention,[237] Article 4(3)(c) of the ICTY Statute, Article 2(3)(c) of the ICTR Statute, and Article 25(3)(e) of the ICC Statute. Unlike the other crimes of encouragement discussed here, for liability to accrue for incitement to commit genocide, it is not necessary to prove that anyone even attempted to commit genocide. Incitement to genocide is an inchoate crime,[238] although sometimes the ICTR has prosecuted defendants under this heading for conduct that has led to the commission of genocide.[239]

The main case in the area is the ICTR's *Media* case.[240] Drawing, *inter alia*, on the Nuremberg IMT's verdicts on Julius Streicher and Hans Frizsche, the Trial Chamber in that

[231] *Blaškić*, ICTY T. Ch. I, 3 March 2000, para. 270; *Orić*, ICTY T. Ch. II, 30 June 2006, para. 274; *Kordić and Čerkez*, ICTY A. Ch., 17 December 2004, para. 27.
[232] *Blaškić*, ICTY T. Ch. I, 3 March 2000, para. 270.
[233] *Gacumbitsi*, ICTR A. Ch., 7 July 2006, para. 129; *Kordić and Čerkez*, ICTY A. Ch., 17 December 2004, para. 27.
[234] *Orić*, ICTY T. Ch. II, 30 June 2006, para. 271. It is questionable whether the implicit assertion that aiding or abetting is *per se* less serious than incitement ('merely') is appropriate.
[235] *Kordić and Čerkez*, ICTY A. Ch., 17 December 2004, para. 32. See similarly *Orić*, ICTY T. Ch. II, 30 June 2006, para. 279, which also asserts that the instigator must accept the intentional commission of the relevant crime. *Quaere* whether this is necessary for crimes for which a lesser mental element is required or consistent with the Appeals Chamber's finding in *Kordić and Čerkez*.
[236] *Meyer* (the 'Abbaye Ardenne' case), IV LRTWC 97, 98.
[237] 1948 Convention on the Prevention and Punishment of the Crime of Genocide.
[238] *Nahimana et al.* (the 'Media case'), ICTR A. Ch., 28 November 2007, para. 678; *Akayesu*, ICTR T. Ch. I, 2 September 1998, para. 562; *Mugesera v. Canada* [2005] 2 SCR 100, paras. 84–5.
[239] See e.g. *Akayesu*, ICTR T. Ch. I, 2 September 1998, paras. 672–5. Such conduct might be better considered abetment or instigation; however, see e.g. *Kalimanzira*, ICTR T. Ch. III, 22 June 2009, paras. 512–13.
[240] *Nahimana et al.* (the 'Media case'), ICTR T. Ch. I, 3 December 2003.

case decided that, in determining liability, the purpose and context of any communication is important.[241] The result was approved by the Appeals Chamber, who also noted that the effect the incitement had on an audience is a relevant factor.[242]

On the basis of the earlier *Akayesu* case, the Trial Chamber in the *Media* case determined that the crime required 'a call for criminal action to a number of individuals in a public place or to members of the general public at large by such means as the mass media, for example, radio or television'.[243] So far, determining what is public has not been too difficult, most prosecutions being based on speeches to large groups of people or the mass media.[244] It has been held that:

Incitement is 'public' when conducted through speeches, shouting or threats uttered in public places or at public gatherings, or through the sale or dissemination, offer for sale or display of written material or printed matter in public places or at public gatherings, or through the public display of placards or posters, or through any other means of audiovisual communication.[245]

As the last part of the quote implies, the Internet and e-mail may raise interesting questions regarding the 'public' requirement.

Interpreting what is direct is not simple. As the Trial Chamber in *Akayesu* said, 'the direct element of incitement should be viewed in the light of its cultural and linguistic content. Indeed, a particular speech may be perceived as "direct" in one country, and not so in another, depending on the audience. The Chamber further recalls that incitement may be direct, and nonetheless implicit.'[246] The Appeals Chamber has largely agreed, noting that simple 'hate speech' may not be enough; the incitement must be to commit genocide, although that call need not be express, so long as it is direct.[247] Particularly difficult issues of culture, context and interpretation arise here, especially when prosecutions are occurring outside the *locus delicti*.[248]

On the authority of the *Akayesu* case, the Trial Chamber in the *Media* case held that the *mens rea* was the:

intent to directly prompt or provoke another to commit genocide. It implies a desire on the part of the perpetrator to create by his actions a particular state of mind necessary to commit such a crime in the minds of the person(s) he is so engaging. That is to say that the person who is inciting to commit genocide must have himself the specific intent to commit genocide, namely, to destroy, in whole or in part, a national, ethnical, racial or religious group, as such.[249]

---

[241] *Ibid.*, paras. 1000–10.   [242] *Nahimana et al.*, ICTR A. Ch., 28 November 2007, paras. 698–700.

[243] *Nahimana et al.*, ICTR T. Ch. I, 3 December 2003, para. 1011.

[244] In *Kalimanzira*, ICTR A. Ch., 28 October 2010, para. 159, it was decided that supervising a roadblock did not amount to direct public incitement, as it did not involve 'public' speech.

[245] *Kalimanzira*, ICTR T. Ch. III, 22 June 2009, para. 515.

[246] *Akayesu*, ICTR T. Ch. I, 2 September 1998, para. 557; see also *Kalimanzira*, ICTR T. Ch. III, 22 June 2009, para. 514.

[247] *Nahimana et al.*, ICTR A. Ch., 28 November 2007, paras. 693, 703. The ICTR has held that songs may suffice: *Bikindi*, ICTR T. Ch. III, 2 December 2008, para. 389.

[248] See e.g. *Nahimana et al.*, ICTR A. Ch., 28 November 2007, paras. 704–15. See also William Schabas, 'Mugesera v. Minister of Citizenship and Immigration' (1999) 93 *American Journal of International Law* 529.

[249] *Nahimana et al.*, ICTR T. Ch. I, 3 December 2003, para. 1012.

15.5 Planning, preparation, attempt and conspiracy

15.5.1 Planning and preparing

Planning or preparing a war of aggression was criminalized in Article 6(a) of the Charter of the Nuremberg IMT and Article 5(a) of the Charter of the Tokyo IMT. Both also contained a clause that read 'leaders, organisers, instigators and accomplices participating in the formulation of a common plan . . . to commit any of the foregoing crimes are responsible for all acts performed by any person in execution of such a plan'. Both Tribunals read this as being limited to crimes against peace, however.

Such crimes are usually considered at the national level to amount to inchoate (incomplete) crimes that are punishable without proof that the crime itself was completed. Article 7(1) of the ICTY Statute, as well as Article 6(1) of the ICTR Statute and Article 6(1) of the SCSL Statute, all criminalize those who 'aided and abetted in the planning, preparation or execution' of an international crime. As aiding and abetting is a secondary form of liability, which requires a primary crime to be committed or attempted to attach to, these instruments imply that planning is a primary offence, which in turn implies that planning and preparation are in themselves enough, and do not require that the crimes planned or prepared actually occurred.[250]

For planning,[251] however, the ICTY Appeals Chamber has held differently, stating that '[t]he *actus reus* of "planning" requires that one or more persons design the criminal conduct constituting one or more statutory crimes that are later perpetrated'.[252] A number of trial chamber decisions, in particular from the ICTR, requiring that the offence occurs, have been criticized as misunderstanding the nature of 'planning',[253] but the definition on point is now settled before the Tribunals.[254] Either way, the planning must have a substantial effect on the commission of the crime,[255] although the planning need not necessarily relate to the commission of a particular offence, but can be of an objective that is to be achieved by the commission of crimes.[256] The perpetrator does not have to be the originator of, or one of the prime movers in, the plan. The question is one of substantial contribution.[257]

The *mens rea* has been said to be fulfilled by 'a person who plans an act or omission with the awareness of the substantial likelihood that a crime will be committed in the execution of that plan . . . Planning with such awareness has to be regarded as accepting that crime.'[258] The ICC Statute does not have any provision similar to Article 7(1) of the ICTY Statute in relation to planning or preparing war crimes, crimes against humanity and genocide, possibly as it was thought that they would come under other heads of liability enumerated

---

[250] For policy reasons in support (on the basis of the severity of international crimes and prevention), see Cassese *et al.*, *Cassese's International Criminal Law*, 204–5.
[251] There is no modern jurisprudence on 'preparing' as a separate crime.
[252] *Kordić and Čerkez*, ICTY A. Ch., 17 December 2004, para. 26. [253] Mettraux, *International Crimes*, 279–80.
[254] *Taylor*, SCSL A. Ch., 26 September 2013, para. 494. [255] *Kordić and Čerkez*, ICTY A. Ch., 17 December 2004, para. 26.
[256] *Boškoški and Tarčulovski*, ICTY A. Ch., 19 May 2010, paras. 171–2; *Taylor*, SCSL A. Ch., 26 September 2013, para. 493.
[257] *Boškoški and Tarčulovski*, ICTY A. Ch., 19 May 2010, para. 154; *Taylor*, SCSL A. Ch., 26 September 2013, para. 494.
[258] *Kordić and Čerkez*, ICTY A. Ch., 17 December 2004, para. 31; *Taylor*, SCSL A. Ch., 26 September 2013, para. 494.

in the Statute.[259] The aggression amendments to the ICC Statute, on the other hand, repeat the planning and preparing language of the Nuremberg and Tokyo IMTs.

15.5.2 *Attempt*

The Statutes of all the international criminal tribunals prior to the ICC Statute are silent on attempt liability other than for genocide.[260] The ICTY Prosecutor has shown an unwillingness to prosecute attempts to commit international crimes, preferring to conceptualize them under other headings of liability (for example, 'violence to life and person' or 'inhumane acts' rather than attempted murder).[261] However, there is sufficient evidence from the post-Second World War era to show such a form of liability exists in custom.[262]

The ICC Statute expressly criminalizes attempts to commit international crimes in Article 25(3)(f): a person is liable who:

Attempts to commit such a crime by taking action that commences its execution by means of a substantial step, but the crime does not occur because of circumstances independent of the person's intentions. However a person who abandons the effort to commit the crime or otherwise prevents the completion of the crime shall not be liable if that person completely and voluntarily gave up the criminal purpose.

This in many ways makes up for the absence of a provision on planning or preparation, although, if those types of liability are in fact inchoate crimes, Article 25(3)(f) may be narrower than them.[263] The formulation at Rome was a compromise, making it difficult to interpret precisely when a person has 'commence[d] its execution by a substantial step'.[264] As can be seen, the ICC Statute recognizes that, if an attempt is abandoned, or a person prevents the crime, they will not be liable for attempt. However, if they abandon their role in the crime, and it is completed by others, it is possible that liability for aiding and abetting or participating in a joint criminal enterprise might still arise.

15.5.3 *Conspiracy*

Conspiracy, in the sense of the inchoate crime of agreeing to commit a crime, which does not have to be proved to occur, was applied by the Nuremberg and Tokyo IMTs to crimes against peace, not war crimes or crimes against humanity.[265] The reason for that limitation was that there was considerable disagreement between the judges on whether or not such a principle

---

[259] Cassese *et al.*, *Cassese's International Criminal Law*, 198.
[260] Art. 4(d) of the ICTY Statute; Art. 2(d) of the ICTR Statute. See generally Ambos, *Treatise*, Chapter VI.
[261] See *Vasiljević*, ICTY T. Ch. I, 29 November 2002. See Antonio Cassese, 'Black Letter Lawyering vs Constructive Interpretation: The Vasiljević Case' (2004) 2 *Journal of International Criminal Justice* 265, 266–71, *contra* Mettraux, *International Crimes*, 293–5.
[262] Cassese, 'Black Letter Lawyering'. See also Commentary, XV LRTWC at 89.   [263] See Cryer, 'General Principles', 253.
[264] Eser, 'Individual Criminal Responsibility', 811–13; Ambos, 'Article 25', 488–9.
[265] Nuremberg IMT, Judgment and Sentences, reprinted in (1947) 41 *American Journal of International Law* 172, 224.

existed in international law.[266] This also led the Nuremberg IMT to take a sensibly narrow view of conspiracy, stating that '[t]he conspiracy must be clearly outlined in its criminal purpose. It must not be too far removed from the time of decision and of action.'[267] The Tokyo IMT, although also limiting its decision to conspiracies to commit crimes against peace, took a very broad interpretation of the concept of conspiracy.[268] Under current international law, conspiracy does not exist as a form of liability for war crimes or crimes against humanity.[269] Conspiracy to commit genocide, however, is a separate charge.[270] It is included in Article 3(b) of the Genocide Convention, and it is clear that the type of conspiracy included is of the inchoate type.[271] The same crime is included in Article 4(3)(b) of the ICTY Statute and Article 2(3)(b) of the ICTR Statute. It is not, however, present in the ICC Statute. According to the ICTR, conspiracy to commit genocide is '[a]n agreement between two or more persons to commit the crime of genocide'.[272] This can be implicit, as well as express.[273] It has also determined, rightly, that, '[w]ith respect to the *mens rea* of the crime of conspiracy to commit genocide … it rests on the concerted intent to commit genocide, that is to destroy, in whole or in part, a national, ethnic, racial or religious group, as such. Thus … the requisite intent for the crime of conspiracy to commit genocide is, *ipso facto*, the intent required for the crime of genocide that is the *dolus specialis* of genocide.'[274]

15.6 Mental elements

It is an important aspect of criminal law that a person must have some form of culpability for his or her conduct. This is usually shown through his or her state of mind when he or she acted (or failed to act). There are various forms of mental element that apply to international crimes, from intention, through recklessness to (arguably) negligence.[275] Different offences, and different forms of liability require different forms of *mens rea*. Hence, for the most part, they are thus dealt with when dealing with the specific offence or principle of liability.

There is little in the general parts of the Statutes of the ICTY, ICTR and SCSL that deals with *mens rea*. Thus, it has had to be dealt with at the level of case law.[276] Perhaps the broadest

---

[266] See Telford Taylor, *The Anatomy of the Nuremberg Trials* (London, 1993) 36, 50.

[267] Nuremberg IMT, Judgment and Sentences, reprinted in (1947) 41 *American Journal of International Law* 172, 222. It must also be noted that the tribunal was dealing with conspiracies which had manifested themselves in later crimes, so was not, strictly speaking, dealing with inchoate conspiracies.

[268] See section 6.4.3.

[269] *Hamdan* v. *Rumsfeld*, 126 S Ct 2749, 2777–85 (2006). The Supreme Court in this case was clear that it was discussing conspiracies that are offences on their own, not forms of participation in completed crimes, see *ibid.*, 2785, footnote 40.

[270] Although it does not merge with the offence if the conspiracy leads to genocide: *Gatete*, ICTR A. Ch., 9 October 2012, paras. 260–4 (double convictions have little point).

[271] Schabas, *Genocide*, 260; *Kajelijeli*, ICTR T. Ch. II, 1 December 2003, para. 788; *Musema*, ICTR T. Ch. I, 27 January 2000, para. 187. It is, however, a continuing offence: *Popović*, ICTY T. Ch., 10 June 2010, para. 876.

[272] *Musema*, ICTR T. Ch. I, 27 January 2000, para. 189; *Kajelijeli*, ICTR T. Ch. II, 1 December 2003, para. 787; *Ntagerura et al.*, ICTR A. Ch., 7 July 2006, para. 92.

[273] *Nahimana et al.* ICTR A. Ch., 28 January 2007, paras. 896–8.   [274] *Musema*, ICTR T. Ch. I, 27 January 2000, para. 192.

[275] Or, in analogous, but not identical civil law terms, *dolus directus*, *dolus indirectus*, *dolus eventualis* and *culpa*. On the issue generally, see Ambos, *Treatise*, Chapter VII. For a very useful comparative and international law approach, see Mohamed Elewa Badar, *The Concept of Mens Rea in International Criminal Law: The Case for a Unified Approach* (Oxford, 2013).

[276] See William Schabas, *The UN International Criminal Tribunals: The Former Yugoslavia, Rwanda and Sierra Leone* (Cambridge, 2006) 292–3.

statement that has been made was that by the Trial Chamber in *Blaškić* that, in relation to grave breaches, 'the *mens rea* . . . includes both guilty intent and recklessness which may be likened to serious criminal negligence'.[277] This is too broad. Criminal negligence is mainly at issue in relation to superior responsibility, and is not a generally applicable form of *mens rea*.[278] The ICTY and ICTR have been surprisingly reticent in setting out the ingredients of intent in the abstract, rather than in the context of specific crimes or modes of liability. Discussions in the case law are also sometimes confused by the use of the term 'intent', not as a term of art, but to refer to *mens rea* generally.[279] The Appeals Chamber in *Čelebići* asserted that an 'intentional act or omission . . . is an act which, judged objectively, is deliberate and not accidental',[280] but this is decidedly unclear, as there are considerable differences between that which is 'deliberate' and that which is 'not accidental'. Intention has been used to mean only deliberate acts,[281] but the case law on point is inconclusive, not least because, as the Tribunals have tended to accept that recklessness suffices for many crimes, they have not drawn the boundaries between intention and recklessness clearly.[282]

When discussing its concept of recklessness (or perhaps *mens rea* in general), the Appeals Chamber in *Blaškić* set down what, although framed in the context of ordering crimes, might be the general standard for recklessness (or *mens rea*) in the ICTY:

> a person who orders an act or omission with the awareness of the substantial likelihood that a crime will be committed in the execution of that order, has the requisite *mens rea* for establishing liability under Article 7(1) pursuant to ordering. Ordering with such awareness has to be regarded as accepting that crime.[283]

It has been argued that the default standard for *mens rea* in the ad hoc Tribunals appears to be recklessness.[284] The practice of the SCSL does little to counteract this assertion.[285] Whether or not this is correct, the ICC Statute takes a different track, setting intention as the default mental element to be applied. Article 30 of the ICC Statute reads:

1. Unless otherwise provided, a person shall be criminally responsible and liable for punishment for a crime within the jurisdiction of the Court only if the material elements are committed with intent and knowledge.
2. For the purposes of this article, a person has intent where:
   (a) In relation to conduct, that person means to engage in the conduct;
   (b) In relation to a consequence, that person means to cause that consequence or is aware that it will occur in the ordinary course of events.

---

[277] *Blaškić*, ICTY T. Ch. I, 3 March 2000, para. 152; see also *Kayishema and Ruzindana*, ICTR T. Ch. II, 21 May 1999, para. 146.

[278] The Secretary-General described superior responsibility as 'imputed responsibility or criminal negligence': Report of the Secretary-General Pursuant to Paragraph 2 of Security Council Resolution 808(1993), UN Doc. S/25704, para. 56. See also below. Some Elements of Crimes (e.g. those to Art. 8(2)(b)(xxvi)) also adopt a 'should have known' standard, which muddies the waters a little, but not greatly. See *Lubanga*, ICC T. Ch. I, 14 March 2012, paras. 1011–12.

[279] *Blaškić*, ICTY T. Ch. I, 3 March 2000, para. 474. The confusion probably arises out of the difference between the meaning of 'intention' in civil and common law countries. In civil law countries, it is a synonym for *mens rea*; in common law countries, it is a specific type of *mens rea*.

[280] *Čelebići* case, ICTY A. Ch., 20 February 2001, para. 426.   [281] *Alekšovski*, ICTY T. Ch. Ibis, 25 June 1999, para. 56.

[282] Although it is clear that neither concept requires motive: see van Sliedregt, *Criminal Responsibility*, 48–9.

[283] *Blaškić*, ICTY A. Ch., 29 July 2004, para. 42.

[284] Werle, *Principles*, 153–4; van Sliedregt, *Criminal Responsibility*, 48–50.   [285] See above.

3. For the purposes of this Article, 'knowledge' means awareness that a circumstance exists or a consequence will occur in the ordinary course of events. 'Know' and 'knowingly' shall be construed accordingly.

One ICC Pre-Trial Chamber has attempted to use the jurisprudence of the ad hoc Tribunals to read subjective recklessness (*dolus eventualis*) into Article 30.[286] The wording of Article 30 and the history of its drafting cannot support that interpretation, as a different Pre-Trial Chamber accepted in the *Bemba Gombo* confirmation of charges decision.[287] As that Chamber opined:

> the words 'will occur' ... [in Article 30] read together with the phrase 'in the ordinary course of events', clearly indicate that the required standard of occurrence is close to certainty. In this regard, the Chamber defines this standard as 'virtual certainty' or 'practical certainty', namely that the consequence will follow, barring an unforeseen or unexpected intervention that prevents its occurrence.[288]

The exclusion of *dolus eventualis* and recklessness was also accepted by the Trial Chamber in *Lubanga*,[289] and represents the more persuasive interpretation of Article 30.[290]

Article 30 sets the mental element bar high. By requiring intention, in the clear subjective sense, the ICC Statute adopts, as a default, a highly culpable form of mental element for all elements of the offences. This may have a specific effect in relation to the offences for which customary international law and many domestic systems differ as to *mens rea* from the provision in the ICC Statute and the ICC Elements of Crimes. An example is in relation to Article 8(2)(b)(i): attacking civilians requires a higher *mens rea* (intention) than that required by customary international law, for which recklessness suffices.[291]

Article 30 applies absent specific provision elsewhere.[292] The drafters of the ICC Statute excluded any lesser mental element, unless the Statute (or the Elements of Crimes) expressly provided for one (as in Article 28); this minimized the chance of the ICC going outside the Statute and Elements of Crimes to determine, for example, that customary international law set a lower standard than those instruments. It has been suggested that it could,[293] but this seems unlikely.[294] The practice of the ICC to date has been to accept lower *mens rea* standards set out in the Elements of Crimes, but not to look outside the Statute or Elements.[295]

The requirement that the defendant is 'aware ... in relation to a consequence that it will occur in the ordinary course of events' seems to leave a lacuna. Awareness that something

---

[286] *Lubanga*, ICC PTC I, 29 January 2007, paras. 350–5.   [287] *Bemba Gombo*, ICC PTC, 15 June 2009, paras. 352–69.
[288] *Ibid.*, para. 362.   [289] *Lubanga*, ICC T. Ch. I, 14 March 2012, paras. 1011–12.   [290] Ambos, *Treatise*, 276–8.
[291] See William Fenrick, 'A First Attempt to Adjudicate Conduct of Hostilities Offences: Comments on Aspects of the ICTY Trial Decision in the Prosecutor v. Tihomir Blaškić' (2000) 13 *Leiden Journal of International Law* 931, 936–43.
[292] As will be seen, precisely where is not necessarily clear; see also Roger Clark, 'The Mental Element in International Criminal Law: The ICC Statute of the International Criminal Court and the Elements of Offences' (2002) 12 *Criminal Law Forum* 291, 321. On Art. 30's default position, see also ICC Elements of Crimes, general introduction, para. 2.
[293] Knut Dörmann, 'War Crimes in the Elements of Crimes' in Horst Fischer, Claus Kreß and Sascha Liider (eds.), *International and National Prosecution of Crimes under International Law: Current Developments* (Berlin, 2001) 95, 98; Wirth, 'Co-Perpetration', 990–5.
[294] Maria Kelt and Hermann von Hebel, 'General Principles of Criminal Law and Elements of Crimes' in Lee, *Elements and Rules*, 29–30; Ambos, *Treatise*, 291; van Sliedregt, *Individual*. 45–50.
[295] E.g. *Lubanga*, ICC PTC I, 29 January 2007, paras. 356–9; *Bemba Gombo*, ICC PTC II, 15 June 2009, paras. 136, 353.

will occur in the ordinary course of events implies that a belief that this is the case must be borne out for a person to fall under Article 30. At the very least, by the time the consequence has manifested itself, there seems to be no necessary reason for this. The culpability of the state of mind is essentially the same.[296]

15.7   Command/superior responsibility[297]

Command responsibility[298] is an inculpatory doctrine specific to international criminal law, which does not have an equivalent general principle of liability at the domestic level.[299] It is a broad form of liability, which is justified by the privileges, honours and responsibilities that command entails.[300] Command responsibility as a whole has a lengthy history, going back roughly 2,500 years to the China of Sun Tzu.[301] The responsibility of a commander extends far beyond criminal liability, and disciplinary or administrative action can be pursued even if there is no criminal liability.[302] Discussion here, however, is specifically on the criminal responsibility of a commander for offences committed by his or her subordinates. An early and clear example of such liability, which is remarkably similar to modern command responsibility, may be found in the French Code instituted by Charles VII of Orléans in 1439, which stated:

The King orders that each captain or lieutenant be held responsible for the abuses, ills and offences committed by members of his company, and that as soon as he receives any complaint concerning any such misdeed or abuse, he bring the offender to justice so that the said offender be punished in a manner commensurate with his offence, according to these ordinances. If he fails to do so or covers up the misdeed or delays taking action, or if, because of his negligence or otherwise, the offender escapes and thus evades punishment, the captain shall be deemed responsible for the offence as if he had committed it himself and be punished in the same way as the offender would have been.[303]

The foundation of the modern law of command responsibility may be found in the Report of the Commission of Inquiry on the Responsibility of the Authors of the War in 1919, which opined that superiors could be held responsible for crimes of their subordinates where they knew of them but did not intervene.[304] The first major modern case on the principle, though, was the *Yamashita* case.[305] The case has proved controversial and many of its factual

---

[296] David Ormerod, *Smith and Hogan's Criminal Law*, 12th edn (Oxford, 2008) 99.
[297] See generally Guénaël Mettraux, *The Law of Command Responsibility* (Oxford, 2009); van Sliedregt, *Individual Responsibility*, Chapter 8; and Ambos, *Treatise*, 197–232.
[298] The terms 'command responsibility' and 'superior responsibility' are functionally synonymous, although the former is sometimes taken as limited to military personnel. It need not be.
[299] Although there are some analogues in limited areas of domestic criminal law.
[300] See e.g. *Hadžihasanović et al.*, ICTY A. Ch., 16 July 2003, para. 14. See also Cryer, 'General Principles', 260–1.
[301] See W. Hays Parks, 'Command Responsibility for War Crimes' (1973) 62 *Military Law Review* 1, 1–20.
[302] *Bagilishema*, ICTR A. Ch., 2 July 2002, para. 36.
[303] Theodor Meron, *Henry's Laws and Shakespeare's Wars* (Oxford, 1993) 149, footnote 40.
[304] 'Report of the Commission on the Responsibility of the Authors of the War' (1920) 14 *American Journal of International Law* 95, 121.
[305] *United States* v. *Yamashita*, 327 US 1 (1945).

findings, and the fairness of the trial, have been subject to considerable critique.[306] The Nuremberg IMT did not deal with command responsibility in this sense in any real way. The Tokyo IMT, however, took a very broad interpretation of the principle, which at times appeared to shade into joint criminal enterprise liability.[307] Command responsibility was included in military manuals after the Second World War,[308] but made its first clear appearance in a treaty in 1977, in Articles 86 and 87 of Additional Protocol I to the Geneva Conventions.

In a provision that is similar to, but not quite the same as, the provisions of Additional Protocol I, Article 7(3)[309] of the ICTY Statute reads:

The fact that [crimes were] committed by a subordinate does not relieve his superior of criminal responsibility if he knew or had reason to know that the subordinate was about to commit such acts or had done so and the superior failed to take the necessary and reasonable measures to prevent such acts or to punish the perpetrators thereof.[310]

Article 28 of the ICC Statute is more detailed, reading:

In addition to other grounds of criminal responsibility under this Statute for crimes within the jurisdiction of the Court:

(a) A military commander or person effectively acting as a military commander shall be criminally responsible for crimes within the jurisdiction of the Court committed by forces under his or her effective command and control, or effective authority and control as the case may be, as a result of his or her failure to exercise control properly over such forces, where:
  (i) That military commander or person either knew or, owing to the circumstances at the time, should have known that the forces were committing or about to commit such crimes; and
  (ii) That military commander or person failed to take all necessary and reasonable measures within his or her power to prevent or repress their commission or to submit the matter to the competent authorities for investigation and prosecution.
(b) With respect to superior and subordinate relationships not described in paragraph (a), a superior shall be criminally responsible for crimes within the jurisdiction of the Court committed by subordinates under his or her effective authority and control, as a result of his or her failure to exercise control properly over such subordinates, where:
  (i) The superior either knew, or consciously disregarded information which clearly indicated, that the subordinates were committing or about to commit such crimes;

---

[306] See e.g. M. Cherif Bassiouni, *Crimes against Humanity in International Criminal Law*, 2nd edn (The Hague, 1999) 427–31; Anne-Marie Prevost, 'Race and War Crimes: The 1945 War Crimes Trial of General Tomoyuki Yamashita' (1992) 14 *Human Rights Quarterly* 303, 318–19; Richard Lael, *The Yamashita Precedent: War Crimes and Command Responsibility* (Wilmington, DE, 1982); Mettraux, *Law of Command*, 5 *et seq.*
[307] Tokyo IMT, reprinted in Neil Boister and Robert Cryer, *Documents on the Tokyo International Military Tribunal* (Oxford, 2008) 48,442–7. This engendered dissents from Judges Bernard (12–18), Röling (Dissenting Opinion of the Member from the Netherlands at 54–61) and Pal (Dissenting Opinion of the Member from India at 1027–225). See Boister and Cryer, *Tokyo International Military Tribunal*, 205–36.
[308] US Department of the Army Field Manual, The Law of Land Warfare, 1956 (FM 27-10) (as revised), para. 501. See also the 1958 British Manual, The Law of War on Land, being Part III of the Manual of Military Law (London, 1958), para. 631.
[309] Which has been taken as applying both to international and non-international armed conflicts as a matter of customary international law: *Hadžihasanović et al.*, ICTY A. Ch., 16 July 2003, paras. 10–31.
[310] Art. 6(1) of the ICTR Statute and Art. 6(1) of the SCSL Statute are essentially the same. The latter, post-dating the ICC Statute, may be a rejection of aspects of the ICC Statute's definition of the concept.

(ii) The crimes concerned activities that were within the effective responsibility and control of the superior; and

(iii) The superior failed to take all necessary and reasonable measures within his or her power to prevent or repress their commission or to submit the matter to the competent authorities for investigation and prosecution.

The Trial Chamber in *Čelebići* helpfully elaborated the requirements of command responsibility under customary law:[311] first, a superior/subordinate relationship; second, the 'mental element'; and, third, a failure to take reasonable measures to prevent or punish violations of international criminal law.[312] This trio has been adopted by the UN tribunals since and is a helpful list of the requirements.[313] To that, the ICC Statute has added another requirement: causation.[314]

15.7.1   Superior/subordinate relationship

Where there are the clear formal chains of command that characterize modern well-disciplined armies, this criterion may appear simple to apply. However, modern conflicts are not always fought on this basis and by such forces.[315] Therefore, and understandably, the Appeals Chamber in *Čelebići* based itself on a test of 'effective control', defined as 'a material ability to prevent or punish criminal conduct'.[316] Substantial influence is not enough;[317] the ICC agrees with this.[318] It is required that 'the accused has to be, by virtue of his position, senior in some sort of formal or informal hierarchy to the perpetrator'.[319] The *de jure* position of the superior is not determinative of this, it is largely factual ability to prevent and punish that counts.[320] Equally, a *de jure* position may be evidence of effective control.[321] Issuance of orders may also be good evidence,[322] but, if they are not obeyed, this

---

[311] The taxonomy, though, finds a basis in Judge Röling's Opinion in the Tokyo IMT, 59–61.

[312] *Čelebići* case, ICTY T. Ch. II, 16 November 1998, para. 344; *Blaškić*, ICTY T. Ch. I, 3 March 2000, para. 294; *Orić*, ICTY T. Ch. II, 30 June 2006, para. 294, added that crimes were committed by those other than the superior. This is true, but does not really add to the specifics of the principle of liability. The Chamber added it only as it had been challenged by the defence; *Orić ibid.*, para. 295. The Chamber asserted that all forms of participation in Art. 7(1) of the ICTY Statute sufficed to fulfil this criterion: paras. 295–306, 328. This is probably correct, as long as it is remembered that the mental element for superior responsibility must still be fulfilled: Werle, *Principles*, 136–7.

[313] See e.g. *Alekšovski*, ICTY T. Ch. I*bis*, 25 June 1999, paras. 69–71; *Kayishema and Ruzindana*, ICTR T. Ch. II, 21 May 1999, para. 209; *Blaškić*, ICTY T. Ch. I, 3 March 2000, para. 294.

[314] Werle, *Principles*, 136–7.

[315] For an excellent discussion of aspects of command responsibility in such contexts, see Sandesh Sivakumaran, 'Command Responsibility in Irregular Groups' (2012) 10 *Journal of International Criminal Justice* 1129.

[316] *Čelebići* case, ICTY A. Ch., 20 February 2001, para. 256. See generally Mettraux, *Law of Command*, Chapter 9.

[317] *Čelebići* case, ICTY A. Ch., 20 February 2001, para. 266.   [318] *Bemba Gombo*, ICC PTC II, 15 June 2009, paras. 414–16.

[319] *Halilović*, ICTY A. Ch., 16 October 2007, para. 59. Otherwise, as the Chamber said, police officers could be considered superiors to all in their jurisdiction owing to their ability to prevent and set punishment in motion; see also, para. 210. There may be an exception for occupation commanders, who do not have to have this type of relationship: see Mettraux, *Command Responsibility*, 153.

[320] *Čelebići* case, ICTY A. Ch., 20 February 2001, paras. 186–98; *Halilović*, ICTY A. Ch., 16 October 2007, para. 59; *Kajelijeli*, ICTR A. Ch., 23 May 2005, para. 85. See also e.g. *United States* v. *List et al.* (the 'Hostages case'), VIII LRTWC 89; Tokyo IMT, reprinted in Neil Boister and Robert Cryer, *Documents on the Tokyo International Military Tribunal* (Oxford, 2008) 48,820.

[321] *Čelebići* case, ICTY A. Ch., 20 February 2001, para. 197; *Hadžihasanović et al.*, ICTY A. Ch., 22 April 2008, para. 21. There is no presumption, however, that *de jure* positions give rise to effective control: *Orić*, ICTY A. Ch., 3 July 2008, paras. 91–2.

[322] This is the case even where that accused's superior has also ordered the offences: *Nizeyimana*, ICTR T. Ch. III, 19 June 2012, para. 1528.

will count the other way.[323] Other factors which are probative in this regard include the capacity to alter command structures and promote or remove people, and the ability to require people to engage or withdraw from hostilities.[324] Payment of salaries and reliance on logistical support lines of reporting are also relevant.[325] In the end, however, the issue must be decided on a case-by-case basis,[326] and it ought to be noted that even the fact that it is necessary to use force to enforce authority does not automatically mean that a person does not have effective control over subordinates.[327]

It is clear that superior responsibility also attaches to civilian superiors.[328] The standard of control is again 'effective control', 'in the sense that he exercised a degree of control over . . . [subordinates] which is similar to the degree of control of military commanders'.[329] Also, as Article 28(b)(ii) of the ICC Statute shows, the crimes must fall within the area of responsibility of a civilian commander. The ICTY has on occasion been criticized for taking a narrow approach to effective control, against a background of fluid levels of control and multiple lines of command.[330]

The ICTY Appeals Chamber, in its split 3:2 decision in *Hadžihasanović et al.*, determined that for superior responsibility to arise the crimes must be committed whilst the superior had effective control over the offenders.[331] This has particular relevance to failure to punish liability. The case has generated considerable debate.[332] The dissenting judges in particular were very critical of the majority, and asserted that the decision was wrong in law.[333] One judge also asserted that it left a lacuna in protection.[334] In relation to this last point, it is relevant that the primary authors of the crimes are still responsible for them. The controversy has continued in the ICTY, with Trial Chambers expressly or implicitly criticizing the majority finding as a matter of law.[335] In *Orić*, the Prosecutor asked the

[323] *Blaškić*, ICTY A. Ch., 29 July 2004, paras. 69 and 399. See also *Strugar*, ICTY A. Ch., 17 July 2008, para. 254; *Halilović*, ICTY A. Ch., 16 October 2007, para. 207. As noted by Mettraux, *Command Responsibility*, 176–8, the nature and type of order is relevant, as is whether the person signing the order is, in essence, just passing it on for his or her superiors. Orders to the person may be relevant evidence of their material abilities, but this depends on the interpretation of the order: *Halilović*, ICTY A. Ch., 16 October 2007, para. 193.
[324] *Bemba Gombo*, ICC PTC II, 15 June 2009, para. 417. See also Mettraux, *Command Responsibility*, 164–70.
[325] *Perišić*, ICTY T. Ch. I, 6 September 2011, para. 1672. For some contextual factors in irregular groups, see *Brima et al.*, SCSL T. Ch. II, 20 June 2007, para. 788.
[326] This is not always simple: see e.g. *Orić*, ICTY A. Ch., 3 July 2008, paras. 28 *et seq*. In addition, a failure to initiate investigations, either because there is no ability to do so, or because a person has failed to take the necessary and reasonable steps international criminal law requires: see *Halilović*, ICTY A. Ch., 16 October 2007, paras. 175–80, 182.
[327] *Hadžihasanović et al.*, ICTY A. Ch., 22 April 2008, para. 228.
[328] *Bagilishema*, ICTR A. Ch., 2 July 2002, para. 52; *Orić*, ICTY T. Ch. II, 30 June 2006, para. 308. This is also provided for expressly in Art. 28(b) of the ICC Statute. See also Tokyo IMT, reprinted in Neil Boister and Robert Cryer, *Documents on the Tokyo International Military Tribunal* (Oxford, 2008) 48,442–7; *United States* v. *Karl Brandt et al.* (the 'Doctors' Trial'), IV LRTWC 91–3. Some are a little uncomfortable about this, e.g. van Sliedregt, *Individual*, 209.
[329] *Bagilishema*, ICTR A. Ch., 2 July 2002, para. 52, overturning the Trial Chamber on point. As the Appeals Chamber noted (*ibid*.), the way authority is exercised may not be the same.
[330] Osiel, 'The Banality of Good', 1774–9. The ICTY has admitted the fluidity of such situations: *Orić*, ICTY T. Ch. II, 30 June 2006, paras. 309–10.
[331] *Hadžihasanović et al.*, ICTY A. Ch., 16 July 2003, paras. 37–56.
[332] See Mettraux, *International Crimes*, 301; *contra* Christopher Greenwood, 'Command Responsibility and the Hadžihasanović Decision' (2004) 2 *Journal of International Criminal Justice* 598. One ICTY Trial Chamber has seemingly doubted it: *Orić*, ICTY T. Ch. II, 30 June 2006, para. 335.
[333] *Hadžihasanović et al.*, ICTY A. Ch., 16 July 2003, Partially Dissenting Opinion of Judge Shahabuddeen, paras. 1–40, Separate and Partially Dissenting Opinion of Judge Hunt, paras. 6–34. Part of the disagreement related to the way in which the nature of superior responsibility is seen: see section 15.7.5.
[334] *Hadžihasanović et al.*, ICTY A. Ch., 16 July 2003, Partially Dissenting Opinion of Judge Hunt, para. 22.
[335] *Orić*, ICTY T. Ch. II, 30 June 2006, para. 335; *Hadžihasanović*, ICTY T. Ch. II, 15 March 2006, para. 199.

Appeals Chamber to revisit the matter. In spite of a bare majority of the judges taking the view that *Hadžihasanović et al.* was wrong, the decision was left undisturbed, as it did not affect the outcome of the case, and Judge Shahabuddeen (a dissenter in the earlier case) preferred to wait for a larger majority to overturn it.[336] This leaves the customary law on point uncertain,[337] and subsequent Trial Chambers have continued to express disquiet about this issue.[338] The ICC Statute, by requiring that offences occur as 'a result of . . . [a superior's] failure to exercise control properly over such forces' leads to the same result as the majority decision in *Hadžihasanović et al.*,[339] but the customary nature or otherwise of this provision was divisive in that case.[340]

15.7.2   *Mental element*

The mental element of command responsibility is one of its most controversial aspects.[341] This is in part because of the broad ambit of this type of liability, which accrues essentially by omission. The discord is not helped by the opaque nature of the finding in the seminal *Yamashita* case, and the fair trial issues that still cast a pall over that proceeding. The fact that the various documents dealing with the matter use different terminology does not help. The ICTY has been at great pains to explain that superior responsibility is not a form of strict liability.[342] The leading authority in the ICTY determined that:

> [A superior] may possess the *mens rea* for command responsibility where: (1) he had actual knowledge, established through direct or circumstantial evidence, that his subordinates were committing or about to commit crimes . . . or (2) where he had in his possession information of a nature, which at the least, would put him on notice of the risk of such offences by indicating the need for additional investigation in order to ascertain whether such crimes were committed or were about to be committed by his subordinates.[343]

It is accepted that actual knowledge can be determined by a direct proof, or with reference to circumstantial evidence.[344] Relevant circumstantial evidence for this purpose includes 'the number, type and scope of illegal acts, time during which the illegal acts occurred, number and types of troops and logistics involved, geographical location, whether the occurrence of the acts is widespread, tactical tempo of operations, *modus operandi* of similar illegal acts, officers and

---

[336] *Orić*, ICTY A. Ch., 3 July 2008, paras. 166–8, Declaration of Judge Shahabuddeen, paras. 2–15.
[337] Mettraux, *Command Responsibility*, 192.   [338] *Ndindiliyimana et al.*, ICTR T. Ch. II, 17 May 2011, paras. 1961–3.
[339] *Bemba Gombo*, ICC PTC II, 15 June 2009, para. 424.
[340] *Hadžihasanović et al.*, ICTY A. Ch., 16 July 2003, para. 53, Judge Shahabuddeen, para. 38, Judge Hunt, paras. 29–33.
[341] See generally Mettraux, *Command Responsibility*, Chapter 10; Ambos, *Treatise*, 220–8.
[342] E.g. *Čelebići* case, ICTY A. Ch., 20 February 2001, paras. 226 and 239.
[343] *Ibid.*, paras. 223 and 241. 'Commission' in this regard includes the various forms of liability: *Blagojević and Jokić*, ICTY A. Ch., 9 May 2007, para. 280; but a finding on the liability of a subordinate on some form of responsibility seems necessary: *Orić*, ICTY A. Ch., 3 July 2008, paras. 47–8.
[344] *Blaškić*, ICTY T. Ch. I, 3 March 2000, para. 307; *Orić*, ICTY T. Ch. II, 30 June 2006, paras. 319–20; *Halilović*, ICTY T. Ch. I, 16 November 2005, para. 66.

staff involved, and location of the commander at the time'.[345] What the superior knew or had reason to know must be crimes, and the type of crimes committed[346] (or that 'might'[347] be about to be committed) by their subordinates; it is not sufficient that they are aware of some general form of criminality.[348] Such information can be relevant for proof that the superior had reason to know of offences;[349] they do not need to know the precise identities of the perpetrators.[350]

The Trial Chamber in the *Blaškić* case, in an opinion which canvassed some jurisprudence not discussed in *Čelebići*, took a broader approach to the 'had reason to know standard' than the latter decision, and came to the conclusion that:

if a commander has exercised due diligence in the fulfilment of his duties yet lacks knowledge that crimes are about to be or have been committed, such lack of knowledge cannot be held against him. However, taking into account his particular position of command and the circumstances prevailing at the time, such ignorance cannot be a defence where the absence of knowledge is the result of negligence in the discharge of his duties: this commander had reason to know within the meaning of the Statute.[351]

Despite considerable academic support,[352] this standard has not prevailed in the ICTY,[353] and any talk of negligence has been disavowed by the Appeals Chamber.[354] The *Čelebići* standard has become the accepted one in the ad hoc Tribunals for both military and civilian superiors.[355]

Article 28 of the ICC Statute, however, sets a different standard for military and non-military superiors, the standard for the former being that the superior 'knew or, owing to the circumstances at the time, should have known that the forces were committing or about to commit such crimes'. For civilians, it is that the civilian superior 'knew, or consciously disregarded information which clearly indicated, that the subordinates were committing or about to commit such crimes'. Commentators have questioned whether this distinction is

---

[345] *Čelebići* case, ICTY A. Ch., 20 February 2001, para. 238; *Limaj et al.*, ICTY T. Ch. II, 30 November 2005, para. 524; *Halilović*, ICTY T. Ch. I, 16 November 2005, para. 66. Prior crimes may be, although are not necessarily, sufficiently alarming to infer that a person had 'reason to know' of later offences: *Hadžihasanović et al.*, ICTY A. Ch., 22 April 2008, para. 261. See also the list in Mettraux, *Command Responsibility*, 214–15.

[346] *Orić*, ICTY T. Ch. II, 30 June 2006, paras. 298–303, took a broad approach, asserting that this included complicity and inchoate offences. This has been severely criticized, however: Ambos, *Treatise*, 213–14.

[347] *Strugar*, ICTY A. Ch., 7 June 2006, para. 304.

[348] *Krnojelac*, ICTY A. Ch., 17 September 2003, para. 155; *Orić*, ICTY A. Ch., 3 July 2008, paras. 169–74; and Mettraux, *Command Responsibility*, 200–2.

[349] *Strugar*, ICTY A. Ch., 7 June 2006, para. 301.

[350] *Blagojević and Jokić*, ICTY A. Ch., 9 May 2007, para. 287. Their existence must be proved, however: *Orić*, ICTY A. Ch., 3 July 2008, para. 35.

[351] *Blaškić*, ICTY T. Ch. I, 3 March 2000, para. 332.

[352] Monica Feria Tinta, 'Commanders on Trial: The Blaškić Case and the Doctrine of Command Responsibility under International Law' (2000) 47 *Netherlands International Law Review* 293, 314–22; Yoram Dinstein, *The Conduct of Hostilities under the Law of International Armed Conflict* (Cambridge, 2004) 24; Robert Kolb, 'The Jurisprudence of the Yugoslav and Rwandan Criminal Tribunals on their Jurisdiction and on International Crimes' (2000) 69 *British Yearbook of International Law* 259, 301. Support is not universal though: see Bing Bing Jia, 'The Doctrine of Command Responsibility: Current Problems' (2000) 3 *Yearbook of International Humanitarian Law* 131, 155–60.

[353] *Blaškić*, ICTY A. Ch., 29 July 2004, paras. 58–64.

[354] *Bagilishema*, ICTR A. Ch., 2 July 2002, paras. 34–5; *Blaškić*, ICTY A. Ch., 29 July 2004, para. 63; *Halilović*, ICTY T. Ch. I, 16 November 2005, para. 71.

[355] *Bagilishema*, ICTR A. Ch., 2 July 2002, paras. 26–37. The ICTR had, on occasion, applied the ICC Statute standard: *Kayishema and Ruzindana*, ICTR T. Ch. II, 21 May 1999, paras. 227–8, and had been criticized for it. See Alexander Zahar, 'Command Responsibility of Civilian Superiors for Genocide' (2001) 14 *Leiden Journal of International Law* 591.

consistent with customary law,[356] and the ICTR Appeals Chamber has at least implicitly rejected the ICC Statute *mens rea* for civilian superiors.[357]

It has been argued that the Statutes of the ad hoc Tribunals and the ICC Statute are broadly consistent on the mental element for military superiors.[358] However, the ICC has adopted a broad approach regarding the *mens rea* for military commanders in the ICC Statute, asserting that 'should have known' is a negligence standard,[359] and that failure to seek out information could lead to liability.[360] In doing so, the Pre-Trial Chamber expressly departed from the standards set elsewhere:

The Chamber is mindful of the fact that the 'had reason to know' criterion embodied in the statutes of the ICTR, ICTY and SCSL sets a different standard to the 'should have known' standard under article 28(a) of the Statute. However, despite such a difference, which the Chamber does not deem necessary to address in the present decision, the criteria or indicia developed by the ad hoc tribunals to meet the standard of 'had reason to know' may also be useful when applying the 'should have known' requirement.[361]

In relation to civilians, however, the ICC Statute clearly sets a higher *mens rea* standard than exists for military superiors and civilian superiors in customary law.[362]

15.7.3 Failure to take measures

The final link in the chain of liability under customary law is the failure or refusal to take 'necessary and reasonable measures' to prevent or punish the offences the superior knew or culpably ought to have known of. It is important to emphasize in this regard that liability may accrue to a superior for a failure to prevent or a failure to punish those crimes. The two types of liability are separate.[363] There is no necessity that a person knew or should have known of the offences before they occurred for failure to punish liability to arise. Similarly, if a superior knew or should have known of impending offences before they occurred, it is no defence to a charge of failing to take adequate measures to suppress them that he chose to allow them to occur, then punished the perpetrators.[364] As has been said, 'a superior's failure to prevent the commission of the crime by a subordinate, where he had the ability to do so, cannot simply be remedied by subsequently punishing the subordinate for the crime'.[365]

[356] See Greg Vetter, 'Command Responsibility of Non-Military Superiors in the International Criminal Court (ICC)' (2000) 25 *Yale Journal of International Law* 89; van Sliedregt, *Criminal Responsibility*, 191–2; Robert Cryer, *Prosecuting International Crimes: Selectivity and the International Criminal Law Regime* (Cambridge, 2005) 321–3.
[357] *Bagilishema*, ICTR A. Ch., 2 July 2002, paras. 26–37.
[358] See Charles Garraway, 'Command Responsibility: Victor's Justice or Just Deserts?' in Richard Burchill, Nigel White and Justin Morris (eds.), *International Conflict and Security Law: Essays in Memory of Hilaire McCoubrey* (Cambridge, 2005) 68, 82–3.
[359] *Bemba Gombo*, ICC PTC II, 15 June 2009, para. 429.   [360] *Ibid.*, paras. 432–3.   [361] *Ibid.*, para. 434.
[362] Mettraux, *Command Responsibility*, 194–6. For further critique, see van Sliedregt, *Individual Responsibility*, 200–2, 209.
[363] *Hadžihasanović et al.*, ICTY A. Ch., 16 July 2003, Judge Shahabuddeen, paras. 35–6. See also *Blaškić*, ICTY A. Ch., 29 July 2004, paras. 78–85; *Halilović*, ICTY T. Ch. I, 16 November 2005, para. 94; *Orić*, ICTY T. Ch. II, 30 June 2006, paras. 325–6.
[364] *Blaškić*, ICTY T. Ch. I, 3 March 2000, para. 336; *Strugar*, ICTY T. Ch. II, 31 January 2005, para. 373; *Halilović*, ICTY T. Ch. I, 16 November 2005, para. 72. See also *Bemba Gombo*, ICC PTC II, 15 June 2009, para. 436.
[365] *Orić*, ICTY T. Ch. II, 30 June 2006, para. 326. In addition, to fail to take measures may be considered tacit acceptance of the crime: see *Halilović*, ICTY T. Ch. I, 16 November 2005, para. 95.

The measures which can be expected were explained by the ICTY Appeals Chamber in *Blaškić* as being those that:

can be taken within the competence of a commander as evidenced by the degree of effective control he wielded over his subordinates . . . What constitutes such measures is not a matter of substantive law but of evidence.[366]

Thus, the measures that can be expected to be taken depend on the precise nature of the control exercised by the superior. As the ICC Statute identifies, this can mean acts intended to prevent or punish where that is possible, and/or, where appropriate, submitting the matter to the appropriate prosecutorial organs.[367] What measures may be expected of a superior relates to what power the superior has, and this requires a contextual analysis.

An ICTY Trial Chamber in the *Orić* case gave some guidance on the yardsticks to be used for failure to prevent: (1) the measures 'depend on the degree of effective control over the conduct of subordinates at the time a superior is expected to act'; (2) measures must be taken to prevent planning or preparation of crimes, not simply their execution; (3) 'the more grievous and/or imminent the potential crimes of subordinates appear to be, the more attentive and quicker the superior is expected to react'; and (4) a superior is not 'obliged to do the impossible'.[368] Relevant actions are issuing special orders to prevent international crimes and ensuring their implementation, where there is information about the possible commission of crimes, investigating their possible commission, protesting and criticizing actions, initiating disciplinary measures and reporting to, and insisting on action from, higher authorities.[369] Turning a 'blind eye' to international crimes is clearly unreasonable in this respect,[370] and the ICTR has said that, where a superior knows of serious offences, 'general statements . . . made about restoring calm and security' are not enough.[371] Basing itself on ICTY jurisprudence, a Pre-Trial Chamber in the ICC has taken the view that the relevant measures include:

(i) to ensure that superior's forces are adequately trained in international humanitarian law; (ii) to secure reports that military actions were carried out in accordance with international law; (iii) to issue orders aiming at bringing the relevant practices into accord with the rules of war; (iv) to take disciplinary measures to prevent the commission of atrocities by the troops under the superior's command.[372]

---

[366] *Blaškić*, ICTY A. Ch., 29 July 2004, para. 72. See e.g. Ambos, *Treatise*, 217–20.

[367] The ICTY has agreed, *Halilović*, ICTY A. Ch., 16 October 2007, para. 182. Formal legal competence to take the necessary measures to prevent or repress the crime is not required: see *Čelebići* case, ICTY T. Ch. II, 16 November 1998, para. 395; cf. ILC 1996 Draft Code of Crimes 38–9.

[368] *Orić*, ICTY T. Ch. II, 30 June 2006, para. 329.

[369] *Ibid.*, para. 331. See also *Halilović*, ICTY T. Ch. I, 16 November 2005, para. 74.

[370] *Orić*, ICTY T. Ch. II, 30 June 2006, para. 331. The Chamber also mentions failing to give instructions not to commit international crimes owing to absences not mandated by 'other overriding obligations'. The Trial Chamber in *Halilović* adds 'failure to secure reports that military actions have been carried out in accordance with international law', and notes that '[t]he Tokyo Trial held that a superior's duty may not be discharged by the issuance of routine orders and that more active steps may be required': ICTY T. Ch. I, 16 November 2005, para. 89.

[371] *Bagosora and Nsengiyumva*, ICTR A. Ch., 14 December 2011, para. 674.

[372] *Bemba Gombo*, ICC PTC II, 15 June 2009, para. 438.

In relation to the duty to punish, the *Orić* Trial Chamber noted that:

the duty to punish commences only if, and when, the commission of a crime by a subordinate can be reasonably suspected. Under these conditions, the superior has to order or execute appropriate sanctions or, if not yet able to do so, he or she must at least conduct an investigation and establish the facts in order to ensure that offenders under his or her effective control are brought to justice. The superior need not conduct the investigation or dispense the punishment in person, but he or she must at least ensure that the matter is investigated and transmit a report to the competent authorities for further investigation or sanction . . . Since the duty to punish aims at preventing future crimes of subordinates, a superior's responsibility may also arise from his or her failure to create or sustain, amongst the persons under his or her control, an environment of discipline and respect for the law.[373]

There are certain circumstances in which the possibility that the duty to punish may be fulfilled by the use of disciplinary sanctions rather than criminal prosecutions 'cannot be excluded',[374] but, for international crimes, these will be rare.[375] What can be expected of irregular groups in regard to punishment is a further complicating factor, although not an insuperable one.[376]

15.7.4 *Causation*

The question of causation is an awkward one in relation to superior responsibility. This is, to a large extent, because superior responsibility is a form of liability for omission, to which causation is difficult, but not impossible, to apply.[377] This has caused considerable confusion as failure to prevent and failure to punish liability are entirely separate forms of liability. For the latter form of liability, causation logically cannot be a requirement.[378] With respect to the former case, the Trial Chamber in *Čelebići*, with which the Appeals Chamber in *Blaškić* agreed,[379] said that it:

found no support for the existence of a requirement of proof of causation as a separate element of superior responsibility . . . This is not to say that, conceptually, the principle of causality is without application to the doctrine of command responsibility insofar as it relates to the responsibility of superiors for their failure to prevent the crimes of their subordinates. In fact, a recognition of a necessary causal nexus may be considered to be inherent in the requirement of crimes committed by subordinates and the superior's failure to take the measures within his powers to prevent them. In this

---

[373] *Orić*, ICTY T. Ch. II, 30 June 2006, para. 336; see also *Halilović*, ICTY T. Ch. I, 16 November 2005, paras. 97–100.

[374] *Hadžihasanović et al.*, ICTY A. Ch., 22 April 2008, para. 33.

[375] *Ibid.*, paras. 149–55. As this case notes though (*ibid.*), if matters are referred on, it will not always be determinative that those authorities do not take sufficient action.

[376] See Sivakumaran, 'Command Responsibility', 1144–50. See further Sandesh Sivakumaran, 'Courts of Armed Opposition Groups: Fair Trials or Summary Justice?' (2009) 7 *Journal of International Criminal Justice* 489.

[377] See generally Otto Triffterer, 'Causality, a Separate Element of the Doctrine of Superior Responsibility as Expressed in Article 28 of the Rome Statute?' (2002) 15 *Leiden Journal of International Law* 179; Darryl Robinson, 'How Command Responsibility Got So Complicated: A Culpability Contradiction, its Obfuscation and a Simple Solution' (2012) 13 *Melbourne Journal of International Law* 1.

[378] *Orić*, ICTY T. Ch. II, 30 June 2006, para. 338.

[379] *Blaškić*, ICTY A. Ch., 29 July 2004, paras. 75–7. See also *Halilović*, ICTY T. Ch. I, 16 November 2005, para. 77.

situation, the superior may be considered to be causally linked to the offences, in that, but for his failure to fulfil his duty to act, the acts of his subordinates would not have been committed.[380]

In the *Orić* case, the Trial Chamber was certain that there was no requirement of causation for either type of superior responsibility, as, 'even with regard to the superior's failure to prevent, a requirement of causation would run counter to the very basis of this type of superior responsibility as criminal liability of omission'.[381] Whether or not this reflects the law, this appears to misunderstand the idea of negative causation, where an omission permits something to occur. Leaving a window open allows the rain in, even if it does not cause a change in the weather. Still, the Appeals Chamber in *Hadžihasanović et al.* reaffirmed its view that no causation requirement exists.[382]

The ICC Statute, by imposing the general requirement for liability that the crimes occur as a result of a failure to supervise subordinates, excludes liability where there is no form of causation, even in the expanded sense that a failure to prevent may facilitate commission. The first decision on point in the ICC posited a low threshold for causation, accepting that there is some connection between the failure to exercise control and the offences, but saying that it only applied to failure to prevent crimes,[383] and:

There is no direct causal link that needs to be established between the superior's omission and the crime committed by his subordinates. Therefore, the Chamber considers that it is only necessary to prove that the commander's omission increased the risk of the commission of the crimes charged in order to hold him criminally responsible under article 28(a) of the Statute.[384]

15.7.5 The nature of superior responsibility

The nature of responsibility attributed to a superior under this principle of liability is controversial.[385] Some domestic legislation (including that of the United Kingdom, which follows Article 28 almost *verbatim*) criminalizes superior responsibility as a form of complicity.[386] Others believe,[387] and the Canadian and German legislation imply, that it is a separate offence of omission, on the ground that it would be unfair to hold a person vicariously liable for the serious crimes of another based on a relaxed mental element. On this view, command responsibility is in essence a more serious form of a dereliction of duty

---

[380] *Čelebići* case, ICTY T. Ch. II, 16 November 1998, paras. 398–9. [381] *Orić*, ICTY T. Ch. II, 30 June 2006, para. 338.
[382] *Hadžihasanović et al.*, ICTY A. Ch., 22 April 2008, para. 39.
[383] *Ibid.*, para. 38. This was in part on the basis that the Chamber treated violation of the duty to control as being, in essence, the same as failure to take reasonable and necessary steps, as required in Art. 28(a)(ii), rather than a violation of the more general duty to control subordinates. The distinction was proposed in *Halilović*, ICTY T. Ch. I, 16 November 2005, para. 80, but criticized by the Appeals Chamber in that case as it 'fosters confusion', *Halilović*, ICTY A. Ch., 16 October 2007, para. 62. It might be more applicable in the ICC given the wording of Art. 28, but the Pre-Trial Chamber in *Bemba Gombo* did not take this route.
[384] *Bemba Gombo*, ICC PTC II, 15 June 2009, paras. 424–5.
[385] See *Halilović*, ICTY T. Ch. I, 16 November 2005, paras. 42–54. Chantal Meloni, *Command Responsibility in International Criminal Law* (The Hague, 2010); Elies van Sliedregt, 'Command Responsibility at the ICTY – Three Generations of Case Law and Still Ambiguity' in Bert Swart, Alexander Zahar and Göran Sluiter (eds.), *The Legacy of the International Criminal Tribunal for Former Yugoslavia* (Oxford, 2011) 377.
[386] International Criminal Court Act 2001, s. 65. [387] Kai Ambos, 'Superior Responsibility' in Cassese, *Commentary*, 850–5.

charge.[388] There was confusion about the basis of liability in the Secretary-General's report relating to the ICTY Statute, which said that command responsibility is a form of 'imputed responsibility or criminal negligence'.[389]

In *Hadžihasanović et al.*, Judge Shahabuddeen challenged the idea that command responsibility is a form of complicity, opining that '[c]ommand responsibility imposes responsibility on a commander for failure to take corrective action in respect of a crime committed by another; it does not make the commander party to the crime committed by that other'.[390] As he accepted, the ambit of superior responsibility is intrinsically linked to its conceptualization.[391] Relying, in part, on Judge Shahabuddeen's opinion, the Trial Chamber in *Halilović* asserted that:

> command responsibility is responsibility for an omission. The commander is responsible for the failure to perform an act required by international law. This omission is culpable because international law imposes an affirmative duty on superiors to prevent and punish crimes committed by their subordinates. Thus 'for the acts of his subordinates' as generally referred to in the jurisprudence of the Tribunal does not mean that the commander shares the same responsibility as the subordinates who committed the crimes, but rather that because of the crimes committed by his subordinates, the commander should bear responsibility for his failure to act. The imposition of responsibility upon a commander for breach of his duty is to be weighed against the crimes of his subordinates; a commander is responsible not as though he had committed the crime himself, but his responsibility is considered in proportion to the gravity of the offences committed.[392]

This is consistent with the fact that the ICTY considers that Article 7(1) and (3) provide distinct categories of criminal liability which exclude cumulative convictions for the same count based on the same facts.[393] Such views have also gained support in the Appeals Chamber. In *Krnojelac*, that Chamber, in an entirely unreasoned, rather 'throwaway' line, said '[i]t cannot be overemphasised that, where superior responsibility is concerned, an accused is not charged with the crimes of his subordinates but with his failure to carry out his duty as a superior to exercise control'.[394] In *Hadžihasanović et al.*, the Chamber 'took into consideration' the views expressed in *Halilović* that command responsibility is a *sui generis* form of omission liability.[395] In the *Orić* appeal judgment, Judge Shahabuddeen, with whom Judges Shomburg and Liu basically agreed, reasserted his view from the earlier *Hadžihasanović et al.* decision, that command responsibility was not liability for the underlying offences.[396] As they decided in that case not to overturn the majority decision

[388] On the 'general duty to prevent' on superiors, see *Halilović*, ICTY T. Ch. I, 16 November 2005, paras. 81–8.

[389] Report of the Secretary-General Pursuant to Paragraph 2 of Security Council Resolution 808, UN Doc. S/25704, para. 56.

[390] *Hadžihasanović et al.*, ICTY A. Ch., 16 July 2003, Judge Shahabuddeen, para. 33. See also *Orić*, ICTY T. Ch. II, 30 June 2006, para. 294.

[391] *Hadžihasanović et al.*, ICTY A. Ch., 16 July 2003, para. 33.   [392] *Halilović*, ICTY T. Ch. I, 16 November 2005, para. 54.

[393] *Blaškić*, ICTY A. Ch., 29 July 2004, para. 91; but see *Čelebići* case, ICTY A. Ch., 20 February 2001, paras. 745–6. See section 17.8.5 and section 19.3.2.

[394] *Krnojelac*, ICTY A. Ch., 13 September 2003, para. 171.   [395] *Hadžihasanović et al.*, ICTY A. Ch., 16 July 2003, para. 39.

[396] *Orić*, ICTY A. Ch., 3 July 2008, Judge Shahabuddeen, paras. 18–19; Separate and Partially Dissenting Opinion of Judge Shomburg, para. 12; Separate and Partially Dissenting Opinion of Judge Liu, para. 27. See Robert Cryer, 'The Ad Hoc Tribunals and Command Responsibility: A Quiet Earthquake' in Shane Darcy and Joseph Powderly (eds.), *Judicial Creativity in International Criminal Tribunals* (Oxford, 2010) 159; Alphons Orie, 'Stare Decisis in the ICTY Appeal: Successor Responsibility in the Hadžihasanović Case' (2012) 10 *Journal of International Criminal Justice* 635.

in the earlier case, the matter cannot be considered settled,[397] not least as the preponderance of case law until recently has supported the view that it is a form of liability relating to the underlying crimes. The Appeals Chamber has most recently attempted to square the circle, providing that, although the culpable conduct in command responsibility is the failure to prevent or punish,[398] 'the seriousness of the superior's conduct in failing to prevent or punish crimes must be measured to some extent by the nature of the crimes to which this relates, i.e. the gravity of the crimes committed by the direct perpetrator(s)'.[399] They further held that:

The Statute does not accord any 'lesser' form of individual criminal responsibility to superior responsibility. Whilst the Appeals Chamber also recognizes that, in appropriate cases, a conviction under Article 6(3) of the Statute may result in a lesser sentence to that imposed in the context of an Article 6(1) conviction it reiterates its view that, in the circumstances of this case, superior responsibility is not to be seen as less grave than criminal responsibility under Article 6(1) of the Statute. The Appeals Chamber also recalls the well-established principle of gradation in sentencing, which holds that leaders and planners should bear heavier criminal responsibility than those further down the scale.[400]

Under the ICC Statute, command responsibility is treated as a form of liability for the underlying offences. Although some elements of Article 28 of the ICC Statute could be read as creating a dereliction of duty-type offence,[401] it quite clearly imputes the crimes of the subordinates to the superior,[402] which is more consistent with a form of complicity. Where there is a duty to intervene, and knowledge of an offence, it can be more easily seen that there is a complicity base for liability on the basis of traditional aiding/abetting ideas.[403]

Whichever way it is formulated in international criminal law, command responsibility is un-nuanced, covering many different forms of liability under one heading. It moves from deliberate failures to intervene despite a duty to do so, which fall close to traditional complicity ideas, to, in essence, conduct which is close to, if not the same as, negligent dereliction of duty.[404] This is recognized by the German law relating to the subject, which deals separately with failure to know of offences in dereliction of duty, failure to report an offence, and knowing tolerance of an offence when there is a duty and an ability to intervene to prevent it.[405] By running all these concepts together, like joint criminal enterprise, the concept of superior responsibility can be criticized from the point of view of the principle of fair labelling, and on the basis that it 'display[s] a measure of insensitivity to the degree

---

[397] For a contrary view, see Mettraux, *Command Responsibility*, Chapter 4.
[398] *Ntabakuze*, ICTR A. Ch., 8 May 2012, para. 282.
[399] *Ibid.*, para. 302. The two steps may be traced back to *Hadžhasanović et al.*, ICTY A. Ch., 22 April 2008, para. 318, which, in turn refers back to the *Čelebići* case, ICTY A. Ch., 20 February 2001, para. 313.
[400] *Ntabakuze*, ICTR A. Ch., 8 May 2012, para. 303.   [401] Ambos, 'Superior Responsibility', 850–5.
[402] Art. 28 provides that the commander 'shall be criminally responsible for crimes within the jurisdiction of the Court committed by forces under his or her effective command and control'. See *Bemba Gombo*, ICC PTC II, 15 June 2009, para. 405.
[403] See the German Code of Crimes against International Law, s. 4.
[404] See Mirjan Damaška, 'The Shadow Side of Command Responsibility' (2001) 49 *American Journal of Comparative Law* 455, 460–71. See generally the symposium at (2007) 5 *Journal of International Criminal Justice* 599–682.
[405] German Code of Crimes against International Law, ss. 13 and 14.

of the actor's own personal culpability',[406] and provides for the negligent commission of intentional offences.[407]

The fact that on occasion the ICTY and ICTR have accepted that command responsibility can lead to a conviction for genocide if the superior knew or had reason to know that subordinates were committing or about to commit genocide,[408] has led some commentators to express a corresponding concern about diluting the seriousness of the label 'genocide'.[409] In the ICC the Tribunals' case law will presumably be followed on point, unless the Court is willing to rely on the 'unless otherwise provided' phrase in Article 30 to eliminate the application of 'negligent' command responsibility for genocide.[410]

Further reading

There are helpful symposia on joint criminal enterprise, command responsibility, and co-perpetration at (2007) 5 *Journal of International Criminal Justice* 67–244; (2007) 5 *Journal of International Criminal Justice* 599–682; and (2011) 9 *Journal of International Criminal Justice* 85–226 respectively.

Kai Ambos, *Treatise on International Criminal Law,* Vol. I, *Foundations and General Part* (Oxford, 2013)
Roberta Arnold and Otto Triffterer, 'Article 28' in Triffterer, *Observers' Notes*, 795
Mohamed Elewa Badar, *The Concept of Mens Rea in International Criminal Law: The Case for a Unified Approach* (Oxford, 2013)
Gideon Boas, James Bischoff and Natalie Reid, *Forms of Responsibility in International Criminal Law* (Cambridge, 2007)
Robert Cryer, *Prosecuting International Crimes: Selectivity and the International Criminal Law Regime* (Cambridge, 2005) Chapter 6
Guénaël Mettraux, *The Law of Command Responsibility* (Oxford, 2009)
Darryl Mundis, 'Crimes of the Commander: Superior Responsibility under Article 7(3) of the ICTY Statute' in Gideon Boas and William A. Schabas (eds.), *International Criminal Law Developments in the Case Law of the ICTY* (The Hague, 2003) 239
Héctor Olásolo, *The Criminal Responsibility of Senior Political and Military Leaders as Principals to International Crimes* (Oxford, 2009)

---

[406] See Damaška, 'The Shadow Side', 456; Chantal Meloni, 'Command Responsibility: Mode of Liability for Subordinates or Separate Offence of the Superior?' (2007) 5 *Journal of International Criminal Justice* 619; Volker Nerlich, 'Superior Responsibility under Article 28 of the Rome Statute: For Exactly What Is the Superior Held Responsible?' (2007) 5 *Journal of International Criminal Justice* 665. For a partial solution, see Robinson, 'Command Responsibility', 30–5.
[407] William A. Schabas, 'General Principles of Criminal Law in the International Criminal Court Statute (Part III)' (1998) 6 *European Journal of Crime, Criminal Law and Criminal Justice* 400, 417.
[408] See e.g. *Blagojević and Jokić*, ICTY T. Ch. I, 17 January 2005, para. 686. In *Ntabakuze*, ICTR A. Ch., 8 May 2012, the majority found that the defendant knew that his subordinates were acting with genocidal intent (paras. 245–9). In their Joint Declaration (para. 1), Judges Liu and Pocar, agreed, but said that it was unnecessary; all that was necessary was that the superior knew or had reason to know that their subordinates were going to commit a crime, rather than their specific *mens rea*. It has been suggested that the majority's approach implies that it is necessary to know of a subordinate's genocidal intent for there to be command responsibility. Patrick Hayden and Katrina A. Kappos, 'Current Developments at the Ad Hoc International Criminal Tribunals' (2013) 11 *Journal of International Criminal Justice* 247, 250. However, the majority were responding to a specific argument from the defence that such knowledge had not been proved, and, for sentencing purposes, the finding is relevant. Hence, this need not be the implication of the majority's view.
[409] See, prior to *Blagojević and Jokić*, ICTY T. Ch. I, 17 January 2005, and in relation to earlier suggestions along the same lines, Mettraux, *International Crimes*, 261–4.
[410] See William A. Schabas, 'The Jelisić Case and the Mens Rea of Genocide' (2001) 14 *Leiden Journal of International Law* 125, 132.

Per Saland, 'International Criminal Law Principles' in Lee, *The Making of the Rome Statute*, 189

William Schabas, 'Hate Speech in Rwanda: The Road to Genocide' (2000) 46 *McGill Law Journal* 141

William Schabas, *The UN International Criminal Tribunals: The Former Yugoslavia, Rwanda and Sierra Leone* (Cambridge, 2006) Chapter 9

Elies van Sliedregt, *The Criminal Responsibility of Individuals for Violations of International Humanitarian Law* (The Hague, 2003)

Elies van Sliedregt, *Individual Criminal Responsibility in International Law* (Oxford, 2012)

16

Defences/Grounds for Excluding Criminal Responsibility

16.1 Introduction

Defences (or, in the carefully calibrated terminology of the ICC Statute, 'grounds for excluding criminal responsibility')[1] are an oft-forgotten aspect of international criminal law. Jurisprudence from the international criminal tribunals (including the ICC) on the matter is sparse, and not always satisfactory. There are a number of reasons for this, one of which also at least partially explains the relative lack of scholarly attention given to most defences in international criminal law.[2] This is the tendency towards a lack of sympathy for defendants in international criminal proceedings. As Albin Eser has said, there are 'certain psychological reservations toward defences. By providing perpetrators of brutal crimes against humanity . . . with defences for their offences, we have effectively lent them a hand in finding grounds for excluding punishability.'[3] Other reasons include the fact that, in international Tribunals, the Prosecutor's choice of defendants rarely includes those who have plausible claims of defences recognized by the law. Defences are, however, a fundamental part of criminal law, and reflect important limitations on the proper scope of punishable conduct. It is the purpose of this chapter to set out and critique the law relating to defences, in both treaty-based and customary international law. This chapter is primarily concerned with substantive defences to international crimes; it does not deal with issues such as immunity, youth, *ne bis in idem* or limitation periods. These are not defences for conduct, but pleas as to the jurisdiction or right of a court to try a person, both of which are separate matters.

16.1.1 The types of defences

At the outset, certain terminological and conceptual matters ought to be clarified. In the common law world, it is usual to speak of 'defences' in the omnibus sense, whereas in civil

---

[1] Although for simplicity's sake this chapter uses 'defences', this should not be taken as representing a position on the doctrinal controversies about the choice of terminology.

[2] Superior orders are an exception to this trend.

[3] Albin Eser, 'Defences in War Crimes Trials' in Yoram Dinstein and Mala Tabory (eds.), *War Crimes in International Law* (The Hague, 1996) 251. For a very useful discussion of this, see Harmen van der Wilt, 'Justification and Excuse in International Criminal Law: An Appraisal of ICTY Jurisprudence' in Bert Swart, Alexander Zahar and Göran Sluiter (eds.), *The Legacy of the International Criminal Tribunal for Former Yugoslavia* (Oxford, 2011) 275.

law jurisdictions a firm distinction is drawn between types of defences, in particular between justifications and excuses.[4] Justifications, broadly speaking, are pleas that the conduct of the defendant was acceptable, and thus necessarily lawful. It is difficult, for example, to argue that a person acting in self-defence has done anything which the law seeks to prevent. 'Excuses', painting again with something of a broad brush, do not seek to defend the conduct of the defendant *per se*, but look to say that, in the particular instance, the defendant ought not be blamed for what he or she did. The boundary between the different types of defences is not especially clear, however,[5] even though the classification does have important consequences, at least in national law. For example, there may be no secondary liability for aiding and abetting justified conduct; the same may not be the case for excused conduct. Also, justifications tend to exclude liability for the conduct in private law, whereas excuses do not necessarily do so.[6] It is not clear that there was agreement on the distinction at Rome, hence the neutral terminology of the ICC Statute, 'grounds for excluding criminal responsibility' rather than 'defences', 'justifications' or 'excuses'. The distinction, nonetheless, remains useful for understanding the appropriate ambit of some defences.[7]

There is another set of 'defences', however, which also require treatment. These are what can be termed 'failure of proof defences'.[8] These defences are usually denials that a person can be held responsible on the basis that the prosecution has failed to show a fundamental element of the offence. As a result, some national legal systems do not treat these issues as defences. These pleas often relate to the presence or otherwise of *mens rea*.[9] Consent is a notable example in relation to offences to which it is relevant. Such defences, depending on the circumstances, may also operate across the excuse/justification divide.[10] They are dealt with in this chapter, as the ICC Statute impliedly treats them as defences.[11] A final introductory point is that defences here are those that serve, as the ICC Statute puts it, to 'exclude criminal responsibility'. Mitigating factors, such as inexperience or pressure not amounting to duress are merely mitigating factors, which go to sentencing rather than responsibility.[12]

16.2   The ICC Statute and defences

Although the ICC Statute is neither a complete, nor an entirely accurate, statement of defences as they exist in international criminal law, it is the first treaty that attempts to

---

[4] See generally Antonio Cassese, 'Justifications and Excuses in International Criminal Law' in Cassese, *Commentary*, 951; Elies van Sliedregt, *Individual Criminal Responsibility in International Law* (Oxford, 2012) 215–17, Kai Ambos, *Treatise on International Criminal Law*: Vol. I, *Foundations and General Part* (Oxford, 2013) 304–7. The distinction is not entirely unknown to the common law, however.

[5] See George Fletcher, *Rethinking Criminal Law* (New York, 1978) 759 *et seq.*; Kent Greenawalt, 'The Perplexing Borders of Justification and Excuse' (1984) 84 *Columbia Law Review* 1897.

[6] See Cassese, 'Justifications', 952–4. As he notes though, international criminal law has yet to make any practical distinction between the two.

[7] See e.g. Kai Ambos, 'Other Grounds for Excluding Criminal Responsibility' in Cassese, *Commentary*, 1003, 1036–7; Illan Rua Wall, 'Duress, International Criminal Law and Literature' (2006) 4 *Journal of International Criminal Justice* 724.

[8] Ambos, *Treatise*, 307–8.

[9] Alibi is sometimes seen as a type of this claim, in that the assertion is that the person did not undertake the conduct, as he or she was not there. In fact, it is slightly different, in that it is a denial of any of the conduct at all.

[10] Cassese, 'Justifications', 953–4, treats some such defences as excuses, but others (consent) as a justification.

[11] See e.g. Art. 32 of the ICC Statute.   [12] See section 19.3.1.

deal with defences in any systematic way.[13] Its provisions were the outcome of compromises between a large number of States, some of which came from the common law tradition, and some from their civil law counterparts. While the provisions therefore leave something to be desired from a criminal law point of view, they provide a sensible structure within which to investigate defences in international criminal law. Article 31 sets out a reasonable proportion of the defences which are applicable to international crimes, providing for defences of insanity, intoxication, self-defence (including defence of others or, exceptionally, property), duress and necessity.

Certain points ought to be noted at the outset. First, as Article 31(1) makes clear, it is not intended to be exhaustive. There are other parts of the Statute (in particular Articles 32 and 33, which deal with mistakes of fact and law and the defence of superior orders respectively) that are also relevant. Second, as the definitions of defences given in the Statute are the outcome of difficult negotiations, Article 31(2) provides that 'the Court shall determine the applicability of the grounds for excluding criminal responsibility provided for in this Statute to the case before it'. It has been argued, by one of its drafters, that this provision recognizes that the ICC has a residual power to refuse to apply a defence to an individual case even where the text of the ICC Statute might require it.[14] This might be criticized on the basis that a person ought to be able to rely on the defences that the Statute ostensibly sets down without the risk that it will be set aside in an individual case. A better way to interpret this provision may be that the ICC has discretion to determine the factual applicability of a defence before entering into serious discussion of it at trial. In other words, the Court may require an 'air of reality' of a defence to be established before permitting detailed argument and evidence to be tendered.[15]

On the other side, Article 31(3) of the ICC Statute recognizes that there are defences applicable to international crimes which it does not enumerate. Article 31(3) reads:

At trial, the Court may consider a ground for excluding criminal responsibility other than those referred to in paragraph 1 where such a ground is derived from applicable law as set forth in Article 21.[16]

Pursuant to this Article, a defendant may plead defences before the ICC which have their basis outside the ICC Statute, i.e. in other applicable treaties, customary law and general principles of law.[17] There are a number of such defences, to which we shall return. However, owing to the hierarchy of sources established in Article 21 (which places the Statute at the apex of authority), arguments that defences contained within Article 31 are narrower than those available under customary law are not admissible under this head, although they may have purchase in arguments about the appropriate application of Article 31(2).

---

[13] See Albin Eser, 'Article 31' in Triffterer, *Observers' Notes*, 863, 865–6.

[14] Per Saland, 'International Criminal Law Principles' in Lee, *The Making of the Rome Statute*, 189, 208–9.

[15] This is particularly relevant where evidence, such as of consent in sexual offences, is sensitive and examination of witnesses can be distressing. See r. 72 of the ICC RPE.

[16] Art. 21 provides (in addition to the ICC Statute, the Elements of Crimes and the RPE) for the use of applicable treaties, principles and rules of international law (i.e. custom) and, 'failing that', general principles of law.

[17] If seeking to do so, the defence must inform the Trial Chamber and Prosecutor in advance, giving them sufficient time to prepare on point: r. 80 of the ICC RPE.

16.3   Mental incapacity[18]

Insanity is a defence which often (although not always) amounts to a claim of lack of proof. It ought to be distinguished from the procedural plea of unfitness to plead.[19] Article 31(1)(a) of the ICC Statute is the first codification of a defence of insanity in international law, and applies when:

The person suffers from a mental disease or defect that destroys that person's capacity to appreciate the unlawfulness or nature of his or her conduct, or capacity to control his or her conduct to conform to the requirements of law.

Although parts of the provision are quite restrictive, Article 31(1)(a) is a fairly uncontroversial formulation of the defence. It encompasses three situations. The first is the *locus classicus* of a mental incapacity plea, which is when a person is unable to understand the nature of his or her conduct. The usual example given to explain this situation is a person who cuts the victim's throat delusionally thinking that it is a loaf of bread.[20] There is no point convicting such a person, who is in need of treatment rather than prison. Article 31(1)(a) also covers the situation where a person is incapable of understanding the unlawfulness of his or her conduct. Such a person may well deserve exemption from liability, but this is not quite the same as exemption under the first head, at least as appreciation of unlawfulness may involve a more subtle analysis than the concept that the drafters were probably trying to codify, which is that the person was incapable of understanding the wrongfulness of the conduct. The final concept recognized by Article 31(1)(a) is that of the 'irresistible impulse', where a person understands the nature and wrongfulness of the conduct, but is unable, owing to mental illness, to stop from acting as he or she did.[21] There is no requirement that the insanity is permanent. It is sufficient that the person's capacity was destroyed at the time of the impugned conduct. As with the other forms of the defence, such a plea will require expert evidence from both sides.[22]

   It is notable that Article 31(1)(a) requires destruction, rather than impairment, of ability. This is a high standard, albeit one which is consistent with the way most domestic jurisdictions deal with the matter. Diminished, as opposed to absent, ability to comprehend the nature or unlawfulness of conduct or comply with the law is no defence in the ICC Statute, nor is it in the jurisprudence of the ad hoc Tribunals, which treats any such claim as one of mitigation of sentence.[23] This is similar to the way the issue was treated in the

---

[18] See generally Peter Krug, 'The Emerging Mental Incapacity Defense in International Criminal Law: Some Initial Questions of Implementation' (2000) 96 *American Journal of International Law* 317.

[19] On which, see Albin Eser, 'Article 31' in Triffterer, *Observers' Notes*, 863, 873.

[20] This is, of course, also a mistake of fact, but it would essentially be impossible to persuade a fact-finder that this belief was honestly held without proof of mental incapacity.

[21] In such an instance, the claim stands on the border of denial of proof (of voluntary action (i.e. *actus reus*)) and excuse.

[22] See Krug, 'The Emerging Mental Incapacity Defense'. In the ICTY, the defence bears the burden of proof (on the balance of probabilities) with respect to this defence: see *Delalić et al.*, ICTY A. Ch., 20 February 2001 (the '*Čelebići* case'), para. 582.

[23] See *ibid.*, paras. 580–90, r. 67(A)(ii)(b) of the ICTY RPE. The Trial Chamber in *Vasiljević*, ICTY T. Ch. I, 29 November 2002, paras. 282–3, defined diminished responsibility as 'an impairment to his capacity to appreciate the unlawfulness of or the nature of his conduct or to control his conduct so as to conform to the requirements of the law'. In *Jelisić*, ICTY T. Ch., 14 December 1999, para. 125, 'personality disorders … [and] borderline, narcissistic and anti-social characteristics' were insufficient to diminish responsibility.

post-Second World War trials in which it was raised,[24] and in the ICC Rules of Procedure and Evidence.[25]

One unfortunate aspect of Article 31(1)(a) is its failure to provide for a special verdict in the eventuality of a person being acquitted on the basis of mental incapacity. This is important: in domestic systems, a person who is acquitted on the basis of lack of mental capacity is necessarily liable to some other form of order, which provides for psychiatric evaluation and treatment.[26] It is to be hoped that some arrangements may be found with the mental health authorities in States supportive of the ICC that will provide for those who have been acquitted by the ICC, but are in need of treatment or confinement on the basis of their disorder.[27]

16.4   Intoxication

There is more of a history than might be thought of international crimes being committed by the intoxicated. In the Second World War, the *Sonderkommandos*, who were forced to work in the concentration camps they were held in, were frequently given intoxicants. Many of the participants in Rwanda's genocide were drunk.[28] Child soldiers are often given drugs or alcohol as a control mechanism, to loosen their inhibitions and increase their ferocity.[29] After the Second World War, at least one case accepted the existence of a partial defence of intoxication, although it was rejected on the facts.[30]

Although it might be queried if those most responsible for international crimes, who are likely to be the defendants before the ICC, will have much resort to the defence,[31] intoxication is dealt with in Article 31(1)(b) of the ICC Statute, which provides for the exclusion of responsibility when:

The person is in a state of intoxication that destroys that person's capacity to appreciate the unlawful-ness or nature of his or her conduct, or capacity to control his or her conduct to conform to the requirements of law, unless the person has become voluntarily intoxicated under such circumstances that the person knew, or disregarded the risk, that, as a result of the intoxication, he or she was likely to engage in conduct constituting a crime within the jurisdiction of the Court.

At the outset, it ought to be noted that chronic alcoholism or addiction to drugs might also lead to a defence under Article 31(1)(a).[32] The nature of the plea here, though, is that, owing to the intoxication, the mental element is not formed; thus it is a plea of failure of proof. However, debate on the defence in Rome was awkward, as some delegations were opposed

---

[24] *Gerbsch*, XIII LRTWC 131, 132, 137. See also Antonio Cassese *et al.*, *Cassese's International Criminal Law*, 3rd edn (Oxford, 2013) 225.
[25] Rule 145(2) of the ICC RPE.
[26] In the United Kingdom, see e.g. the Criminal Procedure (Insanity and Unfitness to Plead) Act 1991.
[27] See William Schabas, *The International Criminal Court: A Commentary on the Rome Statute* (Oxford, 2010) 485.
[28] William Schabas, *Genocide in International Law* (Cambridge, 2008) 398.
[29] Matthew Happold, *Child Soldiers in International Law* (Manchester, 2004) 16–17; Mark Drumbl, *Reimagining Child Soldiers in International Law and Policy* (Oxford, 2012) 80.
[30] *Chusaburo*, III LRTWC 76, 78.   [31] Ambos, 'Other Grounds', 1031; Schabas, *International Criminal Court*, 486.
[32] Geert-Jan Knoops, *Defences in Contemporary International Criminal Law* (New York, 2001) 123.

to its inclusion at all, considering intoxication as an aggravating factor rather than a possible defence.[33] As a result of this, the scope of the defence in Article 31(1)(b) is narrow.

16.4.1   *Voluntary and involuntary intoxication*

The primary focus of the text of the Article is involuntary intoxication, that is to say, when a person unwittingly becomes intoxicated owing to inadvertent consumption of drugs or alcohol. Voluntary intoxication is only a defence when a person did not realize that he or she might engage in conduct prohibited by the Statute whilst intoxicated, and was not at fault by disregarding such a risk.[34] This is, in essence, a recklessness test.[35] Taking drink or drugs to gain 'Dutch courage' will not provide the basis for a defence under this provision as the person will know of at least the risk (and almost inevitably more) that he or she will commit the offence whilst under the influence.[36] Even so, some have questioned whether customary law allows for any defence of voluntary intoxication,[37] and the ICTY has said that even involuntary intoxication only 'could be' a mitigating circumstance, and that voluntary intoxication is often an aggravating factor.[38]

16.4.2   *Destruction of capacity*

The intoxication must have destroyed the person's capacity to understand the nature or unlawfulness of the conduct, or ability to conform to the law's dictates. Impairment, even of a substantial nature, is insufficient to exclude a person's liability.[39] On the language of Article 31(1)(b), it appears that the person must be incapable of understanding or controlling his or her conduct; it does not appear sufficient that the person simply did not do so owing to the intoxication, although it is uncertain if this was the intention of the drafters.

It is not clear precisely how specific the risk of conduct has to be to exclude the defence. 'Conduct constituting a crime within the jurisdiction of the court' could be broad, simply meaning any physical act or omission prohibited in the Statute, for example killing, engaging in inhumane treatment, or inflicting serious injury. Or it could be interpreted more narrowly, meaning that the person must have known or disregarded the risk that he or she would engage in the specific conduct for which he or she is being prosecuted. Also, there is ambiguity about whether the reference to 'conduct' includes the relevant circumstantial elements (for example, that there was an armed conflict, there was a widespread or

---

[33] Saland, 'Principles', 209; Ambos, 'Other Grounds', 1029–30. Most (although not all) domestic systems provide for some form of defence of involuntary intoxication, but some States refuse to accept voluntary intoxication as a defence, on policy grounds. The ICTY has said that, 'in contexts where violence is the norm and weapons are carried, intentionally consuming drugs or alcohol constitutes an aggravating rather than a mitigating factor': *Kvočka*, ICTY T. Ch. I, 2 November 2001, para. 706; *Kvočka*, ICTY A. Ch., 28 February 2005, paras. 707–8.

[34] Where someone is at fault in failing to realize, his or her liability is said to rest on this prior fault.

[35] Van Sliedregt, *Individual Criminal Responsibility*, 229.   [36] Eser, 'Article 31', 877; Ambos, *Treatise*, 329.

[37] Gerhard Werle, *Principles of International Criminal Law*, 2nd edn (Cambridge, 2009) 222; Ambos, *Treatise*, 330.

[38] *Kvočka*, ICTY T. Ch. I, 2 November 2001, para. 706; see van Sliedregt, *Individual Criminal Responsibility*, 233.

[39] See Elies van Sliedregt, *The Criminal Responsibility of Individuals for Violations of International Humanitarian Law* (The Hague, 2003) 249.

systematic attack on the civilian population, or a manifest pattern of similar events), although, given the phrasing of Article 30 of the ICC Statute, they would appear to be included.[40] Still, it is difficult to see the ICC acquitting someone on such a basis.

16.4.3   A complete defence

In common law systems such as the United Kingdom, intoxication is only a defence to certain crimes (known, rather unfortunately in the context of international crimes, as crimes of 'specific intent').[41] Pleas that *mens rea* is not established owing to voluntary intoxication are not admissible in crimes of 'basic intent', which tend to be less serious versions of crimes of 'specific intent' (for example, murder is a crime of specific intent, manslaughter is a crime of basic intent). The result of a plea of intoxication is thus usually a conviction for a less serious offence.[42] The ICC Statute does not adopt such a position. Thus, a drunk offender could entirely escape criminal responsibility on the basis of this provision, although the strict terms of the defence mean that it will be difficult to sustain such a plea.

16.5   Self-defence, defence of others and of property[43]

It has never been questioned that people have the right to defend themselves. Indeed (non-mistaken) self-defence is often considered a paradigmatic justification of conduct.[44] There were a number of cases in which this justification was raised after the Second World War.[45] The ICTY Trial Chamber in *Kordić and Čerkez* accepted that customary law recognized self-defence,[46] an uncontroversial finding made more contentious by the fact that the Chamber asserted that the formulation found in the ICC Statute represented customary law.[47] Article 31(1)(c) provides for an acquittal when:

The person acts reasonably to defend himself or herself or another person or, in the case of war crimes, property which is essential for the survival of the person or another person or property which is essential for accomplishing a military mission, against an imminent and unlawful use of force in a manner proportionate to the degree of danger to the person or the other person or property protected. The fact that the person was involved in a defensive operation conducted by forces shall not in itself constitute a ground for excluding criminal responsibility under this subparagraph.

---

[40]   Eser, 'Article 31', 878 (who considers contextual elements to be included).
[41]   See generally David Ormerod, *Smith and Hogan's Criminal Law*, 13th edn (Oxford, 2011) 314–21. The term could cause confusion owing to its use in international criminal law, in particular when referring to the intention required for genocide.
[42]   In civilian systems, there is often a crime of committing an offence whilst intoxicated; see e.g. German Criminal Code, § 323a.
[43]   See generally van Sliedregt, *Criminal Responsibility*, 254–67.
[44]   See e.g. George Fletcher, *The Grammar of Criminal Law* (Oxford, 2007) Vol. I, 23–7, 50–1.
[45]   See *Tessmann (Willi)*, XV LRTWC 177.   [46]   *Kordić and Čerkez*, ICTY T. Ch. III, 26 February 2001, paras. 448–52.
[47]   Ibid.

16.5.1 *Imminent, unlawful use of force*

The defence here ought not to be confused with self-defence by States under Article 51 of the UN Charter.[48] In addition, this defence is not available in relation to *any* threat. It is limited to action in response to 'an imminent and unlawful use of force'.[49] What is imminent is a matter of appreciation, although Article 31(1)(c) does make clear that a person must not wait for someone else to strike the first blow.[50] 'Unlawful' means that there is no right to defend against someone who is acting lawfully.[51] However, this should not be interpreted as meaning 'criminally'. There have been some suggestions that there is no right to defend against those covered by any of the grounds in Article 31(1).[52] However, at the domestic level, defence against the insane or highly intoxicated is acceptable, and there seems to be no reason to doubt that the same would apply here. Some assistance might usefully be drawn here from the distinction between justifications and excuses. Justified actors are not acting unlawfully, whereas those who are merely excused (the insane and the very intoxicated being two examples) are acting unlawfully, and thus can be defended against. Some suggest that the 'force' can be psychological, as well as physical,[53] but this is not universally accepted.[54]

The expansion of the defence, with respect to war crimes, to protect 'mission essential property'[55] was controversial in the negotiations at Rome. According to Cassese, 'this extension is manifestly outside the *lex lata* and may generate quite a few misgivings'.[56] Given that many States have limited rights to use force to protect, for example, nuclear installations, and UN rules of engagement often provide for defence of mission essential property, this criticism may be a little harsh.[57] On the other hand, Belgium considered this provision contrary to *ius cogens* and therefore issued a declaration on point at the time of its ratification.[58] This defence (in particular, the reference to 'mission essential property') does have links to military necessity, and ought to be limited by that.[59] Nonetheless, some fears that aspects of this provision are open to abuse have some foundation.[60] As the Article

---

[48] *Martić*, ICTY A. Ch., 8 October 2008, para. 268. See also Werle, *Principles*, 203.
[49] *Kordić and Čerkez*, ICTY T. Ch. III, 26 February 2001, para. 451.
[50] Eser, 'Article 31', 881, defines imminent as 'immediately antecedent, presently exercised or still enduring'.
[51] This ought to exclude, for example, attacks on military property which are lawful under IHL. This would obviate the criticism that the defence may delegitimize attacks that are lawful under IHL, thus altering IHL through the back door; for such a critique, see Cassese *et al.*, *Cassese's International Criminal Law*, 213.
[52] Werle, *Principles*, 201. More recently, the ICTY has used the term 'immediate', although whether they intended any difference is unclear, and the reference is brief: *Gotovina*, ICTY T. Ch. I, 15 April 2011, para. 1730. The better view is that they did not intend any difference.
[53] Eser, 'Article 31', 880; Werle, *Principles*, 201; Ambos, *Treatise*, 339.   [54] See Ambos, *Treatise*, 339.
[55] Property essential to the survival of a person may be different here, as parasitic on protection of the person's life: Ambos, *Treatise*, 340.
[56] Antonio Cassese, 'The Rome Statute of the International Criminal Court: Some Preliminary Reflections' (1999) 10 *European Journal of International Law* 144, 154–5.
[57] It might be questioned whether a civilian stealing a truck full of small arms ought to be protected in this situation, although in that situation it is quite possible the person would be considered (or reasonably believed) to be taking an active part in hostilities, thus forfeiting their protection.
[58] See http://untreaty.un.org/ENGLISH/bible/englishinternetbible/partI/chapterXVIII/treaty11.asp. Although incorrect as a matter of law (see Schabas, *International Court*, 489), this is State practice, accompanied by *opinio iuris*, and thus relevant for the determination of customary law, as well as for interpretation of the ICC Statute.
[59] Nobuo Hayashi, 'Requirements of Military Necessity in International Humanitarian Law and International Criminal Law' (2010) 28 *Boston University International Law Journal* 39, 134–8; Werle, *Principles*, 202.
[60] See Ambos, 'Other Grounds', 1033.

clarifies, however, the simple fact that a State is acting in self-defence is not enough in itself to invoke this provision. There does not appear to be any acceptance in this provision of a defence when a person reasonably (but wrongly) believes that there is such an attack.[61]

16.5.2   *Reasonable and proportionate response*

Not every reaction to an attack is acceptable. For a response to be defended on the basis of Article 31(1)(c), it must be reasonable to resort to force, and the level of force must be 'proportionate to the degree of danger' faced.[62] Proportionality is not a test which can be set down with scientific precision in advance. However, in applying the test, 'such considerations as the nature of the weapon in the hands of the accused, the question whether the assailant had any weapon, and so forth, have to be considered'.[63] 'Eagle-eyed' hindsight is to be avoided when appraising proportionality, as a person does not have the luxury of time to weigh things very carefully when there is an imminent or ongoing attack. Article 31(1)(c) does not create a duty to retreat[64] or any specific rules on what the response must be, other than setting down the test of proportionality to the level of danger. This test is to be applied by the court; the defendant's view is not determinative. The ICTY has provided some brief comments on the defence, rejecting it in relation to a charge of killing civilians, on the basis that it considered 'the perpetrators' conduct, even if an immediate illegitimate attack could be assumed, to be disproportionate, where other ways of thwarting any possible danger instead of firing lethal shots were available'.[65] This implies that lethal force should be a last resort, but in cases where the defence is raised much will depend on the facts and what could be considered proportionate in the specific context. The defence is further limited by the language of Article 31(3)(c) (the person 'acts . . . to defend'), which implies that the person must intend to act in defence.[66]

16.6   Duress and necessity

Situations in which international crimes are committed tend to be ones in which there is group activity, and therefore some level of coercion of an offender by colleagues can often be expected.[67] Also in such situations painful choices have at times to be made. Article 31 (1)(d), the first codification at the international level of necessity and duress, decidedly controversially,[68] treats the two together, providing for a defence when:[69]

---

[61]   Eser, 'Article 31', 882, and see section 16.7.1 on mistake of fact. Although see *contra* Cassese *et al.*, *Cassese's International Criminal Law*, 212.
[62]   See van Sliedregt, *Individual Criminal Responsibility*, 236–8.   [63]   *Tessmann (Willi)*, XV LRTWC 177.
[64]   *Tessman* (*ibid.*) could be read as requiring this.   [65]   *Gotovina*, ICTY T. Ch. I, 15 April 2011, para. 1730.
[66]   See also Werle, *Principles*, 202; but see Ambos, *Treatise*, 342, for the view that knowledge suffices.
[67]   Such colleagues may, of course, become liable themselves for offences they encouraged, assisted or participated in.
[68]   Claus Kreß, 'War Crimes Committed in Non-International Armed Conflicts and the Emerging System of International Criminal Justice' (2000) 30 *Israel Yearbook on Human Rights* 103, 152 *et seq.*; Ambos, *Treatise*, 356.
[69]   And has been criticized for doing so, not least as duress is an excuse, and most examples of necessity are justifications: see Eser, 'Article 31', 883.

The conduct which is alleged to constitute a crime within the jurisdiction of the Court has been caused by duress resulting from a threat of imminent death or of continuing or imminent serious bodily harm against that person or another person, and the person acts necessarily and reasonably to avoid this threat, provided that the person does not intend to cause a greater harm than the one sought to be avoided. Such a threat may either be:

(i) Made by other persons; or
(ii) Constituted by other circumstances beyond that person's control.

Although this was the first codification of these defences, one of the most plausible explanations of the way in which the Nuremberg IMT dealt with its provision on superior orders[70] is that it laid down a test for duress.[71] There was also considerable jurisprudence on duress and necessity in other post-Second World War cases,[72] such as *Krupp*,[73] *Flick*,[74] *Krauch*[75] and *von Leeb*.[76] Much of this jurisprudence was canvassed in the ICTY in one of its few fully reasoned decisions on defences, *Erdemović*.[77] In this case, a bare majority of the Appeals Chamber decided that, although there was a defence of duress in international law, it did not apply to cases involving the killing of innocent victims.[78] In particular, as two of the judges determined the matter on avowedly policy-based grounds, and there were strong dissents from two other judges,[79] the finding was controversial.[80] Notably, this aspect of the decision in *Erdemović* was not taken up in the ICC Statute.[81] The requirements of the defence in the ICC Statute are probably customary.[82]

16.6.1 *Imminent threat beyond the control of the accused*

The first requirement is that there is a threat of 'imminent death or of continuing or imminent serious bodily harm'. Thus, it is clear that blackmail or other threats not involving imminent serious violence will not suffice. For the criminal law to permit a person to excuse himself or herself from liability on the basis of threats, those threats must be very serious. Also, the

---

[70] See section 16.7.
[71] See Yoram Dinstein, *The Defence of 'Obedience to Superior Orders' in International Criminal Law* (The Hague, 1965) 147–56.
[72] See Commentary, XV LRTWC 170–5.   [73] X LRTWC 69, 156.   [74] IX LRTWC 1, 19.   [75] X LRTWC 1, 54, 57.
[76] XII LRTWC 1, 144, 149.   [77] *Erdemović*, ICTY A. Ch., 7 October 1997.
[78] *Ibid.*, Separate Opinion of Judge Li, paras. 1–12; Separate Opinion of Judges McDonald and Vohrah, paras. 32–89.
[79] *Ibid.*, Dissenting Opinion of Judge Stephen, paras. 23–67; Dissenting Opinion of Judge Cassese, paras. 11–51.
[80] See e.g. Peter Rowe, 'Duress as a Defence to War Crimes after Erdemović: A Laboratory for a Permanent Court?' (1998) 1 *Yearbook of International Humanitarian Law* 210; David Turns, 'The International Criminal Tribunal for the Former Yugoslavia: The Erdemović Case' (1998) 47 *International and Comparative Law Quarterly* 461; Claus Kreß, 'Zur Methode der Rechtsfindung im Allgemeinen Teil des Völkerstrafrechts: Die Bewertung von Tötungen im Nötigungsnotstand durch die Rechtsmittelkammer des Internationalen Straftribunals für das ehemalige Jugoslawien im Fall Erdemović' (1999) 111 *Zeitschrift für die gesamte Strafrechtswissenschaft* 597; Robert Cryer, 'One Appeal, Four Opinions, Two Philosophies and a Remittal' (1998) 2 *Journal of Armed Conflict Law* 193; Aaron Fichtelberg, 'Liberal Values in International Criminal Law: A Critique of Erdemović' (2008) 6 *Journal of International Criminal Justice* 3. For a rare example of support of the majority, see Yoram Dinstein, 'Defences' in Gabrielle Kirk McDonald and Olivia Swaak-Goldman (eds.), *Substantive and Procedural Aspects of International Criminal Law* (The Hague, 2000) 367, 376.
[81] See Mohamed Shahabuddeen, *International Criminal Justice at the Yugoslav Tribunal: A Judge's Recollection* (Oxford, 2012) 206–10.
[82] There has been an implication that fighting on the 'right side' might be relevant to necessity (*Fofana and Kondewa*, SCSL T. Ch. 2 August 2007, Partially Dissenting Opinion of Judge Thompson, paras. 66–8). However, this must be regarded as incorrect, and inconsistent with the equal applicability of humanitarian law: see Valerie Oosterveld and Andrea Marlowe, 'Prosecutor v. Kamara et al. and Fofana and Kondewa' (2007) 101 *American Journal of International Law* 848, 856–7.

threats must be of imminent danger. It is by no means clear that imminent means the same thing here as in Article 31(1)(c). The threats may be against the accused or others; there is no requirement that there be any particular relationship between the accused and the people threatened. The threat must be real, however, and not simply believed to exist by the defendant.[83]

As recognized by Article 31(1)(d)(ii), the threat must be outside the control of the defendant. The use of the term 'other' in that part of the Article implies that this condition also applies to duress in (i). This would probably exclude the situation where a person had 'courted' the threats by others, such as in the instance where a person had joined a group notorious for its criminality. This condition was considered a part of customary law by Judges Cassese and Stephen in *Erdemović*,[84] and is consistent with national practice.[85]

16.6.2 Necessary and reasonable actions

As with self-defence, pressure, whether from another or by virtue of circumstance, does not suffice to defend *any* reaction. The reactions of the person seeking to use the defence must be both necessary and reasonable in the circumstances to avoid the threat. The test is similar, but not necessarily identical, to that of proportionality in self-defence.[86] This includes the question of whether a reasonable person would have given in to the threats.[87] One issue that does arise, however, is what can be expected of soldiers, who, although frequently in very stressful situations,[88] have undergone military training, and are expected to put themselves in harm's way to protect others,[89] with respect to this aspect of the test. In such circumstances, the test is perhaps best formulated as what would be considered necessary and reasonable by a service member of the experience and rank of the defendant. Such a nuance to the test seems appropriate (after all, the test of reasonableness always begs the question of reasonable to whom?)[90] and finds some support in Judge Cassese's interpretation of the existing jurisprudence on point in *Erdemović*.[91]

16.6.3 Causation

It is an express requirement that the threats caused the impugned conduct. If a person would have acted as he or she did anyway, he or she will not be able to take advantage of this defence. Article 31(1)(d) is silent on whether the threats have to be the sole cause of the defendant's conduct, or whether they only need to be one of a number of causes. This also

---

[83] The *Krupp* case may have seen things differently: *Krupp*, X LRTWC 69, 148. See also Commentary, XV LRTWC 174.
[84] *Erdemović*, ICTY A. Ch., 7 October 1997, Opinion of Judge Cassese, para. 16; Opinion of Judge Stephen, para. 68.
[85] Werle, *Principles*, 208.
[86] The test is described in proportionality terms in *Erdemović*, ICTY A. Ch., 7 October 1997, Opinion of Judge Cassese, para. 16; Opinion of Judges McDonald and Vohrah, para. 37. See also Eser, 'Article 31', 886–7.
[87] Eser, 'Article 31', 885–6.   [88] See Larry May, *War Crimes and Just War* (Cambridge, 2007) Chapter 13.
[89] See e.g. the comments in *R* v. *Dudley and Stevens* (1884–5) LR 14 QBD 273; 287, Werle, *Principles*, 209.
[90] Such a test, it ought to be accepted, may be difficult, albeit not impossible, to apply in the case of civilians or rebel forces.
[91] *Erdemović*, ICTY A. Ch., 7 October 1997, Opinion of Judge Cassese, para. 45.

means, though, that there is nothing in the Article that would require the ICC to take the view that the relevant threat needs to be the sole cause of the conduct.

16.6.4   Mental element

As can be seen from Article 31(1)(d), the intention of the person seeking to rely on either defence must be to bring about the lesser of the two evils. In the words of the *Krupp* case, 'if, in the execution of the illegal act, the will of the accused be not thereby overpowered but instead coincides with the will of those from whom the alleged compulsion emanates, there is no necessity justifying the original conduct'.[92] Owing to the formulation of the mental aspect of this defence in the ICC Statute, 'provided that the person does not intend to cause a greater harm than the one sought to be avoided', it is not absolutely clear whether a distinction between actions undertaken to avoid the harm and their consequences is created.[93] If there is a distinction, then unintended excessive consequences of necessary and reasonable reactions are not to be taken into account. If there is no distinction, then the consequences, as well as the actions of the accused, must be necessary and reasonable. Basing himself on post-Second World War case law, Judge Cassese in the *Erdemović* case took the latter view.[94]

16.7   Mistake of fact and law[95]

Mistakes of fact and law are issues which tend to be dealt with differently by civil and common law systems. Civil law jurisdictions tend to be more generous with regard to mistakes of law, allowing for defences where there are reasonable mistakes relating to various aspects of crimes or defences.[96] Although there might be a trend away from this, in common law systems mistakes generally only provide an excuse when they serve to undermine *mens rea*, making the plea one of failure of proof.[97] Article 32 of the ICC Statute appears to adopt the, perhaps over-strict,[98] common law approach, providing that:

1. A mistake of fact shall be a ground for excluding criminal responsibility only if it negates the mental element required by the crime.
2. A mistake of law as to whether a particular type of conduct is a crime within the jurisdiction of the Court shall not be a ground for excluding criminal responsibility. A mistake of law may, however, be a ground for excluding criminal responsibility if it negates the mental element required by such a crime, or as provided for in article 33.

---

[92] *Krupp*, X LRTWC 69, 149.   [93] Against any distinction, see Ambos, 'Other Grounds', 1040.
[94] *Erdemović*, ICTY A. Ch., 7 October 1997, Opinion of Judge Cassese, para. 16.
[95] See generally Albin Eser, 'Mental Elements – Mistake of Fact and Mistake of Law' in Cassese, *Commentary*, 889, 934–46; van Sliedregt, *Individual Criminal Responsibility* Ch. 10; Ambos, *Treatise*, 368–76; Otto Triffterer, 'Article 32' in Triffterer, *Observers' Notes*, 895. Also, there is a 'grey zone' in which it is difficult to separate mistakes of fact and law: see Thomas Wiegend, 'The Harmonization of General Principles of Criminal Law: The Statutes and Jurisprudence of the ICTY, ICTR and the ICC: An Overview' (2004) 19 *Nouvelles études pénales* 319, 333.
[96] See George Fletcher, *Rethinking Criminal Law* (New York, 1978) 683–91.
[97] In relation to mistakes of law, these are relevant, for example, in relation to the requirement of dishonesty in theft.
[98] Ambos, *Treatise*, 375–6.

16.7.1   Mistake of fact

Article 32(1) is unequivocal. A mistake of fact is only relevant to liability if it serves to show that the defendant did not have the *mens rea*.[99] For example, if a person bombed a civilian bunker believing it was a military command centre, there would not be liability on the basis of this provision. Interestingly, Article 32(1) does not contain any express requirement that the mistake be a reasonable one.[100] One practical limitation, though, is that the less reasonable a belief is, the less likely it is that a claim that a person honestly held that belief will be accepted. Questions may arise about the situation where a person is at fault in making the mistake, such as if he or she was drunk or reckless when he or she decided what he or she believed.

From its terms, it seems that mistakes of fact which, if they were true, would provide the basis of a defence do not fall under Article 32, as they do not relate to *mens rea*.[101] Earlier cases allowed such mistakes to negate responsibility.[102] Beyond this, certain of the Elements of Crimes[103] (and the Statute itself, in Article 28, on command responsibility) exclude mistakes of fact where the person should have known of the relevant facts.[104]

16.7.2   Mistake of law

Like mistakes of fact, mistakes of law, with one exception (which, as we shall see, occurs with respect to superior orders), must negate *mens rea*. This defence does not include mistakes (or ignorance) about whether conduct is criminalized by the ICC Statute,[105] or whether a defence exists in law.[106] Nor does it deal with errors about the ambit of defences. The only acceptable mistake in Article 32(2) is where an element of a crime requires a legal evaluation, and the mistake relates to this, for example where a person takes property under a mistaken belief that he or she is its owner, or may lawfully take it.[107] Aggression could raise difficult issues in this regard, but the definition of the crime requires that there be a manifest violation of the UN Charter. So, even if 'an honest and reasonable belief that a use of force was not unlawful would be irrelevant to the satisfaction of [the] *mens rea* [of]

---

[99]   As such, a good case can be made that it adds little, if anything, to Art. 30's requirements on *mens rea*, Werle, *Principles*, 210.
[100] Cassese *et al.*, *International Criminal Law*, 222, appear to consider that any mistake must be reasonable to found a defence under Art. 32(1).
[101] Eser, 'Mental Elements', 945, argues that Art. 32(1) ought to apply by analogy to mistakes relating to justifications (as opposed to excuses), but the terms of Art. 32(1) do not provide particularly fertile soil for such arguments. See also Werle, *Principles*, 211; Ambos, *Treatise*, 374–5.
[102] See e.g. *United States v. List*, VIII LRTWC 1, 69.   [103] See e.g. Elements of Crimes, Art. 8(2)(b)(xxvi).
[104] Although the distinction ought to have relevance when it comes to describing the relevant conduct of the accused and determining the sentence of any convicted person.
[105] Such a point was made expressly in *Lubanga*, ICC PTC, 29 January 2007, para. 302. See Thomas Weigend, 'Intent, Mistake of Law and Co-Perpetration in the Lubanga Decision on Confirmation of Charges' (2008) 6 *Journal of International Criminal Justice* 471, 474–6.
[106] See Neil Boister, 'Reflections on the Relationship between the Duty to Educate in Humanitarian Law and the Absence of a Defence of Mistakes of Law in the Rome Statute' in Richard Burchill, Nigel White and Justin Morris (eds.), *International Conflict and Security Law* (Cambridge, 2005) 32, 38–43.
[107] For a broad view of what this would cover, see Kevin Jon Heller, 'Mistake of Legal Element, the Common Law, and Article 32 of the Rome Statute' (2008) 6 *Journal of International Criminal Justice* 419; for critique of Heller's view, see van Sliedregt, *Individual Criminal Responsibility*, 283–5.

aggression',[108] reasonable beliefs in legality would relate strongly to the 'manifest' nature of a violation.[109]

It has been suggested that, when the defence is made out, the use of 'may' in Article 33(2) implies that the ICC may convict the defendant nonetheless.[110] However, the fact that this defence is a plea of failure of proof (of *mens rea* in this instance) means this cannot be correct as it would involve convicting someone despite an element of the offence not being established.

16.8   Superior orders

The defence of superior orders has a lengthy history,[111] and reflects the tension between the importance of international law and of military discipline.[112] Originally, the tendency was to accept that orders amounted to a defence for those who carried them out, and thus that liability accrued to the person who ordered the offence, rather than the one who carried that order out.[113] This was not the clearly accepted position, though; even by the late nineteenth century there was significant evidence that the *respondeat superior* principle (i.e. the complete defence of superior orders) had been replaced by the rule that orders only protected a subordinate if they were not manifestly unlawful.[114] Such a position crystallized after the First World War, if not before.[115] The position seemed to change, however, with Article 8 of the Nuremberg IMT Statute, which read:

the fact that the defendant acted pursuant to an order of his government or of a superior shall not free him from responsibility, but may be considered in mitigation of punishment if the Tribunal determines that justice so requires.[116]

The Nuremberg IMT explained that provision as follows:

The provisions of this article are in conformity with the law of all nations. That a soldier was ordered to kill or torture in violation of the international law of war has never been recognised as a defence to such acts of brutality, though, as the Charter here provides, the order may be urged in mitigation of punishment. The true test, which is found in various degrees in the criminal law of most nations, is not the existence of the order, but whether moral choice was in fact possible.[117]

---

[108] Carrie McDougall, *The Crime of Aggression under the Rome Statute of the International Criminal Court* (Cambridge, 2012) 197.
[109] See further Chapter 13.   [110] See Boister, 'Reflections', 39; Eser, 'Mental Elements', 942.
[111] See Dinstein, *Superior Orders*, 93–103; van Sliedregt, *Individual Criminal Responsibility*, 287–92.
[112] See e.g. Martha Minow, 'Living Up to Rules: Holding Soldiers Responsible for Abusive Conduct and the Dilemma of the Superior Orders Defence' (2007) 52 *McGill Law Journal* 1.
[113] Lassa Oppenheim, *International Law* (London, 1906) Vol. II, 264–5.
[114] William Winthrop, *Military Law and Precedents* (Washington DC, 1896) 446–7.
[115] See e.g. *Llandovery Castle* (1922) 16 *American Journal of International Law* 708.
[116] Charter of the International Military Tribunal, annex to the London Agreement on the Prosecution and Punishment of the Major War Criminals of the European Axis Powers, 82 UNTS 279, Art. 8. Art. 6 of the Tokyo IMT Charter is largely the same: see Special Proclamation: Establishment of an International Military Tribunal for the Far East, 19 January 1946, TIAS No. 1589.
[117] Nuremberg IMT, Judgment and Sentences, reprinted in (1947) 41 *American Journal of International Law* 172, 221.

After this, and after General Assembly Resolution 95(1),[118] which affirmed the Nuremberg Charter and judgment, it might be thought that international law no longer permitted superior orders as a defence. However, case law and practice on the point from the period up to the creation of the ICTY was more equivocal.[119] The Genocide Convention, and the Geneva Conventions for example, contain no provision on superior orders, although the Torture Convention excludes reliance on them.[120] Article 7(4) of the ICTY Statute (and Article 6(4) of the ICTR Statute) essentially repeat Article 8 of the Nuremberg IMT Statute. The ICC Statute, on the other hand, takes a different track, largely returning to the 'manifest illegality' test.[121] The ICC Statute has been criticized for this, although such critiques rely on the (controversial) assertion that the Nuremberg IMT Charter reflects customary law.[122] Also, it must be remembered that the person giving the order will be responsible for his or her part in the crime whether or not the defence applies. Against this backdrop, Article 33 adopts a narrow view of the applicability of superior orders as a defence. Article 33 provides:

1. The fact that a crime within the jurisdiction of the Court has been committed pursuant to an order of a government or of a superior, whether military or civilian, shall not relieve that person of criminal responsibility unless:
    (a) That person was under a legal obligation to obey orders of the government or the superior in question;
    (b) The person did not know that the order was unlawful; and
    (c) The order was not manifestly unlawful.
2. For the purposes of this article, orders to commit genocide or crimes against humanity are manifestly unlawful.

As can be seen, Article 33 provides that superior orders are not a defence unless the three cumulative conditions are fulfilled.[123] Where, however, the conditions of defence under Article 33 are not fulfilled, the possibility of mitigation for those who acted under orders is not excluded.[124]

16.8.1   *Obligation to obey*

For the defence to apply, the person obeying the order must be under a legal obligation to obey orders in domestic law. This will be the case for soldiers in all countries, but civilians

---

[118] UN Doc. A/64/Add.1.
[119] Paolu Gaeta, 'The Defence of Superior Orders: The Statute of the International Criminal Court versus Customary International Law' (1999) 10 *European Journal of International Law* 172; *contra* Charles Garraway, 'Superior Orders and the International Criminal Court: Justice Delivered or Justice Denied?' (1999) 836 *International Review of the Red Cross* 785.
[120] Torture Convention 1984, Art. 2.
[121] Art. 6(4) of the SCSL Statute notably returns to the Nuremberg/Tokyo/ICTY/ICTR standard, as do the Statutes of other (varyingly authoritative) internationalized tribunals such as the STL and the ECCC: see Cassese *et al.*, *Cassese's International Criminal Law*, 229.
[122] Cassese, *International Criminal Law*, 228; Gaeta, 'Defence of Superior Orders'. It might be noted that in 1996 the ILC adopted the position that the Nuremberg provision was the relevant standard: see the Draft Code of Crimes against the Peace and Security of Mankind 1996, Art. 5.
[123] Werle, *Principles*, 217. The order must also have a causal link to the commission of the offence: van Sliedregt, *Criminal Responsibility*, 324.
[124] Werle, *Principles*, 218.

may be in a different position in different States. The reference in Article 33(1)(a) to 'orders' is deliberate. In some States, the obligation is only to obey *lawful* orders[125] and it was necessary to generalize the reference (to 'orders'), as otherwise in those States at any time the defence could apply there would be no obligation to obey the particular order. There have been suggestions that a superior/subordinate relationship is required.[126] This is only correct in so far as it could be an aspect of the requirement that there must be a legal obligation on the person to obey orders. This requirement creates an interesting question about the status of orders from rebel authorities and commanders. Owing to the requirement that there be a legal obligation to obey orders, it appears that such orders cannot form the basis of a defence of obedience.[127] Furthermore, it has been asserted that, if a person mistakenly believes himself or herself to be under an obligation to obey an order, a defence of mistake of law may be pleaded.[128] However, according to Article 32, mistakes of law only exculpate if they negate *mens rea* (or as provided in Article 33), and, since such a mistake would not do so, this would not apply here.

16.8.2   Knowledge of unlawfulness

The nature of the defence in the ICC Statute is, as implied by Article 32(2), an expanded form of a mistake of law defence.[129] Therefore, if a person knows that an order is unlawful, he or she cannot use that order as a defence. This undermines one asserted explanation of the defence, namely, that a subordinate is placed in a dilemma with respect to an unlawful order: either to obey and run the risk of criminal liability for an international crime, or to disobey and face liability for a military offence of disobedience.[130] For a person to be placed in such a situation, they would have to know that the order is unlawful, and so would be prohibited from relying on superior orders by Article 33. It is not always easy to determine what the person knew about the legality of the order, however.

16.8.3   Manifest illegality

Ignorance of the unlawfulness of the order is not enough to exempt a subordinate from liability. That ignorance must, in essence, be forgivable or, to put it another way, the subordinate must not be at fault in not knowing that the order was unlawful. The manifest illegality test now exists to help evaluate whether a defendant was culpably ignorant of the illegality of the order.[131] If an order is manifestly illegal, there is no defence that can be based on it, irrespective of whether or not the subordinate knew it was unlawful. It

---

[125]   In the United Kingdom, Armed Forces Act 2006, s.12(1).
[126]   Andreas Zimmermann, 'Superior Orders' in Cassese, *Commentary*, 957, 968.
[127]   *Ibid.*, 969; and see van Sliedregt, *Criminal Responsibility*, 323–4. Ambos is less certain of this: Ambos, *Treatise*, 381.
[128]   See Otto Triffterer, 'Article 33' in Triffterer, *Observers' Notes*, 915, 920–1, but see 926–7.
[129]   But not a plea of failure of proof. See Kreß, 'War Crimes', 150.
[130]   Where the obligation to obey orders is not limited to lawful orders.
[131]   Earlier cases sometimes used the test to determine if, in fact, the person knew the order was unlawful; see Dinstein, *Superior Orders*, 26–37.

must be remembered though that 'no sailor and no soldier can carry with him a library of international law, or have immediate access to a professor in that subject'.[132] Some cases have attempted to provide a definition of manifest illegality. The *Eichmann* case, for example stated that:

The distinguishing mark of a 'manifestly unlawful order' should fly like a black flag above the order given … Not formal unlawfulness, hidden or half-hidden, nor unlawfulness discernible only to the eyes of legal experts, but a flagrant and manifest breach of the law.[133]

The 'High Command' case, however, framed the test as whether the order was 'criminal on its face'.[134] The *Finta* case in Canada said an order could not be relied upon if it was 'so outrageous as to be manifestly unlawful'.[135] It might be questioned, however, whether any of these formulations provide a clear standard. The question remains (analogously to the test of reasonableness in duress): manifest to whom?[136] A different standard may be expected, for example, of fully trained army lawyers or high-ranking officials from that of young, low-ranking soldiers who are on their first tour of duty. The role of culture, propaganda and 'common knowledge' may also be relevant to the extent to which unlawfulness is manifest.[137] Whether or not such considerations are appropriately integrated into the manifest illegality test, and, if they are to be, to what extent, is not without controversy, as in many circumstances succumbing to ideas that international criminal law finds fundamentally objectionable is in itself wrongful.[138] The Canadian War Crimes and Crimes against Humanity Act attempts to deal with this difficulty by providing that:

An accused cannot base their defence … [of superior orders] on a belief that an order was lawful if the belief was based on information about a civilian population or an identifiable group of persons that encouraged, was likely to encourage or attempted to justify the commission of inhumane acts or omissions against the population or group.[139]

16.8.4 Genocide and crimes against humanity

Article 33(2) was intended to ensure that superior orders could be pleaded in cases involving war crimes (or, possibly, aggression) but not genocide or crimes against humanity. The wording, however, is unfortunate, as it focuses on 'orders to commit genocide or crimes against humanity' rather than focusing on the perpetrator's *mens rea*.[140] It also, illegitimately, assumes that every example of a war crime will necessarily be less serious than

---

[132] *Peleus*, 13 ILR 248, 249.   [133] *Attorney-General of Israel v. Eichmann*, 36 ILR 277.   [134] *Von Leeb*, XII LRTWC 1, 74.
[135] *R v. Finta*, 104 ILR 285, 322.
[136] For a discussion of one State's relevant cases, see Ziv Bohrer, 'Clear and Obvious? A Critical Examination of the Superior Orders Defense in Israeli Case Law' (2005–2006) 2 *Israel Defence Force Law Review* 197. See also Larry May, *Crimes against Humanity: A Normative Account* (Cambridge, 2005) 185–7.
[137] See e.g. Mark Osiel, *Mass Atrocity, Ordinary Evil and Hannah Arendt: Criminal Consciousness in Argentina's Dirty War* (New Haven, CT, 2001).
[138] Arne J. Vetlesen, *Evil and Human Agency, Understanding Collective Evildoing* (Cambridge, 2005) Chapter 5.
[139] 2000, c. 24, s. 14(3).
[140] See further Robert Cryer, 'Superior Orders in the International Criminal Court' in Burchill, White and Morris (eds.), *Conflict and Security*, 49, 63–7.

every example of a crime against humanity and (perhaps more legitimately) every example of genocide.[141]

The amendments to the ICC Statute relating to aggression, if and when they come into force, do not exclude the general principles of liability in the Statute and the possibility of superior orders being a defence cannot entirely be excluded. The conditions for liability for aggression, in particular that the defendant be at a 'policy' level and that the violation of the UN Charter be 'manifest', render it very unlikely that such a defence would succeed,[142] even though the concepts of manifest illegality and manifest violation of the Charter in Article 33(1)(c) and Article 8*bis*(1) were not specifically drafted with each other in mind.

16.8.5   *The relationship of superior orders to other defences*

The existence of superior orders may also give rise to other defences, in particular mistake of fact and duress. If an order contains a factual assertion, such as 'bomb the enemy arms cache at' particular coordinates, and it turns out that the building at those coordinates is a hospital, the order forms the factual underpinning for a defence of mistake of fact, rather than superior orders, as the factual basis asserted in the order would undermine *mens rea*. Duress may be relevant because, as Judge Cassese stated in *Erdemović*:

> Superior orders may be issued without being accompanied by any threats to life or limb. In these circumstances, if the superior order is manifestly illegal under international law, the subordinate is under a duty to refuse to obey the order. If, following such a refusal, the order is reiterated under a threat to life or limb, then the defence of duress may be raised, and superior orders lose any legal relevance.[143]

The way in which Article 33 of the ICC Statute is framed renders the defence in the ICC an expanded form of a mistake of law defence. It is expanded as it does not require the mistake of legality to undermine *mens rea*.[144]

16.9   Other 'defences'

There are other defences that may apply in international criminal law which are not directly enumerated in the ICC Statute. The three main defences falling under this head are consent and (more controversially) reprisals and military necessity.[145] The new amendments to the ICC Statute on aggression do not include any new defences to the crime. A justification by a

---

[141] Zimmermann, 'Superior Orders', 972; Triffterer, 'Article 33', 928. See also s. 3 of the German Code of Crimes against International Law, which applies the manifest illegality principle to all crimes.

[142] McDougall, *Crime of Aggression*, 198.

[143] *Erdemović*, ICTY A. Ch., 7 October 1997, Separate and Dissenting Opinion of Judge Cassese, para. 15. Although orders lose their legal relevance, they retain an evidentiary one.

[144] Cryer, 'Superior Orders', 58–60.

[145] *Tu quoque*, a plea that others (in particular, prosecuting States) have committed similar offences, is not a defence in law: *Kupreškic et al.*, ICTY T. Ch. II, 14 January 2000, paras. 515–20; *Kunarac*, ICTY A. Ch., 12 June 2002, para. 87; although, admittedly, it can affect the legitimacy of proceedings. See e.g. Robert Cryer, *Prosecuting International Crimes: Selectivity and the International Criminal Law Regime* (Cambridge, 2005) Chapter 4.

State for a use of force, such as self-defence under Article 51 of the UN Charter, will be pleaded by the defendant not as a separate defence to a charge of aggression but as a failure of proof of an essential element of the crime.

16.9.1   *Consent*

Certain offences, in particular sexual offences, are subject to 'defences' of consent.[146] Indeed, the absence of consent is a definitional aspect of some international crimes. However, as many situations in which international crimes occur are inherently coercive, especially when people are confined, the reality of any consent must be carefully investigated,[147] and assumptions about autonomy that are the norm in domestic law are not necessarily applicable in international criminal law.[148]

The ICTY has been sceptical of claims of consent in the circumstances that surround international crimes, in particular with respect to sexual offences.[149] In the *Kunarac* case, for example, the Appeals Chamber has said that 'the circumstances giving rise to the present appeal and that prevail in most cases charged as either war crimes or crimes against humanity will be almost universally coercive. That is to say, true consent will not be possible.'[150] The ICTR has held that the prosecution must prove that consent was not present.[151] However, owing to the nature of international crimes, it added that 'the Trial Chamber is free to infer non-consent from the background circumstances, such as an ongoing genocide or the detention of the victim' rather than the specific relationship between the defendant and the victim.[152] Similarly, rather than proving that the accused did not know of the lack of consent, it suffices that 'the accused was aware, or had reason to be aware, of the coercive circumstances that undermined the possibility of genuine consent'.[153]

In relation to sexual offences, the ICC Elements of Crimes vitiate any purported consent where certain offences are committed 'by force, or by threat of force or coercion, such as that caused by fear of violence, duress, detention, psychological oppression or abuse of power, against such person or another person, or by taking advantage of a coercive environment, or the invasion was committed against a person incapable of

---

[146] See e.g. William Schabas, *The UN International Criminal Tribunals: The Former Yugoslavia, Rwanda and Sierra Leone* (Cambridge, 2006) 341–3. Outside this context, Art. 52 of Geneva Convention III also only allows certain forms of work to be undertaken by prisoners-of-war if they consent.

[147] *Naletilić and Martinović*, ICTY T. Ch. I, 31 March 2003, para. 519, saw the test as being of 'true' or 'real' consent. In *Kunarac, Kovać and Vuković*, ICTY A. Ch., 12 June 2002, paras. 132–3, the Chamber notes that, in the circumstances of the victim's detention, 'the circumstances . . . were so coercive as to negate any possibility of consent', although it appeared (*ibid.*, para. 131) to consider that consent was not an element of the offence. In most cases relating to international crimes it is difficult to think of situations in which consent would be a genuine issue. See Wolfgang Schomburg and Ines Peterson, 'Genuine Consent to Sexual Violence under International Criminal Law' (2007) 101 *American Journal of International Law* 121, 128–31. More generally, see Noëlle Quinevet, *Sexual Offences in Armed Conflict and International Law* (The Hague, 2005).

[148] Schomburg and Peterson, 'Genuine Consent', 125 *et seq*.

[149] *Ibid.* See also Catharine MacKinnon, 'The ICTR's Legacy on Sexual Violence' (2008) 14 *New England Journal of International and Comparative Law* 101.

[150] *Kunarac, Kovać and Vuković*, ICTY A. Ch., 12 June 2002, para. 130.

[151] *Gacumbitsi*, ICTR A. Ch., 7 July 2006, para. 153.   [152] *Ibid.*, para. 155.

[153] *Ibid.*, para. 157; see also Schomburg and Peterson, 'Genuine Consent', 137–8. In relation to the crime of forced marriage which is not, according to the Special Court for Sierra Leone, inherently a sexual offence, consent was an issue which was, in the circumstances, necessarily excluded: *Prosecutor* v. *Brima Kamara and Kanu*, SCSL A. Ch., 22 February 2008, paras. 187–203.

giving genuine consent'.[154] Owing to the sensitivity of evidence relating to consent, the ICC Rules of Procedure and Evidence set up a special regime for when and how the court is to hear it.[155] This is a careful balance of the facts that almost inevitably surround international crimes, and the (remote) possibility that a defendant might genuinely believe in the existence of consent. Outside this context, the ICC has rejected the defence of consent with respect to the charge of use of child soldiers.[156] Given the soft paternalist justification of the criminalization of child soldiers, which is not inherently illiberal,[157] this is supportable.

16.9.2   *Reprisals*

Reprisals are responses to violations of humanitarian law that would themselves otherwise amount to violations of that law.[158] They are a crude and often dangerous form of law enforcement, but remain lawful in limited situations, and subject to a number of stringent requirements. The ICTY summed up those restrictions as being:

(a) the principle whereby they must be a last resort in attempts to impose compliance by the adversary with legal standards (which entails, amongst other things, that they may be exercised only after a prior warning has been given which has failed to bring about the discontinuance of the adversary's crimes); (b) the obligation to take special precautions before implementing them (they may be taken only after a decision to this effect has been made at the highest political or military level; in other words they may not be decided by local commanders); (c) the principle of proportionality (which entails not only that the reprisals must not be excessive compared to the precedent unlawful act of warfare, but also that they must stop as soon as that unlawful act has been discontinued); and (d) 'elementary considerations of humanity'.[159]

There are prohibitions on reprisals against the wounded, sick and shipwrecked, prisoners-of-war, interned civilians and those in occupied territories,[160] which are considered customary.[161] The prohibitions on reprisals against other civilians and against cultural property, laid down in Articles 51.6 and 53(c) Additional Protocol I, are of a more dubious customary status.[162] The ICTY, in the *Kupreškić* case, asserted that they were customary; however, this conclusion has been the subject of significant academic critique,[163] and the United

---

[154] Elements of Crimes, Art. 8(2)(b)(xxii)–1; this includes, 'natural, induced or age-related incapacity'. Other elements also note that 'genuine consent' can be vitiated through deception: see e.g. Elements of Crimes, Art. 8(2)(b)(xxii)–5.

[155] Rules 70–72. See also r. 96 of the respective RPEs of the ICTY and ICTR.

[156] *Lubanga*, ICC PTC, 29 January 2007, para. 247.

[157] I.e. intervention to trump the choices of a person who is not fully autonomous (e.g. a child). See e.g. Joel Feinberg, *Harm to Self* (Oxford, 1986).

[158] As such, there is no evidence that reprisals could be a defence to crimes against humanity or genocide.

[159] *Kupreškić et al.*, ICTY T. Ch. II, 14 January 2000, para. 535.

[160] Art. 46 of Geneva Convention I; Art. 47 of Geneva Convention II; Art. 13 of Geneva Convention III; Art. 33 of Geneva Convention IV.

[161] Henckaerts and Doswald-Beck, *ICRC Customary Law*, 519–20.

[162] *Kupreškić et al.*, ICTY T. Ch. II, 14 January 2000, paras. 527–35.

[163] Christopher Greenwood, 'Belligerent Reprisals in the Jurisprudence of the International Criminal Tribunal for the Former Yugoslavia' in Horst Fischer, Claus Kreß and Sascha Rolf Lüder (eds.), *International and National Prosecution of Crimes under International Law* (Berlin, 2001) 359. See also Kreß, 'War Crimes', 153 *et seq*.

Kingdom's military manual expressly disavows this conclusion.[164] Another ICTY Trial
Chamber, in the *Martić* case, did not follow the *Kupreškić* decision on point, and was
implicitly upheld on point by the Appeals Chamber, which appraised the relevant actions
with reference to the criteria applicable to lawful reprisals rather than relying upon a blanket
customary ban on reprisals.[165]

16.9.3 *Military necessity*[166]

Military necessity is no longer, if it ever was, a general defence. As was said in the
'Hostages' case, '[m]ilitary necessity or expediency do not justify a violation of positive
rules ... [which are] superior to military necessities of the most urgent nature except where
the regulations themselves specifically provide to the contrary'.[167] Thus, it is only a defence
where rules expressly incorporate it as, for example, Article 8(2)(a)(iv) of the ICC Statute,
and perhaps Article 31(1)(c), do. It is difficult to define in the abstract what is or is not a
matter of military necessity, but two things are reasonably clear: neither mere expediency[168]
nor political necessity[169] is sufficient.[170]

Further reading

Kai Ambos, *Treatise on International Criminal Law*, Vol. I, *Foundations and General Part*
(Oxford, 2013) Chapter 8
Antonio Cassese, *International Criminal Law*, 2nd edn (Oxford, 2008) Chapters 12–13
Roger Clark, 'The Mental Element in International Criminal Law: The Rome Statute of the
International Criminal Court and the Elements of Offences' (2002) 12 *Criminal Law
Forum* 291
Robert Cryer, *Prosecuting International Crimes: Selectivity and the International Criminal
Law Regime* (Cambridge, 2005) Chapter 6
Yoram Dinstein, 'Defences' in Gabrielle Kirk McDonald and Olivia Swaak-Goldman (eds.),
Substantive and Procedural Aspects of International Criminal Law (The Hague,
2000) Vol. I, 367
Albin Eser, 'Article 31' in Triffterer, *Observers' Notes*, 863
Leslie Green, *Superior Orders in National and International Law* (Leiden, 1976)
Frits Kalshoven, *Belligerent Reprisals* (Leiden, 1976)
Matthew Lippman, 'Conundrums of Armed Conflict: Criminal Defences to Violations of the
Humanitarian Law of War' (1996) 15 *Dickinson Journal of International Law* 1
Larry May, *Crimes against Humanity: A Normative Account* (Cambridge, 2005) Chapter 10
Larry May, *War Crimes and Just War* (Cambridge, 2007) Chapter 13
Mark Osiel, *Obeying Orders: Atrocities, Military Discipline and the Law of War* (New
Brunswick, NJ, 1999)

---

[164] Ministry of Defence, *Manual of the Law of Armed Conflict* (Oxford, 2004) 421.
[165] *Martić*, ICTY T. Ch., 12 July 2007, paras. 464–8; *Martić*, ICTY A. Ch., 8 October 2008, paras. 263–7.
[166] See further van Sliedregt, *Criminal Responsibility*, 295–8; Hayashi, 'Military Necessity'. [167] *List*, VIII LRTWC 66–9.
[168] Geoffrey Best, *Humanity in Warfare* (London, 1983) 64. [169] Commentary, XV LRTWC 176.
[170] For a useful and very detailed discussion of the case law on point, see Hayashi, 'Military Necessity'.

Massimo Scaliotti, 'Defences before the International Criminal Court' Parts 1 and 2 (2001) 1 *International Criminal Law Review* 111 and (2002) 2 *International Criminal Law Review* 1

William Schabas, *The UN International Criminal Tribunals: The Former Yugoslavia, Rwanda and Sierra Leone* (Cambridge, 2006) 325–47.

Otto Triffterer, 'Article 33' in Triffterer, *Observers' Notes*, 915

Elies van Sliedregt, *Individual Responsibility in International Criminal Law* (Oxford, 2012) Part 3

Part E

Principles and Procedures
of International Prosecutions

17

Procedures of International Criminal Investigations and Prosecutions

17.1 International criminal procedures

17.1.1 Introduction

From the Nuremberg trials onwards, the need to develop a procedural system for any new international criminal tribunal has been acknowledged.[1] Such a procedural system would be *sui generis* in the sense that it would depart from any one domestic system or legal tradition. But, inevitably, it would incorporate elements from the major domestic legal systems of the world, thus enhancing the perceived legitimacy of the tribunal and its proceedings. As will be further developed in this chapter, different solutions have been chosen.[2]

From being a rather underdeveloped field in the international tribunal discourse, international criminal procedures are now widely discussed and debated. The different procedural schemes are compared and assessed. They influence each other and possibly also domestic law and practice. After all, the quality of the procedural law and the efficiency of the institutional structure in which it is to be interpreted and applied are key to the ability of the court or tribunal to fulfil its mandate and to meet the highest standard of fairness and due process. Hence, international criminal procedures are emerging as a new branch of law and academic discipline.[3]

This chapter will briefly introduce some general features of the criminal procedures of international criminal courts and tribunals, in particular the ICTY, ICTR and ICC. The procedures will thereafter be outlined with a particular focus on the ICC: the ICC is a permanent institution while the others are temporary and in the process of winding down.[4]

---

[1] As late as 1983, however, some argued that, absent substantive international criminal law and international criminal jurisdictions, there were also no international criminal procedures: see Georg Schwarzenberger, 'Province of International Judicial Law' (1983) 1 *Notre Dame International Law Journal* 21.

[2] Apart from the ICTY, ICTR and ICC, one should also note the special and different procedural schemes of the 'internationalized courts', the SCSL, ECCC, and STL. See also Chapter 9.

[3] See Sluiter, *International Criminal Procedure*, 1–7.

[4] For a comparative approach, see instead the earlier editions of this book. See also e.g. Boas, *Practitioner Library*, Vol. III; and Sluiter, *International Criminal Procedure*.

17.1.2   *Different legal traditions*

There is a significant distinction between the criminal procedures of two major domestic legal traditions: the common law tradition (or Anglo-American tradition) and the civil law tradition (or Continental or Romano-Germanic tradition). The dichotomy between the two traditions is commonly used to describe and evaluate the criminal procedures of the international criminal jurisdictions, often with a preference expressed for the legal tradition that the commentator knows best. While the blending of elements from the two legal traditions will be noted here too, in general the emphasis should be placed on whether the procedural solutions meet interests such as fair trial rights or effectiveness and efficiency.

Although these traditions go beyond the system of criminal procedures,[5] the common law model is said to be 'adversarial' or 'accusatorial' and the civil law model 'inquisitorial'. No domestic system represents a pure model, however, and there are considerable differences between systems belonging to the same tradition.[6] Moreover, some systems, for example in Scandinavia, do not really belong to either of the two traditions. In spite of shortcomings,[7] we shall here use the terms 'adversarial' and 'inquisitorial' to describe in a general sense differences attributed to the two traditions, but also, on occasion, we shall resort to the common law and civil law labels.

While both systems aim at finding the truth,[8] the means and methods vary. A fundamental difference is the role of the parties and of the judges. The 'adversarial' model, as the term suggests, is premised on two adversarial parties each bringing its case to court, the prosecution and the defence. Hence, the two parties conduct their own investigations and the role of the judge at trial is (traditionally) like a referee, mainly deciding procedural issues raised by the parties – a system that fits well with jury trials. In the 'inquisitorial' model, by contrast, State agencies are obliged to carry out objective criminal investigations and prosecutions and, essentially, only one case is presented to the court. Defence interests are looked after in the investigation, and there is judicial supervision, often by an examining judge (*juge d'instruction*). The prosecutor and the examining judge instruct the police, and a 'dossier' is assembled for the entire case. The trial judge is a different person from the examining judge, but will have access to the 'dossier'. The judge plays a much more active and intervening role at trial, with an explicit task to 'seek the truth'. These differences have effects throughout the proceedings and have led to different procedures.

Ideally, elements from different domestic legal systems should be incorporated in international procedural rules with a view to creating a coherent whole, providing for fair and yet effective proceedings. For the perception of legitimacy and acceptance, the ICC with a broad

---

[5] Not only legal but also sociological and cultural differences are espoused by the different legal traditions.

[6] Regarding Europe, see e.g. Mireille Delmas-Marty and John R. Spencer (eds.), *European Criminal Procedure* (Cambridge, 2002).

[7] See e.g. Kai Ambos, 'International Criminal Procedure: "Adversarial", "Inquisitorial" or Mixed?' (2003) 3 *International Criminal Law Review* 1 (noting that modern systems depart from the traditional 'inquisitorial' model, where prosecutor and judge are one and the same, and that both models are 'accusatorial' in nature).

[8] It is sometimes said that the civil law system aims at establishing 'objective truth', as a necessary precondition for a just decision, and the common law system rather seeks 'procedural truth', with an emphasis on a just settlement of a dispute; see e.g. Zappalà, *Human Rights*, 16.

geographical jurisdiction may have a greater need for mixed influences than a tribunal for a particular conflict. But blending elements from different legal traditions is not without its problems and adversarial and inquisitorial features are not always compatible. Furthermore, political considerations (and perhaps nationalistic pride) require compromises, which in turn may result in untested solutions or overly flexible rules; procedural efficiency and fair trial rights could thereby be affected.

Apart from the need to achieve broad acceptance, there are other reasons for a mixed model. Adversarial principles are generally attractive for fulfilling the fair trial rights of the accused as laid down in international human rights instruments.[9] On the other hand, procedures that require the suspect or accused to conduct his or her investigation in preparation of a separate case may prove difficult, or even impossible, in international criminal proceedings dependent upon State cooperation.[10] Moreover, the focus on objective truth-finding in inquisitorial systems may better serve, for example, the aim of creating an 'accurate historical record'. A less two-party-centred process also allows the crime victims a more pronounced role, and increased judicial control may enhance the efficiency of the proceedings and the acceptance of broad prosecutorial powers.

17.1.3 *Procedural law of international criminal tribunals and courts*

Special criminal procedures were established for the Nuremberg and Tokyo IMTs, but except for some general principles the procedures were mainly judge-made law. Basic provisions were laid down in the respective Charters.[11] In addition, the Charters provided for Rules of Procedure to be established by each tribunal.[12] The procedures were influenced by domestic procedural principles, primarily from the Anglo-American adversarial system. But the Nuremberg procedures also had some inquisitorial elements, such as allowing trials *in absentia*, giving the defendant a right to explain himself or herself at a preliminary hearing, relaxed rules on admissibility of evidence, and trial by a panel of judges instead of a jury. When assessed by the standards of the day, the criminal procedures were essentially fair.[13] Measured against today's standards, however, the protections were minimal and did not include, for example, a right to remain silent or to appeal against a conviction. The subsequent trials in Germany under Control Council Law No. 10 were conducted under

---

[9] Indeed, the detailed minimum guarantees laid down in Art. 14 of the ICCPR are based on the Anglo-Saxon common law tradition of 'due process of law'; see Manfred Nowak, *UN Covenant on Civil and Political Rights – CCPR Commentary*, 2nd edn (Kehl, Strasbourg and Arlington, VA, 2005) 305.

[10] This may work both ways, however, and sometimes the accused will have much better access to State archives and other information than the international prosecutor (e.g. in the former Yugoslavia). But, in other instances, such as after a regime change (e.g. in Rwanda), the accused could be completely barred from access to the State where the investigation is to be conducted.

[11] Arts. 16 (fair trial rights), 17–25 (powers and trial procedures) and 26–29 (judgment and sentence) of the Nuremberg Charter and Arts. 9–10 (fair trial), 11–15 (powers and trial procedures), and 16–17 (judgment and sentence) of the Tokyo Charter.

[12] Art. 13 of the Nuremberg Charter and Art. 7 of the Tokyo Charter. The Nuremberg Rules, adopted on 29 October 1945, and the Tokyo RPE, promulgated on 25 April 1946, contained a few more detailed procedural provisions.

[13] The argument has been made that the trials as such contravened the principle of legality, but such criticisms are directed more against the substantive law than the criminal procedures; see section 1.5.1.

criminal procedures established by the commanders of the different zones of occupation.[14] Other trials, both in Europe and in the Far East, were conducted by individual States, applying domestic procedural law.

The ICTY and ICTR Statutes, adopted by the Security Council, include only a few basic procedural provisions; further detail was left to the judges to establish in the form of Rules of Procedure and Evidence (RPE). The approach was that the RPE had to reflect 'concepts that are generally recognised as being fair and just in the international arena',[15] and an early ICTY Trial Chamber decision[16] explained that the procedures were a 'unique amalgam of common and civil law features' and did not 'strictly follow the procedure of civil law or common law'. In fact, however, the Tribunals' procedures, which are similar but not identical, are mainly adversarial in nature. The RPE for the Tribunals were experimental[17] and have been amended many times, leading to criticism regarding legal certainty and fairness.[18] Many of the amendments have been in an inquisitorial direction, *inter alia* increasing the judges' controlling powers with the aim of reducing the length of the proceedings.[19] In addition to written law, the ICTY and ICTR judges have resorted to the so-called 'inherent powers' of the Tribunal in seeking out procedures.[20] Notable examples are a decision in *Tadić* on the competence to ascertain the Tribunal's jurisdiction and one in *Blaškić* regarding the issuance of binding orders to States.[21] Inherent powers have also been resorted to for more routine matters such as the withdrawal of counsel[22] and ordering disclosure.[23] In order to wind down the operations of the Tribunals, the Residual Mechanism has been established with a Statute adopted by the Security Council, and RPE, drawing upon the ICTY and ICTR RPE, adopted by the judges.[24] The Mechanism will conduct some trial and appeals proceedings, but may not open new investigations or issue any new indictments except with respect to contempt of court and perjury.[25]

---

[14] Art. III.2 of Control Council Law No. 10. In the United States zone of occupation, general criminal procedures were set forth for example in Ordinance No. 7 of Military Government for Germany, United States Zone, and more specific provisions were adopted by the established military tribunals, e.g. the Rules of Procedure of Military Tribunal I, adopted on 2 November 1946 and later amended. Later, Uniform Rules of Procedure were adopted for all military tribunals in the US zone. See generally Kevin Jon Heller, *The Nuremberg Military Tribunals and the Origins of International Criminal Law* (Oxford, 2011).

[15] Annual Report of the International Tribunal for the Prosecution of Persons Responsible for Serious Violations of International Humanitarian Law Committed in the Territory of the Former Yugoslavia since 1991, UN Doc. A/49/342-S/1994/1007, para. 53 (hereinafter 'First ICTY Report to the UN, 1994').

[16] *Tadić*, ICTY T. Ch. II, 5 August 1996, para. 14. Similarly, *Delalić et al.*, ICTY T. Ch. II, 1 May 1997, para. 15.

[17] See also the First ICTY Report to the UN, 1994, para. 54 (stressing that the Tribunal had little by way of precedent to guide it when drafting the RPE).

[18] On 22 May 2013, the 49th revised version of the ICTY RPE was adopted, and version 21 of the ICTR RPE on 9 February 2010. For a critical view, see e.g. Andreas O'Shea, 'Changing the Rules of the Game in the Middle of Play: The Dilemma of Procedural Development in the Rwanda Tribunal' (2001) 14 *South African Journal of Criminal Justice* 233.

[19] E.g. Daryl Mundis, 'From "Common Law" towards "Civil Law": The Evolution of the ICTY Rules of Procedure and Evidence' (2001) 14 *Leiden Journal of International Law* 367.

[20] E.g. Louise Symons, 'The Inherent Powers of the ICTY and ICTR' (2003) 3 *International Criminal Law Review* 369.

[21] *Tadić*, ICTY A. Ch., 2 October 1995, paras. 14–20 (a power often referred to as '*Kompetenz-Kompetenz*' or '*la compétence de la compétence*'); *Blaškić*, ICTY T. Ch. II, 18 July 1997, paras. 30–40, and ICTY A. Ch., 29 October 1997, paras. 25–31 (also explaining that 'inherent powers' is preferably used for functions that are judicial in nature, while 'implied powers' is often used in relation to expanded competencies).

[22] E.g. *Delalić et al.*, ICTY A. Ch., 24 June 1999.   [23] E.g. *Tadić*, ICTY A. Ch., 15 July 1999, para. 322.

[24] The MICT Statute is attached to SC Res. 1966(2010) of 22 December 2010. The power to adopt RPE is set out in Art. 13 of the MICT Statute, and the first version of the RPE was adopted on 8 June 2012.

[25] Art. 1 of the MICT Statute.

The ICC Statute is a treaty negotiated by States. The ILC draft Statute, much inspired by the procedural law of the ICTY and ICTR, reflected a basically adversarial approach. But, during the negotiations, more inquisitorial features were proposed and incorporated,[26] partly as a reaction against the ICTY and ICTR procedures. Huge efforts were made towards finding solutions satisfactory to the different legal traditions, resulting in agreement on important 'bridges' between the two traditions such as a pre-trial chamber and the procedure in case of admission of guilt. In addition to the very detailed procedural regime they negotiated in the ICC Statute, the States also reserved for themselves the powers to formulate the RPE.[27] This departs from the practice of other international courts and tribunals where the adoption of procedural law is left to the judges, a practice that promotes flexibility but may cause principled objections.[28] The ICC judges were, however, given the power to adopt Regulations of the Court,[29] which in practice also regulate procedural matters of substantive importance. Together with other normative texts, the procedural law of the ICC has become voluminous, multi-layered and complex. As a result of the practical experiences thus far, the Court has initiated a process for procedural improvements – 'Lessons Learned' – which includes proposals for amendments to the RPE and other statutory documents.[30]

While influenced by domestic procedures, the ICTY, ICTR and ICC thus all have mixed systems with adversarial as well as inquisitorial elements, albeit that the procedures are primarily adversarial in nature. Seen as a whole, each procedural system is unprecedented and may be considered as unique (*sui generis*).[31] At least to an extent, the traditional common law and civil law divide has been overcome.[32] But some lawyers are uneasy about the hybrid systems created, which depart from the mature and carefully structured balance of domestic systems.[33] At the ICC, the uncertainty is exacerbated by the fact that

---

[26] On the ICC negotiations, see Silvia Fernàndez de Gurmendi, 'International Criminal Law Procedures: The Process of Negotiations' in Lee, *The Making of the Rome Statute*, 217–27; and Silvia Fernàndez de Gurmendi and Håkan Friman, 'The Rules of Procedure and Evidence of the International Criminal Court' (2000) 3 *Yearbook of International Humanitarian Law* 289, and 'The Rules of Procedure and Evidence and Regulations of the Court' in Doria, *Legal Regime*, 797–824.

[27] Art. 51 of the ICC Statute (which allows the judges to adopt amendments to the RPE under certain conditions, but only on a provisional basis and subject to the approval of the ICC States Parties).

[28] E.g. Claus Kreß, 'The Procedural Texts of the International Criminal Court' (2007) 5 *Journal of International Criminal Justice* 537, 538. See also David Hunt, 'The International Criminal Court: High Hopes, "Creative Ambiguity" and an Unfortunate Mistrust in International Judges' (2004) 2 *Journal of International Criminal Justice* 56.

[29] Art. 52 of the ICC Statute.

[30] The ASP has set up a structure for dealing with amendments, and the Court has produced a 'road map' of procedural issues to be considered: see Study Group on Governance: Lessons Learnt: First Report of the Court to the Assembly of States Parties, ICC-ASP/11/31/Add.1, Annex. On 21 November 2012, the first amendment to the RPE, proposed by the Court, was adopted by the ASP; Res. ICC-ASP//11/Res.2. A proposal by the Court requires the approval of an absolute majority of the judges: Art. 51(2)(b) of the ICC Statute.

[31] E.g. *Delalić et al.*, ICTY T. Ch. II, 1 May 1997, para. 15. See e.g. Patrick Robinson, 'Ensuring Fair and Expeditious Trials at the International Criminal Tribunal for the Former Yugoslavia' (2000) 11 *European Journal of International Law* 569, 574 (the ICTY procedures are 'neither common law accusatorial nor civil law inquisitorial, nor even an amalgam of both; it is *sui generis*'). Similarly, Ambos, 'International Criminal Procedure', 34–5; and Gabrielle Kirk McDonald, 'Trial Procedures and Practice' in McDonald and Goldman, *Substantive and Procedural Aspects*, 556. Cf. Máxime Langer, 'The Rise of Managerial Judging in International Criminal Law' (2005) 53 *American Journal of Comparative Law* 835 (claiming that the ICTY's procedures are neither unique nor represent an undefined hybrid system).

[32] But whether this reflected a real development towards a new, fused procedural tradition more generally or was just the result of the political wish to establish the ICC is a debated issue; see e.g. Mark Findlay, 'Synthesis in Trial Proceedings? The Experience of International Criminal Tribunals' (2001) 50 *International and Comparative Law Quarterly* 26.

[33] E.g. Vladimir Tochilovsky, 'International Criminal Justice: Strangers in the Foreign System' (2004) 15 *Criminal Law Forum* 319.

'technical terms' with a special meaning are avoided.[34] In any case, domestic notions, legal constructs and terms of art should not be 'mechanically imported into international proceedings'; they must be understood against the object and purpose of the international proceedings.[35]

These institutions serve as models for international criminal justice and a source of inspiration for the development of domestic proceedings,[36] as well as for the procedures of the 'internationalized criminal courts'. It is important to bear in mind, however, that these international criminal procedures were never devised to be adopted in States' domestic systems and have been framed against the specific circumstances applicable to the international jurisdictions; they might not always and in every respect represent 'best practice' for States.

17.1.4   Sources of international criminal procedure

As already noted,[37] the primary sources of procedural law in the ICTY, ICTR, the Residual Mechanism and the ICC are their respective Statutes and, secondarily, their Rules of Procedure and Evidence. In addition, there are other legal instruments adopted by the tribunal or court itself.[38] But there is still a need to seek recourse to external sources. The Tribunals have resorted to traditional sources set forth in Article 38 of the ICJ Statute: international treaties, international custom, and 'general principles of law recognized by civilized nations'.[39]

The ICC Statute contains explicit provisions exposing a hierarchy of sources. As a second tier, Article 21(1) provides that 'applicable treaties and the principles and rules of international law' apply 'where appropriate'; a formula that also encompasses customary international law. But domestic procedures are so diverse that it is often difficult to argue customary law status, although to some extent principles are conceived so uniformly that domestic law analogies are relevant. Meaningful conclusions require extensive comparative research, something the Chambers rarely have time or resources to do. Nor is consistent practice among the international criminal jurisdictions sufficient to establish 'customary law', which evolves from State practice and *opinio iuris*. Hence, 'general principles' are a more promising source with respect to procedural law; this is also the third tier of applicable

---

[34] See e.g. Kai Ambos and Dennis Miller, 'Structure and Function of the Confirmation Procedure before the ICC from a Comparative Perspective' (2007) 7 *International Criminal Law Review* 335, 337–40.

[35] See Judge Cassese's Dissenting Opinion in *Erdemović*, ICTY A. Ch., 7 October 1997, paras. 1–6.

[36] E.g. Göran Sluiter, 'The Law of International Criminal Procedure and Domestic War Crimes Trials' (2006) 6 *International Criminal Law Review* 605.

[37] See section 17.1.3 and, concerning the ICC, section 8.5. See also section 1.3.

[38] At the ICC, four legal texts are required by the Statute: the relationship agreement with the UN (Art. 2), the headquarters agreement with the Netherlands (Art. 3(2)), the staff regulations (Art. 44(3)), and the ICC Regulations (Art. 52). Other instruments include the Regulations of the OTP, Regulations of the Registry, the Code of Professional Conduct of Counsel, and the Code of Judicial Ethics. The ICTY and the ICTR have adopted various directives, codes and practice directions.

[39] E.g. *Kupreškić et al.*, ICTY T. Ch. II, 14 January 2000, paras. 539–40. Whether a hierarchy of the sources applies is debated: see Sergey Vasiliev, 'General Rules and Principles of International Criminal Procedure: Definition, Legal Nature, and Identification' in Sluiter and Vasiliev, *International Criminal Procedure*, 74–6.

law according to Article 21(1).[40] The ICC has adopted a strict hierarchy whereby there can be no recourse to any of the now mentioned external sources if the matter is exhaustively dealt with in the Statute or RPE.[41] Further, the ICC has been rather reluctant to accept national practices as applicable to the Court's proceedings.[42]

Another possible source of law is case law. Similar to the common law doctrine of binding precedent (*stare decisis*), the ICTY and ICTR have established that a Trial Chamber is bound to follow the *ratio decidendi* (the ground or reason of the decision) of the Appeals Chamber.[43] But a Trial Chamber is not bound by the decisions of another Trial Chamber, and decisions of another court or tribunal, be it domestic or international, may only have persuasive effect.[44] Formally, the Appeals Chamber is also not bound by its own prior decisions, but in practice it has been reluctant to depart from earlier practice due to concerns of stability in the law. Article 21(2) of the ICC Statute rejects the notion of binding jurisprudence even within the same Court – the Court 'may apply principles and rules of law as interpreted in its previous decisions'. In addition, the Court has often dismissed arguments on procedural matters relating to the practice of the ICTY and ICTR, noting that its own procedural law is quite different concerning, *inter alia*, the role of victims, the Prosecutor and the judges.[45]

Highly relevant for criminal procedures is human rights law. Article 21(3) of the ICC Statute provides for an unprecedented and far-reaching application of 'internationally recognized human rights', not only as a source of law but also as a 'general principle of interpretation'.[46] The question of human rights is discussed in section 17.3.

17.2   Actors in the proceedings and their roles

The organs of the ICTY, ICTR, the Residual Mechanism and the ICC are all organized in a similar way, and the organs have been described briefly in Chapters 7 and 8. Their functions and powers are set out in the applicable Statute and RPE.

17.2.1   *Judges*

The role of the judges at the ICTY and ICTR was from the outset inspired by the adversarial nature of the proceedings. But some provisions allow them a more active role, for

---

[40] One should note, however, that national law is not binding as such, neither are national decisions. See e.g. *Lubanga*, ICC PTC I, 29 January 2007, para. 69; and *Katanga and Ngudjolo Chui*, ICC PTC I, 30 September 2008, para. 91. See also Art. 69(8) of the ICC Statute, preventing the Court from ruling on the application of national law by national authorities when deciding on the relevance or admissibility of evidence, and *Bemba Gombo*, ICC A. Ch., 19 October 2010, para. 66.

[41] E.g. *Situation in the DRC*, ICC A. Ch., 13 July 2006, paras. 32–9; and *Lubanga*, ICC A. Ch., 14 December 2006, para. 34.

[42] E.g. *Lubanga*, ICC A. Ch., 14 December 2006, paras. 28–35 ('abuse of process' doctrine); *Lubanga*, ICC PTC I, 8 November 2006, paras. 35–42, and ICC T. Ch. I, 30 November 2007, para. 41 ('witness proofing'); *Situation in Uganda*, ICC A. Ch., 13 July 2006 (suspensive effect of an appeal).

[43] *Aleksovski*, ICTY A. Ch., 24 March 2000, para. 133. For a critical view and reference to civil law principles, see Alphons Orie, 'Stare Decisis in the ICTY Appeal System? Successor Responsibility in the Hadžhasanović Case' (2012) 10 *Journal of International Criminal Justice* 635, 640–2.

[44] E.g. *Tadić*, ICTY T. Ch. II, 7 May 1997, para. 654; and *Kupreškić et al.*, ICTY T. Ch. II, 14 January 2000, para. 540.

[45] E.g. *Lubanga*, ICC T. Ch. I, 30 November 2007, paras. 43–5. See also *Kony et al.*, ICC PTC II, 28 October 2005, para. 19; and *Ruto et al.*, ICC A. Ch., 24 May 2012, para. 31. See generally Volker Nerlich, 'The Status of ICTY and ICTR Precedent in Proceedings before the ICC' in Stahn and Sluiter, *Emerging Practice*, 305–25.

[46] E.g. *Lubanga*, ICC PTC I, 19 May 2006, para. 7, and 8 November 2006, para. 10. See also *Lubanga*, ICC A. Ch., 14 December 2006, paras. 36–9.

example to order the parties to present additional evidence and *ex officio* to summon a witness. Over time, the judges have become more active in controlling the proceedings as a whole, rather than simply the trial. The introduction of pre-trial judges in the ICTY and more stringent provisions for both Tribunals on preparations for trial mark this development. It has been described as a 'managerial judging system' where the judge acts as an expediting manager of cases, also on their own motion, but the parties remain primarily in charge of running the pre-trial investigation and trial.[47]

The role of the ICC judges, on the other hand, is already by statute more interventionist in nature. Apart from activities regarding preparations for trial and submission of evidence, judges have a certain limited role to play in the criminal investigation. It may be a far cry from the role of an investigative judge in a civil law system, but it reflects additional inquisitorial elements in the criminal procedures. Early and active judicial involvement helps ensure the rights of the suspect or accused, and the protection of other interests, such as the interests of victims or States. It may also assist in obtaining State cooperation. However, finding the appropriate role is difficult and the early practice has exposed palpable tensions between the judges and the prosecution.

Since none of the international criminal jurisdictions has been provided with comprehensive criminal procedures, much is left to the judges to decide. Their role as 'law-makers' has caused considerable debate, both from a principled perspective and in terms of 'creativity versus activism'.[48] While an international lawyer and a common law lawyer may consider a degree of law-making by the judge as natural and necessary, a traditional civil law lawyer would be more reluctant in the area of criminal law and procedures; in part this is due to different understandings of the principle of legality.[49] When accepting judicial development of the law, a distinction is made between the narrower approach of filling lacunae in the law (creativity) and arbitrary rule-creation without real foundation in pre-existing principles and rules (activism).[50]

17.2.2   Prosecutor

True to adversarial principles, the international prosecutor enjoys a high degree of independence, albeit under a varying degree of judicial supervision. The supervision is greater in the ICC than in the ICTY, ICTR and the Residual Mechanism, and the rather interventionist approach adopted by the ICC judges has prompted an intensive discussion concerning judicial control and supervision versus prosecutorial discretion.[51] One crucial difference is

---

[47] See Langer, 'Rise of Managerial Judging'.
[48] See e.g. Shane Darcy and Joseph Powderly (eds.), *Judicial Creativity at the International Criminal Tribunals* (Oxford, 2010).
[49] See e.g. Dov Jacobs, 'Positivism and International Criminal Law: The Principle of Legality as a Rule of Conflict of Theories' in Jean D'Aspremont and Jörg Kammerhofer (eds.), *International Legal Positivism in a Post-Modern World* (Cambridge, forthcoming); and generally Kenneth Gallant, *The Principle of Legality in International Criminal Law* (Cambridge, 2009). Although the principle relates to substantive criminal law rather than to criminal procedure, the distinction may be drawn differently with respect to issues such as jurisdiction, statutes of limitations, etc. See further section 1.5.1.
[50] See e.g. Joseph Powderly, 'Distinguishing Creativity from Activism: International Criminal Law and the "Legitimacy" of Judicial Development of the Law' in Schabas, *Ashgate Research Companion*, 223–50.
[51] See section 17.8.1 and section 17.9.

in the extent of the Prosecutor's powers flowing from the more limited geographical and temporal jurisdiction of the Tribunals compared with the ICC. Each Prosecutor decides on the commencement of the investigation, the conduct of the investigation and prosecution of a crime. The onus to prove the guilt of the accused rests with the Prosecutor. However, the obligations differ, and the prosecutorial role to represent the public interest of prosecuting and punishing the perpetrators of crimes under its jurisdiction is tempered at the ICC by a more active truth-seeking duty.[52] The Prosecutor shapes the practice and legacy of the institution more than any other actor and serves as the public face of international criminal justice.[53] To characterize the Prosecutor merely as an officer of justice would thus not capture his or her entire role and functions.

17.2.3 Defendant and defence counsel

At the ICTY and ICTR, a 'suspect' is a person concerning whom the Prosecutor possesses reliable information which tends to show that he or she may have committed a crime over which the Tribunal has jurisdiction; the 'suspect' becomes an 'accused' upon the confirmation of an indictment.[54] The ICC Statute and RPE avoid the term 'suspect', a choice that creates unnecessary ambiguities, and the term 'accused' applies to someone against whom charges have been confirmed.[55] The Statutes and RPE provide for some fundamental rights for those suspected or accused of a crime. Among the rights of the suspect are the right to remain silent, to legal assistance during questioning, and to interpretation and translations.[56] More extensive rights, reflecting international human rights instruments, are prescribed for the 'accused'.[57] These and other rights are further developed in more detailed statutory provisions and in the jurisprudence.

The adversarial nature of the ICTY and ICTR proceedings presupposes that the defendant may put forward his or her own 'defence case'. In turn, this requires a separate investigation conducted by the defence. Although not inevitable according to the law of the ICC, so far the same procedural model has been followed there as well. Under these circumstances, the assistance of a defence counsel, or rather a defence team, is particularly important. The right to counsel has been consistently enforced by the international jurisdictions. Specific qualifications are required of counsel, although they differ among the international criminal jurisdictions.[58] The Registry has important functions regarding

---

[52] See generally Christopher Keith Hall, 'The Powers and Role of the Prosecutor of the International Criminal Court in the Global Fight against Impunity' (2004) 17 *Leiden Journal of International Law* 121.

[53] See further Luc Reydams, Jan Wouters and Cedric Ryngaert (eds.), *International Prosecutors* (Oxford, 2012).

[54] Rules 2 and 47(H)(ii) of the ICTY RPE and ICTR RPE. See also rr. 2 and 48(H)(ii) of the MICT RPE.

[55] Art. 55(2) of the ICC Statute refers to '[w]here there are grounds to believe that a person has committed a crime within the jurisdiction of the Court', which is the equivalent of a 'suspect'. See Art. 61 of the ICC Statute regarding the 'accused' (cf. 'the person charged' or 'the person'). See also Ambos and Miller, 'Structure and Function', 339–40.

[56] In particular, Art. 18(3) of the ICTY Statute, Art. 17(3) of the ICTR Statute, Art. 16(3) of the MICT Statute, r. 42 of the ICTY RPE and ICTR RPE, r. 40 of the MICT RPE, and Art. 55(2) of the ICC Statute.

[57] Primarily, Art. 21 of the ICTY Statute, Art. 20 of the ICTR Statute, Art. 19 of the MICT Statute, and Art. 67 of the ICC Statute. At the ICC, these rights are applicable, in principle, from the first appearance before the Court: see r. 121(1) of the ICC RPE. Compare with Art. 14 of the ICCPR.

[58] Rule 44 of the ICTY RPE and ICTR RPE, r. 42 of the MICT RPE, r. 22 of the ICC RPE, and regs. 67–68 of the ICC Regulations.

vetting of qualifications and assistance to counsel, and the Chambers exercise some super-vision. But it has been argued that the responsibility for ensuring effective representation largely falls upon the counsel and the burden of verifying and assessing the quality on the defendant.[59]

Almost all defendants at the ICTY and ICTR are represented by counsel, normally appointed and paid for by the Tribunal. However, the issue of self-representation has arisen in several cases. Four political leaders indicted by the ICTY demanded to conduct their own defences, which highlighted the question whether legal assistance could be imposed against the will of the accused. Mandatory representation is accepted in civil law systems,[60] but contrary to the practice in common law systems this does not mean that the accused is prevented from participating actively at the trial. In trying to balance the rights of the accused and the need to ensure fair and expeditious proceedings, the ICTY has taken context-specific decisions rather than decisions of principle.[61] Generally, the Appeals Chamber has upheld a right to self-representation even in cases of blatant abuse by the accused, arguing that the right may be limited only to the minimum extent necessary to ensure reasonably expeditious proceedings.[62] Different tools have been employed, such as *amici curiae* (friends of the court) to assist the court,[63] 'stand-by counsel'[64] or 'privileged associates'.[65] However, the right to self-representation is not absolute, and counsel has sometimes been imposed.[66] A qualified right may be justified since the obstructions could hamper the possibilities to ensure a fair trial and the ability to facilitate the testimony of victims and other witnesses and, thus, undermine the public's confidence in and respect for the legal process.[67] The non-absolute approach has its critics,[68] but others argue that representation by counsel should be the norm and thus that a presumption against self-representation should apply.[69]

The ICC Statute also recognizes the right to legal representation of the suspect's or accused's own choosing, and if necessary free of cost.[70] As in the Tribunals, the Registrar is to establish and maintain a list of counsel from which counsel are to be

---

[59] See Til Gut, Stefan Kirsch, Daryl Mundis and Melinda Taylor, 'Defence Issues' in Sluiter, *International Criminal Procedure*, 1225.

[60] See Mirjan Damaška, 'Assignment of Counsel and Perceptions of Fairness' (2005) 3 *Journal of International Criminal Justice* 3.

[61] See Jarinde Temminck Tuinstra, 'The ICTY's Continuing Struggle with the Right to Self-Representation' in Bert Swart, Alexander Zahar and Göran Sluiter (eds.), *The Legacy of the International Criminal Tribunal for the Former Yugoslavia* (Oxford, 2011) 345–76.

[62] E.g. *Milošević*, ICTY A. Ch., 1 November 2004, paras. 17–18.   [63] *Milošević*, ICTY T. Ch. III, 30 August 2001.

[64] E.g. *Šešelj*, ICTY T. Ch. II, 9 May 2003; *Karadžić*, ICTY T. Ch. III, 15 April 2010 and 21 June 2012.

[65] See *Šešelj*, ICTY T. Ch. III, 10 February 2010 (by entering into a confidentiality agreement with the Registry, two persons could access confidential information, the courtroom, and the accused, on a privileged basis).

[66] *Milošević*, ICTY A. Ch., 1 November 2004; *Šešelj*, ICTY T. Ch. I, 21 August 2006; and *Karadžić*, ICTY T. Ch. III, 5 November 2009. Similarly, *Norman et al.*, SCSL T. Ch. I, 8 June 2004, paras. 8 and 27. See r. 45*ter* of the ICTY RPE, r. 45*quater* of the ICTR RPE, r. 46 of the MICT RPE, Art. 67(1)(d) of the ICC Statute and reg. 76(1) of the ICC Regulations. Cf. *Šešelj*, ICTY A. Ch., 8 December 2006 (the right to self-representation was afforded primacy).

[67] See e.g. Michael Scharf, 'Self-Representation of the Accused before International Tribunals: An Absolute Right or a Qualified Privilege?' in Brown, *Research Handbook*, 284–98, at 297.

[68] E.g. Temminck Tuinstra, 'The ICTY's Continuing Struggle'.

[69] E.g. Gideon Boas, 'Self-Representation before the ICTY' (2011) 9 *Journal of International Criminal Justice* 53.

[70] Arts. 55(2) and 67(1)(d) of the ICC Statute. See also Registry's Single Policy Document on the Court's Legal Aid System, 4 June 2013, Doc. ICC-ASP/12/3.

chosen, but the ICC RPE also allows a counsel not on the list to be chosen if that counsel meets the required qualifications and is willing to be included in the list.[71] So far, all suspects and accused who have been surrendered or otherwise appeared before the ICC have been represented by defence counsel and the issue of self-representation has not yet arisen. In addition, the ICC has established a system with public defence counsel (ad hoc counsel) to assist in the very early stages of an investigation.[72] Such counsel may be appointed from the list or from the independent Office of Public Counsel for the Defence. But representing 'general defence interests' instead of a particular client has its limitations.[73]

17.2.4 *Victims and witnesses*

Victims are afforded a substantially stronger role at the ICC than in proceedings before the ICTY, ICTR and the Residual Mechanism, which includes an independent right to participate in the proceedings and to claim reparations. In all these jurisdictions victims also appear as witnesses; the double–role of (participating) victim–witness poses particular challenges at the ICC. The role of victims is further addressed in Chapter 18.

The term 'witness' is not defined in the rules of the Tribunals or Court, but there is a distinction between 'expert witnesses'[74] and other witnesses.[75] Generally, adversarial and inquisitorial systems view the role of the witness differently. The ICTY and ICTR have opted for an adversarial approach whereby the parties have the primary responsibility for the evidence and, accordingly, each party may call witnesses, who will therefore be either 'prosecution witnesses' or 'defence witnesses'.[76] A more inquisitorial element, however, is the power of the judges to summon witnesses or order their attendance.[77] Such witnesses are sometimes called 'court witnesses'.[78] Similar provisions apply to the ICC,[79] and in practice the trials so far have been divided into prosecution and defence cases. But it has been emphasized in several decisions that witnesses are not attributable to either party but instead are 'witnesses of the Court'.[80] The Trial Chambers have exercised their power to call

---

[71] Rule 22 of the ICC RPE, and regs. 69–76 of the ICC Regulations. See also r. 45 of the ICTY RPE and ICTR RPE, and r. 43 of the MICT RPE.

[72] Reg. 77 of the ICC Regulations. See e.g. *Situation in the DRC*, ICC PTC I, 26 April 2005 ('unique investigative opportunity') and 21 July 2005 (responding to victims' application for participation); and *Situation in Darfur, Sudan*, ICC PTC I, 24 July 2006 (responding to *amicus* briefs).

[73] See Jens Dieckmann and Christina Kerll, 'Representing the "General Interests of the Defence": Boon or Bane? – A Stocktaking of the System of Ad Hoc Counsel at the ICC' (2011) 11 *International Criminal Law Review* 105.

[74] Rule 94*bis* of the ICTY RPE and ICTR RPE, r. 116 of the MICT RPE, and r. 140(3) of the ICC RPE (see also rr. 91 and 191 of the ICC RPE and reg. 44 of the ICC Regulations).

[75] For general surveys and assessments, see Yvonne McDermott, 'Regular Witness Testimony', and Suzannah Linton, 'Testimony of Expert Witnesses, Journalists, ICRC, and UN Staff', both in Sluiter, *International Criminal Procedure*, 859–938.

[76] E.g. r. 65*ter* of the ICTY RPE and ICTR RPE, and r. 70 of the MICT RPE.

[77] Rule 98 of the ICTY RPE and ICTR RPE, and r. 120 of the MICT RPE.

[78] E.g. *Milošević*, ICTY T. Ch. III, 18 February 2004. There are also examples where the Trial Chamber has considered all witnesses as 'witnesses of justice', and not of either of the parties, once they have made the solemn declaration, e.g. *Jelisić*, ICTY T. Ch. I, 11 December 1998.

[79] Arts. 64(6)(b) and 69(3) of the ICC Statute, and rr. 76 and 79 of the ICC RPE.

[80] E.g. *Lubanga*, ICC PTC I, 8 November 2006, para. 26, and ICC T. Ch. I, 30 November 2007, para. 34; *Muthaura et al.*, ICC PTC II, 4 April 2011, para. 10.

(expert) witnesses.[81] The accused may also give testimony as a witness, but only in his or her own defence.

A witness giving testimony under solemn declaration (a neutral term for 'oath') is obliged to speak the truth and does so with criminal liability for false testimony.[82] A protection against self-incrimination is provided for.[83] Certain witness privileges apply.[84] The ICTY and ICTR Trial Chambers may issue a *subpoena ad testificandum* when it is 'necessary for the purpose of an investigation or for the preparation or conduct of the trial'.[85] The ICC Trial Chambers may 'require the attendance and testimony of a witness'.[86] But the enforcement of such orders differs, which is addressed in Chapter 20.

Various measures for the protection of witnesses, and at the ICC also victims, are widely applied, and this triggers important questions regarding fairness and the rights of the suspect or accused (see Chapter 18).

17.2.5   States and international organizations

An international criminal jurisdiction will inevitably take decisions which affect State interests, for example decisions regarding the exercise of jurisdiction or State cooperation. Consequently, there are certain possibilities for States to intervene in the proceedings. In the ICTY, States 'directly affected' by a decision have a right to request a review, and this right has been exercised with respect to, *inter alia*, an order to a State to provide documents,[87] an order to NATO (and SFOR) to provide reports and documents,[88] a request for arrest and surrender,[89]

---

[81] E.g. *Lubanga*, ICC T. Ch. I, 14 March 2012, para. 11; and *Ngudjolo Chui*, ICC T. Ch. II, 18 December 2012, para. 23. Concerning experts, joint instruction by the parties is preferred, e.g. *Lubanga*, ICC T. Ch. I, 10 December 2007, paras. 14–16; and *Bemba Gombo*, ICC T. Ch. III, 12 February 2010, paras. 11–12.

[82] Rules 90–91 of the ICTY RPE and ICTR RPE, rr. 106 and 108 of the MICT RPE, Arts. 69(1) and 70 of the ICC Statute and r. 66 of the ICC RPE.

[83] Rule 90(E) of the ICTY RPE and ICTR RPE, r. 106(E) of the MICT RPE, and rr. 65, 74–75 of the ICC RPE (which also cover incrimination of family members). However, the witness may be compelled to answer incriminating questions under an assurance that the information will not be used for prosecution against him or her.

[84] Rule 97 of the ICTY RPE and ICTR RPE, and r. 119 of the MICT RPE (lawyer–client). Other privileges have evolved in practice, e.g. for a former employee of the ICRC (*Simić et al.*, ICTY T. Ch. III, 27 July 1999), employees and functionaries of the Tribunals (*Delalić et al.*, ICTY T. Ch. II, 8 July 1997), and a war correspondent (*Brđanin and Talić*, ICTY A. Ch., 11 December 2002, reversing ICTY T. Ch. II, 7 June 2002). See also r. 73 of the ICC RPE (a more general formula for privilege and special provisions regarding the ICRC). Privileges also apply for confidential (national security) information: r. 70 of the ICTY RPE and ICTR RPE, r. 76 of the MICT RPE, and Art. 72 of the ICC Statute; see also e.g. *Milošević*, ICTY A. Ch., 23 October 2002 (on r. 70) and the subsequent application, ICTY T. Ch. III, 30 October 2003. See further Emily Ann Herman, 'In Pursuit of Accountability: The Red Cross, War Correspondents, and Evidentiary Privileges in International Criminal Tribunals' (2005) 80 *New York University Law Review* 241. Cf. the interesting decision by the SCSL whereby an international human rights worker was refused witness privileges: *Brima et al.*, SCSL T. Ch. II, 16 September 2005; but reversed on appeal: *Brima et al.*, SCSL A. Ch., 26 May 2006.

[85] Rule 54 of the ICTY RPE and ICTR RPE, and r. 55 of the MICT RPE.

[86] Art. 64(6)(b) of the ICC Statute. In addition, the Pre-Trial Chamber has a general power to issue necessary orders at the request of the Prosecutor or the defence: Art. 57(3)(a)–(b) of the ICC Statute.

[87] *Blaškić*, ICTY A. Ch., 29 October 1997 (Croatia against a *subpoena duces tecum*); and *Kordić and Čerkez*, ICTY A. Ch., 26 March 1999.

[88] *Simić et al.*, ICTY A. Ch., 27 March 2001 (the motions became moot after the prosecution and the accused entered into a plea agreement).

[89] *Bobetko*, ICTY A. Ch., 29 November 2002. Cf. *Gotovina et al.*, ICTY A. Ch., 17 January 2008 (Croatia's request for a review of the decision to deny provisional release was rejected).

and disclosure of confidential information.[90] But a general right to intervene or file statements of interest in the judicial proceedings has been rejected.[91]

Due to their origin, the Tribunals have a particular relationship with the UN Security Council. But, while the Tribunals report to the Security Council, it is important to note that there are no provisions allowing the Council to intervene in their proceedings. As to other international organizations, the ICTY and ICTR have directed binding orders for cooperation, but have also concluded that they are not, formally speaking, obliged to cooperate.[92] The organization as such may also request a review.[93] As previously noted,[94] the ICRC is afforded special privileges.

At the ICC, States are given an even greater scope for intervention owing to the 'trigger mechanisms' and principle of complementarity.[95] A referring State (or the Security Council) may request a review of the Prosecutor's decision not to investigate or to prosecute.[96] Certain decisions may be appealed by an affected State,[97] and States may also seek a ruling on the legality of a request for cooperation and intervene in procedures regarding a failure to cooperate.[98] Of course, the Security Council's power to require the deferral of an investigation or prosecution is a substantive form of intervention.[99]

Additionally, the Chambers of both the Tribunals and the ICC may allow States and organizations (and individuals) to make *amicus curiae* (friend of the court) submissions on legal or other issues.[100] The ICC has used this mechanism for granting States leave to file submissions in proceedings to which the State is not a party or participant.[101]

17.3 International criminal procedures and human rights

17.3.1 *International human rights standards*

In his report on the establishment of the ICTY, the UN Secretary-General underlined, as axiomatic, that internationally recognized human rights standards regarding the rights of the accused be fully respected at all stages of the proceedings.[102] Apart from the argument of principle, this is also a necessary requirement for allowing an international court to prosecute individuals, a matter that is normally intrinsically linked to State sovereignty.[103] Adherence to international human rights standards is also important in order to obtain cooperation by States having obligations under international law to respect human rights.

---

[90] *Milošević*, ICTY A. Ch., 23 October 2002.   [91] *Gotovina and Markač*, ICTY A. Ch., 8 February 2012, paras. 14–17.
[92] E.g. *Simić et al.*, ICTY T. Ch. III, 27 July 1999, para. 78 (Art. 29 of the ICTY Statute does not apply to international organizations). See Chapter 20.
[93] *Milutinović et al.*, ICTY A. Ch., 15 May 2006, para. 11.   [94] See footnote 84 above.
[95] See Chapter 8. See also Arts. 18–19 of the ICC Statute, and *Ruto et al.*, ICC PTC II, 30 May 2011.
[96] *Ibid.*, Art. 53(3) of the ICC Statute.   [97] *Ibid.*, Art. 82(1)(d) and (2).
[98] Regs. 108–109 of the ICC Regulations. See e.g. *Al Bashir*, ICC PTC I, 19 October 2011, and ICC PTC II, 22 February 2013.
[99] See Chapter 8.   [100] Rule 74 of the ICTY RPE and ICTR RPE, r. 83 of the MICT RPE, and r. 103 of the ICC RPE.
[101] E.g. *Gbagbo*, ICC A. Ch., 12 December 2012, paras. 39–43 and PTC I, 14 March 2013 (observations on the defendant's admissibility challenge); and *Ruto and Sang*, ICC T. Ch. V(A), 24 April 2013 and 3 July 2013 (allegations of non-cooperation). Cf. *Ruto et al.*, ICC PTC II, 1 September 2011, para. 8 (request to participate in the confirmation of charges proceedings was rejected).
[102] Report of the Secretary-General Pursuant to Paragraph 2 of Security Council Resolution 808(1993), para. 106.
[103] Antonio Cassese, 'Opinion: The International Criminal Tribunal for the Former Yugoslavia and Human Rights' (1997) 4 *European Human Rights Law Review* 329, 332.

Other reasons that have been advanced for close compliance are the acquisition of trust, which is necessary in order to contribute to reconciliation, and the fact that these courts and tribunals are not subject to external review by any human rights court or UN treaty body.[104]

While the international human rights instruments and jurisprudence thereunder are directed to States, certain principles are integrated into the Statutes and RPE of the international criminal courts and tribunals. As a global treaty with a large number of ratifications, the ICCPR has served as the model.[105] Such principles have also entered into the legal framework more indirectly as principles of the UN or as enshrined in customary international law or general principles of law, regarding which human rights treaties and jurisprudence may serve as authoritative evidence.[106]

After some initial reluctance,[107] the ICTY and ICTR now frequently make reference to international human rights treaties and case law in their decisions.[108] Nevertheless, in some instances the Tribunals have departed from a strict adherence to human rights standards, as developed for domestic proceedings. The Tribunals' unique structure, status and subject-matter jurisdiction have been regarded as justification for this departure.[109] But, even when the outcome can be defended, the method used may be criticized.[110] On the other hand, it may be questioned whether national and international justice should be judged by the same metric.[111]

The ICC Statute contains provisions reflecting international human rights law and directs that the Court must apply applicable treaties and the principles and rules of international law as sources of law (Article 21(1)(b)). Further, the application and interpretation of the law 'must be consistent with internationally recognized human rights' (Article 21(3));[112] this is 'a general rule of consistency', or a rule of interpretation, rather than a source of

---

[104] See Vojin Dimitrijević and Marko Milanović, *Human Rights Provisions in Conventional Sources of International Criminal Law and their Effects on International Criminal Justice* (Venice Commission, 2005) 12.
[105] Particularly Art. 14 of the ICCPR. One should remember, however, that some States made far-reaching reservations with respect to that Article: see Nowak, *UN Covenant*, 306–7.
[106] E.g. *Barayagwiza*, ICTR A. Ch., 3 November 1999, para. 40 (the ECHR and the ACHR and the jurisprudence developed thereunder are persuasive authority as evidence of international custom); and *Kajelijeli*, ICTR A. Ch., 23 May 2005, para. 209 (customary international law is reflected, *inter alia*, in the ICCPR).
[107] E.g. *Tadić*, ICTY T. Ch. II, 10 August 1995, paras. 17–30 (majority considered interpretations of human rights standards made by other judicial bodies to be of limited value due to the Tribunal's unique procedures).
[108] E.g. *Delalić et al.*, ICTY T. Ch. II, 28 April 1997, para. 27 (decisions on provisions of the ICCPR and the ECHR were found 'authoritative and applicable'); see also *Kajelijeli*, ICTR A. Ch., 23 May 2005, para. 209. See generally e.g. Antonio Cassese, 'The Influence of the European Court of Human Rights on International Criminal Tribunals: Some Methodological Remarks' in Morten Bergsmo (ed.), *Human Rights and Criminal Justice for the Downtrodden: Essays in Honour of Asbjørn Eide* (Leiden, 2003) 19–52; and Emanuela Fronza, 'Human Rights and Criminal Law: Reference to the Case Law of Human Rights Bodies by International Criminal Tribunals' in Robert Kolb and Damien Scalia (eds.), *Droit international pénal*, 2nd edn (Munich, 2012) 369–92.
[109] See e.g. *Kunarac et al.*, ICTY T. Ch. II, 22 February 2001, para. 470.
[110] E.g. Gabrielle McIntyre, 'Defining Human Rights in the Arena of International Humanitarian Law: Human Rights in the Jurisprudence of the ICTY' in Gideon Boas and William Schabas (eds.), *International Criminal Law Developments in the Case Law of the ICTY* (Dordrecht, 2003) 193–238; and Patricia Pinto Soares, 'Tangling Human Rights and International Criminal Law: The Practice of International Tribunals and the Call for Rationalized Legal Pluralism' (2012) 23 *Criminal Law Forum* 161.
[111] See Mirjan Damaška, 'Should National and International Justice Be Subjected to the Same Evaluative Framework?' in Sluiter, *International Criminal Procedure*, 1418–22. See also section 1.4.1.
[112] See section 17.1.4. See also *Lubanga*, ICC A. Ch., 14 December 2006, paras. 36–9. On the meaning of this rather ambiguous phrase, see Rebecca Young, '"Internationally Recognized Human Rights" before the International Criminal Court' (2011) 60 *International and Comparative Law Quarterly* 189.

applicable law.[113] Article 21(3) applies to all sources of law, including extraneous ones, and unlike the sources listed in Article 21(1)(b)–(c) it may even serve as a tool to set aside the Court's own statutory provisions.[114] The Court often resorts to international human rights law in practice,[115] and also regional human rights instruments may qualify.[116] It has also referred to human rights law when defining or clarifying procedural concepts such as 'proceedings' or 'reasonable grounds to believe'.[117] Many commentators claim that the ICC represents a clear improvement in the codification of human rights, sometimes going further than international human rights law.

But there is also the criticism that the Court has been too reluctant to act as a supervisor of national law and practice, in particular with respect to arrest and surrender.[118] The high threshold has been retained when challenged, and the Court has concluded that, 'in the absence of any involvement on the part of the Court in the detention . . . the Chamber cannot proceed to a determination of any particular violation of . . . fundamental rights during his detention'.[119]

17.3.2   Independence and impartiality

All human rights treaties require an institutional guarantee in the form of an independent and impartial tribunal or court established by law. This is an integral part of the right of the accused to a fair trial and a general principle of law recognized by all legal systems of the world. Independence requires an institutional and functional separation from the executive and legislative powers as well as from the parties.[120] One problem for the international criminal jurisdictions, however, is their dependence on cooperation by States and others. The dilemma was described in the *Barayagwiza* case, after suspension by the government of Rwanda of cooperation with the ICTR, though well aware of the fact that most of the evidence that the Tribunal needed was located in Rwanda.[121]

The Statutes of the ICTY and ICTR do not address the independence of the Tribunals, and their status as judicial institutions established by the Security Council has led to some discomfort regarding their institutional independence.[122] However, domestic courts are

---

[113] See Young, *ibid.* See also Per Saland, 'International Criminal Law Principles' in Lee, *The Making of the Rome Statute*, 214; Alain Pellet, 'Applicable Law' in Cassese, *Commentary*, 1080–1 (describing Art. 21(3) as a form of 'super-hierarchy'); and William Schabas, *The International Criminal Court: A Commentary on the Rome Statute* (Oxford, 2010) 385.

[114] See e.g. Lorenzo Gradoni, 'The Human Rights Dimension of International Criminal Procedure' in Sluiter, *International Criminal Procedure*, 74–95; and Dapo Akande, 'Sources of International Criminal Law' in Cassese, *Companion*, 41–53. See also *Situation in the DRC*, ICC A. Ch., 13 July 2006, para. 11; and *Katanga and Ngudjolo Chui*, ICC T. Ch. II, 9 June 2011, para. 73. Cf. *Al Bashir*, ICC PTC I, 4 March 2009, para. 44 (application of Art. 21(1)(b)–(c) requires a lacunae in written law). Earlier, however, also Art. 21(3) was assigned a gap-filling function: *Situation in the DRC*, ICC PTC I, 17 January 2006, para. 81.

[115] E.g. *Katanga and Ngudjolo Chui*, ICC A. Ch., 16 July 2010, paras. 51, 78–80 (disclosure); and *Lubanga*, ICC A. Ch., 8 December 2009, para. 84 (recharacterization of charges).

[116] E.g. *Harun and Ali Kushayb*, ICC PTC I, 27 April 2007, para. 28.

[117] E.g. *Situation in the DRC*, ICC PTC I, 17 January 2006, paras. 52–3; *Al Bashir*, ICC A. Ch., 3 February 2010, para. 31.

[118] E.g. Göran Sluiter, 'Human Rights Protection in the ICC Pre-Trial Phase' in Stahn and Sluiter, *Emerging Practice*, 459–75.

[119] *Gbagbo*, ICC PTC I, 15 August 2012, para. 112. In another case, however, a thorough analysis of national seizure measures was conducted: *Lubanga*, ICC PTC I, 29 January 2007, paras. 62–90 (admissibility of evidence).

[120] E.g. *Ringeisen* v. *Austria*, ECtHR, 16 July 1971, para. 95.

[121] *Barayagwiza*, ICTR A. Ch., 3 November 1999 and 31 March 2000 (particularly the Separate Opinions of Judges Vohrah and Nieto-Navia).

[122] E.g. José Alvarez, 'Nuremberg Revisited: The Tadić Case' (1996) 7 *European Journal of International Law* 245, 253–4.

also subject to the exercise of executive and legislative powers, for example as regards budgets and appointments, and this alone does not rule out independence. In an objective sense, the ICTY and ICTR are institutionally and functionally independent. For example, both Tribunals have addressed the legality of their creation,[123] and there are no provisions allowing the Security Council to interfere in individual cases. The impartiality requirement also relates to the judge, who must be both personally and institutionally impartial.[124] The established standard for the assessment of impartiality is that actual bias or an unacceptable appearance of bias – certain interests or circumstances that would lead 'a reasonable observer, properly informed, to reasonably apprehend bias' – reflect partiality and thus that the judge should be disqualified.[125]

The ICC is an independent, treaty-based body and its more comprehensive Statute explicitly addresses the independence and impartiality of the judges and the Prosecutor (and Deputy Prosecutors), as well as the right of the accused to a 'fair hearing conducted impartially'.[126] The Statute provides for both personal and institutional impartiality. With respect to the Security Council, the relationship is essentially of a legal nature, but some have expressed concerns regarding the Council's power to request a deferral of an investigation or prosecution.[127] The non-renewable term in office of the judges and prosecutors is one way of ensuring independence and impartiality. While the Prosecutor's institutional independence and large functional autonomy under the law are adversarial features, the prescribed impartiality is more inquisitorial in nature and indicates a role as 'an officer of justice' rather than a partisan party to the proceedings. There is a case for disqualification when the impartiality of a judge or the Prosecutor when 'the circumstances would lead a reasonable observer, properly informed, to reasonably apprehend bias in the judge' or Prosecutor;[128] thus, the appearance of grounds to doubt his or her impartiality will be sufficient.

Circumstances that may impair a judge's (or prosecutor's) impartiality can be a personal interest in the case (political, financial or other stake in the outcome), a personal connection with a party or counsel, or the judge's public airing of a prejudicing opinion.[129] The procedures for disqualification motions vary in the different courts.[130]

[123] E.g. *Tadić*, ICTY A. Ch., 2 October 1995; and *Kanyabashi*, ICTR T. Ch. II, 18 June 1997, paras. 37–50.

[124] Art. 13 of the ICTY Statute, Art. 12 of the ICTR Statute, and Art. 9 of the MICT Statute. See also rr. 14–15 of the ICTY RPE and ICTR RPE, and rr. 17–18 of the MICT RPE (solemn declaration and disqualification of judges).

[125] *Furundžija*, ICTY A. Ch., 21 July 2000, paras. 177–91. See also *Rutaganda*, ICTR A. Ch., 26 May 2003, paras. 39–49. In one case before the ICTR, the appearance of bias regarding one judge extended to the whole Trial Chamber and the Chamber was reconstituted: *Karemera et al.*, ICTR A. Ch., 28 September 2004 and 22 October 2004, paras. 62–8 (two judges dissenting).

[126] Arts. 36 (qualifications and election of judges), 40 (independence of judges), 41 (excusing and disqualification of judges), 42(5)–(8) (independence, impartiality and disqualification of the Prosecutor), 45 (solemn undertaking) and 67(1) (fair trial rights) of the ICC Statute. See also rr. 5–6 and 33–35 of the ICC RPE, which include, *inter alia*, a duty for a judge or Prosecutor to request to be excused if he or she 'has reason to believe that a ground for disqualification exists in relation to him or her' (r. 35).

[127] See further section 8.9.

[128] *Banda and Jerbo*, ICC Plenary of Judges 5 June 2012, para. 11. On disqualification of the Prosecutor, see *Gadaffi and Al-Senussi*, ICC A. Ch., 12 June 2012 (motion rejected but criticism for inappropriate statements). See further Hirad Abtahi, Odo Ogwuma and Rebecca Young, 'The Composition of Judicial Benches, Disqualification and Excusal of Judges at the International Criminal Court' (2013) 11 *Journal of International Criminal Justice* 379.

[129] See e.g. r. 34(1) of the ICC RPE; *Furundžija* A. Ch., 21 July 2000, paras. 169–215; and *Lubanga*, ICC Plenary, 11 June 2013. See also *Sesay et al.*, SCSL A. Ch., 13 March 2004; and *Norman et al.*, SCSL A. Ch., 28 May 2004.

[130] Compare r. 15(B) of the ICTY RPE, r. 15(B) of the ICTR RPE, r. 18(B) of the MICT RPE, Art. 41(2) of the ICC Statute and rr. 33–34 of the ICC RPE.

17.3.3   *Presumption of innocence*

Another fundamental principle set forth in human rights instruments, and also generally accepted and often constitutionally protected by States, is that the accused shall be presumed innocent until proven guilty according to law.[131] As phrased in those instruments, the principle applies only to an 'accused', and the same restriction is expressed in the ICTY and ICTR Statutes.[132] However, a widely shared opinion is that the presumption should also extend to the investigative stage. The ICC Statute affords this right to 'everyone', and this wording, in spite of the provision being placed in the part dealing with trials, may suggest that it is of general application.[133] A broad application is also reflected in the cautious approach not to prejudge guilt when establishing who is a 'victim' in relation to victim participation in the early stages of the process.[134] Moreover, the principle played a prominent role when a Trial Chamber decided, contrary to an explicit statutory provision, to excuse one accused, the current Deputy President of Kenya, from continuous presence at trial.[135]

The presumption of innocence has many implications. A corollary is the right to remain silent and not be compelled to incriminate oneself or confess guilt, which, broadly interpreted, applies throughout the proceedings. Indeed, this right is provided for 'suspects' at the ICTY and ICTR and generally at the ICC.[136] Silence may not be used as evidence to prove guilt and also not be interpreted as an admission of guilt.[137] Another consequence is that an accused refusing to express an opinion as to his or her guilt or innocence shall be considered as not having admitted any guilt; at the ICTY and ICTR, the judge will then enter a 'plea of not guilty' on behalf of the accused.[138]

Another important effect is that the prosecution must prove the defendant's guilt, and in case of doubt the accused must be found not guilty (*in dubio pro reo*).[139] Hence, the prosecutor has the burden of proof. National systems take different approaches as to the scope of the prosecutor's burden. In common law and other adversarial systems, the standard is referred to as 'guilt beyond a reasonable doubt', and in civil law systems often as 'the judge's innermost conviction' (*l'intime conviction du juge*). The ICTY and ICTR have themselves adopted a common law-inspired approach whereby the Prosecutor is required to prove guilt 'beyond a reasonable doubt',[140] but the onus to establish a defence rests with the

---

[131] Some countries, however, interpret the principle as 'not presumed guilty', e.g. the Italian Constitution.

[132] Art. 21(3) of the ICTY Statute, Art. 20(3) of the ICTR Statute, and Art. 19(3) of the MICT Statute.

[133] Art. 66(1) of the ICC Statute (in Part 6, 'The Trial'). See e.g. *Bemba Gombo*, ICC PTC II, 14 August 2009, para. 37; and *Mbarushimana*, ICC PTC I, 31 January 2011, para. 8.

[134] See Chapter 18.

[135] *Ruto and Sang*, ICC T. Ch. V(A), 18 June 2013, para. 48; cf. Art. 63(1) of the ICC Statute ('[t]he accused shall be present during the trial'). The decision was reversed on appeal.

[136] Rule 42(A)(iii) of the ICTY RPE and ICTR RPE, r. 40(A)(iii) of the MICT RPE, and Art. 55(1)(a) and (2)(b) of the ICC Statute.

[137] Arts. 55(2) and 67(1)(g) of the ICC Statute. See also e.g. *Brđanin*, ICTY T. Ch. II, 1 September 2004, para. 24.

[138] Rule 62 of the ICTY RPE and ICTR RPE, and r. 64 of the MICT RPE.

[139] An interesting question is whether the principle applies only to questions of fact or also to questions of law: see declarations by Judges Shahabuddeen (both) and Schomburg (facts only) in *Limaj et al.*, ICTY A. Ch., 27 September 2007; see Darryl Robinson, 'The Identity Crisis of International Criminal Law' (2008) 21 *Leiden Journal of International Law* 925. A general and far-reaching approach to the principle is taken in *Bemba Gombo*, ICC PTC II, 15 June 2009, para. 31.

[140] Rule 87(A) of the ICTY RPE and ICTR RPE. See also r. 104(A) of the MICT RPE.

accused.[141] In relation to the charges, the accused need only bring evidence 'to suggest a reasonable possibility' in order to induce a reasonable doubt, while the proof required for other issues which the accused might raise has been declared as 'on the balance of probabilities'.[142] In spite of domestic differences, the States agreed that the ICC Statute should establish the Prosecutor's onus and a 'beyond a reasonable doubt' standard for a conviction, but also a right for the accused 'not to have imposed on him or her any reversal of the burden of proof or any onus of rebuttal'.[143] What this right will mean in practice is not entirely clear and it may create problems, for example with respect to the generally accepted presumption of a person's sanity. But some (civil-law-inspired) commentators go further, claiming a burden on the prosecution to disprove defences.[144] In the two judgments handed down so far, the Trial Chambers refer only to the Prosecutor's burden of proof and place no burden upon the defendant.[145] More concrete guidance by the Court is awaited.

17.3.4 Public, fair and expeditious proceedings

The principle of a public hearing allows a public scrutiny of the judicial proceedings and thus a protection against unfairness and arbitrary action by the courts. This principle also applies at the ICTY, ICTR, the Residual Mechanism and the ICC. The respective Statutes provide for public hearings and delivery of the judgment in public.[146] As in domestic proceedings there are exceptions, however, and the provisions of the ICTY and ICTR RPEs are inspired by the exceptions set out in the ICCPR and ECHR. Closed sessions are allowed for reasons of public order or morality, safety, security or non-disclosure of the identity of a protected victim or witness, and the protection of the interests of justice.[147] The ICC Statute provides for two exceptions: protection of the accused, victims and witnesses; and protection of confidential or sensitive evidence.[148] The ICC Trial Chamber in *Lubanga* pledged 'to scrutinise very carefully each and every occasion when it is suggested that there should be a departure from the principle of open justice'.[149] In all international jurisdictions, however, protective measures are applied extensively.

---

[141] E.g. *Delalić et al.*, ICTY A. Ch., 20 February 2001, para. 582. An alibi, however, is not a defence in a proper sense and the defendant is only required to 'raise a reasonable doubt in the Prosecution case': e.g. *Zigiranyirazo*, ICTR A. Ch., 16 November 2009, paras. 17–18.

[142] E.g. *Delalić et al.*, ICTY A. Ch., 20 February 2001, para. 603.

[143] Arts. 66(2)–(3) and 67(1)(i) of the ICC Statute. Cf. Art. 21 of the ICTY Statute, Art. 20 of the ICTR Statute and Art. 19 of the MICT Statute, which simply refer to the accused being proven guilty 'according to the provisions of the present Statute'. The reasonable doubt standard was also defeated with respect to Art. 14 of the ICCPR.

[144] E.g. Salvatore Zappalà, 'The Rights of the Accused' in Cassese, *Commentary*, 1346.

[145] *Lubanga*, ICC T. Ch. I, 14 March 2012, para. 92; *Ngudjolo Chui*, ICC T. Ch. II, 18 December 2012, paras. 34–6.

[146] Arts. 21(2) and 23(2) of the ICTY Statute, Arts. 20(2) and 22(2) of the ICTR Statute, Arts. 19(2) and 21(2) of the MICT Statute, and Arts. 64(7), 67(1) and 74(5) of the ICC Statute. See also rr. 78 and 98*ter* of the ICTY RPE, r. 78 of the ICTR RPE and rr. 92 and 122 of the MICT RPE.

[147] Rule 79 of the ICTY RPE and ICTR RPE, and r. 93 of the MICT RPE; to be compared with Art. 14(1) of the ICCPR and Art. 6(1) of the ECHR.

[148] Art. 64(7) of the ICC Statute, referring to Art. 68 concerning the protection of the accused, victims and witnesses. See also Art. 72(5)(d) (national security information) and r. 72 (relevance or admissibility of evidence in cases of sexual violence) and rr. 87–88 (protective and special measures) of the ICC RPE.

[149] *Lubanga*, ICC T. Ch. I, 4 September 2007 (transcript), p. 6.

The right to a 'fair trial' is a general principle of international law, but different opinions exist as to the closer meaning and actual implementation of the principle. The ICTY, ICTR and ICC have concluded that the right applies both to the defence and to the prosecution.[150] In the ICC where victims also have procedural rights, the concept of 'fairness' becomes more complex. One approach that has been advanced is that fairness is the act of balancing, or finding equilibrium, between the procedural rights of all participants.[151] Another approach is to make a distinction between 'general rights', demanding that all participants are given a genuine opportunity to present their case and respond to evidence, and 'specific fairness', affording the person on trial special rights.[152] The Court has acknowledged, however, that the right to a fair trial first and foremost applies to the defendant and the defence,[153] a prioritization that is also reflected in the statutory provisions on victim participation and protective measures.

A fundamental element of a fair trial, and a general principle of law, is the principle of equality of arms; a principle that should not be confused with the principle of equality before the law, or non-discrimination.[154] Equality of arms is especially important in adversarial proceedings and requires opportunities for each party to prepare and present its case, both on law and on facts, and to respond to the opponent's case. The Tribunals argue a more liberal interpretation than in domestic courts, owing to the difficulties encountered by the parties in tracing and gaining access to evidence,[155] but also establish limitations. A judicial body must ensure that neither party is put at a disadvantage when presenting its case[156] but the application is less far-reaching with respect to preparations. The accused's right to have adequate time and facilities to prepare the defence should be ensured under conditions that do not place him or her at a 'substantial disadvantage' *vis-à-vis* the Prosecutor, but does not imply ensuring parity of resources between the parties, such as the material equality of financial or personal resources.[157] The ICC takes a similar legal stance, but a number of measures have also been introduced to minimize unequal resources.[158] Even so, the defence's lack of institutional status in the ICC is a key equality-of-arms concern among defence counsel.[159]

---

[150] E.g. *Karemera et al.*, ICTR T. Ch. III, 7 December 2004, para. 26; *Milutinović et al.*, ICTY T. Ch. III, 30 August 2006, para. 10; and *Situation in Uganda*, ICC PTC II, 19 December 2007, para. 27. See further Yvonne McDermott, 'Rights in Reverse: A Critical Analysis of Fair Trial Rights under International Criminal Law' in Schabas, *Ashgate Research Companion*, 165–80.

[151] *Situation in the DRC*, ICC PTC I, 31 March 2006, para. 38, and references to ECtHR case law, para. 50.

[152] *Kony et al.*, ICC PTC II, 10 July 2006, para. 24. [153] E.g. *ibid.*, para. 24.

[154] Art. 21(1) of the ICTY Statute, Art. 20(1) of the ICTR Statute, Art. 19(1) of the MICT Statute and Art. 67(1) of the ICC Statute. See also Arts. 14(1) and 26 of the ICCPR. See further e.g. Stefania Negri, 'Equality of Arms: Guiding Light or Empty Shell?' in Bohlander, *International Criminal Justice*, 13–73; and Charles Chernor Jalloh and Amy DiBella, 'Equality of Arms in International Criminal Law: Continuing Challenges' in Schabas, *Ashgate Research Companion*, 251–87.

[155] E.g. *Tadić*, ICTY A. Ch., 15 July 1999, paras. 44 and 52.   [156] *Ibid.*, para. 48.

[157] E.g. *Kayishema and Ruzindana*, ICTR A. Ch., 1 June 2001, paras. 67–9; and *Kordić and Čerkez*, ICTY A. Ch., 17 December 2004, paras. 175–6 (referring to an earlier decision in the same case: ICTY A. Ch., 11 September 2001, paras. 5–9).

[158] E.g. *Lubanga*, ICC T. Ch. I, 14 December 2007, para. 19 ('absolute equality of arms' is impossible to create). The emphasis is rather placed on the sufficiency or adequacy of resources, e.g. *Kony et al.*, ICC PTC II, 19 August 2005, para. 30. See Marc Dubuisson *et al.*, 'Contribution of the Registry to Greater Respect for the Principles of Fairness and Expeditious Proceedings before the International Criminal Court' in Stahn and Sluiter, *Emerging Practice*, 565–84.

[159] Cf. the STL where a Defence Office has been established as a separate organ of the Court. See generally International Bar Association, *Fairness at the International Criminal Court* (August 2011) 10, 32–5.

Other aspects of the equality of arms are the accused's rights to prompt and detailed information about the charges, to disclosure of and access to the Prosecutor's evidence, to defence counsel, to examine witnesses against him or her, and to call witnesses under equal conditions.[160]

Each Statute provides the accused with the right to be tried without 'undue delay'; a right also reflected in all major human rights instruments.[161] The ICTY, ICTR and ICC are often criticized for excessively long proceedings,[162] and many challenges have been launched by accused claiming violations of this right. To no surprise, many critics are coloured by their own legal tradition; common law observers would, for example, question the relaxed practice on admissibility of evidence,[163] and civil law observers argue in favour of even more judicial intervention in the investigation and, based on a 'dossier', at trial.[164] In response, the ICTY and ICTR have amended their practices and rules to achieve more expeditious proceedings but they still remain very long in most cases.[165] Such efforts are also made regarding the ICC. Apart from the fact that the resources are limited, the main reason is that international investigations and prosecutions are very complex, factually, legally and politically, and therefore more time-consuming than most domestic ones. Hence, procedural reforms and practices can only do so much to reduce the length of the proceedings.[166]

17.4   Jurisdiction and admissibility procedures

The Tribunals have established their authority to determine the legality of their creation.[167] Challenges to the Tribunals' jurisdiction, of which there have been many in practice, are dealt with as preliminary motions and carry a right to interlocutory appeal.[168]

The procedures for establishing jurisdiction and admissibility were an important component in reaching an agreement in the ICC negotiations (see Chapter 8). The main rule is that the Court must satisfy itself that it has jurisdiction and it may also, on its own motion, determine the admissibility of a case.[169] This will not be relevant at every stage of the

[160] These rights are also specifically provided for: Art. 21(4) of the ICTY Statute, Art. 20(4) of the ICTR Statute, Art. 19(4) of the MICT Statute and Art. 67(1) of the ICC Statute. The right to call witnesses has been interpreted as placing a positive duty upon the Tribunal to assist the accused with summonses, safe conducts and other measures necessary for obtaining the testimony; see e.g. *Tadić*, ICTY T. Ch. II, 26 June 1996, and *Kupreškić et al.*, ICTY T. Ch. II, 6 October 1998.
[161] Art. 21 of the ICTY Statute, Art. 20 of the ICTR Statute, Art. 19 of the MICT Statute and Art. 67 of the ICC Statute. See also Art. 14(3) of the ICCPR. In addition, Art. 64(3)(c) of the ICC Statute obliges the Trial Chamber to 'confer with the parties and adopt such procedures as are necessary to facilitate the fair and expeditious conduct of the proceedings'.
[162] Reference is sometimes made to the Nuremberg trials which lasted some ten months and covered all of the Second World War in the Western theatre, but this comparison is not entirely relevant due to the development of fair trial rights since the 1940s, including the right to appeals.
[163] E.g. Ian Bryan and Peter Rowe, 'The Role of Evidence in War Crimes Trials: The Common Law and the Yugoslav Tribunal' (1999) 2 *Yearbook of International Humanitarian Law* 307; Peter Murphy, 'No Free Lunch, No Free Proof: The Indiscriminate Admission of Evidence Is a Serious Flaw in International Criminal Trials' (2010) 8 *Journal of International Criminal Justice* 539; and Nancy Amoury Combs, *Fact-Finding without Facts* (Cambridge, 2010).
[164] E.g. Stéphane Bourgon, 'Procedural Problems Hindering Expeditious and Fair Justice' (2004) 2 *Journal of International Criminal Justice* 526.
[165] See Máximo Langer and Joseph Doherty, 'Managerial Judging Goes International, but its Promise Remains Unfulfilled: An Empirical Assessment of the ICTY Reforms' (2011) 36 *Yale Journal of International Law* 241.
[166] See also Alex Whiting, 'In International Criminal Prosecutions, Justice Delayed Can Be Justice Delivered' (2009) 50 *Harvard International Law Journal* 323 (questioning the push for quick investigations and prosecutions of international crimes).
[167] See section 7.2.4.   [168] Rule 72 of the ICTY RPE and the ICTR RPE, and r. 79 of the MICT RPE.
[169] Art. 19(1) of the ICC Statute.

proceedings. In relation to the issuance of arrest warrants, for example, the *proprio motu* power to determine admissibility should only be exercised exceptionally in order to preserve the interests of the suspect.[170] For example, this discretionary power was applied when general information indicated that there was an intention to institute prosecutions and to set up alternative justice mechanisms as part of the peace process in Uganda.[171] The Prosecutor has to consider the issues when deciding whether to proceed with an investigation or prosecution.[172] Upon the commencement of an investigation, the Prosecutor must notify all States with jurisdiction, so that they may if they wish seek a deferral of the ICC investigation while they undertake national proceedings.[173]

Although all investigations so far have been opened with respect to an entire 'situation', the admissibility test is always case-specific.[174] Accordingly, admissibility in early stages (before any particular case is selected) must be examined more generally in relation to 'potential cases'.[175] When the Pre-Trial Chamber assesses whether to authorize the commencement of an investigation, the Prosecutor will have to provide sufficient information for this assessment.[176]

The ICC cannot request national courts to 'defer to its competence'.[177] Hence, States are not prohibited from initiating proceedings after the ICC has done so, unless the ICC has already handed down a final verdict.[178] A challenge to jurisdiction or the admissibility of a case may be made when the ICC process is under way, at any time prior to the commencement of the trial, and exceptionally thereafter.[179] A right to challenge is afforded to: (1) the accused or a person for whom a warrant of arrest or a summons to appear has been issued; (2) any State with concurrent jurisdiction over the crimes and where investigation or prosecution has been commenced; and (3) any State from which acceptance of jurisdiction is required.[180] Certain provisions seek to make the scheme manageable, for example that States must make their challenge at the earliest opportunity and that a person or a State may make a challenge only once.[181] Still, these proceedings tend to be many and lengthy.[182] In

---

[170] *Situation in the DRC*, ICC A. Ch., 13 July 2006, paras. 50–3 (requiring that, e.g. 'an ostensible cause' or 'self-evident factor' impel the exercise of the discretion). Cf. *Lubanga*, ICC PTC I, 10 February 2006, paras. 17–20 (admissibility determination when deciding to issue an arrest warrant). See also Sarah Nouwen, 'Fine-Tuning Complementarity' in Brown, *Research Handbook*, 226–7.

[171] E.g. *Kony et al.*, ICC PTC, 10 March 2009 (including a survey in paras. 15–19), and ICC A. Ch., 16 September 2009 (confirming the decision, although indicating that it might have exercised the discretion differently).

[172] See sections 17.5 and 17.8.1.

[173] Art. 18 of the ICC Statute and rr. 52–57 of the ICC RPE. But this notification procedure does not apply when the Security Council has referred the situation to the Court.

[174] See also Nouwen, 'Fine-Tuning Complementarity', 222. On the distinction between a 'situation' and a 'case', see further section 17.5.

[175] See also section 8.6.7.

[176] *Situation in Kenya*, ICC PTC II, 31 March 2010, paras. 40–50, 181–2; and *Situation in Côte d'Ivoire*, ICC PTC III, 3 October 2010, paras. 191–200.

[177] Cf. Art. 9(2) of the ICTY Statute, Art. 8(2) of the ICTR Statute and Art. 5(2) of the MICT Statute.

[178] See Art. 20(2) of the ICC Statute.

[179] Art. 19(4) of the ICC Statute; see also Arts. 17(1)(c) and 20(3) and rr. 58–60 of the ICC RPE. On the meaning of 'prior to or at the commencement of the trial', see *Katanga and Ngudjolo Chui*, ICC PTC II, 16 June 2009, paras. 29–50.

[180] Art. 19(2) of the ICC Statute. The Prosecutor may also seek a ruling from the Court: *ibid.*, Art. 19(3).

[181] *Ibid.*, Art. 19(4)–(5).

[182] They have been described as a 'complex and burdensome procedural regime', likely to impede the functioning of the ICC; see Leila Sadat and Richard Carden, 'The New International Criminal Court: An Uneasy Revolution' (2000) 88 *Georgetown Law Journal* 381, 417. Libya's challenge to the admissibility of the case against Mr Gaddafi was decided by the Pre-Trial Chamber one year after being filed and after repeated requests for additional information.

order to avoid a complete standstill, the Pre-Trial Chamber may authorize the Prosecutor to perform specific investigative measures in spite of a deferral or a State challenge.[183] A State may postpone the execution of a request for cooperation, which, if court ordered, such as a request for arrest and surrender, requires authorization by the Court.[184] The decisions are subject to interlocutory appeal and the Prosecutor may seek review of a decision declaring the case inadmissible.[185]

The admissibility of a case must be determined on the basis of the facts as they exist at the time of the proceedings concerning the challenge.[186] The allocation of the burden of proof for the questions of unwillingness or inability as well as the factual circumstances concerning domestic investigations, prosecutions and jurisdiction is not settled in the ICC Statute or RPE.[187] The Court has held that a State challenging the admissibility of a case 'bears the burden of proof to show that the case is inadmissible', and that the evidence must have 'a sufficient degree of specificity and probative value'.[188] But 'an evidentiary debate on the State's unwillingness or inability will be meaningful only when doubts arise with regard to the genuineness of the domestic investigations or prosecutions'.[189] The required standard of proof has been explained as 'concrete, tangible and pertinent evidence' which 'shall demonstrate that [the State] is taking concrete and progressive steps toward ascertaining [the suspected or accused person's] responsibility'.[190]

While at the Tribunals a challenge may also relate to the exercise of jurisdiction in the particular case,[191] the ICC does not consider a request that the Court decline jurisdiction due to 'abuse of process' as a jurisdictional challenge.[192] But neither the Tribunals nor the ICC treat the interpretation and existence of a contextual element of a crime as an issue of (subject-matter) jurisdiction since this relates to the substantive merits of the case.[193] As with admissibility challenges, the burden of proof rests with the party bringing the jurisdictional challenge.[194]

[183] Arts. 18(6) and 19(7)–(8) of the ICC Statute and rr. 57 and 61 of the ICC RPE.
[184] Art. 95 of the ICC Statute. See e.g. *Gaddafi and Al-Senussi*, ICC PTC I, 1 June 2012.
[185] Art. 19(6) and (10) of the ICC Statute and rr. 60 and 62 of the ICC RPE.
[186] See *Katanga and Ngudjolo Chui*, ICC A. Ch., 25 September 2010, para. 56.
[187] Different solutions have been advanced, e.g. Simon Young, 'Surrendering the Accused to the International Criminal Court' (2001) 71 *British Yearbook of International Law* 317, 334; Markus Benzing, 'The Complementarity Regime of the International Criminal Court: International Criminal Justice between State Sovereignty and the Fight against Impunity' (2003) 7 *Max Planck Yearbook of United Nations Law* 591; Megan Fairlie, 'Establishing Admissibility in the International Criminal Court: Does the Buck Stop with the Prosecutor, Full Stop?' (2005) 39 *International Lawyer* 817.
[188] *Ruto et al.*, ICC A. Ch., 30 August 2011, paras. 2, 62; and *Muthaura et al.*, ICC A. Ch., 30 August 2011, paras. 2, 61.
[189] *Gaddafi and Al-Senussi*, ICC PTC I, 31 May 2013, paras. 52–3.   [190] *Ibid.*, paras. 54–5.
[191] E.g. *Barayagwiza*, ICTR A. Ch., 3 November 1999, para. 74; *Dragan Nikolić*, ICTY T. Ch. II, 9 October 2002, para. 114, and ICTY A. Ch., 5 June 2003, paras. 28–30, and *Karadžić*, ICTY T. Ch. III, 8 July 2009, paras. 80–8.
[192] *Lubanga*, ICC A. Ch., 14 December 2006, para. 24. Cf. *Lubanga*, ICC PTC I, 3 October 2006; and *Karadžić*, ICTY T. Ch. III, 8 July 2009, paras. 41–4. See section 17.7.3.
[193] *Ruto et al.*, ICC A. Ch., 24 May 2012, paras. 27–30. Similarly, the ICTY and ICTR also opine that factual and evidentiary matters are to be considered at trial and not as part of pre-trial jurisdictional challenges, and make a distinction between challenges to the existence of a crime (jurisdiction) and those relating to the contours or elements of crimes or modes of liability, e.g. *Gotovina et al.*, ICTY A. Ch., 6 June 2007, paras. 15, 18, 21 and 24.
[194] *Mbarushimana*, ICC PTC I, 26 October 2011, para. 4.

17.5   Commencement and discontinuance of a criminal investigation

The ICTY and ICTR have clear jurisdictional mandates as to crimes, persons, territory and time, set out in their respective Statutes (see Chapter 7). Within these parameters, the Prosecutors have initiated investigations *ex officio*, provided there was 'sufficient basis to proceed'.[195] Judicial permission is not required, nor is there an obligation to investigate all crimes that fulfil the jurisdictional criteria.

At the ICC, the requirements for the commencement of an investigation are more complex. Unlike the Tribunals, the ICC will potentially have global jurisdiction, and specified 'trigger mechanisms' are therefore required for bringing a 'situation' before the Court.[196] Upon a referral of the situation, the decision whether to open an investigation rests with the Prosecutor and a positive decision is not subject to judicial review. A decision not to investigate may be reviewed by the Pre-Trial Chamber on its own motion, but only under very limited circumstances.[197] Where there is no referral, the investigation is always subject to approval by the Pre-Trial Chamber, which in turn requires 'a reasonable basis to proceed with an investigation' and a preliminary assessment of jurisdiction.[198] Hence, a system of checks and balances between the Prosecutor and the judiciary has been built into the ICC Statute on the sensitive issue of the commencement of an investigation. Critics argue, however, that this is far from enough and that extended judicial control is required.[199]

Regardless of the trigger mechanism, the ICC Prosecutor must determine whether an investigation may be initiated in accordance with set criteria, namely (1) a reasonable suspicion of a crime under the Court's jurisdiction;[200] (2) the admissibility of the case in accordance with the complementarity principle and the requirement of 'sufficient gravity'; and (3) an assessment of the 'interests of justice'.[201] A process of information gathering and analysis, a 'preliminary examination', precedes the criminal investigation.[202]

Although the drafting of Article 53(1) of the ICC Statute ('shall initiate … unless …') indicates a duty to go ahead if the conditions are met, the conditions in reality provide for a high degree of discretion. Such discretion is known in common law jurisdictions, but foreign to civil law systems where instead the duty approach applies. The solution provides necessary flexibility to set strategies and focus resources, but may be criticized on principled and other grounds.[203] The discretion primarily hinges on a contentious, complex and

---

[195] Art. 18(1) of the ICTY Statute, Art. 17(1) of the ICTR Statute, and Art. 14(1) of the MICT Statute. However, the Residual Mechanism may not open new investigations on the core crimes, Art. 1(5).

[196] See section 8.7.

[197] Art. 53(3) of the ICC Statute. When the Prosecutor was challenged with inaction concerning the referral of one situation, the Pre-Trial Chamber merely concluded that the preliminary examination 'must be completed within a reasonable time' and requested the Prosecutor to inform the referring State about the current status of his examination: *Situation in Central African Republic*, ICC PTC III, 30 November 2006.

[198] *Ibid.*, Art. 15(4). See also reg. 49 of the ICC Regulations; *Situation in Kenya*, ICC PTC II, 31 March 2010; and *Situation in Côte d'Ivoire*, ICC PTC III, 3 October 2011.

[199] E.g. Carsten Stahn, 'Judicial Review of Prosecutorial Discretion: On Experiments and Imperfections' in Sluiter and Vasiliev, *International Criminal Procedure*, 239–71.

[200] This requirement also includes respecting any applicable reservations concerning jurisdiction over war crimes (Art. 124 of the ICC Statute).

[201] Art. 53(1) of the ICC Statute and r. 48 of the ICC RPE.

[202] Procedures have been established in the ICC Regulations of the OTP of 23 April 2009 (ICC-BD 05–07–09).

[203] See section 17.8.1.

undefined 'interests of justice' criterion, which has caused debate.[204] While the Prosecutor must consider the requirement when deciding whether to open an investigation (or seek authorization for one) and has expressed a policy, the Chambers have not yet pronounced on the issue.[205] However, the text and purpose of the ICC Statute clearly favour the pursuit of investigations and prosecutions when the conditions concerning the evidentiary threshold and admissibility are met. Hence, declining to proceed due to 'interests of justice' should be an exceptional decision.

So far, the ICC Prosecutor has commenced investigations into entire 'situations', within which the focus has then been placed on selected incidents. Similar to the ICTY and ICTR, the ICC Prosecutor has followed a prosecutorial policy focusing on those bearing the greatest responsibility for the most serious crimes.[206] Being a policy matter of the utmost importance, the selection of situations and cases has caused intense debates.[207] Central to the selection at the ICC is the 'gravity' of the crimes,[208] and the ICC Prosecutor refers to four elements – the scale, nature, and manner of commission, and the impact of the crimes[209] – which have also been endorsed by Pre-Trial Chambers.[210] At some later point a more specific 'case' arises, but it is a matter of dispute as to when this is.[211] There are indications, however, that a 'case' arises first with an arrest warrant or summons to appear.[212] In order to ensure a coherent system, a settled view on the understanding of 'situations' and 'cases' is

---

[204] Art. 53(1)(c) of the ICC Statute. See e.g. Darryl Robinson, 'Serving the Interests of Justice: Amnesties, Truth Commissions, and the International Criminal Court' (2003) 14 *European Journal of International Law* 481; and Kenneth Rodman, 'Is Peace in the Interest of Justice? The Case for Broad Prosecutorial Discretion at the International Criminal Court' (2009) 22 *Leiden Journal of International Law* 99.

[205] See regs. 29(1) and 31 of the ICC Regulations of the OTP; and ICC OTP, *Policy Paper on the Interests of Justice* (September 2007). Only when the Prosecutor declines to investigate (or prosecute) will the Chamber have to address the issue; see *Situation in Kenya*, ICC PTC II, 31 March 2010, para. 24 (footnotes 35 and 63); and *Situation in Côte d'Ivoire*, ICC PTC III, 3 October 2011, paras. 207–8.

[206] ICC OTP, *Prosecutorial Strategy 2009–2012* (1 February 2010), para. 19. See Fabricio Guariglia, '"Those Most Responsible" versus International Sex Crimes: Competing Prosecution Themes?' in Morten Bergsmo (ed.), *Thematic Prosecution of International Sex Crimes* (Beijing, 2012) 45–58.

[207] On the ICTY, compare Richard Goldstone, 'A View from the Prosecution' (2004) 2 *Journal of International Criminal Justice* 380; and Antonio Cassese, 'The ICTY: A Living and Vital Reality' (2004) 2 *Journal of International Criminal Justice* 587. On the ICC, see e.g. Fabricio Guariglia, 'The Selection of Cases by the Office of the Prosecutor of the International Criminal Court' in Stahn and Sluiter, *Emerging Practice*, 209–17; Margaret deGuzman, 'Choosing to Prosecute: Expressive Selection at the International Criminal Court' (2012) 33 *Michigan Journal of International Law* 265; Kai Ambos and Ignaz Stegmiller, 'Prosecuting International Crimes at the International Criminal Court: Is there a Coherent and Comprehensive Prosecution Strategy?' (2012) 58 *Crime, Law and Social Change* 391. See also Morten Bergsmo (ed.), *Criteria for Prioritizing and Selecting Core International Crimes Cases* (Oslo, 2010); and Margaret deGuzman and William Schabas, 'Initiation of Investigations and Selection of Cases' in Sluiter, *International Criminal Procedure*, 131–69.

[208] See Arts. 17(1)(d) and 53(1)(c) of the ICC Statute.

[209] Reg. 29(2) of the ICC Regulations of the OTP. See also ICC OTP, *Policy Paper on Preliminary Examinations (Draft)* (October 2010), para. 70.

[210] *Situation in Kenya*, ICC PTC II, 31 March 2010, paras. 62, 188–9; and *Situation in Côte d'Ivoire*, ICC PTC III, 3 October 2011, para. 204. Both Chambers concluded that other circumstances could also be taken into account, such as 'any aggravating circumstances', and that the gravity of the 'situation' as well as 'potential cases' should be considered. See also *Abu Garda*, ICC PTC I, 8 February 2010, paras. 31–2. The Prosecutor, on the other hand, appears to have moved towards assessing the gravity of the incidents and not of the situation as a whole: see ICC OTP, *Situation in Mali: Article 53(1) Report* of 16 January 2013, paras. 142–70.

[211] An attempt to explain the distinction is provided in *Lubanga*, ICC PTC I, 17 January 2006, para. 65. See further Rod Rastan, 'What Is a "Case" for the Purpose of the Rome Statute?' (2008) 19 *Criminal Law Forum* 435, and 'Situation and Case: Defining the Parameters' in Carsten Stahn and Mohamed El Zeidy (eds.), *The International Criminal Court and Complementarity: From Theory to Practice* (Cambridge, 2011) 421–59.

[212] E.g. *Situation in the DRC*, ICC PTC I, 9 November 2005.

very important, not least since admissibility determinations in accordance with the complementarity principle are clearly linked to a 'case'.[213]

The jurisdictional scope of the situation, and thus the investigation, may be difficult to define, but only rarely have the Chambers addressed whether a particular case actually is within the boundaries of the situation for which the jurisdiction of the Court was activated.[214] As for temporal jurisdiction, the practice is mixed, and, while one Chamber has determined that the investigation may cover only crimes committed prior to the Prosecutor's application for authorization (under Article 15),[215] others have also included 'any ongoing and continuing crimes'.[216]

Since it covers an entire 'situation', there will come a time when the investigation should be closed because no more crimes will be pursued. Arguably, such a decision should be formalized, but the ICC Statute and RPE are not really designed for the discontinuation of a 'situation' and it is not clear that the relevant provisions apply, including those on judicial review, especially if the decision does not relate to specific suspects or incidents.[217]

17.6   The criminal investigation

Both at the ad hoc Tribunals and at the ICC, the Prosecutor is in charge of the criminal investigation. Each investigation is conducted by a multidisciplinary team (lawyers, investigators, analysts and others). While the ICTY's investigations were led by a senior trial attorney, a feature that departs from the traditional approach in many common law jurisdictions but corresponds to other domestic jurisdictions, the ICC has taken a 'joint team' approach with less clear legal supervision.[218] The investigation seeks to collect evidence regarding individual criminal liability, for sentencing and, at the ICC, for freezing, seizure and forfeiture. The prosecutorial policy of 'focused investigations' at the ICC.[219]

The Prosecutor is given the authority to take necessary measures in the investigation.[220] Although not an investigating body, the Pre-Trial Chamber has some role with respect to the

---

[213] See Chapter 8 and section 17.4.

[214] E.g. *Mbarushimana*, ICC PTC I, 28 September 2010, paras. 5–8, and ICC PTC I, 26 October 2011. See also *Gbagbo*, ICC A. Ch., 12 December 2012. See generally Rod Rastan, 'The Jurisdictional Scope of Situations before the International Criminal Court' (2012) 23 *Criminal Law Forum* 1.

[215] *Situation in Kenya*, ICC PTC II, 31 March 2010, para. 206.

[216] *Situation in Côte d'Ivoire*, ICC PTC III, 3 October 2011, paras. 178–9; *Mbarushimana*, ICC PTC I, 26 October 2011, paras. 6–7; and *Gbagbo*, ICC A. Ch., 12 December 2012, paras. 77–84 (on Art. 12(3) of the ICC Statute).

[217] See Art. 53 of the ICC Statute, read together with rr. 105–106 of the ICC RPE. A review requires a decision by the Prosecutor; see *Situation in the DRC*, ICC PTC I, 26 September 2007 p. 5. On the interpretation of Art. 53(2) on non-prosecution, see Stahn, 'Judicial Review', 270–1.

[218] See ICTY/UNICRI, *ICTY Manual on Developed Practices* (Turin, 2009) 12–13; and reg. 32 of the ICC OTP Regulations. On European systems, see e.g. Eric Mathias, 'The Balance of Power between the Police and the Public Prosecutor' in Delmas-Marty and Spencer, *European Criminal Procedure*, 459–87.

[219] Reg. 34(2) of the ICC OTP Regulations and ICC OTP, *Prosecutorial Strategy 2009–2012* (1 February 2010), paras. 19–21.

[220] Rule 39(ii) of the ICTY RPE and ICTR RPE, r. 36(B) of the MICT RPE and Art. 54(1)(b) of the ICC Statute.

investigation. Limited but important judicial intervention in the investigation, inspired by
civil law systems, is provided for by a so-called 'unique investigative opportunity', whereby
the Chambers may take measures to ensure the efficiency and integrity of the proceedings
and protect the rights of the defence.[221] In addition, the Chamber has certain general
functions which also apply during the investigation.[222] The Chambers have explored
these powers in practice, but it is important to note that the ICC Statute explicitly vests
the responsibility for conducting the investigation in the Prosecutor.[223]

As to the scope of the investigation, the ICC Prosecutor is under an obligation to
'investigate incriminating and exonerating circumstances equally' (a 'principle of objectivity'), which departs from the Prosecutor's function at the ICTY, ICTR and the Residual
Mechanism.[224] It has been argued that this mechanism, properly operated, has the potential
to narrow the scope of the case, reducing the number of charges, and possibly the length of
the subsequent trial;[225] the traditional distinction in adversarial proceedings between a
'prosecution case' and a 'defence case' could also diminish.

Investigative measures include the questioning of individuals (suspects, victims, witnesses, experts and others), the collection of written and other material, exhumation of mass
graves, and other forensic measures. A suspect who is questioned must be given certain
information and has rights to silence, legal assistance, and interpretation.[226] The circumstances surrounding the interview may affect the use at trial of the statement obtained.[227]
The ICC provisions explicitly apply also when national authorities conduct the questioning
on behalf of the Court. Further, the ICC Statute provides for certain fundamental rights of
any person[228] – concerning self-incrimination, coercion, duress and threat, interpretation
and translations, and deprivation of liberty – which reflect generally accepted human rights,
and, as such, will be observed also by the ICTY and ICTR. An important but difficult task,
shared by the prosecution and the Chambers, is to provide for protection of victims and
witnesses (see Chapter 18).

Without an international police force to carry out the investigation and to enforce court
orders, the investigation depends to a large extent upon the cooperation of States and other
entities such as peacekeeping forces (see Chapter 20). The Prosecutor is entitled to seek
cooperation from States and others in the investigation.[229] A Chamber may also issue

---

[221] Art. 56 of the ICC Statute. See also *Situation in the DRC*, ICC PTC I, 26 April 2005.

[222] Art. 57(3) of the ICC Statute. The functions include, *inter alia*, protection and privacy of victims and witnesses, preservation of
evidence, protection of persons who have been arrested or appeared in response to a summons, and protection of national
security information (para. 3(c)). In order to fulfil its functions, the Pre-Trial Chamber may request the Prosecutor to provide
information: reg. 48 of the ICC Regulations.

[223] Art. 42(1) of the ICC Statute. See also *Situation in the DRC*, ICC A. Ch., 19 December 2008, para. 52.

[224] Art. 54(1)(a) of the ICC Statute. In the Tribunals, the Prosecutor is not required actively to investigate circumstances and collect
evidence that speaks in favour of the suspect. Only if such evidence emerges anyway during the investigation must it be
considered and disclosed.

[225] See e.g. ICC OTP, *Informal Expert Paper: Measures Available to the International Criminal Court to Reduce the Length of
Proceedings* (2003), paras. 22–30.

[226] Art. 18(3) of the ICTY Statute, Art. 17(3) of the ICTR Statute, Art. 16(3) of the MICT Statute, r. 42 of the ICTY RPE and ICTR
RPE, rr. 40–41 of the MICT RPE, and Art. 55(2) of the ICC Statute.

[227] E.g. *Halilović*, ICTY A. Ch., 19 August 2005; and *Delalić et al.*, ICTY T. Ch. II, 2 September 1997, para. 55.

[228] Art. 55(1) of the ICC Statute.

[229] Art. 18(2) of the ICTY Statute, Art. 17(2) of the ICTR Statute, Art. 16(2) of the MICT Statute and Art. 54(2)(c) of the ICC
Statute, as well as provisions in the respective RPE.

necessary orders and warrants.[230] The defence may by this means seek a request for cooperation by a State and, in the ICC,[231] an order directed to the Prosecutor regarding specific investigative measures.

Generally, it is valuable that the Court's own investigators undertake, or at least participate in, the investigative measures. Thereby they can ensure various rights and collection of evidence that can later be used in the proceedings, and, sometimes, secure the confidence and cooperation of victims and witnesses. The ICC Prosecutor's right to conduct on-site investigations is circumscribed by specific conditions and confined to non-coercive measures.[232] Exceptionally, the ICC Pre-Trial Chamber may, if the State functions have collapsed, authorize the Prosecutor 'to take specific investigative steps within the territory of a State without having secured the cooperation of that State'.[233]

International criminal investigations are challenging owing to conditions such as restricted access to evidence, lack of cooperation by States and others, security concerns, particularly when the conflict is ongoing, cultural and linguistic barriers, and different views on best practices in multinational teams.[234] The mixed success regarding confirmation of charges and prosecutions has led to criticism and review of the ICC's investigations.[235] Small investigation teams and 'short investigations', aiming at 'expeditious and focused cases',[236] have together with security concerns led not only to narrow prosecutions[237] but also to investigative practices being questioned.[238] Most serious was a heavy reliance upon intermediaries without adequate supervision and control by the prosecution, causing an attempt to stay the proceedings permanently, evidence to be rejected, and victims to lose their participatory rights.[239] The issue is being addressed in the form of guidelines, a code of conduct for intermediaries, and a model contract. Other issues are the reliance upon secondary information gathered by third parties rather than by the investigators, a cautious

---

[230] Rule 54 of the ICTY RPE and ICTR RPE, r. 55 of the MICT RPE and Art. 57(3) of the ICC Statute. An order to a State for production of documents requires a sufficient level of specificity, and a 'fishing expedition' is not allowed; see *Blaškić*, ICTY A. Ch., 29 October 1997, para. 32, later codified in r. 54*bis* of the ICTY RPE and r. 56 of the MICT RPE. See also r. 116 of the ICC RPE.

[231] See *Banda and Jerbo*, ICC T. Ch. IV, 1 July 2011, para. 31. Cf. *Kabiligi*, ICTR T. Ch. III, 1 June 2000, para. 20 (no legal basis for the Chamber to intervene and order supplementary investigations).

[232] Art. 99(4) of the ICC Statute. Cf. Art. 18(2) of the ICTY Statute, Art. 17(2) of the ICTR Statute and Art. 16(3) of the MICT Statute. See further section 20.6.3.

[233] Arts. 54(2) and 57(3)(d) of the ICC Statute and r. 115 of the ICC RPE. For these (controversial) cases there is no explicit restriction to non-coercive measures.

[234] See e.g. Hiroto Fujiwara and Stephan Parmentier, 'Investigations' in Reydams, *International Prosecutors*, 573–5.

[235] See e.g. Elena Bayliss, 'Outsourcing Investigations' (2009) 14 *UCLA Journal of International Law and Foreign Affairs* 121, and *Investigative Management, Strategies, and Techniques of the International Criminal Court's Office of the Prosecutor* (Report 16, American University, Washington College of Law, War Crimes Research Office, Washington DC, October 2012).

[236] ICC OTP, *Prosecutorial Strategy 2009–2012*, 1 February 2010, para. 20; and *Report on the Activities Performed during the First Three Years (June 2003–June 2006)*, 12 September 2006, 7–8.

[237] Also this being criticized, not least with respect to crimes of sexual violence and gender crimes; see e.g. *Lubanga*, ICC T. Ch. I, 14 March 2012, para. 896. See generally Bergsmo, *Thematic Prosecutions*.

[238] In both trial judgments thus far, the Trial Chamber found reason to critically address the investigation in relative detail: *Lubanga*, ICC T. Ch. I, 14 March 2012, paras. 124–68; and *Ngudjolo Chui*, ICC T. Ch. II, 18 December 2012, paras. 115–23.

[239] *Lubanga*, ICC T. Ch. I, 7 March 2011, and ICC T. Ch. I, 14 March 2012, para. 482, 484 (also seriously criticizing the prosecution for having 'delegated its investigative responsibilities'). See also *Lubanga*, ICC T. Ch. I, 31 May 2010 (where the Chamber made specific orders in relation to intermediaries, including ordering the prosecution to call two of them as well as the lead investigator as witnesses).

approach to on-site investigations, and cases being brought forward before they were sufficiently investigated.[240]

There is no time limit as to when the investigation must be concluded, but, 'ideally, it would be desirable for the investigation to be complete by the time of the confirmation hearing'.[241] The Prosecutor has expressed an ambition to be 'nearly trial ready' by the time he seeks an arrest warrant.[242] But generally this has not been the case. Pre-Trial Chambers (and individual judges) have repeatedly expressed discomfort with a possible expansion of the factual ambit of the case after the confirmation process,[243] owing primarily to the perceived function of the confirmation process.

17.7   Coercive measures

17.7.1   Coercive measures in general

In all criminal investigations and proceedings, it must be possible to resort to coercive measures of various kinds. Due to the relationship between the international criminal jurisdictions and domestic jurisdictions, the international Prosecutor will primarily have to resort to the cooperation of States or sometimes other entities, mainly international military or police forces. As already noted, the ICC Prosecutor's powers to conduct measures on site are more circumscribed than those of the ICTY and ICTR Prosecutors, and normally limited to non-coercive measures. While the latter were entitled, under certain conditions, to undertake coercive measures directly on the territory of a State,[244] the ICC Prosecutor will have to go through national authorities or others.[245]

In domestic systems, coercive measures which infringe on the rights and freedoms of individuals are generally subject to judicial review, either before the measure is taken or afterwards. The Chambers of the ICTY, ICTR and the ICC have explicit powers to issue necessary warrants and orders,[246] which may also concern coercive measures. On-site measures by the ICTY and ICTR without the assistance of national authorities have been conducted pursuant to such warrants,[247] but in most cases no warrant was sought.[248] A debated issue is whether international warrants should be required in connection with a

---

[240] See e.g. American University, *Management, Strategies, and Techniques.*
[241] *Lubanga*, ICC A. Ch., 13 October 2006, para. 54; overruling the Pre-Trial Chamber's decision that the investigation is limited to the time before the confirmation hearing (ICC PTC I, 19 May 2006, para. 39). The Appeals Chamber also rejected other asserted restrictions to the Prosecutor's investigative powers (ICC A. Ch., 13 October 2006, paras. 51–6). See also *Mbarushimana*, ICC A. Ch., 30 May 2012, para. 44.
[242] ICC OTP, *Prosecutorial Strategy 2009–2012*, 1 February 2010, para. 20.
[243] E.g. *Mbarushimana*, ICC PTC I, 16 December 2012, paras. 81–2; and *Gbagbo*, ICC PTC I, 3 June 2013, paras. 25 and 37 (cf. Judge Fernandez de Gurmendi's Dissenting Opinion, paras. 7–9, 13–15).
[244] E.g. *Kordić and Čerkez*, ICTY T. Ch. III, 25 June 1999 (the investigation, resulting in the seizure of certain material, 'was perfectly within the Prosecutor's powers as provided for in the Statute'). See section 20.6.3.
[245] See *Blaškić*, ICTY A. Ch., 29 October 1997, para. 55. In case of a failed State, however, the ICC Pre-Trial Chamber may arguably authorize also coercive measures to be directly enforced on the State's territory: Art. 57(3)(d) of the ICC Statute.
[246] Rule 54 of the ICTY RPE and ICTR RPE, r. 55 of the MICT RPE and Art. 57(3) of the ICC Statute.
[247] E.g. *Kordić and Čerkez*, ICTY T. Ch. III, 25 June 1999; *Naletilić and Martinović*, ICTY T. Ch. I, 14 November 2001; and *Karadžić*, ICTY T. Ch. (Duty Judge), 11 September 2003.
[248] See e.g. *Stakić*, ICTY T. Ch. II, 31 July 2002, 2. See generally Amal Alamuddin, 'Collection of Evidence' in Kahn, *Principles of Evidence*, 284–94; and Karel de Meester, Kelly Pitcher, Rod Rastan and Göran Sluiter, 'Investigation, Coercive Measures, Arrest, and Surrender' in Sluiter, *International Criminal Procedure*, 284–98.

request for cooperation.[249] At the ICC, evidence obtained in contravention of the Statute or internationally recognized human rights may be declared inadmissible, which applies also to items seized by national authorities or international peacekeepers.[250] Presumably, a general principle of proportionality applies to coercive measures.[251]

17.7.2 Deprivation or restriction of liberty and surrender of suspects

Deprivation or restriction of liberty infringes on the fundamental rights of the person concerned and is at the same time an essential mechanism for the effective operation of criminal justice systems. These matters are therefore regulated in relative detail for the international criminal tribunals. The scheme of the ICC Statute departs from, and is in part a reaction to, the rules and practices of the ICTY and ICTR.

At the ICTY, ICTR and the Residual Mechanism, the arrest warrant must be issued by a judge following confirmation of the indictment in whole or in part, thus requiring that a '*prima facie* case' exists (see section 17.9.1).[252] The warrant serves as the basis for arrest and surrender. In urgent cases, the Prosecutor may request any State to arrest the suspect provisionally without an arrest warrant, but the subsequent transfer to and provisional arrest at the Tribunal require an order issued by a judge.[253] The rules provide for mandatory detention of the accused upon being transferred to the Tribunal.[254] This common law-inspired model is balanced by provisions on provisional release, which are important in order to respect the fundamental principle that liberty is the general rule and detention the exception.[255] The Trial Chamber may order provisional release if it is satisfied that the accused will appear for trial and, if released, will not pose a danger to any victim, witness or other persons.[256] But the accused must prove that the conditions are met[257] and provisional release is a discretionary power of the Chamber; even if the explicit conditions are met, release will be ordered only when appropriate in the case at hand.[258] An earlier requirement of 'extraordinary circumstances' was, controversially,[259] a major obstacle to release in practice, but, after amending the rules, and improving the relations with the States in the former Yugoslavia, the ICTY has released numerous accused awaiting trial. The ICTR and the Residual Mechanism, however, have not yet done that.

---

[249] See section 20.6.4.   [250] Art. 69(7) of the ICC Statute. See also *Lubanga*, ICC PTC I, 29 January 2007, paras. 62–94.
[251] See e.g. *Stakić*, ICTY T. Ch. II, 5 July 2002, 4; and *Lubanga*, ICC PTC I, 29 January 2007, para. 82. See also Art. 57(3)(a)–(b) of the ICC Statute and r. 116 of the ICC RPE, which may indicate that other requirements such as necessity, specificity, and relevance, also apply to coercive measures.
[252] Rules 47(H)(i) and 54 of the ICTY RPE and ICTR RPE, rr. 48(H)(i) and 57 of the MICT RPE.
[253] Rule 40*bis* of the ICTY RPE and ICTR RPE, and r. 37 of the MICT RPE. Regarding the Prosecutor's obligations, see *Kajelijeli*, ICTR A. Ch., 23 May 2005, paras. 218–33. The Residual Mechanism has re-issued arrest warrants for the ICTR fugitives still at large.
[254] Rule 64 of the ICTY RPE and ICTR RPE, r. 67 of the MICT RPE.
[255] See Art. 9(3) of the ICCPR, Art. 5(1) of the ECHR, Art. 6 of the ACHPR and Art. 7(1) of the ACHR.
[256] Rule 65 of the ICTY RPE and ICTR RPE, r. 68 of the MICT RPE. On the cumulative nature of the conditions, see e.g. *Rukundo*, ICTR T. Ch. III, 15 July 2004, para. 19. See generally Fergal Gaynor, 'Provisional Release in the Law of the International Criminal Tribunal for the Former Yugoslavia' in Doria, *Legal Regime*, 183–207; and de Meester *et al.*, 'Investigation', 312–39.
[257] E.g. *Prlić et al.*, ICTY A. Ch., 8 September 2004, paras. 27–8.
[258] E.g. *Brđanin and Talić*, ICTY T. Ch. II, 25 July 2000, para. 22.
[259] E.g. Judge Patrick Robinson's dissenting opinion in *Krajišnik and Plavšić*, ICTY T. Ch. III, 8 October 2001.

The test for provisional release at the Tribunals does not include an assessment of the strength of the suspicion, and Chambers have refused to review the evidentiary basis for a challenged arrest.[260] But, since the underlying decision to confirm the indictment is not subject to a separate appeal,[261] and no periodic review of detention is required, the practice prevents the accused from challenging the lawfulness of the arrest with respect to the requirement of a 'reasonable suspicion'. Hence, some ICTY Trial Chambers have allowed a review of the evidence 'in a cursory manner' in order to ascertain whether the detention of the accused remains lawful.[262]

The ICC Statute provides a quite different regime. Every request for a person's arrest, including a request for provisional arrest pending a surrender request, must be based on an arrest warrant issued by the Pre-Trial Chamber.[263] A separate procedure applies for issuance of an arrest warrant and the warrant is independent of, and regularly precedes, the indictment. Once arrested, national authorities may release the fugitive pending surrender, but there are certain requirements including ensuring that the State can fulfil its duty to surrender the person to the Court.[264] As to interim release after the surrender to the Court, the Pre-Trial Chamber is required to review its rulings on release or detention periodically on its own motion, and may do so at the request of a party.[265] The obligation to conduct the periodic reviews every 120 days is, according to settled practice, triggered only once the detained person has made one initial request for interim release;[266] it is the first ruling on interim release, not the decision to issue the arrest warrant, which thereafter is subject to the review. In addition, the Pre-Trial Chamber has a responsibility to ensure that detention does not last 'for an unreasonable period prior to trial due to inexcusable delay by the Prosecutor', and thus the detainee may be released in spite of all other prerequisites being met.[267] The Trial Chamber assumes the function of conducting reviews after the confirmation of charges.[268] A decision granting or denying release may be appealed without a requirement that leave be granted.

Specific requirements must be satisfied for the arrest warrant to be issued, namely, 'reasonable grounds to believe' that the person has committed a crime and additional prerequisites regarding a risk that the suspect absconds, obstructs or endangers the investigation or court proceedings, or continues to commit the crime in question or a related crime.[269] The same prerequisites must be assessed when the ICC decides on interim release pending trial and, if any criterion is not met, the person is to be released, with or without

---

[260] E.g. *Brđanin and Talić*, ICTY T. Ch. II, 8 December 1999, para. 16, and ICTY T. Ch. II, 10 December 1999.

[261] E.g. *Bagosora and 28 Others*, ICTR A. Ch., 8 June 1998.

[262] E.g. *Delalić et al.*, ICTY T. Ch. II, 25 September 1996, para. 24. See also McIntyre, 'Defining Human Rights', 211–14.

[263] Arts. 58(5), 91 (arrest and surrender) and 92 (provisional arrest) of the ICC Statute.   [264] *Ibid.*, Art. 59.

[265] Art. 60(3) of the ICC Statute and r. 118(2) of the ICC RPE. See e.g. *Lubanga*, ICC A. Ch., 13 February 2007, paras. 94–100, 134; *Katanga and Ngudjolo Chui*, ICC A. Ch., 9 June 2008, paras. 12, 26–7 (the detention must be assessed anew against the material presented to the Chamber); *Bemba Gombo*, ICC A. Ch., 16 December 2008 (defence access to documents is essential for effective challenge of lawfulness).

[266] E.g. *Lubanga*, ICC A. Ch., 13 February 2007, paras. 94–5; *Bemba Gombo*, ICC A. Ch., 19 November 2010, para. 45.

[267] Art. 60(4) of the ICC Statute. See e.g. *Lubanga*, ICC A. Ch., 13 February 2007, paras. 118–24.

[268] E.g. *Bemba Gombo*, ICC T. Ch. III, 1 April 2010, para. 25.

[269] Art. 58(1) of the ICC Statute. The admissibility of the case is *not* a substantive prerequisite: *Situation in the DRC*, ICC A. Ch., 13 July 2006 (169), para. 42. On the evidentiary standard, see e.g. *Al Bashir*, ICC A. Ch., 3 February 2010, paras. 31, 39; and *Gbagbo*, ICC PTC I, 30 November 2011, para. 27.

conditions.[270] Prosecution evidence concerning the alleged crimes is thus required and assessed as part of the process to issue the arrest warrant,[271] and the question is explicitly relevant in the subsequent reviews. In practice, however, the review focuses primarily on changed circumstances and the Prosecutor is not required to re-establish the facts underlying the warrant.[272] The first interim release was ordered in *Bemba Gombo*, but the decision was reversed since no State that was willing to receive the person and able to enforce the conditions for release was identified.[273] Another difference compared with the Tribunals is that the ICC has the option to issue a summons to appear, instead of an arrest warrant, when this is considered sufficient to ensure the person's appearance before the Court.[274] The summons may be combined with conditions restricting the person's liberty.[275] In sum, the legal conditions for deprivation of liberty are stricter at the ICC, but once in remand the odds for interim release are better at the ICTY.

The ICC Statute, but not the rules of the ICTY, ICTR or Residual Mechanism, provides for compensation for wrongfully arrested or convicted persons; but the Tribunals have an inherent power to award compensation on a discretionary basis.[276] Such compensation is considered very differently in domestic jurisdictions; some have a general right to compensation when deprivation of liberty is not followed by a conviction and others restrict compensation to unlawful arrests. International human rights instruments reflect this divide and require compensation only for 'unlawful arrests'.[277] The ICC provisions go further, and internationally they represent a breakthrough for broader compensation rights.[278]

17.7.3   *Legality of the arrest and violations of procedural rights*

The Statutes of the ICTY, ICTR and the Residual Mechanism make no explicit provision for challenges to the legality of deprivation of liberty of the kind which are available under the common law remedy of *habeas corpus*.[279] Nonetheless, in *Barayagwiza*, the ICTR Appeals Chamber concluded that a detained individual must have recourse to a court to challenge the lawfulness of his detention,[280] a conclusion that has been upheld in subsequent ICTY and

---

[270] Art. 60(2) of the ICC Statute and r. 118 of the ICC RPE (and r. 119 on conditional release).
[271] E.g. *Lubanga*, ICC PTC I, 10 February 2006, paras. 7–15.
[272] E.g. *Bemba Gombo*, ICC A. Ch., 19 November 2010, paras. 51–3.
[273] *Bemba Gombo*, ICC A. Ch., 2 December 2009; cf. PTC II, 14 August 2009. For conclusions similar to those of the Appeals Chamber, see e.g. *Rukundo*, ICTR T. Ch. III, 15 July 2004, para. 19; and *Katanga and Ngudjolo Chui*, ICC T. Ch. II, 17 March 2009, para. 8. See Chapter 20 on the subsequent debate concerning the lack of State cooperation in this regard.
[274] Art. 58(7) of the ICC Statute. See also r. 119 of the ICC RPE. See e.g. *Abu Garda*, ICC PTC I, 7 May 2009; cf. *Harun and Al Kushayb*, ICC PTC I, 27 April 2007, paras. 108–24.
[275] E.g. *Muthaura et al.*, ICC PTC II, 8 March 2011 and 4 April 2011.
[276] Art. 85 of the ICC Statute and rr. 173–175 of the ICC RPE. See *Rwamakuba*, ICTR A. Ch., 13 September 2007, para. 10 (compensation refused to a defendant for having been prosecuted and acquitted); and *Zigiranyirazo*, ICTR T. Ch. III, 18 June 2012, paras. 19–22 (no compensation; also considering Art. 85(3) of the ICC Statute as reflective of customary law).
[277] E.g. Art. 9(5) of the ICCPR. See also Art. 5(4) of the ECHR.
[278] See Stuart Beresford, 'Redressing the Wrongs of the International Justice System: Compensation for Persons Erroneously Detained, Prosecuted, or Convicted by the Ad Hoc Tribunals' (2002) 96 *American Journal of International Law* 628.
[279] The writ of *habeas corpus* is a fundamental feature of the common law jurisdiction, deriving its origins from Magna Carta, and has long been used domestically as a means of testing the validity of executive committals. However, this judicial remedy is peculiar to certain national jurisdictions – and nominally a precept of a sovereign or a head of State (a 'writ') – but not applicable, as such, in international criminal proceedings.
[280] *Barayagwiza*, ICTR A. Ch., 3 November 1999, para. 88.

ICTR decisions where similar motions have been heard.[281] The Chamber found support in the ICTR Statute and RPE, and noted that such a right to a judicial review is also enshrined in international human rights instruments.[282] Violations of other rights may be challenged, such as the rights regarding information of the reasons for the arrest, appearance before a judge, assistance by counsel during questioning, and an initial appearance; the Tribunal may also intervene *proprio motu*.[283] A challenge must be pursued with due diligence and be addressed without delay.[284]

Moreover, when the violation of the accused's rights is considered 'serious and egregious', the *Barayagwiza* decision established that the Tribunals have a discretionary power, based on the so-called abuse of process doctrine,[285] to decline to exercise jurisdiction and hence to dismiss the case.[286] This is an exceptional measure, however, and other more proportionate remedies would be a reduction of an imposed sentence or, if acquitted, compensation.[287] Fairness concerns may also lead to a temporary stay.[288]

As noted above, the ICC Statute explicitly provides for both challenges and *proprio motu* reviews of the legality of the arrest warrant; and a challenge may be launched after the arrest before the person is surrendered to the Court.[289] However, the only remedy according to these provisions is release. Although not considering it a challenge to the jurisdiction of the Court and rejecting the domestic 'abuse of process' doctrine as inapplicable, the ICC Appeals Chamber has nonetheless concluded that the Court has the power, and indeed responsibility, to decline to exercise its jurisdiction: 'Where the breaches of the rights of the accused are such as to make it impossible for him/her to make his/her defence within the framework of his rights, no fair trial can take place and the proceedings can be stayed.'[290] This follows from the obligation to interpret and apply the law in accordance with 'internationally recognized human rights' (Article 20(3)).[291] But a permanent stay is a 'drastic' and 'exceptional' remedy and thus a high threshold applies: it must be 'impossible to piece together the constituent element of a fair trial'.[292] A conditional stay may be imposed if the

---

[281]   E.g. *Brđanin and Talić*, ICTY T. Ch. II, 8 December 1999; and *Kanyabashi*, ICTR T. Ch. II, 23 May 2000.

[282]   See Art. 8 of the Universal Declaration of Human Rights, Art. 9(4) of the ICCPR, Art. 5(4) of the ECHR, Art. 7(6) of the ACHR and Art. 7(1)(a) of the ACHPR. See also the Separate Opinion of Judge Robinson in *Simić et al.*, ICTY T. Ch. III, 18 October 2000.

[283]   E.g. *Kajelijeli*, ICTR A. Ch., 23 May 2005, paras. 208, 251–3.

[284]   E.g. *Semanza*, ICTR A. Ch., 31 May 2000, paras. 112–13, 119, 121.

[285]   The doctrine evolved in English case law and constitutes a feature of common law, but it does not apply in civil law systems; see *Lubanga*, ICC A. Ch., 14 December 2006, paras. 26–33. The doctrine recognizes that serious violations of the accused's fair trial rights may prevent the criminal proceedings, and by weighing in the prior treatment of the accused it rejects another traditional principle (*male captus bene detentus*) which instead allows the court to exercise jurisdiction regardless of procedural irregularities.

[286]   *Barayagwiza*, ICTR A. Ch., 3 November 1999, para. 74. See also *Dragan Nikolić*, ICTY T. Ch. II, 9 October 2002, para. 114, and ICTY A. Ch., 5 June 2003, paras. 28–30; and *Karadžić*, ICTY T. Ch. III, 8 July 2009, paras. 80–8.

[287]   E.g. *Kajelijeli*, ICTR A. Ch., 23 May 2005, paras. 206, 254–5, 320; *Rwamakuba*, ICTR T. Ch. III, 31 January 2007; and *Gatete*, ICTR A. Ch., 9 October 2012, para. 286.

[288]   E.g. *Nahimana et al.*, ICTR A. Ch., 4 August 2004.

[289]   Art. 60 of the ICC Statute, and r. 117(3) of the ICC RPE. See section 17.7.2.

[290]   See *Lubanga*, ICC A. Ch., 14 December 2006, paras. 24, 34–5, 39. A consequence of the non-jurisdictional nature of a challenge is that leave is required for an appeal, see *Gbagbo*, ICC A. Ch., 12 December 2012, para. 101. A motion that is filed too late may be dismissed: see *Katanga and Ngudjolo Chui*, ICC T. Ch. II, 3 December 2009.

[291]   *Lubanga*, ICC A. Ch., 14 December 2006, paras. 36–8.

[292]   *Lubanga*, ICC A. Ch., 8 October 2010, para. 55; see also *Lubanga*, ICC A. Ch., 21 October 2008 (1486) and T. Ch. 7 March 2011, and *Mbarushimana*, ICC PTC I, 1 July 2011, 7–8 (requiring 'gross violations').

unfairness can be cured, for example when disclosure of exculpatory evidence was prevented by the provider of the material.[293] The release of the suspect or accused, however, requires a 'permanent and irreversible stay of the proceedings'.[294] In addition, a reduction in sentence is a possible remedy.[295]

The arrest requires the involvement of both the international and domestic jurisdictions, and a difficult question is how far the international jurisdiction should go in the exercise of its powers to review the legality of the deprivation of liberty. Could the Tribunal or Court also review the legality of domestic measures and, if so, which legal standard should be applied? Furthermore, abductions and the abuse of process doctrine are not concerned merely with violations of individual rights, but may also relate to a violation of rights of another State and thus a breach of international law. One view is that such a breach is always a reason to decline jurisdiction,[296] another that this should be done only if the custodial State colluded in the abduction.[297]

The Tribunals have reviewed domestic measures, by applying the Tribunal's own legal requirements and international human rights standards, when the possible violation, at least to some extent, could be attributed to the Tribunal.[298] In addition, the ICTR Appeals Chamber in *Barayagwiza* did not feel barred from addressing the question of violations of the rights of the accused when these were also attributable to a State;[299] the Prosecutor and the State often have overlapping responsibilities. As clarified in *Kajelijeli*, however, the Tribunal is not competent to pronounce on the responsibility of the State for any violations, only on faults attributable to the Tribunal.[300]

The ICTY has had to consider these issues in cases where the accused was subject to a sealed indictment and apprehended through irregular practices by the prosecution ('luring'),[301] or in the abduction of fugitives from Serbia by unknown individuals and delivery to SFOR, with which the Prosecutor had a confidential cooperation agreement.[302] On setting aside jurisdiction because of a violation of State sovereignty, the Appeals Chamber concluded in *Nikolić* that State practice differs but that sovereign rights (and international human rights) must be weighed against the interest of bringing those accused of 'universally condemned offences' to justice – an 'Eichmann exception'.[303] But a minor intrusion, particularly when the violated State is in default of its cooperation obligations and has not complained, was not sufficient to decline jurisdiction. Moreover, the Chamber questioned whether abductions carried out by private individuals without being instigated,

---

[293] E.g. *Lubanga*, ICC T. Ch. I, 13 June 2008 (1401), and ICC A. Ch., 21 October 2008 (1486), paras. 80–3. Cf. *Kony et al.*, ICC PTC II, 31 October 2008 (request for stay was denied).

[294] *Lubanga*, ICC A. Ch., 21 October 2008 (1487), para. 36.   [295] *Lubanga*, ICC T. Ch., 10 July 2012, paras. 89–90.

[296] E.g. the South African Supreme Court in *State* v. *Ebrahim*, 1991 (2) SA 553.

[297] Regarding UK law, see Colin Warbrick, 'Judicial Jurisdiction and Abuse of Process' (2000) 49 *International and Comparative Law Quarterly* 489. See also *Öcalan* v. *Turkey*, ECtHR, 12 May 2005, paras. 83–90.

[298] E.g. *Barayagwiza*, ICTR A. Ch., 3 November 1999; and *Kajelijeli*, ICTR A. Ch., 23 May 2005. See also *Delalić et al.*, ICTY T. Ch. II, 2 September 1997, confirmed on appeal, ICTY A. Ch., 20 February 2001, paras. 528–64.

[299] *Barayagwiza*, ICTR A. Ch., 3 November 1999, para. 73.   [300] *Kajelijeli*, ICTR A. Ch., 23 May 2005, paras. 219–21, 252.

[301] *Dokmanović* (see *Mrkšić et al.*), ICTY T. Ch. II, 22 October 1997. For a critical view, see Michael Scharf, 'The Prosecutor v. Slavko Dokmanović: Irregular Rendition and the ICTY' (1998) 11 *Leiden Journal of International Law* 369.

[302] E.g. *Simić et al.*, ICTY T. Ch. III, 18 October 2000 (proceedings which were later abandoned due to a plea-bargaining arrangement).

[303] *Dragan Nikolić*, ICTY A. Ch., 5 June 2003, paras. 24–7. Regarding the *Eichmann* case, see Chapter 3. See also section 5.4.7.

acknowledged or condoned by a State, international organization, or other entity, violate State sovereignty at all.

As for the ICC, the Statute provides that the legality of the arrest process in the custodial State is primarily a matter for domestic courts.[304] In *Lubanga*, the Appeals Chamber concluded that the Court's role is not to review the correctness of domestic decisions, but instead 'to see that the process envisaged by [national] law was duly followed and that the rights of the arrestee were properly respected'[305] – a distinction that is not entirely clear. But, for the Court to divest itself of jurisdiction, it is not enough that national authorities or unknown third parties have violated fundamental rights of the suspect or accused; instead, 'concerted action' between those actors and the ICC must be established, and the mere knowledge of the Prosecutor is not proof of the ICC's involvement.[306] Whether the requirement of 'concerted action' will apply also to torture or other serious mistreatment of the person is subject to debate.[307]

17.8   Prosecution and indictment

17.8.1   *Decision whether to prosecute*

The determination whether to prosecute follows adversarial principles, in that the Prosecutor is the only one who may initiate a trial by submitting an indictment; a judge or a victim cannot do so. The Prosecutor is also responsible for its content. However, there are also different forms of judicial review. One review common to all international jurisdictions is the requirement that the indictment be confirmed before the case moves to trial (see section 17.9.1). Of course, the charged question of case selection, as discussed with respect to the commencement of investigations in section 17.5, is equally relevant to prosecution decisions.[308]

At the ICTY and ICTR, the decision whether to prosecute is subject to broad discretion, and, when challenged, the ICTY Appeals Chamber referred only to general limitations, particularly the statutory requirements of prosecutorial independence and equality before the Tribunal; there must be no discriminatory or otherwise unlawful or improper motive.[309] The required standard for prosecuting is a '*prima facie* case'.[310] But no obligation to prosecute exists.[311] Instead, self-adopted prosecutorial policies, which focus on those

---

[304] Art. 59(2)(c) of the ICC Statute. The domestic court is not allowed, however, to consider the legality of the ICC arrest warrant: Art. 59(4).
[305] *Lubanga*, ICC A. Ch., 14 December 2006, para. 41.   [306] *Ibid.*, para. 42.
[307] The Pre-Trial Chamber in *Lubanga*, ICC PTC I, 3 October 2006, p. 10, concluded, with reference to *Nikolić*, ICTY A. Ch., 5 June 2003, para. 30, and other cases, that 'concerted action' is not required (under the 'abuse of process' doctrine) in case of torture or serious mistreatment by national authorities, but it is less clear that the Appeals Chamber adopted this conclusion: ICC A. Ch., 14 December 2006. Compare Göran Sluiter, 'Human Rights Protection in the ICC Pre-Trial Phase' in Stahn and Sluiter, *Emerging Practice*, 471; and Christophe Paulussen, *Male Captus Bene Detentus? Surrendering Suspects to the International Criminal Court* (Antwerp, 2010) 897–900. For a critical review, see Melinda Taylor and Charles Chernor Jalloh, 'Provisional Arrest and Incarceration in the International Criminal Tribunals' (2013) *Santa Clara Journal of International Law* 303.
[308] See generally Robert Cryer, *Prosecuting International Crimes* (Cambridge, 2005).
[309] *Delalić et al.*, ICTY A. Ch., 20 February 2001, paras. 596–618.
[310] Art. 18(4) of the ICTY Statute, Art. 17(4) of the ICTR Statute and Art. 16(4) of the MICT Statute.
[311] Indeed, Trial Chambers have accepted the withdrawal of indictments in cases where the statutory conditions for the indictment were met but the case did not fall under the (new) prosecutorial strategy, e.g. *Sikirica et al.*, ICTY T. Ch., 5 May 1998.

bearing the greatest responsibility, and internal 'selection criteria' have guided the work.[312] An internal review process operated within the Office of the Prosecutor. Judicial screening of new indictments was introduced as part of the ICTY's completion strategy.[313]

The ICC Statute provides guidance in the form of negative criteria: the conditions under which there can be no prosecution.[314] The conditions relate to a suspicion of crime sufficient for an arrest warrant, the admissibility of the case, and an assessment of 'the interests of justice'. A decision not to prosecute is subject to judicial review by the Pre-Trial Chamber under the same terms as a decision not to commence an investigation.[315] The Prosecutor may reconsider a decision not to prosecute.[316] Also, at the ICC the decision whether to prosecute is a discretionary one. A prosecutorial strategy and other external and internal documents guide the selection process.[317] Calls for further judicial intervention into the process have been rejected.[318]

17.8.2 Amendments to and withdrawal of the indictment

As in domestic criminal proceedings, an international indictment may be amended or withdrawn.[319] In accordance with adversarial principles, these measures are, generally, the Prosecutor's prerogative in the ICTY, ICTR and ICC, but the principles and procedures vary. Amendments and clarifications are common at the ICTY and ICTR and the required judicial approval has normally been granted; the main consideration is whether the amendment will cause unfair prejudice to the accused.[320] A 'new charge' requires a new confirmation and support by evidence. Amendments may also be made during trial,[321] but not on appeal.[322]

Post-confirmation, the ICC Prosecutor may amend the charges only with the permission of the Pre-Trial Chamber; a new confirmation is required if the Prosecutor 'seeks to add additional charges or to substitute more serious charges'.[323] But, without a formal hierarchy of crimes (see Chapter 19), the notion of 'more serious charges' will cause difficulties in practice. Moreover, the provisions refer only to amendments 'before the trial has begun' and thus beg the question whether any amendments may be made thereafter. Different

---

[312] On internal selection criteria for the ICTY, see Morten Bergsmo, Kjetil Helvig, Ilia Utlemedze and Gorana Žagovec, *The Backlog of Core International Crimes Case Files in Bosnia and Herzegovina* (Oslo, 2010) 98–111. Cf. Antonio Cassese, 'The ICTY: A Living and Vital Reality' (2004) 2 *Journal of International Criminal Justice* 585, 587 (arguing that a limitation to those most responsible can be inferred from Art. 1 of the ICTY Statute).

[313] Rule 28(A) of the ICTY RPE; see further Chapter 7. For critique, see Daryl Mundis, 'The Judicial Effects of the "Completion Strategies" on the Ad Hoc International Criminal Tribunals' (2005) 99 *American Journal of International Law* 142.

[314] Art. 53(2) of the ICC Statute.   [315] *Ibid.*, Art. 53(3); see section 17.5.   [316] *Ibid.*, Art. 53(4).

[317] See Paul Seils, 'The Selection and Prioritization of Cases by the Office of the Prosecutor of the International Criminal Court' in Bergsmo, *Criteria for Prioritizing and Selecting*, 69–78.

[318] E.g. *Situation in the DRC*, ICC PTC I, 26 September 2007 (a decision to prosecute certain individuals was not an implicit decision not to prosecute others, and thus the decision was not subject to a judicial review).

[319] Rules 50–51 of the ICTY RPE, ICTR RPE and MICT RPE; see also, e.g. *Dragan Nikolić*, ICTY T. Ch. II, 20 October 1995, para. 32; and Art. 61 (4) of the ICC Statute. See generally Håkan Friman, Helen Brady, Matteo Costi, Fabricio Guariglia and Carl-Friedrich Stuckenberg, 'Charges' in Sluiter, *International Criminal Procedure*, 415–23.

[320] E.g. *Naletilić and Martinović*, ICTY T. Ch. I, 14 February 2001. Regarding other circumstances to consider, such as delays, see e.g. *Kovačević*, ICTY A. Ch., 2 July 1998; and *Karemera et al.*, ICTR A. Ch., 19 December 2003.

[321] *Akayesu*, ICTR A. Ch., 1 June 2001, para. 120.   [322] *Niyitegeka*, ICTR A. Ch., 9 July 2004, para. 196.

[323] Art. 61(4) and (9) of the ICC Statute. See *Kenyatta*, ICC PTC II, 21 March 2013 (amendment granted); cf. *Ruto and Sang*, ICC PTC II, 16 August 2013 (amendment rejected when requested shortly before the start of the trial).

interpretations are possible. A complete ban on amendments at trial could result in acquittals on 'technical' grounds, although this may be counteracted by the Chamber's power to 'modify the legal characterisation' of the facts (see section 17.8.4). A post-confirmation withdrawal of charges is not contemplated in the Statute or RPE, but was accepted by a Trial Chamber when the prosecution no longer had a reasonable prospect of securing evidence for a conviction and the accused did not object.[324]

17.8.3   The indictment

Framing an indictment is often a routine task in domestic criminal systems, but not so in the international jurisdictions; the crimes and further requirements for criminal responsibility are not very well defined in law and the indictments often cover multiple alleged perpetrators and events. The form of the indictment and the relationship between the charges and a subsequent judgment vary in different domestic legal systems. Hence, the principles for and form of the indictment have been subject to many challenges in the ICTY and ICTR. True to adversarial trial principles, however, the Chambers have been unwilling, although empowered thereto, to check the form of the indictment *ex officio*.[325] Over time a relatively consistent practice has been established,[326] which is relevant also to the ICC.

  The form of the indictment is important in order to uphold the rights of the accused to a fair hearing, to be informed promptly and in detail of the nature and cause of the charges, and to have adequate time and facilities for the preparation of the defence.[327] The 'nature' of the charge relates to the legal characterization of the charge, that is to say, the alleged offence and form of criminal liability, and the 'cause' to the factual basis or description of the charge. Nonetheless, the statutory requirements for the Tribunals are very general in nature and instead a rich case law has developed.[328] The indictment must include the 'material facts' underpinning the charges, but not the evidence by which such material facts are to be proven. The material facts must be given with enough detail to inform the defendant clearly of the charges and allow preparation of the defence. What constitutes a material fact, however, depends on the nature of the case at hand, and the specificity, such as the identity of the victims, mainly on the nature of the alleged criminal conduct. Defects may be cured by amendments of the indictment or subsequent information, and minor ones may be ignored, as long as the fair trial rights of the accused are not affected. A fundamental defect, however,

---

[324] *Muthaura and Kenyatta*, ICC T. Ch. V, 18 March 2013, para. 11 (majority decision; one judge dissenting with respect to requiring leave by the Court for a withdrawal prior to the trial).

[325] E.g. *Brđanin and Talić*, ICTY T. Ch. II, 20 February 2001, para. 23.

[326] For a survey of the principles in case law, see e.g. *Blaškić*, ICTY A. Ch., 29 July 2004, paras. 207–21; and *Ntakirutimana*, ICTR A. Ch., 13 December 2004, paras. 21–9, 469–77. See also Friman *et al.*, 'Charges', 384–97.

[327] Art. 21(2) and (4)(a)–(b) of the ICTY Statute, Art. 20(2) and (4)(a)–(b) of the ICTR Statute, Art. 19(2) and (4)(a)–(b) of the MICT Statute, and Art. 67(1) (a)–(b) of the ICC Statute. The text of the ICC Statute is different, however, and speaks of, *inter alia*, the 'nature, cause, and content' of the charges.

[328] Art. 18(4) of the ICTY Statute, Art. 17(4) of the ICTR Statute, Art. 16(4) of the MICT Statute, r. 47(C) of the ICTY RPE and ICTR RPE, and r. 48(C) of the MICT RPE. See also e.g. *Milutinović et al.*, ICTY T. Ch. III, 22 March 2006 (with references).

can result in the Trial Chamber disregarding the charge or the Appeals Chamber reversing a conviction.[329]

At the ICC, the accused must be provided with 'a detailed description of the charges' before the confirmation hearing.[330] With the experience and case law of the Tribunals in mind, the ICC Regulations are more detailed concerning the content of the 'document containing the charges' (DCC).[331] The Appeals Chamber has explained the terms 'facts and circumstances' that shall be included and clarified that they do not cover evidence, which is to be provided separately.[332] Owing to the confirmation process, and how it has been applied in practice, the DCC may have to be amended post-confirmation.[333] In case of disparity, the charge of the confirmation decision takes precedence over the charge in the DCC.[334] As we shall see in the following section, the ICC scheme means that it is the Chambers and not the Prosecutor who have assumed the final say concerning the framing of the charges and that the issue of defects is primarily dealt with by a special mechanism for modification of the charges.

17.8 4   The charge and its relationship to the judgment

The indictment is the primary accusatory instrument and establishes the framework for the criminal trial; only what is properly charged may lead to a conviction. Hence, the judges of the Tribunals and the ICC are required to identify, assess and pronounce on each charge (or count) of the indictment, and the ICC Statute clarifies that the judgment 'shall not exceed the facts and circumstances described in the charges and any amendment to the charges'.[335] At the ICC, the *Lubanga* Trial Chamber concluded that 'the power to frame the charges lies at the heart of the Pre-Trial Chamber's functions' and that the result is binding on the Trial Chamber.[336] Thus, the Trial Chamber considered itself bound by the Pre-Trial Chamber's legal findings even if the trial judge disagreed with the finding.[337] This approach may be criticized for unduly restricting the Trial Chamber's latitude to adjudicate the case and might be reversed on appeal.[338]

Other questions are how the legal classification of facts – the nature of the charge – in the indictment should be understood and how Trial Chambers should act in the case of an erroneous legal classification. All the Statutes and RPEs are silent on these matters and different legal traditions take different approaches. Common law jurisdictions place the

---

[329] E.g. *Krnojelac*, ICTY A. Ch., 17 September 2003, paras. 138–42; and *Muhimana*, ICTR A. Ch., 21 May 2007, paras. 217–18, 224–6 (cf. the Dissenting Opinion by Judge Schomburg).

[330] Rule 121(3) of the ICC RPE; see also Art. 61(3) of the ICC Statute.

[331] Reg. 52 of the ICC Regulations. See e.g. *Bemba Gombo*, ICC PTC II, 15 June 2009, paras. 65–70.

[332] *Lubanga*, ICC A. Ch., 8 December 2009, para. 90 (footnote 163).

[333] E.g. *Lubanga*, ICC T. Ch. I, 9 December 2008, para. 13.

[334] Compare *Bemba Gombo*, ICC T. Ch. III, 8 October 2010, para. 12.

[335] Rule 87 of the ICTY RPE and ICTR RPE, r. 104 of the MICT RPE, and Art. 74(2) of the ICC Statute (where 'charges' is used instead of the term 'indictment'; see also Art. 61 of the ICC Statute).

[336] *Lubanga*, ICC T. Ch. I, 13 December 2007, paras. 39–43.

[337] See the Separate Opinion of Judge Fulford, para. 2, in *Lubanga*, ICC T. Ch. I, 14 March 2012.

[338] E.g. Jens Ohlin, 'Lubanga Decision Roundtable: Lubanga and the Control Theory' *Opinio Juris* (15 March 2012), and Thomas Liefländer, 'The Lubanga Judgment of the ICC: More than Just a First Step?' (2012) 1 *Cambridge Journal of International and Comparative Law* 191, 210–11.

emphasis on the 'offence' as categorized by the prosecutor in the indictment. This means that the legal characterization made for a charge is binding on the trial court; it is against the crime charged that the accused raises the defence. An exception is that the trial court may, without amendment, convict for a lesser included offence. As a consequence, the indictment will often present numerous counts in order to avoid an acquittal in case all the factual and legal requirements for a conviction are met but the court finds a crime different from the one charged. The ICTY has opted to follow this model.[339]

In many civil law jurisdictions and mixed jurisdictions, the conduct – the charged acts or omissions – is decisive, not the legal categorization of the 'offence'. The principle *iura novit curia* (the court knows the law) applies and, accordingly, the Prosecutor's legal characterization is not binding but merely a theory (a recommendation). The ICTY Trial Chamber in *Kupreškić et al.* discussed the possible application of this principle, but concluded that it should not be applied.[340] At the ICC, however, an expression of the *iura novit curia* principle has been established in regulation 55 of the ICC Regulations, allowing a Chamber to 'modify the legal characterisation' of the facts;[341] that is to say, to determine that the facts and circumstances pleaded in the charges should be characterized as a different crime or a different form of criminal responsibility than that which the Prosecutor has chosen. This could counteract multiple-count indictments and acquittals on mere 'technical grounds'.

In practice, ICC Chambers have made extensive use of this power. After being incorrectly applied by the Trial Chamber (majority) in *Lubanga*, the Appeals Chamber found regulation 55 to be compatible with the ICC Statute and the defendant's right to a fair trial and clarified the correct application of the regulation.[342] In *Katanga and Ngudjolo*, the Trial Chamber gave notice to the parties on the application of the regulation after the conclusion of the trial hearing – from one mode of criminal responsibility to another – which was upheld by the Appeals Chamber.[343] In *Bemba*, the regulation was applied during trial to allow the Trial Chamber to consider a different form of knowledge as a basis for command responsibility and the trial was temporarily suspended to allow the defence to reconsider its evidence.[344]

---

[339] See *Kupreškić et al.*, ICTY T. Ch., 14 January 2000, paras. 728–48 (including a survey of domestic law).

[340] *Ibid.*, para. 740. The Chamber was prepared to apply a lesser included offence theory and gave some examples which, however, require an established hierarchy of offences and of modes of criminal liability (crimes against humanity more serious than war crimes, perpetration more serious than aiding or abetting, etc.): paras. 744–6. The issue was raised but not considered in *Aleksovski*, ICTY A. Ch., 24 March 2000, para. 55. Cf. *Karemera et al.*, ICTR T. Ch. III, 13 February 2004, para. 47 (the Trial Chamber indicated that it would apply the principle of *iura novit curia* at the close of the proceedings). Similarly, *Ntagerura et al.*, ICTR T. Ch. III, 25 February 2004, paras. 36–8.

[341] Any such recharacterization is subject to safeguards ensuring the participants, particularly the accused, opportunities to respond and make preparations. The accused may also, if necessary, re-examine witnesses or call new evidence. See Carsten Stahn, 'Modification of the Legal Characterization of Facts in the ICC System: A Portrayal of Regulation 55' (2005) 16 *Criminal Law Forum* 1; and Friman *et al.*, 'Charges', 408–11, 430–4.

[342] *Lubanga*, ICC A. Ch., 8 December 2009, reversing ICC T. Ch. I, 14 July 2009 (minority opinion by Judge Fulford, 17 July 2009). See also in the same case, ICC T. Ch. I, 8 January 2010.

[343] *Katanga and Ngudjolo Chui*, ICC T. Ch. II, 21 November 2012 (Judge van der Wyngaert dissenting) and ICC A. Ch., 27 March 2013 (Judge Tarfusser dissenting, *inter alia* being concerned about the defendant's fair trial rights).

[344] *Bemba Gombo*, ICC T. Ch. III, 21 September 2012 and 13 December 2012; the defence was denied leave to appeal the decision: ICC T. Ch. III, 6 January 2013. This was preceded by a confirmation process where the Pre-Trial Chamber restricted the charges with respect to command responsibility which in turn caused the Trial Chamber to order an amended DCC: *Bemba Gombo*, ICC PTC II, 15 June 2009, and ICC T. Ch. III, 20 July 2010, para. 121.

Very controversially, the modification provisions have also been applied, albeit just once, by a Pre-Trial Chamber when confirming charges; the Chamber substituted charges of war crimes in a non-international armed conflict for the same offences in an international armed conflict during a certain time period.[345] This is difficult to reconcile with Article 61(7) of the ICC Statute,[346] and forced the Prosecutor to prosecute something other than that which he planned to do (based on available evidence). The Trial Chamber did not consider itself competent to annul or amend the confirmed charges, but allowed the parties to present evidence relating to both classifications of the conflict.[347] By applying regulation 55 (again) the Trial Chamber convicted for crimes committed in a non-international armed conflict.[348] This is unlikely to happen again, and other Chambers have rejected outright the application of regulation 55 in the confirmation process,[349] but the case highlights tensions between the confirmation process and the functions and powers of the Prosecutor and the Trial Chamber.[350]

17.8.5 *Concurrence of offences: alternative and cumulative charges*

International crimes are more complex than most crimes under domestic law. Multiple acts by many perpetrators and over a long period of time are often the case. Overlapping crimes are also common; the same killing or rape could, depending on the surrounding (contextual) facts, simultaneously be considered as genocide, crimes against humanity and war crimes. This concurrence of offences (*concursus delictorum*) gives rise to both theoretical and practical difficulties,[351] but the Statutes and RPE provide little assistance, and here too the common law and civil law approaches vary.

The ICTY and ICTR have long accepted cumulative charges and, when challenged, the Trial Chambers have concluded that this is a matter to be resolved at trial, particularly in sentencing.[352] In turn, this triggers the question of cumulative convictions, and, after some initial uncertainty, consistent principles now apply in both Tribunals. The Appeals Chamber in *Delalić et al.* held that only distinct crimes justify multiple convictions.[353] Cumulative convictions entered under different statutory provisions but based on the same conduct are permissible only if both statutory provisions involved have a materially distinct element not

---

[345] *Lubanga*, ICC PTC I, 29 January 2007. Requests for leave to appeal the decision were later denied.

[346] See e.g. Michela Miraglia, 'Admissibility of Evidence, Standard of Proof, and Nature of the Decision in the ICC Confirmation of Charges in Lubanga' (2008) 6 *Journal of International Criminal Justice* 489, 501–3; and Rastan, 'What Is a "Case"', 444–6. Cf. Ambos and Miller, 'Structure and Function', 358–60. For the better solution of requesting the Prosecutor to reconsider the charges, see e.g. *Bemba Gombo*, ICC PTC III, 3 March 2009.

[347] *Lubanga*, ICC T. Ch. I, 13 December 2007. See also ICC T. Ch. I, 19 December 2008 (order for amended DCC).

[348] *Lubanga*, ICC T. Ch. I, 14 March 2012, para. 566; see also ICC T. Ch. I, 13 December 2007 and 12 April 2011.

[349] E.g. *Ruto and Sang*, ICC PTC II, 19 August 2011, paras. 7–8, and ICC T. Ch. V, 28 December 2012, paras. 13–19; see also ICC T. Ch. V, 20 November 2012.

[350] See generally Dov Jacobs, 'A Shifting Scale of Power: Who Is in Charge of the Charges at the International Criminal Court?' in Schabas, *Ashgate Research Companion*, 205–22.

[351] See Carl-Friedrich Stuckenberg, 'Multiplicity of Offences: Concursus Delictorum' in Fischer, *International and National Prosecution*, 559–604.

[352] E.g. *Delalić et al.*, ICTY T. Ch. II, 2 October 1996, para. 24; and *Kanyabashi*, ICTR T. Ch. II, 31 May 2000, paras. 5.5–5.7. See section 19.3.2.

[353] *Delalić et al.*, ICTY A. Ch., 20 February 2001, paras. 412–13. See also *Musema*, ICTR A. Ch., 16 November 2001, paras. 358–70. But cf. *Kupreškić et al.*, ICTY T. Ch. II, 14 January 2000, paras. 637–748.

contained within the other. An element is materially distinct from another if it requires proof of a fact not required by the other element.[354] If this test is met, cumulative convictions must be imposed; this is not a discretionary decision.[355] If not, a single conviction must be entered; the more specific offence is to have preference over the more general one. The contextual elements for the different crimes are also to be taken into account, meaning that cumulative convictions for the same conduct, such as murder/killing, are permissible as different crimes (under different Articles of the Statute). More complicated is the test for different charges relating to the same conduct under the same Article. For example, cumulative convictions are not permitted for persecution as a crime against humanity and for other underlying crimes against humanity, unless each offence has a materially distinct element, which, however, the ICTY Appeals Chamber has concluded that many of them have.[356]

When cumulative charges and cumulative convictions are allowed, there is little need for alternative charges. However, different forms of criminal responsibility cannot be imposed cumulatively for the same conduct and thus these forms may be pleaded in the alternative in the ICTY and ICTR.[357]

The pleading practice of the ICC is still developing. The Pre-Trial Chamber in *Bemba* rejected cumulative charges, arguing that the practice was detrimental to the rights of the defence and that the possibility to modify the charges in accordance with regulation 55 has reduced the need to resort to it.[358] However, the Pre-Trial Chamber did endorse the test adopted by the ICTY and ICTR, and cumulative charges, based on this test, have been accepted subsequently in other cases.[359] The issue of cumulative convictions has not yet arisen at the ICC.

17.9   Pre-trial proceedings: preparations for trial

17.9.1   *First appearance and confirmation of charges*

As with many domestic jurisdictions, a formal first appearance hearing is held at the ICTY, ICTR and ICC as soon as the suspect has arrived at the Tribunal or Court.[360] The Chamber will check that the person has been served with the indictment (ICTY/ICTR) or arrest warrant (ICC) and that certain rights are respected. At the ICTY and ICTR, one main function is to charge the accused formally and allow him or her to enter a plea to the charges (immediately or at a further appearance). A date for trial will be set in case of a plea of not

---

[354] This test serves two purposes: to ensure that the accused is convicted only for distinct offences and that the convictions fully reflect his or her criminality: *Kordić and Čerkez*, ICTY A. Ch., 17 December 2004, para. 1033.
[355] E.g. *Strugar*, ICTY A. Ch., 17 July 2008, para. 324.
[356] E.g. *Kordić and Čerkez*, ICTY A. Ch., 17 December 2004, paras. 1039–44.
[357] E.g. *Stanisić*, ICTY T. Ch. II, 19 July 2005, para. 6. For example, superior responsibility is considered subsidiary to other modes of liability, and commission excludes a conviction for also planning the crime; a superior position or participation in planning will instead be factors in sentencing: see *Blaškić*, ICTY A. Ch., 29 July 2004, para. 91; and *Kajelijeli*, ICTR A. Ch., 23 May 2005, para. 81.
[358] *Bemba Gombo*, ICC PTC II, 15 June 2009, paras. 202–9; see also PTC III, 10 June 2008, para. 25.
[359] E.g. *Al Bashir*, ICC PTC I, 4 March 2009, paras. 95–6; *Ruto et al.*, ICC PTC II, 23 January 2012, paras. 279–81.
[360] Rule 62 of the ICTY RPE and ICTR RPE, r. 64 of the MICT RPE, Art. 60(1) of the ICC Statute and r. 121 of the ICC RPE.

guilty, whereas a guilty plea leads to simplified trial proceedings (see section 17.11). In the ICC proceedings, on the other hand, it is not required that the person is formally charged at this stage and the main purpose, apart from the assurance of rights, is instead to set a date for the confirmation of charges.

Another common feature of many, but not all, domestic systems is a judicial pre-trial review of the indictment to ensure that the charges concern criminal acts and that there is evidence of sufficient strength for prosecution. Judicial confirmation of the indictment is also required at the ICTY, ICTR, the Residual Mechanism and the ICC.[361] It is meant to protect suspects against unsubstantiated prosecutions, which is particularly important when the crimes are inherently very serious and the proceedings often attract public attention.[362] The Tribunal's review proceedings are simple and *ex parte*. The relatively low threshold for confirmation is a '*prima facie* case': a credible case which, if not contradicted by the defence, would be a sufficient basis to convict the accused on the charge.[363] In principle, the indictments are to be made public, but it is possible to keep the indictment under seal, *inter alia* to facilitate an arrest or to protect confidential information.[364]

The ICC has a much more elaborate and adversarial confirmation procedure with a robust disclosure process and a hearing. This is a public process, which is unrelated to the issuance of arrest warrants. The Prosecutor must support the charges with sufficient evidence, at this stage normally documentary or summary evidence. But the accused is also entitled to challenge the Prosecutor's evidence and to present his or her own evidence, which has prompted concerns that the proceedings could lead to an additional 'mini-trial' unless the Pre-Trial Chamber exercises sufficient control. The ICC Statute requires 'substantial grounds to believe' that the person has committed the crime charged, an evidentiary threshold held to be higher than the '*prima facie*' standard applied by the Tribunals.[365] The Chamber is to assess each charge and either confirm or dismiss it, but it may also request the Prosecutor to consider providing further evidence, conducting further investigation, or amending a charge 'because the evidence submitted appears to establish a different crime'; with the latter mechanism there should be no need for the Chamber to re-qualify the charges itself (see section 17.8.4).[366] Upon confirmation, a case at the ICC is transferred from the Pre-Trial Chamber to the Trial Chamber.

In practice, ICC confirmation processes have been long, the hearings have lasted days with witnesses being examined, and have resulted in very long and detailed decisions. While the process has indeed served a screening purpose, the charges against almost one-third of the accused having been rejected, it has also been seriously questioned.[367] The process

---

[361] Art. 19 of the ICTY Statute, Art. 18 of the ICTR Statute, Art. 18 of the MICT Statute and Art. 61 of the ICC Statute.
[362] The indictment (and any subsequent amendment to it) is to be served upon the accused: r. 53*bis* of the ICTY RPE and ICTR RPE, r. 54 of the MICT RPE and r. 121 of the ICC RPE.
[363] See e.g. *Milošević*, ICTY (Judge May), 22 November 2001, paras. 11–15.
[364] Rules 52–53 of the ICTY RPE, ICTR RPE and MICT RPE.
[365] Art. 61(6)–(7) of the ICC Statute. See *Mbarushimana*, ICC A. Ch., 30 May 2012, para. 43.
[366] *Bemba Gombo*, ICC PTC III, 3 March 2009; and *Gbagbo*, ICC PTC I, 3 June 2013.
[367] For a critical view, see e.g. Miraglia, 'Admissibility of Evidence', 489–503. For a more positive view, see e.g. Volker Nerlich, 'The Confirmation of Charges Process at the International Criminal Court: Advance or Failure?' (2012) 10 *Journal of International Criminal Justice* 1339.

provides added protection for the suspect and an opportunity for victim participation, but it is also lengthy and contributes too little to the preparations for trial. More seriously, the role of the Pre-Trial Chamber, *vis-à-vis* the Prosecutor as well as the Trial Chamber, is far from settled and is subject to very different interpretations, as is the actual implementation of the evidentiary requirement for confirmation.[368] Hence, the debate will continue as to whether this model for review, as currently designed, is the most appropriate one.

The confirmation of the indictment at the Tribunals is designed to precede the arrest and surrender of the accused, while the opposite is true at the ICC. But, since the actual apprehension and surrender of suspects and accused is a serious obstacle to international criminal proceedings, special confirmation proceedings *in absentia* have been introduced; at the Tribunals they are conducted with a view to issuing an international arrest warrant to all States and establishing that a State has failed to cooperate, but at the ICC they have no discernible objective.[369] In *Karadžić and Mladić*, it was also suggested that the proceedings have stigmatizing and reparative effects and contribute to a true historical record.[370] While the first two results might be true, the third is debatable since only the prosecution case is presented and the accused could be unrepresented. Indeed, a confirmation *in absentia* does not substitute for a trial and cannot result in a verdict. Moreover, the conclusions reached in a decision of this kind should arguably only be preliminary in nature and cannot prevent different conclusions at trial.[371]

17.9.2   *Preparations for trial*

The preparations for trial include the resolution of many legal issues, such as challenges to jurisdiction, matters relating to evidence, protective measures and, at the ICC, the admissibility of a case.[372] Most of the litigation, however, is devoted to disclosure of evidence, at the ICC followed by matters concerning participation of victims. A controversial issue, where the different legal traditions provide different answers, is whether the parties may prepare witnesses in substance before giving evidence ('witness proofing'). Whereas it is allowed in the ICTY and ICTR, the ICC has prohibited the Prosecutor from this practice.[373] However, so-called 'witness familiarization' is accepted by all. Another important issue is the joinder

---

[368] This has been highlighted, *inter alia*, in a number of dissenting opinions, e.g. Judge Fernández de Gurmendi's dissent in *Gbagbo*, ICC PTC I, 3 June 2013; leave to appeal the decision limited the scope for the Appeals Chamber to settle the issues authoritatively: see PTC I, 31 July 2013 (with dissenting opinion). On evidence, see also *Mbarushimana*, ICC A. Ch., 30 May 2012.

[369] Rule 61 of the ICTY RPE and ICTR RPE, r. 63 of the MICT RPE, Art. 61(2) of the ICC Statute and rr. 123–126 of the ICC RPE. At the ICC, the procedure was a compromise for States wishing a possibility to conduct trials *in absentia*: see section 17.12.

[370] *Karadžić and Mladić*, ICTY T. Ch. I, 11 July 1996, para. 3.

[371] See also Christopher Greenwood, 'The Development of International Humanitarian Law by the International Criminal Tribunal for the Former Yugoslavia' (1998) 2 *Max Planck Yearbook of United Nations Law* 97, 113.

[372] Rules 54, 72–73 of the ICTY RPE and ICTR RPE, rr. 55, 70, 79–80 of the MICT RPE, Arts. 64 and 68–69 of the ICC Statute, and numerous provisions in the ICC RPE and ICC Regulations.

[373] *Lubanga*, ICC PTC I, 8 November 2006 and ICC T. Ch. I, 23 May 2008; cf. *Limaj et al.*, ICTY T. Ch. III, 10 December 2004, *Milutinović et al.*, ICTY T. Ch. III, 12 December 2006 and *Karemera et al.*, ICTR A. Ch., 11 May 2007, para. 7 (the two latter reacting to the ICC's practice). See Sergey Vasiliev, 'Proofing the Ban on "Witness Proofing": Did the ICC Get It Right?' (2009) 20 *Criminal Law Forum* 193; and Kai Ambos, '"Witness Proofing" before the ICC: Neither Legally Admissible nor Necessary' in Stahn and Sluiter, *Emerging Practice*, 599–614.

or severance of trials against multiple accused.[374] Joinder has been ordered in many ICTY and ICTR cases concerning crimes committed in the course of 'the same transaction'.[375] Joint trials may promote judicial economy, avoid duplication of evidence and repeated witness appearances, and ensure the consistency of verdicts, but a concern is prejudice to the accused.[376]

In the interest of efficiency, the ICTY, ICTR and ICC have developed different procedural tools, such as pre-trial (or pre-appeal) judges,[377] status conferences,[378] and pre-trial and pre-defence conferences.[379] The ICC has also a detailed pre-confirmation scheme.[380] A common feature is that the judges have assumed an increasingly active and controlling role. This even includes powers to restrict the number of witnesses at trial and the time available to the respective party for presenting evidence at trial.[381] Still, much time and effort are devoted to preliminary issues. In *Lubanga*, for example, the Trial Chamber had held 54 status conferences and delivered 275 written and 347 oral decisions at the time of the verdict.[382]

17.9.3 *Disclosure of evidence*

A fundamental feature of a fair trial, and a manifestation of 'equality of arms', is the disclosure of the prosecutor's evidence to the accused, allowing the latter to prepare for trial. In an inquisitorial system, this is done easily since all the material collected during the investigation – incriminating and exonerating – is collected in a 'dossier' which, in principle, is available to the accused. In an adversarial system, however, disclosure is more complicated and premised on separate prosecution and defence cases. While the prosecutor normally has extensive disclosure obligations, including for material that is favourable to the accused, defence disclosure is more restricted and is often postponed until the prosecutor has presented his or her evidence at trial. The defendant has the right to remain silent. Another difference is the extent to which the evidence should be disclosed to the court before the trial. Such disclosure allows the judges to prepare and control the trial more actively, as well as fulfilling a truth-finding function, but could taint the court's impartiality (or at least be perceived to do so). Where a 'dossier' is collected, the material is also made available to the court.

---

[374] Rules 48, 49 and 82 of the ICTY RPE, rr. 48, 48*bis*, 49 and 82 of the ICTR RPE, rr. 49 and 97 of the MICT RPE, Art. 64(5) of the ICC Statute and r. 136 of the ICC RPE.

[375] Rule 2 of the ICTY RPE and ICTR RPE; see also *Milošević*, ICTY A. Ch., 18 April 2002, para. 20. Concerning the ICC, see *Katanga and Ngudjolo Chui*, ICC PTC I, 10 March 2008 and ICC A. Ch., 9 June 2008.

[376] For a review of the jurisprudence, see *Popović et al.*, ICTY T. Ch. III, 21 September 2005. For a critical view on the joinder decision in *Milošević*, see Gideon Boas, *The Milošević Trial* (Cambridge, 2007) 115–21.

[377] Rules 65*ter* and 107of the ICTY RPE. rr. 70 and 135 of the MICT RPE, Arts. 39(2)(b)(iii) and 57(2)(b) of the ICC Statute, rr. 7 and 132*bis* of the ICC RPE, reg. 47 of the ICC Regulations.

[378] Rule 65*bis* of the ICTY RPE and ICTR RPE, r. 69 of the MICT RPE, r. 132 of the ICC RPE, reg. 54 of the ICC Regulations.

[379] Rules 73*bis* and 73*ter* of the ICTY RPE and ICTR RPE; rr. 81–82 of the MICT RPE, reg. 54 of the ICC Regulations.

[380] Rule 121 of the ICC RPE.

[381] E.g. *Milošević*, ICTY A. Ch., 16 May 2002 (time limit etc. for the prosecution case), and ICTY T. Ch. III, 25 February 2004 (time limit etc. for the defence case). See also ICC T. Ch. III, 17 September 2003 (time for preparation of the defence case), upheld on appeal, ICTY A. Ch., 20 January 2004, and ICTY T. Ch. III, 17 October 2003 (time limits for examination of a witness). Regarding limitations, however, see *Orić*, ICTY A. Ch., 20 July 2005.

[382] *Lubanga*, ICC T. Ch. I, 14 March 2012, paras. 10–11.

Disclosure at the ICTY and ICTR is construed against their primarily adversarial procedures. The Prosecutor has extensive, and continuous, obligations concerning pre-trial disclosure: the material supporting the indictment, copies of statements of all witnesses whom
the Prosecutor intends to call to testify at trial, and copies of all statements offered in
evidence in lieu of a witness testimony.[383] The defence must also be permitted to inspect the
Prosecutor's material.[384] The obligation to disclose also extends to exculpatory and other
relevant material in the custody or control of the Prosecutor,[385] a provision which has
triggered numerous claims of violations at both Tribunals. However, certain information and
material are exempt from disclosure[386] and the Trial Chamber may allow non-disclosure of
specific information. Defence disclosure is also provided with respect to a defence of alibi or
any special defence (such as diminished or lack of mental responsibility) before the
commencement of the defence case.[387] Failure by the defence to disclose does not prevent
it from raising a defence or presenting evidence. The Prosecutor may seek clarifications on
disclosure from the Trial Chamber[388] and the accused may obtain an order to the Prosecutor
to meet the disclosure obligations. In the case of violations, the trial may be reopened in
order to allow the presentation of additional evidence,[389] and sanctions may be imposed.[390]
On the controversial question whether the evidence should also be disclosed to the Trial
Chamber, the ICTY Appeals Chamber has established that this is a discretionary matter for
the Trial Chamber.[391]

Disclosure is briefly touched upon in the ICC Statute and further developed in the RPE
and jurisprudence. Controversial questions in the negotiations were whether full disclosure
of the evidence for trial should take place before or after the confirmation hearing and
whether the Chambers should have access to a 'dossier'.[392] The RPE leave room for
different interpretations. But it is important to note that the confirmation and the trial
serve different purposes and that the evidentiary requirements differ, which is also reflected
in the rules on pre-confirmation disclosure.[393] In practice, separate disclosure has taken
place for the confirmation process and for the trial.

The ICC Chambers play a significant role in the disclosure process and are empowered to
order disclosure for the purpose of the confirmation of charges. The Trial Chamber is also

---

[383] Rules 66, 92*bis* and 94*bis* of the ICTY RPE and ICTR RPE, rr. 71, 110 and 116 of the MICT RPE. See generally the
contributions by Vladimir Tochilovsky and Mark Klamberg, in Sluiter, *International Criminal Procedure*, 1083–107.

[384] The Prosecutor also has a right to inspect and copy evidence in the defence's custody which is to be presented as evidence at trial
(r. 67 of the ICTY and ICTR RPE, r. 72 of the MICT RPE), but only the ICTR RPE (r. 67(C)) make this right automatically
reciprocal to an inspection request by the defence.

[385] Rule 68 of the ICTY RPE and ICTR RPE and r. 73 of the MICT RPE. See e.g. *Blaškić*, ICTY A. Ch., 29 July 2004, paras.
263–9.

[386] Rule 70 of the ICTY RPE and ICTR RPE and r. 76 of the MICT RPE.

[387] Rule 67 of the ICTY RPE and ICTR RPE and r. 72 of the MICT RPE. Regarding the timing of the defence disclosure, see also
r. 65*ter* of the ICTY RPE and r. 70 of the MICT RPE.

[388] E.g. *Krajišnik and Plavšić*, ICTY T. Ch. III, 1 August 2001.

[389] See *Furundžija*, ICTY T. Ch. II, 10 December 1998, para. 22.

[390] Rules 46 and 68*bis* of the ICTY RPE, r. 46 of the ICTR RPE, rr. 47 and 74 of the MICT RPE; e.g. *Krstić*, ICTY A. Ch., 19 April
2004, paras. 210–15; and *Blaškić*, ICTY A. Ch., 29 July 2004, para. 295.

[391] *Blagojević et al.*, ICTY A. Ch., 8 April 2003, paras. 11–19.

[392] For opposing views, see the contributions by Helen Brady and Gilbert Bitti in Fischer, *International and National Prosecution*,
261–88.

[393] Regarding the confirmation hearing, see Art. 61(5) of the ICC Statute and r. 121(3) of the ICC RPE.

empowered to provide for disclosure of documents and information not previously disclosed.[394] Disclosure takes place between the parties and there has not (so far) been any all-embracing 'dossier'. The RPE provide for disclosure by the prosecution and, regarding material offered in evidence, by the defence as well as on inspection by the other party of material subject to disclosure.[395] Exceptions from disclosure are also available;[396] different schemes for redactions have been ordered by the Chambers for protection purposes.[397] The Statute places an important obligation upon the Prosecutor to disclose 'evidence' that is exculpatory, mitigating, or which may affect the credibility of prosecution evidence.[398] However, the disclosure obligation has been expanded to cover exculpatory 'material',[399] as is the case at the Tribunals. The relationship between the obligation and the protection of confidential information, equally sanctioned under the Statute, was put to the test in *Lubanga* (see section 20.6.2).[400] The conflict between the obligation to disclose and the obligation to preserve confidentiality led to a stay of the trial.[401] But it was also affirmed that the disclosure obligations do not override confidentiality, and the issue was resolved when the Prosecutor secured the permission of the providers to submit the undisclosed material to the Trial Chamber for an *ex parte* review.[402] The same issue has arisen in *Banda and Jerbo*, where the Trial Chamber considered appropriate counter-balancing measures following refusal of disclosure by one provider.[403]

17.10 Evidentiary rules

At the ICTY, ICTR, the Residual Mechanism and the ICC, the procedures are adversarial in the sense that the parties are primarily responsible for putting evidence before the court, but the judges may provide for additional evidence.[404] Issues concerning the role of the witness, the burden and standard of proof, collection of evidence, evidence in the confirmation process, and disclosure have already been touched upon[405] and the presentation of evidence follows in section 17.12. The challenges of gathering evidence through State cooperation are discussed in Chapter 20.

Domestic systems provide for rules on evidence, particularly rules regarding the admission and exclusion of evidence. While many adversarial systems, particularly those with jury trials, tend to have strict and technical provisions, inquisitorial systems do not and

---

[394] Arts. 61(3) (Pre-Trial Chamber) and 64(3)(c) (Trial Chamber) of the ICC Statute. Extensive instructions for disclosure have been issued by the Pre-Trial and Trial Chambers in each case.

[395] Rules 76–79 of the ICC RPE. On the test for inspection (r. 77), see *Banda and Jerbo*, ICC A. Ch., 28 August 2013.

[396] *Ibid.*, rr. 81–82.   [397] E.g. *Ruto and Sang*, ICC T. Ch. V, 27 September 2012.   [398] Art. 67(2) of the ICC Statute.

[399] E.g. *Lubanga*, ICC T. Ch. I, 13 June 2008, para. 59.

[400] Art. 67(2) versus Art. 54(3)(e) of the ICC Statute. See e.g. Ambos and Miller, 'Structure and Function', 341–4; Sabine Swoboda, 'The ICC Disclosure Regime – A Defence Perspective' (2008) 19 *Criminal Law Forum* 449; Larry D. Johnson, 'The Lubanga Case and Cooperation between the UN and the ICC' (2012) 10 *Journal of International Criminal Justice* 887.

[401] *Lubanga*, ICC T. Ch. I, 13 June 2008 and ICC A. Ch., 21 October 2008 (1486).

[402] See *Lubanga*, ICC A. Ch., 21 October 2008 (1486), para. 48, and T. Ch. I, 23 January 2009. See also r. 83 of the ICC RPE.

[403] *Banda and Jerbo*, ICC T. Ch. IV, 23 November 2011, 26 October 2012 (407) and 21 June 2013.

[404] At the ICC, the judges (actively seeking the 'truth') may order the production of exculpatory as well as incriminating evidence: see *Katanga and Ngudjolo Chui*, ICC A. Ch., 16 July 2010, para. 86.

[405] See section 17.2.4, 17.3.3, 17.6, 17.9.1 and 17.9.3.

instead admit most evidence to be presented at trial.[406] The former approach seeks to protect the fact-finder from unreliable or improper evidence. The latter places the emphasis on the court weighing the totality of the evidence (a principle of 'free evaluation of evidence') and providing the findings in a reasoned opinion. Regardless of the system, however, a high evidentiary standard is important for the legitimacy of any court; in *Kupreškić et al.*, the Trial Chamber stated: 'we have had to shoulder the heavy burden of establishing incredible facts by means of credible evidence'.[407]

The approach to evidence at the Tribunals has been described as flexible, liberal and unhindered by technical rules found in national and particularly common law systems.[408] Professional judges try both fact and law and there is no need to protect jurors from lay prejudice. The same is true for the ICC. The complex factual situations, a large amount of evidence, and difficulties in obtaining it, are all reasons for flexibility, but this also raises issues of fairness and efficiency of the proceedings.[409] But the amount of evidence can be reduced if the parties agree on alleged facts and thus limit the contested issues.[410]

There are a few rules for the Tribunals but a rich jurisprudence,[411] which has also influenced the ICC law. The Trial Chambers are not to be bound by national rules of evidence.[412] Instead, the Tribunals are instructed to apply the rules 'which will best favour a fair determination of the matter' and 'are consonant with the spirit of the Statute and the general principles of law'.[413] They have the discretion to 'admit any relevant evidence which it deems to have probative value' and to exclude evidence 'if its probative value is substantially outweighed by the need to ensure a fair trial'.[414] In order to be relevant (to an allegation or issue in the trial) and probative (whether it tends to prove an issue) the evidence must be 'reliable', which in turn depends upon many circumstances, for example the origin, content, corroboration, truthfulness, voluntariness and trustworthiness of the evidence.[415] The ICC Statute is less extensive. It provides that the judgment shall be based 'only on evidence submitted and discussed before it at trial', but the Trial Chambers have adopted a liberal interpretation and also included evidence 'discussed' in written submissions that were part of the trial record.[416] No legal requirement of corroboration may be required.[417] Generally, the 'probative value of the evidence and any prejudice that such evidence may

[406] E.g. Mirjan Damaška, 'Free Proof and its Detractors' (1995) 43 *American Journal of Comparative Law* 343; Jackson and Summers, *Internationalization of Criminal Evidence*, 3–76.
[407] *Kupreškić et al.*, ICTY T. Ch. II, 14 January 2000, para. 758; see also ICTY A. Ch., 23 October 2001, paras. 34–40 (on domestic principles).
[408] Richard May and Marieke Wierda, 'Evidence before the ICTY' in Richard May *et al.* (eds.), *Essays on ICTY Procedure and Evidence* (The Hague, 2001) 251.
[409] For critical views, see e.g. Patricia Wald, 'To Establish Incredible Events by Credible Evidence: The Use of Affidavit Testimony in Yugoslavia War Crimes Tribunal Proceedings' (2001) 42 *Harvard International Law Review* 535. See also footnote 163.
[410] Rule 69 of the ICC RPE. See e.g. *Banda and Jerbo*, ICC T. Ch. IV, 28 September 2011.
[411] The 'guidelines' issued in *Brđanin and Talić*, ICTY T. Ch. II, 15 February 2002, are instructive.
[412] Rule 89(A) of the ICTY RPE and ICTR RPE, r. 105(A) of the MICT RPE, Art. 69(8) of the ICC Statute and r. 63(5) of the ICC RPE.
[413] Rule 89(B) of the ICTY RPE and ICTR RPE, and r. 105(B) of the MICT RPE.
[414] Rule 89(C)–(D) of the ICTY RPE and r. 105(C)–(D) of the MICT RPE. Cf. the ICTR RPE which only set out the first part on admission: r. 89(C).
[415] E.g. *Tadić*, ICTY T. Ch. II, 5 August 1996, paras. 15–19; and *Musema*, ICTR T. Ch. I, 27,1.2000, paras. 38–42.
[416] Art. 74(2) of the ICC Statute. See, *Lubanga*, ICC T. Ch. I, 14 March 2012, para. 98; *Ngudjolo Chui*, ICC T. Ch. II, 18 December 2012, para. 44.
[417] Rule 63(3) of the ICC RPE.

cause to a fair trial or to a fair evaluation of the testimony of a witness' are decisive factors for a ruling on admissibility or relevance.[418] In addition, evidence before the ICC as well as the Tribunals may be excluded because of the means by which it was obtained.[419]

With no lay judges and an obligation to provide reasons for the factual findings, a presumption in favour of admission of evidence exists in the Tribunals and the ICC; the evidence should rather be weighed at trial than weeded out beforehand.[420] For example, the Tribunals and the ICC have usually accepted hearsay evidence but also assessed it with caution.[421] The ICC has also shown a generous attitude to admitting indirect material such as reports by the UN and non-governmental organizations and news reports.[422] But the suggestion to dispose of any admissibility assessment, in favour of the evaluation of the evidence, was rejected by the ICC Appeals Chamber.[423]

With respect to certain evidence in cases of sexual assault, the opposite presumption applies or the evidence is banned altogether.[424] The issue of 'consent' with respect to crimes of sexual violence committed in coercive circumstances requires special attention; in such a situation, a claim of consent is rarely credible.[425] But the issue is difficult both in substance and with respect to the conflation of material and procedural aspects. The ICC RPE provide that consent cannot be inferred from silence or lack of resistance, nor can it be inferred from words or conduct of a victim incapable of giving genuine consent.[426] The special exclusionary rules are meant to reinforce the law concerning 'consent', but also to protect the victims from spurious lines of questioning.

Another issue that has provoked much debate and litigation is the use of written witness statements in lieu of oral testimony, which is now allowed at the Tribunals regarding 'proof of a matter other than the acts and conduct of the accused as charged in the indictment'.[427] The ICC may also permit video-recorded or audio-recorded testimony, documents and written transcripts;[428] but how the Court will deal with already adjudicated facts and

---

[418] Art. 69(4) of the ICC Statute.

[419] Rule 95 of the ICTY RPE and ICTR RPE; r. 117 of the MICT RPE; Art. 69(7) of the ICC Statute. While the ICTY has seldom applied this rule, the ICTR has done so more often, but has also concluded that not all unlawfully obtained evidence must automatically be excluded; e.g. *Karemera et al.*, ICTR T. Ch. III, 2 November 2007 and 25 January 2008; cf. *Halilović*, ICTY A. Ch., 16 October 2007, paras. 28–41, and Separate Opinions by Judges Meron and Schomburg. For critique of the apparently higher standard for exclusion required at the ICC, see e.g. Alexander Zahar and Göran Sluiter, *International Criminal Law* (Oxford, 2008) 382.

[420] On general considerations concerning the evaluation of evidence, see e.g. *Brđanin*, ICTY T. Ch. II, 1 September 2004, paras. 20–36; *Lubanga*, ICC T. Ch. I, 14 March 2012, paras. 93–118; and *Ngudjolo Chui*, ICC T. Ch. II, 18 December 2012, paras. 33–72.

[421] E.g. *Alekšovski*, ICTY A. Ch., 16 February 1999, para. 15; *Ndindabahizi*, ICTR A. Ch., 16 January 2007, para. 115; *Lubanga*, ICC PTC I, 29 January 2007, para. 106; *Ngudjolo Chui*, ICC T. Ch. II, 18 December 2012, paras. 56.

[422] E.g. *Bemba Gombo*, ICC T. Ch. III, 8 October 2012 and 27 June 2013 (Judge Ozaki partly dissenting).

[423] *Bemba Gombo*, ICC A. Ch., 3 May 2011, paras. 37–8; cf. ICC T. Ch. III, 19 November 2010 (1022) (majority), para. 35.

[424] Rule 96 of the ICTY RPE and ICTR RPE, r. 118 of the MICT RPE, and rr. 70–72 of the ICC RPE. See further Donald Piragoff, 'Evidence' in Lee, *Elements and Rules*, 369–91.

[425] On consent, see e.g. *Kunarac et al.*, ICTY A. Ch., 12 June 2002, paras. 127–9, 131.   [426] Rule 70 of the ICC RPE.

[427] Rule 92*bis* of the ICTY RPE and ICTR RPE, and r. 110 of the MICT RPE. Other rules address depositions, written statements and transcripts from other proceedings, evidence of a consistent pattern of conduct and judicial notice of notorious facts and adjudicated facts or documentary evidence from other proceedings: rr. 71, 92*ter* to 92*quinquies* and 93–94 of the ICTY RPE and ICTR RPE and rr. 77, 111–115 of the MICT RPE.

[428] Art. 69(2) of the ICC Statute and rr. 47, 67 and 68 of the ICC RPE. See e.g. *Lubanga*, ICC T. Ch. I, 13 June 2008 (1399) (written evidence) and 15 January 2009 (prior recorded witness statements); *Katanga and Ngudjolo Chui*, ICC T. Ch. II, 3 September 2010 (prior recorded testimony).

material from other proceedings is a matter for jurisprudence.[429] While there is still a preference for oral testimony in principle, the ICTY in particular has been prepared to depart from this in the interest of shorter trials.[430] Such a preference is also expressed in the ICC Statute, but some advocate a greater reliance upon written statements here too.[431] Although there are certain inherent problems with witness evidence,[432] the major advantage is that examination at trial is possible, including by way of video-link,[433] and alternatives should therefore be confined to evidence that does not relate to the conduct or *mens rea* of the accused. But it has also been said that the acceptance of written statements as the norm is '[t]he single most important procedural development during the life of the ICTY' and that '[i]t is extremely doubtful that the work of the ICTY could have been completed without that development'.[434]

17.11   Admission of guilt, guilty pleas and plea bargaining

Common law and civil law systems take very different approaches when the accused confesses to the crimes charged. The law of the ICTY and ICTR, on the one hand, and the ICC, on the other, reflect these differences. The Tribunals have adopted the common law approach of a formal review of the 'guilty plea' and, if accepted by the Chamber, a finding of guilt and a move to a sentencing hearing, that is to say, simplified proceedings.[435] The test is whether it was a voluntary, informed and unequivocal plea, and whether there is a sufficient factual basis for the crime and the participation of the accused in it. The crucial difference between the two views is whether the court must accept the facts as the parties have agreed them or whether it will conduct a further inquiry and perhaps require additional evidence. Although the ICTY and ICTR Chambers are required to satisfy themselves as to the facts, the factual basis is often limited and the Chambers are reluctant to call for additional evidence. More recent ICTY practice, however, reveals a more thorough examination of the agreed facts and the consistency with the admitted crimes.[436]

---

[429] On judicial notice of facts of common knowledge and on agreements between the parties regarding evidence, see Art. 69(6) of the ICC Statute and r. 69 of the ICC RPE. A request to admit portions of witness statements, as they appeared in a judgment, was rejected after the submission of the final trial briefs in *Katanga and Ngudjolo Chui*, ICC T. Ch. II, 14 May 2012.

[430] Compare r. 89(F) of the ICTY RPE and r. 90(1) of the ICTR RPE; the ICTY, but not the ICTR, has departed from the primary reliance on oral testimony. See also *Milošević*, ICTY T. Ch. III, 21 March 2002 and ICTY A. Ch., 30 September 2003 (including a dissenting opinion). See further Steven Kay, 'The Move from Oral Evidence to Written Evidence' (2004) 2 *Journal of International Criminal Justice* 495; and Boas, *Practitioner Library*, Vol. III, 352–7.

[431] Art. 69(2) of the ICC Statute; and Donald Piragoff, 'Article 69' in Triffterer, *Observers' Notes*, 1312. See, *Expediting Proceedings at the International Criminal Court* (Report 14, American University, Washington College of Law, War Crimes Research Office, Washington DC, June 2011) 35–45.

[432] E.g. Robert Cryer, 'Witness Evidence before International Criminal Tribunals' (2003) 2 *Law and Practice of International Courts and Tribunals* 411, 417–38; and Combs, *Fact-Finding*, 14–20.

[433] See e.g. *Bemba Gombo*, ICC T. Ch. III, 3 February 2012, paras. 5–11.

[434] Iain Bonamy, 'Making War Crimes Trials Work – Balancing Fairness and Expedition' in Gideon Boas, William Schabas and Michael Scharf (eds.), *International Criminal Justice: Legitimacy and Coherence* (Cheltenham, UK, and Northampton, MA, 2012) 44, 57.

[435] Rules 62*bis* and 62*ter* of the ICTY RPE, rr. 62 and 62*bis* of the ICTR RPE, rr. 64–65 of the MICT RPE. Cf. Art. 20(3) of the ICTY Statute, Art. 19(3) of the ICTR Statute and Art. 18(3) of the MICT Statute, which direct that, regardless of the plea, there be a 'trial'.

[436] See e.g. *Babić*, ICTY A. Ch., 18 July 2005, paras. 8–10; and *Deronjić*, ICTY A. Ch., 20 July 2005, paras. 12–19. Cf. *Jelisić*, ICTY A. Ch., 5 July 2001, para. 87 (unless cogent reasons indicate otherwise, the sentence should be based on the agreed facts).

Closely connected is the issue of agreements between the parties regarding matters of guilt and sentencing – 'plea bargaining' – which has long existed in many common law jurisdictions.[437] Regardless of the approach to confessions, however, negotiations and agreements on the disposition of criminal cases are now accepted in many legal systems, including in civil law jurisdictions.[438] But many differences exist, and a fundamental one is whether the agreement under certain conditions is binding on the court. 'Negotiated justice' is debated, and, while proponents often highlight the judicial economy of plea bargaining, opponents focus instead on inequality before the law and the risk of materially incorrect verdicts.[439]

The ICTY and ICTR have long accepted plea bargaining, but the attraction of this tool depends on a predictable outcome for the accused, particularly a sentencing rebate, and here the jurisprudence is inconsistent.[440] While it is clear that the Chamber is not bound by any agreement between the parties, many sentencing recommendations have been accepted and the Trial Chamber in *Todorović* concluded that a timely plea would normally result in a rebate.[441] But, in later decisions, ICTY Trial Chambers have departed from such recommendations and the Appeals Chamber has avoided giving express support to a rebate,[442] which in turn has discouraged new plea agreements.

During the ICC negotiations, the issue of guilty pleas was extensively discussed. As a compromise, the Statute provides a formula leaning more towards the civil law view that a confession is merely one piece of evidence, but it still allows simplified proceedings in case of 'an admission of guilt'.[443] The assessment of the 'admission of guilt' by the Trial Chamber is similar to that of the Tribunals but with a stronger focus on the submitted facts and any evidence. The Chamber may also, in 'the interests of justice', decide on a more complete presentation of the facts of the case by requesting the Prosecutor to present additional evidence or ordering a trial under the ordinary trial procedures. Plea bargaining was also a hotly contested issue in the negotiations and some expressed strong reservations. A provision was inserted in the Statute that no agreement between the parties is to be binding on the Court.[444] But the provision does not prevent plea bargaining as such, and certain powers of the Prosecutor, albeit under a level of Court control, could leave room for such agreements. Whether the ICC will accept the practical necessity of some form of plea bargaining in spite of the principled concerns and likely criticism is not yet known. But,

---

[437] One should note, however, that not all common law jurisdictions allow plea bargaining and that among those allowing the practice there are important differences.

[438] See Jenia Iontcheva Turner and Thomas Weigend, 'Negotiated Justice' in Sluiter, *International Criminal Procedure*, 1400–5.

[439] See *Erdemović*, ICTY A. Ch., 7 October 1997, paras. 17–21, and the Dissenting Opinion of Judge Cassese. See further e.g. Michael Bohlander, 'Plea-Bargaining before the ICTY' in May *et al.*, *Essays on ICTY Procedure*, 151–63; Henri Bosly, 'Admission of Guilt before the ICC and in Continental Systems' (2004) 2 *Journal of International Criminal Justice* 1040; Nancy Amoury Combs, *Guilty Pleas in International Criminal Law: Constructing a Restorative Justice Approach* (Stanford, CA, 2007); Mark Harmon, 'Plea Bargaining: The Uninvited Guest at the International Criminal Tribunal for the Former Yugoslavia' in Doria, *Legal Regime*, 163–82.

[440] On concerns about such rebates, see section 19.3.1; and Turner and Weigend, 'Negotiated Justice', 1377–89.

[441] *Todorović*, ICTY T. Ch. I, 31 July 2001, para. 80. See also *Bisengimana*, ICTR T. Ch. II, 13 April 2006, para. 126.

[442] See *Dragan Nikolić*, ICTY A. Ch., 4 February 2005, paras. 55–6.

[443] Art. 65 of the ICC Statute and r. 139 of the ICC RPE.

[444] Art. 54(3)(d) of the ICC Statute, on agreements with individuals, and Arts. 53(3) and 61(4) and (9), relating to decisions not to pursue a prosecution. See Turner and Weigend, 'Negotiated Justice', 1389–92.

as one commentator suggests, it would be desirable to conduct as many trials as possible, and resort to bargaining only when absolutely necessary.[445]

17.12   Trial and judgment

Generally, the trial hearings before the Tribunals and the ICC have been lengthy. In part this is due to the basically adversarial nature of the trial whereby the prosecution and the defence present separate 'cases'. Initially, the parties before the Tribunals were allowed to make different dispositions and adapt their evidence depending on the development of the trial, and with little intervention by the Chambers. Today, however, this has changed and the preparations and trial management in the Tribunals and the ICC are now much more rigorous and under stricter judicial control (see also section 17.9).

In principle, the trial is to be public, but closed sessions are allowed for specified reasons: public order and morality, safety and security of a victim or witness, protection of confidential or sensitive information, or the protection of the interests of justice.[446] Disruptive persons, including the accused, may be removed from the courtroom.[447] Unlike many civil law jurisdictions, neither the ICTY and ICTR nor the ICC may proceed with the trial in the absence of the accused (trials *in absentia*).[448] While some criticize this choice, particularly in light of the difficulties of apprehending the accused, others consider this to be a fundamental precondition for a fair trial and the issue was much discussed in the ICC negotiations.[449]

The trial itself follows a straightforward scheme: opening statements, presentation of evidence, closing arguments, deliberations, and judgment.[450] Sentencing and reparations proceedings are discussed in Chapters 18 and 19. In the ICTY and ICTR, this follows the two-case model, prosecution first and defence thereafter. So far, this has also been the practice at the ICC, although this is not inevitable owing to the presiding judge's broad powers to give directions for the conduct of the proceedings.[451] This considerable discretion could potentially result in fundamentally different approaches being taken in different cases, and in turn affect the perceived fairness of the Court proceedings and the right of all accused to equal treatment, but this has not happened and could be reduced by practice directives or harmonization in other forms.[452]

---

[445] Mirjan Damaška, 'Negotiated Justice in International Criminal Courts' (2004) 2 *Journal of International Criminal Justice* 1018.

[446] Rules 78–79 of the ICTY RPE and ICTR RPE, rr. 92–93 of the MICT RPE and Arts. 63 and 64(7) of the ICC Statute.

[447] Rule 80 of the ICTY RPE and ICTR RPE, r. 94 of the MICT RPE and Arts. 63(2) and 71 of the ICC Statute.

[448] Art. 21(4)(d) of the ICTY Statute, Art. 20(4)(d) of the ICTR Statute, Art. 19(4)(d) of the MICT Statute and Art. 63 of the ICC Statute.

[449] See Håkan Friman, 'Rights of Persons Suspected or Accused of a Crime' in Lee, *The Making of the Rome Statute*, 255–61; and William Schabas, 'In Absentia Proceedings before International Criminal Courts' in Sluiter and Vasiliev, *International Criminal Procedure*, 335–80. See also section 17.9.1.

[450] Rules 84–87 of the ICTY RPE, rr. 84–88 of the ICTR RPE, rr. 100–104 of the MICT RPE, Art. 64(8) of the ICC Statute and rr. 140–142 of the ICC RPE.

[451] Art. 64(8)(b) of the ICC Statute and r. 140 of the ICC RPE.

[452] See Reinhold Gallmetzer, 'The Trial Chamber's Discretionary Power to Devise the Proceedings before It and its Exercise in the Trial of Thomas Lubanga Dyilo' in Stahn and Sluiter, *Emerging Practice*, 501–24. See generally Sergey Vasiliev, 'Structure of Contested Trial' in Sluiter, *International Criminal Procedure*, 569–600 (ICTY and ICTR) and 600–22 (ICC).

Unless the Trial Chamber decides otherwise, the presentation of evidence in Tribunal trials follows a true adversarial model: prosecution evidence, defence evidence, prosecution evidence in rebuttal, defence evidence in rejoinder, evidence ordered by the Chamber, evidence regarding sentencing.[453] In each case, examination-in-chief, cross-examination, and re-examination are to be allowed, and the judge may ask questions at any stage.[454] The Chamber is to exercise control over the mode and order of interrogating witnesses, with a view to efficiency, and the cross-examination is limited in scope.[455] The ICC scheme, on the other hand, leaves room for a different approach inspired by inquisitorial principles: less of a distinction, or none at all, between prosecution and defence witnesses, and a less strict scheme for examination beginning with a free statement and questions by the judges, not the parties. There are some minimum rules, however, which provide for an examination model quite similar to that of the Tribunals.[456] As was noted in section 17.2.4, the term 'witnesses of the Court' has often been used, which, together with the ICC Trial Chambers' directions for the presentation of evidence and the subject-matter and form of judicial questioning,[457] point towards a more tempered adversarial approach. One Trial Chamber has expressed a preference for neutral questions, but without completely precluding the use of 'leading questions', while others have not.[458] Before the Tribunals and the ICC, the accused may appear as a witness in his or her own defence, which departs from the practice in civil law jurisdictions, but he or she is also allowed to make unsworn statements at trial.[459]

In line with the adversarial two-case model at the ICTY and ICTR, there is room for the accused to request a judgment after the presentation of the prosecution case, a so-called mid-trial acquittal.[460] The Chamber may also enter such a judgment *proprio motu*. The rationale is that the accused has 'no case to answer' due to insufficient evidence, but the assessment of evidence at mid-trial could potentially affect the perception of the judges' impartiality. Attempting to overcome this, the test is explained as: 'whether there is evidence (if accepted) upon which a reasonable tribunal of fact *could* be satisfied beyond reasonable doubt of the guilt of the accused on the particular charge in question'.[461] This procedure is not provided for the ICC, but the Court might argue, like early ICTY decisions, an 'inherent power' to dismiss charges due to insufficient evidence.[462]

The judgment must contain reasons, which allows a subsequent review of the legal and factual findings.[463] As majority decisions are permitted, both majority and minority

---

[453] Rule 85 of the ICTY RPE and ICTR RPE and r. 102 of the MICT RPE.
[454] In particular, the cross-examination is considered a cornerstone for the common law trial model, sometimes even called 'the greatest legal engine ever invented for the discovery of truth'; see John H. Wigmore, *A Treatise on the Anglo-American System of Evidence at Trials in Common Law*, 3rd edn (Boston, 1940) 29, § 1367.
[455] Rule 90 of the ICTY RPE and ICTR RPE and r. 106 of the MICT RPE.   [456] Rule 140 of the ICC RPE.
[457] E.g. *Lubanga*, ICC T. Ch. I, 18 March 2010, paras. 33–47 (also including 'leading questions').
[458] E.g. *Bemba Gombo*, ICC T. Ch. III, 19 November 2010 (1023), para. 15, and 15 December 2010, para. 19. Cf. *Lubanga*, ICC T. Ch. I, 16 September 2009, para. 23; and *Katanga and Ngudjolo Chui*, ICC T. Ch. II, 20 November 2009 (Annex), paras. 66–7, 71. In *Ruto and Sang*, no general directions on the mode of questioning were given (ICC T. Ch. V(A), 9 August 2013, para. 18) but even so some instructions on cross-examination (ICC T. Ch. V(A), 3 September 2013, para. 19).
[459] Rule 84*bis* of the ICTY RPE, r. 84 of the ICTR RPE, r. 101 of the MICT RPE and Art. 67(1)(h) of the ICC Statute.
[460] Rule 98*bis* of the ICTY RPE and ICTR RPE and r. 121 of the MICT RPE.
[461] E.g. *Delalić et al.*, ICTY A. Ch., 20 February 2001, para. 434.
[462] *Tadić*, ICTY T. Ch. II, 13 September 1996. See also Friman *et al.*, 'Charges', 425–7, 487.
[463] Art. 23 of the ICTY Statute, r. 98*ter* of the ICTY RPE, Art. 22 of the ICTR Statute, r. 88 of the ICTR RPE, Art. 21 of the MICT Statute, r. 122 of the MICT RPE, Art. 74 of the ICC Statute and r. 144 of the ICC RPE.

opinions are to be included. While the ICC Statute clearly strives towards unanimity, in practice many decisions include separate opinions.

17.13   Appeals proceedings

17.13.1 Appeal against judgment and sentence

The Nuremberg and Tokyo IMTs did not provide for appeals, but today anyone convicted of a crime is entitled to a review of the conviction and sentence by a higher court.[464] The ICTY, ICTR and ICC all allow appeals.

Like most civil law jurisdictions, appeals are not restricted to convictions or sentences, but also extend to acquittals. In many common law jurisdictions, on the contrary, acquittals are considered final immediately and are not subject to appeal. The latter model stresses the protection of the individual against repeated charges by the State,[465] the former is more concerned with achieving a materially correct verdict. A safeguard in domestic jurisdictions where acquittals are subject to appeals is a prohibition against *reformatio in peius* (worsening of an earlier verdict), which prevents changes regarding the verdict or sentence to the detriment of the accused if only he or she appeals; such a change is possible only where the prosecutor appeals. The ICC Statute sets out this principle, and the Tribunals have applied it too.[466] In practice, however, the principle is straightforward concerning penalties but hard to apply regarding convictions since no formal hierarchical order is established between the different crimes (see section 19.3).

On appeal, the Appeals Chamber may affirm, reverse or revise the appealed decision.[467] Alternatively, it may set aside the judgment and order a new trial before a different Trial Chamber.[468] Detailed procedures are set forth for each jurisdiction.[469]

17.13.2 Grounds of appeal and standard of review

At the ICTY and ICTR, appeals against trial judgments, as appeals against sentencing judgments, are appeals *sensu stricto*, that is to say, of a corrective nature, and not new trials (trials *de novo*).[470] The process is limited to correcting errors of law invalidating the decision

---

[464] E.g. Art. 14(5) of the ICCPR.
[465] In common law jurisdictions, an appeal against an acquittal would contravene the principle of protection against double jeopardy, at least if it relates to facts established by a jury, but exceptions also exist; see e.g. Rafael Nieto-Navia and Barbara Roche, 'The Ambit of the Powers under Article 25 of the ICTY Statute: Three Issues of Recent Interest' in May *et al.*, *Essays on ICTY Procedure*, 473–94.
[466] Art. 83(2) of the ICC Statute; *Bralo*, ICTY A. Ch., 2 April 2007, para. 85; and *Muvunyi*, ICTR A. Ch., 29 August 2008, para. 170.
[467] Art. 25(2) of the ICTY Statute, Art. 24(2) of the ICTR Statute, Art. 23(2) of the MICT Statute and Art. 81(2) of the ICC Statute.
[468] Rule 117(C) of the ICTY RPE, r. 118(C) of the ICTR RPE, r. 144(C) of the MICT RPE and Art. 81(2) of the ICC Statute. Examples include *Erdemović*, ICTY A. Ch., 7 October 1997 (invalid guilty plea), *Tadić*, ICTY A. Ch., 10 September 1999 (re-sentencing after reversal of acquittal) and *Muvunyi*, ICTR A. Ch., 29 August 2008 (insufficient reasoning in the judgment).
[469] Rules 107–118 of the ICTY RPE, rr. 107–119 of the ICTR RPE, rr. 131–145 of the MICT RPE, rr. 149–158 of the ICC RPE and regs. 57–65 of the ICC Regulations.
[470] Art. 25 of the ICTY Statute, Art. 24 of the ICTR Statute and Art. 23 of the MICT Statute; also e.g. *Kupreškić et al.*, ICTY A. Ch., 23 October 2001, paras. 22 and 408.

and errors of fact resulting in a 'miscarriage of justice'. The threshold for intervening in factual determinations is high and requires that the Trial Chamber's conclusion is one 'which no reasonable trier of fact could have reached',[471] leading to a 'grossly unfair outcome in judicial proceedings, as when the defendant is convicted despite a lack of evidence on an essential element of the crime'.[472] In principle, the same standards apply regardless of whether the prosecution or the defence lodges the appeal.[473] Against the limited scope of the appeals process, the ICTY and ICTR Appeals Chambers have also established an inherent power, deriving from their judicial function, to ensure that justice is done by assuming a discretionary power to correct an error of law on their own motion if the interests of justice so require.[474] Consequently, the burden of proof on appeals is not absolute regarding points of law, but the party must at least identify the alleged error, present arguments and explain how the error invalidates the decision.[475]

In earlier decisions, the ICTY Appeals Chamber avoided assuming the role of trier of fact after having established an error of law, and instead ordered a retrial by a Trial Chamber. But, being increasingly faced with additional evidence on appeal,[476] and mindful of the long trials and limited resources, the Appeals Chamber became less hesitant. Hence, in *Blaškić*, it decided not only to correct errors of law but also to apply the correct legal standard to the case at hand.[477] Critics would argue, however, that the parties are thereby deprived of the right to appeal the subsequent factual findings.

As to sentencing, both Tribunals have taken the view that the Appeals Chamber should not revise the sentence unless the Trial Chamber has committed a 'discernible error' in exercising its discretion or has failed to follow applicable law.[478]

The ICC Statute lists the grounds of appeal as procedural error, error of fact, and error of law, and, as an additional ground in case of conviction, 'any other ground that affects the fairness or reliability of the proceedings or decision'.[479] Regarding sentences, the main ground of appeal is disproportion between the crime and the sentence.[480] In addition, however, a reversal, amendment or remittal to a new trial before a Trial Chamber requires that the 'proceedings were unfair in a way that affected the reliability of the decision or sentence' or that 'the decision or sentence . . . was materially affected by error of fact or law or procedural error'.[481] Hence, the standard of review is further qualified. The Appeals Chamber is not restricted by the appeals, and may on its own motion raise the question to set aside a conviction or reduce a sentence.[482]

The ICC Statute leaves the Appeals Chamber with broad discretion as to procedures; the Appeals Chamber has all the powers of the Trial Chamber and evidence may be presented in

---

[471] E.g. *Tadić*, ICTY A. Ch., 15 July 1999, para. 64; and *Akayesu*, ICTR A. Ch., 1 June 2001, para. 178.

[472] *Furundžija*, ICTY A. Ch., 21 July 2000, para. 37.　　[473] E.g. *Mrkšić and Šljvančanin*, ICTY A. Ch., 5 May 2009, para. 15.

[474] E.g. *Delalić et al.*, ICTY A. Ch., 8 April 2003, para. 16; and *Kambanda*, ICTR A. Ch., 19 October 2000, para. 98.

[475] E.g. *Krnojelac*, ICTY A. Ch., 17 September 2003, para. 10; and *Ntakirutimana*, ICTR A. Ch., 13 December 2004, para. 7.

[476] Rule 115 of the ICTY RPE and ICTR RPE and r. 142 of the MICT RPE.

[477] *Blaškić*, ICTY A. Ch., 29 July 2004, para. 24. See also *Kordić and Čerkez*, ICTY A. Ch., 17 December 2004, para. 24.

[478] E.g. *Tadić*, ICTY A. Ch., 26 January 2000, para. 22; and *Musema*, ICTR A. Ch., 16 November 2001, para. 395.

[479] Art. 81(1) of the ICC Statute; see also Christopher Staker, 'Article 81' in Triffterer, *Observers' Notes*, 1466.

[480] Arts. 81(2) and 83(3) of the ICC Statute.　　[481] *Ibid.*, Art. 83(2).

[482] *Ibid.*, Art. 81(2); similarly, see *Erdemović*, ICTY A. Ch., 7 October 1997, para. 39 (exercising an 'inherent power').

the appeals proceedings.[483] Although it could be argued that the scheme leaves room for a trial *de novo*, the enumerated grounds for an appeal rather point towards a corrective procedure with a possibility of admitting additional evidence.[484] So far, the Appeals Chamber has dealt only with interlocutory appeals, primarily on procedural issues.

17.13.3 Interlocutory appeals

Interlocutory appeals are not provided for in the ICTY and ICTR Statutes, but they were soon accepted in practice and are now provided for in the RPE.[485] Such appeals are also allowed at the ICC.[486] But, since interlocutory appeals are time- and resource-consuming, only certain decisions are subject to such review. Decisions on jurisdiction, traditionally quite strictly defined in ICTY and ICTR jurisprudence,[487] and in the ICC also decisions concerning the admissibility of the case, are always subject to separate appeals. The ICC Statute also allows interlocutory appeals against decisions concerning provisional release and certain Pre-Trial Chamber-ordered measures during the investigation. All other decisions require leave to appeal (or certification) by the Chamber issuing the challenged decision.[488] In turn, leave to appeal normally requires that the decision 'involves an issue that would significantly affect the fair and expeditious conduct of the proceedings or the outcome of the trial' and for which 'an immediate resolution by the Appeals Chamber may materially advance the proceedings'.[489] Initially, the ICC Pre-Trial and Trial Chambers were very restrictive on granting leave, but inconsistent approaches to various procedural issues have prompted a more generous practice, allowing the Appeals Chamber to provide authoritative determinations.[490] In part owing to the current rules on motions and responses, interlocutory appeals at the ICC often last for many months.

As to the standard of review, a successful interlocutory appeal at the Tribunals requires a finding that the Trial Chamber erred. The Tribunals have taken a deferential approach to the exercise of discretionary powers, restricting the review to whether the discretion was correctly exercised, rather than to whether the Appeals Chamber agrees in substance.[491] A matter determined in an interlocutory decision is not open for reconsideration unless 'a clear error of reasoning has been demonstrated or if it is necessary to do so to prevent an injustice'.[492] Similarly, the ICC Appeals Chamber has accepted that the grounds for an ordinary appeal – procedural error, error of fact, and error of law – may be transposed to

---

[483] Art. 83(1)–(2) of the ICC Statute; see also r. 149 of the ICC RPE.

[484] See Helen Brady, 'Appeal and Revision' in Lee, *The Making of the Rome Statute*, 585–6; and Alphons Orie, 'Accusatorial v. Inquisitorial Approaches in International Criminal Proceedings Prior to the Establishment of the ICC and in the Proceedings before the ICC' in Cassese, *Commentary*, 1490–1.

[485] E.g. *Tadić*, ICTY A. Ch., 2 October 1995, paras. 4–6; rr. 72–73 of the ICTY RPE and ICTR RPE, r. 132 of the MICT RPE.

[486] Art. 82 of the ICC Statute and rr. 154–158 of the ICC RPE.

[487] However, a more generous practice is discernible in more recent decisions, e.g. *Boškoski and Tarćulovski*, ICTY A. Ch., 22 July 2005, para. 5.

[488] See *Situation in the DRC*, ICC A. Ch., 13 July 2006 (168) (no extraordinary review available).

[489] Rules 72(B)(ii) and 73(B) of the ICTY RPE and ICTR RPE, rr. 79(B)(ii) and 80(B) of the MICT RPE and Art. 82(1)(d) of the ICC Statute.

[490] Supportive of a restrictive practice, e.g. Schabas, *Commentary*, 939; more critical, Håkan Friman, 'Interlocutory Appeals in the Early Practice of the International Criminal Court' in Stahn and Sluiter, *Emerging Practice*, 553–61.

[491] E.g. *Milošević*, ICTY A. Ch., 1 November 2004, paras. 9–10.   [492] E.g. *Kajelijeli*, ICTR A. Ch., 23 May 2005, paras. 201–7.

interlocutory appeals and explained the 'issues' that may be appealed if leave to appeal is granted.[493] Regarding the standard of review, the Chamber has emphasized that it is corrective in nature and not *de novo*; it will intervene against a legal error which 'materially affects' the impugned decision, and against a factual error if the Chamber 'misappreciated the facts, took into account irrelevant facts or failed to take into account relevant facts'.[494] Unless a clear factual error is demonstrated, the Appeals Chamber will defer to the Pre-Trial or Trial Chamber's factual finding.[495] The Appeals Chamber has a discretionary right to order that the appeal shall have suspensive effect, but the threshold for doing so is high.[496]

17.14 Revision

The Statutes of the ICTY, ICTR, the Residual Mechanism and the ICC make provision for review proceedings, an exceptional remedy against miscarriage of justice, which goes beyond mere errors of fact or law.[497] There are some important differences between the ICTY and ICTR on the one hand and the ICC on the other. While the Tribunals allow either party to seek revision, thus allowing the Prosecutor to apply in relation to an acquittal,[498] revision at the ICC applies only to a conviction or sentence.[499] Moreover, the Tribunals have extended the scope to all final decisions, not only those which include a verdict of conviction or acquittal but also, for example, final decisions resulting in the dismissal of the case with prejudice to the Prosecutor.[500]

The strict requirements for a review by the Tribunals are: (1) a 'new fact'; (2) the new fact was not known to the applicant at the time of the original proceedings; (3) the failure to discover the new fact was not due to the applicant's lack of due diligence; and (4) the new fact could have been a decisive factor in reaching the original decision.[501] In extraordinary circumstances, however, review may be granted by the Tribunal although the fact was known to or discoverable by the applicant; this is in order to prevent a miscarriage of justice.[502] Similarly, revision at the ICC requires that 'new evidence', which was not available at the time of the trial for reasons not wholly or partially attributable to the moving party, is sufficiently important so that the verdict is likely to have turned out differently. In addition, however, the ICC Statute allows revision when decisive evidence at trial turns out to be false, forged or falsified, or in case of serious misconduct or breach of duty by a participating judge.

[493] E.g. *Situation in the DRC*, ICC A. Ch., 13 July 2006 (168 on Art. 82(1)(d); and 169 on Art. 82(1)(a)). See Franziska Eckelmans, 'The First Jurisprudence of the Appeals Chamber of the ICC' in Stahn and Sluiter, *Emerging Practice*, 527–52.
[494] E.g. *Kony et al.*, ICC A. Ch., 16 September 2009, para. 48; and *Ruto et al.*, ICC A. Ch., 30 August 2011, para. 56.
[495] E.g. *Ruto et al.*, ICC A. Ch., 30 August 2011, para. 57.   [496] E.g. *Bemba Gombo*, ICC A. Ch., 9 July 2010.
[497] Art. 26 of the ICTY Statute, Art. 25 of the ICTR Statute, Art. 24 of the MICT Statute and Art. 84 of the ICC Statute. The Residual Mechanism may also review ICTY and ICTR judgments.
[498] The Prosecutor may seek revision within one year after the final judgment; for the convicted person there is no time limit: r. 119 of the ICTY RPE, r. 120 of the ICTR RPE and r. 146 of the MICT RPE.
[499] Art. 84(1) of the ICC Statute.
[500] E.g. *Barayagwiza*, ICTR A. Ch., 31 March 2000, paras. 45–50; and *Delalić et al.*, ICTY A. Ch., 25 April 2002, para. 5. See Jean Galbraith, 'New Facts in ICTY and ICTR Review Proceedings' (2008) 21 *Leiden Journal of International Law* 131.
[501] *Barayagwiza*, ICTR A. Ch., 31 March 2000, para. 41; and *Delalić et al.*, ICTY A. Ch., 25 April 2002, para. 8.
[502] *Barayagwiza*, ICTR A. Ch., 31 March 2000, para. 65; and *Tadić*, ICTY A. Ch., 30 July 2002, para. 27.

The procedures also differ.[503] At the Tribunals, both admissibility of the application for revision and any review of the earlier decision are normally adjudicated by the original Chamber. At the ICC, however, a two-step approach applies whereby the Appeals Chamber first determines admissibility and, if the application succeeds, the revision itself is conducted by this or another Chamber.

17.15 Offences against the administration of justice

The ICTY, ICTR, the Residual Mechanism and the ICC all have provisions on prosecution and punishment of offences directed against the administration of justice. Since the ICTY and ICTR Statutes are silent on the matter, this is considered an inherent power derived from the judicial function of the Tribunals.[504] For the Residual Mechanism and the ICC, however, the power is laid down in the Statutes.[505] While the list of qualifying acts in the provisions of the ICTY, ICTR and the Residual Mechanism is not exhaustive, the list of offences for the ICC is.[506] Another important difference is that prosecution and punishment of these offences is a shared responsibility between the ICC and the States Parties.[507]

At the Tribunals, the rules refer to 'contempt of court' and specify the criminal offences, penalties and the procedures. The ICC provisions, however, make a distinction between 'offences against the administration of justice' – with a broader scope than the Tribunals' contempt provisions – and lesser 'misconduct before the Court'. The maximum penalty for offences against the administration of justice is a prison sentence, a fine, or a combination of the two; misconduct at the ICC may lead to a fine and other measures.[508] Separate provisions apply for misconduct of counsel[509] and for perjury.[510]

17.16 Some concluding observations

A comprehensive assessment of the procedural law of the international criminal jurisdictions is a huge task and beyond the scope of this book. The principles are discussed throughout the chapter; many of them, however, stem from the dichotomy between the different legal traditions, or adversarial and inquisitorial features. Indeed, most qualitative assessments of the international criminal procedures are coloured by the commentator's own domestic legal background. Nonetheless, some commentators react to the preoccupation with the common law/civil law divide and the description of the systems as hybrids, and

---

[503] Rules 119–122 of the ICTY RPE; rr. 120–123 of the ICTR RPE; rr. 146–148 of the MICT RPE, Art. 84(2) of the ICC Statute, rr. 159–161 of the ICC RPE and reg. 66 of the ICC Regulations.
[504] Rule 77 of the ICTY RPE and ICTR RPE. See also e.g. *Tadić*, ICTY A. Ch., 31 January 2000, para. 13.
[505] Art. 1(4) of the MICT Statute, r. 90 of the MICT RPE, Arts. 70 and 71 of the ICC Statute and rr. 162–172 of the ICC RPE.
[506] E.g. *Marijačić and Rebić*, ICTY T. Ch. III, 7 October 2005, para. 31.   [507] Art. 70(4) of the ICC Statute.
[508] The ICC may also order forfeiture: r. 166(2) of the ICC RPE.
[509] Rule 46 of the ICTY RPE and ICTR RPE; concerning the ICC, see reg. 29 of the ICC Regulations; Arts. 30–34 of the Code of Professional Conduct for Counsel (ICC-ASP/4/Res.1) of 2 December 2005, and Chapter 5, ss. 1–2, of the Code of Conduct of the Office of the Prosecutor of 5 September 2013.
[510] Rule 91 of the ICTY RPE and ICTR RPE and r. 108 of the MICT RPE. Perjury is also one offence under Art. 70(1) of the ICC Statute.

argue that the procedural law should be viewed in its own right.[511] This, it is hoped, would facilitate a clearer application of principles developed in the specific international context instead of through the lens of one's own domestic legal experience.[512] While this approach has merit, it is probably too early to consider this a discrete body of law owing to the multiplicity of jurisdictional forums and procedural differences that exist between them.[513] Nonetheless, it has been argued that a clearer methodology or theory for international criminal procedure is necessary.[514]

Another common yardstick is found in international human rights standards and principles, which again are subject to different interpretations and preferences as how best to be implemented. But the particular circumstances and challenges that exist, not least concerning international cooperation, must also be considered. Accordingly, it might be unreasonable to assess procedural fairness against exactly the same yardstick as domestic systems.

The ICTY and ICTR, beginning with very little guidance, have shown that international criminal proceedings can be conducted in accordance with high procedural and human rights standards, including extensive protection of the rights of the accused. However, the length of the proceedings has long been a target of criticism and the major internal remedy has been a shift from purely adversarial principles to stronger and more invasive intervention by the judges. While this development has generally been welcomed, the actual success has been questioned, and some empirical research indicates that the reforms have instead lengthened the process.[515]

For the ICC, on the other hand, inquisitorial features and a stronger role for victims were present from the outset; a novel set-up to which neither the Tribunals nor most domestic analogies provide real guidance. Some would argue that these procedures are more fair, others that they are less so and instead rather confusing. Clearly, the proper distribution of roles and powers between the Pre-Trial Chamber, Trial Chamber and prosecution has not been settled. Nor are issues such as the distinction between 'situations' and 'cases', admissibility assessments, restrictions on disclosure, and participation of victims, resolved. Investigative practices can be improved. The pre-trial process, including the confirmation proceedings with separate disclosure and a hearing, has been described as 'a gigantic enterprise, with an almost unmanageable amount of documentation, filings and litigation'.[516] Although the first case of a new jurisdiction must be allowed more time to settle matters, the *Lubanga* case has proven to be more difficult and run longer than the first cases before the ICTY (*Tadić*), ICTR (*Akayesu*) and SCSL (*Norman et al.*).

---

[511] E.g. John Jackson, 'Finding the Best Epistemic Fit for International Criminal Tribunals: Beyond the Common Law–Civil Law Dichotomy' (2009) 7 *Journal of International Criminal Justice* 17.

[512] E.g. Boas, *Practitioner Library*, Vol. III, 14–17.   [513] See Sluiter, *International Criminal Procedure*, 3–7.

[514] See Safferling, *International Criminal Procedure*, Chapter 3. Cf. Mireille Delmas-Marty, 'Interactions between National and International Criminal Law in the Preliminary Phase of the Trial at the ICC' (2006) 4 *Journal of International Criminal Justice* 2 ('common denominators' in national systems should suffice for resolving procedural problems).

[515] See Langer and Doherty, 'Managerial Judging Goes International'.

[516] William Schabas and Carsten Stahn, '(Symposium) Introductory Note: Legal Aspects of the Lubanga Case' (2008) 19 *Criminal Law Forum* 431, 432.

Similar crimes and broadly similar conditions have been addressed by different procedural solutions, but none of them has conclusively provided an optimal process. Creating a good international code of criminal procedure is, to be sure, a daunting task.

It is thus safe to conclude that international criminal procedures will always be faced with critical comments and calls for amendments, just as in a domestic setting, although there the demands for dramatic shifts are less commonplace. The most common line of critique is that the process is far too slow and unacceptably long, in particular when the suspect or accused is deprived of his or her liberty. It is argued that the success of the international criminal jurisdictions depends upon a more expeditious process. But it is important to acknowledge that the cases are legally and factually complex which, together with the conditions for investigations and prosecutions, must be factored into expectations. Investigating and prosecuting too quickly and narrowly, as a means for expediency, may even counteract some goals of the international criminal process.[517] It has been observed with respect to the ICTY that an already strengthened and legitimated institution may be a prerequisite for an advantageous procedural reform.[518]

So, while there is a widespread view that a reform of the ICC's criminal procedures is necessary, and various initiatives are under way, a good balance between expediency and other interests must be attempted. Since there is little appetite among the States Parties to conduct a broad review of procedures, another obstacle may be to find a workable and acceptable format for reform. The current structure whereby amendments are initiated by the ICC judges (the 'Lessons Learned' process) has an ambitious scope and offers qualitative proposals based on experience, but it can hardly be expected to produce the more general and radical reform that might be needed. In other words, it is a challenge both in substance and in process. The criminal procedures form a system where one element impacts on other parts and thus a comprehensive, rather than piecemeal, review should be welcomed; and why not approach the international criminal procedures in their own context rather than through the lens of common law or civil law preferences?

Further reading

Reports on ICC procedures by the American University, Washington College of Law, War Crimes Research Office, are available at www.wcl.american.edu/warcrimes.

Boas, *Practitioner Library*, Vol. III
Michael Bohlander (ed.), *International Criminal Justice: A Critical Analysis of Institutions and Procedures* (London, 2007)
Cassese, *Commentary*, Chapters 28–38
Antonio Cassese (ed.), *The Oxford Companion to International Criminal Justice* (Oxford, 2009)

---

[517] See Whiting, 'International Criminal Prosecutions'.
[518] See Nancy Amoury Combs, 'Legitimizing International Criminal Justice: The Importance of Process Control' (2012) 33 *Michigan Journal of International Law* 321.

Silvia Fernándes de Gurmendi and Håkan Friman, 'The Rules of Procedure and Evidence and the Regulations of the Court' in Doria, *Legal Regime*, 797–824

Horst Fischer, Claus Kreß and Sascha Rolf Lüder (eds.), *International and National Prosecution of Crimes under International Law* (Berlin, 2001)

John Jackson and Sarah Summers, *The Internationalization of Criminal Evidence: Beyond Common Law and Civil Law Traditions* (Cambridge, 2012)

Karim Kahn, Rodney Dixon and Sir Adrian Fulford (eds.), *Archbold International Criminal Courts: Practice, Procedure and Evidence*, 4th edn (London, 2013)

Karim Kahn, Caroline Buisman and Christopher Gosnell (eds.), *Principles of Evidence in International Criminal Justice* (Oxford, 2010)

Lee, *Elements and Rules*

Christoph Safferling, *International Criminal Procedure* (Oxford, 2012)

William A. Schabas, *The International Criminal Court: A Commentary on the Rome Statute* (Oxford, 2010)

Sluiter, *International Criminal Procedure*

Sluiter and Vasiliev, *International Criminal Procedure*

Stahn and Sluiter, *Emerging Practice*

Vladimir Tochilovsky, *The Law and Jurisprudence of the International Criminal Tribunals and Courts: Procedure and Human Rights Aspects* (forthcoming, 2014)

Salvatore Zappalà, *Human Rights in International Criminal Proceedings* (Oxford, 2003)

18

Victims in the International Criminal Process

18.1   Introduction

Traditionally, the accused is at the very centre of the criminal process and he or she is afforded rights and protection in order to ensure a fair process. The opposing party is the prosecutor, in modern criminal systems primarily a public prosecutor representing the public interest in prosecuting crimes. But where does that leave the victim who also has interests in the process? Domestic systems address this issue in different ways.[1] Generally speaking, an adversarial process, based upon two opposing parties, leaves little room for providing the victim with a strong and independent participatory role. Also, where private prosecutions are allowed, or where victims may play a subsidiary prosecutorial role when a public prosecution is instituted, the two-party process is basically retained. On the other hand, the more active role of the judge in an inquisitorial process, and consequently a less clear-cut two-party design, leaves a greater scope for victims to participate in their own right. Regardless of the system, however, victims play an important role as witnesses in the criminal process,[2] a role that may be compromised if the victim also has an independent function in the same process.

Domestic systems also vary with respect to the victim's right to obtain compensation from the perpetrator of the crime. Often this is considered as a civil claim to be pursued in a separate civil process, but there are also examples where such claims can be handled within the criminal proceedings.[3] Quite apart from this, certain criminal sanctions may be of a compensatory nature, for example orders for restitution of property.

Internationally, there is an increasing focus on the role of victims of crime and thus a debate as to how victim-related interests can be met. But opinions differ and different schools of thought are more, or less, sympathetic to such interests; retributive and utilitarian thinking tends to place the accused at the forefront, while restorative justice theories allow

---

[1] For examples (France, the Netherlands, Germany and the United Kingdom), see Claude Jorda and Jérome de Hemptinne, 'The Status and Role of the Victim' in Cassese, *Commentary*, 1401–2. See also Mikaela Heikkilä, *International Criminal Tribunals and Victims of Crimes* (Åbo, 2004) 43–56; and generally Mireille Delmas-Marty and John R. Spencer (eds.), *European Criminal Procedure* (Cambridge, 2002).

[2] In most domestic systems, the victim will be treated like other witnesses, including being required to give evidence under oath. But, in some systems, for example in Sweden, where the accused may not be heard under oath, a sworn statement by the victim is also not allowed for fairness sake.

[3] Again, Sweden may serve as an example.

for a greater role for victims.[4] A milestone was the UN Victims Declaration, adopted by the UN General Assembly in 1985.[5] Twenty years later, the General Assembly adopted the so-called 'Van Boven/Bassiouni Principles' on victims' right to a remedy and to reparation for gross violations of international human rights and international humanitarian law.[6] Guidelines on child victims and witnesses of crime have been adopted by ECOSOC.[7] Regional instruments have also been developed, for example within the Council of Europe[8] and the European Union.[9]

When the international criminal jurisdictions were established, different models were contemplated. Clearly, one important objective behind the creation of these jurisdictions was to provide redress to the victims of atrocities. However, redress may take different forms and be provided in different forums, not necessarily by the international criminal jurisdictions.[10] The procedures of the ICTY and ICTR were from the outset clearly adversarial in nature, and thus the role of the victims was rather limited; their primary function was to give evidence as a witness. They are not even parties to the proceedings with respect to restitution of property.[11] This largely auxiliary role has been criticized as insufficient if, as France stated at the time of adoption of the ICTY Statute, one of the rationales behind the institution is to bring justice to the victims.[12]

Hence, the relatively extensive scheme provided for victims in the ICC Statute – protection, participation and reparations – was not inevitable. On the contrary, the issues and how best to address them were controversial during the negotiations.[13] The questions have garnered enormous attention and the comments by observers have been mixed too. Many have hailed the victims-related provisions as a substantial advance when compared with the law and practice of the predecessors of the ICC.[14] The scheme has been described as

---

[4] E.g. Heikkilä, *International Criminal Tribunals*, 23–42.

[5] Declaration of Basic Principles for Victims of Crime and Abuse of Power, GA Res. 40/34 of 29 November 2005.

[6] Basic Principles and Guidelines on the Right to a Remedy and Reparations for Victims of Gross Violations of International Human Rights Law and Serious Violations of International Humanitarian Law, GA Res. 2005/35 of 16 December 2005. See also Marten Zwanenburg, 'The Van Boven/Bassiouni Principles: An Appraisal' (2006) 24 *Netherlands Quarterly of Human Rights* 641.

[7] Guidelines on Justice in Matters involving Child Victims and Witnesses of Crime of 22 July 2005.

[8] See e.g. the European Convention on the Compensation of Victims of Violent Crimes of 24 November 1983 (ETS 116), and Recommendation of the Committee of Ministers to Member States on the Position of the Victim in the Framework of Criminal Law and Procedure of 28 June 2005 (R(85)11).

[9] The most recent instruments are the Council Directive relating to compensation to crime victims (2004/80/EC of 29 April 2004); and the Directive of the European Parliament and of the Council establishing minimum standards on the rights, support and protection of victims of crime, and replacing Council Framework Decision 2001/220/JHA (2012/29/EU of 25 October 2012). A proposed Regulation on mutual recognition of protection measures in civil matters is currently under discussion.

[10] E.g. the victims played a very limited role in the Nuremberg trials: see Sam Garkawe, 'The Role and Rights of Victims at the Nuremberg International Military Tribunal' in Herbert Reginbogin *et al.* (eds.), *The Nuremberg Trials: International Criminal Law since 1945* (Munich, 2006) 86–94.

[11] Rule 105 of the ICTY RPE and ICTR RPE and r. 129 of the MICT RPE (the question of restitution may be raised by the Prosecutor or by the Trial Chamber *proprio motu*). See generally Sam Garkawe, 'Victims and the International Criminal Court: Three Major Issues' (2003) 3 *International Criminal Law Review* 345.

[12] E.g. Jorda and de Hemptinne, 'Status and Role of the Victim', 1387–98. Cf. Antonio Cassese, 'The International Criminal Tribunal for the Former Yugoslavia and Human Rights' (1997) 4 *European Human Rights Law Review* 329 (envisaging a greater role for victims in the ICTY process). See generally Eric Stover, *The Witnesses: War Crimes and the Promise of Justice in The Hague* (Philadelphia, 2007).

[13] On the negotiations, see Christopher Muttukumaru, 'Reparations to Victims' in Lee, *The Making of the Rome Statute*, 262–70; and Gilbert Bitti and Håkan Friman, 'Participation of Victims in the Proceedings' in Lee, *Elements and Rules*, 456–74.

[14] See e.g. Theo van Boven, 'Victims' Rights and Interests in the International Criminal Court' in Doria, *Legal Regime*, 895–906.

representing a move away from the exercise of purely retributive justice.[15] But there are also critics, some of whom warn that the scheme for victims, particularly their rights to participate, is a potentially harmful experiment in a still fragile system.[16] Yet others suggest that the scheme might be insufficient owing to the tension between the necessary selectivity in international prosecutions and an increasing recognition of the rights of all victims to a remedy and to reparations in international human rights law.[17]

It has very wisely been argued that, while the ICC procedures should indeed allow for effective victim participation, the limitations on restoring every victim's sense of self-respect should be honestly acknowledged in order to avoid raising false hopes.[18] In fact, an ambition that the ICC should provide justice to individual victims[19] could easily cause unrealistic expectations, since it would most likely be unattainable in practice. However, the ICC should not be seen as the only forum for redress for the victims of atrocities. Just because the Court is there, that does not mean it can take on all the roles undertaken at the national level by large parts of government structures. Other initiatives, whether national or international, could also, and perhaps even better, serve interests such as establishing a historical record and promoting reconciliation; criminal proceedings clearly have limitations in this sense. The Court has adopted a strategic plan for outreach activities and a comprehensive strategy in relation to victims.[20]

More recent internationalized courts also recognize victims' rights.[21] The Extraordinary Chambers in the Courts of Cambodia (ECCC) underline reconciliation as an important aim and provide for extensive victim participation in the proceedings and a right to claim moral and collective reparations.[22] Moreover, the Special Tribunal for Lebanon Statute contains provisions on victim participation, which are based on the ICC Statute, but here civil claims for reparations are to be placed before ordinary national courts.[23] In both cases, the principles have support in domestic (French-influenced) law.

---

[15] See e.g. Silvia Fernández de Gurmendi and Håkan Friman, 'The Rules of Procedure and Evidence of the International Criminal Court' (2001) 3 *Yearbook of International Humanitarian Law* 289, 312. See also Funk, *Victims' Rights and Advocacy.*

[16] See e.g. Alexander Zahar and Göran Sluiter, *International Criminal Law* (Oxford, 2007) 75–6.

[17] See e.g. Cécile Aptel, 'Prosecutorial Discretion at the ICC and Victims' Right to Remedy' (2012) 10 *Journal of International Criminal Justice* 1357. For scepticism concerning connecting redress to international criminal justice, see Conor McCarthy, 'Victim Redress and International Criminal Justice' (2012) 10 *Journal of International Criminal Justice* 351.

[18] Emily Haslam, 'Victim Participation at the International Criminal Court: A Triumph of Hope over Experience?' in Dominic McGoldrick *et al.* (eds.), *The Permanent International Criminal Court* (Oxford, 2004) 319. See also *Victim Participation before the International Criminal Court* (Report 1, American University, Washington College of Law, War Crimes Research Office, Washington DC, November 2007) 44–6.

[19] See e.g. David Donat-Cattin, 'The Role of Victims in ICC Proceedings' in F. Lattanzi and W. Schabas (eds.), *Essays on the Rome Statute of the International Criminal Court* (Il Sirente, 1999) Vol. I, 252.

[20] The first comprehensive strategy was adopted by the Court in 2009 and amended in 2012: Court Revised Strategy in Relation to Victims, ICC-ASP/11/38 of 5 November 2012. See also Report of the Court on the Revised Strategy in Relation to Victims: Past, Present and Future, ICC-ASP/11/40 of 5 November 2012.

[21] Apart from those mentioned in the text, the courts in East Timor (UNTAET Regulation 2000/30 on Transitional Rules of Criminal Procedure) and Kosovo (Provisional Criminal Procedure Code) also allow victim participation in the proceedings.

[22] See e.g. Brianne McGonigle, 'Two for the Price of One: Attempts by the Extraordinary Chambers in the Courts of Cambodia to Combine Retributive and Restorative Justice Principles' (2009) 22 *Leiden Journal of International Law* 127. See also *Nuon Chea*, ECCC PTC, 20 March 2008; and David S. Sokol, 'Reduced Victim Participation: A Misstep by the Extraordinary Chambers in the Courts of Cambodia' (2011) 10 *Washington University Global Studies Law Review* 167.

[23] Arts. 17 and 25 of the STL Statute. See e.g. Jérôme de Hemptinne, 'Challenges Raised by Victims' Participation in the Proceedings of the Special Tribunal for Lebanon' (2010) 8 *Journal of International Criminal Justice* 165.

18.2 Definition of victims

The ICC Rules include a general definition of 'victims', which is influenced by the 1985 UN Victims Declaration and intended for all purposes (protection, participation and reparations).[24] It distinguishes between 'natural persons' and 'organizations or institutions'.

A victim is someone who has suffered 'harm', but this notion is not defined and may be understood in a number of different ways. The Court has resorted to the Van Boven/Bassiouni Principles for guidance,[25] and also to the practice of international human rights courts. 'Harm' to natural persons[26] denotes hurt, injury and damage and the definition covers material, physical and psychological (or emotional) harm, but only in so far as the harm is suffered personally by the victim ('personal harm').[27] Although the harm must be suffered personally, not only 'direct victims' but also 'indirect victims', such as family members of someone killed or of a child soldier, are covered by the definition.[28] The harm must relate to a crime within the jurisdiction of the Court in substantive, territorial and temporal terms; the question of nexus between the 'harm' and a crime actually investigated or prosecuted by the Court is addressed below in relation to participation. What evidence may be sufficient will be determined on a case-by-case basis.[29]

Legal persons may qualify as victims too, but the definition requires that they have sustained direct harm and that this relates to certain property such as a hospital or a school.[30]

18.3 Protection of victims and witnesses

Protection of victims and witnesses is a difficult and demanding task for any criminal jurisdiction, and is particularly so for an international one.[31] Apart from a great reliance upon live evidence, the nature of the crimes and the fact that the tribunals are international and highly public, necessitated the development of thorough victim/witness protection regimes. In addition, the ICC often conducts its initial investigations during ongoing violent conflicts, which makes the question of protection even more important and challenging. But these institutions have a more limited range of possible protective measures than national

---

[24] Rule 85 of the ICC RPE. See generally Silvia Fernández de Gurmendi, 'Definition of Victims and General Principle' in Lee, *Elements and Rules*, 427–34; and Tatiana Bachvarova, 'Victims' Eligibility before the International Criminal Court in Historical and Comparative Context' (2011) 11 *International Criminal Law Review* 665.

[25] *Lubanga*, ICC T. Ch. I, 18 January 2008, para. 92 (cf. Judge Blattmann's dissent, paras. 4–5), and ICC A. Ch., 11 July 2008, paras. 20 and 33.

[26] Practice varies concerning whether deceased persons are included or not: see *Situation in Darfur*, ICC PTC I, 14 December 2007, para. 36 (excluded); and *Bemba Gombo*, ICC PTC III, 12 December 2008, para. 40 (included).

[27] *Lubanga*, ICC A. Ch., 11 July 2008, paras. 31–2. Hence, personal harm, not collective harm, is decisive for the right to participate: *ibid.*, paras. 35 and 37. The Appeals Chamber's definition is broader than that of, for example, the ICTY (r. 2(A) of the ICTY RPE) and the STL (r. 2(A) of the STL RPE), but also limited since it excludes suffering due to the substantial impairment of rights; see further Matthew Gillet, 'Victim Participation at the International Criminal Court' (2009) 16 *Australian International Law Journal* 29, 34–6.

[28] *Lubanga*, ICC A. Ch., 11 July 2008, para. 32 (cf. Judge Pikis' dissent, para. 3). See also *Lubanga*, ICC T. Ch. I, 18 January 2008, para. 91, and ICC T. Ch. I, 8 April 2009.

[29] *Kony et al.*, ICC A. Ch., 23 February 2009, para. 38.

[30] Rule 85(b) of the ICC RPE. See also e.g. *Situation in the DRC*, ICC PTC I, 18 August 2011, paras. 10, 30–4.

[31] See generally e.g. John R. W. D. Jones, 'Protection of Victims and Witnesses' in Cassese, *Commentary*, 1355–70; and Daniela Kravetz, 'The Protection of Victims in War Crimes Trials' in Bonacker and Safferling, *Victims of International Crimes*, 149–64.

authorities; the international jurisdictions do not have their own police forces and are dependent upon State authorities, peacekeeping forces or others in order to offer the more robust forms of protection.[32]

The protection of victims and witnesses is regulated in the Statutes and Rules of Procedure and Evidence[33] and a rich jurisprudence on this has developed. While the granting of protective measures is primarily a responsibility of the Chambers at the Tribunals, the Prosecutor and the Chambers, and also the Registrar and Registry, share the responsibility at the ICC; the Pre-Trial Chambers have been particularly active, including during the investigation.[34] Special units for victim and witness issues, including protective measures and security arrangements, are also established in the respective Registries.[35] In order to avoid 'secondary victimization', specialized Registry units also provide support measures that are similar to social welfare services.[36]

Factors such as the victim's age, gender, health and the nature of the crime, particularly sexual crimes, may add to his or her vulnerability and thus prompt protective measures.[37] But in practice the need for protective measures goes far beyond that. Most of the crimes, as well as the circumstances within which the Tribunals and Court operate, are such that witnesses and victims are very anxious and may refuse to collaborate unless various protective measures are taken. Coercing a person to appear and give evidence is seldom a realistic option.[38] Hence, there is abundant use of protective measures.

The protection may be motivated by security or privacy reasons.[39] Protective measures which are to be enforced out of court are possible only to a limited extent; witness protection programmes, including relocation, require assistance by States and others and must be used sparingly. A cheaper, and possibly more effective, alternative is to develop prosecutorial investigation plans and practices whereby contacts with vulnerable witnesses and victims are avoided to the greatest possible extent. Such investigative practices, as adopted by the ICC Prosecutor, including extensive use of indirect evidence and intermediaries and limited on-site activities by ICC investigators, have not been very successful, however, and have been criticized.[40]

In the proceedings, measures may be taken to prevent disclosure to the public (screening, voice or image distortion, pseudonyms and a ban on photography), and postponed disclosure, closed sessions and testimony by video-link may be employed. Apart from the actual witnesses, family members and even potential witnesses may also be afforded protection.[41]

---

[32] See Chapter 20.
[33] Arts. 20(1) and 22 of the ICTY Statute, Arts. 19(1) and 21 of the ICTR Statute, rr. 39(ii), 69, 75 and 79 of the ICTY RPE and ICTR RPE, Arts. 54(1)(b) and (3)(f), 57(3)(c), 64(6)(e) and 68 of the ICC Statute, and rr. 87–88 of the ICC RPE.
[34] See Håkan Friman, 'Protection of Victims and Witnesses' in André Klip and Göran Sluiter (eds.), *Annotated Leading Cases of International Criminal Tribunals* (Antwerp, 2010) Vol. XXIII, 297–302.
[35] Rule 34 of the ICTY RPE and ICTR RPE, Arts. 43(6) and 68(4) of the ICC Statute and rr. 16–19 of the ICC RPE.
[36] See e.g. Stover, *The Witnesses*, 79–91.   [37] See Art. 60(1) of the ICC Statute.   [38] See section 20.2.3.
[39] The ICTY, ICTR and ICC have concluded special (confidential) agreements with States for the purpose of witness protection.
[40] See e.g. *Investigative Management, Strategies, and Techniques of the International Criminal Court's Office of the Prosecutor* (Report 16, American University, Washington College of Law, War Crimes Research Office, Washington DC, October 2012). See also Caroline Buisman, 'Delegating Investigations: Lessons to Be Learned from the Lubanga Judgment' (2013) 11 *Northwestern Journal of International Human Rights* 30.
[41] See e.g. *Ngirabatware*, ICTR T. Ch. II, 6 May 2009.

By an extensive interpretation of non-disclosure provisions, the ICC Appeals Chamber extended the application of protection measures to 'persons at risk on account of the activities of the Court' and thus to identification of 'innocent third parties' and Court staff.[42]

Protection programmes must be available to both the prosecution and the defence and be perceived as neutral. Hence, the responsibility for these matters, including relocation, is placed upon special units with the Registry. The ICC Appeals Chamber rejected the Prosecutor's attempt to 'preventively relocate' witnesses unilaterally and concluded that the relevant Chamber was the final arbiter in case of disagreement between the Prosecutor and the Registry.[43] Nonetheless, the process of accepting witnesses into the ICC's Protection Programme is cumbersome and time-consuming, which in turn has been a major cause for disclosure complications and delays.[44]

Clearly, all these measures impact on important fair trial principles, and a careful balancing of interests is required.[45] Protection from public identification deviates from the principle of a public trial. Even more problematic are measures withholding the identity from the accused, which must be construed so that rights such as having adequate time and facilities for the preparation of the defence and examining witnesses are respected. A particularly controversial measure is the use of anonymous witnesses, that is to say, witnesses whose identity is not known to both parties. An early ICTY decision allowed this practice, clearly influenced by the Tribunal's impotence concerning physical protection, but it was sharply criticized, particularly by proponents of adversarial procedures,[46] and the practice has not been repeated, probably not least as one of the anonymous witnesses was shown to have fabricated his testimony. At the ICC, it is clear that the identity of witnesses may be withheld from disclosure to the defence, but different interpretations are possible as to whether witnesses may remain anonymous at trial.[47] The better view, however, is that the identity may be withheld only 'prior to the commencement of the trial'.[48] For example, identities may be withheld during the confirmation process, although on an exceptional basis only.[49]

---

[42] *Katanga*, ICC A. Ch., 13 May 2008 (Judge Pikis dissenting).

[43] *Katanga and Ngudjolo Chui*, ICC A. Ch., 26 November 2008 (but the Appeals Chamber did not rule out that 'temporary emergency measures' might have to be taken by the Prosecutor; para. 103).

[44] See e.g. *Katanga and Ngudjolo Chui*, ICC PTC I, 25 April 2008 (ICC-01/04-01/07-428), paras. 61–2; and *Expediting Proceedings at the International Criminal Court* (Report 14, American University, Washington College of Law, War Crimes Research Office, Washington DC, June 2011) 61–70.

[45] For a critical view of ICTR practice, see Göran Sluiter, 'The ICTR and the Protection of Witnesses' (2005) 3 *Journal of International Criminal Justice* 962; similar criticisms can be raised against the ICTY and ICC as well.

[46] *Tadić*, ICTY T. Ch. II, 10 August 1995 (Judge Stephen dissenting). See also Monroe Leigh, 'The Yugoslav Tribunal: Anonymity Is Inconsistent with Due Process' (1996) 90 *American Journal of International Law* 235 (and (1997) 99 *American Journal of International Law* 80); Christine Chinkin, 'Due Process and Witness Anonymity' (1997) 99 *American Journal of International Law* 75; Olivia Swaak-Goldman, 'The ICTY and the Right to a Fair Trial: A Critique of the Critics' (1997) 10 *Leiden Journal of International Law* 215; and Natasha Affolder, 'Tadić, the Anonymous Witness and the Sources of International Procedural Law' (1998) 19 *Michigan Journal of International Law* 445.

[47] On non-disclosure, see e.g. *Lubanga*, ICC A. Ch., 11 July 2008. See also Claus Kreß, 'Witnesses in Proceedings before the International Criminal Court: An Analysis in the Light of Comparative Criminal Procedure' in Horst Fischer *et al.* (eds.), *International and National Prosecutions of Crimes under International Law* (Berlin, 2001) 309, 364–82 (arguing that the ICC judges are left with a policy choice).

[48] Art. 68(5) of the ICC Statute and r. 81(4) of the ICC RPE.   [49] E.g. *Lubanga*, ICC A. Ch., 13 October 2006, paras. 34–9.

Quite another matter is to what extent participating victims, who are not witnesses but at least sometimes could be considered as 'accusers', may have their identities protected from the prosecution and defence. Such anonymity has not been ruled out by the ICC.[50]

18.4   Victim participation in ICC criminal proceedings

Unlike in the ICTY and ICTR, the ICC Statute and RPE provide for victim participation in proceedings in pursuance of their own personal interests, both in certain specific instances and generally, although the latter is a right with explicit caveats.[51] Importantly, the exercise of this right – where, when and how – is to be firmly controlled by the relevant Chamber, thus having the challenging task of balancing the victims' rights so that a 'second prosecution' to the detriment of the accused and the prosecution is avoided. Victims in the ICC are not given a status like that of a *partie civile* known to many civil law systems. It is also necessary to find practical and pragmatic solutions in light of the potentially very large number of affected victims. In *Bemba*, for example, more than 5,200 victims have been granted the right to participate in the trial proceedings. Hence, jurisprudence in this area is particularly important and has been steadily developing. These issues have occupied, and continue to occupy, considerable time and effort on the part of all involved in the process. Serious questions have thus been raised concerning the sustainability, and even the meaningfulness, of the regime.[52] The Assembly of States Parties has underlined the 'need to consider reviewing the victim participation system with a view to ensuring its sustainability, effectiveness and efficiency' and requested the Court to conduct such a review.[53]

This general right of participation should be distinguished from participation with respect to protective measures and reparations.[54] On such matters victims may initiate proceedings themselves and hence are parties to them, including a right to appeal decisions. Beyond that, and in relation to the general right to participate, victims are not considered parties and their rights as 'participants' are more confined.

The early decisions, and comments concerning them,[55] understandably related primarily to victim participation in the investigation and pre-trial stages. The first and very influential decision by a Pre-Trial Chamber on point was handed down in January 2006 in the *Situation in the Democratic Republic of the Congo*,[56] rapidly followed by several other Pre-Trial Chamber decisions. The first decision concerning trial proceedings was made by the Trial Chamber in the subsequent *Lubanga* case in January 2008.[57] Being interlocutory matters,

---

[50] E.g. *Lubanga*, ICC T. Ch. I, 18 January 2008, paras. 130–1.

[51] Arts. 15(3), 19(3) and 68(3) of the ICC Statute. See also rr. 89–93 of the ICC RPE.

[52] E.g. Christine Van den Wyngaert, 'Victims before International Criminal Courts: Some Views and Concerns of an ICC Trial Judge' (2011) 44 *Case Western Reserve Journal of International Law* 475.

[53] Res. ICC-ASP/10/Res.5, para. 49.   [54] See *Situation in the DRC*, ICC A. Ch., 19 December 2008, para. 50.

[55] See e.g. Carsten Stahn, Hector Olásolo and Kate Gibson, 'Participation of Victims in the Pre-Trial Proceedings of the ICC' (2006) 4 *Journal of International Criminal Justice* 219; Christine Chung, 'Victims' Participation at the International Criminal Court: Are Concessions of the Court Clouding the Promise?' (2008) 6 *Northwestern Journal of International Human Rights* 459; Sergey Vasiliev, 'Article 68(3) and Personal Interests of Victims in the Emerging Practice of the ICC' in Stahn and Sluiter, *Emerging Practice*; and Håkan Friman, 'The International Criminal Court and Participation of Victims: A Third Party to the Proceedings?' (2009) 22 *Leiden Journal of International Law* 485.

[56] *Situation in the DRC*, ICC PTC I, 17 January 2006.   [57] *Lubanga*, ICC T. Ch. I, 18 January 2008.

the decisions on victim participation require leave to appeal and the very restrictive practice adopted in this regard meant that for a long time the Appeals Chamber was prevented from addressing the issues beyond the question of victim participation in the appeals proceedings as such.[58] The practice of the different Chambers, however, became inconsistent and leave to appeal was granted in a few instances, allowing the Appeals Chamber to give guidance for the future practice of Pre-Trial and Trial Chambers. Greater clarity and consistency has now begun to evolve, but the law on victim participation is still developing, and more recently with particular attention paid to effectiveness.

18.4.1   *Purposes of participation*

The purposes behind the participatory rights afforded to victims are not explicitly laid out in the ICC Statute and must therefore be established by the Court. Ideally, the answer should inform when and how, and perhaps where, participation ought to take place, as well as guide the substantive content of victims' rights of participation. The objectives should be realistic, possible to implement and achieve in practice, and consistent with the rights of the defence and the overall procedural system. This is addressed in the Court's overall strategy in relation to victims which also contains a detailed list of the rights and prerogatives of victims in various parts of the proceedings, as established in the Court's founding documents and practice. But neither the strategy nor the sources of the listed rights are based on a fully consistent and comprehensive analysis of the purposes of victims' participation.

Obvious purposes would be to contribute to the prosecution and obtain restitution or reparation and other forms of satisfaction.[59] But participatory rights may have further aims: fairness to the victim who has suffered harm, avoiding secondary victimization and victim alienation, treating the victim with dignity and respect, and ensuring that the truth is exposed and that a just punishment is imposed.[60] Victim participation could also contribute to making the offender more conscious of the serious injury and suffering they have inflicted on others. Even broader restorative and reconciliatory aims could be claimed in which the interest of bringing the process closer to those who have suffered could be an important component.[61] Nonetheless, not all victims are necessarily in favour of prosecutions. Hence, merely linking the participatory rights to interests in seeking a conviction and obtaining reparations is arguably too narrow an approach; after all, the explicit general purpose is to enable the victims to present their 'views and concerns'.[62]

---

[58] See e.g. *Lubanga*, ICC A. Ch., 13 June 2007. For a critical view, see e.g. Håkan Friman, 'Interlocutory Appeals in the Early Practice of the International Criminal Court' in Stahn and Sluiter, *Emerging Practice*, 553–61.

[59] See e.g. Salvatore Zappalà, *Human Rights in International Criminal Proceedings* (Oxford, 2003) 221.

[60] See Heikkilä, *International Criminal Tribunals*, 141–2 (with further references). See also *Katanga and Ngudjolo Chui*, ICC PTC I, 13 May 2008, paras. 31–44.

[61] See e.g. Hans-Peter Kaul, 'Victims' Rights and Peace' in Bonacker and Safferling, *Victims of International Crimes*, 223–9.

[62] Art. 68(3) of the ICC Statute.

18.4.2   *Conditions for participation and legal representation*

Article 68(3) of the ICC Statute provides for victim participation as a right. Nonetheless, the ICC Chambers have considerable discretion regarding when and how this may be done. The assessment encompasses whether: (1) those seeking participation are 'victims'; (2) their 'personal interests' are affected; (3) the participation is 'appropriate'; and (4) the manner of participation is not prejudicial to or inconsistent with the rights of the accused and a fair and impartial trial. In practice, the Chambers have adopted a rather cumbersome two-step process with, first, an authorization of the individual victim's right to participate in a 'situation' or a 'case' and, second, applications and determinations concerning the actual participation. The burden of satisfying the Chamber that the conditions are met rests with the victim, although the Court has been at pains to make the task a reasonable one. But experience shows that the admissions process could and should be made more efficient.[63] One response is the more collective approach to victims' applications to participate that is being developed in *Gbagbo* and further developed in *Ntaganda*.[64] Further options for reforming the applications system are also considered.[65]

The evidentiary standard has been described differently by different Chambers, but it now seems to be a combination of a *prima facie* test and a freer assessment (similar to the French *intime conviction*).[66] For certain facts, such as identity, a higher standard may be required.[67]

A 'victim' must meet the criteria of the definition (see section 18.2) and thus be a natural person (or a legal person as specified in the definition) and have suffered 'harm' which ensued from a crime within the jurisdiction of the Court.[68] Moreover, a causal link between the crime and the harm is required, which may be difficult to establish.[69] In the early stages of the process, only the Prosecutor knows which incidents are being investigated, and at a later stage the assessment of the linkage could affect the presumption of innocence. A relaxed evidentiary standard and an explicitly preliminary and non-prejudicial determination of this causal link have not satisfied all critics.[70] One problem is that a victim of a particular offence which is neither investigated nor prosecuted may participate in the proceedings regarding the 'situation'. Once a 'case' is identified, the nexus must be between the 'harm' and the crime that the perpetrator is actually suspected or accused of (in the arrest

---

[63] E.g. Lucia Catani, 'Victims at the International Criminal Court: Some Lessons Learned from the Lubanga Case' (2012) 10 *Journal of International Criminal Justice* 905, 917–21.

[64] *Gbagbo*, ICC PTC III, 6 February 2012, 5 April 2012 and 4 June 2012; and *Ntaganda*, ICC PTC II, 28 May 2013. See also *Situation in Uganda*, ICC PTC II, 9 March 2012. Some commentators have also suggested that the class action mechanism in US federal law could be employed: see e.g. Christodoulos Kaoutzanis, 'Two Birds with One Stone: How the Use of the Class Action Device for Victim Participation in the International Criminal Court Can Improve Both the Fights against Impunity and Victim Participation' (2010) 17 *UC Davis Journal of International Law* 111.

[65] Report of the Court on the Review of the System for Victims to Apply to Participate in Proceedings, ICC-ASP/11/22 of 5 November 2012.

[66] See e.g. *Katanga and Ngudjolo Chui*, ICC PTC I, 2 April 2008, 8–9. See, however, more recent decisions plainly referring to a *prima facie* test, e.g. *Gbagbo*, ICC PTC III, 4 June 2012, paras. 21, 23, 27 and 31.

[67] See e.g. *Kony et al.*, ICC A. Ch., 23 February 2009, paras. 35–8.

[68] See e.g. *Situation in the DRC*, ICC PTC I, 17 January 2006, para. 79. A particular problem arising in Lubanga was the withdrawal of some victims' right to participate after they had given unreliable evidence as witnesses; *Lubanga*, ICC T. Ch. I, 14 March 2012, paras. 484, 1363 (cf. Judge Odio Benito's Dissenting Opinion, paras. 24–35).

[69] On the difficulties of establishing harm and even the identity of the victim, see Kaul, 'Victims' Rights and Peace', 223–9.

[70] *Ibid.*, paras. 94–101. For example, some argue that the Court should refrain from an adjudication of harm in the participation process: American University, Washington College of Law, *Victim Participation*, 63.

warrant or indictment). The *Lubanga* Trial Chamber's decision to construe 'personal interests' without requiring such a link, was rejected by the Appeals Chamber.[71]

The notion of 'personal interests' is decisive for participation and should be closely linked to the rationale behind the participation scheme as such. Yet no clear guidance has been given as to the interpretation of this term. Furthermore, the interests may shift during the course of the process. During the 'situation' phase, the interests are considered as quite general and primarily having 'their crimes' investigated and the perpetrator identified.[72] To confine the interests to receiving reparations is clearly too narrow.[73] Another possible, albeit not uncontroversial, interest could be with respect to sentencing.[74] But there are limitations and the Appeals Chamber has emphasized that the interests of the victims must not be regarded as the same as those belonging to the role assigned to the Prosecutor.[75] The suggestion that victim participation may be used by the judges to 'exert some pressure on the Prosecutor to proceed with an investigation' is thus highly doubtful.[76]

The participation of victims must be 'appropriate'. This issue should be considered primarily against the objectives of participation. Other circumstances may also be relevant, however; one Pre-Trial Chamber found victim participation inappropriate at the time owing to the current security situation.[77] Often, however, the issue has been assessed with respect to the manner in which participation may take place,[78] which in fact relates to the fourth condition of safeguarding the rights of the accused and the fairness of the proceedings. This last requirement presupposes a delicate balancing act. A number of defence rights might be affected by victim participation, not least the right to be tried without undue delay.[79] Preserving the equilibrium between the prosecution and the defence is also a challenge. Another difficulty is reconciling the roles of a participating victim who is also a witness.[80]

Legal representation is both a carrot and a stick; common legal representation may be necessary, and thus be ordered by the Court, to make a large number of victims manageable; but a legal representative is guaranteed more extensive participation than an unrepresented victim.[81] A Chamber may direct that victims be legally represented and the Office of Legal

---

[71] *Lubanga*, ICC T. Ch. I, 18 January 2008, paras. 93–5 (Judge Blattmann dissenting) and ICC A. Ch., 11 July 2008, paras. 58–66. See further Gillet, 'Victim Participation', 36–9.

[72] See e.g. *Situation in the DRC*, ICC PTC I, 17 January 2006, paras. 63–4 and 72. See also *Bemba Gombo*, ICC PTC III, 12 December 2008, para. 90 (noting, *inter alia*, that the victims' and prosecution's interests do not always coincide).

[73] *Lubanga*, ICC T. Ch. I, 18 January 2008, para. 98. Cf. *Lubanga*, ICC A. Ch., 16 May 2008, paras. 42–6 (highlighting protection and reparations as examples of personal interests) and Separate Opinions by Judges Pikis and Song.

[74] See e.g. Elisabeth Baumgartner, 'Aspects of Victim Participation in the Proceedings of the International Criminal Court' (2008) 90 (870) *International Review of the Red Cross* 409, 434–7.

[75] *Lubanga*, ICC A. Ch., 19 December 2008, paras. 52–3.

[76] See Jérôme de Hemptinne and Francesco Rindi, 'ICC Pre-Trial Chamber Allows Victims to Participate in the Investigation Phase of Proceedings' (2006) 4 *Journal of International Criminal Justice* 342, 346. Nonetheless, various efforts were made by victim representatives and trial judges to put pressure on the Prosecutor to prosecute crimes of sexual violence in *Lubanga*; this is further discussed in Chapter 17.

[77] *Lubanga*, ICC PTC I, 20 October 2006, paras. 10–11.

[78] See e.g. *Lubanga*, ICC PTC I, 17 January 2006, paras. 56–60. For a better elaboration of 'appropriateness', see Judge Blattmann's Separate and Dissenting Opinion in *Lubanga*, ICC T. Ch. I, 18 January 2008.

[79] See e.g. Jorda and de Hemptinne, 'Status and Role of the Victim', 1393; Heikkilä, *International Criminal Tribunals*, 152; Catani, 'Victims', 915–7; and Salvatore Zappalà, 'The Rights of Victims v. the Rights of the Accused' (2010) 8 *Journal of International Criminal Justice* 137.

[80] See e.g. *Lubanga*, ICC T. Ch. I, 5 June 2008. For the view that the dual status of victim and witness should not be allowed, see Jorda and de Hemptinne, 'Status and Role of the Victim', 1409.

[81] Rule 91 of the ICC RPE.

Counsel for victims has been established.[82] Various Chambers have indicated that victims' common views might best be expressed through a common legal representative,[83] and so far all participating victims have been represented collectively. But, while 129 victims were represented by seven representatives in *Lubanga*, in March 2011 the then 366 victims in *Katanga and Ngudjolo* and the 1,366 victims in *Bemba* were in each case divided into two groups with one common representative per group.[84] Apart from the obvious difficulties to manage, consult with and represent large groups, the interests within a group may diverge.[85] While conflicting interests may motivate separate representation,[86] efficiency and economy may restrict the number of legal representatives. There is no simple solution to such conundrums.

With reference to the large number of victims as well as 'unprecedented security concerns and other difficulties', the Trial Chamber in *Ruto and Sang* and *Muthaura and Kenyatta* opted for a new approach.[87] It was decided that the ordinary application process should only apply to victims who wished to present their views and concerns individually by appearing directly before the Chamber, in person or via video-link; other victims, who wanted to participate without appearing before the Chamber, were to be permitted to present their views and concerns only through a common legal representative upon a simple registration process.[88] Subsequently, the Chamber appointed one legal representative for all victims in the respective case.[89] The differentiated procedure for direct individual participation and participation through a common legal representative is a quite radical step towards a more manageable process, but one which does not come without representational costs.

18.4.3   Participation in different stages of the process

Victim participation is not confined to any particular stage of the process but is likely to have substantive differences at the different stages. To establish the modalities is fully within the domain of judicial discretion. The Court has held that the participation should be 'meaningful' as opposed to 'purely symbolic'.[90]

Victims may provide the Prosecutor with information for the purpose of a criminal investigation, but this is not a formal report of a crime (*notitia criminis*) which automatically triggers an investigation. The information may, however, contribute to the Prosecutor seeking authorization to commence an investigation under Article 15 of the ICC Statute

---

[82] *Ibid.*, r. 90 and regs. 79–82 of the ICC Regulations. See also *Katanga and Ngudjolo Chui*, ICC T. Ch. II, 22 July 2009.
[83] E.g. *Lubanga*, ICC T. Ch. I, 18 January 2008, para. 116.
[84] *Katanga and Ngudjolo Chui*, ICC T. Ch. II, 22 July 2009; and *Bemba Gombo*, ICC T. Ch. III, 10 November 2010.
[85] See Emily Haslam and Rod Edmunds, 'Common Legal Representation at the International Criminal Court: More Symbolic than Real?' (2012) 12 *International Criminal Law Review* 871.
[86] Rule 90(4) of the ICC RPE.
[87] *Ruto and Sang*, ICC T. Ch. V, 3 October 2012, para. 24; and *Muthaura and Kenyatta*, ICC T. Ch. V, 3 October 2012, para. 23.
[88] *Ruto and Sang*, ICC T. Ch. V, 3 October 2012, para. 25; and *Muthaura and Kenyatta*, ICC T. Ch. V, 3 October 2012, para. 24.
[89] *Muthaura and Kenyatta*, ICC T. Ch. V, 20 November 2012; and *Ruto and Sang*, ICC T. Ch. V, 23 November 2012 (one judge dissenting in the latter case regarding whom to appoint).
[90] E.g. *Lubanga*, ICC T. Ch. I, 18 January 2008, para. 85, and ICC A. Ch., 11 July 2008, para. 97.

and participation in the Pre-Trial Chamber's authorization process is explicitly spelled out.[91] Victims may also apply to participate in any review, in accordance with Article 53(3), of the Prosecutor's decision not to investigate or prosecute, but they are not competent to seek such a review.[92]

Although Article 68(3) refers to participation in 'the proceedings', it was established early on that participation in the investigation stage is possible.[93] But the conduct of the investigation falls under the Prosecutor's authority and participation at this stage is therefore confined to judicial proceedings, including when these affect the investigation.[94] Instead of allowing participation generally during the investigation of a situation, the question is to be addressed with respect to particular procedural activities.[95] One Pre-Trial Chamber has further clarified a predetermined framework for participation in different scenarios where judicial proceedings are to be conducted.[96] The nature of the participation in the early stages of the process has been framed in vague terms like 'to be heard' and 'to file documents'.[97] The added value of this, compared with not seeking a formal authorization to participate, is questionable. More far-reaching forms of participation, such as requesting specific proceedings or requesting the Prosecutor to provide information on 'the status of the investigation', which were indicated in older decisions,[98] are incompatible with the statutory scheme and more recent Appeals Chamber decisions.

Once a suspect is identified and a 'case' established, which is normally when a warrant of arrest or summons to appear is issued, many assessments become more straightforward, not the least with respect to the required nexus between the harm and the relevant crimes. The participation is continuous but the Chambers generally require discrete applications for participation in specific procedural activities. Arrest proceedings, confirmation hearings and the trial are instances where typically victims' interests are at stake and participation thus takes place. The ICC Statute specifically provides that victims may submit observations in proceedings with respect to jurisdiction or admissibility.[99]

The ICC RPE provide only limited guidance as to what the participation right might entail. Apart from notifications from the Court and possible invitations to submit

---

[91] See *Situation in Côte d'Ivoire*, ICC PTC III, 6 July 2011 and 3 October 2011, paras. 19–20 (applying less strict conditions for participation owing to the low evidentiary threshold in Art. 15).

[92] The presumed interest of victims to take part in such reviews is indicated by the notification requirements in r. 92(2) of the ICC RPE.

[93] *Lubanga*, ICC PTC I, 17 January 2006, paras. 28–54.

[94] *Situation in the DRC*, ICC A. Ch., 19 December 2008, paras. 45 and 52–6 (reversing the Pre-Trial Chamber decision). See also *Situation in Darfur*, ICC A. Ch., 2 February 2009.

[95] E.g. *Situation in the DRC* PTC I, 11 April 2011, paras. 9–13; and *Situation in Libya*, ICC PTC I, 24 January 2012. Cf. *Katanga and Ngudjolo Chui*, ICC PTC I, 13 May 2008, paras. 45–51 (rejecting such a 'casuistic approach'). See also Friman, 'Participation of Victims', 223–6.

[96] *Situation in Kenya*, ICC PTC II, 3 November 2010; *Situation in the Central African Republic*, ICC PTC II, 11 November 2010; and *Situation in Uganda*, ICC PTC II, 9 March 2012.

[97] See e.g. *Lubanga*, ICC PTC I, 17 January 2006, para. 71.

[98] *Ibid.*, para. 75; and *Situation in the DRC*, ICC PTC I, 26 September 2007.

[99] Art. 19(3) of the ICC Statute. Observations by victims were provided when the admissibility of the case was challenged in *Katanga and Ngudjolo Chui* (ICC T. Ch. II, 16 June 2009), but not in *Kony et al.* (ICC PTC II, 10 March 2009) where instead two NGOs made *amicus curiae* submissions under r. 103 of the ICC RPE. In other instances, the participating victims were represented by the Office of Public Counsel for Victims; e.g. *Ruto et al.*, ICC PTC II, 4 April 2011; and *Gbagbo*, ICC PTC III, 15 June 2012.

observations, there is a presumption that unrepresented victims are confined to written interventions, while a more active participation (attending hearings, making oral interventions etc.) is foreseen for legal representatives.[100] But a much more ambitious scheme for participation has been worked out by the Chambers in practice, which includes access to documents (including confidential ones), making submissions, attending public and sometimes closed sessions, making oral and written interventions, and even examination of witnesses.[101] A right to pose questions to witnesses at trial is laid down in the ICC RPE, inspired by judicial economy and the wish to avoid recalling witnesses to subsequent reparations proceedings, but this has been extended through jurisprudence to a right to tender and examine evidence pertaining to guilt or innocence, as well as to challenge the admissibility of evidence.[102] In another controversial ruling, the majority of the *Lubanga* Trial Chamber admitted a request by victim representatives to consider a legal re-characterization of the charges in accordance with regulation 55 of the ICC Regulations. Although only an 'early notice' of the possibility of the Chamber taking this course of action, the application should have been dismissed, as the strong dissent by one judge concluded, as later did the Appeals Chamber.[103]

Victims are entitled to appeal decisions on matters that they may initiate, in particular on reparations and possibly also protective measures. In other appeals proceedings, the general provisions on victim participation apply and the key question is whether their 'personal interests' are affected by the matter under appeal. For example, a limited right of participation was granted in the appeal against a decision to refuse interim release.[104]

18.5   Reparations to victims

The ICTY and ICTR Statutes do not provide for reparations to victims, and the rule on compensation in the RPE relates to domestic proceedings.[105] The ICC, however, does have the power to order reparations directly to, or in respect of, victims[106] – a contentious matter

---

[100] Rules 91–93 of the ICC RPE.

[101] A comprehensive analysis is provided in *Katanga and Ngudjolo Chui*, ICC PTC I, 13 May 2008, paras. 127–45. The Pre-Trial Chamber distinguished between anonymous and non-anonymous victims (*ibid.*, paras. 182–4), granting the former more limited rights, but this distinction has not been upheld by other Chambers; see e.g. *Bemba Gombo*, ICC PTC III, 12 December 2008, paras. 99, 103–5. See also *Gbagbo*, ICC PTC III, 4 June 2012, paras. 46–60 (participatory rights prior to and at the confirmation hearing). On access to confidential material, see e.g. *Ruto et al.*, ICC PTC II, 23 September 2011.

[102] Rule 91(3) of the ICC RPE; *Lubanga*, ICC T. Ch. I, 18 January 2008, paras. 108–9, 119–22, upheld by the majority of the Appeals Chamber, ICC A. Ch., 11 July 2008, para. 93 (Judges Pikis and Kirsch recording strong dissents). See also *Katanga and Ngudjolo Chui*, ICC PTC I, 13 May 2008, paras. 30–44, 101–3 (concluding a right for victims to call evidence, but not evidence not furnished by the parties for the purpose of confirmation of charges), and ICC A. Ch., 16 July 2009 (elaborating on the role of victims in this respect and on disclosure). For analysis and criticism, see e.g. Friman, 'International Criminal Court and Participation of Victims', 492–8.

[103] *Lubanga*, ICC T. Ch. I, 14 July 2009 and minority opinion (dissent) by Judge Fulford, 17 July 2009, and ICC A. Ch., 8 December 2009. See also section 17.8.4.

[104] See *Lubanga*, ICC A. Ch., 13 February 2007; also concluding that a new application must be made and thus that the right to participate does not automatically transfer to the appeals proceedings (*ibid.*, paras. 38–43; cf. the Dissenting Opinion of Judge Song).

[105] Rule 106 of the ICTY RPE and ICTR RPE as well as r. 130 of the MICT RPE, which also provide that the judgment of the Tribunal (or Mechanism) 'shall be final and binding as to the criminal responsibility of the convicted person for such injury'. However, whether this provision binds States is debatable: see e.g. Zappalà, *Human Rights*, 227–8.

[106] Art. 75 of the ICC Statute. See also rr. 94–99 of the ICC RPE.

in political as well as in legal terms.[107] Reparations may include restitution, compensation and rehabilitation. It is left to the judges to establish principles and determine the scope and extent of any damage, loss or injury; so far no general principles have been established and it appears that this will occur on a case-by-case basis. The Van Boven/Bassiouni Principles may provide guidance on the principles and the different forms of reparation.[108] Also international mass-claims processes and domestic compensation schemes may provide inspiration.[109] While it could be argued that reparations are a penal sanction – as they presuppose a conviction – they are rather of a civil nature;[110] an order will normally follow upon a request, albeit that the ICC in exceptional circumstances may act upon its own motion. Both individual and collective awards are foreseen and the special Trust Fund for Victims (TFV) is the main conduit for the latter.[111] In addition, the TFV itself may provide support for physical or psychological rehabilitation or material support for the benefit of victims or their families, although this must not be inconsistent with the judicial activities of the Court and is thus subject to the relevant Chamber's approval.[112] The TFV collects court-ordered fines and forfeitures, but also voluntary contributions from States and private donations; the operational costs are paid for by the ICC's budget.[113] Reparations are subject to separate proceedings including appeals.[114] In order to secure future reparations, the Court may request States to freeze assets.[115] The Pre-Trial Chambers have regularly, and on their own motion, made such requests when issuing arrest warrants.[116]

The first decision on reparations was rendered in *Lubanga* where the Trial Chamber established principles and procedures to be followed, but did not rule on individual claims.[117] After written submissions by the parties and the victims (labelled as 'participants'), the TFV, as well as UNICEF and four NGOs as *amici curiae*,[118] the Chamber held that the right to reparations is well established in global and regional human rights treaties and other instruments, including those of international humanitarian law.[119] It expressed different objectives of reparations:

---

[107] See e.g. Muttukumaru, 'Reparations to Victims', 262–70.

[108] Although guidance from 'soft law' was controversial, the Rome Conference Working Group referred explicitly to the Van Boven/Bassiouni Principles in its report; footnote 5 to Art. 73 in UN Doc. A/CONF/F.183/C.l/WGPM/L.2/Add.7 of 13 July 1998. See also Peter Lewis and Håkan Friman, 'Reparations to Victims' in Lee, *Elements and Rules*, 477–8. Successive ICTY Presidents have noted the lack of compensation to victims as a shortcoming and have proposed, *inter alia*, the establishment of a claims commission.

[109] See e.g. Marc Henzelin, Veijo Heiskanen and Guénaël Mettraux, 'Reparations to Victims before the International Criminal Court: Lessons from International Mass Claims Processes' (2006) 17 *Criminal Law Forum* 317; and Frédéric Mégret, 'Justifying Compensation by the International Criminal Court's Victims Trust Fund: Lessons from Domestic Compensation Schemes' (2010) 36 *Brooklyn Journal of International Law* 146.

[110] Cf. Birte Timm, 'The Legal Position of Victims in the Rules of Procedure and Evidence' in Horst Fischer *et al.* (eds.), *International and National Prosecution of Crimes under International Law* (Berlin, 2001) 306–8.

[111] Arts. 75(2) and 79 of the ICC Statute and rr. 98 and 221 of the ICC RPE. A board of directors has been appointed and Regulations of the Trust Fund for Victims (ICC-ASP/4/Res.3 of 3 December 2005) have been adopted.

[112] Reg. 50 of the Trust Fund Regulations. See *Situation in Uganda*, ICC PTC II, 19 March 2008 (approval of proposed trust fund activities in Uganda). See also Anne-Marie de Brouwer and Marc Groenhuijsen, 'The Role of Victims in International Criminal Proceedings' in Sluiter and Vasiliev, *International Criminal Procedure*, 190–5.

[113] See further www.trustfundforvictims.org.

[114] Arts. 76(3) and 82(4) of the ICC Statute and rr. 91(4) and 94–97 of the ICC RPE.   [115] Art. 57(3)(e) of the ICC Statute.

[116] See e.g. *Lubanga*, ICC PTC I, 10 February 2006, paras. 130–41. See further section 20.6.4.

[117] *Lubanga*, ICC T. Ch. I, 7 August 2012.

[118] See *Lubanga*, ICC T. Ch. I, 20 April 2012. The various submissions, summarized in the judgment (*ibid.*), demonstrate the wide variety of viewpoints that exist concerning redress to victims of international crimes.

[119] *Lubanga*, ICC T. Ch. I, 7 August 2012, para. 185.

Reparations fulfil two main purposes that are enshrined in the Statute: they oblige those responsible for serious crimes to repair the harm they caused to the victims and they enable the Chamber to ensure that offenders account for their acts. Furthermore, reparations can be directed at particular individuals, as well as contributing more broadly to the communities that were affected. Reparations in the present case must – to the extent achievable – relieve the suffering caused by these offences; afford justice to the victims by alleviating the consequences of the wrongful acts; deter future violations; and contribute to the effective reintegration of former child soldiers. Reparations can assist in promoting reconciliation between the convicted person, the victims of the crimes and the affected communities (without making Mr Lubanga's participation in this process mandatory).[120]

In the Chamber's view, reparations should be applied in a broad and flexible manner and honouring principles of dignity, non-discrimination, and non-stigmatization of victims.[121] Possible beneficiaries are direct and indirect victims and reparations are not confined to those who participated in the trial proceedings.[122] Individual and collective reparations may be awarded concurrently, but given the uncertainty of the total number of victims and the limited number of individual claimants the Chamber favoured 'a collective approach that ensures that reparations reach those victims who are currently unidentified'.[123] Victims should receive 'appropriate, adequate and prompt reparations' and the modalities of reparations in Article 75 should not be considered exclusive; reparations like 'those with a symbolic, preventative or transformative value' may also be appropriate.[124] With respect to the crimes in question, it must be established that the crimes were the 'proximate cause' of the harm for which reparations are sought, and the Court will apply a 'balance of probabilities' standard, while the TFV, concerning reparations awarded from its own resources, is allowed 'a wholly flexible approach to determining factual matters'.[125]

The Chamber identified the TFV as the principal agency to deal with reparations, subject to monitoring and oversight by a differently composed Chamber, and recommended that a multidisciplinary team of experts is retained to provide assistance to the Court in certain areas.[126] A five-step process, which includes local consultations, was devised.[127] The scheme was clearly influenced by Lubanga's indigence and thus that any reparations would have to be financed by the TFV. Hence, the Chamber transmitted all individual claims to the TFV without any closer examination and declined to issue any specific orders to the TFV on the implementation of reparations to be funded using voluntary contributions.[128]

[120] *Ibid.*, para. 179 (footnotes omitted).   [121] *Ibid.*, paras. 180 and 187–93.
[122] *Ibid.*, para. 194 (further developed in, paras. 195–201).
[123] *Ibid.*, paras. 219–20. Collective reparations should address the harm the victims suffered on an individual and collective basis and the Court should consider medical services, general rehabilitation, housing, education, and training (para. 221).
[124] *Ibid.*, paras. 222 and 242; various forms of reparations are further elaborated in paras. 223–41.   [125] *Ibid.*, paras. 247–54.
[126] *Ibid.*, paras. 260–6.   [127] *Ibid.*, para. 282.
[128] While the Registry had argued that the Court could order the TFV to use its 'other resources' for court-ordered reparations, the TFV strongly disagreed. The Chamber sided with the Registry in principle (*ibid.*, paras. 269–73), underlined its monitoring and oversight functions, but refrained from making orders about the use of TFV's 'other resources' (para. 287).

18.6 An assessment

The focus on victims is far greater in the ICC than in the ICTY and ICTR, and this trend has continued in subsequent internationalized courts. An assessment of the fundamental issue of whether this is valuable, or instead a detraction from the 'core mandate' of prosecuting international crimes, goes back to the question of the objectives of international criminal justice.[129] Apart from the element of restorative justice that victims' rights encompass, some would add that this involvement could boost the legitimacy of the international criminal process and thus of the relevant court. But such effects will occur only if both the scheme and the expectations of it are well managed. A proper balancing *vis-à-vis* the rights of the accused is also necessary. A further complication, which must be taken into account, is that not all victims share the same interests; a general assumption that they all support prosecution, or any particular process or outcome, would be an oversimplification.

Although there are domestic systems that combine far-reaching victims' rights with a basically adversarial criminal process, from which the Court may seek inspiration, the ICC victim participation scheme is novel in international criminal tribunals. Ensuring it is a daunting and resource-intensive task that has resulted in a huge number of decisions. Difficulties have included large numbers of victims, detailed application requirements and assessments, and multiple decisions in the same 'situation' or 'case', some of them early on and rather hypothetical in nature. While the prosecution, defence counsel and Appeals Chamber have been rather restrained, most Pre-Trial and Trial Chambers have taken a more radical approach with the apparent aim of providing for meaningful forms of victim participation. The, still developing, practice exposes serious questions concerning the role of the victims and its relationship to the parties, the rights of the accused, and trial efficiency, and also whether the participatory rights in practice can be more than merely symbolic. It may also be asked to what extent individual victims, and not only more lawyers, ought to and do get involved in the judicial process. It is always difficult to backtrack from a laid course, but in order to find a workable system the Court will need to test different options and allow the scheme to evolve reflexively.

The ICC reparations regime is also an unprecedented and often praised restorative justice element in international criminal law. But the scheme is not yet fully developed and it requires further elaboration. It is not intended to prejudice any other international or domestic reparations options that may exist. Whether an individual right to compensation from the State exists for violations of international human rights law or international humanitarian law is a hotly contested issue, but good arguments can be made in support of such a right.[130] In any case, the resources available for reparations will most likely be small, and one challenge for the Court is to avoid the reparations regime being perceived as nothing more than an illusion. Although the *Lubanga* decision was explicitly confined to the

---

[129] See Chapter 2.
[130] See Roland Bank and Elke Schwager, 'Is there a Substantive Right to Compensation for Individual Victims of Armed Conflicts against a State under International Law?' (2006) 49 *German Yearbook of International Law* 367.

case at hand, the established principles and procedures,[131] if upheld on appeal, will undoubtedly be very important for later ICC cases, and probably beyond that as well.[132]

As for protective measures for victims and witnesses, their extensive use is an unfortunate necessity in all international criminal jurisdictions. But it is important to be vigilant so that they do not become merely routine, and to ensure that the rights of the accused are respected.

For the ICC, the policy choice of a victim-oriented approach was made when its Statute was adopted and it is now up to the Court to implement the measures in the best possible way. Victim participation, reparations and protection are closely linked to each other but also to the broader substantive and procedural schemes. Measures to provide protection, to increase the efficiency of the participation regime, and to safeguard the fair trial rights of the accused where many victims participate, all potentially counteract one of the main objectives behind an increased role for victims in the international process: to allow them to be involved, heard and seen. This objective is also important for other desired effects, such as promotion of rehabilitation, reconciliation, as well as exposure of truth and crimes that have traditionally been ignored or obscured (like sexual crimes and child soldiering). A fine balance of different interests is required and further refinements of the practice and law are to be expected.

Considering the difficulties with regard to victim participation, and other shortcomings of the ICC, it might be easy to dismiss the victims-centric approach as well intended but unrealistic and argue that it should be abandoned. But it is also convincingly argued that the need to provide redress to victims of atrocities – to provide 'restorative justice to those who traditionally have remained voiceless outsiders to the legal process' – is possible and should be pursued, which in turn requires real and meaningful reform as well as better comprehension of the issues and advocacy by practitioners and others.[133] It is clear that the Court is set to take this challenge seriously, and the victims-related issues are highlighted in the 'Lessons Learned' process for procedural reform that the judges are currently undertaking.[134]

Further reading

Useful reviews and analysis of ICC practice concerning victims are provided in a series of reports by the American University, Washington College of Law, War Crimes Research Office, www.wcl.american.edu/warcrimes/icc/icc_reports.cfm.

Tatiana Bachvarova, 'Victims' Eligibility before the International Criminal Court in Historical and Comparative Context' (2011) 11 *International Criminal Law Review* 665

---

[131] *Lubanga*, ICC T. Ch. I, 7 August 2012, para. 181.
[132] See Dinah Shelton, 'Introductory Note to the International Criminal Court: Situation in the Democratic Republic of the Congo, Prosecutor v. Thomas Lubanga Dyilo, Decision Establishing the Principles and Procedures to Be Applied to Reparations' (2012) 51 ILM 971.
[133] Funk, *Victims' Rights and Advocacy* (quotation at 4).   [134] See further Chapter 17.

Elisabeth Baumgartner, 'Aspects of Victim Participation in the Proceedings of the International Criminal Court' (2008) 90 (870) *International Review of the Red Cross* 409

Gilbert Bitti and Håkan Friman, 'Participation of Victims in the Proceedings' in Lee, *Elements and Rules*, 456–74

Thorsten Bonacker and Christoph Safferling (eds.), *Victims of International Crimes: An Interdisciplinary Discourse* (The Hague, 2013)

Helen Brady, 'Protective and Special Measures for Victims and Witnesses' in Lee, *Elements and Rules*, 434–56

Pascale Chifflet, 'The Role and Status of the Victim' in Gideon Boas and William Schabas (eds.), *International Criminal Law Developments in the Case Law of the ICTY* (Leiden, 2003) 75–111

Christine Chung, 'Victims' Participation at the International Criminal Court: Are Concessions of the Court Clouding the Promise?' (2008) 6 *Northwestern Journal of International Human Rights* 459

Anne-Marie De Brouwer, 'Reparations to Victims of Sexual Violence: Possibilities at the International Criminal Court and at the Trust Fund for Victims and their Families' (2007) 20 *Leiden Journal of International Law* 207

Eva Dwertmann, *The Reparation System of the International Criminal Court: Its Implementation, Possibilities and Limitations* (Leiden, 2010)

Christine Evans, *The Right to Reparation in International Law for Victims of Armed Conflict* (Cambridge, 2012)

Carla Ferstman, Mariana Goetz and Alan Stephens (eds.), *Reparations for Victims of Genocide, War Crimes and Crimes against Humanity* (Leiden, 2009)

Håkan Friman, 'Participation of Victims before the ICC: A Critical Assessment of the Early Developments' in Sluiter and Vasiliev, *International Criminal Procedure*, 205–36

Håkan Friman, 'The International Criminal Court and Participation of Victims: A Third Party to the Proceedings?' (2009) 22 *Leiden Journal of International Law* 485

T. Markus Funk, *Victims' Rights and Advocacy at the International Criminal Court* (Oxford, 2010)

Emily Haslam, 'Victim Participation at the International Criminal Court: A Triumph of Hope over Experience?' in Dominic McGoldrick *et al.* (eds.), *The Permanent International Criminal Court* (Oxford, 2004) 315–34

Mikaela Heikkilä, *International Criminal Tribunals and Victims of Crimes* (Åbo, 2004)

Claude Jorda and Jérôme de Hemptinne, 'The Status and Role of Victims' in Cassese, *Commentary*, 1387–419

Peter Lewis and Håkan Friman, 'Reparations to Victims' in Lee, *Elements and Rules*, 474–91

Conor McCarthy, *Reparations and Victim Support in the International Criminal Court* (Cambridge, 2012)

Brianne McGonigle Leyh, *Procedural Justice? Victim Participation in International Criminal Proceedings* (Cambridge, 2011)

Carsten Stahn, Hector Olásolo and Kate Gibson, 'Participation of Victims in the Pre-Trial Proceedings of the ICC' (2006) 4 *Journal of International Criminal Justice* 219

Theo van Boven, 'Victims' Rights and Interests in the International Criminal Court' in Doria, *Legal Regime*, 895–906

Sergey Vasiliev, 'Article 68(3) and Personal Interests of Victims in the Emerging Practice of the ICC' in Stahn and Sluiter, *Emerging Practice*, 635–90

19

Sentencing and Penalties

19.1   International punishment of crimes

International humanitarian law and criminal law treaties provide for individual criminal responsibility for certain violations of their provisions, but they give virtually no guidance as to applicable penalties or other sentencing issues. For example, the Genocide Convention merely provides that penalties shall be 'effective' and the Torture Convention that the penalties shall be 'appropriate' and take into account the 'grave nature' of the offence.[1] Customary law is no better. However, the principle of legality includes a prohibition against the retroactive creation of punishments (*nulla poena sine lege*)[2] and for that reason also an international criminal jurisdiction requires regulation of penalties;[3] an effort that is fraught with difficulties since States take very different views on appropriate criminal penalties. Consequently, international provisions on penalties and sentencing are rather general, leaving tribunals with wide discretion, triggering concerns amongst many on the basis of the legality principle.[4]

The Nuremberg and Tokyo Tribunals had the power to impose 'death or such other punishment as shall be determined by it to be just'.[5] At Nuremberg, twelve of the accused were sentenced to death, three to life imprisonment and four to fixed-term prison sentences. The Tokyo trial produced seven death sentences, eleven of life imprisonment and two of fixed-term imprisonment. The national military tribunals operating in Germany (under Control Council Law No. 10) and in the Far East had the same sentencing powers.[6] To dispel concerns about retroactivity, the penalties were considered rooted in customary

---

[1] Art. 5 of the 1948 Genocide Convention; Art. 4(2) of the 1984 Torture Convention. The requirement of effective punishment is also reflected elsewhere, e.g. the 1949 Geneva Conventions (Art. 49 of Geneva Convention I; Art. 50 of Geneva Convention II; Art. 129 of Geneva Convention III; Art. 146 of Geneva Convention IV).

[2] See Kai Ambos, 'Nulla Poena Sine Lege in International Criminal Law' in Roelof Haveman and Olaoluwa Olusanya (eds.), *Sentencing and Sanctioning in Supranational Criminal Law* (Antwerp, 2006) 17. See section 1.5.2.

[3] It has been questioned whether the penalty regulations of the ICTY, ICTR and ICC meet the legality principle: see Damien Scalia, *Du principe de légalité des peines en droit international pénal* (Brussels, 2011).

[4] On the discussions concerning the ICTY, see William Schabas, 'Sentencing by International Tribunals: A Human Rights Approach' (1997) 7 *Duke Journal of Comparative and International Law* 461.

[5] Art. 27 of the Nuremberg Charter and Art. 16 of the Tokyo Charter. In addition, the Nuremberg Tribunal could deprive the convicted person of stolen property: Art. 28 of the Nuremberg Charter.

[6] On the Far East, see Neil Boister and Robert Cryer, *The Tokyo International Military Tribunal: A Reappraisal* (Oxford, 2008) Chapter 9. On the European trials, see Kevin Jon Heller, *The Nuremberg Military Tribunals and the Origins of International Criminal Law* (Oxford, 2011) Chapter 14.

international law.[7] None of these Tribunals developed sentencing guidelines of use for later tribunals. In fact, sentencing considerations occupied very little room in the judgments and, even then, only briefly on mitigating factors.[8]

When the ICTY and ICTR were established, the development of international human rights standards in general, and the gradual international rejection of capital punishment in particular, had an impact. Capital punishment is highly controversial and State practice ranges from extensive use to complete abolition. This divide is also reflected in international human rights treaties. The ICCPR and ECHR restrict, but do not prohibit, the penalty, while additional protocols to those treaties provide for prohibitions which, by way of reservations, may be set aside in time of war;[9] however, Protocol No. 13 to the ECHR prohibits capital punishment in all circumstances.[10] States may therefore be treaty-bound to abolish the death penalty, and an emerging abolitionist norm in customary international law has been asserted,[11] but a universally accepted prohibition does not exist today.

The only applicable penalty for the core crimes at the post-Nuremberg/Tokyo tribunals is a term of imprisonment, for life or a defined period.[12] In response to concerns regarding the principle of legality, the Statutes of the ICTY and ICTR provide that the respective Tribunal shall have recourse to the general practice regarding prison sentences in the courts of the former Yugoslavia and Rwanda. In practice, however, both Tribunals have established that there is no obligation to conform to national practice, only to take it into account and explain any departure from it.[13] The principle also applies when the relevant domestic law prescribes a less severe penalty than the law of the Tribunal.[14] Nonetheless, the Tribunals have addressed the principle of legality with reference to more severe penalties (capital punishment) in domestic law.[15] In the case of the former Yugoslavia, however, the death

---

[7] For a critical view, see e.g. William Schabas, 'War Crimes, Crimes against Humanity, and the Death Penalty' (1997) 60 *Albany Law Review* 733 at 735.

[8] See Bradley Smith, *Recalling Judgment at Nuremberg* (New York, 1977) Chapters 7–9. As to the Tokyo judgment, Judge Röling developed his views in his Dissenting Opinion: see Bernard Röling and Antonio Cassese, *The Tokyo Trial and Beyond* (Oxford, 1993) 64.

[9] Art. 6 of the ICCPR and Art. 2 of the ECHR; Second Optional Protocol to the ICCPR, 15 December 1989; and Protocol No. 6 to the ECHR, 28 April 1983.

[10] See also *Öcalan* v. *Turkey*, ECtHR, 12 May 2005, paras. 150–75; and *Al-Saldoon and Mufdhi* v. *United Kingdom*, ECtHR, 2 March 2010, paras. 115–43.

[11] See e.g. William Schabas, *The Abolition of the Death Penalty in International Law*, 3rd edn (Cambridge, 2002). The argument has also been made that abolitionist States must not directly or indirectly facilitate the death penalty elsewhere: see e.g. Bharat Malkani, 'The Obligation to Refrain from Assisting the Use of the Death Penalty' (2013) 62 *International and Comparative Law Quarterly* 523.

[12] Art. 24 of the ICTY Statute, Art. 23 of the ICTR Statute, Art. 22 of the MICT Statute, as well as r. 101 of the ICTY RPE and ICTR RPE and r. 125 of the MICT RPE. The Tribunals may also order the return of property and proceeds of crime to their rightful owners, but this penalty has not yet been applied. For contempt of court, fines may also be imposed: r. 77 of the ICTY RPE and ICTR RPE, Art. 22(1) of the MICT Statute, and rr. 90 and 108 of the MICT RPE.

[13] See e.g. *Kunarac et al.*, ICTY T. Ch. II, 22 February 2001, para. 829; *Krstić*, ICTY A. Ch., 19 April 2004, para. 260; and *Semanza*, ICTR A. Ch., 20 May 2005, para. 377. It has also been noted in this context that very important differences often exist between international and national prosecutions, particularly concerning the nature, scope and scale of the offences. See also Yuval Shany, 'Seeking Domestic Help: The Role of Domestic Criminal Law in Legitimizing the Work of International Criminal Tribunals' (2013) 11 *Journal of International Criminal Justice* 5, 20–3.

[14] See e.g. *Dragan Nikolić*, ICTY A. Ch., 4 February 2005, paras. 77–86; and *Semanza*, ICTR A. Ch., 20 May 2005, para. 393.

[15] See e.g. *Tadić*, ICTY T. Ch. II, 14 July 1997, para. 9. For a critical view, see e.g. Dirk Van Zyl Smit, *Taking Life Imprisonment Seriously in National and International Law* (The Hague, 2002) 180–3.

penalty had already been abolished in the early 1990s, and replaced by a maximum of forty years' imprisonment, and in Rwanda it was replaced by life imprisonment in 2007.[16]

The issue of applicable penalties was also controversial in the ICC negotiations.[17] Some States, a number of them strong supporters of the Court generally, insisted on the death penalty as a prerequisite for the Court's credibility and its deterrent function. But many other States could not accept this penalty, arguing, *inter alia*, their other treaty commitments. Life imprisonment represented a compromise solution. But, again, concerns were raised from a human rights perspective, some States also referring to constitutional prohibitions of indefinite imprisonment. The solution was imprisonment for a fixed term not exceeding thirty years or, when justified by the extreme gravity of the crime and the individual circumstances of the convicted person, life imprisonment.[18] An aspect of the compromise was the insertion of a provision to ensure that the penalties which the ICC may impose will not affect any powers by States to impose penalties that are allowed in their national law, penalties either more lenient or more severe than those applicable at the ICC.[19] This is a step away from the idea of a more coherent international criminal justice system with harmonized penalties for international crimes as one element,[20] but it was a necessary compromise.

The ICC may also impose fines and order forfeiture of proceeds, property and assets derived directly or indirectly from the relevant crime. It is noteworthy that forfeiture does not include instrumentalities of crime; for example, forfeiture of military equipment would be very sensitive. While forfeiture is a post-conviction measure, the ICC may also seek to obtain, from a State, provisional measures for the purpose of forfeiture;[21] victims may ultimately benefit if the money or other property is subsequently forfeited and transferred to the Trust Fund for victims.

19.2   Purposes of sentencing

The purposes of sentencing, and indeed the purposes of punishment as such, are a relatively undeveloped aspect of international criminal law. Classical objectives in municipal systems are retribution, deterrence, public protection (incapacitation), rehabilitation and social integration of the offender. As discussed in Chapter 2, however, the objectives of punishment in general, and for the purpose of international criminal justice in particular, are the subject of very different opinions. All of them have their strengths and pitfalls, particularly in the context of international criminal justice. Some consider that retribution (or 'just desert') is the appropriate philosophical and policy ground for inter-national punishment.[22] Others dispute this, however, advocating a more restorative approach

---

[16] See e.g. *Milutinović et al.*, ICTY T. Ch. III, 26 February 2009, paras. 1159–60; and *Kanyarukiga*, ICTR T. Ch., 6 June 2008, paras. 94–6.

[17] See e.g. Rolf Einar Fife, 'Penalties' in Lee, *The Making of the Rome Statute*, 319–43.

[18] Art. 77 of the ICC Statute. Offences against the administration of justice may be punished by a maximum five-year sentence, or a fine, or both; *ibid.*, Art. 70(3).

[19] *Ibid.*, Art. 80.   [20] See e.g. M. Cherif Bassiouni, *Introduction to International Criminal Law* (New York, 2002) 682.

[21] Arts. 57(3)(e) and 93(1)(k) of the ICC Statute, and r. 99 of the ICC RPE.

[22] See e.g. Bassiouni, *Introduction to International Criminal Law*, 681.

in international sentencing and arguing that this will better serve peace and reconciliation efforts.[23] Deterrence presents special difficulties in this context. Broader aims such as rehabilitation and social integration are difficult to pursue; the range of penalties is limited and the enforcement is outsourced to States. In the absence of consensus regarding the objectives of punishment and how to balance different objectives against each other, the ICTY, ICTR and ICC are provided with very little guidance as to the purposes of sentencing.

As primary purposes for sentencing, the ICTY and ICTR have consistently emphasized retribution and general deterrence,[24] although retribution appears to be considered the most important goal of punishment.[25] Retribution should be seen as 'just desert' and not as revenge or vengeance.[26] But other objectives are also emphasized, such as special deterrence (concerning the defendant),[27] rehabilitation,[28] 'protection of society, stigmatisation and public reprobation',[29] and reconciliation.[30] However, as the ICTY has said:

The other three aims that sentencing usually promotes, namely, rehabilitation, social defence and restoration have not yet achieved the same dominance as retribution and deterrence in the sentencing history of this Tribunal, even though, in the opinion of the Trial Chamber, they are important for achieving the goals of this Tribunal. Such factors have tended to be dealt with as mitigating or aggravating factors, with social defence intermingling with the understanding that this Tribunal has of the aim of deterrence.[31]

More recently, the Tribunals have concluded that rehabilitation has not played a predominant role in sentencing in light of the serious nature of the crimes committed under the Tribunal's jurisdiction.[32]

Inconsistency in sentencing exists, revealing an absence of agreed principles, and it could affect the legitimacy of the judicial institution.[33] It has also been noted that the pragmatic rationales behind plea bargaining in the Tribunals are at odds with the general purposes of punishment; sentencing rebates depart from the idea of punishment based on the gravity of

---

[23] See e.g. Ralph Henham, 'Some Issues for Sentencing in the International Criminal Court' (2003) 52 *International and Comparative Law Quarterly* 81.

[24] See e.g. *Delalić et al.*, ICTY A. Ch., 20 February 2001, para. 806; and *Serushago*, ICTR T. Ch. I, 15 February 1999, para. 20. On deterrence, see section 2.2.2.

[25] The ICTY Appeals Chamber has held that deterrence should not be given 'undue prominence' in sentencing: see e.g. *Mrkšić and Šljivančanin*, ICTY A. Ch., 5 May 2009, para. 415. See further Mark Drumbl, 'Collective Violence and Individual Punishment: The Criminality of Mass Atrocity' (2005) 99 *Northwestern University Law Review* 539.

[26] See section 2.2.1 and *Kordić and Čerkez*, ICTY A. Ch., 17 December 2004, para. 1075.

[27] *Ibid.*, paras. 1076–7; cf. *Dragan Nikolić*, ICTY A. Ch., 4 February 2005, paras. 45–7 (may be considered but is merely one factor in sentencing).

[28] But rehabilitation should not be given 'undue weight', see e.g. *Delalić et al.*, ICTY A. Ch., 20 February 2001, para. 806; cf. *Kunarac et al.*, ICTY T. Ch. II, 22 February 2001, para. 844 (questioning rehabilitation as a sentencing purpose). Cf. *Erdemović*, ICTY T. Ch. I, 29 November 1996, para. 111 (considering the 'corrigible personality' as a mitigating factor), and see section 2.2.4.

[29] See section 2.2.5 and *Ntakirutimana*, ICTR T. Ch. I, 21 February 2003, paras. 881–2; cf. *Kunarac et al.*, ICTY T. Ch., 22 February 2001, para. 843 (protection of society not very relevant).

[30] *Kamuhanda*, ICTR T. Ch. II, 22 January 2004, paras. 753–4, and ICTR A. Ch., 19 September 2005, para. 351 (see also the Preamble to the ICTR Statute); *Momir Nikolić*, ICTY T. Ch. I, 2 December 2003, para. 93.

[31] *Brđanin*, ICTY T. Ch. II, 1 September 2004, para. 1092.

[32] E.g. *Krajišnik*, ICTY A. Ch., 17 March 2009, para. 806; and *Popović et al.*, ICTY T. Ch. II, 10 June 2010, para. 2130.

[33] See e.g. Ralph Henham, *Punishment and Process in International Criminal Trials* (Aldershot, 2005) 16–24; and Jens Ohlin, 'Towards a Unique Theory of International Criminal Sentencing' in Sluiter and Vasiliev, *International Criminal Procedure* Chapter 10.

the crime (retribution) and could weaken its deterrent function.[34] Another source of criticism is that the sentences are lenient when compared with domestic practice, but this comparison relates to ordinary crimes such as murder, and domestic sentencing practice differs greatly.[35]

The ICC has, to date, sentenced one person,[36] so issues of consistency have not yet arisen. The Trial Chamber, in its sentencing decision, referred to the applicable law, including parts of the Preamble to the ICC Statute, but avoided general statements concerning the purposes of sentencing.

19.3   Sentencing practice

The ICTY and ICTR have emphasized that sentencing is an essentially discretionary procedure; no sentencing scales for the different crimes have been provided either in their Statutes or case law. Consequently, the ICTY Appeals Chamber has repeatedly refused to set down a definite list of sentencing guidelines.[37] While emphasizing the principle of equal treatment, that is to say, consistency, the Appeals Chamber has also concluded that a comparison with the sentences imposed in other cases before the Tribunal is often of limited assistance; the previous decision must relate to the same offence and the circumstances be substantially similar.[38] The Tribunals have paid limited attention to each other's sentencing practice. While noting that decisions of other international courts and tribunals are not part of the directly applicable law, the ICC Trial Chamber in *Lubanga* nevertheless took into account the practice of the SCSL regarding the same type of offences.[39]

The ICTY and ICTR have underlined that the primary goal in sentencing is to ensure that the final or aggregate sentence reflects the totality of the criminal conduct and overall culpability of the offender.[40] The most important factor in sentencing at the Tribunals is the gravity of the offence, including considerations regarding the form and degree of the participation of the accused in the crimes and the circumstances of the case.[41] In the absence of a formal hierarchy of crimes, advocated by some as being necessary for sentencing,[42] the Tribunals have taken a case-by-case approach. Due to the special *mens rea* requirement, however, genocide has generally been regarded as more serious than

---

[34] See e.g. Ralph Henham and Mark Drumbl, 'Plea Bargaining at the International Criminal Tribunal for the Former Yugoslavia' (2005) 16 *Criminal Law Forum* 56–9.

[35] See e.g. Mark Harmon and Fergal Gaynor, 'Ordinary Sentences for Extraordinary Crimes' (2007) 5 *Journal of International Criminal Justice* 683; cf. Marisa Bassett, 'Defending Sentencing: Past Criticism to the Promise of the ICC' (2009) 16 *Human Rights Brief* 22. On difficulties with domestic analogies, see also section 2.1 and 2.2.1.

[36] *Lubanga*, ICC T. Ch. I, 10 July 2012.

[37] See e.g. *Furundžija*, ICTY A. Ch., 21 July 2000, para. 238; *Delalić et al.*, ICTY A. Ch., 20 February 2001, para. 715; and *Krstić*, ICTY A. Ch., 19 April 2004, para. 242.

[38] See e.g. *Delalić et al.*, ICTY A. Ch., 20 February 2001, paras. 719–20; *Kamuhanda*, ICTR A. Ch., 19 September 2005, paras. 361–2; *Momir Nikolić*, ICTY A. Ch., 8 March 2006, paras. 38–54; *Strugar*, ICTY A. Ch., 17 July 2008, paras. 336 and 348; *Ntabakuze*, ICTR A. Ch., 8 May 2012, paras. 297–300; and *Stanišić and Župljanin*, ICTY T. Ch. II, 27 March 2013, para. 888.

[39] *Lubanga*, ICC T. Ch. I, 10 July 2012, paras. 12–15.

[40] E.g. *Martić*, ICTY A. Ch., 8 October 2008, para. 350; and *Ntabakuze*, ICTR A. Ch., 8 May 2012, para. 267.

[41] Art. 24(2) of the ICTY Statute, Art. 23(2) of the ICTR Statute and Art. 22(3) of the MICT Statute; and see e.g. *Delalić et al.*, ICTY A. Ch., 20 February 2001, paras. 731 and 741; and *Blaškić*, ICTY A. Ch., 29 July 2004, para. 683.

[42] See e.g. Allison Marston Danner, 'Constructing a Hierarchy of Crimes in International Criminal Law Sentencing' (2001) 87 *Virginia Law Review* 415.

crimes against humanity and war crimes.[43] Similarly, persecution has been considered 'inherently very serious', justifying a more severe penalty.[44] Although not uncontroversial, crimes against humanity and war crimes are seen by the Tribunals as equally serious in principle.[45] This has led to much debate, with some arguing that there is a hierarchy based upon the inherent gravity of the different crimes, while others consider that other circumstances, such as the quantum of suffering inflicted, are more important than the characterization of the offence.[46] However, the Tribunals' broad acceptance of cumulative convictions reduces the legal importance of a hierarchy of crimes.[47]

The form of responsibility is also important and, for example, both Tribunals have established that aiding and abetting generally warrants lower sentences than co-perpetration;[48] although this is a conclusion that the SCSL Appeals Chamber, paying close attention to ICTY and ICTR practice, has rejected as unsupported, *inter alia*, in customary international law.[49] Further, the ICTY and ICTR have rejected the argument that superior responsibility as such should be seen as less grave than other forms of individual criminal responsibility.[50] There have been suggestions in the jurisprudence of the ICC that Article 25(3) of the ICC Statute established a hierarchy of modes of liability (descending from Article 25(3)(a)–(d)), but such suggestions have been controversial, even within the Court, and are not backed up by the negotiating history of the Statute.[51] But abstract rankings and comparisons are not decisive; the punishment always depends on the facts of the case. In addition, the Tribunals are required to take into account the individual circumstances of the accused and give credit for time already spent in detention.[52]

Similar provisions and principles are applicable to the ICC, although the RPE give some further direction.[53] The *Lubanga* Trial Chamber thoroughly analysed the gravity of the crimes, the large-scale and widespread nature of the crimes, the degree of participation

---

[43] See e.g. *Kambanda*, ICTR T. Ch. I, 4 September 1998, paras. 16 and 42; *Krstić*, ICTY T. Ch. I, 2 August 2001, para. 700, and ICTY A. Ch., 19 April 2004, paras. 36–7 and 275. Cf. *Serushago*, ICTR T. Ch. I, 5 February 1999, paras. 13–14 (considering genocide and crimes against humanity to be of an equally grave nature).

[44] See e.g. *Blaškić*, ICTY T. Ch. I, 3 March 2000, para. 785; *Todorović*, ICTY T. Ch. I, 31 July 2001, para. 31.

[45] See e.g. *Tadić*, ICTY A. Ch., 26 January 2000, para. 69; and *Kayishema and Ruzindana*, ICTR A. Ch., 1 June 2001, para. 367. Earlier decisions, however, considered crimes against humanity as more serious and carrying a higher penalty than war crimes: see e.g. *Tadić*, ICTY T. Ch. II, 14 July 1997, para. 73; *Erdemović*, ICTY A. Ch., 7 October 1997 (majority), paras. 20–6; and *Kambanda*, ICTR T. Ch. I, 4 September 1998, para. 4.

[46] For proponents of a hierarchy, see e.g. Jan Christoph Nemitz, 'The Law of Sentencing in International Criminal Law: The Purposes of Sentencing and the Applicable Method for the Determination of the Sentence' (2001) 4 *Yearbook of International Humanitarian Law* 87; and Olaoluwa Olusanya, 'Do Crimes against Humanity Deserve a Higher Sentence than War Crimes?' (2004) 4 *International Criminal Law Review* 431. Against, see e.g. Mark Harmon and Fergal Gaynor, 'Ordinary Sentences for Extraordinary Crimes' (2007) 5 *Journal of International Criminal Justice* 683.

[47] See section 17.8.5.

[48] See e.g. *Vasiljević*, ICTY A. Ch., 25 February 2004, para. 182; and *Kajelijeli*, ICTR T. Ch. II, 1 December 2003, para. 963.

[49] *Taylor*, SCSL A. Ch., 26 September 2013, paras. 666–70; cf. *Sesay et al.*, SCSL T. Ch. I, 8 April 2009, para. 20, *Taylor*, SCSL T. Ch. II, 26 April 2012, para. 94, and 30 May 2013, para. 21 (all following the ICTY and ICTR practice).

[50] *Ntabakuze*, ICTR A. Ch., 8 May 2012, para. 303. But special circumstances may motivate a lesser sentence for superior responsibility: see *Milošević (Dragomir)*, ICTY A. Ch., 12 November 2009, para. 334.

[51] For a hierarchy, see *Lubanga*, ICC PTC I, 29 January 2007, paras. 330–5 and ICC T. Ch. I, 14 March 2007, paras. 996–9, as well as *Katanga and Ngudjolo Chui*, ICC PTC I, 26 September 2008, paras. 506–8. Against, see Judge Fulford's Dissenting Opinion in *Lubanga*, ICC T. Ch. I, 14 March 2012, paras. 8–9, and Judge Van den Wyngaert's Concurring Opinion in *Ngudjolo Chui*, ICC T. Ch. II, 18 December 2012, paras. 22–30. See further Chapter 15.

[52] Art. 24(2) of the ICTY Statute, Art. 23(2) of the ICTR Statute and r. 101 of the respective RPE. See also Art. 22(3) of the MICT Statute and r. 125 of the MICT RPE.

[53] Art. 78 of the ICC Statute and r. 145 of the ICC RPE. As a consequence of Art. 81(2)(a) on appeals, the sentence must be in proportion to the crime: *Lubanga*, ICC T. Ch. I, 10 July 2012, para. 26.

and intent of the accused, and his individual circumstances.[54] The Chamber rejected the Prosecutor's suggestion to apply a 'consistent baseline' for sentences, arguing that such an approach would undermine the principle that the sentence should be proportional to the crime.[55] Three concurrent sentences of thirteen years (conscription of child soldiers), twelve years (enlistment of child soldiers) and fourteen years (using children to participate actively in hostilities) of imprisonment, and thus a joint sentence of fourteen years, were imposed.[56]

The sentencing practice of the ICTY and ICTR has been criticized for being inconsistent, both within the same Tribunal and between them.[57] In spite of the general seriousness of the crimes, the final sentences imposed by the ICTY and ICTR have had a very broad span, being from three years to life. Life sentences have been meted out in a number of ICTR cases regarding genocide and, more rarely, by the ICTY for genocide and/or crimes against humanity.[58] Although reasons can be identified for the apparent tendency of the ICTR to impose much longer sentences than the ICTY, it has been argued that the ICTY's sentences are surprisingly low and that this is owing to proportionality being assessed with respect to the offenders rather than the gravity of the offences.[59] But the ICTR's sentences have also been criticized as being too lenient.[60] Nonetheless, recent studies conclude that the sentencing of the Tribunals is fairly structured and logical, and exposes certain patterns: high-ranked perpetrators in influential positions receive longer sentences; more extensive criminal activities are punished more severely than isolated single acts; crimes against humanity generate longer sentences than war crimes;[61] and instigators are punished more severely than all other participants in the atrocities.[62]

19.3.1 *Aggravating and mitigating circumstances*

While the ICTY and ICTR Trial Chambers are required to consider any aggravating and mitigating circumstances in passing sentence, neither their Statutes nor the RPE

---

[54] *Lubanga*, ICC T. Ch. I, 10 July 2012, paras. 36–56.   [55] *Ibid.*, paras. 92–3.

[56] *Ibid.* In dissent, Judge Odio Benito argued for three concurrent sentences of fifteen years each (Dissent, paras. 24–7). For a critical view, see Mark Drumbl, 'The Effects of the Lubanga Case on Understanding and Preventing Child Soldiering' (2012) 15 *Yearbook of International Humanitarian Law* 87.

[57] E.g. see John R. W. D. Jones and Steven Powles, *International Criminal Practice*, 3rd edn (Oxford, 2003) 778–80. For the contrary view, see Frederik Harhoff, 'Sense and Sensibility in Sentencing: Taking Stock of International Criminal Punishment' in Ola Engdahl and Pål Wrange (eds.), *Law at War: The Law as It Was and the Law as It Should Be* (Leiden, 2008) 121, 134–7.

[58] See e.g. *Akayesu*, ICTR A. Ch., 1 June 2001; *Stakić*, ICTY T. Ch. II, 31 July 2003 (life imprisonment replaced on appeal by a fixed-term sentence of forty years: ICTY A. Ch., 22 March 2006); *Galić*, ICTY A. Ch., 30 November 2006, paras. 455–6 (a twenty-year sentence increased after appeal to life imprisonment); *Lukić and Lukić*, ICTY T. Ch., 20 July 2009 and ICTY A. Ch., 4 December 2012; and *Tolimir*, ICTY T. Ch., 12 December 2012.

[59] See Jens Ohlin, 'Proportional Sentences at the ICTY' in Bert Swart, Alexander Zahar and Göran Sluiter (eds.), *The Legacy of the International Criminal Tribunal for the Former Yugoslavia* (Oxford, 2011) 322–41.

[60] E.g. Sam Szoke-Burke, 'Avoiding Belittlement of Human Suffering: A Retributivist Critique of ICTR Sentencing Practices' (2012) 10 *Journal of International Criminal Justice* 561.

[61] Interestingly, this finding runs counter to the rhetorical position on the abstract relationship between the two crimes.

[62] B. Hola, A. L. Smeulers and C. C. J. H. Bijleveld, 'Is ICTY Sentencing Predictable? An Empirical Analysis of ICTY Sentencing Practice' (2009) 22 *Leiden Journal of International Law* 79; and, by the same authors, 'Consistency of International Sentencing: ICTY and ICTR Case Study' (2012) 9 *European Journal of Criminology* 539. See also Uwe Ewald, '"Predictably Irrational" – International Sentencing and its Discourse against the Backdrop of Preliminary Empirical Findings on ICTY Sentencing Practices' (2010) 10 *International Criminal Law Review* 365; and James Meernik, 'Sentencing Rationales and Judicial Decision Making at the International Criminal Tribunals' (2011) 92 *Social Science Quarterly* 588.

exhaustively define those factors.[63] Instead, both the factors and their relative weight are left for judicial discretion.[64] The RPE of the ICC, although inspired by the Tribunals' case law, are more detailed.[65] In the Tribunals and the ICC, the Prosecutor must establish any aggravating circumstances 'beyond a reasonable doubt'.[66] The defendant is required to prove mitigating circumstances on a lower – 'balance of probabilities' – standard.[67]

The aggravating factors developed by the ICTY and ICTR in their jurisprudence include[68] the scale of the crimes, the length of time during which it continued, the age, number and suffering of the victims, the nature of the perpetrator's involvement, premeditation and discriminatory intent, abuse of power and position as a superior. The main rule is that only circumstances directly related to the offence may be considered as aggravating.[69] But a factor may not be aggravating if it forms an element of the actual crime or has been taken into account as an aspect of the gravity of the crime (i.e. there is no 'double-counting').[70] Similarly, the ICC RPE mention abuse of power or official capacity, particularly defenceless victims, multiple victims, particular cruelty, and discrimination. Relevant prior convictions must also be taken into account;[71] and 'double-counting' is not applied.[72] In *Lubanga*, the majority of the Trial Chamber found no aggravating circumstances, but one judge held that the harm caused to the child victims and their families should be considered in aggravation.

The only mitigating circumstance expressed in the ICTY, ICTR and the Residual Mechanism (the Mechanism for International Criminal Tribunals, or MICT) RPE is substantial cooperation with the Prosecutor before or after conviction.[73] A related issue is whether and to what extent a guilty plea should be a mitigating factor.[74] Usually, such pleas have been linked to an agreement between the accused and the prosecution, which may include non-binding recommendations to the court as to the sentence. In order to encourage guilty pleas – for reasons of judicial economy, concerns for victims, or otherwise – it is important that the accused can expect a sentencing discount. While guilty pleas have generally been considered in mitigation, the Chambers have avoided declaring a guaranteed discount and have instead adopted an individualized approach to the mitigating effect

---

[63] Rule 101 of the ICTY RPE and ICTR RPE, and r. 125 of the MICT RPE. See e.g. *Musema*, ICTR A. Ch., 16 November 2001, para. 395.

[64] E.g. the ICTR has concluded that the existence of a mitigating circumstance does not automatically imply a reduction of sentence or preclude a life sentence; see e.g. *Ntabakuze*, ICTR A. Ch., 8 May 2012, para. 280.

[65] R. 145(2) of the ICC RPE.

[66] See e.g. *Delalić et al.*, ICTY A. Ch., 20 February 2001, para. 763; *Kajelijeli*, ICTR A. Ch., 23 May 2005, para. 294; and *Lubanga*, ICC T. Ch. I, 10 July 2012, paras. 32–3.

[67] The circumstance must be 'more probable than not': see e.g. *Delalić et al.*, ICTY A. Ch., 20 February 2001, para. 590; and *Kajelijeli*, ICTR A. Ch., 23 May 2005, para. 294. See also *Lubanga*, ICC T. Ch. I, 10 July 2012, para. 34.

[68] See e.g. *Blaškić*, ICTY A. Ch., 29 July 2004, para. 686.

[69] See e.g. *Stakić*, ICTY T. Ch. II, 31 July 2003, para. 911; and *Simba*, ICTR A. Ch., 27 November 2007, para. 82; cf. *Delalić et al.*, ICTY A. Ch., 20 February 2001, paras. 780–9 (also conduct at trial, indicating a lack of remorse, was considered as an aggravating factor).

[70] *Blaškić*, ICTY A. Ch., 29 July 2004, para. 693; *Deronjic*, ICTY A. Ch., 20 July 2005, paras. 106–7; *Momir Nikolić*, ICTY A. Ch., 8 March 2006, paras. 57–67; *Simba*, ICTR A. Ch., 27 November 2007, para. 320.

[71] R. 145(2) of the ICC RPE.   [72] *Lubanga*, ICC T. Ch. I, 10 July 2012, para. 35.

[73] Rule 101(B)(ii) of the ICTY and ICTR RPE and r. 125(B)(ii) of the MICT RPE; see e.g. *Jokić*, ICTY T. Ch. I, 18 March 2004, paras. 93–6, and ICTY A. Ch., 30 August 2005, paras. 87–9; and *Zelenović*, ICTY A. Ch., 31 October 2007, para. 24 (the cooperation need not be substantial for mitigation).

[74] See further section 17.11.

of the plea.[75] Hence, there are examples where the Tribunal has found that the aggravating circumstances outweighed the mitigating effect of a guilty plea,[76] and also departed from the sentencing recommendations.[77] Cooperation with the Court may also be a mitigating factor at the ICC.[78]

Other mitigating factors include[79] an expression of remorse,[80] voluntary surrender, assistance to detainees or victims, and personal circumstances such as good character,[81] age, comportment in detention, and family circumstances, but only exceptionally poor health. Hence, many mitigating circumstances relate to conduct subsequent to the crime, and this is also acknowledged when a Tribunal has attached significant weight to the contributions of the accused to peace.[82] But factors directly related to the crime in question are also of importance, such as indirect or limited participation[83] and circumstances falling short of constituting grounds for excluding criminal liability (duress and diminished mental responsibility); again, 'double-counting' is not allowed (see above in this section).[84] Similar factors apply for the ICC.[85] Importantly, the ICTR has also established that the sentence may be reduced as a remedy for violations of the convicted person's fundamental rights during the proceedings.[86]

The relative significance of the role of the accused may have an impact on the penalty. But the Tribunals have stated that a high position should not automatically aggravate, nor should a low rank or subordinate function mitigate, the sentence.[87] In fact, a superior position as such is not an aggravating factor, since this may constitute an element of the crime, but the abuse of such a position may well be.[88] But the fact that the accused otherwise had a high level of authority, or the status of being known and respected, such as a priest, may be considered aggravating.[89]

---

[75] See Henham and Drumbl, 'Plea Bargaining'; and Pascale Chifflet and Gideon Boas, 'Sentencing Coherence in International Criminal Law: The Cases of Biljana Plavšić and Miroslav Bralo' (2012) 23 *Criminal Law Forum* 135.

[76] See e.g. *Kambanda*, ICTR T. Ch. I, 4 September 1998, paras. 60–2, and ICTR A. Ch., 19 October 2000, paras. 125–6.

[77] See e.g. *Dragan Nikolić*, ICTY T. Ch. II, 18 December 2003, and ICTY A. Ch., 4 February 2005 (a sentence of twenty-three years imposed when the recommendation was fifteen years; reduced to twenty years on appeal). For more on these issues, see the symposia in (2004) 2 *Journal of International Criminal Justice* 1018–81 and (2005) 3 *Journal of International Criminal Justice* 649–94.

[78] Rule 145(2)(a)(ii) of the ICC RPE; and *Lubanga*, ICC T. Ch. I, 10 July 2012, paras. 90–1.

[79] See e.g. *Blaškić*, ICTY A. Ch., 29 July 2004, para. 696.

[80] To be understood in the context of reconciliation, see e.g. Alan Tieger, 'Remorse and Mitigation in the International Criminal Tribunal for the Former Yugoslavia' (2003) 16 *Leiden Journal of International Law* 777; and Henham and Drumble, 'Plea Bargaining'.

[81] Generally of limited importance; see e.g. *Semanza*, ICTR A. Ch., 20 May 2005, para. 398. Cf. *Tadić*, ICTY T. Ch. II, 14 July 1997, para. 59 (good character was considered to aggravate more than mitigate: 'for such a man to have committed these crimes requires an even greater evil will on his part than for a lesser man').

[82] See e.g. *Krajišnik and Plavšić*, ICTY T. Ch. III, 27 February 2003, paras. 85–94; and *Babić*, ICTY A. Ch., 18 July 2005, paras. 55–9.

[83] See e.g. *Babić*, ICTY A. Ch., 18 July 2005, paras. 39–40.

[84] See e.g. *Limaj et al.*, ICTY A. Ch., 27 September 2007, para. 143.

[85] Rule 145(2) of the ICC RPE. See also *Lubanga*, ICC T. Ch. I, 10 July 2012, paras. 83–7 (necessity, peaceful motives and demobilization orders were ruled out as mitigating factors in the case at hand).

[86] E.g. *Semanza*, ICTR A. Ch., 31 May 2000 and 20 May 2005, para. 389; and *Kajelijeli*, ICTR A. Ch., 23 May 2005, paras. 320–4.

[87] See e.g. *Delalić et al.*, ICTY A. Ch., 20 February 2001, para. 847; and *Krstić*, ICTY T. Ch. I, 2 August 2001, para. 709. See further Guénaël Mettraux, *International Crimes and the Ad Hoc Tribunals* (Oxford, 2005) 353–5.

[88] See e.g. *Kayishema and Ruzindana*, ICTR A. Ch., 1 June 2001, paras. 358–9; *Stakić*, ICTY A. Ch., 22 March 2006, para. 411.

[89] See e.g. *Rugambarara*, ICTR T. Ch. II, 16 November 2007, para. 26; and *Seromba*, ICTR A. Ch., 12 March 2008, para. 230.

It is not clear whether, and if so to what extent, the accused's motive may influence the sentence. Interestingly, an SCSL Trial Chamber considered a political motive, namely, to support the democratically elected regime, as an important mitigating factor, and the accused therefore received relatively short prison terms. The Appeals Chamber disagreed, holding that allowing a 'just cause' to mitigate the sentence would contravene the sentencing purpose of affirmative prevention, and thus it avoided the conflation of *ius in bello* with *ius ad bellum* that was the implication of the Trial Chamber's determination.[90]

19.3.2 Cumulative or joint sentences

As explained in section 17.8.5, the ICTY and ICTR allow cumulative charges and convictions based on the same underlying conduct; this practice ought not to prejudice the accused, and therefore raises the question of sentencing. The jurisprudence of both Tribunals establishes that a Chamber has discretion to impose sentences which are either global, concurrent, or consecutive; this has subsequently also been clarified in the RPEs.[91] Consequently, the practice is not consistent. Regardless of method, however, the final or aggregated sentence should reflect the totality of the culpable conduct in a just and appropriate way. The difficulty is in determining what is just and appropriate.

The ICC Statute provides that a separate sentence is to be pronounced for each crime, together with a joint sentence specifying the total period of imprisonment.[92] The joint sentence must not be less than the highest individual sentence or exceed the maximum sentence according to the Statute.

19.4   Sentencing procedures

Initially, the ICTY Trial Chambers addressed sentencing separately and subsequent to conviction.[93] However, in December 2000 the ICTY RPE were amended to allow for guilt and sentencing to be determined in a single judgment,[94] which is now the practice in both Tribunals. The ICC Statute also provides for unified trials, but a bifurcated trial will be conducted if either party so requests;[95] reparations claims should normally be heard at a sentencing or separate hearing. A unified trial means that the defendant cannot apply a different strategy for the purpose of sentencing. In *Lubanga*, the ICC Trial Chamber early on indicated a bifurcated trial but allowed evidence relating to sentence during the trial for

---

[90] *Fofana and Kondewa*, SCSL T. Ch. I, 9 October 2007, paras. 80 and 86, and SCSL A. Ch., 28 May 2008, paras. 533–4 (concurring with *Kordić and Čerkez*, ICTY A. Ch., 17 December 2004, para. 1082). Moreover, the Sierra Leonean judges of both Chambers dissented and voted to acquit on the same ground. See the discussion in section 12.1.3.

[91] Rule 87(C) of the ICTY RPE and ICTR RPE and r. 104(C) of the MICT RPE; see *Delalić et al.*, ICTY A. Ch., 20 February 2001, para. 429; and *Kambanda*, ICTR A. Ch., 19 October 2000, paras. 102–12 (interpreting r. 101 of the respective RPE).

[92] Art. 78(3) of the ICC Statute.

[93] See e.g. *Erdemović*, ICTY T. Ch. I, 29 November 1996; and *Tadić*, ICTY T. Ch. II, 14 July 1997.

[94] Rule 87 of the ICTY RPE. See also r. 85 of the ICTR RPE and r. 104 of the MICT RPE. The Tokyo IMT was criticized for its unified trial: see Boister and Cryer, *Tokyo Tribunal*, 250.

[95] Art. 76 of the ICC Statute and r. 143 of the ICC RPE. In addition, the Trial Chamber on its own motion may decide to hold a separate sentencing hearing.

reasons of efficiency and economy.[96] Separate sentencing hearings are contemplated also in the other cases that have reached the trial stage. In case of an accepted guilty plea at the Tribunals or admission of guilt at the ICC, the case moves to a sentencing hearing.[97]

A sentence may be appealed separately both at the Tribunals and at the ICC,[98] and an appeal against a conviction or acquittal may also lead to a revision of sentence. Due to the corrective nature of the ICTY and ICTR appeals proceedings, the normal test will be whether the Trial Chamber has committed a 'discernible error' in the exercise of its sentencing discretion, something that the appellant must demonstrate.[99] If a conviction or acquittal is revised on appeal, however, the Appeals Chamber will either refer the matter back to the Trial Chamber for sentencing[100] or itself impose a new sentence.[101] At the ICTY and ICTR, time-limited sentences have occasionally been replaced by life imprisonment.[102] A different test applies for the ICC – whether 'the sentence is disproportionate to the crime' – and the determination of a new sentence on appeal is a matter for the Appeals Chamber unless a retrial is ordered.[103] As yet there is no ICC practice on point.

19.5   Pardon, early release and review of sentence

The prisoner may be eligible for pardon, commutation of the sentence or early release in the State where it is served (see section 19.6) but the Tribunal retains control over the sentence and therefore retains the final say on the matter.[104] Although not provided in the Statutes or the RPEs, the Tribunals apply the same rules to prisoners who have not been transferred to a State but still remain in the Tribunal's detention centre in The Hague or Arusha.[105] The Tribunal will consider, *inter alia*, the gravity of the crimes, the prisoner's demonstration of rehabilitation, any substantial cooperation with the Prosecutor, and personal circumstances. The functions of the ICTY and ICTR with respect to, *inter alia*, pardon and commutation of sentences are now performed by the Residual Mechanism.[106] Consistency with the earlier practice of the ICTY and ICTR is desired, which is important for achieving equal treatment

---

[96] *Lubanga*, ICC T. Ch. I, 29 January 2008, para. 32, and 18 March 2010, para. 38. See also *Bemba Gombo*, ICC T. Ch. III, 19 November 2010 (1023), para. 13.

[97] Rules 62*bis* and 100 of the ICTY RPE, rr. 62(B) and 100 of the ICTR RPE, rr. 65 and 124 of the MICT RPE and (indirectly) Art. 76(2) of the ICC Statute.

[98] See section 17.13.

[99] See e.g. *Delalić et al.*, ICTY A. Ch., 20 February 2001, para. 725; and *Semanza*, ICTR A. Ch., 20 May 2005, para. 374.

[100] See e.g. *Tadić*, ICTY A. Ch., 15 July 1999, para. 27.

[101] See e.g. *Blaškić*, ICTY A. Ch., 29 July 2004, para. 726; and *Ntabakuze*, ICTR A. Ch., 8 May 2012, paras. 313–16.

[102] *Gacumbitsi*, ICTR A. Ch., 7 July 2006, para. 206; and *Galić*, ICTY A. Ch., 30 November 2006, paras. 454–5; in both cases, judges presented dissenting opinions and separate opinions on this matter.

[103] Art. 83 of the ICC Statute.

[104] Art. 28 of the ICTY Statute, Art. 27 of the ICTR Statute, rr. 123–125 of the ICTY RPE, and rr. 124–126 of the ICTR RPE. See also ICTY, Practice Direction on the Procedure for the Determination of Applications for Pardon, Commutation of Sentence and Early Release of Persons Convicted by the International Tribunal (IT/146, 7 April 1999). See e.g. *Furundžija*, ICTY President, 29 July 2004.

[105] In accordance with Practice Directions, the respective President takes a decision, which is not subject to appeal; see e.g. *Simić et al.*, ICTY President, 21 January 2004; and *Rutaganira*, ICTR A. Ch., 24 August 2006 (where an appeal against the President's decision was dismissed).

[106] Art. 26 of the MICT Statute and rr. 149–151 of the MICT RPE.

of similarly situated prisoners, but the Residual Mechanism also adheres to the ICTY practice of early release upon the completion of two-thirds of the sentence.[107]

As part of the compromise reached at the Rome Conference regarding applicable penalties, the ICC Statute makes provision for an automatic review of sentences.[108] The review must take place when two-thirds of the sentence has been served, or twenty-five years of life imprisonment, and a decision not to reduce the sentence must be reviewed at regular intervals. The grounds for reduction of sentence relate to post-conviction co-operation or change of circumstances and the mechanism serves essentially the same purpose as an early release or a pardon.

19.6   Enforcement

A sentence imposed by a Tribunal or the ICC will be served in a State which has declared its willingness to enforce the sentence.[109] This is a voluntary undertaking by States and may have conditions attached, for example regarding the nationality of the prisoner, acceptance of only a limited number of prisoners, or retention of a right to accept or reject in each individual case. Separate enforcement agreements with States have been concluded.[110] The Tribunal President or the (collective) ICC Presidency designates the State of enforcement in the individual case.[111] While the ICC will seek and take into account the views of the convicted person, no such role is afforded him or her at the Tribunals.[112] The enforcement of ICTY and ICTR sentences has been taken over by the Residual Mechanism, which has also stepped into the enforcement agreements with States concluded by the Tribunals.[113]

The enforcing State may not modify the length of the sentence. Consequently, the State may not release the convicted person due to pardon, commutation of sentence and early release, without the approval of the Tribunal or Court.[114] Disapproval of an impending domestic measure may cause a transfer of the enforcement to another State.[115] The conditions of imprisonment will be in accordance with domestic law, but subject to the

---

[107] E.g. *Bisengimana*, MICT President, 11 December 2012, paras. 17 and 20; and *Serushago*, MICT President, 13 December 2012, paras. 16–18. Cf. *Bagaragaza*, ICTR President, 24 October 2011 (early release after three-quarters of the sentence had been served).

[108] Art. 110 of the ICC Statute and rr. 223–224 of the ICC RPE.

[109] Art. 27 of the ICTY Statute, Art. 26 of the ICTR Statute and Art. 103 of the ICC Statute. While the ICTY convicts serve their sentences in a number of European States, the ICTR prisoners have been transferred to Mali and Benin. The SCSL has transferred all convicted persons, except Charles Taylor, to Rwanda under an agreement of 18 March 2009. The enforcement of sentences and their oversight was also a big issue concerning the Nuremberg and Tokyo Tribunals; see e.g. Boister and Cryer, *Tokyo Tribunal*, 261–9. See generally Róisín Mulgrew, *Towards the Development of the International Penal System* (Cambridge, 2013) 33–102.

[110] Up to August 2013, the ICC had concluded agreements with eight States: Austria, Belgium, Colombia, Denmark, Finland, Mali, Serbia, and the United Kingdom. See further Hirad Abtahi and Steven Arrigg Koh, 'The Emerging Enforcement Practice of the International Criminal Court' (2012) 45 *Cornell International Law Journal* 1.

[111] Rule 103 of the ICTY RPE and ICTR RPE, rr. 198–206 of the ICC RPE and regs. 113–115 of the ICC Regulations.

[112] Rule 203 of the ICC RPE; cf. *Kvočka et al.* ICTY President, 31 May 2006.

[113] SC Res. 1966(2010) of 22 December 2010, Art. 25 of the MICT Statute and rr. 127–128 of the MICT RPE.

[114] Art. 28 of the ICTY Statute, Art. 27 of the ICTR Statute, Art. 26 of the MICT Statute and Arts. 105(1) and 110(1) of the ICC Statute. Hence, Art. 103(2) of the ICC Statute, and the Tribunal enforcement agreements, provide for notifications and consultations on matters which could affect the terms or extent of the imprisonment. See also r. 149 of the MICT RPE.

[115] See Art. 104 of the ICC Statute and rr. 209–210 of the ICC RPE. Transfer for this reason may also be ordered by the ICTY and ICTR but is not explicitly provided for in the Statutes or RPEs.

supervision of the respective Tribunal or Court.[116] The ICC Statute additionally requires compliance with 'widely accepted international treaty standards governing treatment of prisoners' and no better or worse treatment than other prisoners convicted of similar offences.[117] Hence, there is a division of responsibility between the Tribunal or Court and the enforcing State, whereby the supervisory role of the former concerns the welfare of the prisoner and the length of the sentence to be served – a division that appears straightforward but which may be complex and create tensions in practice.[118]

The ICC Statute also provides for the obligatory enforcement of fines, forfeiture orders and reparation orders by national authorities at the request of the Court.[119] Here, too, the State of enforcement must not modify the fines or orders. Enforcement by national authorities is also foreseen concerning restitution of property or the proceeds thereof to victims at the ICTY and ICTR.[120]

The ICC Statute distinguishes between international cooperation (Part 9) and enforcement (Part 10) in spite of the close relationship between the two. While enforcement of prison sentences differs in that it is voluntary, enforcement of the other specified orders is not and it has been argued that certain cooperation provisions of Part 9 should apply by analogy to obligations regarding the latter too.[121] But, as far as the enforcement of sentences is concerned, there is little appetite among States to move away from the voluntary scheme and ad hoc determinations in the individual case and towards a compulsory system which, depending upon its finer details, could require them to commit substantial resources and accept politically sensitive prisoners.[122]

Further reading

Penalties and sentencing

Stuart Beresford, 'Unshackling the Paper Tiger – The Sentencing Practices of the Ad Hoc International Criminal Tribunals for the Former Yugoslavia and Rwanda' (2001) 1 *International Criminal Law Review* 33

Nadia Bernaz, 'Sentencing and Penalties' in Schabas and Barnaz, *Routledge Handbook* (London, 2011) 289–303

Jan Philipp Book, *Appeal and Sentence in International Criminal Law* (Berlin, 2011)

Andrea Carcano, 'Sentencing and the Gravity of the Offence in International Criminal Law' (2002) 51 *International and Comparative Law Quarterly* 583

Silvia D'Ascoli, *Sentencing in International Criminal Law: The Approach of the Two Ad Hoc Tribunals and Future Perspectives for the International Criminal Court* (Oxford, 2011)

Rolf Einar Fife, 'Penalties' in Lee, *The Making of the Rome Statute*, 319–43

---

[116] Art. 27 of the ICTY Statute, Art. 26 of the ICTR Statute, Art. 25 of the MICT Statute and Art. 106 of the ICC Statute. On internal and external oversight, see Mulgrew, *International Penal System*, 131–43.

[117] Art. 106(2) of the ICC Statute. Similarly, a standards requirement is included in the Tribunal enforcement agreements.

[118] See Mulgrew, *International Penal System*, 45–84.

[119] *Ibid.*, Arts. 75 and 109. See also rr. 212 and 217–222 of the ICC RPE and reg. 116 of the ICC Regulations.

[120] Rule 105 of the ICTY RPE and ICTR RPE and r. 129 of the MICT RPE.

[121] See further Claus Kreß and Göran Sluiter, 'Enforcement' in Cassese, *Commentary*, 1752 and 1831.

[122] See Mulgrew, *International Penal System*, 33–5.

Rolf Einar Fife, 'Penalties' in Lee, *Elements and Rules*, 555–73

Mark Harmon and Fergal Gaynor, 'Ordinary Sentences for Extraordinary Crimes' (2007) 5 *Journal of International Criminal Justice* 683

Ralph Henham and Mark Drumbl, 'Plea Bargaining at the International Criminal Tribunal for the Former Yugoslavia' (2005) 16 *Criminal Law Forum* 49

Jan Christoph Nemitz, 'The Law of Sentencing in International Criminal Law: The Purposes of Sentencing and the Applicable Method for the Determination of the Sentence' (2001) 4 *Yearbook of International Humanitarian Law* 87

William A. Schabas, 'Penalties' in Cassese, *Commentary*, 1497–534

William A. Schabas, *The UN International Criminal Tribunals: The Former Yugoslavia, Rwanda and Sierra Leone* (Cambridge, 2006) Chapter 14

Dirk Van Zyl Smit, 'International Imprisonment' (2005) 54 *International and Comparative Law Quarterly* 357

Enforcement of penalties

Denis Abels, *Prisoners of the International Community* (The Hague, 2012) Chapter 7

Hirad Abtahi and Steven Arrigg Koh, 'The Emerging Enforcement Practice of the International Criminal Court' (2012) 45 *Cornell International Law Journal* 1

Claus Kreß and Göran Sluiter, 'Enforcement' in Cassese, *Commentary*, Chapters 43–5

Róisín Mulgrew, *Towards the Development of the International Penal System* (Cambridge, 2013)

David Tolbert and Åsa Rydberg, 'Enforcement of Sentences' in Richard May *et al.* (eds.), *Essays on ICTY Procedure and Evidence: In Honour of Gabrielle Kirk McDonald* (The Hague, 2001) 533–43

Part F

Relationship between National and
International Systems

20

State Cooperation with the International Courts and Tribunals

20.1   Characteristics of the cooperation regimes

State cooperation with the Tribunals and the ICC – the 'external part' of the judicial process – departs in many important ways from State-to-State cooperation in criminal matters (see Chapter 5). The obligations *vis-à-vis* the international jurisdictions are more far-reaching[1] since these jurisdictions are created by the international community to investigate and prosecute the most serious crimes of international concern. As regards the Tribunals, and Security Council referrals of situations to the ICC, they also explicitly form part of international efforts to preserve or restore international peace and security. In addition, traditional restrictions on cooperation can be renounced since the international jurisdictions must act in accordance with the highest international standards of procedures and protection of individual rights.

The successful operation of these institutions is completely dependent upon international cooperation. They may not and cannot themselves implement their decisions, such as an arrest warrant, on the territory of a State, and they do not have their own police force.[2] As the ICTY Appeals Chamber concluded in its landmark decision in *Blaškić*, enforcement powers must be expressly provided and cannot be regarded as inherent in an international criminal tribunal.[3] Cooperation is therefore at the heart of effective international criminal proceedings, but this dependence has led to many difficulties in practice.[4]

The *Blaškić* decision found that inter-State and State–Tribunal cooperation follows different models:[5] the former is 'horizontal' and the latter 'vertical' in nature. This characterization is now commonly used. The distinction is based on the stricter obligations to the

---

[1] Compare, however, the SCSL, which cannot demand that any State, except Sierra Leone, cooperate unless the State has entered into a separate cooperation agreement with the Court.

[2] Of course, this was not the case for the Nuremberg and Tokyo IMTs, which were established by occupying powers.

[3] *Blaškić*, ICTY A. Ch., 29 October 1997, para. 25.

[4] See e.g. Mark Harmon and Fergal Gaynor, 'Prosecuting Massive Crimes with Primitive Tools: Three Difficulties Encountered by Prosecutors in International Criminal Proceedings' (2004) 2 *Journal of International Criminal Justice* 403; and Yolanda Gamarra and Alejandra Vicente, 'United Nations Member States' Obligations towards the ICTY: Arresting and Transferring Lukić, Gotovina and Zelenenović' (2008) 8 *International Criminal Law Review* 627.

[5] *Blaškić*, ICTY A. Ch., 29 October 1997, paras. 47 and 54.

international jurisdictions, non-reciprocity and the right of the requesting party (that is to say, the Court or Tribunal) unilaterally to interpret and determine the duties of cooperation.[6]

The ICC is the creation of all States Parties and acceptance of even stricter obligations to cooperate than with respect to the Tribunals could therefore be expected. But in fact the opposite is true. The general duty to cooperate set out in the ICTY and ICTR Statutes[7] is binding on all UN Member States by virtue of Chapter VII of the UN Charter and it contains no qualifications or exceptions: a truly vertical scheme. The same applies to the Residual Mechanism, which as of 1 July 2013 has taken over most functions of the ICTY and ICTR.[8] In the following, the term 'Tribunals' also includes the Residual Mechanism unless otherwise indicated.

The State-negotiated ICC scheme, on the other hand, also contains a duty to cooperate but it is in some respects closer to inter-State cooperation. In particular, the regime is based on requests instead of orders, certain grounds for postponement or refusal exist, and the scope for on-site investigations and compelling individuals to give evidence is limited. The weaknesses of the ICC cooperation regime, sometimes referred to as a middle ground between a vertical and a horizontal model, are often criticized.[9]

20.2   Obligation to cooperate

20.2.1   *States*

The ICTY, ICTR and the Residual Mechanism are subsidiary organs of the Security Council, and thus of the UN, but being judicial institutions they are of 'a special kind' and have been given powers by the Security Council to make decisions that are binding on sovereign States.[10] The duty to cooperate is explicitly laid down in the Statutes (see section 20.1) and corresponds to the general principle that the Tribunals have primacy over national courts. In accordance with the principle that an international treaty cannot impose obligations on third States without their consent (*pacta tertiis non nocent*),[11] this duty is confined to UN Member States and other States that have accepted obligations of cooperation. But the ICTY has gone further and decided, *inter alia*, that self-proclaimed and non-recognized entities which exercise governmental functions must also cooperate.[12] In addition, there are duties of cooperation under the Dayton Peace Agreement and other agreements: the Dayton

---

[6] See Göran Sluiter, *International Criminal Adjudication and the Collection of Evidence: Obligations of States* (Antwerp, 2002) 82–8.

[7] Art. 29 of the ICTY Statute and Art. 28 of the ICTR Statute, which derive their authority from SC Res. 827(1993) and 955(1994). According to the wording, the Tribunal may choose between issuing an 'order' or a 'request', both being equally binding on the States; see Sluiter, *International Criminal Adjudication*, 147–50.

[8] Art. 28 of the MICT Statute; see further Chapter 7. The cooperation provision is almost identical to that of the ICTY and the ICTR, but it explicitly extends also to contempt and perjury offences and adds rules on assistance to national authorities in the countries of the former Yugoslavia and Rwanda.

[9] See e.g. Bert Swart, 'General Problems' in Cassese, *Commentary*, 1589–605; and Hans-Peter Kaul and Claus Kreß, 'Jurisdiction and Cooperation in the Statute of the International Criminal Court: Principles and Compromises' (1999) 2 *Yearbook of International Humanitarian Law* 143, 158–61.

[10] See *Blaškić*, ICTY T. Ch. II, 18 July 1997, paras. 18–23.

[11] Art. 35 of the 1969 Vienna Convention on the Law of Treaties.

[12] E.g. *Karadžić and Mladić*, ICTY T. Ch. I, 11 July 1996, para. 98. See also r. 2 of the ICTY RPE regarding the definition of a 'State'. For a critical view, see Sluiter, *International Criminal Adjudication*, 54–5.

Peace Agreement imposes on the signatories, States of the former Yugoslavia and the Bosnian Serb entity, obligations supplementary to the ICTY Statute on important issues such as unrestricted access to areas over which the signatory exercises control.

The Tribunal Statutes provide a non-exhaustive list, which means that the duty is not confined to particular forms of cooperation. Grounds for refusal traditional to inter-State cooperation are not permitted.[13] But there are nonetheless limitations to the duty; for example, it does not cover relocation of acquitted persons.[14] The Tribunal decides the scope of the duty in the particular case and it may issue binding orders to States and, as we shall see in section 20.2.3, to individuals, 'as may be necessary for the purposes of an investigation or for the preparations or conduct of the trial'.[15] The Appeals Chamber in *Blaškić* concluded that the term 'binding order' should be used with respect to States, not 'subpoena' which requires that the injunction is accompanied by a threat of penalty.[16] The assistance will normally be provided in accordance with national law; the Tribunals sometimes make clear that there is room for some discretion as to how the State is to meet a specific request.[17]

The ICC is an independent and autonomous intergovernmental organization with international legal personality and powers to request cooperation from the States Parties.[18] The Statute explicitly requires these States to 'cooperate fully with the Court' and to ensure that national law allows all specified forms of cooperation.[19] The provisions should serve as general interpretive principles for the specific obligations set out in the Statute.[20] The duty to 'cooperate fully' is explicitly confined to cooperation in accordance with the provisions of the Statute, which means that the ICC cannot demand cooperation beyond what the Statute requires. However, there is a catch-all provision at the end of the list of measures for assistance other than arrest and surrender.[21] States may also provide additional cooperation voluntarily. The duty of implementation requires that States make any necessary domestic changes so that they are able to provide all the required forms of cooperation, but allows the States Parties to design the procedures in keeping with their legal and constitutional systems (see section 20.9). Some grounds for refusal are explicitly laid down in the Statute; in light of the negotiating history these should be considered as exhaustive.[22] There may be additional obligations to cooperate in other agreements, including those concluded by the Court with individual States to enhance cooperation.[23]

---

[13] Compare Chapter 5.   [14] *Ntagerura*, ICTY A. Ch., 18 November 2008, para. 14.

[15] Rule 54 of the ICTY RPE and ICTR RPE and r. 55 of the MICT RPE.

[16] *Blaškić*, ICTY A. Ch., 29 October 1997, para. 25.   [17] See e.g. *Gotovina et al.*, ICTY T. Ch. I, 16 September 2008.

[18] Art. 4 and Part 9 of the ICC Statute.   [19] *Ibid.*, Arts. 86 and 88.

[20] Claus Kreß, 'Penalties, Enforcement and Cooperation in the International Criminal Court' (1998) 6 *European Journal of Crime, Criminal Law and Criminal Justice* 442, 450.

[21] Art. 93(1)(l) of the ICC Statute.

[22] See Phakiso Mochochoko, 'International Cooperation and Judicial Assistance' in Lee, *The Making of the Rome Statute*, 305–17.

[23] See Art. 54(3)(d) of the ICC Statute and reg. 107 of the ICC Regulations; and see Report of the International Criminal Court for 2005–2006 (UN Doc. A/61/217 of 3 August 2006), paras. 52–6.

Although not beyond dispute, the duty to cooperate with the ICC (and Part 9 of the Statute) is triggered first when an investigation is formally commenced.[24] It thereafter covers subsequent proceedings; certain obligations apply after the final verdict, for example the temporary transfer of a prisoner to the Court for testimony.[25]

20.2.2   *Conflicting international obligations of States*

Another important aspect of the different regimes is the relationship between the State's cooperation duties towards the Tribunal or Court and other international obligations. Since the duties *vis-à-vis* the Tribunals have their legal force in the UN Charter, these will normally prevail over the State's obligations under other international agreements, at least agreements between UN Member States.

The situation is more complex regarding the ICC. If the Security Council imposes cooperation obligations when referring a situation to the Court, and thus acts under Chapter VII of the UN Charter, the equivalent primacy over other international obligations should apply.[26] This is how the ICC has interpreted the not entirely clear cooperation provisions in the Security Council resolution concerning the *Situation in Darfur, Sudan*.[27] In other instances general international principles for contradictory treaty obligations will apply, such as *lex posterior* (the treaty later in time prevails) and *lex specialis* (the more specific treaty prevails). To what extent such interpretations favour the Court will depend on the circumstances. Hence, the obligations *vis-à-vis* the ICC do not have a general primacy. Two types of conflicts are addressed in the Statute: competing requests for cooperation; and immunities and similar obstacles. On competing requests, the Statute sets out a complex system whereby the existence of an admissibility decision by the Court (on the ground of complementarity) and the origin of the competing request (from a State Party or third State) are important factors for the resolution of the conflict.[28]

The provision on conflicts regarding immunities (for example, State immunity, diplomatic immunity, or safe conduct) and similar obstacles (for example, exclusive jurisdiction in status of forces agreements or conditioned re-extradition in extradition agreements) is Article 98; it has turned out to be controversial.[29] From a cooperation perspective, however, it is important to note that the provision, as drafted, is directed to the ICC: '[t]he Court may not proceed with a request' unless a waiver of immunity or consent for surrender has been

---

[24] See Informal Expert Paper: *Fact-Finding and Investigative Functions of the Office of the Prosecutor, Including International Cooperation* (2003), paras. 22–9, available on the website of the ICC at www.icc-cpi.int.

[25] Rule 193 of the ICC RPE.

[26] See also e.g. Dan Sarooshi, 'The Peace and Justice Paradox: The International Criminal Court and the UN Security Council' in Dominic McGoldrick *et al.* (eds.), *The Permanent International Criminal Court: Legal and Policy Issues* (Oxford, 2003) 95, 104.

[27] SC Res. 1593(2005) of 31 March 2005; *Situation in Darfur* (*Al Bashir* arrest warrant case), ICC PTC I, 4 March 2009, paras. 244–7; see also Matthias Neuner, 'The Darfur Referral of the Security Council and the Jurisdiction of the International Criminal Court' (2005) 8 *Yearbook of International Humanitarian Law* 320; Robert Cryer, 'Sudan, Resolution 1593, and International Criminal Justice' (2006) 19 *Leiden Journal of International Law* 195; and Dapo Akande, 'The Effect of the Security Council Resolutions and Domestic Proceedings on State Obligations to Cooperate with the ICC' (2012) 10 *Journal of International Criminal Justice* 299.

[28] Art. 90 of the ICC Statute. See also Art. 93(9) on other forms of cooperation.   [29] See section 8.11.1, 21.5.2 and 21.5.4.

obtained. Hence, the requested State may raise the issue of conflicting obligations before the Court,[30] but the conflict is not a ground for refusal if the Court still insists on the request.[31] If the requested State continues to resist, however, the issue may be subject to adjudication by the Court in non-compliance proceedings.[32] In addition, nothing prevents a non-State Party from seeking a remedy against a violation by the requested State of the agreement between them. When issuing an arrest warrant against the President of Sudan, the Pre-Trial Chamber did not address the issue of Article 98 although the request for arrest and surrender was sent to numerous States and thus issues of immunity or conflicting treaty obligations could possibly arise.[33] Nor has this issue been addressed when the Court has decided on non-cooperation against States receiving visits of the President.[34]

20.2.3 Individuals

The Tribunals have on occasion issued binding orders to individuals to appear and give evidence. These orders are 'subpoenas' (*subpoena ad testificandum*) since non-compliance may result in liability for contempt. Lacking explicit support in the Statutes, the practice has been based on 'inherent powers'.[35] By jurisprudence, and now also in the RPE, it is clarified that such orders may only be issued by a Chamber.[36] The orders, as well as any sanctions, must be enforced by national authorities, and most States will require that a domestic order be issued. Some States attribute direct effect to the order issued by the Tribunal, meaning that the Tribunal order serves as the basis for a domestic compulsory process. According to the Appeals Chamber in *Blaškić*, States have a duty, when requested, to arrest, compel under threat of a domestic penalty to surrender evidence, or bring a witness to the Tribunal to testify.[37] These are far-reaching obligations that depart from the general practice among States, which does not recognize a duty to testify across national borders.[38] In practice, however, only a few States have introduced legislation providing for forcible transfer of witnesses to the Tribunals, and the Tribunals have framed their requests for State assistance in very cautious terms.[39]

Here, the traditional act of State doctrine is to be observed and the Tribunal may not address binding orders to State officials for cooperation in their official capacity; such orders

---

[30] Rule 195 of the ICC RPE.
[31] See also Art. 119(1) of the ICC Statute: 'Any dispute concerning the judicial functions of the Court shall be settled by the direction of the Court.'
[32] Reg. 109 of the ICC Regulations.
[33] *Al Bashir* arrest warrant case, ICC PTC I, 4 March 2009. See sections 21.5.2 to 21.5.4.
[34] For a critical view, see Dire Tladi, 'The ICC Decisions on Chad and Malawi: On Cooperation, Immunities, and Article 98' (2013) 11 *Journal of International Criminal Justice* 199.
[35] *Blaškić*, ICTY A. Ch., 29 October 1997, paras. 47 and 55. See Anne-Laure Chaumette, 'The ICTY's Power to Subpoena Individuals, to Issue Binding Orders to International Organisations and to Subpoena their Agents' (2004) 4 *International Criminal Law Review* 357. Art. 1(4)(a) of the MICT Statute empowers the Mechanism to hold a person in contempt but the Statute does not explicitly authorize subpoenas.
[36] Rule 54 of the ICTY RPE and ICTR RPE and r. 56 of the MICT RPE. See e.g. *Mrkšić et al.*, ICTY A. Ch., 30 July 2003; and *Krstić*, ICTY A. Ch., 1 July 2003.
[37] *Blaškić*, ICTY A. Ch., 29 October 1997, para. 27.
[38] A special scheme exists among the Nordic countries, however, but it does not include effective sanctions in case of non-compliance by the witness.
[39] See Sluiter, *International Criminal Adjudication*, 253–68.

must instead be made to the State.[40] The orders may, however, be addressed to officials when acting in their 'private capacity', but still the Tribunal will normally proceed via national authorities and only exceptionally address itself directly to the individual.[41] Nonetheless, an unqualified immunity of this kind could go too far[42] and subsequently the 'State official' exception has been further restricted to apply 'only in relation to the production of documents in their custody in their official capacity'; it does not cover what the official has seen or heard in the course of exercising official functions.[43] The ICTY and ICTR have dismissed claims of immunity, *inter alia*, regarding the then British Prime Minister Blair and German Chancellor Schröder, and have issued a subpoena to the Rwandan Defence Minister.[44] Members of international peacekeeping or peace-enforcing forces with a UN mandate are also compellable.[45]

The ICC Statute gives conflicting messages as to whether the Court may compel an individual to cooperate, the suspect or accused of course being excluded.[46] The cooperation obligation of Part 9 does not extend to private individuals. But another provision authorizes the Trial Chamber to 'require the attendance and testimony of witnesses', although the RPE restrict the 'compellability of witnesses' to those who actually appear before the Court.[47] Read together with the provision that States are required to assist with the 'voluntary appearance' of witnesses and experts,[48] it appears that the ICC might have the power to order a witness to appear before the Court but cannot demand that a State deliver a witness who does not comply. The Court might request non-voluntary transfer of a witness under the catch-all provision. But this requires that no 'existing fundamental legal principle of general application' in the requested State would be violated, which could well be argued to preclude coercive measures without an explicit authorization in national law. The lack of power to bring witnesses before the Court is a serious weakness in the ICC cooperation regime.[49]

As in ordinary inter-State regimes, the Tribunal or Court, instead of issuing a subpoena, may order the temporary transfer of a witness who is already detained in a State.[50] If a subpoena fails to secure the appearance of the witness, for example when the non-appearance is because of a medical condition, compelled testimony by video-link can be an alternative.[51]

---

[40] *Blaškić*, ICTY A. Ch., 29 October 1997, paras. 39–44.   [41] *Ibid.*, paras. 46–51 and 53–6.

[42] For criticism, see e.g. Susan Lamb, 'The Powers of Arrest of the International Criminal Tribunal for the Former Yugoslavia' (1999) 70 *British Yearbook of International Law* 165, 217–18.

[43] *Krstić*, ICTY A. Ch., 1 July 2003, paras. 24, 26–8.

[44] *Milošević*, ICTY T. Ch. III, 9 December 2005; and *Bagosora et al.*, ICTR T. Ch. I, 11 September 2006. Cf. the SCSL, which avoided the issue of immunity when refusing to subpoena the President of Sierra Leone: *Norman et al.*, SCSL A. Ch., 11 September 2006, paras. 40–4 (but Judge Robertson, dissenting, addressed the issue). For further discussion of immunities, see Chapter 21.

[45] See e.g. *Simić et al.*, ICTY T. Ch. I, 18 October 2000, paras. 62–3; and *Bagosora et al.*, ICTR T. Ch. III, 14 July 2006.

[46] On the binding effect of the ICC Statute, as a treaty, on individuals, see Marko Milanović, 'Is the Rome Statute Binding on Individuals? (And Why We Should Care)' (2011) 9 *Journal of International Criminal Justice* 25.

[47] Art. 64(6)(b) of the ICC Statute and r. 65 of the ICC RPE.   [48] Art. 93(1)(e) of the ICC Statute.

[49] See also Claus Kreß and Kimberly Prost, 'Article 87' in Triffterer, *Observers' Notes*, 1576; and Göran Sluiter, '"I Beg You, Please Come Testify" – The Problematic Absence of Subpoena Powers at the ICC' (2009) 12 *New Criminal Law Review* 590.

[50] Rule 90*bis* of the ICTY RPE and ICTR RPE, r. 107 of the MICT RPE and Art. 93(1)(f) and (7) of the ICC Statute. See e.g. *Karemera et al.*, ICTR T. Ch. III, 9 April 2009.

[51] See e.g. *Haradinaj et al.*, ICTY T. Ch. I, 14 September 2007. See also Art. 69(2) of the ICC Statute.

However, a subpoena power is not necessarily a recipe for success. For example, in *Haradinaj et al.*, a subpoenaed key witness refused to appear and the Appeals Chamber refused the Prosecutor's request for more time to secure his testimony.[52] In the ICC, another difficulty has occurred when defence witnesses who were transferred from detention in their home State requested asylum in the Netherlands. While the ICC is obliged to return the temporarily transferred detainee to the State once the purposes of the transfer have been fulfilled, the Court is not competent to consider the asylum request and it is thus in the hands of the host State (the Netherlands) for the resolution of this matter;[53] but the detention remains with the Court during the asylum process.[54] Complications of this kind might discourage States from cooperating with the Court and further hamper its ability to obtain live evidence. Possible solutions are increased reliance upon testimony by video-link or pre-recorded testimony.

20.3 Non-States Parties and international organizations

In practice, cooperation with non-States Parties has not been much of an issue for the Tribunals owing to the practically universal membership of the UN; Switzerland, a non-member at the time of the Tribunals' creation, declared that it would cooperate voluntarily. Neither has the application of the duty of cooperation, laid down in the ICTY Statute, to the newly independent States after the break-up of the former Yugoslavia, been challenged with reference to non-membership in the UN, which would have involved difficult issues of State succession.[55] All but one of these States were UN members when the ICTY was established; Serbia and Montenegro considered itself the successor State, although this was not accepted by the UN with respect to membership.[56]

The explicit duty to cooperate set out in the ICC Statute is confined to States Parties, but special provisions authorize the Court to invite non-States Parties to cooperate in accordance with separate arrangements.[57] In addition, non-States Parties which accept the jurisdiction of the ICC in individual cases must also cooperate with the Court in accordance with Part 9 of the ICC Statute.[58] Finally, the Security Council may, when referring a situation to the ICC, require that UN Member States cooperate with the Court, regardless of whether those States are parties to the ICC Statute or not. This was done with respect to Sudan (Darfur) and Libya, although not for UN Member States generally, when the situations in those countries

---

[52] *Haradinaj et al.*, ICTY A. Ch., 19 October 2009, para. 41. See also *Kabashi*, ICTY T. Ch. I, 16 September 2011.

[53] See *Lubanga*, ICC T. Ch. I, 5 August 2011. See also *Katanga and Ngudjolo Chui*, ICC T. Ch. II, 9 June 2011.

[54] *Lubanga*, ICC T. Ch. I, 15 August 2011, 25 October 2011 and 15 December 2011. See also *Djokaba Lambi Longa* v. *The Netherlands*, ECtHR, 9 October 2012. However, the ICC did not consider itself competent to review the detention as such since this is a matter for the transferring State: see *Katanga and Ngudjolo Chui*, ICC T. Ch. II, 1 March 2012, para. 18. See also Göran Sluiter, 'Shared Responsibility in International Criminal Justice' (2012) 10 *Journal of International Criminal Justice* 661.

[55] These issues were raised, however, with respect to the ICTY's jurisdiction over crimes committed in Kosovo: see *Milutinović et al.*, ICTY T. Ch. III, 6 May 2003.

[56] The question of the UN membership of Serbia and Montenegro was extraordinarily complicated and was described as a 'rather confused and complex state of affairs': see ICJ in *Case Concerning Legality of Use of Force* (*Serbia and Montenegro* v. *United Kingdom*), 15 December 2004, paras. 53–77. See also ICJ in *Case Concerning the Application of the Convention on the Prevention and Punishment of the Crime of Genocide* (*Croatia* v. *Serbia*), 18 November 2008, paras. 43–51.

[57] Art. 87(5) of the ICC Statute.   [58] *Ibid.*, Art. 12(3).

were referred to the Court.[59] Quite apart from this, it has been argued that there may be a customary law duty to ensure compliance with international humanitarian law, which in turn could translate into a duty to cooperate with the ICC in a given case,[60] although such an argument has by no means been universally accepted.[61] Of course, non-States Parties may also choose to cooperate, which was the case when the United States and Rwanda assisted in the voluntary surrender of the fugitive Bosco Ntaganda to the ICC in March 2013.

The cooperation of entities other than States has proved indispensable in practice. For example, international forces have carried out most of the arrests for the ICTY. Such action was controversial and there was initial resistance to authorizing, let alone requiring, IFOR to arrest indicted war criminals.[62] Nonetheless, an authorization to arrest was given to IFOR, but only under restrictive conditions, and it took some time before the first arrest was made. Contributing to this increased willingness to assist was a practice of 'sealed indictments' which reduced the risks to troops effectuating the arrests.[63] It has been debated whether the ICTY Statute allows arrest by bodies other than States and whether IFOR (later SFOR) had a duty to arrest:[64] the ICTY itself has given an affirmative answer to the former question[65] and a negative answer to the latter.[66] Arrest warrants have sometimes been issued directly to non-State entities instead of States.[67] It is truly an anomaly, however, that the international community imposed a duty on States to cooperate with the ICTY but provided the relevant international forces (IFOR/SFOR and KFOR) with only a permission to do so. Requests have also been made to international organizations for other purposes, for example assistance with exhumation.[68]

Due mainly to US opposition to the Court, the mandate of the UN peacekeeping forces in the Democratic Republic of the Congo (MONUC) initially did not refer to the ICC; more robust assistance in arresting war criminals was only to be provided to the DRC authorities and courts. But later MONUC was given an explicit mandate to cooperate with international efforts to bring perpetrators to justice.[69] In practice, however, MONUC had provided assistance to the Court for a long time, including in the arrest of suspects in the *Situation of the DRC*. Today explicit references to the ICC by the Security Council are no longer avoided; newer resolutions contain explicit cooperation mandates to peacekeeping

---

[59] SC Res. 1593(2005) of 31 March 2005 and SC Res. 1970(2011) of 26 February 2011. See also *Gaddafi and Al-Senussi*, ICC PTC I, 28 August 2013, paras. 13–15 (Mauretania, which was not a party to the Statute, had no duty to cooperate with the ICC).

[60] Claus Kreß and Kimberly Prost, 'Article 87' in Triffterer, *Observers' Notes*, 1061–2; Zhu Wenqi, 'On Cooperation by States Not Party to the International Criminal Court' (2006) 88 (861) *International Review of the Red Cross* 87.

[61] Henckaerts and Doswald-Beck, *ICRC Customary Law*, 618–21.

[62] See Richard Holbrook, *To End a War*, 2nd edn (New York, 1998) 221–2.

[63] See Gary Jonathan Bass, *Stay the Hand of Vengeance: The Politics of War Crimes Tribunals* (Princeton, NJ, 2000) 265–7.

[64] See e.g. John R. W. D. Jones, 'The Implications of the Dayton Peace Agreement for the International Criminal Tribunals for the Former Yugoslavia' (1996) 7 *European Journal of International Law* 226; Gary Sharp, 'International Obligations to Search for and Arrest War Criminals: Government Failure in the Former Yugoslavia' (1997) 7 *Duke Journal of Comparative and International Law* 411; Paolo Gaeta, 'Is NATO Authorized or Obliged to Arrest Persons Indicted by the International Criminal Tribunal for the Former Yugoslavia?' (1998) 9 *European Journal of International Law* 174; Lamb, 'Powers of Arrest', 165–244; and Han-Ru Zhou, 'The Enforcement of Arrest Warrants by International Forces' (2006) 4 *Journal of International Criminal Justice* 202.

[65] See r. 59*bis* of the ICTY RPE.   [66] (1996) *Yearbook of the ICTY*, 229.

[67] See e.g. *Dokmanović*, ICTY T. Ch. II, 22 October 1997, para. 3 (arrest warrant issued to the United Nations Transitional Administration for Eastern Slavonia, Baranja and Western Sirmium, UNTAES).

[68] E.g. *Haradinaj et al.*, ICTY T. Ch. II, 19 October 2006 (UNMIK).

[69] Cf. SC Res. 1565(2004) of 1 October 2004 and 1856(2008) of 22 December 2008.

missions[70] and calls to States to continue their close cooperation with the Court.[71] In Sudan, on the contrary, any links between the ICC and the international peacekeeping mission (UNAMID) have been avoided and UNAMID's mandate contains no reference to international criminal investigations or prosecutions.[72]

Intergovernmental organizations may have international legal personality, separate from that of the constituent States. Regardless of this, the ICTY, by using a 'purposive interpretation' of its Statute, has found itself competent to issue binding orders to such organizations. In *Simić et al.*, for example, such an order was issued not only to the participating States of SFOR but also to SFOR, as a collective State enterprise, and its responsible authority, the North Atlantic Council.[73] Binding orders have also been directed to others.[74] The ICC, on the other hand, applies the same scheme to intergovernmental organizations as to non-States Parties, and cooperation thus depends on a voluntary commitment.[75] For example, a cooperation agreement has been concluded with the European Union.[76] A special relationship exists between the ICC and the United Nations and matters having an impact on cooperation are addressed in a Relationship Agreement.[77] A separate agreement was concluded concerning MONUC.[78] The difficult issue of how to deal with confidentiality is discussed in section 20.6.2. One organization, the ICRC, has been granted special treatment, motivated by the special status drawn from its mandate under the Geneva Conventions. In *Simić et al.*, the ICTY found that in order to discharge its mandate the ICRC must have a right not to disclose information relating to its activities.[79] The ICC has followed suit with an absolute privilege provision.[80] The ICRC may thus prevent disclosure of information or testimonies by present and past ICRC officials or employees. The ICC has concluded that it may seek cooperation from intergovernmental organizations also without a prior agreement, when the requirements of specificity, relevance, and necessity are met.[81]

---

[70] SC Res. 2098(2013) of 28 March 2013 (DRC; MONUSCO), which also welcomes an instance of successful State cooperation with the ICC. See also SC Res. 2100(2013) of 25 April 2013 (Mali, MINUSMA).

[71] *Ibid.* See also SC Res. 2095(2013) of 14 March 2013 (Libya) and SC Res. 2101(2013) of 25 April 2013 (Côte d'Ivoire).

[72] SC Res. 1769(2007) of 31 July 2007; the earlier African Union mission (AMIS) also had no mandate to cooperate with the ICC. In more recent resolutions, the Security Council is merely '*emphasizing* the need to bring to justice the perpetrators of such crimes, and *urging* the Government of Sudan to comply with its obligations in this respect'; e.g. SC Res. 2063(2012) of 31 July 2012.

[73] ICTY T. Ch. III, 18 October 2000, paras. 46–9, 58. One should note, however, that SFOR was different from regular UN peacekeeping forces since it consisted of different State-led forces remaining under the control of their respective governments.

[74] See e.g. *Kordić*, ICTY T. Ch. III, 4 August 2000 (the European Community Monitoring Mission); and *Haradinaj et al.*, ICTY A. Ch., 10 March 2006 (UNMIK); cf. *Kovačević*, ICTY T. Ch. II, 23 June 1998 (refusal to issue an order to the OSCE). See also Chaumette, 'The ICTY's Power to Subpoena', 413–17.

[75] Art. 87(6) of the ICC Statute.

[76] Agreement between the International Criminal Court and the European Union on Cooperation and Assistance of 10 April 2006 (ICC-PRES/01-01-06).

[77] Art. 2 of the ICC Statute and the Relationship Agreement between the International Criminal Court and the United Nations of 4 October 2004 (ICC-ASP/3/Res.1).

[78] Memorandum of Understanding between the UN and the ICC Concerning Co-operation between MONUC and the ICC, 8 November 2005. See Rod Rastan, 'Testing Co-operation: The International Criminal Court and National Authorities' (2008) 21 *Leiden Journal of International Law* 444–6.

[79] *Simić et al.*, ICTY T. Ch. III, 27 July 1999, paras. 72–4 (but with one judge dissenting).   [80] Rule 73(4) of the ICC RPE.

[81] *Banda and Jerbo*, ICC T. Ch. IV, 1 July 2011 (170) and 21 December 2011 (cooperation request to the African Union).

20.4   Authority to seek cooperation and defence rights

As in inter-State cooperation, there is a certain inequality between the powers of the prosecution and the defence to seek cooperation, and this is a source of criticism.[82] While the Prosecutor has certain powers to seek cooperation independently on behalf of the international jurisdiction, including provisional arrest and seizure of evidence in urgent cases,[83] the defence is directed to go through a judge.[84] Such court orders have been issued by all the international criminal jurisdictions and some States even require them in order to provide assistance in accordance with national law.[85] In case the State refuses to implement an order to produce documents requested by the defence, ICTR Trial Chambers have sometimes ordered the prosecution to obtain the documents instead.[86] The problem is more pronounced in adversarial proceedings where each party prepares its case, than in inquisitorial ones where the prosecution has a duty to investigate exonerating circumstances actively.[87] Difficulties in obtaining cooperation, and thus in preparing its case, may even cause the defence to seek a stay of the proceedings with reference to a violation of fair trial rights.[88] Considering the potential for a less adversarial process, this could turn out to be less of a problem at the ICC than in the Tribunal proceedings.[89] Also, the Prosecutor may turn to the relevant Chamber for the grant or authorization of necessary warrants or orders.[90] This happens less frequently, for example concerning documentary evidence that a State has not produced.[91] Moreover, the ICTY judges may issue an arrest warrant directly to the Prosecutor.[92] In the same vein, it has been suggested that the ICC Prosecutor may retain the right to determine where and when to request an arrest to be executed, although the underlying arrest warrant will always be issued by the Pre-Trial Chamber.[93] But in practice the Chambers have rejected this argument and instead made the requests themselves.[94]

Another issue is to what extent fair trial rights and other procedural standards must be respected by national authorities when acting on behalf of the Tribunal or Court and what remedies are available when such rights or standards are violated. This is discussed in more detail in Chapter 17, but it should now be noted that the ICC Statute lays down some

---

[82] See e.g. Mark Ellis, 'Achieving Justice Before the International War Crimes Tribunal: Challenges for the Defence Counsel' (1997) 7 *Duke Journal of Comparative and International Law* 519, 533–6.

[83] Rules 39–40 of the ICTY RPE and ICTR RPE rr. 36–37 of the MICT RPE and Art. 54(3)(c)–(d) of the ICC Statute.

[84] Rule 54 of the ICTY RPE and ICTR RPE r. 55 of the MICT RPE, Art. 57(3)(b) of the ICC Statute and r. 116 of the ICC RPE.

[85] See e.g. *Setako*, ICTR T. Ch. I, 31 March 2009, para. 4; and *Katanga and Ngudjolo Chui*, ICC PTC II, 25 August 2008. Cf. *Banda and Jerbo*, ICC PTC I, 17 November 2010 (a cooperation request to Sudan concerning defence investigation on-site was not considered 'necessary' in the pre-confirmation phase of the process).

[86] Rule 98 of the ICTR RPE (additional evidence); see e.g. *Bagilishema*, ICTR T. Ch. I, 8 June 2000, paras. 18–19.

[87] See sections 17.2.2 and 17.6.   [88] E.g. *Banda and Jerbo*, ICC T. Ch. IV, 26 October 2012 (410).

[89] See *Katanga and Ngudjolo Chui*, ICC PTC I, 25 April 2008, where the majority found the defence request partially unnecessary since the documents were available from the prosecution; cf. the Dissenting Opinion of Judge Ušacka.

[90] Rule 54 of the ICTY RPE and ICTR RPE r. 55 of the MICT RPE and Art. 57(3)(a) of the ICC Statute.

[91] See e.g. *Gotovina et al.*, ICTY T. Ch. I, 16 September 2008; cf. *Gotovina et al.*, ICTY T. Ch. I, 26 July 2010, paras. 29 and 135 (an order required the Chamber's assessment whether it was sufficiently certain that the requested document was created, if it still existed, and if its whereabouts were ascertainable).

[92] Rule 59*bis* of the ICTY RPE.   [93] Informal Expert Paper: *Fact-Finding and Investigative Functions*, para. 82.

[94] See e.g. *Situation in Uganda*, ICC PTC II, 8 July 2005; and *Lubanga*, ICC PTC I, 24 February 2006. For a critical view, see Håkan Friman, 'Cooperation with the International Criminal Court: Some Thoughts of Improvements Under the Current Regime' in Mauro Politi and Federica Gioia (eds.), *The International Criminal Court and National Jurisdictions* (Aldershot, 2008) 93–102. See also Rastan, 'Testing Co-operation', 447–9.

procedural rights relating to the questioning of a suspect which are explicitly applicable also when it is being conducted by national authorities.[95]

20.5   Arrest and surrender

The duty to assist with arrest and surrender is explicitly mentioned in the Statutes of the ICTY, ICTR and the Residual Mechanism and further reinforced in the respective RPE.[96] The basis is normally an arrest warrant issued by a Tribunal judge, but in urgent cases the Prosecutor may request provisional arrest to be followed up by a judge-made order for surrender.[97] The special confirmation proceedings *in absentia* at the Tribunals are provided with a view to issuing an international arrest warrant to all States.[98] Both an international and, according to case law, a regular arrest warrant may be combined with an order to freeze the assets of the accused.[99]

In spite of the lack of grounds for refusal, States have sometimes refused cooperation on grounds of national law. For example, a US court refused to extradite an accused to the ICTR claiming that there was no extradition treaty, as required by national law.[100] The Federal Republic of Yugoslavia initially refused to transfer indictees to the ICTY on the basis of a constitutional prohibition against extradition of nationals.[101] Moreover, some domestic implementation laws contain double-criminality requirements.[102] But such traditional grounds for refusing extradition are not compatible with the Tribunal cooperation regime.[103]

The fact remains that the national law of many States prohibits 'extradition' under certain circumstances, most notably concerning nationals in many civil law jurisdictions. These strongly held exceptions were advanced in the ICC negotiations and, in order to create a regime which excludes any explicit grounds for refusal, compromises were required. One element of the agreed regime was to distinguish between 'surrender' (to the Court) and 'extradition' (to a State), and thereby avoid a potential application of ordinary extradition principles and national requirements (see section 20.7).[104] Another element was to satisfy the evidentiary requirements that apply to extradition in many common law jurisdictions. While the judicial authorities of the requested State may not examine the legality of the warrant itself or rule on a *habeas corpus* challenge, the Statute indirectly acknowledges that the State, as part of its surrender procedures, may test evidence and that the Court must support its request with documents, statements or information to meet the requirements.[105] But the Statute also requires that national requirements for surrender should not be more

---

[95] Art. 55(2) of the ICC Statute.   [96] In rr. 57–61 of the MICT RPE, more detailed provisions have been added.
[97] Rules 40 and 40*bis* of the ICTY RPE and ICTR RPE.   [98] So-called 'Rule 61 proceedings': see section 17.9.1.
[99] Rule 61(D) of the ICTY RPE and ICTR RPE and r. 63(D) of the MICT RPE; *Milošević*, ICTY (Judge Hunt), 24 May 1999, paras. 26–9.
[100] See Göran Sluiter, 'To Cooperate or Not to Cooperate? The Case of the Failed Transfer of Ntakirutimana to the Rwanda Tribunal' (1998) 11 *Leiden Journal of International Law* 383; and Mary Coombs, 'International Decisions: In Re Surrender of Ntakirutimana' (2000) 94 *American Journal of International Law* 171.
[101] ICTY Report to the United Nations 1997, UN Doc. A/52/375 and S/1997/729, para. 189.   [102] See section 5.3.2.
[103] See r. 58 of the ICTY RPE and ICTR RPE and r. 60 of the MICT RPE.
[104] Art. 102 of the ICC Statute. See Michael Plachta, '"Surrender" in the Context of the International Criminal Court and the European Union' (2004) 19 *Nouvelles études pénales* 465.
[105] Art. 91(2) and (4) of the ICC Statute; see Kaul and Kreß, 'Jurisdiction and Cooperation', 165–6.

burdensome, and should if possible be less burdensome, than those applicable to inter-State extradition. A State that normally applies evidentiary requirements for extradition but has made exceptions concerning requests from certain States, will therefore arguably be prevented from applying such requirements *vis-à-vis* the ICC.

Other issues were resolved in the Statute by introducing postponements or consultations.[106] By containing these detailed provisions, the Statute may satisfy any national requirement that there must be an extradition treaty before a person may be transferred.

For the ICC, arrest and surrender or provisional arrest will always be based on an arrest warrant issued by the Pre-Trial Chamber. National authorities will enforce the request by applying national procedures, but the Statute sets forth some minimum requirements concerning the national arrest proceedings, and prescribes a division of competences, consultations regarding provisional release, and speedy execution of the request.[107] In practice, most decisions to issue arrest warrants have been lengthy and have included a detailed assessment of the various matters, including the alleged crimes, jurisdiction and, in some cases, the complementarity principle.[108] An arrest warrant may be combined with a request for identification, tracing, and seizing or freezing assets and property belonging to the suspect, which has regularly been done and sometimes also led to assets being frozen.[109]

Somewhat surprisingly in view of the strictly limited subject-matter jurisdiction of the ICC, there was strong support for including the rule of specialty in the ICC Statute.[110] Hence, if there are amendments to the charges, a waiver may have to be obtained from the surrendering State.[111] The consent of the person surrendered is not required. When raised in *Mbarushimana*, the Pre-Trial Chamber allowed wide room for inclusion of new crimes in the subsequent charging document without violating the principle.[112] The Tribunals, on the other hand, have rejected the rule by reference to the fact that States cannot refuse surrender on any ground.[113] The same argument could be made for the ICC, but still the specialty rule applies explicitly and may create practical problems.

A notable omission in the cooperation regimes relates to accepting and guaranteeing the return of a suspect or accused who is granted interim release by the Tribunal or Court. The ICC Appeals Chamber in *Bemba* concluded that the identification of a State that is willing and able to accept the person is a precondition for conditional release and thus that the

---

[106] Art. 89(2) (*ne bis in idem* challenge), Art. 89(4) (domestic proceeding concerning other crimes) and Art. 95 (general provision on postponement) of the ICC Statute.

[107] *Ibid.*, Arts. 89(1), 58 and 59 of the ICC Statute.

[108] However, the issue of admissibility should only exceptionally be addressed in connection to the issuance of an arrest warrant: see *Situation in the DRC*, ICC A. Ch., 13 July 2006 (169), paras. 53–4; see section 17.4.

[109] Art. 57(3)(e) of the ICC Statute; *Lubanga*, ICC PTC I, 24 February 2006, paras. 130–41. In one case, a bank account was seized and frozen in Portugal, but, since most of the money seemed to have disappeared, the Court requested the national authorities to investigate the matter: see *Bemba Gombo*, ICC PTC III, 17 November 2008.

[110] Art. 101 of the ICC Statute.

[111] Unlike most extradition instruments, however, the provision is drafted in such a way that it only targets a different 'conduct or course of conduct' but does not apply to a different legal qualification of the charged facts: see Peter Wilkitzki, 'Article 101' in Triffterer, *Observers' Notes*, 1638.

[112] *Mbarushimana*, ICC PTC I, 16 December 2011, paras. 86–92.

[113] *Kovačević*, ICTY A. Ch., 2 July 1998, para. 37. However, the rule of specialty might apply if the case and accused are later referred from the Tribunal to a national jurisdiction; see *Milan Lukić*, ICTY Referral Bench, 5 April 2007, para. 45. See also Gamarra and Vicente, 'UN Member States' Obligations', 644–6.

release depends upon State cooperation.[114] But States have no obligation to provide such cooperation. To resolve this, the ICC is seeking to enter into separate agreements with States on interim release, but unsurprisingly the response from States has been very limited. As the experience of the ICTY has shown, ad hoc arrangements in individual cases provide a more realistic approach.

In practice, the Office of the Prosecutor takes various measures to trace those who are subject to arrest warrants; the ICC Prosecutor is 'invited' to transmit the collected information to the Chamber and the Registry, but only 'as far as his confidentiality obligations allow'.[115] The ICC Office of the Prosecutor has full access to all Interpol databases. But so far the ICC Office of the Prosecutor, unlike the ICTY, has not considered it necessary to establish a special 'tracking unit'; security and political reasons are the major obstacles to securing arrests, not difficulties in establishing the whereabouts of fugitives.

20.6   Other forms of legal assistance

As already mentioned, the cooperation obligation of the ICTY and ICTR Statutes is not restricted to specified forms of cooperation; it is up to the Tribunal to decide what is required for the case at hand. Requests and orders for various measures have been issued and the Tribunals have established some general principles. For example, a request for an order to produce documents must be relatively specific, explain why the documents are relevant for trial, not be unduly onerous, and allow sufficient time for compliance.[116] Normally, the applicant must approach the State for assistance before seeking a court order for the production of documents.[117]

Article 93 of the ICC Statute, on the other hand, sets out various forms of assistance that are to be provided, and measures other than those listed are available under the 'catch-all' provision (see section 20.2.1). The drafting of the Statute, and indeed early practice, suggest that the Court makes the requests and the requested State thereafter performs the investigative acts or other measures on behalf of the Court.

20.6.1   Grounds for refusal

No grounds for refusal are provided with respect to cooperation with the Tribunals. Apart from the national security exception (see the next section), only one ground for refusal for 'other forms' of assistance was retained in the ICC regime: if the requested measure is prohibited on the basis of 'an existing fundamental legal principle of general application' in the requested State.[118] Arguably, a strict interpretation should apply and it may even be that

---

[114] See *Bemba Gombo*, ICC A. Ch., 2 December 2009, paras. 106–7; cf. *Bemba Gombo*, ICC PTC II, 14 August 2009.
[115] E.g. *Mbarushimana*, ICC PTC I, 28 September 2010. Cf. the ad hoc Tribunals, where the OTP is more directly involved in the enforcement of arrest warrants.
[116] Rule 54*bis* of the ICTY RPE; and *Blaškić*, ICTY A. Ch., 29 October 1997, para. 32. See also r. 56 of the MICT RPE.
[117] *Karadžić*, ICTY T. Ch. III, 19 May 2010, para. 16. Cf. *Gatete*, ICTR T. Ch. III, 23 November 2009, para. 26 (applying r. 98 of the ICTR RPE).
[118] Art. 93(3) of the ICC Statute; on national security, see Art. 93(4).

the principle must be of a constitutional character.[119] But all other grounds for declining assistance that normally apply in inter-State cooperation,[120] such as a double-criminality requirement, are disallowed. Nevertheless, the requested State may seek consultation, modification or postponement of the cooperation, and thus cause disruption and delays, on a number of additional grounds, such as a competing request, an ongoing domestic case, lack of information, or immunity.

20.6.2   *National security objections*

Orders or requests directed to States or individuals may give rise to national security concerns; the question arises whether the relevant national law of a State should constitute an obstacle to cooperation. Clearly, a national security exception can jeopardize efficient cooperation and even the rights of the accused (if the information is exculpatory in nature). But it is at the same time unrealistic to believe that a State will readily reveal sensitive secrets, or even admit to their existence, even though the information could be indispensable to the case.[121] Hence, both the ICTY RPE and the ICC Statute contain compromise solutions in order to protect national security interests.

The Appeals Chamber in *Blaškić* rejected Croatia's claim that it is for the State to determine its national security needs and that such needs may serve as a ground for refusal. The Chamber decided that a right to refuse by reference to *ordre public*, which is a general cooperation principle, would therefore not be 'fully in keeping with the Statute'.[122] But, since national security concerns may well be legitimate, the Chamber devised a number of mechanisms to protect sensitive information in the Tribunal proceedings,[123] which were later codified.[124] They apply also when the information is provided in the form of testimony.[125] For information provided by international organizations, their relationship to Member States and others comes into play. For example, the ICTY has ruled that NATO is not required to divulge intelligence information provided to it by States and other entities without the provider's consent.[126]

The ICC Statute allows a State to deny cooperation on national security grounds.[127] The State itself determines when such interests are affected, but it must comply with detailed procedures that are inspired by the *Blaškić* scheme and aimed at ensuring sufficient protection so that the information can be made available. Nevertheless, it is ultimately the Chamber that determines whether a State has complied with its duty to cooperate, and, if it

---

[119] See Kreß, 'Penalties, Enforcement and Cooperation', 456–7.   [120] See further Chapter 5.
[121] See Grant Dawson and Joakim Dungel, 'Compulsion of Information from States and Due Process in Cases before the International Criminal Tribunal for the Former Yugoslavia' (2007) 20 *Leiden Journal of International Law* 115.
[122] *Blaškić*, ICTY A. Ch., 29 October 1997, paras. 61–6.   [123] *Ibid.*, paras. 67–9.
[124] Rules 54*bis* and 70 of the ICTY RPE. See André Klip, 'Confidentiality Restrictions' (2012) 10 *Journal of International Criminal Justice* 645.
[125] *Milošević*, ICTY A. Ch., 23 October 2002.
[126] *Milutinović et al.*, ICTY A. Ch., 15 May 2006, paras. 16 and 19–20, reversing the opposite conclusion reached by the Trial Chamber in ICTY T. Ch. III, 17 November 2005.
[127] Arts. 72, 73 and 93(4)–(6) of the ICC Statute. See further Donald Piragoff, 'Protection of National Security Information' in Lee, *The Making of the Rome Statute*, 270–94.

decides that it has not, the Court may refer the matter to the Assembly of States Parties or the Security Council. Apart from this, the Chamber may make certain inferences at trial.[128]

As with the Tribunals, sensitive information may also be transmitted to the Court on the condition that it be used solely for the purpose of generating new evidence and, thus, not be subject to disclosure without the consent of the provider.[129] This may cause difficulties with respect to the rights of the accused. A telling example is the *Lubanga* case where the conflict between the provider's confidentiality requirement and the accused's right to exculpatory disclosure led the Trial Chamber to stay the proceedings and order the release of the accused.[130] The prosecution was found to have entered into confidentiality agreements, routinely and in inappropriate circumstances, with the UN and others.[131] The matter was finally resolved after arrangements were made to allow the judges to review the material and make an assessment in accordance with Article 67(2) of the ICC Statute. But the Appeals Chamber also held that the confidentiality agreement must be respected and hence that other counter-balancing measures must be considered if the provider does not agree to disclosure.[132] At the Tribunals, the opposite approach applies and the exculpatory disclosure rules are explicitly made subject to confidentiality provisions *vis-à-vis* the information provider.[133]

20.6.3 On-site investigations and trials

On-site investigations are often crucial for the criminal investigation and not only when the State is uncooperative. Having direct access to sites, victims and witnesses will generally be conducive to an effective and complete investigation. For example, potential witnesses may be reluctant to speak in the presence of national authorities in view of their recent experience; to be meaningful, the questioning would have to be conducted by the international investigators alone. Their involvement on site will also offer an assurance that the investigative measures are taken in accordance with international standards and procedures, which in turn may preclude later challenges by the accused.

In the Tribunals, the Prosecutor's power to conduct on-site investigations is expressly laid down in the Statutes;[134] the Prosecutor may seek assistance from State authorities, but the consent of the State is not required. Coercive measures may be taken, such as search and seizure.[135] In practice, however, State permission or other involvement will often be sought

[128] Art. 72(7) of the ICC Statute.   [129] *Ibid.*, Arts. 54(3)(e) and 93(8).
[130] *Lubanga*, ICC T. Ch. I, 13 June 2008 (1401) (staying the proceedings) and 3 September 2008 (refusing to lift the stay), ICC A. Ch., 21 October 2008 (1486) (confirming the stay), and ICC T. Ch. I, 18 November 2008 (lifting the stay). See also Larry D. Johnson, 'The Lubanga Case and Cooperation between the UN and the ICC' (2012) 10 *Journal of International Criminal Justice* 887.
[131] *Lubanga*, ICC T. Ch. I, 13 June 2008 (1401), para. 72.
[132] *Lubanga*, ICC A. Ch., 21 October 2008 (1486), paras. 3, 43–8.
[133] Rule 68 of the ICTY RPE, r. 73 of the MICT Statute and (less explicit) r. 68 of the ICTR RPE.
[134] Art. 18(2) of the ICTY Statute and Art. 17(2) of the ICTR Statute and Art. 16(2) of the MICT Statute.
[135] See e.g. *Kordić and Čerkez*, ICTY T. Ch. III, 25 June 1999.

and one may note that only a few domestic implementation laws authorize the Prosecutor to act independently on national territory.[136]

The ICC Statute contains provisions empowering the ICC Prosecutor to undertake certain measures on the territory of a State Party without making a request for assistance by State authorities. But, being controversial, this power is normally confined to non-compulsory measures, for example taking voluntary witness statements, and may require consultations and sometimes adherence to reasonable, State-imposed conditions.[137] Exceptionally, the Pre-Trial Chamber may also authorize specific on-site measures to be taken without securing cooperation in the case of a 'failed State' that is clearly unable to execute a request;[138] arguably these also include coercive measures.

Considering the importance of on-site investigations, the scope under the ICC Statute is very narrow and reflects the horizontal approach to cooperation; the ICC is seen as a separate entity, not an extension of the national jurisdiction, and the Court's activities on the State territory are therefore an intrusion on the sovereignty of the State. However, it is not ruled out that the Prosecutor may make a request for assistance in the form of an on-site investigation which goes further than what is explicitly set out in the Statute.[139] In practice, however, the Prosecutor has been very restrictive with respect to on-site investigations out of concerns for the safety and security of those assisting the Court and the investigators. This has also led to extensive use of intermediaries for contacts with witnesses and victims, a practice that was roundly criticized in the *Lubanga* trial judgment.[140] As noted by commentators,[141] defence teams have sometimes been more active to investigate on site than the prosecution.

While the ICTY and ICTR have conducted their trials in The Hague and Arusha, the ICC has considered holding them, wholly or partly, in the country concerned.[142] In part, this may be driven by outreach considerations – to bring justice closer to those most concerned. Amendments to the RPE are being prepared to simplify (and clarify) the decision-making process. Nonetheless, on-site trials will still require the consent of the State in question and an agreement on the terms and conditions for the ICC's judicial operations on the territory of that State, including on sensitive issues such as the exercise of coercive powers.

---

[136] See e.g. German, Norwegian and Swiss law (but special permission is required). Also without legislation, some States, e.g. Sweden, allow certain measures to be taken, such as obtaining voluntary witness statements.

[137] Art. 99(4) of the ICC Statute.   [138] *Ibid.*, Art. 57(3)(d) and r. 115 of the ICC RPE.

[139] See Informal Expert Paper: *Fact-Finding and Investigative Functions*, para. 57.

[140] *Lubanga*, ICC T. Ch. I, 14 March 2012.

[141] E.g. Caroline Buisman, 'Delegating Investigations: Lessons to Be Learned from the Lubanga Judgment' (2013) 11 *Northwestern Journal of International Human Rights* 30.

[142] E.g. in *Ruto and Sang*, ICC T. Ch. V(A), 3 June 2013, the Chamber recommended to the Presidency to allow the trial to be held in Kenya, but the judges of the Court decided in a plenary session on 15 July 2013 that the trial should be conducted in The Hague. See also *Lubanga*, ICC T. Ch. I, 8 May 2008 (Annex 2, dated 24 April 2008, para. 105) where the idea of an *in situ* trial was considered but rejected.

20.6.4   *Assistance regarding coercive measures*

An issue of controversy is whether the ICC may, or should, issue a warrant in connection with a request to national authorities for assistance involving coercive measures. The basic principle is that the request must be executed in accordance with national procedures in the requested State, while procedures prescribed in the request must also be followed.[143] Normally, national law will require a domestic judicial warrant for coercive measures, or a judicial review, and this should be sufficient. But there could be instances where there is no such judicial supervision or a review that departs from international human rights standards and the standards applicable to the international jurisdiction in question. Some therefore argue that all coercive measures taken on behalf of an international criminal tribunal or court ought to be subject to a warrant issued by that tribunal or court, or, in urgent cases, a subsequent review of the measure.[144] In Tribunal practice, judge-made warrants for coercive measures other than arrest have sometimes been issued when the measures were to be taken without the assistance of national authorities,[145] including ordering the State to permit the measures to be taken.[146] However, no general requirement of international warrants or reviews in case of State cooperation has been adopted in written law or in practice.[147] Instead, the major forms of judicial supervision by the Tribunal or Court are conducted *ex post facto* with respect to an alleged abuse of process or admissibility of evidence (see further in Chapter 17). Consequently, the ICC has so far issued requests, and not warrants, to States concerning identification, tracing, seizure and freezing of property for the purpose of eventual forfeiture.[148]

20.7   Domestic implementation

When international law creates obligations for States, it is not permissible to raise the objection that national law, constitutional or otherwise, prevents the honouring of the obligations.[149] Therefore, States must make sure that national law allows them to comply with their international obligations, either by direct application of international rules or by implementing legislation. This is required with respect both to the Tribunals and the ICC;[150] a request cannot be refused with reference to the absence of procedures under national law.[151] It also corresponds with the principle that requests be executed in accordance with

---

[143] Art. 99(1) of the ICC Statute.
[144] See Sluiter, *International Criminal Adjudication*, 125–8. See also Christoph Safferling, *Towards an International Criminal Procedure* (Oxford, 2001) 108–14, 125–8; and Karel de Meester, 'Coercive Measures, Privacy Rights and Judicial Supervision in International Criminal Investigations: In Need of Further Regulation?' in Sluiter and Vasiliev, *International Criminal Procedure*, 273–309.
[145] See e.g. *Kordić and Čerkez*, ICTY T. Ch. III, 25 June 1999; and *Naletilić and Martinović*, ICTY T. Ch. I, 14 November 2001.
[146] See e.g. *Karadžić*, ICTY T. Ch. (Duty Judge), 11 September 2003.
[147] Both principled and practical objections could be advanced. Pre-authorization may not be possible or be time-consuming and post-authorization could be sensitive if it involves international judicial supervision of domestic measures, including the application of national law and perhaps even its compliance with international human rights standards.
[148] Art. 93(1)(k) of the ICC Statute.   [149] See *Blaškić*, ICTY T. Ch. II, 18 July 1997, para. 84.
[150] SC Res. 827(1993) and 955(1994); and Art. 88 of the ICC Statute.
[151] See e.g. Claus Kreß and Kimberly Prost, 'Article 88' in Triffterer, *Observers' Notes*, 1534.

domestic procedures. But, while national law may govern procedures, it will lead to violations of the respective Statutes if it inhibits the cooperation required.[152] Cooperation with the ICC must also be provided in the manner specified in the request, unless this is specifically prohibited by national law.[153]

In practice, however, only a few States have introduced implementing legislation or concluded that the cooperation rules have direct effect in the domestic system. Such legislation, where it exists, provides a basis, *inter alia*, for arrest and surrender, assistance concerning evidence and witnesses, and enforcement of penalties; but the scope of cooperation and the means for providing assistance vary and States have often resorted to inter-State practices and principles.[154] The lack of domestic legislation may create serious problems in practice. Reliance on the ordinary law on extradition and mutual legal assistance to other States may not be sufficient, in light of the significant differences between the cooperation rules and normal inter-State practice. Special legislation could also speed up the process considerably.[155] With respect to the ICC, various efforts are being made to encourage and assist States to legislate.[156] It has been suggested that the ICC itself should provide such assistance, but great care is required since the Court is the counter-party and may have to assess compliance with the cooperation duties under the Statute.[157] It should be noted that States have provided substantive assistance also without domestic legislation on cooperation; for example, a number of African States have arrested and handed over accused persons to the ICTR.[158] The ICC has reported that cooperation from States Parties has been generally forthcoming,[159] even if many States still lack implementing legislation. Some special agreements have been concluded with 'situation States' which enhance the cooperation in practice but do not replace the obligation with respect to implementation.[160]

The ICC Statute is a complex instrument and domestic implementation is a challenging task. Apart from legal and technical issues, the cooperation obligations have triggered questions concerning national constitutional compatibility.[161] The debates have mainly taken place concerning the ICC, but many of the same issues are also relevant with respect to the Tribunals. Common problems relate to extradition of nationals and constitutional immunities, in relation to the obligation to arrest and surrender suspects to the Tribunal or the ICC.[162] Other areas of controversy are the powers to conduct on-site investigations, life imprisonment, national amnesties and pardons. Importantly, the States cannot avoid such

---

[152] See Broomhall, *International Justice*, 155.   [153] See Rastan, 'Testing Co-operation', 434–5.

[154] For criticism, see e.g. Antonio Cassese, 'On Current Trends towards Criminal Prosecution and Punishment of Breaches of International Humanitarian Law' (1998) 9 *European Journal of International Law* 2, 13–14.

[155] On the Spanish process to surrender Gotovina to the ICTY (three days after his arrest), see Gamarra and Vicente, 'UN Member States' Obligations', 648–9.

[156] For a collection of such legislation, see www.legal-tools.org.

[157] See Informal Expert Paper: *Fact-Finding and Investigative Functions*, para. 16.

[158] See Broomhall, *International Justice*, 154.

[159] E.g. *Report on the Activities of the Court*, ICC-ASP/11/21 of 9 October 2012, paras. 81–3.   [160] See also section 20.2.1.

[161] See Helen Duffy, 'Overview of Constitutional Issues and Recent State Practice' in Claus Kreß, Bruce Broomhall, Flavia Lattanzi and Valeria Santori (eds.), *The Rome Statute and Domestic Legal Orders* (Baden-Baden, 2005) Vol. II, 498–514; Darryl Robinson, 'The Rome Statute and its Impact on National Law' in Cassese, *Commentary*, 1849–60; and the Venice Commission, *Report on Constitutional Issues Raised by the Ratification of the Rome Statute of the International Court*, 45th Plenary Meeting on 15–16 December 2000.

[162] See e.g. Zsuzsanna Deen-Racsmány, 'Lessons of the European Arrest Warrant for Domestic Implementation of the Obligation to Surrender Nationals to the International Criminal Court' (2007) 20 *Leiden Journal of International Law* 167.

problems by making reservations to their obligations of cooperation.[163] On the other hand, constitutional amendments are often difficult politically, if indeed they are possible at all, and require lengthy processes. A few States, such as France, Germany and Mexico, amended their constitutions before ratifying the ICC Statute, but most States have not and have instead interpreted the international instruments and the constitution as compatible with each other.

20.8   Non-compliance

The ICTY and ICTR Statutes do not address the issue of non-compliance with the duty of cooperation, but again the *Blaškić* decision provides answers. The Appeals Chamber found that an international tribunal must have powers to make all judicial determinations that are necessary for the exercise of its primary jurisdiction, including making a finding of non-compliance and reporting this to the Security Council.[164] But the Tribunal may not recommend or suggest how the Security Council could or should address the matter. Similarly, the ICC may make a finding of non-compliance and refer the matter to the Assembly of States Parties or, when the Security Council has referred the underlying situation, to the Security Council.[165] A breach by a non-State Party of a legally binding cooperation agreement or arrangement may also be reported. As noted in section 8.10, ICC Chambers have deliberated on a number of instances of non-compliance and reported those to the Security Council and the Assembly of States Parties.

Having the power to make findings of non-cooperation is important for the credibility of the institution, but also a sensitive matter for States, and the potential consequences are not spelled out at all. Measures such as public condemnation and even collective economic sanctions could be contemplated, but other considerations, such as the need to maintain support for the international jurisdiction, may well prevail.[166] Moreover, the State might cooperate partially and a finding of non-cooperation is likely to close the door to further cooperation and inhibit positive developments in that respect.

In practice, the Security Council has failed to respond effectively to reports of non-compliance by the ICTY; collective action by States, such as threats to withhold financial aid, has been more successful.[167] As a result, high-level accused have been obtained and the ICTY has no unenforced arrest warrants: Slobodan Milošević was surrendered to the Tribunal in 2001, Karadžić in 2008, and Mladić and Hadžić in 2011. The ICTR has also experienced instances of non-cooperation, including at times by the government of Rwanda.[168] The Residual Mechanism has retained jurisdiction over three ICTR fugitives and re-issued arrest warrants against them.

---

[163] See Art. 120 of the ICC Statute.   [164] *Blaškić*, ICTY A. Ch., 29 October 1997, paras. 33–7.

[165] Art. 87(7) of the ICC Statute. The Assembly of States Parties has adopted procedures for dealing with cases of non-compliance, Res. ICC-ASP/10/Res.5 of 21 December 2011.

[166] See Bruce Broomhall, *International Justice and the International Criminal Court* (Oxford, 2003) 156–7.

[167] Gabrielle Kirk McDonald, 'Problems, Obstacles and Achievements of the ICTY' (2004) 2 *Journal of International Criminal Justice* 558, 562–7.

[168] See e.g. Erik Møse, 'Main Achievements of the ICTR' (2005) 3 *Journal of International Criminal Justice* 920, 939–40.

The ICC also experiences non-compliance with its arrest warrants, most notably in the situations referred to the Court by the Security Council (Darfur and Libya). In addition, no arrest warrants issued in the *Situation in Uganda*, as far back as in 2005, have been enforced, but here the reason is rather the difficulties for any national authorities to arrest the fugitives.

But the potential tools available are manifold[169] and international pressure and Security Council action towards the arrest and surrender to the SCSL of the former Liberian President, Charles Taylor, in 2006 show that if there is a will there is also hope.[170] However, the Council's response so far to the ICC Prosecutor's reports that Sudan has failed to comply with its cooperation obligations in accordance with Security Council Resolution 1593(2005) was merely a Presidential Statement urging the government of Sudan and others to cooperate fully with the Court.[171] No action has (yet) been taken by the Security Council upon the ICC Chambers' reports of non-compliance.

20.9   Cooperation and the ICC complementarity principle

The ICC cooperation regime is influenced by the fundamental complementarity principle; domestic investigations and prosecutions have priority in principle. The regulation of issues such as competing requests (see section 20.2.2), challenges concerning *ne bis in idem* (or double jeopardy),[172] and simultaneous proceedings in the requested State concerning other crimes,[173] bear evidence of this. Generally, a decision by the Court on admissibility is decisive of the matter since that decision determines whether the Court will go ahead with its investigation or prosecution. A complementarity challenge by a State has the effect that the Prosecutor must suspend the investigation. However, authority to take certain measures may be sought from the Chamber; in addition, the State's duty to cooperate remains in effect until the Court orders otherwise, as does an arrest warrant.[174] In line with this, a *ne bis in idem* challenge before a national court may cause the requested State to postpone surrender pending an admissibility decision by the ICC, but the execution of the arrest warrant may not be postponed.[175]

---

[169] See Michael Scharf, 'The Tools for Enforcing International Criminal Justice in the New Millennium: Lessons from the Yugoslav Tribunal' (2000) 49 *DePaul Law Review* 925.

[170] See SC Res. 1638(2005) of 11 November 2005.

[171] Seventh Report of the Prosecutor of the International Criminal Court to the UN Security Council pursuant to UNSCR 1593(2005) of 5 June 2008, repeated in subsequent reports to the Council; Presidential Statement of 16 June 2008 (S/PRST/ 2008/21).

[172] Art. 89(2) of the ICC Statute.

[173] *Ibid.*, Arts. 89(4) and 94. It has been suggested that, as an alternative to an admissibility challenge, there could be a burden-sharing whereby the ICC and national authorities would pursue different crimes and the proceedings be coordinated by sequencing: see Carsten Stahn, 'Libya, the International Criminal Court and Complementarity' (2012) 10 *Journal of International Criminal Justice* 325, 340–3.

[174] Arts. 19(7)–(9) and 58(4) of the ICC Statute. See also *Gaddafi and Al-Senussi*, ICC PTC I, 4 April 2012, 1 June 2012 and 14 June 2013.

[175] Art. 89(2) of the ICC Statute. See Informal Expert Paper: *Fact-Finding and Investigative Functions*, paras. 45–7; but cf. Bert Swart, 'Arrest and Surrender' in Cassese, *Commentary*, 1694–5.

The Statute also provides for some, limited, assistance that the ICC may grant a State, which is a logical supplement to the complementarity principle.[176] Moreover, the ICC may transfer the suspect or accused to a State that has made a successful admissibility challenge, but only with the approval of the originally surrendering State.[177] Clearly, the negotiating States were more hesitant about transferring information and suspects to other States than to the ICC. Nonetheless, cooperation among States is truly important for the prosecution of the Statute crimes where there is more than one State willing and able to take jurisdiction, a situation that is more likely to arise with the growth of universal jurisdiction. This is not, however, addressed by the Statute.

It has been suggested that the provisions of the ICC Statute on consultations could be used to reach agreements on sequencing between international and national proceedings and hence to resolve complementarity conflicts.[178] But so far this has not happened in practice.

20.10   An assessment

The dependence upon cooperation by States and others has led to the metaphorical description of each Tribunal as a 'giant without arms or legs'.[179] The distinction between 'horizontal' and 'vertical' cooperation schemes depicts a fundamental difference in approach; the 'vertical' model attributes greater powers to the international jurisdiction and imposes greater duties on the States. The scheme of the Tribunals is more 'vertical' than that of the ICC, and the latter is weaker on issues such as arrest by peacekeeping forces, investigations on site and powers to bring witnesses before the Court. But, although it contributes to explaining the normative framework, the distinction does little to explain why cooperation is successful or not in practice. Both models currently provide for indirect rather than direct enforcement, and compliance with the cooperation obligations depends primarily upon factors that are unrelated to the judicial functions of the Tribunal or Court. In view of the difficulties of conducting international investigations and trials, and the weak sanctions regimes, neither system can be effective unless States are truly willing (and able) to assist. A breach of international obligations may come with a price, but the alternative price for complying may be higher and more direct (for example, in domestic public opinion).

Both the Tribunals and the ICC are faced with instances of non-compliance or a bare minimum of cooperation. For example, the relationship between the ICTR and the government of Rwanda has been troubled at times, with Rwanda suspending cooperation when the Tribunal ordered the release of an accused.[180] In the former Yugoslavia, the willingness to cooperate with

---

[176] Art. 93(10) of the ICC Statute. See Federica Gioia, '"Reverse Cooperation" and the Architecture of the Rome Statute: A Vital Part of the Relationship between States and the ICC?' in Maria Chiara Malaguti (ed.), *ICC and International Cooperation in Light of the Rome Statute* (Lecce, Italy, 2007) 75–101. See also Art. 28(3) of the MICT Statute and rr. 87–88 of the MICT RPE, which, in line with the added emphasis on the referral of cases to national jurisdictions, explicitly provide for assistance to national authorities in the former Yugoslavia and Rwanda.

[177] Rule 185 of the ICC RPE.

[178] Carsten Stahn, 'Libya, the International Criminal Court and Complementarity' (2012) 10 *Journal of International Criminal Justice* 325.

[179] Cassese, 'On Current Trends', 13.

[180] The decision in *Barayagwiza*, ICTR A. Ch., 3 November 1999, was subsequently reversed: ICTR A. Ch., 31 March 2000; see sections 17.3.2 and 17.7.3.

the ICTY has varied over time, but more recent changes of government have improved cooperation. Over time, however, the Tribunals have been rather successful in obtaining cooperation.[181]

The ICC encounters even more complex situations. It operates in many conflicts which are still ongoing and this complicates all forms of cooperation. Although the practice of 'self-referrals' of situations by States[182] includes a particular commitment to cooperate with the Court, something that the ICC Prosecutor has stressed as important,[183] practical and other circumstances may prevent effective cooperation. When the territorial State has not sought the Court's intervention, where the investigation is triggered by a Security Council referral or the Prosecutor's *proprio motu* power, constructive assistance has been even less forthcoming, as examples with respect to Sudan, Libya and Kenya show. The ICC's activities, and hence the need for cooperation, will in many cases occur when the State most concerned is unwilling or unable to take appropriate action itself – a paradoxical effect of the complementarity principle.

The ICC Assembly of States Parties has repeatedly emphasized the importance of timely and effective cooperation of States, but also encouraged adequate and clear mandates in Security Council resolutions referring situations to the Court and follow-up to such referrals.[184] The States Parties at the Kampala Review Conference in 2010 adopted a Declaration on Cooperation,[185] and the Assembly has put forward recommendations to improve cooperation. The efforts relate not only to formal kinds of legal cooperation but also to other assistance measures, including witness relocation and public and diplomatic support.

In practice, the international tribunals and courts are often cautious not to rush to depict States as uncooperative.[186] They have no real influence over and should not expect much visible action from the bodies that could impose sanctions. Instead, strong political support and more informal forms of pressure tend to be more important and effective. Hence, the decision of the African Union not to cooperate with the ICC concerning the arrest warrant against Al Bashir is potentially very damaging;[187] it is politically hazardous in spite of the fact that the linkage made between non-cooperation, Article 98, and the Security Council's inaction on the AU's request for a deferral in accordance with Article 16 of the ICC Statute, is nonsensical from a legal point of view.

The ICC cooperation regime may be strengthened and improved over time, but it is unrealistic to expect that the indirect model for enforcement will be replaced, and it will therefore remain the weakest link of the Court's procedural framework. This is very unfortunate since it may affect not only the efficiency but also the legitimacy of the Court. Quite apart from the appearance

---

[181] See e.g. Viktor Peskin, *International Justice in Rwanda and the Balkans: Virtual Trials and the Struggle for State Cooperation* (Cambridge, 2008) 237.

[182] See section 8.7.4, which also notes risks arising from self-referrals.

[183] Remarks by former ICC Prosecutor, Luis Moreno-Ocampo, at the 27th meeting of the Committee of Legal Advisers on Public International Law (CADHI), Strasbourg, 18–19 March 2004.

[184] E.g. Res. ICC-ASP/11/Res.15 of 21 November 2012.   [185] Declaration on Cooperation, RC/Decl.2 of 8 June 2010.

[186] Although non-compliance has been reported, for example by the ICTY; see Kirk McDonald, 'Problems', 562–7.

[187] E.g. Decision by the 13th Ordinary Session of the AU Assembly, 3 July 2009, Doc. Assembly/AU/13(XIII), and subsequent decisions. In addition, the AU has requested deferral of the proceedings regarding Kenya by the Security Council, but without taking a decision on non-cooperation with the ICC. See section 8.11.2.

of impotence in cases on non-compliance, the restraints can cause selectivity with respect to investigations and prosecutions, and frustrate efforts against persons with links to a government.[188]

Further reading

Michele Caianiello, 'Models of Judicial Cooperation with Ad Hoc Tribunals and with the Permanent International Criminal Court in Europe' in Stefano Ruggeri (ed.), *Transnational Inquiries and the Protection of Fundamental Rights in Criminal Proceedings* (Berlin and Heidelberg, 2013) 111–23

Cassese, *Commentary*, Chapters 39–42

Yolanda Gamarra and Alejandra Vicente, 'United Nations Member States' Obligations towards the ICTY: Arresting and Transferring Lukić, Gotovina and Zelenenović' (2008) 8 *International Criminal Law Review* 627

Thomas Henquet, 'Mandatory Compliance Powers vis-à-vis States by the Ad Hoc Tribunals and the International Criminal Court: A Comparative Analysis' (1999) 12 *Leiden Journal of International Law* 969

Claus Kreß, Bruce Broomhall, Flavia Lattanzi and Valeria Santori (eds.), *The Rome Statute and Domestic Legal Orders* (Baden-Baden, 2005) Vol. II

Roy S. Lee (ed.), *States' Responses to Issues Arising from the ICC Statute: Constitutional, Sovereignty, Judicial Cooperation and Criminal Law* (New York, 2005)

Valerie Oosterveld, Mike Perry and John McManus, 'The Cooperation of States with the International Criminal Court' (2002) 25 *Fordham International Law Journal* 767

Viktor Peskin, *International Justice in Rwanda and the Balkans: Virtual Trials and the Struggle for State Cooperation* (Cambridge, 2008)

Rod Rastan, 'Testing Co-operation: The International Criminal Court and National Authorities' (2008) 21 *Leiden Journal of International Law* 431

Göran Sluiter, *International Criminal Adjudication and the Collection of Evidence: Obligations of States* (Antwerp, 2002)

Dagmar Stroh, 'State Cooperation with the International Criminal Tribunals for the Former Yugoslavia and for Rwanda' (2001) 5 *Max Planck Yearbook of United Nations Law* 249

Triffterer, *Observers' Notes*

Patricia M. Wald, 'Apprehending War Criminals: Does International Cooperation Work?' (2012) 27 *American University International Law Review* 229.

---

[188] See e.g. Richard Goldstone and Nicole Fritz, '"In the Interests of Justice" and Independent Referral: The ICC Prosecutor's Unprecedented Powers' (2000) 13 *Leiden Journal of International Law* 655, 658; and Louise Arbour and Morten Bergsmo, 'Conspicuous Absence of Jurisdictional Overreach' (1999) 1 *International Law Forum/Forum de droit international* 13, 18.

21

Immunities

21.1   Introduction

21.1.1   Overview

The international law of immunities has ancient roots, extending back not hundreds, but thousands, of years.[1] In order to maintain channels of communication and thereby prevent and resolve conflicts, societies needed to have confidence that their envoys could have safe passage, particularly in times when emotions and distrust were at their highest. Domestic and international law developed to provide for inviolability of a foreign State's representatives and immunities from the exercise of jurisdiction over those representatives.

While immunities are valuable in preventing interference with representatives, and thereby maintaining the conduct of international relations, they can also frustrate prosecutions for very serious crimes. In recent decades, with the advent of the human rights movement, States have taken stronger and stronger steps to prosecute international criminals. This emboldened State practice has brought to the fore many hidden or unresolved questions as to the boundaries between principles of accountability and immunity.

While international priorities are shifting in favour of justice and accountability, it would be an oversimplification to assume that international criminal law has simply superseded immunities law. Commentators have at times assumed that no immunity of any kind may be raised in response to allegations of genocide, crimes against humanity or war crimes.[2] However, such a view overlooks the different kinds of immunities, and is contradicted by the great bulk of State practice and jurisprudence.[3] Even the landmark precedents that narrowed immunities also explicitly affirmed that some immunities would still apply even with regard to allegations of serious international crimes.[4]

---

[1] Linda S. Frey and Marsha L. Frey, *The History of Diplomatic Immunity* (Columbus, OH, 1999); J. Craig Barker, *The Abuse of Diplomatic Privileges and Immunities: A Necessary Evil?* (Aldershot, 1996) 14–31; Montell Ogdon, *Juridical Bases of Diplomatic Immunity* (Washington DC, 1936) 8–20; Grant V. McLanahan, *Diplomatic Immunity* (New York, 1989) 18–25.

[2] See e.g. Andrea Bianchi, 'Immunity versus Human Rights: The Pinochet Case' (1999) 10 *European Journal of International Law* 237; Amnesty International, *Universal Jurisdiction: The Duty of States to Enact and Implement Legislation*, (September 2001, AI Index IOR 53/2001) Chapter 14.

[3] See sections 21.3 and 21.4.

[4] Reference is often made to Art. 27 of the ICC Statute and the *Pinochet* decision. However, as discussed in section 21.5, the ICC Statute explicitly contemplates that there are immunities for which waiver is still neeeded. Further, as discussed in section 21.2, each Law Lord in *Pinochet* emphasized that a current head of State would retain immunity even against charges of torture or crimes against humanity.

A recurring argument against immunity is that the prohibitions of international crimes are *ius cogens*, and therefore any immunities must give way to the 'higher value' of ensuring prosecution.[5] Such arguments have been considered and rejected in an extensive line of national cases in various countries as well as at the European Court of Human Rights and the International Court of Justice.[6] As was recently observed by the House of Lords in the *Jones* case,[7] the argument depends on a false conflict: *ius cogens* prohibits *committing* the crimes; it does not mean that all international laws regarding *prosecution* cease to apply. The State respecting the immunity of another State is not committing a crime and hence is not in conflict with *ius cogens*.[8] This principle was more recently reaffirmed by the ICJ in the *Germany* v. *Italy* case.[9]

As was explained by three judges of the ICJ in the *Yerodia* case (discussed below), the objective that serious crimes must be punished:

does not *ipso facto* mean that immunities are unavailable whenever impunity would be the outcome . . . immunities serve other purposes which have their own intrinsic value and . . . international law seeks the accommodation of this value with the fight against impunity, and not the triumph of one norm over the other. A State may exercise the criminal jurisdiction which it has under international law, but in doing so it is subject to other legal obligations.[10]

Thus, a more sophisticated approach is needed in order to understand this area of law. It will be necessary to appreciate the underlying principles and protected values, to distinguish between 'functional' immunity and 'personal' immunity, and to distinguish between national and international courts.

The interplay of international criminal law and immunities is complex, and the jurisprudence and authorities have been described as perplexing, contradictory, confused or incoherent.[11] However, if one keeps in mind the above-mentioned distinctions and the underlying purposes of the rules, one will find that a fairly consistent and coherent set of rules is emerging. It is nonetheless a complex area with many controversies; this chapter will strive to introduce the intricacies in as clear a manner as possible.

This chapter discusses the immunities of individuals in relation to criminal prosecution for international crimes, in national and international courts. Personal immunities in civil proceedings and questions of State immunity are not discussed here. Nor does this chapter

---

[5] See e.g. Bianchi, 'Immunity', 265.

[6] See e.g. *Al-Adsani* v. *United Kingdom*, ECtHR, 21 November 2001; *Tachiona* v. *Mugabe*, 169 F Supp 2d 259 (SDNY, 2001); *Jones* v. *Kingdom of Saudi Arabia* [2006] UKHL 26; [2006] 2 WLR 1424, considering and rejecting arguments based on *ius cogens*, as well as the ICJ *Yerodia* decision, discussed in section 21.4.2.

[7] *Jones* v. *Kingdom of Saudi Arabia* [2006] UKHL 26; [2006] 2 WLR 1424, paras. 24–8 and 43–63.

[8] Hazel Fox, *The Law of State Immunity* (Oxford, 2004); Lee Caplan, 'State Immunity, Human Rights and Jus Cogens: A Critique of the Normative Hierarchy Theory' (2003) 97 *American Journal of International Law* 741; Andrea Gattini, 'War Crimes and State Immunity in the *Ferrini* Decision' (2005) 3 *Journal of International Criminal Justice* 224. But see Lorna McGregor, 'Torture and State Immunity: Deflecting Impunity, Distorting Sovereignty' (2007) 18 *European Journal of International Law* 903 (noting that formalistic arguments should not obscure the fact that upholding immunity can lead to impunity).

[9] *Jurisdictional Immunities of the State* (*Germany* v. *Italy*: *Greece Intervening*), ICJ General List 143, 2 March 2012.

[10] Joint Separate Opinion of Judges Higgins, Kooijmans and Buergenthal, para. 79, in the *Yerodia* judgment, discussed in section 21.4.2.

[11] Rosanne van Alebeek, 'The Pinochet Case: International Human Rights Law on Trial' (2001) 71 *British Yearbook of International Law* 29, 47; J. Craig Barker, 'The Future of Former Head of State Immunity after Ex Parte Pinochet' (1999) 48 *International and Comparative Law Quarterly* 937, 938.

deal with immunities of heads of State or high officials in their own countries, which are governed primarily by national law.

21.1.2   Functional and personal immunity

With respect to immunity from prosecution, a fundamental distinction must be made between 'functional immunity' (also known as immunity *ratione materiae*) and 'personal immunity' (also known as immunity *ratione personae*).

Functional immunity protects *conduct* carried out on behalf of a State. It is linked to a maxim of sovereign equality, that a State's policies and actions cannot be judged without some form of consent by that State. If State A could bring criminal proceedings against the individual officials who carried out official functions of State B, then State A would be doing indirectly what it cannot do directly, namely, acting as the arbiter of the conduct of another State. Functional immunity attaches to a comparatively large class of officials – all who carry out State functions. Significantly, functional immunity does not provide complete protection of the person, it only covers conduct that was an official act of a State. Thus, for example, criminal activity carried out in a private capacity remains subject to prosecution. As will be discussed below, an exception to functional immunity has emerged whereby international crimes may also be prosecuted.

Personal immunity is not limited to any particular conduct; it provides complete immunity of the *person* of certain office-holders while they carry out important representative functions. Personal immunity is granted only to a comparatively small set of people, such as heads of State and diplomats accredited to a host country. It is temporary, in that it lasts only for as long as the person is serving in that representative role. There is no exception based on the seriousness of the alleged crime, or whether the acts were private or official, because the rationale is unconnected to the nature of the charge. The rationale was stated in 1740 by Wicquefort:

> if Princes had the Liberty of Proceeding against the Embassador who negotiates with them on any Account, or under any Colour whatsoever, the Person of the Embassador would never be in Safety; because those who should have a Mind to make away with Him would never want a Pretext.[12]

To sum up, personal immunity is absolute, but it only attaches to a limited set of official roles and it endures only while the person enjoys the official position which attracts the immunity. Conversely, functional immunity protects only conduct carried out in the course of the individual's duties, but does not drop away when a person's role comes to an end, since it protects the conduct, not the person. For both types of immunity, the purpose is not to benefit the individual,[13] but to protect official acts (functional immunity) or to facilitate international relations (personal immunity). It is the State which is the real beneficiary of the

---

[12] A. van Wicquefort, *The Embassador and his Functions*, 2nd edn (London, 1740) (translated into English by John Digby) 251, quoted in Ogdon, *Juridical Bases*, 128–9.

[13] Vienna Convention on Diplomatic Relations 1961, Preamble, paras. 2–4.

immunity, and it is the State which may waive it, irrespective of the wishes of the person claiming the immunity.

The existence of immunity does not mean that there is a lack of substantive legal responsibility, but rather that a foreign State is procedurally prevented from bringing proceedings against the alleged offender. Thus, immunities are not a 'defence' as such.[14] As merely procedural bars, immunities may be waived by the State concerned.

21.1.3   Examples of immunities

The most well-developed and well-defined area of immunities is that of diplomatic immunities. Centuries of State practice with diplomatic relations have produced considerable precision as to the rules. The law is now codified in the Vienna Convention on Diplomatic Relations 1961. While serving in a host country, diplomatic agents enjoy *personal* immunity: they are immune from criminal jurisdiction, their person is inviolable and they may not be arrested or detained.[15] After their term of service in the host country has ended, diplomats continue to enjoy *functional* immunity for acts in the exercise of their functions.[16] If the diplomat commits a serious crime, the options available to the host State are to request a waiver of immunity from the sending State[17] or to declare the diplomat *persona non grata*.[18] After the diplomat's term is over, the diplomat enjoys only functional immunity, and thus the host authorities may prosecute the diplomat for any crimes committed in a non-official capacity, if they can acquire custody of him or her. Other members of a diplomatic mission enjoy lesser degrees of immunity,[19] as do consular officials.[20]

The contours of head of State immunity are less well defined. There is no codifying convention and State practice on point is limited. The lack of State practice is probably in part a reflection of the immunity and in part due to the reluctance of States to interfere with heads of State.[21] Even the conceptual foundations of the immunity are unclear.[22] It is widely accepted, however, that heads of State enjoy at least the same immunities as ambassadors: absolute personal immunity while in office,[23] and afterwards functional immunity for official acts carried out while in office.[24]

---

[14] A claim to functional immunity may also bring with it a claim under the 'act of State doctrine', under which national courts of one State may decline to examine the acts of another State. This is a matter of substantive law and, along with the fact that it applies only to particular conduct, probably explains why functional immunity is sometimes referred to as a substantive defence: Hazel Fox, *The Law of State Immunity*, 2nd edn (Oxford, 2008) 93–7.

[15] Arts. 29 and 31 of the Vienna Convention on Diplomatic Relations 1961.   [16] *Ibid.*, Art. 39(1).   [17] *Ibid.*, Art. 32.

[18] *Ibid.*, Art. 9.   [19] *Ibid.*, Art. 37(3).   [20] Vienna Convention on Consular Relations 1963.

[21] In one exception, French authorities issued a witness summons to the head of State of Djibouti, a matter brought to the ICJ by Djibouti in *Certain Questions of Mutual Assistance in Criminal Matters (Djibouti v. France)*, 4 June 2008. The Court held that, as the summons was only an invitation, there was no violation by France of its obligations to Djibouti.

[22] Some treat it as a type of State immunity and others as a type of diplomatic immunity, but neither of these analogies is entirely apt, so it seems most accurate to regard head of State immunity as a separate category. Diplomatic immunity provides the closer analogy, although a head of State is not posted in the host State. See e.g. Jerrold Mallory, 'Resolving the Confusion over Head of State Immunity: The Defined Right of Kings' (1986) 86 *Columbia Law Review* 169; Jürgen Bröhmer, *State Immunity and the Violation of Human Rights* (The Hague, 1997) 29–32.

[23] Charles Lewis, *State and Diplomatic Immunity*, 3rd edn (London, 1999) 125; *R v. Bow Street Metropolitan Stipendiary Magistrate, ex parte Pinochet Ugarte (No. 3)* [1999] 2 All ER 97, HL, at 111, 119–20, 152, 168–9, 179 and 181.

[24] Lord Gore Booth (ed.), *Satow's Guide to Diplomatic Practice*, 5th edn (London, 1979) 9.

While head of State immunity is well established, the position of heads of government and other ministers has not always been so clear.[25] In *Democratic Republic of the Congo* v. *Belgium*, the International Court of Justice upheld personal immunity for ministers of foreign affairs, analogous to that of heads of State.[26] This conclusion is understandable in that the post fulfils similar representative roles. Similar principles undoubtedly apply to a head of government, such as a prime minister – whose representative function is more sensitive than a minister of foreign affairs and, in many systems, the head of State.[27] As will be discussed in section 21.4.2, it is unclear whether other ministers enjoy this immunity as well.[28]

In addition, State representatives travelling to participate in meetings of international organizations enjoy immunities provided in the relevant treaties, which typically include personal immunity.[29] Furthermore, when a State hosts a major summit or meeting outside the context of an international organization (such as a G8 summit), it is typical practice to extend immunity to visiting delegates.[30] The Convention on Special Missions (1969) sought to provide a general regime for visits of officials to another State, with the consent of that State, 'for the purpose of dealing with it on specific questions or performing in relation to it a specific task'.[31] That convention has not been widely ratified,[32] but there is some State practice regarding it as customary international law.[33]

Certain officials of international organizations, such as the United Nations or the International Criminal Court, enjoy immunities as provided in specific conventions.[34] In general, personal immunity is granted sparingly and reserved for the highest officials. Most officials receive only functional immunity even while on official missions.[35]

While this chapter is focused on criminal proceedings, a brief word should be offered with respect to State immunity from *civil* proceedings. Under the customary law principle of State immunity, a State (and hence its assets) may not be subjected to civil proceedings in foreign courts, unless it chooses to submit to such courts. However, this immunity is subject to many exceptions. For example, a State is not immune in relation to its commercial activities, or for acts causing death or injury that are committed in the territory of the

---

[25] Arthur Watts, 'The Legal Position in International Law of Heads of State, Heads of Government and Foreign Ministers' (1994-III) 247 *Hague Recueil* 97–113.

[26] See section 21.4.2.   [27] Watts, 'Legal Position', 97–113.

[28] See the discussion of *Yerodia* in section 21.4.2; and see the *Mofaz* case, concluding that a Minister of Defence enjoys personal immunity but expressing doubts with respect to several other types of minister, reproduced (2004) 53 *International and Comparative Law Quarterly* 769.

[29] See e.g. in the context of the UN, the Convention on the Privileges and Immunities of the United Nations 1946, 1 UNTS 15.

[30] See e.g. a typical Canadian regulation, the G8 Summit Privileges and Immunities Order, 2002, PC 2002-828.

[31] Convention on Special Missions 1969, Art. 1(a).

[32] The immunities are analogous to those in the Vienna Convention on Diplomatic Relations 1961: Convention on Special Missions 1969, Arts. 29 and 31. While some commentators believe that aspects of it may reflect customary law (Watts, 'Legal Position', 38), others have concluded that it goes beyond State practice in the extent of immunity it confers: *United States* v. *Sissoko* (1997) 121 IR 599.

[33] Examples of State practice to this effect, including of UK courts and the UK government, are canvassed in Dapo Akande and Sangeeta Shah, 'Immunities of State Officials, International Crimes, and Foreign Domestic Courts' (2011) 21 *European Journal of International Law* 815; see also the *Khurts Bat* case ([2011] EWHC 2029 (Admin)).

[34] See e.g. Convention on the Privileges and Immunities of the United Nations 1946; Agreement on Privileges and Immunities of the International Criminal Court 2002.

[35] See e.g. Convention on the Privileges and Immunities of the United Nations 1946, Art. V, ss. 18–19, granting full diplomatic immunities to the Secretary-General and Assistant Secretary-Generals and functional immunity to other staff.

forum State. There have been many proposals for a 'human rights' or 'international crime' exception to State immunity, although such proposals have met with little success at this time.[36]

21.1.4   *Underlying rationales and values*

Historically, various rationales have been put forward in support of immunities. Some of these were legal fictions, such as 'extraterritoriality' (the fiction that the premises of the mission represented an extension of the sending State's territory), 'personal representation' (that the ambassador is equivalent to his or her head of State) or 'personification' (that the head of State personifies the State).[37] Respect for the 'dignity' of the head of State or the sending State has also been a major consideration,[38] as has political expediency – the desire to avoid controversy with other nations.[39]

In the last century, and especially in recent decades, there has been a considerable demystification in this area, such that legal fictions are no longer plausible bases for immunities.[40] Moreover, with increasing emphasis on human rights, neither dignity nor political expediency is a compelling reason to preclude *a priori* accountability for serious international crimes.

With respect to functional immunity, the remaining rationale is the principle that one State may not sit in judgment on another State (also known as *par in parem non habet iudicium*). This is an attribute of sovereign equality. This is why international law insists that disputes between States may only be brought to appropriate forums with the agreement of States. If a State could prosecute officials for acts of another State, it would indirectly be passing judgment on another State, and could even use prosecutions to force changes in policies of the other State. As is discussed below, however,[41] an exception has emerged for some or all serious international crimes.

The rationale for personal immunity is its value in facilitating international relations. The ICJ has described the inviolability of diplomatic envoys as the most fundamental prerequisite for the conduct of relations between States.[42] The institution of diplomacy is 'an instrument essential for effective co-operation in the international community, and for enabling States, irrespective of their differing constitutional and social systems, to achieve

---

[36] *Princz* v. *Federal Republic of Germany*, 26 F 3d 1166 (DC Cir. 1994); *Al-Adsani* v. *Government of Kuwait* (1996) 107 ILR 536, Court of Appeal of England; *Al-Adsani* v. *United Kingdom*, ECtHR, 21 November 2001; *Tachiona* v. *Mugabe*, 169 F Supp 2d 259 (SDNY, 2001); *Jones* v. *Kingdom of Saudi Arabia* [2006] UKHL 26; [2006] 2 WLR 1424; but see the anomalous Greek case concerning the Distomo massacre, discussed in Ilias Bantekas, 'Prefecture of Voiotia v. Federal Republic of Germany' (1998) 92 *American Journal of International Law* 765, which was doubted in subsequent Greek cases and rejected by the German Supreme Court in *Distomo Massacre* (2003) 42 ILM 1030. Italian cases, such as *Ferrini*, held that they could set aside the immunities of Germany, but Germany brought the question before the ICJ, which held that in doing so Italy breached international law by failing to respect Germany's State immunity. The Court rejected arguments for a human rights exception, a *ius cogens* exception, and a 'last resort' exception: *Jurisdictional Immunities of the State* (*Germany* v. *Italy: Greece Intervening*), ICJ General List 143, 2 March 2012.
[37] See Ogdon, *Juridical Bases*, 63–165; Robert Jennings and Arthur Watts, *Oppenheim's International Law*, 9th edn (London, 1992) 1034.
[38] See *Schooner Exchange* v. *M'Fadden*, 11 US 116 (1812) 137.
[39] See e.g. *Tachiona* v. *Mugabe*, 169 F Supp 2d 259, 290–1 (SDNY, 2001).   [40] See e.g. Watts, 'Legal Position', 35–6.
[41] Section 21.2.   [42] *United States Diplomatic and Consular Staff in Iran* (*US* v. *Iran*), Merits (1980) ICJ Reports 3, para. 91.

mutual understanding and to resolve their differences by peaceful means'.[43] The existing system of diplomatic relations has made possible global summits, the creation of international organizations and the development of treaties creating today's corpus of laws. It has enabled diplomats to work in antagonistic States to protect nationals and to avert or end conflicts. It also enables UN human rights rapporteurs and international prosecutors to carry out their work in States that might welcome pretexts to frustrate their work.[44]

Unfortunately, immunities have also had many perverse effects, shielding persons responsible for spectacular abuses and crimes. This has often led to public outcry. Recently, with the increased prioritization of human rights and the rule of law, governments have become more assertive and immunities have rightly come under scrutiny and pressure.

Two main methods have been employed to rebalance the goals served by immunities with the goal of ending impunity. Both methods were foreshadowed by the Nuremberg Charter, but it is only recently that international practice has followed up on these ideas. The first method was to declare that functional immunity, which protects State conduct from scrutiny, does not extend to international crimes (see sections 21.2 and 21.3). That solution is not transposable to personal immunity, because such immunity is not based on any authorization of the act, but rather aims to preclude any pretext to interfere with high representatives (see section 21.4). However, Nuremberg serves as a precedent on how to deal with this problem as well: the creation of international criminal tribunals authorized to set aside even personal immunity. We shall look below at different ways that personal immunity may be relinquished before international courts (section 21.5) as well as the more controversial claim that immunities are simply inapplicable before international courts (section 21.6).

21.2   Functional immunity and national courts

Issues of immunity can arise before national courts in different ways. A State may wish to prosecute a current or former official of another State, may wish to request extradition, or may receive a request for extradition.[45] Traditionally, national governments and courts were so cautious and deferential in the area of immunities that controversial efforts at prosecution simply did not arise. In recent times, this has begun to change.[46]

21.2.1   The Pinochet precedent

In 1998, Senator Augusto Pinochet, former head of State of Chile, was visiting the United Kingdom when Spain issued a request for his extradition. The charges included torture and conspiracy to torture. Pinochet was arrested by British authorities. He applied to have the

---

[43] *Ibid.*

[44] See e.g. *Difference Relating to Immunity from Legal Process of a Special Rapporteur of the Commission on Human Rights*, Advisory Opinion (1999) ICJ Reports 100.

[45] Examples of the first scenario are the *Mugabe* and *Qaddafi* cases (see section 21.4.1); an example of the second scenario is the Belgian case against Yerodia (see section 21.4.2); and the *Pinochet* case (see section 21.2.1) is an example of the third scenario.

[46] Michael Byers, 'The Law and Politics of the Pinochet Case' (2000) 10 *Duke Journal of Comparative and International Law* 415.

warrants quashed, *inter alia*, on the ground that as a former head of State he was entitled to immunity.

In the first hearing of the immunity issue, at the level of the Divisional Court, three judges, applying a classically deferential approach to immunities, unanimously upheld Senator Pinochet's claim and quashed the warrant.[47] The court applied the established proposition that a former head of State 'ceases to enjoy any immunity in respect of *personal or private* acts but continues to enjoy immunity in respect of *public* acts performed by him as head of State'.[48] Since Pinochet was charged 'not with personally torturing or murdering victims or causing their disappearance, but with using the power of the State of which he was head to that end',[49] the judges concluded that they could hardly be described as 'private' acts and therefore had to be official acts. They rejected the argument that serious international crimes could not be functions of a head of State.[50] The judges rejected an exception restricted to serious international crimes, because it would be unclear where to draw the line.[51] The Nuremberg Charter, the ICTY Statute and the ICTR Statute were distinguished on the grounds that 'these were international tribunals, established by international agreement. They did not therefore violate the principle that one sovereign State will not implead another in relation to its sovereign acts.'[52]

At the first House of Lords hearing, following the intervention of *amici curiae* and a more detailed review of developments in international law, three out of five judges were persuaded that former head of State immunity did not cover such serious international crimes.[53] The essence of the decision was that the commission of certain serious international crimes is condemned by all States as illegal and therefore cannot also be protected by international law as an 'official function'. However, a rehearing was necessitated by the possible appearance of bias of one of the judges in the first hearing, who had some (fairly slender) affiliations with Amnesty International, one of the intervenors.[54]

In the final House of Lords decision, six out of seven judges confirmed that the immunity of a former head of State did not prevent his extradition for torture.[55] Each of the judges in the final decision issued a separate opinion, and the reasoning within each opinion was not always clear. As a result, the judgment is one of those gems of the common law system in which, however important the decision, it is difficult to identify a *ratio decidendi*. Commentators tend to emphasize different passages and offer different interpretations, and thereby arrive at different views as to the basis of the decision. It is beyond the scope of this introductory text to provide a detailed analysis, but the following observations illustrate the open questions concerning the rationale as well as the scope of the decision.

The most cautious interpretation, restricted to the terms of the 1984 Torture Convention, is that, where official involvement is a necessary element of a crime, there cannot be

---

[47] *Re Pinochet Ugarte* [1998] All ER (D) 629; [1998] EWJ No. 2878 (Queen's Bench Division, 1998) (Quicklaw).
[48] *Ibid.*, para. 56 (Quicklaw citation) (emphasis added).   [49] *Ibid.*, para. 58.   [50] *Ibid.*, paras. 63–5 and 80.   [51] *Ibid.*
[52] *Ibid.*, para. 68.
[53] *R v. Bow Street Metropolitan Stipendiary Magistrate, ex parte Pinochet Ugarte (No. 1)* [1998] 4 All ER 897, HL.
[54] *R v. Bow Street Metropolitan Stipendiary Magistrate, ex parte Pinochet Ugarte (No. 2)* [1999] 1 All ER 577, HL.
[55] *R v. Bow Street Metropolitan Stipendiary Magistrate, ex parte Pinochet Ugarte (No. 3)* [1999] 2 All ER 97, HL (hereinafter 'Pinochet (No. 3)').

immunity by reason of official involvement; otherwise the crime would be vacated of content.[56] As noted by Lord Millett, '[t]he offence is one which could only be committed in circumstances which would normally give rise to the immunity ... International law cannot be supposed to have established a crime having the character of *ius cogens* and at the same time to have provided an immunity which is co-extensive with the obligation it seeks to impose.'[57] Support for this reading can be found in the opinions of Lords Browne-Wilkinson, Saville and Phillips.[58]

Another reading is that international crimes cannot constitute 'official functions' and hence do not give rise to functional immunity. Such a reading may be supported from passages of Lord Browne-Wilkinson and Lord Hutton.[59] However, the approach of denying the official character of the acts does not appear to find support among a majority of the judges. Several judges noted that the mere fact that conduct is criminal does not *per se* change its governmental character.[60] In any event, such an approach would create contradictions, given that, for the crime of torture, official participation is an element of the crime, so official character would have to be asserted in order to gain jurisdiction and then denied in order to avoid immunity. To say such crimes are not 'official' is also counterfactual when the crimes are in fact committed through the apparatus of the State; moreover, such an approach could obscure State responsibility for the act.[61]

A more sophisticated variation on that reading is that international crimes are not a type of official conduct that attracts functional immunity.[62] Functional immunity protects certain conduct, but it would be contradictory for international law to protect conduct and at the same time condemn it and require its prosecution.[63] On this view, one would interpret the speeches of Lords Browne-Wilkinson and Hutton not as denying any official character of the acts, but as indicating that these acts 'could not rank *for immunity purposes* as performance of an official function' (emphasis added).[64] Lord Phillips appears to come into this camp: 'where international crime is concerned, that principle [that one State cannot judge another] cannot prevail'; 'no immunity *ratione materiae* could exist for ... a crime contrary to international law'.[65] Lord Hope may also be interpreted as not permitting functional immunity for serious international crimes: 'the obligations which were recognized by

---

[56] See e.g. Colin Warbrick, Elena Martin Salgado and Nicholas Goodwin, 'The Pinochet Cases in the United Kingdom' (1999) 2 *Yearbook of International Humanitarian Law* 91; Barker, 'Future of Former Head of State Immunity'; Eileen Denza, 'Ex Parte Pinochet: Lacuna or Leap?' (1999) 48 *International and Comparative Law Quarterly* 949; van Alebeek, 'Pinochet Case'; Dapo Akande, 'International Law Immunities and the International Criminal Court' (2004) 98 *American Journal of International Law* 407, 415.

[57] *Pinochet (No. 3)* at 179.   [58] *Ibid.*, 114–15 (Browne-Wilkinson), 169 (Saville) and 190 (Phillips).

[59] *Ibid.*, 113 (Browne-Wilkinson) and 166 (Hutton).   [60] *Ibid.*, 172 (Millett), 147 (Hope), 119 (Goff) and 187 (Phillips).

[61] Antonio Cassese, 'When May Senior State Officials Be Tried for International Crimes? Some Comments on the Congo v. Belgium Case' (2002) 13 *European Journal of International Law* 853; Marina Spinedi, 'State Responsibility v. Individual Responsibility for International Crimes: Tertium Non Datur?' (2002) 13 *European Journal of International Law* 895; Barker, 'Future of Former Head of State Immunity', 943 and 948.

[62] See e.g. Christine Chinkin, 'Regina v. Bow Street Stipendiary Magistrate, Ex Parte Pinochet Ugarte (No. 3)' (1999) 93 *American Journal of International Law* 703; Steffen Wirth, 'Immunities, Related Problems, and Article 98 of the Rome Statute' (2001) 12 *Criminal Law Forum* 429; Claus Kreß, 'War Crimes Committed in Non-International Armed Conflict and the Emerging System of International Criminal Justice' (2000) 30 *Israel Yearbook on Human Rights* 103, 158–9.

[63] Note that such reasoning would not apply to personal immunity, because personal immunity does not protect *conduct*, it protects persons in particular high representative *roles* from interference on any grounds.

[64] *Pinochet (No. 3)* at 114 (Browne-Wilkinson) and 166 (Hutton).   [65] *Ibid.*, 190.

customary law in the case of such serious international crimes . . . are so strong as to override any objection . . . on the ground of immunity *ratione materiae*'.[66] Passages by Lord Millett may also fall within this camp, as he cites with approval the *Eichmann* case as authority that official authority is no bar to the exercise of jurisdiction for certain international crimes, and then refers to *ius cogens* crimes on a large scale, including murder.[67]

In addition to these differing interpretations of the *legal basis* for loss of immunity, there are differing possibilities as to the *scope* of the rule. On the first approach mentioned above, the scope would be limited to torture and other crimes specifically requiring official participation as an element of the crime;[68] on the latter approaches, the rule is broader, potentially covering all serious international crimes. Some judges indicated that a single act of torture would not suffice to override functional immunity, and that it would have to constitute a crime against humanity, that is to say, 'widespread or systematic torture as an instrument of State policy'.[69]

The basis of the *Pinochet* decision, and thus the extent of its implications, remains shrouded in some uncertainty. For the purposes of UK law, the decision has been interpreted narrowly in a subsequent House of Lords case, as being confined to the wording of the Torture Convention (and presumably other treaties like the Enforced Disappearances Convention), which defines the crime by reference to official status and thus removes the immunity by necessary implication.[70] For the purposes of international law, the decision is often placed within a line of authorities limiting the availability of functional immunity for core crimes.

21.2.2 The scope of the exception to functional immunities

A considerable body of international cases, national cases, other State practice and academic commentary supports the view that functional immunity does not preclude prosecution for serious international crimes, which is consistent with the broader reading of *Pinochet*. However, as will be discussed in this section, the failure of the ICJ to mention the principle, as well as a few outlying cases, means that the proposition is not free from doubt.

Authorities indicating no functional immunities for core crimes

As the Nuremberg judgment observed:

The principle of international law which, under certain circumstances, protects the representative of a State cannot be applied to acts which are condemned as criminal by international law. The authors of these acts cannot shelter themselves behind their official position in order to be freed from punishment . . . individuals have duties which transcend the national obligations of obedience

---

[66] *Ibid.*, 152.   [67] *Ibid.*, 176–7.   [68] Warbrick *et al.*, 'The Pinochet Cases', 113–14.
[69] *Pinochet (No. 3)* at 144–5 and 150–1 (Hope); see also 177 (Millett) and 188 (Phillips). At least one judge felt that a single act of torture would suffice (presumably with respect to States Parties to the Torture Convention): *ibid.*, 166 (Lord Hutton).
[70] See *Jones* v. *Kingdom of Saudi Arabia* [2006] UKHL 26; [2006] 2 WLR 1124, paras. 19 and 79–81.

imposed by the individual State. He who violates the laws of war cannot obtain immunity while acting in pursuance of the authority of the State, if the State in authorizing action moves outside its competence under international law.[71]

The legal theory underlying this proposition is compelling. First, functional immunity protects State conduct from scrutiny, but it would be incongruous for international law to protect the very conduct which it criminalizes and for which it imposes duties to prosecute. Second, the State cannot complain that its sovereignty is being restricted or that a policy is being imposed on it, when the prohibited conduct is recognized by all as an international crime. Third, from the perspective of the perpetrator, State agents are normally able to pass responsibility for dubious activities to the State that authorized them, but, in the case of serious international crimes, 'individuals have international duties which transcend the national obligations of obedience',[72] and hence they are rightly held to account. Finally, it is also sound in terms of balancing the underlying values; where an individual possesses only functional immunity, international law already reflects that such an individual is no longer playing a high representative role which necessitates absolute immunity.

The proposition was endorsed by the International Law Commission and the General Assembly as principle III of the Nuremberg principles[73] and has subsequently been reconfirmed by the International Law Commission.[74]

The principle was applied in subsequent national cases. In *Eichmann*, the Israeli Supreme Court rejected a plea by Eichmann that he was carrying out official activities and held that:

There is no basis for the doctrine when the matter pertains to acts prohibited by the law of nations, especially when they are international crimes of the class of 'crimes against humanity' (in the wide sense) . . . such acts . . . are completely outside the 'sovereign' jurisdiction of the State that ordered or ratified their commission, and therefore those who participated in such acts must personally account for them and cannot shelter behind the official character of their task or mission.[75]

More recently, in *Bouterse*, the Amsterdam Court of Appeal held with respect to the former head of State of Suriname that serious international crimes such as crimes against humanity did not constitute 'official functions' for the purpose of functional immunity.[76] In addition, a Belgian court in the *Sharon* case, Spanish authorities requesting extradition of Pinochet, and a Spanish court in the *Castro* case, all indicated that there was no functional immunity for

---

[71] Nuremberg IMT, Judgment and Sentences, reprinted in (1947) 41 *American Journal of International Law* 172, 221.

[72] Trial of the Major War Criminals before the International Military Tribunal, Vol. I, Nuremberg 1947, p. 223.

[73] Affirmation of the Principles of International Law recognized by the Charter of the Nuremberg Tribunal, Resolution 95(I) of the United Nations General Assembly, 11 December 1946; Principles of the Nuremberg Tribunal, Report of the International Law Commission Covering its Second Session, 5 June–29 July 1950, Doc. A/1316, pp. 11–14 and commentaries in *Yearbook of the International Law Commission* (1950) Vol. II, 374–8.

[74] See e.g. draft Code of Crimes against the Peace and Security of Mankind, *Yearbook of the International Law Commission* (1996) Vol. II (Part Two), Art. 7.

[75] *Attorney-General of Israel* v. *Eichmann* (1968) 36 ILR 277, 308–10. The discussion was in the context of 'act of State', but, as noted by Lord Millett in *Pinochet (No. 3)* at 176, the principles are the very same.

[76] *Bouterse* (2000) 51 *Nederlandse Jurisprudentie* 302. An appeal was granted by the Supreme Court on other, jurisdictional, grounds.

serious international crimes, as did a committee of jurists appointed by the African Union recommending prosecution of Hassan Habré, former head of State of Chad.[77]

The proposition has also been supported by international criminal tribunals. For example, in *Blaškić*, the ICTY recognized functional immunity as a 'well-established rule of customary international law', with the exception that those responsible for 'war crimes, crimes against humanity and genocide ... cannot invoke immunity from national or international jurisdiction even if they perpetrated such crimes while acting in their official capacity'.[78]

The proposition is also supported in much of the literature.[79]

An open question?

While the trend of these authorities seems clear, there are a few judgments that leave a possibility of doubt.[80] The most important of these is the failure of the ICJ to mention such an exception in the *Democratic Republic of the Congo* v. *Belgium* case (discussed in section 21.4). In a paragraph of *obiter dicta*, the ICJ mentioned that a former foreign minister may be tried for acts committed during his or her period of office in a *private capacity*.[81] This appears to omit the exception that former officials can also be tried for any acts which constitute serious international crimes, whether in a 'private capacity' or not. The omission was conspicuous, and it was extensively criticized by commentators.[82] The omission was also puzzling in that both parties to the dispute – DRC and Belgium – agreed that functional immunity is not a bar to prosecution for international crime.[83] As already discussed (in section 21.2.1), one solution might be to say that international crimes are not 'official' acts but rather 'private' acts,[84] but such a solution raises its own problems.[85] As the paragraph was merely *obiter dicta*, providing a series of examples rather than a closed list, most subsequent national decisions have continued to assert an exception for international crimes.[86]

---

[77] See 'Immunity of State Officials from Criminal Jurisdiction, Memorandum by the Secretariat', UN Doc. A/CN.4/596, 31 March 2008, paras. 180–90; Antonio Cassese, 'The Belgian Court of Cassation v. The International Court of Justice: The Sharon and Others Case' (2003) 1 *Journal of International Criminal Justice* 437, 443–50.

[78] *Blaškić*, ICTY A. Ch., 24 October 1997, para. 41. See also *Furundžija*, ICTY T. Ch. II, 10 December 1998, para. 140.

[79] See e.g. *Princeton Principles on Universal Jurisdiction* (Princeton University, 2001) 48–50; Paola Gaeta, 'Official Capacity and Immunities' in Cassese, *Commentary*, 981; Cassese, 'Senior State Officials'; Steffen Wirth, 'Immunity for Core Crimes? The ICJ's Judgment in the Congo v. Belgium Case' (2002) 13 *European Journal of International Law* 877; Hugh King, 'Immunities and Bilateral Agreements: Issues Arising from Articles 27 and 98 of the Rome Statute' (2006) *New Zealand Journal of Public and International Law* 269; Watts, 'Legal Position', 4; Akande and Shah, 'Immunities of State Officials', 839–46. But see Ingrid Wuerth, '*Pinochet's* Legacy Reassessed' (2012) 106 *American Journal of International Law* 731.

[80] A special rapporteur of the International Law Commission, examining the topic of immunities, also expressed doubt about an international crimes exception to functional immunity: UN Doc. A/CN.4/654, 31 May 2012, para. 21.

[81] *Case Concerning the Arrest Warrant of 11 April 2000* (*Democratic Republic of the Congo* v. *Belgium*), ICJ Reports 2002, para. 61.

[82] See e.g. Cassese, 'Senior State Officials'; Wirth, 'Immunity for Core Crimes?'; David Koller, 'Immunities of Foreign Ministers: Paragraph 61 of the Yerodia Judgment as It Pertains to the Security Council and the International Criminal Court' (2004) 20 *American University International Law Review* 7; Paolo Gaeta, 'Ratione Materiae Immunities of Former Heads of State and International Crimes: The Hissène Habré Case' (2003) 1 *Journal of International Criminal Justice* 186; Chanakra Wickremasinghe, 'Arrest Warrant of 11 April 2000' (2003) 52 *International and Comparative Law Quarterly* 775; King, 'Immunities and Bilateral Agreements'.

[83] Cassese, 'Senior State Officials', 872.

[84] The Joint Separate Opinion of Judges Higgins, Kooijmans and Buergenthal in the *Yerodia* case (see footnote 104 below) at para. 85, suggests that international crimes should not be seen as 'official acts'.

[85] See section 21.2.1. [86] Examples are listed above in this section.

Nonetheless, in 2007 French authorities decided not to proceed with torture allegations against Donald Rumsfeld, citing advice from the Ministry of Foreign Affairs that under 'rules of customary law established by the International Court of Justice', immunity for official functions continues after termination of their functions.[87] The case may be authority against the exception for international crimes. On the other hand, observers have suggested that the decision was not entirely untouched by politics, given that the position taken in relation to Rumsfeld is irreconcilable with the earlier French request for the extradition of Pinochet.

Another case raises possible doubts about the parameters of the exception. An Italian case, *Lozano*, dealt with a US serviceman in Iraq who opened fire on a car speeding towards a checkpoint, killing an Italian agent and wounding another officer and a reporter.[88] The court specifically affirmed a general exception that functional immunity does not prevail against international crimes.[89] The significant finding was that Lozano's conduct was not a war crime, given the car's rapid approach to the checkpoint.[90] However, that court also made reference to high thresholds, requiring that war crimes be 'odious or inhuman' or involve scale or planning, which might be seen as an additional requirement to set aside functional immunity for war crimes or (more likely) as a simple misstatement of the elements of war crimes.[91]

21.3   Functional immunity and international courts

The reasoning in the foregoing authorities is based on the nature of functional immunity, and not on the nature of the jurisdiction trying the crime. Thus, the same reasoning would apply in any forum, including international courts. The ICTY has confirmed that international law offers no functional immunity for genocide, crimes against humanity or war crimes.[92] Many former officials have been tried before international courts and tribunals.

In addition to benefiting from any inherent inapplicability of functional immunity to international crimes, international tribunals are also granted certain powers to set aside immunities, as is discussed in section 21.5.

21.4   Personal immunity and national courts

21.4.1   *State practice and jurisprudence*

While inroads have been made into *functional* immunity, State practice and jurisprudence have consistently upheld *personal* immunity, regardless of the nature of the charges. For

---

[87] See UN, 'Immunity of State Officials', para. 188.
[88] Antonio Cassese, 'The Italian Court of Cassation Misapprehends the Notion of War Crimes' (2008) 6 *Journal of International Criminal Justice* 1077.
[89] *Ibid.*, 1082.   [90] *Ibid.*, 1084.
[91] *Ibid.*, 1085–8. Such a requirement would not be entirely unprecedented; several passages in *Pinochet* arguably required 'widespread or systematic' crimes: see section 21.2.
[92] See e.g. *Blaškić*, ICTY A. Ch., 24 October 1997, para. 41.

example, even in the *Pinochet* decision, all of the Law Lords agreed that, if Pinochet were still a serving head of State, he could not be arrested. A serving head of State has personal immunity and, '[t]he nature of the charge is irrelevant; his immunity is personal and absolute'.[93] 'He is not liable to be arrested or detained on any ground whatever.'[94]

To understand the divergent treatment of functional and personal immunity, one must recall their purposes. Functional immunity relates to the conduct and its authorization by a State, whereas personal immunity flows from a completely different rationale, unconnected with the alleged conduct. Its purpose is to preclude any pretext for interference with a State representative, in order to allow international relations between potentially distrustful States. Thus, personal immunity cannot be set aside without the consent of the relevant State.

The possibility of creating exceptions to personal immunity has been considered but rejected over the years, even in situations of great pressure or incentive to prosecute, including cases of espionage, drug smuggling, murder[95] and plots against monarchs.[96] In each case, the conclusion reached was that, despite all of the problems with immunities, the benefits of upholding the existing system of diplomatic immunities and diplomatic communication outweighed the disadvantages.[97]

Judicial decisions have confirmed that there is no exception to personal immunity. In 1946, a Canadian case held that a foreign diplomat could not be arrested or detained even after threatening the security of the State, because, '[i]f the diplomat violates the law of nations, it does not follow that the other State has the right to do likewise'.[98]

This view has been upheld in recent cases in the context of serious international crimes. In March 2001, the French Cour de Cassation held in the *Qaddafi* case that a serving head of State is immune from prosecution in national courts in relation to serious acts of terrorism.[99] The Spanish Audienco Nacional reached a similar conclusion with respect to allegations of international crimes by Fidel Castro,[100] and the same result was reached in a UK court in a case against President Mugabe.[101] State practice has adhered to the same line. For example, when lobbied by NGOs to arrest the serving Israeli ambassador, Carmi Gillon, on allegations that he was previously responsible for torture, Denmark refused, on the basis of its obligation to respect diplomatic immunity.[102]

[93] *Pinochet (No. 3)* at 179 (Millett).   [94] *Ibid.*, 171 (Millett).
[95] The murder of policewoman Yvonne Fletcher in the United Kingdom in 1984 provoked a massive outcry and a parliamentary review of diplomatic immunities. The review concluded, however, that attempts to renegotiate the Vienna Convention would create more problems than they would solve. See Barker, *A Necessary Evil?*, 135–52.
[96] In 1571 and in 1584, when ambassadors in England were detected in plots against the Crown, some urged that foreign ambassadors should lose their immunity for treason and high crimes. In the end, these arguments did not prevail and the diplomats were expelled. Similar practices were followed in other countries. See Ogdon, *Juridical Bases*, 56–9.
[97] In the United States, proposals for legislation to remove diplomatic immunity for drunk driving and violent crimes have been rejected, on the grounds that complete immunity is essential for diplomatic relations, as otherwise other States could bring false charges. See Barker, *A Necessary Evil?*, 232.
[98] *Rose v. R* (1947) 3 DLR 618, 645.   [99] *Qadaffi* (2001) 125 ILR 456.   [100] *Castro* (1999) 32 ILM 596.
[101] Reproduced in Colin Warbrick, 'Immunity and International Crimes in English Law' (2004) 53 *International and Comparative Law Quarterly* 769.
[102] Jacques Hartmann, 'The Gillon Affair' (2005) 45 *International and Comparative Law Quarterly* 745.

21.4.2   The ICJ **Yerodia** *decision*

In April 2000, a Belgian judge issued an international arrest warrant against Abdulaye
Yerodia Ndombasi, who was at the time serving as the minister for foreign affairs for the
Democratic Republic of the Congo (DRC). The DRC brought the matter to the ICJ, arguing
that Belgium had failed to recognize the immunity of a serving minister of foreign affairs.
The ICJ held, by thirteen votes to three, that Belgium had breached its international legal
duties to the DRC 'in that they failed to respect the immunity from criminal jurisdiction and
the inviolability which the incumbent Minister for Foreign Affairs of the Democratic
Republic of the Congo enjoyed under international law'.[103] The personal immunity enjoyed
by a foreign minister could not be set aside by a national court by charging him or her with
war crimes or crimes against humanity.[104] The ICJ examined the non-immunity provisions
of the Nuremberg Charter, and the Statutes of the ICTY, ICTR and ICC, and found that these
did not suggest any exception in customary international law in regard to national courts.[105]

The judgment emphasized that the temporary status of personal immunity did not mean
impunity for serious crimes. First, persons may be tried in their home courts; second, they
may be prosecuted if the State waives the immunity; third, they may be prosecuted, once
they cease to hold office, for crimes committed in a private capacity; and, fourth, they may
be prosecuted before international criminal courts where such courts have jurisdiction.[106]

The outcome of the decision is consistent with the line of national decisions and State
practice upholding absolute personal immunity. Nevertheless, there are elements of the
decision which have been questioned. First, by observing that former high officials may be
tried for 'private' acts once they cease to hold office, the ICJ seemed to omit the exception
that serious international crimes may also be prosecuted.[107] Second, in the view of some
commentators, it unjustifiably extended head of State immunity to what may be a wide range
of ministers, without sufficient argument or reference to authority.[108] Third, the ICJ asserted
that such ministers enjoy personal immunity even when on 'private visits', without a
demonstration that State practice supports such a view.

Which ministers enjoy personal immunity?

The ICJ recognized immunity for heads of State, heads of government and ministers of
foreign affairs, and left a door open for other ministers. Jurisprudence has to date been
cautious in extending personal immunity to other ministers. In the *Mofaz* case, a UK court
found that the role of a minister of defence was one attracting personal immunity, but
expressed doubt that ministers of culture, sport or education would qualify.[109] Other cases
indicate that neither Solicitors-General nor ministers of State qualify, nor do leaders of
provinces and sub-States.[110] An ongoing work by the International Law Commission on

---

[103] *Case Concerning the Arrest Warrant of 11 April 2000* (*Democratic Republic of the Congo* v. *Belgium*), Judgment, 14 February
2002, (2002) ICJ Reports (hereinafter '*Yerodia*'), para. 75.
[104] *Ibid.*, paras. 56–8.   [105] *Ibid.*, para. 58.   [106] *Ibid.*, para. 61.   [107] Discussed in section 21.2.2.
[108] Akande, 'International Law Immunities', 412.
[109] *Mofaz*, reproduced (2004) 53 *International and Comparative Law Quarterly* 769.
[110] UN, 'Immunity of State Officials', paras. 132–6.

immunity has suggested that personal immunity is indeed restricted to the 'troika' of heads of State, heads of government and foreign ministers.[111]

Are personal immunities established for private visits?

The *Yerodia* judgment indicated that personal immunity must be recognized even on private visits, on the grounds that the consequences of being arrested for the performance of one's functions would be the same.[112] However, the ICJ did not conduct its usual review of State practice and *opinio iuris*; a review of State practice might have led to more nuanced conclusions. The comments were *obiter dicta* and, given that many judges dissented from or distanced themselves from this particular finding, it seems not to have commanded a majority.[113] Thus, this issue is still open for clarification in State practice.[114]

On the one hand, the sparse previous authorities refer to such immunities *on an official visit*.[115] If an analogy is drawn from the law of diplomatic immunities, personal immunity is not accorded during holidays in third countries, but only during transit between the home country and the host country.[116] Further, where the host State has not invited the official or consented to the visit, the rationale of an implied undertaking to bestow full immunity is not applicable.[117] Moreover, the rationale on which the ICJ based its conclusion, which was that exposure to proceedings 'could deter the Minister from travelling internationally *when required to do so for the purposes of the performance of his or her official functions*'[118] is inapplicable to holiday travel. The competing values could be balanced differently by suggesting that officials fearful of arrest should curtail private travel.

On the other hand, the arrest of a President even during a private visit does engage many of the same problems and considerations. An ongoing work on immunity by the ILC suggests that personal immunity should persist during private travel.[119] If the immunity is limited to the 'troika' of three types of high official, the resulting restriction on territorial State sovereignty and on accountability is arguably modest.

---

[111] UN Doc. A/CN.4/661, 4 April 2013, paras. 56–68. The ILC noted that other high officials may still benefit from 'special missions' immunity granted for official visits.

[112] *Yerodia*, para. 55.

[113] Seven out of thirteen judges dissented from or expressed doubts about this finding. See Darryl Robinson, 'The Impact of the Human Rights Accountability Movement on the International Law of Immunities' (2002) 40 *Canadian Yearbook of International Law* 151, 188–9.

[114] For discussion, see Watts, 'Legal Position', 72–4; Salvatore Zappala, 'Do Heads of State in Office Enjoy Immunity from Jurisdiction for International Crimes? The Ghaddafi Case before the French *Cour de Cassation*' (2001) 12 *European Journal of International Law* 595, 606; Koller, 'Immunities of Foreign Ministers', 15–16; UN, 'Immunities of State Officials', para. 128.

[115] Convention on Special Missions 1969, Art. 21; US Restatement (Third) of Foreign Relations Law § 464, footnote 14.

[116] Vienna Convention on Diplomatic Relations 1961, Art. 40.

[117] On the idea of implied undertaking, see R. Y. Jennings and A. Watts (eds.), *Oppenheim's International Law*, 9th edn (London, 1992) 1034. In the *Yerodia* case (para. 68), even Belgium recognized that 'immunity from enforcement must, in our view, be accorded to all State representatives welcomed as such onto the territory of Belgium (on "official visits") ... such welcome includes an undertaking by the host State and its various components to refrain from taking any coercive measures against its guest and the invitation cannot become a pretext for ensnaring the individual concerns in what would then have to be labelled a trap.'

[118] *Yerodia*, para. 55 (emphasis added). [119] UN Doc. A/CN.4/661, 4 April 2013.

21.5   Personal immunity and international courts

As may be seen from the foregoing, authorities have consistently rejected any exception to personal immunity in domestic courts based on the nature of the charges. Personal immunity may only be overcome through consent of the State concerned. This raises the unsettling prospect of an accountability gap with respect to such persons while they are in office. Fortunately, States have devised means of reducing this accountability gap: to create international tribunals and to empower them to supersede even their personal immunities.

In the case of the Nuremberg and Tokyo Tribunals, both Japan and Germany had surrendered. Hence, the Allies stood in the position of national legislators and, in that position, they could legislate away immunity before the Tokyo and Nuremberg Tribunals. In the case of the ad hoc Tribunals, immunities are overridden by virtue of the paramount obligation to comply with Chapter VII decisions of the Security Council. In the case of the ICC, States Parties relinquish their immunities by treaty. These avenues for relinquishing immunity will be discussed in this section. Particular attention will be given to complexities that arise in Security Council referrals to the ICC, including the controversies around the ICC's arrest warrant against Omar Al Bashir, President of Sudan.

Section 21.5.4 will examine an alternative theory, raised in the *Taylor* case, that immunities are simply inapplicable before international courts, by virtue of their 'international' character.

21.5.1   *Security Council decisions and the international tribunals*

One way to remove personal immunity is through a Chapter VII Security Council decision, because all States have consented in advance to comply with Chapter VII decisions. The UN Charter grants the Security Council a broad discretion to determine what measures are appropriate to maintain or restore international peace and security, whether involving use of force (Article 42) or not (Article 41). All UN Member States are obliged to carry out such measures (Articles 25 and 48),[120] and the obligation is paramount even over other treaty commitments.[121]

When creating the ad hoc Tribunals, the Security Council incorporated the principle that the official position of a defendant is no bar before the tribunals,[122] and ordered all States to cooperate fully with requests from the Tribunals, including requests for surrender. No exception was created for surrender requests relating to persons otherwise enjoying immunities. A UN Member State receiving a request for surrender is obliged to comply with that request, even if the request conflicts with a duty to respect immunities. By the same token, the State otherwise enjoying the immunities is estopped from raising those immunities as a

---

[120] For further discussion on the power of the Security Council to create Tribunals, see Chapter 7.
[121] See UN Charter, Arts. 25, 41, 49 and especially at 103: 'In the event of a conflict between the obligations of the Members of the United Nations under the present Charter and their obligations under any other international agreement, their obligations under the present Charter shall prevail.'
[122] Art. 7(2) of the ICTY Statute; Art. 6(2) of the ICTR Statute.

shield, by virtue of its obligations under the UN Charter.[123] The legal analysis is the same where the Security Council orders States to cooperate with the ICC, as will be discussed in section 21.5.3.

The situation is less straightforward with respect to the Federal Republic of Yugoslavia (FRY), which was the recipient of orders to surrender its head of State, because it was not recognized as a UN Member State. However, it was a party to the Dayton Accords, which imposed an obligation to cooperate with the ICTY.[124]

Both Tribunals have carried out proceedings with respect to high governmental officials. In 1998, the ICTR convicted former Prime Minister Jean Kambanda, sentencing him to life imprisonment for genocide and crimes against humanity.[125] In 1999, the ICTY issued the first indictment against a serving head of State, Slobodan Milošević.[126] Although Milošević died of a heart attack before the completion of his trial,[127] his indictment, arrest and trial remain a valuable precedent on the authority of a Security Council tribunal over heads of State.

21.5.2 *Relinquishment directly to the ICC*

The ICC Statute offers another solution to the problem of personal immunity. In the present stage of development of international relations, States are apparently unwilling to allow other States to set aside personal immunities; however, a great many States have been willing to create an impartial international court with jurisdiction over serious international crimes, to invest it with safeguards against abuse, and to relinquish even their personal immunities to that court.

States can relinquish their immunities *vis-à-vis* the ICC by ratifying the ICC Statute. States Parties to the ICC Statute are obliged to cooperate with the ICC and to surrender individuals in accordance with the terms of the Statute, without reservation.[128] Article 27(2) specifies that '[i]mmunities or special personal rules which may attach to the official capacity of a person … shall not bar the Court from exercising its jurisdiction'.[129] Thus, States Parties accept that the immunities their officials may enjoy under international law will not bar prosecution before the ICC. This provision has required many States to amend domestic legislation and even their constitutions in order to ratify the ICC Statute.[130]

---

[123] Koller, 'Immunities of Foreign Ministers', 35–6; Gaeta, 'Official Capacity and Immunities', 989.

[124] Dayton Peace Accords, 21 November 1995, Art. IX. On approaches to this question, as well as the interpretation that the UN Charter is of a *sui generis* character that binds third party States, see Chapter 7.

[125] *Kambanda*, ICTR T. Ch. I, 4 September 1998.

[126] *Milošević*, ICTY Indictment (Judge Hunt), 24 May 1999; *Milošević*, ICTY T. Ch. III, 8 November 2001, paras. 26–53.

[127] See Chapter 7.

[128] Art. 86 (obligation to cooperate), Art. 89 (surrender of persons to the court) and Art. 120 (no reservations) of the ICC Statute.

[129] *Ibid.*, Art. 27(1): 'official capacity as a Head of State or Government, a member of a Government or parliament, an elected representative or a government official shall in no case exempt a person from criminal responsibility under this Statute'. See Otto Triffterer, 'Article 27' in Triffterer, *Observers' Notes*, 501.

[130] See e.g. Claus Kreß and Flavia Lattanzi (eds.), *The Rome Statute and Domestic Legal Orders* (Rome, 2000) Vol. I; Darryl Robinson, 'The Rome Statute and its Impact on National Laws' in Cassese, *Commentary*, 1849.

In addition, States may also undertake the obligation to cooperate fully through unilateral declarations (see, for example, Articles 12(3) and 87(5) of the ICC Statute). This obligation places them in the same position as States Parties, for the reasons given in the previous paragraph. Furthermore, as will be explored in section 21.5.3, an order of the Security Council can have the same effect.

Article 27 is not the only provision on immunities in the ICC Statute. Article 98(1) provides that the ICC will not proceed with requests for surrender:

> which would require the requested State to act inconsistently with its obligations under international law with respect to the State or diplomatic immunity of a person or property of a third State, unless the Court can first obtain the cooperation of that third State for the waiver of the immunity.[131]

Article 27 and Article 98(1) must be read together to understand the Statute regime.[132] At first glance, they appear contradictory, with one rejecting immunities and the other upholding immunities.[133] The provisions apply at different stages. Article 98(1) deals with a specific situation where a State Party (or other State obliged to cooperate) is requested to surrender a person, but that person is protected by immunities bestowed by a third State. In such a case, the requested State would be placed in a position of conflicting obligations: for example, either to breach a duty to carry out ICC requests or to breach a duty to respect immunities of a State not party to the ICC Statute.

The interplay of Articles 27 and 98(1) therefore creates a regime wherein States Parties agree to relinquish all immunities in relation to ICC requests concerning their own officials, while still respecting the existing immunities of States which have not joined the ICC Statute system. It is worth recalling here that the only relevant immunities would be personal immunities, since functional immunity does not protect conduct which amounts to a core crime.[134]

We can consider three scenarios: a State Party[135] surrendering (1) its own official, (2) an official of another State Party, or (3) an official of a non-State Party. In the first scenario, concerning the State's own official, Article 98(1) does not apply, since it refers to obligations to a 'third State'. The State is obliged to cooperate without reservation (Article 86).

The second scenario is where a State Party is asked to surrender an official with personal immunity bestowed by *another* State Party. It is generally accepted that it would not be necessary for the requested State first to obtain the waiver of the other State Party.[136] There are different interpretive routes by which this conclusion is reached.[137] The most convincing

---

[131] Similarly, Art. 98(2) of the ICC Statute respects obligations under international agreements pursuant to which the consent of a sending State is required to surrender a person of that State to the court. The controversy over the interpretation of Art. 98(2) is discussed in Chapter 8. See generally Kimberly Prost and Angelika Schlunck, 'Article 98' in Triffterer, *Observers' Notes*, 1131.

[132] Triffterer, 'Article 27', 509.   [133] Gaeta, 'Official Capacity', 992–6.   [134] See section 21.2 and 21.3.

[135] References here to 'State Party' also include other States subject to the same obligation to cooperate fully with the Court.

[136] The relationship between Arts. 27 and 98 was discussed in informal meetings at the ICC Preparatory Commission, on the basis of an informal paper by Canada and the United Kingdom, with the conclusion being reached that, '[h]aving regard to the terms of the Statute, the Court shall not be required to obtain a waiver of immunity with respect to the surrender by one State Party of a head of State or government, or diplomat, of another State Party'. See Broomhall, *International Justice*, 144. This view has been endorsed by an ICC Pre-Trial Chamber in its decisions concerning Malawi and Chad, discussed below (section 21.5.4): *Al Bashir*, ICC PTC I, 13 December 2011, para. 18.

[137] Some interpret 'third State' in Art. 98(1) as referring only to non-States Parties. However, this view overlooks that the Statute consistently uses the term 'State not party to this Statute' to describe non-States Parties, and that 'third State' is routinely used in cooperation treaties to refer to a State other than the requesting and requested States.

view is that there are no 'obligations under international law' owed to States Parties hindering surrender, because they have relinquished immunities when they accepted the obligations to the ICC (including Articles 88 and 27).[138] The same analysis applies where the third State has voluntarily placed itself in the position of a State Party through a unilateral declaration (Articles 12(3) and 87(5)).

The third scenario concerns an official enjoying personal immunity bestowed by a *non-State Party*. If that State has not relinquished its immunities in favour of the ICC regime, then personal immunity persists. Article 98(1) requires respect for any immunities existing under international law. This does not mean there can be no prospect for surrender. First, even officials of non-States Parties will lose their immunity if the Security Council under Chapter VII orders full cooperation, as will be discussed in section 21.5.3. Second, prosecution is possible if the non-State Party agrees to waive the immunity. Third, once the official is no longer serving in a capacity that entails personal immunity, he or she will only have functional immunity, and hence be liable to prosecution for core crimes on the basis discussed in section 21.2 above.

21.5.3   *Security Council decisions and the ICC*

Many controversies have arisen as to the correct legal analysis where the Security Council has referred a situation to the ICC under Chapter VII, and the ICC proceeds against a person with personal immunity bestowed by a State not party to the ICC Statute. This has arisen in the Darfur situation, which was referred to the Court by the Security Council under Chapter VII. In March 2009, a Pre-Trial Chamber of the ICC issued an arrest warrant against Omar Al Bashir, President of Sudan.[139] The same scenario arose when the Security Council referred the Libya situation, and the ICC issued a warrant for Muammar Qaddafi, but Qaddafi was killed in Libya after his capture. The Al Bashir warrant has triggered a vigorous international legal debate about the status of immunities in such a situation.

Consistently with the foregoing sections, this section will proceed on the premise that personal immunity may only be set aside with the direct or indirect consent of the State concerned. (An alternative view, that immunities are simply not opposable against an international court, is discussed below.) As explained above, a Chapter VII resolution provides the necessary authority, since States have accepted a paramount obligation to comply with such decisions. In particular, this section suggests that (1) where the Security Council orders a State to 'cooperate fully' with a court and (2) the court's statute provides that it does not defer to the immunities of States that are obliged to cooperate, this has been sufficient to override immunities.

By requiring a State to cooperate fully, the Security Council creates the same situation as was described in section 21.5.1: the Security Council has subjected the State to a regime

---

[138] See Broomhall, *International Justice*, 144–5; Wirth, 'Immunities, Related Problems', 456–7; Gaeta, 'Official Capacity', 993–5.
[139] *Al Bashir*, ICC PTC I, 4 March 2009.

which overrides its immunities.[140] The obligation to 'cooperate fully' imposes obligations identical to those of a State Party. Thus, the *source* of the obligation is the Chapter VII order to cooperate fully, and the *content* of the obligation is defined by the ICC Statute, because the Security Council has incorporated it by reference. The Council can impose obligations on Member States which may be identical to those found in a treaty.[141]

One popular objection to the loss of immunity of officials of non-States Parties is that the ICC Statute is simply a treaty, and hence its provisions, including Article 27, only bind States Parties. It is also argued that the mere fact that a situation was triggered by Security Council referral does not alter the legal positions of States.[142] These arguments are correct as far as they go, but they miss the basis for the obligation on non-States Parties. The legal obligation does not arise from the Statute. Nor does it arise from the mere fact of the referral. The obligation arises from the decision of the Security Council, acting under Chapter VII, requiring the State to cooperate fully.[143]

Another objection is that the Security Council can order States to relinquish immunities *vis-à-vis* a tribunal of its own creation, but not *vis-à-vis* a treaty creation such as the ICC.[144] However, no such limitation appears in Articles 41 or 42 of the Charter, nor has a conceptual underpinning for such a limitation been offered. Further, such arguments would require a return to costly and redundant tribunals to address immunities, and thus would contradict a major purpose of the Court, which was to avoid the need for the Council to create new ad hoc tribunals for each situation.[145] Instead the Council can compel Member States to cooperate with the Court under Chapter VII, just as it compelled cooperation with other tribunals.[146]

A more plausible objection is that the obligation to 'cooperate fully' is not sufficiently explicit to entail a loss of personal immunity.[147] Such issues will only be resolved conclusively through future practice, but a few counter-arguments can be made here. First, the obligation to cooperate must include not only Part 9 but also many other important Articles throughout the Statute.[148] Second, 'cooperate fully' was precisely the term used in the resolutions creating the ICTY and ICTR, and the formula has hitherto been considered

---

[140] Marko Milanovic, 'ICC Prosecutor Charges the President of Sudan with Genocide, Crimes against Humanity and War Crimes in Darfur' (28 July 2008) 12 *ASIL Insights*, available at www.asil.org/insights.cfm.

[141] See e.g. SC Res. 1373(2001). The Council can also impose obligations on Member States overriding any that arise from a treaty; see e.g. *Case Concerning Questions of Interpretation and Application of the 1971 Montreal Convention Arising from the Aerial Incident at Lockerbie* (*Libya* v. *USA*), Provisional Measures, ICJ, 14 April 1992, para. 42.

[142] Gaeta, 'President Al Bashir', 322–5; Dire Tladi, 'The ICC Decisions on Chad and Malawi: On Cooperation, Immunities, and Article 98' (2013) 11 *Journal of International Criminal Justice* 199, 211.

[143] Dapo Akande, 'The Legal Nature of Security Council Referrals to the ICC and its Impact on Al Bashir's Immunities' (2009) 7 *Journal of International Criminal Justice* 333, 341–2.

[144] Gaeta, 'President Al Bashir', 326, 330.

[145] Lionel Yee, 'The International Criminal Court and the Security Council' in Lee, *The Making of the Rome Statute*, 146.

[146] Claus Kreß and Kimberly Prost, 'Article 87' in Triffterer, *Observers' Notes* at 1523 and 1525. The Statute expressly contemplates that the facility of the Court is available to the Security Council and that a Council reference of a situation to the Court can entail a wider personal and territorial jurisdiction, further cooperation and different arrangements for funding: Arts. 13, 53(3), 87(5)(b), 87(7) and 115.

[147] In this vein it could be argued the Council decision imposes only Part 9 of the ICC Statute on a State, but not Art. 27, and hence immunities are not relinquished. A related argument might be that a State is obliged to waive its immunities under the Council resolution, but that if it fails to do so, other States still face conflicting obligations.

[148] As an incomplete list, see Arts. 3(3), 4(3), 4(4), 18(5), 19(8), 19(11), 27(2), 48, 54(2), 56, 57(3), 59, 64(6), 75(5) and 109.

perfectly sufficient to remove immunities.[149] In the context of the ICC, the most obvious interpretation of 'cooperate fully' is that a State must cooperate, in accordance with the terms of the Statute, to the same extent as if it were a State Party.[150] If 'cooperate fully' means cooperation *less* than that required of a State Party, it is profoundly unclear what that inferior extent of cooperation might be.[151] Moreover, it would seem incompatible with the adverb 'fully'.

Finally, one additional complication arises because of the narrow wording of Resolution 1593, which did not issue an order to all Member States. Instead it only ordered 'the Government of Sudan and all other parties to the conflict in Darfur' to cooperate fully, and 'urged' other States and organizations to cooperate fully.[152] What is the legal position if President Al Bashir travels to the territory of a *non-State Party?* States Parties are obliged to carry out an arrest, but non-States Parties are merely 'urged' to cooperate with the Court. They have no *obligation* to arrest Al Bashir or surrender him to the Court. Would a non-State Party be *permitted* to do so? The most plausible view is that the above analysis would still apply: Sudan has no immunity opposable to the ICC by virtue of the Council resolution, and thus arrest and surrender would not be a wrongful act about which Sudan could complain.[153]

These questions are certainly complex and controversial, and it will be valuable to have them clarified through practice and jurisprudence.

21.5.4 *The Taylor theory: is personal immunity irrelevant before international courts?*

An alternative theory is that immunities, including personal immunities, are simply not opposable to international courts. This theory has the advantage of simplicity: it facilitates international prosecution, it avoids the need to find any form of consent, and it vastly simplifies the Article 98 analysis, because it recognizes immunity for no one. However the theory has significant difficulties, as will be discussed here.

The 'international courts' theory

In June 2003, the Special Court for Sierra Leone (SCSL) issued a warrant for the arrest of Charles Taylor, who at the time was the President of Liberia. Lawyers for Charles Taylor made an application to declare the warrant null and void, on the grounds that he was a serving head of State, enjoying absolute immunity; that exceptions to this immunity can only be derived from other rules of international law such as Security Council resolutions under Chapter VII; and that the SCSL did not have Chapter VII powers.

---

[149] SC Res. 827(1993), para. 4, and SC Res. 935(1994), para. 2, both of which have been read in conjunction with the relevant Statute provisions denying immunities.

[150] Akande, 'Legal Nature of Security Council Referrals', 342.

[151] On the potential vagaries of 'cooperate fully', see Göran Sluiter, 'Obtaining Cooperation from Sudan – Where Is the Law?' (2008) 6 *Journal of International Criminal Justice* 871.

[152] SC Res. 1593(2005), para. 2.   [153] Akande, 'Legal Nature of Security Council Referrals', 344–5.

In May 2004, the SCSL issued its decision, holding that the SCSL was an 'international court' and as such not barred from prosecuting serving heads of State.[154] The SCSL relied on passages in *Pinochet* and *Yerodia* which made reference to the possibility of prosecution before international courts. The SCSL interpreted those passages as meaning that personal immunities are simply inapplicable before any tribunal that can be characterized as 'international'. Although the Security Council imposed no Chapter VII obligations upon States to cooperate with the SCSL, the SCSL held that it was created by an agreement between the UN and Sierra Leone, and therefore it was an 'international' court,[155] and hence personal immunity was no barrier to prosecution.

The same approach was adopted more recently, in 2011, by an ICC Pre-Trial Chamber (the 'Malawi decision'). That decision concerned the failure of Malawi, an ICC State Party, to execute the arrest warrant against President Al Bashir while he was visiting Malawi.[156] (A similar decision was issued against Chad.)[157] Malawi argued that Sudan is not a party to the ICC Statute, and hence Article 27, waiving immunity, is not applicable to Sudan.[158] The Pre-Trial Chamber rejected the argument. The Chamber noted the line of cases in which international courts had prosecuted heads of State, noted the growing number of States Parties to the ICC, and held that a 'critical mass' had been reached, wherein customary international law immunities no longer apply in this context.[159] The Chamber held that 'when cooperating with this Court and therefore acting on its behalf, States Parties are instruments for the enforcement of the *jus puniendi* of the international community'.[160]

The *outcome*, though not the reasoning, of both decisions is satisfactory. For the SCSL, Taylor was no longer a head of State at the time of the decision, having stepped down in August 2003, and hence he no longer enjoyed personal immunity. For the Malawi decision, the Chapter VII resolution by the Security Council placed Sudan under the same obligations as a State Party. Thus, in both cases there are sound legal grounds to support the conclusion that there was no immunity.

Grounds for scepticism about the 'international courts' theory

The legal theory advanced in *Taylor* has been accepted by some[161] and doubted by many.[162] The reasoning in the Malawi decision has also been met with significant scepticism.[163] The African Union criticized the decision for changing customary international law, rendering Article 98 redundant, and failing to engage with the effect of a Security Council resolution

---

[154] *Taylor*, SCSL A. Ch., 31 May 2004 (hereinafter '*Taylor*'), paras. 51–3. [155] *Taylor*, paras. 34–42.
[156] *Al Bashir* (ICC-02/05-01/09), ICC PTC I, 12 December 2011 (the 'Malawi decision').
[157] *Al Bashir* (ICC-02/05-01/09), ICC PTC I, 13 December 2011 (the 'Chad decision').   [158] Malawi decision, para. 8.
[159] *Ibid.*, para. 42.   [160] *Ibid.*, para. 46.
[161] Paola Gaeta, 'Does President Al Bashir Enjoy Immunity from Arrest?' (2009) 7 *Journal of International Criminal Justice* 315; UN, 'Immunities of State Officials', para. 87.
[162] Zsuzsanna Deen-Racsmány, 'Prosecutor v. Taylor: The Status of the Special Court for Sierra Leone and its Implications for Immunity' (2005) 18 *Leiden Journal of International Law* 299; Micaela Frulli, 'The Question of Charles Taylor's Immunity' (2004) 2 *Journal of International Criminal Justice* 1118; Koller, 'Immunities of Foreign Ministers'; King, 'Immunities and Bilateral Agreements'.
[163] However, contrary to the general trend, see the thoughtful defence by Claus Kreß, 'The International Criminal Court and Immunities under International Law for States Not Party to the Court's Statute' in Morten Bergsmo and Ling Yan (eds.), *State Sovereignty and International Criminal Law* (FICHL Publication Series No. 15, Beijing, 2012) 223–65.

on immunities.[164] The following are some reasons for scepticism about the 'international courts' theory.

First, the *Taylor* decision places inordinate weight on one passage in the *Yerodia* case. The ICJ, in explaining that immunity did not necessarily lead to impunity, noted that 'an incumbent ... Minister for Foreign Affairs may be subject to criminal proceedings before certain international courts, where they have jurisdiction'.[165] The *Taylor* decision interprets this passage as meaning that, as long as a court is 'international', it can disregard personal immunity. A more plausible reading is that the ICJ was simply addressing concerns that its ruling would secure impunity for leaders, and it was listing possible avenues of recourse. In other words, the ICJ was simply observing that there are international courts with the power to supersede personal immunities in accordance with known principles of law (for example, relinquishment through treaty or Chapter VII powers).

Second, the SCSL argued that personal immunity is rooted in the 'principle that one sovereign State does not adjudicate on the conduct of another State', which 'has no relevance to international criminal tribunals which are not organs of a State but derive their mandate from the international community'.[166] This statement misidentifies the rationale for personal immunity. The principle *par in parem non habet iudicium* is the basis for *functional* immunity, not personal immunity. Personal immunity exists to protect international relations by precluding any basis to interfere with high representatives without the consent of their sending State.

Third, it is in any event rather facile to sidestep immunity by asserting that a tribunal is not a State. An international tribunal is a creation of States. If neither the United Kingdom nor Canada has the power to ignore the personal immunity of a third State without consent, then the two together cannot create an international court and bestow upon it a power that they do not possess. The problem remains whether it is two States, or twenty, or sixty: they cannot bestow a power that they do not possess.[167]

The theory supporting *Taylor* emphasizes that international courts are in a 'vertical relationship' with States, ranking hierarchically above States and hence not subject to the same limitations.[168] However, international courts only acquire that vertical relationship (the ability to issue orders to States) in so far as States grant them that position, by treaty or other means such as Chapter VII.[169] A claim that one is acting 'on behalf of the international community', which is a rather amorphous concept, does not expand one's powers.

The *Taylor* judgment also emphasized that international courts have limited jurisdiction and safeguards against abuse, and that their collective judgment reduces the potential destabilizing effects of unilateral action.[170] These are indeed good *policy* arguments as to

---

[164] AU Press Release of 9 January 2012, quoted in Kreß, *ibid.*   [165] *Yerodia*, para. 61.   [166] *Taylor*, para. 51.
[167] *Nemo dat quod non habet.*   [168] Gaeta, 'President Al Bashir', 320–2.
[169] Note that this is a very different question from jurisdiction. To acquire jurisdiction over the nationals of a State does not require the consent of the State. See Chapter 8. There are many possible bases on which jurisdiction may be acquired; we deal here with the separate question of obtaining authority to set aside immunities.
[170] See e.g. *Taylor*, para. 51; similar possibilities are suggested in Ryszard Piotrowicz, 'Immunities of Foreign Ministers and their Exposure to Universal Jurisdiction' (2002) 76 *Austin Law Journal* 290, 293.

why such an exception might be desirable, but it does not explain the *legal* basis or origin for the alleged exception. As one commentator has noted, not only does this purported exception 'violate the principle of *pacta tertiis*, but it also ignores the fact that fairness [of the tribunal] has nothing to do with the creation of immunities'.[171] The safeguards and stability may help explain why States are willing to relinquish immunities, but they do not in themselves override immunities.

As for the ICC Malawi and Chad decisions, the Chamber points to a practice of international tribunals prosecuting heads of State, but in each of those prior cases the State concerned had directly or indirectly relinquished immunity. The Chamber argues that 120 States have ratified the Statute and thereby renounced their immunities, but that certainly does not prove that all other States have also lost their immunities. The Pre-Trial Chamber decision has been criticized for essentially disregarding Article 98 of the Statute.[172]

Finally, State practice seems to have been predicated on the need for relinquishment of personal immunity. Hence, we see the existence of Article 98 in the ICC Statute and the emphasis on the Chapter VII powers of the ad hoc Tribunals, as discussed in the previous sections.[173] For these reasons, the more plausible view is that under existing international law, 'it is not the international nature of the court as such but the waiver by the parties (and the Security Council's Chapter VII powers . . .) that accounts for the irrelevance of immunities before it'.[174]

Reasons for open-mindedness

There are, however, some reasons for a modest open-mindedness to the possibility of an 'international courts exception'. If further judicial rulings consistently support the proposition that personal immunity is no barrier before international courts, and that proposition is supported by State practice and *opinio iuris*, then such a rule could certainly become custom.[175]

21.6   Conclusion

As may be seen, the interplay of the law of accountability and the law of immunity is complex and controversial. However, as long as one recalls the purpose of functional and personal immunity, an underlying coherence in the law can be found. Functional immunity is more easily dealt with, because many authorities indicate that the immunity does not extended to serious international crime. However there are some uncertainties as to the parameters of that rule. Personal immunity has proved more resilient, allowing no exception

---

[171] Koller, 'Immunities of Foreign Ministers', 32.

[172] Dire Tladi, 'The ICC Decisions on Chad and Malawi: On Cooperation, Immunities, and Article 98' (2013) 11 *Journal of International Criminal Justice* 199.

[173] Another indicator of State practice is national legislation such as the United Kingdom's International Criminal Court Act 2001, s. 23(1) and (2). The legislation of some other countries (such as Canada) is consistent with this position but defers the issue entirely to the ICC.

[174] Deen-Racsmány, 'Prosecutor v. Taylor', 318; see also King, 'Immunities and Bilateral Agreements'.

[175] For the most thoughtful and thought-provoking arguments for the 'international courts' position, see Kreß, 'The International Criminal Court and Immunities'.

based on the nature of the crimes alleged. States have, however, relinquished personal immunity to some international jurisdictions; for example by ratifying the ICC Statute or by virtue of their obligations to the Security Council under Chapter VII of the UN Charter. The interplay of Articles 27 and 98 of the ICC Statute attracts controversy, but it appears that States bound by the ICC system lose their immunities but still respect the personal immunities of officials of States that are not bound. An alternative view is that personal immunity is never opposable to an international court.

Further reading

Dapo Akande, 'International Law Immunities and the International Criminal Court' (2004) 98 *American Journal of International Law* 407

Dapo Akande, 'The Legal Nature of Security Council Referrals to the ICC and its Impact on Al Bashir's Immunities' (2009) 7 *Journal of International Criminal Justice* 332

J. Craig Barker, *The Abuse of Diplomatic Privileges and Immunities: A Necessary Evil?* (Aldershot, 1996)

J. Craig Barker, 'The Future of Former Head of State Immunity after Ex Parte Pinochet' (1999) 48 *International and Comparative Law Quarterly* 937

Bruce Broomhall, *International Justice and the International Criminal Court: Between Sovereignty and the Rule of Law* (Oxford, 2003) Chapter 7

Antonio Cassese, 'When May Senior State Officials Be Tried for International Crimes? Some Comments on the Congo v. Belgium Case' (2002) 13 *European Journal of International Law* 853

Zsuzsanna Deen-Racsmány, 'Prosecutor v. Taylor: The Status of the Special Court for Sierra Leone and its Implications for Immunity' (2005) 18 *Leiden Journal of International Law* 299

Eileen Denza, 'Ex Parte Pinochet: Lacuna or Leap?' (1999) 48 *International and Comparative Law Quarterly* 949

Joanne Foakes, *The Position of Heads of State and Senior Officials in International Law* (Oxford, 2013)

Linda S. Frey and Marsha L. Frey, *The History of Diplomatic Immunity* (Columbus, OH, 1999)

Micaela Frulli, 'The Question of Charles Taylor's Immunity' (2004) 2 *Journal of International Criminal Justice* 1118

Paola Gaeta, 'Official Capacity and Immunities' in Cassese, *Commentary*, 975

Paola Gaeta, 'Does President Al Bashir Enjoy Immunity from Arrest?' (2009) 7 *Journal of International Criminal Justice* 315

David Koller, 'Immunities of Foreign Ministers: Paragraph 61 of the Yerodia Judgment as It Pertains to the Security Council and the International Criminal Court' (2004) 20 *American University International Law Review* 7

Claus Kreß, 'The International Criminal Court and Immunities under International Law for States Not Party to the Court's Statute' in Morten Bergsmo and Ling Yan (eds.), *State Sovereignty and International Criminal Law* (FICHL Publication Series No. 15, Beijing, 2012)

Rosanne Van Alebeek, *The Immunities of States and their Officials in International Criminal Law and International Human Rights Law* (Oxford, 2008) Chapter 5

Colin Warbrick, 'Immunity and International Crimes in English Law' (2004) 53 *International and Comparative Law Quarterly* 769

Colin Warbrick, Elena Martin Salgado and Nicholas Goodwin, 'The Pinochet Cases in the United Kingdom' (1999) 2 *Yearbook of International Humanitarian Law* 91

Arthur Watts, 'The Legal Position in International Law of Heads of State, Heads of Government and Foreign Ministers' (1994-III) 247 *Hague Recueil*

Steffen Wirth, 'Immunities, Related Problems, and Article 98 of the Rome Statute' (2001) 12 *Criminal Law Forum* 429

Steffen Wirth, 'Immunity for Core Crimes? The ICJ's Judgment in the Congo v. Belgium Case' (2002) 13 *European Journal of International Law* 877

22

Alternatives and Complements to Criminal Prosecution

22.1   Introduction

It is probably fair to say that most international criminal lawyers have an expressed (or unexpressed) preference for criminal prosecutions as the default response to the commission of international crimes. It is also the case that there has been something of a swing away from the 'politics of impunity' towards an 'age of accountability', or 'justice cascade' in international law.[1] However, many people hold out greater goals for international criminal justice than prosecutions for their own sake, and as was seen in Chapter 2, there is truth in the proposition that '[c]riminal prosecution … does some things rather well, other things only passably well, and makes an utter hash of still others'.[2] Thus, it is unsurprising that there have been other models suggested for dealing with international crimes, on the basis that they are said to fulfil more completely at least some of the purposes of trials, and incur fewer of the problems. Not all of them are mutually exclusive,[3] and indeed there is currently much debate on 'sequencing' of responses to international crime, where different responses are adopted over time to different situations, depending on their feasibility.[4] This chapter will provide an overview of the responses, alongside some of their positive and negative features.[5]

None of the mechanisms discussed in this chapter are in and of themselves perfect. Each has 'incompleteness and inescapable inadequacy' as a response to international crimes.[6] Just

---

[1] See e.g. Address of the UN Secretary-General, Ban Ki-moon, to the Review Conference of the International Criminal Court, 'The Age of Accountability', 31 May 2010; Leila Sadat, *The International Criminal Court and the Transformation of International Law: Justice for the New Millennium* (New York, 2002) Chapter 3; Katherine Sikkink, *The Justice Cascade: How Human Rights Prosecutions Are Changing World Politics* (New York, 2011); *Case Concerning the Arrest Warrant of 11 April 2000 (Democratic Republic of the Congo* v. *Belgium)* (2002) ICJ Reports, 3, 14 February 2002, Separate Opinion of Judges Higgins, Kojimans and Buergenthal, para. 51; *Case Concerning Questions Relating to the Obligation to Extradite or Prosecute (Belgium* v. *Senegal)*, Request for the Indication of Provisional Measures Order of 29 May 2009, ICJ General List 144, Dissenting Opinion of Judge Cançado Trindade, paras. 30–45.
[2] Mark Osiel, 'Ever Again: Legal Remembrance of Administrative Massacre' (1995) 144 *University of Pennsylvania Law Review* 463, 700.
[3] Obviously, amnesties and prosecutions are inconsistent, although amnesties do not have to cover all people or all offences.
[4] Laurel Fletcher, Harvey Weinstein with Jaimie Rowen, 'Context, Timing and the Dynamics of Transitional Justice: A Historical Perspective' (2009) 31 *Human Rights Quarterly* 163; Juan Mendez, 'Foreword' in Francesca Lessa and Leigh Payne (eds.), *Amnesty in the Age of Human Rights Accountability* (Cambridge, 2012) xvii, xxvii.
[5] See further e.g. W. Michael Reisman, 'Institutions and Practices for Restoring and Maintaining Public Order' (1995) 6 *Duke Journal of International and Comparative Law* 175; Martha Minow, *Between Vengeance and Forgiveness* (Boston, 1998); Ruti Teitel, *Transitional Justice* (New York, 2002).
[6] Minow, *Between Vengeance*, 5. See also Katherine Francke, 'Gendered Subjects of Transitional Justice' (2006) *Columbia Journal of Gender and Law* 813: 'Transitional justice will always be both incomplete and messy' (*ibid.*, 813).

because other mechanisms perform certain roles in a fashion that prosecutions cannot, does not mean that they are necessarily the most appropriate response to international crimes in any particular situation. The circumstances that attend decisions about that are too varied to take a 'one size fits all' approach to what ought to be done.[7] The political, economic, cultural and religious aspects of each situation have affected each response, and the outcomes of the approaches taken.[8] Care must therefore be taken when transposing 'lessons' directly from one context to another.

In appraising the way in which international crimes are dealt with, it must be remembered that, when decisions are being made about what to do about international crimes, practical limits, such as funding, political possibility and the available infrastructure, are important.[9] This is particularly the case for transitional societies or those emerging from conflicts. As was said in relation to the South African transition (which was itself by no means uncontroversial):

> the Constitution seeks to … facilitate the transition to a new democratic order, committed to 'reconciliation between the people of South Africa and the reconstruction of society'. The question is how this can be done effectively with the limitations of our resources and the legacy of the past … The families of those whose fundamental human rights were invaded by torture and abuse are not the only victims who have endured 'untold suffering and injustice' in consequence of the crass inhumanity of apartheid which so many have had to endure for so long. Generations of children born and yet to be born will suffer the consequences of poverty, of malnutrition, of homelessness, of illiteracy and disempowerment generated and sustained by the institutions of apartheid and its manifest effects on life and living for so many. The country has neither the resources nor the skills to reverse fully these massive wrongs … Those negotiators of the Constitution and leaders of the nation who were required to address themselves to these agonising problems must have been compelled to make hard choices. They could have chosen to direct that the limited resources of the state be spent by giving preference to the formidable delictual claims of those who had suffered from acts of murder, torture or assault perpetrated by servants of the state, diverting to that extent, desperately needed funds in the crucial areas of education, housing and primary health care … They were entitled to permit the claims of … school children and the poor and the homeless to be preferred.[10]

This is an important point. Equally, however, it must be noted that the language of necessity, appropriateness or feasibility is open to abuse,[11] and it often ignores the broader aspects of international crimes. One of the reasons which may justify a separate regime of international criminal accountability is that crimes which are thought to affect all humanity need to be dealt with sensitively as to both the national and international effects of such crimes. The

---

[7] See Mark Drumbl, *Atrocity, Punishment and International Law* (Cambridge, 2007).

[8] See on one aspect e.g. Thomas Brudholm and Thomas Cushman, *The Religious in Responses to Mass Atrocity* (Cambridge, 2009).

[9] See Secretary-General's Report on the Rule of Law and Transitional Justice in Post-Conflict Societies, 23 August 2004, UN Doc. S/2004/616, para. 3; Jon Elster, *Closing the Books: Transitional Justice in Historical Perspective* (Cambridge, 2004) Chapter 7; Stanley Cohen, 'State Crimes of Previous Regimes: Knowledge, Accountability and the Policing of the Past' (1995) 20 *Law and Social Inquiry* 7, 8.

[10] *Azanian People's Organization (AZAPO) and Others* v. *President of the Republic of South Africa* (1996) 4 SA 562 (CC), paras. 42–5.

[11] Susan Dwyer, 'Reconciliation for Realists' (1999) 13 *Ethics and International Affairs* 81.

international community of States has, at least at the level of rhetoric, affirmed the un-acceptability of impunity for such crimes.[12] It must also be remembered that transitional societies are not the only societies that need to deal with issues relating to international criminal law. It is all too easy to assume that international criminal law is only an issue for such States. Many stable, democratic States also have nationals, including State officials, who have committed international crimes.

22.2   Amnesties

Probably the most well-known, and controversial, alternative to prosecutions are amnes-ties.[13] An amnesty has been usefully, albeit incompletely, defined by Mark Freeman as 'an extraordinary legal measure whose primary function is to remove the prospect and con-sequences of criminal liability for designated individuals or classes of persons in respect of designated types of offences irrespective of whether the persons concerned have been tried for such offences in a court of law'.[14] Amnesties come in all shapes and sizes, and not all are express.[15] They can also, for example, block civil claims. Amnesties have a lengthy history in international law. The Treaty of Westphalia, which was considered by many to usher in the modern era in international law and order, contained an amnesty.[16] More recently, they were frequently employed in Latin America during and after the military dictatorship there, often as the price paid for the leaders of those dictatorships to hand over power to civilian governments.[17] Probably the most famous amnesty process is the South African one.[18]

As mentioned above, there are various types of amnesties, which range from those granted by regimes to themselves, such as that in Chile, to those which are voted upon by the population. Although the latter are usually thought, with some justification, to have greater legitimacy than the former, it must also be said that the consent of the population in such instances is often coerced, as the alternative is the continuation in power of an abusive regime.[19] A further distinction must be made between 'blanket' amnesties, which prevent legal proceedings against all persons without distinction, and those, such as the South African amnesty legislation, which required certain conduct (often full confession of crimes) and/or certain motivations for the crimes (usually political ones) before an amnesty was granted.[20] They remain a frequent, and controversial, feature of conflict settlement.[21]

---

[12] See e.g. SC Res. 1012 (28 August 1995), 1545 (21 May 2004), 1556 (11 June 2004) and 1564 (18 September 2004); and GA Res. 60/147.

[13] For detailed studies, see Louise Mallinder, *Amnesty, Human Rights and Political Transitions: Bridging the Peace and Justice Divide* (Oxford, 2008); Mark Freeman, *Necessary Evils: Amnesties and the Search for Justice* (Cambridge, 2009).

[14] Freeman, *Necessary Evils*, 13.

[15] *Ibid.*, 13–14. Furthermore, they can be factual, rather than legal, as where exile is offered, as was the case, for a time, for Charles Taylor in Nigeria. A similar fate was suggested for General Gaddafi prior to the coalition involvement in Libya in 2011. For critique, see Michael Scharf, 'From the eXile? Files: An Essay on Trading Justice for Peace' (2006) 63 *Washington and Lee Law Review* 339.

[16] Scott Veitch, 'The Legal Politics of Amnesty' in Emilios Christodoulidis and Scott Veitch (eds.), *Lethe's Law: Justice, Law and Ethics in Reconciliation* (Oxford, 2001) 33.

[17] For discussion, see Elster, *Closing the Books*, 62 *et seq.*

[18] Which has generated a huge literature; see e.g. Charles Villa-Vincencio and Erik Doxtader, *The Provocations of Amnesty* (Cape Town, 2003).

[19] Mark Osiel, *Mass Atrocity, Collective Memory and the Law* (New Brunswick, NJ, 1997) 138.

[20] See e.g. Veitch, 'The Legal Politics of Amnesty', 37–8.

[21] See Mallinder, *Amnesty*. The reasons for their frequency are a matter of some controversy: see e.g. Katherine Sikkink, 'The Age

22.2.1   *International law and amnesties*

There are a number of claims that amnesties for international crimes are always unlawful.[22] One claim is that amnesties are contrary to the duty to prosecute international crimes. The question of whether or not there is a duty to prosecute all international crimes was canvassed in Chapter 4. In brief, however, leaving aside treaty-based obligations to prosecute international crimes, it is difficult to prove a duty to prosecute every instance of an international crime on the basis of customary law, human rights obligations, or the *ius cogens* prohibitions that are encapsulated in parts of international criminal law.[23]

The question of duties to prosecute does not quite exhaust that of the legality of amnesties, although the issues are closely related. The question is whether there is an exception to any existing duty to prosecute when an amnesty is said to be necessary to re-establish peace.[24] Human rights bodies have not been very sympathetic to such claims, and are taking more and more measures to require, and oversee, prosecutions.[25] The Human Rights Committee has said that amnesties for State officials for torture are 'generally incompatible' with obligations to investigate, prosecute and prevent human rights violations, although the word 'generally' introduces some doubt into the matter.[26] The ICTY has gone further, asserting that the *ius cogens* prohibition on torture also delegitimizes any amnesty for torture.[27] This was also part of the decision of the European Court of Human Rights in *Ouid Dah*, where the Court agreed that amnesties for torture are generally incompatible with the international prohibition of that crime.[28] The African Commission on Human and Peoples' Rights determined that a Zimbabwean 'clemency order' which prevented prosecution of various serious human rights violations violated the African Charter on Human and Peoples' Rights.[29] The Inter-American Human Rights Court and Commission have been the most strident in declaring amnesties unlawful.[30] The probable high-water mark of its practice was the *Barrios Altos* case.[31] In this case, the Inter-American Court of Human

---

of Accountability: The Global Rise of Individual Accountability' in Lessa and Payne, *Amnesty*, 19, 20–1; Louise Mallinder, 'Amnesties' Challenge to the Global Accountability Norm? Interpreting Regional and International Trends in Amnesty Enactment' in Lessa and Payne, *Amnesty*, 69.

[22] Diane Orentlicher, 'Settling Accounts, The Duty to Prosecute Human Rights Violations of a Former Regime' (1991) 100 *Yale Law Journal* 2537.

[23] See further section 4.3.

[24] See e.g. Anja Siebert-Fohr, *Prosecuting Serious Human Rights Violations* (Oxford, 2009) 37 *et seq.*; and, on the State responsibility aspects of the question, Freeman, *Necessary Evils*, 65–8.

[25] See Alexandra Huneeus, 'International Criminal Law by Other Means: The Quasi-Criminal Jurisdiction of the Human Rights Courts' (2013) 107 *American Journal of International Law* 1.

[26] General Comment 20, Compilation of General Comments and General Recommendations Adopted by Human Rights Treaty Bodies, UN Doc. HRI\GEN\I\Rev.1 (1994) at 30.

[27] *Furundžija*, ICTY T. Ch. II, 10 December 1998, para. 155. See also *Karadžić*, ICTY T. Ch., 17 December 08; and Benjamin Brockman-Hawe, 'Decision on the Accused's Second Motion for Inspection and Disclosure: Immunity Issue' (2009) 58 *International and Comparative Law Quarterly* 726, 730–2. For critique of the ICTY here, see Mark Freeman and Max Pensky, 'The Amnesty Controversy in International Law' in Lessa and Payne, *Amnesty*, 42, 59–60.

[28] *Ould Dah* v. *France*, ECtHR, 17 March 2009, at 17.

[29] *Zimbabwe Human Rights NGO Forum* v. *Zimbabwe* (2006) AHRLR 128. Other examples include *Degli and Others* v. *Togo* (2000) AHRLR 317.

[30] See e.g. Inter-American Commission on Human Rights, El Salvador Report, 'State's Responsibility for 1983 Las Hajas Massacre', Report No. 26/92, 24 September 1992, para. 169. See generally Siebert-Fohr, *Prosecuting*, Chapter 3.

[31] *Barrios Altos* case (*Chumbipuma Aguirre et al.* v. *Peru*), Inter-American Court of Human Rights, 14 March 2001. See also *Gomes Lund et al.* v. *Brazil*, Inter-American Court of Human Rights, 24 November 2010.

Rights expressly said that the amnesty granted to State agents by the Peruvian government was invalid, and that:

This Court considers that all amnesty provisions, provisions on prescription and the establishment of measures designed to eliminate responsibility are inadmissible, because they are intended to prevent the investigation and punishment of those responsible for serious human rights violations such as torture, extrajudicial, summary or arbitrary execution and forced disappearance, all of them prohibited because they violate non-derogable rights recognized by international human rights law.[32]

This is a strong statement, and the case has been interpreted by some as sounding the death knell for all amnesties.[33] This may overstate what is probably the most assertive of all the international courts' decisions on point, and it has not been adopted by other international courts. The case ought also to be read against the backdrop of the nature of the (self) amnesties that were granted, the fact that they were not aimed at reconciliation, related to developed States, and did not involve mass participation in international crimes.[34]

At first sight, one international treaty provision, Article 6(5) of Additional Protocol II relating to non-international armed conflict, appears to argue in favour of amnesties. It reads as follows:

At the end of hostilities, the authorities in power shall endeavour to grant the broadest possible amnesty to persons who have participated in the armed conflict, or those deprived of their liberty for reasons related to the armed conflict, whether they are interned or detained.

But, in 1999, when interpreting this provision, the ICRC asserted that it was not intended to cover international crimes, in spite of the fact that this was not clear in 1977 when the Protocol was drafted.[35]

Claims that amnesties are always contrary to international law are therefore probably in advance of the current law, although UN policy is now formally against amnesties for international crimes.[36] The current position on amnesties in international law was summed up by the Special Court for Sierra Leone in the *Kallon and Kamara* decision:

that there is a crystallising international norm that a government cannot grant amnesty for serious violations of crimes under international law is amply supported by materials placed before the Court [but the view] that it has crystallised may not be entirely correct . . . it is accepted that such a norm is developing under international law.[37]

---

[32] *Ibid.*, para. 41.

[33] Lisa LaPlante, 'Outlawing Amnesty: The Return of Criminal Justice to Transitional Justice Schemes' (2008–9) 48 *Virginia Journal of International Law* 915.

[34] Siebert-Fohr, *Prosecuting*, 109; Robert Cryer, 'Accountability in Post-Conflict Societies: A Matter of Judgment, Practice or Principle?' in Nigel White and Dirk Klaasen (eds.), *The United Nations and Human Rights Protection in Post-Conflict Situations* (Manchester, 2005) 267, 269–70; Freeman, *Necessary Evils*, 48–50.

[35] Mallinder, *Amnesty*, 125–6.

[36] UN practice since the late 1990s (but not before) has been to say that amnesties are not acceptable: see Report of the Secretary-General on the Establishment of a Special Court for Sierra Leone UN Doc. S/2000/915, 4 October 2000, para. 24. For discussion and critique, see Freeman, *Necessary Evils*, 88–108.

[37] *Kallon and Kamara*, SCSL A. Ch., 13 March 2004, para. 82.

Similarly, a Trial Chamber of the Extraordinary Chambers in the Courts of Cambodia (ECCC) has said, 'an emerging consensus prohibits amnesties in relation to serious international crimes, based on a duty to investigate and prosecute these crimes and to punish their perpetrators'.[38] A complete prohibition may not yet have completely emerged, but the scope for lawful amnesties has narrowed.[39]

22.2.2 *The ICC and amnesties*[40]

The Preamble to the ICC Statute affirms 'that the most serious crimes of concern to the international community as a whole must not go unpunished', and that States Parties are 'determined to put an end to impunity for the perpetrators of such crimes'; it recalled 'that it is the duty of every State to exercise its criminal jurisdiction over those responsible for international crimes'.[41] Although these provisions do not create legal obligations, a failure to do anything about crimes committed by nationals of, or on the territory of, States Parties to the ICC Statute could well lead to the ICC exercising its powers to prosecute offenders itself.[42] A domestic amnesty does not bind the ICC nor its Prosecutor. The early practice of the ICC, in particular in relation to Uganda, has raised the issue of amnesties.[43] The ICC's Office of the Prosecutor took a tough line in this regard early on, refusing to take the possibility of an amnesty into account. Its current practice seems to follow this, with the Office of the Prosecutor criticizing the possibility of amnesties in Libya,[44] and making clear in the Colombia situation that the Office 'would view with concern any measures that appear designed to shield or hinder the establishment of criminal responsibility of individuals for crimes within the jurisdiction of the Court'.[45]

Although the possibility of the Prosecutor deciding to take account of amnesties may remain, the Office of the Prosecutor has taken the view that the 'interests of justice' required the ICC to prosecute international crimes rather than refraining from doing so on political grounds.[46] In taking that view, the Office of the Prosecutor stated that the drafters of the ICC Statute clearly chose prosecution as the appropriate response to international crimes.[47] Hence, when the Prosecutor is dealing with a matter, '[t]he issue is no longer about whether

---

[38] *Ieng Sary*, ECCC T. Ch., 3 November 2011, para. 53.
[39] Although see Christine Bell, *On the Law of Peace: Peace Agreements and the Lex Pacificatoria* (Oxford, 2008) 240–1; Freeman, *Necessary Evils, passim.*
[40] See generally Mallinder, *Amnesty*, 279–91; Freeman, *Necessary Evils*, 73–88; and section 8.6.5. For the view that the ICC Statute implies or creates a duty to prosecute, see Payam Akhavan, 'Whither National Courts? The Rome Statute's Missing Half, towards an Express and Enforceable Obligation for the Domestic Repression of International Crimes' (2010) 8 *Journal of International Criminal Justice* 1045.
[41] ICC Statute, Preamble, paras. 4–6.   [42] See section 8.6.5.
[43] See section 8.12; and William W. Burke-White and Scott Kaplan, 'Shaping the Contours of Domestic Justice: The International Criminal Court and an Admissibility Challenge in the Uganda Situation' in Stahn and Sluiter, *Emerging Practice*, 79.
[44] Statement of the Prosecutor of the International Criminal Court to the Security Council, 7 November 2012, UN Doc. S.PV/6855, 3.
[45] *Situation in Colombia*, Interim Report, November 2012, para. 205.
[46] See e.g. Darryl Robinson, 'Serving the Interests of Justice: Amnesties, Truth Commissions and the International Criminal Court' (2003) 14 *European Journal of International Law* 481; Michael P. Scharf, 'The Amnesty Exception to the Jurisdiction of the International Criminal Court' (1999) 32 *Cornell International Law Journal* 507.
[47] ICC Office of the Prosecutor, Policy Paper on the Interests of Justice, September 2007, at 3–4.

we agree or disagree with the pursuit of justice in moral or practical terms: it is the law', and non-prosecution is a 'last resort'.[48]

While the reason that many assert for the necessity of amnesties is the so-called 'peace versus justice' dilemma,[49] the Office of the Prosecutor has taken the position that the 'interests of justice' are not the same as the interests of peace, and its mandate does not cover the latter. Those considerations were, to the Office of the Prosecutor, the domain of the political organs of the UN, in particular the Security Council, which has the power to defer (for renewable one-year periods) investigations and prosecutions under Article 16 of the ICC Statute.[50] Whether this amounts to an abdication of responsibility, or a sensible means of ensuring that the ICC is seen as being apolitical, is perhaps an open question.[51]

22.2.3 *Domestic jurisdictions and amnesties*

Domestic amnesties do not bind States other than the granting State in their exercise of extraterritorial jurisdiction; legislation in one State does not alter the jurisdiction of another.[52] It was in part for this reason that the Special Court for Sierra Leone declared that it was not unlawful for the United Nations to refuse to accept the amnesty contained in the 1999 Lomé Peace Accord and thus grant the Court jurisdiction over international crimes from 1996:

Where jurisdiction is universal, a State cannot deprive another of its jurisdiction to prosecute the offender by the grant of amnesty. It is for this reason unrealistic to regard as universally effective the grant of an amnesty by a State in regard to grave international crimes in which universal jurisdiction exists. A State cannot bring into oblivion and forgetfulness a crime, such as a crime against international law, which other States are entitled to keep alive and remember.[53]

The Court had, as mentioned above (see section 22.2.1), noted that amnesties were not contrary to customary law, but took the view that it was not an abuse of process for the Court to ignore the amnesty given its perilous status under international law and the fact that the Court was not part of the Sierra Leonean justice system.[54]

The extent to which amnesties granted within a jurisdiction preclude action by municipal courts in that jurisdiction depends, *inter alia*, on the status of international law in the domestic legal order, and the consistency or otherwise of the amnesty with international law.[55] It is undeniable that judges in some countries are increasingly unlikely to accept

---

[48] *Ibid.*, 4, 8–9.   [49] See section 2.3.1.   [50] See section 8.9.
[51] See e.g. Jens David Ohlin, 'Peace, Security and Prosecutorial Discretion' in Carsten Stahn and Göran Sluiter (eds.), *The Emerging Practice of the International Criminal Court* (Leiden, 2009) 185; Steven Roach, *Politicizing the International Criminal Court: The Convergence of Politics, Ethics and Law* (New York, 2006). It bears remembering that, as Martti Koskenniemi has said, institutions enact, rather than replace politics: Martti Koskenniemi, *The Gentle Civilizer of Nations: The Rise and Fall of International Law 1870–1960* (Cambridge, 2002) 177. The Prosecutor's point was, however, that the politics have been, and are still to be, determined by others, not by the ICC.
[52] In *Ould Dah* v. *France*, ECtHR, 17 March 2009, the European Court of Human Rights decided that a Mauritanian amnesty for torture occurring in Mauritania did not prevent France from prosecuting torture there; see section 22.2.1.
[53] *Kallon and Kamara*, SCSL A. Ch., 13 March 2004, para. 67.
[54] *Ibid.* And see José Doria, 'The Work of the Special Court for Sierra Leone through its Jurisprudence' in José Doria *et al.* (eds.), *The Legal Regime of the International Criminal Court: Essays in Honour of Igor Blishchenko* (The Hague, 2009) 229, 243. See also Chapter 9.
[55] Mallinder, *Amnesty*, 204. For a detailed survey of court decisions on point, see *ibid.*, Chapter 4.

amnesties. For example, there are a number of examples of domestic courts, after many years of accepting amnesties, coming around to the view that they are unconstitutional, not relevant to the particular charge, or otherwise inapplicable. For example, in 2005 the Argentine Supreme Court declared the amnesties relating to the 'Dirty War' in the 1970s and 1980s to be unconstitutional.[56] In this case, although the Congress had already repealed the amnesty, the Supreme Court, relying on international law, made clear that the amnesty was also unlawful. In other examples, courts have restrictively interpreted amnesties. For example, in Chile, the Supreme Court has determined that neither amnesties nor statutes of limitation apply to offences involving disappearances, since they are 'continuing' offences, and therefore not susceptible to being amnestied.[57]

The ECCC has determined that State practice 'demonstrates at a minimum a retroactive right for third States, internationalised and domestic courts to evaluate amnesties and to set them aside or limit their scope should they be deemed incompatible with international norms'.[58] This may go a little far. Third States and internationalized courts (which are not grounded solely in the domestic legal order) are simply not bound by other States' domestic amnesties, rather than having a right to set them aside or interpret them. Also, many (although not all) domestic courts in the country of the crime have overturned or limited amnesties on the basis of their constitutional provisions, rather than international law directly, but the result is often the same. Still, it bears remembering that the majority of domestic decisions on point have upheld amnesties early after their passage, only later becoming willing to challenge or limit them.[59]

22.2.4 *Appraisal of amnesties*

Amnesties are controversial both in law and policy.[60] Those who speak in their favour often claim that it is necessary to have amnesties to bring to an end conflicts, and that to insist on anything more is to condemn others to death or other serious human rights violations, as combatants and others will refuse to relinquish their weapons or power without promises of non-prosecution.[61] Others see the grant of amnesties as giving in to blackmail,[62] and fostering a culture of impunity which encourages the future commission of international crimes.[63] It has also been said that amnesties do not lead to peace, and that 'warlords and political leaders capable of committing human rights atrocities are not deterred by amnesties obtained, but emboldened'.[64] Granting amnesties, therefore, is considered by many to

---

[56] *Simón*, Decision of 14 June 2005, Case No. 17.768. See Christine Bakker, 'A Full Stop to Amnesty in Argentina' (2005) 3 *Journal of International Criminal Justice* 1106.
[57] *Sepúlveda*, 17 November 2004. See Fannie Lafontaine, 'No Amnesty or Statute of Limitation for Enforced Disappearances: The Sandoval Case before the Supreme Court of Chile' (2005) 3 *Journal of International Criminal Justice* 469. For an example of a narrow reading from an internationalized tribunal, see *Ieng Sary*, ECCC PTC, 17 October 2008, para. 61.
[58] *Ieng Sary*, ECCC T. Ch., 3 November 2011, para. 53.   [59] Mallinder, *Amnesty*, 206.
[60] See e.g. Freeman, *Necessary Evils*, 17–32.
[61] Anonymous, 'Human Rights in Peace Negotiations' (1996) 18 *Human Rights Quarterly* 249.
[62] Mallinder, *Amnesty*, 1–2.   [63] See Anja Sibert-Fohr, *Prosecuting Serious Human Rights Violations* (Oxford, 2009) 281–2.
[64] Leila Nadya Sadat, 'The Effect of Amnesties before Domestic and International Tribunals: Morality, Law and Politics' in Edel Hughes, William Schabas and Ramesh Thakur (eds.), *Atrocities and International Accountability: Beyond Transitional Justice* (Tokyo, 2007) 225, 227.

undermine the deterrent function of international criminal law (to the extent that it has one),[65] and to represent an ugly political compromise. Sometimes this compromise is also seen as one between elites who bargain away the rights of victims with little regard for them.[66] In part, this has led to calls for 'transitional justice from below', where the calls of those outside political elites are given greater respect,[67] although it is accepted that this can also be exclusionary.[68]

As a result, many approach amnesties with a deeply sceptical raised eyebrow.[69] Still, even if the time for 'blanket' amnesties may now be over, there are other forms of amnesty, such as the South African amnesty, that are accompanied by other processes that may render them more acceptable, and it is important not to treat all amnesties as the same. Conditional amnesties, that require truth telling, or apply to the less responsible, or are democratically legitimated in the State that passes them, are more likely to be acceptable than those that do not.[70]

It is often said (but not empirically proved) that amnesties promote reconciliation between previously antagonistic parties, and allow populations to 'move on' from the past.[71] However, on the other side it is argued that 'it is difficult to imagine how society can liberate itself from a past in which impunity, lawlessness and abuse of power have prevailed, unless respect for the basic principle of individual criminal responsibility is resurrected'.[72] This is often reduced to the phrase 'no peace without justice' (or, more recently, 'no lasting peace without justice'). Whether this is empirically true is a matter of contention.

The matter is made more complex by loose talk about reconciliation (often from perpetrators, rather than victims).[73] Reconciliation is not a simple notion.[74] For example, it is often assumed that reconciliation is a social process, whereas it is at least as much an individual one, between victim and perpetrator.[75] Also, it must be acknowledged that reconciliation, and its partner, forgiveness, often draw upon religious (often, although by no means exclusively, Christian) notions, which are not necessarily universalizable.[76] Indeed, some question the philosophical appropriateness of forgiveness at all, or at least

---

[65] See Mallinder, *Amnesty*, 17.

[66] Richard A. Wilson, *The Politics of Truth and Reconciliation in South Africa: Legitimizing the Post-Apartheid State* (Cambridge, 2001); Richard Burchill, 'From East Timor to Timor-Leste: A Demonstration of the Limits of International Law in the Pursuit of Justice' in Doria, *Legal Regime*, 255, 288–9. Desmond Tutu's response is that the delegations which negotiated the amnesty in South Africa included victims, who were entitled to speak on behalf of all the victims: Desmond Tutu, *No Future without Forgiveness* (London, 1999) 52–4.

[67] See Kieran McEvoy and Lorna McGregor, *Transitional Justice from Below: Grassroots Activism and the Struggle for Change* (Oxford, 2008).

[68] Kieran McEvoy and Lorna McGregor, 'Transitional Justice from Below: An Agenda for Research, Policy and Praxis' in McEvoy and McGregor, *Transitional Justice*, 9–10.

[69] As Freeman and Pensky, two advocates for the continued relevance of amnesty accept, they are 'potentially serious failures of justice': Freeman and Pensky, 'Amnesty', 43.

[70] See Mallinder, *Amnesty*, Chapters 2–4 and 10; John Dugard, 'Dealing with the Crimes of a Past Regime: Is Amnesty Still an Option?' (1999) 12 *Leiden Journal of International Law* 1001.

[71] Andreas O'Shea, *Amnesty for Crime in International Law and Practice* (The Hague, 2002) 23–33.

[72] Lyal S. Sunga, 'Ten Principles for Reconciling Truth Commissions and Criminal Proceedings' in Doria, *Legal Regime*, 1071.

[73] Stanley Cohen, *States of Denial: Knowing About Atrocities and Suffering* (Cambridge, 2001) 238–9.

[74] See e.g. Laura Olson, 'Provoking the Dragon on the Patio: Matters of Transitional Justice: Penal Repression vs Amnesties' (2006) 88 *International Review of the Red Cross* 275, 277.

[75] Arne J. Vetlesen, *Evil and Human Agency: Understanding Collective Evildoing* (Cambridge, 2005) 272–81.

[76] Thomas Brudholm, 'On the Advocacy of Forgiveness after Mass Atrocities' in Brudholm and Cushman, *The Religious*, 124. For a more sanguine view, see Daniel Philpott, 'When Faith Meets History: The Influence of Religion on Transitional Justice' in *ibid.*, 174.

in all circumstances.[77] What is certain is that reconciliation, like friendship, cannot be forced upon people, and some victims will not wish to be reconciled with their persecutors, in particular in the absence of remorse.[78] Equally, there is no doubt that forgiveness has accompanied amnesties in certain circumstances.[79]

Alongside forgiveness, there is also the possibility of forgetfulness, in particular, of victims. After all, the term 'amnesty', as is often pointed out, shares a common Latin root, *amnestia*, with forgetfulness – amnesia.[80] With this comes the risk of increased denial or relativization of international crimes.[81] Not all amnesty processes provide for revelations about what has been done, and, as such, can lead to a refusal to acknowledge the suffering of victims, or the extent of wrongdoing. This can be non-accidental: as Stanley Cohen has said: 'social control is . . . possible by transforming . . . or obliterating the past . . . not by opening the past to scrutiny, but closing it and deliberately setting up barriers to memory. This mode of policing the past calls not for the recovery of memory, but its eradication',[82] or by simple 'slippage' when things are not acknowledged.[83] This strategy is not necessarily effective, in particular where, as in South America, long-standing victims' rights advocates have kept the suffering of the victims visible, and, as time has gone on, amnesties and the like have been repealed.[84]

Still, international law has not yet developed so far as to prohibit all amnesties in all situations. There is also political support for them in some States; for example, prior to the Iraq war in 2003, the United States offered Saddam Hussein exile and non-prosecution if he were to stand down as President of Iraq,[85] and there have been reports of similar offers being made to Colonel Gadaffi in 2011.[86] In spite of the fact that the language of forgiving and forgetting comes easier to the mouths of perpetrators than victims, there have been political defences of amnesties as being necessary measures in post-conflict situations, at least with respect to lower-ranking offenders, and where resources outstrip the possibility of prosecuting any more than a small number of defendants.[87] As a result, amnesties and the criticisms of them are likely to continue to be a feature of responses to international crimes for the foreseeable future.

22.3   Truth commissions

In part because of the possibility that amnesties will lead to forgetfulness or denial, one of the activities which often accompany them is the setting up of a truth commission.[88] A truth

---

[77] See the discussion in Brudholm and Cushman, *The Religious*; and Charles Griswold, *Forgiveness: A Philosophical Investigation* (Cambridge, 2007).

[78] Antje du Bois-Pedain, *Transitional Amnesty in South Africa* (Cambridge, 2007) 232–43, 286–93; Brudholm and Cushman, *The Religious*, 132–5; Olson, 'Provoking the Dragon', 277.

[79] For examples in South Africa, see Tutu, *No Future.*   [80] See e.g. Mallinder, *Amnesty*, 4.   [81] E.g. see *ibid.*, 243.

[82] Cohen, *States of Denial*, 243.   [83] *Ibid.*, 222.

[84] LaPlante, 'Outlawing Amnesty', 950–6. On an African analogue, in relation to Hissène Habré, see *Case Concerning Questions Relating to the Obligation to Extradite or Prosecute (Belgium v. Senegal)*, Request for the Indication of Provisional Measures Order of 29 May 2009, ICJ General List 144, Dissenting Opinion of Judge Cançado Trindade, paras. 30–45.

[85] See Mallinder, *Amnesty*, Chapter 8.

[86] William Schabas, *Unimaginable Atrocities: Justice, Politics, Rights at the War Crimes Tribunal* (Oxford, 2012) 176.

[87] *Ibid., passim.*

[88] Albie Sachs, *The Strange Alchemy of Life and Law* (Oxford, 2009) 84. On truth commissions, see generally Priscilla Hayner, *Unspeakable Truths: Confronting State Terror and Atrocity*, 2nd edn (London, 2011); Priscilla Hayner, 'Fifteen Truth Commissions – A Comparative Study' (1994) 16 *Human Rights Quarterly* 597; Minow, *Between Vengeance*, Chapter 4.

commission has been defined as a body that '(1) is focused on the past, rather than ongoing, events; (2) investigates a pattern of events that took place over a period of time; (3) engages directly and broadly with the affected population, gathering information on their experiences; (4) is a temporary body, with the aim of concluding with a final report; and (5) is officially authorised by the state under review'.[89] They are better than prosecutions at achieving certain aims,[90] and they have been set up as an alternative to prosecutions, especially where the clandestine nature of many of the offences means that they are difficult, if not impossible, to prove to the relevant criminal standard. They are also a means of attempting to get beyond the 'closing of ranks' that can make prosecution of offences by those in close-knit groups, such as particular regiments or teams, so difficult. The idea behind many truth commissions is that people will be more willing to tell about their activities if they are not to be prosecuted for them. This can be important, for example when people have 'disappeared' and relatives of the victims are caught in limbo, not knowing the fate of their family members. Truth commissions can also enable more victims to be able to tell their story than is possible in a court, with all its procedural restrictions. Some commissions, such as the Guatemalan commission, have the authority to make recommendations for reforms, although they are not always taken up.[91] This is indicative of a broader issue; truth commissions are usually only given a mandate to recommend action, and they are not normally given any authority to oversee or ensure their implementation.[92]

The terms of reference setting up a commission will define the time frame and sometimes the kinds of conduct to be investigated. Their mandates and terms of reference are usually the outcome of negotiations between the relevant parties,[93] and can reflect their relative power. One of the main purposes of truth commissions is to acknowledge the harm that was done to the victims, by writing an official report setting out the violations of their rights. This is thought not only to counter later denials,[94] but also to provide a form of healing for victims,[95] and provide the basis for societal reconciliation. The South African Truth and Reconciliation report named names, whilst the Argentine commission did not have the authority to do so.[96] Where names are named, it is more important to have some form of procedural protection for those giving evidence or admitting crimes.[97] For example, some truth commissions that identified perpetrators gave them advance notice of this and a chance to respond.[98]

There are other possible limits on the reports they issue. The South African report, for example, only had the mandate to deal with political violence. It could not, therefore, deal

---

[89] Hayner, *Unspeakable Truths*, 11–12. Mark Freeman, *Truth Commissions and Procedural Fairness* (Cambridge, 2006) 18 defines them as 'an ad hoc, autonomous, and victim centred commission of inquiry set up in and authorised by a state for the primary purposes of (1) investigating and reporting on the principal causes and consequences of broad and relatively recent patterns of severe violence or repression that occurred in the state during determinate periods of abusive rule or conflict, and (2) making recommendations for their redress and future prevention'.

[90] See generally Alison Bisset, *Truth Commissions and Criminal Courts* (Cambridge, 2012) Chapter 1; Report of the Special Rapporteur on the Promotion of Truth, Justice, Reparation and Guarantees of Non-Recurrence, Pablo de Grieff, A/HRC/24/42, 28 August 2013.

[91] Hayner, *Unspeakable Truths*, Chapter 10.

[92] Report of the Special Rapporteur on the Promotion of Truth, paras. 44, 71–9.

[93] On the various aspects of mandates of truth commissions, see Report of the Special Rapporteur on the Promotion of Truth, paras. 32–52.

[94] Cohen, *States of Denial*, Chapter 10.   [95] Minow, *Between Vengeance*, 66–74.

[96] Hayner, *Unspeakable Truths*, Chapter 8.   [97] See Freeman, *Truth Commissions*.   [98] *Ibid.*, Chapter 7.

with issues such as land dispossessions, forcible transfers and other aspects of apartheid.[99] As a result, it could only tell part of the story of apartheid. It could not deal with the use and abuse of the legal and political system in creating and maintaining the apartheid system. In contrast, the Liberian Truth and Reconciliation Commission, although intended to focus primarily on the post-1979 history of that country's conflict, also looked into issues such as corruption, misgovernment and the role of third party States.[100] The general trend is towards broader mandates,[101] which, whilst welcome at some levels, can stretch the limited resources of commissions.

The quality of a commission's report depends in part on how good the information available to the commission is. It can be difficult to persuade perpetrators to come forward to testify about their role in repressions, or victims to speak about sensitive matters such as sexual offences committed against them.[102] The confessions of perpetrators can also be framed in a manner which amounts, in fact, to a form of denial.[103] This was, in part, avoided in South Africa by making amnesty applications contingent on attending the commission and telling the full story. There have been some prosecutions for those who refused to testify, or who did not completely disclose their actions.[104] However, some important witnesses such as ex-President P. W. Botha refused to testify before the commission.

The evidence-taking engaged in by a commission often requires people to incriminate themselves and, therefore, truth commissions sometimes stand in place of prosecutions. This does not, however, have to be the case.[105] For example, the Truth and Reconciliation Commission in Sierra Leone took place at the same time as the Special Court for Sierra Leone.[106] Relations between the two were strained, however, and the Commission was critical of the Special Court in its report, in particular of the fact that the Special Court was not willing to allow Sam Hinga Norman, being tried before that court, to testify before the Commission in the manner it preferred.[107] This is indicative of the difficult problems that relate to the extent to which testimony and other forms of evidence can be used later on in prosecutions, at home, abroad and before international criminal tribunals, although the latter two will not be bound directly by any promise of confidentiality or non-use granted by the territorial State.[108] The Liberian Truth and Reconciliation Commission's final report recommended prosecutions of some of those responsible for gross violations of human rights or serious violations of humanitarian law,[109] although these have not yet materialized.

---

[99] *Ibid.*, 73–4.

[100] Truth and Reconciliation Commission of Liberia, Final Report, Vol. II, available at www.trcofliberia.org/reports/final, Chapter 6, 261, 243–51.

[101] Report of the Special Rapporteur on the Promotion of Truth, paras. 35. 40.   [102] Hayner, *Unspeakable Truths*, 77–8.

[103] Cohen, *States of Denial*, Chapter 4.   [104] Sachs, *Strange Alchemy*, 78.

[105] See generally Bisset, *Truth Commissions*; Sunga, 'Ten Principles'.

[106] See William Schabas, 'Internationalized Courts and their Relationship with Alternative Accountability Mechanisms: The Case of Sierra Leone' in Cesare Romano *et al.* (eds.), *Internationalized Criminal Courts* (Oxford, 2004) 157.

[107] *Witness to Truth: Report of the Truth and Reconciliation Commission for Sierra Leone* (Accra, 2004) Vol. 3b, Chapter 6: *Norman*, SCSL A. Ch., 28 November 2003.

[108] See generally Bisset, *Truth Commissions*, Chapters 3–5.

[109] Truth and Reconciliation Commission of Liberia, Final Report, Vol. II, 268. It also recommended non-prosecution (but not amnesty) for some perpetrators, on the basis that they had cooperated fully with the Commission: *ibid.*, 268–9, 288.

There are questions about the extent to which the reports of truth commissions can reflect any form of 'objective truth', if such a concept exists, and whether they can lead to an agreed history between old enemies.[110] Given the orientation of truth commissions towards victims, they tend not to have the rules of procedure and evidence that are considered necessary in courts to ensure reliability and verification of testimony.[111] Whilst this is understandable and correct, it may impact upon the truth that the report seeks to set out.[112]

It has also been questioned whether truth telling does lead to reconciliation,[113] or an ability to move beyond the past.[114] Similarly, it has been doubted whether truth and reconciliation are congruent goals.[115] Most, though, accept that truth has a role to play in reconciliation, although few would say that truth alone can achieve such a goal.[116] Much again can depend on what is reported on; commissions which exclude the roles of bystanders and of those who benefited from the system that committed such crimes have been criticized on the basis that they cannot provide for reconciliation, as they exclude a large part of society from their gaze.[117]

Sometimes, as occurred in South Africa, as part of the attempt to promote reconciliation and help provide victims with some form of healing, victims are given the opportunity to attend the hearings and discuss the revelations made by the perpetrators. Some scholars are of the view that truth commissions are particularly well suited to provide healing for victims.[118] Much depends on the attitude of perpetrators, and the engagement that they have with the process ranges from the full to the essentially grudging and formal. Albie Sachs writes of the South African Truth and Reconciliation hearings that:

instead of coming forward and speaking from the heart and crying and being open, most of the perpetrators came in neatly pressed suits, expressing tight body language, with their lawyers next to them, and read prepared statements as though they were in a court of law. Their admissions were important but tended to be limited to a factual acknowledgement of unlawful conduct coupled with a rehearsed apology, rather than encompassing an emotional and convincing acknowledgement of wrongdoing.[119]

Others have used truth and reconciliation hearings as political platforms.[120] Rather like in the case of testifying in criminal proceedings, the extent to which victims are assisted by the process depends on individual reactions, and these are not easily extrapolated into general statements about victims as a whole. Some victims in South Africa issued a court challenge

---

[110] Tutu, *No Future*, 33; François du Bois, 'Nothing but the Truth: The South African Alternative to Corrective Justice in Transitions to Democracy' in Christodoulidis and Veitch, *Lethe's Law*, 91.

[111] See Freeman, *Truth Commissions*.

[112] Anne Orford, 'Commissioning the Truth' (2006) 15 *Columbia Journal of Gender and Law* 851, 859–60.

[113] Hayner, *Unspeakable Truths*, 155–61.

[114] It is possible that the idea that truth allows people to move on is at least in part a religious notion: see e.g. John 8:23: 'And ye shall know the truth, and the truth shall make you free.' It is notable that the South African Truth and Reconciliation Commission often began its hearings with prayers (Sachs, *Strange Alchemy*, 75). See also Minow, *Between Vengeance*, 55.

[115] Hayner, *Unspeakable Truths*, 182–3.   [116] See e.g. Minow, *Between Vengeance*, 79–83.

[117] Rama Maini, 'Does Power Trump Morality? Reconciliation or Transitional Justice?' in Hughes, Schabas and Thakur, *Atrocities*, 27, 36.

[118] Minow, *Between Vengeance*, 61–79.

[119] Sachs, *Strange Alchemy*, 86–7. A similar problem was noted by the Truth and Reconciliation Commission of Liberia, Final Report, Vol. II, v.

[120] Minow, *Between Vengeance*, 83.

to the Truth and Reconciliation Commission and the amnesty process, although it was rejected by the South African Constitutional Court.[121]

Truth commissions, as has been said, are both high risk and 'inherently political enterprises'.[122] They are set up for reasons that are both good and bad. They may well be created in some circumstances to ensure that victims are given acknowledgment of their suffering, or as a means of attempting to prevent the recurrence of the crimes.[123] In others, though, 'a cynical government may hope that a truth commission will help exhaust public interest in greater measures of political and legal accountability'.[124] Such critiques have been made in relation to the recommendation of the East Timor Truth and Reconciliation Commission that there be no further prosecutions.[125] Truth commissions are considered by some to be an *ersatz* response to international crimes. This is a harsh evaluation: truth commissions do not always replace prosecutions, and can go at least part of the way to fulfilling goals that prosecutions cannot, particularly for victims.[126] Much, of course, depends on how well the process is designed and run,[127] and 'a poorly executed truth commission may be worse than no truth commission at all'.[128]

22.4   Lustration

One way of dealing with large-scale administrative complicity in international crimes is lustration, that is to say, the purging of public servants who are thought to be responsible for international crimes.[129] This was a frequently used mechanism in Eastern Europe after the collapse of Communism there in the late 1980s. There are elements of this approach to international crimes in the removal of members of the Ba'ath party from the Iraqi public service and judiciary. Lustration may be seen as a means of removing corrupt or inefficient staff, but the main purpose is often a form of punishment. Although it can deal in some ways with large-scale complicity, the fact that it is a form of punishment (or is intended to be) is problematic, because it involves serious consequences for people, but is almost always done on a mass basis, without individual hearings to determine what precise responsibility a lustrated person bears. In many totalitarian societies, party membership is necessary for a career in the civil service, and many join essentially as an administrative convenience, and are not personally involved in wrongdoing. As a result, it is questionable whether lustration is consistent with human rights law, in particular the right to have rights and duties at law

---

[121] See *Azanian People's Organization (AZAPO) and Others* v. *President of the Republic of South Africa* (1996) 4 SA 562 (CC).
[122] Freeman, *Truth Commissions*, 37.   [123] *Ibid.*, 38.   [124] *Ibid.*, 37.   [125] Burchill, 'From East Timor', 289.
[126] Minow, *Between Vengeance*, 55–90.
[127] For some of the factors that are relevant in this regard, see Report of the Special Rapporteur on the Promotion of Truth, paras. 53–70.
[128] Maini, 'Does Power Trump Morality?', 34. The Secretary-General's Report on the Rule of Law and Transitional Justice, para. 51, takes the view that truth commissions are best formed through consultative processes on mandates and commissioner selection and that, to be successful, they must enjoy real independence and have credible commissioner criteria and processes, strong public information and communication strategies, be gender- and victim-sensitive and provide for reparations. They also need international support.
[129] See generally Teitel, *Transitional Justice*, Chapter 5; Stanley Cohen, 'State Crimes of Previous Regimes: Knowledge, Accountability and the Policing of the Past' (1995) 20 *Law and Social Inquiry* 7.

determined by a judicial process.[130] Punishment is only appropriate following criminal proceedings.[131] Notwithstanding this, the Liberian Truth and Reconciliation Commission recommended that people whom it had found responsible for grave crimes ought to be barred from public office.[132] The United Nations has undertaken vetting proceedings, for example in Kosovo; however, these are designed as individuated processes, where individuals are identified who have engaged in wrongdoing and are given opportunities to answer allegations against them. This is to ensure that the processes are compatible with international human rights law standards.[133]

22.5   Reparations and civil claims

International crimes, where attributable to States, have been the subject of reparations. Germany, for example, has paid over US$60 billion to victims in reparations for the Holocaust. Reparations have also been given to some of those who were the victims of the Argentine junta in the 1970s and 1980s.[134] There is a human right to a remedy for violations of human rights, which may involve some form of financial recompense.[135] The levels of such reparations are often controversial, however, and many societies in which international crimes are committed do not have large funds to finance reparations programmes. Even so, the symbolic function of reparations can be important.[136]

There may also be the possibility of bringing private civil actions against those responsible for international crimes, either in the State where the activity occurred, or in a third State.[137] The United States is perhaps the most well known of those third States, owing to its Alien Tort Claims Act and the *Filartiga* jurisprudence on it, which permit non-US nationals to bring tort actions against certain violators of international law.[138] However, recent developments in case law on the Act have limited the extraterritorial reach of such claims considerably.[139] In other countries, such claims may be excluded through lack of jurisdiction or because of immunities attaching to State officials. Civil claims may mean quite a lot to victims, as the continued attempts by 'comfort women' to obtain compensation from Japan show.[140] The problem with such claims, even where they succeed, is that it is difficult to enforce the judgments,[141] and they rely on the person sued having money. Evidence gathering is also difficult, and bringing such claims can be expensive. In the absence of a legal aid programme, or lawyers willing to work *pro bono*, such actions can be beyond the

---

[130] Art. 14 of the ICCPR; *Casanovas v. France*, HRC, 19 July 1994.

[131] Joel Feinberg, *Doing and Deserving* (1970) 95–118, reprinted in Antony Duff and David Garland (eds.), *A Reader on Punishment* (Oxford, 1994) 71.

[132] Truth and Reconciliation Commission of Liberia, Final Report, Vol. II, 269–70.

[133] Secretary-General's Report on the Rule of Law and Transitional Justice, paras. 52–3.

[134] See Hayner, *Unspeakable Truths*, Chapter II; Teitel, *Transitional Justice*, Chapter 4.   [135] Art. 2(3) of the ICCPR.

[136] Minow, *Between Vengeance*, 100, 102–5.

[137] Although amnesties may limit the possibility of civil actions in the *locus delicti*.

[138] *Filartiga* v. *Peña-Irala*, 630 F 2d 876 (1980); *Sosa* v. *Alvarez-Machain*, 542 US 692 (2004).

[139] *Kiobel* v. *Royal Dutch Petroleum*, 135 S Ct 1659 (2013). The precise extent to which they have done so is, however, uncertain.

[140] Kelly Askin, 'Comfort Women – Shifting Blame and Stigma from Victims to Victimizers' (2001) 1 *International Criminal Law Review* 5.

[141] Which may be disappointing for victims expecting to obtain anything other than moral satisfaction from the proceedings.

means of victims. Also, financial measures may not bring the same satisfaction to victims as would the criminal prosecution of the offenders.

22.6   Local justice mechanisms

In part because of the increasing acceptance of cultural diversity in relation to the implementation of international criminal law,[142] there has been an increase in interest in local justice mechanisms. Local justice has been said to have 'three key attributes, (1) it focuses on groups rather than individuals, (2) it seeks compromise and community "harmony", and (3) it emphasises restitution over other forms of punishment'.[143] The practices of local justice are probably too varied to be defined easily in such a way, however, as they run the gamut of responses from the *gacaca* trials in Rwanda, which are in essence a form of semi-formal court proceeding,[144] to the ceremonial reintegration ceremony *mato oput* in northern Uganda which involves the drinking of a bitter root-based drink. It is possible to see the South African Truth and Reconciliation Commission as being in part inspired by local justice ideas, in particular the concept of humaneness and community known in South Africa as *ubuntu*. The Commission has frequently been defended on this basis.[145]

Local justice mechanisms are supported by many, on the basis that they 'may have greater legitimacy and capacity than devastated formal systems, and they promise local ownership, access and efficiency'.[146] In addition, some take the view that such local justice mechanisms can provide a more comprehensive and individuated response to conflicts.[147] Support for local justice mechanisms is often linked to calls for the ICC to show respect for their activities, to avoid being seen as culturally insensitive.[148] The ICC Prosecutor's paper on the interests of justice has recognized a role for local justice mechanisms.[149] However, care must be taken not to accept uncritically, 'romanticize'[150] or 'sentimentalize'[151] local justice mechanisms, which, in spite of their positive aspects, can, in fact, also be government led, questionable on human rights grounds, and can reproduce local hierarchies rather than respond to the needs of all.[152] Some may also not be appropriate for international crimes, as they were not developed for such serious offences, or their procedures cannot be invoked,

---

[142] See section 2.4.
[143] Lars Waldorf, 'Mass Justice for Mass Atrocity: Rethinking Local Justice as Transitional Justice' (2006) 79 *Temple Law Review* 1, 9.
[144] See Phil Clarke, *The Gacaca Courts, Post-Genocide Justice and Reconciliation in Rwanda: Justice without Lawyers* (Cambridge, 2010); Paul Bornkamm, *Rwanda's Gacaca Courts: Between Retribution and Reparation* (Oxford, 2012); Gerald Gahima, *Transitional Justice in Rwanda* (London, 2013) Chapter 6.
[145] See e.g. Minow, *Between Vengeance*, 51.   [146] Waldorf, 'Mass Justice', 4.
[147] Lorna McGregor, 'International Law as a Tiered Process: Transitional Justice at the Local, National and International Level' in McEvoy and McGregor, *Transitional Justice*, 47, 61.
[148] Drumbl, *Atrocity*, Chapter 5 and 187–94; Karami Maxine Clarke, *Fictions of Justice: The International Criminal Court and the Challenge of Legal Pluralism in Sub-Saharan Africa* (Cambridge, 2009) is a forceful assertion of such a view.
[149] See ICC Office of the Prosecutor, Policy Paper on the Interests of Justice, 8, available on the website of the ICC at www.icc-cpi.int.
[150] See P. McAuliffe, 'Romanticization versus Integration? Indigenous Justice in Rule of Law Reconstruction and Transitional Justice Discourse' (2013) 5 *Göttingen Journal of International Law* 41.
[151] Drumbl, *Atrocity*, 148.
[152] McGregor, 'International Law', 61–3; Mark Drumbl, 'Collective Violence and Individual Punishment: The Criminality of Mass Atrocity' (2005) 99 *Northwestern University Law Review* 539, 549; Tim Allen, *Trial Justice: The International Criminal Court and the Lord's Resistance Army* (London, 2007) Chapter 6; MacAuliffe, 'Romanticization'.

for example when the victims (or perpetrators) are dead or unknown,[153] and it can be a fine line between local and parochial. At the same time, 'in exploring the relationship between indigenous processes and formal justice mechanisms, the debate should not regress to a stark neo-colonialist versus cultural relativism stand-off ... [and] in considering options for transitional justice, the choice between local and international approaches should not be viewed as exclusive'.[154]

Further reading

M. Cherif Bassiouni (ed.), *Post-Conflict Justice* (Ardsley, NY, 2002)

Christine Bell, *On the Law of Peace: Peace Agreements and the Lex Pacificatoria* (Oxford, 2008) Chapter 12

Alison Bisset, *Truth Commissions and Criminal Courts* (Cambridge, 2012)

Phil Clarke, *The Gacaca Courts, Post-Genocide Justice and Reconciliation in Rwanda: Justice without Lawyers* (Cambridge, 2010)

Stanley Cohen, *States of Denial* (Cambridge, 2001)

David Dyzenhaus, *Judging Judges, Judging Ourselves: Truth, Reconciliation and the Apartheid Legal Order* (Oxford, 1998)

Mark Freeman, *Necessary Evils: Amnesties and the Search for Justice* (Cambridge, 2009)

Neil Kritz, *Transitional Justice: How Emerging Democracies Reckon with Former Regimes* (Washington DC, 1995)

Louise Mallinder, *Amnesty, Human Rights and Political Transitions: Bridging the Peace and Justice Divide* (Oxford, 2008)

Carlos Nino, 'The Duty to Punish Past Abuses of Human Rights Put into Context: The Case of Argentina' (1991) 100 *Yale Law Journal* 2619

Laura Olsen, 'Measures Complementing Prosecution' (2002) 84 *International Review of the Red Cross* 173

Steven Ratner, 'New Democracies, Old Atrocities: An Inquiry in International Law' (1999) 87 *Georgetown Law Journal* 707

Naomi Roht-Arriaza, 'State Responsibility to Investigate and Prosecute Grave Human Rights Violations in International Law' (1990) 78 *California Law Review* 449

Carsten Stahn, 'United Nations Peace-Building, Amnesties and Alternative Forms of Justice: A Change in Practice?' (2002) 845 *International Review of the Red Cross* 191

---

[153] Lino Owor Ogora, *Moving Forward: Traditional Justice and Victim Participation in Northern Uganda* (Wynberg, 2009) 9–10.

[154] McGregor, 'International Law', 72.

23

The Future of International Criminal Law

23.1   Introduction

International criminal law has developed at an unprecedented rate since the early 1990s and is now an established part of the international scene and of the academic curriculum. It is too early to issue any final judgments, but it is the purpose of this chapter to evaluate recent developments as far as possible, and to look tentatively to the future of international criminal law.

23.2   International courts and tribunals

The catalyst for the revival of international criminal law was the creation of the ad hoc Tribunals by the Security Council in the early to mid 1990s. Although the project for an international criminal court had received some increased attention since its re-inclusion on the General Assembly's agenda in 1989, this was not seen as likely to bear fruit. However, the creation of the ad hoc Tribunals showed that such tribunals could be established in a reasonably short time, and the focus of debate shifted from the question whether such tribunals were a realistic possibility to how they could be improved.

The ad hoc Tribunals were criticized almost from the start as being expensive and bureaucratic,[1] as well as producing what some consider to be show trials.[2] Nonetheless, these experiments (as that is what they were at their beginnings)[3] have to be credited not only with a reasonable level of success in their own proceedings,[4] but also with providing the impetus for the creation of what many thought was a near impossibility in the international legal order, a permanent international criminal court.[5]

The progression from Nuremberg to the ICC has been described as a long road ending in the triumph of the Rome Conference, hence the frequent use of the title 'From Nuremberg to

---

[1] Ralph Zacklin, 'The Failings of the Ad Hoc Tribunals' (2004) 2 *Journal of International Criminal Justice* 541, 542–3.
[2] See the discussion in Martti Koskenniemi, 'Between Impunity and Show Trials' (2002) 6 *Max Planck Yearbook of United Nations Law* 1.
[3] Which many thought would never get beyond the paper stage: see Antonio Cassese, 'The ICTY: A Living and Vital Reality' (2004) 2 *Journal of International Criminal Justice* 585, 585–6.
[4] See sections 7.2.5 and 7.3.5.   [5] Ian Brownlie, *Principles of International Law*, 5th edn (Oxford, 1998) 568.

The Hague' in writings on international criminal law.[6] It was claimed that the ICC would lead to the 'end of impunity' and it was hailed as something of a panacea for international ills.[7] But the euphoria which accompanied the adoption of the ICC Statute has given way to a hard-headed, sometimes cynical, realism about what can be achieved by an international court. Much of the discourse around the ICC and the other institutions has a critical note. Critical reflection is of course to be welcomed, but at times it fails to acknowledge the complexities of the challenges. The success of the Court hinges on careful, meaningful examination not of any single aspect but of the interplay of investigative practices, resources, expectations, operational environment, cooperation and support, judicial standards, judicial qualifications, and procedures.

The ICC suffers from many inherent disadvantages. Its Statute does not create a supranational criminal law enforcement regime. It does not establish a self-contained police force to investigate international crimes or to enforce its arrest warrants. The Statute has not been universally ratified and a number of States are either ambivalent about or opposed to the Court. Compared to the Tribunals, the Court has fewer resources (on a per-situation basis) and less reliable political backing and yet faces higher expectations. The Court has worked in situations of ongoing violence, insecurity, and political difficulty, without reliable external support on the ground. Whereas judges in the early days of the Tribunals were arguably too flexible and pro-prosecution, today if anything the pendulum has swung the other way, and some judges are applying legal and evidentiary standards that are arguably problematically high.[8]

A major controversy surrounding the ICC is that all seven situations currently under investigation are in Africa. This focus on one continent has led to understandable grievance as well as less convincing accusations that the Court is a neocolonial tool of the North against the South.[9] As well as the resolutions adopted by the African Union urging non-cooperation with the Court,[10] some African leaders have spoken out against the Court, and in September 2013 the Kenyan Parliament proposed withdrawing from the ICC Statute. Many regard the Court's selection of situations as evidence that the Court is reluctant to pursue the powerful, and hence that it is not truly upholding the rule of law. The Prosecutors respond that they have selected situations based on the Statute criteria: that these are the gravest admissible situations within the Court's territorial and temporal jurisdiction.[11] A careful examination of the evidence shows that neither hypothesis (impartial standards or

---

[6] Koskenniemi, 'Between Impunity', 34–5.

[7] On this discussion, see Bruce Broomhall, *International Justice and the International Criminal Court: Between Sovereignty and the Rule of Law* (Oxford, 2003) 1–2.

[8] See sections 7.2.4 and 11.2.3. See also Chapter 17.

[9] See the discussions in Nicholas Waddell and Phil Clark (eds.), *Courting Conflict? Justice, Peace and the ICC in Africa* (London, Royal African Society, 2008); Ifeonu Eberechi, 'Rounding Up the Usual Suspects: Exclusion, Selectivity, and Impunity in the Enforcement of International Criminal Justice and the African Union's Emerging Resistance' (2011) 4 *African Journal of Legal Studies* 51; Tim Murithi, 'The African Union and the International Criminal Court: An Embattled Relationship?' (Institute for Justice and Reconciliation Policy Brief, 8 March 2013); Dire Tladi, 'The African Union and the International Criminal Court: The Battle for the Soul of International Law' (2009) 34 *South African Yearbook of International Law* 57. See also section 8.11.2.

[10] See sections 8.11.2 and 20.10.

[11] See e.g. ICC OTP, 'Draft Policy Paper on Preliminary Examinations', 4 October 2012, available on the website of the ICC at www.icc-cpi.int.

political agenda) can be disproven.[12] And the fact that some States are presently beyond the reach of the ICC is not a fact of the Court's creation.[13]

The criticisms of bias against Africa and responses to them are addressed in Chapter 8 of this volume. There remains a need for a more holistic approach to the selection of situations for investigation. Even if we assume that situations have been selected so far based on reasonable and confirmable indicators of the gravity of each situation, that approach has not forestalled accusations of politicization. The Statute seems to permit an approach that also looks to other considerations, such as the 'interests of justice'.[14] It is imperative, in order to 'guarantee lasting respect for ... international justice',[15] that the Court address crimes in more than one region.

Other trends are more positive. Given the inertia that frequently attends treaty ratification, few would have predicted that over 120 States would have ratified the ICC Statute by 2013. Early fears that the Court would have little to investigate, because no State with a recent history of crimes would ratify, have also proved unfounded. Since its creation, the Court has investigated seven situations – a breadth comparable to all other international tribunals combined. The Court has completed investigations of many cases, persons have been arrested, and several trials are underway. The Court has issued arrest warrants against three heads of State, and one – Laurent Gbagbo – is in custody and facing proceedings before the Court. Another indicted head of State, Uhuru Kenyatta of Kenya, has been cooperating with the Court. There is anecdotal evidence that the first proceedings are having a deterrent effect.

Moreover, the African view on the ICC is more nuanced than the current controversies suggest. For example, thirty-four African States are States Parties and many continue to cooperate with the Court in practice; the initiative for five of the eight situations came from the State in question; much of the core of the frustration relates more to the Security Council than to the Court; and various measures show a will to combat impunity for international crimes.[16] It should also be noted that the United States has been engaging much more constructively with the ICC in recent years.

As David Luban has aptly noted, if one compares the current state of international criminal law to the euphoric projections of the late 1990s, there seems to have been a loss of momentum; however, if one uses any earlier period as a benchmark, the current state of international criminal law is quite remarkable.[17]

---

[12] Kai Ambos, 'Expanding the Focus of the "African Criminal Court"' in Schabas, *Ashgate Research Companion*, 499.
[13] Phoebe Murungi, *Politicization of the International Criminal Court? A Study of the UN Security Council's Power of Intervention in the ICC's Jurisdiction under the Rome Statute – Article 16* (Lambert Academic Publishing, 2012).
[14] Art. 53 of the ICC Statute.   [15] *Ibid.* Preamble, para. 11.
[16] Max Du Plessis, Antoinette Louw and Ottilia Maunganidze, *African Efforts to Close the Impunity Gap* (Institute for Security Studies Paper 241, Pretoria, November 2012). Among the efforts are also the provisional measures ordered by the African Court of Human and Peoples' Rights to safeguard the rights of Saif al-Islam Gaddafi; *In the Matter of African Commission of Human and Peoples' Rights* v. *Libya*, 15 March 2013.
[17] David Luban, 'After the Honeymoon: Reflections on the Current State of International Criminal Justice' (2013) 11 *Journal of International Criminal Justice* 505, 506–7.

23.3 National prosecutions of international crimes

The site of most international criminal law enforcement is intended to be national systems, not international courts. International tribunals have arisen because of the failure, or the absence, of national justice efforts. One of the major roles which international judicial mechanisms have is the promotion of the more effective use of national criminal justice systems. The international courts and tribunals cannot deal with any but a handful of cases, and national systems must take a greater part in the prosecution of international crimes if international criminal law is to be effectively enforced.

This is particularly the case for the ICC. Owing to the principle of complementarity,[18] it is sometimes said that the ICC will have succeeded if it never has to prosecute anyone itself.[19] Such assertions are arguably overstated: the ICC presumably must conduct its own proceedings in order to fulfil its didactic and catalytic functions. Nonetheless, there is a great deal of truth in the claim that a major role of the ICC is to ensure that domestic jurisdictions act against international crimes. The role of the Prosecutor is structured so that the Court can act as a considerable incentive for States to prosecute international crimes. Where it is appropriate, the Prosecutor may also assist genuine national efforts, for example through the passing of evidence. The Prosecutor has stated that the policy of the Office of the Prosecutor is to engage with governments to ensure prosecution of crimes within the jurisdiction of the ICC.[20] In addition, ratification of the ICC Statute has prompted a reasonable number of States (although not enough) to adopt domestic criminal legislation covering the core international crimes.[21] Given the traditional failure of States to implement international crimes into their domestic law,[22] this in itself is a development worthy of note.

Universal jurisdiction has come under attack in recent years, and this has led, to some extent, to a retrenchment of universal jurisdiction in theory and in practice.[23] Nonetheless, this retrenchment has occurred because universal jurisdiction has moved from the warm greenhouse of aspiration to the cold light of day-to-day international law. Universal jurisdiction, in some form or another, has been implemented into more States' domestic law than was the case in 1998. The existence of such jurisdiction and its possible exercise have had some impact on other States, which have looked to prosecute the commission of international crimes by their own nationals, in part to pre-empt such claims. There have also been some significant exercises of universal jurisdiction at the domestic level, which are sometimes forgotten in the debate over the precise ambit of the permission which international law grants to States to assert it.[24] But, as the 2009 statement of the African Union criticizing

---

[18] See section 8.6.
[19] ICC OTP, 'Draft Policy Paper on Preliminary Examinations', 4 October 2012, 4, available on the website of the ICC at www.icc-cpi.int; and see section 8.6.
[20] *Ibid.*, 3.   [21] See section 4.4.
[22] Menno Kamminga, 'Final Report on the Exercise of Universal Jurisdiction in Relation to Gross Human Rights Abuses' in International Law Association, *Report of the Sixty-Ninth Conference* (London, 2000) 403, 412–14.
[23] See section 3.5.4.   [24] *Ibid.*

the 'abuse' of universal jurisdiction shows, the political controversies about the exercise of universal jurisdiction have not gone away.[25]

The problems which States have in cooperating with one another in prosecuting international crimes may, it is hoped, become less significant with the conclusion of new and more effective agreements on inter-State cooperation, including those at the regional level.[26] A potential treaty on crimes against humanity, affirming obligations of prevention, prosecution and cooperation, would be a valuable advance.[27] And the further clarifications on the interpretation and delineation of the obligation to prosecute or to extradite (*aut dedere aut judicare*) by the ICJ and the International Law Commission are welcome in this regard.[28]

One continuing area of controversy is that of immunities, as is shown, *inter alia*, by the negative reaction of the African Union to the indictment by the ICC of President Al Bashir.[29] The ICJ in the *Yerodia* case has shown that international criminal law is still subject to aspects of the law on immunity.[30] National (and international) courts have recognized that certain immunities still exist under general international law. Many issues of the parameters of immunity and accountability remain to be determined.[31] Immunities reflect other important values of the international legal order, and international criminal law cannot yet be regarded as a trump card.[32] As a result, triumphalism about international criminal law would be misplaced.

23.4   Engraining a commitment to accountability

One of the significant impacts of international criminal law is at the level of the ideas, attitudes and habits of international actors. In a statement released just after the Rome Conference, which adopted the Statute for the ICC, Amnesty International claimed:

The true significance of the adoption of the Statute may well lie, not in the actual institution itself in its early years, which will face enormous obstacles, but in the revolution in legal and moral attitudes towards the worst crimes in the world. No longer will these crimes be simply political events to be addressed by diplomacy at the international level, but crimes which all states have a duty to punish themselves, or, if they fail to fulfil this duty, by the international community in accordance with the rule of law.[33]

This assertion contains more than a grain of truth. The creation of the ICC reflects, and contributes greatly to, a significant cultural turn to accountability. Twenty years ago, most of those accused of international crimes could sleep soundly, fairly sure that they would not be

---

[25] Decision on the Report of the Commission on the Abuse of Universal Jurisdiction (Assembly/AU/14/(XI)), annexed to Letter from the AU Permanent Observer to the President of the Security Council, UN Doc. S/2008/465. Tanzania having referred the matter to the General Assembly, the Sixth Committee has been considering the question in a desultory manner.

[26] See Chapters 5 and 20.   [27] See section 11.1.2.   [28] See sections 4.3.1 and 5.4.

[29] Decision of the African States Parties to the ICC Statute of the International Criminal Court (Assembly/AU/13 (XIII)).

[30] On the ambit of these, see Chapter 21.   [31] *Ibid.*

[32] As Judge ad hoc Van den Wyngaert noted, the majority opinion in *Yerodia* did not even use the term: *Case Concerning the Arrest Warrant of 11 April 2000* (*Democratic Republic of the Congo* v. *Belgium*), 14 February 2002, (2002) ICJ Reports, Dissenting Opinion of Judge ad hoc Van den Wyngaert, para. 6.

[33] Quoted in William Pace and Mark Thieroff, 'Participation of Non-Governmental Organizations' in Lee, *The Making of the Rome Statute*, 396.

required to stand trial for their conduct. It is unlikely that Augusto Pinochet or Hissène Habré thought that international law would be brought to bear upon them. Both of them, to different extents, have been proved wrong, even if, on the basis of what had occurred since Nuremberg and Tokyo, their opinion had an empirical basis.

The ad hoc international criminal tribunals may well have been created out of motives that were, at best, mixed,[34] but the idea they contained, that of accountability for international crimes, was one which caught on. Ideas are important in international relations,[35] and this one caught the eye both of States and of many non-governmental actors. As has been said, '[w]hat started out in 1993 as mostly a public relations ploy, namely to create an ad hoc tribunal to appear to be doing something about human rights violations in Bosnia without major risk, by 1998 had become an important global movement for international criminal justice'.[36]

A resulting challenge for States today is to determine the place of justice in their foreign relations policy. It is notable that criminal justice has been structured into the work of the relevant UN agencies, and, whenever the UN has a say in a post-conflict situation, accountability for international crimes appears on the agenda. This does not guarantee a particular response, but the fact that justice weighs in the scales is a transformation from the politics of impunity from which even the UN was not immune as recently as 1994.[37] The importance of international justice has been accepted by what some consider to be the primary international organ of *realpolitik*, the Security Council. For example, in Resolution 1265(1999), the Security Council emphasized 'the responsibility of States to end impunity and to prosecute those responsible for genocide, crimes against humanity and serious violations of international humanitarian law'. It must be conceded, by way of reminder, that 'present signals are not universally positive'[38] and the power of ideas is not always determinative. Nor should one underestimate the capacity for States to maintain a distinction between their public rhetoric and private positions.

States have had to engage with the peace and justice dilemma in relation to the early cases at the ICC. On occasion, there has been a lack of enthusiasm for the enforcement of arrest warrants when that is perceived, rightly or wrongly, to pose a threat to peace processes. The apparently conflicting requirements of peace and justice have been seen in the ICC warrants against the leaders of the Lord's Resistance Army in Uganda and those in Sudan and this has led to criticisms of the Prosecutor or the Court as a whole. But this is a matter which the international community as a whole must address, including the role of the Security Council in seeking deferrals if there is an instance when prosecutions should temporarily give way to peace and security.

Having asserted the importance of international criminal law, States and others may (and, indeed, will, according to a constructivist account) begin to internalize the values they have

---

[34] See section 2.4.   [35] See Alexander Wendt, *Social Theory of International Relations* (Cambridge, 1999).
[36] David Forsythe, *Human Rights in International Relations* (Cambridge, 2000) 221.
[37] See Michael Scharf, 'Swapping Amnesty for Peace, Was there a Duty to Prosecute International Crimes in Haiti?' (1996) 31 *Texas International Law Journal* 1.
[38] Broomhall, *International Justice*, 3.

espoused, even if initially only rhetorically, and act upon them.[39] Once States prosecute international crimes, even if it is on the basis that if they do not do so the ICC will or that they will be criticized internationally or domestically, this will have an effect on the way they perceive their interests. The more that international crimes are prosecuted, the more that doing so becomes normalized and States are likely to do so simply on the basis that it is what is done in relation to international crimes.[40]

There have been suggestions that the current trend towards international criminal liability runs the risk of removing focus for liability from States.[41] There are a number of answers to such critiques. Where the conduct of those committing international crimes is attributable to a State, through the normal rules of State responsibility,[42] such responsibility is concurrent, rather than exclusive.[43] Pragmatically speaking, the reason for the rise of individual liability is also that State responsibility has not proved efficacious in achieving any of the specific aims of international criminal law. Hence, Leila Sadat has suggested that individual criminal liability has been revived, at least as much as for any other reason, out of a frustration with other mechanisms of ensuring accountability.[44] Such a view is more than adequately supported by the classic statement of the Nuremberg IMT that 'crimes against international law are committed by men, not abstract entities, and only by punishing individuals who commit such crimes can the provisions of international law be enforced'.[45] In the end, the critique ought to be seen not as undermining the importance of individual liability, but as a reminder that it is not the only form of responsibility relevant to international crimes.

23.5   The development of substantive international criminal law

International criminal law is a relatively new discipline and it does not pretend to be a complete system of criminal law. The law has inconsistencies and incoherencies and must continue to evolve and develop.[46] The ICC Statute is not the final word; Article 10 of the Statute recognizes that the law may continue to develop.[47] There is scope for further

---

[39] Robert Cryer, 'State Sovereignty vs International Criminal Law: Another Round?' (2005) 16 *European Journal of International Law* 979, 994–6.

[40] *Ibid.*

[41] See the careful case made in Hazel Fox, 'The ICJ's Treatment of Acts of the State, and in Particular, the Attribution of Acts of Individuals to the State' in Nisuke Ando, Edward McWhinney and Rüdiger Wolfrum (eds.), *Liber Amoricorum Shigeru Oda* (The Hague, 2001) 147.

[42] Which is frequently, although not inevitably, the case. For details on such rules, see James Crawford, *The International Law Commission's Articles on State Responsibility: Introduction, Text and Commentaries* (Cambridge, 2002).

[43] See e.g. André Nollkaemper, 'Concurrence between Individual Responsibility and State Responsibility in International Law' (2003) 52 *International and Comparative Law Quarterly* 615.

[44] Leila Sadat, *The International Criminal Court and the Transformation of International Law: Justice for the New Millennium* (New York, 2002) Chapter 3.

[45] Nuremberg IMT, Judgment and Sentences, reprinted in (1947) 41 *American Journal of International Law* 172, 221.

[46] Broomhall, for example, correctly notes that '[b]ecause the judgement of states, individually and collectively, is subject to diverse extra-legal influences, the process of international criminalisation will always be less orderly than its conceptual formulation' (Broomhall, *International Justice*, 39).

[47] Robert Cryer, 'Of Custom, Treaties, Scholars and the Gavel: The Impact of the International Criminal Tribunals on the ICRC Customary Law Study' (2006) 11 *Journal of Conflict and Security Law* 239, 257–62.

development, within limits, by other courts and even by the ICC, although the ICC's interpretive mandate is more 'hemmed in' than others have been.[48]

The multiplicity of courts and institutions raises the possibility of fragmentation, as different tribunals develop differing jurisprudence on international criminal law. This raises challenges not only for coherence, but also for determining the precise customary law position on controversial questions.[49] There are already areas of divergence on substantive law between the founding documents of the ad hoc Tribunals and the ICC Statute.[50] Although the ICC has shown respect towards the jurisprudence of the ad hoc Tribunals, there are already some significant differences with respect to substantive international criminal law on, for example, genocide, joint criminal enterprise and superior responsibility.[51] There are also differences between international law and some national laws.[52] This may be unfortunate, although it must be said that there is far more evidence in support of propositions of customary international law than was previously the case. Some of the remaining problems can be mitigated by careful study of the law, which involves an appreciation of the relative authoritativeness of the various sources and evidences of custom on point.

One area in which further legal development can be anticipated is with respect to war crimes, and particularly the continued assimilation of the rules applicable in international and non-international armed conflict. Some take a very broad approach to the extent to which the two have already coalesced.[53] The ICTY has implied such a view, by suggesting that '[w]hat is inhumane, and consequently proscribed, in international wars, cannot but be inhumane and inadmissible in civil strife'.[54] On the other hand, not all of the rules applicable to international armed conflict are easily applied to their civil war counterparts.[55] Thus, the ICTY, in the same case, averred that there has not been 'a full and mechanical transplant' of the rules.[56] Where it is possible to do so, however, the case for unifying the law relating to international and non-international armed conflicts, both in treaty and customary international law, is very strong.[57] The first Review Conference of the ICC, held in Kampala in

---

[48] See William Schabas, 'Interpreting the Statutes of the Ad Hoc Tribunals' in Lai Chand Vohrah *et al.* (eds.), *Man's Inhumanity to Man: Essays in Honour of Antonio Cassese* (The Hague, 2003) 847, 887.

[49] This problem arises not only between criminal tribunals but also with the International Court of Justice in the context of State responsibility. For discussion of the different rulings of the ICJ (in the *Nicaragua* case) and the ICTY (in *Tadić*) on the meaning of 'effective' or 'overall' control for the purpose of responsibility for the acts of others, see Report of the Study Group of the ILC, 'Fragmentation of International Law: Difficulties Arising from the Diversification and Expansion of International Law' (GAOR A/CN.4/L.682, 13 April 2006), paras. 49–52. The ICJ has reiterated its support for the *Nicaragua* test and criticized the ICTY on point; see *Case Concerning the Application of the Convention on the Prevention and Punishment of the Crime of Genocide (Bosnia and Herzegovina v. Serbia and Montenegro)*, ICJ, 26 February 2007, paras. 402–6.

[50] Compare e.g. Art. 7 of the ICC Statute with Art. 5 of the ICTY Statute, Art. 3 of the ICTR Statute and Art. 2 of the SCSL Statute.

[51] On genocide, compare *Situation in Darfur* (*Al Bashir* arrest warrant case), ICC PTC I, 4 March 2009, paras. 117–33, with *Krstić*, ICTY A. Ch., 19 April 2004, para. 224. On command responsibility, see *Bemba Gombo*, ICC PTC I, 15 June 2009, paras. 432–4. As seen in Chapter 15, the ICC has preferred co-perpetration to joint criminal enterprise in its early practice.

[52] See e.g. Australia and the International Criminal Court (Consequential Amendments) Act 2002, s. 268.115.

[53] See Henckaerts and Doswald-Beck, *ICRC Customary Law.*   [54] *Tadić*, ICTY A. Ch., 2 October 1995, para. 119.

[55] Marco Sassoli and Laura Olsen, 'Prosecutor v. Tadić' (1999) 93 *American Journal of International Law* 571, 575–7.

[56] *Tadić*, ICTY A. Ch., 2 October 1995, para. 126.

[57] Colin Warbrick and Peter Rowe, 'The International Criminal Tribunal for Yugoslavia: The Decision of the Appeals Chamber on the Interlocutory Appeal on Jurisdiction in the Tadić Case' (1996) 45 *International and Comparative Law Quarterly* 691, 698.

2010, continued this trend by recognizing violations of certain weapons prohibitions as war crimes in non-international armed conflict.[58]

Another area of international criminal law where suggestions have been made for change is the harmonization of war crimes and crimes against humanity. An eminent authority in the area, Leslie Green, has suggested that the two crimes ought to be amalgamated.[59] The fact that the contextual elements for the two crimes reflect different (if overlapping) situations militates against the advisability of this position.[60] Still, there may be room for harmonization of the physical elements of similar offences, such as unlawful confinement and arbitrary imprisonment. The expansion of international criminal law into some areas that it does not adequately cover, such as the intentional or reckless creation of mass starvation, would also seem appropriate,[61] and go some way to accepting the reality of structural as well as direct violence. That said, further expansion should be supported by credible legal methods, and one must also recall that 'there might be a fundamental incompatibility between the political agendas of States and the process of codifying, in a progressive manner [international criminal law]'.[62]

A further area of development relates to the crime of aggression, over which the ICC will be able to exercise jurisdiction once the amendments agreed at the Kampala Review Conference in 2010 have come into force.[63] While it is to be expected that prosecutions will be rare, the definition of the crime for the purpose of the ICC Statute and the threat of prosecution will have to be taken into account in the future by governments when taking decisions about the use of armed force against other States.

Finally, another area in which there may be further development is that of corporate liability for criminal conduct. The ad hoc Tribunals and the ICC have jurisdiction only over natural persons. There was support at the Rome Conference for including legal entities, but it did not prove possible to reach agreement.[64] Financial gain – whether from the acquisition of natural resources or from arms trading – may be either the cause of atrocities committed in conflicts or the reason for their continuation, and accountability would be increased if it were possible to prosecute directly the companies participating in such atrocities. This is an area which deserves more study in relation to both international and national jurisdictions.[65]

23.6   The path forward (or back?)

At the time of writing, the African Union is threatening a withdrawal from the ICC Statute by African States, the Kenyan Parliament has voted to withdraw from the Statute, certain

---

[58] See section 12.3.6.
[59] Leslie Green, 'Grave Breaches or Crimes against Humanity?' (1997–8) 8 *US Air Force Academy Journal of Legal Studies* 19.
[60] William Fenrick, 'Should Crimes against Humanity Replace War Crimes?' (1999) 37 *Columbia Journal of Transnational Law* 767.
[61] So long as it is carefully defined. See David Marcus, 'Famine Crimes in International Law' (2004) 97 *American Journal of International Law* 245.
[62] Sadat, *Justice for the New Millennium*, 261; see also Broomhall, *International Justice*, 18, 131.   [63] See Chapter 13.
[64] See Per Saland, 'International Criminal Law Principles' in Lee, *The Making of the Rome Statute*, 199.
[65] See the workshop in (2008) 6 *Journal of International Criminal Justice* 899.

governments, in particular of Sudan and Libya, are refusing to comply with orders by the ICC, proceedings before the ICTY are in doubt because of the disqualification of a judge, the staff of the ECCC are on strike because of lack of pay and the funding of the Chambers is at risk, the Special Tribunal for Lebanon is unlikely ever to be able to have a trial in the presence of defendants, and the Security Council is refusing to refer a situation of mass atrocities (in Syria) to the ICC. Some of these facts will change, but the position of international criminal justice is not secure and needs continuing support from the international community.

One trend that can be seen in international criminal law is a movement away from ad hoc international tribunals. The critiques of ad hoc tribunals, not least of having to 'reinvent the wheel' by establishing a new institution for each new situation, have taken hold. The referral of the situations in Darfur and Libya to the ICC, rather than setting up an ad hoc tribunal at the global or local level, signals a watershed. Of course, other mechanisms, such as international tribunals for matters outside ICC jurisdiction (Lebanon), or national courts with extensive international assistance, may remain an important part of the landscape.[66]

The ICC is, to a very considerable extent, reliant on the willingness of States to assist the Court in every form of cooperation and enforcement, including provision of intelligence, arrest of suspects and acceptance of convicted persons for imprisonment.[67] The ICC will fail unless it is properly resourced and properly supported.[68] If it is to make any difference, the role of the Court and its needs and capabilities will have to become a part of the general policy of States in strengthening or restoring international peace and security. To achieve this, the ICC must prove itself as viable and credible by providing not only fair but also efficient proceedings as well as investigations which are appropriate for the complex crimes at hand and sufficient for a conviction of those most responsible for the offence.[69] In this sense, the Court could and should improve. But the expectations with respect to efficiency must be realistic and the yardstick for procedural fairness should not necessarily be exactly the same as for domestic criminal proceedings.[70]

The ICC should not, however, be regarded as the exclusive locus of international criminal law. Domestic proceedings have many advantages over international ones, including the benefit for the victims of having the trial in their own country, and local enforcement mechanisms such as police and prison systems. Often, however, domestic proceedings may need the legitimacy that an international *imprimatur* can ensure. The best way forward for international criminal law, in our view, is for there to be a synergy between international and domestic efforts to ensure accountability for international crimes.[71] International

---

[66] See Chapter 9.
[67] See e.g. Hans-Peter Kaul, 'Construction Site for More Justice: The International Criminal Court After Two Years' (2005) 99 *American Journal of International Law* 370, 383.
[68] A serious failure in this respect is the refusal of the Security Council to allow UN funding of the Darfur referral; see Robert Cryer, 'Sudan, Resolution 1593 and International Criminal Justice' (2006) 19 *Leiden Journal of International Law* 195, 206–8. The same applies to the Libya referral.
[69] See Chapter 17.
[70] Mirjan Damaška, 'Reflections on Fairness in International Criminal Justice' (2012) 10 *Journal of International Criminal Justice* 611.
[71] See also William W. Burke-White, 'A Community of Courts: Toward a System of International Criminal Law Enforcement' (2002) 24 *Michigan Journal of International Law* 1.

assistance for national prosecutions of international crimes will continue and, it is to be hoped, lead to further entrenchment of international criminal law in the area, and maybe even globally.

Too much should not be claimed for international criminal law. The purposes of an international trial which are sometimes advanced – for example, recording history, reconciling communities, telling the victims' story – may sometimes run counter to the interests at the centre of a criminal trial, namely, to determine guilt or innocence while respecting the rights of the accused; further, history may actually be distorted in the process.[72] The necessary selection of serious cases also means that ambitions of this kind will only partially be satisfied. There are additional approaches to bringing reconciliation in conflict situations and post-conflict societies.[73] More work needs to be done on the particular difficulties of delivering non-judicial forms of justice and how to calibrate criminal justice mechanisms with other forms of justice. The broader aspects of this programme require a detailed examination of the complex causes of mass crimes, including the role of those financing and profiting from atrocities.[74] International criminal law is not a panacea, and simply referring a situation to the ICC is not a substitute for action. International criminal law should work within a broader framework of, *inter alia*, peacebuilding, demobilization, institutional reform, fact-finding, education, and removal of the financial incentives that often underlie mass atrocity.

International courts and tribunals operate in an international legal system which is made up of sovereign States. Just as it is still only an aspiration that all States should accept the rule of law in international relations generally (and thus, for example, subordinate their policy on the use of force to international law), so there are still huge difficulties in achieving the rule of law in international criminal justice, in the sense of the consistent and impartial enforcement of the law.[75] That would require more States accepting that their policy be shaped 'on a basis that is less responsive to geopolitical realism, and more in line with legal/moral factors and a genuine commitment to global humane governance as a long-term goal'.[76] In many ways the development of international criminal law is a metonym for the extent to which an international community can be said to exist.[77] The evidence of whether international society has developed into an international community is mixed.[78]

All that said, between the late 1940s and the early 1990s international criminal law was a field of law which was rarely seen as relevant by many international lawyers or governments, and which was rarely studied or written on, let alone taught as a separate subject.[79] Now it is a major area of study and practice. Twenty years ago, few would have thought that a textbook like this would be useful, or necessary. Even less would it have been predicted

---

[72] Mark Osiel, *Mass Atrocity, Collective Memory, and the Law* (New Brunswick, NJ, 1997).   [73] See section 2.3.
[74] For acceptance of such a view, see e.g. SC Res. 1306(2000) on 'blood diamonds'.
[75] Broomhall, *International Justice*, 53–4.
[76] Richard Falk, 'Telford Taylor and the Legacy of Nuremberg' (1999) 37 *Columbia Journal of Transnational Law* 693, 716.
[77] Frédéric Mégret, 'Epilogue to an Endless Debate: The International Court's Third Party Jurisdiction and the Looming Revolution of International Law' (2001) 12 *European Journal of International Law* 247.
[78] See Hedley Bull, *The Anarchical Society: A Study of Order in World Politics*, 2nd edn (London, 1995).
[79] The most notable exception to this trend was the voluminous writings on the subject by M. Cherif Bassiouni.

that a second and third edition would already have proven necessary to keep pace with rapid developments in this field. It is our hope that, by aiding understanding of the law, this book will contribute in a small way to the objectives of international criminal law as a whole, including the pursuit of justice and the deterrence of the atrocities that continue to plague our world.

Index